T0137222

Lecture Notes in Computer Science 11214

Commenced Publication in 1973
Founding and Former Series Editors:
Gerhard Goos, Juris Hartmanis, and Jan van Leeuwen

More information about this series at http://www.springer.com/series/7412

Vittorio Ferrari · Martial Hebert
Cristian Sminchisescu · Yair Weiss (Eds.)

Computer Vision – ECCV 2018

15th European Conference
Munich, Germany, September 8–14, 2018
Proceedings, Part X

 Springer

Editors
Vittorio Ferrari
Google Research
Zurich
Switzerland

Cristian Sminchisescu
Google Research
Zurich
Switzerland

Martial Hebert
Carnegie Mellon University
Pittsburgh, PA
USA

Yair Weiss
Hebrew University of Jerusalem
Jerusalem
Israel

ISSN 0302-9743   ISSN 1611-3349 (electronic)
Lecture Notes in Computer Science
ISBN 978-3-030-01248-9   ISBN 978-3-030-01249-6 (eBook)
https://doi.org/10.1007/978-3-030-01249-6

Library of Congress Control Number: 2018955489

LNCS Sublibrary: SL6 – Image Processing, Computer Vision, Pattern Recognition, and Graphics

This Springer imprint is published by the registered company Springer Nature Switzerland AG
The registered company address is: Gewerbestrasse 11, 6330 Cham, Switzerland

Foreword

It was our great pleasure to host the European Conference on Computer Vision 2018 in Munich, Germany. This constituted by far the largest ECCV event ever. With close to 2,900 registered participants and another 600 on the waiting list one month before the conference, participation more than doubled since the last ECCV in Amsterdam. We believe that this is due to a dramatic growth of the computer vision community combined with the popularity of Munich as a major European hub of culture, science, and industry. The conference took place in the heart of Munich in the concert hall Gasteig with workshops and tutorials held at the downtown campus of the Technical University of Munich.

One of the major innovations for ECCV 2018 was the free perpetual availability of all conference and workshop papers, which is often referred to as open access. We note that this is not precisely the same use of the term as in the Budapest declaration. Since 2013, CVPR and ICCV have had their papers hosted by the Computer Vision Foundation (CVF), in parallel with the IEEE Xplore version. This has proved highly beneficial to the computer vision community.

We are delighted to announce that for ECCV 2018 a very similar arrangement was put in place with the cooperation of Springer. In particular, the author's final version will be freely available in perpetuity on a CVF page, while SpringerLink will continue to host a version with further improvements, such as activating reference links and including video. We believe that this will give readers the best of both worlds; researchers who are focused on the technical content will have a freely available version in an easily accessible place, while subscribers to SpringerLink will continue to have the additional benefits that this provides. We thank Alfred Hofmann from Springer for helping to negotiate this agreement, which we expect will continue for future versions of ECCV.

September 2018

Horst Bischof
Daniel Cremers
Bernt Schiele
Ramin Zabih

Preface

Welcome to the proceedings of the 2018 European Conference on Computer Vision (ECCV 2018) held in Munich, Germany. We are delighted to present this volume reflecting a strong and exciting program, the result of an extensive review process. In total, we received 2,439 valid paper submissions. Of these, 776 were accepted (31.8%): 717 as posters (29.4%) and 59 as oral presentations (2.4%). All oral presentations were presented as posters as well. The program selection process was complicated this year by the large increase in the number of submitted papers, +65% over ECCV 2016, and the use of CMT3 for the first time for a computer vision conference. The program selection process was supported by four program co-chairs (PCs), 126 area chairs (ACs), and 1,199 reviewers with reviews assigned.

We were primarily responsible for the design and execution of the review process. Beyond administrative rejections, we were involved in acceptance decisions only in the very few cases where the ACs were not able to agree on a decision. As PCs, and as is customary in the field, we were not allowed to co-author a submission. General co-chairs and other co-organizers who played no role in the review process were permitted to submit papers, and were treated as any other author is.

Acceptance decisions were made by two independent ACs. The ACs also made a joint recommendation for promoting papers to oral status. We decided on the final selection of oral presentations based on the ACs' recommendations. There were 126 ACs, selected according to their technical expertise, experience, and geographical diversity (63 from European, nine from Asian/Australian, and 54 from North American institutions). Indeed, 126 ACs is a substantial increase in the number of ACs due to the natural increase in the number of papers and to our desire to maintain the number of papers assigned to each AC to a manageable number so as to ensure quality. The ACs were aided by the 1,199 reviewers to whom papers were assigned for reviewing. The Program Committee was selected from committees of previous ECCV, ICCV, and CVPR conferences and was extended on the basis of suggestions from the ACs. Having a large pool of Program Committee members for reviewing allowed us to match expertise while reducing reviewer loads. No more than eight papers were assigned to a reviewer, maintaining the reviewers' load at the same level as ECCV 2016 despite the increase in the number of submitted papers.

Conflicts of interest between ACs, Program Committee members, and papers were identified based on the home institutions, and on previous collaborations of all researchers involved. To find institutional conflicts, all authors, Program Committee members, and ACs were asked to list the Internet domains of their current institutions. We assigned on average approximately 18 papers to each AC. The papers were assigned using the affinity scores from the Toronto Paper Matching System (TPMS) and additional data from the OpenReview system, managed by a UMass group. OpenReview used additional information from ACs' and authors' records to identify collaborations and to generate matches. OpenReview was invaluable in refining conflict definitions and in generating quality matches. The only glitch is that, once the matches were generated, a small percentage of papers were unassigned because of discrepancies between the OpenReview conflicts and the conflicts entered in CMT3. We manually assigned these papers. This glitch is revealing of the challenge of using multiple systems at once (CMT3 and OpenReview in this case), which needs to be addressed in future.

After assignment of papers to ACs, the ACs suggested seven reviewers per paper from the Program Committee pool. The selection and rank ordering were facilitated by the TPMS affinity scores visible to the ACs for each paper/reviewer pair. The final assignment of papers to reviewers was generated again through OpenReview in order to account for refined conflict definitions. This required new features in the OpenReview matching system to accommodate the ECCV workflow, in particular to incorporate selection ranking, and maximum reviewer load. Very few papers received fewer than three reviewers after matching and were handled through manual assignment. Reviewers were then asked to comment on the merit of each paper and to make an initial recommendation ranging from definitely reject to definitely accept, including a borderline rating. The reviewers were also asked to suggest explicit questions they wanted to see answered in the authors' rebuttal. The initial review period was five weeks. Because of the delay in getting all the reviews in, we had to delay the final release of the reviews by four days. However, because of the slack included at the tail end of the schedule, we were able to maintain the decision target date with sufficient time for all the phases. We reassigned over 100 reviews from 40 reviewers during the review period. Unfortunately, the main reason for these reassignments was reviewers declining to review, after having accepted to do so. Other reasons included technical relevance and occasional unidentified conflicts. We express our thanks to the emergency reviewers who generously accepted to perform these reviews under short notice. In addition, a substantial number of manual corrections had to do with reviewers using a different email address than the one that was used at the time of the reviewer invitation. This is revealing of a broader issue with identifying users by email addresses that change frequently enough to cause significant problems during the timespan of the conference process.

The authors were then given the opportunity to rebut the reviews, to identify factual errors, and to address the specific questions raised by the reviewers over a seven-day rebuttal period. The exact format of the rebuttal was the object of considerable debate among the organizers, as well as with prior organizers. At issue is to balance giving the author the opportunity to respond completely and precisely to the reviewers, e.g., by including graphs of experiments, while avoiding requests for completely new material or experimental results not included in the original paper. In the end, we decided on the two-page PDF document in conference format. Following this rebuttal period, reviewers and ACs discussed papers at length, after which reviewers finalized their evaluation and gave a final recommendation to the ACs. A significant percentage of the reviewers did enter their final recommendation if it did not differ from their initial recommendation. Given the tight schedule, we did not wait until all were entered.

After this discussion period, each paper was assigned to a second AC. The AC/paper matching was again run through OpenReview. Again, the OpenReview team worked quickly to implement the features specific to this process, in this case accounting for the existing AC assignment, as well as minimizing the fragmentation across ACs, so that each AC had on average only 5.5 buddy ACs to communicate with. The largest number was 11. Given the complexity of the conflicts, this was a very efficient set of assignments from OpenReview. Each paper was then evaluated by its assigned pair of ACs. For each paper, we required each of the two ACs assigned to certify both the final recommendation and the metareview (aka consolidation report). In all cases, after extensive discussions, the two ACs arrived at a common acceptance decision. We maintained these decisions, with the caveat that we did evaluate, sometimes going back to the ACs, a few papers for which the final acceptance decision substantially deviated from the consensus from the reviewers, amending three decisions in the process.

We want to thank everyone involved in making ECCV 2018 possible. The success of ECCV 2018 depended on the quality of papers submitted by the authors, and on the very hard work of the ACs and the Program Committee members. We are particularly grateful to the OpenReview team (Melisa Bok, Ari Kobren, Andrew McCallum, Michael Spector) for their support, in particular their willingness to implement new features, often on a tight schedule, to Laurent Charlin for the use of the Toronto Paper Matching System, to the CMT3 team, in particular in dealing with all the issues that arise when using a new system, to Friedrich Fraundorfer and Quirin Lohr for maintaining the online version of the program, and to the CMU staff (Keyla Cook, Lynnetta Miller, Ashley Song, Nora Kazour) for assisting with data entry/editing in CMT3. Finally, the preparation of these proceedings would not have been possible without the diligent effort of the publication chairs, Albert Ali Salah and Hamdi Dibeklioğlu, and of Anna Kramer and Alfred Hofmann from Springer.

September 2018   Vittorio Ferrari
                                                     Martial Hebert
                                           Cristian Sminchisescu
                                                        Yair Weiss

Organization

General Chairs

Horst Bischof   Graz University of Technology, Austria
Daniel Cremers   Technical University of Munich, Germany
Bernt Schiele   Saarland University, Max Planck Institute for Informatics, Germany
Ramin Zabih   CornellNYCTech, USA

Program Committee Co-chairs

Vittorio Ferrari   University of Edinburgh, UK
Martial Hebert   Carnegie Mellon University, USA
Cristian Sminchisescu   Lund University, Sweden
Yair Weiss   Hebrew University, Israel

Local Arrangements Chairs

Björn Menze   Technical University of Munich, Germany
Matthias Niessner   Technical University of Munich, Germany

Workshop Chairs

Stefan Roth   TU Darmstadt, Germany
Laura Leal-Taixé   Technical University of Munich, Germany

Tutorial Chairs

Michael Bronstein   Università della Svizzera Italiana, Switzerland
Laura Leal-Taixé   Technical University of Munich, Germany

Website Chair

Friedrich Fraundorfer   Graz University of Technology, Austria

Demo Chairs

Federico Tombari   Technical University of Munich, Germany
Joerg Stueckler   Technical University of Munich, Germany

Publicity Chair

Giovanni Maria   University of Catania, Italy
  Farinella

Industrial Liaison Chairs

Florent Perronnin   Naver Labs, France
Yunchao Gong   Snap, USA
Helmut Grabner   Logitech, Switzerland

Finance Chair

Gerard Medioni   Amazon, University of Southern California, USA

Publication Chairs

Albert Ali Salah   Boğaziçi University, Turkey
Hamdi Dibeklioğlu   Bilkent University, Turkey

Area Chairs

Kalle Åström   Lund University, Sweden
Zeynep Akata   University of Amsterdam, The Netherlands
Joao Barreto   University of Coimbra, Portugal
Ronen Basri   Weizmann Institute of Science, Israel
Dhruv Batra   Georgia Tech and Facebook AI Research, USA
Serge Belongie   Cornell University, USA
Rodrigo Benenson   Google, Switzerland
Hakan Bilen   University of Edinburgh, UK
Matthew Blaschko   KU Leuven, Belgium
Edmond Boyer   Inria, France
Gabriel Brostow   University College London, UK
Thomas Brox   University of Freiburg, Germany
Marcus Brubaker   York University, Canada
Barbara Caputo   Politecnico di Torino and the Italian Institute
                         of Technology, Italy
Tim Cootes   University of Manchester, UK
Trevor Darrell   University of California, Berkeley, USA
Larry Davis   University of Maryland at College Park, USA
Andrew Davison   Imperial College London, UK
Fernando de la Torre   Carnegie Mellon University, USA
Irfan Essa   GeorgiaTech, USA
Ali Farhadi   University of Washington, USA
Paolo Favaro   University of Bern, Switzerland
Michael Felsberg   Linköping University, Sweden

Sanja Fidler	University of Toronto, Canada
Andrew Fitzgibbon	Microsoft, Cambridge, UK
David Forsyth	University of Illinois at Urbana-Champaign, USA
Charless Fowlkes	University of California, Irvine, USA
Bill Freeman	MIT, USA
Mario Fritz	MPII, Germany
Jürgen Gall	University of Bonn, Germany
Dariu Gavrila	TU Delft, The Netherlands
Andreas Geiger	MPI-IS and University of Tübingen, Germany
Theo Gevers	University of Amsterdam, The Netherlands
Ross Girshick	Facebook AI Research, USA
Kristen Grauman	Facebook AI Research and UT Austin, USA
Abhinav Gupta	Carnegie Mellon University, USA
Kaiming He	Facebook AI Research, USA
Martial Hebert	Carnegie Mellon University, USA
Anders Heyden	Lund University, Sweden
Timothy Hospedales	University of Edinburgh, UK
Michal Irani	Weizmann Institute of Science, Israel
Phillip Isola	University of California, Berkeley, USA
Hervé Jégou	Facebook AI Research, France
David Jacobs	University of Maryland, College Park, USA
Allan Jepson	University of Toronto, Canada
Jiaya Jia	Chinese University of Hong Kong, SAR China
Fredrik Kahl	Chalmers University, USA
Hedvig Kjellström	KTH Royal Institute of Technology, Sweden
Iasonas Kokkinos	University College London and Facebook, UK
Vladlen Koltun	Intel Labs, USA
Philipp Krähenbühl	UT Austin, USA
M. Pawan Kumar	University of Oxford, UK
Kyros Kutulakos	University of Toronto, Canada
In Kweon	KAIST, South Korea
Ivan Laptev	Inria, France
Svetlana Lazebnik	University of Illinois at Urbana-Champaign, USA
Laura Leal-Taixé	Technical University of Munich, Germany
Erik Learned-Miller	University of Massachusetts, Amherst, USA
Kyoung Mu Lee	Seoul National University, South Korea
Bastian Leibe	RWTH Aachen University, Germany
Aleš Leonardis	University of Birmingham, UK
Vincent Lepetit	University of Bordeaux, France and Graz University of Technology, Austria
Fuxin Li	Oregon State University, USA
Dahua Lin	Chinese University of Hong Kong, SAR China
Jim Little	University of British Columbia, Canada
Ce Liu	Google, USA
Chen Change Loy	Nanyang Technological University, Singapore
Jiri Matas	Czech Technical University in Prague, Czechia

Yasuyuki Matsushita	Osaka University, Japan
Dimitris Metaxas	Rutgers University, USA
Greg Mori	Simon Fraser University, Canada
Vittorio Murino	Istituto Italiano di Tecnologia, Italy
Richard Newcombe	Oculus Research, USA
Minh Hoai Nguyen	Stony Brook University, USA
Sebastian Nowozin	Microsoft Research Cambridge, UK
Aude Oliva	MIT, USA
Bjorn Ommer	Heidelberg University, Germany
Tomas Pajdla	Czech Technical University in Prague, Czechia
Maja Pantic	Imperial College London and Samsung AI Research Centre Cambridge, UK
Caroline Pantofaru	Google, USA
Devi Parikh	Georgia Tech and Facebook AI Research, USA
Sylvain Paris	Adobe Research, USA
Vladimir Pavlovic	Rutgers University, USA
Marcello Pelillo	University of Venice, Italy
Patrick Pérez	Valeo, France
Robert Pless	George Washington University, USA
Thomas Pock	Graz University of Technology, Austria
Jean Ponce	Inria, France
Gerard Pons-Moll	MPII, Saarland Informatics Campus, Germany
Long Quan	Hong Kong University of Science and Technology, SAR China
Stefan Roth	TU Darmstadt, Germany
Carsten Rother	University of Heidelberg, Germany
Bryan Russell	Adobe Research, USA
Kate Saenko	Boston University, USA
Mathieu Salzmann	EPFL, Switzerland
Dimitris Samaras	Stony Brook University, USA
Yoichi Sato	University of Tokyo, Japan
Silvio Savarese	Stanford University, USA
Konrad Schindler	ETH Zurich, Switzerland
Cordelia Schmid	Inria, France and Google, France
Nicu Sebe	University of Trento, Italy
Fei Sha	University of Southern California, USA
Greg Shakhnarovich	TTI Chicago, USA
Jianbo Shi	University of Pennsylvania, USA
Abhinav Shrivastava	UMD and Google, USA
Yan Shuicheng	National University of Singapore, Singapore
Leonid Sigal	University of British Columbia, Canada
Josef Sivic	Czech Technical University in Prague, Czechia
Arnold Smeulders	University of Amsterdam, The Netherlands
Deqing Sun	NVIDIA, USA
Antonio Torralba	MIT, USA
Zhuowen Tu	University of California, San Diego, USA

Tinne Tuytelaars	KU Leuven, Belgium
Jasper Uijlings	Google, Switzerland
Joost van de Weijer	Computer Vision Center, Spain
Nuno Vasconcelos	University of California, San Diego, USA
Andrea Vedaldi	University of Oxford, UK
Olga Veksler	University of Western Ontario, Canada
Jakob Verbeek	Inria, France
Rene Vidal	Johns Hopkins University, USA
Daphna Weinshall	Hebrew University, Israel
Chris Williams	University of Edinburgh, UK
Lior Wolf	Tel Aviv University, Israel
Ming-Hsuan Yang	University of California at Merced, USA
Todd Zickler	Harvard University, USA
Andrew Zisserman	University of Oxford, UK

Technical Program Committee

Hassan Abu Alhaija	Peter Anderson	Arunava Banerjee
Radhakrishna Achanta	Juan Andrade-Cetto	Atsuhiko Banno
Hanno Ackermann	Mykhaylo Andriluka	Aayush Bansal
Ehsan Adeli	Anelia Angelova	Yingze Bao
Lourdes Agapito	Michel Antunes	Md Jawadul Bappy
Aishwarya Agrawal	Pablo Arbelaez	Pierre Baqué
Antonio Agudo	Vasileios Argyriou	Dániel Baráth
Eirikur Agustsson	Chetan Arora	Adrian Barbu
Karim Ahmed	Federica Arrigoni	Kobus Barnard
Byeongjoo Ahn	Vassilis Athitsos	Nick Barnes
Unaiza Ahsan	Mathieu Aubry	Francisco Barranco
Emre Akbaş	Shai Avidan	Adrien Bartoli
Eren Aksoy	Yannis Avrithis	E. Bayro-Corrochano
Yağız Aksoy	Samaneh Azadi	Paul Beardlsey
Alexandre Alahi	Hossein Azizpour	Vasileios Belagiannis
Jean-Baptiste Alayrac	Artem Babenko	Sean Bell
Samuel Albanie	Timur Bagautdinov	Ismail Ben
Cenek Albl	Andrew Bagdanov	Boulbaba Ben Amor
Saad Ali	Hessam Bagherinezhad	Gil Ben-Artzi
Rahaf Aljundi	Yuval Bahat	Ohad Ben-Shahar
Jose M. Alvarez	Min Bai	Abhijit Bendale
Humam Alwassel	Qinxun Bai	Rodrigo Benenson
Toshiyuki Amano	Song Bai	Fabian Benitez-Quiroz
Mitsuru Ambai	Xiang Bai	Fethallah Benmansour
Mohamed Amer	Peter Bajcsy	Ryad Benosman
Senjian An	Amr Bakry	Filippo Bergamasco
Cosmin Ancuti	Kavita Bala	David Bermudez

Jesus Bermudez-Cameo
Leonard Berrada
Gedas Bertasius
Ross Beveridge
Lucas Beyer
Bir Bhanu
S. Bhattacharya
Binod Bhattarai
Arnav Bhavsar
Simone Bianco
Adel Bibi
Pia Bideau
Josef Bigun
Arijit Biswas
Soma Biswas
Marten Bjoerkman
Volker Blanz
Vishnu Boddeti
Piotr Bojanowski
Terrance Boult
Yuri Boykov
Hakan Boyraz
Eric Brachmann
Samarth Brahmbhatt
Mathieu Bredif
Francois Bremond
Michael Brown
Luc Brun
Shyamal Buch
Pradeep Buddharaju
Aurelie Bugeau
Rudy Bunel
Xavier Burgos Artizzu
Darius Burschka
Andrei Bursuc
Zoya Bylinskii
Fabian Caba
Daniel Cabrini Hauagge
Cesar Cadena Lerma
Holger Caesar
Jianfei Cai
Junjie Cai
Zhaowei Cai
Simone Calderara
Neill Campbell
Octavia Camps

Xun Cao
Yanshuai Cao
Joao Carreira
Dan Casas
Daniel Castro
Jan Cech
M. Emre Celebi
Duygu Ceylan
Menglei Chai
Ayan Chakrabarti
Rudrasis Chakraborty
Shayok Chakraborty
Tat-Jen Cham
Antonin Chambolle
Antoni Chan
Sharat Chandran
Hyun Sung Chang
Ju Yong Chang
Xiaojun Chang
Soravit Changpinyo
Wei-Lun Chao
Yu-Wei Chao
Visesh Chari
Rizwan Chaudhry
Siddhartha Chaudhuri
Rama Chellappa
Chao Chen
Chen Chen
Cheng Chen
Chu-Song Chen
Guang Chen
Hsin-I Chen
Hwann-Tzong Chen
Kai Chen
Kan Chen
Kevin Chen
Liang-Chieh Chen
Lin Chen
Qifeng Chen
Ting Chen
Wei Chen
Xi Chen
Xilin Chen
Xinlei Chen
Yingcong Chen
Yixin Chen

Erkang Cheng
Jingchun Cheng
Ming-Ming Cheng
Wen-Huang Cheng
Yuan Cheng
Anoop Cherian
Liang-Tien Chia
Naoki Chiba
Shao-Yi Chien
Han-Pang Chiu
Wei-Chen Chiu
Nam Ik Cho
Sunghyun Cho
TaeEun Choe
Jongmoo Choi
Christopher Choy
Wen-Sheng Chu
Yung-Yu Chuang
Ondrej Chum
Joon Son Chung
Gökberk Cinbis
James Clark
Andrea Cohen
Forrester Cole
Toby Collins
John Collomosse
Camille Couprie
David Crandall
Marco Cristani
Canton Cristian
James Crowley
Yin Cui
Zhaopeng Cui
Bo Dai
Jifeng Dai
Qieyun Dai
Shengyang Dai
Yuchao Dai
Carlo Dal Mutto
Dima Damen
Zachary Daniels
Kostas Daniilidis
Donald Dansereau
Mohamed Daoudi
Abhishek Das
Samyak Datta

Achal Dave
Shalini De Mello
Teofilo deCampos
Joseph DeGol
Koichiro Deguchi
Alessio Del Bue
Stefanie Demirci
Jia Deng
Zhiwei Deng
Joachim Denzler
Konstantinos Derpanis
Aditya Deshpande
Alban Desmaison
Frédéric Devernay
Abhinav Dhall
Michel Dhome
Hamdi Dibeklioğlu
Mert Dikmen
Cosimo Distante
Ajay Divakaran
Mandar Dixit
Carl Doersch
Piotr Dollar
Bo Dong
Chao Dong
Huang Dong
Jian Dong
Jiangxin Dong
Weisheng Dong
Simon Donné
Gianfranco Doretto
Alexey Dosovitskiy
Matthijs Douze
Bruce Draper
Bertram Drost
Liang Du
Shichuan Du
Gregory Dudek
Zoran Duric
Pınar Duygulu
Hazım Ekenel
Tarek El-Gaaly
Ehsan Elhamifar
Mohamed Elhoseiny
Sabu Emmanuel
Ian Endres

Aykut Erdem
Erkut Erdem
Hugo Jair Escalante
Sergio Escalera
Victor Escorcia
Francisco Estrada
Davide Eynard
Bin Fan
Jialue Fan
Quanfu Fan
Chen Fang
Tian Fang
Yi Fang
Hany Farid
Giovanni Farinella
Ryan Farrell
Alireza Fathi
Christoph Feichtenhofer
Wenxin Feng
Martin Fergie
Cornelia Fermuller
Basura Fernando
Michael Firman
Bob Fisher
John Fisher
Mathew Fisher
Boris Flach
Matt Flagg
Francois Fleuret
David Fofi
Ruth Fong
Gian Luca Foresti
Per-Erik Forssén
David Fouhey
Katerina Fragkiadaki
Victor Fragoso
Jan-Michael Frahm
Jean-Sebastien Franco
Ohad Fried
Simone Frintrop
Huazhu Fu
Yun Fu
Olac Fuentes
Christopher Funk
Thomas Funkhouser
Brian Funt

Ryo Furukawa
Yasutaka Furukawa
Andrea Fusiello
Fatma Güney
Raghudeep Gadde
Silvano Galliani
Orazio Gallo
Chuang Gan
Bin-Bin Gao
Jin Gao
Junbin Gao
Ruohan Gao
Shenghua Gao
Animesh Garg
Ravi Garg
Erik Gartner
Simone Gasparin
Jochen Gast
Leon A. Gatys
Stratis Gavves
Liuhao Ge
Timnit Gebru
James Gee
Peter Gehler
Xin Geng
Guido Gerig
David Geronimo
Bernard Ghanem
Michael Gharbi
Golnaz Ghiasi
Spyros Gidaris
Andrew Gilbert
Rohit Girdhar
Ioannis Gkioulekas
Georgia Gkioxari
Guy Godin
Roland Goecke
Michael Goesele
Nuno Goncalves
Boqing Gong
Minglun Gong
Yunchao Gong
Abel Gonzalez-Garcia
Daniel Gordon
Paulo Gotardo
Stephen Gould

Venu Govindu
Helmut Grabner
Petr Gronat
Steve Gu
Josechu Guerrero
Anupam Guha
Jean-Yves Guillemaut
Alp Güler
Erhan Gündoğdu
Guodong Guo
Xinqing Guo
Ankush Gupta
Mohit Gupta
Saurabh Gupta
Tanmay Gupta
Abner Guzman Rivera
Timo Hackel
Sunil Hadap
Christian Haene
Ralf Haeusler
Levente Hajder
David Hall
Peter Hall
Stefan Haller
Ghassan Hamarneh
Fred Hamprecht
Onur Hamsici
Bohyung Han
Junwei Han
Xufeng Han
Yahong Han
Ankur Handa
Albert Haque
Tatsuya Harada
Mehrtash Harandi
Bharath Hariharan
Mahmudul Hasan
Tal Hassner
Kenji Hata
Soren Hauberg
Michal Havlena
Zeeshan Hayder
Junfeng He
Lei He
Varsha Hedau
Felix Heide

Wolfgang Heidrich
Janne Heikkila
Jared Heinly
Mattias Heinrich
Lisa Anne Hendricks
Dan Hendrycks
Stephane Herbin
Alexander Hermans
Luis Herranz
Aaron Hertzmann
Adrian Hilton
Michael Hirsch
Steven Hoi
Seunghoon Hong
Wei Hong
Anthony Hoogs
Radu Horaud
Yedid Hoshen
Omid Hosseini Jafari
Kuang-Jui Hsu
Winston Hsu
Yinlin Hu
Zhe Hu
Gang Hua
Chen Huang
De-An Huang
Dong Huang
Gary Huang
Heng Huang
Jia-Bin Huang
Qixing Huang
Rui Huang
Sheng Huang
Weilin Huang
Xiaolei Huang
Xinyu Huang
Zhiwu Huang
Tak-Wai Hui
Wei-Chih Hung
Junhwa Hur
Mohamed Hussein
Wonjun Hwang
Anders Hyden
Satoshi Ikehata
Nazlı Ikizler-Cinbis
Viorela Ila

Evren Imre
Eldar Insafutdinov
Go Irie
Hossam Isack
Ahmet Işcen
Daisuke Iwai
Hamid Izadinia
Nathan Jacobs
Suyog Jain
Varun Jampani
C. V. Jawahar
Dinesh Jayaraman
Sadeep Jayasumana
Laszlo Jeni
Hueihan Jhuang
Dinghuang Ji
Hui Ji
Qiang Ji
Fan Jia
Kui Jia
Xu Jia
Huaizu Jiang
Jiayan Jiang
Nianjuan Jiang
Tingting Jiang
Xiaoyi Jiang
Yu-Gang Jiang
Long Jin
Suo Jinli
Justin Johnson
Nebojsa Jojic
Michael Jones
Hanbyul Joo
Jungseock Joo
Ajjen Joshi
Amin Jourabloo
Frederic Jurie
Achuta Kadambi
Samuel Kadoury
Ioannis Kakadiaris
Zdenek Kalal
Yannis Kalantidis
Sinan Kalkan
Vicky Kalogeiton
Sunkavalli Kalyan
J.-K. Kamarainen

Martin Kampel
Kenichi Kanatani
Angjoo Kanazawa
Melih Kandemir
Sing Bing Kang
Zhuoliang Kang
Mohan Kankanhalli
Juho Kannala
Abhishek Kar
Amlan Kar
Svebor Karaman
Leonid Karlinsky
Zoltan Kato
Parneet Kaur
Hiroshi Kawasaki
Misha Kazhdan
Margret Keuper
Sameh Khamis
Naeemullah Khan
Salman Khan
Hadi Kiapour
Joe Kileel
Chanho Kim
Gunhee Kim
Hansung Kim
Junmo Kim
Junsik Kim
Kihwan Kim
Minyoung Kim
Tae Hyun Kim
Tae-Kyun Kim
Akisato Kimura
Zsolt Kira
Alexander Kirillov
Kris Kitani
Maria Klodt
Patrick Knöbelreiter
Jan Knopp
Reinhard Koch
Alexander Kolesnikov
Chen Kong
Naejin Kong
Shu Kong
Piotr Koniusz
Simon Korman
Andreas Koschan

Dimitrios Kosmopoulos
Satwik Kottur
Balazs Kovacs
Adarsh Kowdle
Mike Krainin
Gregory Kramida
Ranjay Krishna
Ravi Krishnan
Matej Kristan
Pavel Krsek
Volker Krueger
Alexander Krull
Hilde Kuehne
Andreas Kuhn
Arjan Kuijper
Zuzana Kukelova
Kuldeep Kulkarni
Shiro Kumano
Avinash Kumar
Vijay Kumar
Abhijit Kundu
Sebastian Kurtek
Junseok Kwon
Jan Kybic
Alexander Ladikos
Shang-Hong Lai
Wei-Sheng Lai
Jean-Francois Lalonde
John Lambert
Zhenzhong Lan
Charis Lanaras
Oswald Lanz
Dong Lao
Longin Jan Latecki
Justin Lazarow
Huu Le
Chen-Yu Lee
Gim Hee Lee
Honglak Lee
Hsin-Ying Lee
Joon-Young Lee
Seungyong Lee
Stefan Lee
Yong Jae Lee
Zhen Lei
Ido Leichter

Victor Lempitsky
Spyridon Leonardos
Marius Leordeanu
Matt Leotta
Thomas Leung
Stefan Leutenegger
Gil Levi
Aviad Levis
Jose Lezama
Ang Li
Dingzeyu Li
Dong Li
Haoxiang Li
Hongdong Li
Hongsheng Li
Hongyang Li
Jianguo Li
Kai Li
Ruiyu Li
Wei Li
Wen Li
Xi Li
Xiaoxiao Li
Xin Li
Xirong Li
Xuelong Li
Xueting Li
Yeqing Li
Yijun Li
Yin Li
Yingwei Li
Yining Li
Yongjie Li
Yu-Feng Li
Zechao Li
Zhengqi Li
Zhenyang Li
Zhizhong Li
Xiaodan Liang
Renjie Liao
Zicheng Liao
Bee Lim
Jongwoo Lim
Joseph Lim
Ser-Nam Lim
Chen-Hsuan Lin

Shih-Yao Lin
Tsung-Yi Lin
Weiyao Lin
Yen-Yu Lin
Haibin Ling
Or Litany
Roee Litman
Anan Liu
Changsong Liu
Chen Liu
Ding Liu
Dong Liu
Feng Liu
Guangcan Liu
Luoqi Liu
Miaomiao Liu
Nian Liu
Risheng Liu
Shu Liu
Shuaicheng Liu
Sifei Liu
Tyng-Luh Liu
Wanquan Liu
Weiwei Liu
Xialei Liu
Xiaoming Liu
Yebin Liu
Yiming Liu
Ziwei Liu
Zongyi Liu
Liliana Lo Presti
Edgar Lobaton
Chengjiang Long
Mingsheng Long
Roberto Lopez-Sastre
Amy Loufti
Brian Lovell
Canyi Lu
Cewu Lu
Feng Lu
Huchuan Lu
Jiajun Lu
Jiasen Lu
Jiwen Lu
Yang Lu
Yujuan Lu

Simon Lucey
Jian-Hao Luo
Jiebo Luo
Pablo Márquez-Neila
Matthias Müller
Chao Ma
Chih-Yao Ma
Lin Ma
Shugao Ma
Wei-Chiu Ma
Zhanyu Ma
Oisin Mac Aodha
Will Maddern
Ludovic Magerand
Marcus Magnor
Vijay Mahadevan
Mohammad Mahoor
Michael Maire
Subhransu Maji
Ameesh Makadia
Atsuto Maki
Yasushi Makihara
Mateusz Malinowski
Tomasz Malisiewicz
Arun Mallya
Roberto Manduchi
Junhua Mao
Dmitrii Marin
Joe Marino
Kenneth Marino
Elisabeta Marinoiu
Ricardo Martin
Aleix Martinez
Julieta Martinez
Aaron Maschinot
Jonathan Masci
Bogdan Matei
Diana Mateus
Stefan Mathe
Kevin Matzen
Bruce Maxwell
Steve Maybank
Walterio Mayol-Cuevas
Mason McGill
Stephen Mckenna
Roey Mechrez

Christopher Mei
Heydi Mendez-Vazquez
Deyu Meng
Thomas Mensink
Bjoern Menze
Domingo Mery
Qiguang Miao
Tomer Michaeli
Antoine Miech
Ondrej Miksik
Anton Milan
Gregor Miller
Cai Minjie
Majid Mirmehdi
Ishan Misra
Niloy Mitra
Anurag Mittal
Nirbhay Modhe
Davide Modolo
Pritish Mohapatra
Pascal Monasse
Mathew Monfort
Taesup Moon
Sandino Morales
Vlad Morariu
Philippos Mordohai
Francesc Moreno
Henrique Morimitsu
Yael Moses
Ben-Ezra Moshe
Roozbeh Mottaghi
Yadong Mu
Lopamudra Mukherjee
Mario Munich
Ana Murillo
Damien Muselet
Armin Mustafa
Siva Karthik Mustikovela
Moin Nabi
Sobhan Naderi
Hajime Nagahara
Varun Nagaraja
Tushar Nagarajan
Arsha Nagrani
Nikhil Naik
Atsushi Nakazawa

Gernot Riegler
Hayko Riemenschneider
Tammy Riklin Raviv
Ergys Ristani
Tobias Ritschel
Mariano Rivera
Samuel Rivera
Antonio Robles-Kelly
Ignacio Rocco
Jason Rock
Emanuele Rodola
Mikel Rodriguez
Gregory Rogez
Marcus Rohrbach
Gemma Roig
Javier Romero
Olaf Ronneberger
Amir Rosenfeld
Bodo Rosenhahn
Guy Rosman
Arun Ross
Samuel Rota Bulò
Peter Roth
Constantin Rothkopf
Sebastien Roy
Amit Roy-Chowdhury
Ognjen Rudovic
Adria Ruiz
Javier Ruiz-del-Solar
Christian Rupprecht
Olga Russakovsky
Chris Russell
Alexandre Sablayrolles
Fereshteh Sadeghi
Ryusuke Sagawa
Hideo Saito
Elham Sakhaee
Albert Ali Salah
Conrad Sanderson
Koppal Sanjeev
Aswin Sankaranarayanan
Elham Saraee
Jason Saragih
Sudeep Sarkar
Imari Sato
Shin'ichi Satoh

Torsten Sattler
Bogdan Savchynskyy
Johannes Schönberger
Hanno Scharr
Walter Scheirer
Bernt Schiele
Frank Schmidt
Tanner Schmidt
Dirk Schnieders
Samuel Schulter
William Schwartz
Alexander Schwing
Ozan Sener
Soumyadip Sengupta
Laura Sevilla-Lara
Mubarak Shah
Shishir Shah
Fahad Shahbaz Khan
Amir Shahroudy
Jing Shao
Xiaowei Shao
Roman Shapovalov
Nataliya Shapovalova
Ali Sharif Razavian
Gaurav Sharma
Mohit Sharma
Pramod Sharma
Viktoriia Sharmanska
Eli Shechtman
Mark Sheinin
Evan Shelhamer
Chunhua Shen
Li Shen
Wei Shen
Xiaohui Shen
Xiaoyong Shen
Ziyi Shen
Lu Sheng
Baoguang Shi
Boxin Shi
Kevin Shih
Hyunjung Shim
Ilan Shimshoni
Young Min Shin
Koichi Shinoda
Matthew Shreve

Tianmin Shu
Zhixin Shu
Kaleem Siddiqi
Gunnar Sigurdsson
Nathan Silberman
Tomas Simon
Abhishek Singh
Gautam Singh
Maneesh Singh
Praveer Singh
Richa Singh
Saurabh Singh
Sudipta Sinha
Vladimir Smutny
Noah Snavely
Cees Snoek
Kihyuk Sohn
Eric Sommerlade
Sanghyun Son
Bi Song
Shiyu Song
Shuran Song
Xuan Song
Yale Song
Yang Song
Yibing Song
Lorenzo Sorgi
Humberto Sossa
Pratul Srinivasan
Michael Stark
Bjorn Stenger
Rainer Stiefelhagen
Joerg Stueckler
Jan Stuehmer
Hang Su
Hao Su
Shuochen Su
R. Subramanian
Yusuke Sugano
Akihiro Sugimoto
Baochen Sun
Chen Sun
Jian Sun
Jin Sun
Lin Sun
Min Sun

Qing Sun
Zhaohui Sun
David Suter
Eran Swears
Raza Syed Hussain
T. Syeda-Mahmood
Christian Szegedy
Duy-Nguyen Ta
Tolga Taşdizen
Hemant Tagare
Yuichi Taguchi
Ying Tai
Yu-Wing Tai
Jun Takamatsu
Hugues Talbot
Toru Tamak
Robert Tamburo
Chaowei Tan
Meng Tang
Peng Tang
Siyu Tang
Wei Tang
Junli Tao
Ran Tao
Xin Tao
Makarand Tapaswi
Jean-Philippe Tarel
Maxim Tatarchenko
Bugra Tekin
Demetri Terzopoulos
Christian Theobalt
Diego Thomas
Rajat Thomas
Qi Tian
Xinmei Tian
YingLi Tian
Yonghong Tian
Yonglong Tian
Joseph Tighe
Radu Timofte
Massimo Tistarelli
Sinisa Todorovic
Pavel Tokmakov
Giorgos Tolias
Federico Tombari
Tatiana Tommasi

Chetan Tonde
Xin Tong
Akihiko Torii
Andrea Torsello
Florian Trammer
Du Tran
Quoc-Huy Tran
Rudolph Triebel
Alejandro Troccoli
Leonardo Trujillo
Tomasz Trzcinski
Sam Tsai
Yi-Hsuan Tsai
Hung-Yu Tseng
Vagia Tsiminaki
Aggeliki Tsoli
Wei-Chih Tu
Shubham Tulsiani
Fred Tung
Tony Tung
Matt Turek
Oncel Tuzel
Georgios Tzimiropoulos
Ilkay Ulusoy
Osman Ulusoy
Dmitry Ulyanov
Paul Upchurch
Ben Usman
Evgeniya Ustinova
Himanshu Vajaria
Alexander Vakhitov
Jack Valmadre
Ernest Valveny
Jan van Gemert
Grant Van Horn
Jagannadan Varadarajan
Gul Varol
Sebastiano Vascon
Francisco Vasconcelos
Mayank Vatsa
Javier Vazquez-Corral
Ramakrishna Vedantam
Ashok Veeraraghavan
Andreas Veit
Raviteja Vemulapalli
Jonathan Ventura

Matthias Vestner
Minh Vo
Christoph Vogel
Michele Volpi
Carl Vondrick
Sven Wachsmuth
Toshikazu Wada
Michael Waechter
Catherine Wah
Jacob Walker
Jun Wan
Boyu Wang
Chen Wang
Chunyu Wang
De Wang
Fang Wang
Hongxing Wang
Hua Wang
Jiang Wang
Jingdong Wang
Jinglu Wang
Jue Wang
Le Wang
Lei Wang
Lezi Wang
Liang Wang
Lichao Wang
Lijun Wang
Limin Wang
Liwei Wang
Naiyan Wang
Oliver Wang
Qi Wang
Ruiping Wang
Shenlong Wang
Shu Wang
Song Wang
Tao Wang
Xiaofang Wang
Xiaolong Wang
Xinchao Wang
Xinggang Wang
Xintao Wang
Yang Wang
Yu-Chiang Frank Wang
Yu-Xiong Wang

Zhaowen Wang
Zhe Wang
Anne Wannenwetsch
Simon Warfield
Scott Wehrwein
Donglai Wei
Ping Wei
Shih-En Wei
Xiu-Shen Wei
Yichen Wei
Xie Weidi
Philippe Weinzaepfel
Longyin Wen
Eric Wengrowski
Tomas Werner
Michael Wilber
Rick Wildes
Olivia Wiles
Kyle Wilson
David Wipf
Kwan-Yee Wong
Daniel Worrall
John Wright
Baoyuan Wu
Chao-Yuan Wu
Jiajun Wu
Jianxin Wu
Tianfu Wu
Xiaodong Wu
Xiaohe Wu
Xinxiao Wu
Yang Wu
Yi Wu
Ying Wu
Yuxin Wu
Zheng Wu
Stefanie Wuhrer
Yin Xia
Tao Xiang
Yu Xiang
Lei Xiao
Tong Xiao
Yang Xiao
Cihang Xie
Dan Xie
Jianwen Xie

Jin Xie
Lingxi Xie
Pengtao Xie
Saining Xie
Wenxuan Xie
Yuchen Xie
Bo Xin
Junliang Xing
Peng Xingchao
Bo Xiong
Fei Xiong
Xuehan Xiong
Yuanjun Xiong
Chenliang Xu
Danfei Xu
Huijuan Xu
Jia Xu
Weipeng Xu
Xiangyu Xu
Yan Xu
Yuanlu Xu
Jia Xue
Tianfan Xue
Erdem Yörük
Abhay Yadav
Deshraj Yadav
Payman Yadollahpour
Yasushi Yagi
Toshihiko Yamasaki
Fei Yan
Hang Yan
Junchi Yan
Junjie Yan
Sijie Yan
Keiji Yanai
Bin Yang
Chih-Yuan Yang
Dong Yang
Herb Yang
Jianchao Yang
Jianwei Yang
Jiaolong Yang
Jie Yang
Jimei Yang
Jufeng Yang
Linjie Yang

Michael Ying Yang
Ming Yang
Ruiduo Yang
Ruigang Yang
Shuo Yang
Wei Yang
Xiaodong Yang
Yanchao Yang
Yi Yang
Angela Yao
Bangpeng Yao
Cong Yao
Jian Yao
Ting Yao
Julian Yarkony
Mark Yatskar
Jinwei Ye
Mao Ye
Mei-Chen Yeh
Raymond Yeh
Serena Yeung
Kwang Moo Yi
Shuai Yi
Alper Yılmaz
Lijun Yin
Xi Yin
Zhaozheng Yin
Xianghua Ying
Ryo Yonetani
Donghyun Yoo
Ju Hong Yoon
Kuk-Jin Yoon
Chong You
Shaodi You
Aron Yu
Fisher Yu
Gang Yu
Jingyi Yu
Ke Yu
Licheng Yu
Pei Yu
Qian Yu
Rong Yu
Shoou-I Yu
Stella Yu
Xiang Yu

Yang Yu
Zhiding Yu
Ganzhao Yuan
Jing Yuan
Junsong Yuan
Lu Yuan
Stefanos Zafeiriou
Sergey Zagoruyko
Amir Zamir
K. Zampogiannis
Andrei Zanfir
Mihai Zanfir
Pablo Zegers
Eyasu Zemene
Andy Zeng
Xingyu Zeng
Yun Zeng
De-Chuan Zhan
Cheng Zhang
Dong Zhang
Guofeng Zhang
Han Zhang
Hang Zhang
Hanwang Zhang
Jian Zhang
Jianguo Zhang
Jianming Zhang
Jiawei Zhang
Junping Zhang
Lei Zhang
Linguang Zhang
Ning Zhang
Qing Zhang

Quanshi Zhang
Richard Zhang
Runze Zhang
Shanshan Zhang
Shiliang Zhang
Shu Zhang
Ting Zhang
Xiangyu Zhang
Xiaofan Zhang
Xu Zhang
Yimin Zhang
Yinda Zhang
Yongqiang Zhang
Yuting Zhang
Zhanpeng Zhang
Ziyu Zhang
Bin Zhao
Chen Zhao
Hang Zhao
Hengshuang Zhao
Qijun Zhao
Rui Zhao
Yue Zhao
Enliang Zheng
Liang Zheng
Stephan Zheng
Wei-Shi Zheng
Wenming Zheng
Yin Zheng
Yinqiang Zheng
Yuanjie Zheng
Guangyu Zhong
Bolei Zhou

Guang-Tong Zhou
Huiyu Zhou
Jiahuan Zhou
S. Kevin Zhou
Tinghui Zhou
Wengang Zhou
Xiaowei Zhou
Xingyi Zhou
Yin Zhou
Zihan Zhou
Fan Zhu
Guangming Zhu
Ji Zhu
Jiejie Zhu
Jun-Yan Zhu
Shizhan Zhu
Siyu Zhu
Xiangxin Zhu
Xiatian Zhu
Yan Zhu
Yingying Zhu
Yixin Zhu
Yuke Zhu
Zhenyao Zhu
Liansheng Zhuang
Zeeshan Zia
Karel Zimmermann
Daniel Zoran
Danping Zou
Qi Zou
Silvia Zuffi
Wangmeng Zuo
Xinxin Zuo

Contents – Part X

Human Sensing

Poster Session

Bayesian Semantic Instance Segmentation in Open Set World

Trung Pham$^{(\boxtimes)}$, B. G. Vijay Kumar, Thanh-Toan Do, Gustavo Carneiro, and Ian Reid

School of Computer Science, The University of Adelaide, Adelaide, Australia
{trung.pham,vijay.kumar,thanh-toan.do,gustavo.carneiro,
ian.reid}@adelaide.edu.au

Abstract. This paper addresses the semantic instance segmentation task in the open-set conditions, where input images can contain known and unknown object classes. The training process of existing semantic instance segmentation methods requires annotation masks for all object instances, which is expensive to acquire or even infeasible in some realistic scenarios, where the number of categories may increase boundlessly. In this paper, we present a novel open-set semantic instance segmentation approach capable of segmenting all known and unknown object classes in images, based on the output of an object detector trained on known object classes. We formulate the problem using a Bayesian framework, where the posterior distribution is approximated with a simulated annealing optimization equipped with an efficient image partition sampler. We show empirically that our method is competitive with state-of-the-art supervised methods on known classes, but also performs well on unknown classes when compared with unsupervised methods.

Keywords: Instance segmentation · Open-set conditions

1 Introduction

In recent years, scene understanding driven by multi-class semantic segmentation [10,13,16], object detection [19] or instance segmentation [7] has progressed significantly thanks to the power of deep learning. However, a major limitation of these deep learning based approaches is that they only work for a set of known object classes that are used during supervised training. In contrast, autonomous systems often operate under *open-set* conditions [23] in many application domains, i.e. they will inevitably encounter object classes that were not part of the training dataset. For instance, state-of-the-art methods such as Mask-RCNN [7] and YOLO9000 [19] fail to detect such unknown objects. This behavior is detrimental to the performance of autonomous systems that would ideally need to understand scenes holistically, i.e., reasoning about all objects that appear in the scene and their complex relations.

V. Ferrari et al. (Eds.): ECCV 2018, LNCS 11214, pp. 3–18, 2018.
https://doi.org/10.1007/978-3-030-01249-6_1

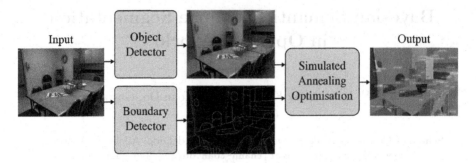

Fig. 1. Overview of semantic instance segmentation in a open-set environment. Our method segments all image regions irrespective of whether they have been detected or undetected, or are from a known or unknown class

Semantic instance segmentation based scene understanding has recently attracted the interest of the field [3,25]. The ultimate goal is to decompose the input image into individual objects (e.g., car, human, chair) and stuffs (e.g., road, floor) along with their semantic labels. Compared with semantic segmentation and object detection, the accuracy and robustness of semantic instance segmentation lags significantly. Recent efforts (e.g., [7]) follow a *detect-and-segment* approach—first detect objects in an image, then generate a segmentation mask for each instance. Such an approach might label a pixel with multiple object instances, and completely fails to segment unknown objects, and even known, but miss-detected objects. More importantly, current instance segmentation methods require annotation masks for all object instances during training, which is too expensive to acquire for new classes. A much cheaper alternative consists of the bounding box annotation of new classes (a mere two mouse clicks, compared to the multiple clicks required for annotating segmentation masks).

In this paper, we propose a novel Bayesian semantic instance segmentation approach that is capable of segmenting all object instances irrespective of whether they have been detected or undetected and are from a known or an unknown training class. Such a capability is vitally useful for many vision-based robotic systems. Our proposed approach generates a global pixelwise image segmentation conditioned on a set of detections of known object classes (in terms of either bounding boxes or masks) instead of generating a segmentation mask for each detection (e.g., [7]). The segmentation produced by our approach not only keeps the benefits of the ability to segment known objects, but also retains the generality of an approach that can handle unknown objects via perceptual grouping. The outcome of our algorithm is a set of regions which are perceptually grouped and are each associated either to a known (object) detection or an unknown object class. To best of our knowledge, such a segmentation output has never been achieved before.

We formulate the instance segmentation problem using a Bayesian framework, where the likelihood is measured using image boundaries, a geometric bounding box model for pixel locations and optionally a mask model. These models compete with each other to explain different image regions. Intuitively, the boundary model explains unknown regions while bounding box and mask models describe regions where known objects are detected. The prior model simply penalizes the number of regions and enforces object compactness.

Nonetheless, finding the segmentation that maximizes the posterior distribution over a very large image partition space is non-trivial. Gibbs sampling [9] could be employed but it might take too long to converge. One of the main contributions of this work is an efficient image partition sampler that quickly generates high-quality segmentation proposals. Our image partition sampler is based on a boundary-driven region hierarchy, where regions of the hierarchy are likely representations of object instances. The boundary is estimated using a deep neural network [12]. To sample a new image partition, we simply select one region of the hierarchy, and "paste" it to the current segmentation. This operation will automatically realize either the split, merge or split-and-merge move between different segmentations depending on the selected region. Finally, the image partitioner is equipped with a Simulated Annealing optimization [28] to approximate the optimal segmentation.

We evaluate the effectiveness of our open-set instance segmentation approach on several datasets including indoor NYU [24] and general COCO [11]. Experimental results confirm that our segmentation method, with only bounding box supervision, is competitive with the state-of-the-art supervised instance segmentation methods (e.g., [7,8]) when tested on known object classes, while it is able to segment miss-detected and unknown objects. Our segmentation approach also outperforms other unsupervised segmentation methods when tested on unknown classes. Figure 1 demonstrates an overview and an example outcome of our segmentation method.

2   Related Work

Supervised Instance Segmentation: State-of-the-art supervised instance segmentation methods (e.g., [4,7,29]) follow a detect-and-segment approach— first detect objects in an image, then generate a segmentation mask for each instance. For example, the Mask-RCNN method [7] extends the Faster-RCNN [21] object detection network by adding another semantic segmentation branch for predicting a segmentation mask for each detected instance. Earlier methods [17,18] are based on segment proposals. For instance, DeepMask [17] and Sharp-Mask [18] learn to generate segment proposals which are then classified into semantic categories using Fast-RCNN. In contrast, the FCIS method [29] jointly predicts, for each location in the image, an object class, a bounding box and a segmentation mask. The methods in [20,22] employ Recurrent Neural Networks (RNN) to sequentially predict an object binary mask at each step.

Another group of supervised instance segmentation methods is based on clustering. In [5], the idea is first computing the likelihood that two pixels belong to the same object (using a deep neural network), then use these likelihoods to segment the image into object instances. Instead of predicting similarities between pixels, the method in [2] predicts a energy value for each pixel, the energy surface is then used to partition the image into object instances using the watershed transform algorithm.

The common drawback of existing instance segmentation methods is that they require a strong supervisory signal, consisting of the annotation masks of the known objects that are used during training. In contrast, our Bayesian instance segmentation approach does not necessarily require such object annotation masks, while being capable of segmenting all object instances irrespective of whether they have been detected or not and are from a known or unknown class.

Unsupervised Segmentation: In contrast to learning based segmentation, unsupervised segmentation methods [6,15,26] are able to discover unknown objects without the strong supervisory training signal mentioned above. These methods, however, often make strong assumptions about visual objects (e.g., they tend to have similar color, texture and share strong edges) and consequently rely on low-level image cues such as color, depth, texture and edges for segmentation. As a result, their results tend to be relatively inaccurate. In contrast, our segmentation approach combines the best of both worlds using a unified formulation. In particular, our method exploits the prior object locations (for example given by an object detector) to improve the overall image segmentation. At the same time, our method does not require expensive segmentation masks of all object instances for training.

3   Open-Set Semantic Instance Segmentation

Let $\mathbf{I} : \Omega \rightarrow \mathbb{R}$ be an input image defined on a discrete pixel grid $\Omega = \{v_1, v_2, \dots\}$, i.e., $\mathbf{I}_v$ is the color or intensity at pixel v. The goal of semantic instance segmentation is to decompose the image $\mathbf{I}_\Omega$ into individual object instance regions (e.g., chair, monitor) and stuff regions (e.g., floor, ceiling) along with their semantic labels. In particular, one seeks a partition of the image into k *non-overlap* regions

$$\cup_{i=1}^k R_i = \Omega, \quad R_i \cap R_j = \emptyset, \; \forall i \neq j, \tag{1}$$

and the assignment of each region $R \in \Omega$ to a semantic label l_R. Unlike the semantic segmentation task, here a region should not contain more than one object instance of the same class. A region, however, may not be contiguous since occlusions can break regions into disconnected segments.

Recently, the supervised *detect-and-segment* approach has become increasingly popular due to its simplicity. First, a deep-learning based object detector is applied to the input image to generate m detections in terms of bounding boxes $\mathcal{D}$. Then, a semantic segmentation network is applied to each bounding box to generate a segmentation mask for each instance, resulting in m regions $\{R_1, R_2, \dots, R_m\}$. However, it is clear that the condition in (1) is not necessarily satisfied because

$$\cup_{i=1}^m R_i \subseteq \Omega, \quad R_i \cap R_j = \emptyset, \; \neg\forall i \neq j. \tag{2}$$

This means that not all pixels in the image are segmented and two segmentation masks can overlap. While the second problem can be resolved using a pixel voting mechanism, the first problem is more challenging to be addressed. In *open-set* world, an image might capture objects that are unknown to the detector, so pixels belonging to these unknown object instances will not be labelled by this *detect-and-segment* approach. Miss-detected objects are not segmented either.

Ideally, one needs a model that is able to segment all individual objects (and "stuff") in an image regardless of whether they have been detected or not. In other words, all known and unknown object instances should be segmented. However, unknown and miss-detected objects will be assigned an "unknown" label.

Toward that goal, in this work, we propose a segmentation model that performs image segmentation globally (i.e., guaranteeing the condition $\cup_{i=1}^{k} R_i = \Omega$) so that each R_i is a coherent region. The segmentation process also optimally assigns labels to these regions using the detection set $\mathcal{D}$. In the next section, we discuss our Bayesian formulation to achieve this goal.

4   Bayesian Formulation

Similar to the unsupervised Bayesian image segmentation formulation in [27], our image segmentation solution S has the following structure:

$$S = ((R_1, t_1, \theta_1), (R_2, t_2, \theta_2), \ldots, (R_k, t_k, \theta_k)), \tag{3}$$

where each region R_i is "explained" by a model type t_i with parameters θ_i. More precise definitions of t_i and θ_i will be given below. The number of regions k is also unknown. In a Bayesian framework, the quality of a segmentation S is measured as the density of a posterior distribution:

$$p(S|\mathbf{I}) \propto p(\mathbf{I}|S)p(S) \quad S \in \mathcal{S}, \tag{4}$$

where $p(\mathbf{I}|S)$ is the likelihood and $p(S)$ is the prior, and $\mathcal{S}$ is the solution space. In the following, we will discuss the likelihood and prior terms used in our work.

4.1   The Likelihood Models

We assume that object regions in the image are mutually independent, forming the following likelihood term:

$$p(\mathbf{I}|S) = \prod_{i=1}^{k} p(\mathbf{I}_{R_i}|t_i, \theta_i). \tag{5}$$

The challenge is to define a set of robust image models that explain complex visual patterns of object classes. The standard machine learning approach is to learn an image model for each object category using training images that have been manually annotated (i.e., segmented). Unfortunately, in open-set problems, as the number of object categories increases boundlessly, manually annotating training data for all possible object classes becomes infeasible.

In this work, we consider three types of image models to explain image regions: boundary/contour model ($\mathcal{C}$), bounding box model ($\mathcal{B}$), and mask model ($\mathcal{M}$) i.e., $t \in \{\mathcal{C}, \mathcal{B}, \mathcal{M}\}$. We use the boundary to describe unknown regions. More complicated models such as Gaussian mixture could also be used, but they have higher computational cost. The bounding box and mask models are used for known objects.

Boundary/Contour Model ($\mathcal{C}$). Objects in the image are often isolated by their contours. Assume that we have a method (e.g., COB [12]) that is able to estimate a contour probability map from the image. Given a region R, we can define its external boundary score $c_{ex}(R)$ as the lowest probability on the boundary, whereas its internal boundary score $c_{in}(R)$ is highest probability among internal pixels. The likelihood of the region R being an object is defined as:

$$p(\mathbf{I}_R | c_{ex}(R), c_{in}(R)) \propto \left[\exp\left(-\frac{|c_{ex}(R) - 1|^2}{\sigma_{ex}^2} \right) \times \exp\left(-\frac{|c_{in}(R) - 0|^2}{\sigma_{in}^2} \right) \right]^{|R|} \tag{6}$$

where σ_{ex} and σ_{in} are standard deviation parameters. According to (6), a region with strong external boundary (≈ 1) and weak internal boundary (≈ 0) is more likely to represent an object. We used $\sigma_{in} = 0.4$ and $\sigma_{ex} = 0.6$.

Bounding Box Model ($\mathcal{B}$). Given an object detection $\mathbf{d}$ represented by a bounding box $\mathbf{b} = [c_x, c_y, w, h]$, object class c, and detection score s, the likelihood of a region R being from the object $\mathbf{d}$ is:

$$p(\mathbf{I}_R | \mathbf{b}) \propto \mathrm{IoU}(\mathbf{b}_R, \mathbf{b}) \times s \times \prod_{v \in R} \exp\left(-\frac{|v_x - c_x|^2}{\sigma_w^2} \right) \exp\left(-\frac{|v_y - c_y|^2}{\sigma_h^2} \right) \tag{7}$$

where $\mathbf{b}_R$ is the minimum bounding box covering the region R, IoU(.) computes the intersection-over-union between two bounding boxes, $[v_x, v_y]$ is the location of pixel v in the image space. σ_w and σ_h, standard deviations from the center of the bounding box, are functions of bounding box width w and height h respectively. To avoid bigger bounding boxes with higher detection scores taking all the pixels, we encourage smaller bounding boxes by setting $\sigma_w = w^\alpha$ and $\sigma_h = h^\alpha$, where α is a constant smaller than 1. In our experiments, we set $\alpha = 0.8$.

Mask Model ($\mathcal{M}$). Similarly, given an object detection $\mathbf{d}$ represented by a segmentation mask $\mathbf{m}$, object class c, and detection score s, the likelihood of a region R being from the object $\mathbf{d}$ is:

$$p(\mathbf{I}_R | \mathbf{m}) \propto [\mathrm{IoU}(R, \mathbf{m}) \times s]^{|R|}, \tag{8}$$

where IoU() computes the intersection-over-union between two regions. Note that the mask model is optional in our framework.

4.2   The Prior Model

Our prior segmentation model is defined as:

$$p(S) \propto \exp(-\gamma k) \times \prod_{i=1}^{k} \exp\left(-|R_i|^{0.9}\right) \times \exp\left(-\rho(R_i)\right), \tag{9}$$

where k is the number of regions, and γ is a constant parameter. In (9), the first term $\exp(-\gamma k)$ penalizes the number of regions k, and the second term $\exp(-|R_i|^{0.9})$ encourages large regions. The function $\rho(R_i)$, calculating the ratio of the total number of pixels in the region R and the area of its convex hull, encourages compact regions. In our experiments, we set $\gamma = 100$.

5   MAP Inference Using Simulated Annealing

Having defined the model for the semantic instance segmentation problem, the next challenge is to quickly find an optimal segmentation S^* that maximizes the posterior probability over the solution space S

$$S^* = \underset{S \in S}{\operatorname{argmax}}\, p(S|\mathbf{I}), \tag{10}$$

or analogously minimizing the energy $E(S, \mathbf{I}) = -\log(p(S|\mathbf{I}))$. The segmentation S defined in (3) can be decomposed as $S = (k, \pi_k, (t_1, \theta_1), (t_2, \theta_2), \ldots, (t_k, \theta_k))$, where $\pi_k = (R_1, R_2, \ldots, R_k)$ is a partition of the image domain Ω into exactly k non-overlap regions. Given a partition π_k, it is easy to compute the optimal t_i and θ_i for each region $R_i \in \pi_k$ by comparing the likelihoods of R_i given different image models. However, the more difficult part is the estimation of the partition π_k. Given an image domain Ω, we can partition it into a minimum of 1 region and maximum of $|\Omega|$ regions. Let ω_{π_k} be the set of all possible partitions π_k of the image into k regions, then the full partition space is:

$$\mathcal{P} = \cup_{k=1}^{|\Omega|} \omega_{\pi_k}. \tag{11}$$

It is clearly infeasible to examine all possible partitions π_k with different values of k. We mitigate this problem by resorting to the Simulated Annealing (SA) optimization approach [28] to approximate the global optimum of the energy function $E(S, \mathbf{I})$.

5.1   Simulated Annealing

Algorithm 1 details our simulated annealing approach to minimizing the energy function $E(S, \mathbf{I}) = -\log(p(S|\mathbf{I}))$. Our algorithm performs a series of "moves" between image partitions $(\pi_k \rightarrow \pi_{k'})$ of different k to explore the complex partition space $\mathcal{P}$, defined in (11). The model parameters (t_i, θ_i) for each region R_i are computed deterministically at each step. A proposed segmentation is accepted probabilistically in order to avoid local minima.

Algorithm 1. Simulated Annealing for Open-set Bayesian Instance Segmentation

---

Input: A set of detections (bounding boxes or masks), initial segmentation S, $E(S, \mathbf{I})$, and temperature T.

Output: Optimal segmentation S^*.

1: $S^* = S$.

2: Sample a neighbor partition $\pi_{k'}$ near the last partition π_k.

3: Update parameters (t_i, θ_i) $i = 1, 2, \ldots, k'$.

4: Create a new solution $S = (k', \pi_{k'}, (t_1, \theta_1), \ldots, (t_{k'}, \theta_{k'}))$.

5: Compute $E(S, \mathbf{I})$

6: With probability $\exp\left(\frac{E(S^*, \mathbf{I}) - E(S, \mathbf{I})}{T}\right)$, $S^* = S$.

7: $T = 0.99T$ and repeat from Step 2 until the stopping criteria is true.

A crucial component of Algorithm 1 is the sampling of new partition $\pi_{k'}$ near by the current partition π_k (Line 2). The sooner good partitions are sampled, the faster Algorithm 1 reaches the optimal S^*. In Sect. 5.2, we propose an efficient partition sampling method based on a region hierarchy.

5.2 Efficient Partition Sampling

The key component of our Simulated Annealing based instance segmentation approach is an efficient image partition generator based on a boundary-driven region hierarchy.

Boundary-Driven Region Hierarchy. A region hierarchy is a multi-scale representation of an image, where regions are groups of pixels with similar characteristics (i.e., colors, textures). Similar regions at lower levels are iteratively merged into bigger regions at higher levels. A region hierarchy can be efficiently represented using a single Ultrametric Contour Map (UCM) [1]. A common way to construct an image region hierarchy is based on image boundaries, which can be either estimated using local features such as colors, or predicted using deep convolutional networks (e.g., [12]). In this work, we use the COB network proposed in [12] for the object boundary estimation due to its superior performance compared to other methods.

Let $\mathcal{R}$ denote the region hierarchy (tree). One important property of $\mathcal{R}$ is that one can generate valid image partitions by either selecting various levels of the tree or performing tree cuts [14]. Conditioned on $\mathcal{R}$, the optimal tree cut can be found exactly using Dynamic Programming, as done in [14]. Unfortunately, regions of the hierarchy $\mathcal{R}$ might not represent accurately all complete objects in the image due to imperfect boundary estimation. Also, occlusion might cause objects to split into different regions of the tree. As a result, the best partition obtained by the optimal tree cut may be far away from the optimal partition π_k^*. Below, we show how to sample higher-quality image partitions based on the initial region hierarchy $\mathcal{R}$.

Fig. 2. Intermediate segmentation results when the Algorithm 1 progresses. Left is the initialized segmentation. Right is the final result when the algorithm converges. In each image, bounding boxes represent detected objects returned by the trained detector. Notice black bounding boxes are currently rejected by the algorithm

Image Partition Proposal. Let $\pi_k = (R_1, R_2, \ldots, R_k) \subset \mathcal{R}$ be the current image partition, a new partition can be proposed by first randomly sampling a region $R \in \mathcal{R} \setminus \pi_k$, then "paste" it onto the current partition π_k. Let $\mathcal{A}_R \subset \pi_k$ be a subset of regions that overlap with R, where $|\mathcal{A}_R|$ denotes the number of regions in $\mathcal{A}_R$. The following scenarios can happen:

- $R = \cup \mathcal{A}_R$. Regions in $\mathcal{A}_R$ will be merged into a single region R.
- $|\mathcal{A}_R| = 1, R \subset \mathcal{A}_R$. $\mathcal{A}_R$ will be split into two subregions: R and $\mathcal{A}_R \setminus R$.
- $|\mathcal{A}_R| > 1, R \subset \cup \mathcal{A}_R$. Each region in $\mathcal{A}_R$ will be split by R into two subregions, one of which will be merged into R. This is a split-and-merge process.

It can be seen that the above "sample-and-paste" operation naturally realizes the split, merge, and split-and-merge processes probabilistically, allowing the exploration of partition spaces of difference cardinalities. Note that the last two moves may generate new region candidates that are not in the original region hierarchy $\mathcal{R}$. These regions are added into $\mathcal{R}$ in the next iteration. Figure 2 demonstrates the progressive improvement of the segmentation during Simulated Annealing optimisation.

Occlusion Handling. The above "sample-and-paste" process is unlikely to be able to merge regions that are spatially separated. Because of occlusion, spatially isolated regions might be from the same object instance. Given a current partition π_k and a detection represented by either a bounding box **b** or a mask **m**, we create more region candidates by sampling pairs of regions in π_k that overlap with **b** or **m**. These regions are added into $\mathcal{R}$ in the next iteration.

6 Experimental Evaluation

In all below experiments, we run the Algorithm 1 for 3000 iterations. For each image, we run the COB network [12] and compute a region hierarchy of 20 levels, in which level 10 will be used as the initialized segmentation.

Fig. 3. Baseline (top row) vs our method (second row) with bounding box supervision. Testing images are from the NYU dataset. Bounding boxes represent detected objects. Note that not all detected object instances are used in the final segmentation. Black bounding boxes are detections rejected by the methods

6.1   Baselines

Since we are not aware of any previous work solving the same problem as ours, we develop a simple baseline for comparisons. Noting that the input to our method is an image, and possibly a set of object detections or masks returned either by an object detection (e.g., Faster-RCNN) or an instance segmentation method (e.g., Mask-RCNN) trained on known classes. In some cases, no known objects are detected in the image. For the baseline method, we first apply an unsupervised segmentation method to decompose the image into a set of non-overlap regions. If a set of detections (bounding boxes) is given, we classify each segmented region into these detected objects using intersection-over-union scores. If the maximum score is smaller than 0.25, we assign that region to an unknown class. When a set of object masks is given, we overwrite these masks onto the segmentation. Masks are sorted (in ascending order) using detection scores to ensure that high confidence masks will be on top.

We develop the unsupervised segmentation by thresholding the UCMs, computed from the boundary maps estimated by the COB network [12]. We use different thresholds for the baseline method, including the best threshold computed using ground-truth data. As reported in [12,14], this segmentation method greatly outperforms other existing unsupervised image segmentation methods, making it a strong baseline for comparison.

6.2   Open-Set Datasets

For evaluation, we create a testing environment which includes both known and unknown object classes. In computer vision, the COCO dataset has been widely used for training and testing the object detection and instance segmentation methods. This dataset has annotations (bounding boxes and masks) of 80 object classes. We select these 80 classes as known classes. Moreover, the popular NYU

Fig. 4. Baseline (top row) vs our method (second row) with mask supervision. Testing images are from the NYU dataset. Bounding boxes represents detected objects

dataset has annotations of 894 classes, in which 781 are objects and 113 are stuffs. We observe (manually check) that 60 classes from the COCO dataset actually appear in the NYU dataset. Consequentially, we select the NYU dataset as the testing set with 60 known and 721 unknown for benchmarking our method and baseline method.

6.3 Ablation Studies

We compare our method against the baseline in three different settings: (1) No supervision, (2) Bounding box supervision and (3) Mask supervision. In the first case, we assume that there is no training data available for training the object detection or instance segmentation networks. In the second case, we assume that known object classes are annotated with only bounding boxes so that one can train an object detector (i.e., Faster-RCNN). It is worth mentioning that while our method can be guided by a given set of bounding boxes (if available), the baseline method does not use the given bounding boxes for segmentation at all because the object segmentation and object labeling are carried sequentially. Finally, in the last setting, if known object instances are carefully annotated with binary masks, one can train an instance segmentation network (i.e., Mask-RCNN), which is then applied onto testing images to return a set of segmentation masks together with their categories. The predicted segmentation masks are taken as input to the baseline and our method. In all our experiments, we use Detectron[1], which implements Mask-RCNN method, to generate bounding boxes and segmentation masks. We select the model trained on the COCO dataset.

Evaluation. For each image, we first run the Hungarian matching algorithm to associate ground truth regions to predicted regions based on IoU scores. We then compute, given an IoU threshold, precision and recall rates, which will be

---

[1] https://github.com/facebookresearch/Detectron.

Table 1. Quantitative comparison results on 654 NYU RGB-D testing images between our method and the baseline method with different supervision information. The baseline method is tested with different thresholds. We report F-1 scores for known and unknown classes at 0.5 and 0.75 IoU thresholds respectively

Method	Supervision	Known		Unknown	
		F_1^{50}	F_1^{75}	F_1^{50}	F_1^{75}
Baseline (0.3)	None/BBoxes	40.1	21.1	47.8	26.3
Baseline (0.3)	Masks	10.6	5.1	19.5	10.9
Baseline (0.4)	None/BBoxes	47.4	26.1	45.2	26.7
Baseline (0.4)	Masks	7.3	3.8	13.25	7.9
Our method	None	45.6	22.6	55.7	32.2
Our method	BBoxes	48.6	23.1	54.2	30.4
Our method	Masks	51.1	25.9	53.8	30.3

Table 2. Comparison results on 80 known classes tested on 5k COCO validation images. $mIoU_w$ is weighted by the object sizes

Method	Supervision	mAP	$mIoU_w$	mIoU
Baseline	Weakly (Boxes)	10.1	26.6	25.2
Our method	Weakly (Boxes)	20.0	33.6	32.3
Mask-RCNN	Fully (Boxes and Masks)	30.5	38.7	37.3

summarised via F-1 scores. Note that we evaluate known and unknown object classes separately. Table 1 reports comparison results tested on NYU images using F-1 scores at different IoU thresholds. Firstly, it is clear that our method performs much better than the baseline when both methods are not guided by detections, even when the baseline is provided the best threshold (0.4) computed using ground truth. Moreover, when guided by bounding boxes and masks, our accuracies on known object classes increase significantly as expected. In contrast, the baseline method's accuracies decrease greatly when masks are used because the given masks are greedily overwritten onto the unsupervised segmentation results. These results confirm the efficacies of our global Bayesian image segmentation approach compared to the greedy baseline method.

Figures 3 and 4 demonstrate the qualitative comparison results between our method and the baseline. It can be seen that the baseline method fails to segment objects correctly (either under-segmentation or over-segmentation). In contrast, our method, guided by the given bounding boxes, performs much better. More importantly, the baseline method does not take the given bounding boxes into segmentation, it can not suppress multiple duplicated detections (with different classes) at the same location, unlike our method.

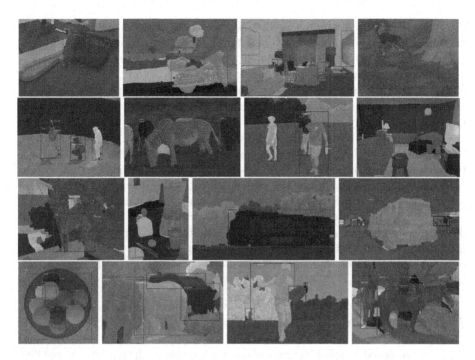

Fig. 5. Example instance segmentation results of our method on COCO dataset. Bounding boxes represents detected objects. In these examples, our method only uses bounding box supervision. Notice that our method segments not only detected objects, but also other miss-detected and unknown objects

6.4   Weakly Supervision Segmentation of Known Objects

Existing instance segmentation methods (e.g., Mask-RCNN) require ground-truth instance masks for training. However, annotating segmentation masks for all object instances is very expensive. Nonetheless, our semantic instance segmentation method does not require mask annotations for training. Here, we compare our weakly supervision instance segmentation of known objects against the fully supervised Mask RCNN method. Recently, Hu et al. [8] have proposed a learning transfer method, named Mask^{X}RCNN, for instance segmentation when only a subset of known object classes has mask annotations. We are, however, unable to compare with Mask^{X}RCNN as neither its pre-trained model nor predicted segmentation masks are publicly available.

Evaluation. While our method outputs one instance label per pixel, Mask RCNN returns a set of overlap segmentation masks per image. Therefore, the two methods can be not practically compared. To be fair, we post-process the Mask RCNN's results to ensure that one pixel is assigned to only one instance (via pixel voting based on detection scores). We measure the segmentation accuracies using Mean Intersection over Union (mIoU) metric. We first run the Hungarian matching algorithm to match predicted regions to ground-truth regions. The "matched" IoU scores are then averaged over all object instances and semantic categories. We also report Mean Average Precision (mAP) scores as Mask RCNN does. However, we note that mAP metric is only suitable for problems where an output is a set of ranked items. In contrast, our method returns, for each image, a single pixelwise segmentation where each pixel is assigned to a single object instance without any ranking.

Table 2 reports the comparison results. It can be seen that our method, though only requiring bounding box supervision, is competitive with respect to Mask RCNN, which requires ground-truth segmentation masks of all known object instances for training. This again indicates the efficacy of our method for the *open-set* instance segmentation problem where it is expensive, if not impossible, to annotate segmentation masks for all object instances. Figure 5 demonstrates example semantic instance segmentation results from our method using images from COCO dataset. Notice that our method is not only able to segment known objects but also unknown objects and stuffs such as grass, sky with high accuracies.

7   Discussion and Conclusion

We have presented a global instance segmentation approach that has a capability to segment all object instances and stuffs in the scene regardless of whether these objects are known or unknown. Such a capability is useful for autonomous robots working in *open-set* conditions [23], where the robots will unavoidably encounter novel objects that were not part of the training dataset.

Different from state-of-the-art supervised instance segmentation methods [4, 7,19,29], our approach does not perform segmentation on each detection independently, but instead segments the input image globally. The outcome is a set of coherent regions which are perceptually grouped and are each associated either to a known detection or unknown object instance. We formulate the instance segmentation problem in a Bayesian framework, and approximate the optimal segmentation using a Simulated Annealing approach.

We envision that *open-set* instance segmentation will soon become a hot research topic in the field. We thus believe the proposed method and the experimental setup proposed will serve as a strong baseline for future methods to be proposed in the field (e.g., end-to-end learning mechanisms).

Moreover, existing supervised learning methods which require a huge amount of precise mask annotations for all object instances for training, which is very expensive to extend to new object categories. Our approach offers an alternative, which is based on a more natural incremental annotation strategy to deal with new classes. This strategy consists of explicitly identifying unknown objects from images and training new object models using the labels provided by an "oracle" (such as a human).

Acknowledgements. This research was supported by the Australian Research Council through the Centre of Excellence for Robotic Vision (CE140100016) and by Discover Project (DP180103232).

References

1. Arbelaez, P.: Boundary extraction in natural images using ultrametric contour maps. In: 2006 Conference on Computer Vision and Pattern Recognition Workshop (CVPRW 2006), pp. 182–182, June 2006. https://doi.org/10.1109/CVPRW.2006.48
2. Bai, M., Urtasun, R.: Deep watershed transform for instance segmentation. In: 2017 IEEE Conference on Computer Vision and Pattern Recognition, CVPR 2017, Honolulu, HI, USA, 21–26 July 2017, pp. 2858–2866 (2017)
3. Cordts, M., et al.: The cityscapes dataset for semantic urban scene understanding. In: Proceedings of the IEEE Conference on Computer Vision and Pattern Recognition, pp. 3213–3223 (2016)
4. Dai, J., He, K., Sun, J.: Instance-aware semantic segmentation via multi-task network cascades. In: CVPR (2016)
5. Fathi, A., et al.: Semantic instance segmentation via deep metric learning. CoRR abs/1703.10277 (2017)
6. Felzenszwalb, P.F., Huttenlocher, D.P.: Efficient graph-based image segmentation. Int. J. Comput. Vis. **59**(2), 167–181 (2004)
7. He, K., Gkioxari, G., Dollár, P., Girshick, R.: Mask R-CNN. arXiv preprint arXiv:1703.06870 (2017)
8. Hu, R., Dollár, P., He, K., Darrell, T., Girshick, R.B.: Learning to segment every thing. CoRR abs/1711.10370 (2017). http://arxiv.org/abs/1711.10370
9. Kim, C.J., Nelson, C.R., et al.: State-Space Models with Regime Switching: Classical and Gibbs-Sampling Approaches with Applications, vol. 1. MIT Press, Cambridge (1999)
10. Lin, G., Milan, A., Shen, C., Reid, I.: RefineNet: multi-path refinement networks for high-resolution semantic segmentation. In: CVPR, July 2017
11. Lin, T.Y., et al.: Microsoft COCO: common objects in context. In: Fleet, D., Pajdla, T., Schiele, B., Tuytelaars, T. (eds.) ECCV 2014. LNCS, vol. 8693, pp. 740–755. Springer, Cham (2014). https://doi.org/10.1007/978-3-319-10602-1_48
12. Maninis, K., Pont-Tuset, J., Arbeláez, P., Gool, L.V.: Convolutional oriented boundaries: from image segmentation to high-level tasks. IEEE Trans. Pattern Anal. Mach. Intell. (TPAMI) **40**(4), 819–833 (2017)
13. Milan, A., et al.: Semantic segmentation from limited training data. CoRR abs/1709.07665 (2017)
14. Pham, T., Do, T.T., Sünderhauf, N., Reid, I.: SceneCut: joint geometric and object segmentation for indoor scenes. In: 2018 IEEE International Conference on Robotics and Automation (ICRA) (2018)
15. Pham, T.T., Eich, M., Reid, I.D., Wyeth, G.: Geometrically consistent plane extraction for dense indoor 3D maps segmentation. In: IEEE/RSJ International Conference on Intelligent Robots and Systems, pp. 4199–4204 (2016)
16. Pham, T.T., Reid, I.D., Latif, Y., Gould, S.: Hierarchical higher-order regression forest fields: an application to 3D indoor scene labelling. In: 2015 IEEE International Conference on Computer Vision (ICCV), pp. 2246–2254 (2015)
17. Pinheiro, P.O., Collobert, R., Dollár, P.: Learning to segment object candidates. In: NIPS (2015)

18. Pinheiro, P.O., Lin, T.-Y., Collobert, R., Dollár, P.: Learning to refine object segments. In: Leibe, B., Matas, J., Sebe, N., Welling, M. (eds.) ECCV 2016. LNCS, vol. 9905, pp. 75–91. Springer, Cham (2016). https://doi.org/10.1007/978-3-319-46448-0_5

19. Redmon, J., Farhadi, A.: YOLO9000: better, faster, stronger. CoRR abs/1612.08242 (2016)

20. Ren, M., Zemel, R.S.: End-to-end instance segmentation with recurrent attention. In: CVPR (2017)

21. Ren, S., He, K., Girshick, R., Sun, J.: Faster R-CNN: towards real-time object detection with region proposal networks. In: Advances in Neural Information Processing Systems (NIPS) (2015)

22. Romera-Paredes, B., Torr, P.H.S.: Recurrent instance segmentation. In: Leibe, B., Matas, J., Sebe, N., Welling, M. (eds.) ECCV 2016. LNCS, vol. 9910, pp. 312–329. Springer, Cham (2016). https://doi.org/10.1007/978-3-319-46466-4_19

23. Scheirer, W.J., de Rezende Rocha, A., Sapkota, A., Boult, T.E.: Toward open set recognition. IEEE Trans. Pattern Anal. Mach. Intell. **35**(7), 1757–1772 (2013)

24. Silberman, N., Hoiem, D., Kohli, P., Fergus, R.: Indoor segmentation and support inference from RGBD images. In: Fitzgibbon, A., Lazebnik, S., Perona, P., Sato, Y., Schmid, C. (eds.) ECCV 2012. LNCS, vol. 7576, pp. 746–760. Springer, Heidelberg (2012). https://doi.org/10.1007/978-3-642-33715-4_54

25. Sünderhauf, N., Pham, T.T., Latif, Y., Milford, M., Reid, I.D.: Meaningful maps with object-oriented semantic mapping. In: IEEE/RSJ International Conference on Intelligent Robots and Systems (2017)

26. Trevor, A.J.B., Gedikli, S., Rusu, R.B., Christensen, H.I.: Efficient organized point cloud segmentation with connected components (2013)

27. Tu, Z., Zhu, S.C.: Image segmentation by data-driven Markov chain monte carlo. IEEE Trans. Pattern Anal. Mach. Intell. **24**(5), 657–673 (2002)

28. Van Laarhoven, P.J., Aarts, E.H.: Simulated annealing. In: Van Laarhoven, P.J., Aarts, E.H. (eds.) Simulated Annealing: Theory and Applications, pp. 7–15. Springer, Dordrecht (1987). https://doi.org/10.1007/978-94-015-7744-1_2

29. Li, Y., Qi, H., Dai, J., Ji, X., Wei, Y.: Fully convolutional instance-aware semantic segmentation (2017)

BOP: Benchmark for 6D Object Pose Estimation

Tomáš Hodaň[1]([✉]), Frank Michel[2], Eric Brachmann[3], Wadim Kehl[4],
Anders Glent Buch[5], Dirk Kraft[5], Bertram Drost[6], Joel Vidal[7],
Stephan Ihrke[2], Xenophon Zabulis[8], Caner Sahin[9], Fabian Manhardt[10],
Federico Tombari[10], Tae-Kyun Kim[9], Jiří Matas[1], and Carsten Rother[3]

[1] CTU in Prague, Prague, Czech Republic
hodantom@cmp.felk.cvut.cz
[2] TU Dresden, Dresden, Germany
[3] Heidelberg University, Heidelberg, Germany
[4] Toyota Research Institute, Los Altos, USA
[5] University of Southern Denmark, Odense, Denmark
[6] MVTec Software, Munich, Germany
[7] Taiwan Tech, Taipei, Taiwan
[8] FORTH Heraklion, Heraklion, Greece
[9] Imperial College London, London, UK
[10] TU Munich, Munich, Germany

Abstract. We propose a benchmark for 6D pose estimation of a rigid object from a single RGB-D input image. The training data consists of a texture-mapped 3D object model or images of the object in known 6D poses. The benchmark comprises of: (i) eight datasets in a unified format that cover different practical scenarios, including two new datasets focusing on varying lighting conditions, (ii) an evaluation methodology with a pose-error function that deals with pose ambiguities, (iii) a comprehensive evaluation of 15 diverse recent methods that captures the status quo of the field, and (iv) an online evaluation system that is open for continuous submission of new results. The evaluation shows that methods based on point-pair features currently perform best, outperforming template matching methods, learning-based methods and methods based on 3D local features. The project website is available at bop.felk.cvut.cz.

1 Introduction

Estimating the 6D pose, i.e. 3D translation and 3D rotation, of a rigid object has become an accessible task with the introduction of consumer-grade RGB-D sensors. An accurate, fast and robust method that solves this task will have a big impact in application fields such as robotics or augmented reality.

Many methods for 6D object pose estimation have been published recently, e.g. [2,18,21,24,25,27,34,36], but it is unclear which methods perform well and

---

T. Hodaň and F. Michel—Authors have been leading the project jointly.

V. Ferrari et al. (Eds.): ECCV 2018, LNCS 11214, pp. 19–35, 2018.
https://doi.org/10.1007/978-3-030-01249-6_2

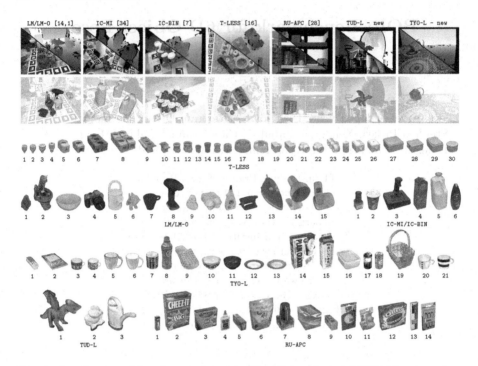

Fig. 1. A collection of benchmark datasets. Top: Example test RGB-D images where the second row shows the images overlaid with 3D object models in the ground-truth 6D poses. Bottom: Texture-mapped 3D object models. At training time, a method is given an object model or a set of training images with ground-truth object poses. At test time, the method is provided with one test image and an identifier of the target object. The task is to estimate the 6D pose of an instance of this object.

in which scenarios. The most commonly used dataset for evaluation was created by Hinterstoisser et al. [14], which was not intended as a general benchmark and has several limitations: the lighting conditions are constant and the objects are easy to distinguish, unoccluded and located around the image center. Since then, some of the limitations have been addressed. Brachmann et al. [1] added ground-truth annotation for occluded objects in the dataset of [14]. Hodaň et al. [16] created a dataset that features industry-relevant objects with symmetries and similarities, and Drost et al. [8] introduced a dataset containing objects with reflective surfaces. However, the datasets have different formats and no standard evaluation methodology has emerged. New methods are usually compared with only a few competitors on a small subset of datasets.

This work makes the following contributions:

1. **Eight datasets in a unified format**, including two new datasets focusing on varying lighting conditions, are made available (Fig. 1). The datasets contain: (i) texture-mapped 3D models of 89 objects with a wide range of sizes, shapes and reflectance properties, (ii) 277K training RGB-D images showing

isolated objects from different viewpoints, and (iii) 62K test RGB-D images of scenes with graded complexity. High-quality ground-truth 6D poses of the modeled objects are provided for all images.

2. **An evaluation methodology** based on [17] that includes the formulation of an industry-relevant task, and a pose-error function which deals well with pose ambiguity of symmetric or partially occluded objects, in contrast to the commonly used function by Hinterstoisser et al. [14].

3. **A comprehensive evaluation** of 15 methods on the benchmark datasets using the proposed evaluation methodology. We provide an analysis of the results, report the state of the art, and identify open problems.

4. **An online evaluation system** at bop.felk.cvut.cz that allows for continuous submission of new results and provides up-to-date leaderboards.

1.1   Related Work

The progress of research in computer vision has been strongly influenced by challenges and benchmarks, which enable to evaluate and compare methods and better understand their limitations. The Middlebury benchmark [31,32] for depth from stereo and optical flow estimation was one of the first that gained large attention. The PASCAL VOC challenge [10], based on a photo collection from the internet, was the first to standardize the evaluation of object detection and image classification. It was followed by the ImageNet challenge [29], which has been running for eight years, starting in 2010, and has pushed image classification methods to new levels of accuracy. The key was a large-scale dataset that enabled training of deep neural networks, which then quickly became a game-changer for many other tasks [23]. With increasing maturity of computer vision methods, recent benchmarks moved to real-world scenarios. A great example is the KITTI benchmark [11] focusing on problems related to autonomous driving. It showed that methods ranking high on established benchmarks, such as the Middlebury, perform below average when moved outside the laboratory conditions.

Unlike the PASCAL VOC and ImageNet challenges, the task considered in this work requires a specific set of calibrated modalities that cannot be easily acquired from the internet. In contrast to KITTY, it was not necessary to record large amounts of new data. By combining existing datasets, we have covered many practical scenarios. Additionally, we created two datasets with varying lighting conditions, which is an aspect not covered by the existing datasets.

2   Evaluation Methodology

The proposed evaluation methodology formulates the 6D object pose estimation task and defines a pose-error function which is compared with the commonly used function by Hinterstoisser et al. [13].

2.1   Formulation of the Task

Methods for 6D object pose estimation report their predictions on the basis of two sources of information. Firstly, at training time, a method is given a training set $T = \{T_o\}_{o=1}^n$, where o is an object identifier. Training data T_o may have different forms, e.g. a 3D mesh model of the object or a set of RGB-D images showing object instances in known 6D poses. Secondly, at test time, the method is provided with a test target defined by a pair (I, o), where I is an image showing at least one instance of object o. The goal is to estimate the 6D pose of one of the instances of object o visible in image I.

If multiple instances of the same object model are present, then the pose of an arbitrary instance may be reported. If multiple object models are shown in a test image, and annotated with their ground truth poses, then each object model may define a different test target. For example, if a test image shows three object models, each in two instances, then we define three test targets. For each test target, the pose of one of the two object instances has to be estimated.

This task reflects the industry-relevant bin-picking scenario where a robot needs to grasp a single arbitrary instance of the required object, e.g. a component such as a bolt or nut, and perform some operation with it. It is the simplest variant of the 6D localization task [17] and a common denominator of its other variants, which deal with a single instance of multiple objects, multiple instances of a single object, or multiple instances of multiple objects. It is also the core of the 6D detection task, where no prior information about the object presence in the test image is provided [17].

2.2   Measuring Error

A 3D object model is defined as a set of vertices in $\mathbb{R}^3$ and a set of polygons that describe the object surface. The object pose is represented by a 4×4 matrix $\mathbf{P} = [\mathbf{R}, \mathbf{t}; 0, 1]$, where $\mathbf{R}$ is a 3×3 rotation matrix and $\mathbf{t}$ is a 3×1 translation vector. The matrix $\mathbf{P}$ transforms a 3D homogeneous point $\mathbf{x}_m$ in the model coordinate system to a 3D point $\mathbf{x}_c$ in the camera coordinate system: $\mathbf{x}_c = \mathbf{P}\mathbf{x}_m$.

Visible Surface Discrepancy. To calculate the error of an estimated pose $\hat{\mathbf{P}}$ w.r.t. the ground-truth pose $\bar{\mathbf{P}}$ in a test image I, an object model $\mathcal{M}$ is first rendered in the two poses. The result of the rendering is two distance maps[1] $\hat{S}$ and $\bar{S}$. As in [17], the distance maps are compared with the distance map S_I of the test image I to obtain the visibility masks $\hat{V}$ and $\bar{V}$, i.e. the sets of pixels where the model $\mathcal{M}$ is visible in the image I (Fig. 2). Given a misalignment tolerance τ, the error is calculated as:

---

[1] A distance map stores at a pixel p the distance from the camera center to a 3D point $\mathbf{x}_p$ that projects to p. It can be readily computed from the depth map which stores at p the Z coordinate of $\mathbf{x}_p$ and which can be obtained by a Kinect-like sensor.

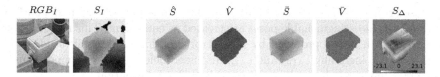

Fig. 2. Quantities used in the calculation of e_{VSD}. Left: Color channels RGB_I (only for illustration) and distance map S_I of a test image I. Right: Distance maps $\hat{S}$ and $\bar{S}$ are obtained by rendering the object model $\mathcal{M}$ at the estimated pose $\hat{\mathbf{P}}$ and the ground-truth pose $\bar{\mathbf{P}}$ respectively. $\hat{V}$ and $\bar{V}$ are masks of the model surface that is visible in I, obtained by comparing $\hat{S}$ and $\bar{S}$ with S_I. Distance differences $S_\Delta(p) = \hat{S}(p) - \bar{S}(p)$, $\forall p \in \hat{V} \cap \bar{V}$, are used for the pixel-wise evaluation of the surface alignment.

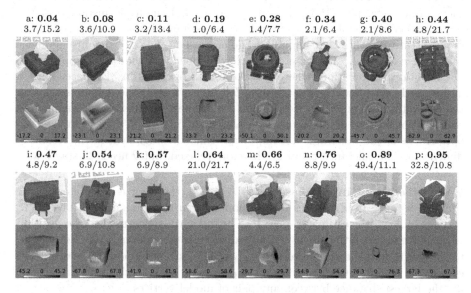

Fig. 3. Comparison of e_{VSD} (bold, $\tau = 20\,\mathrm{mm}$) with $e_{\mathrm{ADI}}/\theta_{\mathrm{AD}}$ (mm) on example pose estimates sorted by increasing e_{VSD}. Top: Cropped and brightened test images overlaid with renderings of the model at (i) the estimated pose $\hat{\mathbf{P}}$ in blue, and (ii) the ground-truth pose $\bar{\mathbf{P}}$ in green. Only the part of the model surface that falls into the respective visibility mask is shown. Bottom: Difference maps S_Δ. Case (b) is analyzed in Fig. 2. (Color figure online)

$$e_{\mathrm{VSD}}(\hat{S}, \bar{S}, S_I, \hat{V}, \bar{V}, \tau) = \operatorname*{avg}_{p \in \hat{V} \cup \bar{V}} \begin{cases} 0 & \text{if } p \in \hat{V} \cap \bar{V} \wedge |\hat{S}(p) - \bar{S}(p)| < \tau \\ 1 & \text{otherwise.} \end{cases} \tag{1}$$

Properties of e_{VSD}. The object pose can be ambiguous, i.e. there can be multiple poses that are indistinguishable. This is caused by the existence of multiple fits of the visible part of the object surface to the entire object surface. The visible part is determined by self-occlusion and occlusion by other objects and the multiple surface fits are induced by global or partial object symmetries.

Pose error e_{VSD} is calculated only over the visible part of the model surface and thus the indistinguishable poses are treated as equivalent. This is a desirable property which is not provided by pose-error functions commonly used in the literature [17], including e_{ADD} and e_{ADI} discussed below. As the commonly used pose-error functions, e_{VSD} does not consider color information.

Definition (1) is different from the original definition in [17] where the pixel-wise cost linearly increases to 1 as $|\hat{S}(p) - \bar{S}(p)|$ increases to τ. The new definition is easier to interpret and does not penalize small distance differences that may be caused by imprecisions of the depth sensor or of the ground-truth pose.

Criterion of Correctness. An estimated pose $\hat{\mathbf{P}}$ is considered correct w.r.t. the ground-truth pose $\bar{\mathbf{P}}$ if the error $e_{\text{VSD}} < \theta$. If multiple instances of the target object are visible in the test image, the estimated pose is compared to the ground-truth instance that minimizes the error. The choice of the misalignment tolerance τ and the correctness threshold θ depends on the target application. For robotic manipulation, where a robotic arm operates in 3D space, both τ and θ need to be low, e.g. $\tau = 20\,\text{mm}$, $\theta = 0.3$, which is the default setting in the evaluation presented in Sect. 5. The requirement is different for augmented reality applications. Here the surface alignment in the Z dimension, i.e. the optical axis of the camera, is less important than the alignment in the X and Y dimension. The tolerance τ can be therefore relaxed, but θ needs to stay low.

Comparison to Hinterstoisser et al. In [14], the error is calculated as the average distance from vertices of the model $\mathcal{M}$ in the ground-truth pose $\bar{\mathbf{P}}$ to vertices of $\mathcal{M}$ in the estimated pose $\hat{\mathbf{P}}$. The distance is measured to the position of the same vertex if the object has no indistinguishable views (e_{ADD}), otherwise to the position of the closest vertex (e_{ADI}). The estimated pose $\hat{\mathbf{P}}$ is considered correct if $e \leq \theta_{\text{AD}} = 0.1d$, where e is e_{ADD} or e_{ADI}, and d is the object diameter, i.e. the largest distance between any pair of model vertices.

Error e_{ADI} can be un-intuitively low because of many-to-one vertex matching established by the search for the closest vertex. This is shown in Fig. 3, which compares e_{VSD} and e_{ADI} on example pose estimates of objects that have indistinguishable views. Overall, (f)–(n) yield low e_{ADI} scores and satisfy the correctness criterion of Hinterstoisser et al. These estimates are not considered correct by our criterion. Estimates (a)–(e) are considered correct and (o)–(p) are considered wrong by both criteria.

3   Datasets

We collected six publicly available datasets, some of which we reduced to remove redundancies[2] and re-annotated to ensure a high quality of the ground truth. Additionally, we created two new datasets focusing on varying lighting conditions, since this variation is not present in the existing datasets. An overview of the datasets is in Fig. 1 and a detailed description follows.

---

[2] Identifiers of the selected images are available on the project website.

3.1   Training and Test Data

The datasets consist of texture-mapped 3D object models and training and test RGB-D images annotated with ground-truth 6D object poses. The 3D object models were created using KinectFusion-like systems for 3D surface reconstruction [26,33]. All images are of approximately VGA resolution.

For training, a method may use the 3D object models and/or the training images. While 3D models are often available or can be generated at a low cost, capturing and annotating real training images requires a significant effort. The benchmark is therefore focused primarily on the more practical scenario where only the object models, which can be used to render synthetic training images, are available at training time. All datasets contain already synthesized training images. Methods are allowed to synthesize additional training images, but this option was not utilized for the evaluation in this paper. Only T-LESS and TUD-L include real training images of isolated, i.e. non-occluded, objects.

Table 1. Parameters of the datasets. Note that if a test image shows multiple object models, each model defines a different test target – see Sect. 2.1.

Dataset	Objects	Training images/obj.		Test images		Test targets	
		Real	Synt.	Used	All	Used	All
LM [14]	15	–	1313	3000	18273	3000	18273
LM-O [1]	8	–	1313	200	1214	1445	8916
IC-MI [34]	6	–	1313	300	2067	300	2067
IC-BIN [7]	2	–	2377	150	177	200	238
T-LESS [16]	30	1296	2562	2000	10080	9819	49805
RU-APC [28]	14	–	2562	1380	5964	1380	5911
TUD-L - new	3	>11000	1827	600	23914	600	23914
TYO-L - new	21	–	2562	–	1680	–	1669
Total	89			7450	62155	16951	110793

To generate the synthetic training images, objects from the same dataset were rendered from the same range of azimuth/elevation covering the distribution of object poses in the test scenes. The viewpoints were sampled from a sphere, as in [14], with the sphere radius set to the distance of the closest object instance in the test scenes. The objects were rendered with fixed lighting conditions and a black background.

The test images are real images from a structured-light sensor – Microsoft Kinect v1 or Primesense Carmine 1.09. The test images originate from indoor scenes with varying complexity, ranging from simple scenes with a single isolated object instance to very challenging scenes with multiple instances of several objects and a high amount of clutter and occlusion. Poses of the modeled objects were annotated manually. While LM, IC-MI and RU-APC provide annotation for instances of only one object per image, the other datasets provide ground-truth for all modeled objects. Details of the datasets are in Table 1.

3.2   The Dataset Collection

LM/LM-O [1,14]. LM (a.k.a. Linemod) has been the most commonly used dataset for 6D object pose estimation. It contains 15 texture-less household objects with discriminative color, shape and size. Each object is associated with a test image set showing one annotated object instance with significant clutter but only mild occlusion. LM-O (a.k.a. Linemod-Occluded) provides ground-truth annotation for all other instances of the modeled objects in one of the test sets. This introduces challenging test cases with various levels of occlusion.

IC-MI/IC-BIN [7,34]. IC-MI (a.k.a. Tejani et al.) contains models of two texture-less and four textured household objects. The test images show multiple object instances with clutter and slight occlusion. IC-BIN (a.k.a. Doumanoglou et al., scenario 2) includes test images of two objects from IC-MI, which appear in multiple locations with heavy occlusion in a bin-picking scenario. We have removed test images with low-quality ground-truth annotations from both datasets, and refined the annotations for the remaining images in IC-BIN.

T-LESS [16]. It features 30 industry-relevant objects with no significant texture or discriminative color. The objects exhibit symmetries and mutual similarities in shape and/or size, and a few objects are a composition of other objects. T-LESS includes images from three different sensors and two types of 3D object models. For our evaluation, we only used RGB-D images from the Primesense sensor and the automatically reconstructed 3D object models.

RU-APC [28]. This dataset (a.k.a. Rutgers APC) includes 14 textured products from the Amazon Picking Challenge 2015 [6], each associated with test images of a cluttered warehouse shelf. The camera was equipped with LED strips to ensure constant lighting. From the original dataset, we omitted ten objects which are non-rigid or poorly captured by the depth sensor, and included only one from the four images captured from the same viewpoint.

TUD-L/TYO-L. Two new datasets with household objects captured under different settings of ambient and directional light. TUD-L (TU Dresden Light) contains training and test image sequences that show three moving objects under eight lighting conditions. The object poses were annotated by manually aligning the 3D object model with the first frame of the sequence and propagating the initial pose through the sequence using ICP. TYO-L (Toyota Light) contains 21 objects, each captured in multiple poses on a table-top setup, with four different table cloths and five different lighting conditions. To obtain the ground truth poses, manually chosen correspondences were utilized to estimate rough poses which were then refined by ICP. The images in both datasets are labeled by categorized lighting conditions.

4   Evaluated Methods

The evaluated methods cover the major research directions of the 6D object pose estimation field. This section provides a review of the methods, together with a description of the setting of their key parameters. If not stated otherwise, the image-based methods used the synthetic training images.

4.1   Learning-Based Methods

Brachmann-14 [1]. For each pixel of an input image, a regression forest predicts the object identity and the location in the coordinate frame of the object model, a so called "object coordinate". Simple RGB and depth difference features are used for the prediction. Each object coordinate prediction defines a 3D-3D correspondence between the image and the 3D object model. A RANSAC-based optimization schema samples sets of three correspondences to create a pool of pose hypotheses. The final hypothesis is chosen, and iteratively refined, to maximize the alignment of predicted correspondences, as well as the alignment of observed depth with the object model. The main parameters of the method were set as follows: maximum feature offset: 20 px, features per tree node: 1000, training patches per object: 1.5M, number of trees: 3, size of the hypothesis pool: 210, refined hypotheses: 25. Real training images were used for TUD-L and T-LESS.

Brachmann-16 [2]. The method of [1] is extended in several ways. Firstly, the random forest is improved using an auto-context algorithm to support pose estimation from RGB-only images. Secondly, the RANSAC-based optimization hypothesizes not only with regard to the object pose but also with regard to the object identity in cases where it is unknown which objects are visible in the input image. Both improvements were disabled for the evaluation since we deal with RGB-D input, and it is known which objects are visible in the image. Thirdly, the random forest predicts for each pixel a full, three-dimensional distribution over object coordinates capturing uncertainty information. The distributions are estimated using mean-shift in each forest leaf, and can therefore be heavily multimodal. The final hypothesis is chosen, and iteratively refined, to maximize the likelihood under the predicted distributions. The 3D object model is not used for fitting the pose. The parameters were set as: maximum feature offset: 10 px, features per tree node: 100, number of trees: 3, number of sampled hypotheses: 256, pixels drawn in each RANSAC iteration: 10K, inlier threshold: 1 cm.

Tejani-14 [34]. Linemod [14] is adapted into a scale-invariant patch descriptor and integrated into a regression forest with a new template-based split function. This split function is more discriminative than simple pixel tests and accelerated via binary bit-operations. The method is trained on positive samples only, i.e. rendered images of the 3D object model. During the inference, the class distributions at the leaf nodes are iteratively updated, providing occlusion-aware segmentation masks. The object pose is estimated by accumulating pose regression votes from the estimated foreground patches. The baseline evaluated in this paper implements [34] but omits the iterative segmentation/refinement step and does not perform ICP. The features and forest parameters were set as in [34]: number of trees: 10, maximum depth of each tree: 25, number of features in both the color gradient and the surface normal channel: 20, patch size: 1/2 the image, rendered images used to train each forest: 360.

Kehl-16 [22]. Scale-invariant RGB-D patches are extracted from a regular grid attached to the input image, and described by features calculated using a convolutional auto-encoder. At training time, a codebook is constructed from descriptors of patches from the training images, with each codebook entry holding information about the 6D pose. For each patch descriptor from the test image, k-nearest neighbors from the codebook are found, and a 6D vote is cast using neighbors whose distance is below a threshold t. After the voting stage, the 6D hypothesis space is filtered to remove spurious votes. Modes are identified by mean-shift and refined by ICP. The final hypothesis is verified in color, depth and surface normals to suppress false positives. The main parameters of the method with the used values: patch size: 32×32 px, patch sampling step: 6 px, k-nearest neighbors: 3, threshold t: 2, number of extracted modes from the pose space: 8. Real training images were used for T-LESS.

4.2 Template Matching Methods

Hodaň-15 [18]. A template matching method that applies an efficient cascade-style evaluation to each sliding window location. A simple objectness filter is applied first, rapidly rejecting most locations. For each remaining location, a set of candidate templates is identified by a voting procedure based on hashing, which makes the computational complexity largely unaffected by the total number of stored templates. The candidate templates are then verified as in Linemod [14] by matching feature points in different modalities (surface normals, image gradients, depth, color). Finally, object poses associated with the detected templates are refined by particle swarm optimization (PSO). The templates were generated by applying the full circle of in-plane rotations with 10° step to a portion of the synthetic training images, resulting in 11–23K templates per object. Other parameters were set as described in [18]. We present also results without the last refinement step (Hodaň-15-nr).

4.3 Methods Based on Point-Pair Features

Drost-10 [9]. A method based on matching oriented point pairs between the point cloud of the test scene and the object model, and grouping the matches using a local voting scheme. At training time, point pairs from the model are sampled and stored in a hash table. At test time, reference points are fixed in the scene, and a low-dimensional parameter space for the voting scheme is created by restricting to those poses that align the reference point with the model. Point pairs between the reference point and other scene points are created, similar model point pairs searched for using the hash table, and a vote is cast for each matching point pair. Peaks in the accumulator space are extracted and used as pose candidates, which are refined by coarse-to-fine ICP and re-scored by the relative amount of visible model surface. Note that color information is not used. It was evaluated using function find_surface_model from HALCON 13.0.2 [12]. The sampling distances for model and scene were set to 3% of the object diameter, 10% of points were used as the reference points, and the normals were computed using the mls method. Points further than 2 m were discarded.

Drost-10-Edge. An extension of [9] which additionally detects 3D edges from the scene and favors poses in which the model contours are aligned with the edges. A multi-modal refinement minimizes the surface distances and the distances of reprojected model contours to the detected edges. The evaluation was performed using the same software and parameters as Drost-10, but with activated parameter train_3d_edges during the model creation.

Vidal-18 [35]. The point cloud is first sub-sampled by clustering points based on the surface normal orientation. Inspired by improvements of [15], the matching strategy of [9] was improved by mitigating the effect of the feature discretization step. Additionally, an improved non-maximum suppression of the pose candidates from different reference points removes spurious matches. The most voted 500 pose candidates are sorted by a surface fitting score and the 200 best candidates are refined by projective ICP. For the final 10 candidates, the consistency of the object surface and silhouette with the scene is evaluated. The sampling distance for model, scene and features was set to 5% of the object diameter, and 20% of the scene points were used as the reference points.

4.4   Methods Based on 3D Local Features

Buch-16 [3]. A RANSAC-based method that iteratively samples three feature correspondences between the object model and the scene. The correspondences are obtained by matching 3D local shape descriptors and are used to generate a 6D pose candidate, whose quality is measured by the consensus set size. The final pose is refined by ICP. The method achieved the state-of-the-art results on earlier object recognition datasets captured by LIDAR, but suffers from a cubic complexity in the number of correspondences. The number of RANSAC iterations was set to 10000, allowing only for a limited search in cluttered scenes. The method was evaluated with several descriptors: 153d SI [19], 352d SHOT [30], 30d ECSAD [20], and 1536d PPFH [5]. None of the descriptors utilize color.

Buch-17 [4]. This method is based on the observation that a correspondence between two oriented points on the object surface is constrained to cast votes in a 1-DoF rotational subgroup of the full group of poses, SE(3). The time complexity of the method is thus linear in the number of correspondences. Kernel density estimation is used to efficiently combine the votes and generate a 6D pose estimate. As Buch-16, the method relies on 3D local shape descriptors and refines the final pose estimate by ICP. The parameters were set as in the paper: 60 angle tessellations were used for casting rotational votes, and the translation/rotation bandwidths were set to 10 mm/22.5°.

5 Evaluation

The methods reviewed in Sect. 4 were evaluated by their original authors on the datasets described in Sect. 3, using the evaluation methodology from Sect. 2.

5.1 Experimental Setup

Fixed Parameters. The parameters of each method were fixed for all objects and datasets. The distribution of object poses in the test scenes was the only dataset-specific information used by the methods. The distribution determined the range of viewpoints from which the object models were rendered to obtain synthetic training images.

Pose Error. The error of a 6D object pose estimate is measured with the pose-error function e_{VSD} defined in Sect. 2.2. The visibility masks were calculated as in [17], with the occlusion tolerance δ set to 15 mm. Only the ground truth poses in which the object is visible from at least 10% were considered in the evaluation.

Performance Score. The performance is measured by the recall score, i.e. the fraction of test targets for which a correct object pose was estimated. Recall scores per dataset and per object are reported. The overall performance is given by the average of per-dataset recall scores. We thus treat each dataset as a separate challenge and avoid the overall score being dominated by larger datasets.

Subsets Used for the Evaluation. We reduced the number of test images to remove redundancies and to encourage participation of new, in particular slow, methods. From the total of 62K test images, we sub-sampled 7K, reducing the number of test targets from 110K to 17K (Table 1). Full datasets with identifiers of the selected test images are on the project website. TYO-L was not used for the evaluation presented in this paper, but it is a part of the online evaluation.

5.2 Results

Accuracy. Tables 2 and 3 show the recall scores of the evaluated methods per dataset and per object respectively, for the misalignment tolerance $\tau = 20$ mm and the correctness threshold $\theta = 0.3$. Ranking of the methods according to the recall score is mostly stable across the datasets. Methods based on point-pair features perform best. Vidal-18 is the top-performing method with the average recall of 74.6%, followed by Drost-10-edge, Drost-10, and the template matching method Hodaň-15, all with the average recall above 67%. Brachmann-16 is the best learning-based method, with 55.4%, and Buch-17-ppfh is the best method based on 3D local features, with 54.0%. Scores of Buch-16-si and Buch-16-shot are inferior to the other variants of this method and not presented.

Table 2. Recall scores (%) for $\tau = 20\,\text{mm}$ and $\theta = 0.3$. The recall score is the percentage of test targets for which a correct object pose was estimated. The methods are sorted by their average recall score calculated as the average of the per-dataset recall scores. The right-most column shows the average running time per test target.

# Method	LM	LM-O	IC-MI	IC-BIN	T-LESS	RU-APC	TUD-L	Average	Time (s)
1. Vidal-18	87.83	59.31	95.33	96.50	66.51	36.52	80.17	74.60	4.7
2. Drost-10-edge	79.13	54.95	94.00	92.00	67.50	27.17	87.33	71.73	21.5
3. Drost-10	82.00	55.36	94.33	87.00	56.81	22.25	78.67	68.06	2.3
4. Hodan-15	87.10	51.42	95.33	90.50	63.18	37.61	45.50	67.23	13.5
5. Brachmann-16	75.33	52.04	73.33	56.50	17.84	24.35	88.67	55.44	4.4
6. Hodan-15-nopso	69.83	34.39	84.67	76.00	62.70	32.39	27.83	55.40	12.3
7. Buch-17-ppfh	56.60	36.96	95.00	75.00	25.10	20.80	68.67	54.02	14.2
8. Kehl-16	58.20	33.91	65.00	44.00	24.60	25.58	7.50	36.97	1.8
9. Buch-17-si	33.33	20.35	67.33	59.00	13.34	23.12	41.17	36.81	15.9
10. Brachmann-14	67.60	41.52	78.67	24.00	0.25	30.22	0.00	34.61	1.4
11. Buch-17-ecsad	13.27	9.62	40.67	59.00	7.16	6.59	24.00	22.90	5.9
12. Buch-17-shot	5.97	1.45	43.00	38.50	3.83	0.07	16.67	15.64	6.7
13. Tejani-14	12.10	4.50	36.33	10.00	0.13	1.52	0.00	9.23	1.4
14. Buch-16-ppfh	8.13	2.28	20.00	2.50	7.81	8.99	0.67	7.20	47.1
15. Buch-16-ecsad	3.70	0.97	3.67	4.00	1.24	2.90	0.17	2.38	39.1

Table 3. Recall scores (%) per object for $\tau = 20\,\text{mm}$ and $\theta = 0.3$.

# Method	LM 1	2	3	4	5	6	7	8	9	10	11	12	13	14	15	LM-O 1	5	6	8	9	10	11	12	TUD-L 1	2	3
1. Vidal-18	89	96	91	94	92	96	89	89	87	97	59	69	93	92	90	66	81	46	65	73	43	26	64	79	88	74
2. Drost-10-edge	77	97	94	40	98	94	83	96	45	94	68	66	72	88	79	47	82	46	75	42	44	36	57	85	88	90
3. Drost-10	86	83	89	84	93	87	86	92	66	96	53	67	79	91	80	62	75	39	70	57	46	26	57	73	90	74
4. Hodan-15	91	97	79	97	91	97	73	69	90	97	81	79	99	74	95	54	66	40	26	73	37	44	68	27	63	48
5. Brachmann-16	92	93	76	84	86	90	44	72	85	79	46	67	94	60	66	64	65	44	68	71	3	32	61	81	95	91
6. Hodan-15-nr	91	57	40	89	66	87	59	49	92	90	65	63	71	54	79	47	35	24	12	63	9	32	53	12	52	20
7. Buch-17-ppfh	77	65	0	94	84	60	24	59	75	67	24	39	75	47	62	59	85	70	57	55	60	17	5	55	89	63
8. Kehl-16	60	52	81	25	79	68	17	68	42	91	45	42	78	83	46	39	47	24	30	48	14	13	49	0	23	0
9. Buch-17-si	40	43	1	63	81	47	12	8	36	43	18	3	46	19	43	54	63	11	2	16	9	1	3	2	74	48
10. Brachmann-14	74	70	77	75	88	66	11	81	69	66	50	75	92	75	49	50	48	27	44	60	6	30	62	0	0	0
11. Buch-17-ecsad	31	2	2	19	66	3	3	0	9	49	1	0	3	7	6	29	29	0	0	7	8	1	0	1	62	10
12. Buch-17-shot	3	4	11	9	9	4	1	3	2	10	1	0	10	12	14	2	7	0	0	1	1	1	0	1	33	17
13. Tejani-14	36	0	36	0	1	0	1	11	1	70	27	0	0	0	0	26	2	0	1	0	0	10	0	0	0	0
14. Buch-16-ppfh	11	0	1	22	3	7	2	7	18	12	4	3	9	12	14	4	0	0	2	11	1	1	1	2	0	0
15. Buch-16-ecsad	2	0	0	9	5	0	0	4	5	8	0	0	17	3	5	1	3	0	2	2	0	0	0	0	1	0

# Method	IC-MI 1	2	3	4	5	6	-BIN 2	4	T-LESS 1	2	3	4	5	6	7	8	9	10	11	12	13	14	15	16	17	18
1. Vidal-18	80	100	100	98	100	94	100	93	43	46	68	65	69	71	76	76	92	69	68	84	55	47	54	85	82	79
2. Drost-10-edge	78	100	100	100	98	84	100	84	53	44	61	67	71	73	75	89	72	64	81	53	46	55		85	88	78
3. Drost-10	76	100	98	100	96	96	100	74	34	46	63	63	68	64	54	48	59	54	51	69	43	45	53	80	79	68
4. Hodan-15	100	100	100	74	98	100	100	81	66	67	72	72	61	60	52	61	86	72	56	55	54	21	59	81	81	79
5. Brachmann-16	42	98	70	88	64	78	84	29	8	10	21	4	46	19	52	22	12	7	3	3	0	0		5	3	54
6. Hodan-15-nr	100	100	92	62	60	94	72	80	64	67	71	73	62	57	49	56	85	70	57	55	60	23	60	82	81	77
7. Buch-17-ppfh	88	100	94	100	100	88	100	50	1	7	0	5	25	16	4	35	37	48	4	10	4	0		12	34	49
8. Kehl-16	22	100	70	72	96	30	71	17	7	10	18	24	23	10	0	2	11	17	5	1	0	9	12	56	52	22
9. Buch-17-si	62	100	94	62	52	34	97	21	0	1	17	17	9	3	1	4	0	8	2	0	0	0	0	20	26	12
10. Brachmann-14	96	100	66	72	46	92	28	20	0	0	1	0	0	0	0	1	0	0	0	0	0	0	0	0	1	2
11. Buch-17-ecsad	66	88	0	56	34	0	95	23	0	0	0	0	0	0	1	1	0	0	0	0	0	0	0	1	0	8
12. Buch-17-shot	52	88	38	36	40	4	66	11	0	0	1	0	1	5	0	2	1	0	0	1	0	1	1	2	1	3
13. Tejani-14	42	36	0	40	26	74	4	16	0	0	0	0	0	0	0	0	0	0	0	0	0	0	0	0	0	0
14. Buch-16-ppfh	28	34	20	6	24	8	4	1	1	6	3	1	24	4	10	13	10	13	3	8	1	0	0	5	32	13
15. Buch-16-ecsad	4	4	8	4	2	0	5	3	0	1	0	0	0	0	0	1	0	0	0	0	0	0	0	0	0	2

# Method	T-LESS 19	20	21	22	23	24	25	26	27	28	29	30	RU-APC 1	2	3	4	5	6	7	8	9	10	11	12	13	14
1. Vidal-18	57	43	62	69	85	66	43	58	62	69	69	85	39	38	42	54	53	43	4	82	32	0	48	47	20	8
2. Drost-10-edge	55	47	55	56	84	59	47	69	61	80	84	89	0	20	35	47	35	39	0	89	28	0	48	21	15	3
3. Drost-10	53	35	60	61	81	57	28	51	32	60	81	71	0	11	29	45	33	29	26	71	10	0	47	9	0	0
4. Hodan-15	59	27	57	50	74	59	47	72	45	73	74	85	4	36	59	24	47	46	52	97	28	28	34	52	17	0
5. Brachmann-16	38	1	39	19	61	1	16	27	17	13	6	5	6	64	25	21	32	41	47	37	1	0	18	40	0	5
6. Hodan-15-nr	58	27	55	50	73	60	49	72	40	72	76	85	4	39	50	24	41	15	43	91	25	33	31	39	16	1
7. Buch-17-ppfh	31	25	36	35	71	46	64	51	4	44	49	58	16	5	17	51	27	6	57	24	8	10	55	5	11	0
8. Kehl-16	35	5	26	27	71	36	28	51	34	54	86	69	19	14	46	38	54	40	4	80	3	5	3	37	7	5
9. Buch-17-si	11	21	18	11	37	4	52	53	3	35	32	53	24	49	16	39	3	4	32	54	14	9	43	15	17	5
10. Brachmann-14	0	0	0	0	1	0	1	1	0	0	0	0	6	80	42	19	31	33	52	89	19	1	0	40	7	0
11. Buch-17-ecsad	16	11	16	8	27	20	51	31	0	32	22	3	1	2	0	1	3	8	23	34	5	8	2	0	3	1
12. Buch-17-shot	6	6	8	2	28	3	17	13	0	11	7	6	0	0	0	0	0	0	0	1	0	0	0	0	0	0
13. Tejani-14	0	0	0	0	0	0	0	0	0	0	0	2	1	0	0	3	9	0	5	0	0	3	0	0	0	0
14. Buch-16-ppfh	3	3	8	8	16	2	24	4	5	11	6	1	0	0	6	19	2	12	34	8	0	0	38	2	5	0
15. Buch-16-ecsad	2	1	3	0	10	0	12	1	2	4	1	1	0	3	5	0	1	1	11	13	0	0	3	2	0	1

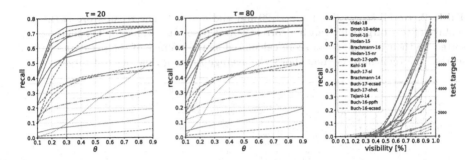

Fig. 4. Left, middle: Average of the per-dataset recall scores for the misalignment tolerance τ fixed to 20 mm and 80 mm, and varying value of the correctness threshold θ. The curves do not change much for $\tau > 80$ mm. Right: The recall scores w.r.t. the visible fraction of the target object. If more instances of the target object were present in the test image, the largest visible fraction was considered.

Figure 4 shows the average of the per-dataset recall scores for different values of τ and θ. If the misalignment tolerance τ is increased from 20 mm to 80 mm, the scores increase only slightly for most methods. Similarly, the scores increase only slowly for $\theta > 0.3$. This suggests that poses estimated by most methods are either of a high quality or totally off, i.e. it is a hit or miss.

Speed. The average running times per test target are reported in Table 2. However, the methods were evaluated on different computers[3] and thus the presented running times are not directly comparable. Moreover, the methods were optimized primarily for the recall score, not for speed. For example, we evaluated Drost-10 with several parameter settings and observed that the running time can be lowered by a factor of ~5 to 0.5 s with only a relatively small drop of the average recall score from 68.1% to 65.8%. However, in Table 2 we present the result with the highest score. Brachmann-14 could be sped up by sub-sampling the 3D object models and Hodaň-15 by using less object templates. A study of such speed/accuracy trade-offs is left for future work.

Open Problems. Occlusion is a big challenge for current methods, as shown by scores dropping swiftly already at low levels of occlusion (Fig. 4, right). The big gap between LM and LM-O scores provide further evidence. All methods perform on LM by at least 30% better than on LM-O, which includes the same but partially occluded objects. Inspection of estimated poses on T-LESS test images confirms the weak performance for occluded objects. Scores on TUD-L show that varying lighting conditions present a serious challenge for methods that rely on synthetic training RGB images, which were generated with fixed lighting. Methods relying only on depth information (e.g. Vidal-18, Drost-10) are noticeably more robust under such conditions. Note that Brachmann-16 achieved a high

---

[3] Specifications of computers used for the evaluation are on the project website.

score on TUD-L despite relying on RGB images because it used real training images, which were captured under the same range of lighting conditions as the test images. Methods based on 3D local features and learning-based methods have very low scores on T-LESS, which is likely caused by the object symmetries and similarities. All methods perform poorly on RU-APC, which is likely because of a higher level of noise in the depth images.

6 Conclusion

We have proposed a benchmark for 6D object pose estimation that includes eight datasets in a unified format, an evaluation methodology, a comprehensive evaluation of 15 recent methods, and an online evaluation system open for continuous submission of new results. With this benchmark, we have captured the status quo in the field and will be able to systematically measure its progress in the future. The evaluation showed that methods based on point-pair features perform best, outperforming template matching methods, learning-based methods and methods based on 3D local features. As open problems, our analysis identified occlusion, varying lighting conditions, and object symmetries and similarities.

Acknowledgements. We gratefully acknowledge Manolis Lourakis, Joachim Staib, Christoph Kick, Juil Sock and Pavel Haluza for their help. This work was supported by CTU student grant SGS17/185/OHK3/3T/13, Technology Agency of the Czech Republic research program TE01020415 (V3C – Visual Computing Competence Center), and the project for GAČR, No. 16-072105: Complex network methods applied to ancient Egyptian data in the Old Kingdom (2700–2180 BC).

References

1. Brachmann, E., Krull, A., Michel, F., Gumhold, S., Shotton, J., Rother, C.: Learning 6D object pose estimation using 3D object coordinates. In: Fleet, D., Pajdla, T., Schiele, B., Tuytelaars, T. (eds.) ECCV 2014. LNCS, vol. 8690, pp. 536–551. Springer, Cham (2014). https://doi.org/10.1007/978-3-319-10605-2_35
2. Brachmann, E., Michel, F., Krull, A., Yang, M.Y., Gumhold, S., Rother, C.: Uncertainty-driven 6D pose estimation of objects and scenes from a single RGB image. In: CVPR (2016)
3. Buch, A.G., Petersen, H.G., Krüger, N.: Local shape feature fusion for improved matching, pose estimation and 3D object recognition. SpringerPlus 5(1), 297 (2016)
4. Buch, A.G., Kiforenko, L., Kraft, D.: Rotational subgroup voting and pose clustering for robust 3D object recognition. In: ICCV (2017)
5. Buch, A.G., Kraft, D.: Local point pair feature histogram for accurate 3D matching. In: BMVC (2018)
6. Correll, N., et al.: Lessons from the Amazon picking challenge. arXiv e-prints (2016)
7. Doumanoglou, A., Kouskouridas, R., Malassiotis, S., Kim, T.K.: Recovering 6D object pose and predicting next-best-view in the crowd. In: CVPR (2016)
8. Drost, B., Ulrich, M., Bergmann, P., Härtinger, P., Steger, C.: Introducing MVTec ITODD - a dataset for 3D object recognition in industry. In: ICCVW (2017)

9. Drost, B., Ulrich, M., Navab, N., Ilic, S.: Model globally, match locally: Efficient and robust 3D object recognition. In: CVPR (2010)
10. Everingham, M., Van Gool, L., Williams, C.K., Winn, J., Zisserman, A.: The PASCAL visual object classes (VOC) challenge. IJCV **88**(2), 303–338 (2010)
11. Geiger, A., Lenz, P., Urtasun, R.: Are we ready for autonomous driving? The KITTI vision benchmark suite. In: CVPR (2012)
12. MVTec HALCON. https://www.mvtec.com/halcon/
13. Hinterstoisser, S., et al.: Gradient response maps for real-time detection of texture-less objects. TPAMI **34**(5), 876–888 (2012)
14. Hinterstoisser, S., et al.: Model based training, detection and pose estimation of texture-less 3D objects in heavily cluttered scenes. In: Lee, K.M., Matsushita, Y., Rehg, J.M., Hu, Z. (eds.) ACCV 2012. LNCS, vol. 7724, pp. 548–562. Springer, Heidelberg (2013). https://doi.org/10.1007/978-3-642-37331-2_42
15. Hinterstoisser, S., Lepetit, V., Rajkumar, N., Konolige, K.: Going further with point pair features. In: Leibe, B., Matas, J., Sebe, N., Welling, M. (eds.) ECCV 2016. LNCS, vol. 9907, pp. 834–848. Springer, Cham (2016). https://doi.org/10.1007/978-3-319-46487-9_51
16. Hodaň, T., Haluza, P., Obdržálek, Š., Matas, J., Lourakis, M., Zabulis, X.: T-LESS: an RGB-D dataset for 6D pose estimation of texture-less objects. In: WACV (2017)
17. Hodaň, T., Matas, J., Obdržálek, Š.: On evaluation of 6D object pose estimation. In: Hua, G., Jégou, H. (eds.) ECCV 2016. LNCS, vol. 9915, pp. 606–619. Springer, Cham (2016). https://doi.org/10.1007/978-3-319-49409-8_52
18. Hodaň, T., Zabulis, X., Lourakis, M., Obdržálek, Š., Matas, J.: Detection and fine 3D pose estimation of texture-less objects in RGB-D images. In: IROS (2015)
19. Johnson, A.E., Hebert, M.: Using spin images for efficient object recognition in cluttered 3D scenes. TPAMI **21**(5), 433–449 (1999)
20. Jørgensen, T.B., Buch, A.G., Kraft, D.: Geometric edge description and classification in point cloud data with application to 3D object recognition. In: VISAPP (2015)
21. Kehl, W., Manhardt, F., Tombari, F., Ilic, S., Navab, N.: SSD-6D: making RGB-based 3D detection and 6D pose estimation great again. In: ICCV (2017)
22. Kehl, W., Milletari, F., Tombari, F., Ilic, S., Navab, N.: Deep Learning of Local RGB-D Patches for 3D Object Detection and 6D Pose Estimation. In: Leibe, B., Matas, J., Sebe, N., Welling, M. (eds.) ECCV 2016. LNCS, vol. 9907, pp. 205–220. Springer, Cham (2016). https://doi.org/10.1007/978-3-319-46487-9_13
23. Krizhevsky, A., Sutskever, I., Hinton, G.E.: ImageNet classification with deep convolutional neural networks. In: NIPS (2012)
24. Krull, A., Brachmann, E., Michel, F., Ying Yang, M., Gumhold, S., Rother, C.: Learning analysis-by-synthesis for 6D pose estimation in RGB-D images. In: ICCV (2015)
25. Michel, F., et al.: Global hypothesis generation for 6D object pose estimation. In: CVPR (2017)
26. Newcombe, R.A., et al.: KinectFusion: real-time dense surface mapping and tracking. In: ISMAR (2011)
27. Rad, M., Lepetit, V.: BB8: a scalable, accurate, robust to partial occlusion method for predicting the 3D poses of challenging objects without using depth. In: ICCV (2017)
28. Rennie, C., Shome, R., Bekris, K.E., De Souza, A.F.: A dataset for improved RGBD-based object detection and pose estimation for warehouse pick-and-place. Rob. Autom. Lett. **1**(2), 1179–1185 (2016)

29. Russakovsky, O., et al.: ImageNet large scale visual recognition challenge. IJCV **115**(3), 211–252 (2015)
30. Salti, S., Tombari, F., Di Stefano, L.: SHOT: unique signatures of histograms for surface and texture description. Comput. Vis. Image Underst. **125**, 251–264 (2014)
31. Scharstein, D., Szeliski, R.: A taxonomy and evaluation of dense two-frame stereo correspondence algorithms. IJCV **47**(1–3), 7–42 (2002)
32. Scharstein, D., Pal, C.: Learning conditional random fields for stereo. In: CVPR (2007)
33. Steinbrücker, F., Sturm, J., Cremers, D.: Volumetric 3D mapping in real-time on a CPU. In: ICRA (2014)
34. Tejani, A., Tang, D., Kouskouridas, R., Kim, T.-K.: Latent-class hough forests for 3D object detection and pose estimation. In: Fleet, D., Pajdla, T., Schiele, B., Tuytelaars, T. (eds.) ECCV 2014. LNCS, vol. 8694, pp. 462–477. Springer, Cham (2014). https://doi.org/10.1007/978-3-319-10599-4_30
35. Vidal, J., Lin, C.Y., Martí, R.: 6D pose estimation using an improved method based on point pair features. In: ICCAR (2018)
36. Wohlhart, P., Lepetit, V.: Learning descriptors for object recognition and 3D pose estimation. In: CVPR (2015)

3D Vehicle Trajectory Reconstruction in Monocular Video Data Using Environment Structure Constraints

Sebastian Bullinger[1]([✉]) [iD], Christoph Bodensteiner[1], Michael Arens[1], and Rainer Stiefelhagen[2]

[1] Fraunhofer IOSB, Ettlingen, Germany
{sebastian.bullinger,christoph.bodensteiner,
michael.arens}@iosb.fraunhofer.de
[2] Karlsruhe Institute of Technology, Karlsruhe, Germany
rainer.stiefelhagen@kit.edu

Abstract. We present a framework to reconstruct three-dimensional vehicle trajectories using monocular video data. We track two-dimensional vehicle shapes on pixel level exploiting instance-aware semantic segmentation techniques and optical flow cues. We apply Structure from Motion techniques to vehicle and background images to determine for each frame camera poses relative to vehicle instances and background structures. By combining vehicle and background camera pose information, we restrict the vehicle trajectory to a one-parameter family of possible solutions. We compute a ground representation by fusing background structures and corresponding semantic segmentations. We propose a novel method to determine vehicle trajectories consistent to image observations and reconstructed environment structures as well as a criterion to identify frames suitable for scale ratio estimation. We show qualitative results using drone imagery as well as driving sequences from the Cityscape dataset. Due to the lack of suitable benchmark datasets we present a new dataset to evaluate the quality of reconstructed three-dimensional vehicle trajectories. The video sequences show vehicles in urban areas and are rendered using the path-tracing render engine Cycles. In contrast to previous work, we perform a quantitative evaluation of the presented approach. Our algorithm achieves an average reconstruction-to-ground-truth-trajectory distance of 0.31 m using this dataset. The dataset including evaluation scripts will be publicly available on our website (Project page: http://s.fhg.de/trajectory).

Keywords: Vehicle trajectory reconstruction
Instance-aware semantic segmentation · Structure-from-motion

1 Introduction

1.1 Trajectory Reconstruction

Three-dimensional vehicle trajectory reconstruction has many relevant use cases in the domain of autonomous systems and augmented reality applications. There

© Springer Nature Switzerland AG 2018
V. Ferrari et al. (Eds.): ECCV 2018, LNCS 11214, pp. 36–51, 2018.
https://doi.org/10.1007/978-3-030-01249-6_3

are different platforms like drones or wearable systems where one wants to achieve this task with a minimal number of devices in order to reduce weight or lower production costs. We propose a novel approach to reconstruct three-dimensional vehicle motion trajectories using a single camera as sensor.

The reconstruction of object motion trajectories in monocular video data captured by moving cameras is a challenging task, since in general it cannot be solely solved exploiting image observations. Each observed object motion trajectory is scale ambiguous. Additional constraints are required to identify a motion trajectory consistent to environment structures. [3,14,26] assume that the camera is mounted on a driving vehicle, i.e. the camera has specific height and a known pose. [17–19,31] solve the scale ambiguity by making assumptions about object and camera motion trajectories. We follow Ozden's principle of non-accidental motion trajectories [18] and introduce a new object motion constraint exploiting semantic segmentation and terrain geometry to compute consistent object motion trajectories.

In many scenarios, objects cover only a minority of pixels in video frames. This increases the difficulty of reconstructing object motion trajectories using image data. In such cases, current state-of-the-art Structure from Motion (SfM) approaches treat vehicle observations most likely as outliers and reconstruct background structures instead. Previous works, e.g. [12,13], tackle this problem by considering multiple video frames to determine moving parts in the video. They apply motion segmentation or keypoint tracking to detect moving objects. These kind of approaches are vulnerable to occlusion and require objects to move in order to separate them from background structures.

Our method exploits recent results in instance-aware semantic segmentation and rigid Structure from Motion techniques. Thus, our approach extends naturally to stationary vehicles. In addition, we do not exploit specific camera pose constraints like a fixed camera-ground-angle or a fixed camera-ground-distance. We evaluate the presented vehicle trajectory reconstruction algorithm in UAV scenarios, where such constraints are not valid.

1.2   Related Work

Semantic segmentation or scene parsing is the task of providing semantic information at pixel-level. Early semantic segmentation approaches using ConvNets, e.g. Farabet et al. [6], exploit patchwise training. Long et al. [24] applied Fully Convolutional Networks for semantic segmentation, which are trained end-to-end. Recently, [5,10,15] proposed instance-aware semantic segmentation approaches.

The field of Structure from Motion (SfM) can be divided into iterative and global approaches. Iterative or sequential SfM methods [16,23,25,27,30] are more likely to find reasonable solutions than global SfM approaches [16,27]. However, the latter are less prone to drift.

The determination of the correct scale ratio between object and background reconstruction requires additional constraints. Ozden et al. [18] exploit the non-accidentalness principle in the context of independently moving objects.

Yuan et al. [31] propose to reconstruct the 3D object trajectory by assuming that the object motion is perpendicular to the normal vector of the ground plane. Kundu et al. [12] exploit motion segmentation with multibody VSLAM to reconstruct the trajectory of moving cars. They use an instantaneous constant velocity model in combination with Bearing only Tracking to estimate consistent object scales. Park et al. propose an approach in [19] to reconstruct the trajectory of a single 3D point tracked over time by approximating the motion using a linear combination of trajectory basis vectors. Previous works, like [12,18,19,31] show only qualitative results.

1.3   Contribution

The core contributions of this work are as follows. (1) We present a new framework to reconstruct the three-dimensional trajectory of vehicles in monocular video data leveraging state-of-the-art semantic segmentation and structure from motion approaches. (2) We propose a novel method to compute vehicle motion trajectories consistent to image observations and environment structures including a criterion to identify frames suitable for scale ratio estimation. (3) In contrast to previous work, we quantitatively evaluate the reconstructed vehicle motion trajectories. (4) We created a new vehicle trajectory benchmark dataset due to the lack of publicly available video data of vehicles with suitable ground truth data. The dataset consists of photo-realistic rendered videos of urban environments. It includes animated vehicles as well as set of predefined camera and vehicle motion trajectories. 3D vehicle and environmental models used for rendering serve as ground truth. (5) We will publish the dataset and evaluation scripts to foster future object motion reconstruction related research.

1.4   Paper Overview

The paper is organized as follows. Section 2 describes the structure and the components of the proposed pipeline. In Sect. 2.1 we derive an expression for a one-parameter family of possible vehicle motion trajectories combining vehicle and background reconstruction results. Section 2.2 describes a method to approximate the ground locally. In Sect. 2.3 we describe a method to compute consistent vehicle motion trajectories. In Sect. 4 we provide an qualitative and quantitative evaluation of the presented algorithms using driving sequences, drone imagery and rendered video data. Section 5 concludes the paper.

2   Object Motion Trajectory Reconstruction

Figure 1 shows the elements of the proposed pipeline. We use the approach presented in [2] to track two-dimensional vehicle shapes in the input video on pixel level. We detect vehicle shapes exploiting the instance-aware semantic segmentation method presented in [15] and associate extracted object shapes of subsequent frames using the optical flow approach described in [11]. Without loss of

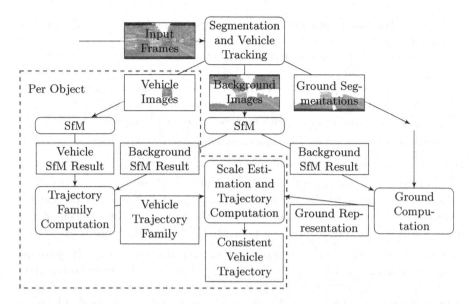

Fig. 1. Overview of the trajectory reconstruction pipeline. Boxes with corners denote computation results and boxes with rounded corners denote computation steps, respectively.

generality, we describe motion trajectory reconstructions of single objects. We apply SfM [16,23] to object and background images as shown in Fig. 1. Object images denote images containing only color information of single object instance. Similarly, background images show only background structures. We combine object and background reconstructions to determine possible, visually identical, object motion trajectories. We compute a consistent object motion trajectory exploiting constraints derived from reconstructed terrain ground geometry.

2.1 Object Trajectory Representation

In order to estimate a consistent object motion trajectory we apply SfM simultaneously to vehicle/object and background images as shown in Fig. 1. We denote the corresponding SfM results with $sfm^{(o)}$ and $sfm^{(b)}$. Let $\mathbf{o}_j^{(o)} \in \mathcal{P}^{(o)}$ and $\mathbf{b}_k^{(b)} \in \mathcal{P}^{(b)}$ denote the 3D points contained in $sfm^{(o)}$ or $sfm^{(b)}$, respectively. The superscripts o and b in $\mathbf{o}_j^{(o)}$ and $\mathbf{b}_k^{(b)}$ describe the corresponding coordinate frame. The variables j and k are the indices of points in the object or the background point cloud, respectively. We denote the reconstructed intrinsic and extrinsic parameters of each registered input image as virtual camera. Each virtual camera in $sfm^{(o)}$ and $sfm^{(b)}$ corresponds to a certain frame from which object and background images are extracted. We determine pairs of corresponding virtual cameras contained in $sfm^{(o)}$ and $sfm^{(b)}$. In the following, we consider only camera pairs, whose virtual cameras are contained in $sfm^{(o)}$

and $sfm^{(b)}$. Because of missing image registrations this may not be the case for all virtual cameras.

We reconstruct the object motion trajectory by combining information of corresponding virtual cameras. Our method is able to determine the scale ratio using a single camera pair. For any virtual camera pair of an image with index i the object SfM result $sfm^{(o)}$ contains information of object point positions $o_j^{(o)}$ relative to virtual cameras with camera centers $c_i^{(o)}$ and rotations $R_i^{(o)}$. We express each object point $o_j^{(o)}$ in camera coordinates $o_j^{(i)}$ of camera i using $o_j^{(i)} = R_i^{(o)} \cdot (o_j^{(o)} - c_i^{(o)})$. The background SfM result $sfm^{(b)}$ contains the camera center $c_i^{(b)}$ and the corresponding rotation $R_i^{(b)}$, which provide pose information of the camera with respect to the reconstructed background. Note that the camera coordinate systems of virtual cameras in $sfm^{(o)}$ and $sfm^{(b)}$ are equivalent. We use $c_i^{(b)}$ and $R_i^{(b)}$ to transform object points to the background coordinate system using $o_{j,i}^{(b)} = c_i^{(b)} + R_i^{(b)^T} \cdot o_j^{(i)}$. In general, the scale ratio of object and background reconstruction does not match due to the scale ambiguity of SfM reconstructions [9]. We tackle this problem by treating the scale of the background as reference scale and by introducing a scale ratio factor r to adjust the scale of object point coordinates. The overall transformation of object points given in object coordinates $o_j^{(o)}$ to object points in the background coordinate frame system $o_{j,i}^{(b)}$ of camera i is described according to Eq. (1).

$$o_{j,i}^{(b)} = c_i^{(b)} + r \cdot R_i^{(b)^T} \cdot R_i^{(o)} \cdot (o_j^{(o)} - c_i^{(o)}) := c_i^{(b)} + r \cdot v_{j,i}^{(b)} \qquad (1)$$

with

$$v_{j,i}^{(b)} = R_i^{(b)^T} \cdot R_i^{(o)} \cdot (o_j^{(o)} - c_i^{(o)}) = o_{j,i}^{(b)} - c_i^{(b)}. \qquad (2)$$

Given the scale ratio r, we can recover the full object motion trajectory computing Eq. (2) for each virtual camera pair. We use $o_{j,i}^{(b)}$ of all cameras and object points as object motion trajectory representation. The ambiguity mentioned in Sect. 1 is expressed by the unknown scale ratio r.

2.2   Terrain Ground Approximation

Further camera or object motion constraints are required to determine the scale ratio r introduced in Eq. (2). In contrast to previous work [3,14,18,19,26,31] we assume that the object category of interest moves on top of the terrain. We exploit semantic segmentation techniques to estimate an approximation of the ground surface of the scene. We apply the ConvNet presented in [24] to determine ground categories like street or grass for all input images on pixel level. We consider only stable background points, i.e. 3D points that are observed at least four times. We determine for each 3D point a ground or non-ground label by accumulating the semantic labels of corresponding keypoint measurement pixel positions. This allows us to determine a subset of background points, which represent the ground of the scene. We approximate the ground surface locally using plane representations. For each frame i we use corresponding estimated camera parameters and object point observations to determine a set of ground points P_i close to the object. We build a kd-tree containing all ground measurement positions of the current frame. For each object point observation, we determine the num_b closest background measurements. In our experiments, we set num_b to 50. Let $card_i$ be the cardinality of P_i. While $card_i$ is less than num_b, we add the next background observation of each point measurement. This results in an equal distribution of local ground points around the vehicle. We apply RANSAC [7] to compute a local approximation of the ground surface using P_i. Each plane is defined by a corresponding normal vector $\mathbf{n}_i$ and an arbitrary point $\mathbf{p}_i$ lying on the plane.

2.3 Scale Estimation Using Environment Structure Constraints

In Sect. 2.3, we exploit priors of object motion to improve the robustness of the reconstructed object trajectory. We assume that the object of interest moves on a locally planar surface. In this case the distance of each object point $\mathbf{o}_{j,i}^{(b)}$ to the ground is constant for all cameras i. The reconstructed trajectory shows this property only for the true scale ratio and non-degenerated camera motion. For example, a degenerate case occurs when the camera moves exactly parallel to a planar object motion. For a more detailed discussion of degenerated camera motions see [18].

Scale Ratio Estimation Using a Single View Pair. We use the term *view* to denote cameras and corresponding local ground planes. The signed distance of an object point $\mathbf{o}_{j,i}^{(b)}$ to the ground plane can be computed according to $d_{j,i} = \mathbf{n}_i \cdot (\mathbf{o}_{j,i}^{(b)} - \mathbf{p}_i)$, where $\mathbf{p_i}$ is an arbitrary point on the local ground plane and $\mathbf{n_i}$ is the corresponding normal vector. If the object moves on top of the approximated terrain ground the distance $d_{j,i}$ is be independent of a specific camera i. Thus, for a specific point and different cameras the relation shown in Eq. (3) holds.

$$\mathbf{n}_i \cdot (\mathbf{o}_{j,i}^{(b)} - \mathbf{p}_i) = \mathbf{n}_{i'} \cdot (\mathbf{o}_{j,i'}^{(b)} - \mathbf{p}_{i'}). \tag{3}$$

Substituting Eq. (1) in Eq. (3) results in (4)

$$\mathbf{n}_i \cdot (\mathbf{c}_i^{(b)} + r \cdot \mathbf{v}_{j,i}^{(b)} - \mathbf{p}_i) = \mathbf{n}_{i'} \cdot (\mathbf{c}_{i'}^{(b)} + r \cdot \mathbf{v}_{j,i'}^{(b)} - \mathbf{p}_{i'}) \tag{4}$$

Solving Eq. (4) for r yields Eq. (5)

$$r = \frac{\mathbf{n}_{i'} \cdot (\mathbf{c}_{i'}^{(b)} - \mathbf{p}_{i'}) - \mathbf{n}_i \cdot (\mathbf{c}_i^{(b)} - \mathbf{p}_i)}{(\mathbf{n}_i \cdot \mathbf{v}_{j,i}^{(b)} - \mathbf{n}_{i'} \cdot \mathbf{v}_{j,i'}^{(b)})}. \tag{5}$$

Equation (5) allows us to determine the scale ratio r between object and background reconstruction using the extrinsic parameters of two cameras and corresponding ground approximations.

Scale Ratio Estimation Using View Pair Ranking. The accuracy of the estimated scale ratio r in Eq. (5) is subject to the condition of the parameters of the particular view pair. For instance, if the numerator or denominator is close to zero, small errors in the camera poses or ground approximations may result in negative scale ratios. In addition, wrongly estimated local plane normal vectors may disturb camera-plane distances. We tackle these problems by combining two different view pair rankings. The first ranking uses for each view pair the difference of the camera-plane distances, i.e. $|\mathbf{n}_{i'} \cdot (\mathbf{c}_{i'}^{(b)} - \mathbf{p}_{i'}) - \mathbf{n}_i \cdot (\mathbf{c}_i^{(b)} - \mathbf{p}_i)|$. The second ranking reflects the quality of the local ground approximation w.r.t. the object reconstruction. A single view pair allows to determine $|\mathcal{P}^{(o)}|$ different scale ratios. For a view pair with stable camera registrations and well reconstructed local planes the variance of the corresponding scale ratios is small. This allows us to determine ill conditioned view pairs. The second ranking uses the scale ratio difference to order the view pairs. We sort the view pairs by weighting both ranks equally.

This ranking is crucial to deal with motion trajectories close to degenerated cases. In contrast to other methods, this ranking allows to estimate consistent vehicle motion trajectories, even if the majority of local ground planes are badly reconstructed. Concretely, this approach allows to determine a consistent trajectory using a single suitable view pair.

Let vp denote the view pair with the lowest overall rank. The final scale ratio is determined by using a least squares method w.r.t. all equations of vp according to Eq. (6). Let i and i' denote the image indices corresponding to vp.

$$
\begin{bmatrix}
\cdots \\
\mathbf{n}_i \cdot \mathbf{v}_{j,i}^{(b)} - \mathbf{n}_{i'} \cdot \mathbf{v}_{j,i'}^{(b)} \\
\cdots \\
\mathbf{n}_i \cdot \mathbf{v}_{j+1,i}^{(b)} - \mathbf{n}_{i'} \cdot \mathbf{v}_{j+1,i'}^{(b)} \\
\cdots
\end{bmatrix} \cdot r =
\begin{bmatrix}
\cdots \\
\mathbf{n}_{i'}(\mathbf{c}_{i'}^{(b)} - \mathbf{p}_{i'}) - \mathbf{n}_i \cdot (\mathbf{c}_i^{(b)} - \mathbf{p}_i) \\
\cdots \\
\mathbf{n}_{i'}(\mathbf{c}_{i'}^{(b)} - \mathbf{p}_{i'}) - \mathbf{n}_i \cdot (\mathbf{c}_i^{(b)} - \mathbf{p}_i) \\
\cdots
\end{bmatrix}
\tag{6}
$$

2.4   Scale Estimation Baseline Using Intersection Constraints

The baseline is motivated by the fact, that some of the reconstructed points at the bottom of a vehicle should lie in the proximity of the ground surface of the environment. Consider for example 3D points triangulated at the wheels of a vehicle. This approach works only if at least one camera-object-point-ray intersects the local ground surface approximations. For each camera we use Eq. (2) to generate a set of direction vectors $\mathbf{v}_{j,i}^{(b)}$. For non-orthogonal direction vectors $\mathbf{v}_{j,i}^{(b)}$ and normal vectors $\mathbf{n}_i$ we compute the ray-plane-intersection parameter for each camera-object-point-pair according to Eq. (7)

$$
r_{j,i} = (\mathbf{p}_i - \mathbf{c}_i^{(b)}) \cdot \mathbf{n}_i \cdot (\mathbf{v}_{j,i}^{(b)} \cdot \mathbf{n}_i)^{-1}.
\tag{7}
$$

Let r_i denote the smallest ray-plane-intersection parameter of image i. This parameter corresponds to a point at the bottom of the vehicle lying on the planar approximation of the ground surface. Substituting r in Eq. (1) with r_i results in a vehicle point cloud being on top of the local terrain approximation corresponding to image i. Thus, r_i represents a value close to the scale ratio of object and background reconstruction. To increase the robustness of the computed scale ratio, we use the median r of all image specific scale ratios r_i to determine the final scale ratio.

$$r = \text{median}(\{\min(\{r_{j,i} \mid j \in \{1, \ldots, |\mathcal{P}^{(o)}|\}\}) \mid i \in \mathcal{I}\}), \tag{8}$$

Here, $\mathcal{I}$ denotes the set of images indices. Cameras without valid intersection parameter r_i are not considered for the computation of r.

3   Virtual Object Motion Trajectory Dataset

To quantitatively evaluate the quality of the reconstructed object motion trajectory we require accurate object and environment models as well as object and camera poses at each time step. The simultaneous capturing of corresponding ground truth data with sufficient quality is difficult to achieve. For example, one could capture the environment geometry with LIDAR sensors and the camera/object pose with an additional system. However, the registration and synchronization of all these different modalities is a complex and cumbersome process. The result will contain noise and other artifacts like drift. To tackle these issues we exploit virtual models. Previously published virtually generated and virtually augmented datasets, like [8, 20, 21, 28], provide data for different application domains and do not include three-dimensional ground truth information. We build a virtual world including an urban environment, animated vehicles as well as predefined vehicle and camera motion trajectories. This allows us to compute spatial and temporal error free ground truth data. We exploit procedural generation of textures to avoid artificial repetitions. Thus, our dataset is suitable for evaluating SfM algorithms.

3.1   Trajectory Dataset

We use the previously created virtual world to build a new vehicle trajectory dataset. The dataset consists of 35 sequences capturing five vehicles in different urban scenes. Figure 2 shows some example images. The virtual video sequences cover a high variety of vehicle and camera poses. The vehicle trajectories reflect common vehicle motions include vehicle acceleration, different curve types and motion on changing slopes. We use the path-tracing render engine Cycles [1] to achieve photo realistic rendering results. We observed that the removal of artificial path-tracing artifacts using denoising is crucial to avoid degenerated SfM reconstructions.

The dataset includes 6D vehicle and camera poses for each frame as well as ground truth meshes of corresponding vehicle models. In contrast to measured ground truth data, virtual ground truth data is free of noise and shows no spatial registration or temporal synchronization inaccuracies. The dataset

Fig. 2. Frames from sequences contained in the presented virtual vehicle trajectory dataset.

contains semantic segmentations of vehicles, ground and background to separate the reconstruction task from specific semantic segmentation and tracking approaches. In addition to the virtual data, the dataset also includes the computed reconstruction results. We will make our evaluation scripts publicly available to foster future analysis of vehicle trajectory estimation.

3.2   Virtual World

We used Blender [1] to create a virtual world consisting of a city surrounded by a countryside. We exploit procedural generation to compute textures of large surfaces, like streets and sidewalks, to avoid degenerated Structure from Motion results caused by artificial texture repetitions. The virtual world includes different assets like trees, traffic lights, streetlights, phone booths, bus stops and benches. We collected a set of publicly available vehicle assets to populate the scenes. We used skeletal animation, also referred to as rigging, for vehicle animation. This includes wheel rotation and steering w.r.t. the motion trajectory as well as consistent vehicle placement on uneven ground surfaces. The animation of wheels is important to avoid unrealistic wheel point triangulations. We adjusted the scale of vehicles and virtual environment using Blender's unit system. This allows us to set the virtual space in relation to the real world. The extent of the generated virtual world corresponds to one square kilometer. We exploit environment mapping to achieve realistic illumination. With Blender's built-in tools, we defined a set of camera and object motion trajectories. This allows us to determine the exact 3D pose of cameras and vehicles at each time step.

4   Experiments and Evaluation

Figure 3 shows qualitative results using driving sequences from the Cityscapes dataset [4] as well as real and virtual drone footage. For sequences with

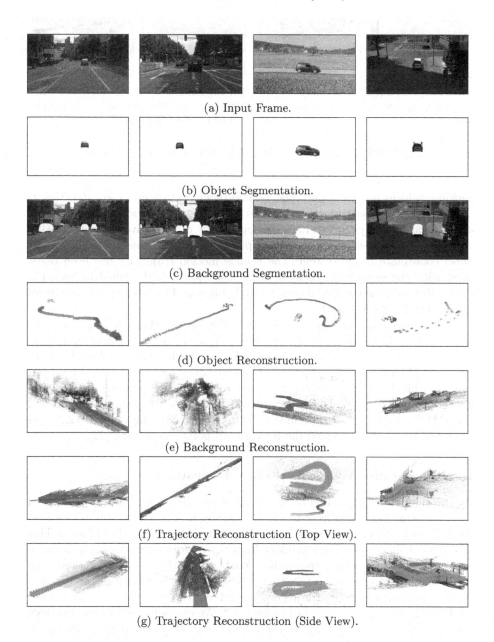

(a) Input Frame.

(b) Object Segmentation.

(c) Background Segmentation.

(d) Object Reconstruction.

(e) Background Reconstruction.

(f) Trajectory Reconstruction (Top View).

(g) Trajectory Reconstruction (Side View).

Fig. 3. Vehicle trajectory reconstruction using two sequences (first two columns) from the Cityscape dataset [4], one sequence captured by a drone (third column) as well as one virtually generated sequence of our dataset (last column). Object segmentations and object reconstructions are shown for one of the vehicles visible in the scene. The reconstructed cameras are shown in red. The vehicle trajectories are colored green, blue and pink. (Color figure online)

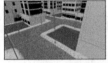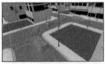

(a) Example of a registered vehicle trajec-   (b) Example of a vehicle trajectory with
tory in the ground truth coordinate frame   the corresponding ground truth vehicle
system.   model at selected frames.

Fig. 4. Vehicle trajectory registration for quantitative evaluation.

multiple vehicle instances only one vehicle segmentation and reconstruction is shown. However, the trajectory reconstruction results contain multiple reconstructed vehicle trajectories. Figure 4 depicts the quantitative evaluation using our dataset. Figure 4a shows the object point cloud transformed into the virtual world coordinate frame system. The vehicle motion trajectory has been registered with the virtual environment using the approach described in Sect. 4.2. Figure 4b shows the overlay of transformed points and the corresponding virtual ground truth vehicle model.

To segment the two-dimensional vehicle shapes, we follow the approach presented in [2]. In contrast to [2], we used [15] and [11] to segment and track visible objects, respectively. We considered the following SfM pipelines for vehicle and background reconstructions: Colmap [23], OpenMVG [16], Theia [27] and VisualSfM [30]. Our vehicle trajectory reconstruction pipeline uses Colmap for vehicle and OpenMVG for background reconstructions, since Colmap and OpenMVG created in our experiments the most reliable vehicle and background reconstructions. We enhanced the background point cloud using [22].

4.1   Quantitative Vehicle Trajectory Evaluation

We use the dataset presented in Sect. 3 to quantitatively evaluate the proposed vehicle motion trajectory reconstruction approach. The evaluation is based on vehicle, background and ground segmentations included in the dataset. This allows us to show results independent from the performance of specific instance segmentation and tracking approaches. We compare the proposed method with the baseline presented in Sect. 2.4 using 35 sequences contained in the dataset. We automatically register the reconstructed vehicle trajectory to the ground truth using the method described in Sect. 4.2. We compute the shortest distance of each vehicle trajectory point to the vehicle mesh in ground truth coordinates. For each sequence we define the trajectory error as the average trajectory-point-mesh distance. Figure 5 shows for each sequence the trajectory error in meter. The average trajectory error per vehicle using the full dataset is shown in Table 1. Overall, we achieve a trajectory error of 0.31 m. The error of the vehicle trajectory reconstructions reflects four types of computational inaccuracies: deviations of camera poses w.r.t. vehicle and background point clouds, wrong triangulated vehicle points as well as scale ratio discrepancies. Figure 5 compares the

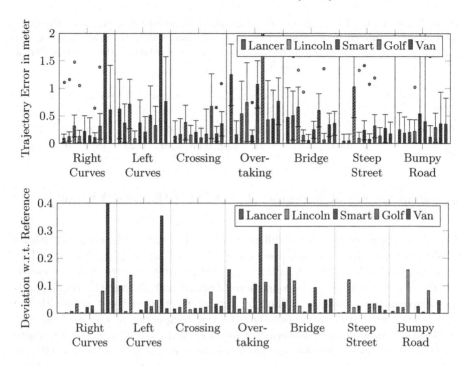

Fig. 5. Quantitative evaluation of the trajectory reconstruction computed by our proposed method (plain colored bars) and the *baseline* (dashed bars). We evaluate seven different vehicle trajectories (*Right Curves, . . .*) and five different vehicle models (*Lancer, . . .*). The top figure shows the trajectory error in meter, which reflects deviations of camera poses w.r.t. vehicle and background point clouds, wrong triangulated vehicle points as well as scale ratio discrepancies. The circles show the trajectory error of the most distant points. The intervals denote the standard deviation of the trajectory errors. The reference scale ratios used in the bottom figure are only subject to the registration of the background reconstruction and the virtual environment. The figure is best viewed in color.

estimated scale ratios of the proposed and the baseline method w.r.t. the reference scale ratio. The reference scale ratio computation is described in Sect. 4.3. The overall estimated scale ratio deviation w.r.t. the reference scale per vehicle is shown in Table 1. The provided reference scale ratios are subject to the registration described in Sect. 4.2. Wrongly reconstructed background camera poses may influence the reference scale ratio. The *van* vehicle reconstruction was only partial successful on the sequences *crossing*, *overtaking* and *steep street*. The SfM algorithm registered 19%, 60% and 98% of the images, respectively. The vehicle reconstruction of the *smart* model contained 74% of the *crossing* input vehicle images. Here, we use the subset of registered images to perform the evaluation. The camera and the vehicle motion in *bumpy road* simulate a sequence close to a degenerated case, i.e. Eq. (5) is ill conditioned for all view pairs.

Table 1. Summary of the conducted evaluation. The second column shows the deviation of the estimated scale ratio w.r.t to the reference scale ratio. The third column contains the average distances of the full dataset in meter. Overall, the trajectory error of the baseline and our approach is 0.77 m and 0.31 m.

Scale ratio Est. type	Average scale ratio deviation					Average trajectory error [m]				
	Lancer	Lincoln	Smart	Golf	Van	Lancer	Lincoln	Smart	Golf	Van
Baseline	0.05	0.07	**0.01**	0.08	0.13	0.42	0.53	**0.25**	0.95	1.68
Ours	**0.04**	**0.04**	0.04	**0.06**	**0.08**	**0.20**	**0.23**	0.33	**0.33**	**0.47**

4.2 Registration of Background Reconstruction and Virtual Environment

A common approach to register different coordinate systems is to exploit 3D-3D correspondences. To determine points in the virtual environment corresponding to background reconstruction points one could create a set of rays from each camera center to all visible reconstructed background points. The corresponding environment points are defined by the intersection of these rays with the mesh of the virtual environment. Due to the complexity of our environment model this computation is in terms of memory and computational effort quite expensive. Instead, we use the algorithm presented in [29] to estimate a similarity transformation $\mathbf{T}_s$ between the cameras contained in the background reconstruction and the virtual cameras used to render the corresponding video sequence. This allows us to perform 3D-3D-registrations of background reconstructions and the virtual environment as well as to quantitatively evaluate the quality of the reconstructed object motion trajectory. We use the camera centers as input for [29] to compute an initial reconstruction-to-virtual-environment transformation. Depending on the shape of the camera trajectory there may be multiple valid similarity transformations using camera center positions. In order to find the semantically correct solution we enhance the original point set with camera pose information, i.e. we add points reflecting up vectors $\mathbf{u}_i^{(b)} = \mathbf{R}_i^{(b)^T} \cdot (0,1,0)^T$ and forward vectors $\mathbf{f}_i^{(b)} = \mathbf{R}_i^{(b)^T} \cdot (0,0,1)^T$. For the reconstructed cameras, we adjust the magnitude of these vectors using the scale computed during the initial similarity transformation. We add the corresponding end points of up $\mathbf{c}_i^{(b)} + m \cdot \mathbf{u}_i^{(b)}$ as well as viewing vectors $\mathbf{c}_i^{(b)} + m \cdot \mathbf{f}_i^{(b)}$ to the camera center point set. Here, m denotes the corresponding magnitude.

4.3 Reference Scale Ratio Computation

As explained in Sect. 4.1 the presented average trajectory errors in Fig. 5 are subject to four different error sources. To evaluate the quality of the scale ratio estimation between object and background reconstruction we provide corresponding reference scale ratios. The scale ratios between object reconstruction, background reconstruction and virtual environment are linked via the relation

$r_{(ov)} = r_{(ob)} \cdot r_{(bv)}$, where $r_{(ov)}$ and $r_{(bv)}$ are the scale ratios between object and background reconstructions and virtual environment, respectively. The scale ratios $r_{(ob)}$ in Fig. 5 express the spatial relation of vehicle and background reconstructions. The similarity transformation $\mathbf{T}_s$ defined in Sect. 4.2 implicitly contains information about the scale ratio $r_{(bv)}$ between background reconstruction and virtual environment. To compute $r_{(ov)}$ we use corresponding pairs of object reconstruction and virtual cameras. We use the extrinsic parameters of the object reconstruction camera to transform all 3D points in the object reconstruction into camera coordinates. Similarly, the object mesh with the pose of the corresponding frame is transformed into the camera coordinates leveraging the extrinsic camera parameters of the corresponding virtual camera. The ground truth pose and shape of the object mesh is part of the dataset. In camera coordinates we generate rays from the camera center (i.e. the origin) to each 3D point $\mathbf{o}_j^{(i)}$ in the object reconstruction. We determine the shortest intersection $\mathbf{m}_j^{(i)}$ of each ray with the object mesh in camera coordinates. This allows us to compute the reference scale ratio $r_{(ov)}^{ref}$ according to Eq. (9) and the reference scale ratio $r_{(ob)}^{ref}$ according to $r_{(ob)}^{ref} = r_{(ov)}^{ref} \cdot r_{(bv)}^{-1}$.

$$r_{(ov)}^{ref} = \mathrm{med}(\{\mathrm{med}(\{\|\mathbf{m}_j^{(i)}\| \cdot \|\mathbf{o}_j^{(i)}\|^{-1} | j \in \{1,\dots,n_J\}\}) | i \in \{1,\dots,n_I\}\}). \quad (9)$$

The reference scale ratio $r_{(ob)}^{ref}$ depends on the quality of the estimated camera poses in the background reconstruction, i.e. $r_{(bv)}$, and may slightly differ from the true scale ratio.

5   Conclusions

This paper presents a pipeline to reconstruct the three-dimensional trajectory of vehicles using monocular video data. We propose a novel constraint to estimate consistent object motion trajectories and demonstrate the effectiveness of our approach showing vehicle trajectory reconstructions using drone footage and driving sequences from the Cityscapes dataset. Due to the lack of 3D object motion trajectory benchmark datasets with suitable ground truth data, we present a new virtual dataset to quantitatively evaluate object motion trajectories. The dataset contains rendered videos of urban environments and accurate ground truth data including semantic segmentations, object meshes as well as object and camera poses for each frame. The proposed algorithm achieves an average reconstruction-to-ground-truth distance of 0.31 m evaluating 35 trajectories. In future work, we will analyze the performance of the proposed pipeline in more detail with focus on minimal object sizes, object occlusions and degeneracy cases. In addition, we intend to integrate previously published scale estimation approaches. These will serve together with our dataset as benchmark references for future vehicle/object motion trajectory reconstruction algorithms.

References

1. Blender Online Community: Blender - a 3D modelling and rendering package (2016). http://www.blender.org
2. Bullinger, S., Bodensteiner, C., Arens, M.: Instance flow based online multiple object tracking. In: IEEE International Conference on Image Processing (ICIP). IEEE (2017)
3. Chhaya, F., Reddy, N.D., Upadhyay, S., Chari, V., Zia, M.Z., Krishna, K.M.: Monocular reconstruction of vehicles: combining SLAM with shape priors. In: IEEE International Conference on Robotics and Automation (ICRA). IEEE (2016)
4. Cordts, M., et al.: The cityscapes dataset for semantic urban scene understanding. In: IEEE Conference on Computer Vision and Pattern Recognition (CVPR). IEEE (2016)
5. Dai, J., He, K., Sun, J.: Instance-aware semantic segmentation via multi-task network cascades. In: IEEE Conference on Computer Vision and Pattern Recognition (CVPR). IEEE (2016)
6. Farabet, C., Couprie, C., Najman, L., LeCun, Y.: Learning hierarchical features for scene labeling. IEEE Trans. Pattern Anal. Mach. Intell. (PAMI) $35(8)$, 1915–1929 (2013)
7. Fischler, M.A., Bolles, R.C.: Random sample consensus: a paradigm for model fitting with applications to image analysis and automated cartography. ACM Commun. $24(6)$, 381–395 (1981)
8. Gaidon, A., Wang, Q., Cabon, Y., Vig, E.: Virtual worlds as proxy for multi-object tracking analysis. In: IEEE Conference on Computer Vision and Pattern Recognition (CVPR). IEEE (2016)
9. Hartley, R.I., Zisserman, A.: Multiple View Geometry in Computer Vision, 2nd edn. Cambridge University Press, Cambridge (2004). ISBN 0521540518
10. He, K., Gkioxari, G., Dollar, P., Girshick, R.: Mask R-CNN. In: IEEE International Conference on Computer Vision (ICCV). IEEE (2017)
11. Ilg, E., Mayer, N., Saikia, T., Keuper, M., Dosovitskiy, A., Brox, T.: Flownet 2.0: evolution of optical flow estimation with deep networks. In: IEEE Conference on Computer Vision and Pattern Recognition (CVPR). IEEE (2017)
12. Kundu, A., Krishna, K.M., Jawahar, C.V.: Realtime multibody visual slam with a smoothly moving monocular camera. In: IEEE International Conference on Computer Vision (ICCV). IEEE (2011)
13. Lebeda, K., Hadfield, S., Bowden, R.: 2D or not 2D: bridging the gap between tracking and structure from motion. In: Cremers, D., Reid, I., Saito, H., Yang, M.-H. (eds.) ACCV 2014. LNCS, vol. 9006, pp. 642–658. Springer, Cham (2015). https://doi.org/10.1007/978-3-319-16817-3_42
14. Lee, B., Daniilidis, K., Lee, D.D.: Online self-supervised monocular visual odometry for ground vehicles. In: IEEE International Conference on Robotics and Automation (ICRA). IEEE (2015)
15. Li, Y., Qi, H., Dai, J., Ji, X., Wei, Y.: Fully convolutional instance-aware semantic segmentation. In: IEEE Conference on Computer Vision and Pattern Recognition (CVPR). IEEE (2017)
16. Moulon, P., Monasse, P., Marlet, R., et al.: OpenMVG: an open multiple view geometry library (2013)
17. Namdev, R.K., Krishna, K.M., Jawahar, C.V.: Multibody VSLAM with relative scale solution for curvilinear motion reconstruction. In: IEEE International Conference on Robotics and Automation (ICRA). IEEE (2013)

18. Ozden, K.E., Cornelis, K., Eycken, L.V., Gool, L.J.V.: Reconstructing 3D trajectories of independently moving objects using generic constraints. Comput. Vis. Image Underst. **96**(3), 453–471 (2004)

19. Park, H.S., Shiratori, T., Matthews, I., Sheikh, Y.: 3D trajectory reconstruction under perspective projection. Int. J. Comput. Vis. **115**(2), 115–135 (2015)

20. Richter, S.R., Vineet, V., Roth, S., Koltun, V.: Playing for data: ground truth from computer games. In: Leibe, B., Matas, J., Sebe, N., Welling, M. (eds.) ECCV 2016. LNCS, vol. 9906, pp. 102–118. Springer, Cham (2016). https://doi.org/10.1007/978-3-319-46475-6_7

21. Ros, G., Sellart, L., Materzynska, J., Vazquez, D., Lopez, A.M.: The synthia dataset: a large collection of synthetic images for semantic segmentation of urban scenes. In: IEEE Conference on Computer Vision and Pattern Recognition (CVPR). IEEE (2016)

22. Schönberger, J.L., Zheng, E., Frahm, J.-M., Pollefeys, M.: Pixelwise view selection for unstructured multi-view stereo. In: Leibe, B., Matas, J., Sebe, N., Welling, M. (eds.) ECCV 2016. LNCS, vol. 9907, pp. 501–518. Springer, Cham (2016). https://doi.org/10.1007/978-3-319-46487-9_31

23. Schönberger, J.L., Frahm, J.M.: Structure-from-motion revisited. In: IEEE Conference on Computer Vision and Pattern Recognition (CVPR). IEEE (2016)

24. Shelhamer, E., Long, J., Darrell, T.: Fully convolutional networks for semantic segmentation. IEEE Trans. Pattern Anal. Mach. Intell. (PAMI) **39**(4), 640–651 (2017)

25. Snavely, N., Seitz, S.M., Szeliski, R.: Photo tourism: exploring photo collections in 3D. ACM Trans. Graph. **25**(3), 835–846 (2006)

26. Song, S., Chandraker, M., Guest, C.C.: High accuracy monocular SFM and scale correction for autonomous driving. IEEE Trans. Pattern Anal. Mach. Intell. (PAMI) **38**(4), 730–743 (2016)

27. Sweeney, C.: Theia Multiview Geometry Library: Tutorial & Reference. University of California Santa Barbara (2014)

28. Tsirikoglou, A., Kronander, J., Wrenninge, M., Unger, J.: Procedural modeling and physically based rendering for synthetic data generation in automotive applications. CoRR (2017)

29. Umeyama, S.: Least-squares estimation of transformation parameters between two point patterns. IEEE Trans. Pattern Anal. Mach. Intell. (PAMI) **13**(4), 376–380 (1991)

30. Wu, C.: VisualSFM: a visual structure from motion system (2011)

31. Yuan, C., Medioni, G.G.: 3D reconstruction of background and objects moving on ground plane viewed from a moving camera. In: IEEE Computer Society Conference on Computer Vision and Pattern Recognition (CVPR). IEEE (2006)

Pairwise Body-Part Attention for Recognizing Human-Object Interactions

Hao-Shu Fang[1]📍, Jinkun Cao[1], Yu-Wing Tai[2], and Cewu Lu[1(✉)]📍

[1] Shanghai Jiao Tong University, Shanghai, China
fhaoshu@gmail.com, {caojinkun,lucewu}@sjtu.edu.cn
[2] Tencent YouTu Lab, Shanghai, China
yuwingtai@tencent.com

Abstract. In human-object interactions (HOI) recognition, conventional methods consider the human body as a whole and pay a uniform attention to the entire body region. They ignore the fact that normally, human interacts with an object by using some parts of the body. In this paper, we argue that different body parts should be paid with different attention in HOI recognition, and the correlations between different body parts should be further considered. This is because our body parts always work collaboratively. We propose a new pairwise body-part attention model which can learn to focus on crucial parts, and their correlations for HOI recognition. A novel attention based feature selection method and a feature representation scheme that can capture pairwise correlations between body parts are introduced in the model. Our proposed approach achieved **10%** relative improvement (36.1 mAP → 39.9 mAP) over the state-of-the-art results in HOI recognition on the HICO dataset. We will make our model and source codes **publicly available**.

Keywords: Human-object interactions · Body-part correlations · Attention model

1 Introduction

Recognizing Human-Object Interactions (HOI) in a still image is an important research problem and has applications in image understanding and robotics [1,44,48]. From a still image, HOI recognition needs to infer the possible interactions between the detected human and objects. Our goal is to evaluate the probabilities of certain interactions on a predefined HOI list.

Conventional methods consider the problem of HOI recognition at holistic body level [21,40,52] or very coarse part level (e.g., head, torso, and legs) [11] only. However, studies in cognitive science [4,35] have already found that our visual attention is non-uniform, and humans tend to focus on different body

---

Cewu Lu is a member of MoE Key Lab of Artificial Intelligence, AI Institute, Shanghai Jiao Tong University, and SJTU-SenseTime AI lab.

V. Ferrari et al. (Eds.): ECCV 2018, LNCS 11214, pp. 52–68, 2018.
https://doi.org/10.1007/978-3-030-01249-6_4

(a) Conventional HOI recognition model   (b) Our model

Fig. 1. Given an image, a person holding a mug in his/her hand, conventional model (a) infers the HOI from the whole body feature. In contrast, our model (b) explicitly focuses on discriminative body parts and the correlations between objects and different body parts. In this example, the upper and lower arms which hold a mug form an acute angle across all of the above images.

parts according to different context. As shown in Fig. 1, although the HOI label are the same across all examples, the body gestures are all different except for the arm which holds a mug. This motivates us to introduce a non-uniform attention model which can effectively discover the most informative body parts for HOI recognition.

However, simply building attention on body parts can not capture important HOI semantics, since it ignores the correlations between different body parts. In Fig. 1, the upper and lower arms and the hand work collaboratively and form an acute angle due to physical constraints. Such observation motivates us to further focus on the correlations between multiple body parts. In order to make a practical solution, we consider the joint correlations between each pair of body parts. Such pairwise sets define a new set of correlation feature maps whose features should be extracted simultaneously. Specifically, we introduce pairwise ROI pooling which pools out the joint feature maps of pairwise body parts, and discards the features of other body parts. This representation is robust to irrelevant human gestures and the detected HOI labels have significantly less false positives, since the irrelevant body parts are filtered. With the set of pairwise features, we build an attention model to automatically discover discriminative pairwise correlations of body parts that are meaningful with respect to each HOI label. By minimizing the end-to-end loss, the system is forced to select the most representative pairwise features. In this way, our trained pairwise attention module is able to extract meaningful connections between different body parts.

To the best of our knowledge, our work is the first attempt to apply the attention mechanism to human body part correlations for recognizing human-object interactions.

We evaluate our model on the HICO dataset [5] and the MPII dataset [2]. Our method achieves the state-of-the-art result, and outperforms the previous methods by **10%** relatively in mAP on HICO dataset.

2   Related Work

Our work is related to two active areas in computer vision: human-object interactions and visual attention.

Human-Object Interactions. Human-object interactions (HOI) recognition is a sub-task of human actions recognition but also a crucial task in understanding the actual human action. It can resolve the ambiguities in action recognition when two persons have almost identical pose and provide a higher level of semantic meaning in the recognition label. Early researches in action recognition consider video inputs. Representative works include [16,41,42]. In action recognition from still images, previous works attempt to use human pose to recognize human action [21,28,40,43,47,52].

However, considering human pose solely is ambiguous since there is no motion cue in a still image. Human-object interactions are introduced in order to resolve such ambiguities. With additional high level contextual information, it has demonstrated success in improving performance of action recognition [8,20,32,51]. Since recognizing the small object is difficult, some works [36,50,54] attempt to ease the object recognition by recognizing discriminative image patches. Other lines of work include utilizing high level attributes in images [26,53], exploring the effectiveness of BoF method [6], incorporating color information [24] and semantic hierarchy [33] to assist HOI recognition.

Recently, deep learning based methods [11–13,29] give promising results on this task. Specifically, Gkioxari *et al.* [11] develop a part based model to make fine-grained action recognition based on the input of both whole-person and part bounding boxes. Mallya and Lazebnik [29] propose a simple network that fuses features from a person bounding box and the whole image to recognize HOIs.

Comparing to the aforementioned methods, especially the deep learning based methods, our method differs mainly in the following aspects. Firstly, our method explicitly considers human body parts and their pairwise correlations, while Gkioxari *et al.* [11] only consider parts at a coarse level (i.e., head, torso and legs) and the correlations among them are ignored, and Mallya *et al.* [29] only consider bounding boxes of the whole person. Secondly, we propose an attention mechanism to learn to focus on specific parts of body and the spatial configurations, which has not been discussed yet in the previous literatures.

Attention Model. Human perception focuses on parts of the field of view to acquire detailed information and ignore those irrelevant. Such attention mechanism has been studied for a long time in computer vision community. Early works motivated by human perception are saliency detection [15,19,22]. Recently, there have been works that try to incorporate attention mechanism into deep learning framework [7,25,31]. Such attempt has been proved to be very effective in many vision tasks including classification [45], detection [3], image captioning [38,46,55] and image-question-answering [49]. Sharma *et al.* [37] first applied attention model to the area of action recognition by using LSTM [18] to focus on important parts of video frames. Several recent works [10,27,39] are partly

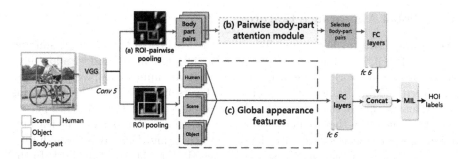

Fig. 2. Overview of our framework. The model first extracts visual features of human, object and scene from a set of proposals. We encode the features of different body parts and their pairwise correlations using ROI-pairwise pooling (a). Then our pairwise body-part attention module (b) will select the feature maps of those discriminative body-part pairs. The global appearance features (c) from the human, object and scene will also contribute to the final predictions. Following [29], we adopt MIL to address the problem of multi-person co-occurrence in an image. See text for more details.

related to our paper. In [27,39], a LSTM network is used to learn to focus on informative joints of skeleton within each frame to recognize actions in videos. Their method differs from ours that their model learns to focus on discriminative joints of 3D skeleton in an action sequence. In [10], the authors introduce an attention pooling mechanism for action recognition. But their attention is applied to the whole image instead of explicitly focusing on human body parts and the correlations among body parts as we do.

3   Our Method

Our approach utilizes both global and local information to infer the HOI labels.

The global contextual information has been well studied by many previous works [8,20,32,51], focusing on utilizing the features of person, object and scene. In Sect. 3.1, we review the previous deep learning model [29] that utilizes features of person and scene. Based on the model from [29], we further incorporate object features. This forms a powerful base network which efficiently captures global information. Note that our improved base network has already achieved better performance than the model presented by [29].

In Sect. 3.2, we describe our main algorithm to incorporate pairwise body parts correlations into the deep neural network. Specifically, we propose a simple yet efficient pooling method called ROI-pairwise pooling which encodes both local features of each body part and the pairwise correlations between them. An attention model is developed to focus on discriminative pairwise features. Finally, we present the combination of global features and our local pairwise correlation features in Sect. 3.3. Figure 2 shows an overview of our network architecture.

3.1 Global Appearance Features

Scene and Human Features. To utilize the features of the whole person and the scene for HOI recognition, [29] proposed an effective model and we adopt it to build our base network. As shown in Fig. 2, given an input image, we resized and forwarded it through the VGG convolutional layers until the *Conv5* layer. On this shared feature maps, the ROI pooling layer extracts ROI features for each person and the scene given their bounding boxes. For each detected person, the features of him/her are concatenated with the scene features and forwarded through fully connected layers to estimate the scores of each HOI on the predefined list. In the HICO dataset, there can be multiple persons in the same image. Each HOI label is marked as positive as long as the corresponding HOI is observed. To address the issue of multiple persons, the *Multiple Instance Learning*(MIL) framework [30] is adopted. The inputs of MIL layer are the predictions for each person in the image, and the output of it is a score array which takes the maximum score of each HOI among all the input predictions. Since MIL is not the major contribution of our work, we refer readers to [29, 30] for more details of MIL and how it is applied in HOI recognition.

Incorporating Object Features. In order to have a coherent understanding of the HOI in context, we further improve the baseline method by incorporating object features, which is ignored in [29].

Feature Representation. Given an object bounding box, a simple solution is to extract the corresponding feature maps and then concatenate them with the existing features of human and scene. However, such method does not have much improvement for the task of HOI recognition. This is because the relative locations between object and human are not encoded. So instead, we set our ROI as a union box of detected human and object. Our experiments (Sect. 4.2) show that such representation is effective.

Handling Multiple Objects. In HICO dataset, there can be multiple persons and multiple objects in an image. For each person, multiple objects can co-appear around him/her. To solve this problem, we sample multiple union boxes of different objects and the person, and the ROI pooling is applied to each union box respectively. The total number of sampled objects around a person is fixed in our implementation. Implementing details will be explained in Sect. 4.

The extracted features of objects are concatenated together with the features of human and scene. This builds a strong base network for capturing well global appearance features.

3.2 Local Pairwise Body-Part Features

In this subsection, we will describe how to obtain pairwise body-part features using our pairwise body-part attention module.

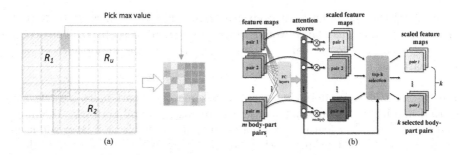

Fig. 3. (a) Illustration of the ROI-pairwise pooling layer. The R_1 and R_2 each represent a bounding box of different body parts. The ROI-pairwise pooling layer extracts the union area feature of R_1 and R_2. The remaining areas are discarded. For each sampled grid location in the ROI-pairwise pooling, the maximum value within the grid area is sampled. (b) Pipeline of the pairwise body-part attention module. From the pairwise body part feature maps pooled by the ROI-pairwise pooling layer, we apply FC layers to estimate the attention score. The attention score is then multiplied with the body part feature maps. Finally, we introduce the feature selection layer which selects the top k most important body part pairs and their scaled feature maps are propagated to the next step.

ROI-Pairwise Pooling. Given a pair of body parts, we want to extract their joint feature maps while preserving their relative spatial relationships. Let us denote the ROI pair by $R_1(r_1, c_1, h_1, w_1)$, $R_2(r_2, c_2, h_2, w_2)$, and their union box by $R_u(r_u, c_u, h_u, w_u)$, where (r, c) specifies the top-left corner of the ROI and (h, w) specifies the height and width. An intuitive idea is to set the ROI as the union box of the body-part pair and use ROI pooling layer to extract the features. However, when the two body parts are far from each other, e.g., the wrist and the ankle, their union box would cover a large area of irrelevant body-part. These irrelevant features will confuse the model during training. To avoid it, we assign activation outside (two) body-part boxes as zero to eliminate those irrelevant features. Then, to ensure the uniform size of R_u representation, we convert the feature map of union box R_u into a fixed size of $H \times W$ feature. It works in a uniformly max-pooling manner: we first divide the $h_u \times w_u$ into $H \times W$ grids, then for each grid, the maximum value inside that grid cell is pooled into the corresponding output cell. Figure 3(a) illustrates the operation of our ROI-pairwise pooling.

With ROI-pairwise pooling layer, both the joint features of two body parts and their relative location are encoded. Note that the number of body-part pairs are usually big ($C(n, 2)$ for n parts) and many pairwise body parts are rarely correlated. We automatically discover those discriminative correlations by proposing an attention module.

Attention Module. Figure 3(b) illustrates the pipeline of our attention module. Our attention module takes the feature maps of all possible pairwise body-part pairs $P = \{p_1, p_2, ..., p_m\}$ after the ROI-pairwise pooling as input, where

$m = C(n, 2)$ is the number of body-part pairs. For each pairwise body-part p_i, the fully connected layer would regress an attention score s_i. The scores $S = \{s_1, s_2, ..., s_m\}$ for m pairwise body-parts indicate the importance of each body-part pair.

Feature Selection. As aforementioned, only some body part pairs are relevant to HOI and irrelevant ones may cause over-fitting of neural network. Assuming that we need to select features of k body-part pairs, our selection layer will keep the feature maps that belong to the body-part pairs with top-k score and drop the remaining. The selected set can be expressed as:

$$\Phi = \{p_i | s_i \text{ ranks top } k \text{ in } S\}. \tag{1}$$

Attention Allocation. Different feature maps always have equal value scale, yet they offer different contributions on HOI recognition. So, we should re-scale the feature maps to reflect their indeed influence. Mathematically, it is modeled as multiplying the corresponding attention score, which can be expressed as:

$$f_j = p_{c(j)} \times s_{c(j)}, \tag{2}$$

where $c(j)$ is the index for the jth element in Φ and f_j represents the jth re-scaled feature maps.

Discussion. We only allow k pairwise features to represent an interaction. S is forced to assign large value to some pairwise body parts related with input interaction to achieve better accuracy. Therefore, S enables attention mechanism without human supervision. In the experiment Sect. 4.4, we verify that the learned attention score is in accord with human perception.

Training. Since Eq. (1) is not a differentiable function, it has no parameter to be updated and only conveys gradients from the latter layer to the former one during back-propagation. When only the top k pairwise feature maps are selected, the gradients of the feature maps that are selected by the feature selection layer will be copied from latter layer to the former layer. The gradients of the dropped feature maps will be discarded by setting the corresponding values to zero. Since Eq. (2) can be derived easily, the attention scores are updated automatically during back-propagation and our attention module is trained in an end-to-end manner.

Combining the ROI-pairwise pooling layer and the attention module, our pairwise body-part attention module has the following properties:

- Both local features of each body part and the higher level spatial relationships between body parts are taken into consideration.
- For different HOI, our novel pairwise body-part attention module will automatically discover the discriminative body parts and pairwise relationships.

3.3   Combining Global and Local Features

After obtaining the selected pairwise body-part features and the global appearance features, we forwarded them through the last FC layers respectively to estimate the final predictions. The prediction is applied for every detected person instances.

4   Experiment

We report our experimental results in this section. We first describe the experimental setting and the details in training our baseline model. Then, we compare our results with those of state-of-the-art methods. Ablation studies are carried to further analyze the effectiveness of each component of our network. Finally, some analyses will be given at the end of this section.

4.1   Setting

Dataset. We conduct experiments on two frequently used datasets, namely, HICO and MPII dataset. **HICO dataset** [5] is currently the largest dataset for HOI recognition. It contains 600 HOI labels in total and multiple labels can be simultaneously presented in an image. The ground truth labels are given at image level without any bounding box or location information. Also, multiple persons can appear in the same image, and the activities they perform may or may not be the same. Thus the label can be regarded as an aggregation over all HOI activities in an image. The training set contains 38,116 images and the testing set contains 9,658 images. We randomly sample 10,000 images from the training set as our validation set. **MPII dataset** [2] contains 15,205 training images and 5708 test images. Unlike HICO dataset, all person instances in an image are assumed to take the same action and each image is classified into only one of 393 action classes. Following [29], we sample 6,987 images from the training set as validation set.

HICO. We use Faster RCNN [34] detector to obtain human and object bounding boxes. For each image, 3 human proposals and 4 object proposals will be sampled to fit the GPU memory. If the number of human or objects is less than expected, we pad the remaining area with zero. For the human body parts, we first use pose estimator [9] to detect all human keypoints and then define 10 body parts based on keypoints. The selected representative human body parts of our method are shown in Fig. 5(a). Each part is defined as a regular bounding box with side length proportional to the size of detected human torso. For body-part pairs, the total number of the pair-wise combination between different body parts is $45(C(10,2))$.

We first try to reproduce Mallya and Lazebnik [29]'s result as our baseline. However, with the best of our effort, we can only achieve 35.6 mAP, while the reported result from Mallya and Lazebnik is 36.1 mAP. We use this model as our baseline model. During training, we follow the same setting as [29], with an initial learning rate of 1e-5 for 30000 iterations and then 1e-6 for another 30000 iterations. The batch size is set to 10. Similar to the work in [14,29], the network is fine-tuned until *conv3* layer. We train our model using Caffe framework [23] on a single Nvidia 1080 GPU. In the testing period, one forward pass takes 0.15s for an image.

Since the HOI labels in the HICO dataset are highly imbalanced, we adopt a weighted sigmoid cross entropy loss

$$\text{loss}(I, y) = \sum_{i=1}^{C} w_p^i \cdot y^i \cdot \log(\hat{y}^i) + w_n^i \cdot (1 - y^i) \cdot \log(1 - \hat{y}^i), \tag{3}$$

where C is the number of independent classes, w_p and w_n are weight factors for positive and negative examples, $\hat{y}$ is model's prediction and y is the label for image I. Following [29], we set $w_p = 10$ and $w_n = 1$.

MPII. Since all persons in an image are performing the same action, we directly train our model on each person instead of using MIL. The training set of MPII contains manually labeled human keypoints. For testing set, we ran [9] to get human keypoints and proposals. The detector [34] is adopted to obtain object bounding boxes in both training and testing sets. Similar to the setting for HICO dataset, we sample a maximum of 4 object proposals per image. During training, we set our initial learning rate as 1e-4, with a decay of 0.1 for every 12000 iterations and stop at 40000 iterations. For MPII dataset, we do not use the weighted loss function for fair comparison with [29].

4.2   Results

We compare our performance on HICO testing set in Table 1 and on MPII testing set in Table 2. By selectively focusing on human body parts and their correlations, our VGG16 based model achieves **37.6** mAP on HICO testing set and

Table 1. Comparison with previous results on the HICO test set. The result of R*CNN is directly copied from [29].

Method	Full Im	Bbox/Pose	MIL	Wtd Loss	mAP
AlexNet+SVM [5]	✓				19.4
R*CNN [14]		✓	✓		28.5
Mallya and Lazebnik [29]	✓	✓	✓		33.8
Pose Regu. Attn. Pooling [10]	✓	✓			34.6
Ours	✓	✓	✓		**37.5**
Mallya and Lazebnik, weighted loss [29]	✓	✓	✓	✓	36.1
Ours, weighted loss	✓	✓	✓	✓	**39.9**

Table 2. Comparison with previous results on the MPII test set. The results on test set are obtained by e-mailing our predictions to the author of [2]

Method	Full Img	Bbox	Pose	Val (mAP)	Test (mAP)
Dense Trajectory + Pose [2]	✓		✓	-	5.5
R*CNN, VGG16 [14]		✓		21.7	26.7
Mallya and Lazebnik, VGG16 [29]	✓	✓		-	32.2
Ours, VGG16	✓	✓	✓	**30.9**	**36.8**
Pose Reg. Attn. Pooling, Res101 [10]	✓		✓	30.6	36.1
Ours, Res101	✓	✓	✓	**32.0**	**37.5**

Elbow-Ankle
body-part pair
for skateboard jumping

Wrist-Knee, Wrist-Ankle
body-part pair
for bycicle riding

(a) Our model is able to discover correlations between different body-parts and tends to pick similar body-part pairs for each HOI. The body part pairs with the highest attention score are shown in the red boxes.

sit on a bench

straddle a bicycle, ride a bicycle,
sit on a bicycle, hold a bicycle

hold a kite, launch a kite

hold a tie, wear a tie
tie a tie, adjust a tie

hold a horse, ride a horse,
run a horse, straddle a horse

carry a backpack,
wear a backpack

grind a snowboard,
jump a snowboard, ride a snowboard,
stand on a snowboard

jump a skateboard,
ride a skateboard,
flip a skateboard

guitar, classical, folk, sitting

golf

violin, sitting

child care

(b) Some examples of our model's predictions. The first two rows are results from HICO dataset and the last row is results from MPII dataset. The detected human bounding boxes are shown in the green boxes and the body part pairs with the highest attention score are shown in the red boxes. Predicted HOIs are given underneath.

Fig. 4. Results of our model's predictions.

36.8 mAP on MPII testing set. Using a weighted loss function, we can further achieve **39.9** mAP on HICO testing set. Since [10] use ResNet101 [17] as their base model, we also perform an experiment on MPII dataset by replacing our VGG16 base network with the ResNet101 for fair comparison with [10]. We can see that our VGG16 based model has already achieved better performance than [10] on HICO and MPII dataset, and by using the same base model, we outperform [10] by 1.4 mAP on MPII dataset. These results show that the information from body-parts and their correlations is important in recognizing human-object interactions, and it allows us to achieve the state-of-the-art performances on both datasets.

Figure 4 shows some qualitative results produced by our model. We visualize the body-part pairs with the highest attention score in the red boxes. More results are given in supplementary material.

4.3   Ablative Studies

To evaluate the effectiveness of each component in our network, we conduct several experiments on HICO dataset and the results are shown in Table 3.

Table 3. Performance of the baseline networks on the HICO test set. "union box" refers to the features of an object which are extracted from the area of union box of human and object. "tight box" refers to the features of an object which are extracted from the exact area of the object tight box. "w/o attention" refers to the method without attention mechanism.

	Method	mAP
(a)	Baseline	35.6
(b)	Union box	**37.0**
	Tight box	36.3
(c)	Body parts, w/o attention	38.0
(d)	Body-part pairs, w/o attention	38.9
	Body-part pairs, with attention	**39.9**
	Body parts & pairs, with attention	39.1

Incorporating Object Information. As shown in Table 3(b), our improved baseline model with object features can achieve higher mAP than the baseline method without using object features. It shows that object information is important for HOI recognition. From the table, we can see that using the features from the union box instead of the tight box can achieve higher mAP. Note that our improved baseline model has already achieved the state-of-the-art results with 0.9 mAP higher than the results reported by [29].

Improvements from Body Parts Information. We evaluate the performance improvement with additional body-parts information. The feature maps of 10 body parts are directly concatenated with the global appearance features, without taking the advantages of attention mechanism or body-part correlations. As can be seen in Table 3(c), we further gain an improvement of 1.0 mAP.

Pairwise Body-Part Attention. To evaluate the effectiveness of each component of our pairwise body-part attention model, a series of experiments have been carried out and results are reported in Table 3(d).

Firstly, we consider the correlations of different body parts. The feature maps of the 45 body-part pairs are concatenated with the global appearance features to estimate HOI labels. With body-part pairwise information considered, our model can achieve **38.9** mAP. It demonstrates that exploiting spatial relationships between body parts benefits the task of HOI recognition.

Then, we add our attention module upon this network. For our feature selection layer, we set k as 20. The influence of the value of k will be discussed in the analysis in Sect. 4.4. With our pairwise body-part attention model, the performance of our model further yields **39.9** mAP even though the fully connected layers receive less information from fewer parts.

We also conduct an experiment by simultaneously learning to focus on discriminative body parts and body-part pairs. The candidates for our attention model are the feature maps of 10 body parts and 45 body-part pairs. However, the final result drops slightly to 39.1 mAP. One possible reason is that our ROI-pairwise pooling has already encoded local features of each single body part. The extra information of body parts may have distracted our attention network.

4.4   Analysis

Parameter for Feature Selection Layer. In our feature selection layer, we need to decide k, the number of body part pairs that we propagate to the next

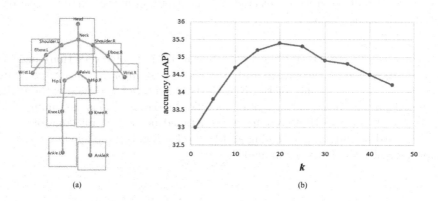

(a)   (b)

Fig. 5. (a) Our defined human body-parts. Each bounding box denotes a defined body part. (b) The relationship between recognition accuracy and the number of selected pairwise body part feature maps in the feature selection layer.

Table 4. Some HOIs and their corresponding most selected body-part pairs chosen by our model. The "l" and "r" flags denote for left and right.

HOI	Selected correlations		
chase-bird	l.knee-r.wrist	r.elbow-neck	r.ankle-r.elbow
board-car	r.ankle-l.elbow	r.ankle-r.elbow	r.elbow-neck
hug-person	l.elbow-neck	r.elbow-neck	r.wrist-neck
jump-bicycle	l.wrist-pelvis	r.ankle-pelvis	r.elbow-neck
adjust-tie	r.wrist-neck	l.wrist-neck	l.elbow-neck

step. We perform an experiment to evaluate the effect of k. We train our pairwise body part attention model on HICO training set with different value of k. The performances on validation set are reported in Fig. 5(b). When k increases, the performance of our model increases until $k = 20$. After that, the performance of our model starts to drop. When k equals to 45, it is equivalent to not using the feature selection layer. The performance in this case is 1.2 mAP lower than the highest accuracy. This indicates that rejecting irrelevant body-part pairs is important.

Evaluation of Attention. To see how close the attention of our model is to human's attention, we list out different HOIs and their corresponding body-part pairs that are selected most frequently by our trained attention module. Some examples are presented in Table 4. The entire list is provided in supplementary material. We invite 30 persons to judge whether the choice of the selected pairs are relevant to the given HOI labels. If half of the persons agree that a selected body part pair is important to decide the HOI labels, we regard the selected body part pair as correct. In our setting, the top-k accuracy means the correct body part pair appears in the first k predictions of attention module. Our top-1 accuracy achieves 0.28 and top-5 accuracy achieves 0.76. It is interesting to see that the body part pairs selected by our attention module match with our intuition to some extent.

Improvements by HOI Class. To see which kinds of interactions become less confused due to the incorporation of body part information, we compare the results on 20 randomly picked HOIs in HICO dataset with and without the proposed pairwise body-part attention module. The comparisons are summarized in Table 5. When the HOIs require more detailed body part information, such as surfboard holding, apple buying and bird releasing, our model shows a great improvement over the baseline model.

Table 5. We randomly pick 20 categories in HICO dataset and compare our results with results from Mallya and Lazebnik [29]. The evaluation metric is mAP. The full set of results can be found in the supplementary materials.

HOI	[29]	Ours	HOI	[29]	Ours
Cat scratching	47.7	**50.9**	Train boarding	37.1	**48.2**
Umbrella carrying	83.7	**86.9**	Apple buying	19.3	**59.0**
Keyboard typing on	**71.6**	68.3	Cake lighting	16.3	**24.1**
Boat inspecting	21.1	**31.9**	Cup inspecting	1.0	**1.5**
Oven cleaning	**22.1**	13.1	Fork licking	4.4	**5.3**
Surfboard holding	52.9	**63.6**	Bird releasing	14.5	**51.3**
Dining table eating at	86.6	**86.9**	Car parking	**28.9**	26.3
Sandwich no interaction	74.2	**85.2**	Horse jumping	**87.0**	86.9
Motorcycle washing	57.7	**64.8**	Spoon washing	14.5	**15.3**
Airplane loading	**64.1**	60.0	Toilet repairing	11.4	**22.6**

5 Conclusions

In this paper, we have proposed a novel pairwise body part attention model which can assign different attention to different body-part pairs. To achieve our goal, we have introduced the ROI pairwise pooling, and the pairwise body-part attention module which extracts useful body part pairs. The pairwise feature maps selected by our attention module are concatenated with background, human, and object features to make the final HOI prediction. Our experimental results show that our approach is robust, and it significantly improves the recognition accuracy especially for the HOI labels which require detailed body part information. In the future, we shall investigate the possibility of including multi-person interactions into the HOI recognition.

Acknowledgement. This work is supported in part by the National Key R&D Program of China No. 2017YFA0700800, National Natural Science Foundation of China under Grants 61772332 and SenseTime Ltd.

References

1. Aksoy, E.E., Abramov, A., Dörr, J., Ning, K., Dellen, B., Wörgötter, F.: Learning the semantics of object-action relations by observation. Int. J. Rob. Res. **30**(10), 1229–1249 (2011)
2. Andriluka, M., Pishchulin, L., Gehler, P., Schiele, B.: 2D human pose estimation: new benchmark and state of the art analysis. In: IEEE Conference on Computer Vision and Pattern Recognition (CVPR), June 2014
3. Ba, J., Mnih, V., Kavukcuoglu, K.: Multiple object recognition with visual attention. arXiv preprint arXiv:1412.7755 (2014)

4. Boyer, T.W., Maouene, J., Sethuraman, N.: Attention to body-parts varies with visual preference and verb-effector associations. Cogn. Process. **18**(2), 195–203 (2017)
5. Chao, Y.W., Wang, Z., He, Y., Wang, J., Deng, J.: Hico: a benchmark for recognizing human-object interactions in images. In: ICCV (2015)
6. Delaitre, V., Laptev, I., Sivic, J.: Recognizing human actions in still images: a study of bag-of-features and part-based representations. In: BMVC (2010)
7. Denil, M., Bazzani, L., Larochelle, H., de Freitas, N.: Learning where to attend with deep architectures for image tracking. Neural Comput. **24**(8), 2151–2184 (2012)
8. Desai, C., Ramanan, D., Fowlkes, C.: Discriminative models for static human-object interactions. In: CVPR'w (2010)
9. Fang, H.S., Xie, S., Tai, Y.W., Lu, C.: RMPE: regional multi-person pose estimation. In: ICCV (2017)
10. Girdhar, R., Ramanan, D.: Attentional pooling for action recognition. In: NIPS (2017)
11. Gkioxari, G., Girshick, R., Malik, J.: Actions and attributes from wholes and parts. In: ICCV (2015)
12. Gkioxari, G., Hariharan, B., Girshick, R., Malik, J.: R-CNNs for pose estimation and action detection. arXiv preprint arXiv:1406.5212 (2014)
13. Gkioxari, G., Girshick, R., Dollár, P., He, K.: Detecting and recognizing human-object intaractions. arXiv preprint arXiv:1704.07333 (2017)
14. Gkioxari, G., Girshick, R., Malik, J.: Contextual action recognition with R* CNN. In: ICCV (2015)
15. Goferman, S., Zelnik-Manor, L., Tal, A.: Context-aware saliency detection. TPAMI **34**(10), 1915–1926 (2012)
16. Han, D., Bo, L., Sminchisescu, C.: Selection and context for action recognition. In: ICCV (2009)
17. He, K., Zhang, X., Ren, S., Sun, J.: Deep residual learning for image recognition. arXiv preprint arXiv:1512.03385 (2015)
18. Hochreiter, S., Schmidhuber, J.: Long short-term memory. Neural Comput. **9**(8), 1735–1780 (1997)
19. Hou, X., Zhang, L.: Saliency detection: a spectral residual approach. In: CVPR (2007)
20. Hu, J.F., Zheng, W.S., Lai, J., Gong, S., Xiang, T.: Recognising human-object interaction via exemplar based modelling. In: ICCV (2013)
21. Ikizler, N., Cinbis, R.G., Pehlivan, S., Duygulu, P.: Recognizing actions from still images. In: ICPR (2008)
22. Itti, L., Koch, C., Niebur, E.: A model of saliency-based visual attention for rapid scene analysis. TPAMI **20**(11), 1254–1259 (1998)
23. Jia, Y., et al.: Caffe: convolutional architecture for fast feature embedding. arXiv preprint arXiv:1408.5093 (2014)
24. Khan, F.S., Anwer, R.M., van de Weijer, J., Bagdanov, A.D., Lopez, A.M., Felsberg, M.: Coloring action recognition in still images. IJCV **105**(3), 205–221 (2013)
25. Larochelle, H., Hinton, G.E.: Learning to combine foveal glimpses with a third-order Boltzmann machine. In: NIPS (2010)
26. Liu, J., Kuipers, B., Savarese, S.: Recognizing human actions by attributes. In: CVPR (2011)
27. Liu, J., Wang, G., Hu, P., Duan, L.Y., Kot, A.C.: Global context-aware attention LSTM networks for 3D action recognition. In: CVPR (2017)
28. Maji, S., Bourdev, L., Malik, J.: Action recognition from a distributed representation of pose and appearance. In: CVPR (2011)

29. Mallya, A., Lazebnik, S.: Learning models for actions and person-object inter-actions with transfer to question answering. In: Leibe, B., Matas, J., Sebe, N., Welling, M. (eds.) ECCV 2016. LNCS, vol. 9905, pp. 414–428. Springer, Cham (2016). https://doi.org/10.1007/978-3-319-46448-0_25

30. Maron, O., Lozano-Pérez, T.: A framework for multiple-instance learning (1998)

31. Mnih, V., Heess, N., Graves, A., et al.: Recurrent models of visual attention. In: NIPS (2014)

32. Prest, A., Schmid, C., Ferrari, V.: Weakly supervised learning of interactions between humans and objects. TPAMI **34**(3), 601–614 (2012)

33. Ramanathan, V., et al.: Learning semantic relationships for better action retrieval in images. In: CVPR (2015)

34. Ren, S., He, K., Girshick, R., Sun, J.: Faster R-CNN: towards real-time object detection with region proposal networks. In: NIPS (2015)

35. Ro, T., Friggel, A., Lavie, N.: Attentional biases for faces and body parts. Vis. Cogn. **15**(3), 322–348 (2007)

36. Sharma, G., Jurie, F., Schmid, C.: Expanded parts model for human attribute and action recognition in still images. In: CVPR (2013)

37. Sharma, S., Kiros, R., Salakhutdinov, R.: Action recognition using visual attention (2015)

38. Shih, K.J., Singh, S., Hoiem, D.: Where to look: focus regions for visual question answering. In: CVPR (2016)

39. Song, S., Lan, C., Xing, J., Zeng, W., Liu, J.: An end-to-end spatio-temporal attention model for human action recognition from skeleton data. In: AAAI (2017)

40. Thurau, C., Hlaváč, V.: Pose primitive based human action recognition in videos or still images. In: CVPR (2008)

41. Wang, H., Kläser, A., Schmid, C., Liu, C.L.: Action recognition by dense trajecto-ries. In: CVPR (2011)

42. Wang, H., Schmid, C.: Action recognition with improved trajectories. In: ICCV (2013)

43. Wang, Y., Jiang, H., Drew, M.S., Li, Z.N., Mori, G.: Unsupervised discovery of action classes. In: CVPR (2006)

44. Wörgötter, F., Aksoy, E.E., Krüger, N., Piater, J., Ude, A., Tamosiunaite, M.: A simple ontology of manipulation actions based on hand-object relations. IEEE Trans. Auton. Mental Dev. **5**(2), 117–134 (2013)

45. Xiao, T., Xu, Y., Yang, K., Zhang, J., Peng, Y., Zhang, Z.: The application of two-level attention models in deep convolutional neural network for fine-grained image classification. In: CVPR (2015)

46. Xu, K., et al.: Show, attend and tell: Neural image caption generation with visual attention. In: ICML, vol. 14 (2015)

47. Yang, W., Wang, Y., Mori, G.: Recognizing human actions from still images with latent poses. In: CVPR (2010)

48. Yang, Y., Fermuller, C., Aloimonos, Y.: Detection of manipulation action conse-quences (MAC). In: CVPR (2013)

49. Yang, Z., He, X., Gao, J., Deng, L., Smola, A.: Stacked attention networks for image question answering. In: CVPR (2016)

50. Yao, B., Fei-Fei, L.: Grouplet: a structured image representation for recognizing human and object interactions. In: CVPR (2010)

51. Yao, B., Fei-Fei, L.: Modeling mutual context of object and human pose in human-object interaction activities. In: CVPR (2010)

52. Yao, B., Fei-Fei, L.: Action recognition with exemplar based 2.5D graph matching. In: Fitzgibbon, A., Lazebnik, S., Perona, P., Sato, Y., Schmid, C. (eds.) ECCV 2012. LNCS, vol. 7575, pp. 173–186. Springer, Heidelberg (2012). https://doi.org/10.1007/978-3-642-33765-9_13
53. Yao, B., Jiang, X., Khosla, A., Lin, A.L., Guibas, L., Fei-Fei, L.: Human action recognition by learning bases of action attributes and parts. In: ICCV (2011)
54. Yao, B., Khosla, A., Fei-Fei, L.: Combining randomization and discrimination for fine-grained image categorization. In: CVPR (2011)
55. You, Q., Jin, H., Wang, Z., Fang, C., Luo, J.: Image captioning with semantic attention. In: CVPR (2016)

Exploiting Temporal Information for 3D Human Pose Estimation

Mir Rayat Imtiaz Hossain$^{(\boxtimes)}$ and James J. Little$^{(\boxtimes)}$

Department of Computer Science, University of British Columbia, Vancouver, Canada
{rayat137,little}@cs.ubc.ca

Abstract. In this work, we address the problem of 3D human pose estimation from a sequence of 2D human poses. Although the recent success of deep networks has led many state-of-the-art methods for 3D pose estimation to train deep networks end-to-end to predict from images directly, the top-performing approaches have shown the effectiveness of dividing the task of 3D pose estimation into two steps: using a state-of-the-art 2D pose estimator to estimate the 2D pose from images and then mapping them into 3D space. They also showed that a low-dimensional representation like 2D locations of a set of joints can be discriminative enough to estimate 3D pose with high accuracy. However, estimation of 3D pose for individual frames leads to temporally incoherent estimates due to independent error in each frame causing jitter. Therefore, in this work we utilize the temporal information across a sequence of 2D joint locations to estimate a sequence of 3D poses. We designed a sequence-to-sequence network composed of layer-normalized LSTM units with shortcut connections connecting the input to the output on the decoder side and imposed temporal smoothness constraint during training. We found that the knowledge of temporal consistency improves the best reported result on Human3.6M dataset by approximately 12.2% and helps our network to recover temporally consistent 3D poses over a sequence of images even when the 2D pose detector fails.

Keywords: 3D human pose · Sequence-to-sequence networks
Layer normalized LSTM · Residual connections

1 Introduction

The task of estimating 3D human pose from 2D representations like monocular images or videos is an open research problem among the computer vision and graphics community for a long time. An understanding of human posture and limb articulation is important for high level computer vision tasks such as human

Electronic supplementary material The online version of this chapter (https://doi.org/10.1007/978-3-030-01249-6_5) contains supplementary material, which is available to authorized users.

© Springer Nature Switzerland AG 2018
V. Ferrari et al. (Eds.): ECCV 2018, LNCS 11214, pp. 69–86, 2018.
https://doi.org/10.1007/978-3-030-01249-6_5

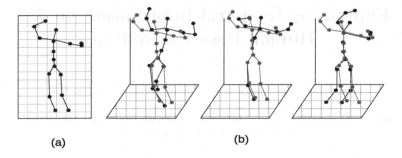

(a)   (b)

Fig. 1. (a) 2D position of joints, (b) Different 3D pose interpretations of the same 2D pose. Blue points represent the ground truth 3D locations of joints while the black points indicate other possible 3D interpretations. All these 3D poses project to exactly same 2D pose depending on the position and orientation of the camera projecting them onto 2D plane. (Color figure online)

action or activity recognition, sports analysis, augmented and virtual reality. A 2D representation of human pose, which is considered to be much easier to estimate, can be used for these tasks. However, 2D poses can be ambiguous because of occlusion and foreshortening. Additionally poses that are totally different can appear to be similar in 2D because of the way they are projected as shown in Fig. 1. The depth information in 3D representation of human pose makes it free from such ambiguities and hence can improve performance for higher level tasks. Moreover, 3D pose can be very useful in computer animation, where the articulated pose of a person in 3D can be used to accurately model human posture and movement. However, 3D pose estimation is an ill-posed problem because of the inherent ambiguity in back-projecting a 2D view of an object to the 3D space maintaining its structure. Since the 3D pose of a person can be projected in an infinite number of ways on a 2D plane, the mapping from a 2D pose to 3D is not unique. Moreover, obtaining a dataset for 3D pose is difficult and expensive. Unlike the 2D pose datasets where the users can manually label the keypoints by mouse clicks, 3D pose datasets require a complicated laboratory setup with motion capture sensors and cameras. Hence, there is a lack of motion capture datasets for images in-the-wild.

Over the years, different techniques have been used to address the problem of 3D pose estimation. Earlier methods used to focus on extracting features, invariant to factors such as background scenes, lighting, and skin color from images and mapping them into 3D human pose [2–5]. With the success of deep networks, recent methods tend to focus on training a deep convolutional neural network (CNN) end-to-end to estimate 3D poses from images directly [6–16]. Some approaches divided the 3D pose estimation task into first predicting the joint locations in 2D using 2D pose estimators [17,18] and then back-projecting them to estimate the 3D joint locations [19–24]. These results suggest the effectiveness of decoupling the task of 3D pose estimation where 2D pose estimator abstracts the complexities in the image. In this paper, we also adopt the decoupled approach to 3D pose estimation. However, predicting 3D pose for each

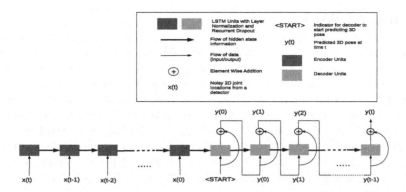

Fig. 2. Our model. It is a sequence-to-sequence network [1] with residual connections on the decoder side. The encoder encodes the information of a sequence of 2D poses of length t in its final hidden state. The final hidden state of the encoder is used to initialize the hidden state of decoder. The $\langle START \rangle$ symbol tells the decoder to start predicting 3D pose from the last hidden state of the encoder. Note that the input sequence is reversed as suggested by Sutskever et al. [1]. The decoder essentially learns to predict the 3D pose at time (t) given the 3D pose at time $(t-1)$. The residual connections help the decoder to learn the perturbation from the previous time step.

frame individually can lead to jitter in videos because the errors in each frame are independent of each other. Therefore, we designed a sequence-to-sequence network [1] with shortcut connections on the decoder side [25] that predicts a sequence of temporally consistent 3D poses given a sequence of 2D poses. Each unit of our network is a Long Short-Term Memory (LSTM) [26] unit with layer normalization [27] and recurrent dropout [28]. We also imposed a temporal smoothness constraint on the predicted 3D poses during training to ensure that our predictions are smooth over a sequence.

Our network achieves the state-of-the-art result on the Human3.6M dataset improving the previous best result by approximately 12.2%. We also obtained the lowest error for every action class in Human3.6M dataset [29]. Moreover, we observed that our network predicted meaningful 3D poses on Youtube videos, even when the detections from the 2D pose detector were extremely noisy or meaningless. This shows the effectiveness of using temporal information. In short our contributions in this work are:

- Designing an efficient sequence-to-sequence network that achieves the state-of-the-art results for every action class of Human3.6M dataset [29] and can be trained very fast.
- Exploiting the ability of sequence-to-sequence networks to take into account the events in the past, to predict temporally consistent 3D poses.
- Effectively imposing temporal consistency constraint on the predicted 3D poses during training so that the errors in the predictions are distributed smoothly over the sequence.
- Using only the previous frames to understand temporal context so that it can be deployed online and real-time.

2   Related Work

Representation of 3D Pose. Both model-based and model-free representations of 3D human pose have been used in the past. The most common model-based representation is a skeleton defined by a kinematic tree of a set of joints, parameterized by the offset and rotational parameters of each joint relative to its parent. Several 3D pose methods have used this representation [10,22,30,31]. Others model 3D pose as a sparse linear combination of an over-complete dictionary of basis poses [19–21]. However, we have chosen a model-free representation of 3D pose, where a 3D pose is simply a set of 3D joint locations relative to the root node like several recent approaches [8,9,23,24]. This representation is much simpler and low-dimensional.

Estimating 3D Pose from 2D Joints. Lee and Chen [32] were the first to infer 3D joint locations from their 2D projections given the bone lengths using a binary decision tree where each branch corresponds to two possible states of a joint relative to its parent. Jiang [33] used the 2D joint locations to estimate a set of hypothesis 3D poses using Taylor's algorithm [34] and used them to query a large database of motion capture data to find the nearest neighbor. Gupta et al. [35] and Chen and Ramanan [36] also used this idea of using the detected 2D pose to query a large database of exemplar poses to find the nearest nearest neighbor 3D pose. Another common approach to estimating 3D joint locations given the 2D pose is to separate the camera pose variability from the intrinsic deformation of the human body, the latter of which is modeled by learning an over-complete dictionary of basis 3D poses from a large database of motion capture data [19–22,37]. A valid 3D pose is defined by a sparse linear combination of the bases and by transforming the points using transformation matrix representing camera extrinsic parameters. Moreno-Nouguer [23] used the pair-wise distance matrix of 2D joints to learn a distance matrix for 3D joints, which they found invariant up to a rigid similarity transform with the ground truth 3D and used multi-dimensional scaling (MDS) with pose-priors to rule out the ambiguities. Martinez et al. [24] designed a fully connected network with shortcut connections every two linear layers to estimate 3D joint locations relative to the root node in the camera coordinate space.

Deep Network Based Methods. With the success of deep networks, many have designed networks that can be trained end-to-end to predict 3D poses from images directly [6–10,14,15,38–40]. Li et al. [8] and Park et al. [14] designed CNNs to jointly predict 2D and 3D poses. Mehta et al. [9] and Sun et al. [15] used transfer learning to transfer the knowledge learned for 2D human pose estimation to the task of 3D pose estimation. Pavlakos et al. [7] extended the stacked-hourglass network [18] originally designed to predict 2D heatmaps of each joint to make it predict 3D volumetric heatmaps. Tome et al. [40] also extended a 2D pose estimator called Convolutional Pose Machine (CPM) [17] to make it predict 3D pose. Rogesz and Schmid [39] and Varol et al. [38] augmented the training data with synthetic images and trained CNNs to predict 3D poses from real images. Sun et al. [15] designed a unified network that can regress both 2D and 3D poses at the same time given an image. Hence during training time, in-the-wild images which do not have any ground truth 3D poses can be combined with the data with ground truth 3D poses. A similar idea of exploiting in-the-wild images to learn pose structure was used by Fang et al. [41]. They learned a pose grammar that encodes the possible human pose configurations.

Using Temporal Information. Since estimating poses for each frame individually leads to incoherent and jittery predictions over a sequence, many approaches tried to exploit temporal information [11,20,42–44]. Andriluka et al. [42] used tracking-by-detection to associate 2D poses detected in each frame individually and used them to retrieve 3D pose. Tekin et al. [43] used a CNN to first align bounding boxes of successive frames so that the person in the image is always at the center of the box and then extracted 3D HOG features densely over the spatio-temporal volume from which they regress the 3D pose of the central frame. Mehta et al. [11] implemented a real-time system for 3D pose estimation that applies temporal filtering across 2D and 3D poses from previous frames to predict a temporally consistent 3D pose. Lin et al. [13] performed a multi-stage sequential refinement using LSTMs to predict 3D pose sequences using previously predicted 2D pose representations and 3D pose. We focus on predicting temporally consistent 3D poses by learning the temporal context of a sequence using a form of sequence-to-sequence network. Unlike Lin et al. [13] our method does not need multiple stages of refinement. It is simpler and requires fewer parameters to train, leading to much improved performance.

3   Our Approach

Network Design. We designed a sequence-to-sequence network with LSTM units and residual connections on the decoder side to predict a temporally coherent sequence of 3D poses given a sequence of 2D joint locations. Figure 2 shows the architecture of our network. The motivation behind using a sequence-to-sequence network comes from its application on the task of Neural Machine Translation (NMT) by Sutskever et al. [1], where their model translates a sentence in one language to a sentence in another language e.g. English to French. In a language translation model, the input and output sentences can have different lengths. Although our case is analogous to the NMT, the input and output sequences always have the same length while the input vectors to the encoder and decoder have different dimensions.

The encoder side of our network takes a sequence of 2D poses and encodes them in a fixed size high dimensional vector in the hidden state of its final LSTM unit. Since the LSTMs are excellent in memorizing events and information from the past, the encoded vector stores the 2D pose information of all the frames. The initial state of the decoder is initialized by the final state of the encoder. A $\langle START \rangle$ token is passed as initial input to the decoder, which in our case is a vector of ones, telling it to start decoding. Given a 3D pose estimate y_t at a time step t each decoder unit predicts the 3D pose for next time step y_{t+1}. Note that the order of the input sequence is reversed as recommended by Sutskever et al. [1]. The shortcut connections on the decoder side cause each decoder unit to estimate the amount of perturbation in the 3D pose from the previous frame instead of having to estimate the actual 3D pose for each frame. As suggested by He et al. [25], such a mapping is easier to learn for the network.

We use layer normalization [27] and recurrent dropout [28] to regularize our network. Ba et al. [27] came up with the idea of layer normalization which estimates the normalization statistics (mean and standard deviation) from the summed inputs to the recurrent neurons of hidden layer on a *single* training example to regularize the RNN units. Similarly, Zaremba et al. [28] proposed the idea of applying dropout only on the non-recurrent connections of the network with a certain probability p while always keeping the recurrent connections intact because they are necessary for the recurrent units to remember the information from the past.

Loss Function. Given a sequence of 2D joint locations as input, our network predicts a sequence of 3D joint locations relative to the root node (central hip). We predict each 3D pose in the camera coordinate space instead of predicting them in an arbitrary global frame as suggested by Martinez et al. [24].

We impose a temporal smoothness constraint on the predicted 3D joint locations to ensure that the prediction of each joint in one frame does not differ too much from its previous frame. Because the 2D pose detectors work on individual frames, even with the minimal movement of the subject in the image, the detections from successive frames may vary, particularly for the joints which move fast or are prone to occlusion. Hence, we made an assumption that the subject does not move too much in successive frames given the frame rate is high enough. Therefore, we added the L2 norm of the first order derivative on the 3D joint locations with respect to time to our loss function during training. This constraint helps us to estimate 3D poses reliably even when the 2D pose detector fails for a few frames within the temporal window without any post-processing.

Empirically we found that certain joints are more difficult to estimate accurately e.g. wrist, ankle, elbow compared to others. To address this issue, we partitioned the joints into three disjoint sets **torso_head**, **limb_leg** and **limb_arm** based on their contribution to overall error. We observed that the joints connected to the torso and the head e.g. hips, shoulders, neck are always predicted with high accuracy compared to those joints belonging to the limbs and therefore put them in the set **torso_head**. The joints of the limbs, especially the joints on the arms, are always more difficult to predict due to their high range of motion and occlusion. We put the knees and the ankles in the set **limb_leg** and the elbow and wrist in **limb_arm**. We multiply the derivatives of each set of joints with different scalar values based on their contribution to the overall error.

Therefore our loss function consists of the sum of two separate terms: Mean Squared Error (MSE) of N different sequences of 3D joint locations; and the mean of the L2 norm of the first order derivative of N sequences of 3D joint locations with respect to time, where the joints are divided into three disjoint sets.

The MSE over N sequences, each of T time-steps, of 3D joint locations is given by

$$\mathbf{L}(\hat{\mathbf{Y}}, \mathbf{Y}) = \frac{1}{NT} \sum_{i=1}^{N} \sum_{t=1}^{T} \left\| \hat{\mathbf{Y}}_{i,t} - \mathbf{Y}_{i,t} \right\|_2^2. \tag{1}$$

Here, $\hat{\mathbf{Y}}$ denotes the estimated 3D joint locations while $\mathbf{Y}$ denotes 3D ground truth.

The mean of L2 norm of the first order derivative of N sequences of 3D joint locations, each of length T, with respect to time is given by

$$\left\| \nabla_t \hat{\mathbf{Y}} \right\|_2^2 = \frac{1}{N(T-1)} \sum_{i=1}^{N} \sum_{t=2}^{T} \left\{ \eta \left\| \hat{\mathbf{Y}}_{i,t}^{\mathbf{TH}} - \hat{\mathbf{Y}}_{i,t-1}^{\mathbf{TH}} \right\|_2^2 \right.$$
$$\left. + \rho \left\| \hat{\mathbf{Y}}_{i,t}^{\mathbf{LL}} - \hat{\mathbf{Y}}_{i,t-1}^{\mathbf{LL}} \right\|_2^2 + \tau \left\| \hat{\mathbf{Y}}_{i,t}^{\mathbf{LA}} - \hat{\mathbf{Y}}_{i,t-1}^{\mathbf{LA}} \right\|_2^2 \right\}. \tag{2}$$

In the above equation, $\hat{\mathbf{Y}}^{\mathbf{TH}}$, $\hat{\mathbf{Y}}^{\mathbf{LL}}$ and $\hat{\mathbf{Y}}^{\mathbf{LA}}$ denotes the predicted 3D locations of joints belonging to the sets **torso_head**, **limb_leg** and **limb_arm** respectively. The η, ρ and τ are scalar hyper-parameters to control the significance of the derivatives of 3D locations of each of the three set of joints. A higher weight is assigned to the set of joints which are generally predicted with higher error.

The overall loss function for our network is given as

$$\mathbf{L} = \min_{\hat{\mathbf{Y}}} \alpha \mathbf{L}(\hat{\mathbf{Y}}, \mathbf{Y}) + \beta \left\| \nabla_t \hat{\mathbf{Y}} \right\|_2^2. \tag{3}$$

Here α and β are scalar hyper-parameters regulating the importance of each of the two terms in the loss function.

4 Experimental Evaluation

Datasets and Protocols. We perform quantitative evaluation on the Human 3.6M [29] dataset and on the HumanEva dataset [45]. Human 3.6M, to the best of our knowledge, is the largest publicly available dataset for human 3D pose estimation. The dataset contains 3.6 million images of 7 different professional actors performing 15 everyday activities like walking, eating, sitting, making a phone call. The dataset consists of 2D and 3D joint locations for each corresponding image. Each video is captured using 4 different calibrated high resolution cameras. In addition to 2D and 3D pose ground truth, the dataset also provides ground truth for bounding boxes, the camera parameters, the body proportion of all the actors and high resolution body scans or meshes of each actor. HumanEva, on the other hand, is a much smaller dataset. It has been largely used to benchmark previous work over the last decade. Most of the methods report results on two different actions and on three actors. For qualitative evaluation, we used the some videos from Youtube and the Human3.6M dataset.

Table 1. Results showing the errors action-wise on Human3.6M [29] under Protocol #1 (no rigid alignment or similarity transform applied in post-processing). Note that our results reported here are for sequence of length 5. SA indicates that a model was trained for each action, and MA indicates that a single model was trained for all actions. GT indicates that the network was trained on ground truth 2D pose. The bold-faced numbers represent the best result while underlined numbers represent the second best.

Protocol #1	Direct.	Discuss	Eating	Greet	Phone	Photo	Pose	Purch.	Sitting	SitingD	Smoke	Wait	WalkD	Walk	WalkT	Avg
LinKDE [29] (SA)	132.7	183.6	132.3	164.4	162.1	205.9	150.6	171.3	151.6	243.0	162.1	170.7	177.1	96.6	127.9	162.1
Tekin et al [43] (SA)	102.4	147.2	88.8	125.3	118.0	182.7	112.4	129.2	138.9	224.9	118.4	138.8	126.3	55.1	65.8	125.0
Zhou et al [20] (MA)	87.4	109.3	87.1	103.2	116.2	143.3	106.9	99.8	124.5	199.2	107.4	118.1	114.2	79.4	97.7	113.0
Park et al [14] (SA)	100.3	116.2	90.0	116.5	115.3	149.5	117.6	106.9	137.2	190.8	105.8	125.1	131.9	62.6	96.2	117.3
Nie et al [12] (MA)	90.1	88.2	85.7	95.6	103.9	103.0	92.4	90.4	117.9	136.4	98.5	94.4	90.6	86.0	89.5	97.5
Mehta et al [9] (MA)	57.5	68.6	59.6	67.3	78.1	82.4	56.9	69.1	100.0	117.5	69.4	68.0	76.5	55.2	61.4	72.9
Mehta et al [11] (MA)	62.6	78.1	63.4	72.5	88.3	93.8	63.1	74.8	106.6	138.7	78.8	73.9	82.0	55.8	59.6	80.5
Lin et al [13] (MA)	58.0	68.2	63.3	65.8	75.3	93.1	61.2	65.7	98.7	127.7	70.4	68.2	72.9	50.6	57.7	73.1
Tome et al [40] (MA)	65.0	73.5	76.8	86.4	86.3	110.7	68.9	74.8	110.2	173.9	84.9	85.8	86.3	71.4	73.1	88.4
Tekin et al [16]	54.2	61.4	60.2	61.2	79.4	78.3	63.1	81.6	70.1	107.3	69.3	70.3	74.3	51.8	63.2	69.7
Pavlakos et al [7] (MA)	67.4	71.9	66.7	69.1	72.0	77.0	65.0	68.3	83.7	96.5	71.7	65.8	74.9	59.1	63.2	71.9
Martinez et al. [24] (MA)	51.8	56.2	58.1	59.0	69.5	78.4	55.2	58.1	74.0	94.6	62.3	59.1	65.1	49.5	52.4	62.9
Fang et al. [41] (MA) 17j	50.1	54.3	57.0	57.1	66.6	73.3	53.4	55.7	72.8	88.6	60.3	57.7	62.7	47.5	50.6	60.4
Sun et al. [15] (MA) 17j	52.8	54.8	54.2	54.3	61.8	67.2	53.1	53.6	71.7	86.7	61.5	53.4	61.6	47.1	53.4	59.1
Baseline 1 ([24] + median filter)	51.8	55.3	59.1	58.5	66.4	79.2	54.7	55.8	73.2	89.0	61.6	59.5	65.9	49.5	53.5	62.2
Baseline 2 ([24] + mean filter)	50.9	54.9	58.2	57.9	65.6	78.9	53.7	55.8	73.5	89.9	60.9	59.2	65.1	49.2	52.8	61.8
Our network (MA)	44.2	46.7	52.3	49.3	59.9	59.4	47.5	46.2	59.9	65.6	55.8	50.4	52.3	43.5	45.1	51.9
Martinez et al. [24] (GT) (MA)	37.7	44.4	40.3	42.1	48.2	54.9	44.4	42.1	54.6	58.0	45.1	46.4	47.6	36.4	40.4	45.5
Our network (GT) (MA)	35.2	40.8	37.2	37.4	43.2	44.0	38.9	35.6	42.3	44.6	39.7	39.7	40.2	32.8	35.5	39.2

We follow the standard protocols of the Human3.6M dataset used in the literature. We used subjects 1, 5, 6, 7, and 8 for training, and subjects 9 and 11 for testing and the error is evaluated on the predicted 3D pose without any transformation. We refer this as protocol #1. Another common approach used by many to evaluate their methods is to align the predicted 3D pose with the ground truth using a similarity transformation (Procrustes analysis). We refer this as protocol #2. We use the average error per joint in millimeters between the estimated and the ground truth 3D pose relative to the root node as the error metric. For the HumanEva dataset, we report results on each subject and action separately after performing rigid alignment with the ground truth data, following the protocol used by the previous methods.

2D Detections. We fine-tuned a model of stacked-hourglass network [18], initially trained on the MPII dataset [46] (a benchmark dataset for 2D pose estimation), on the images of the Human3.6M dataset to obtain 2D pose estimations for each image. We used the bounding box information provided with the dataset to first compute the center of the person in the image and then cropped a 440×440 region across the person and resized it to 256×256. We fine-tuned the network for 250 iterations and used a batch size of 3 and a learning rate of $2.5e - 4$.

Baselines. Since many of the previous methods are based on single frame predictions, we used two baselines for comparison. To show that our method is much better than naive post processing, we applied a mean filter and a median filter on the 3D pose predictions of Martinez et al. [24]. We used a window size of 5 frames and a stride length of 1 to apply the filters. Although non-rigid structure from motion (NRSFM) is one of the most general approaches for any 3D reconstruction problem from a sequence of 2D correspondences, we did not use

Table 2. Results showing the errors action-wise on Human3.6M [29] dataset under protocol #2 (Procrustes alignment to the ground truth in post-processing). Note that the results reported here are for sequence of length 5. The 14j annotation indicates that the body model considers 14 body joints while 17j means considers 17 body joints. (SA) annotation indicates per-action model while (MA) indicates single model used for all actions. The bold-faced numbers represent the best result while underlined numbers represent the second best. The results of the methods are obtained from the original papers, except for (*), which were obtained from [22].

Protocol #2	Direct.	Discuss	Eating	Greet	Phone	Photo	Pose	Purch.	Sitting	SitingD	Smoke	Wait	WalkD	Walk	WalkT	Avg
Akhter & Black [21]* (MA) 14j	199.2	177.6	161.8	197.8	176.2	186.5	195.4	167.3	160.7	173.7	177.8	181.9	176.2	198.6	192.7	181.1
Ramakrishna et al [19]* (MA) 14j	137.4	149.3	141.6	154.3	157.7	158.9	141.8	158.1	168.6	175.6	160.4	161.7	150.0	174.8	150.2	157.3
Zhou et al [20]* (MA) 14j	99.7	95.8	87.9	116.8	108.3	107.3	93.5	95.3	109.1	137.5	106.0	102.2	106.5	110.4	115.2	106.7
Rogez et al [9] (MA)	–	–	–	–	–	–	–	–	–	–	–	–	–	–	–	87.3
Nie et al [12] (MA)	62.8	69.2	79.6	78.8	80.8	86.9	72.5	73.9	96.1	106.9	88.0	70.7	76.5	71.9	76.5	79.5
Mehta et al [9] (MA) 14j	–	–	–	–	–	–	–	–	–	–	–	–	–	–	–	54.6
Bogo et al [22] (MA) 14j	62.0	60.2	67.8	76.5	92.1	77.0	73.0	75.3	100.3	137.3	83.4	77.3	86.8	79.7	87.7	82.3
Moreno-Noguer [23] (MA) 14j	66.1	61.7	84.5	73.7	65.2	67.2	60.9	67.3	103.5	74.6	92.6	69.6	71.5	78.0	73.2	74.0
Tekin et al [16] (MA) 17j	–	–	–	–	–	–	–	–	–	–	–	–	–	–	–	50.1
Pavlakos et al [7] (MA) 17j	–	–	–	–	–	–	–	–	–	–	–	–	–	–	–	51.9
Martinez et al [24] (MA) 17j	39.5	43.2	46.4	47.0	51.0	56.0	41.4	40.6	56.5	69.4	49.2	45.0	49.5	38.0	43.1	47.7
Fang et al [41] (MA) 17j	_38.2_	_41.7_	_43.7_	_44.9_	_48.5_	_55.3_	_40.2_	_38.2_	_54.5_	_64.4_	_47.2_	_44.3_	_47.3_	_36.7_	_41.7_	_45.7_
Baseline 1 ([24] + median filter)	44.1	46.3	49.6	50.3	53.2	60.9	43.7	43.5	61.2	74.4	53.0	48.6	54.7	43.0	48.5	51.7
Baseline 2 ([24] + mean filter)	43.1	45.0	48.8	49.0	52.1	59.4	43.5	42.4	59.7	70.9	51.2	46.9	52.4	40.3	46.0	50.0
Our network (MA) 17j	**36.9**	**37.9**	**42.8**	**40.3**	**46.8**	**46.7**	**37.7**	**36.5**	**48.9**	**52.6**	**45.6**	**39.6**	**43.5**	**35.2**	**38.5**	**42.0**

it as a baseline because Zhou et al. [20] did not find NRSFM techniques to be effective for 3D human pose estimation. They found that the NRSFM techniques do not work well with slow camera motion. Since the videos in the Human3.6M dataset [29] are captured by stationary cameras, the subjects in the dataset do not rotate that much to provide alternative views for NRSFM algorithm to perform well. Another reason is that human pose reconstruction is a specialized problem in which constraints from human body structure apply.

Data Pre-processing. We normalized the 3D ground truth poses, the noisy 2D pose estimates from stacked-hourglass network and the 2D ground truth [18] by subtracting the mean and dividing by standard deviation. We do not predict the 3D location of the root joint i.e. central hip joint and hence zero center the 3D joint locations relative to the global position of the root node. To obtain the ground truth 3D poses in camera coordinate space, an inverse rigid body transformation is applied on the ground truth 3D poses in global coordinate space using the given camera parameters. To generate both training and test sequences, we translated a sliding window of length T by one frame. Hence there is an overlap between the sequences. This gives us more data to train on, which is always an advantage for deep learning systems. During test time, we initially predict the first T frames of the sequence and slide the window by a stride length of 1 to predict the next frame using the previous frames.

Training Details. We trained our network for 100 epochs, where each epoch makes a complete pass over the entire Human 3.6M dataset. We used the Adam [47] optimizer for training the network with a learning rate of $1e-5$ which is decayed exponentially per iteration. The weights of the LSTM units are initialized by Xavier uniform initializer [48]. We used a mini-batch batch size of

32 i.e. 32 sequences. For most of our experiments we used a sequence length of 5, because it allows faster training with high accuracy. We experimented with different sequence lengths and found sequence length 4, 5 and 6 to generally give better results, which we will discuss in detail in the results section. We trained a single model for all the action classes. Our code is implemented in Tensorflow. We perform cross-validation on the training set to select the hyper-parameter values α and β of our loss function to 1 and 5 respectively. Similarly, using cross-validation, the three hyper-parameters of the temporal consistency constraint η, ρ and τ, are set to $1, 2.5$ and 4 respectively. A single training step for sequences of length 5 takes only 34 ms approximately, while a forward pass takes only about 16ms on NVIDIA Titan X GPU. Therefore given the 2D joint locations from a pose detector, our network takes about 3.2 ms to predict 3D pose per frame.

4.1   Quantitative Results

Evaluation on Estimated 2D Pose. As mentioned before, we used a sequence length of 5 to perform both qualitative and quantitative evaluation of our network. The results on Human3.6M dataset [29] under protocol #1 are shown in Table 1. From the table we observe that our model achieves the lowest error for every action class under protocol #1, unlike many of the previous state-of-the-art methods. Note that we train a single model for all the action classes unlike many other methods which trained a model for each action class. Our network significantly improves the state-of-the-art result of Sun et al. [15] by approximately 12.1% (by 7.2 mm). The results under protocol #2, which aligns the predictions to the ground truth using a rigid body similarity transform before computing the error, is reported in Table 2. Our network improves the reported state-of-the-art results by 8.09% (by 3.7 mm) and achieves the lowest error for each action in protocol #2 as well. From the results, we observe the effectiveness of exploiting temporal information across multiple sequences. By using the information of temporal context, our network reduced the overall error in estimating 3D joint locations, especially on actions like *phone, photo, sit* and *sitting down* on which most previous methods did not perform well due to heavy occlusion. We also observe that our method outperforms both the baselines by a large margin on both the protocols. This shows that our method learned the temporal context of the sequences and predicted temporally consistent 3D poses, which naive post-processing techniques like temporal mean and median filters over frame-wise prediction failed to do.

Like most previous methods, we report the results on action classes *Walking* and *Jogging* of the HumanEva [45] dataset in Table 3. We obtained the lowest error in four of the six cases and the lowest average error for the two actions. We also obtained the second best result on subject 2 of action *Walking*. However, HumanEva is a smaller dataset than Human3.6M and the same subjects appear in both training and testing.

Table 3. Results on the HumanEva [45] dataset, and comparison with previous work. The bold-faced numbers represent the best result while underlined numbers represent the second best.

	Walking			Jogging			
	S1	S2	S3	S1	S2	S3	Avg
Radwan et al. [49]	75.1	99.8	93.8	79.2	89.8	99.4	89.5
Wang et al. [37]	71.9	75.7	85.3	62.6	77.7	54.4	71.3
Simo-Serra et al. [50]	65.1	48.6	73.5	74.2	46.6	32.2	56.7
Bo et al. [51]	46.4	30.3	64.9	64.5	48.0	38.2	48.7
Kostrikov et al. [52]	44.0	30.9	41.7	57.2	35.0	33.3	40.3
Yasin et al. [53]	35.8	32.4	41.6	46.6	41.4	35.4	38.9
Moreno-Noguer [23]	19.7	**13.0**	**24.9**	39.7	20.0	21.0	26.9
Pavlakos et al. [7]	22.1	21.9	<u>29.0</u>	29.8	23.6	26.0	25.5
Lin et al. [13]	26.5	20.7	38.0	41.0	29.7	29.1	30.8
Martinez et al. [24]	19.7	17.4	46.8	<u>26.9</u>	18.2	18.6	24.6
Fang et al. [41]	<u>19.4</u>	16.8	37.4	30.4	<u>17.6</u>	<u>16.3</u>	<u>22.9</u>
Ours	**19.1**	<u>13.6</u>	43.9	**23.2**	**16.9**	**15.5**	**22.0**

Evaluation on 2D Ground Truth. As suggested by Martinez et al. [24], we also found that the more accurate the 2D joint locations are, the better are the estimates for 3D pose. We trained our model on ground truth 2D poses for a sequence length of 5. The results under protocol #1 are reported in Table 1. As seen from the table, our model improves the lower bound error of Martinez et al. [24] by almost 13.8%.

The results on ground truth 2D joint input for protocol #2 are reported in Table 4. When there is no noise in 2D joint locations, our network performs better than the models by Martinez et al. [24] and Moreno-Nouguer [23]. These results suggest that the information of temporal consistency from previous frames is a

Table 4. Performance of our system trained with ground truth 2D pose of Human3.6M [29] dataset and tested with different levels of additive Gaussian noise **(Top)** and on 2D pose predictions from stacked-hourglass [18] pose detector **(Bottom)** under protocol #2.

	Moreno-Nouguer [23]	Martinez et al. [24]	Ours
GT/GT	62.17	37.10	**31.67**
GT/GT + $\mathcal{N}(0,5)$	67.11	46.65	**37.46**
GT/GT + $\mathcal{N}(0,10)$	79.12	52.84	**49.41**
GT/GT + $\mathcal{N}(0,15)$	96.08	**59.97**	61.80
GT/GT + $\mathcal{N}(0,20)$	115.55	**70.24**	73.65

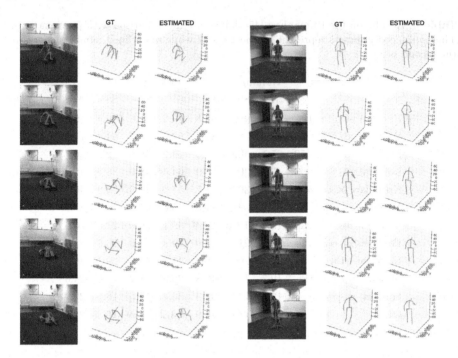

Fig. 3. Qualitative results on Human3.6M videos. The images on the **left** are for subject 11 and action *sitting down*. On the **right** the images are for subject 9 and action *phoning*. 3D poses in the center is the ground truth and on the right is the estimated 3D pose.

valuable cue for the task of estimating 3D pose even when the detections are noise free.

Robustness to Noise. We carried out some experiments to test the tolerance of our model to different levels of noise in the input data by training our network on 2D ground truth poses and testing on inputs corrupted by different levels of Gaussian noise. Table 4 shows how our final model compares against the models by Moreno-Nouguer [23] and Martinez et al. [24]. Our network is significantly more robust than Moreno-Nouguer's model [23]. When compared against Martinez et al. [24] our network performs better when the level of input noise is low i.e. standard deviation less than or equal to 10. However, for higher levels of noise our network performs slightly worse than Martinez et al. [24]. We would like to attribute the cause of this to the temporal smoothness constraint imposed during training which distributes the error of individual frames over the entire sequence. However, its usefulness can be observed in the qualitative results (See Figs. 5 and 3).

Ablative Analysis. To show the usefulness of each component and design decision of our network, we perform an ablative analysis. We follow protocol #1 for

Table 5. Ablative and hyperparameter sensitivity analysis.

	Error (mm)	Δ
Ours	51.9	— —
w/o weighted joints	52.3	0.4
w/o temporal consistency constraint	52.7	0.8
w/o recurrent dropout	58.3	6.4
w/o layer normalized LSTM	61.1	9.2
w/o layer norm and recurrent dropout	59.5	7.6
w/o residual connections	102.4	50.5
w non-fine tuned SH [18]	55.6	3.7
w CPM detections [17] (14 joints)	66.1	14.2

performing ablative analysis and trained a single model for all the actions. The results are reported in Table 5. We observe that the biggest improvement in result is due the residual connections on the decoder side, which agrees with the hypothesis of He et al. [25]. Removing the residual connections massively increases the error by 50.5 mm. When we do not apply layer normalization on LSTM units, the error increases by 9.2 mm. On the other hand when dropout is not performed, the error raises by 6.4 mm. When both layer normalization and recurrent dropout are not used the results get worse by 7.6 mm. Although the temporal consistency constraint may seem to have less impact (only 0.8 mm) quantitatively on the performance of our network, it ensures that the predictions over a sequence are smooth and temporally consistent which is apparent from our qualitative results as seen in Figs. 5 and 3.

To show the effectiveness of our model on detections from different 2D pose detectors, we also experimented with the detections from CPM [17] and from stacked-hourglass [18] (SH) module which is not fine-tuned on Human3.6M dataset. We observe that even for the non-fine tuned stacked hourglass detections, our model achieves the state-of-the-art results. For detections from CPM, our model achieves competitive accuracy for the predictions.

Performance on Different Sequence Lengths. The results reported so far have been for input and output sequences of length 5. We carried out experiments to see how our network performs for different sequence lengths ranging from 2 to 10. The results are shown in Fig. 4. As can be seen, the performance of our network remains stable for sequences of varying lengths. Even for a sequence length of 2, which only considers the previous and the current frame, our model generates very good results. Particularly the best results were obtained for length 4, 5 and 6. However, we chose sequence length 5 for carrying out our experiments as a compromise between training time and accuracy.

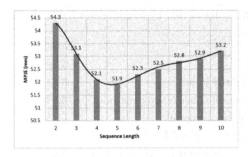

Fig. 4. Mean Per Joint Error (MPJE) in mm of our network for different sequence lengths.

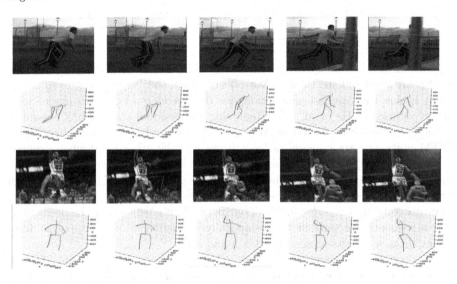

Fig. 5. Qualitative results on Youtube videos. Note on the sequence at the top, our network managed to predict meaningful 3D poses even when the 2D pose detections were poor using temporal information of the past.

4.2   Qualitative Analysis

We provide qualitative results on some videos of Human3.6M and Youtube. We apply the model trained on the Human3.6M dataset on some videos gathered from Youtube, The bounding box for each person in the Youtube video is labeled manually and for Human3.6M the ground truth bounding box is used. The 2D poses are detected using the stacked-hourglass model fine-tuned on Human3.6M data. The qualitative result for Youtube videos is shown in Fig. 5 and for Human3.6M in Fig. 3. The real advantage of using the temporal smoothness constraint during training is apparent in these figures. For Fig. 5, we can see that even when the 2D pose estimator breaks or generates extremely noisy detections, our system can recover temporally coherent 3D poses by exploiting the temporal consistency information. A similar trend can also be found for Human3.6M videos in Fig. 3, particularly for the action *sitting down* of subject 11. We have provided more qualitative results in the supplementary material.

5 Conclusion

Both the quantitative and qualitative results for our network show the effectiveness of exploiting temporal information over multiple sequences to estimate 3D poses which are temporally smooth. Our network achieved the best accuracy till date on all of the 15 action classes in the Human3.6M dataset [29]. Particularly, most of the previous methods struggled with actions which have a high degree of occlusion like *taking photo, talking on the phone, sitting* and *sitting down*. Our network has significantly better results on these actions. Additionally we found that our network is reasonably robust to noisy 2D poses. Although the contribution of temporal smoothness constraint is not apparent in the ablative analysis in Table 5, its effectiveness is clearly visible in the qualitative results, particularly on challenging Youtube videos (see Fig. 5).

Our network effectively demonstrates the power of using temporal context information which we achieved using a sequence-to-sequence network that can be trained efficiently in a reasonably quick time. Also our network makes predictions from 2D poses at 3 ms per frame on average which suggests that, given the 2D pose detector is real time, our network can be applied in real-time scenarios.

References

1. Sutskever, I., Vinyals, O., Le, Q.V.: Sequence to sequence learning with neural networks. In: Advances in neural information processing systems (NIPS), pp. 3104–3112 (2014)
2. Agarwal, A., Triggs, B.: 3D human pose from silhouettes by relevance vector regression. In: IEEE Conference on Computer Vision and Pattern Recognition (CVPR) (2004)
3. Mori, G., Malik, J.: Recovering 3D human body configurations using shape contexts. IEEE Trans Pattern Anal. Mach. Intell. (TPAMI) **28**(7), 1052–1062 (2006)
4. Bo, L.F., Sminchisescu, C., Kanaujia, A., Metaxas, D.N.: Fast algorithms for large scale conditional 3D prediction. In: IEEE Conference on Computer Vision and Pattern Recognition (CVPR), pp. 1–8 (2008)
5. Shakhnarovich, G., Viola, P.A., Darrell, T.J.: Fast pose estimation with parameter-sensitive hashing. In: IEEE International Conference on Computer Vision (ICCV) (2003)
6. Tekin, B., Katircioglu, I., Salzmann, M., Lepetit, V., Fua, P.: Structured prediction of 3D human pose with deep neural networks. In: British Machine Vision Conference (BMVC) (2016)
7. Pavlakos, G., Zhou, X., Derpanis, K.G., Daniilidis, K.: Coarse-to-fine volumetric prediction for single-image 3D human pose. In: IEEE Conference on Computer Vision and Pattern Recognition (CVPR) (2017)

8. Li, S., Chan, A.B.: 3D human pose estimation from monocular images with deep convolutional neural network. In: Cremers, D., Reid, I., Saito, H., Yang, M.-H. (eds.) ACCV 2014. LNCS, vol. 9004, pp. 332–347. Springer, Cham (2015). https://doi.org/10.1007/978-3-319-16808-1_23

9. Mehta, D., Rhodin, H., Casas, D., Sotnychenko, O., Xu, W., Theobalt, C.: Monocular 3D human pose estimation using transfer learning and improved CNN supervision. arXiv preprint arXiv:1611.09813 (2016)

10. Zhou, X., Sun, X., Zhang, W., Liang, S., Wei, Y.: Deep kinematic pose regression. In: Hua, G., Jégou, H. (eds.) ECCV 2016. LNCS, vol. 9915, pp. 186–201. Springer, Cham (2016). https://doi.org/10.1007/978-3-319-49409-8_17

11. Mehta, D., et al.: VNect: real-time 3D human pose estimation with a single RGB camera. ACM Trans. Graph. **36**(4), 44 (2017)

12. Nie, B.X., Wei, P., Zhu, S.C.: Monocular 3D human pose estimation by predicting depth on joints. In: IEEE International Conference on Computer Vision (ICCV) (2017)

13. Lin, M., Lin, L., Liang, X., Wang, K., Chen, H.: Recurrent 3D pose sequence machines. In: IEEE Conference on Computer Vision and Pattern Recognition (CVPR) (2017)

14. Park, S., Hwang, J., Kwak, N.: 3D human pose estimation using convolutional neural networks with 2D pose information. In: Hua, G., Jégou, H. (eds.) ECCV 2016. LNCS, vol. 9915, pp. 156–169. Springer, Cham (2016). https://doi.org/10.1007/978-3-319-49409-8_15

15. Sun, X., Shang, J., Liang, S., Wei, Y.: Compositional human pose regression. In: IEEE International Conference on Computer Vision (ICCV) (2017)

16. Tekin, B., Marquez Neila, P., Salzmann, M., Fua, P.: Learning to fuse 2D and 3D image cues for monocular body pose estimation. In: International Conference on Computer Vision (ICCV) (2017)

17. Wei, S.E., Ramakrishna, V., Kanade, T., Sheikh, Y.: Convolutional pose machines. In: IEEE Conference on Computer Vision and Pattern Recognition (CVPR) (2016)

18. Newell, A., Yang, K., Deng, J.: Stacked hourglass networks for human pose estimation. In: European Conference on Computer Vision (ECCV) (2016)

19. Ramakrishna, V., Kanade, T., Sheikh, Y.: Reconstructing 3D human pose from 2D image landmarks. In: Fitzgibbon, A., Lazebnik, S., Perona, P., Sato, Y., Schmid, C. (eds.) ECCV 2012. LNCS, vol. 7575, pp. 573–586. Springer, Heidelberg (2012). https://doi.org/10.1007/978-3-642-33765-9_41

20. Zhou, X., Zhu, M., Leonardos, S., Derpanis, K.G., Daniilidis, K.: Sparseness meets deepness: 3D human pose estimation from monocular video. In: IEEE Conference on Computer Vision and Pattern Recognition (CVPR), pp. 4966–4975 (2016)

21. Akhter, I., Black, M.J.: Pose-conditioned joint angle limits for 3D human pose reconstruction. In: IEEE Conference on Computer Vision and Pattern Recognition (CVPR), pp. 1446–1455 (2015)

22. Bogo, F., Kanazawa, A., Lassner, C., Gehler, P., Romero, J., Black, M.J.: Keep it SMPL: automatic estimation of 3D human pose and shape from a single image. In: Leibe, B., Matas, J., Sebe, N., Welling, M. (eds.) ECCV 2016. LNCS, vol. 9909, pp. 561–578. Springer, Cham (2016). https://doi.org/10.1007/978-3-319-46454-1_34

23. Moreno-Noguer, F.: 3D human pose estimation from a single image via distance matrix regression. In: IEEE Conference on Computer Vision and Pattern Recognition (CVPR) (2017)

24. Martinez, J., Hossain, R., Romero, J., Little, J.J.: A simple yet effective baseline for 3D human pose estimation. In: IEEE International Conference on Computer Vision (ICCV) (2017)

25. He, K., Zhang, X., Ren, S., Sun, J.: Deep residual learning for image recognition. In: IEEE conference on Computer Vision and Pattern Recognition (CVPR), pp. 770–778 (2016)
26. Hochreiter, S., Schmidhuber, J.: Long short-term memory. Neural Comput. **9**(8), 1735–1780 (1997)
27. Ba, J.L., Kiros, J.R., Hinton, G.E.: Layer normalization. arXiv preprint arXiv:1607.06450 (2016)
28. Zaremba, W., Sutskever, I., Vinyals, O.: Recurrent neural network regularization. arXiv preprint arXiv:1409.2329 (2014)
29. Ionescu, C., Papava, D., Olaru, V., Sminchisescu, C.: Human3.6M: large scale datasets and predictive methods for 3D human sensing in natural environments. IEEE Trans. Pattern Anal. Mach. Intell. (T-PAMI) **36**(7), 1325–1339 (2014)
30. Barron, C., Kakadiaris, I.A.: Estimating anthropometry and pose from a single uncalibrated image. Compu. Vis. Image Underst. (CVIU) **81**(3), 269–284 (2001)
31. Parameswaran, V., Chellappa, R.: View independent human body pose estimation from a single perspective image. In: IEEE Conference on Computer Vision and Pattern Recognition (CVPR) (2004)
32. Lee, H.J., Chen, Z.: Determination of 3D human body postures from a single view. Comput. Vis., Graph. Image Process. **30**, 148–168 (1985)
33. Jiang, H.: 3D human pose reconstruction using millions of exemplars. In: IEEE International Conference on Pattern Recognition (ICPR), pp. 1674–1677. IEEE (2010)
34. Taylor, C.J.: Reconstruction of articulated objects from point correspondences in a single uncalibrated image. In: IEEE Conference on Computer Vision and Pattern Recognition (CVPR), vol. 1, pp. 677–684. IEEE (2000)
35. Gupta, A., Martinez, J., Little, J.J., Woodham, R.J.: 3D pose from motion for cross-view action recognition via non-linear circulant temporal encoding. In: IEEE Conference on Computer Vision and Pattern Recognition (CVPR) (2014)
36. Chen, C.H., Ramanan, D.: 3D human pose estimation = 2D pose estimation + matching. In: IEEE Conference on Computer Vision and Pattern Recognition (CVPR) (2017)
37. Wang, C., Wang, Y., Lin, Z., Yuille, A.L., Gao, W.: Robust estimation of 3D human poses from a single image. In: IEEE Conference on Computer Vision and Pattern Recognition (CVPR) (2014)
38. Varol, G., et al.: Learning from synthetic humans. In: IEEE Conference on Computer Vision and Pattern Recognition (CVPR) (2017)
39. Rogez, G., Schmid, C.: MoCap-guided data augmentation for 3D pose estimation in the wild. In: Advances in Neural Information Processing Systems (NIPS) (2016)
40. Tome, D., Russell, C., Agapito, L.: Lifting from the deep: convolutional 3D pose estimation from a single image. In: IEEE Conference on Computer Vision and Pattern Recognition (CVPR), pp. 2500–2509 (2017)
41. Fang, H., Xu, Y., Wang, W., Liu, X., Zhu, S.C.: Learning knowledge-guided pose grammar machine for 3D human pose estimation. arXiv preprint arXiv:1710.06513 (2017)
42. Andriluka, M., Roth, S., Schiele, B.: Monocular 3D pose estimation and tracking by detection. In: IEEE Conference on Computer Vision and Pattern Recognition (CVPR), pp. 623–630. IEEE (2010)
43. Tekin, B., Rozantsev, A., Lepetit, V., Fua, P.: Direct prediction of 3D body poses from motion compensated sequences. In: Proceedings of the IEEE Conference on Computer Vision and Pattern Recognition (CVPR), pp. 991–1000 (2016)

44. Du, Y., et al.: Marker-less 3D human motion capture with monocular image sequence and height-maps. In: Leibe, B., Matas, J., Sebe, N., Welling, M. (eds.) ECCV 2016. LNCS, vol. 9908, pp. 20–36. Springer, Cham (2016). https://doi.org/10.1007/978-3-319-46493-0_2

45. Sigal, L., Balan, A.O., Black, M.J.: HUMANEVA: synchronized video and motion capture dataset and baseline algorithm for evaluation of articulated human motion. Int. J. Comput. Vis. (IJCV) **87**(1–2), 4 (2010)

46. Andriluka, M., Pishchulin, L., Gehler, P., Schiele, B.: 2D human pose estimation: new Benchmark and state of the art analysis. In: IEEE Conference on Computer Vision and Pattern Recognition (CVPR) (2014)

47. Kingma, D., Ba, J.: Adam: a method for stochastic optimization. In: ICLR (2015)

48. Glorot, X., Bengio, Y.: Understanding the difficulty of training deep feedforward neural networks. In: Proceedings of the Thirteenth International Conference on Artificial Intelligence and Statistics, pp. 249–256 (2010)

49. Radwan, I., Dhall, A., Goecke, R.: Monocular image 3D human pose estimation under self-occlusion. In: IEEE International Conference on Computer Vision (ICCV) (2013)

50. Simo-Serra, E., Quattoni, A., Torras, C., Moreno-Noguer, F.: A joint model for 2D and 3D pose estimation from a single image. In: IEEE Conference on Computer Vision and Pattern Recognition (CVPR) (2013)

51. Bo, L., Sminchisescu, C.: Twin Gaussian processes for structured prediction. Int. J. Comput. Vis. (IJCV) **87**(1–2), 28 (2010)

52. Kostrikov, I., Gall, J.: Depth sweep regression forests for estimating 3D human pose from images. In: British Machine Vision Conference (BMVC) (2014)

53. Yasin, H., Iqbal, U., Kruger, B., Weber, A., Gall, J.: A dual-source approach for 3D pose estimation from a single image. In: IEEE Conference on Computer Vision and Pattern Recognition (CVPR), pp. 4948–4956 (2016)

Recovering 3D Planes from a Single Image via Convolutional Neural Networks

Fengting Yang[(✉)] and Zihan Zhou

The Pennsylvania State University, University Park, USA
{fuy34,zzhou}@ist.psu.edu

Abstract. In this paper, we study the problem of recovering 3D planar surfaces from a single image of man-made environment. We show that it is possible to directly train a deep neural network to achieve this goal. A novel plane structure-induced loss is proposed to train the network to simultaneously predict a plane segmentation map and the parameters of the 3D planes. Further, to avoid the tedious manual labeling process, we show how to leverage existing large-scale RGB-D dataset to train our network without explicit 3D plane annotations, and how to take advantage of the semantic labels come with the dataset for accurate planar and non-planar classification. Experiment results demonstrate that our method significantly outperforms existing methods, both qualitatively and quantitatively. The recovered planes could potentially benefit many important visual tasks such as vision-based navigation and human-robot interaction.

Keywords: 3D reconstruction · Plane segmentation · Deep learning

1 Introduction

Automatic 3D reconstruction from a single image has long been a challenging problem in computer vision. Previous work have demonstrated that an effective approach to this problem is exploring structural regularities in man-made environments, such as planar surfaces, repetitive patterns, symmetries, rectangles and cuboids [5,12,14,15,21,28,33]. Further, the 3D models obtained by harnessing such structural regularities are often attractive in practice, because they provide a high-level, compact representation of the scene geometry, which is desirable for many applications such as large-scale map compression, semantic scene understanding, and human-robot interaction.

In this paper, we study how to recover 3D planes – arguably the most common structure in man-made environments – from a single image. In the literature, several methods have been proposed to fit a scene with a piecewise planar model.

Electronic supplementary material The online version of this chapter (https://doi.org/10.1007/978-3-030-01249-6_6) contains supplementary material, which is available to authorized users.

© Springer Nature Switzerland AG 2018
V. Ferrari et al. (Eds.): ECCV 2018, LNCS 11214, pp. 87–103, 2018.
https://doi.org/10.1007/978-3-030-01249-6_6

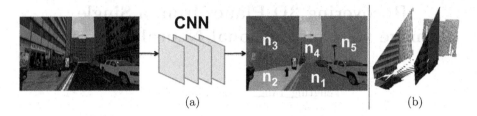

CNN

(a)   (b)

Fig. 1. We propose a new, end-to-end trainable deep neural network to recover 3D planes from a single image. **(a)** Given an input image, the network simultaneously predicts (i) a plane segmentation map that partitions the image into planar surfaces plus non-planar objects, and (ii) the plane parameters $\{\mathbf{n}_j\}_{j=1}^m$ in 3D space. **(b)** With the output of our network, a piecewise planar 3D model of the scene can be easily created.

These methods typically take a *bottom-up* approach: First, geometric primitives such as straight line segments, corners, and junctions are detected in the image. Then, planar regions are discovered by grouping the detected primitives based on their spatial relationships. For example, [3,6,27,34] first detect line segments in the image, and then cluster them into several classes, each associated with a prominent vanishing point. [21] further detects junctions formed by multiple intersecting planes to generate model hypotheses. Meanwhile, [9,11,16] take a learning-based approach to predict the orientations of local image patches, and then group the patches with similar orientations to form planar regions.

However, despite its popularity, there are several inherent difficulties with the bottom-up approach. *First*, geometric primitives may not be reliably detected in man-made environments (e.g., due to the presence of poorly textured or specular surfaces). Therefore, it is very difficult to infer the geometric properties of such surfaces. *Second*, there are often a large number of irrelevant features or outliers in the detected primitives (e.g., due to presence of non-planar objects), making the grouping task highly challenging. This is the main reason why most existing methods resort to rather restrictive assumptions, e.g., requiring "Manhattan world" scenes with three mutually-orthogonal dominant directions or a "box" room model, to filter outliers and produce reasonable results. But such assumptions greatly limit the applicability of those methods in practice.

In view of these fundamental difficulties, we take a very different route to 3D plane recovery in this paper. Our method does not rely on grouping low-level primitives such as line segments and image patches. Instead, inspired by the recent success of convolutional neural networks (CNNs) in object detection and semantic segmentation, we design a novel, end-to-end trainable network to directly identify all planar surfaces in the scene, and further estimate their parameters in the 3D space. As illustrated in Fig. 1, the network takes a single image as input, and outputs (i) a segmentation map that identifies the planar surfaces in the image and (ii) the parameters of each plane in the 3D space, thus effectively creating a piecewise planar model for the scene.

One immediate difficulty with our learning-based approach is the lack of training data with annotated 3D planes. To avoid the tedious manual labeling process, we propose a novel plane structure-induced loss which essentially casts our problem as one of single-image depth prediction. Our key insight here is that, if we can correctly identify the planar regions in the image and predict the plane parameters, then we can also accurately infer the depth in these regions. In this way, we are able to leverage existing large-scale RGB-D datasets to train our network. Moreover, as pixel-level semantic labels are often available in these datasets, we show how to seamlessly incorporate the labels into our network to better distinguish planar and non-planar objects.

In summary, **the contributions of this work** are: (i) We design an effective, end-to-end trainable deep neural network to directly recover 3D planes from a single image. (ii) We develop a novel learning scheme that takes advantage of existing RGB-D datasets and the semantic labels therein to train our network without extra manual labeling effort. Experiment results demonstrate that our method significantly outperforms, both qualitatively and quantitatively, existing plane detection methods. Further, our method achieves real-time performance at the testing time, thus is suitable for a wide range of applications such as visual localization and mapping, and human-robot interaction.

2   Related Work

3D Plane Recovery from a Single Image. Existing approaches to this problem can be roughly grouped into two categories: geometry-based methods and appearance-based methods. *Geometry-based methods* explicitly analyze the geometric cues in the 2D image to recover 3D information. For example, under the pinhole camera model, parallel lines in 3D space are projected to converging lines in the image plane. The common point of intersection, perhaps at infinity, is called the vanishing point [13]. By detecting the vanishing points associated with two sets of parallel lines on a plane, the plane's 3D orientation can be uniquely determined [3,6,27]. Another important geometric primitive is the junction formed by two or more lines of different orientations. Several work make use of junctions to generate plausible 3D plane hypotheses or remove impossible ones [21,34]. And a different approach is to detect rectangular structures in the image, which are typically formed by two sets of orthogonal lines on the same plane [26]. However, all these methods rely on the presence of strong regular structures, such as parallel or orthogonal lines in a Manhattan world scene, hence have limited applicability in practice.

To overcome this limitation, *appearance-based methods* focus on inferring geometric properties of an image from its appearance. For example, [16] proposes a diverse set of features (e.g., color, texture, location and shape) and uses them to train a model to classify each superpixel in an image into discrete classes such as "support" and "vertical (left/center/right)". [11] uses a learning-based method to predict continuous 3D orientations at a given image pixel. Further, [9] automatically learns meaningful 3D primitives for single image understanding.

Our method also falls into this category. But unlike existing methods which take a bottom-up approach by grouping local geometric primitives, our method trains a network to directly predict global 3D plane structures. Recently, [22] also proposes a deep neural network for piecewise planar reconstruction from a single image. But its training requires ground truth 3D planes and does not take advantage of the semantic labels in the dataset.

Machine Learning and Geometry. There is a large body of work on developing machine learning techniques to infer pixel-level geometric properties of the scene, mostly in the context of depth prediction [7,30] and surface normal prediction [8,18]. But few work has been done on detecting mid/hight-level 3D structures with supervised data. A notable exception which is also related to our problem is the line of research on indoor room layout estimation [5,14,15,20,28]. In these work, however, the scene geometry is assumed to follow a simple "box" model which consists of several mutually orthogonal planes (e.g., ground, ceiling, and walls). In contrast, our work aims to detect 3D planes under arbitrary configurations.

3   Method

3.1   Difficulty in Obtaining Ground Truth Plane Annotations

As most computer vision problems, a large-scale dataset with ground truth annotations is needed to effectively train the neural network for our task. Unfortunately, since the planar regions often have complex boundaries in an image, manual labeling of such regions could be very time-consuming. Further, it is unclear how to extract precise 3D plane parameters from an image.

To avoid the tedious manual labeling process, one strategy is to automatically convert the per-pixel depth maps in existing RGB-D datasets into planar surfaces. To this end, existing multi-model fitting algorithms can be employed to cluster 3D points derived from the depth maps. However, this is not an easy task either. Here, the fundamental difficulty lies in the choice of a proper threshold in practice to distinguish the inliers of a model instance (e.g., 3D points on a particular plane) from the outliers, *regardless of which algorithm one chooses.*

To illustrate this difficulty, we use the SYNTHIA dataset [29] which provides a large number of photo-realistic synthetic images of urban scenes and the corresponding depth maps (see Sect. 4.1 for more details). The dataset is generated by rendering a virtual city created using the Unity game development platform. Thus, the depth maps are noise-free. To detect planes from the 3D point cloud, we apply a popular multi-model fitting method called J-Linkage [31]. Similar to the RANSAC technique, this method is based on sampling consensus. We refer interested readers to [31] for a detailed description of the method.

A key parameter of J-Linkage is a threshold ϵ which controls the maximum distance between a model hypothesis (i.e., a plane) and the data points belonging to the hypothesis. In Fig. 2, we show example results produced by J-Linkage with

(a)   (b)   (c)   (d)

Fig. 2. Difficulty in obtaining ground truth plane annotations. (**a–b**): Original image and depth map. (**c–d**): Plane fitting results generated by J-Linkage with $\epsilon = 0.5$ and $\epsilon = 2$, respectively.

different choices of ϵ. As one can see in Fig. 2(c), when a small threshold ($\epsilon = 0.5$) is used, the method breaks the building facade on the right into two planes. This is because the facade is not completely planar due to small indentations (e.g., the windows). When a large threshold ($\epsilon = 2$) is used (Fig. 2(d)), the stairs on the building on the left are incorrectly grouped with another building. Also, some objects (e.g., cars, pedestrians) are merged with the ground. If we use these results as ground truth to train a deep neural network, the network will also likely learn the systematic errors in the estimated planes. And the problem becomes even worse if we want to train our network on real datasets. Due to the limitation of existing 3D acquisition systems (e.g., RGB-D cameras and LIDAR devices) and computational tools, the depth maps in these datasets are often noisy and of limited resolution and limited reliable range. Clustering based on such depth maps is prone to errors.

3.2 A New Plane Structure-Induced Loss

The challenge in obtaining reliable labels motivates us to develop alternative training schemes for 3D plane recovery. Specifically, we ask the following question: Can we leverage the wide availability of large-scale RGB-D and/or 3D datasets to train a network to recognize geometric structures such as planes *without* obtaining ground truth annotations about the structures?

To address this question, our key insight is that, if we can recover 3D planes from the image, then we can use these planes to (partially) explain the scene geometry, which is generally represented by a 3D point cloud. Specifically, let $\{I_i, D_i\}_{i=1}^n$ denote a set of n training RGB image and depth map pairs with known camera intrinsic matrix K.[1] Then, for any pixel $\mathbf{q} \doteq [x, y, 1]^T$ (in homogeneous coordinates) on image I_i, it is easy to compute the corresponding 3D point as $Q = D_i(\mathbf{q}) \cdot K^{-1}\mathbf{q}$. Further, let $\mathbf{n} \in \mathbb{R}^3$ represents a 3D plane in the scene. If Q lies on the plane, then we have $\mathbf{n}^T Q = 1$.[2]

---

[1] Without loss of generality, we assume a constant K for all images in the dataset.

[2] A common way to represent a 3D plane is $(\tilde{\mathbf{n}}, d)$ where $\tilde{\mathbf{n}}$ is a normal vector and d is the distance to the camera center. In this paper, we choose a more succinct parametrization: $\mathbf{n} \doteq \tilde{\mathbf{n}}/d$. Note that $\mathbf{n}$ can uniquely identify a 3D plane, assuming the plane is not through the camera center (which is valid for real world images).

With the above observation, assuming there are m planes in the image I_i, we can now train a network to simultaneously output (i) a per-pixel probability map S_i, where $S_i(\mathbf{q})$ is an $(m+1)$-dimensional vector with its j-th element $S_i^j(\mathbf{q})$ indicating the probability of pixel $\mathbf{q}$ belonging to the j-th plane,[3] and (ii) the plane parameters $\Pi_i = \{\mathbf{n}_i^j\}_{j=1}^m$, by minimizing the following objective function:

$$\mathcal{L} = \sum_{i=1}^{n} \sum_{j=1}^{m} \left(\sum_{\mathbf{q}} S_i^j(\mathbf{q}) \cdot |(\mathbf{n}_i^j)^T Q - 1| \right) + \alpha \sum_{i=1}^{n} \mathcal{L}_{reg}(S_i), \qquad (1)$$

where $\mathcal{L}_{reg}(S_i)$ is a regularization term preventing the network from generating a trivial solution $S_i^0(\cdot) \equiv 1$, i.e., classifying all pixels as non-planar, and α is a weight balancing the two terms.

Before proceeding, we make two important observations about our formulation Eq. (1). *First*, the term $|(\mathbf{n}_i^j)^T Q - 1|$ measures the deviation of a 3D scene point Q from the j-th plane in I_i, parameterized by $\mathbf{n}_i^j$. In general, for a pixel $\mathbf{q}$ in the image, we know from perspective geometry that the corresponding 3D point must lie on a ray characterized by $\lambda K^{-1}\mathbf{q}$, where λ is the depth at $\mathbf{q}$. If this 3D point is also on the j-th plane, we must have

$$(\mathbf{n}_i^j)^T \cdot \lambda K^{-1}\mathbf{q} = 1 \implies \lambda = \frac{1}{(\mathbf{n}_i^j)^T \cdot K^{-1}\mathbf{q}}. \qquad (2)$$

Hence, in this case, λ can be regarded as the depth at $\mathbf{q}$ constrained by $\mathbf{n}_i^j$. Now, we can rewrite the term as:

$$|(\mathbf{n}_i^j)^T Q - 1| = |(\mathbf{n}_i^j)^T D_i(\mathbf{q}) \cdot K^{-1}\mathbf{q} - 1| = |D_i(\mathbf{q})/\lambda - 1|. \qquad (3)$$

Thus, the term $|(\mathbf{n}_i^j)^T Q - 1|$ essentially compares the depth λ induced by the j-th predicted plane with the ground truth $D_i(\mathbf{q})$, and penalizes the difference between them. In other words, our formulation casts the 3D plane recovery problem as a depth prediction problem.

Second, Eq. (1) couples plane segmentation and plane parameter estimation in a loss that encourages consistent explanations of the visual world through the recovered plane structure. It mimics the behavior of biological agents (e.g., humans) which also employ structural priors for 3D visual perception of the world [32]. This is in contrast to alternative methods that rely on ground truth plane segmentation maps and plane parameters as direct supervision signals to tackle the two problems separately.

3.3   Incorporating Semantics for Planar/Non-planar Classification

Now we turn our attention to the regularization term $\mathcal{L}_{reg}(S_i)$ in Eq. (1). Intuitively, we wish to use the predicted planes to explain as much scene geometry as possible. Therefore, a natural choice of $\mathcal{L}_{reg}(S_i)$ is to encourage plane predictions by minimizing the cross-entropy loss with constant label 1 at each pixel.

---

[3] In this paper, we use $j = 0$ to denote the "non-planar" class.

Specifically, let $p_{plane}(\mathbf{q}) = \sum_{j=1}^{m} S_i^j(\mathbf{q})$ be the sum of probabilities of pixel $\mathbf{q}$ being assigned to each plane, we write

$$\mathcal{L}_{reg}(S_i) = \sum_{\mathbf{q}} -1 \cdot \log(p_{plane}(\mathbf{q})) - 0 \cdot \log(1 - p_{plane}(\mathbf{q})). \tag{4}$$

Note that, while the above term effectively encourages the network to explain every pixel in the image using the predicted plane models, it treats all pixels equally. However, in practice, some objects are more likely to form meaningful planes than others. For example, a building facade is often regarded as a planar surface, whereas a pedestrian or a car is typically viewed as non-planar. In other words, if we can incorporate such high-level semantic information into our training scheme, the network is expected to achieve better performance in differentiating planar vs. non-planar surfaces.

Motivated by this observation, we propose to further utilize the semantic labels in the existing datasets. Take the SYNTHIA dataset as an example. The dataset provides precise pixel-level semantic annotations for 13 classes in urban scenes. For our purpose, we group these classes into "planar" = {building, fence, road, sidewalk, lane-marking} and "non-planar" = {sky, vegetation, pole, car, traffic signs, pedestrians, cyclists, miscellaneous}. Then, let $z(\mathbf{q}) = 1$ if pixel $\mathbf{q}$ belongs to one of the "planar" classes, and $z(\mathbf{q}) = 0$ otherwise, we can revise our regularization term as:

$$\mathcal{L}_{reg}(S_i) = \sum_{\mathbf{q}} -z(\mathbf{q}) \cdot \log(p_{plane}(\mathbf{q})) - (1 - z(\mathbf{q})) \cdot \log(1 - p_{plane}(\mathbf{q})). \tag{5}$$

Note that the choices of planar/non-planar classes are dataset- and problem-dependent. For example, one may argue that "sky" can be viewed as plane at infinity, thus should be included in the "planar" classes. Regardless the particular choices, we emphasize that here we provide a flexible way to incorporate high-level semantic information (generated by human annotators) to the plane detection problem. This is in contrast to traditional geometric methods that solely rely on a single threshold to distinguish planar vs. non-planar surfaces.

3.4   Network Architecture

In this paper, we choose a *fully convolutional network* (FCN), following its recent success in various pixel-level prediction tasks such as semantic segmentation [2, 23] and scene flow estimation [25]. Figure 3 shows the overall architecture of our proposed network. To simultaneously estimate the plane segmentation map and plane parameters, our network consists of two prediction branches, as we elaborate below.

Plane Segmentation Map. To predict the plane segmentation map, we use an encoder-decoder design with skip connections and multi-scale side predictions, similar to the DispNet architecture proposed in [25]. Specifically, the encoder

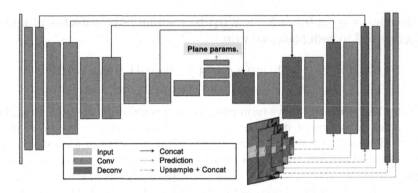

Fig. 3. Network architecture. The width and height of each block indicates the channel and the spatial dimension of the feature map, respectively. Each reduction (or increase) in size indicates a change by a factor of 2. The first convolutional layer has 32 channels. The filter size is 3 except for the first four convolutional layers (7, 7, 5, 5).

takes the whole image as input and produces high-level feature maps via a convolutional network. The decoder then gradually upsamples the feature maps via deconvolutional layers to make final predictions, taking into account also the features from different encoder layers. The multi-scale side predictions further allow the network to be trained with deep supervision. We use ReLU for all layers except for the prediction layers, where the softmax function is applied.

Plane Parameters. The plane parameter prediction branch shares the same high-level feature maps with the segmentation branch. The branch consists of two stride-2 convolutional layers ($3 \times 3 \times 512$) followed by a $1 \times 1 \times 3\,\mathrm{m}$ convolutional layer to output the parameters of the m planes. Global average pooling is then used to aggregate predictions across all spatial locations. We use ReLU for all layers except for the last layer, where no activation is applied.

Implementation Details. Our network is trained from scratch using the publicly available Tensorflow framework. By default, we set the weight in Eq. (1) as $\alpha = 0.1$, and the number of planes as $m = 5$. During training, we adopt the Adam [17] method with $\beta_1 = 0.99$ and $\beta_2 = 0.9999$. The batch size is set to 4, and the learning rate is set to 0.0001. We also augment the data by scaling the images with a random factor in [1, 1.15] followed by a random cropping. Convergence is reached at about 500K iterations.

4   Experiments

In this section, we conduct experiments to study the performance of our method, and compare it to existing ones. All experiments are conducted on one Nvidia

GTX 1080 Ti GPU device. At testing time, our method runs at about 60 frames per second, thus are suitable for potential real-time applications[4].

4.1 Datasets and Ground Truth Annotations

SYNTHIA: The recent SYNTHIA dataset [29] comprises more than 200,000 photo-realistic images rendered from virtual city environments with precise pixel-wise depth maps and semantic annotations. Since the dataset is designed to facilitate autonomous driving research, all frames are acquired from a virtual car as it navigates in the virtual city. The original dataset contains seven different scenarios. For our experiment, we select three scenarios (SEQS-02, 04, and 05) that represents city street views. For each scenario, we use the sequences for all four seasons (spring, summer, fall, and winter). Note that, to simulate real traffic conditions, the virtual car makes frequent stops during navigation. As a result, the dataset has many near-identical frames. We filter these redundant frames using a simple heuristic based on the vehicle speed. Finally, from the remaining frames, we randomly sample 8,000 frames as the training set and another 100 frames as the testing set.

For quantitative evaluation, we need to label all the planar regions in the test images. As we discussed in Sect. 3.1, automatic generation of ground truth plane annotations is difficult and error-prone. Thus, we adopt a semi-automatic method to interactively determine the ground truth labels with user input. To label one planar surface in the image, we ask the user to draw a quadrilateral region within that surface. Then, we fit a plane to the 3D points (derived from the ground truth depth map) that fall into that region to obtain the plane parameters *and* an instance-specific estimate of the variance of the distance distribution between the 3D points and the fitted plane. Note that, with the instance-specific variance estimate, we are able to handle surfaces with varying degrees of deviation from a perfect plane, but are commonly regarded as "planes" by humans. Finally, we use the plane parameters and the variance estimate to find all pixels that belong to the plane. We repeat this process until all planes in the image are labeled.

Cityscapes: Cityscapes [4] contains a large set of real street-view video sequences recorded in different cities. From the 3,475 images with publicly available fine semantic annotations, we randomly select 100 images for testing, and use the rest for training. To generate the planar/non-planar masks for training, we label pixels in the following classes as "planar" = {ground, road, sidewalk, parking, rail track, building, wall, fence, guard rail, bridge, and terrain}.

In contrast to SYNTHIA, the depth maps in Cityscapes are highly noisy because they are computed from stereo correspondences. Fitting planes on such data is extremely difficult even with user input. Therefore, to identify planar

---

[4] Please refer to supplementary materials for additional experiment results about (i) the choice of plane number and (ii) the effect of semantic labels.

surfaces in the image, we manually label the boundary of each plane using polygons, and further leverage the semantic annotations to refine it by ensuring that the plane boundary aligns with the object boundary, if they overlap.

4.2 Methods for Comparison

As discussed in Sect. 2, a common approach to plane detection is to use geometric cues such as vanishing points and junction features. However, such methods all make strong assumptions on the scene geometry, e.g., a "box"-like model for indoor scenes or a "vertical-ground" configuration for outdoor scenes. They would fail when these assumptions are violated, as in the case of SYNTHIA and Cityscapes datasets. Thus, we do not compare to these methods. Instead, we compare our method to the following *appearance-based methods*:

Depth + Multi-model Fitting: For this approach, we first train a deep neural network to predict pixel-level depth from a single image. We directly adopt the DispNet architecture [25] and train it from scratch with ground truth depth data. Following recent work on depth prediction [19], we minimize the berHu loss during training.

To find 3D planes, we have then applied two different multi-model fitting algorithms, namely J-Linkage [31] and RansaCov [24], on the 3D points derived from the predicted depth map. We call the corresponding methods **Depth + J-Linkage** and **Depth + RansaCov**, respectively. For fair comparison, we only keep the top-5 planes detected by each method. As mentioned earlier, a key parameter in these methods is the distance threshold ϵ. We favor them by running J-Linkage or RansaCov multiple times with various values of ϵ and retaining the best results.

Geometric Context (GC) [16]: This method uses a number of hand-crafted local image features to predict discrete surface layout labels. Specifically, it trains decision tree classifiers to label the image into three main geometric classes {support, vertical, sky}, and further divide the "vertical" class into five subclasses {left, center, right, porous, solid}. Among these labels, we consider the "support" class and "left", "center", "right" subclasses as four different planes, and the rest as non-planar.

To retrain their classifiers using our training data, we translate the labels in SYNTHIA dataset into theirs[5] and use the source code provided by the authors[6]. We found that this yields better performance on our testing set than the pretrained classifiers provided by the authors. We do not include this method in the experiment on Cityscapes dataset because it is difficult to determine the orientation of the vertical structures from the noisy depth maps.

---

[5] sky→sky, {road, sidewalk, lane-marking}→support, and the rest→vertical. For the "building" and "fence" classes in the SYNTHIA dataset, we fit 3D planes at different orientations to determine the appropriate subclass label (i.e., left/center/right).

[6] http://dhoiem.cs.illinois.edu/.

Fig. 4. Plane segmentation results on SYNTHIA. **From left to right:** Input image; Ground truth; Depth + J-Linkage; Depth + RansaCov; Geometric Context; Ours.

Finally, we note that there is another closely related work [11], which also detects 3D planes from a single image. Unfortunately, the source code needed to train this method on our datasets is currently unavailable. And it is reported in [11] that its performance on plane detection is on par with that of GC. Thus, we decided to compare our method to GC instead.

4.3   Experiment Results

Plane Segmentation. Figure 4 shows example plane segmentation results on SYNTHIA dataset. We make several important observations below.

First, Neither Depth + J-Linkage nor Depth + RansaCov performs well on the test images. In many cases, they fail to recover the individual planar surfaces (except the ground). To understand the reason, we show the 3D point cloud derived from the predicted depth map in Fig. 5. As one can see, the point cloud tends to be very noisy, making the task of choosing a proper threshold ϵ in the multi-model fitting algorithm extremely hard, if possible at all – if ϵ is small, it would not be able to tolerate the large noises in the point cloud; if ϵ is large, it would incorrectly merge multiple planes/objects into one cluster. Also, these methods are unable to distinguish planar and non-planar objects due to lack of ability to reason about the scene semantics.

Second, GC does a relatively good job in identifying major scene categories (e.g., separating the ground, sky from buildings). However, it has difficulty in determining the orientation of vertical structures (e.g., Fig. 4, first and fifth rows). This is mainly due to the coarse categorization (left/center/right) used by this method. In complex scenes, such a discrete categorization is often ineffective and ambiguous. Also, recall that GC is unable to distinguish planes that have the same orientation but are at different distances (e.g., Fig. 4, fourth row), not to mention finding the precise 3D plane parameters.

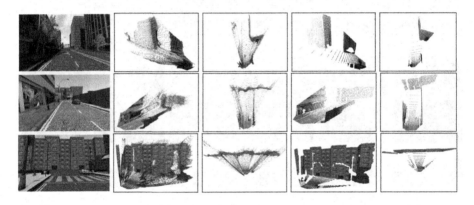

Fig. 5. Comparison of 3D models. **First column:** Input image. **Second and third columns:** Model generated by depth prediction. **Fourth and fifth columns:** Model generated by our method.

Table 1. Plane segmentation results. **Left:** SYNTHIA. **Right:** Cityscapes.

Method	RI	VOI	SC	Method	RI	VOI	SC
Depth+J-Linkage	0.825	1.948	0.589	Depth+J-Linkage	0.713	2.668	0.450
Depth+RansaCov	0.810	2.274	0.550	Depth+RansaCov	0.705	2.912	0.431
Geo. Context [16]	0.846	1.626	0.636	Ours (w/o fine-tuning)	0.759	1.834	0.597
Ours	**0.925**	**1.129**	**0.797**	Ours (w/ fine-tuning)	**0.884**	**1.239**	**0.769**

Third, our method successfully detects most prominent planes in the scene, while excluding non-planar objects (e.g., trees, cars, light poles). This is no surprise because our supervised framework implicitly encodes high-level semantic information as it learns from the labeled data provided by humans. Interestingly, one may observe that, in the last row of Fig. 4, our method classifiers the unpaved ground next to the road as non-planar. This is because such surfaces are not considered part of the road in the original SYNTHIA labels. Figure 5 further shows some piecewise planar 3D models obtained by our method.

For quantitative evaluation, we use three popular metrics [1] to compare the plane segmentation maps obtained by an algorithm with the ground truth: Rand index (RI), variation of information (VOI), and segmentation covering (SC). Table 1(left) compares the performance of all methods on SYNTHIA dataset. As one can see, our method outperforms existing methods by a significant margin w.r.t all evaluation metrics.

Table 1(right) further reports the segmentation accuracies on Cityscapes dataset. We test our method under two settings: (i) directly applying our model trained on SYNTHIA dataset, and (ii) fine-tuning our network on Cityscapes dataset. Again, our method achieves the best performance among all methods. Moreover, fine-tuning on the Cityscapes dataset significantly boost the performance of our network, despite that the provided depth maps are very noisy. Finally, we show example segmentation results on Cityscapes in Fig. 6.

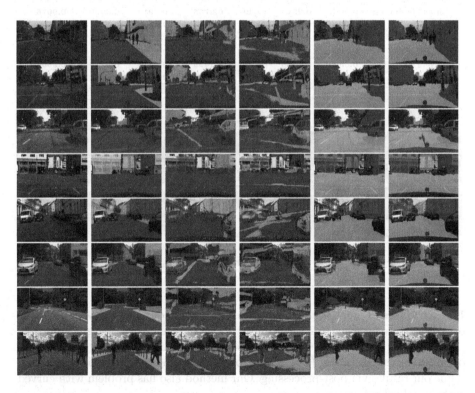

Fig. 6. Plane segmentation results on Cityscapes. **From left to right:** Input image; Ground truth; Depth + J-Linkage; Depth + RansaCov; Ours (w/o fine-tuning); Ours (w/ fine-tuning).

Depth Prediction. To further evaluate the quality of the 3D planes estimated by our method, we compare the depth maps derived from the 3D planes with those obtained via standard depth prediction pipeline (see Sect. 4.2 for details). Recall that our method outputs a per-pixel probability map $S(\mathbf{q})$. For each pixel $\mathbf{q}$ in the test image, we pick the 3D plane with the maximum probability to compute our depth map. We exclude pixels which are considered as "non-planar" by our method, since our network is not designed to make depth predictions in that case.

As shown in Table 2, our method achieves competitive results on both datasets, but the accuracies are slightly lower than those of standard depth prediction pipeline. The decrease in accuracy may be partly attributed to that our method is designed to recover large planar structures in the scene, therefore ignores small variations and details in the scene geometry.

Table 2. Depth prediction results.

Method	Abs Rel	Sq Rel	RMSE	RMSE log	$\delta < 1.25$	$\delta < 1.25^2$	$\delta < 1.25^3$
SYNTHIA							
Train set mean	0.3959	3.7348	10.6487	0.5138	0.3420	0.6699	0.8221
DispNet+berHu loss	0.0451	**0.2226**	**1.6491**	**0.0755**	**0.9912**	**0.9960**	**0.9976**
Ours	**0.0431**	0.3643	2.2405	0.0954	0.9860	0.9948	0.9966
Cityscapes							
Train set mean	0.2325	4.6558	15.4371	0.5093	0.6127	0.7352	0.8346
DispNet+berHu loss	**0.0855**	**0.7488**	**5.1307**	**0.1429**	**0.9222**	**0.9776**	**0.9907**
Ours	0.1042	1.4938	6.8755	0.1869	0.8909	0.9672	0.9862

Fig. 7. Failure examples.

Failure Cases. Figure 7 shows typical failure cases of our method, which include occasionally separating one plane into two (first column) or merging multiple planes into one (second column). Interestingly, for the formal case, one can still obtain a decent 3D model (Fig. 5, last row), suggesting opportunities to further refine our results via post-processing. Our method also has problem with curved surfaces (third column).

Other failures are typically associated with our assumption that there are at most $m = 5$ planes in the scene. For example, in Fig. 7, fourth column, the building on the right has a large number of facades. And it becomes even more difficult when multiple planes are at great distance (fifth column). We leave adaptively choosing the plane number in our framework for future work.

5 Conclusion

This paper has presented a novel approach to recovering 3D planes from a single image using convolutional neural networks. We have demonstrated how to train the network, without 3D plane annotations, via a novel plane structure-induced loss. In fact, the idea of exploring structure-induced loss to train neural networks is by no means restricted to planes. We plan to generalize the idea to detect other geometric structures, such as rectangles and cuboids.

Another promising direction for future work would be to improve the generalizability of the networks via unsupervised learning, as suggested by [10]. For example, it is interesting to probe the possibility of training our network without depth information, which is hard to obtain in many real world applications.

Acknowledgement. This work is supported in part by a startup fund from Penn State and a hardware donation from Nvidia.

References

1. Arbelaez, P., Maire, M., Fowlkes, C., Malik, J.: Contour detection and hierarchical image segmentation. IEEE Trans. Pattern Anal. Mach. Intell. **33**(5), 898–916 (2011)
2. Badrinarayanan, V., Kendall, A., Cipolla, R.: SegNet: a deep convolutional encoder-decoder architecture for image segmentation. IEEE Trans. Pattern Anal. Mach. Intell. **39**(12), 2481–2495 (2017)
3. Barinova, O., Konushin, V., Yakubenko, A., Lee, K.C., Lim, H., Konushin, A.: Fast automatic single-view 3-d reconstruction of urban scenes. In: Forsyth, D., Torr, P., Zisserman, A. (eds.) ECCV 2008. LNCS, vol. 5303, pp. 100–113. Springer, Heidelberg (2008). https://doi.org/10.1007/978-3-540-88688-4_8
4. Cordts, M., et al.: The cityscapes dataset for semantic urban scene understanding. In: CVPR, pp. 3213–3223 (2016)
5. Dasgupta, S., Fang, K., Chen, K., Savarese, S.: DeLay: robust spatial layout estimation for cluttered indoor scenes. In: CVPR, pp. 616–624 (2016)
6. Delage, E., Lee, H., Ng, A.Y.: Automatic single-image 3d reconstructions of indoor manhattan world scenes. In: Thrun, S., Brooks, R., Durrant-Whyte, H. (eds.) Robotics Research. ISRR, vol. 28, pp. 305–321. Springer, Heidelberg (2005). https://doi.org/10.1007/978-3-540-48113-3_28
7. Eigen, D., Puhrsch, C., Fergus, R.: Depth map prediction from a single image using a multi-scale deep network. In: NIPS, pp. 2366–2374 (2014)
8. Fouhey, D.F., Gupta, A., Hebert, M.: Data-driven 3D primitives for single image understanding. In: ICCV, pp. 3392–3399 (2013)
9. Fouhey, D.F., Gupta, A., Hebert, M.: Unfolding an Indoor origami world. In: Fleet, D., Pajdla, T., Schiele, B., Tuytelaars, T. (eds.) ECCV 2014. LNCS, vol. 8694, pp. 687–702. Springer, Cham (2014). https://doi.org/10.1007/978-3-319-10599-4_44

10. Garg, R., Kumar, B.G.V., Carneiro, G., Reid, I.: Unsupervised CNN for single view depth estimation: geometry to the rescue. In: Leibe, B., Matas, J., Sebe, N., Welling, M. (eds.) ECCV 2016. LNCS, vol. 9912, pp. 740–756. Springer, Cham (2016). https://doi.org/10.1007/978-3-319-46484-8_45

11. Haines, O., Calway, A.: Recognising planes in a single image. IEEE Trans. Pattern Anal. Mach. Intell. **37**(9), 1849–1861 (2015)

12. Han, F., Zhu, S.C.: Bottom-Up/Top-Down image parsing by attribute graph grammar. In: ICCV, pp. 1778–1785 (2005)

13. Hartley, R., Zisserman, A.: Multiple View Geometry in Computer Vision. Cambridge University Press, Cambridge (2000)

14. Hedau, V., Hoiem, D., Forsyth, D.A.: Recovering the spatial layout of cluttered rooms. In: ICCV, pp. 1849–1856 (2009)

15. Hedau, V., Hoiem, D., Forsyth, D.: Thinking inside the box: using appearance models and context based on room geometry. In: Daniilidis, K., Maragos, P., Paragios, N. (eds.) ECCV 2010. LNCS, vol. 6316, pp. 224–237. Springer, Heidelberg (2010). https://doi.org/10.1007/978-3-642-15567-3_17

16. Hoiem, D., Efros, A.A., Hebert, M.: Recovering surface layout from an image. Int. J. Comput. Vis. **75**(1), 151–172 (2007)

17. Kingma, D.P., Ba, J.: Adam: a method for stochastic optimization. CoRR abs/1412.6980 (2014)

18. Ladický, L., Zeisl, B., Pollefeys, M.: Discriminatively trained dense surface normal estimation. In: Fleet, D., Pajdla, T., Schiele, B., Tuytelaars, T. (eds.) ECCV 2014. LNCS, vol. 8693, pp. 468–484. Springer, Cham (2014). https://doi.org/10.1007/978-3-319-10602-1_31

19. Laina, I., Rupprecht, C., Belagiannis, V., Tombari, F., Navab, N.: Deeper depth prediction with fully convolutional residual networks. In: 3DV, pp. 239–248 (2016)

20. Lee, C., Badrinarayanan, V., Malisiewicz, T., Rabinovich, A.: RoomNet: End-to-End room layout estimation. In: ICCV, pp. 4875–4884 (2017)

21. Lee, D.C., Hebert, M., Kanade, T.: Geometric reasoning for single image structure recovery. In: CVPR, pp. 2136–2143 (2009)

22. Liu, C., Yang, J., Ceylan, D., Yumer, E., Furukawa, Y.: PlaneNet: piece-wise planar reconstruction from a single RGB image. In: CVPR (2018)

23. Long, J., Shelhamer, E., Darrell, T.: Fully convolutional networks for semantic segmentation. In: CVPR, pp. 3431–3440 (2015)

24. Magri, L., Fusiello, A.: Multiple models fitting as a set coverage problem. In: CVPR, pp. 3318–3326 (2016)

25. Mayer, N., et al.: A large dataset to train convolutional networks for disparity, optical flow, and scene flow estimation. In: CVPR, pp. 4040–4048 (2016)

26. Micusík, B., Wildenauer, H., Kosecka, J.: Detection and matching of rectilinear structures. In: CVPR (2008)

27. Micusík, B., Wildenauer, H., Vincze, M.: Towards detection of orthogonal planes in monocular images of indoor environments. In: ICRA, pp. 999–1004 (2008)

28. Ramalingam, S., Pillai, J.K., Jain, A., Taguchi, Y.: Manhattan junction catalogue for spatial reasoning of indoor scenes. In: CVPR, pp. 3065–3072 (2013)

29. Ros, G., Sellart, L., Materzynska, J., Vázquez, D., López, A.M.: The SYNTHIA dataset: a large collection of synthetic images for semantic segmentation of urban scenes. In: CVPR, pp. 3234–3243 (2016)

30. Saxena, A., Sun, M., Ng, A.Y.: Make3D: learning 3D scene structure from a single still image. IEEE Trans. Pattern Anal. Mach. Intell. **31**(5), 824–840 (2009)

31. Toldo, R., Fusiello, A.: Robust multiple structures estimation with J-linkage. In: Forsyth, D., Torr, P., Zisserman, A. (eds.) ECCV 2008. LNCS, vol. 5302, pp. 537–547. Springer, Heidelberg (2008). https://doi.org/10.1007/978-3-540-88682-2_41

32. Witkin, A.P., Tenenbaum, J.M.: On the role of structure in vision. In: Beck, J., Hope, B., Rosenfeld, A. (eds.) Human and Machine Vision, pp. 481–543. Academic Press, Cambridge (1983)

33. Xiao, J., Russell, B.C., Torralba, A.: Localizing 3D cuboids in single-view images. In: NIPS, pp. 755–763 (2012)

34. Yang, H., Zhang, H.: Efficient 3D room shape recovery from a single panorama. In: CVPR (2016)

stagNet: An Attentive Semantic RNN for Group Activity Recognition

Mengshi Qi[1], Jie Qin[2,3], Annan Li[1], Yunhong Wang[1(✉)], Jiebo Luo[4], and Luc Van Gool[2]

[1] Beijing Advanced Innovation Center for Big Data and Brain Computing, School of Computer Science and Engineering, Beihang University, Beijing, China
yhwang@buaa.edu.cn
[2] Computer Vision Laboratory, ETH Zurich, Zurich, Switzerland
[3] Inception Institute of Artificial Intelligence, Abu Dhabi, UAE
[4] Department of Computer Science, University of Rochester, Rochester, USA

Abstract. Group activity recognition plays a fundamental role in a variety of applications, *e.g.* sports video analysis and intelligent surveillance. How to model the spatio-temporal contextual information in a scene still remains a crucial yet challenging issue. We propose a novel attentive semantic recurrent neural network (RNN), dubbed as stagNet, for understanding group activities in videos, based on the spatio-temporal attention and semantic graph. A semantic graph is explicitly modeled to describe the spatial context of the whole scene, which is further integrated with the temporal factor via structural-RNN. Benefiting from the 'factor sharing' and 'message passing' mechanisms, our model is capable of extracting discriminative spatio-temporal features and capturing inter-group relationships. Moreover, we adopt a spatio-temporal attention model to attend to key persons/frames for improved performance. Two widely-used datasets are employed for performance evaluation, and the extensive results demonstrate the superiority of our method.

Keywords: Group activity recognition · Spatio-temporal attention Semantic graph · Scene understanding

1 Introduction

Understanding dynamic scenes in sports and surveillance videos has a wide range of applications, such as tactics analysis and abnormal behavior detection. How to recognize/understand group activities within the scene, such as 'team spiking' in a volleyball match [23] (see Fig. 1), is an important yet challenging issue, due to cluttered backgrounds and confounded relationships, *etc.*

Extensive efforts [4,5,28,31,33,38,39,44,51] have been made to address the above issue in the computer vision community. Fundamentally, spatio-temporal relations between people [17,23,25] are important cues for group activity recognition. There are two major issues in representing such information. One is the

© Springer Nature Switzerland AG 2018
V. Ferrari et al. (Eds.): ECCV 2018, LNCS 11214, pp. 104–120, 2018.
https://doi.org/10.1007/978-3-030-01249-6_7

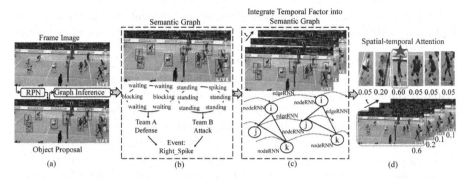

Fig. 1. Pipeline of the semantic graph-based group activity recognition. From left to right: (a) object proposals are extracted from raw frames by a region proposal network [14]; (b) the semantic graph is constructed from text labels and visual data; (c) temporal factor is integrated into the graph by using a structural-RNN, and the semantic graph is inferred via message passing and factor sharing mechanisms; (d) finally, a spatio-temporal attention mechanism is adopted for detecting key persons/frames (denoted with a red star) to further improve the performance. (Color figure online)

representation of visual appearance, which plays an important role in identifying people and describing their action dynamics. The other is the representation of spatial and temporal movement, which describes the interaction between people.

Traditional approaches for modeling the spatio-temporal information in group activity recognition can be summarized as a combination of hand-crafted features and probabilistic graph models. Hand-crafted features used in group activity recognition include motion boundary histograms (MBH) [16], histogram of gradients (HOG) [15], the cardinality kernel [19], *etc.* Markov Random Fields (MRFs) [8] and Conditional Random Fields (CRFs) [26] have been adopted to model the inter-object relationships.

An obvious limitation of the above approaches is that the low-level features they adopted fall short of representing complex group activities and dynamic scenes. With the success of convolutional neural networks (ConvNets) [20,27,42], deep feature representations have demonstrated their capabilities in representing complex visual appearance and achieved great success in many computer vision tasks. However, typical ConvNets regard a single frame of a video as input and output a holistic feature vector. With such architectures, spatial and temporal relations between consecutive frames cannot be explicitly discerned. The spatio-temporal relations [17,23,25] among the people are important cues for group activity recognition in the scene. They consist of the spatial appearance and temporal action of the individuals and their interaction. Recurrent Neural Networks (RNNs) [11,22] are able to capture the temporal features from the video, and to represent dynamic temporal actions from the sequential data. Therefore, it is highly desirable to explore a RNN based network architecture that is capable of capturing the crucial spatio-temporal contextual information.

Moreover, automatically describing the semantic contents in the scene is helpful for better understanding the overall hierarchical structure of the scene (*e.g.* sports matches and surveillance videos). Yet, this task is very difficult, because the semantic description not only captures the personal action, but also expresses how these people relate to each other and how the whole group event occurs. If the above RNN based network can also describe the semantics in the scene, we can have a substantially clearer understanding of the dynamic scene.

In this paper, to address the above-mentioned issues, we propose a novel attentive semantic recurrent neural network named *stagNet* for group activity recognition, based on the spatial-temporal attention and semantic graph. In particular, individual activities and their spatial relations are inferred and represented by an explicit semantic graph, and their temporal interactions are integrated by a structural-RNN model. The network is further enhanced by a spatio-temporal attention mechanism to attach various levels of importance to different persons/frames in video sequences. More importantly, the semantic graph and spatio-temporal attention is collaboratively learned in an end-to-end fashion. The main contributions of this paper include:

- We construct a novel semantic graph to explicitly represent individuals' actions, their spatial relations, and group activity with a 'message passing' mechanism. To the best of our knowledge, we are the first to output a semantic graph for understanding group activities.
- We extend our semantic graph model to the temporal dimension via a structural-RNN, by adopting the 'factor sharing' mechanism in RNN.
- A spatio-temporal attention mechanism, which places emphasis on the key persons/frames in the video, is further integrated for better performance.
- Experiments on two benchmark datasets show that the performance of our framework is competitive with that of the state-of-the-art methods.

2   Related Work

Group Activity Recognition. Traditional approaches [2,3,5,28,35,41,44,51] usually extract hand-crafted spatio-temporal features (*e.g.* MBH and HOG), followed by graph models for group activity recognition. Lan *et al.* [28] introduced an adaptive structure algorithm to model the latent structure. Amer *et al.* [5] formulated Hierarchical Random Field (HiRF) to model grouping nodes and the hidden variables in a scene. Shu *et al.* [44] conducted joint inference of groups, events and human roles with spatio-temporal AND-OR graph [4]. However, these approaches employed shallow features that could not encode higher-level information, and often lost temporal relationship information.

Recently, several deep models [6,17,23,30,43,50] have been proposed for group activity recognition. Deng *et al.* [17] proposed a joint graphical model learned by gates between edges and nodes. Wang *et al.* [50] proposed a recurrent interaction context framework, which unified the features of individual person, intra-group and inter-group interactions. However, most of these works either extracted individual features regardless of the scene context or captured the context in an implicit manner without any semantic information. In this paper, we attempt to *explicitly* model the scene context via an intuitive spatio-temporal *semantic* graph [37] with RNNs. Moreover, we adopt a spatio-temporal attention model to attend to key persons/frames in the scene for better performance.

Deep Structure Model. Many researches have been conducted to make deep neural networks more powerful by integrating graph models. Chen *et al.* [10] combined Markov Random Fields (MRFs) with deep learning to estimate complex representations. Liu *et al.* [32] addressed semantic image segmentation by solving MRFs using Deep Parsing Network. In [29,49,55], structured-output learning was performed using deep neural networks for human pose estimation. Zheng *et al.* [57] integrated CRF-based probabilistic graphic model with RNN for semantic segmentation. Zhang *et al.* [56] improved object detection with deep ConvNets based on Bayesian optimization [46]. Most of these works were task-specific, however, they might fail to handle spatio-temporal modeling and extract interaction information from dynamic scenes. In [25], the Structural-RNN was proposed by combining high-level spatio-temporal graphs and Recurrent Neural Networks. Inspired by [25], we explicitly exploit a semantic spatio-temporal structure graph by injecting specific semantic information, such as inter-object and intra-person relationships, and space-time dynamics in the scene.

Attention Mechanism. Attention mechanisms [7,9,24,34,53,54] have been successfully applied in the field of vision and language. An early work [24] introduced the saliency-based visual attention model for scene recognition. Mnih *et al.* [34] were the first to integrate RNNs with visual attention, and their model could extract selected regions by sequence. The mechanism proposed by [9] could capture visual attention with deep neural networks on special objects in images. Xu *et al.* [53] introduced two kinds of attention mechanisms for image caption. A temporal attention mechanism was proposed in [54] to select the most relevant frames based on text-generation RNNs. In this work, we integrate our spatio-temporal semantic graph and spatio-temporal attention into a joint framework, which is collaboratively trained in an end-to-end manner to attend to more relevant persons/frames in the video.

3   The Proposed Approach

The framework of the proposed approach for group activity recognition is illustrated in Figs. 1 and 2. We utilize two-layer RNN and integrate two kinds of RNN units (*i.e.* nodeRNN and edgeRNN) into our framework, which is trained in an end-to-end fashion. In particular, the first part is to construct the semantic graph from input frames, and then we integrate the temporal factor by using a structural RNN. The inference is achieved via 'message-passing' and 'factor sharing' mechanisms. Finally, we adopt a spatio-temporal attention mechanism to detect key persons and frames to further improve the performance.

3.1 Semantic Graph

In this subsection, we introduce the semantic graph and the mapping from visual data to the graph. We inference the semantic graph to predict person's affiliations based on their positions and visual appearance. As shown in Fig. 1(b), the semantic graph is built by parsing a scene with multiple people into a set of bounding boxes associated with the corresponding spatial positions. Each bounding box of a specific person is defined as a node of the graph. The graph edge that describes pairwise relations is determined by the spatial distance and temporal correlation, which will be introduced in Sect. 3.2.

To generate a set of person-level proposals (bounding boxes) from the t-th frame I^t in video I, we employ the region proposal network (RPN), which is part of the region-based fully convolutional networks [14]. The RPN outputs position-sensitive score maps as the relative position, and connects a position-sensitive region-of-interest (RoI) pooling layer on top of the fully convolutional layer. These proposals are regarded as input of the graph inference procedure. Throughout the graph modeling, three types of information are inferred: (1) the personal action label for each person, (2) the inter-group relationships in each frame, and (3) the group activity label of the whole scene.

In frame I^t, we denote a set of K bounding boxes as $B_{I^t} = (x_{t,1}, ..., x_{t,K})$, and the inter-person relationship set as R (e.g. whether two players belong to the same team on the Volleyball dataset). Given the group activity or scene labels set C_{scene}, and personal action labels set C_{action}, we denote $y^t \in C_{scene}$ as the scene class label, $x_i^{act} \in C_{action}$ as the action class label of the i-th person proposal, x_i^{pos} as its spatial coordinates, and $x_{i \to j} \in R$ as the predicted relationship between the i-th and j-th proposal boxes. Meanwhile, we denote the set of all variables to be $x = \{x_i^{act}, x_i^{pos}, x_{i \to j} \mid i = 1, ..., K; j = 1, ..., K; j \neq i\}$. Specifically, the semantic graph is built up by finding the optimal x^* and y^{t*} that maximize the following probability function:

$$<x^*, y^{t*}> = \arg\max_{x, y^t} Pr(x, y^t \mid I^t, B_{I^t}),$$

$$Pr(x, y^t \mid I^t, B_{I^t}) = \prod_{i,j \in K} \prod_{j \neq i} Pr(y^t, x_i^{act}, x_i^{pos}, x_{i \to j} \mid I^t, B_{I^t}). \qquad (1)$$

In the following, we will introduce how to infer the frame-wise semantic graph structure in detail.

3.2 Graph Inference

Inspired by [52], the graph inference is performed by using the mean field and computing the hidden states with Long Short-Term Memory (LSTM) network [22], which is an effective recurrent neural network. Let the semantic graph be $G = (S, V, E)$, where S is the scene node, and V and E are the object nodes and edges respectively. Specifically, S represents the global scene information in a video frame, an object node $v_i \in V$ ($i = 1, ..., K$) indicates the person-level proposal, and the edge E corresponds to the spatial configuration of object

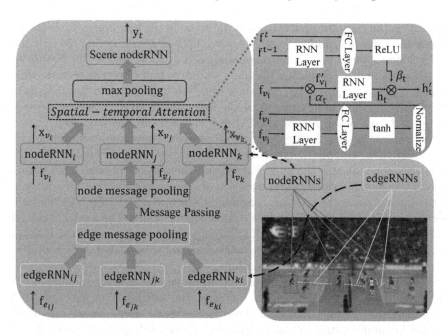

Fig. 2. Illustration of our nodeRNN and edgeRNN model. The model first extracts visual features of nodes and edges from a set of object proposals, and then takes the visual features as initial input to the nodeRNNs and edgeRNNs. We introduce the node/edge message pooling to update the hidden states of nodeRNNs and edgeRNNs. The input of nodeRNNs is the output of the edgeRNNs, and nodeRNNs also output the labels of personal actions. The max pooling is performed subsequently. Furthermore, a spatio-temporal attention mechanism is incorporated into our architecture. Finally, the top-most nodeRNN (*i.e.* Scene nodeRNN) outputs the label of group activity.

nodes V in the frame. In the mean field inference, we approximate $Pr(x, y^t \mid \cdot)$ by $Q(x, y^t \mid \cdot)$, which only depends on the current states of each node and edge. The hidden state of the LSTM unit is the current state of each node and edge in the semantic graph. We define h^t as the current hidden state of scene node, and h_{v_i} and $h_{e_{ij}}$ as the current hidden state of node i and edge $i \to j$, respectively. Notably, all the nodeRNNs share the same set of parameters and all the edgeRNNs share another set of parameters. The solution to $Q(x, y^t \mid I^t, B_{I^t})$ can be obtained by computing the mean field distribution as follows:

$$
Q(x, y^t \mid I^t, B_{I^t})
$$
$$
= \prod_{i=1}^{K} Q(x_i^{act}, x_i^{pos}, y^t \mid h_{v_i}, h^t) Q(h_i \mid f_{v_i}) Q(h^t \mid f^t)
$$
$$
\prod_{j \neq i} Q(x_{i \to j} \mid h_{e_{ij}}) Q(h_{e_{ij}} \mid f_{e_{ij}}), \tag{2}
$$

where f^t is the convolutional feature of the scene in the t-th frame, f_{v_i} is the feature of the i-th node, and $f_{e_{ij}}$ is the feature of the edge connecting the i-th node and j-th node, which is the unified bounding box over two nodes. The feature $f_{e_{ij}}$ has six elements by computing the basic distances and direction vectors, which include $<|dx|, |dy|, |dx + dy|, \sqrt{(dx)^2 + (dy)^2}, \arctan(dy, dx), \arctan2(dy, dx)>$. All of these features are extracted by the RoI pooling layer. Then the messages aggregated from other previous LSTM units are fed into the next step.

As shown in Fig. 2, the edgeRNNs provide contextual information for the nodeRNNs, and the max pooling is performed over the nodeRNNs. The nodeRNN concatenates the node feature and the outputs of edge-RNN accordingly. The edgeRNN passes the summation of all edge features that are connected to the same node as the message. The edgeRNNs and nodeRNNs take the visual features as initial input and produce a set of hidden states. The model iteratively updates the hidden states of the RNN. Finally, the hidden states of the RNN are used to predict the frame-wise scene label, personal action label, person position information and inter-group relationships.

Message passing [52] can iteratively improve the efficacy of inference in the semantic graph. In the graph topology, the neighbors of the egdeRNNs are nodeRNNs. Passing messages through the whole graph involves two subgraphs: *i.e.* node-centric sub-graph and edge-centric sub-graph respectively. For node-centric sub-graph, the nodeRNN receives messages from its neighboring edgeRNNs. Similarly, for edge-centric sub-graph, the edgeRNN gets messages from its adjacent nodeRNNs. We adopt an aggregation function called message pooling to learn adaptive weights for modeling the importance of passed messages. We compute the weight factors for each incoming message and aggregate the messages via a total weight for representation. It is demonstrated that this method is more effective than average pooling or max pooling [52].

Specifically, we denote the update message input to the i-th node v_i as m_{v_i}, and the message to the edge between the i-th and j-th node e_{ij} as $m_{e_{ij}}$, respectively. Then, we compute the message passed into the node considering its own hidden state h_{v_i} and the hidden states of its connected edges $h_{e_{ij}}$ and $h_{e_{ji}}$, and obtain the message passed into the edge with respect to the hidden state of its adjacent nodes h_{v_i} and h_{v_j}. Formally, m_{v_i} and $m_{e_{ij}}$ are computed as

$$m_{v_i} = \sum_{j:i \to j} \sigma(U_1^T [h_{v_i}, h_{e_{ij}}]) h_{e_{ij}} + \sum_{j:j \to i} \sigma(U_2^T [h_{v_i}, h_{e_{ji}}]) h_{e_{ji}},$$
$$m_{e_{ij}} = \sigma(W_1^T [h_{v_i}, h_{e_{ji}}]) h_{v_i} + \sigma(W_2^T [h_{v_j}, h_{e_{ij}}]) h_{v_j}, \tag{3}$$

where W_1, W_2, U_1 and U_2 are parameters to be learned, σ is a sigmoid function, and $[\cdot, \cdot]$ means the concatenation of two hidden vectors. Finally, we utilize these messages to update the hidden states of nodeRNN and edgeRNN iteratively. Once finishing updating, the hidden states are then employed to predict personal action categories, bounding box offsets and relationship types.

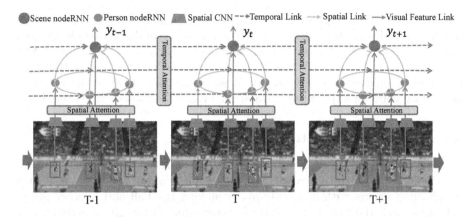

Fig. 3. Hierarchical semantic RNN structure for a volleyball match. Given object proposals and tracklets of all players, we feed them into spatial CNN, followed by a RNN to represent each player's action and appearance of the whole scene. Then we adopt structural-RNN to establish temporal links for a sequence of frames. Furthermore, we integrate the LSTM based spatio-temporal attention mechanism into the model. The output layer classifies the whole team's group activity.

3.3 Integrating Temporal Factors

With the semantic graph of a frame, temporal factors are further integrated to form the spatio-temporal semantic graph (see Fig. 1(c)). Particularly, we adopt the structural-RNN [25] to model the spatio-temporal semantic graph. Based on the graph definition in Sects. 3.1 and 3.2, we add a temporal edge E_T, such that $G = (S, V, E_S, E_T)$, where E_S refers to the spatial edge. The node $v_i \in V$ and edge $e \in E_S \cup E_T$ in the spatio-temporal semantic graph enrolls over time. Specifically, the nodes at adjacent time steps, *e.g.* the node v_i at time t and time $t + 1$ are connected with the temporal edge $e_{ii} \in E_T$. Denote the node label as y_v^t and the corresponding feature vectors for node and edge are denoted as f_v^t, f_e^t at time t, respectively. We introduce a 'factor sharing' mechanism, which indicates that the nodes denoting the same person and the edges representing the same relationship tend to share factors (*e.g.* parameters, original hidden states of RNNs) across different video frames. Figure 3 shows an example of structural-RNN across three time steps in a volleyball game video. Please refer to [25] for more technical details about structural-RNN.

We define two kinds of edges (edgeRNN) in the spatio-temporal graph. One is spatial-edgeRNN representing the spatial relationship. It is formed by the spatial message pooling in each frame and computed from the neighbor player's nodeRNN using the Euclidean distance. The other is temporal-edgeRNN that connects neighbor frames of the same player to represent the temporal information. It is formed by sharing factors between players' nodeRNNs in a video sequence. We incorporate the features of the spatial edgeRNNs between two consecutive frames into the temporal edgeRNN, resulting in 12 additional features.

During the training phase, the errors of predicting the labels of scene nodes and object nodes are back-propagated through the sceneRNNs, nodeRNNs and edgeRNNs. The passed messages represent the interactions between nodeRNNs and edgeRNNs. The nodeRNN is connected to the edgeRNN, and outputs the personal action labels. Every edgeRNN simultaneously models the semantic interaction between adjacent nodes and the evolution of interaction over time.

3.4   Spatio-Temporal Attention Mechanism

The group activity involves multiple persons, but only few of them play decisive roles in determining the activity. For example, the 'winning point' in a volleyball match often occurs with a specific player spiking the ball and another player failing to catch the ball. For a better understanding of the group activity, it is necessary to attend higher levels of importance to key persons. Inspired by [40, 47], we attend to a set of features of different regions at each time step, which contain key persons or objects, with a spatio-temporal soft attention mechanism. With the attention model, we can focus on specific persons in specific frames to improve the recognition accuracy of the group activity.

Since person-level attention is often affected by the evolution and state of the group activity, the context information needs to be taken into consideration. Particularly, we combine the proposals of the same person with KLT trackers [36]. The whole representation of a player can be extracted by incorporating the context information from a sequence of frames.

Person-Level Spatial Attention. We apply a spatial attention model to assign weights to different persons via LSTM networks. Specifically, given one frame that involves K players $x_t = (x_{t,1}, ..., x_{t,K})$, we define the scores $s_t = (s_{t,1}, ..., s_{t,K})^T$ as the importance of all person-level actions in each frame:

$$s_t = W_s \tanh(W_{xs}x_t + U_{hs}h_{t-1}^s + b_s), \tag{4}$$

where W_s, W_{xs}, U_{hs} are the learnable parameter matrices, and b_s is the bias vector. h_{t-1}^s is the hidden variable from an LSTM unit. For the k-th person, the spatial attention weight is computed as a normalization of the scores:

$$\alpha_{t,k} = \frac{\exp(s_{t,k})}{\sum_{i=1}^{K} \exp(s_{t,i})}. \tag{5}$$

Subsequently, the input to the LSTM unit is updated as $x_t' = (x_{t,1}', ..., x_{t,K}')^T$, where $x_{t,k}' = \alpha_{t,k}x_{t,k}$. Then the representation of the attended player can be used as the input to the RNN nodes in the spatio-temporal semantic graph described in Sect. 3.1.

Frame-Level Temporal Attention. We adopt a temporal attention model to discover the key frames. For T frames in a video, the temporal attention model is composed of an LSTM layer, a fully connected layer and a nonlinear ReLU unit. The temporal attention weight of the t-th frame can be computed as

$$\beta_t = \text{ReLU}(W_{x\beta}x_t + U_{h\beta}h_{t-1}^\beta + b_\beta), \tag{6}$$

where x_t is the current input and h_{t-1}^β is the hidden variables at time step t-1. The temporal attention weight controls how much information of every frame can be used for the final recognition. Receiving the output z_t of the main LSTM network and the temporal attention weight β_t at each time step t, the important scores for C_{scene} classes are the weighted summation w.r.t. all time steps:

$$o = \sum_{t=1}^{T} \beta_t \cdot z_t, \tag{7}$$

where $o = (o_1, o_2, \cdots, o_{C_{scene}})^T$. The probability that a video I belongs to the i-th class is

$$p(C_{scene}^i | I) = \frac{e^{o_i}}{\sum_{j=1}^{C_{scene}} e^{o_j}}. \tag{8}$$

3.5   Joint Objective Function

Finally, we formulate the overall objective function with a regularized cross-entropy loss, and combine the semantic graph modeling and the spatio-temporal attention network learning as

$$L = -\sum_{i=1}^{C_{scene}} y^i \log \hat{y}^i - \frac{1}{K}\sum_{i=1}^{K} x_i^* \log \hat{x_i^*} +$$

$$\lambda_1 \sum_{k=1}^{K}(1 - \frac{\sum_{t=1}^{T}\alpha_{t,k}}{T})^2 + \frac{\lambda_2}{T}\sum_{t=1}^{T}\|\beta_t\|_2 + \lambda_3\|W\|_1, \tag{9}$$

where y^i and x_i^* denote the ground-truth label of group activity and personal action, respectively. If a video sequence is classified as the i-th category, $y^i = 1$ and $y^j = 0$ for $j \neq i$. $\hat{y}^i = p(C_{scene}^i|I)$ is the probability that a sequence is classified as the i-th category. $\hat{x}_i^* = p(C_{action}^i|B_{I^t})$ is the probability that a personal action belongs to the i-th category. For classification, we perform max pooling over the hidden representations followed by a softmax classifier. λ_1, λ_2 and λ_3 denote regularization terms. The third regularization term ensures to attend to more persons in the spatial space, and the fourth term regularizes the learned temporal attention via ℓ_2 normalization. The last term regularizes all the parameters of the spatio-temporal attention mechanism [47].

4   Experiments

We evaluate our framework on two widely-adopted benchmarks, *i.e.* the Collective Activity dataset for group activity recognition, and the Volleyball dataset for group activity recognition and personal action recognition.

Collective Activity. [13] contains 44 video clips (about 2,500 frames captured by low-resolution cameras), in which there are five group activities: *crossing, waiting, queueing, walking* and *talking*, and six individual actions: *N/A, crossing, waiting, queueing, walking* and *talking*. The group activity label is predicted based on the majority of people's actions. Following the same experimental setting in [28], we use the tracklet data provided in [12]. The scene is modeled as a bag of individual action context feature descriptors, and we select 1/3 of the video clips for testing and the rest for training.

Volleyball. [23] contains 55 volleyball videos with 4,830 annotated frames. Each player is labeled with a bounding box and one of the nine personal action labels: *waiting, setting, digging, falling, spiking, blocking, jumping, moving* and *standing*. The whole frame is annotated with one of the eight group activity labels: *right set, right spike, right pass, right winpoint, left winpoint, left pass, left spike* and *left set*. Following [23], we choose 2/3 of the videos for training and the remaining 1/3 for testing. Particularly, we split all the players in each frame into two groups using the strategy in [23], and define four additional team-level activities: *attack, defense, win* and *lose*. The labeled data are beneficial for training our semantic RNN model.

4.1   Implementation Details

Our model is implemented using the TensorFlow [1] library. We adopt the VGG-16 model [45] pre-trained on ImageNet, which is then fine-tuned on the Collective Activity and Volleyball datasets, respectively. Based on [14], we only employ the convolution layers of VGG-16 and concatenate a 1024-d 1×1 convolutional layer. As such, each frame is represented by a 1024-d feature vector. Specifically, a person bounding box is represented as a 2805-d feature vector, which includes 1365-d appearance information and 1440-d spatial information. Based on the RPN detector [14], the appearance features can be extracted by feeding the cropped and resized bounding box through the backbone network, and utilizing spatially pooling to obtain the response map from a lower layer. To represent the bounding box at multiple scales, we follow [14] and employ spatial pyramid pooling [14], with respect to a 32×32 spatial histogram.

The LSTM layers used as nodes and edges contain 1024-d hidden units, and they are trained by adding a softmax loss on top of the output at each time step. We use a softmax layer to produce the score maps for the group activity class and action class. The batch size for training the bottom layer of LSTM and fully connected layer of RPN is 8, and the training is performed within 20,000 iterations. The top layer of LSTM is trained in 10,000 iterations with a batch size of 32. For optimization, we adopt RMSprop [21] with a learning rate ranging from 0.00001 to 0.001 for mini-batch gradient descent. In practice, we set $\{\lambda_1, \lambda_2, \lambda_3\}$ as $\{0.001, 0.0001, 0.0001\}$ for Collective Activity, and $\{0.01, 0.001, 0.00001\}$ for Volleyball. Besides, the training and output semantic graph in our paper is recorded as a JavaScript Object Notation (JSON) file, which is a popular tool for extracting structure data.

4.2   Compared Methods

We compare our approach with VGG-16 Network [45], LRCN [18], HDTM [23], Contextual Model [28], Deep Structure Model [17], Cardinality Kernel [19], CERN [43] and SSU [6]. Particularly, in Table 1, 'VGG-16-Image' and 'LRCN-Image' utilize the holistic image features in a single frame for recognition. 'VGG-16-Person' and 'LRCN-Person' predict group activities with features pooled over all fixed-size individual person-level features. 'HDTM' and 'CERN' conduct experiments on the Volleyball Dataset using the grouping strategy, which divides all persons into one or two groups. 'SSU-temporal' models adopted two kinds of detection methods on the Volleyball Dataset, with one using the ground truth (GT) bounding boxes, and the other using Markov Random Fields (MRF) based detection. Note that 'LRCN', 'HDTM' and 'Deep Structure Model' adopt the AlexNet [27] as the backbone, and 'SSU' employs the Inception-V3 [48] framework, while 'CERN' and our model utilize the VGG-16 architecture.

4.3   Results and Analysis

Results on the Collective Activity Dataset. The experimental results of group activity recognition are shown in Table 1. As can be seen, our model

Table 1. Performance comparison of our method and the state-of-the-art approaches.

Methods	Semantic?	Accuracy		
		Collective Activity	Volleyball (Group)	Volleyball (Personal)
VGG-16-Image [45]	×	68.3	71.7	-
VGG-16-Person [45]	×	71.2	73.5	-
LRCN-Image [18]	×	64.2	63.1	-
LRCN-Person [18]	×	64.0	67.6	-
HDTM (1 group) [23]	×	81.5	70.3	75.9
HDTM (2 groups) [23]	×	-	81.9	-
Contextual Model [28]	×	79.1	-	-
Deep Structure Model [17]	×	80.6	-	-
Cardinality kernel [19]	×	83.4	-	-
CERN-1 (1 group) [43]	×	84.8	34.4	69.0
CERN-2 (1 group) [43]	×	87.2	73.5	-
CERN-2 (2 groups) [43]	×	-	83.3	-
SSU-temporal (MRF) [6]	×	-	87.1	-
SSU-temporal (GT) [6]	×	-	89.9	82.4
Ours w/o attention (PRO)	√	85.6	85.7	79.6
Ours w/ attention (PRO)	√	87.9	87.6	-
Ours w/o attention (GT)	√	87.7	87.9	81.9
Ours w/ attention (GT)	√	89.1	89.3	-

'PRO' and 'GT' indicate that we use proposal-based and ground-truth bounding boxes [23], respectively. The best performance is highlighted in red and the second best in blue.

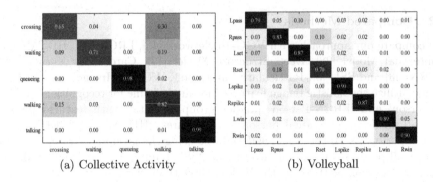

(a) Collective Activity   (b) Volleyball

Fig. 4. Confusion matrices for the two group activity datasets.

with the attention model achieves the best performance among the compared state-of-the-art methods, regardless of using the proposal-based or ground-truth bounding boxes. For instance, our model achieves ≈15% higher in accuracy than image-level and person-level classification methods, mostly because of our RNN-based semantic graph with the iteratively message passing scheme. Meanwhile, our method is the only one that incorporates semantics into the model. The improved performance also indicates that the spatio-temporal semantic graph is beneficial for improving the recognition performance. Note that the cardinality kernel approach [19] achieves the best performance among non-deep learning methods. This approach predicts the group activity label by directly counting the numbers of individual actions based on hand-crafted features. In addition, we draw the confusion matrix based on our model with the spatio-temporal attention in Fig. 4(a). We can observe that nearly 100% recognition accuracies can be obtained in terms of 'queueing' and 'talking', proving the effectiveness of our framework. However, there are also some failure cases, which is probably due to that some action classes share high similarities, such as 'walking' and 'crossing'. More training data are needed for distinguishing these action categories.

Results on the Volleyball Dataset. The recognition results of our method and the state-of-the-art ones are shown in Table 1. As we can see, the group activity and personal action recognition accuracies of our model are superior to most state-of-the-art methods, and also highly competitive to the best 'SSU' method. It should be noted that 'SSU' obtains the bounding boxes by a much more sophisticated multi-scale method and adopts the more advanced Inception-V3 as the backbone. In contrast, we just employ the basic VGG-16 model, and the 'ground-truth' bounding boxes provided by [23] are obtained with a relatively simple strategy. Hence, it can be expected that our performance could be further improved by adopting more advanced backbone networks. Besides, our model outperforms other RNNs based methods by about 5–8% w.r.t. group activity recognition, since our semantic graph with structural-RNN can capture spatio-temporal relationships. Integrating the attention model can further improve the recognition performance, indicating that key persons' visual features are crucial

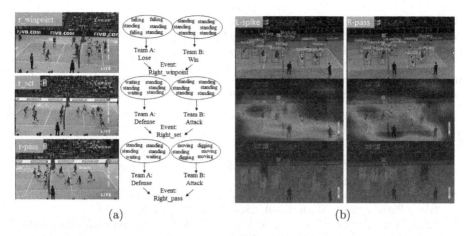

(a)   (b)

Fig. 5. Visualization of results on the Volleyball dataset. (a) Semantic graphs obtained by our method. (b) From top to bottom: group activity and personal action recognition results; attention heat maps using proposal-based bounding boxes; attention heat maps using ground-truth bounding boxes. The important persons are denoted with red stars. The attention weights decrease along with the colors changing from red to blue. (Color figure online)

for recognizing the whole scene label. It is also worth noting that all the other methods, including 'SSU', could not extract the semantic structural information to describe the scene context. On the contrary, our method can output the semantic description of the scene owing to our semantic graph model. We visually depict the recognition results in Fig. 5, including semantic graphs and attention heat maps. In addition, the confusion matrix using our method is shown in Fig. 4(b). As we can see from the figure, our method can achieve promising recognition accuracies ($\geq$87%) in terms of the majority of group activities.

5   Conclusion

In this paper, we presented a novel RNN framework (*i.e.* stagNet) with semantic graph and spatio-temporal attention for group activity recognition. The stagNet could explicitly extract spatio-temporal inter-object relationships in a dynamic scene with a semantic graph. Through the inference procedure of nodeRNNs and edgeRNNs, our model could simultaneously predict the label of the scene and inter-person relationships. By further integrating the spatio-temporal attention mechanism, our framework attended to important persons or frames in the video, leading to enhanced recognition performance. Extensive results on two widely-adopted benchmarks showed that our framework achieved competitive results to the state-of-the-art methods, whilst uniquely outputting the semantic description of the scene.

Acknowledgements. This work was partly supported by the National Natural Science Foundation of China (No. 61573045) and the Foundation for Innovative Research Groups through the National Natural Science Foundation of China (No. 61421003). Jiebo Luo would like to thank the support of New York State through the Goergen Institute for Data Science and NSF Award (No. 1722847). Mengshi Qi acknowledges the financial support from the China Scholarship Council.

References

1. Abadi, M., et al.: TensorFlow: large-scale machine learning on heterogeneous distributed systems. arXiv (2016)
2. Amer, M.R., Todorovic, S.: Sum product networks for activity recognition. IEEE Trans. Pattern Anal. Mach. Intell. **38**(4), 800–813 (2016)
3. Amer, M.R., Todorovic, S., Fern, A., Zhu, S.C.: Monte carlo tree search for scheduling activity recognition. In: ICCV. IEEE (2013)
4. Amer, M.R., Xie, D., Zhao, M., Todorovic, S., Zhu, S.-C.: Cost-sensitive top-down/bottom-up inference for multiscale activity recognition. In: Fitzgibbon, A., Lazebnik, S., Perona, P., Sato, Y., Schmid, C. (eds.) ECCV 2012. LNCS, vol. 7575, pp. 187–200. Springer, Heidelberg (2012). https://doi.org/10.1007/978-3-642-33765-9_14
5. Amer, M.R., Lei, P., Todorovic, S.: HiRF: hierarchical random field for collective activity recognition in videos. In: Fleet, D., Pajdla, T., Schiele, B., Tuytelaars, T. (eds.) ECCV 2014. LNCS, vol. 8694, pp. 572–585. Springer, Cham (2014). https://doi.org/10.1007/978-3-319-10599-4_37
6. Bagautdinov, T., Alahi, A., Fleuret, F., Fua, P., Savarese, S.: Social scene understanding: end-to-end multi-person action localization and collective activity recognition. In: CVPR. IEEE (2017)
7. Bahdanau, D., Cho, K., Bengio, Y.: Neural machine translation by jointly learning to align and translate. In: ICLR (2015)
8. Bengio, Y., LeCun, Y., Henderson, D.: Globally trained handwritten word recognizer using spatial representation, convolutional neural networks, and hidden Markov models. In: NIPS. MIT Press (1994)
9. Cao, C., Liu, X., Yang, Y., Yu, Y.: Look and think twice: capturing top-down visual attention with feedback convolutional neural networks. In: ICCV. IEEE (2015)
10. Chen, L.C., Schwing, A.G., Yuille, A.L., Urtasun, R.: Learning deep structured models. In: ICLR (2014)
11. Cho, K., Van Merriënboer, B., Bahdanau, D., Bengio, Y.: On the properties of neural machine translation: encoder-decoder approaches. arXiv (2014)
12. Choi, W., Savarese, S.: A unified framework for multi-target tracking and collective activity recognition. In: Fitzgibbon, A., Lazebnik, S., Perona, P., Sato, Y., Schmid, C. (eds.) ECCV 2012. LNCS, vol. 7575, pp. 215–230. Springer, Heidelberg (2012). https://doi.org/10.1007/978-3-642-33765-9_16
13. Choi, W., Shahid, K., Savarese, S.: What are they doing?: collective activity classification using spatio-temporal relationship among people. In: ICCV Workshops. IEEE (2009)
14. Dai, J., Li, Y., He, K., Sun, J.: R-FCN: object detection via region-based fully convolutional networks. In: NIPS. MIT Press (2016)
15. Dalal, N., Triggs, B.: Histograms of oriented gradients for human detection. In: CVPR. IEEE (2005)

16. Dalal, N., Triggs, B., Schmid, C.: Human detection using oriented histograms of flow and appearance. In: Leonardis, A., Bischof, H., Pinz, A. (eds.) ECCV 2006. LNCS, vol. 3952, pp. 428–441. Springer, Heidelberg (2006). https://doi.org/10.1007/11744047_33

17. Deng, Z., Vahdat, A., Hu, H., Mori, G.: Structure inference machines: recurrent neural networks for analyzing relations in group activity recognition. In: CVPR. IEEE (2016)

18. Donahue, J., Hendricks, L.A., Guadarrama, S., Rohrbach, M.: Long-term recurrent convolutional networks for visual recognition and description. In: CVPR. IEEE (2015)

19. Hajimirsadeghi, H., Yan, W., Vahdat, A., Mori, G.: Visual recognition by counting instances: a multi-instance cardinality potential kernel. In: CVPR. IEEE (2015)

20. He, K., Zhang, X., Ren, S., Sun, J.: Deep residual learning for image recognition. In: CVPR. IEEE (2016)

21. Hinton, G., Srivastava, N., Swersky, K.: Neural networks for machine learning-lecture 6a-overview of mini-batch gradient descent

22. Hochreiter, S., Schmidhuber, J.: Long short-term memory. Neural Comput. **9**(8), 1735–1780 (1997)

23. Ibrahim, M.S., Muralidharan, S., Deng, Z., Vahdat, A., Mori, G.: A hierarchical deep temporal model for group activity recognition. In: CVPR. IEEE (2016)

24. Itti, L., Koch, C., Niebur, E.: A model of saliency-based visual attention for rapid scene analysis. IEEE Trans. Pattern Anal. Mach. Intell. **20**(11), 1254–1259 (1998)

25. Jain, A., Zamir, A.R., Savarese, S., Saxena, A.: Structural-RNN: deep learning on spatio-temporal graphs. In: CVPR. IEEE (2016)

26. Krahenbuhl, P., Koltun, V.: Efficient inference in fully connected CRFs with Gaussian edge potentials. In: NIPS. MIT Press (2011)

27. Krizhevsky, A., Sutskever, I., Hinton, G.E.: ImageNet classification with deep convolutional neural networks. In: NIPS. MIT Press (2012)

28. Lan, T., Wang, Y., Yang, W., Robinovitch, S.N., Mori, G.: Discriminative latent models for recognizing contextual group activities. IEEE Trans. Pattern Anal. Mach. Intell. **34**(8), 1549–62 (2012)

29. Li, S., Zhang, W., Chan, A.B.: Maximum-margin structured learning with deep networks for 3D human pose estimation. In: ICCV. IEEE (2015)

30. Li, X., Chuah, M.C.: SBGAR: semantics based group activity recognition. In: CVPR. IEEE (2017)

31. Liu, J., Carr, P., Collins, R.T., Liu, Y.: Tracking sports players with context-conditioned motion models. In: CVPR. IEEE (2013)

32. Liu, Z., Li, X., Luo, P., Loy, C.C., Tang, X.: Semantic image segmentation via deep parsing network. In: ICCV. IEEE (2015)

33. Lu, W.L., Ting, J.A., Little, J.J., Murphy, K.P.: Learning to track and identify players from broadcast sports videos. IEEE Trans. Pattern Anal. Mach. Intell. **35**(7), 1704–1716 (2013)

34. Mnih, V., Heess, N., Graves, A., Kavukcuoglu, K.: Recurrent models of visual attention. In: NIPS. MIT Press (2014)

35. Mori, G.: Social roles in hierarchical models for human activity recognition. In: CVPR. IEEE (2012)

36. Munkres, J.: Algorithms for the assignment and transportation problems. J. Soc. Ind. Appl. Math. **5**(1), 32–38 (1957)

37. Qi, M., Wang, Y., Li, A.: Online cross-modal scene retrieval by binary representation and semantic graph. In: MM. ACM (2017)

38. Qin, J., et al.: Binary coding for partial action analysis with limited observation ratios. In: CVPR (2017)
39. Qin, J., et al.: Zero-shot action recognition with error-correcting output codes. In: CVPR (2017)
40. Ramanathan, V., Huang, J., Abu-El-Haija, S., Gorban, A., Murphy, K., Li, F.F.: Detecting events and key actors in multi-person videos. In: CVPR. IEEE (2016)
41. Ryoo, M.S., Aggarwal, J.K.: Stochastic representation and recognition of high-level group activities: describing structural uncertainties in human activities. Int. J. Comput. Vis. **93**(2), 183–200 (2011)
42. Shaoqing, R., Kaiming, H., Ross, G., Jian, S.: Faster R-CNN: towards real-time object detection with region proposal networks. IEEE Trans. Pattern Anal. Mach. Intell. **39**(6), 1137 (2017)
43. Shu, T., Todorovic, S., Zhu, S.C.: CERN: confidence-energy recurrent network for group activity recognition. In: CVPR. IEEE (2017)
44. Shu, T., Xie, D., Rothrock, B., Todorovic, S.: Joint inference of groups, events and human roles in aerial videos. In: CVPR. IEEE (2015)
45. Simonyan, K., Zisserman, A.: Very deep convolutional networks for large-scale image recognition. arXiv preprint arXiv:1409.1556 (2014)
46. Snoek, J., Larochelle, H., Adams, R.P.: Practical Bayesian optimization of machine learning algorithms. In: NIPS, vol. 4, pp. 2951–2959 (2012)
47. Song, S., Lan, C., Xing, J., Zeng, W., Liu, J.: An end-to-end spatio-temporal attention model for human action recognition from skeleton data. In: AAAI. AAAI (2017)
48. Szegedy, C., Vanhoucke, V., Ioffe, S., Shlens, J., Wojna, Z.: Rethinking the inception architecture for computer vision. In: CVPR (2016)
49. Tompson, J., Jain, A., Lecun, Y., Bregler, C.: Joint training of a convolutional network and a graphical model for human pose estimation. In: NIPS. MIT Press (2014)
50. Wang, M., Ni, B., Yang, X.: Recurrent modeling of interaction context for collective activity recognition. In: CVPR. IEEE (2017)
51. Wang, Z., Shi, Q., Shen, C., Anton, V.D.H.: Bilinear programming for human activity recognition with unknown MRF graphs. In: CVPR. IEEE (2013)
52. Xu, D., Zhu, Y., Choy, C.B., Fei-Fei, L.: Scene graph generation by iterative message passing. In: CVPR. IEEE (2017)
53. Xu, K., et al.: Show, attend and tell: neural image caption generation with visual attention. In: ICML. ACM (2015)
54. Yao, L., Torabi, A., Cho, K., Ballas, N.: Describing videos by exploiting temporal structure. In: ICCV. IEEE (2015)
55. Zhang, N., Paluri, M., Ranzato, M., Darrell, T., Bourdev, L.: PANDA: pose aligned networks for deep attribute modeling. In: CVPR. IEEE (2014)
56. Zhang, Y., Sohn, K., Villegas, R., Pan, G., Lee, H.: Improving object detection with deep convolutional networks via Bayesian optimization and structured prediction. In: CVPR. IEEE (2015)
57. Zheng, S., et al.: Conditional random fields as recurrent neural networks. In: ICCV. IEEE (2015)

Learning Class Prototypes via Structure Alignment for Zero-Shot Recognition

Huajie Jiang[1,2,3,4], Ruiping Wang[1,4(✉)], Shiguang Shan[1,4], and Xilin Chen[1,4]

[1] Key Laboratory of Intelligent Information Processing of Chinese Academy of Sciences (CAS), Institute of Computing Technology, CAS, Beijing 100190, China
huajie.jiang@vipl.ict.ac.cn, {wangruiping,sgshan,xlchen}@ict.ac.cn
[2] Shanghai Institute of Microsystem and Information Technology, CAS, Shanghai 200050, China
[3] ShanghaiTech University, Shanghai 200031, China
[4] University of Chinese Academy of Sciences, Beijing 100049, China

Abstract. Zero-shot learning (**ZSL**) aims to recognize objects of novel classes without any training samples of specific classes, which is achieved by exploiting the semantic information and auxiliary datasets. Recently most **ZSL** approaches focus on learning visual-semantic embeddings to transfer knowledge from the auxiliary datasets to the novel classes. However, few works study whether the semantic information is discriminative or not for the recognition task. To tackle such problem, we propose a coupled dictionary learning approach to align the visual-semantic structures using the class prototypes, where the discriminative information lying in the visual space is utilized to improve the less discriminative semantic space. Then, zero-shot recognition can be performed in different spaces by the simple nearest neighbor approach using the learned class prototypes. Extensive experiments on four benchmark datasets show the effectiveness of the proposed approach.

Keywords: Zero-shot learning · Visual-semantic structures
Coupled dictionary learning · Class prototypes

1 Introduction

Object recognition has made tremendous progress in recent years. With the emergence of large-scale image database [28], deep learning approaches [13,17, 29,31] show their great power to recognize objects. However, such supervised learning approaches require large numbers of images to train robust recognition models and can only recognize a fixed number of categories, which limits their flexibility. It is well known that collecting large numbers of images is difficult.

Electronic supplementary material The online version of this chapter (https://doi.org/10.1007/978-3-030-01249-6_8) contains supplementary material, which is available to authorized users.

On one hand, the numbers of images often follow a long-tailed distribution [41] and it is hard to collect images for some rare categories. On the other hand, some fine-grained annotations require expert knowledge [33], which increases the difficulty of the annotation task. All these challenges motivate the rise of zero-shot learning, where no labeled examples are needed to recognize one category.

Zero-shot learning aims at recognizing objects that have not been seen in the training stage, where auxiliary datasets and semantic information are needed to perform such tasks. It is mainly inspired by the human's behavior to recognize new objects. For example, children have no problem recognizing *zebra* if they are told that *zebra* looks like a *horse* (auxiliary datasets) but has *stripes* (semantic information), even though they have never seen *zebra* before. Current **ZSL** approaches generally involve three steps. First, choose a semantic space to build up the relations between seen (auxiliary dataset) and unseen (test) classes. Recently the most popular semantic information includes attributes [9,19] that are manually defined and wordvectors [2,10] that are automatically extracted from the auxiliary text corpus. Second, learn general visual-semantic embeddings from the auxiliary dataset, where the images and class semantics could be projected into a common space [1,5]. Third, perform the recognition task in the common space by different metric learning approaches.

Traditional **ZSL** approaches usually use fixed semantic information and pay much attention to learning more robust visual-semantic embeddings [1,10,15, 19,24,38]. However, most of these approaches ignore the fact that the semantic information, whether human-defined or automatically extracted, is incomplete and may be not discriminative enough to classify different classes because the descriptions about classes are limited. As is shown in Fig. 1, some classes may locate quite close to each other in the semantic space due to the incomplete descriptions, *i.e. cat* and *dog*, thus it may be less effective to perform recognition task in this space. Since images are real reflections of different categories, they may contain more discriminative information that could not be described. Moreover, the semantic information is obtained independently from visual samples so the class structures between the visual space and semantic space are not consistent. In such cases, the visual-semantic embeddings would be too complicated to learn. Even if the embeddings are properly learned, they have large probabilities to overfit the seen classes and have less expansibility to the unseen classes.

In order to tackle such problems, we propose to learn the class prototypes by aligning the visual-semantic structures. The novelty of our framework lies in three aspects. First, different from traditional approaches which learn image embeddings, we perform the structure alignment on the class prototypes, which are automatically learned, to conduct the recognition task. Second, a coupled dictionary learning framework is proposed to align the class structures between visual space and semantic space, where the discriminative property lying in the visual space and the extensive property existing in the semantic space are merged in an aligned space. Third, semantic information of unseen classes is utilized for domain adaptation, which increases the expansibility of our model to the unseen

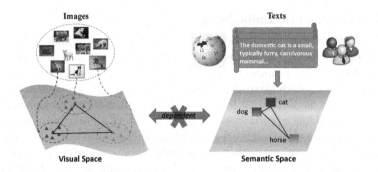

Fig. 1. Illustration diagram that shows the inconsistency of visual feature space and semantic space. The semantic information is manually defined or automatically extracted, which is independent of visual samples. The black lines in the two spaces show the similarities between different classes.

classes. In order to demonstrate the effectiveness of the proposed approach, we perform experiments on four popular datasets for zero-shot recognition, where excellent results are achieved.

2   Related Work

In this section, we review related works on zero-shot learning in three aspects, *i.e.* semantic information, visual-semantic embeddings, zero-shot recognition.

2.1   Semantic Information

Semantic information plays an important role in zero-shot learning. It builds up the relations between seen and unseen classes, thus making it possible for zero-shot recognition. Recently, the most popular semantic information includes attributes [1,3,9,14,19] and wordvectors [2,7,22]. Attributes are general descriptions of objects which can be shared among different classes. For example, *furry* can be shared among different animals. Thus it is possible to learn such attributes by some auxiliary classes and apply them to the novel classes for recognition. Wordvectors are automatically extracted from large numbers of text corpus, where the distances between different wordvectors show the relations between different classes, thus they are also capable of building up the relations between seen and unseen classes.

Since the knowledge that could be collected is limited, the semantic information obtained in general purpose is usually less discriminative to classify different classes in specific domains. To tackle such problem, we propose to utilize the discriminative information lying in the visual space to improve the semantic space.

2.2   Visual-Semantic Embeddings

Visual-semantic embedding is the key to zero-shot learning and most existing ZSL approaches focus on learning more robust visual-semantic embeddings. In the early stage, [9,19] propose to use attribute classifiers to perform ZSL task. Such methods learn each attribute classifier independently, which is not applicable to large-scale datasets with lots of attributes. In order to tackle such problems, label embedding approaches emerge [1,2], where all attributes are considered as a whole for a class and label embedding functions are learned to maximize the compatibility of images with corresponding class semantics. To improve the performance of such embedding models, [35] proposes latent embedding models, where multiple linear embeddings are learned to approximate non-linear embeddings. Furthermore, [10,22,26,30,34,38] exploit deep neural networks to learn more robust visual-semantic transformations.

Although some works pay attention to learning more complicated embedding functions, some other works deal with the visual-semantic transformation problem from different views. [23] forms the semantic information of unseen samples by a convex combination of seen-class semantics. [39,40] utilize the class similarities and [14] proposes discriminative latent attributes to form more effective embedding space. [4] synthesizes the unseen-class classifiers by sharing the structures between the semantic space and the visual space. [5,20] predicts the visual exemplars by learning embedding functions from the semantic space to the visual space. [3] exploits metric learning techniques, where relative distance is utilized, to improve the embedding models. [27] views the image classifier as a function of corresponding class semantic and uses additional regularizer to learn the embedding functions. [16] utilizes the auto-encoder framework to learn the visual-semantic embeddings. [8] uses low rank constraints to learn semantic dictionaries and [37] proposes a matrix tri-factorization approach with manifold regularizations. To tackle the embedding domain shift problem, [11,15] use the transfer learning techniques to extend ZSL into transductive settings, where the unseen-class samples are also utilized in the training process.

Different from such existing approaches which learn image embeddings or synthesize image classifiers, we propose to learn the class prototypes by jointly aligning the class structures between the visual space and the semantic space.

2.3   Zero-Shot Recognition

The most widely used approaches for zero-shot recognition are probability models [19] and nearest neighbour classifiers [1,14,39]. To make use of the rich intrinsic structures on the semantic manifold, [12] proposes semantic manifold distance to recognize the unseen class samples and [4] directly synthesizes the image classifiers of unseen classes in the visual space by sharing the structures between the semantic space and the visual space. Considering more real conditions, [6] expands the traditional ZSL problem to the generalized ZSL problem, where the seen classes are also considered in the test procedure. Recently, [36] proposes more reasonable data splits for different datasets and evaluates the performance of different approaches under such experiment settings.

3   Approaches

The general idea of the proposed approach is to learn the class prototypes by sharing the structures between the visual space and the semantic space. However, the structures between these two spaces may be inconsistent, since the semantic information is obtained independently of the visual examples. In order to tackle such problem, we propose a coupled dictionary learning (**CDL**) framework to simultaneously align the visual-semantic structures. Thus the discriminative information in the visual space and the relations in the semantic space can be shared to benefit each other. Figure 2 shows the framework of our approach. There are three key submodules of the proposed framework: prototype learning, structure alignment, and domain adaptation.

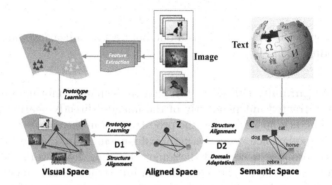

Fig. 2. Coupled dictionary learning framework to align the visual-semantic structure. The solid shapes represent the seen-class prototypes and the dotted shapes denote the prototypes of unseen classes. Black lines show the relationships between different classes. The brown characters are corresponding to the formulation of equations.

3.1   Problem Formulation

Assume a labeled training dataset contains K seen classes with n_s labeled samples $\mathcal{S} = \{(x_i, y_i) | x_i \in \mathcal{X}, y_i \in \mathcal{Y}^s\}_{i=1}^{n_s}$, where $x_i \in \mathbb{R}^d$ represents the image feature and y_i denotes the class label in $\mathcal{Y}^s = \{s_1, ..., s_K\}$. In addition, a disjoint class label set $\mathcal{Y}^u = \{u_1, ..., u_L\}$, which consists L unseen classes, is provided, *i.e.* $\mathcal{Y}^u \bigcap \mathcal{Y}^s = \varnothing$, but the corresponding images are missing. Given the class semantics $\mathcal{C} = \{\mathcal{C}^s \bigcup \mathcal{C}^u\}$, the goal of **ZSL** is to learn image classifiers $f_{zsl} : \mathcal{X} \to \mathcal{Y}^u$.

3.2   Framework

As is shown in Fig. 2, our framework contains three submodules: prototype learning, structure alignment and domain adaptation.

Prototype Learning. The structure alignment approach proposed by our framework is performed on the class prototypes. In order to align the class structures between the visual space and the semantic space, we must first obtain the class prototypes in both spaces. In the semantic space, we denote the class prototypes of seen/unseen classes as $C_s \in \mathbb{R}^{m \times K} / C_u \in \mathbb{R}^{m \times L}$, where m is the dimension of the semantic space. Here, C_s/C_u can be directly set as $\mathcal{C}^s/\mathcal{C}^u$. However, in the visual space, only the seen-class samples $X_s \in \mathbb{R}^{d \times n_s}$ and their corresponding labels Y_s are provided, so we should first learn the class prototypes $P_s \in \mathbb{R}^{d \times K}$ in the visual space, where d is the dimension of the visual space. The basic idea for prototype learning is that samples should locate near their corresponding class prototypes in the visual space, so the loss function can be formulated as:

$$\mathcal{L}_p = \min_{P_s} \|X_s - P_s H\|_F^2, \tag{1}$$

where each column in $H \in \mathbb{R}^{K \times n_s}$ is a one-hot vector indicating the class label of corresponding image.

Structure Alignment. Due to the fact that the semantic information of classes is defined or extracted independently of the images, directly sharing the structures in the semantic space to form the prototypes of unseen classes in the visual space is not a good choice, where structure alignment should be performed first. Therefore, we propose a coupled dictionary learning framework to align the visual-semantic structures. The basic idea for our structure alignment approach is to find some bases in each space to represent each class and enforce the new representation to be the same in the two spaces, thus the structures can be aligned. The loss function is formulated as:

$$\mathcal{L}_s = \min_{P_s, D_1, D_2, Z_s} \|P_s - D_1 Z_s\|_F^2 + \lambda \|C_s - D_2 Z_s\|_F^2,$$
$$s.t. \quad \|d_1^i\|_2^2 \le 1, \quad \|d_2^i\|_2^2 \le 1, \forall i. \tag{2}$$

where P_s and C_s are the prototypes of seen classes in the visual and semantic space respectively. $D_1 \in \mathbb{R}^{d \times n_b}$ and $D_2 \in \mathbb{R}^{m \times n_b}$ are the bases in corresponding spaces, where d, m are the dimensions of visual space and semantic space respectively and n_b is the number of bases. $Z_s \in \mathbb{R}^{n_b \times K}$ is the common new representation of seen classes, and it just plays the key role to align the two spaces. λ is a parameter controlling the relative importance of the visual space and semantic space. d_1^i denotes the i-th column of D_1 and d_2^i is the i-th column of D_2. By exploring new representation bases in each space to reformulate each class, we obtain the same class representations for the visual and semantic spaces, thus the class structures in the two spaces will be consistent.

Domain Adaptation. In the structure alignment process, only seen-class prototypes are utilized and this may cause the domain shift problem [11]. In other words, a general structure alignment approach learned on seen classes may not be appropriate for the unseen classes, since there are some differences between seen and unseen classes. To tackle such problem, we further propose a domain adaptation term, which automatically learns the unseen-class prototypes in the visual space and uses the unseen prototypes to assist the structure learning process. The loss function can be formulated as:

$$\mathcal{L}_u = \min_{P_u, D_1, D_2, Z_u} \|P_u - D_1 Z_u\|_F^2 + \lambda \|C_u - D_2 Z_u\|_F^2 ,$$
$$s.t. \quad \|d_1^i\|_2^2 \leq 1, \quad \|d_2^i\|_2^2 \leq 1, \forall i. \tag{3}$$

where $P_u \in \mathbb{R}^{d \times L}$ and $C_u \in \mathbb{R}^{m \times L}$ are the prototypes of unseen classes in the visual and semantic space respectively, and $Z_u \in \mathbb{R}^{n_b \times L}$ is the common new representation of unseen classes.

In a whole, our full objective can be formulated as:

$$\mathcal{L} = \mathcal{L}_s + \alpha \mathcal{L}_u + \beta \mathcal{L}_p, \tag{4}$$

where α and β are the parameters controlling the relative importance.

3.3 Optimization

The final loss function of the proposed framework can be formulated as:

$$\mathcal{L} = \min_{P_s, P_u, D_1, D_2, Z_s, Z_u} (\|P_s - D_1 Z_s\|_F^2 + \lambda \|C_s - D_2 Z_s\|_F^2) +$$
$$\alpha(\|P_u - D_1 Z_u\|_F^2 + \lambda \|C_u - D_2 Z_u\|_F^2) + \beta(\|X_s - P_s H\|_F^2),$$
$$s.t. \quad \|d_1^i\|_2^2 \leq 1, \quad \|d_2^i\|_2^2 \leq 1, \forall i. \tag{5}$$

It is obvious that Eq. 5 is not convex for P_s, P_u, D_1, D_2, Z_s and Z_u simultaneously, but it is convex for each of them separately. We thus employ an alternating optimization method to solve the problem.

Initialization. In our framework, we set the number of dictionary bases n_b as the number of seen classes K and enforces each column of Z to be the similarities to all seen classes. First, we initialize $Z_u \in \mathbb{R}^{K \times L}$ as the similarities of unseen classes to the seen classes, *i.e.* cosine distances between unseen and seen class prototypes in the semantic space. Second, we get D_2 by the second term of Eq. 3, which has closed-form solution. Third, we get Z_s by the second term of Eq. 2. Next, we initialize P_s as the mean of samples in each class. Then, we get D_1 by the first term of Eq. 2. In the end, we get P_u by the first term in Eq. 3. In this way, all the variables in our framework are initialized.

Joint Optimization. After all variables in our framework are initialized separately, we jointly optimize them as follows:

(1) Fix D_1, Z_s and update P_s. The subproblem can be formulated as:

$$\arg\min_{P_s} \|P_s - D_1 Z_s\|_F^2 + \beta \|X_s - P_s H\|_F^2 \tag{6}$$

(2) Fix P_s, D_1, D_2 and update Z_s by Eq. 2.
(3) Fix P_s, P_u, Z_s, Z_u and update D_1. The subproblem can be formulated as:

$$\arg\min_{D_1} \|P_s - D_1 Z_s\|_F^2 + \alpha \|P_u - D_1 Z_u\|_F^2 \quad s.t. \quad \|\boldsymbol{d}_1^i\|_2^2 \le 1, \forall i. \tag{7}$$

(4) Fix Z_s, Z_u and update D_2. The subproblem can be formulated as:

$$\arg\min_{D_1} \|C_s - D_2 Z_s\|_F^2 + \alpha \|C_u - D_2 Z_u\|_F^2 \quad s.t. \quad \|\boldsymbol{d}_2^i\|_2^2 \le 1, \forall i. \tag{8}$$

(5) Fix P_u, D_1, D_2 and update Z_u by Eq. 3.
(6) Fix D_1, Z_u and update P_u by the first term of Eq. 3.

In our experiments, we set the maximum iterations as 100 and the optimization always converges after tens of iterations, usually less than 50.[1]

3.4   Zero-Shot Recognition

In the proposed framework, we can obtain the prototypes of unseen classes in different spaces (*i.e.* visual space P_u, aligned space Z_u, semantic space C_u), where we can perform zero-shot recognition task using nearest neighbour approach.

Recognition in the Visual Space. In the test process, we can directly compute the similarities Sim_v of test samples (X_i) to the unseen class prototypes (P_u), *i.e.* cosine distance, and classify the images to the classes corresponding to their most similar prototypes.

Recognition in the Aligned Space. To perform recognition task in this space, we must first obtain the representations of images in this space by

$$\arg\min_{Z_i} \|X_i - D_1 Z_i\|_F^2 + \gamma \|Z_i\|_F^2 \tag{9}$$

where X_i represents the test images and Z_i is the corresponding representation in the aligned space. Then we can obtain the similarities Sim_a of test samples (Z_i) to the unseen-class prototypes (Z_u) and use the same recognition approach as that in the visual space.

---

[1] Source code of CDL is available at http://vipl.ict.ac.cn/resources/codes.

Recognition in the Semantic Space. First, we should get the semantic representations of images by $C_i = D_2 Z_i$. Then the similarities Sim_s can be obtained by computing the distances between the test samples (C_i) and the unseen-class prototypes (C_u). The recognition task can be performed the same way as that in the visual space.

Combining Multiple Spaces. Due to the fact that the visual space is discriminative, the semantic space is more generative, and the aligned space is a compromise, combining multiple spaces would improve the performance. In our framework, we simply combine the similarities obtained in each space, *i.e.* combining the visual space and aligned space by $Sim_{va} = Sim_v + Sim_a$, and use the same nearest neighbour approach to perform recognition task.

3.5 Difference from Relevant Works

Among prior works, the most relevant one to ours is [4], where the structures in the semantic space and visual space are also utilized. However, the key ideas of the two works are quite different. [4] uses fixed semantic information and directly shares its structure to the visual space to form unseen classifiers. It doesn't consider whether the two spaces are consistent or not since the semantic information is obtained independently of the visual exemplars. While our approach focuses on aligning the visual-semantic structure and then shares the aligned structures to form unseen-class prototypes in different spaces. Moreover, [4] learns visual classifiers independently of the semantic information while our approach automatically learns the class prototypes in the visual space by jointly leveraging the semantic information. Furthermore, to make the model more suitable to the unseen classes to tackle the challenging domain shift problem, which is not addressed in [4], we propose to utilize the unseen-class semantics to make domain adaptation. Another work [34] also uses structure constraints to learn visual-semantic embeddings. However, it deals with the sample structure, where the distances among samples are preserved. While our approach aligns the class structures, which aims to learn more robust class prototypes.

4 Experiments

4.1 Datasets and Settings

Datasets. Following the new data splits proposed by [36], we perform experiments on four bench-mark **ZSL** datasets, *i.e.* aPascal & aYahoo (aPY) [9], Animals with Attributes (AwA) [19], Caltech-UCSD Birds-200-2011 (CUB) [32], SUN Attribute (SUNA) [25], to verify the effectiveness of the proposed framework. The statistics of all datasets are shown in Table 1.

Table 1. Statistics for attribute datasets: aPY , AwA , CUB and SUNA in terms of image numbers (*Img*), attribute numbers (*Attr*), training + validation seen class numbers (*Seen*) and unseen class numbers (*Unseen*)

Dataset	*Img*	*Attr*	*Seen*	*Unseen*
aPY [9]	15,339	64	15 + 5	12
AwA [19]	30,475	85	27 + 13	10
CUB [32]	11,788	312	100 + 50	50
SUNA [25]	14,340	102	580 + 65	72

Settings. To make fair comparisons, we use the class semantics and image features provided by [36]. Specifically, the attribute vectors are utilized as the class semantics and the image features are extracted by the 101-layered ResNet [13]. Parameters $(\lambda, \alpha, \beta, \gamma)$ in the proposed framework are fine-tuned in the range $[0.001, 0.01, 0.1, 1, 10]$ using the train and validation splits provided by [36]. More details about the parameters can be seen in the supplementary material. We use the average per-class top-1 accuracy to measure the performance of our models.

4.2   Evaluations of Different Spaces

The proposed framework involves three spaces, *i.e.* visual space (v), aligned space (a) and semantic space (s). As is described above, zero-shot recognition can be performed in each space independently or in the combined space, and the recognition results are shown in Fig. 3. It can be seen that the performance in the visual space is higher than that in the semantic space, which indicates that the incomplete semantic information is usually less discriminative. By aligning the visual-semantic structures, the discriminative property of the semantic space improves a lot, which can be inferred from the comparisons between the aligned space and the semantic space. Moreover, the recognition performance will be further improved by combining the visual space and the aligned space, since the visual space is more discriminative and the aligned space is more extensive. For AwA, the best performance is obtained in the visual space. Perhaps the visual space is discriminative enough and it is not complementary with other spaces, so combining it with others will pull down its performance.

4.3   Comparison with State-of-the-Art

To demonstrate the effectiveness of the proposed framework, we compare our method with several popular approaches and the recognition results on the four datasets are shown in Table 2. We report our results in the best space for each dataset, as is analyzed in Sect. 4.2. It can be seen that our framework achieves the best performance on three datasets and is comparable to the best approach on CUB, which indicates the effectiveness of our framework. SAE [16] gets poor

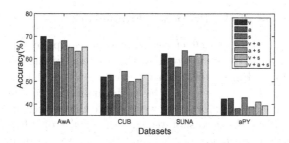

Fig. 3. Zero-shot recognition results via different evaluation spaces, *i.e.* visual space (v), aligned space (a), semantic space (s), combination of visual space and aligned space (v + a) and other combinations, as is described in Sect. 3.4.

performance on aPY probably due to that it is not robust to the weak relations between seen and unseen classes. We owe the success of **CDL** to the structure alignment procedure. Different from other approaches, where fixed semantic information is utilized to perform the recognition task, we automatically adjust the semantic space by aligning the visual-semantic structures. Since the visual space is more discriminative and the semantic space is more extensive, it will benefit each other by aligning the structures for the two spaces. Compared with [4], we get slightly lower result on CUB and this may be caused by the less discriminative class structures. CUB is a fine-grained dataset, where most classes are very similar, so less discriminative class relations could be obtained in the visual space. While [4] learns more complicated image classifiers to enhance the discriminative property in the visual space.

Table 2. Zero-shot recognition results on aPY, AwA, CUB and SUNA (%)

Method	aPY	AwA	CUB	SUNA
DAP [19]	33.8	44.1	40.0	39.9
IAP [19]	36.6	35.9	24.0	19.4
CONSE [23]	26.9	45.6	34.3	38.8
CMT [30]	28.0	39.5	34.6	39.9
SSE [39]	34.0	60.1	43.9	51.5
LATEM [35]	35.2	55.1	49.3	55.3
ALE [1]	39.7	59.9	54.9	58.1
DEVISE [10]	39.8	54.2	52.0	56.5
SJE [2]	32.9	65.6	53.9	53.7
EZSL [24]	38.3	58.2	53.9	54.5
SYNC [4]	23.9	54.0	**55.6**	56.3
SAE [16]	8.3	53.0	33.3	40.3
CDL (Ours)	**43.0**	**69.9**	54.5	**63.6**

4.4 Effectiveness of the Proposed Framework

In order to demonstrate the effectiveness of each component proposed in our framework, we compare our approach with different submodels. The recognition task is performed in the best space according to the datasets. Specifically, for CUB, SUNA, aPY, we evaluate the performance by combining the visual space and the aligned space; for AwA, we evaluate the performance in the visual space. Figure 4 shows the zero-shot recognition results of different submodels. By comparing the performance of "NA" and "CDL", we can figure out that the models will improve a lot by aligning the visual-semantic structures and the less discriminative semantic space will be improved with the help of discriminative visual space. However, if the seen-class prototypes are fixed, it becomes difficult to align the structures between the two spaces and the models degrade seriously, which can be seen through the comparisons of "CDL" and "CDL-Pr". Moreover, the models will be more suitable to the unseen classes by utilizing the unseen-class semantic information to adapt the learning procedure, which is indicated by the comparisons of "CDL" and "CDL-Ad".

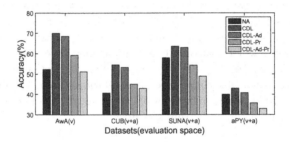

Fig. 4. Comparisons of different baseline methods. NA: not aligning the visual-semantic structure, as is done in the initialization period. CDL: The proposed framework. CDL-Ad: CDL without the adaptation term (second term). CDL-Pr: CDL without the prototype learning term (third term), where P_s is fixed as the means of visual samples in each class. CDL-Ad-Pr: CDL without the adaptation term and the prototype learning term.

4.5 Visualization of the Class Structures

In order to have an intuitive understanding of structure alignment, we visualize the class prototypes in the visual space and semantic space on aPY, since the classes in aPY are more easy to understand. In the visual space, we obtain the class prototypes by the mean feature vector of all samples belonging to each class. In the semantic space, we get the class prototypes directly from the semantic representations. Then we use multidimensional scaling (MDS) approach [18] to visualize the class prototypes, where the relations of all classes are preserved. The original class structures in the semantic space and the visual space are shown in the first row of Fig. 5. To make the figure more intuitive, we manually gathered the classes into three groups, *i.e.* Vehicle, Animal and House. We can figure out that the class structures in the semantic space are not discriminative enough, as can be seen by the tight structures among animals, while those in the visual space are more discriminative. Moreover, the structures between these two space are seriously inconsistent, so directly sharing the structures from the semantic space to the visual space to synthesize the unseen-class prototypes will degrade the model. Therefore, we propose to learn the representation bases in each space to reformulate the class prototypes and align the class structures in a common space. It can be seen that the semantic structures become more discriminative after structure alignment. For example, in the original semantic space, *dog* and *cat* are mostly overlapped and they are separated after structure alignment with the help of their relations in the visual space. Thus the aligned semantic space becomes more discriminative to different classes. Moreover, the aligned structures in the two spaces become more consistent than those in the original spaces.

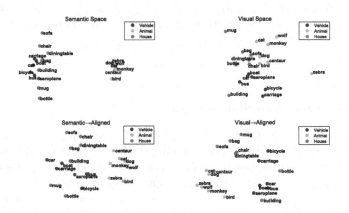

Fig. 5. Visualization of the seen-class prototypes in the semantic space and visual space before and after structure alignment on aPY. To make it intuitive, the classes are manually clustered into three groups, *i.e.* Vehicle, Animal and House.

4.6   Visualization of Class Prototypes

The prototype of one class should locate near the samples belonging to the corresponding class. In order to check whether the prototypes are properly learned, we visualize the prototypes and corresponding samples in the visual space. To have more intuitive understanding, we choose 10 seen classes and 5 unseen classes from AwA. Then we use t-SNE [21] to project the visual samples and class prototypes to a 2-D plane. The visualization results are shown in Fig. 6. It can be seen that most prototypes locate near the samples belonging to the same classes.

Although the unseen prototypes deviate from the centers of corresponding samples due to the fact that no corresponding images are provided for training, they are still discriminative enough to classify different classes, which shows the expansibility of our structure alignment approach for prototype learning. More visualization results can be seen in the supplementary material.

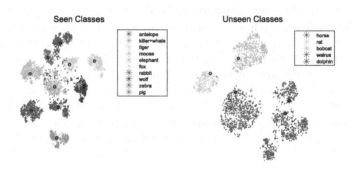

Fig. 6. Visualization of class prototypes on AwA in the feature space by t-SNE. The prototypes are represented by "*" with colors corresponding to the classes. To make them visible, we use black circles to mark them.

4.7   Generalized Zero-Shot Learning

To demonstrate the effectiveness of the proposed framework, we also apply our method to the generalized zero-shot learning (**GZSL**) task, where the seen class are also considered in the test procedure. The task for **GZSL** is to learn images classifiers $f_{gzsl} : \mathcal{X} \rightarrow \mathcal{Y}^s \bigcup \mathcal{Y}^u$. We adopt the data splits provided by [36] and compare our method with several popular approaches. Table 3 shows the generalized zero-shot recognition results on the four datasets. It can be seen that most approaches get low accuracy on the unseen-class samples because of overfitting the seen classes, while our framework gets better results on the unseen classes and achieves more balanced results between the seen and unseen classes. By jointly aligning the visual-semantic structures and utilizing the semantic information of unseen classes to make an adaption, our model has less tendency to overfit the seen classes.

Table 3. Generalized zero-shot learning results on aPY, AwA, CUB and SUNA. ts = Top-1 accuracy of the test unseen-class samples, tr = Top-1 accuracy of the test seen-class samples, H = harmonic mean (CMT*: CMT with novelty detection). We measure top-1 accuracy in %.

Method	aPY			AwA			CUB			SUNA		
	ts	tr	H	ts	tr	H	ts	tr	H	ts	tr	H
DAP [19]	4.8	78.3	9.0	0.0	**88.7**	0.0	1.7	67.9	3.3	4.2	25.1	7.2
IAP [19]	5.7	65.6	10.4	2.1	78.2	4.1	0.2	72.8	0.4	1.0	37.8	1.8
CONSE [23]	0.0	**91.2**	0.0	0.4	88.6	0.8	1.6	72.2	3.1	6.8	39.9	11.6
CMT [30]	1.4	85.2	2.8	0.9	87.6	1.8	7.2	49.8	12.6	8.1	21.8	11.8
CMT* [30]	10.9	74.2	19.0	8.4	86.9	15.3	4.7	60.1	8.7	8.7	28.0	13.3
SSE [39]	0.2	78.9	0.4	7.0	80.5	12.9	8.5	46.9	14.4	2.1	36.4	4.0
LATEM [35]	0.1	73.0	0.2	7.3	71.7	13.3	15.2	57.3	24.0	14.7	28.8	19.5
ALE [1]	4.6	73.7	8.7	16.8	76.1	27.5	23.7	62.8	**34.4**	**21.8**	33.1	26.3
DEVISE [10]	4.9	76.9	9.2	13.4	68.7	22.4	**23.8**	53.0	32.8	16.9	27.4	20.9
SJE [2]	3.7	55.7	6.9	11.3	74.6	19.6	23.5	59.2	33.6	14.1	30.5	19.8
EZSL [24]	2.4	70.1	4.6	6.6	75.6	12.1	12.6	63.8	21.0	11.0	27.9	15.8
SYNC [4]	7.4	66.3	13.3	8.9	87.3	16.2	11.5	**70.9**	19.8	7.9	**43.3**	13.4
SAE [16]	0.4	80.9	0.9	1.8	77.1	3.5	7.8	54.0	13.6	8.8	18.0	11.8
CDL (Ours)	**19.8**	48.6	**28.1**	**28.1**	73.5	**40.6**	23.5	55.2	32.9	21.5	34.7	**26.5**

5   Conclusions

In this paper, we propose a coupled dictionary learning framework to align the visual-semantic structures for zero-shot learning, where unseen-class prototypes are learned by sharing the aligned structures. Extensive experiments on four bench-mark datasets show the effectiveness of the proposed approach. The success of **CDL** should be owing to three characters. First, instead of using the fixed semantic information to perform recognition task, our structure alignment approach shares the discriminative property lying in the visual space and the extensive property lying in the semantic space, which benefits each other and improves the incomplete semantic space. Second, by utilizing the unseen-class semantics to adapt the learning procedure, our model is more suitable for the unseen classes. Third, the class prototypes are automatically learned by sharing the aligned structures, which makes it possible to directly perform recognition task using simple nearest neighbour approach. Moreover, we combine the information of multiple spaces to improve the recognition performance.

Acknowledgements. This work is partially supported by Natural Science Foundation of China under contracts Nos. 61390511, 61772500, 973 Program under contract No. 2015CB351802, Frontier Science Key Research Project CAS No. QYZDJ-SSW-JSC009, and Youth Innovation Promotion Association CAS No. 2015085.

References

1. Akata, Z., Perronnin, F., Harchaoui, Z., Schmid, C.: Label-embedding for attribute-based classification. In: Proceedings of Computer Vision and Pattern Recognition, pp. 819–826 (2013)
2. Akata, Z., Reed, S., Walter, D., Lee, H., Schiele, B.: Evaluation of output embeddings for fine-grained image classification. In: Proceedings of Computer Vision and Pattern Recognition, pp. 2927–2936 (2015)
3. Bucher, M., Herbin, S., Jurie, F.: Improving semantic embedding consistency by metric learning for zero-shot classiffication. In: Leibe, B., Matas, J., Sebe, N., Welling, M. (eds.) ECCV 2016. LNCS, vol. 9909, pp. 730–746. Springer, Cham (2016). https://doi.org/10.1007/978-3-319-46454-1_44
4. Changpinyo, S., Chao, W.L., Gong, B., Sha, F.: Synthesized classifiers for zero-shot learning. In: Proceedings of Computer Vision and Pattern Recognition, pp. 5327–5336 (2016)
5. Changpinyo, S., Chao, W.L., Sha, F.: Predicting visual exemplars of unseen classes for zero-shot learning. In: Proceedings of International Conference on Computer Vision, pp. 3496–3505 (2017)
6. Chao, W.-L., Changpinyo, S., Gong, B., Sha, F.: An empirical study and analysis of generalized zero-shot learning for object recognition in the wild. In: Leibe, B., Matas, J., Sebe, N., Welling, M. (eds.) ECCV 2016. LNCS, vol. 9906, pp. 52–68. Springer, Cham (2016). https://doi.org/10.1007/978-3-319-46475-6_4
7. Demirel, B., Cinbis, R.G., Ikizler-Cinbis, N.: Attributes2Classname: a discriminative model for attribute-based unsupervised zero-shot learning. In: Proceedings of International Conference on Computer Vision, pp. 1241–1250 (2017)
8. Ding, Z., Shao, M., Fu, Y.: Low-rank embedded ensemble semantic dictionary for zero-shot learning. In: Proceedings of Computer Vision and Pattern Recognition, pp. 6005–6013 (2017)
9. Farhadi, A., Endres, I., Hoiem, D., Forsyth, D.: Describing objects by their attributes. In: Proceedings of Computer Vision and Pattern Recognition, pp. 1778–1785 (2009)
10. Frome, A., et al.: Devise: a deep visual-semantic embedding model. In: Proceedings of Advances in Neural Information Processing Systems, pp. 2121–2129 (2013)
11. Fu, Y., Hospedales, T.M., Xiang, T., Gong, S.: Transductive multi-view zero-shot learning. IEEE Trans. Pattern Anal. Mach. Intell. **37**, 2332–2345 (2015)
12. Fu, Z.Y., Xiang, T.A., Kodirov, E., Gong, S.: Zero-shot object recognition by semantic manifold distance. In: Proceedings of Computer Vision and Pattern Recognition, pp. 2635–2644 (2015)
13. He, K., Zhang, X., Ren, S., Sun, J.: Deep residual learning for image recognition. In: Proceedings of Computer Vision and Pattern Recognition, pp. 770–778 (2016)
14. Jiang, H., Wang, R., Shan, S., Yang, Y., Chen, X.: Learning discriminative latent attributes for zero-shot classification. In: Proceedings of International Conference on Computer Vision, pp. 4233–4242 (2017)
15. Kodirov, E., Xiang, T., Fu, Z.Y., Gong, S.: Unsupervised domain adaptation for zero-shot learning. In: Proceedings of International Conference on Computer Vision, pp. 2452–2460 (2015)
16. Kodirov, E., Xiang, T., Gong, S.: Semantic autoencoder for zero-shot learning. In: Proceedings of Computer Vision and Pattern Recognition, pp. 4447–4456 (2017)
17. Krizhevsky, A., Sutskever, I., Hinton, G.E.: Imagenet classification with deep convolutional neural networks. In: Proceedings of Advances in Neural Information Processing Systems, pp. 1097–1105 (2012)

18. Kruskal, J.B.: Multidimensional scaling by optimizing goodness of fit to a non-metric hypothesis. Psychometrika **29**(1), 1–27 (1964)
19. Lampert, C.H., Nickisch, H., Harmeling, S.: Learning to detect unseen object classes by between-class attribute transfer. In: Proceedings of Computer Vision and Pattern Recognition, pp. 951–958 (2009)
20. Long, Y., Liu, L., Shen, F., Shao, L., Li, X.: Zero-shot learning using synthesised unseen visual data with diffusion regularisation. IEEE Trans. Pattern Anal. Mach. Intell. **40**(10), 2498–2512 (2018)
21. van der Maaten, L., Hinton, G.E.: Visualizing data using t-SNE. J. Mach. Learn. Res. **9**, 2579–2605 (2008)
22. Morgado, P., Vasconcelos, N.: Semantically consistent regularization for zero-shot recognition. In: Proceedings of Computer Vision and Pattern Recognition, pp. 2037–2046 (2017)
23. Norouzi, M., et al.: Zero-shot learning by convex combination of semantic embeddings. In: Proceedings of International Conference on Learning Representations (2014)
24. Paredes, B.R., Torr, P.: An embarrassingly simple approach to zero-shot learning. In: Proceedings of International Conference on Machine Learning, pp. 2152–2161 (2015)
25. Patterson, G., Xu, C., Su, H., Hays, J.: The SUN attribute database: beyond categories for deeper scene understanding. Int. J. Comput. Vis. **108**(1–2), 59–81 (2014)
26. Reed, S.E., Akata, Z., Schiele, B., Lee, H.: Learning deep representations of fine-grained visual descriptions. In: Proceedings of Computer Vision and Pattern Recognition, pp. 49–58 (2016)
27. Romera-Paredes, B., Torr, P.H.S.: An embarrassingly simple approach to zero-shot learning. In: Proceedings of International Conference on Machine Learning (2015)
28. Russakovsky, O., et al.: Imagenet large scale visual recognition challenge. Int. J. Comput. Vis. **115**(3), 211–252 (2015)
29. Simonyan, K., Zisserman, A.: Very deep convolutional networks for large-scale image recognition. CoRR abs/1409.1556 (2014)
30. Socher, R., Ganjoo, M., Sridhar, H., Bastani, O., Manning, C.D., Ng, A.Y.: Zero-shot learning through cross-modal transfer. In: Proceedings of Advances in Neural Information Processing Systems, pp. 935–943 (2013)
31. Szegedy, C., et al.: Going deeper with convolutions. In: Proceedings of Computer Vision and Pattern Recognition, pp. 1–9 (2015)
32. Wah, C., Branson, S., Welinder, P., Perona, P., Belongie, S.: The caltech-UCSD birds-200-2011 dataset. Technical report (2011)
33. Wah, C., Branson, S., Welinder, P., Perona, P., Belongie, S.J.: The caltech-UCSD birds-200-2011 dataset. Technical Report CNS-TR-2011-001, California Institute of Technology (2011)
34. Wang, L., Li, Y., Lazebnik, S.: Learning deep structure-preserving image-text embeddings. In: Proceedings of Computer Vision and Pattern Recognition, pp. 5005–5013 (2016)
35. Xian, Y., Akata, Z., Sharma, G., Nguyen, Q.N., Hein, M., Schiele, B.: Latent embeddings for zero-shot classification. In: Proceedings of Computer Vision and Pattern Recognition, pp. 69–77 (2016)
36. Xian, Y., Schiele, B., Akata, Z.: Zero-shot learning - the good, the bad and the ugly. In: Proceedings of Computer Vision and Pattern Recognition (2017)

37. Xu, X., Shen, F., Yang, Y., Zhang, D., Shen, H.T., Song, J.: Matrix tri-factorization with manifold regularizations for zero-shot learning. In: Proceedings of Computer Vision and Pattern Recognition, pp. 2007–2016 (2017)
38. Zhang, L., Xiang, T., Gong, S.: Learning a deep embedding model for zero-shot learning. In: Proceedings of Computer Vision and Pattern Recognition, pp. 3010–3019 (2017)
39. Zhang, Z., Saligrama, V.: Zero-shot learning via semantic similarity embedding. In: Proceedings of International Conference on Computer Vision, pp. 4166–4174 (2015)
40. Zhang, Z., Saligrama, V.: Zero-shot learning via joint latent similarity embedding. In: Proceedings of Computer Vision and Pattern Recognition, pp. 6034–6042 (2016)
41. Zhu, X., Anguelov, D., Ramanan, D.: Capturing long-tail distributions of object subcategories. In: Proceedings of Computer Vision and Pattern Recognition, pp. 915–922 (2014)

CurriculumNet: Weakly Supervised Learning from Large-Scale Web Images

Sheng Guo[1,2], Weilin Huang[1,2(✉)], Haozhi Zhang[1,2], Chenfan Zhuang[1,2], Dengke Dong[1,2], Matthew R. Scott[1,2], and Dinglong Huang[1,2]

[1] Malong Technologies, Shenzhen, China
{sheng,whuang,haozhang,fan,dongdk,mscott,dlong}@malong.com
[2] Shenzhen Malong Artificial Intelligence Research Center, Shenzhen, China

Abstract. We present a simple yet efficient approach capable of training deep neural networks on large-scale weakly-supervised web images, which are crawled raw from the Internet by using text queries, without any human annotation. We develop a principled learning strategy by leveraging curriculum learning, with the goal of handling a massive amount of noisy labels and data imbalance effectively. We design a new learning curriculum by measuring the complexity of data using its distribution density in a feature space, and rank the complexity in an unsupervised manner. This allows for an efficient implementation of curriculum learning on large-scale web images, resulting in a high-performance CNN the model, where the negative impact of noisy labels is reduced substantially. Importantly, we show by experiments that those images with highly noisy labels can surprisingly improve the generalization capability of model, by serving as a manner of regularization. Our approaches obtain state-of-the-art performance on four benchmarks: WebVision, ImageNet, Clothing-1M and Food-101. With an ensemble of multiple models, we achieved a top-5 error rate of 5.2% on the WebVision challenge [18] for 1000-category classification. This result was the top performance by a wide margin, outperforming second place by a nearly 50% relative error rate. Code and models are available at: https://github.com/MalongTech/CurriculumNet.

Keywords: Curriculum learning · Weakly supervised · Noisy data Large-scale · Web images

1 Introduction

Deep convolutional networks have rapidly advanced numerous computer vision tasks, providing state-of-the-art performance on image classification [8,9,14,31,34,37], object detection [20,22,27,28], sematic segmentation [4,10,11,23], etc. They produce strong visual features by training the networks in a fully-supervised manner using large-scale manually annotated datasets, such as ImageNet [5], MS-COCO [21] and PASCAL VOC [6]. Full and clean human annotations are of crucial importance to achieving a high-performance model, and

© Springer Nature Switzerland AG 2018
V. Ferrari et al. (Eds.): ECCV 2018, LNCS 11214, pp. 139–154, 2018.
https://doi.org/10.1007/978-3-030-01249-6_9

Fig. 1. Image samples of the WebVision dataset [19] from the categories of *Carton*, *Dog*, *Taxi* and *Banana*. The dataset was collected from the Internet by using text queries generated from the 1,000 semantic concepts of the ImageNet benchmark [5]. Each category includes a number of mislabeled images as shown on the right.

better results can be reasonably expected if a larger dataset is provided with noise-free annotations. However, obtaining massive and clean annotations are extremely expensive and time-consuming, rendering the capability of deep models unscalable to the size of collected data. Furthermore, it is particularly hard to collect clean annotations for tasks where expert knowledge is required, and labels provided by different annotators are possibly inconsistent.

An alternative solution is to use the web as a source of data and supervision, where a large amount of web images can be collected automatically from the Internet by using input queries, such as text information. These queries can be considered as natural annotations of the images, providing weak supervision of the collected data, which is a cheap way to increase the scale of the dataset near-infinitely. However, such annotations are highly unreliable, and often include a massive amount of noisy labels. Past work has shown that these noisy labels could significantly affect the performance of deep neural networks on image classification [39]. To address this problem, recent approaches have been developed by proposing robust algorithms against noisy labels [30]. Another solution is to develop noise-cleaning methods that aim to remove or correct the mislabelled examples in training data [32]. However, the noise-cleansing methods often suffer from the main difficulty in distinguishing mislabeled samples from hard samples, which are critical to improving model capability. Besides, semi-supervised methods have also been introduced by using a small subset of manually-labeled images, and then the models trained on this subset are generalized to a larger dataset with unlabelled or weakly-labelled data [36]. Unlike these approaches, we do not aim to propose a noise-cleaning, noise-robust or semi-supervised algorithm. Instead, we investigate improving model capability of standard neural networks by introducing a new training strategy.

In this work, we study the problem of learning convolutional networks from large-scale images with a massive amount of noisy labels, such as the WebVision challenge [18], which is a 1000-category image classification task having the same categories as ImageNet [5]. The labels are provided by simply using the queries text generated from the 1,000 semantic concepts of ImageNet [5], *without any manual annotation*. Several image samples are presented in Fig. 1. Our goal is to provide a solution able to handle massive noisy labels and data imbalance effectively. We design a series of experiments to investigate the impact of noisy labels on the performance of deep networks, when the amount of training images is sufficiently large. We develop a simple but surprisingly efficient training strategy that allows for improving model generalization and overall capability of the standard deep networks, by leveraging highly noisy labels. We observe that training a CNN from scratch using both clean and noisy data is more effective than just using the clean one. The contributions of this work are three-fold:

- We propose CurriculumNet by developing an efficient learning strategy with curriculum learning. This allows us to train high-performance CNN models from large-scale web images with massive noisy labels, which are obtained without any human annotation.
- We design a new learning curriculum by ranking data complexity using distribution density in an unsupervised manner. This allows for an efficient implementation of curriculum learning tailored for this task, by directly exploring highly noisy labels.
- We conduct extensive experiments on a number of benchmarks, including WebVision [19], ImageNet [5], Clothing1M [39] and Food101 [2], where the proposed CurriculumNet obtains state-of-the-art performance. The CurriculumNet, with an ensemble of multiple models, achieved the top performance with a top-5 error rate of 5.2%, on the WebVision Challenge at CVPR 2017, outperforming the other results by a large margin.

2 Related Work

We give a brief review on recent studies developed for dealing with noisy annotations on image classification. For a comprehensive overview of label noise taxonomy and noise robust algorithms we refer to [7].

Recent approaches to learn from noisy web data can be roughly classified into two categories. (1) Methods aim to directly learn from noisy labels. This group of approaches mainly focus on noise-robust algorithms [16,25,39], and label cleansing methods which aim to remove or correct mislabeled data [3,15]. However, they generally suffer from the main challenge of identifying mislabeled samples from hard training samples, which are crucial to improve model capability. (2) Semi-supervised learning approaches have also been developed to handle these

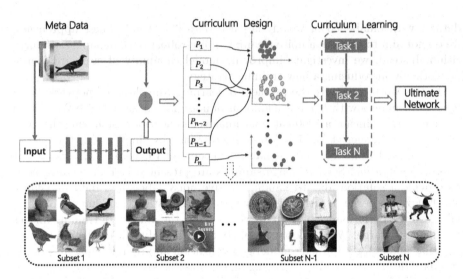

Fig. 2. Pipeline of the proposed CurriculumNet. The training process includes three main steps: initial features generation, curriculum design and curriculum learning.

shortcomings, by combining the noisy labels with a small set of clean labels [26,38,40]. A transfer learning approach solves the label noise by transferring correctness of labels to other classes [17]. The models trained on this subset are generalized to a larger dataset with unlabelled or weakly-labelled data [36]. Unlike these approaches, we do not propose a noise-cleansing or noise-robust or semi-supervised algorithm. Instead, we investigate improving model capability of the standard neural networks, by introducing a new training strategy that alleviates negative impact of the noisy labels.

Convolutional neural networks have recently been applied to training a robust model with noisy data [15,17,25,30,39]. Xiao *et al.* [39] introduced a general framework to train CNNs with a limited amount of human annotation, together with millions of noisy data. A behavior of CNNs on the training set with highly noisy labels was studied in [30]. MentorNet [15] improved the performance of CNNs trained on noisy data, by learning an additional network that weights the training examples. Our method differs from these approaches by directly considering the mislabeled samples in our training process, and we show by experiments that with an efficient training scheme, a standard deep network is robust against the noisy labels.

Our work is closely related to the work of [13], which is able to model noise arising from missing, but visually present labels. The method in [13] is conditioned on the input image, and was designed for multiple labels per image. It does not take advantage of cleaning labels, and the focus is on missing labels, while our approach works reliably on the highly noisy labels, without any cleaned (manual annotation). Our learning curriculum is designed in a completely unsupervised manner.

3   Methodology

In this section, we present details of the proposed CurriculumNet motivated by human learning, in which the model starts from learning easier aspects of a concept, and then gradually includes more complicated tasks into the learning process [1]. We introduce a new method to design a learning curriculum in an unsupervised manner. Then CNNs are trained by following the designed curriculum, where the amount of noisy labels is increased gradually.

3.1   Overview

Pipeline of CurriculumNet is described in Fig. 2. It contains three main steps: (i) initial features generation, (ii) curriculum design and (iii) curriculum learning. First, we use all training data to learn an initial model which is then applied to computing a deep representation (e.g., fully-convolutional (fc) features) from each image in the training set. Second, the initial model aims to roughly map all training images into a feature space where the underlying structure and relationship of the images in each category can be discovered, providing an efficient approach that defines the complexity of the images. We explore the defined complexity to design a learning curriculum where all images in each category are split into a number of subsets ordered by complexity. Third, based on the designed curriculum, we employ curriculum learning which starts training CNNs from an easy subset which combines the easy subsets over all categories. It is assumed to have more clean images with correct labels in the easy subset. Then the model capability is improved gradually by continuously adding the data with increasing complexity into the training process.

3.2   Curriculum Design

Curriculum learning was originally proposed in [1]. It was recently applied to dealing with noise and outliers. One of the main issues to deliver advances of this learning idea is to design an efficient learning curriculum that is specific for our task. The designed curriculum should be able to discover meaningful underlying local structure of the large-scale noisy data in a particular feature space, and our goal is to design a learning curriculum able to rank the training images from easy to complex in an unsupervised manner. We apply a density based clustering algorithm that measures the complexity of training samples using data distribution density. Unlike previous approaches which were developed to handle noisy labels in small-scale or moderate-scale datasets, we design a new learning curriculum that allows our training strategy with a standard CNN to work practically on large-scale datasets, e.g., the WebVision database which contains over 2,400,000 web images with massive noisy labels.

Specifically, we aim to split the whole training set into a number of subsets, which are ranked from an easy subset having clean images with more reliable labels, to a more complex subset containing massive noisy labels. Inspired by recent clustering algorithms described in [29], we conduct the following procedures *in each category*. First, we train an initial model from the whole training set by using an Inception_v2 architecture [14]. Then all images in each category are projected into a deep feature space, by using the fc-layer features of the initial model, $P_i \rightarrow f(P_i)$ for each image P_i. Then we calculate a Euclidean distance matrix $D \subseteq \mathbb{R}^{n \times n}$ as,

$$D_{ij} = \|f(P_i) - f(P_j)\|^2 \tag{1}$$

where n is the number of images in current category, and D_{ij} indicates a similarity value between P_i and P_j (A smaller D_{ij} means higher similarity between P_i and P_j).

We first calculate a local density (ρ_i) for each image:

$$\rho_i = \sum_j X(D_{ij} - d_c) \tag{2}$$

where

$$X(d) = \begin{cases} 1 & d < 0 \\ 0 & \text{other} \end{cases}$$

where d_c is determined by sorting n^2 distances in $D \subseteq \mathbb{R}^{n \times n}$ from small values to large ones, and select a number which is ranked at $k\%$. This result is insensitive to the value of k between 50 and 70, and we empirically set $k = 60$ in all our experiments. ρ_i is the number of samples whose distances to i is smaller than d_c. It is natural to assume that a group of clean images with correct labels often have relatively similar visual appearance, and these images are projected closely to each other, leading to a large value of local density. By contrast, noisy images often have a significant visual diversity, resulting in a sparse distribution with a smaller value of the density.

Then we define a distance (δ_i) for each image:

$$\delta_i = \begin{cases} min_{j:\rho_j > \rho_i}(D_{ij}) & if\ \exists j\ s.t.\ \rho_j > \rho_i \\ max(D_{ij}) & \text{otherwise} \end{cases} \tag{3}$$

If there exists an image I_j having $\rho_j > \rho_i$, δ_i is $D_{i\hat{j}}$ where $\hat{j}$ is the sample nearest to i among the data. Otherwise, if δ_i is the largest one among all density, ρ_j is the distance between i and the data point which is farthest from i. Then a data point with the highest local density has the maximum value of δ, and is selected as cluster center for this category.

As we have computed a cluster center for the category, a closer data point to the cluster center, has a higher confidence to have a correct label. Therefore, we simply proceed with the k-mean algorithm to divide data points into a number of clusters, according to their distances to the cluster center, D_{cj}, where c is the cluster center. Figure 3 (left) is an $\delta - \rho$ figure for all images in the category of cat from the WebVision dataset.

We generate three clusters in each category, and simply use the images within each cluster as a data subset. As each cluster has a density value measuring data

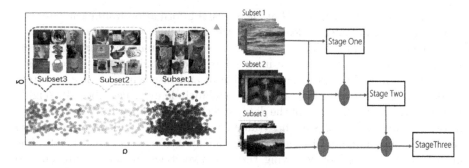

Fig. 3. Left: the sample of the cat category with three subsets. Right: learning process with designed curriculum.

distribution within it, and relationship between different clusters. This provides a natural way to define the complexity of the subsets, giving a simple rule for designing a learning curriculum. A subset with a high density value means all images are close to each other in feature space, suggesting that these images have a strong similarity. We define this subset as a *clean* one, by assuming most of the labels are correct. The subset with a small density value means the images have a large diversity in visual appearance, which may include more irrelevant images with incorrect labels. This subset is considered as *noisy* data. Therefore, we generate a number of subsets in each category, arranged from clean, noisy, to highly noisy ones, which are ordered with increasing complexity. Each category has the same number of subsets, and we combine them over all categories, which form our final learning curriculum that implements training sequentially on the clean, noisy and highly noisy subsets. Figure 3 (left) show data distribution of the three subsets in the category of "cat" from the WebVision dataset, with a number of sample images. As seen, images from the clean subset have very close visual appearance, while the highly noisy subset contains a number of random images which are completely different from those in the clean subset.

3.3 Curriculum Learning

The learning process is performed by following the nature of the underlying data structure. That is, the designed curriculum is able to discover the underlying data structure based on visual appearance, in an unsupervised manner. We design a learning strategy which relies on the intuition - tasks are ordered by increasing difficulty, and training is proceeded sequentially from easier tasks to harder ones. We develop a multi-stage learning process that trains a standard neural network more efficiently with the enhanced capability for handling massive noisy labels.

Training details are described in Fig. 3 (right), where a convolutional model is trained through three stages by continuously mixing training subsets from the clean subset to the highly noisy one. Firstly, a standard convolutional architecture, such as Inception_v2 [14], is used. The model is trained by only using the clean data, where images within each category have close visual appearance. This allows the model to learn basic but clear visual information from each category, serving as the fundamental features for the following process. Secondly, when the model trained in the first stage converges, we continue the learning process by adding the noisy data, where images have more significant visual diversity, allowing the model to learn more meaningful and discriminative features from harder samples. Although the noisy data may include incorrect labels, it roughly preserves the main structure of the data, and thus leads to performance improvement. Thirdly, the model is further trained by adding the highly noisy data which contains a large number of visually irrelevant images with incorrect labels. The deep features learned by following the first two-stage curriculum are able to capture the main underlying structure of the data. We observe that the highly noisy data added in the last stage does not impact negatively to the learned data structure. By contrast, it improves the generalization capability of the model, and allows the model to avoid over-fitting over the clean data, by providing a manner of regularization. A final model is obtained when the training converges in the last stage, where the three subsets are all combined. In addition, when samples from different subsets are combined in the second and third stages, we set different loss weights to the training samples of different subsets as 1, 0.5 and 0.5 for the clean, noisy and highly noisy subsets, respectively.

3.4   Implementation Details

Training Details: The scale of WebVision data [19] is significantly larger than that of ImageNet [5], it is important to consider the computational cost when extensive experiments are conducted in evaluation and comparisons. In our experiments, we employ the inception architecture with batch normalization (bn-inception) [14] as our standard architecture. The bn-inception model is trained by adopting the proposed density-ranking curriculum leaning. The network weights are optimized with mini-batch stochastic gradient decent (SGD), where the batch size is set to 256, and Root Mean Square Propagation (RMSprop) algorithm [14] is adopted. The learning rate starts from 0.1, and decreases by a factor of 10 at the iterations of $30 \times 10^4, 50 \times 10^4, 60 \times 10^4, 65 \times 10^4, 70 \times 10^4$. The whole training process stop at 70×10^4 iterations. To reduce the risk of over-fitting, we use common data augmentation technologies which include random cropping, scale jittering, and ratio jittering. We also add a dropout operation with a ratio of 0.2 after the global pooling layer.

Selective Data Balance: By comparing with ImageNet, another challenge of the WebVision data [18] is that the training images in different categories are highly unbalanced. For example, a large-scale category can have over 10,000 images, while a small-scale category only contains less than 400 images. CNN models, directly trained with random sampling on such unbalanced classes, will have a bias towards the large categories. To alleviate this problem, we develop a two-level data balance approach: subset-level balance and category-level balance. In the subset-level balance, training samples are selected in each min-batch as follows: (256, 0, 0), (128, 128, 0) and (128, 64, 64) for stage 1–3, respectively. For the category-level balance, in each mini-batch, we first random select 256 (in stage 1) or 128 (in stage 2 and 3) categories from the 1000 classes, and then we randomly select only one sample from each selected category. Notice that the category-level balance is only implemented on the clean subset. The performance was dropped down when we applied it to the noisy or highly noisy subset. Because we randomly collect a single sample from each category in the category-level balance, it is possible to obtain a single but completely irrelevant sample from the noisy or highly noisy subset, which would negatively affect the training.

Multi-scale Convolutional Kernels: We also apply multi-scale convolutional kernels in the first convolutional layer, with three different kernel sizes: 5×5, 7×7 and 9×9. Then we concatenate three convolutional maps generated by three types of filters, which form the final feature maps of the first convolutional layer. The multi-scale filters enhance the low-level features in the first layer, leading to about 0.5% performance improvements on top-5 errors on the WebVision data.

4 Experimental Results and Comparisons

The proposed CurriculumNet is evaluated on four benchmarks: WebVision [19], ImageNet [5], Clothing1M [39] and Food101 [2]. Particularly, we investigate the learning capability on large-scale web images without human annotation.

4.1 Datasets

WebVision dataset [19] is an object-centric dataset, and is larger than ImageNet [5] for object recognition and classification. The images are crawled from both Flickr and Google images search, by using queries generated from the 1,000 semantic concepts of the ILSVRC 2012. Meta information along with those web images (e.g., title, description, tags, etc.) are also crawled. The dataset for the WebVision 2017 contains 1,000 object categories (the same with the ImageNet). The training data contains 2,439,574 images in total, but without any human annotation. It includes massive noisy labels, as shown in Fig. 1. There are 50,000 manually-labeled images are used as validation set, and another 50,000 manually-labeled images for testing. The evaluation measure is based on top-5 error, where each algorithm provides a list of at most 5 object categories to match the ground truth.

Clothing1M dataset [39] is a large-scale fashion dataset, which includes 14 clothes categories. It contains 1 million noisy labeled images and 74,000 manually annotated images. We call the annotated images the clean set, which is divided into training data, validation data and testing data, with numbers of 50,000, 14,000, and 10,000 images, respectively. There are some images that overlap between the clean set and the noisy set. The dataset was designed for learning robust models from noisy data without human supervision.

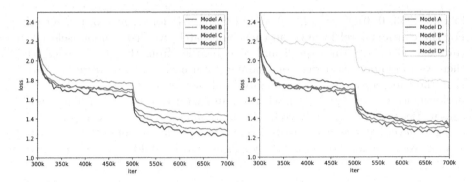

Fig. 4. Testing loss of four different models with BN-Inception architecture, (left) Density-based curriculum, and (right) K-mean based curriculum.

Food-101 dataset [2] is a standard benchmark to evaluate recognition accuracy of visual food. It contains 101 classes, with 101,000 real-world food images in total. The numbers of training and testing images are 750 and 250 per category, respectively. This is a clean dataset with full manual annotations provided. To conduct experiments with noisy data, we manually add 20% noisy images into the training set, which are randomly collected from the training set of ImageNet [5], and each image is randomly assigned a label from 101 categories from the Food-101.

4.2   Experiments and Comparisons

We conducted extensive experiments to evaluate the efficiency of the proposed approaches. We compare various training schemes by using the BN-Inception.

On Training Strategy. We evaluate four different training strategies by using a standard Inception_v2 architecture, resulting in four models, which are described as follows.

- **Model-A**: the model is trained by directly using the whole training set.
- **Model-B**: the model is trained by only using the clean subset.
- **Model-C**: the model is trained by using the proposed learning strategy, with a 2-subset curriculum: clean and noisy subsets.
- **Model-D**: the model is trained by using the proposed learning strategy, with a 3-subset curriculum: clean, noisy and highly noisy subsets.

Test loss of four models (on the validation set of WebVision) are compared in Fig. 4, where the proposed CurriculumNet with a 2-subset curriculum and a 3-subset curriculum (Model-C and Model-D) have better convergence rates. Top 1 and Top 5 results of four models on the validation set of WebVision are reported in Table 1. The results are mainly consistent with the test loss presented in Fig. 4. The proposed method, with 3-subset curriculum learning,

Table 1. Top-1 and Top-5 errors (%) of four different models with BN-Inception architecture on validation set. The models are trained on the WebVision training set and tested on the WebVision and ILSVRC validation sets under various models.

Method	WebVision		ImageNet	
	Top-1	Top-5	Top-1	Top-5
Model-A	30.16	12.43	36.00	16.20
Model-B	30.28	12.98	37.09	16.42
Model-C	28.44	11.38	35.66	15.24
Model-D	**27.91**	**10.82**	**35.24**	**15.11**

significantly outperforms the model trained on all data, with improvements of $30.16\% \rightarrow 27.91\%$ and $12.43\% \rightarrow 10.82\%$ on Top 1 and Top 5 errors, respectively. These improvements are significant on such a large-scale challenge. Consistent improvements are obtained on the validation set of ImageNet, where the models were trained on the WebVision data. In all 1000 categories, our approaches lead to performance improvements on 668 categories, while only 195 categories reduced their Top 5 results, and the results of the remaining 137 categories were unchanged.

On Highly Noisy Data or Training Labels. We further investigate the impact of highly noisy data to the proposed learning strategy. We used different percentages of data from the highly noisy subset for 3-subset curriculum learning, ranging from 0% to 100%. Results are reported in Table 2. As shown, the best results on both Top 1 and Top 5 are achieved at 50% of the highly noisy data. This suggests that, by using the proposed training method, even the highly noisy data can improve model generalization capability, by increasing the amount of the training data with more significant diversity, demonstrating the efficiency of the proposed approach. Increasing the amount of highly noisy data further did not improvement the performance, but with very limited negative affect.

To provide more insights and give deeper analysis on the impact of label noise, we applied the most recent ImageNet-trained SEnet [12] (which has a Top 5 error of 4.47% on ImageNet) to classify all images from the training set of the WebVision data. *We assume the output label of each image by SEnet is correct, and compute the rate of correct labels in each category.* We observed that the average noise rate over the whole training set of the WebVision data is high to 52% (Top 1), indicating that a large amount of incorrect labels is included. We further compute the average noise rates for three subsets of the designed learning curriculum, which are 65%, 39% and 15%, respectively. These numbers are consistent with the increasing complexity of the three subsets, and suggest that most of the images in the third subset are highly noisy.

We calculate the number of categories in 10 different intervals of the correct rates of the training labels, as shown in Fig. 5 (left). There are 12 categories having a correct rate that is lower than 10%. We further compute the average

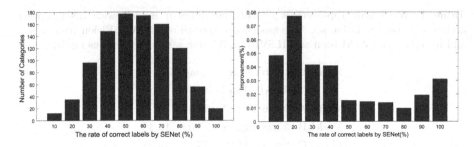

Fig. 5. Numbers of categories (left), and performance improvements (right) in 10 different rate intervals of the training labels.

performance gain in each interval, as show in Fig. 5 (right). We found that the categories with lower correct rates (e.g., < 40%) have larger performance gains (> 4%), and the most significant improvement happens in the interval of 10%–20%, which has an improvement of 7.7%.

On Different Clustering Algorithms. The proposed clustering based curriculum learning can generalize well to other clustering algorithms. We verify it by comparing our density based curriculum design with K-means based clustering on the proposed 3-subset CurriculumNet. As shown in Fig. 4 (right), the Model-B* which is trained using the clean subset by K-means has a significantly lower performance, which means that training without the proposed curriculum learning is highly sensitive to the quality. By adopting the proposed method, Model-D* significantly improves the performance, from 16.6% to 11.5% (Top 5), which is comparable to Model-D. These results demonstrate the strong robustness of the proposed CurriculumNet, allowing for various qualities of the data generated by different algorithms.

Final Results on the WebVision Challenge. We further evaluate the performance of CurriculumNet (Model-D) by using various network architectures, including Inception_v2 [14], Inception_v3 [35], Inception_v4 [33] and Inception_resnet_v2 [33]. Results are reported in Table 3. As can be found, the Inception_v3 outperforms the Inception_v2 substantially, from 10.82% to 7.88% on the Top 5, while a more complicated model, such as Inception_v4 and Inception_resnet_v2, only has similar performance with a marginal performance gain obtained.

Our final results were obtained with ensemble of six models. We had the best performance at a Top 5 error of 5.2% on the WebVision challenge 2017 [18]. It outperforms the 2nd one by a margin of about 2.5%, which is about 50% relative error, and thus is significant for this challenging task. The 5.2% Top 5 error is also comparable to human performance on the ImageNet, but our method obtained this result by using weakly-supervised training data without any human annotation.

Table 2. Performance (%) of model-D by using various percentages of data from the highly noisy subset.

Noise data (%)	Top1	Top5
0	28.44	11.38
25%	28.17	10.93
50%	**27.91**	**10.82**
75%	28.48	11.07
100%	28.33	10.94

Table 3. Performance (%) of model-D by using various networks.

Networks	Top1	Top5
Inception_v2	27.91	10.82
Inception_v3	22.21	7.88
Inception_v4	21.97	6.64
Inception_resnet_v2	**20.70**	**6.38**

Comparisons with the State-of-the-Art Methods. Our method is evaluated by comparing it with recent state-of-the-art approaches developed specifically for learning from label noise, such as CleanNet [17], FoodNet [24] and Patrini et al.'s approach [25]. Experiments and comparisons are conducted on four benchmarks: WebVision [19], ImageNet [5], Clothing1M [39] and Food101 [2]. Model-D with Inception_v2 is used in all our experiments. By following [17], we use the training set of WebVision to train the models, and test on the validation sets of the WebVision and ILSVRC, both of which has the same 1000 categories. On the Clothing1M, we conduct two groups of experiments by following [17], we first apply our curriculum-based training method to one million noisy data, and then use 50 K clean data to fine-tune the trained model. We compare both results against CleanNet [17] and the approach of Patrini et al. [25].

Full results are presented in Table 4. CurriculumNet improves the performance of our baseline significantly in all four databases. Furthermore, our results compare favorably against recent CleanNet on all datasets, with consistent improvements ranged from about 1.5% to 3.3%. Particularly, CurriculumNet reduces Top 5 error of the CleanNet from 12.2% to 10.8% on the WebVision data. In addition, CurriculumNet also outperforms Patrini et al.'s approach (19.6%→18.5%) [25] on the Clothing1M. On the Food101, CurriculumNet, trained with 20% additional noise data with *completely random labels*, achieved substantial improvements over both CleanNet (16.0%→12.7%) and FoodNet (27.9%→12.7%) [24]. These remarkable improvements confirm the advances of CurriculumNet, demonstrating strong capability for learning from massive amount of noisy labels.

Train with More Clean Data: WebVision+ImageNet. We evaluate the performance of CurriculumNet by increasing the amount of clean data in the training set of WebVision. Since ImageNet data is fully cleaned and manually annotated, a straightforward approach is to simply combine the training sets of WebVision and ImageNet data. We implement CurriculumNet with Inception_v2

Table 4. Comparisons with most recent results on the Webvision, ImageNet, Clothes-1M and Food101 databases. For the Webvision and ImageNet, the models are trained on WebVision training set and tested on WebVision and ILSVRC validation sets.

Method	WebVision Top-1 (Top-5)	ImageNet Top-1 (Top-5)	Clothing1M Top-1	Food101 Top-1
Baseline [17]	32.2 (14.2)	41.1 (20.2)	24.8	18.3
CleanNet [17]	29.7 (12.2)	36.6 (15.4)	20.1	–
MentorNet [15]	29.2 (12.0)	37.5 (17.0)	–	–
Our Baseline	30.3 (13.0)	37.1 (16.4)	24.2	15.0
CurriculumNet	**27.9 (10.8)**	**35.2 (15.1)**	**18.5**	**12.7**

Table 5. Performance on the validation sets of ImageNet and WebVision. Models are trained on the training set of ImageNet, WebVision or ImageNet+WebVision.

Training data	WebVision Top-1	Top-5	ImageNet Top-1	Top-5
ImageNet	32.8	13.9	26.9	8.6
ImageNet+WebVision	25.3	9.0	25.6	7.4
CurriculumNet (WebVision)	27.9	10.8	35.2	15.1
CurriculumNet (WebVision+ImageNet)	**24.7**	**8.5**	**24.8**	**7.1**

by considering ImageNet data as an additional clean subset, and test the results on the validation sets of both databases. Results are reported in Table 5.

We summarize key observations as follows. (i) By combining WebVision data into ImageNet data, the performance is generally improved due to the increased amount of training data. (ii) Performance of the proposed CurriculumNet is improved significantly on both validation sets by increasing the amount of the clean data (ImageNet), such as 10.8%→8.5% on WebVision, and 15.1%→7.1% on ImageNet. (iii) By using both WebVision and ImageNet as training data, CurriculumNet is able to improve the performance on both validation sets. For example, it reduces the Top 5 error of WebVision from 9.0% to 8.5% with a same training set. (iv) On ImageNet, CurriculumNet boosts the performance from a Top 5 error of 8.6% to 7.1%, by leveraging additional noisy data (e.g., WebVision). This performance gain is significant on ImageNet, which further confirms the strong capability of CurriculumNet on learning from noisy data.

5   Conclusion

We have presented CurriculumNet - a new training strategy able to train CNN models more efficiently on large-scale weakly-supervised web images, where no human annotation is provided. By leveraging the idea of curriculum learning, we propose a novel learning curriculum by measuring data complexity using cluster density. We show by experiments that the proposed approaches have strong capability for dealing with massive noisy labels. They not only reduce the negative affect of noisy labels, but also, notably, improve the model generalization ability by using the highly noisy data. The proposed CurriculumNet achieved the state-of-the-art performance on the Webvision, ImageNet, Clothing-1M and Food-101 benchmarks. With an ensemble of multiple models, it obtained a Top 5 error of 5.2% on the Webvision Challenge 2017, which outperforms the other submissions by a large margin of about 50% relative error rate.

References

1. Bengio, Y., Louradour, J., Collobert, R., Weston, J.: Curriculum learning. In: ICML, pp. 41–48. ACM (2009)
2. Bossard, L., Guillaumin, M., Van Gool, L.: Food-101 – mining discriminative components with random forests. In: Fleet, D., Pajdla, T., Schiele, B., Tuytelaars, T. (eds.) ECCV 2014. LNCS, vol. 8694, pp. 446–461. Springer, Cham (2014). https://doi.org/10.1007/978-3-319-10599-4_29
3. Brodley, C.E., Friedl, M.A.: Identifying mislabeled training data. CoRR abs/1106.0219 (1999)
4. Chen, L.C., Papandreou, G., Kokkinos, I., Murphy, K., Yuille, A.L.: DeepLab: semantic image segmentation with deep convolutional nets, atrous convolution, and fully connected CRFs. CoRR abs/1606.00915 (2016)
5. Deng, J., Dong, W., Socher, R., Li, L., Li, K., Li, F.: ImageNet: a large-scale hierarchical image database. In: CVPR, pp. 248–255 (2009)
6. Everingham, M., Gool, L.V., Williams, C., Winn, J., Zisserman, A.: The pascal visual object classes challenge 2007 (voc 2007) results (2007, 2008). In: URL http://www.pascal-network.org/challenges/VOC/voc2007/workshop/index.html
7. Frénay, B., Verleysen, M.: Classification in the presence of label noise: a survey. IEEE Trans. Neural Netw. Learn. Syst. **25**(5), 845–869 (2014)
8. Guo, S., Huang, W., Wang, L., Qiao, Y.: Locally-supervised deep hybrid model for scene recognition. IEEE Trans. Image Process. (TIP) **26**, 808–820 (2017)
9. He, K., Zhang, X., Ren, S., Sun, J.: Deep residual learning for image recognition. In: CVPR (2016)
10. He, K., Gkioxari, G., Dollár, P., Girshick, R.: Mask R-CNN. In: ICCV, pp. 2980–2988 (2017)
11. Hong, S., Noh, H., Han, B.: Decoupled deep neural network for semi-supervised semantic segmentation. In: NIPS, pp. 1495–1503 (2015)
12. Hu, J., Shen, L., Sun, G.: Squeeze-and-excitation networks. In: CVPR (2018)
13. Misra, I., Lawrence Zitnick, C., Mitchell, M., Girshick, R.: Seeing through the human reporting bias: visual classifiers from noisy human-centric labels. In: CVPR (2016)
14. Ioffe, S., Szegedy, C.: Batch normalization: accelerating deep network training by reducing internal covariate shift. CoRR abs/1502.03167 (2015)
15. Jiang, L., Zhou, Z., Leung, T., Li, L.J., Fei-Fei, L.: MentorNet: regularizing very deep neural networks on corrupted labels. CoRR abs/1712.05055 (2017)
16. Larsen, J., Nonboe, L., Hintz-Madsen, M., Hansen, L.K.: Design of robust neural network classifiers. In: ICASSP (1998)

17. Lee, K.H., He, X., Zhang, L., Yang, L.: CleanNet: transfer learning for scalable image classifier training with label noise. CoRR abs/1711.07131 (2017)
18. Li, W., et al.: WebVision challenge: visual learning and understanding with web data. CoRR abs/1705.05640 (2017)
19. Li, W., Wang, L., Li, W., Agustsson, E., Van Gool, L.: WebVision database: visual learning and understanding from web data. CoRR abs/1708.02862 (2017)
20. Lin, T.Y., Goyal, P., Girshick, R., He, K., Dollar, P.: Focal loss for dense object detection, pp. 2980–2988 (2017)
21. Lin, T.-Y., et al.: Microsoft COCO: common objects in context. In: Fleet, D., Pajdla, T., Schiele, B., Tuytelaars, T. (eds.) ECCV 2014. LNCS, vol. 8693, pp. 740–755. Springer, Cham (2014). https://doi.org/10.1007/978-3-319-10602-1_48
22. Liu, W., et al.: SSD: single shot multibox detector. In: Leibe, B., Matas, J., Sebe, N., Welling, M. (eds.) ECCV 2016. LNCS, vol. 9905, pp. 21–37. Springer, Cham (2016). https://doi.org/10.1007/978-3-319-46448-0_2
23. Long, J., Shelhamer, E., Darrell, T.: Fully convolutional networks for semantic segmentation. In: CVPR, pp. 3431–3440 (2015)
24. Pandey, P., Deepthi, A., Mandal, B., Puhan, N.: FoodNet: recognizing foods using ensemble of deep networks. IEEE Signal Process. Lett. **24**(12), 1758–1762 (2017)
25. Patrini, G., Rozza, A., Menon, A.K., Nock, R., Qu, L.: Making deep neural networks robust to label noise: a loss correction approach, pp. 1944–1952 (2017)
26. Fergus, R., Weiss, Y., Torralba, A.: Semi-supervised learning in gigantic image collections. In: NIPS (2009)
27. Redmon, J., Divvala, S., Girshick, R., Farhadi, A.: You only look once: unified, real-time object detection. In: CVPR, pp. 779–788 (2016)
28. Ren, S., He, K., Girshick, R., Sun, J.: Faster R-CNN: towards real-time object detection with region proposal networks. In: NIPS, pp. 91–99 (2015)
29. Rodriguez, A., Laio, A.: Clustering by fast search and find of density peaks. Science **344**(6191), 1492–1496 (2014)
30. Rolnick, D., Veit, A., Belongie, S., Shavit, N.: Deep learning is robust to massive label noise. CoRR abs/1705.10694 (2017)
31. Simonyan, K., Zisserman, A.: Very deep convolutional networks for large-scale image recognition. CoRR abs/1409.1556 (2014)
32. Sukhbaatar, S., Fergus, R.: Learning from noisy labels with deep neural networks. CoRR abs/1406.2080 (2014)
33. Szegedy, C., Ioffe, S., Vanhoucke, V., Alemi, A.A.: Inception-v4, inception-resnet and the impact of residual connections on learning. In: AAAI, pp. 4278–4284 (2017)
34. Szegedy, C., et al.: Going deeper with convolutions. In: CVPR, pp. 1–9 (2015)
35. Szegedy, C., Vanhoucke, V., Ioffe, S., Shlens, J., Wojna, Z.: Rethinking the inception architecture for computer vision. In: CVPR, pp. 2818–2826 (2016)
36. Veit, A., Alldrin, N., Chechik, G., Krasin, I., Gupta, A., Belongie, S.: Learning from noisy large-scale datasets with minimal supervision. In: CVPR (2017)
37. Wang, L., Guo, S., Huang, W., Xiong, Y., Qiao, Y.: Knowledge guided disambiguation for large-scale scene classification with multi-resolution CNNs. IEEE Trans. Image Process. (TIP) **26**, 2055–2068 (2017)
38. Chen, X., Shrivastava, A., Gupta, A.: Neil: extracting visual knowledge from web data. In: ICCV (2013)
39. Xiao, T., Xia, T., Yang, Y., Huang, C., Wang, X.: Learning from massive noisy labeled data for image classification. In: CVPR, pp. 2691–2699 (2015)
40. Zhu, X.: Semi-supervised learning literature survey. CoRR abs/1106.0219 (2005)

DDRNet: Depth Map Denoising and Refinement for Consumer Depth Cameras Using Cascaded CNNs

Shi Yan[1], Chenglei Wu[2], Lizhen Wang[1], Feng Xu[1], Liang An[1], Kaiwen Guo[3], and Yebin Liu[1(✉)]

[1] Tsinghua University, Beijing, China
liuyebin@mail.tsinghua.edu.cn
[2] Facebook Reality Labs, Pittsburgh, USA
[3] Google Inc, Mountain View, CA, USA

Abstract. Consumer depth sensors are more and more popular and come to our daily lives marked by its recent integration in the latest Iphone X. However, they still suffer from heavy noises which limit their applications. Although plenty of progresses have been made to reduce the noises and boost geometric details, due to the inherent illness and the real-time requirement, the problem is still far from been solved. We propose a cascaded Depth Denoising and Refinement Network (DDRNet) to tackle this problem by leveraging the multi-frame fused geometry and the accompanying high quality color image through a joint training strategy. The rendering equation is exploited in our network in an unsupervised manner. In detail, we impose an unsupervised loss based on the light transport to extract the high-frequency geometry. Experimental results indicate that our network achieves real-time single depth enhancement on various categories of scenes. Thanks to the well decoupling of the low and high frequency information in the cascaded network, we achieve superior performance over the state-of-the-art techniques.

Keywords: Depth enhancement · Consumer depth camera
Unsupervised learning · Convolutional neural networks
DynamicFusion

1 Introduction

Consumer depth cameras have enabled lots of new applications in computer vision and graphics, ranging from live 3D scanning to virtual and augmented reality. However, even with tremendous progresses in improving the quality and resolution, current consumer depth cameras still suffer from heavy sensor noises.

During the past decades, in view of the big quality gap between depth sensors and traditional image sensors, researchers have made great efforts to leverage RGB images or videos to bootstrap the depth quality. While RGB-guided filtering methods show the effectiveness [22,34], a recent trend is on investigating

© Springer Nature Switzerland AG 2018
V. Ferrari et al. (Eds.): ECCV 2018, LNCS 11214, pp. 155–171, 2018.
https://doi.org/10.1007/978-3-030-01249-6_10

the light transport in the scene for depth refinement with RGB images, which is able to capture high frequency geometry and reduce the texture-copy artifacts [3,12,43,46]. Progresses have also been made to push these methods to run in real time [30,44]. In these traditional methods, before refinement, a smooth filtering is usually carried out on the raw depth to reduce the sensor noise. However, this simple spatial filtering may alter the low-dimensional geometry in a non-preferred way. This degeneration can never be recovered in the follow-up refinement step, as only high-frequency part of the depth is modified.

To attack these challenges, we propose a new cascaded CNN structure to perform depth image denoising and refinement in order to lift the depth quality in low frequency and high frequency simultaneously. Our network consists of two parts, with the first focusing on denosing while the second aiming at refinement. For the denoising net, we train a CNN with a structure similar to U-net [36]. Our first contribution is on how to generate training data. Inspired by the recent progress on depth fusions [11,19,26], we generate reference depth maps from the fused 3D model. With fusion, heavy noise present in single depth map can be reduced by integrating the truncated signed distant function (TSDF). From this perspective, our denoising net is learning a deep fusion step, which is able to achieve better depth accuracy than heuristic smoothing.

Our second contribution is the refinement net, structured in our cascade end-to-end framework, which takes the output from the denoising net and refine it to add high-frequency details. Recent progresses in deep learning have demonstrated the power of deep nets to model complex functions between visual components. One challenge to train a similar net to add high-frequency details is that there is no ground truth depth map with desired high-frequency details. To solve this, we propose a new learning-based method for depth refinement using CNNs in an unsupervised way. Different from traditional methods, which define the loss directly on the training data, we design a generative process for RGB images using the rendering equation [20] and define our loss on the intensity difference between the synthesized image and the input RGB image. Scene reflectance is also estimated through a deep net to reduce the texture-copy artifacts. As the rendering procedure is fully differentiable, the image loss can be effectively back propagated throughout the network. Therefore, through these two components in our DDR-Net, a noisy depth map is enhanced both in low frequency and high frequency.

We extensively evaluate our proposed cascaded CNNs, demonstrating that our method can produce depth map with higher quality in both low and high frequency, compared with the state-of-the-art methods. Moreover, the CNN-based network structure enables our algorithm to run in real-time. And with the progress of deep-net-specific hardware, our method is promising to be deployed on mobile phones. Applications of our enhanced depth stream in the Dynamic-Fusion systems [11,26,47] are demonstrated, which improve the reconstruction performance of the dynamic scenes.

2   Related Work

Depth Image Enhancement. As RGB images usually capture a higher resolution than depth sensors, many methods in the past have focused on leveraging the

RGB images to enhance the depth data. Some heuristic assumptions are usually made about the correlation between color and depth. For example, some work assume that the RGB edges are coinciding with depth edges or discontinuities. Diebel and Thrun [9] upsample the depth with a Markov-Random Field. Depth upsampling with color image as input can be formulated as an optimization problem which maximizes the correlation between RGB edges and depth discontinuities [31]. Another way to implement this heuristics is through filtering [23], e.g. with joint bilateral upsampling filter [22]. Yang et al. [45] propose a depth upsampling method by filtering a cost space joint-bilaterally with a stereo image to achieve the resolution upsampling. Similar joint reconstruction ideas with stereo images and depth data are investigate by further constraining the depth refinement with photometric consistency from stereo matching [50]. With the development of modern hardwares and also the improvements in filtering algorithms, variants of joint-bilateral or multilateral filtering for depth upsampling can run in real-time [6,10,34]. As all of these methods are based on the heuristic assumption between color and depth, even producing plausible results, refined depth maps are not metrically accurate, and texture-copy artifacts are inevitable as texture variations are frequently mistaken for geometric detail.

Depth Fusion. With multiple frames as input, different methods have been proposed to fuse them to improve the depth quality or obtain a better quality scan. Cue et al. [8] has proposed a multi-frame superresolution technique to estimate higher resolution depth images from a stack of aligned low resolution images. Taking into account the sensors' noise characteristics, the signed distance function is employed with an efficient data structure to scan scenes with an RGBD camera [16]. KinectFusion [27] is the first method to show real-time hand-held scanning of large scenes with a consumer depth sensor. Better data structures that exploit spatial sparsity in surface scans, e.g. hierarchical grids [7] or voxel hashing schemes [28], have been proposed to scan larger scenes in real time. These fusion methods are able to effectively reduce the noises in the scanning by integrating the TSDF. Recent progresses have extended the fusion to dynamic scenes [11,26]. The scan from these depth fusion methods can achieve very clean 3D reconstruction, which improves the accuracy of the original depth map. Based on this observation, we employ depth fusion to generate a training data for our denoising net. By feeding lots of the fused depth as our training data to the the network, our denoising net effectively learns the fusion process. In this sense, our work is also related to Riegler et al. [35], where they designed an OctNet to perform the learning on signed distance function. Differently, our denoising net directly works on depth and by special design of our loss function, our net can effectively reduce the noise in the original depth map. Besides, high frequency geometric detail is not dealt with in OctNet, while by our refinement net we can achieve detailed depth maps.

Depth Refinement with Inverse Rendering. To model the relation between color and depth in a physically correct way, inverse rendering methods have been proposed to leverage RGB images to improve depth quality by investigating the light transport process. Shape-from-shading (SfS) techniques have been investigated on how to extract the geometric detail from a single image [17,49]. One challenge to directly apply SfS is that the light and reflectance are usually unknown when capturing the depth map. Recent progresses have shown that SfS can refine coarse image-based geometry models [4], even if they were captured under general uncontrolled lighting with multi-view cameras [42,43] or an RGBD camera [12,46]. In these work, illumination and albedo distributions, as well as refined geometry are estimated via inverse rendering optimization. Optimizing all these unknowns are very challenging by traditional optimization schemes. For instance, if the reflectance is not properly estimated, the texture-copy artifact can still exist. In our work, we employ a specifically structured network to tackle the challenge of reflectance and geometry separation problem. Our network structure can be seen as a regularizer which constrain the inverse rendering loss to back propagate only learnable gradient to train our refinement net. Also with a better reflectance estimation method than previous work, the reflectance influence can be further alleviated, resulting in a CNN network which extracts only geometry-related information to improve the depth quality.

Learning-Based and Statistical Methods. Data driven methods are another category to solve the depth upsampling/refinement problem. Data-driven priors are also helpful for solving the inverse rendering problem. Barron and Malik [2] jointly solve reflectance, shape and illumination, based on priors derived statistically from images. Similar concepts were also used for offline intrinsic image decomposition of RGB-D data [1]. Khan *et al.* [21] learn weighting parameters for complex SfS models to aid facial reconstruction. Wei and Hirzinger [40] use deep neural networks to learn aspects of the physical model for SfS. Note that even our method is also learning based, our refinement net does not take any training data. Instead, the refinement net relies on a pre-defined generative process and thus an inverse rendering loss for the training process. The closest idea to our paper is the encoder-decoder structure used for image-based face reconstruction [33,38]. They take the traditional rendering pipeline as a generative process, defined as a fixed decode. Then, a reconstruction loss can be optimized to train the encoder, which directly regress from a input RGB image. However, these methods all require a predefined geometry and reflectance subspace, usually modeled by linear embedding, to help train a meaningful encode, while our method can work with general scenes captured by RGBD sensor.

3   Method

We propose a new framework for jointly training a denoising net and a refinement net from a consumer-level camera to improve depth map both in low frequency and high frequency. The proposed pipeline features our novelties both in training data creation and cascaded CNNs architecture design. Obtaining ground-truth high-quality depth data for training is very challenging. We thus have formulated the depth improvement problem into two regression tasks, while each one

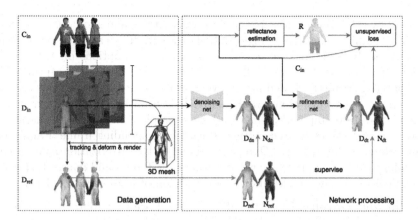

Fig. 1. The pipeline of our method. The black lines are the forward pass during test, the gray lines are supervise signal, and the orange lines are related to the unsupervised loss. Note that every loss function has a input mask W, which is omitted in this figure. D_{dn} and D_{dt} are denoised and refined output. N_{ref}, N_{dt} are reference normal map and refined normal map, normals are only used for the training, not for the inference. (Color figure online)

focuses on lifting the quality in different frequency domains. This also enables us to combine supervised and unsupervised learning to solve the issue of lacking ground truth training data. For denoising part, a function $\mathcal{D}$ mapping a noisy depth map D_{in} to a smoothed one D_{dn} with high-quality low frequency is learned by a CNN with the supervision of near-groundtruth depth maps D_{ref}, created from a state of the art of dynamic fusion. For refinement part, an unsupervised shading-based criterion is developed based on inverse rendering to train and a function $\mathcal{R}$ to map D_{dn} and the corresponding RGB image C_{in} to an improved depth map D_{dt} with rich geometric details. The albedo map for each frame is also estimated the CNN used in [25]. We concurrently train cascaded CNNs from supervised depth data and unsupervised shading cues to achieve state-of-the-art performance on the task of single image depth enhancement. The detailed pipeline can be visualized in Fig. 1.

3.1   Dataset

Previous methods usually take a shortcut to obtain the training data by synthesizing [37,39]. However, what if noise characteristic varies from sensor to sensor, or even the noise source is untraceable? In this case, how to generate ground-truth (or near-ground-truth) depth map becomes a major problem.

Data Generation. In order to learn the real noise distribution of different consumer depth cameras, we need to collect a training dataset of raw depth data with corresponding target depth maps, which act as the supervised signal of our denoising net. To achieve this, we use the non-rigid dynamic fusion pipeline proposed by [11], which is able to reconstruct complete and good quality geometries of dynamic scenes from single RGB-D camera. The captured scene could be static or dynamic and we do not impose any assumptions on the type of motions. Besides, the camera is allowed to move freely during the capture. The reconstructed geometry is well aligned with input color frames. To this end, we first capture a sequence of synchronized RGB-D frames $\{D_t, C_t\}$. Then we run the non-rigid fusion pipeline [11] to produce a complete and improved mesh, and deform it using the estimated motion to each corresponding frame. Finally the target reference depth map $\{D_{ref,t}\}$ is generated by rasterization at each corresponding view point. Besides, we also produce a foreground mask $\{W_t\}$ using morphological filtering, which indicates the region of interest in the depth.

Content and Novelty. Using the above method, we contribute a new dataset of human bodies, including color image, raw depths with real noises and the corresponding reference depths with sufficient quality. Our training dataset contains 36840 views of aligned RGB-D data along with high quality D_{ref} rendered from fused model, among which 11540 views are from structured light depth sensor and 25300 views are from time-of-flight depth sensor. Our validation dataset contains 4010 views. Training set contains human bodies with various clothes poses under different lighting conditions. Moreover, to verify how our method generalized to other scenes, objects such as furniture and toys are also included in the test set. Existing public datasets, *eg.* Face Warehouse, Biwi Kinect face and D3DFACS, lack geometry details, thus do not meet our requirement for surface refinement. ScanNet consists of a huge amount of 3D indoor scenes, but has no human body category. Our dataset fills the blank in human body surface reconstruction. Dataset and training code will be public available.

3.2   Depth Map Denoising

The denoising net $\mathcal{D}$ is trained to remove the sensor noise in depth map D_{in} given the reference depth map D_{ref}. Our denoising net architecture is inspired by Disp-Net [24] with skip connections and multi-scale predictions, as shown in Fig. 2. The denoising net consists of three parts: encoder, nonlinearity and decoder. The encoder aims to successively extract low-resolution high-dimensional features from D_{in}. To add nonlinearity to the network without performance degradation, several residual blocks with pre-activation are stacked sequentially between encoder and decoder part. The decoder part upsamples encoded feature maps to the original size, together with skip connections from the encoder part. These skip connections is useful to preserve geometry details in D_{in}. The whole denoising net adopts the residual learning strategy to extract the latent clean image from noisy observation. Not only does this direct pass set a good initialization, it turns out that residual learning is able to speed up the training process of deep CNN as well. Instead of the "unpooling + convolution" operation, our upsampling uses transpose convolution with trainable kernels. Note that the combination of bilinear up-sampling and transpose convolution in our upsampling pass help to inhibit checkerboard artifacts [29,41]. Our denoising net is

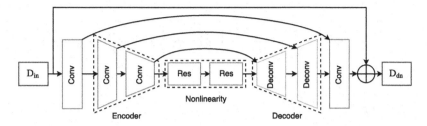

Fig. 2. The structure of our denoising net consists of encoder, nonlinear and decoder. There are three upsampling levels and one direct skip to keep captured value.

fully convolutional with receptive field up to 256. As a result, it is able to handle almost all types of consumer sensor inputs with different size.

The first loss for our denoising net is defined on the depth map itself. For example, per-pixel L1 and L2 loss on depth are used for our reconstruction term:

$$\ell_{rec}(D_{dn}, D_{ref}) = \|D_{dn} - D_{ref}\|_1 + \|D_{dn} - D_{ref}\|_2, \tag{1}$$

where $D_{dn} = \mathcal{D}(D_{in})$ is the output denoised depth map, and D_{ref} is the reference depth map. It is known that L2 and L1 loss may produce blurry results, however they accurately capture the low frequencies [18] which meets our purpose.

However, with only the depth reconstruction constraint, the high-frequency noise in small local patch could still remain after passing denoising net. To prevent this, we design a *normaldot* term to remove the high-frequency noise further. Specifically, this term is designed to constrain the normal direction of the denoised depth map to be consistent with the reference normal direction. We define the dot production of reference normal N_{ref}^i and tangential direction as the second loss term for our denoising net. Since each neighbouring depth point j ($j \in \mathcal{N}(i)$) could potentially define a 3D tangential direction, we sum over all possible directions, and the final normaldot term is formulated as:

$$\ell_{dot}(D_{dn}, N_{ref}) = \sum_{i} \sum_{j \in \mathcal{N}(i)} \left[< P^i - P^j, N_{ref}^i > \right]^2, \tag{2}$$

where P^i is the 3D coordinate of D_{dn}^i. This term explicitly drives the network to consider the dependence between neighboring pixels $\mathcal{N}(i)$, and to learn locally the joint distributions of the neighboring pixels. Therefore, the final loss function for training the denoising net is defined as:

$$\mathcal{L}_{dn}(D_{dn}, D_{ref}) = \lambda_{rec}\ell_{rec} + \lambda_{dot}\ell_{dot}, \tag{3}$$

where $\lambda_{rec}, \lambda_{dot}$ defines the strength of each loss term.

In order to get N_{ref} from the depth map D_{ref}, a *depth to normal* (d2n) layer is proposed, which calculate normal vector given depth map and intrinsic parameters. For each pixel, it takes the surrounding 4 pixels to estimate one normal vector. The d2n layer is fully differentiable and has been employed several times in our end-to-end framework as shown in Fig. 1.

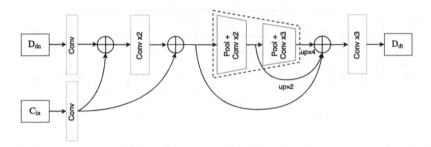

Fig. 3. Refinement net structure. The convolved feature maps from D_{dn} are complemented with the corresponding feature maps from C_{in} possessing the same resolution.

3.3   Depth Map Refinement

Although denoising net is able to effectively remove the noises, the denoised depth map, even getting improved in low frequency, still lacks details compared with RGB images. To add high-frequency details to the denoised depth map, we adopt a relatively small fully convolutional network based on hypercolumn architecture [14,33].

Denote the single channel intensity map of color image C_{in} as I. [1] The hypercolumn descriptor for a pixel is extracted by concatenating the features at its spatial location in several layers, from both D_{dn} and I of the corresponding color image with high-frequency details. We first combine the spectral features from D_{dn} and I, then fuse these features in the spatial domain by max-pooling and convolutional down-sampling, which end with multi-scale fused feature maps. The pooling and convolution operation after hypercolumn extraction constructs a new set of sub-bands by fusing the local features of other hypercolumns in the vicinity. This transfers fine structure from color map domain to depth map domain. Three post-fusion convolutional layers is introduced to learn a better channel coupling. *tanh* function is used as the last activation to limit the output to the same range of the input. In brief, high frequency features in the color image are extracted, and used as guidance, to extrude local detailed geometry from the denoised surfaces by the proposed refinement net shown in Fig. 3. As high frequency details are mainly inferred from small local patches, a shallow network with relative small reception field has enough capacity. Without post-processing as in other two-stage pipelines [37], our refinement net generates high-frequency details on depth map in a single forward pass.

Many SfS-based refinement approaches [13,44] demonstrate that color images can be used to estimate the incident illumination, which is parameterized by the rendering process of an image. For Lambertian surface and low-frequency illumination, we can express the reflected irradiance B as the function of the

---

[1] Intensity image I plays the same role as C_{in}. We study I for simplicity.

Fig. 4. Estimated albedo map and relighted result using estimated lighting coefficients and uniform albedo. The estimation is in line with the actual incident illumination.

surface normal N, the lighting condition l and the albedo R as follows:

$$B(l, N, R) = R \sum_{b=1}^{9} l_b H_b(N), \tag{4}$$

where $H_b : \mathbb{R}^3 \mapsto \mathbb{R}$ is the basis function of spherical harmonics(SH) that takes unit surface normal N as input. $l = [l_1, \cdots, l_9]^T$ are the nine 2nd order SH coefficients which represent the low-frequency scene illumination.

Based on Eq. 4, a per-pixel shading loss is designed. It penalizes both intensity and gradient of the difference value between the rendered image and the corresponding intensity image:

$$\ell_{sh}(N_{dt}, N_{ref}, I) = \|B(l^*, N_{dt}, R) - I\|_2 + \lambda_g \|\nabla B(l^*, N_{dt}, R) - \nabla I\|_2, \tag{5}$$

where N_{dt} represents the normal map of the regressed depth from the refinement net, λ_g is the weight to balance shading loss term, R is the albedo map estimated using Nestmeyer's "CNN + filter" method [25]. Then, the light coefficients l^* can be computed by solving the least squares problem:

$$l^* = \arg \min_{l} \|B(l, N_{ref}, R) - I\|_2^2. \tag{6}$$

Here N_{ref} is calculated by the aforementioned d2n layer in Sect. 3.2. To show the effectiveness of our estimated illumination, a per-pixel albedo image is calculated by $R_I = I / \sum_{b=1}^{9} l_b H_b(N_{ref})$, as shown in Fig. 4. Note that pixels at grazing angles are excluded in the lighting estimation, as both shading and depth are unreliable in these regions. Additionally, to constrain the refined depth to be close to the reference depth map, a fidelity term is added:

$$\ell_{fid}(D_{dt}, D_{ref}) = \|D_{dt} - D_{ref}\|_2. \tag{7}$$

Furthermore, a smoothness term is added to regularize the refined depth. More specifically, we minimize the anisotropic total variation of the depth:

$$\ell_{smo}(D_{dt}) = \sum_{i,j} |D_{dt}^{i+1,j} - D_{dt}^{i,j}| + |D_{dt}^{i,j+1} - D_{dt}^{i,j}|. \tag{8}$$

With all the above terms, the final loss for our refinement net is expressed as:

$$\mathcal{L}_{dt}(D_{dt}, D_{ref}, I) = \lambda_{sh}\ell_{sh} + \lambda_{fid}\ell_{fid} + \lambda_{smo}\ell_{smo}, \tag{9}$$

where $\lambda_{sh}, \lambda_{fid}, \lambda_{smo}$ defines the strength of each loss term. The last two additional terms are necessary, because they constrain the output depth map to be smooth and also close to our reference depth, as the shading loss would not be able to constrain the low frequency component.

3.4   End-to-End Training

We train our cascaded net jointly. To do so, we define total loss as:

$$\mathcal{L}_{total} = \mathcal{L}_{dn} + \lambda\mathcal{L}_{dt} \tag{10}$$

where λ is set to 1 during training. The denoising net is supervised by temporally fused reference depth map, and the refinement CNN is trained in an unsupervised manner. By incorporating supervision signals in both the middle and the output of the network, we achieve a steady convergence during the training phase. In the forward pass, each batch of input depth maps is propagated through the denoising net, and reconstruction L1/L2 term and *normaldot* term are added to $\mathcal{L}_{total}$. Then, the denoised depth maps, together with the corresponding color images, are fed to our refinement net. Shading, fidelity and smooth terms are added to $\mathcal{L}_{total}$. In the backward pass, the gradient of the loss $\mathcal{L}_{total}$ are back-propagated through both network. All the hyper-parameters λ are fixed during training.

There are two types of consumer depth camera data in our training and validation set: structured light (K1) and time-of-flight (K2). We train the variants of our model on K1/K2 dataset respectively. To augment our training set, each RGB-D map are randomly cropped, flipped and re-scaled to the resolution of 256×256. Considering that depth map is 2.5D in nature, the intrinsic matrix should be changed accordingly during data augmentation. This enables the network to learn more object-independent statistics and to work with sensors of different intrinsic parameters. For efficiency, we implement our d2n layer as a single CUDA layer. We choose *Adam* optimizer to compute gradients, with 0.9 and 0.999 exponential decay rate for the 1st and 2nd moment estimates. Base learning-rate is set to 0.001 and batch-size is 32. All convolution weights are initialized by Xavier algorithm, and weight decay is used for regularization.

4   Experiments

In this section, we evaluate the effectiveness of our cascade depth denoising and refinement framework, and analyze the contribution from each loss term. To the best of our knowledge, there is no public dataset for human body that contains raw and ground-truth depth maps with rich details from consumer depth cameras. We thus compare the performance of all available method on our own validation set, qualitatively and quantitatively.

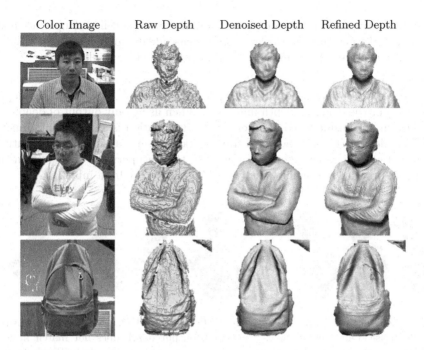

Fig. 5. Qualitative results on validation set. From left to right: RGB image, raw depth map, output of denoising net D_{dn} and output of refinement net D_{dt}. D_{dn} captures the low-dimensional geometry without noise, D_{dt} shows fine-grained details. Although trained on human body dataset, our model also produce high-quality depth map on general objects in arbitrary scenes, *eg.* the backpack sequence.

4.1 Evaluation

To verify the generalization ability of our trained network, we also evaluate on other objects other than human body, which can be seen in Figs. 5 and 8. One can see that although refined in an unsupervised manner, our results are comparable to the fused depth map [11] obtained using consumer depth camera only, and preserve thin structures such as fingers and folds in clothes better.

4.2 Ablation Study

The Role of Cascade CNN. To verify the necessity of our cascade CNNs, we replace our denoising net by a traditional preprocessing procedure, *eg.* bilateral filter, and still keep the refinement net to refine the filtered depth. We call this two-stage method as "Base+Ours refine", and it is trained from scratch with shading, fidelity and smoothness loss. As we can see in the middle of Fig. 6, "Base+Ours refine" is not able to preserve distinctive structures of clothes in the presence of widespread structured noise. Unwanted high frequency noise leads to inaccurate estimation of illuminance, therefore shading loss term will keep fluctuating during training. This training process will end up with non-optimal model parameters. However, in our cascade design, denoising net sets a good initialization for refinement net and achieves better result.

Supervision of Refinement Net. For our refinement net, there are two choices for regularization depth map in fidelity loss formulation, using reference depth map D_{ref} or the denoised depth map D_{dn}. When using only output of denoising net D_{dn} in an unsupervised manner, scene illumination is also estimated using D_{dn}. We denote this unsupervised framework as "Ours unsupervised". Output of these two choices are shown in Fig. 7. In the unsupervised case, refinement net could produce reasonable result, but D_{dt} may stray from input.

Fig. 6. Left: normal map of D_{in}. Middle: Base+Ours refine, bilateral filter can't remove wavelet noise, refinement result suffers from high-frequency. Right: Ours.

Fig. 7. Left: C_{in} and D_{in}. Middle: Ours unsupervised, output depth does not match input value in stripes area in the cloth. Right: Ours with more reliable result.

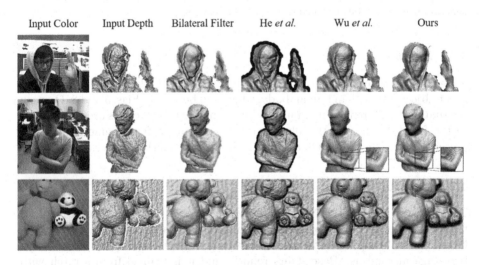

| Input Color | Input Depth | Bilateral Filter | He *et al.* | Wu *et al.* | Ours |

Fig. 8. Comparison of color-assisted depth map enhancement between bilateral filter, He *et al.* [15], Wu *et al.* [44] and our method. The closeup of the finger region demonstrates the effectiveness of unsupervised shading term in our refinement net loss.

4.3   Comparison with Other Methods

Compared with other non-data-driven methods, deep neural networks allow us to optimize non-linear loss and to add data-driven regularization, while keeping the inference time constant. Figure 8 shows examples of the qualitative comparison of different methods for depth map enhancement. Our method outperforms other methods by capturing cleaner structure of the geometry and high-fidelity details.

Quantitative Comparison. To evaluate quantitatively, we need a dataset with ground truth depth map. Multi-view stereo and laser scanner are able to capture static scene with high resolution and quality. We thus obtain ground truth depth value by multi-view stereo [32] (for K1) and Mantis Vision's F6 laser scanner (for K2). Meanwhile, we collect the input of our method, the RGB-D image of the same scene by a consumer depth camera. The size of validation set is limited due to the high scan cost. Therefore, we also contribute a larger validation set labeled with the near-ground-truth depth obtained using mentioned method in Sect. 3.1. After reconstruction, the ground truth 3D model is rescaled and aligned with our reprojected enhanced depth map, using iterative closest point (ICP) [5]. Then the root mean squared error (RMSE) and the mean absolute error (MAE) between these two point clouds are calculated in Euclidean space. We also report the angular difference of normals, and the percentages of normal difference less than 3.0, 5.0, and 10.0°. Two sets of model are trained/evaluated on K1 and K2 data respectively. Quantitative comparison with other methods are summarized in Tables 1 and 2. Results shows that our method substantially outperforms other methods in terms of both metrics on the validation set.

Table 1. Quantitative comparison results on K1 validation set, error metrics in mm.

Method	Near-GT set		GT set	
	MAE	RMSE	MAE	RMSE
Bilateral [22]	15.9	4.8	15.1	3.7
He et al. [15]	46.5	14.7	41.1	15.2
Wu et al. [44]	14.5	4.3	15.7	4.4
Ours	**10.9**	4.1	**11.0**	**3.6**
Base+Ours refine	15.7	**4.1**	15.8	4.4
Ours unsupervised	16.1	5.2	14.9	5.5

Runtime Performance. At test time, our whole processing procedure includes data pre-processing and cascade CNN predicting. The preprocessing steps include: depth-to-color alignment, morphological transformation, and resampling if necessary. The forward pass takes 10.8 ms (256 × 256 input) or 20.4 ms (640 × 480 input) on TitanX, 182.56 ms or 265.8 ms per frame on Intel Core i7-6900K CPU. It is worth mentioning that without denoising CNN, a variant of our method, "Base+Ours refine" reaches a speed of 9.6ms per frame for 640 × 480 inputs.

Table 2. Average score of depth and normal error and on our K2 validation set.

Method	Depth difference					Normal difference				
	Seq. 1	Seq. 2	Seq. 3	Seq. 4	Seq. 5	Mean ↓	Median ↓	3.0↑	5.0↑	10.0↑
Wu *et al.* [44]	27.60	22.19	21.34	22.41	25.67	11.20	5.02	29.81	50.24	76.62
Or-El *et al.* [30]	27.14	25.42	22.89	21.31	26.08	10.03	4.12	35.43	56.57	79.99
Ours D_{dn}	19.03	**19.25**	18.49	**18.37**	18.76	**9.36**	**3.40**	**45.33**	**66.79**	**84.69**
Ours D_{dt}	**18.97**	19.41	**18.38**	18.50	**18.61**	9.55	3.54	43.77	64.98	83.69

4.4 Limitation

Similar to other real-time methods, we consider simplified light transport model. This simplification is effective but will impose intensity image's texture on depth map. With the learning framework, texture-copy artifacts can be alleviated due to the fact that network can balance fidelity and shading loss term during training. Another limitation comes with non-diffuse surface assumption, as we only consider second order spherical harmonics representation.

5   Applications

It is known that real-time single frame depth enhancement is applicable for low-latency system without temporal accumulation. We compare the result using depth refined by our method with result using raw depth, on Dynamic Fusion [11] and DoubleFusion [48]. The temporal window in fusion systems would smooth out noise, but it will also wipe out high-frequency details. The time in TSDF fusion blocks the whole system from tracking detailed motions. In contrast, our method runs on single frame and provide timely update of fast changing surface details (*eg.* deformation of clothes and body gestures), as shown in red circles in Fig. 9 and the supplementary video. Moreover, real-time single frame depth enhancement could help tracking and recognition tasks under interactive scenarios.

Fig. 9. Application on DynamicFusion (left) and DoubleFusion (right) using our enhanced depth stream. Left: color image, Middle: fused geometry using raw depth stream, Right: "instant" geometry using our refined depth stream.

6 Conclusion

We presented the first end-to-end trainable network for depth map denoising and refinement for consumer depth cameras. We proposed a near-groundtruth training data generation pipeline, based on the depth fusion techniques. Enabled by the separation of low/high frequency parts in network design, as well as the collected fusion data, our cascaded CNNs achieves state-of-the-art result in real-time. Compared with available methods, our method achieved higher quality reconstruction in terms of both low dimensional geometry and high frequency details, which leads to superior performance quantitatively and qualitatively. Finally, with the popularity of integrating depth sensors into cellphones, we believe that our deep-net-specific algorithm is able to run on these portable devices for various quantitative measurement and qualitative visualization applications.

Acknowledgement. This work is supported by the National key foundation for exploring scientific instrument of China No. 2013YQ140517, and the National NSF of China grant No. 61522111, No. 61531014, No. 61671268 and No. 61727808.

References

1. Barron, J.T., Malik, J.: Intrinsic scene properties from a single RGB-D image. In: Proceedings of CVPR, pp. 17–24. IEEE (2013)
2. Barron, J.T., Malik, J.: Shape, illumination, and reflectance from shading. Technical report, EECS, UC Berkeley, May 2013
3. Beeler, T., Bickel, B., Beardsley, P.A., Sumner, B., Gross, M.H.: High-quality single-shot capture of facial geometry. ACM Trans. Graph. **29**(4), 40:1–40:9 (2010)
4. Beeler, T., Bradley, D., Zimmer, H., Gross, M.: Improved reconstruction of deforming surfaces by cancelling ambient occlusion. In: Fitzgibbon, A., Lazebnik, S., Perona, P., Sato, Y., Schmid, C. (eds.) ECCV 2012. LNCS, vol. 7572, pp. 30–43. Springer, Heidelberg (2012). https://doi.org/10.1007/978-3-642-33718-5_3
5. Besl, P.J., McKay, N.D.: Method for registration of 3-D shapes. In: Robotics-DL Tentative, pp. 586–606. International Society for Optics and Photonics (1992)
6. Chan, D., Buisman, H., Theobalt, C., Thrun, S.: A noise-aware filter for real-time depth upsampling. In: ECCV Workshop on Multi-camera & Multi-modal Sensor Fusion (2008)
7. Chen, J., Bautembach, D., Izadi, S.: Scalable real-time volumetric surface reconstruction. ACM Trans. Graph. **32**(4), 113:1–113:16 (2013)
8. Cui, Y., Schuon, S., Thrun, S., Stricker, D., Theobalt, C.: Algorithms for 3D shape scanning with a depth camera. IEEE Trans. Pattern Anal. Mach. Intell. **35**(5), 1039–1050 (2013)
9. Diebel, J., Thrun, S.: An application of Markov random fields to range sensing. In: Proceedings of the 18th International Conference on Neural Information Processing Systems, NIPS 2005, pp. 291–298. MIT Press, Cambridge (2005)
10. Dolson, J., Baek, J., Plagemann, C., Thrun, S.: Upsampling range data in dynamic environments. In: 2010 IEEE Computer Society Conference on Computer Vision and Pattern Recognition, pp. 1141–1148, June 2010

11. Guo, K., Xu, F., Yu, T., Liu, X., Dai, Q., Liu, Y.: Real-time geometry, albedo, and motion reconstruction using a single RGB-D camera. ACM Trans. Graph. **36**(3), 32:1–32:13 (2017)

12. Han, Y., Lee, J.Y., Kweon, I.S.: High quality shape from a single RGB-D image under uncalibrated natural illumination. In: Proceedings of ICCV (2013)

13. Han, Y., Lee, J.Y., Kweon, I.S.: High quality shape from a single RGB-D image under uncalibrated natural illumination. In: IEEE International Conference on Computer Vision, pp. 1617–1624 (2013)

14. Hariharan, B., Arbelaez, P., Girshick, R., Malik, J.: Hypercolumns for object segmentation and fine-grained localization, pp. 447–456 (2014)

15. He, K., Sun, J., Tang, X.: Guided image filtering. IEEE Trans. Pattern Anal. Mach. Intell. **35**(6), 1397–1409 (2013)

16. Henry, P., Krainin, M., Herbst, E., Ren, X., Fox, D.: RGB-D mapping: using kinect-style depth cameras for dense 3D modeling of indoor environments. Int. J. Robot. Res. **31**(5), 647–663 (2012)

17. Horn, B.K.: Obtaining shape from shading information. In: The Psychology of Computer Vision, pp. 115–155 (1975)

18. Isola, P., Zhu, J.Y., Zhou, T., Efros, A.A.: Image-to-image translation with conditional adversarial networks (2016)

19. Izadi, S., et al.: KinectFusion: real-time 3D reconstruction and interaction using a moving depth camera. In: Proceedings of UIST, pp. 559–568. ACM (2011)

20. Kajiya, J.T.: The rendering equation. In: Proceedings of the 13th Annual Conference on Computer Graphics and Interactive Techniques, SIGGRAPH 1986, pp. 143–150. ACM, New York (1986)

21. Khan, N., Tran, L., Tappen, M.: Training many-parameter shape-from-shading models using a surface database. In: Proceedings of ICCV Workshop (2009)

22. Kopf, J., Cohen, M.F., Lischinski, D., Uyttendaele, M.: Joint bilateral upsampling. ACM Trans. Graph. **26**(3), 96 (2007)

23. Lindner, M., Kolb, A., Hartmann, K.: Data-fusion of PMD-based distance-information and high-resolution RGB-images. In: 2007 International Symposium on Signals, Circuits and Systems, vol. 1, pp. 1–4, July 2007

24. Mayer, N., et al.: A large dataset to train convolutional networks for disparity, optical flow, and scene flow estimation. In: Computer Vision and Pattern Recognition, pp. 4040–4048 (2016)

25. Nestmeyer, T., Gehler, P.V.: Reflectance adaptive filtering improves intrinsic image estimation. In: CVPR, pp. 1771–1780 (2017)

26. Newcombe, R.A., Fox, D., Seitz, S.M.: Dynamicfusion: reconstruction and tracking of non-rigid scenes in real-time. In: 2015 IEEE Conference on Computer Vision and Pattern Recognition (CVPR), pp. 343–352, June 2015

27. Newcombe, R.A., Izadi, S., et al.: KinectFusion: real-time dense surface mapping and tracking. In: IEEE International Symposium on Mixed and Augmented Reality (ISMAR), pp. 127–136 (2011)

28. Nießner, M., Zollhöfer, M., Izadi, S., Stamminger, M.: Real-time 3D reconstruction at scale using voxel hashing. ACM Trans. Graph. (TOG) **32**(6), 169 (2013)

29. Odena, A., Dumoulin, V., Olah, C.: Deconvolution and checkerboard artifacts. Distill (2016)

30. Or El, R., Rosman, G., Wetzler, A., Kimmel, R., Bruckstein, A.M.: RGBD-fusion: real-time high precision depth recovery. In: The IEEE Conference on Computer Vision and Pattern Recognition (CVPR), June 2015

31. Park, J., Kim, H., Tai, Y.W., Brown, M.S., Kweon, I.: High quality depth map upsampling for 3D-TOF cameras. In: 2011 International Conference on Computer Vision, pp. 1623–1630, November 2011
32. RealityCapture (2017). https://www.capturingreality.com/
33. Richardson, E., Sela, M., Or-El, R., Kimmel, R.: Learning detailed face reconstruction from a single image. In: CVPR (2017)
34. Richardt, C., Stoll, C., Dodgson, N.A., Seidel, H.P., Theobalt, C.: Coherent spatiotemporal filtering, upsampling and rendering of RGBZ videos. Comput. Graph. Forum **31**(2pt1), 247–256 (2012)
35. Riegler, G., Ulusoy, A.O., Bischof, H., Geiger, A.: OctNetFusion: learning depth fusion from data. In: 2017 International Conference on 3D Vision (3DV), pp. 57–66. IEEE (2017)
36. Ronneberger, O., Fischer, P., Brox, T.: U-net: convolutional networks for biomedical image segmentation. In: Navab, N., Hornegger, J., Wells, W.M., Frangi, A.F. (eds.) MICCAI 2015. LNCS, vol. 9351, pp. 234–241. Springer, Cham (2015). https://doi.org/10.1007/978-3-319-24574-4_28
37. Sela, M., Richardson, E., Kimmel, R.: Unrestricted facial geometry reconstruction using image-to-image translation (2017)
38. Tewari, A., et al.: MoFA: model-based deep convolutional face autoencoder for unsupervised monocular reconstruction. In: The IEEE International Conference on Computer Vision (ICCV), vol. 2, p. 5 (2017)
39. Varol, G., et al.: Learning from synthetic humans. In: CVPR (2017)
40. Wei, G., Hirzinger, G.: Learning shape from shading by a multilayer network. IEEE Trans. Neural Netw. **7**(4), 985–995 (1996)
41. Wojna, Z., et al.: The devil is in the decoder (2017)
42. Wu, C., Stoll, C., Valgaerts, L., Theobalt, C.: On-set performance capture of multiple actors with a stereo camera. ACM Trans. Graph. (TOG) **32**(6), 161 (2013)
43. Wu, C., Varanasi, K., Liu, Y., Seidel, H., Theobalt, C.: Shading-based dynamic shape refinement from multi-view video under general illumination, pp. 1108–1115 (2011)
44. Wu, C., Zollhöfer, M., Nießner, M., Stamminger, M., Izadi, S., Theobalt, C.: Real-time shading-based refinement for consumer depth cameras. ACM Trans. Graph. (TOG) **33**(6), 200 (2014)
45. Yang, Q., Yang, R., Davis, J., Nister, D.: Spatial-depth super resolution for range images. In: 2007 IEEE Conference on Computer Vision and Pattern Recognition, pp. 1–8, June 2007
46. Yu, L., Yeung, S., Tai, Y., Lin, S.: Shading-based shape refinement of RGB-D images, pp. 1415–1422 (2013)
47. Yu, T., et al.: BodyFusion: real-time capture of human motion and surface geometry using a single depth camera. In: The IEEE International Conference on Computer Vision (ICCV). IEEE, October 2017
48. Yu, T., et al.: DoubleFusion: real-time capture of human performance with inner body shape from a depth sensor. In: IEEE Conference on Computer Vision and Pattern Recognition (CVPR) (2018)
49. Zhang, Z., Tsa, P.S., Cryer, J.E., Shah, M.: Shape from shading: a survey. IEEE PAMI **21**(8), 690–706 (1999)
50. Zhu, J., Wang, L., Yang, R., Davis, J.: Fusion of time-of-flight depth and stereo for high accuracy depth maps. In: 2008 IEEE Conference on Computer Vision and Pattern Recognition, pp. 1–8, June 2008

ELEGANT: Exchanging Latent Encodings with GAN for Transferring Multiple Face Attributes

Taihong Xiao[iD], Jiapeng Hong, and Jinwen Ma[✉]

Department of Information Science, School of Mathematical Sciences and LMAM,
Peking University, Beijing 100871, China
jwma@math.pku.edu.cn

Abstract. Recent studies on face attribute transfer have achieved great success. A lot of models are able to transfer face attributes with an input image. However, they suffer from three limitations: (1) incapability of generating image by exemplars; (2) being unable to transfer multiple face attributes simultaneously; (3) low quality of generated images, such as low-resolution or artifacts. To address these limitations, we propose a novel model which receives two images of opposite attributes as inputs. Our model can transfer exactly the same type of attributes from one image to another by exchanging certain part of their encodings. All the attributes are encoded in a disentangled manner in the latent space, which enables us to manipulate several attributes simultaneously. Besides, our model learns the residual images so as to facilitate training on higher resolution images. With the help of multi-scale discriminators for adversarial training, it can even generate high-quality images with finer details and less artifacts. We demonstrate the effectiveness of our model on overcoming the above three limitations by comparing with other methods on the CelebA face database. A pytorch implementation is available at https://github.com/Prinsphield/ELEGANT.

Keywords: Face attribute transfer · Image generation by exemplars Attributes disentanglement · Generative adversarial networks

1 Introduction

The task of transferring face attributes is a type of conditional image generation. A source face image is modified to contain the targeted attribute, while the person identity should be preserved. As an example shown in Fig. 1, the bangs attribute is manipulated (added or removed) without changing the person identity. For each pair of images, the right image is purely generated from the left one, without the corresponding images in the training set.

A lot of methods have been proposed to accomplish this task, but they still suffer from different kinds of limitations.

V. Ferrari et al. (Eds.): ECCV 2018, LNCS 11214, pp. 172–187, 2018.
https://doi.org/10.1007/978-3-030-01249-6_11

Gardner *et al.* [3] has proposed a method called Deep Manifold Traversal that was able to approximate the natural image manifold and compute the attribute vector from the source domain to the target domain by using maximum mean discrepancy (MMD) [6]. By this method, the attribute vector is a linear combination of the feature representations of training images extracted from VGG-19 [22] network. However, it suffers from unbearable time and memory cost, and thus is not useful in practice.

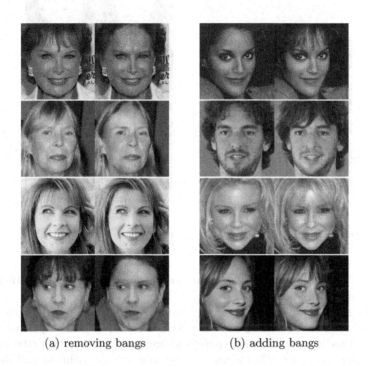

(a) removing bangs   (b) adding bangs

Fig. 1. Results of ELEGANT in transferring the **bangs** attribute. Out of four images in a row, the bangs style of the first image is transferred to the last one.

Under the Linear Feature Space assumptions [1], one can transfer face attribute in a much simpler manner [24]: adding an attribute vector to the original image in the feature space, and then obtaining the solution in the image space inversely from the computed feature. For example, transferring a no-bangs image B to a bangs image A would be formulated as $A = f^{-1}(f(B) + v_{bangs})$, where f is a mapping (usually deep neural networks) from the image space to the feature space, and the attribute vector v_{bangs} can be computed as the difference between the cluster centers of features of bangs images and no-bangs images. The universal attribute vector is applicable to a variety of faces, leading to the same style of bangs in the generated face images. But there are many styles of bangs. Figure 1 would be a good illustration of different styles of bangs. Some kinds of bangs are thick enough to cover the entire forehead, some tend to go

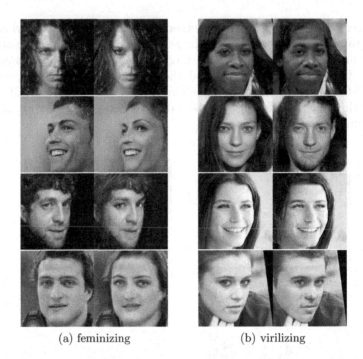

(a) feminizing   (b) virilizing

Fig. 2. Results of ELEGANT in transferring the **gender** attribute.

either left or right side, exposing the other half forehead, and some others may divide from the middle, etc.

To address the diversity issue, the Visual Analogy-Making [19] has used a pair of reference images to specify the attribute vector. Such a pair of images consists of two images of the same person where one has one certain attribute and the other one does not. This method could increase the richness and diversity of generated images, however, it is usually hard to obtain a large quantity of such paired images. For example, if transferring the attribute gender over face images, we need to obtain both male and female images of a same person, which is impossible. (See Fig. 2).

Recently, more and more methods based on GANs [5] have been proposed to overcome this difficulty [10,18,31]. The task of face attribute transfer can be viewed as a kind of image-to-image translation problem. Images with/without one certain attribute lies in different image domains. The dual learning approaches [7,11,21,28,32] have been further exploited to map between source image domain and target image domain. The maps between the two domains are continuous and inverse to each other under the cycle consistency loss. According to the Invariance of Domain Theorem[1], the intrinsic dimensions of two image domains should be the same. This leads to a contradiction, because

---

[1] https://en.wikipedia.org/wiki/Invariance_of_domain.

(a) removing eyeglasses   (b) adding eyeglasses

Fig. 3. Results of ELEGANT in transferring the `eyeglasses` attribute. In each row, the type of eyeglasses in the first image is transferred to the last one.

the intrinsic dimensions of two image domains are not always the same. Taking transferring eyeglasses (Fig. 3) as an example, domain A contains face images wearing eyeglasses, and domain B contains face images wearing no eyeglasses. The intrinsic dimension of A is larger than that of B due to the variety of eyeglasses.

Some other methods [15,23,30] are actually the variants of combinations of GAN and VAE. These models employ the autoencoder structure for image generation instead of using two maps interconnecting two image domains. They successfully bypass the problem of unequal intrinsic dimensions. However, most of these models are limited to manipulating only one face attribute each time.

To control multiple attributes simultaneously, lots of conditional image generation methods [2,13,18,29] receive image labels as conditions. Admittedly, these models could transfer several attributes at the same time, but fail to generate images by exemplars, that is, generating images with exactly the same attributes in another reference image. Consequently, the style of attributes in the generated image might be similar, thus lacking of richness and diversity.

BicycleGAN [33] introduces a noise term to increase the diversity, but fails to generate images of specified attributes. TD-GAN [25] and DNA-GAN [27] can generate images by exemplars. But TD-GAN requires explicit identity information in the label so as to preserve the person identity, which limits its applica-

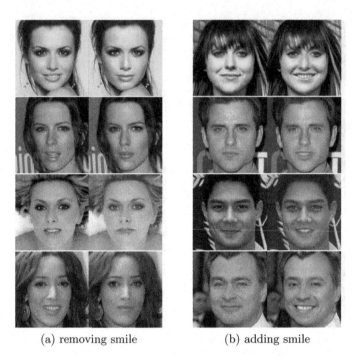

(a) removing smile   (b) adding smile

Fig. 4. Results of ELEGANT in transferring the `smiling` attribute. In each row, the style of smiling of the first image is transplanted into the last one.

tion in many datasets without labeled identity information. DNA-GAN suffers from the training difficulty on high-resolution images. There also exist many other methods [14], however, their results are not visually satisfying, either low-resolution or lots of artifacts in the generated images.

2   Purpose and Intuition

As discussed above, there are many approaches to transferring face attributes. However, most of them suffer from one or more following limitations:

1. Incapability of generating image by exemplars;
2. Being unable to transfer multiple face attributes simultaneously;
3. Low quality of generated images, such as low-resolution or artifacts.

To overcome these three limitations, we propose a novel model integrated with different advantages for multiple face attribute transfer.

To generate images by exemplars, a model must receive a reference for conditional image generation. Most of previous methods [2,13,17,18] use labels directly for guiding conditional image generation. But the information provided by a label is very limited, which is not commensurate with the diversity of images of that label. Various kinds of smiling face images can be classified into `smiling`,

(a) black hair to non-black   (b) non-black hair to black

Fig. 5. Results of ELEGANT in transferring the `black hair` attribute. In each row, the color of the first image turns to be the color of the third one, apart from turning the color of the third image into black. (Color figure online)

but cannot be generated inversely from the same label `smiling`. So we set the latent encodings of images as the reference as the encodings of an image can be viewed as a unique identifier of an image given the encoder. The encodings of reference images are added to inputs so as to guide the generation process. In this way, the generated image will have exactly the same style of attributes in the reference images.

For manipulating multiple attributes simultaneously, the latent encodings of an image can be divided into different parts, where each part encodes information of a single attribute [27]. In this way, multiple attributes are encoded in a disentangled manner. When transferring several certain face attributes, the encodings parts corresponding to those attributes should be changed.

To improve the quality of generated images, we adopt the idea of residual learning [8,21] and multi-scale discriminators [26]. The local property of face attributes is unique in the task of face attributes transfer, contrast to the task of image style transfer [4], where the image style is a holistic property. Such property allows us to modify only a local part of the image so as to transfer face attributes, which helps alleviate the training difficulty. The multi-scale discriminators can capture different levels of information that is useful for the generation of both holistic content and local details.

3   Our Method

In this section, we formally propose our method ELEGANT, the abbreviation of Exchanging Latent Encodings with GAN for Transferring multiple face attributes.

3.1   The ELEGANT Model

The ELEGANT model receives two sets of training images as inputs: a positive set and a negative set. In our convention, the image A from the positive set has the attribute, whereas the image B from the negative set does not. As shown in Fig. 6, image A has the attribute smiling and image B does not. The positive set and negative set need not to be paired. (The person from the positive set needs not to be the same as the one from the negative set.)

All of n transferred attributes are predefined. It is not naturally guaranteed that each attribute is encoded into different parts. Such disentangled representations have to be learned. We adopt the *iterative training strategy*: training the model with respect to a particular attribute each time by feeding with a pair of images with opposite attribute and go over all attributes repeatedly.

When training ELEGANT about the i-th attribute smiling at this iteration, a set of smiling images and another set of non-smiling images are collected as inputs. Formally, the attribute labels of A and B are required to be in this form $Y^A = (y_1^A, \ldots, 1_i, \ldots, y_n^A)$ and $Y^B = (y_1^B, \ldots, 0_i, \ldots, y_n^B)$, respectively.

An encoder was then used to obtain the latent encodings of images A and B, denoted by z_A and z_B, respectively.

$$z_A = \text{Enc}(A) = [a_1, \ldots, a_i, \ldots, a_n], \qquad z_B = \text{Enc}(B) = [b_1, \ldots, b_i, \ldots, b_n] \quad (1)$$

where a_i (or b_i) is the feature tensor that encodes the smiling information of image A (or B). In practice, we split the tensor z_A (or z_B) into n parts along with its channel dimension. Once obtained z_A and z_B, we exchange the i-th part in their latent encodings so as to obtain novel encodings z_C and z_D.

$$z_C = [a_1, \ldots, b_i, \ldots, a_n], \qquad z_D = [b_1, \ldots, a_i, \ldots, b_n] \quad (2)$$

We expect that z_C is the encoding of the non-smiling version of image A, and z_D the encodings of the smiling version of image B. As shown in Fig. 6, A and B are both reference images for each other, C and D are generated by swapping the latent encodings.

Then we need to design a reasonable structure to decipher the latent encodings into images. As discussed in Sect. 2, it would be much better to learn the residual images rather than the original image. So we recombine the latent encodings and employ a decoder to do this job.

$$\text{Dec}([z_A, z_A]) = R_A, \quad A' = A + R_A \qquad \text{Dec}([z_C, z_A]) = R_C, \quad C = A + R_C \tag{3}$$

$$\text{Dec}([z_B, z_B]) = R_B, \quad B' = B + R_B \qquad \text{Dec}([z_D, z_B]) = R_D, \quad D = B + R_D \tag{4}$$

where R_A, R_B, R_C and R_D are residual images, A' and B' are reconstructed images, C and D are images of novel attributes, $[z_C, z_A]$ denotes the concatenation of encodings z_C and z_A. The concatenation could be replaced by difference of two encodings, but we still use the form of concatenation, because the subtraction operation could be learnt by the Dec.

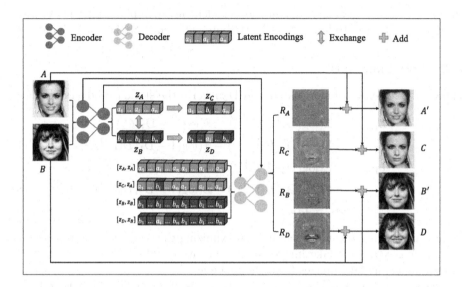

Fig. 6. The ELEGANT model architecture.

Besides, we use the U-Net [20] structure for better visual results. The structures of Enc and Dec are symmetrical, and their intermediary layers are connected by shortcuts, as displayed in Fig. 6. These shortcuts bring the original images as a context condition, so as to generate seamless novel attributes.

The Enc and Dec together act as the generator. We also need discriminators for adversarial training. However, the receptive field of a single discriminator is limited when the input image size becomes large. To address this issue, we adopt multi-scale discriminators [26]: two discriminators having identical network structures whereas operating at different image scales. We denote the discriminator operating at a larger scale by D_1 and the other one by D_2. D_1 has a smaller receptive field compared with D_2. Therefore, D_1 is specialized in guiding the Enc and Dec to produce finer details, whereas D_2 is adept in handling the holistic image content so as to avoid generating grimaces.

The discriminators should also receive image labels as conditional inputs. There are n attributes in total. The output of discriminators in each iteration reflects how real-looking the generated images are with respect to one attribute. It is necessary to let discriminators know which attribute they are dealing with in each iteration. Mathematically, it would be a conditional form. For example, $D_1(A|Y^A)$ represents the output score by D_1 for image A given its label Y^A. We should pay attention to the attribute labels of C and D, since they have novel attributes.

$$Y^A = (y_1^A, \ldots, 1_i, \ldots, y_n^A) \quad Y^B = (y_1^B, \ldots, 0_i, \ldots, y_n^B) \qquad (5)$$

$$Y^C = (y_1^A, \ldots, 0_i, \ldots, y_n^A) \quad Y^D = (y_1^B, \ldots, 1_i, \ldots, y_n^B) \qquad (6)$$

where Y^C differs from Y^A only in the i-th element, by replacing 1 with 0, since we do not expect C to have the i-th attribute. The same applies to Y^D and Y^B.

3.2 Loss Functions

The multi-scale discriminators D_1 and D_2 receive the standard adversarial loss

$$\begin{aligned}
L_{D_1} = &- \mathbb{E}(\log(D_1(A|Y^A))) - \mathbb{E}(\log(1 - D_1(C|Y^C))) \\
&- \mathbb{E}(\log(D_1(B|Y^B))) - \mathbb{E}(\log(1 - D_1(D|Y^D)))
\end{aligned} \qquad (7)$$

$$\begin{aligned}
L_{D_2} = &- \mathbb{E}(\log(D_2(A|Y^A))) - \mathbb{E}(\log(1 - D_2(C|Y^C))) \\
&- \mathbb{E}(\log(D_2(B|Y^B))) - \mathbb{E}(\log(1 - D_2(D|Y^D)))
\end{aligned} \qquad (8)$$

$$L_D = L_{D_1} + L_{D_2} \qquad (9)$$

When minimizing L_D, we are actually maximizing the scores for real images and minimizing scores for fake images in the meantime. This drives D_1 and D_2 to discriminate the fake images from the real ones.

As for the Enc and Dec, there are two types of losses. The first type is the reconstruction loss,

$$L_{reconstruction} = ||A - A'|| + ||B - B'|| \qquad (10)$$

which measures how well the original input is reconstructed after a sequence of encoding and decoding. The second type is the standard adversarial loss

$$\begin{aligned}
L_{adv} = &- \mathbb{E}(\log(D_1(C|Y^C))) - \mathbb{E}(\log(D_1(D|Y^D))) \\
&- \mathbb{E}(\log(D_2(C|Y^C))) - \mathbb{E}(\log(D_2(D|Y^D)))
\end{aligned} \qquad (11)$$

which measures how realistic the generated images are. The total loss for the generator is

$$L_G = L_{reconstruction} + L_{adv}. \qquad (12)$$

4 Experiments

In this section, we carry out different types of experiments to validate the effectiveness of our method in overcoming three limitations. First of all, we introduce the dataset and our model in details.

The CelebA [16] dataset is a large-scale face database including 202599 face images of 10177 identities, each with 40 attributes annotations and 5 landmark

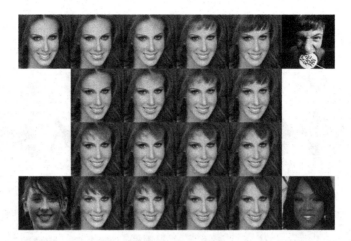

Fig. 7. Interpolation results of different bangs. The top-left is the original one, and those at the other three corners are reference images of different styles of bangs. The rest 16 images in the center are interpolation results.

locations. We use the 5-point landmarks to align all face images and crop them into 256×256. All of the following experiments are performed at this scale.

The encoder is equipped with 5 layers of Conv-Norm-LeakyReLU block, and the decoder has 5 layers of Deconv-Norm-LeakyReLU block. The multi-scale discriminators uses 5 layers of Conv-Norm-LeakyReLU blocks followed by a fully connected layer. All networks are trained using Adam [12] initialized with learning rate 2e-4, $\beta_1 = 0.5$ and $\beta_2 = 0.999$. All input images are normalized into the range $[-1, 1]$, and the last layer of decoder is clipped into the range $[-2, 2]$ using $2 \cdot \tanh$, since the maximum difference between the input image and the output image is 2. After adding the residual to the input image, we clip the output image value into $[-1, 1]$ to avoid the out-of-range error.

It is worth mentioning that the Batch-Normalization (BN) layer should be avoided. ELEGANT receives two batches of images with opposite attribute as inputs, thus the moving mean and moving variance of two batches of images in each layer should make a big difference. If using BN, these running statistics in each layer will always oscillate. To overcome this issue, we replace the BN by ℓ_2-normalization, $\hat{x} = \frac{x}{||x||_2} \cdot \alpha + \beta$, where α and β are learnable parameters. Without computing moving statistics, ELEGANT converges stably and swaps face attributes effectively.

4.1   Face Image Generation by Exemplars

In order to demonstrate that our model can generate face images by exemplars, we choose UNIT [15], CycleGAN [32] and StarGAN [2] for comparison. As shown in Fig. 8, ELEGANT can generate different face images with exactly the same style of attribute in the reference images, whereas other methods are only able to

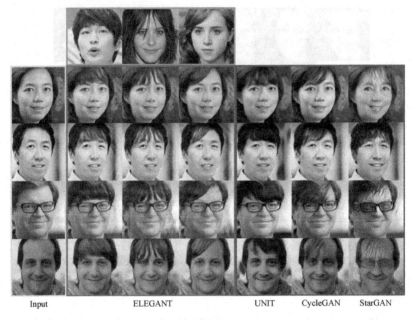

Input   ELEGANT   UNIT   CycleGAN   StarGAN

(a) bangs

Input   ELEGANT   UNIT   CycleGAN   StarGAN

(b) smiling

Fig. 8. Face image generation by exemplars. The yellow and green box are the input images outside the training data and the reference images, respectively. Images in the red and blue box are the results of ELEGANT and other models. (Color figure online)

generate a common style of attribute for any input images. (The style of bangs is the same in each column in the blue box.)

An important drawback of StarGAN should be pointed out here. StarGAN could be trained to transfer multiple attributes, but when transferring only one certain attribute, it may change other attributes. For example, in the last column of Fig. 8(a), Fei-Fei Li and Andrew Ng become younger when adding bangs to them. This is because StarGAN requires an unambiguous label for the input image, and these two images are both labeled as 1 in the attribute young. However, both of them are middle-aged and cannot be simply labeled as either young or old.

The mechanism of exchanging latent encodings in the ELEGANT model effectively addresses this issue. ELEGANT focuses on the attribute that we are dealing with and does not require labels for the input images at testing phase. Moreover, ELEGANT could learn the subtle difference between different bangs style in the reference images, as displayed in Fig. 7.

4.2   Dealing with Multiple Attributes Simultaneously

We compare ELEGANT with DNA-GAN [27], because both of them are able to manipulate multiple face attributes and generate images by exemplars. Two models are performed on the same face images and reference images with respect to three attributes. As shown in Fig. 9, the ELEGANT is visually much better than DNA-GAN, particularly in producing finer details (zooming in for a closer look). The improvement compared with DNA-GAN is mainly the result of the residual learning and multi-scale discriminators.

Residual learning reduces training difficulty. DNA-GAN suffers from unstable training, especially on high resolution images. On one hand, this difficulty comes from an imbalance between the generator and discriminator. At the early stage of DNA-GAN training, the generator outputs nonsense so that the discriminator could easily learn how to tell generated images from real ones, which would break the balance quickly. However, ELEGANT adopts the idea of residual learning, thus the outputs of the generator are almost the same as original images at the early stage. In this way, the discriminator cannot be well trained so fast, which would help stabilize the training process. On the other hand, the burden of the generator becomes heavier than that of the discriminator as the image size goes larger. Because the output space of the generator gets larger (e.g., $256 \times 256 \times 3$), whereas the discriminator only needs to output a number as usual. However, ELEGANT effectively reduces the dimension of generator's output space by learning residual images, where a small number of pixels need to be modified.

Multi-scale discriminators improve the quality of generated images. One discriminator operating at the smaller input scale can guide the overall image content generation, and the other operating at the larger input scale can help the generator to produce finer details. (Already discussed in Sect. 3.1).

Moreover, DNA-GAN utilizes an additional part to encode face id and background information. It is a good idea, but brings the problem of trivial solutions: two input images can be directly swapped so as to satisfy the loss constraints.

ELEGANT   DNA-GAN

(a) Bangs and Smiling

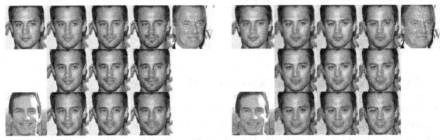

(b) Smiling and Mustache

(c) Bangs and Mustache

Fig. 9. Multiple Attributes Interpolation. The left and right columns are results of ELEGANT and DNA-GAN, respectively. For each picture, the top-left, bottom-left and top-right images are the original image, reference images of the first and the second attributes. The original image gradually owns two different attributes of the reference images in two directions.

Xiao *et al.* [27] have proposed the so called annihilating operation to address this issue. But this operation leads to a distortion on the parameter spaces, which brings additional difficulty to training. ELEGANT learns the residual images that account for the changes so that the face id and background information are automatically preserved. Moreover, it removes the annihilating operation and the additional part in the latent encodings, which makes the whole framework more elegant and easy to understand.

4.3   High-Quality Generated Images

As displayed in Figs. 1, 2, 3, 4 and 5, we present the results of ELEGANT with respect to different attributes in a large size for a close look. Moreover, we use the Fréchet Inception Distance [9] (FID) to measure the quality of generated images. FID measures the distance of two distributions by

$$d^2 = ||\mu_1 - \mu_2||^2 + \mathrm{Tr}(C_1 + C_2 - 2(C_1 C_2)^{1/2}). \tag{13}$$

where (μ_1, C_1) and (μ_2, C_2) are means and covariance matrices of two distributions. As shown in Table 1, we compute the FID between the distribution of real images and generated images with respect to different attributes. ELEGANT achieves competitive results compared with other methods.

The FID score is only for reference due to two reasons. ELEGANT and DNA-GAN can generate images by exemplars, which is much more general and difficult than other types of image translation methods. So it would be still unfair to them using any kind of qualitative measures. Besides, the reasonable qualitative measure for GAN is undetermined.

Table 1. FID of Different Methods with respect to five attributes. The $+$ $(-)$ represents the generated images by adding (removing) the attribute.

FID	bangs		smiling		mustache		eyeglasses		male	
	+	−	+	−	+	−	+	−	+	−
UNIT	135.41	137.94	120.25	125.04	119.32	131.33	111.49	139.43	152.16	154.59
CycleGAN	**27.81**	33.22	**23.23**	**22.74**	43.58	55.49	**36.87**	**48.82**	60.25	**46.25**
StarGAN	59.68	71.07	51.36	78.87	99.03	176.18	70.40	142.35	70.14	206.21
DNA-GAN	79.27	76.89	77.04	72.35	126.33	127.66	75.02	75.96	121.04	118.67
ELEGANT	30.71	**31.12**	25.71	24.88	**37.51**	**49.13**	47.35	60.71	**59.37**	56.80

5   Conclusions

We have established a novel model ELEGANT for transferring multiple face attributes. The model encodes different attributes into disentangled parts and generate images with novel attributes by exchanging certain parts of latent encodings. Under the observation that only local part of the image should be modified to transfer face attribute, we adopt the residual learning to facilitate training on high-resolution images. A U-Net structure design and multi-scale discriminators further improve the image quality. Experimental results on CelebA face database demonstrate that ELEGANT successfully overcomes three common limitations existing in most of other methods.

Acknowledgement. This work was supported by High-performance Computing Platform of Peking University.

References

1. Bengio, Y., Mesnil, G., Dauphin, Y., Rifai, S.: Better mixing via deep representations. In: International Conference on Machine Learning, pp. 552–560 (2013)
2. Choi, Y., Choi, M., Kim, M., Ha, J.W., Kim, S., Choo, J.: StarGAN: unified generative adversarial networks for multi-domain image-to-image translation. In: IEEE Conference on Computer Vision and Pattern Recognition (CVPR) (2018)
3. Gardner, J.R., et al.: Deep manifold traversal: changing labels with convolutional features. arXiv preprint arXiv:1511.06421 (2015)
4. Gatys, L.A., Ecker, A.S., Bethge, M.: A neural algorithm of artistic style. Nature Communications (2015)
5. Goodfellow, I., et al.: Generative adversarial nets. In: Advances in Neural Information Processing Systems, pp. 2672–2680 (2014)
6. Gretton, A., Borgwardt, K.M., Rasch, M.J., Schölkopf, B., Smola, A.: A kernel two-sample test. J. Mach. Learn. Res. **13**(Mar), 723–773 (2012)
7. He, D., et al.: Dual learning for machine translation. In: Advances in Neural Information Processing Systems, pp. 820–828 (2016)
8. He, K., Zhang, X., Ren, S., Sun, J.: Deep residual learning for image recognition. In: Proceedings of the IEEE Conference on Computer Vision and Pattern Recognition, pp. 770–778 (2016)
9. Heusel, M., Ramsauer, H., Unterthiner, T., Nessler, B., Hochreiter, S.: GANs trained by a two time-scale update rule converge to a local Nash equilibrium. In: Advances in Neural Information Processing Systems, pp. 6629–6640 (2017)
10. Isola, P., Zhu, J.Y., Zhou, T., Efros, A.A.: Image-to-image translation with conditional adversarial networks. arXiv preprint (2017)
11. Kim, T., Cha, M., Kim, H., Lee, J.K., Kim, J.: Learning to discover cross-domain relations with generative adversarial networks. In: Precup, D., Teh, Y.W. (eds.) Proceedings of the 34th International Conference on Machine Learning. Proceedings of Machine Learning Research, 06–11 August 2017, PMLR, International Convention Centre, Sydney, Australia, vol. 70, pp. 1857–1865 (2017), http://proceedings.mlr.press/v70/kim17a.html
12. Kingma, D.P., Ba, J.L.: Adam: a method for stochastic optimization. In: International Conference on Learning Representations (2015)
13. Lample, G., Zeghidour, N., Usunier, N., Bordes, A., Denoyer, L., et al.: Fader networks: manipulating images by sliding attributes. In: Advances in Neural Information Processing Systems, pp. 5963–5972 (2017)
14. Li, M., Zuo, W., Zhang, D.: Deep identity-aware transfer of facial attributes. arXiv preprint arXiv:1610.05586 (2016)
15. Liu, M.Y., Breuel, T., Kautz, J.: Unsupervised image-to-image translation networks. In: Advances in Neural Information Processing Systems, pp. 700–708 (2017)
16. Liu, Z., Luo, P., Wang, X., Tang, X.: Deep learning face attributes in the wild. In: Proceedings of International Conference on Computer Vision (ICCV) (2015)
17. Lu, Y., Tai, Y.W., Tang, C.K.: Conditional cycleGAN for attribute guided face image generation. arXiv preprint arXiv:1705.09966 (2017)
18. Perarnau, G., van de Weijer, J., Raducanu, B., Álvarez, J.M.: Invertible conditional GANs for image editing. arXiv preprint arXiv:1611.06355 (2016)

19. Reed, S.E., Zhang, Y., Zhang, Y., Lee, H.: Deep visual analogy-making. In: Advances in Neural Information Processing Systems, pp. 1252–1260 (2015)
20. Ronneberger, O., Fischer, P., Brox, T.: U-Net: convolutional networks for biomedical image segmentation. In: Navab, N., Hornegger, J., Wells, W.M., Frangi, A.F. (eds.) MICCAI 2015. LNCS, vol. 9351, pp. 234–241. Springer, Cham (2015). https://doi.org/10.1007/978-3-319-24574-4_28
21. Shen, W., Liu, R.: Learning residual images for face attribute manipulation. In: IEEE Conference on Computer Vision and Pattern Recognition (CVPR), pp. 1225–1233. IEEE (2017)
22. Simonyan, K., Zisserman, A.: Very deep convolutional networks for large-scale image recognition. In: International Conference on Learning Representations (2015)
23. Taigman, Y., Polyak, A., Wolf, L.: Unsupervised cross-domain image generation. arXiv preprint arXiv:1611.02200 (2016)
24. Upchurch, P., Gardner, J., Bala, K., Pless, R., Snavely, N., Weinberger, K.Q.: Deep feature interpolation for image content changes. arXiv preprint arXiv:1611.05507 (2016)
25. Wang, C., Wang, C., Xu, C., Tao, D.: Tag disentangled generative adversarial network for object image re-rendering. In: Proceedings of the Twenty-Sixth International Joint Conference on Artificial Intelligence. IJCAI, pp. 2901–2907 (2017)
26. Wang, T.C., Liu, M.Y., Zhu, J.Y., Tao, A., Kautz, J., Catanzaro, B.: High-resolution image synthesis and semantic manipulation with conditional GANs. In: IEEE Conference on Computer Vision and Pattern Recognition (CVPR) (2018)
27. Xiao, T., Hong, J., Ma, J.: DNA-GAN: learning disentangled representations from multi-attribute images. In: International Conference on Learning Representations, Workshop (2018)
28. Yi, Z., Zhang, H., Tan, P., Gong, M.: DualGAN: unsupervised dual learning for image-to-image translation. In: The IEEE International Conference on Computer Vision (ICCV), October 2017
29. Zhao, B., Chang, B., Jie, Z., Sigal, L.: Modular generative adversarial networks. arXiv preprint arXiv:1804.03343 (2018)
30. Zhou, S., Xiao, T., Yang, Y., Feng, D., He, Q., He, W.: GeneGAN: learning object transfiguration and attribute subspace from unpaired data. In: Proceedings of the British Machine Vision Conference (BMVC) (2017). http://arxiv.org/abs/1705.04932
31. Zhu, J.-Y., Krähenbühl, P., Shechtman, E., Efros, A.A.: Generative visual manipulation on the natural image manifold. In: Leibe, B., Matas, J., Sebe, N., Welling, M. (eds.) ECCV 2016. LNCS, vol. 9909, pp. 597–613. Springer, Cham (2016). https://doi.org/10.1007/978-3-319-46454-1_36
32. Zhu, J.Y., Park, T., Isola, P., Efros, A.A.: Unpaired image-to-image translation using cycle-consistent adversarial networks. In: Proceedings of International Conference on Computer Vision (ICCV) (2017)
33. Zhu, J.Y., et al.: Toward multimodal image-to-image translation. In: Advances in Neural Information Processing Systems, pp. 465–476 (2017)

Dynamic Filtering with Large Sampling Field for ConvNets

Jialin Wu[1,2](✉) (iD), Dai Li[1], Yu Yang[1], Chandrajit Bajaj[2], and Xiangyang Ji[1]

[1] The Department of Automation, Tsinghua University, Beijing 100084, China
{lidai15,yang-yu16}@mails.tsinghua.edu.cn, xyji@tsinghua.edu.cn
[2] The University of Texas at Austin, Austin, TX 78712, USA
{jialinwu,bajaj}@cs.utexas.edu

Abstract. We propose a dynamic filtering strategy with large sampling field for ConvNets (LS-DFN), where the position-specific kernels learn from not only the identical position but also multiple sampled neighbour regions. During sampling, residual learning is introduced to ease training and an attention mechanism is applied to fuse features from different samples. Such multiple samples enlarge the kernels' receptive fields significantly without requiring more parameters. While LS-DFN inherits the advantages of DFN [5], namely avoiding feature map blurring by positionwise kernels while keeping translation invariance, it also efficiently alleviates the overfitting issue caused by much more parameters than normal CNNs. Our model is efficient and can be trained end-to-end via standard back-propagation. We demonstrate the merits of our LS-DFN on both sparse and dense prediction tasks involving object detection, semantic segmentation and flow estimation. Our results show LS-DFN enjoys stronger recognition abilities in object detection and semantic segmentation tasks on VOC benchmark [8] and sharper responses in flow estimation on FlyingChairs dataset [6] compared to strong baselines.

Keywords: Large sampling field · Object detection
Semantic segmentation · Flow estimation

1 Introduction

Convolutional Neural Networks have recently made significant progress in both sparse prediction tasks including image classification [11,15,29], object detection [3,9,22] and dense prediction tasks such as semantic segmentation [2,16,18], flow estimation [7,13,27], *etc.* Generally, deeper [11,25,28] architectures provide richer features due to more trainable parameters and larger receptive fields.

J. Wu, D. Li and Y. Yang—Equal contribution.

Electronic supplementary material The online version of this chapter (https://doi.org/10.1007/978-3-030-01249-6_12) contains supplementary material, which is available to authorized users.

V. Ferrari et al. (Eds.): ECCV 2018, LNCS 11214, pp. 188–203, 2018.
https://doi.org/10.1007/978-3-030-01249-6_12

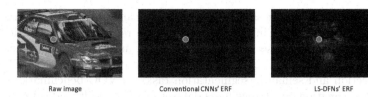

Raw image   Conventional CNNs' ERF   LS-DFNs' ERF

Fig. 1. Visualization of the effective receptive field (ERF). Yellow circle denotes the position on the object and the red region denotes the corresponding ERF. (Color figure online)

Most neural network architectures mainly adopt spatially shared kernels which work well in general cases. However, during training process, the gradients at each spatial position may not share the same descend direction, which can minimize loss at each position. These phenomena are quite ubiquitous when multiple objects appear in a single image in object detection or multiple object with different motion direction in flow estimation, which make the spatially shared kernels more likely to produce blurred feature maps.[1] The reason is that even though the kernels are far from optimal for every position, the global gradients, which are the spatially summation of the gradients over entire feature maps, can be close to zero. Because they are used in the update process, the back-propagation process should nearly not make progress.

Adopting position-specific kernels can alleviate the unshareable descend direction issue and take advantage of the gradients at each position (*i.e.* local gradients) since kernel parameters are not spatially shared. In order to keep the translation invariance, Brabandere *et al.* [5] propose a general paradigm called Dynamic Filter Networks (DFN) and verify them on moving MNIST dataset [26]. However, DFN [5] only generates the dynamic position-specific kernels for their own positions. As a result, the kernels can only receive the gradients from the identical position (*i.e.* square of kernel size), which is usually more unstable, noisy and harder to converge than normal CNN.

Meanwhile, properly enlarging receptive field is one of the most important concerns when designing CNN architectures. In many neural network architectures, adopting stacked convolutional layers with small kernels (*i.e.* 3×3) [25] is more preferable than larger kernels (*i.e.*7×7) [15], because the former one obtains the same receptive fields with fewer parameters. However, it has been shown that the effective receptive fields (ERF) [20] only occupies a fraction of the full theoretical receptive field due to some weak connections and some unactivated ReLU units. In practice, it has been shown that adopting dilation strategies [1] can further improve performance [3,16], which means that enlarging receptive fields in a single layer is still beneficial.

Therefore, we propose LS-DFN to alleviate the unshareable descend direction problem by utilizing dynamic position-specific kernels, and to enlarge the limited ERF by dynamic sampling convolution. As shown in Fig. 1, with ResNet-50 as

---

[1] Please see the examples and detailed analysis in the Supplementary Material.

pretrained model, adding a single LS-DFN layer can significantly enlarge the ERF, which further results in the improvement on representation abilities. On the other hand, since our kernels at each position are dynamically generated, LS-DFNs also benefit from the local gradients. We evaluate our LS-DFNs via object detection and semantic segmentation tasks on VOC benchmark [8] and optical flow estimation on FlyingChairs dataset [6]. The results indicate that the LS-DFNs are general and beneficial for both sparse and dense prediction tasks. We observe improvements over strong baseline models in both tasks without heavy burden in terms of running time using GPUs.

2   Related Work

Dynamic Filter Networks. Dynamic Filter Networks [5] are originally proposed by Brabandere *et al.* to provide custom parameters for different input data. This architecture is powerful and more flexible since the kernels are dynamically conditioned on inputs. Recently, several task-oriented objectives and extensions have been developed. Deformable convolution [4] can be seen as an extension of DFNs that discovers geometric-invariant features. Segmentation-aware convolution [10] explicitly takes advantage of prior segmentation information to refine feature boundaries via attention masks. Different from the models mentioned above, our LS-DFNs aim at constructing large receptive fields and receiving local gradients to produce sharper and more semantic feature maps.

Receptive Field. Wenjie *et al.* propose the concept of effective receptive field (ERF) and the mathematical measure using partial derivatives. The experimental results verify that the ERF usually occupies only a small fraction of the theoretical receptive field [20] which is the input region that an output unit depends on. Therefore, this has attracted lots of research especially in deep learning based computer vision. For instance, Chen *et al.* [1] propose dilated convolution with hole algorithm and achieve better results on semantic segmentation. Dai *et al.* [4] propose to dynamically learn the spatial offset of the kernels at each position so that those kernels can observe wider regions in the bottom layer with irregular shapes. However, some applications such as large motion estimation and large object detection even require larger ERF.

Residual Learning. Generally, residual learning reduces the difficulties of directly learning the objectives by learning their residual discrepancy of an identity function. ResNets [11] are proposed to learn residual features of identity mapping via short-cut connection and helps deepen CNNs to over 100 layers easily. There have been plenty of works adopting residual learning to alleviate the problem of divergence and generate richer features. Kim *et al.* [14] adopt residual learning to model multimodal data in visual QA. Long *et al.* [19] learn residual transfer networks for domain adaptation. Besides, Fei Wang *et al.* [29] apply residual learning to alleviate the problem of repeated features in attention model. We apply residual learning strategy to learn residual discrepancy for identical convolutional kernels. By doing so, we can ensure valid gradients' backpropagation so that the LS-DFNs can easily converge in real-world datasets.

Attention Mechanism. For the purpose of recognizing important features in deep learning unsupervisedly, attention mechanism has been applied to lots of vision tasks including image classification [29], semantic segmentation [10], action recognition [24,31], *etc.* In soft attention mechanisms [24,29,32], weights are generated to identify the important parts from different features using prior information. Sharma *et al.* [24] use previous states in LSTMs as prior information to have the network focus on more meaningful contents in the next frame and get better results for action recognition. Wang *et al.* [29] benefit from lower-level features and learn attention for higher-level feature maps in a residual manner. In contrast, our attention mechanism aims at combining features from multiple samples via learning weights for each positions' kernels at each sample.

3   Largely Sampled Dynamic Filtering

Firstly, we present the overall structure of our LS-DFN in Sect. 3.1, then introduce largely sampling strategies in Sect. 3.2. This design allows kernels at each position to take advantage of larger receptive fields and local gradients. Furthermore, attention mechanisms are utilized to enhance the performance of LS-DFNs as demonstrated in Sect. 3.3. Finally, Sect. 3.4 explains implementation details of our LS-DFNs, *i.e.* parameters reducing and residual learning techniques.

3.1   Network Overview

We introduce the LS-DFNs' overall architecture in Fig. 2. Our LS-DFNs consist of three branches: (1) the feature branch firstly produces C (*e.g.* 128) channels intermediate features; (2) the kernel branch, implemented as a convolution layers with $C'(C + k^2)$ channels where k is kernel size, generates position-specific kernels to sample multiple neighbour regions in feature branches and produces C' (*e.g.* 32) output channels' features; (3) the attention branch, implemented as convolution layers with $C'(s^2 + k^2)$ channels where s is the sampling size, outputs attention weights for each position's kernels and each sampling region. The LS-DFNs output feature maps with C' channels and preserve the original spatial dimensions H and W.

3.2   Largely Sampled Dynamic Filtering

This subsection demonstrates the proposed largely sampled dynamic filtering enjoying both large receptive fields and the local gradients. In particular, the LS-DFNs firstly generate position-specific kernels by the kernel branch. After that, LS-DFNs further convolve these generated kernels with features from multiple neighbor regions in the feature branch to obtain large receptive fields.

Denoting $\mathbf{X}^l$ as the feature maps from l^{th} layer(or intermediate features from feature branch) with shape (C, H, W), normal convolutional layer with spatially shared kernels $\mathbf{W}$ can be formulated as

$$\mathbf{X}_{y,x}^{l+1,v} = \sum_{u=1}^{C} \sum_{j=0}^{k-1} \sum_{i=0}^{k-1} \mathbf{X}_{y+j,x+i}^{l,u} \mathbf{W}_{y,x,j,i}^{v,u} \tag{1}$$

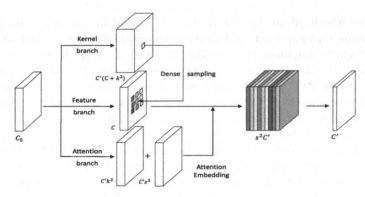

Fig. 2. Overview of the LS-DFN block. Our model consists of three branches: (1) the kernel branch generates position-specific kernels; (2) the feature branch generates features to be position-specifically convolved; (3) the attention branch generates attention weights. Same color indicates features correlated to the same spatial sampled regions.

where u, v denote the indices of the input and output channels, x, y denote the spatial coordinates and k indicates the kernel size.

In contrast, the LS-DFNs treat generated features in kernel branch, which is spatially dependent, as convolutional kernels. This scheme requires the kernel branch to generate kernels $\mathcal{W}(X^l)$ from X^l, which can maps the C-channel features in the feature branch to C'-channel ones[2]. Detailed kernel generation methods will be described in Sect. 3.4 and the supplementary material.

Aiming at larger receptive fields and more stable gradients, we not only convolve the generated position-specific kernels with features at the identical positions in the feature branch, but also sample their s^2 neighbor regions as additional features as shown in Eq. 2. Therefore, we have more learning samples for each position-specific kernel than DFN [5], resulting in more stable gradients. Also, since we obtain more diverse kernels (*i.e* position-specific) than conventional CNNs, we can robustly enrich the feature space.

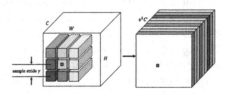

Fig. 3. Illustration of our sampling strategy. The red dot denotes the sampling point. Same color indicates features correlated to the same spatial sampled regions. (Color figure online)

As shown in Fig. 3, each position (*e.g* the red dot) outputs its own kernels in the kernel branch and uses the generated kernels to sample the corresponding multiple neighbour regions (*i.e* the cubes in different colors) in the feature branch. Assuming we have s^2 sampled regions for each position with sample stride γ, kernel size k, the sampling strategy outputs feature maps with shape (s^2, C', H, W) which obtain approximately $(s\gamma)^2$ times larger receptive fields.

---

[2] $\mathcal{W}(X^l)$ is kernels generated from X^l, and we omit (X^l) when there is no ambiguity.

Largely sampled dynamic filtering thus can be formulated as

$$\hat{\mathbf{X}}_{\alpha,\beta,y,x}^{l+1,v} = \sum_{u=1}^{C}\sum_{i=0}^{k-1}\sum_{j=0}^{k-1}\mathbf{X}_{\hat{y}+j,\hat{x}+i}^{l,u}\mathcal{W}_{y,x,j,i}^{v,u}, \tag{2}$$

where $\hat{x} = x+\alpha\gamma$ and $\hat{y} = y+\beta\gamma$ denote the coordinates of the center in sampled neighbor regions. $\mathcal{W}$ denotes the position-specific kernels generated by the kernel branch. And (α,β) is the index of sampled region with sampling stride γ. And when $s = 1$, that LS-DFNs reduce to the origin DFN.

3.3   Attention Mechanism

We present our methods to fuse features from multiple sampled regions at each position $\hat{\mathbf{X}}_{\alpha,\beta,y,x}^{l+1,v}$. A direct solution is to stack s^2 sampled features to form a (s^2C', H, W) tensor or perform a pooling operation on the sample dimension (*i.e* first dimension of $\hat{\mathbf{X}}^{l+1}$) as outputs. However the first choice violates translation invariance and the second choice is not aware of which samples are more important.

To address this issue, we present an attention mechanism to fuse those features via learning attention weights for each position's kernel at each sample. Since the attention weights are also position-specific, the resolution of output feature maps can be potentially preserved. Also, our attention mechanism benefits from residual learning.

Considering s^2 sampled regions and kernel size k in each position, we should have $s^2 \times k^2 \times C'$ attention weights for each position for $\hat{\mathbf{X}}^{l+1}$, which means

$$\widetilde{\mathbf{X}}_{\alpha,\beta,y,x}^{l+1,v} = \sum_{u=1}^{C}\sum_{j=0}^{k-1}\sum_{i=0}^{k-1}\mathbf{X}_{\hat{y}+j,\hat{x}+i}^{l,u}\mathcal{W}_{y,x,j,i}^{v,u}\mathbf{A}_{\hat{y},\hat{x},j,i}^{v,\alpha,\beta}, \tag{3}$$

where $\widetilde{\mathbf{X}}$ denotes weighted features.

However, Eq. 3 requires $s^2k^2C'HW$ attention weights, which is computationally costly and easily leads to overfitting. We thus split this task into learning position attention weights $\mathbf{A}^{pos} \in \mathbb{R}^{k^2 \times C' \times H \times W}$ for kernels at each position and learning sampling attention weights $\mathbf{A}^{sam} \in \mathbb{R}^{s^2 \times C' \times H \times W}$ at each sampled region. Then Eq. 3 becomes

$$\widetilde{\mathbf{X}}_{\alpha,\beta,y,x}^{l+1,v} = \mathbf{A}_{\alpha,\beta,y,x}^{sam,v}\sum_{u=1}^{C}\sum_{j=0}^{k-1}\sum_{i=0}^{k-1}\mathbf{X}_{\hat{y}+j,\hat{x}+i}^{l,u}\mathcal{W}_{y,x,j,i}^{v,u}\mathbf{A}_{\hat{y},\hat{x},j,i}^{pos,v}, \tag{4}$$

where $\hat{y}, \hat{x}$ share the same representations in Eq. 2.

Specifically, we use two CNN sub-branches to generate the attention weights for samples and positions respectively. The sampling attention sub-branch has $C' \times s^2$ output channels and the position attention sub-branch has $C' \times k^2$ output channels. The sample attention weights are generated from the sampling

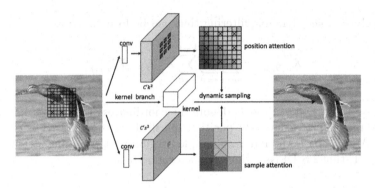

Fig. 4. At each position, we separately learn attention weights for each kernel and for each sample. Then, we combine features from multiple samples via these learned attention weights. Boxes with crosses denote the position to generate attention weights and red one denotes sampling position and black ones denote sampled positions.

position denoted by the red box with cross in Fig. 4 to coarsely predict the importance according to that position. And the position attention weights are generated from each sampled regions denoted by black boxes with cross to model fine-grained local detailed importance based on the sampled local features. Further, we manually add 1 to each attention weight to take advantage of residual learning.

Therefore, the number of attention weights will be reduced from $s^2k^2C'HW$ to $(s^2+k^2)C'HW$ as shown in Eq. 4. Obtaining Eq. 4, we finally combine different samples via attention mechanism as

$$\mathbf{X}_{y,x}^{l+1,v} = \sum_{\alpha=0}^{s-1}\sum_{\beta=0}^{s-1} \widetilde{\mathbf{x}}_{\alpha,\beta,y,x}^{l+1,v}. \tag{5}$$

Noting that feature maps from previous normal convolutional layers might still be noisy, the position attention weights help to filter such noise when applying largely sampled dynamic filtering to such feature maps. And the sample attention weights indicate how much contribution each neighbor region makes.

3.4   Dynamic Kernels Implementation Details

Reducing Parameter. Given that directly generating the position-specific kernels $\mathcal{W}$ with shape same as conventional CNN will require the shape of the kernels to be $(C'Ck^2, H, W)$ as shown in Eq. 2. Since C and C' can be relatively large (*e.g* up to 128 or 256), the required output channels in the kernel branch (*i.e* $C'Ck^2$) can easily get up to hundreds of thousands, which is computationally costly. Recently, several works have focused on reducing kernel parameters (*e.g* MobileNet [12]) by factorizing kernels into different parts to make CNNs efficient in modern mobile devices. Inspired by them and based on our LS-DFNs' case, we describe our proposed parameter reduction method. And we provide the evaluation and comparison with state-of-art counterparts in the supplementary material.

Inspecting that activated output feature maps in a layer usually share similar geometric characteristics across channels, we propose a novel kernel structure that splits the original kernel into two separate parts for the purpose of parameter reduction. As illustrated in Fig. 5, on the one hand, the $C \times 1 \times 1$ part $\mathcal{U}$ at each position, which will be placed into the spatial center of each $k \times k$ kernel, is used to model the differ-

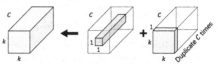

Fig. 5. Illustration of our parameter reducing method. In the first part, $C \times 1 \times 1$ weights are placed in the center of the corresponding kernel and in the second part k^2 weights are duplicated C times.

ence across channels. On the other hand, the $1 \times k \times k$ part $\mathcal{V}$ at each position is used to model the shared geometric characteristics within each channel.

Combining the above two parts together, our method generates kernels that map C-channel feature maps to C'-channel ones with kernel size k by only $C'(C + k^2)$ parameters at each position instead of $C'Ck^2$. Formally, the convolutional kernels used in Eq. 2 become

$$\mathcal{W}^{v,u}_{y,x,j,i} = \begin{cases} \mathcal{U}^{v,u}_{y,x} + \mathcal{V}^{v}_{y,x,j,i} & j = i = \lfloor \frac{k-1}{2} \rfloor \\ \mathcal{U}^{v,u}_{y,x} & \text{otherwise} \end{cases}. \tag{6}$$

Residual Learning. Equation 6 directly generates kernels, which easily leads to divergence in noisy real-world datasets. The reason is that only if the convolutional layers in kernel branch are well trained can we have good gradients back to feature branch and vice versa. Therefore, it's hard to train both of them from scratch simultaneously. Further, since kernels are not shared spatially, gradients at each position are more likely to be noisy, which makes kernel branch even harder to train and further hinders the training process of feature branch.

We adopt residual learning to address this issue, which learns the residual discrepancies of identical convolutional kernels. In particular, we add $\frac{1}{C}$ to each central position of the kernels as

$$\mathcal{W}^{v,u}_{y,x,j,i} = \begin{cases} \mathcal{U}^{v,u}_{y,x} + \mathcal{V}^{v}_{y,x,j,i} + \frac{1}{C} & j = i = \lfloor \frac{k-1}{2} \rfloor \\ \mathcal{U}^{v,u}_{y,x} & \text{otherwise} \end{cases}. \tag{7}$$

Initially, since the outputs of the kernel branch are close to zero, LS-DFN approximately averages features from feature branch. It guarantees gradients are sufficient and reliable for back propagation to the feature branch, which inversely benefits the training process of the kernel branch.

4 Experiments

We evaluate our LS-DFNs via object detection, semantic segmentation and optical flow estimation tasks. Our experiment results show that firstly with larger receptive fields, LS-DFN is more powerful on object recognition tasks. Secondly, with position-specific dynamic kernels and local gradients, LS-DFN produces much sharper optical flow. Besides, the comparison between ERF of the LS-DFNs and conventional CNNs is also presented in Sect. 4.1. This also verifies our aforementioned design target that LS-DFNs have larger ERF.

In the following subsections, we use $w/$ denotes with, w/o denotes without, $\mathcal{A}$ denotes attention mechanism and $\mathcal{R}$ denotes residual learning, C' denotes the number of dynamic features. Since C' in our LS-DFN is relatively small (*e.g.* 24) compared with conventional CNNs' settings, we optionally apply a post-conv layer to increase dimension to C_1 channels to match the conventional CNNs.

4.1 Object Detection

We use *PASCAL VOC* datasets [8] for object detection tasks. Following the protocol in [9], we train our LS-DFNs on the union of VOC 2007 trainval and VOC 2012 trainval and test on VOC 2007 and 2012 test sets. For evaluation, we use the standard mean average precision (mAP) scores with IoU thresholds at 0.5.

When applying our LS-DFN, we insert it into object detection networks such as R-FCN and CoupleNet. In particular, it is inserted right between the feature extractor and the detection head, producing C' dynamic features. It is noting that these dynamic features just serve as complementary features, which are concatenated with original features before fed into detection head. For R-FCN, we adopt ResNet as feature extractor and 7×7 bin R-FCN [7] with OHEM [32] as detection head. During training process, following [4], we resize images to have a shorter side of 600 pixels and adopt SGD optimizer. Following [17], we use pre-trained and fixed RPN proposals. Concretely, the RPN network is trained separately as in the first stage of the procedure in [22]. We train 110k iterations on single GPU with learning rate 10^{-3} in the first 80k and 10^{-4} in the next 30k.

As shown in Table 1, LS-DFN improves R-FCN baseline model's mAP over 1.5% with only $C' = 24$ dynamic features. This implies that the position-specific dynamic features are good supplement to the original feature space. And even though CoupleNets [33] have already explicitly considered global information with large receptive fields, experimental results demonstrate that adding our LS-DFN block is still beneficial.

Evaluation on Effective Receptive Field. We evaluate the effective receptive fields (ERF) in the subsection. As illustrated in Fig. 6, with ResNet-50 as backbone network, single additional LS-DFN layer provides much larger ERF than vanilla models thanks to the large sampling strategy. With larger ERFs, the networks can effectively observe larger region at each position thus can gather information and recognize objects more easily. Further, Table 1 experimentally verified the improvements on recognition abilities provided by our proposed LS-DFNs.

Table 1. Evaluation of the LS-DFN models on VOC 2007 and 2012 detection dataset. We use $s = 3$, $C' = 24$, $\gamma = 1$, $C_1 = 256$ with ResNet-101 as pre-trained networks in experiments when adding LS-DFN layers.

	mAP (%) on VOC12	mAP (%) on VOC07
R-FCN [3]	77.6	79.5
R-FCN+LS-DFN	**79.2**	**81.2**
Deform. Conv. [4]	-	80.6
CoupleNet [33]	80.4	81.7
CoupleNet+LS-DFN	**81.7**[†]	**82.3**

http://host.robots.ox.ac.uk:8080/anony-mous/BBHLEL.html

Table 2. Evaluation of numbers of samples s. The listed results are trained with residual learning and the post-conv layer is not applied. The experiments use R-FCN baseline and adopt ResNet-50 as pre-trained networks.

	$s = 1$	$s = 3$	$s = 5$
$C' = 16, w/\mathcal{A}$	72.1	78.2	78.1
$C' = 24, w/\mathcal{A}$	72.5	78.6	78.6
$C' = 32, w/\mathcal{A}$	72.9	78.6	78.5

Table 3. Evaluation of attention mechanism with different sample strides and numbers of dynamic features. The post-conv layer is not applied. The experiments use R-FCN baseline and adopt ResNet-50 as pre-trained networks.

	$\gamma = 1$		$\gamma = 2$	
	$w/\mathcal{A}$	$w/o\ \mathcal{A}$	$w/\mathcal{A}$	$w/o\ \mathcal{A}$
$C' = 16$	77.8	77.4	78.2	77.4
$C' = 24$	78.1	77.4	78.6	77.3
$C' = 32$	78.6	77.6	78.0	77.3

Table 4. Evaluaion of residual learning strategy in LS-DFN. $\mathcal{F}$ indicates that the model fails to converge and the post-conv layer is not applied. The experiments use R-FCN baseline and adopt ResNet-50 as pretrained networks.

		$w/\mathcal{A}$	$w/o\ \mathcal{A}$
$C' = 24$	$w/\mathcal{R}$	78.68	77.4
	$w/o\ \mathcal{R}$	68.1	$\mathcal{F}$
$C' = 32$	$w/\mathcal{R}$	78.6	77.6
	$w/o\ \mathcal{R}$	68.7	$\mathcal{F}$

Ablation Study on Sampling Size. We perform experiments to verify the advantages of applying more sampled regions in LS-DFN.

Table 2 evaluates the effect of sampling in the neighbour regions. In simple DFN model [5], where $s = 1$, though attention and residual learning strategy are adopted, the accuracy is still lower than R-FCN baseline (77.0%). We argue the reason is that simple DFN model has limited receptive field. Besides, kernels at each position only receive gradients on the identical position which easily leads to overfitting. With more sampled regions, we not only enlarge receptive field in feed-forward step, but also stabilize the gradients in back-propagation process. As shown in Table 2, when we take 3×3 samples, the mAP score surpluses original R-FCN [3] by 1.6% and gets saturated with respect to s when attention mechanism is applied.

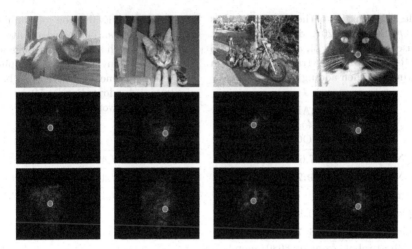

Fig. 6. Visualization on the effective receptive fields. The yellow circles denote the position on the objects. The first row presents input images. The second row contains the ERF figure from vanilla ResNet-50 model. The third row contains figures of the ERF with LS-DFNs. Best view in color.

Ablation Study on Attention Mechanism. We verify the effectiveness of the attention mechanism in Table 3 with different sample strides γ and number of dynamic feature channels C'. In the experiments without attention mechanism, max pooling in channel dimension is adopted. We observe that, in nearly all cases, the attention mechanism helps improve mAP by more than 0.5% in VOC2007 detection tasks. Especially as the number of dynamic feature channels C' increases (*i.e.* 32), the attention mechanism provides more benefits, increasing the mAP by 1%, which indicates that the attention mechanism can further strengthen our LS-DFNs.

Ablation Study on Residual Learning. We perform experiments to verify that with different numbers of dynamic feature channels, residual learning contributes a lot to the convergence of our LS-DFNs. As shown in Table 4, without utilizing residual learning, dynamic convolution models can hardly converge in real-world datasets. Even though they converge, the mAP is lower than expected. When our LS-DFNs learn in a residual fashion, however, the mAP increase about 10% on average.

Runtime Analysis. Since the computation at each position and sampled regions can be done in a parallel fashion, the running time for the LS-DFN models could have potential of only slightly slower than two normal convolutional layers with kernel size s^2.

4.2   Semantic Segmentation

We adopt the DeepLabV2 with CRF as the baseline model. The added LS-DFN layer receives input features from res5b layer in ResNet-101 and its output

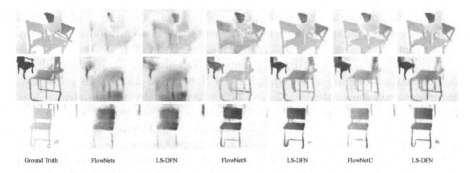

Ground Truth   FlowNetS   LS-DFN   FlowNetS   LS-DFN   FlowNetC   LS-DFN

Fig. 7. Examples of Flow estimation on FlyingChairs dataset. The columns with LS-DFN denote the results of a LS-DFN added to the eir left columns. With LS-DFN, much sharper and more detailed optical flow can be estimated.

Table 5. Performance comparison on the PASCAL VOC 2012 semantic segmentation test set. The average IoU (%) for each class and the overall IoU is reported.

Methods	Bg	Aero	Bike	Bird	**Boat**	Bottle	Bus	Car	Cat	**Chair**	Cow
DeepLabV2 + CRF	-	92.6	**60.4**	**91.6**	63.4	76.3	95.0	88.4	92.6	32.7	88.5
...w/o atrous +LS-DFN	95.3	92.3	57.2	91.1	68.8	76.8	95.0	88.8	92.1	35.0	88.5
...+ SegAware [10]	95.3	92.4	58.5	91.3	65.6	76.8	95.0	88.7	92.1	34.7	88.5
...+ LS-DFN[a]	**95.5**	**94.0**	58.5	91.3	**69.2**	**78.2**	95.4	**89.6**	**92.9**	38.4	89.9

Methods	Table	Dog	Horse	Motor	Person	Plant	Sheep	Sofa	Train	Tv	**All**
DeepLabV2 + CRF	67.6	89.6	92.1	87.0	**87.4**	63.3	88.3	60.0	86.8	74.5	79.7
... w/o atrous + LS-DFN	68.7	89.0	92.2	**87.1**	87.1	63.3	88.4	64.1	88.0	74.8	80.4
... + SegAware [10]	68.7	89.0	92.2	87.0	87.1	**63.4**	88.4	60.9	86.3	74.9	79.8
... + LS-DFN[a]	**70.2**	90.8	93.1	87.0	**87.4**	**63.4**	**89.5**	64.9	**88.9**	**75.8**	**81.1**

[a] http://host.robots.ox.ac.uk:8080/anonymous/5SYVME.html

features are concatenated to the res5c layer. For hyperparameters, we adopt $C' = 24$, $s = 5$, $\gamma = 3$, $k = 3$ and a 1×1 256-channel post-conv layer with shared weights at all three input scales. Following SegAware [10], we initialize the network with ImageNet model, then train on COCO trainval sets, and finetune on the augmented PASCAL images.

We report the segmentation results in Table 5. Our model achieves 81.2% overall IoU accuracy which is 1.4% superior to SegAware DeepLab-V2. Furthermore, the results on large objects like boat and sofa[3] are significantly improved (i.e. 3.6% in boat and 4.2% in sofa). The reason is that the LS-DFN layer is capable of significantly enlarging the effective receptive fields (ERF) so that the pixels inside the objects can utilize a much wider context, which is important since the visual clues of determining the correct categories for the pixels can be far away from the pixels themselves.

---

[3] We observe most boat and sofa instances occupy large area in images in PASCAL VOC test set.

It's worth noting that the performance of the chair category is also significantly improved thanks to the reduced false positive classification where many pixels in sofa instances are originally classified as chairs'.

We use $w/oatrous + \text{LS-DFN}$ to denote the DeepLabV2 model where all the dilated convolutions are replaced by LS-DFN block in Table 5. In particular, the different dilation rates 6, 12, 18, 24 are replaced by sample strides $\gamma = 2, 4, 6, 8$ in the LS-DFN layers. And all branches are implemented as single conv layers with $k = 3$, $s = 5$, $C' = 21$ for classification. Compared with original DeepLabV2 model, we observe a considerable improvement (*i.e.* from 79.7% to 80.4%) indicating that the LS-DFN layers are able to better model the contextual information within the large receptive fields thanks to the dynamic sampling kernels.

4.3   Optical Flow Estimation

We perform experiments on optical flow estimation using the FlyingChairs dataset [6]. This dataset is a synthetic one with optical flow ground truth and widely used in deep learning methods to learn the motion information. It consists of 22872 image pairs and corresponding flow fields. In experiments we use FlowNets(S) and FlowNetC [13] as our baseline models, though other complicated models are also applicable. All of the baseline models are fully-convolutional networks which firstly downsample input image pairs to learn semantic features then upsample the features to estimate optical flow.

In experiments, our LS-DFN model is inserted in a relative shallower layer to produce sharper optical flow images. Specifically, we adopt the third conv layer, where image pairs are merged into a single branch volume in FlowNetC model. We also use skip-connection to connect the LS-DFN outputs to the corresponding upsampling layer. In order to capture large displacement, we apply more samples in our LS-DFN layer. Concretely, we use 7×7 or 9×9 samples with a sample stride of 2 in our experiments. We follow similar training process in [7] for fair comparison[4]. As shown in Fig. 7, our LS-DFN models are able to output sharper and more accurate optical flow. We argue this is due to the large receptive fields and dynamic position-specific kernels. Since each position estimates optical flow with its own kernels, our LS-DFN can better identify the contours of the moving objects.

As shown in Fig. 8, LS-DFN model successfully relaxes the constraint of sharing kernels spatially and converges to a lower training loss in both FlowNets and FlowNetC models. That further indicates the advantages of local gradients when doing dense prediction tasks.

We use average End-Point-Error (aEPE) to quantitatively measure the performance of the optical flow estimation. As shown in Table 6, with a single LS-DFN layer added, the aEPEs decrease in all baseline models by a large margin. In FlowNets model, aEPE decreases by 0.79 which demonstrates the increased learning capacity and robustness of our LS-DFN model. Even though SegAware

---

[4] We use 300k iterations with double batchsize.

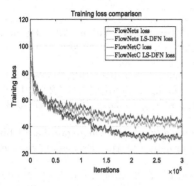

Fig. 8. Training loss of flow estimation. We use moving average with window size of 2k iterations when plotting the loss curve.

Table 6. aEPE and running time evaluation of optical flow estimation.

Model	aEPE	Time
Spynet [21]	2.63	-
EpicFlow [23]	2.94	-
DeepFlow [30]	3.53	-
PWC-Net [27]	2.26	-
FlowNetS [13]	3.67	6 ms
FlowNetS + LS-DFN, $s = 7$	**2.88**	23 ms
FlowNetS [13]	2.78	16 ms
FlowNetS + SegAware [10]	2.36	-
FlowNetS + LS-DFN, $s = 7$	**2.34**	34 ms
FlowNetC [13]	2.19	25 ms
FlowNetC + LS-DFN, $s = 7$	2.11	43 ms
FlowNetC + LS-DFN, $s = 9$	**2.06**	51 ms

attention model [10] explicitly takes advantage of boundary information which requires additional training data, our LS-DFN can still slightly outperforms them using FlowNetS as baseline model. With $s = 9$ and $\gamma = 2$, we have approximately 40 times larger receptive fields which allow the FlowNet models to easily capture large displacements in flow estimation task in FlyingChairs dataset.

5   Conclusion

This work introduces Dynamic Filtering with Large Sampling Field (LS-DFN) to learn dynamic position-specific kernels and takes advantage of very large receptive fields and local gradients. Thanks to the large ERF in a single layer, LS-DFNs have better performance in most general tasks. With local gradients and dynamic kernels, LS-DFNs are able to produce much sharper output features, which is beneficial especially in dense prediction tasks such as optical flow estimation.

Acknowledgements. Supported by National Key R&D Program of China under contract No.2017YFB1002202, Projects of International Cooperation and Exchanges NSFC with No. 61620106005, National Science Fund for Distinguished Young Scholars with No. 61325003, Beijing Municipal Science & Technology Commission Z181100008918014 and Tsinghua University Initiative Scientific Research Program.

References

1. Chen, L.C., Papandreou, G., Kokkinos, I., Murphy, K., Yuille, A.L.: DeepLab: semantic image segmentation with deep convolutional nets, atrous convolution, and fully connected CRFs. arXiv preprint arXiv:1606.00915 (2016)
2. Dai, J., He, K., Li, Y., Ren, S., Sun, J.: Instance-sensitive fully convolutional networks. In: Leibe, B., Matas, J., Sebe, N., Welling, M. (eds.) ECCV 2016. LNCS, vol. 9910, pp. 534–549. Springer, Cham (2016). https://doi.org/10.1007/978-3-319-46466-4_32
3. Dai, J., Li, Y., He, K., Sun, J.: R-FCN: object detection via region-based fully convolutional networks. In: Advances in Neural Information Processing Systems, pp. 379–387 (2016)
4. Dai, J., et al.: Deformable convolutional networks. arXiv preprint arXiv:1703.06211 (2017)
5. De Brabandere, B., Jia, X., Tuytelaars, T., Van Gool, L.: Dynamic filter networks. In: Neural Information Processing Systems (NIPS) (2016)
6. Dosovitskiy, A., et al.: FlowNet: Learning optical flow with convolutional networks. In: IEEE International Conference on Computer Vision (ICCV) (2015). http://lmb.informatik.uni-freiburg.de//Publications/2015/DFIB15
7. Dosovitskiy, A., et al.: FlowNet: Learning optical flow with convolutional networks. In: Proceedings of the IEEE International Conference on Computer Vision, pp. 2758–2766 (2015)
8. Everingham, M., Van Gool, L., Williams, C.K.I., Winn, J., Zisserman, A.: The pascal visual object classes (VOC) challenge. Int. J. Comput. Vis. **88**(2), 303–338 (2010)
9. Girshick, R.: Fast R-CNN. In: The IEEE International Conference on Computer Vision (ICCV), December 2015
10. Harley, A.W., Derpanis, K.G., Kokkinos, I.: Segmentation-aware convolutional networks using local attention masks. arXiv preprint arXiv:1708.04607 (2017)
11. He, K., Zhang, X., Ren, S., Sun, J.: Deep residual learning for image recognition. In: The IEEE Conference on Computer Vision and Pattern Recognition (CVPR), June 2016
12. Howard, A.G., et al.: MobileNets: efficient convolutional neural networks for mobile vision applications. CoRR abs/1704.04861 (2017)
13. Ilg, E., Mayer, N., Saikia, T., Keuper, M., Dosovitskiy, A., Brox, T.: FlowNet 2.0: evolution of optical flow estimation with deep networks. arXiv preprint arXiv:1612.01925 (2016)
14. Kim, J.H., et al.: Multimodal residual learning for visual QA. In: Advances in Neural Information Processing Systems, pp. 361–369 (2016)
15. Krizhevsky, A., Sutskever, I., Hinton, G.E.: Imagenet classification with deep convolutional neural networks. In: Pereira, F., Burges, C.J.C., Bottou, L., Weinberger, K.Q. (eds.) Advances in Neural Information Processing Systems 25, pp. 1097–1105. Curran Associates, Inc. (2012). http://papers.nips.cc/paper/4824-imagenet-classification-with-deep-convolutional-neural-networks.pdf
16. Li, Y., Qi, H., Dai, J., Ji, X., Wei, Y.: Fully convolutional instance-aware semantic segmentation. arXiv preprint arXiv:1611.07709 (2016)
17. Lin, T.Y., Dollár, P., Girshick, R., He, K., Hariharan, B., Belongie, S.: Feature pyramid networks for object detection. arXiv preprint arXiv:1612.03144 (2016)
18. Long, J., Shelhamer, E., Darrell, T.: Fully convolutional networks for semantic segmentation. In: The IEEE Conference on Computer Vision and Pattern Recognition (CVPR), June 2015

19. Long, M., Zhu, H., Wang, J., Jordan, M.I.: Unsupervised domain adaptation with residual transfer networks. In: Advances in Neural Information Processing Systems, pp. 136–144 (2016)
20. Luo, W., Li, Y., Urtasun, R., Zemel, R.S.: Understanding the effective receptive field in deep convolutional neural networks. In: NIPS (2016)
21. Ranjan, A., Black, M.J.: Optical flow estimation using a spatial pyramid network. arXiv preprint arXiv:1611.00850 (2016)
22. Ren, S., He, K., Girshick, R., Sun, J.: Faster R-CNN: towards real-time object detection with region proposal networks. In: Advances in Neural Information Processing Systems, pp. 91–99 (2015)
23. Revaud, J., Weinzaepfel, P., Harchaoui, Z., Schmid, C.: EpicFlow: edge-preserving interpolation of correspondences for optical flow. In: Proceedings of the IEEE Conference on Computer Vision and Pattern Recognition, pp. 1164–1172 (2015)
24. Sharma, S., Kiros, R., Salakhutdinov, R.: Action recognition using visual attention. arXiv preprint arXiv:1511.04119 (2015)
25. Simonyan, K., Zisserman, A.: Very deep convolutional networks for large-scale image recognition. arXiv preprint arXiv:1409.1556 (2014)
26. Srivastava, N., Mansimov, E., Salakhudinov, R.: Unsupervised learning of video representations using LSTMs. In: International Conference on Machine Learning, pp. 843–852 (2015)
27. Sun, D., Yang, X., Liu, M.Y., Kautz, J.: PWC-Net: CNNs for optical flow using pyramid, warping, and cost volume. arXiv preprint arXiv:1709.02371 (2017)
28. Szegedy, C., et al.: Going deeper with convolutions. In: Proceedings of the IEEE Conference on Computer Vision and Pattern Recognition, pp. 1–9 (2015)
29. Wang, F., et al.: Residual attention network for image classification. arXiv preprint arXiv:1704.06904 (2017)
30. Weinzaepfel, P., Revaud, J., Harchaoui, Z., Schmid, C.: DeepFlow: large displacement optical flow with deep matching. In: Proceedings of the IEEE International Conference on Computer Vision, pp. 1385–1392 (2013)
31. Wu, J., Wang, G., Yang, W., Ji, X.: Action recognition with joint attention on multi-level deep features. arXiv preprint arXiv:1607.02556 (2016)
32. Xu, K., et al.: Show, attend and tell: neural image caption generation with visual attention. In: International Conference on Machine Learning, pp. 2048–2057 (2015)
33. Zhu, Y., Zhao, C., Wang, J., Zhao, X., Wu, Y., Lu, H.: CoupleNet: coupling global structure with local parts for object detection

Pose Guided Human Video Generation

Ceyuan Yang[1]([⊠]), Zhe Wang[2], Xinge Zhu[1], Chen Huang[3], Jianping Shi[2], and Dahua Lin[1]

[1] CUHK-SenseTime Joint Lab, CUHK, Shatin, Hong Kong S.A.R.
yangceyuan@sensetime.com
[2] SenseTime Research, Beijing, China
[3] Carnegie Mellon University, Pittsburgh, USA

Abstract. Due to the emergence of Generative Adversarial Networks, video synthesis has witnessed exceptional breakthroughs. However, existing methods lack a proper representation to explicitly control the dynamics in videos. Human pose, on the other hand, can represent motion patterns intrinsically and interpretably, and impose the geometric constraints regardless of appearance. In this paper, we propose a pose guided method to synthesize human videos in a disentangled way: *plausible motion prediction* and *coherent appearance generation*. In the first stage, a Pose Sequence Generative Adversarial Network (PSGAN) learns in an adversarial manner to yield pose sequences conditioned on the class label. In the second stage, a Semantic Consistent Generative Adversarial Network (SCGAN) generates video frames from the poses while preserving coherent appearances in the input image. By enforcing semantic consistency between the generated and ground-truth poses at a high feature level, our SCGAN is robust to noisy or abnormal poses. Extensive experiments on both human action and human face datasets manifest the superiority of the proposed method over other state-of-the-arts.

Keywords: Human video generation · Pose synthesis
Generation adversarial network

1 Introduction

With the emergence of deep convolution networks, a large amount of generative models have been proposed to synthesize images, such as Variational Auto-Encoders [1] and Generative Adversarial Networks [2]. Meanwhile, video generation and video prediction tasks [3–6] have found big progress as well. Among them, the task of human video generation attracts increasing attention lately. One reason is that human video synthesis allows for many human-centric applications like avatar animation. On the other hand, generation of human videos/frames can act as a data augmentation method which largely relieves the

Electronic supplementary material The online version of this chapter (https:// doi.org/10.1007/978-3-030-01249-6_13) contains supplementary material, which is available to authorized users.

© Springer Nature Switzerland AG 2018
V. Ferrari et al. (Eds.): ECCV 2018, LNCS 11214, pp. 204–219, 2018.
https://doi.org/10.1007/978-3-030-01249-6_13

burden of manual annotations. This will speed up the development of a wide range of video understanding tasks such as action recognition.

Human video generation is a non-trivial problem itself. Unlike static image synthesis, the human video generation task not only needs to take care of the temporal smoothness constraint but also the uncertainty of human motions. Therefore, a proper representation of human pose and its dynamics plays an important role in the considered problem. Recent works attempted to model video dynamics separately from appearances. For instance, in [7] each frame is factorized into a stationary part and a temporally varying component. Vondrick *et al.* [8] untangled the foreground scene dynamics from background with a two-stream generative model. Saito *et al.* [9] generated a set of latent variables (each corresponds to an image frame) and learned to transform them into a video. Tulyakov *et al.* [10] generated a sequence of video frames from a sequence of random vectors, each consists of a content part and a motion part. All these methods show the promise of separate modeling of motion dynamics and appearances. However, motions cannot be controlled explicitly in these methods. The motion code is usually sampled from a random latent space, with no physical meaning about the targeted motion pattern.

Here we argue that for human video generation, to model human dynamics effectively and control motions explicitly, the motion representation should be interpretable and accessible. Inspired by the action recognition literature [11–14], human body skeletons are favorable in that they characterize the geometric body configuration regardless of the appearance difference, and their dynamics capture motion patterns interpretably. It is also worth noting that human skeletons can be easily obtained by many state-of-the-art human pose estimators (*e.g.* [15]).

Therefore, we propose a pose guided method to synthesize human videos. The method consists of two stages: *plausible motion prediction* and *coherent appearance generation*, generating the pose dynamics and corresponding human appearances separately. In the first stage, human pose is used to model various motion patterns. The Pose Sequence Generative Adversarial Network (PSGAN) is proposed to learn such patterns explicitly, conditioned on different action labels. In the second stage, a Semantic Consistent Generative Adversarial Network (SCGAN) is proposed to generate video frames given the generated pose sequence in the first stage and input image. Meanwhile, the semantic consistency between the generated and ground-truth poses is also enforced at a high feature level, in order to alleviate the influence of some noisy or abnormal poses. Experiments will show the efficacy and robustness of our method when generating a wide variety of human action and facial expression videos. Figure 1 illustrates the overall framework. We summarize the major contributions of as follows:

- We propose a Pose Sequence Generative Adversarial Network (PSGAN) for plausible motion prediction based on human pose, which allows us to model the dynamics of human motion explicitly.
- Semantic Consistent Generative Adversarial Network (SCGAN) is designed to synthesize coherent video frames given the generated pose and input image, with an effective mechanism for handling abnormal poses.

- Qualitative and quantitative results on human action and facial expression datasets show the superiority of the proposed method over prior arts. The controlled experiments also show our flexibility to manipulate human motions as well as appearances. Codes will be made publicly available.

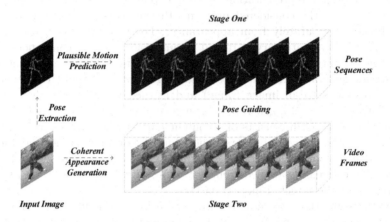

Fig. 1. The framework of our method. In the first stage, we extract the corresponding pose for an input image and feed the pose into our PSGAN to generate a pose sequence. In the second stage, SCGAN synthesizes photo-realistic video frames given the generated poses and input image

2   Related Work

Deep generative models have been extensively studied to synthesize natural images, typically using Variational Auto-Encoders (VAEs) [1] and Generative Adversarial Networks (GANs) [2]. Many follow-up works aim to improve the training of GANs [2] and thus enhance the generated image quality. The authors of [16] noted that the uncertainty of data distribution is likely to cause model collapse, and proposed to use convolutional networks to stabilize training. The works in [17,18] handle the problem of GAN training instability as well.

Another direction is to explore image generation in a conditioned manner. The pioneer work in [19] proposes a conditional GAN to generate images controlled by class labels or attributes. More recently, Ma *et al.* [20] proposed a pose guided person generation network to synthesize person images in arbitrary new poses. StackGAN [21] is able to generate photo-realistic images from some text descriptions. The works in [22–24] further generalize to learn to translate data from one domain to another in an unsupervised fashion. StarGAN [25] even allows to perform image-to-image translation among multiple domains with only a single model. Our proposed PSGAN and SCGAN are also designed conditional, generating a human pose sequence given an action label and then generating video frames given the pose sequence and input image. Our two conditional models are able to generate a continuous human video at one time rather than static images only. The SCGAN can also alleviate the impact of abnormal poses by learning semantic pose representations.

The task of video generation is intrinsically a much more challenging one than the image synthesis task, due to the requirement of foreground dynamics modeling and temporal smoothness constraint. During the past few years, it is with the access to powerful GPUs and the advent of deep convolution networks that video generation and video prediction [3–6] have gained large momentum as well. As an example, one GAN model with a spatio-temporal convolutional architecture is proposed in [8] to model the foreground scene dynamics in videos. Tulyakov *et al.* [10] also decomposed motion and content for video generation. In [26] future-frame predictions are made consistent with the pixel-wise flows in videos through a dual learning mechanism. Other works introduce recurrent networks into video generation (*e.g.* [27,28]). In line with these works, our method separately models the motion and appearance as well, using the PSGAN and SCGAN respectively. This enables us to control the motion patterns explicitly and interpretably, which to the best of our knowledge, is the first attempt in human video generation.

3 Methodology

3.1 Framework Overview

Given an input image of human body or face and a target action class (*e.g.*, *Skip*, *TaiChi*, *Jump*), our goal is to synthesize a video of human action or facial expression belonging to the target category and starting with the input image. We wish to explicitly control the motion patterns in the generated video while maintaining appearance coherence with the input. We here propose to generate human videos in a disentangled way: *plausible motion prediction* and *coherent appearance generation*. Figure 1 illustrates the overall framework of our method.

Similar to the action recognition literature [11–14], we use the human skeletons or human pose for representations of motion dynamics. Our method consists of two stages. In the first stage, we extract the pose from input image and the Pose Sequence GAN (PSGAN) is proposed to generate a temporally smooth pose sequence conditioned on the pose of input image and the target action class. In the second stage, we focus on appearance modeling and propose a Semantic Consistent GAN (SCGAN) to generate realistic and coherent video frames conditioned on the input image and pose sequence from stage one. The impact of noisy/abnormal poses is alleviated by maintaining semantic consistency between generated and ground-truth poses in high-level representation space. Details will be elaborated in the following sections.

3.2 Plausible Motion Prediction

In the first stage, the human pose extracted from input image together with the target action label is fed into our PSGAN to generate a sequence of poses.

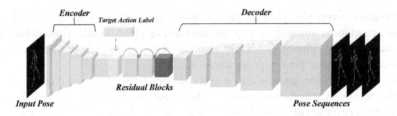

Fig. 2. Network architecture of our Pose Sequence GAN (PSGAN). PSGAN takes the input pose and target action label as input, and synthesizes pose sequences in an encoder-decoder manner. After the last residual block (red), the feature map is extended with a time dimension and then fed into the decoder which is composed of a series of fractionally-strided spatio-temporal convolution layers (Color figure online)

Obviously this is an ill-posed one-to-many problem with infinite possibilities. Our PSGAN learns from example pose sequences in the training set to mimic plausible motion patterns. Thus our learning objective is the modeling of rich motion patterns instead of the precise pose coordinates.

Pose Extraction. To extract the initial pose from input image, a state-of-the-art pose estimator in [15] is adopted to produce the coordinates of 18 key points. The pose is encoded by 18 heatmaps rather than coordinate vectors of the key points. Each heatmap is filled with 1 within a radius of 4 pixels around the corresponding key point and 0 elsewhere. Consequently, pose is actually represented as a $C = 18$ channel tensor. In this way, there is no need to learn how to map the key points into body part locations.

Pose Sequence GAN. Given the initial pose and the target action label, our PSGAN aims to synthesize a meaningful pose sequence at one time. As shown in Fig. 2, PSGAN adopts an encoder-decoder architecture. The $C \times W \times H$-sized pose is first encoded through several convolutional layers. The target action label is also inputted in the form of n-dimensional one-hot vector where n denotes the number of action types. After a few residual blocks, the two signals are embedded into common feature maps in the latent space. These feature maps will finally go through the decoder with a extended time dimension. The output is a $C \times T \times W \times H$-sized tensor via a series of fractionally-strided spatio-temporal convolution layers, where T denotes the number of time steps in the sequence. For the sake of better temporal modeling, the LSTM module [29] is integrated into our network as well. In summary, we define a generator G that transforms an input pose p into a pose sequence $\hat{P}$ conditioned on the target action label a, i.e., $G(p, a) \Rightarrow \hat{P}$. We train the generator G in an adversarial way - it competes with a discriminator D as the PatchGAN [30] which classifies local patches from the ground-truth and generated poses as real or fake.

LSTM Embedding. As is mentioned above, the decoder outputs a $C \times T \times W \times H$ tensor. It can be regarded as T tensors with size $C \times W \times H$, all of which are fed into a one-layer LSTM module for temporal pose modeling. Our experiments will demonstrate that the LSTM module stabilizes training and improves the quality of generated pose sequences.

Objective Function. As in [2], the objective functions of our PSGAN can be formulated as follows:

$$\mathcal{L}_{adv}^{D} = \mathbb{E}_{P}[\log D(P)] + \mathbb{E}_{p,a}[\log(1 - D(G(p,a)))], \qquad (1)$$

$$\mathcal{L}_{adv}^{G} = \mathbb{E}_{p,a}[\log(D(G(p,a)))], \qquad (2)$$

where $\mathcal{L}_{adv}^{D}$ and $\mathcal{L}_{adv}^{G}$ denote the adversarial loss terms for discriminator D and generator G, respectively. The discriminator D aims to distinguish between the generated pose sequence $G(p,a)$ and ground-truth P. Moreover, we find adding a reconstruction loss term can stabilize the training process. The reconstruction loss is given below:

$$\mathcal{L}_{rec} = \lambda_{rec}||(P - G(p,a)) \odot (\alpha M + 1)||_1, \qquad (3)$$

where M denotes the mask for each of the key point heatmap, $\odot$ denotes pixels-wise multiplication and λ_{rec} is the weight for this $L1$ loss. The introduction of mask M is due to the heatmap sparsity and imbalance of each key point, which makes learning difficult. We use the ground-truth P as mask M to mask out the small region around each key point for loss computation. Note when the scaling factor $\alpha = 0$, this loss term is reduced to unweighted $L1$ loss.

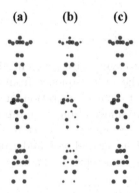

Fig. 3. Examples of abnormal poses. (a–c) show the ground-truth pose, generated poses with bigger/smaller key point responses, and with missing key points respectively

Abnormal Poses. Figure 3 shows some bad pose generation results where some key points seem bigger/smaller (b) than the ground-truth (a), or some key points seem missing (c) because of their weak responses. We call such cases as abnormal poses. For human beings however, abnormal poses might look weird at the first glance, but would hardly prevent us from imagining what the "true" pose is. This requires our network to grasp the semantic implication of human pose, and to alleviate the influence of small numerical differences.

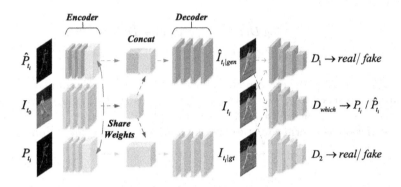

Fig. 4. Network architecture of our SCGAN in the second stage, where $\hat{P}_{t_i}, P_{t_i}, I_{t_i}$ respectively denote the pose generated by our method in stage one, ground-truth pose and the original image. Our generator has an encoder-decoder architecture and generates video frames conditioned on human poses P and the input image I_{t_0}. Discriminators D_1 and D_2 aim to distinguish whether the generated images are real, while D_{which} aims to tell which pose the frame is generated from (Color figure online)

3.3   Coherent Appearance Generation

In the second stage, we aim to synthesize coherent video frames conditioned on the input image as well as the pose sequence from stage one. Since the noisy or abnormal poses will affect image generation in this stage, those methods (*e.g.* [20]) to directly generate images from pose input may be unstable or even fail. Therefore, we propose a Semantic Consistent GAN (SCGAN) to impose semantic consistency between generated pose and ground-truth at a high feature level. By only imposing the consistency at high feature level, SCGAN can be robust to noisy pose inputs.

Conditional Generation. Our conditional image generation process is actually similar to that in recent work [20] which can generate person images controlled by pose. However, we have a major difference with this work: in [20] images are generated in two stages by synthesizing a coarse image first and then refining it; while our SCGAN generates results in one step, for all video frames over time at once. Specifically, given the input image I_{t_0} at time t_0 and the target pose P_{t_i} at time t_i, our generator $G(I_{t_0}, P_{t_i}) \Rightarrow \hat{I}_{t_i}$ is supposed to generate image $\hat{I}_{t_i}$ to keep the same appearance in I_{t_0} but on the new pose P_{t_i}. We design the discriminator D again to tell real image from fake to improve the image generation quality.

Semantic Consistency. As discussed before, the noisy or abnormal pose prediction $\hat{P}_{t_i}$ from the first stage will affect image generation in the second stage. Unfortunately, the ground-truth pose P_{t_i} does not exist during inference for pose correct purposes - it is only available for training. Therefore, it is necessary to teach training to properly handle abnormal poses with the guidance of ground-truth pose, in order to generalize to testing scenarios.

Through the observation of heatmaps of those abnormal poses, we find that they are often due to the small differences in corresponding key point responses, which will not contribute to large loss and thus incur small back-propagation gradients. As a matter of fact, there is no need to push the limit of the pose generation accuracy by PSGAN since the small errors should not affect how people interpret pose globally. Considering the pose prediction difference is inevitably noisy at the input layer or low-level feature layer, we propose to enforce the semantic consistency between abnormal poses and the ground-truth at the high-level feature layer.

Figure 4 shows our Semantic Consistent GAN that encapsulates this idea. We share weights in the last convolutional layer of two pose encoder networks (the yellow block), aiming to impose semantic consistent in the high-level feature space. Moreover, we generate video frames from both predicted pose and ground-truth pose to gain tolerance to pose noise. A new discriminator D_{which} is used to distinguish which pose the generated video frame is conditioned on. We further utilize the $L1$ reconstruction loss to stabilize the training process.

Full Objective Function. As shown in Fig. 4, our final objective is to generate video frames from two pose streams and keep their semantic consistency in an adversarial way. Specifically, G_1 generates the image $I_{t_i|gen}$ at time t_i conditioned on input image I_{t_0} and the pose $\hat{P}_{t_i}$ generated by PSGAN. G_2 generates $I_{t_i|gt}$ in the same way but uses the ground-truth pose for image generation.

$$G_1(I_{t_0}, \hat{P}_{t_i}) \Rightarrow I_{t_i|gen}, \tag{4}$$

$$G_2(I_{t_0}, P_{t_i}) \Rightarrow I_{t_i|gt}. \tag{5}$$

There are three discriminators defined as follows: D_1 and D_2 aim to distinguish between real image and fake when using predicted pose and ground-truth pose respectively; D_{which} aims to judge which pose the generated image is conditioned on. Then we easily arrive at the full objective function for our model training as follows:

$$\mathcal{L}_{D_{which}} = \mathbb{E}[\log(D_{which}(I_{t_i|gt}))] + \mathbb{E}[\log(1 - D_{which}(I_{t_i|gen}))], \quad (6)$$

$$\mathcal{L}_{D_1} = \mathbb{E}[\log(D_1(I_{t_i}))] + \mathbb{E}[\log(1 - D_1(I_{t_i|gen}))], \quad (7)$$

$$\mathcal{L}_{D_2} = \mathbb{E}[\log(D_2(I_{t_i}))] + \mathbb{E}[\log(1 - D_2(I_{t_i|gt}))], \quad (8)$$

$$\mathcal{L}_{G_1} = \mathbb{E}[\log(D_1(I_{t_i|gen}))] + \mathbb{E}[\log(D_{which}(I_{t_i|gen}))], \quad (9)$$

$$\mathcal{L}_{G_2} = \mathbb{E}[\log(D_2(I_{t_i|gt}))]. \quad (10)$$

Since the ground-truth pose guided images $I_{t_i|gt}$ is *real* for D_{which}, the gradient of D_{which} is not propagated back to G_2 in Eq. (10).

3.4   Implementation Details

For our detailed network architecture, all of the generators (G, G_1, G_2) apply 4 convolution layers with a kernel size of 4 and the stride of 2 for downsampling. In the decoding step of stage one, transposed convolution layers with stride of 2 are adopted for upsampling, while normal convolutions layers together with interpolation operations take place of transposed convolution layers in the second stage. The feature map of the red block in Fig. 2 is extended with a time dimension $(C \times W \times H \Rightarrow C \times 1 \times W \times H)$ for the decoder of PSGAN. The discriminators (D, D_1, D_2, D_{which}) are PatchGANs [30] to classify whether local image patches are real or fake. Besides, ReLU [31] serves as the activation function after each layer and the instance normalization [32] is used in all networks. Several residual blocks [33] are leveraged to encode the concatenated feature representations jointly. For the last layer we apply tanh activation function. In addition, we use standard GRU in our PSGAN, without further investigating how the different structures of LSTM can improve pose sequence generation.

We implement all models using PyTorch, and use an ADAM [34] optimizer with a learning rate of 0.001 in all experiments. The batch size in stage one is 64, and 128 in the second stage. All reconstruction loss weights are empirically set to 10. The scaling factor α in Eq. (3) is chosen from 0 to 100, which only affects the convergence speed. We empirically set the scaling factor as 10 and 20 on the human action and facial expression dataset respectively. The PSGAN is trained to generate pose sequences. In the second stage, both the generated and ground-truth poses are utilized to train the SCGAN to learn robust handling of noisy poses. Only the generated pose is fed into SCGAN for inference.

4   Experiments

In this section, we present video generation results on both human action and facial datasets. Qualitative and quantitative comparisons are provided to show our superiority over other baselines and state-of-the-arts. User study is also conducted with a total of 50 volunteers to support our improvements. Ablation study for our two generation stages (for pose and video) is further included to show their efficacy.

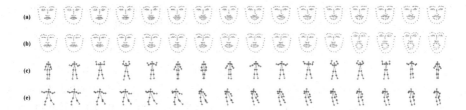

Fig. 5. Example pose sequences generated by our PSGAN with class labels of *Happy* (a), *Surprise* (b), *Wave* (c) and *TaiChi* (d), respecitvely

4.1 Datasets

Our experiments are conducted not only on the human action dataset but also on facial expression dataset, where facial landmarks act as the pose to guide the generation of facial expression videos. Accordingly, we collected the Human Action Dataset and Human Facial Dataset as detailed below. For all experiments, the RGB images are scaled to 128 × 128 pixels while pose images are scaled to 64 × 64 pixels.

- Human Action Dataset comes from the UCF101 [35] and Weizmann Action database [36], including 198848 video frames of 90 persons performing 22 actions. Human pose is extracted by the method in [15] with 18 key points.
- Human Facial Dataset is from the $CK+$ dataset [37]. We consider 6 facial expressions: *angry, disgust, fear, happy, sadness* and *surprise*, corresponding to 60 persons and 60000 frames. The facial pose is annotated with 68 key points.

4.2 Evaluation of Pose Generation

Qualitative Evaluation. As mentioned in Sect. 3.3, our PSGAN focuses on the generation of various pose motions. For qualitative comparisons, we follow the post-processing step in [15] to locate the maximum response region in each pose heatmap. Note such pose-processing is only used for visualization purposes. Figure 5 shows some examples of the generated pose sequences for both human face and body. We can see that the pose sequences change in a smooth and typical way under each action scenario.

Quantitative Comparison. Recall that our final video generator is tolerant to the tiny pose difference in stage one. Therefore, we measure the quality of generated pose sequences by calculating the average pairwise $L2$ distance rather than Euclidean norm between the generated and the ground-truth poses. Smaller distance indicates better pose quality.

We compare three of our PSGAN variants: (1) PSGAN trained with the $L1$-norm loss rather than adversarial loss, (2) PSGAN trained without the LSTM module, and (3) the full PSGAN model with a GRU module. Table 1 indicates

Table 1. Quantitative comparison of pose generation baselines

Average $L2$	Action	Facial exp.
Ground-truth	0	0
PSGAN-$L1$	0.0124	0.0078
PSGAN w/o LSTM	0.0072	0.0062
PSGAN	**0.0064**	**0.0051**

Table 2. User study of pose generation baselines on human action dataset

Distribution of ranks	1	2	3	4
Ground-truth	0.38	0.36	0.12	0.14
PSGAN-$L1$	0.09	0.08	0.32	0.51
PSGAN w/o LSTM	0.21	0.16	0.43	0.20
PSGAN	0.32	0.40	0.13	0.15

that it is better to train our pose generator with the adversarial loss than with the simple $L1$-norm loss. Also important is the temporal modeling by the GRU or LSTM module that improves the quality of pose sequences.

User Study. Table 2 includes the user study results for our three PSGAN variants on human action dataset. For each variant, we generate 25 pose sequences with 20 actions and the time step of 32. All generated pose sequences are shown to 50 users in a random order. Users are then asked to rank the baselines based on their quality from 1 to 4 (best to worst). The distribution for the ranks of each baseline is calculated for comparison. As shown in Table 2, our full PSGAN model has the highest chance to rank top. While the variants of PSGAN w/o LSTM and PSGAN-$L1$ tend to rank lower, indicating the importance of temporal and adversarial pose modeling again.

4.3   Evaluation of Video Generation

Qualitative Comparison. Given the generated pose sequence in the first stage and the input image, our SCGAN is responsible for the generation of photo-realistic video frames. We mainly compare our method with state-of-the-art video generation methods VGAN [8] and MoCoGAN [10]. They are trained on the same human action and facial datasets with hyper-parameters tuned to their best performance. The visual results for example action and facial expression classes *Wave*, *Taichi* and *Superised* are shown in Fig. 6.

It is clear that our method generates much sharper and more realistic video frames than VGAN and MoCoGAN. For the simple action *Wave*, our method performs better or equally well with the strong competitors. For the difficult action *TaiChi* with complex motion patterns, our advantage is evident - the pose dynamics are accurately captured and rendered to visually pleasing images. This confirms the necessity of our pose-guided video generation which benefits from explicit pose motion modeling rather than using a noise vector in VGAN and MoCoGAN. Our supplementary material provides more visual results.

Quantitative Comparison. Table 3 shows the measures of Inception Score [38] (IS) (and its variance) for different methods. Larger IS value indicates better

Table 3. Comparison of IS for video generation baselines

IS	Action	Facial exp.
VGAN [8]	2.73 ± 0.21	1.68 ± 0.17
MoCoGAN [10]	4.02 ± 0.27	1.83 ± 0.08
Ours	**5.70 ± 0.19**	**1.92 ± 0.12**

Table 4. User study for video generation baselines

Winning percentage	Action	Facial exp.
Ours/MCGAN [10]	0.83/0.17	0.86/0.14
Ours/VGAN [8]	0.88/0.12	0.93/0.07

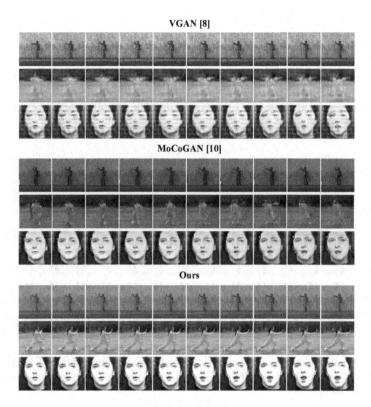

Fig. 6. Generated video frames for example action and facial expression classes *Wave*, *Taichi* and *Superised* by VGAN [8], MoCoGAN [10] and our method

performance. Such quantitative results are in line with our visual evaluations where our method outperforms others by a large margin.

User Study. We further conduct a user study where each method generates 50 videos for comparisons. Results are provided to users in pairs and in random order. The users are then asked to select the winner (looks more realistic) from the paired methods and we calculate the winning percentage for each method. Table 4 demonstrates that most of the time users would choose our method as the winner over MoCoGAN and VGAN.

Table 5. SSIM and LPIPS measures for our training alternatives

SSIM/LPIPS	Action	Facial exp.
Static	0.66/0.063	0.77/0.025
SCGAN-gen	0.73/0.083	0.89/0.038
SCGAN-gt	0.89/0.040	0.92/0.024
SCGAN	0.87/0.041	0.91/0.026

Controlled Generation Results. Figure 7 validates our capability of explicit pose modeling and good generalization ability by controlled tests: generate different action videos with a fixed human appearance, and generate videos with a fixed action for different humans. Successes are found for both human action (a–c) and facial expression (d–f) cases, showing the benefits of separate modeling for pose and appearance.

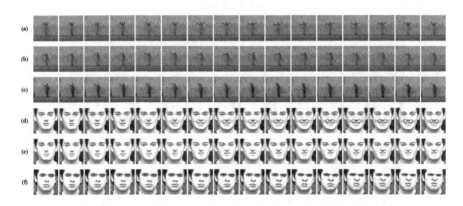

Fig. 7. Controlled video generation with pose and appearance: different poses for the same human (a–b for body, d–e for face), and same pose on different humans (b–c for body, e–f for face)

4.4 Ablation Study

One major feature of our human video generator is its reliance on generated pose $\hat{P}_{t_i}$. It is worth noting that there is no ground-truth pose P_{t_i} during inference. Only for training, we use the available P_{t_i} to enforce the semantic consistency with respect to generated pose $\hat{P}_{t_i}$. To highlight the impact of the semantic consistency constraint, we compare several training alternatives as follows:

- Static generator: video generation by repeating the first frame
- SCGAN-gen: video generation guided by generated pose $\hat{P}_{t_i}$ only.
- SCGAN-gt: video generation guided by ground-truth pose P_{t_i} only.
- SCGAN: video generation guided by both $\hat{P}_{t_i}$ and P_{t_i} as shown in Fig. 4.

The baseline of static generator simply constructs a video by repeating the first frame thus involves no predictions. It acts as a performance lower bound here. Sometimes its performance can be not too bad in those short videos or videos with little change (generating a static video will not be heavily penalized in these cases).

Figure 8 visually compares the baselines of SCGAN-gen and SCGAN. The full SCGAN model can generate sharper and more photo-realistic results, especially in the **mouth** (facial expression) and **waist** (human action) regions. This suggests the efficacy of enforcing semantic consistency between the generated and ground-truth poses. Using the generated pose only can be noisy and thus hinder the final video quality.

We also evaluate performance by computing the SSIM (structural similarity index measure) [39] and LPIPS (Learned Perceptual Image Patch Similarity) scores [40]. The SSIM score focuses on structural similarity between the generated image and ground-truth, while the LPIPS score cares more about perceptual similarity. Higher SSIM score and smaller LPIPS score indicates better performance.

Table 5 shows that SCGAN indeed outperforms SCGAN-gen quantitatively and stands close to the SCGAN-gt using ground-truth pose. The semantic consistency constraint plays a key role in this improvement, because it can alleviate the influence of abnormal poses during the pose guided image generation process. When compared to the static video generator, our method outperforms by generating a variety of motion patterns.

Fig. 8. Visual comparisons of SCGAN (a) and SCGAN-gen (b) on facial expression and human action datasets

5   Conclusion and Future Work

This paper presents a novel method to generate human videos in a disentangled way. We show the important role of human pose for this task, and propose a pose-guided method to generate realistic human videos in two stages. Quantitative and qualitative results on human action and face datasets demonstrate the superiority of our method, which is also shown to be able to manipulate human pose and appearance explicitly. Currently, our method is limited to cropped human or face images since the detectors are missing. In the future, we will integrate detectors as an automatic pre-processing step which will enable multi-person video generation.

Acknowledgement. This work is partially supported by the Big Data Collaboration Research grant from SenseTime Group (CUHK Agreement No. TS1610626).

References

1. Kingma, D.P., Welling, M.: Auto-encoding variational bayes. In: ICLR (2014)
2. Goodfellow, I., et al.: Generative adversarial nets. In: NIPS. (2014)
3. Srivastava, N., Mansimov, E., Salakhudinov, R.: Unsupervised learning of video representations using LSTMs. In: ICML (2015)
4. Finn, C., Goodfellow, I., Levine, S.: Unsupervised learning for physical interaction through video prediction. In: NIPS (2016)
5. Mathieu, M., Couprie, C., LeCun, Y.: Deep multi-scale video prediction beyond mean square error. In: ICLR (2016)
6. Oh, J., Guo, X., Lee, H., Lewis, R.L., Singh, S.: Action-conditional video prediction using deep networks in atari games. In: NIPS (2015)
7. Denton, E.L., et al.: Unsupervised learning of disentangled representations from video. In: NIPS (2017)
8. Vondrick, C., Pirsiavash, H., Torralba, A.: Generating videos with scene dynamics. In: NIPS (2016)
9. Saito, M., Matsumoto, E., Saito, S.: Temporal generative adversarial nets with singular value clipping. In: ICCV (2017)
10. Tulyakov, S., Liu, M.Y., Yang, X., Kautz, J.: MoCoGAN: decomposing motion and content for video generation. arXiv preprint arXiv:1707.04993 (2017)
11. Hodgins, J.K., O'Brien, J.F., Tumblin, J.: Perception of human motion with different geometric models. IEEE Trans. Vis. Comput. Graph. **4**, 307–316 (1998)
12. Yan, S., Xiong, Y., Lin, D.: Spatial temporal graph convolutional networks for skeleton-based action recognition. In: AAAI (2018)
13. Du, Y., Wang, W., Wang, L.: Hierarchical recurrent neural network for skeleton based action recognition. In: CVPR (2015)
14. Vemulapalli, R., Arrate, F., Chellappa, R.: Human action recognition by representing 3D skeletons as points in a lie group. In: CVPR (2014)
15. Cao, Z., Simon, T., Wei, S.E., Sheikh, Y.: Realtime multi-person 2D pose estimation using part affinity fields. In: CVPR (2017)
16. Radford, A., Metz, L., Chintala, S.: Unsupervised representation learning with deep convolutional generative adversarial networks. In: ICLR (2015)
17. Arjovsky, M., Chintala, S., Bottou, L.: Wasserstein GAN. arXiv preprint arXiv:1701.07875 (2017)
18. Gulrajani, I., Ahmed, F., Arjovsky, M., Dumoulin, V., Courville, A.C.: Improved training of Wasserstein GANs. In: NIPS (2017)
19. Mirza, M., Osindero, S.: Conditional generative adversarial nets. arXiv preprint arXiv:1411.1784 (2014)
20. Ma, L., Jia, X., Sun, Q., Schiele, B., Tuytelaars, T., Van Gool, L.: Pose guided person image generation. In: NIPS (2017)
21. Zhang, H., et al.: StackGAN: text to photo-realistic image synthesis with stacked generative adversarial networks. In: ICCV (2017)
22. Zhu, J.Y., Park, T., Isola, P., Efros, A.A.: Unpaired image-to-image translation using cycle-consistent adversarial networks. In: ICCV (2017)
23. Yi, Z., Zhang, H., Tan, P., Gong, M.: DualGAN: unsupervised dual learning for image-to-image translation. In: ICCV (2017)

24. Kim, T., Cha, M., Kim, H., Lee, J., Kim, J.: Learning to discover cross-domain relations with generative adversarial networks. arXiv preprint arXiv:1703.05192 (2017)

25. Choi, Y., Choi, M., Kim, M., Ha, J.W., Kim, S., Choo, J.: StarGAN: unified generative adversarial networks for multi-domain image-to-image translation. In: CVPR (2018)

26. Liang, X., Lee, L., Dai, W., Xing, E.P.: Dual motion GAN for future-flow embedded video prediction. In: ICCV (2017)

27. Fragkiadaki, K., Levine, S., Felsen, P., Malik, J.: Recurrent network models for human dynamics. In: ICCV. IEEE (2015)

28. Zhou, Y., Berg, T.L.: Learning temporal transformations from time-lapse videos. In: Leibe, B., Matas, J., Sebe, N., Welling, M. (eds.) ECCV 2016. LNCS, vol. 9912, pp. 262–277. Springer, Cham (2016). https://doi.org/10.1007/978-3-319-46484-8_16

29. Hochreiter, S., Schmidhuber, J.: Long short-term memory. Neural Comput. **9**, 1735–1780 (1997)

30. Isola, P., Zhu, J.Y., Zhou, T., Efros, A.A.: Image-to-image translation with conditional adversarial networks. In: CVPR (2017)

31. Nair, V., Hinton, G.E.: Rectified linear units improve restricted Boltzmann machines. In: ICML (2010)

32. Ulyanov, D., Vedaldi, A., Lempitsky, V.S.: Instance normalization: the missing ingredient for fast stylization. arXiv preprint arXiv:1607.08022 (2016)

33. He, K., Zhang, X., Ren, S., Sun, J.: Deep residual learning for image recognition. In: CVPR (2016)

34. Kingma, D.P., Ba, J.: Adam: a method for stochastic optimization. In: ICLR (2014)

35. Soomro, K., Zamir, A.R., Shah, M.: UCF101: a dataset of 101 human actions classes from videos in the wild. arXiv preprint arXiv:1212.0402 (2012)

36. Blank, M., Gorelick, L., Shechtman, E., Irani, M., Basri, R.: Actions as space-time shapes. In: ICCV. IEEE (2005)

37. Lucey, P., Cohn, J.F., Kanade, T., Saragih, J., Ambadar, Z., Matthews, I.: The extended Cohn-Kanade dataset (CK+): a complete dataset for action unit and emotion-specified expression. In: 2010 IEEE Computer Society Conference on Computer Vision and Pattern Recognition Workshops (CVPRW). IEEE (2010)

38. Salimans, T., Goodfellow, I., Zaremba, W., Cheung, V., Radford, A., Chen, X.: Improved techniques for training GANs. In: NIPS (2016)

39. Wang, Z., Bovik, A.C., Sheikh, H.R., Simoncelli, E.P.: Image quality assessment: from error visibility to structural similarity. In: IEEE TIP (2004)

40. Zhang, R., Isola, P., Efros, A.A., Shechtman, E., Wang, O.: The unreasonable effectiveness of deep features as a perceptual metric. In: CVPR (2018)

Characterizing Adversarial Examples Based on Spatial Consistency Information for Semantic Segmentation

Chaowei Xiao[1]($\boxtimes$), Ruizhi Deng[2], Bo Li[3,4], Fisher Yu[4], Mingyan Liu[1], and Dawn Song[4]

[1] University of Michigan, Ann Arbor, USA
xiaocw@umich.edu
[2] Simon Fraser University, Burnaby, Canada
[3] UIUC, Champaign, USA
[4] UC Berkeley, Berkeley, USA

Abstract. Deep Neural Networks (DNNs) have been widely applied in various recognition tasks. However, recently DNNs have been shown to be vulnerable against adversarial examples, which can mislead DNNs to make arbitrary incorrect predictions. While adversarial examples are well studied in classification tasks, other learning problems may have different properties. For instance, semantic segmentation requires additional components such as dilated convolutions and multiscale processing. In this paper, we aim to characterize adversarial examples based on spatial context information in semantic segmentation. We observe that spatial consistency information can be potentially leveraged to detect adversarial examples robustly even when a strong adaptive attacker has access to the model and detection strategies. We also show that adversarial examples based on attacks considered within the paper barely transfer among models, even though transferability is common in classification. Our observations shed new light on developing adversarial attacks and defenses to better understand the vulnerabilities of DNNs.

Keywords: Semantic segmentation · Adversarial example · Spatial consistency

1 Introduction

Deep Neural Networks (DNNs) have been shown to be highly expressive and have achieved state-of-the-art performance on a wide range of tasks, such as speech recognition [20], image classification [24], natural language understanding [54], and robotics [32]. However, recent studies have found that DNNs are vulnerable

Electronic supplementary material The online version of this chapter (https://doi.org/10.1007/978-3-030-01249-6_14) contains supplementary material, which is available to authorized users.

© Springer Nature Switzerland AG 2018
V. Ferrari et al. (Eds.): ECCV 2018, LNCS 11214, pp. 220–237, 2018.
https://doi.org/10.1007/978-3-030-01249-6_14

to *adversarial examples* [7–9,17,31,38,40,45,47]. Such examples are intentionally perturbed inputs with small magnitude adversarial perturbation added, which can induce the network to make arbitrary incorrect predictions at test time, even when the examples are generated against different models [5,27,33,46]. The fact that the adversarial perturbation required to fool a model is often small and (in the case of images) imperceptible to human observers makes detecting such examples very challenging. This undesirable property of deep networks has become a major security concern in real-world applications of DNNs, such as self-driving cars and identity recognition systems [16,37]. Furthermore, both white-box and black-box attacks have been performed against DNNs successfully when an attacker is given full or zero knowledge about the target systems [2,17,45]. Among black-box attacks, transferability is widely used for generating attacks against real-world systems which do not allow white-box access. Transferability refers to the property of adversarial examples in classification tasks where one adversarial example generated against a local model can mislead another unseen model without any modification [33].

Given these intriguing properties of adversarial examples, various analyses for understanding adversarial examples have been proposed [29,30,42,43], and potential defense/detection techniques have also been discussed mainly for the image classification problem [13,21,30]. For instance, image pre-processing [14], adding another type of random noise to the inputs [48], and adversarial retraining [17] have been proposed for defending/detecting adversarial examples when classifying images. However, researchers [4,19] have shown that these defense or detection methods are easily attacked again by attackers with or even without knowledge of the defender's strategy. Such observations bring up concerns about safety problems within diverse machine learning based systems.

In order to better understand adversarial examples against different tasks, in this paper we aim to analyze adversarial examples in the semantic segmentation task instead of classification. We hypothesize that adversarial examples in different tasks may contain unique properties that provide in-depth understanding for such examples and encourage potential defensive mechanisms. Different from image classification, in semantic segmentation, each pixel will be given a prediction label which is based on its surrounding information [12]. Such spatial context information plays a more important role for segmentation algorithms, such as [23,26,50,55]. Whether adversarial perturbation would break such spatial context is unknown to the community. In this paper we propose and conduct image spatial consistency analysis, which randomly selects overlapping patches from a given image and checks how consistent the segmentation results are for the overlapping regions. Our pipeline of spatial consistency analysis for adversarial/benign instances is shown in Fig. 1. We find that in segmentation task, adversarial perturbation can be weakened for separately selected patches, and therefore adversarial and benign images will show very different behaviors in terms of the spatial consistency information. Moreover, since such spatial consistency is highly random, it is hard for adversaries to take such constraints into account when performing adaptive attacks. This renders the system less brittle even facing the sophisticated adversaries, who have full knowledge about the model as well as the detection/defense method applied.

We use image scale transformation to perform detection of adversarial examples as a baseline, which has been used for detection in classification tasks [39]. We show that by randomly scaling the images, adversarial perturbation can be destroyed and therefore adversarial examples can be detected. However, when the attacker knows the detection strategy (adaptive attacker), even without the exact knowledge about the scaling rate, attacker can still perform adaptive attacks against the detection mechanism, which is similar with the findings in classification tasks [4]. On the other hand, we show that by incorporating spatial consistency check, existing semantic segmentation networks can detect adversarial examples (average AUC 100%), which are generated by the state-of-the-art attacks considered in this paper, regardless of whether the adversary knows the detection method. Here, we allow the adversaries to have full access to the model and any detection method applied to analyze the robustness of the model against adaptive attacks. We additionally analyze the defense in a black-box setting, which is more practical in real-world systems.

In this paper, our goal is to further understand adversarial attacks by conducting spatial consistency analysis in the semantic segmentation task, and we make the following contributions:

1. We propose the spatial consistency analysis for benign/adversarial images and conduct large scale experiments on two state-of-the-art attack strategies against both DRN and DLA segmentation models with diverse adversarial targets on different dataset, including Cityscapes and real-world autonomous driving video dataset.
2. We are the first to analyze spatial information for adversarial examples in segmentation models. We show that spatial consistency information can be potentially leveraged to distinguish adversarial examples. We also show that spatial consistency check mechanism induce a high degree of randomness and therefore is robust against adaptive adversaries. We evaluate image scaling and spatial consistency, and show that spatial consistency outperform standard scaling based method.
3. In addition, we empirically show that adversarial examples generated by the attack methods considered in our studies barely transfer among models, even when these models are of the same architecture with different initialization, different from the transferability phenomena in classification tasks.

2   Related Work

Semantic Segmentation has received long lasting attention in the computer vision community [25]. Recent advances in deep learning [24] also show that deep convolutional networks can achieve much better results than traditional methods [28]. Yu et al. [50] proposed using dilated convolutions to build high-resolution feature maps for semantic segmentation. They can improve the performance significantly compared to upsampling approaches [1,28,34]. Most of the

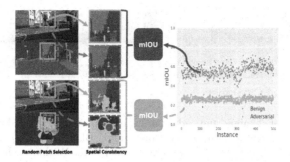

Fig. 1. Spatial consistency analysis for adversarial and benign instances in semantic segmentation.

recent state-of-the-art approaches are based on dilated convolutions [44,51,55] and residual networks [18]. Therefore, in this work, we choose dilated residual networks (DRN) [51] and deep layer aggregation (DLA) [52] as our target models for attacking and defense.

Adversarial Examples for Semantic Segmentation have been studied recently in addition to adversarial examples in image classification. Xie et al. proposed a gradient based algorithm to attack pixels within the whole image iteratively until most of the pixels have been misclassified into the target class [49], which is called dense adversary generation (DAG). Later an optimization based attack algorithm has been studied by introducing a surrogate loss function called Houdini in the objective function [10]. The Houdini loss function is made up of two parts. The first part represents the stochastic margin between the score of actual and predicted targets, which reflects the confidence of model prediction. The second part is the task loss, which is independent with the model and corresponds to the actual task. The task loss enables Houdini algorithm to generate adversarial examples in different tasks, including image segmentation, human pose estimation, and speech recognition.

Various detection and defense methods have also been studied against adversarial examples in image classification. For instance, adversarial training [17] and its variations [30,41] have been proposed and demonstrated to be effective in classification task, which is hard to adapt for the segmentation task. Currently no defense or detection methods have been studied in image segmentation.

3 Spatial Consistency Based Method

In this section, we will explore the effects that spatial context information has on benign and adversarial examples in segmentation models. We conduct different experiments based on various models and datasets, and due to the space limitation, we will use a small set of examples to demonstrate our discoveries and relegate other examples to the supplementary materials. Figure 2 shows the

(a) Cityscapes   (b) BDD

Fig. 2. Samples of benign and adversarial examples generated by Houdini on Cityscapes [11] (targeting on Kitty/Pure) and BDD100K [53] (targeting on Kitty/Scene). We select DRN as our target model here. Within each subfigure, the first column shows benign images and corresponding segmentation results, and the second and third columns show adversarial examples with different adversarial targets.

benign and adversarial examples targeting diverse adversarial targets: "Hello Kitty" (Kitty) and random pure color (Pure) on Cityscapes; and "Hello Kitty" (Kitty) and a real scene without any cars (Scene) on BDD video dataset, respectively. In the rest of the paper, we will use the format "attack method | target" to label each adversarial example. Here we consider both DAG [49] and Houdini [10] attack methods.

(a) Benign example   (b) Heatmap of benign image

(c) DAG | Kitty   (d) DAG | Pure   (e) Houdini | Kitty   (f) Houdini | Pure

Fig. 3. Heatmap of per-pixel self-entropy on Cityscapes dataset against DRN model. (a) and (b) show a benign image and its corresponding per-pixel self-entropy heatmap. (c)–(f) show the heatmaps of the adversarial examples generated by DAG and Houdini attacks targeting "Hello Kitty" (Kitty) and random pure color (Pure).

3.1   Spatial Context Analysis

To quantitatively analyze the contribution of spatial context information to the segmentation task, we first evaluate the entropy of prediction based on different spatial context. For each pixel m within an image, we randomly select K patches

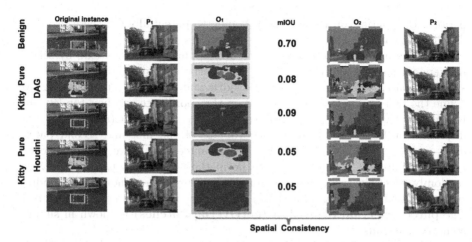

Fig. 4. Examples of spatial consistency based method on adversarial examples generated by DAG and Houdini attacks targeting on Kitty and Pure. First column shows the original image and corresponding segmentation results. Column P_1 and P_2 show two randomly selected patches, while column O_1 and O_2 represent the segmentation results of the overlapping regions from these two patches, respectively. The mIOU between O_1 and O_2 are reported. It is clear that the segmentation results of the overlapping regions from two random patches are very different for adversarial images (low mIOU), but relatively consistent for benign instance (high mIOU).

$\{P_1, P_2, ..., P_K\}$ which contain m. Afterwards, within each patch P_i, the pixel m will be assigned with a confidence vector based on Softmax prediction, so pixel m will correspond to K vectors in total. We discretize each vector to a one-hot vector and sum up these K one-hot vectors to obtain vector $\mathcal{V}_m$. Each component $\mathcal{V}_m[j]$ of the vector represents the number of times pixel m is predicted to be class j. We then normalize $\mathcal{V}_m$ by dividing K. Finally, for each pixel m, we calculate its self-entropy

$$\mathcal{H}(m) = -\sum_j \mathcal{V}_m[j] \log \mathcal{V}_m[j]$$

and therefore calculate the self entropy for each vector. We utilize such entropy information of each pixel to convey the consistency of different surrounding patches and plot this information in the heatmaps in Fig. 3. It is clear that for benign instances, the boundaries of original objects have higher entropy, indicating that these are places harder to predict and can gain more information by considering different surrounding spatial context information (Fig. 4).

3.2 Patch Based Spatial Consistency

The fact that surrounding spatial context information shows different spatial consistency behaviors for benign and adversarial examples motivates us to perform the spatial consistency check hoping to potentially tell these two data distributions apart.

First, we introduce how to generate overlapping spatial contexts by selecting random patches and then validate the spatial consistency information. Let s be the patch size and w, h be the width and height of an image $\mathbf{X}$. We define the first and second patch based on the coordinates of their top-left and bottom-right vertices $(u_1, u_2, u_3, u_4), (v_1, v_2, v_3, v_4)$, where Let $(d_{u_1,v_1}, d_{u_2,v_2})$ be displacement between the top-left coordinate of the first and second patch: $d_{u_1,v_1} = v_1 - u_1, d_{u_2,v_2} = v_2 - u_2$. To guarantee that there is enough overlap, we require (d_{u_1,v_1} and d_{u_2,v_2}) to be in the range ($b_{\mathbf{low}}, b_{\mathbf{upper}}$). Here we randomly select the two patches, aiming to capture diverse enough surrounding spatial context, including information both near and far from the target pixel. The **patch selection algorithm (getOverlapPatches)** is shown in supplementary materials.

Next we show how to apply the spatial consistency based method to a given input and therefore recognize adversarial examples. The detailed algorithm is shown in Algorithm 1. Here K denotes the number of overlapping regions for which we will check the spatial consistency. We use the mean Intersection Over Union (mIOU) between the overlapping regions O_1, O_2 from two patches P_1, P_2 to measure their spatial consistency. The mIOU is defined as $\frac{1}{n_{cls}} \sum_i n_{ii}/(\sum_j n_{ij} + \sum_j n_{ji} - n_{ii})$, where n_{ij} denotes the number of pixels predicted to be class i in O_1 and class j in O_2, and n_{cls} is the number of the unique classes appearing in both O_1 and O_2. **getmIOU** is a function that computes the mIOU given patches P_1, P_2 along with their overlapping regions O_1 and O_2 shown in supplementary materials.

4   Scale Consistency Analysis

We have discussed how spatial consistency can be utilized to potentially characterize adversarial examples in segmentation task. In this section, we will discuss another baseline method: image scale transformation, which is another natural factor considered in semantic segmentation [22,28]. Here we focus on image blur operation by applying Gaussian blur to given images [6], which is studied for detecting adversarial examples in image classification [39]. Similarly, we will analyze the effects of image scaling on benign/adversarial samples. Since spatial context information is important for segmentation task, scaling or performing segmentation on small patches may damage the global information and therefore affect the final prediction. Here we aim to provide quantitative results to understand and explore how image scale transformation would affect adversarial perturbation.

4.1   Scale Consistency Property

Scale theory is commonly applied in image segmentation task [35], and therefore we train scale resilient models to obtain robust ones, which we perform attacks

---

Algorithm 1. Spatial Consistency Check Algorithm

---

input: Input image $\mathbf{X}$;
number of overlapping regions K;
patch size s;
segmentation model f;
bound $b_{\text{low}}, b_{\text{upper}}$;
output: Spatial consistency threshold c;

Initialization : $\mathbf{cs} \leftarrow [], w \leftarrow x.width, h \leftarrow x.height$;

1 **for** $k \leftarrow 0$ **to** K **do**
2    $\quad (u_1, u_2, u_3, u_4), (v_1, v_2, v_3, v_4) \leftarrow \mathbf{getOverlapPatches}(s, w, h, b_{\text{low}}, b_{\text{upper}})$;
3    $\quad P_1 = X[u1 : u3, u2 : u4], P_2 = X[v_1 : v_3, v_3 : v_4]$;
     $\quad$ /* get prediction result of two random patches from f */;
4    $\quad pred^1 \leftarrow \text{argmax}_c f_c(P_1), pred^2 \leftarrow \text{argmax}_c f_c(P_2)$;
     $\quad$ /* get prediction of the overlap area between two patches   */;
5    $\quad p_1 \leftarrow \{pred_{i,j}^1 | \forall (i,j) \in pred^1, i > v_1 - u_1, j > v_2 - u_2\}$;
6    $\quad p_2 \leftarrow \{pred_{i,j}^2 | \forall (i,j) \in pred^2, i < s - (v_1 - u_1), j < s - (v_2 - u_2)\}$;
     $\quad$ /* get consistency value (mIOU) from two patches   */;
7    $\quad \mathbf{cs} \xleftarrow{+} \mathbf{getmIOU}(p1, p2)$;
8 **end**
9 $c \leftarrow \mathbf{Mean(cs)}$;
   Return: c

---

against. On these scale resilient models, we first analyze how image scaling affect segmentation results for benign/adversarial samples. We applied the DAG [49] and Houdili [10] attacks against the DRN and DLA models with different adversarial targets. The images and corresponding segmentation results before and after scaling are shown in Fig. 5. We apply Gaussian kernel with different standard deviations (std) to scale both benign and adversarial instances. It is clear that when we apply Gaussian blurring with higher std (3 and 5), adversarial perturbation is harmed and the segmentation results are not longer adversarial targets for scale transformed adversarial examples as shown in Fig. 5(a)–(e).

5   Experimental Results

In this section, we conduct comprehensive large scale experiments to evaluate the image spatial and scale consistency information for benign and adversarial examples generated by different attack methods. We will also show that the spatial consistency based detection method is robust against sophisticated adversaries with knowledge about defenders, while scale transformation method is not.

5.1   Implementation Details

Datasets. We apply both Cityscapes [11] and BDD100K [53] in our evaluation. We show results on the validation set of both datasets, which contains 500 high

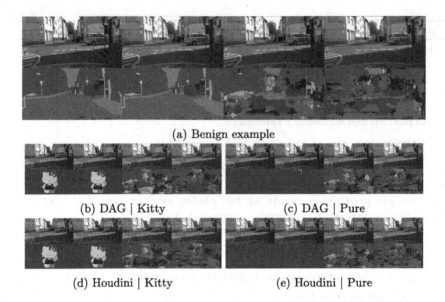

(a) Benign example

(b) DAG | Kitty   (c) DAG | Pure

(d) Houdini | Kitty   (e) Houdini | Pure

Fig. 5. Examples of images and corresponding segmentation results before/after image scaling on Cityscapes against DRN model. For each subfigure, the first column shows benign/adversarial image, while the later columns represent images after scaling by applying Gaussian kernel with std as 0.5, 3, and 5, respectively. (a) shows benign images before/after image scaling and the corresponding segmentation results; (b)–(e) present similar results for adversarial images generated by DAG and Houdini attacks targeting on Kitty and Pure.

resolution images with a combined 19 categories of segmentation labels. These two datasets are both outdoor datasets containing instance-level annotations, which would raise real-wold safety concerns if they were attacked. Comparing with other datasets such as Pascal VOC [15] and CamVid [3], these two dataset are more challenging due to the relatively high resolution and diverse scenes within each image.

Semantic Segmentation Models. We apply Dilated residual networks (DRN) [51] and Deep Layer Aggregation (DLA) [52] as our target models. More specifically, we select DRN-D-22 and DLA-34. For both models, we use 512 crop size and 2 random scale during training to obtain scale resilient models for both the BDD and Cityscapes datasets. The mIOU of these two models on pristine training data are shown in Table 1. More result on different models can be found in supplementary materials.

Adversarial Examples. We generate adversarial examples based on two state-of-the-art attack methods: DAG [49] and Houdini [10] using our own implementation of the methods. We select a complex image, Hello Kitty (Kitty), with different background colors and a random pure color (Pure) as our targets on Cityscapes dataset. Furthermore, in order to increase the diversity, we also select a real-world driving scene (Scene) without any cars from the BDD training dataset as another malicious target on BDD. Such attacks potentially show that every image taken in the real world can be attacked to the same scene without any car showing on the road, which raises great security concerns for future autonomous driving systems. Furthermore, we also add three additional adversarial targets, including "ECCV 2018", "Remapping", and "Color strip" in supplementary materials to increase the diversity of adversarial targets.

We generate 500 adversarial examples for Cityscapes and BDD100K datasets against both DRN and DLA segmentation models targeting on various malicious targets (More results can be found in supplementary materials).

5.2 Spatial Consistency Analysis

To evaluate the spatial consistency analysis quantitatively for segmentation task, we leverage it to build up a simple detector to demonstrate its property. Here we perform patch based spatial consistency analysis, and we select patch size and region bound as $s = 512$, $b_{low} = 32, b_{upper} = 64$. We select the number of overlapping regions as $K \in \{1, 5, 10, 50\}$. Here we first select some benign instances, and calculate the normalize mIOU of overlapping regions from two random patches. We record the lower bound of theses mIOU as the threshold of the detection method. Note that when reporting detection rate in the rest of the paper, we will use the threshold learned from a set of benign training data; while we also report Area Under Curve (AUC) of Receiver Operating Characteristic Curve (ROC) curve of a detection method to evaluate its overall performance. Therefore, given an image, for each overlapping region of two random patches, we will calculate the normalize mIOU and compare with the threshold calculated before. If it is larger, the image is recognized as benign; vice versa. This process is illustrated in Algorithm 1. We report the detection results in terms of AUC in Table 1 for adversarial examples generated in various settings as mentioned above. We observed that such simple detection method based on spatial consistency information can achieve AUC as nearly 100% for adversarial examples that we studied here. In addition, we also select s with a random number between 384 to 512 (too small patch size will affect the segmentation accuracy even on benign instances, so we tend not to choose small patches on the purpose of control variable) and show the result in supplementary materials. We observe that random patch sizes achieve similar detection result.

5.3 Image Scale Analysis

As a baseline, we also utilize image scale information to perform as a simple detection method and compare it with the spatial consistency based method. We apply Gaussian kernel to perform the image scaling based detection, and select $\mathbf{std}_{detect} \in \{0.5, 3, 5\}$ as the standard deviation of Gaussian kernel. We compute the normalize mIOU between the original and scalled images. Similarly, the detection results of corresponding AUC are shown in Table 1. It is demonstrated

Table 1. Detection results (AUC) of image spatial (Spatial) and scale consistency (Scale) based methods on Cityscapes dataset. The number in parentheses of the Model shows the number of parameters for the target mode, and mIOU shows the performance of segmentation model on pristine data. We color all the AUC less than 80% with red.

Method		Model	mIOU	Detection				Detection Adap			
				DAG		Houdini		DAG		Houdini	
				Pure	Kitty	Pure	Kitty	Pure	Kitty	Pure	Kitty
Scale (std)	0.5	DRN (16.4M)	66.7	100%	95%	100%	99%	100%	67%	100%	78%
	3.0			100%	100%	100%	100%	100%	0%	97%	0%
	5.0			100%	100%	100%	100%	100%	0%	71%	0%
	0.5	DLA (18.1M)	74.5	100%	98%	100%	100%	100%	75%	100%	81%
	3.0			100%	100%	100%	100%	100%	24%	100%	34%
	5.0			100%	100%	100%	100%	97%	0%	95%	0%
Spatial (K)	1	DRN (16.4M)	66.7	91%	91%	94%	92%	98%	94%	92%	94%
	5			100%	100%	100%	100%	100%	100%	100%	100%
	10			100%	100%	100%	100%	100%	100%	100%	100%
	50			100%	100%	100%	100%	100%	100%	100%	100%
	1	DLA (18.1M)	74.5	96%	98%	97%	97%	99%	99%	100%	100%
	5			100%	100%	100%	100%	100%	100%	100%	100%
	10			100%	100%	100%	100%	100%	100%	100%	100%
	50			100%	100%	100%	100%	100%	100%	100%	100%

that detection method based on image scale information can achieve similarly high AUC compared with spatial consistency based method.

5.4 Adaptive Attack Evaluation

Regarding the above detection analysis, it is important to evaluate *adaptive attacks*, where adversaries have knowledge of the detection strategy.

As Carlini and Wagner suggest [4], we conduct attacks with full access to the detection model to evaluate the adaptive adversary based on Kerckhoffs principle [36]. To perform adaptive attack against the image scaling detection mechanism, instead of attacking the original model, we add another convolutional layer after the input layer of the target model similarly with [4]. We select std $\in \{0.5, 3, 5\}$ to apply adaptive attack, which is the same with the detection model. To guarantee that the attack methods will converge, when performing the adaptive attacks, we select 0.06 for the upper bound for adversarial perturbation, in terms of L_2 distance (pixel values are in range [0,1]), since larger than that the perturbation is already very visible. The detection results against such adaptive attacks are shown in Table 1 on Cityscapes (We omit the results on BDD to supplementary materials). Results on adaptive attack show that the image scale based detection method is easily to be attacked (AUC of detection drops dramatically), which draws similar conclusions as in classification task [4]. We show the qualitative results in Fig. 6(a), and it is obvious that even under large std of Gaussian kernel, the adversarial example can still be fooled into the malicious target (Kitty).

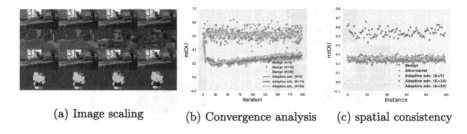

(a) Image scaling   (b) Convergence analysis   (c) spatial consistency

Fig. 6. Performance of adaptive attack. (a) shows adversarial image and corresponding segmentation result for adaptive attack against image scaling. The first two rows show benign images and the corresponding segmentation results; the last two rows show the adaptive adversarial images and corresponding segmentation results under different std of Gaussian kernel (0.5, 3, 5 for column 2–4). (b) and (c) show the performance of adaptive attack against spatial consistency based method with different K. (b) presents mIOU of overlapping regions for benign and adversarial images during along different iterations. (c) shows mIOU for overlapping regions of benign and adversarial instances at iteration 200.

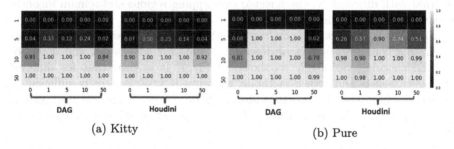

(a) Kitty   (b) Pure

Fig. 7. Detection performance of spatial consistency based method against adaptive attack with different K on Cityscapes with DRN model. X-axis indicates the number of patches selected to perform the adaptive attack (0 means regular attack). Y-axis indicates the number of overlapping regions selected for during detection.

Next, we will apply adaptive attack against the spatial consistency based method. Due to the randomness of the approach, we propose to develop a strong adaptive adversary that we can think of by randomly select K patches (the same value of K used by defender). Then the adversary will try to attack both the whole image and the selected K patches to the corresponding part of malicious target. The detailed attack algorithm is shown in the supplementry materials. The corresponding detection results of the spatial consistency based method against such adaptive attacks on Cityscapes are shown in Table 1. It is interesting to see that even against such strong adaptive attacks, the spatial consistency based method can still achieve nearly 100% detection results. We hypothesize that it is because of the high dimension randomness induced by the spatial consistency based method since the search space for patches and the overlapping regions is pretty high. Figure 6(b) analyzes the convergence of such adaptive

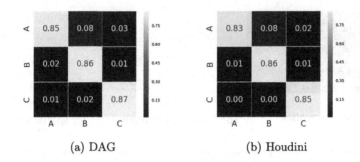

(a) DAG   (b) Houdini

Fig. 8. Transferability analysis: cell (i, j) shows the normalized mIoU value or pixel-wise attack success rate of adversarial examples generated against model j and evaluate on model i. Model A,B,C are DRN (DRN-D-22) with different initialization. We select "Hello Kitty" as target

attack against spatial consistency based method. From Fig. 6(b) and (c), we can see that with different K, the selected overlapping regions still remain inconsistent with high probability.

Since the spatial consistency based method can induce large randomness, we generate a confusion matrix of detection results for adversaries and detection method choosing various K as shown in Fig. 7. It is clear that for different malicious targets and attack methods, choosing $K = 50$ is already sufficient to detect sophisticated attacks. In addition, based on our empirical observation, attacking with higher K increases the computation complexity of adversaries dramatically.

5.5 Transferability Analysis

Given the common properties of adversarial examples for both classifier and segmentation tasks, next we will analyze whether transferability of adversarial examples exists in segmentation models considering they are particularly sensitive to spatial and scale information. *Transferability* is demonstrated to be one of the most interesting properties of adversarial examples in classification task, where adversarial examples generated against one model is able to mislead the other model, even if the two models are of different architectures. Given this property, transferability has become the foundation of a lot of black-box attacks in classification task. Here we aim to analyze whether adversarial examples in segmentation task still retain high transferability. First, we train three DRN models with the same architecture (DRN-D-22) but different initialization and generate adversarial images with the same target.

Each adversarial image has at least 96% pixel-wise attack success rate against the original model. We evaluate both the DAG and Houdini attacks and evaluate the transferability using normalized mIoU excluding pixels with the same label for the ground truth adversarial target. We show the transferability evaluation among different models in the confusion matrices in Fig. 8[1]. We observe that the transferability rarely appears in the segmentation task. More results on different network architectures and data sets are in the supplementary materials.

As comparison with classification task, for each network architecture we train a classifier on it and evaluate the transferability results as shown in supplementary materials. As a control experiments, we observe that classifiers with the same architecture still have high transferability aligned with existing findings, which shows that the low transferability is indeed due to the natural of segmentation instead of certain network architectures.

This observation here is quite interesting, which indicates that black-box attacks against segmentation models may be more challenging. Furthermore, the reason for such low transferability in segmentation is possibly because adversarial perturbation added to one image could have focused on a certain region, while such spatial context information is captured differently among different models. We plan to analyze the actual reason for low transferability in segmentation in the future work.

6 Conclusions

Adversarial examples have been heavily studied recently, pointing out vulnerabilities of deep neural networks and raising a lot of security concerns. However, most of such studies are focusing on image classification problems, and in this paper we aim to explore the spatial context information used in semantic segmentation task to better understand adversarial examples in segmentation scenarios. We propose to apply spatial consistency information analysis to recognize adversarial examples in segmentation, which has not been considered in either image classification or segmentation as a potential detection mechanism. We show that such spatial consistency information is different for adversarial and benign instances and can be potentially leveraged to detect adversarial examples even when facing strong adaptive attackers. These observations open a wide door for future research to explore diverse properties of adversarial examples under various scenarios and develop new attacks to understand the vulnerabilities of DNNs.

Acknowledgments. We thank Warren He, George Philipp, Ziwei Liu, Zhirong Wu, Shizhan Zhu and Xiaoxiao Li for their valuable discussions on this work. This work was supported in part by Berkeley DeepDrive, Compute Canada, NSERC and National Science Foundation under grants CNS-1422211, CNS-1616575, CNS-1739517, JD Grapevine plan, and by the DHS via contract number FA8750-18-2-0011.

---

[1] Since the prediction of certain classes presents low IoU value due to imperfect segmentation, we eliminate K classes with the lowest IoU values to avoid side effects. In our experiments, we set K to be 13.

References

1. Badrinarayanan, V., Kendall, A., Cipolla, R.: SegNet: a deep convolutional encoder-decoder architecture for image segmentation. IEEE Trans. Pattern Anal. Mach. Intell. **39**(12), 2481–2495 (2017)
2. Bhagoji, A.N., He, W., Li, B., Song, D.: Exploring the space of black-box attacks on deep neural networks. arXiv preprint arXiv:1712.09491 (2017)
3. Brostow, G.J., Shotton, J., Fauqueur, J., Cipolla, R.: Segmentation and recognition using structure from motion point clouds. In: Forsyth, D., Torr, P., Zisserman, A. (eds.) ECCV 2008. LNCS, vol. 5302, pp. 44–57. Springer, Heidelberg (2008). https://doi.org/10.1007/978-3-540-88682-2_5
4. Carlini, N., Wagner, D.: Adversarial examples are not easily detected: bypassing ten detection methods. In: Proceedings of the 10th ACM Workshop on Artificial Intelligence and Security, pp. 3–14. ACM (2017)
5. Carlini, N., Wagner, D.A.: Towards evaluating the robustness of neural networks. In: 2017 IEEE Symposium on Security and Privacy, SP 2017, San Jose, CA, USA, 22–26 May 2017, pp. 39–57 (2017). https://doi.org/10.1109/SP.2017.49
6. Chan, T.F., Wong, C.K.: Total variation blind deconvolution. IEEE Trans. Image Process. **7**(3), 370–375 (1998)
7. Chen, H., Zhang, H., Chen, P.Y., Yi, J., Hsieh, C.J.: Attacking visual language grounding with adversarial examples: a case study on neural image captioning. In: Proceedings of the 56th Annual Meeting of the Association for Computational Linguistics, Long Papers, vol. 1, pp. 2587–2597 (2018)
8. Chen, P.Y., Sharma, Y., Zhang, H., Yi, J., Hsieh, C.J.: EAD: elastic-net attacks to deep neural networks via adversarial examples. arXiv preprint arXiv:1709.04114 (2017)
9. Chen, P.Y., Zhang, H., Sharma, Y., Yi, J., Hsieh, C.J.: ZOO: zeroth order optimization based black-box attacks to deep neural networks without training substitute models. In: Proceedings of the 10th ACM Workshop on Artificial Intelligence and Security, pp. 15–26. ACM (2017)
10. Cisse, M., Adi, Y., Neverova, N., Keshet, J.: Houdini: fooling deep structured prediction models. arXiv preprint arXiv:1707.05373 (2017)
11. Cordts, M., et al.: The cityscapes dataset for semantic urban scene understanding. In: Proceedings of the IEEE Conference on Computer Vision and Pattern Recognition, pp. 3213–3223 (2016)
12. Cui, W., Wang, Y., Fan, Y., Feng, Y., Lei, T.: Localized FCM clustering with spatial information for medical image segmentation and bias field estimation. J. Biomed. Imaging **2013**, 13 (2013)
13. Das, N., et al.: Keeping the bad guys out: protecting and vaccinating deep learning with JPEG compression. arXiv preprint arXiv:1705.02900 (2017)
14. Dziugaite, G.K., Ghahramani, Z., Roy, D.M.: A study of the effect of JPG compression on adversarial images. arXiv preprint arXiv:1608.00853 (2016)
15. Everingham, M., Eslami, S.M.A., Van Gool, L., Williams, C.K.I., Winn, J., Zisserman, A.: The pascal visual object classes challenge: a retrospective. Int. J. Comput. Vis. **111**(1), 98–136 (2015)
16. Evtimov, I., et al.: Robust physical-world attacks on machine learning models. arXiv preprint arXiv:1707.08945 (2017)
17. Goodfellow, I.J., Shlens, J., Szegedy, C.: Explaining and harnessing adversarial examples. arXiv preprint arXiv:1412.6572 (2014)

18. He, K., Zhang, X., Ren, S., Sun, J.: Deep residual learning for image recognition. In: Proceedings of the IEEE Conference on Computer Vision and Pattern Recognition, pp. 770–778 (2016)
19. He, W., Wei, J., Chen, X., Carlini, N., Song, D.: Adversarial example defense: ensembles of weak defenses are not strong. In: 11th USENIX Workshop on Offensive Technologies (WOOT 2017). USENIX Association, Vancouver (2017). https://www.usenix.org/conference/woot17/workshop-program/presentation/he
20. Hinton, G., et al.: Deep neural networks for acoustic modeling in speech recognition: the shared views of four research groups. IEEE Signal Process. Mag. **29**(6), 82–97 (2012)
21. Hosseini, H., Chen, Y., Kannan, S., Zhang, B., Poovendran, R.: Blocking transferability of adversarial examples in black-box learning systems. arXiv preprint arXiv:1703.04318 (2017)
22. Johnson, B., Xie, Z.: Unsupervised image segmentation evaluation and refinement using a multi-scale approach. ISPRS J. Photogramm. Remote. Sens. **66**(4), 473–483 (2011)
23. Krähenbühl, P., Koltun, V.: Efficient inference in fully connected CRFs with Gaussian edge potentials. In: Advances in Neural Information Processing Systems, pp. 109–117 (2011)
24. Krizhevsky, A., Sutskever, I., Hinton, G.E.: ImageNet classification with deep convolutional neural networks. In: Advances in Neural Information Processing Systems, pp. 1097–1105 (2012)
25. Leung, T., Malik, J.: Representing and recognizing the visual appearance of materials using three-dimensional textons. Int. J. Comput. Vis. **43**(1), 29–44 (2001)
26. Lin, G., Shen, C., Van Den Hengel, A., Reid, I.: Efficient piecewise training of deep structured models for semantic segmentation. In: Proceedings of the IEEE Conference on Computer Vision and Pattern Recognition, pp. 3194–3203 (2016)
27. Liu, Y., Chen, X., Liu, C., Song, D.: Delving into transferable adversarial examples and black-box attacks. arXiv preprint arXiv:1611.02770 (2016)
28. Long, J., Shelhamer, E., Darrell, T.: Fully convolutional networks for semantic segmentation. In: Proceedings of the IEEE Conference on Computer Vision and Pattern Recognition, pp. 3431–3440 (2015)
29. Ma, X., et al.: Characterizing adversarial subspaces using local intrinsic dimensionality. arXiv preprint arXiv:1801.02613 (2018)
30. Madry, A., Makelov, A., Schmidt, L., Tsipras, D., Vladu, A.: Towards deep learning models resistant to adversarial attacks. arXiv preprint arXiv:1706.06083 (2017)
31. Nguyen, A., Yosinski, J., Clune, J.: Deep neural networks are easily fooled: high confidence predictions for unrecognizable images. In: 2015 IEEE Conference on Computer Vision and Pattern Recognition (CVPR), pp. 427–436. IEEE (2015)
32. Noda, K., Arie, H., Suga, Y., Ogata, T.: Multimodal integration learning of robot behavior using deep neural networks. Robot. Auton. Syst. **62**(6), 721–736 (2014)
33. Papernot, N., McDaniel, P., Goodfellow, I.: Transferability in machine learning: from phenomena to black-box attacks using adversarial samples. arXiv preprint arXiv:1605.07277 (2016)
34. Ronneberger, O., Fischer, P., Brox, T.: U-Net: convolutional networks for biomedical image segmentation. In: Navab, N., Hornegger, J., Wells, W.M., Frangi, A.F. (eds.) MICCAI 2015. LNCS, vol. 9351, pp. 234–241. Springer, Cham (2015). https://doi.org/10.1007/978-3-319-24574-4_28
35. Saha, P.K., Udupa, J.K., Odhner, D.: Scale-based fuzzy connected image segmentation: theory, algorithms, and validation. Comput. Vis. Image Underst. **77**(2), 145–174 (2000)

36. Shannon, C.E.: Communication theory of secrecy systems. Bell Labs Tech. J. **28**(4), 656–715 (1949)
37. Sharif, M., Bhagavatula, S., Bauer, L., Reiter, M.K.: Accessorize to a crime: real and stealthy attacks on state-of-the-art face recognition. In: Proceedings of the 2016 ACM SIGSAC Conference on Computer and Communications Security, pp. 1528–1540. ACM (2016)
38. Szegedy, C., et al.: Intriguing properties of neural networks. arXiv preprint arXiv:1312.6199 (2013)
39. Tabacof, P., Valle, E.: Exploring the space of adversarial images. In: 2016 International Joint Conference on Neural Networks (IJCNN), pp. 426–433. IEEE (2016)
40. Tong, L., Li, B., Hajaj, C., Xiao, C., Vorobeychik, Y.: Hardening classifiers against evasion: the good, the bad, and the ugly. CoRR, abs/1708.08327 (2017)
41. Tramèr, F., Kurakin, A., Papernot, N., Boneh, D., McDaniel, P.: Ensemble adversarial training: attacks and defenses. arXiv preprint arXiv:1705.07204 (2017)
42. Weng, T.W., et al.: Towards fast computation of certified robustness for ReLU networks. arXiv preprint arXiv:1804.09699 (2018)
43. Weng, T.W., et al.: Evaluating the robustness of neural networks: an extreme value theory approach. In: International Conference on Learning Representations (2018). https://openreview.net/forum?id=BkUHlMZ0b
44. Wu, Z., Shen, C., van den Hengel, A.: Wider or deeper: revisiting the resnet model for visual recognition. arXiv preprint arXiv:1611.10080 (2016)
45. Xiao, C., Li, B., Zhu, J.Y., He, W., Liu, M., Song, D.: Generating adversarial examples with adversarial networks. In: Proceedings of the Twenty-Seventh International Joint Conference on Artificial Intelligence, IJCAI 2018, pp. 3905–3911. International Joint Conferences on Artificial Intelligence Organization, July 2018. https://doi.org/10.24963/ijcai.2018/543
46. Xiao, C., Sarabi, A., Liu, Y., Li, B., Liu, M., Dumitras, T.: From patching delays to infection symptoms: using risk profiles for an early discovery of vulnerabilities exploited in the wild. In: 27th USENIX Security Symposium (USENIX Security 2018). USENIX Association, Baltimore (2018). https://www.usenix.org/conference/usenixsecurity18/presentation/xiao
47. Xiao, C., Zhu, J.Y., Li, B., He, W., Liu, M., Song, D.: Spatially transformed adversarial examples. In: International Conference on Learning Representations (2018). https://openreview.net/forum?id=HyydRMZC-
48. Xie, C., Wang, J., Zhang, Z., Ren, Z., Yuille, A.: Mitigating adversarial effects through randomization. In: International Conference on Learning Representations (2018)
49. Xie, C., Wang, J., Zhang, Z., Zhou, Y., Xie, L., Yuille, A.: Adversarial examples for semantic segmentation and object detection. In: International Conference on Computer Vision. IEEE (2017)
50. Yu, F., Koltun, V.: Multi-scale context aggregation by dilated convolutions. In: International Conference on Learning Representations (ICLR) (2016)
51. Yu, F., Koltun, V., Funkhouser, T.: Dilated residual networks. In: Computer Vision and Pattern Recognition (CVPR) (2017)
52. Yu, F., Wang, D., Darrell, T.: Deep layer aggregation. arXiv preprint arXiv:1707.06484 (2017)
53. Yu, F., et al.: BDD100K: a diverse driving video database with scalable annotation tooling. arXiv preprint arXiv:1805.04687 (2018)

54. Zeng, D., Liu, K., Lai, S., Zhou, G., Zhao, J.: Relation classification via convolutional deep neural network. In: Proceedings of COLING 2014, the 25th International Conference on Computational Linguistics: Technical Papers, pp. 2335–2344 (2014)
55. Zhao, H., Shi, J., Qi, X., Wang, X., Jia, J.: Pyramid scene parsing network. In: IEEE Conference on Computer Vision and Pattern Recognition (CVPR), pp. 2881–2890 (2017)

Joint Task-Recursive Learning for Semantic Segmentation and Depth Estimation

Zhenyu Zhang[1], Zhen Cui[1(✉)], Chunyan Xu[1], Zequn Jie[2], Xiang Li[1], and Jian Yang[1(✉)]

[1] PCA Lab, Key Lab of Intelligent Perception and Systems for High-Dimensional Information of Ministry of Education, and Jiangsu Key Lab of Image and Video Understanding for Social Security, School of Computer Science and Engineering, Nanjing University of Science and Technology, Nanjing, China
{zhangjesse,zhen.cui,cyx,xiang.li.implus,jyang}@njust.edu.cn
[2] Tencent AI Lab, Shenzhen, China
zequn.nus@gmail.com

Abstract. In this paper, we propose a novel joint Task-Recursive Learning (TRL) framework for the closing-loop semantic segmentation and monocular depth estimation tasks. TRL can recursively refine the results of both tasks through serialized task-level interactions. In order to mutually-boost for each other, we encapsulate the interaction into a specific Task-Attentional Module (TAM) to adaptively enhance some counterpart patterns of both tasks. Further, to make the inference more credible, we propagate previous learning experiences on both tasks into the next network evolution by explicitly concatenating previous responses. The sequence of task-level interactions are finally evolved along a coarse-to-fine scale space such that the required details may be reconstructed progressively. Extensive experiments on NYU-Depth v2 and SUN RGB-D datasets demonstrate that our method achieves state-of-the-art results for monocular depth estimation and semantic segmentation.

Keywords: Depth estimation · Semantic segmentation Recursive learning · Recurrent neural network · Deep learning

1 Introduction

Semantic segmentation and depth estimation from single monocular images are two challenging tasks in computer vision, due to lack of reliable cues of a scene, large variations of scene types, cluttered backgrounds, pose changing and occlusions of objects. Recently, driven by deep learning techniques, the study on them

Electronic supplementary material The online version of this chapter (https://doi.org/10.1007/978-3-030-01249-6_15) contains supplementary material, which is available to authorized users.

V. Ferrari et al. (Eds.): ECCV 2018, LNCS 11214, pp. 238–255, 2018.
https://doi.org/10.1007/978-3-030-01249-6_15

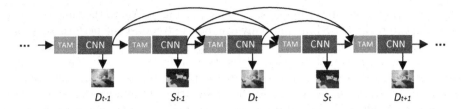

Fig. 1. Illustration of our main idea. The two tasks (i.e., depth estimation and semantic segmentation) are progressively refined to form a task alternate state sequence. At time slice t, we denote the task states as D_t and S_t respectively. Previous task-related experiences and information of the other task are adaptively propagate into the next new state (D_t) via a designed task-interactive module called Task-Attentional Module (TAM). The evolution-alternate process of the dual tasks is finally framed into the proposed task-recursive learning.

has seen great progress and starts to benefit some potential applications such as scene understanding [1], robotics [2], autonomous driving [3] and simultaneous localization and mapping (SLAM) system [4]. Despite the successes of deep learning (especially CNNs) on monocular depth estimation [5–9] and semantic segmentation [10–13], most of these methods emphasize to learn robust regression yet scarcely consider the interactions between them. Actually, the two tasks have some common characteristics, which can be utilized for each other. For example, semantic segmentation and depth of a scene can both reveal the layout and object shapes/boundaries. The recent work in the literature [14] also indicated that leveraging the depth information from RGB-D data may facilitate the semantic segmentation. Therefore, a joint learning of both tasks should be considered to reciprocally promote for each other.

Existing joint learning of two tasks falls into the category of multi-task learning, which has been extensively studied in the past few decades [15]. It involves many cross tasks, such as detection and classification [16,17], depth estimation and image decomposition [18], image segmentation and classification [19], and also depth estimation and semantic segmentation [20–22], etc. But such existing joint learning methods mainly belong to the shallow task-level interaction. For example, a shared deep network is utilized to extract the common features for both tasks, and bifurcates from a high-level layer to perform the two tasks individually [16–19,21,22]. As such, in these methods, less interaction is taken due to the relative independency between tasks. However, it is well known that human learning system benefits from an iterative/looping interactive process between different tasks [23]. Taking a simplest commonsense case, alternately reading and writing can promptly improve human capability in the both aspects. Therefore, we argue whether task-alternate learning (such as cross segmentation and depth estimation) can go deeper with the breakthrough of deep learning.

To address such problem, in this paper, we propose a novel joint Task-Recursive Learning (TRL) framework to closely-loop semantic segmentation and depth estimation on indoor scenes. The interactions between both tasks are serialized as a newly-created time axis, as shown in Fig. 1. Along the time dimension, the two tasks $\{D, S\}$ are mutually collaborate to boost the performance for each other. In each interaction, the historical experiences of previous states (i.e., features of the previous time steps of the two tasks) will be selectively propagated and help to estimate the new state, as ploted by the arc and horizontal black arrows. To properly propagate the information stream, we design a Task-Attentional Module (TAM) to correlate the two tasks, where the useful common information related to the current task will be enhanced while suppressing task-irrelevant information. Thus the learning process of the two tasks can be easily modularized into a sequence network called task-recursive learning network in this paper. Besides, considering the difficulty of high-resolution pixel-level prediction, we derive the recursive task learning on a sequence of coarse-to-fine scales, which would progressively refine the details of the estimation results. Extensive experiments demonstrate that our proposed task-recursive learning can benefit the two tasks for each other. In summary, the contributions of this paper are three folds:

- Propose a novel joint Task-Recursive Learning (TRL) framework for semantic segmentation and depth estimation. Serializing the problems as a task-alternate time sequence, TRL can progressively refine and mutually boost the two tasks through properly propagating the information stream.
- Design a Task-Attentional Module (TAM) to enclose the interaction of the two tasks, which thus can be used in those conventional networks as a general layer or module.
- Validate the effectiveness of the deeply task-alternate mechanism, and achieve some new state-of-the-art results of for the dual tasks of depth estimation and semantic segmentation on NYU Depth V2 and SUN RGBD datasets.

2   Related Work

Depth Estimation: Many works have been proposed for monocular depth estimation. Eigen et al. [5, 24] proposed a multi-stage CNN to resolve the monocular depth prediction. Liu et al. [25] and Li et al. [26] utilized CRF models to capture local image texture and guide the network learning process. Recently, Laina et al. [7] proposed a fully convolutional network with up-projection to achieve an efficient upsampling process. Xu et al. [6] employed multi-scale continuous CRFs as a deep sequential network. In contrast to these methods, our approach focuses on the dual-task learning, and attempts to utilize segmentation cues to promote depth prediction.

Semantic Segmentation: Most methods [10,11,27–29] conducted semantic segmentation from single RGB image. As the large RGBD dataset was released, some approaches [30,31] attempted to fuse depth information for better segmentation. Recently, Cheng et al. [32] computed the affinity matrices from RGB images and HHA depth images for better upsampling important locations. Different from these RGBD based methods, our method does not directly use ground truth of depth, but the estimated depth for semantic segmentation, which thus essentially falls into the category of RGB image segmentation.

Multi-task Learning: The generic multi-task learning problem [15] has been studied for a long history, and numerous methods were developed in different research areas such as representation learning [33–35], transfer learning [36,37], computer vision [16,17,19,38–40]. Here the most related works are those multi-task learning methods of computer vision. For examples, the literatures [21, 22] utilized CNN with hierarchical CRFs and multi-decoder to obtain depth estimation and semantic segmentation. In the literature [19], a cross-stitch unit was proposed to better interact two tasks. The recent proposed Ubernet [40] attempted to give a solution for various tasks on diverse datasets with limited memory. Different from these previous works, our proposed TRL takes multi-task learning as a deep manner of task interactions. Specifically, depth estimation and semantic segmentation are mutually boosted and refined in a general recursive architecture.

3   Approach

3.1   Motivation

Here we focus on the interactive learning problem of two tasks including depth estimation and semantic segmentation from a monocular RGB image. Our motivation mainly comes from two folds: (i) human learning benefits from an iterative/looping interactive process between tasks [23]; (ii) Such a couple of tasks are complementary to some extent besides sharing some common information. Therefore, our aim is to make the task-level alternate interaction go deeper, so as to let the two tasks mutually boosted. The main idea is illustrated in Fig. 1. We define the task-alternate learning processes as a series of state transformation along the time axis. Formally, we denote the states of depth estimation and semantic segmentation tasks as D_p and S_p at time step p respectively, and the corresponding responses as f_D^p and f_S^p. Suppose the previous obtained experiences as $\mathcal{F}_D^{p-1:p-k} = \{f_D^{p-1}, f_D^{p-2}, \ldots, f_D^{p-k}\}$ and $\mathcal{F}_S^{p-1:p-k} = \{f_S^{p-1}, f_S^{p-2}, \ldots, f_S^{p-k}\}$, then we formulate the dual-task learning at the time clip p as

$$\begin{cases} D^p = \Phi_D^p(\mathcal{T}(\mathcal{F}_D^{p-1:p-k}, \mathcal{F}_S^{p-1:p-k}), \Theta_D^p) \\ S^p = \Phi_S^p(\mathcal{T}(\mathcal{F}_D^{p:p-k+1}, \mathcal{F}_S^{p-1:p-k}), \Theta_S^p) \end{cases}, \tag{1}$$

where $\mathcal{T}$ is the interactive function (designed as task-attentional module below), Φ_D^p and Φ_S^p are transformation functions to predict the next state with the parameters Θ_D^p and Θ_S^p to be learnt. As the time slice p, the depth estimation D_p is on the conditions of previous k-order experiences $\mathcal{F}_D^{p-1:p-k}$ and $\mathcal{F}_S^{p-1:p-k}$, and the segmentation S_t is dependent on $\mathcal{F}_D^{p:p-k+1}$ and $\mathcal{F}_S^{p-1:p-k}$. In this way, those historical experiences from both tasks will be propagated along the time

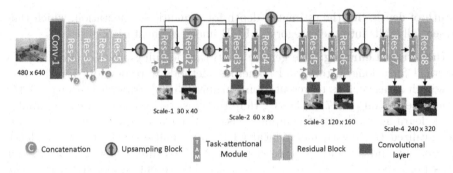

Fig. 2. The overview of our Task-Recursive Learning (TRL) network. The TRL network is an encoder-decoder architecture, which is composed of a series of residual blocks, upsampling blocks and Task-attentional Modules. The input RGB image is firstly fed into a ResNet to encode multi-level features, and then these features are fed into the task-recursive decoding process to estimate depth and semantic segmentation. In the decoder, the two tasks are alternately processed by adaptively evolving previous experiences of both tasks (i.e., the previous features of depth and segmentation), so as to boost and benefit for each other during the learning process. To estimate the current task state, the previous features of the two tasks are fed into a TAM to enhance the common information. To better refine the predicted details, we progressively execute the two tasks in a coarse-to-fine scale space.

sequences by using TAM. That means, the dual-task interactions will go deeper along the sequence of states. As a general idea, the framework can be adapted to other dual-task applications and even multi-task learning. We give the formulation of multi-task learning in the supplemental materials. In this paper we simply set $k = 1$ in Eq. 1, i.e., a short-term dependency.

3.2   Network Architecture

Overview: The entire network architecture is shown in Fig. 2. We use the sophisticated ResNet [41] to encode the input image. The gray cubes from Res-2 to Res-5 are multi-scale response maps extracted from ResNet. The next decoding process is designed to solve the dual tasks based on the task-recursive idea. The decoder is composed of upsampling blocks, task-attentional modules and residual-blocks. The upsampling blocks upscale the convolutional features to required scales for pixel-level prediction. The detailed architecture will be introduced in the following subsection. For the pixel-level prediction, we introduce residual-blocks (blue cubes) to decode the previous features, which are the mirror type of the corresponding ones in the encoder but only have two bottle-necks in each residual block. The Res-d1, Res-d3, Res-d5 and Res-d7 focus on depth estimation, while the rest ones focus on semantic segmentation. The TAM is designed to perform the interaction of two tasks. During the interaction, the previous information will be selectively enhanced to adapt to the current task. For example, the TAM before Res-d5 receives inputs from two sources: one is

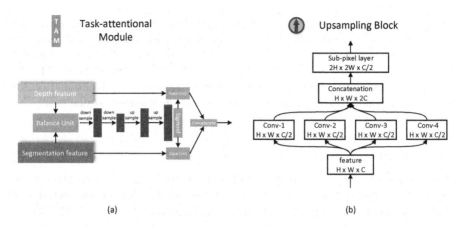

Fig. 3. The overview of our upsampling-block and task-attentional module.

the features upsampled from Res-d4 with segmentation information, and the other is the features upsampled from Res-d3 with depth information. During the interaction, the information of two inputs will be selectively enhanced to propagate to the next task. As the interaction times increase, the results of the two tasks are progressively refined in a mutual-boosting scheme. Another import strategy is taking a coarse-to-fine process to progressively reconstruct details and produce fine-grained predictions of high resolution. Concretely, we concatenate the different-scale features of encoder to the corresponding residual block, as indicated by the green arrows. The upsampling block and the task-attentional module will be described in the following subsections.

Task-Attentional Module. As discussed in the Sect. 1, semantic segmentation and depth estimation results of a scene have many common patterns, e.g., they can both reveal the object edges, boundaries or layouts. To better mine and utilize the common information, we design a task-attentional module to enhance the correlated information of the two tasks. As illustrated in Fig. 2, the TAM is used before each residual block and takes depth/segmentation features from previous residual blocks as inputs. The designed TAM are presented in Fig. 3(a). The input depth/segmentation features are firstly fed into a balance unit to balance the contribution of the features of two sources. If we use f_d and $f_s \in \mathrm{R}^{H \times W \times C}$ to denote the received depth and segmentation features respectively, the balance unit can be formulated as:

$$B = \mathrm{Sigmoid}(\Psi_1(\mathrm{concat}(f_d, f_s), \Theta_1)),$$
$$f_b = \Psi_2(\mathrm{concat}(B \cdot f_d, (1 - B) \cdot f_s), \Theta_2), \qquad (2)$$

where Ψ_1 and Ψ_2 are two convolutional layers with parameters Θ_1 and Θ_2, respectively. $B \in \mathrm{R}^{H \times W \times C}$ is the learnt balancing tensor, and $f_b \in \mathrm{R}^{H \times W \times C}$ is the balanced output of the balance unit. In this way, f_b combines the balanced information from the two sources. Next, the balanced output will be fed into a series of conv-deconvolutional layers, as illustrated by the yellow cubs in Fig. 3(a). Such a mechanism is designed to get different spatial attentions by using the receptive field variation, as demonstrated in the residual attention [42]. After a Sigmoid transformation, we get an attentional map $M \in R^{H \times W \times C}$, which is expected to have higher responses on the common patterns. Finally, the attentional tensor M is used to generate the gated depth/segmentation features, formally,

$$f_d^g = (1 + M) \cdot f_d,$$
$$f_s^g = (1 + M) \cdot f_s. \tag{3}$$

Thus the feature f_d and f_s may be enhanced through the learned attentional map M. The gated features f_d^g and f_s^g are further fused by concatenation followed by one convolutional layer. The output of TAM is denoted as $f_{TAM} \in R^{H \times W \times C}$. The task-attentional module can benefit our task-recursive learning method as experimentally analysed in Sect. 4.2.

Upsampling Blocks: The upsampling blocks are designed to match the scale variations during the task-recursive learning. The architecture of upsampling block is shown in Fig. 3(b). The features with size of $H \times W \times C$ are firstly fed into four parallel convolutional layers with different receptive fields (i.e., conv-1 to conv-4 in Fig. 3). These four convolutional layers are designed to capture different local structures. Then the responses produced from the four convolutional layers are concatenated to a tensor feature with size of $H \times W \times 2C$. Finally, the sub-pixel operation in [43] is applied to spatially upscale the feature. Formally, given a tensor feature T and a coordinate $[h, w, c]$, the sub-pixel operator can be defined as:

$$\mathcal{P}(T_{h,w,c}) = T_{\lfloor h/r \rfloor, \lfloor w/r \rfloor, c \cdot r \cdot \mathrm{mod}(w,r) + c \cdot \mathrm{mod}(h,r)}, \tag{4}$$

where r is the scale factor. After such sub-pixel operation, the output of one upsampling block is the feature of size $2H \times 2W \times C/2$, when we set $r = 2$. The upsampling blocks are more effective than the general deconvolution, as verified in the experiments in Sect. 4.2.

3.3   Training Loss

We impose the supervised loss constraint on each scale to obtain multi-scale predictions. For depth estimation, we use inverse Huber loss defined in [7] as the loss function, which can be formulated as:

$$\mathcal{L}^D(d_i) = \begin{cases} |d_i|, & |d_i| \leq c, \\ \frac{d_i^2 + c^2}{2c}, & |d_i| > c, \end{cases} \tag{5}$$

where d_i is the difference between prediction and ground truth at each pixel i, and c is a threshold with $c = \frac{1}{5} \max(d_i)$ as default. Such a loss function can provide more obvious gradients at the locations where the depth difference is low, and thus can help to better train the network. The loss function for semantic segmentation is a cross-entropy loss, denoted as $\mathcal{L}^S$. For a better optimization of our proposed dual-task network, we use the strategy proposed in [22] to balance the two tasks. Suppose the network predicts N pairs (w.r.t. N scales) of depth maps and semantic segmentation maps, the total loss function can be defined as:

$$\mathcal{L}(\Theta, \sigma_1, \sigma_2) = \frac{1}{\sigma_1^2} \sum_{n=1}^{N} \mathcal{L}_n^D + \frac{1}{\sigma_2^2} \sum_{n=1}^{N} \mathcal{L}_n^S + \log(\sigma_1^2) + \log(\sigma_2^2), \qquad (6)$$

where Θ is the parameter of network, σ_1 and σ_2 are the balancing weights to the two tasks. Please note that the balancing weights are also optimized as parameters during training. In practice, to avoid a potential division by zero, we redefine $\delta = \log \sigma^2$. Thus the total loss can be rewritten as:

$$\mathcal{L}(W, \delta_1, \delta_2) = \exp(-\delta_1) \sum_{n=1}^{N} \mathcal{L}_n^D + \exp(-\delta_2) \sum_{n=1}^{N} \mathcal{L}_n^S + \delta_1 + \delta_2. \qquad (7)$$

4   Experiments

4.1   Experimental Settings

Dataset: We evaluate the effectiveness of our proposed method on NYU Depth V2 [1] and SUN RGBD [44] datasets. The NYU Depth v2 dataset [1] consists of RGB-D images of 464 indoor scenes. There are 1449 images with semantic labels, 795 of them are used for training and the remaning 654 images for testing. We randomly select 4k images of the raw data from official training scenes. These 4k images have the corresponding depth maps but no semantic labels. Before training our network, we first train a ResNet-50 based DeconvNet [11] for 40-class semantic segmentation using the given 795 images. Then we use the predictions of the trained DeconvNet on the 4k images as coarse semantic labels to train our network. Finally we fine-tune the network on the 795 images of standard training split. The SUN RGBD dataset [44] contains 10355 RGB-D images with semantic labels of which 5285 for training and 5050 for testing. We use the 5285 images with depth and semantic labels to train our network, and the 5050 images for evaluation. The semantic labels are divided into 37 classes. Following the settings in [6,7,24,32], we use the same data augmentation strategies including cropping, scaling, flipping and rotating, to increase the diversity of data. As the largest outputs are half size of the input images, we upsample the predicted segmentation results and depth maps to the original size for comparison.

Implementation Details: We implement the proposed model using Pytorch on a single Nvidia P40 GPU. We build our network based on ResNet-18, ResNet-50 and ResNet-101, and each model is pre-trained on the ImageNet classification task [45]. ReLU activating function and Batch normalization are applied behind every convolutional layers, except for the final convolutional layers before the predictions. In the upsampling blocks, we set conv-1, conv-2, conv-3 and conv-4 with 1×1, 3×3, 5×5 and 7×7 kernel sizes, respectively. Note that we use 3×3 convolution with dilation $= 2$ to efficiently get a 7×7 receptive field. For the parameters of training loss, we simply use initial values of $\delta_1 = \delta_2 = 0.5$ of Eq. 7 for all scenes, and find that different initial values have no large effects on the performance. Initial learning rate is set to 10^{-5} for the pre-trained convolution layers and 0.01 for the other layers. For NYU Depth v2 dataset, we train our model on 4k unique images with coarse semantic labels and depth ground truth in 40K batch iterations, and then fine-tune the model with a learning rate of 0.001 on 795 images with depth and segmentation ground truth in 10K batch iterations. For the SUN-RGBD dataset, we train our model with 50K batch iterations on the initial learning rates, and fine-tune the non-pretrained layers for 30K batch iterations with a learning rate of 0.001. The momentum and weight decay are set to 0.9 and 0.0005 respectively, and the network is trained using SGD with batch size of 16. As there are many missing values in the depth ground truth maps, following the literatures [7, 24], we mask out the pixels that have missing depths both in the training and testing phases.

Metrics: Similar to the previous works [6, 7, 24], we evaluate our depth prediction results with the following metrics:

- average relative error (rel): $\frac{1}{n} \sum_i \frac{|\tilde{x}_i - x_i|}{x_i}$;
- root mean squared error (rms): $\sqrt{\frac{1}{n} \sum_i (\tilde{x}_i - x_i)^2}$;
- root mean squared error in log space (rms(log)): $\sqrt{\frac{1}{n} \sum_i (\log \tilde{x}_i - \log x_i)^2}$;
- accuracy with threshold (δ): % of $\tilde{x}_i$ s.t. $\max(\frac{\tilde{x}_i}{x_i}, \frac{x_i}{\tilde{x}_i}) = \delta$ $\delta = 1.25, 1.25^2, 1.25^3$;

where $\tilde{x}_i$ is the predicted depth value at the pixel i, n is the number of valid pixels and x_i is the ground truth.

For the evaluation of semantic segmentation results, we follow the recent works [27, 32, 46] and use the common metrics including pixel accuracy (pixel-acc), mean accuracy (mean-acc) and mean intersection over union (mean-IoU).

4.2   Ablation Study

In this section, we conduct several experiments to evaluate the effectiveness of our proposed method. The concrete ablation studies are introduced in the following.

Analysis on Tasks: We first analyse the benefit of jointly predicting depth and segmentation of one image. The experiments use the same network architecture as our ResNet-18 based network and are trained on NYU Depth v2 and SUN-RGBD datasets for depth estimation and segmentation respectively. As illustrated in Table 1, our proposed TRL network obviously benefits for each other under the joint learning of depth estimation and semantic segmentation. For NYU Depth v2 dataset, compared to the gain on depth estimation, semantic segmentation has a larger gain after the dual-task learning, i.e., the improvement

Table 1. Joint task learning v.s. single task learning on NYU depth V2 and SUN-RGBD datasets.

	NYU-D				SUN-RGBD			
Metric	rms	rel	mean-acc	IoU	rms	rel	mean-acc	IoU
Depth only	0.547	0.172	-	-	0.517	0.163	-	-
Segmentation only	-	-	51.2	42.0	-	-	54.1	43.5
TRL-jointly	**0.510**	**0.156**	**55.3**	**45.0**	**0.468**	**0.140**	**56.3**	**46.3**

Table 2. Comparisons of different network architectures and baselines on NYU depth v2 dataset.

Method	rms	rel	mean-acc	IoU
Baseline-I	0.545	0.171	53.5	43.2
TRL w/o TAM	0.526	0.153	54.0	43.6
TRL w/o exp-TAM	0.540	0.167	52.5	42.2
TRL w/o gate unit	0.515	0.160	55.0	44.7
TRL scale-1	0.597	0.202	50.1	40.3
TRL scale-2	0.572	0.198	51.9	41.0
TRL scale-3	0.541	0.166	53.2	43.8
TRL-ResNet18	0.510	0.156	55.3	45.0
TRL-ResNet50	0.501	0.144	56.3	46.4
TRL-ResNet101	**0.492**	**0.138**	**56.9**	**46.8**

about 4.1% on mean class accuracy and 3.0% on IoU. One possible reason should be more data of 4k depth images than semantic labels of 795 images. In contrast, for SUN-RGBD dataset, all training samples are with depth and semantic ground truth, i.e., the training samples for both tasks are balanced. We can observe that the performance on both tasks can be promoted for each other under the framework of proposed task-recursive learning.

Architectures and Baselines: We conduct experiments to analyse the effect of different network architectures. We set the baseline network with the same encoder but two parallel decoders. Each decoder corresponds to one task, which contains four residual blocks using the same type to the original TRL network decoder. To softly share the parameters and interact the two tasks, similar to the method in [19], we use the cross-stitch unit to fuse features at each scale. To evaluate the effectiveness of the task-attentional module, further, we perform an experiment without TAMs. To verify the importance of historical experience at previous stages, we also train a TRL network without any earlier experience (i.e., not considering the TAMs and the features from previous residual blocks). Besides, we also evaluate the prediction ability of other three scales (from scale-1 to scale-3) to show the effectiveness of the coarse-to-fine mechanism. All these

Fig. 4. Visual exhibition of the learned attentional maps. (a) input image; (b) segmentation ground truth; (c) depth ground truth; (d) learned attentional map. We can find that the attentional maps give high attention to objects, edges and boundaries which are very salient in both ground truth maps, i.e., more attention to the useful common information.

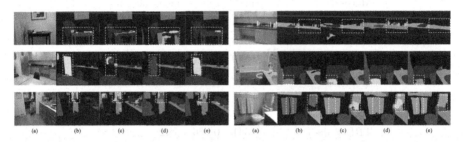

Fig. 5. Visual comparisons between TRL and baselines on NYU depth V2 and SUN RGBD. (a) input image; (b) ground truth; (c) results of baseline; (d) results of TRL w/o TAMs; (e) results of the TRL network. It can be observed that the predictions results of our proposed TRL contain less errors and suffer less class ambiguity.

experimental models take ResNet-18 as infrastructure. Externally, we also train ResNet-50 and ResNet-101 based TRL networks to analyse the effect of deeper encoding networks.

As reported in Table 2, our proposed TRL network signaficantly performs better than the baseline on both tasks. Compared with the TRL network without TAMs, TRL can obtain a superior performance on both tasks. It indicates that TAMs can potentially take some common patterns of the two tasks to promote the performance. For this, we also visually exhibit the learned attentional map M from the TAMs. As observed in Fig. 4, the attentional maps have higher attention to objects, edges and boundaries, which are very obvious according to both ground truth maps. These features commonly exist in the two tasks, and thus can make TAMs capture such common information to promote both tasks. For the case without the historical experience mechanism, i.e., TRL w/o exp-TAMs, the original TRL can obtain an accumulative gain of 21.4% on the two tasks, which demonstrates that the experience mechanism is also crucial for the task-recursive learning process. In the cast that TAM has no gate unit, i.e., TRL w/o gate unit, the resulting accuracies are slightly decreased. When the scale increases, i.e., the coarse-to-fine manner, the performances are

Table 3. Comparisons with the state-of-the-art depth estimation approaches on NYU depth v2 dataset.

Method	rms	rel	rms(log)	δ_1	δ_2	δ_3
Li [26]	0.821	0.232	-	0.621	0.886	0.968
Liu [25]	0.824	0.230	-	0.614	0.883	0.971
Wang [21]	0.745	0.220	0.262	0.605	0.890	0.970
Eigen [5]	0.877	0.214	0.285	0.611	0.887	0.971
Roy [47]	0.744	0.187	-	-	-	-
Eigen [24]	0.641	0.158	0.214	0.769	0.950	0.988
Cao [48]	0.615	0.148	-	0.800	0.956	0.988
Xu-4.7k [6]	0.613	0.143	-	0.789	0.946	0.984
Xu-95k [6]	0.586	**0.121**	-	0.811	0.954	0.987
Laina [7]	0.573	0.127	0.194	0.811	0.953	0.988
TRL-ResNet18	0.510	0.156	0.187	0.804	0.951	0.990
TRL-ResNet50	**0.501**	0.144	**0.181**	**0.815**	**0.962**	**0.992**

gradually improved on both tasks. An obvious reason is that details can be better reconstructed in those fine scale space. Further, when more sophisticated and deeper encoders are employed, ResNet-50 and ResNet-101, the proposed TRL network can improve the performance, which can be easily understood as the same observations in other literatures.

For a visual analysis, we show some prediction results of baselines and TRL in Fig. 5. From the figure, we can observe that the segmentation results of the two baselines suffer obvious classification error, especially as shown in the white bounding boxes. In contrast, the prediction results of TRL suffer less class ambiguity and are more reasonable visually. More ablation study and visual results can be found in our supplementary material.

4.3   Comparisons with the State-of-the-Art Methods

In this section we compare our method with several state-of-the-art approaches on both tasks. The experiments are conducted on NYU Depth V2 and SUN-RGBD datasets, which will be discussed below.

Depth Estimation: We compare our depth estimation performance on NYU depth V2 dataset, and summarize the results in Table 3. As observed from this table, our TRL network with ResNet-50 achieves the best performance on the rms, rms(log) and the δ-accuracy metrics, while this version with ResNet-18 also obtains satisfactory results. Compared with the recent method [7], our TRL is slightly inferior in the rel metric, but significantly superior in other metrics, where a total 7.67% relative gain is achieved. It is worth noting that the method in literature [7] used a larger training set which contains 12k unique image and

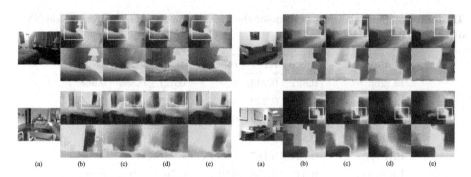

Fig. 6. Qualitative comparison with some state-of-the-art approaches on NYU depth v2 dataset. (a) input RGB image; (b) ground truth; (c) results of [24]; (d) results of [6]; (e) results of our TRL with ResNet-50. It can be easily observed that our predictions contain more details and less noise than these compared methods.

Table 4. Comparisons the state-of-the-art semantic segmentation methods on NYU depth v2 dataset.

Method	data	pixel-acc	mean-acc	IoU
FCN [10]	RGB	60.0	49.2	29.2
Context [49]	RGB	70.0	53.6	40.6
Eigen *et al.* [24]	RGB	65.6	45.1	34.1
B-SegNet [27]	RGB	68.0	45.8	32.4
RefineNet-101 [46]	RGB	72.8	57.8	44.9
Deng *et al.* [50]	RGBD	63.8	-	31.5
He *et al.* [31]	RGBD	70.1	53.8	40.1
LSTM [51]	RGBD	-	49.4	-
Cheng *et al.* [32]	RGBD	71.9	**60.7**	45.9
3D-GNN [52]	RGBD	-	55.7	43.1
RDF-50 [53]	RGBD	74.8	60.4	**47.7**
TRL-ResNet18	RGB	74.3	55.5	45.0
TRL-ResNet50	RGB	**76.2**	56.3	46.4

depth pairs, but our model uses only 4k unique images (less than 12k) and still gets a better performance. Compared with the method in [6], we have the same observation that our TRL is slightly poor in rel metric but has obviously better results in all other metrics. Please note that the method in [6] attempted to use more training images (95k) to promote the performance of depth estimation. Nevertheless, if the training data is reduced to 4.7k, the accuracies have an obvious degradation for the method in [6]. In contrast, under the nearly equal size of training data, our TRL can still achieve the best performance in most metrics.

Table 5. Comparison with the state-of-the-art semantic segmentation methods on SUN-RGBD dataset.

Method	data	pixel-acc	mean-acc	IoU
Context [49]	RGB	78.4	53.4	42.3
B-SegNet [27]	RGB	71.2	45.9	30.7
RefineNet-101 [46]	RGB	80.4	57.8	45.7
RefineNet-152 [46]	RGB	80.6	58.5	45.9
LSTM [51]	RGBD	-	48.1	-
Cheng *et al.* [32]	RGBD	-	58.0	-
CFN [54]	RGBD	-	-	48.1
3D-GNN [52]	RGBD	-	57.0	45.9
RDF-152 [53]	RGBD	81.5	**60.1**	47.7
TRL-ResNet18	RGB	81.1	56.3	46.3
TRL-ResNet50	RGB	83.6	58.2	49.6
TRL-ResNet101	RGB	**84.3**	58.9	**50.3**

In addition, to provide a visual observation, we show some visual comparison examples in Fig. 6. The prediction results of the methods in [6,24] usually have much noise, especially at the object boundaries, curtains, sofa and bed. On the contrary, our predictions have less noise and better match the geometry of the scenes. Therefore, these experimental results can demonstrate that our proposed approach is more effective than the state-of-the-art method by borrowing semantic segmentation information.

RGBD Semantic Segmentation: We compare our TRL method with the state-of-the-art approaches on NYU Depth V2 and SUN RGBD datasets. For NYU Depth V2 dataset, as summarized in Table 4, our TRL network with ResNet-50 achieve the best pixel accuracies, but is slightly poor in mean class accuracy metric than the method in [32] and mean IoU metric than the method in [53]. It may be attributed to the imperfect depth predictions. Actually, the methods in [32,53] used the depth ground truth as the input, and carefully designed some depth-RGB feature fusion strategies to make the segmentation prediction better benefit from the depth ground truth. In contrast, our TRL method uses only RGB images as the input and conduct semantic segmentation based on estimated image depth, not depth ground truth. Although our TRL itself can obtain impressive depth estimation results, the depth estimation is still not as precise as ground truth, which usually results into more or less errors in the segmentation prediction process. Meanwhile, as the number of samples with semantic labels is limited in training for NYU Depth V2 dataset (795 images), the performance may be affected for our method.

For SUN-RGBD dataset, as reported in Table 5, our TRL network with ResNet-101 can reach the best performance in pixel-accuracy and mean IoU metrics. It is worth noting that the number of training samples with semantic labels is 5285 in SUN-RGBD, which is more than NYU Depth V2. Thus the performances on the two tasks are totally better than those on NYU Depth V2 for most methods, including our TRL network. Compared with the method in [53], our TRL with ResNet-50 has a total 2.1% gain for all metrics, while the version with ResNet-101 obtains a total 4.3% gain. Note that, the method in [53] used the stronger ResNet-152 and more precise depth (i.e., ground truth) as inputs, while our TRL network uses only RGB images as the input. Overall, our TRL outperforms the current state-of-the-art methods in most evaluation metrics except the mean accuracy metric, in which ours is slightly poor but comparable.

5 Conclusions

In this paper, a novel end-to-end task-recursive learning framework had been proposed for jointly predicting depth map and semantic segmentation from one RGB image. The task-recursive learning network alternately refined the two tasks as a recursive sequence of time states. To better leverage the correlated and common patterns of depth and semantic segmentation, we also designed a task-attentional module. The module can adaptively mine the common information of the two tasks, encourage both interactive learning, and finally benefit for each other. Comprehensive benchmark evaluations demonstrated the superiority of our task-recursive network on jointly dealing with depth estimation and semantic segmentation. Meantime, we also reported some new state-of-the-art results on NYU-Depth v2 and SUN RGB-D datasets. In future, we will generalize the framework into the joint learning on more tasks.

Acknowledgement. The authors would like to thank the anonymous reviewers for their critical and constructive comments and suggestions. This work was supported by the National Natural Science Fund of China under Grant Nos. U1713208, 61472187, 61602244 and 61772276, the 973 Program No. 2014CB349303, the fundamental research funds for the central universities No. 30918011321, and Program for Changjiang Scholars.

References

1. Silberman, N., Hoiem, D., Kohli, P., Fergus, R.: Indoor segmentation and support inference from RGBD images. In: Fitzgibbon, A., Lazebnik, S., Perona, P., Sato, Y., Schmid, C. (eds.) ECCV 2012. LNCS, vol. 7576, pp. 746–760. Springer, Heidelberg (2012). https://doi.org/10.1007/978-3-642-33715-4_54
2. Michels, J., Saxena, A., Ng, A.Y.: High speed obstacle avoidance using monocular vision and reinforcement learning. In: ICML, pp. 593–600 (2005)
3. Hadsell, R., et al.: Learning long-range vision for autonomous off-road driving. J. Field Robot. **26**(2), 120–144 (2009)
4. Tateno, K., Tombari, F., Laina, I., Navab, N.: CNN-SLAM: real-time dense monocular SLAM with learned depth prediction. In: CVPR, vol. 2, pp. 6565–6574 (2017)

5. Eigen, D., Puhrsch, C., Fergus, R.: Depth map prediction from a single image using a multi-scale deep network. In: NIPS, pp. 2366–2374 (2014)
6. Xu, D., Ricci, E., Ouyang, W., Wang, X., Sebe, N.: Multi-scale continuous CRFs as sequential deep networks for monocular depth estimation. In: CVPR, vol. 1, pp. 161–169 (2017)
7. Laina, I., Rupprecht, C., Belagiannis, V., Tombari, F., Navab, N.: Deeper depth prediction with fully convolutional residual networks. In: 3DV, pp. 239–248 (2016)
8. Zhang, Z., Xu, C., Yang, J., Gao, J., Cui, Z.: Progressive hard-mining network for monocular depth estimation. IEEE Trans. Image Process. **27**(8), 3691–3702 (2018)
9. Zhang, Z., Xu, C., Yang, J., Tai, Y., Chen, L.: Deep hierarchical guidance and regularization learning for end-to-end depth estimation. Pattern Recognit. **83**, 430–442 (2018)
10. Long, J., Shelhamer, E., Darrell, T.: Fully convolutional networks for semantic segmentation. IEEE Trans. Pattern Anal. Mach. Intell. **39**(4), 640–651 (2017)
11. Noh, H., Hong, S., Han, B.: Learning deconvolution network for semantic segmentation. In: ICCV, pp. 1520–1528 (2015)
12. Li, X., et al.: FoveaNet: perspective-aware urban scene parsing. In: ICCV, pp. 784–792 (2017)
13. Wei, Y., et al.: Learning to segment with image-level annotations. Pattern Recognit. **59**, 234–244 (2016)
14. Wang, J., Wang, Z., Tao, D., See, S., Wang, G.: Learning common and specific features for RGB-D semantic segmentation with deconvolutional networks. In: Leibe, B., Matas, J., Sebe, N., Welling, M. (eds.) ECCV 2016. LNCS, vol. 9909, pp. 664–679. Springer, Cham (2016). https://doi.org/10.1007/978-3-319-46454-1_40
15. Caruana, R.: Multitask learning. Mach. Learn. **28**(1), 41–75 (1997)
16. Girshick, R.: Fast R-CNN. In: ICCV, pp. 1440–1448 (2015)
17. He, K., Gkioxari, G., Dollr, P., Girshick, R.: Mask R-CNN. In: IEEE International Conference on Computer Vision (2017)
18. Kim, S., Park, K., Sohn, K., Lin, S.: Unified depth prediction and intrinsic image decomposition from a single image via joint convolutional neural fields. In: Leibe, B., Matas, J., Sebe, N., Welling, M. (eds.) ECCV 2016. LNCS, vol. 9912, pp. 143–159. Springer, Cham (2016). https://doi.org/10.1007/978-3-319-46484-8_9
19. Misra, I., Shrivastava, A., Gupta, A., Hebert, M.: Cross-stitch networks for multi-task learning. In: CVPR, pp. 3994–4003 (2016)
20. Shi, J., Pollefeys, M.: Pulling things out of perspective. In: CVPR, pp. 89–96 (2014)
21. Wang, P., Shen, X., Lin, Z., Cohen, S.: Towards unified depth and semantic prediction from a single image. In: CVPR, pp. 2800–2809 (2015)
22. Kendall, A., Gal, Y., Cipolla, R.: Multi-task learning using uncertainty to weigh losses for scene geometry and semantics. arXiv:1705.07115 (2017)
23. Borst, J.P., Taatgen, N.A., Van Rijn, H.: The problem state: a cognitive bottleneck in multitasking. J. Exp. Psychol. Learn. Mem. Cogn. **36**(2), 363 (2010)
24. Eigen, D., Fergus, R.: Predicting depth, surface normals and semantic labels with a common multi-scale convolutional architecture. In: ICCV, pp. 2650–2658 (2015)
25. Liu, F., Shen, C., Lin, G., Reid, I.: Learning depth from single monocular images using deep convolutional neural fields. IEEE Trans. Pattern Anal. Mach. Intell. **38**(10), 2024–2039 (2016)
26. Li, B., Shen, C., Dai, Y., van den Hengel, A., He, M.: Depth and surface normal estimation from monocular images using regression on deep features and hierarchical CRFs. In: CVPR, pp. 1119–1127 (2015)

27. Kendall, A., Badrinarayanan, V., Cipolla, R.: Bayesian SegNet: model uncertainty in deep convolutional encoder-decoder architectures for scene understanding. arXiv preprint arXiv:1511.02680 (2015)
28. Wei, Y., Xiao, H., Shi, H., Jie, Z., Feng, J., Huang, T.S.: Revisiting dilated convolution: a simple approach for weakly-and semi-supervised semantic segmentation. In: CVPR, pp. 7268–7277 (2018)
29. Jin, X., Chen, Y., Jie, Z., Feng, J., Yan, S.: Multi-path feedback recurrent neural networks for scene parsing. In: AAAI, vol. 3, p. 8 (2017)
30. Gupta, S., Girshick, R., Arbeláez, P., Malik, J.: Learning rich features from RGB-D images for object detection and segmentation. In: Fleet, D., Pajdla, T., Schiele, B., Tuytelaars, T. (eds.) ECCV 2014. LNCS, vol. 8695, pp. 345–360. Springer, Cham (2014). https://doi.org/10.1007/978-3-319-10584-0_23
31. He, Y., Chiu, W.C., Keuper, M., Fritz, M.: STD2P: RGBD semantic segmentation using spatio-temporal data-driven pooling. arXiv preprint arXiv:1604.02388 (2016)
32. Cheng, Y., Cai, R., Li, Z., Zhao, X., Huang, K.: Locality-sensitive deconvolution networks with gated fusion for RGB-D indoor semantic segmentation. In: CVPR, vol. 3, pp. 1475–1483 (2017)
33. Amit, Y., Fink, M., Srebro, N., Ullman, S.: Uncovering shared structures in multi-class classification. In: Proceedings of the Twenty-Fourth International Conference on Machine Learning, pp. 17–24 (2007)
34. Evgeniou, T., Pontil, M.: Regularized multi-task learning. In: Tenth ACM SIGKDD International Conference on Knowledge Discovery and Data Mining, pp. 109–117 (2004)
35. Jalali, A., Ravikumar, P.D., Sanghavi, S., Chao, R.: A dirty model for multi-task learning. In: NIPS, pp. 964–972 (2010)
36. Razavian, A.S., Azizpour, H., Sullivan, J., Carlsson, S.: CNN features off-the-shelf: an astounding baseline for recognition. In: CVPR Workshops, pp. 512–519 (2014)
37. Yosinski, J., Clune, J., Bengio, Y., Lipson, H.: How transferable are features in deep neural networks? In: NIPS, pp. 3320–3328 (2014)
38. Wang, X., Fouhey, D.F., Gupta, A.: Designing deep networks for surface normal estimation. In: CVPR, pp. 539–547 (2014)
39. Gebru, T., Hoffman, J., Li, F.F.: Fine-grained recognition in the wild: a multi-task domain adaptation approach. arXiv:1709.02476 (2017)
40. Kokkinos, I.: UberNet: training a 'universal' convolutional neural network for low-, mid-, and high-level vision using diverse datasets and limited memory. In: CVPR, pp. 5454–5463 (2017)
41. He, K., Zhang, X., Ren, S., Sun, J.: Deep residual learning for image recognition. In: CVPR, pp. 770–778 (2016)
42. Wang, F., et al.: Residual attention network for image classification. In: CVPR, pp. 6450–6458 (2017)
43. Shi, W., et al.: Real-time single image and video super-resolution using an efficient sub-pixel convolutional neural network. In: CVPR, pp. 1874–1883 (2016)
44. Song, S., Lichtenberg, S.P., Xiao, J.: Sun RGB-D: a RGB-D scene understanding benchmark suite. In: CVPR, pp. 567–576 (2015)
45. Deng, J., Dong, W., Socher, R., Li, L.J., Li, K., Fei-Fei, L.: ImageNet: a large-scale hierarchical image database. In: CVPR, pp. 248–255 (2009)
46. Lin, G., Milan, A., Shen, C., Reid, I.: RefineNet: multi-path refinement networks for high-resolution semantic segmentation. In: CVPR, vol. 1, pp. 5168–5177 (2017)
47. Roy, A., Todorovic, S.: Monocular depth estimation using neural regression forest. In: CVPR, pp. 5506–5514 (2016)

48. Cao, Y., Wu, Z., Shen, C.: Estimating depth from monocular images as classification using deep fully convolutional residual networks. In: IEEE Transactions on Circuits and Systems for Video Technology (2017)
49. Lin, G., Shen, C., van den Hengel, A., Reid, I.: Efficient piecewise training of deep structured models for semantic segmentation. In: CVPR, pp. 3194–3203 (2016)
50. Deng, Z., Todorovic, S., Latecki, L.J.: Semantic segmentation of RGBD images with mutex constraints. In: ICCV, pp. 1733–1741 (2015)
51. Li, Z., Gan, Y., Liang, X., Yu, Y., Cheng, H., Lin, L.: LSTM-CF: unifying context modeling and fusion with LSTMs for RGB-D scene labeling. In: Leibe, B., Matas, J., Sebe, N., Welling, M. (eds.) ECCV 2016. LNCS, vol. 9906, pp. 541–557. Springer, Cham (2016). https://doi.org/10.1007/978-3-319-46475-6_34
52. Xiaojuan, Q., Renjie, L., Jiaya, J., Sanya, F., Raquel, U.: 3D graph neural networks for RGBD semantic segmentation. In: ICCV, pp. 5209–5218 (2017)
53. Seong-Jin, P., Ki-Sang, H., Seungyong, L.: RDFNet: RGB-D multi-level residual feature fusion for indoor semantic segmentation. In: ICCV, pp. 4990–4999 (2017)
54. Di, L., Guangyong, C., Daniel, C.O., Pheng-Ann, H., Hui, H.: Cascaded feature network for semantic segmentation of RGB-D images. In: ICCV, pp. 1320–1328 (2017)

Fast, Accurate, and Lightweight Super-Resolution with Cascading Residual Network

Namhyuk Ahn⬤, Byungkon Kang⬤, and Kyung-Ah Sohn^(✉)⬤

Department of Computer Engineering, Ajou University, Suwon, South Korea
{aa0dfg,byungkon,kasohn}@ajou.ac.kr

Abstract. In recent years, deep learning methods have been successfully applied to single-image super-resolution tasks. Despite their great performances, deep learning methods cannot be easily applied to real-world applications due to the requirement of heavy computation. In this paper, we address this issue by proposing an accurate and lightweight deep network for image super-resolution. In detail, we design an architecture that implements a *cascading mechanism* upon a residual network. We also present variant models of the proposed cascading residual network to further improve efficiency. Our extensive experiments show that even with much fewer parameters and operations, our models achieve performance comparable to that of state-of-the-art methods.

Keywords: Super-resolution · Deep convolutional neural network

1 Introduction

Super-resolution (SR) is a computer vision task that reconstructs a high-resolution (HR) image from a low-resolution (LR) image. Specifically, we are concerned with single image super-resolution (SISR), which performs SR using a single LR image. SISR is generally difficult to achieve due to the fact that computing the HR image from an LR image is a many-to-one mapping. Despite such difficulty, SISR is a very active area because it can offer the promise of overcoming resolution limitations, and could be used in a variety of applications such as video streaming or surveillance system.

Recently, convolutional neural network-based (CNN-based) methods have provided outstanding performance in SISR tasks [6,19,23]. From the SRCNN [6] that has three convolutional layers to MDSR [25] that has more than 160 layers, the depth of the network and the overall performance have dramatically grown over time. However, even though deep learning methods increase the quality of the SR images, they are not suitable for real-world scenarios. From this point of view, it is important to design lightweight deep learning models that are practical for real-world applications. One way to build a lean model is reducing the number of parameters. There are many ways to achieve this [11,18], but the most simple

© Springer Nature Switzerland AG 2018
V. Ferrari et al. (Eds.): ECCV 2018, LNCS 11214, pp. 256–272, 2018.
https://doi.org/10.1007/978-3-030-01249-6_16

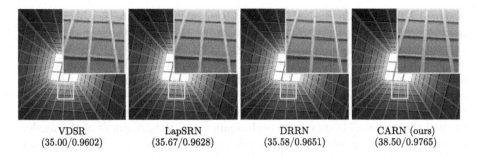

| VDSR | LapSRN | DRRN | CARN (ours) |
| (35.00/0.9602) | (35.67/0.9628) | (35.58/0.9651) | (38.50/0.9765) |

Fig. 1. Super-resolution result of our methods compared with existing methods.

and effective approach is to use a *recursive network*. For example, DRCN [20] uses a recursive network to reduce redundant parameters, and DRRN [34] improves DRCN by adding a residual architecture to it. These models decrease the number of model parameters effectively when compared to the standard CNN and show good performance. However, there are two downsides to these models: (1) They first upsample the input image before feeding it to the CNN model, and (2) they increase the depth or the width of the network to compensate for the loss due to using a recursive network. These points enable the model to maintain the details of the image when reconstructed, but at the expense of the increased number of operations and inference time.

Most of the works that aim to build a lean model focused primarily on reducing the number of parameters. However, as mentioned above, the number of operations is also an important factor to consider in real-world scenarios. Consider a situation where an SR system operates on a mobile device. Then, the execution speed of the system is also of crucial importance from a user-experience perspective. Especially the battery capacity, which is heavily dependent on the amount of computation performed, becomes a major problem. In this respect, reducing the number of operations in the deep learning architectures is a challenging and necessary step that has largely been ignored until now. Another scenario relates to applying SR methods to video streaming services. The demand for streaming media has skyrocketed and hence requires large storage to store massive multimedia data. It is therefore imperative to compress data using lossy compression techniques before storing. Then, an SR technique can be applied to restore the data to the original resolution. However, because latency is the most critical factor in streaming services, the decompression process (i.e., super-resolution) has to be performed in real-time. To do so, it is essential to make the SR methods lightweight in terms of the number of operations.

To handle these requirements and improve the recent models, we propose a Cascading residual network (CARN) and its variant CARN-Mobile (CARN-M). We first build our CARN model to increase the performance and extend it to CARN-M to optimize it for speed and the number of operations. Following the FSRCNN [7], CARN family take the LR images and compute the HR counterparts as the output of the network. The middle parts of our models are designed based on the ResNet [13]. The ResNet architecture has been widely used in deep learning-based SR methods [25,34] because of the ease of training and superior performance. In addition to the ResNet architecture, CARN uses a *cascading mechanism* at both the local and the global level to incorporate the features from multiple layers. This has the effect of reflecting various levels of input representations in order to receive more information. In addition to the CARN model, we also provide the CARN-M model that allows the designer to tune the trade-off between the performance and the *heaviness* of the model. It does so by means of the efficient residual block (residual-E) and recursive network architecture, which we describe in more detail in Sect. 3.

In summary, our main contributions are as follows: (**1**) We propose CARN, a neural network based on the cascading modules, which achieves high performance on SR task (Fig. 1). Our cascading modules, effectively boost the performance via multi-level representation and multiple shortcut connections. (**2**) We also propose CARN-M for efficient SR by combining the efficient residual block and the recursive network scheme. (**3**) We show through extensive experiments, that our model uses only a modest number of operations and parameters to achieve competitive results. Our CARN-M, which is the more lightweight SR model, shows comparable results to others with much fewer operations.

2 Related Work

Since the success of AlexNet [22] in image recognition task [5], many deep learning approaches have been applied to diverse computer vision tasks [9,26,29,39]. The SISR task is one such task, and we present an overview of the deep learning-based SISR in Sect. 2.1. Another area we deal with in this paper is model compression. Recent deep learning models focus on squeezing model parameters and operations for application in low-power computing devices, which has many practical benefits in real-world applications. We briefly review in Sect. 2.2.

2.1 Deep Learning Based Image Super-Resolution

Recently, deep learning based models have shown dramatic improvements in the SISR task. Dong et al. [6] first proposed a deep learning-based SR method, SRCNN, which outperformed traditional algorithms. However, SRCNN has a large number of operations compared to its depth, since network takes upsampled images as input. Taking a different approach from SRCNN, FSRCNN [7] and ESPCN [32] upsample images at the end of the networks. By doing so, it leads to the reduction in the number of operations compared to the SRCNN. However, the overall performance could be degraded if there are not enough layers after the upsampling process. Moreover, they cannot manage multi-scale training, as the input image size differs for each upsampling scale.

Despite the fact that the power of deep learning comes from *deep* layers, the aforementioned methods have settled for shallow layers because of the difficulty in training. To better harness the depth of deep learning models, Kim et al. [19]

proposed VDSR, which uses *residual learning* to map the LR images **x** to their residual images **r**. Then, VDSR produces the SR images **y** by adding the residual back into the original, *i.e.*, $\mathbf{y} = \mathbf{x} + \mathbf{r}$. On the other hand, LapSRN [23] uses a Laplacian pyramid architecture to increase the image size gradually. By doing so, LapSRN effectively performs SR on extremely low-resolution cases with a fewer number of operations compared to VDSR.

Another issue of deep learning-based SR is how to reduce the parameters and operation. For example, DRCN [20] uses a recursive network to reduce parameters by engaging in redundant usages of a small number of parameters. DRRN [34] improves DRCN by combining the recursive and residual network schemes to achieve better performance with fewer parameters. However, DRCN and DRRN use very deep networks to compensate for the loss of performance and hence these require heavy computing resources. Hence, we aim to build a model that is lightweight in both size and computation. We will briefly discuss previous works that address such model efficiency issues in the following section.

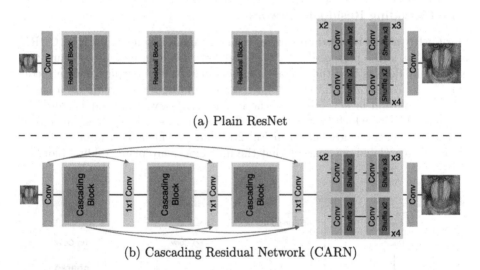

(a) Plain ResNet

(b) Cascading Residual Network (CARN)

Fig. 2. Network architectures of plain ResNet (**top**) and the proposed CARN (**bottom**). Both models are given an LR image and upsample to HR at the end of the network. In the CARN model, each residual block is changed to a cascading block. The blue arrows indicate the global cascading connection. (Color figure online)

2.2   Efficient Neural Network

There has been rising interest in building small and efficient neural networks [11,15,18]. These approaches can be categorized into two groups: **(1)** Compressing pretrained networks, and **(2)** designing small but efficient models. Han et al. [11] proposed deep compressing techniques, which consist of pruning, vector quantization, and Huffman coding to reduce the size of a pretrained network. In the latter category, SqueezeNet [18] builds an AlexNet-based architecture and achieves comparable performance level with 50× fewer parameters. MobileNet [15] builds an efficient network by applying depthwise separable convolution introduced in Sifre et al. [33]. Because of this simplicity, we also apply this technique in the residual block with some modification to achieve a lean neural network.

3   Proposed Method

As mentioned in Sect. 1, we propose two main models: CARN and CARN-M. CARN is designed to be a high-performing SR model while suppressing the number of operations compared to the state-of-the-art methods. Based on CARN, we design CARN-M, which is a much more efficient SR model in terms of both parameters and operations.

3.1   Cascading Residual Network

Our CARN model is based on ResNet [13]. The main difference between CARN and ResNet is the presence of local and global cascading modules. Figure 2(b) graphically depicts how the global cascading occurs. The outputs of intermediary layers are *cascaded* into the higher layers, and finally converge on a single 1 × 1 convolution layer. Note that the intermediary layers are implemented as cascading blocks, which host local cascading connections themselves. Such local cascading operations are shown in Fig. 2(c) and (d). Local cascading is almost identical to a global one, except that the unit blocks are plain residual blocks.

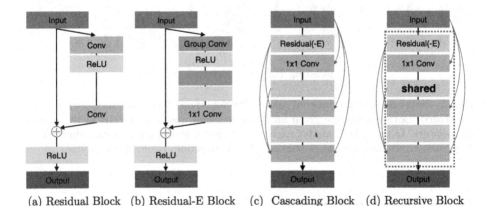

(a) Residual Block   (b) Residual-E Block   (c) Cascading Block   (d) Recursive Block

Fig. 3. Simplified structures of (a) residual block (b) efficient residual block (residual-E), (c) cascading block and (d) recursive cascading block. The ⊕ operations in (a) and (b) are element-wise addition for residual learning.

To express the implementation formally, let f be a convolution function and τ be an activation function. Then, we can define the i-th residual block R_i, which has two convolutions followed by a residual addition, as

$$R_i(H^{i-1}; W_R^i) = \tau(f(\tau(f(H^{i-1}; W_R^{i,1})); W_R^{i,2}) + H^{i-1}). \tag{1}$$

Here, H^i is the output of the i-th residual block, W_R^i is the parameter set of the residual block, and $W_R^{i,j}$ is the parameter of the j-th convolution layer in the i-th block. With this notation, we denote the output feature of the final residual block of ResNet as H^u, which becomes the input to the upsampling block.

$$H^u = R_u \left(\dots \left(R_1 \left(f\left(\boldsymbol{X}; W_c \right); W_R^1 \right) \right) \dots; W_R^u \right). \tag{2}$$

Note that because our model has a single convolution layer before each residual block, the first residual block gets $f(\boldsymbol{X}; W_c)$ as input, where W_c is the parameter of the convolution layer.

In contrast to ResNet, our CARN model has a local cascading block illustrated in block (c) of Fig. 3 instead of a plain residual block. In here, we denote $B^{i,j}$ as the output of the j-th residual block in the i-th cascading block, and W_c^i as the set of parameters of the i-th local cascading block. Then, the i-th local cascading block B_{local}^i is defined as

$$B_{local}^i \left(H^{i-1}; W_l^i \right) \equiv B^{i,U}, \tag{3}$$

where $B^{i,U}$ is defined recursively from the $B^{i,u}$'s as:

$$B^{i,0} = H^{i-1}$$
$$B^{i,u} = f\left(\left[I, B^{i,0}, \dots, B^{i,u-1}, R^u \left(B^{i,u-1}; W_R^u \right) \right]; W_c^{i,u} \right) \quad \text{for } u = 1, \dots, U.$$

Finally, we can define the output feature of the final cascading block H^b by combining both the local and global cascading. Here, H^0 is the output of the first convolution layer. And we fix $u = b = 3$ for our CARN and CARN-M.

$$H^0 = f\left(\boldsymbol{X}; W_c \right)$$
$$H^b = f\left(\left[H^0, \dots, H^{b-1}, B_{local}^u \left(H^{b-1}; W_B^b \right) \right] \right) \quad \text{for } b = 1, \dots, B. \tag{4}$$

The main difference between CARN and ResNet lies in the cascading mechanism. As shown in Fig. 2, CARN has global cascading connections represented as the blue arrows, each of which is followed by a 1×1 convolution layer. Cascading on both the local and global levels has two advantages: (1) The model incorporates features from multiple layers, which allows learning multi-level representations. (2) Multi-level cascading connection behaves as multi-level shortcut connections that quickly propagate information from lower to higher layers (and vice-versa, in case of back-propagation).

CARN adopts a multi-level representation scheme as in [24,27], but we apply this arrangement to a variety of feature levels to boost performance, as shown in Eq. 4. By doing so, our model reconstructs the LR image based on multi-level features. This facilitates the model to restore the details and contexts of the image simultaneously. As a result, our models effectively improve not only primitive objects but also complex objects.

Another reason for adopting the cascading scheme is two-fold: First, the propagation of information follows multiple paths [16,31]. Second, by adding extra convolution layers, our model can learn to choose the right pathway with the given input information flows. However, the strength of multiple shortcuts is degraded when we use only one of local or global cascading, especially the local connection. We elaborate the details and present a case study on the effects of cascading mechanism in Sect. 4.4.

3.2   Efficient Cascading Residual Network

To improve the efficiency of CARN, we propose an efficient residual (residual-E) block. We use a similar approach to the MobileNet [15], but use group convolution instead of depthwise convolution. Our residual-E block consists of two 3×3 group and one pointwise convolution, as shown in Fig. 3(b). The advantage of using group convolution over the depthwise convolution is that it makes the efficiency of the model tunable. The user can choose the group size appropriately since the group size and performance are in a trade-off relationship. The analysis on the cost efficiency of using the residual-E block is as follows.

Let K be the kernel size and C_{in}, C_{out} be the number of input and output channels. Because we retain the feature resolution of the input and output by padding, we can denote F to be both the input and output feature size. Then, the cost of a plain residual block is as $2 \times (K \cdot K \cdot C_{in} \cdot C_{out} \cdot F \cdot F)$. Note that we only count the cost of convolution layers and ignore the addition or activation because both the plain and the efficient residual blocks have the same amount of cost in terms of addition and activation.

Let G be the group size. Then, the cost of a residual-E block, which consist of two group convolutions and one pointwise convolution, is as given in Eq. 5.

$$2 \times \left(K \cdot K \cdot C_{in} \cdot \frac{C_{out}}{G} \cdot F \cdot F \right) + C_{in} \cdot C_{out} \cdot F \cdot F \qquad (5)$$

By changing the plain residual block to our efficient residual block, we can reduce the computation by the ratio of

$$\frac{2 \times \left(K \cdot K \cdot C_{in} \cdot \frac{C_{out}}{G} \cdot F \cdot F \right) + C_{in} \cdot C_{out} \cdot F \cdot F}{2 \times (K \cdot K \cdot C_{in} \cdot C_{out} \cdot F \cdot F)} = \frac{1}{G} + \frac{1}{2K^2}. \qquad (6)$$

Because our model uses a kernel of size 3×3 for all group convolutions, and the number of channels is constantly 64, using an efficient residual block instead of a standard residual block can reduce the computation from 1.8 up to 14 times depending on the group size. To find the best trade-off between performance and computation, we performed an extensive case study in Sect. 4.4.

To further reduce the parameters, we apply a technique similar to the one used by the recursive network. That is, we make the parameters of the Cascading blocks shared, effectively making the blocks recursive. Figure 3(d) shows our block after applying the recursive scheme. This approach reduces the parameters by up to three times of their original number.

3.3   Comparison to Recent Models

Comparison to SRDenseNet. SRDenseNet [36] uses dense block and skip connection. The differences from our model are: **(1)** We use global cascading, which is more general than the skip connection. In SRDenseNet, all levels of features are combined at the end of the final dense block, but our global cascading scheme connects all blocks, which behaves as multi-level skip connection. **(2)** SRDenseNet preserves local information of dense block via concatenation operations, while we gather it progressively by 1×1 convolution layers. The use of additional 1×1 convolution layers results in a higher representation power.

Comparison to MemNet. The motivation of MemNet [35] and ours is similar. However, there are two main differences from our mechanism. **(1)** Inside of the memory blocks of MemNet, the output features of each recursive units are concatenated at the end of the network and then fused with 1×1 convolution. On the other hand, we fuse the features at every possible point in the local block, which can boost up the representation power via the additional convolution layers and nonlinearity. In general, this representation power is often not met because of the difficulty of training. However, we overcome this problem by using both local and global cascading mechanisms. We will discuss the details on Sect. 4.4. **(2)** MemNet takes upsampled images as input so the number of multi-adds is larger than ours. The input to our model is a LR image and we upsample it at the end of the network in order to achieve computational efficiency.

4   Experimental Results

4.1   Datasets

There exist diverse single image super-resolution datasets, but the most widely used ones are the 291 image set by Yang et al. [38] and the Berkeley Segmentation Dataset [2]. However, because these two do not have sufficient images for training a deep neural network, we additionally use the DIV2K dataset [1]. The DIV2K dataset is a newly-proposed high-quality image dataset, which consists of 800 training images, 100 validation images, and 100 test images. Because of the richness of this dataset, recent SR models [4,8,25,30] use DIV2K as well. We use the standard benchmark datasets such as Set5 [3], Set14 [38], B100 [28] and Urban100 [17] for testing and benchmarking.

4.2   Implementation and Training Details

We use the RGB input patches of size 64×64 from the LR images for training. We sample the LR patches randomly and augment them with random horizontal flips and 90° rotation. We train our models with the ADAM optimizer [21] by setting $\beta_1 = 0.9$, $\beta_2 = 0.999$, and $\epsilon = 10^{-8}$ in 6×10^5 steps. The minibatch size is 64, and the learning rate begins with 10^{-4} and is halved every 4×10^5 steps. All the weights and biases are initialized by $\theta \sim U(-k, \ k)$ with $k = 1/\sqrt{c_{in}}$ where, c_{in} is the number of channels of input feature map.

The most well-known and effective weight initialization methods are given by Glorot et al. [10] and He et al. [12]. However, such initialization routines tend to set the weights of our multiple narrow 1×1 convolution layers very high, resulting in an unstable training. Therefore, we sample the initial values from a uniform distribution to alleviate the initialization problem.

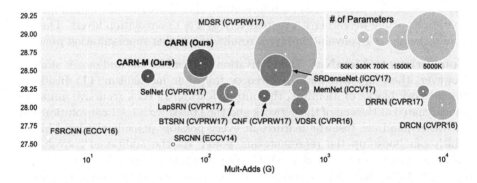

Fig. 4. Trade-off between performance vs. number of operations and parameters on Set14 ×4 dataset. The x-axis and the y-axis denote the Multi-Adds and PSNR, and the size of the circle represents the number of parameters. The Mult-Adds is computed by assuming that the resolution of HR image is 720p.

To train our model in a multi-scale manner, we first set the scaling factor to one of ×2, ×3, and ×4 because our model can only process a single scale for each batch. Then, we construct and argument our input batch, as described above. We use the L1 loss as our loss function instead of the L2. The L2 loss is widely used in the image restoration task due to its relationship with the peak signal-to-noise ratio (PSNR). However, in our experiments, L1 provides better convergence and performance. The downside of the L1 loss is that the convergence speed is relatively slower than that of L2 without the residual block. However, this drawback could be mitigated by using a ResNet style model.

4.3   Comparison with State-of-the-Art Methods

We compare the proposed CARN and CARN-M with state-of-the-art SR methods on two commonly-used image quality metrics: PSNR and the structural similarity index (SSIM) [37]. One thing to note here is that we represent the number of operations by Mult-Adds. Mult-Adds is the number of composite multiply-accumulate operations for a single image. We assume the HR image size to be 720p (1280 × 720) to calculate Multi-Adds. In Fig. 4, we compare our CARN family against the various benchmark algorithms in terms of the Mult-Adds and the number of the parameters on the Set14 ×4 dataset. Here, our CARN model outperforms all state-of-the-art models that have less than 5M parameters. Especially, CARN has the similar number of parameters to that of DRCN [20], SelNet [4] and SRDenseNet [36], but we outperform all three models. The MDSR [25] achieves better performance than ours, which is not surprising because MDSR has 8M parameters which are nearly six times more parameters than ours. The CARN-M model also outperforms most of the benchmark methods and shows comparable results against the heavy models.

Moreover, our models are most efficient in terms of the computation cost: CARN shows second best results with 90.9G Mult-Adds, which is on par with SelNet [4]. This efficiency mainly comes from the *late-upsample* approach that many recent models [7, 23, 36] used. In addition, our novel cascading mechanism shows increased performance compared to the models with the same manner. For example, CARN outperforms SelNet by a margin of 0.11 PSNR using almost identical computation resources. Also, the CARN-M model obtains comparable results against computationally-expensive models, while only requiring the similar number of the operations with respect to SRCNN.

Table 1 also shows the quantitative comparisons of the performances over the benchmark datasets. Note that MDSR is excluded from this table, because we only compare models that have roughly similar number of parameters as ours; MDSR has a parameter set whose size is four times larger than that of the second-largest model. Our CARN exceeds all the previous methods on numerous benchmark dataset. CARN-M model achieves comparable results using very few operations. We would also like to emphasize that although CARN-M has more parameters than SRCNN or DRRN, it is tolerable in real-world scenarios. The sizes of SRCNN and CARN-M are 200 KB and 1.6 MB, respectively, all of which are acceptable on recent mobile devices.

To make our models even more lightweight, we apply the multi-scale learning approach. The benefit of using multi-scale learning is that it can process multiple scales using a single trained model. This helps us alleviate the burden of heavy-weight model size when deploying the SR application on mobile devices; CARN(-M) only needs a single fixed model for multiple scales, whereas even the state-of-the-art algorithms require to train separate models for each supported scale. This property is well-suited for real-world products because the size of the applications has to be fixed while the scale of given LR images could vary. Using the multi-scale learning to our models increases the number of parameters, since the network has to contain possible upsampling layers. On the other hand, VDSR and DRRN do not require this extra burden, even if multi-scale learning is performed, because they upsample the image before processing it.

In Fig. 6, we visually illustrate the qualitative comparisons over three datasets (Set14, B100 and Urban100) for ×4 scale. It can be seen that our model works better than others and accurately reconstructs not only stripes and line patterns, but also complex objects such as hand and street lamps.

Table 1. Quantitative results of deep learning-based SR algorithms. Red/blue text: best/second-best.

Scale	Model	Params	MultAdds	Set5 PSNR/SSIM	Set14 PSNR/SSIM	B100 PSNR/SSIM	Urban100 PSNR/SSIM
2	SRCNN [6]	57K	52.7G	36.66/0.9542	32.42/0.9063	31.36/0.8879	29.50/0.8946
	FSRCNN [7]	12K	6.0G	37.00/0.9558	32.63/0.9088	31.53/0.8920	29.88/0.9020
	VDSR [19]	665K	612.6G	37.53/0.9587	33.03/0.9124	31.90/0.8960	30.76/0.9140
	DRCN [20]	1,774K	9,788.7G	37.63/0.9588	33.04/0.9118	31.85/0.8942	30.75/0.9133
	CNF [30]	337K	311.0G	37.66/0.9590	33.38/0.9136	31.91/0.8962	-
	LapSRN [23]	813K	29.9G	37.52/0.9590	33.08/0.9130	31.80/0.8950	30.41/0.9100
	DRRN [34]	297K	6,796.9G	37.74/0.9591	33.23/0.9136	32.05/0.8973	31.23/0.9188
	BTSRN [8]	410K	207.7G	37.75/-	33.20/-	32.05/-	31.63/−
	MemNet [35]	677K	623.9G	37.78/0.9597	33.28/0.9142	32.08/0.8978	31.31/0.9195
	SelNet [4]	974K	225.7G	37.89/0.9598	33.61/0.9160	32.08/0.8984	-
	CARN (ours)	1,592K	222.8G	37.76/0.9590	33.52/0.9166	32.09/0.8978	31.51/0.9312
	CARN-M (ours)	412K	91.2G	37.53/0.9583	33.26/0.9141	31.92/0.8960	30.83/0.9233
3	SRCNN [6]	57K	52.7G	32.75/0.9090	29.28/0.8209	28.41/0.7863	26.24/0.7989
	FSRCNN [7]	12K	5.0G	33.16/0.9140	29.43/0.8242	28.53/0.7910	26.43/0.8080
	VDSR [19]	665K	612.6G	33.66/0.9213	29.77/0.8314	28.82/0.7976	27.14/0.8279
	DRCN [20]	1,774K	9,788.7G	33.82/0.9226	29.76/0.8311	28.80/0.7963	27.15/0.8276
	CNF [30]	337K	311.0G	33.74/0.9226	29.90/0.8322	28.82/0.7980	-
	DRRN [34]	297K	6,796.9G	34.03/0.9244	29.96/0.8349	28.95/0.8004	27.53/0.8378
	BTSRN [8]	410K	176.2G	34.03/-	29.90/-	28.97/−	27.75/−
	MemNet [35]	677K	623.9G	34.09/0.9248	30.00/0.8350	28.96/0.8001	27.56/0.8376
	SelNet [4]	1,159K	120.0G	34.27/0.9257	30.30/0.8399	28.97/0.8025	-
	CARN (ours)	1,592K	118.8G	34.29/0.9255	30.29/0.8407	29.06/0.8034	27.38/0.8404
	CARN-M (ours)	412K	46.1G	33.99/0.9236	30.08/0.8367	28.91/0.8000	26.86/0.8263
4	SRCNN [6]	57K	52.7G	30.48/0.8628	27.49/0.7503	26.90/0.7101	24.52/0.7221
	FSRCNN [7]	12K	4.6G	30.71/0.8657	27.59/0.7535	26.98/0.7150	24.62/0.7280
	VDSR [19]	665K	612.6G	31.35/0.8838	28.01/0.7674	27.29/0.7251	25.18/0.7524
	DRCN [20]	1,774K	9,788.7G	31.53/0.8854	28.02/0.7670	27.23/0.7233	25.14/0.7510
	CNF [30]	337K	311.0G	31.55/0.8856	28.15/0.7680	27.32/0.7253	-
	LapSRN [23]	813K	149.4G	31.54/0.8850	28.19/0.7720	27.32/0.7280	25.21/0.7560
	DRRN [34]	297K	6,796.9G	31.68/0.8888	28.21/0.7720	27.38/0.7284	25.44/0.7638
	BTSRN [8]	410K	165.2G	31.85/-	28.20/-	27.47/-	25.74/-
	MemNet [35]	677K	623.9G	31.74/0.8893	28.26/0.7723	27.40/0.7281	25.50/0.7630
	SelNet [4]	1,417K	83.1G	32.00/0.8931	28.49/0.7783	27.44/0.7325	-
	SRDenseNet [36]	2,015K	389.9G	32.02/0.8934	28.50/0.7782	27.53/0.7337	26.05/0.7819
	CARN (ours)	1,592K	90.9G	32.13/0.8937	28.60/0.7806	27.58/0.7349	26.07/0.7837
	CARN-M (ours)	412K	32.5G	31.92/0.8903	28.42/0.7762	27.44/0.7304	25.63/0.7688

Table 2. Effects of the global and local cascading modules measured on the Set14 ×4 dataset. CARN-NL represents CARN without local cascading and CARN-NG without global cascading. CARN is our final model.

	Baseline	CARN-NL	CARN-NG	CARN
Local cascading			✓	✓
Global cascading		✓		✓
# Params.	1,444K	1,481K	1,555K	1,592K
PSNR	28.43	28.45	28.42	**28.52**

4.4 Model Analysis

To further investigate the performance behavior of the proposed methods, we analyze our models via ablation study. First, we show how local and global cascading modules affect the performance of CARN. Next, we analyze the trade-off between performance vs. parameters and operations.

Cascading Modules. Table 2 presents the ablation study on the effect of local and global cascading modules. In this table, the baseline is ResNet, CARN-NL is CARN without local cascading and CARN-NG is CARN without global cascading. The network topologies are all same, but because of the 1×1 convolution layer, the overall number of parameters is increased by up to 10%.

We see that the model with only global cascading (CARN-NL) shows better performance than the baseline because the global cascading mechanism effectively carries mid- to high-level frequency signals from shallow to deep layers. Furthermore, by gathering all features before the upsampling layers, the model can better leverage multi-level representations. By incorporating multi-level representations, the CARN model can consider a variety of information from many different receptive fields when reconstructing the image.

Somewhat surprisingly, using only local cascading blocks (CARN-NG) harms the performance. As discussed in He et al. [14], multiplicative manipulations such as 1×1 convolution on the shortcut connection can hamper information propagation, and thus lead to complications during optimization. Similarly, cascading connections in the local cascading blocks of CARN-NG behave as shortcut connections inside the residual blocks. Because these connections consist of concatenation and 1×1 convolutions, it is natural to expect performance degradation. That is, the advantage of multi-level representation is limited to the inside of each local cascading block. Therefore, there appears to be no benefit of using the cascading connection because of the increased number of multiplication operations in the cascading connection. However, CARN uses both local and global cascading levels and outperforms all three models. This is because the global cascading mechanism eases the information propagation issues that CARN-NG suffers from. In detail, information propagates globally via global cascading, and information flows in the local cascading blocks are fused with the ones that come through global connections. By doing so, information is transmitted by multiple shortcuts and thus mitigates the vanishing gradient problem. In other words, the advantage of multi-level representation is leveraged by the global cascading connections, which help the information to propagate to higher layers.

Efficiency Trade-Off. Figure 5 depicts the trade-off study of PSNR vs. parameters, and PSNR vs. operations in relation to the efficient residual block and recursive network. In this experiment, we evaluate all possible group sizes of the efficient residual block for both the recursive and non-recursive cases. In both graphs, the blue line represents the model that does not use the recursive scheme and the orange line is the model that uses recursive cascading block.

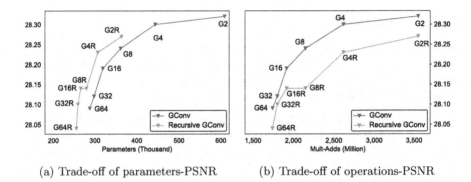

(a) Trade-off of parameters-PSNR   (b) Trade-off of operations-PSNR

Fig. 5. Results of using efficient residual block and recursive network in terms of PSNR vs. parameters (**left**) and PSNR vs. operations (**right**). We evaluate all models on Set14 with ×4 scale. *GConv* represents the group size of group convolution and *R* means the model with the recursive network scheme (i.e., *G4R* represents group four with recursive cascading blocks). (Color figure online)

Although all efficient models perform worse than the CARN, which shows 28.70 PSNR, the number of parameters and operations are decreased dramatically. For example, the *G64* shows a five-times reduction in both parameters and operations. However, unlike the comparable result that is shown in Howard et al. [15], the degradation of performance is more pronounced in our case.

Next, we observe the case which uses the recursive scheme. As illustrated in Fig. 5b, there is no change in the Mult-Adds but the performance worsens, which seems reasonable given the decreased number of parameters in the recursive scheme. On the other hand, Fig. 5a shows that using the recursive scheme makes the model achieve better performance with fewer parameters. Based on these observations, we decide to choose the group size as four in the efficient residual block and use the recursive network scheme as our CARN-M model. By doing so, CARN-M reduces the number of parameters by five times and the number of operations by nearly four times with a loss of 0.29 PSNR compared to CARN.

Fig. 6. Visual qualitative comparison on ×4 scale datasets.

5   Conclusion

In this work, we proposed a novel cascading network architecture that can perform SISR accurately and efficiently. The main idea behind our architecture is to add multiple cascading connections starting from each intermediary layer to the others. Such connections are made on both the local (block-wise) and global (layer-wise) levels, which allows for the efficient flow of information and gradient. Our experiments show that employing both types of connections greatly outperforms those using only one or none at all.

We wish to further develop this work by applying our technique to video data. Many streaming services require large storage to provide high-quality videos. In conjunction with our approach, one may devise a service that stores low-quality videos that go through our SR system to produce high-quality videos on-the-fly.

Acknowledgement. This research was supported through the National Research Foundation of Korea (NRF) funded by the Ministry of Education: NRF-2016R1D1A1B03933875 (K.-A. Sohn) and NRF-2016R1A6A3A11932796 (B. Kang).

References

1. Agustsson, E., Timofte, R.: NTIRE 2017 challenge on single image super-resolution: dataset and study. In: Proceedings of the Conference on Computer Vision and Pattern Recognition (CVPR) Workshops (2017)
2. Arbelaez, P., Maire, M., Fowlkes, C., Malik, J.: Contour detection and hierarchical image segmentation. IEEE Trans. Pattern Anal. Mach. Intell. **33**(5), 898–916 (2011)
3. Bevilacqua, M., Roumy, A., Guillemot, C., Alberi-Morel, M.: Low-complexity single-image super-resolution based on nonnegative neighbor embedding. In: Proceedings of the British Machine Vision Conference (BMVC) (2012)
4. Choi, J.S., Kim, M.: A deep convolutional neural network with selection units for super-resolution. In: Proceedings of the Conference on Computer Vision and Pattern Recognition (CVPR) Workshops (2017)
5. Deng, J., Dong, W., Socher, R., Li, L.J., Li, K., Fei-Fei, L.: ImageNet: a large-scale hierarchical image database. In: Proceedings of the Conference on Computer Vision and Pattern Recognition (CVPR) (2009)
6. Dong, C., Loy, C.C., He, K., Tang, X.: Learning a deep convolutional network for image super-resolution. In: Fleet, D., Pajdla, T., Schiele, B., Tuytelaars, T. (eds.) ECCV 2014. LNCS, vol. 8692, pp. 184–199. Springer, Cham (2014). https://doi.org/10.1007/978-3-319-10593-2_13
7. Dong, C., Loy, C.C., Tang, X.: Accelerating the super-resolution convolutional neural network. In: Leibe, B., Matas, J., Sebe, N., Welling, M. (eds.) ECCV 2016. LNCS, vol. 9906, pp. 391–407. Springer, Cham (2016). https://doi.org/10.1007/978-3-319-46475-6_25
8. Fan, Y., et al.: Balanced two-stage residual networks for image super-resolution. In: Proceedings of the Conference on Computer Vision and Pattern Recognition (CVPR) Workshops (2017)
9. Girshick, R.: Fast R-CNN. In: Proceedings of the International Conference on Computer Vision (ICCV) (2015)

10. Glorot, X., Bengio, Y.: Understanding the difficulty of training deep feedforward neural networks. In: Proceedings of the International Conference on Artificial Intelligence and Statistics (2010)

11. Han, S., Mao, H., Dally, W.J.: Deep compression: compressing deep neural networks with pruning, trained quantization and Huffman coding. In: Proceedings of the International Conference on Learning Representations (ICLR) (2016)

12. He, K., Zhang, X., Ren, S., Sun, J.: Delving deep into rectifiers: surpassing human-level performance on imagenet classification. In: Proceedings of the International Conference on Computer Vision (ICCV) (2015)

13. He, K., Zhang, X., Ren, S., Sun, J.: Deep residual learning for image recognition. In: Proceedings of the Conference on Computer Vision and Pattern Recognition (CVPR) (2016)

14. He, K., Zhang, X., Ren, S., Sun, J.: Identity mappings in deep residual networks. In: Leibe, B., Matas, J., Sebe, N., Welling, M. (eds.) ECCV 2016. LNCS, vol. 9908, pp. 630–645. Springer, Cham (2016). https://doi.org/10.1007/978-3-319-46493-0_38

15. Howard, A.G., et al.: MobileNets: efficient convolutional neural networks for mobile vision applications. arXiv preprint arXiv:1704.04861 (2017)

16. Huang, G., Liu, Z., van der Maaten, L., Weinberger, K.Q.: Densely connected convolutional networks. In: Proceedings of the Conference on Computer Vision and Pattern Recognition (CVPR) (2017)

17. Huang, J.B., Singh, A., Ahuja, N.: Single image super-resolution from transformed self-exemplars. In: Proceedings of the Conference on Computer Vision and Pattern Recognition (CVPR) (2015)

18. Iandola, F.N., Han, S., Moskewicz, M.W., Ashraf, K., Dally, W.J., Keutzer, K.: SqueezeNet: AlexNet-level accuracy with 50x fewer parameters and <0.5 MB model size. arXiv preprint arXiv:1602.07360 (2016)

19. Kim, J., Kwon Lee, J., Mu Lee, K.: Accurate image super-resolution using very deep convolutional networks. In: Proceedings of the Conference on Computer Vision and Pattern Recognition (CVPR) (2016)

20. Kim, J., Kwon Lee, J., Mu Lee, K.: Deeply-recursive convolutional network for image super-resolution. In: Proceedings of the Conference on Computer Vision and Pattern Recognition (CVPR) (2016)

21. Kingma, D.P., Ba, J.: Adam: a method for stochastic optimization. In: Proceedings of the International Conference on Learning Representations (ICLR) (2015)

22. Krizhevsky, A., Sutskever, I., Hinton, G.E.: ImageNet classification with deep convolutional neural networks. In: Proceedings of the Conference on Neural Information Processing Systems (NIPS) (2012)

23. Lai, W.S., Huang, J.B., Ahuja, N., Yang, M.H.: Deep Laplacian pyramid networks for fast and accurate super-resolution. In: Proceedings of the Conference on Computer Vision and Pattern Recognition (CVPR) (2017)

24. Lee, J., Nam, J.: Multi-level and multi-scale feature aggregation using pretrained convolutional neural networks for music auto-tagging. IEEE Signal Process. Lett. **24**(8), 1208–1212 (2017)

25. Lim, B., Son, S., Kim, H., Nah, S., Lee, K.M.: Enhanced deep residual networks for single image super-resolution. In: Proceedings of the Conference on Computer Vision and Pattern Recognition (CVPR) Workshops (2017)

26. Liu, W., et al.: SSD: single shot multibox detector. In: Leibe, B., Matas, J., Sebe, N., Welling, M. (eds.) ECCV 2016. LNCS, vol. 9905, pp. 21–37. Springer, Cham (2016). https://doi.org/10.1007/978-3-319-46448-0_2

27. Long, J., Shelhamer, E., Darrell, T.: Fully convolutional networks for semantic segmentation. In: Proceedings of the Conference on Computer Vision and Pattern Recognition (CVPR) (2015)
28. Martin, D., Fowlkes, C., Tal, D., Malik, J.: A database of human segmented natural images and its application to evaluating segmentation algorithms and measuring ecological statistics. In: Proceedings of the International Conference on Computer Vision (ICCV) (2001)
29. Noh, H., Hong, S., Han, B.: Learning deconvolution network for semantic segmentation. In: Proceedings of the International Conference on Computer Vision (ICCV) (2015)
30. Ren, H., El-Khamy, M., Lee, J.: Image super resolution based on fusing multiple convolution neural networks. In: Proceedings of the Conference on Computer Vision and Pattern Recognition (CVPR) Workshops (2017)
31. Ronneberger, O., Fischer, P., Brox, T.: U-Net: convolutional networks for biomedical image segmentation. In: Navab, N., Hornegger, J., Wells, W.M., Frangi, A.F. (eds.) MICCAI 2015. LNCS, vol. 9351, pp. 234–241. Springer, Cham (2015). https://doi.org/10.1007/978-3-319-24574-4_28
32. Shi, W., et al.: Real-time single image and video super-resolution using an efficient sub-pixel convolutional neural network. In: Proceedings of the Conference on Computer Vision and Pattern Recognition (CVPR) (2016)
33. Sifre, L., Mallat, S.: Rigid-motion scattering for image classification. Ph.D. thesis, Citeseer (2014)
34. Tai, Y., Yang, J., Liu, X.: Image super-resolution via deep recursive residual network. In: Proceedings of the Conference on Computer Vision and Pattern Recognition (CVPR) (2017)
35. Tai, Y., Yang, J., Liu, X., Xu, C.: MemNet: a persistent memory network for image restoration. In: Proceedings of the International Conference on Computer Vision (ICCV) (2017)
36. Tong, T., Li, G., Liu, X., Gao, Q.: Image super-resolution using dense skip connections. In: Proceedings of the International Conference on Computer Vision (ICCV) (2017)
37. Wang, Z., Bovik, A.C., Sheikh, H.R., Simoncelli, E.P.: Image quality assessment: from error visibility to structural similarity. IEEE Trans. Image Process. 13(4), 600–612 (2004)
38. Yang, J., Wright, J., Huang, T.S., Ma, Y.: Image super-resolution via sparse representation. IEEE Trans. Image Process. 19(11), 2861–2873 (2010)
39. Zhang, R., Isola, P., Efros, A.A.: Colorful image colorization. In: Leibe, B., Matas, J., Sebe, N., Welling, M. (eds.) ECCV 2016. LNCS, vol. 9907, pp. 649–666. Springer, Cham (2016). https://doi.org/10.1007/978-3-319-46487-9_40

ExFuse: Enhancing Feature Fusion for Semantic Segmentation

Zhenli Zhang[1]([✉])[iD], Xiangyu Zhang[2][iD], Chao Peng[2][iD], Xiangyang Xue[1][iD], and Jian Sun[2][iD]

[1] Fudan University, Shanghai, China
{zhenlizhang14,xyxue}@fudan.edu.cn
[2] Megvii Inc., Beijing, China
{zhangxiangyu,pengchao,sunjian}@megvii.com

Abstract. Modern semantic segmentation frameworks usually combine low-level and high-level features from pre-trained backbone convolutional models to boost performance. In this paper, we first point out that a simple fusion of low-level and high-level features could be less effective because of the gap in semantic levels and spatial resolution. We find that introducing semantic information into low-level features and high-resolution details into high-level features is more effective for the later fusion. Based on this observation, we propose a new framework, named ExFuse, to bridge the gap between low-level and high-level features thus significantly improve the segmentation quality by 4.0% in total. Furthermore, we evaluate our approach on the challenging PASCAL VOC 2012 segmentation benchmark and achieve 87.9% mean IoU, which outperforms the previous state-of-the-art results.

Keywords: Semantic segmentation · Convolutional neural networks

1 Introduction

Most state-of-the-art semantic segmentation frameworks [2–6,12,22,26,28,35, 38,40] follow the design of Fully Convolutional Network (FCN) [25]. FCN has a typical encoder-decoder structure – semantic information is firstly embedded into the feature maps via encoder then the decoder takes responsibility for generating segmentation results. Usually the encoder is the pre-trained convolutional model to extract image features and the decoder contains multiple upsampling components to recover resolution. Although the top-most feature maps of the encoder could be highly semantic, its ability to reconstruct precise details in segmentation maps is limited due to insufficient resolution, which is very common in modern backbone models such as [15,16,20,31,33,37]. To address this, an "U-Net" architecture is proposed [28] and adopted in many recent work [2,12,22,25,26,28]. The core idea of *U-Net* is to gradually fuse high-level low-resolution features from top layers with low-level but high-resolution features from bottom layers, which

V. Ferrari et al. (Eds.): ECCV 2018, LNCS 11214, pp. 273–288, 2018.
https://doi.org/10.1007/978-3-030-01249-6_17

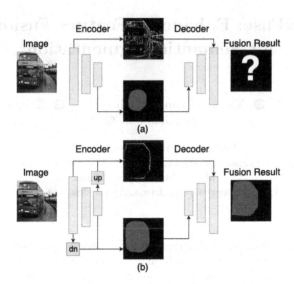

Fig. 1. Fusion of low-level and high-level features. (a) "Pure" low-level high-resolution and "pure" high-level low-resolution features are difficult to be fused because of the significant semantic and resolution gaps. (b) Introducing semantic information into low-level features or spatial information into high-level features benefits the feature fusion. "dn" and "up" blocks represent *abstract* up/down-sampling feature embedding.

is expected to be helpful for the decoder to generate high-resolution semantic results.

Though the great success of U-Net, the working mechanism is still unknown and worth further investigating. Low-level and high-level features are complementary by nature, where low-level features are rich in spatial details but lack semantic information and vice versa. Consider the extreme case that "pure" low-level features only encode low-level concepts such as points, lines or edges. Intuitively, the fusion of high-level features with such "pure" low-level features helps little, because low-level features are too noisy to provide sufficient high-resolution semantic guidance. In contrast, if low-level features include more semantic information, for example, encode relatively clearer semantic boundaries, then the fusion becomes easy – fine segmentation results could be obtained by aligning high-level feature maps to the boundary. Similarly, "pure" high-level features with little spatial information cannot take full advantage of low-level features; however, with additional high-resolution features embedded, high-level features may have chance to refine itself by aligning to the nearest low-level boundary. Figure 1 illustrates the above concepts. Empirically, the semantic and resolution overlap between low-level and high-level features plays an important role in the effectiveness of feature fusion. In other words, feature fusion could be enhanced by introducing more semantic concepts into low-level features or by embedding more spatial information into high-level features.

Motivated by the above observation, we propose to boost the feature fusion by bridging the semantic and resolution gap between low-level and high-level feature maps. We propose a framework named *ExFuse*, which addresses the gap from the following two aspects: (1) to introduce more semantic information into low-level features, we suggest three solutions – *layer rearrangement, semantic supervision* and *semantic embedding branch*; (2) to embed more spatial information into high-level features, we propose two novel methods: *explicit channel resolution embedding* and *densely adjacent prediction*. Significant improvements are obtained by either approach and a total increase of 4% is obtained by the combination. Furthermore, we evaluate our method on the challenging PASCAL VOC 2012 [10] semantic segmentation task. In the test dataset, we achieve the score of 87.9% mean IoU, surpassing the previous state-of-the-art methods.

Our contributions can be summerized as follows:

- We suggest a new perspective to boost semantic segmentation performance, i.e. bridging the semantic and resolution gap between low-level and high-level features by more effective feature fusion.
- We propose a novel framework named ExFuse, which introduces more semantic information into low-level features and more spatial high-resolution information into high-level features. Significant improvements are obtained from the enhanced feature fusion.
- Our fully-equipped model achieves the new state-of-the-art result on the test set of PASCAL VOC 2012 segmentation benchmark.

2   Related Work

Feature Fusion in Semantic Segmentation. Feature fusion is frequently employed in semantic segmentation for different purposes and concepts. A lot of methods fuse low-level but high-resolution features and high-level low-resolution features together [2,12,22,25,26,28]. Besides, *ASPP* module is proposed in DeepLab [4–6] to fuse multi-scale features to tackle objects of different size. Pyramid pooling module in PSPNet [40] serves the same purpose through different implementation. BoxSup [8] empirically fuses feature maps of bounding boxes and segmentation maps to further enhance segmentation.

Deeply Supervised Learning. To the best of our knowledge, deeply supervised training is initially proposed in [21], which aims to ease the training process of very deep neural networks since depth is the key limitation for training modern neural networks until batch normalization [18] and residual networks [15] are proposed. Extra losses are utilized in GoogleNet [33] for the same purpose. Recently, PSPNet [40] also employs this method to ease the optimization when training deeper networks.

Upsampling. There are mainly three approaches to upsample a feature map. The first one is bilinear interpolation, which is widely used in [4–6,40]. The second

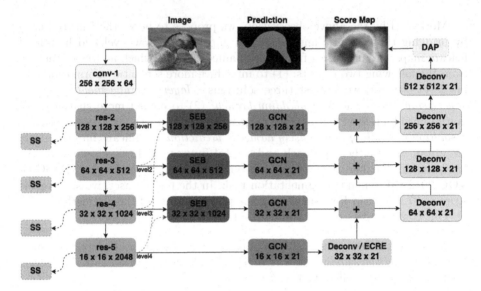

Fig. 2. Overall architecture of our approach. Components with solid boxes belong to the backbone *GCN* framework [26], while others with dashed lines are proposed in this work. Similar to [26], *Boundary Refinement* blocks are actually used but omitted in the figure. Numbers ($H \times W \times C$) in blocks specify the output dimension of each component. **SS** – semantic supervision. **ECRE** – explicit channel resolution embedding. **SEB** – semantic embedding branch. **DAP** – densely adjacent prediction. (Color figure online)

method is deconvolution, which is initially proposed in FCN [25] and utilized in later work such as [2,3,22,26,28]. The third one is called "sub-pixel convolution", which derives from [1,30] in super resolution task and is widely broadcast to other tasks such as semantic segmentation. For instance, [35] employs it to replace the traditional deconvolution operation.

3   Approach

In this work we mainly focus on the feature fusion problem in "U-Net" segmentation frameworks [2,12,22,25,26,28]. In general, *U-Net* have an encoder-decoder structure as shown in Fig. 1. Usually the encoder part is based on a convolutional model pretrained on large-scale classification dataset (e.g. ImageNet [9]), which generates low-level but high-resolution features from the bottom layers and high-level low-resolution features from the top layers. Then the decoder part mixes up the features to predict segmentation results. A common way of feature fusion [2,12,14,22,26–28] is to formulate as a residual form:

$$\mathbf{y}_l = Upsample(\mathbf{y}_{l+1}) + \mathcal{F}(\mathbf{x}_l) \tag{1}$$

where $\mathbf{y}_l$ is the fused feature at l-th level; $\mathbf{x}_l$ stands for the l-th feature generated by the encoder. Features with larger l have higher semantic level but lower spatial resolution and vice versa (see Fig. 2).

In Sect. 1 we argue that feature fusion could become less effective if there is a large semantic or resolution gap between low-level and high-level features. To study and verify the impact, we choose one of the start-of-the-art "U-Net" frameworks – *Global Convolutional Network (GCN)* [26] – as our backbone segmentation architecture (see Fig. 2 for details). In GCN, 4 different semantic levels of feature maps are extracted from the encoder network, whose spatial resolutions, given the 512×512 input, are $\{128, 64, 32, 16\}$ respectively. To examine the effectiveness of feature fusion, we select several subsets of feature levels and use them to retrain the whole system. Results are shown in Table 1. It is clear that even though the segmentation quality increases with the fusion of more feature levels, the performance tends to saturate quickly. Especially, the lowest two feature levels (1 and 2) only contribute marginal improvements (0.24% for ResNet 50 and 0.05% for ResNeXt 101), which implies the fusion of low-level and high-level features is rather ineffective in this framework.

In the following subsections we will introduce our solutions to bridge the gap between low-level and high-level features – embedding more semantic information into low-level features and more spatial resolution clues into high-level features. First of all, we introduce our baseline settings:

Table 1. *GCN* [26] segmentation results using given feature levels. Performances are evaluated by standard mean IoU(%) on PASCAL VOC 2012 validation set. Lower feature level involves less semantic but higher-resolution features and vice versa (see Fig. 2). The feature extractor is based on pretrained ResNet50 [15] and ResNeXt101 [37] model. Performance is evaluated in mIoU.

Feature levels	ResNet 50 (%)	ResNeXt 101 (%)
$\{4\}$	70.04	73.79
$\{3, 4\}$	72.17	75.97
$\{2, 3, 4\}$	72.28	75.98
$\{1, 2, 3, 4\}$	72.41	76.02

Baseline Settings. The overall semantic segmentation framework follows the fully-equipped *GCN* [26] architecture, as shown in Fig. 2. For the backbone encoder network, we use ResNeXt 101 [37] model pretrained on ImageNet by default[1] unless otherwise mentioned. We use two public-available semantic segmentation benchmarks – *PASCAL VOC 2012* [10] and *Semantic Boundaries Dataset* [13] – for training and evaluate performances on PASCAL VOC 2012 validation set, which is consistent with many previous work [2–6,12,22,25–27,35,38,40]. The performance is measured by standard mean intersection-over-union (mean IoU). Other training and test details or hyper-parameters are

---

[1] Though ResNeXt 101 performs much better than ResNet 101 [15] on ImageNet classification task (21.2% vs. 23.6% in top-1 error), we find there are no significant differences on the semantic segmentation results (both are 76.0% mIoU).

exactly the same as [26]. Our reproduced GCN baseline score is 76.0%, shown in Table 3 (#1).

3.1 Introducing More Semantic Information into Low-Level Features

Our solutions are inspired by the fact: for convolutional neural networks, feature maps close to semantic supervisions (e.g. classification loss) tend to encode more semantic information, which has been confirmed by some visualization work [39]. We propose three methods as follows:

Layer Rearrangement. In our framework, features are extracted from the tail of each stage in the encoder part (res-2 to res-5 in Fig. 2). To make low-level features (res-2 or res-3) 'closer' to the supervisions, one straight-forward approach is to arrange more layers in the early stages rather than the latter. For example, ResNeXt 101 [37] model has $\{3, 4, 23, 3\}$ building blocks for Stage 2–5 respectively; we rearrange the assignment into $\{8, 8, 9, 8\}$ and adjust the number of channels to ensure the same overall computational complexity. Experiment shows that even though the ImageNet classification score of the newly designed model is almost unchanged, its segmentation performance increases by 0.8% (Table 3, compare #2 with #3), which implies the quality of low-level feature might be improved.

Semantic Supervision. We come up with another way to improve low-level features, named *Semantic Supervision (SS)*, by assigning auxiliary supervisions directly to the early stages of the encoder network (see Fig. 2). To generate semantic outputs in the auxiliary branches, low-level features are forced to encode more semantic concepts, which is expected to be helpful for later feature fusion. Such methodology is inspired by *Deeply Supervised Learning* used in some old classification networks [21,33] to ease the training of deep networks. However, more sophisticated classification models [15–17,32,34,37] suggest end-to-end training without auxiliary losses, which is proved to have no convergence issue even for models over 100 layers. Our experiment also shows that for ResNet or ResNeXt models deeply supervised training is useless or even harms the classification accuracy (see Table 2). Therefore, our *Semantic Supervision* approach mainly focuses on improving the quality of low-level features, rather than boosting the backbone model itself.

Figure 3 shows the detailed structure of our Semantic Supervision block. When pretraining the backbone encoder network, the components are attached to the tail of each stage as auxiliary supervisions (see Fig. 2). The overall classification loss equals to a weighted summation of all auxiliary branches. Then after pretraining, we remove these branches and use the remaining part for fine tuning. Experiment shows the method boosts the segmentation result by 1.1%. Moreover, we find that if features are extracted from the second convolutional layer in the auxiliary module for fine tuning (Fig. 3), more improvement (1.5%)

Table 2. Effects of *Semantic Supervision (SS)*. Classification scores are evaluated on ImageNet 2012 validation set.

Model	Cls err (top-1, %)	Seg mIoU (%)
Res50	24.15	72.4
SS Res50	24.77	73.5

is obtained (see Table 3, compare #1 with #2), which supports our intuition that feature maps closer to the supervision tend to encode more semantic information.

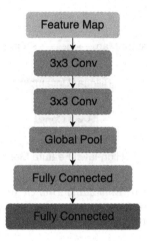

Fig. 3. Details of *Semantic Supervision (SS)* component in our pipeline.

It is worth noting that the recent semantic segmentation work *PSPNet* [40] also employs deeply supervised learning and reports the improvements. Different from ours, the architecture of [40] do not extract feature maps supervised by the auxiliary explicitly; and their main purpose is to ease the optimization during training. However, in our framework we find the improvements may result from different reasons. For instance, we choose a relatively shallower network ResNet 50 [15] and pretrain with or without semantic supervision. From Table 2, we find the auxiliary losses do not improve the classification score, which implies ResNet 50 is unlikely to suffer from optimization difficulty. However, it still boosts the segmentation result by 1.1%, which is comparable to the deeper case of ResNeXt 101 (1.0%). We believe the enhancement in our framework mainly results from more "semantic" low-level features.

Semantic Embedding Branch. As mentioned above, many "U-Net" structures involve low-level feature as the residue to the upsampled high-level feature. In Eq. 1 the residual term $\mathcal{F}(\mathbf{x}_l)$ is a function of low-level but high-resolution feature, which is used to fill the spatial details. However, if the low-level feature contains little semantic information, it is insufficient to recover the semantic resolution. To address the drawback, we generalize the fusion as follows:

$$\mathbf{y}_l = Upsample\,(\mathbf{y}_{l+1}) + \mathcal{F}(\mathbf{x}_l, \mathbf{x}_{l+1}, \dots, \mathbf{x}_L) \qquad (2)$$

where L is the number of feature levels. Our insight is to involve more semantic information from high-level features to guide the resolution fusion.

The detailed design of function $\mathcal{F}\,(\cdot)$ is illustrated in Fig. 4, named *Semantic Embedding Branch, (SEB)*. We use the component for features of Level 1-3 (see Fig. 2). In our experiment SEB improves the performance by 0.7% (Table 3, compare #3 with #5).

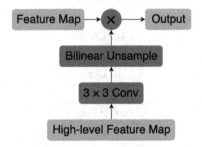

Fig. 4. Design of the *Semantic Embedding Branch* in Fig. 2. The "×" sign means element-wise multiplication. If there are more than one groups of high-level features, the component outputs the production of each feature map after upsampling.

3.2   Embedding More Spatial Resolution into High-Level Features

For most backbone feature extractor networks, high-level features have very limited spatial resolution. For example, the spatial size of top-most feature map in ResNet or ResNeXt is 7×7 for 224×224 input size. To encode more spatial details, a widely used approach is *dilated strategy* [4–6,35,38,40], which is able to enlarge feature resolution without retraining the backbone network. However, since high-level feature maps involve a lot of channels, larger spatial size significantly increases the computational cost. So in this work we mainly consider another direction – we do not try to increase the "physical" resolution of the feature maps; instead, **we expect more resolution information encoded within channels**. We propose the following two methods:

Explicit Channel Resolution Embedding. In our overall framework, segmentation loss is only connected to the output of decoder network (see Fig. 2), which is considered to have less impact on the spatial information of high-level features by intuition. One straight-forward solution is to borrow the idea of *Semantic Supervision* (Sect. 3.1) – we could add an auxiliary supervision branch

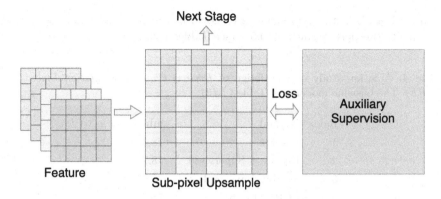

Fig. 5. Illustration of the design of *Explicit Channel Resolution Embedding (ECRE)* module in Fig. 2.

to the high-level feature map, upsample and force it to learn fine segmentation map. Following the insight, firstly we try adding an extra segmentation loss to the first deconvolution module (the light-blue component in Fig. 2), however, no improvements are obtained (Table 4, #2).

Table 3. Ablation experiments of the methods in Sect. 3. Performances are evaluated by standard mean IoU(%) on PASCAL VOC 2012 validation set. The baseline model is [26] (our impl.) **SS** – semantic supervision. **LR** – layer rearrangement. **ECRE** – explicit channel resolution embedding. **SEB** – semantic embedding branch. **DAP** – densely adjacent prediction.

Index	Baseline	SS	LR	ECRE	SEB	DAP	mIoU (%)
1	✓						76.0
2	✓	✓					77.5
3	✓	✓	✓				78.3
4	✓	✓	✓	✓			78.8
5	✓	✓	✓		✓		79.0
6	✓	✓	✓		✓	✓	79.6
7	✓	✓	✓	✓	✓	✓	**80.0**

Why does the auxiliary loss fail to work? Note that the purpose of the supervision is to embed high resolution information "explicitly" into feature map channels. However, since deconvolution layer includes weights, the embedding becomes implicit. To overcome this issue, we adopt a parameter-free upsampling method – *Sub-pixel Upsample* [1,30] – to replace the original deconvolution. Since sub-pixel upsample enlarge the feature map just by reshaping the spatial and channel dimensions, the auxiliary supervision is able to *explicitly* impact the features. Details of the component are shown in Fig. 5. Experiment shows that it enhances the performance by 0.5% (see Tables 4 and 3).

Table 4. Ablation study on the design of *Explicit Channel Resolution Embedding, (ECRE)*. The baseline model is in Table 3 (#3)

Index	Method	mIoU (%)
1	Baseline	78.3
2	Deconv + Supervised	78.2
3	Sub-pixel upsample only	77.6
4	ECRE (Fig. 5)	**78.8**

Moreover, to demonstrate that the improvement is brought by explicit resolution embedding rather than sub-pixel upsampling itself, we also try to replace the deconvolution layer only without auxiliary supervision. Table 4 (#3) shows the result, which is even worse than the baseline.

Densely Adjacent Prediction. In the decoder upstream of the original architecture (Fig. 2), feature point at the spatial location (i, j) mainly takes responsibility for semantic information at the same place. To encode as much spatial information into channels, we propose a novel mechanism named *Densely Adjacent Prediction (DAP)*, which allows to predict results at the adjacent position, e.g. $(i-1, j+1)$. Then to get the final segmentation map, result at the position (i, j) can be generated by averaging the associated scores. Formally, given the window size $k \times k$, we divide the feature channels into $k \times k$ groups, then DAP works as follows:

$$\mathbf{r}_{i,j} = \frac{1}{k \times k} \sum_{0 \le l,m < k} \mathbf{x}^{(l \times k + m)}_{i+l-\lfloor k/2 \rfloor, j+m-\lfloor k/2 \rfloor} \tag{3}$$

where $\mathbf{r}_{i,j}$ denotes the result at the position (i, j) and $\mathbf{x}^{(c)}_{i,j}$ stands for the features at the position (i, j) belonging to channel group c. In Fig. 6 we illustrate the concept of DAP.

We use DAP on the output of our decoder (see Fig. 2). In our experiment we set $k = 3$. Note that DAP requires the number of feature channels increased by $k \times k$ times, so we increase the output channels of each deconvolution block to 189 ($21 \times 3 \times 3$). For fair comparison, we also evaluate the baseline model with the same number of channels. Results are shown in Table 5. It is clear that DAP improves the performance by 0.6% while the counterpart model without DAP only obtains marginal gain, which implies DAP may be helpful for feature maps to embed more spatial information.

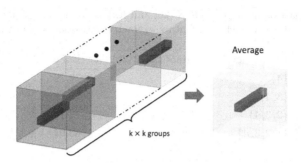

Fig. 6. Illustration of *Densely Adjacent Prediction (DAP)* component in Fig. 2.

Table 5. Ablation study on the effect of *Densely Adjacent Prediction (DAP)*. The baseline model is in Table 3 (#5)

Index	Method	mIoU (%)
1	Baseline	79.0
2	Baseline (more channels)	79.1
3	DAP (Fig. 6)	**79.6**

3.3 Discussions

Is Feature Fusion Enhanced? At the beginning of Sect. 3 we demonstrate that feature fusion in our baseline architecture (*GCN* [26]) is ineffective. Only marginal improvements are obtained by fusing low-level features (Level 1 and 2), as shown in Table 1. We attribute the issue to the semantic and resolution gap between low-level and high-level features. In Sects. 3.1 and 3.2, we propose a series of solutions to introduce more semantic information into low-level features and more spatial details into high-level features.

Despite the improved performance, a question raises: is feature fusion in the framework *really* improved? To justify this, similar to Table 1 we compare several subsets of different feature levels and use them to train original baseline (GCN) and our proposed model (*ExFuse*) respectively. For the ExFuse model, all the 5 approaches in Sects. 3.1 and 3.2 are used. Table 6 shows the results. We find that combined with low-level feature maps (Level 1 and 2) the proposed ExFuse still achieves considerable performance gain (~1.3%), while the baseline model cannot benefit from them. The comparison implies our insights and methodology enhance the feature fusion indeed.

Table 6 also shows that the proposed model is much better than the baseline in the case that only top-most feature maps (Level 4) are used, which implies the superior high-level feature quality to the original model. Our further study shows that methods in Sect. 3.2 contribute most of the improvement. Empirically we conclude that boosting high-level features not only benefits feature fusion, but also contributes directly to the segmentation performance.

Table 6. Comparison of original GCN [26] and ExFuse on segmentation results using given feature levels. The backbone feature extractor networks are both ResNeXt 101.

Feature levels	Original GCN [26] (%)	ExFuse (%)
{4}	73.79	77.29
{3, 4}	75.97	78.69
{2, 3, 4}	75.98	79.11
{1, 2, 3, 4}	76.02	80.04

Could the Perspective and Techniques Generalize to Other Computer Vision Tasks? Since U-Net structure is widely applied to other vision tasks such as low-level vision [29] and detection [23], a question raises naturally: could the proposed perspective and techniques generalize to other tasks? We carefully conducted ablation experiments and observe positive results. We leave detailed discussion for future work.

4   PASCAL VOC 2012 Experiment

In the last section we introduce our methodology and evaluate their effectiveness via ablation experiments. In this section we investigate the fully-equipped system and report benchmark results on PASCAL VOC 2012 test set.

To further improve the feature quality, we use deeper ResNeXt 131 as our backbone feature extractor, in which *Squeeze-and-excitation* modules [17] are also involved. The number of building blocks for Stage 2-5 is {8, 8, 19, 8} respectively, which follows the idea of Sect. 3.1. With ResNeXt 131, we get 0.8% performance gain and achieve 80.8% mIoU when training with 10582 images from *PASCAL VOC 2012* [10] and *Semantic Boundaries Dataset (SBD)* [13], which is 2.3% better than *DeepLabv3* [6] at the same settings.

Table 7. Strategies and results on PASCAL VOC 2012 validation set

Index	ResNeXt 131	COCO	Flip	mIoU (%)
1	(ResNeXt 101)			80.0
2	✓			80.8
3	✓	✓		85.4
4	✓	✓	✓	**85.8**

Following the same procedure as [2, 4–6, 12, 22, 26, 35, 40], we employ Microsoft COCO dataset [24] to pretrain our model. COCO has 80 classes and we only retain images including the same 20 classes in PASCAL VOC 2012 and all other classes are regarded as background. Training process has 3 stages. In stage-1, we mix up all images in COCO, SBD and standard PASCAL VOC 2012. In stage-2, we utilize SBD and PASCAL VOC 2012 training images. Finally for stage-3, we only employ standard PASCAL VOC 2012 training set. We keep image crop size unchanged during the whole training procedure and all other settings are exactly the same as [26]. COCO pretraining brings about another 4.6% increase in performance, as shown in Table 7 (#2 and #3).

We further average the score map of an image with its horizontal flipped version and eventually get a 85.8% mIoU on PASCAL VOC 2012 validation set, which is 2.3% better than DeepLabv3+ [7] (Table 7 #4).

Resembling [6], we then freeze the batch normalization parameters and fine tune our model on official PASCAL VOC 2012 *trainval* set. In particular, we duplicate the images that contain hard classes (namely bicycle, chair, dining table, potted plant and sofa). Finally, our ExFuse framework achieves **87.9%** mIoU on PASCAL VOC 2012 test set without any DenseCRF [19] post-processing, which surpasses previous state-of-the-art results, as shown in Table 8. For fair comparison, we also evaluate our model using a standard ResNet101 and it achieves 86.2% mIoU, which is better than DeepLabv3 at the same setting.

Table 8. Performance on PASCAL VOC 2012 test set

Method	mIOU
Tusimple [35]	83.1
Large_Kernel_Matters [26]	83.6
Multipath_RefineNet [22]	84.2
ResNet_38_MS_COCO [36]	84.9
PSPNet [40]	85.4
DeepLabv3 [6]	85.7
SDN [11]	86.6
DeepLabv3+ (Xception) [7]	87.8
ExFuse_ResNet101 (ours)	**86.2**
ExFuse_ResNeXt131 (ours)	**87.9**

Figure 7 visualizes some representative results of the GCN [26] baseline and our proposed ExFuse framework. It is clear that the visualization quality of our method is much better than the baseline. For example, the boundary in ExFuse is more precise than GCN.

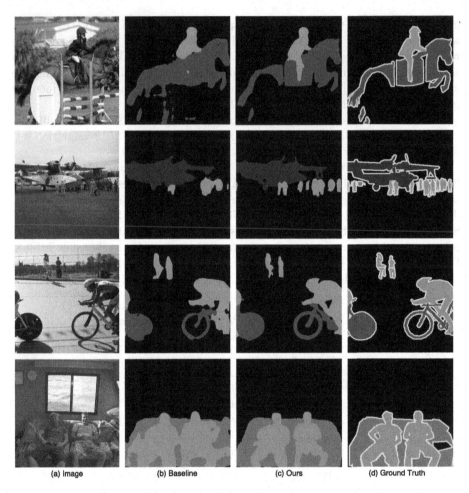

(a) Image   (b) Baseline   (c) Ours   (d) Ground Truth

Fig. 7. Examples of semantic segmentation results on PASCAL VOC 2012 validation set. (b) is our GCN [26] baseline which achieves 81.0% mIoU on val set. (c) is our method which achieves 85.4% on val set, as shown in Table 7 #3.

5 Conclusions

In this work, we first point out the ineffective feature fusion problem in current *U-Net* structure. Then, we propose our *ExFuse* framework to tackle this problem via bridging the gap between high-level low-resolution and low-level high-resolution features. Eventually, better feature fusion is demonstrated by the performance boost when fusing with original low-level features and the overall segmentation performance is improved by a large margin. Our *ExFuse* framework also achieves new state-of-the-art performance on PASCAL VOC 2012 benchmark.

References

1. Aitken, A., Ledig, C., Theis, L., Caballero, J., Wang, Z., Shi, W.: Checkerboard artifact free sub-pixel convolution: a note on sub-pixel convolution, resize convolution and convolution resize (2017)
2. Amirul Islam, M., Rochan, M., Bruce, N.D.B., Wang, Y.: Gated feedback refinement network for dense image labeling. In: The IEEE Conference on Computer Vision and Pattern Recognition (CVPR), July 2017
3. Badrinarayanan, V., Kendall, A., Cipolla, R.: SegNet: a deep convolutional encoder-decoder architecture for scene segmentation. IEEE Trans. Pattern Anal. Mach. Intell. **PP**(99), 1 (2017)
4. Chen, L.C., Papandreou, G., Kokkinos, I., Murphy, K., Yuille, A.L.: Semantic image segmentation with deep convolutional nets and fully connected CRFs. Comput. Sci. (4), 357–361 (2014)
5. Chen, L.C., Papandreou, G., Kokkinos, I., Murphy, K., Yuille, A.L.: DeepLab: semantic image segmentation with deep convolutional nets, atrous convolution, and fully connected CRFs. IEEE Trans. Pattern Anal. Mach. Intell. **PP**(99), 1 (2016)
6. Chen, L.C., Papandreou, G., Schroff, F., Adam, H.: Rethinking atrous convolution for semantic image segmentation (2017)
7. Chen, L.C., Zhu, Y., Papandreou, G., Schroff, F., Adam, H.: Encoder-decoder with atrous separable convolution for semantic image segmentation (2018)
8. Dai, J., He, K., Sun, J.: BoxSup: exploiting bounding boxes to supervise convolutional networks for semantic segmentation. In: IEEE International Conference on Computer Vision, pp. 1635–1643 (2015)
9. Deng, J., Dong, W., Socher, R., Li, L.J., Li, K., Li, F.F.: ImageNet: a large-scale hierarchical image database. In: IEEE Conference on Computer Vision and Pattern Recognition, CVPR 2009, pp. 248–255 (2009)
10. Everingham, M., Gool, L., Williams, C.K., Winn, J., Zisserman, A.: The pascal visual object classes (VOC) challenge. Int. J. Comput. Vis. **88**(2), 303–338 (2010)
11. Fu, J., Liu, J., Wang, Y., Lu, H.: Stacked deconvolutional network for semantic segmentation (2017)
12. Ghiasi, G., Fowlkes, C.C.: Laplacian pyramid reconstruction and refinement for semantic segmentation. In: Leibe, B., Matas, J., Sebe, N., Welling, M. (eds.) ECCV 2016. LNCS, vol. 9907, pp. 519–534. Springer, Cham (2016). https://doi.org/10.1007/978-3-319-46487-9_32
13. Hariharan, B., Arbelaez, P., Bourdev, L., Maji, S., Malik, J.: Semantic contours from inverse detectors. In: International Conference on Computer Vision, pp. 991–998 (2011)
14. Hariharan, B., Arbelaez, P., Girshick, R., Malik, J.: Hypercolumns for object segmentation and fine-grained localization, pp. 447–456 (2014)
15. He, K., Zhang, X., Ren, S., Sun, J.: Deep residual learning for image recognition. In: Computer Vision and Pattern Recognition, pp. 770–778 (2016)
16. He, K., Zhang, X., Ren, S., Sun, J.: Identity mappings in deep residual networks. In: Leibe, B., Matas, J., Sebe, N., Welling, M. (eds.) ECCV 2016. LNCS, vol. 9908, pp. 630–645. Springer, Cham (2016). https://doi.org/10.1007/978-3-319-46493-0_38
17. Hu, J., Shen, L., Sun, G.: Squeeze-and-excitation networks. arXiv preprint arXiv:1709.01507 (2017)
18. Ioffe, S., Szegedy, C.: Batch normalization: accelerating deep network training by reducing internal covariate shift, pp. 448–456 (2015)

19. Krähenbühl, P., Koltun, V.: Efficient inference in fully connected CRFs with Gaussian edge potentials. In: Advances in Neural Information Processing Systems, pp. 109–117 (2011)
20. Krizhevsky, A., Sutskever, I., Hinton, G.E.: Imagenet classification with deep convolutional neural networks. In: International Conference on Neural Information Processing Systems, pp. 1097–1105 (2012)
21. Lee, C.Y., Xie, S., Gallagher, P., Zhang, Z., Tu, Z.: Deeply-supervised nets. Eprint Arxiv, pp. 562–570 (2014)
22. Lin, G., Milan, A., Shen, C., Reid, I.: RefineNet: multi-path refinement networks for high-resolution semantic segmentation (2016)
23. Lin, T.Y., Dollár, P., Girshick, R., He, K., Hariharan, B., Belongie, S.: Feature pyramid networks for object detection (2016)
24. Lin, T.-Y., et al.: Microsoft COCO: common objects in context. In: Fleet, D., Pajdla, T., Schiele, B., Tuytelaars, T. (eds.) ECCV 2014. LNCS, vol. 8693, pp. 740–755. Springer, Cham (2014). https://doi.org/10.1007/978-3-319-10602-1_48
25. Long, J., Shelhamer, E., Darrell, T.: Fully convolutional networks for semantic segmentation. In: Computer Vision and Pattern Recognition, pp. 3431–3440 (2015)
26. Peng, C., Zhang, X., Yu, G., Luo, G., Sun, J.: Large kernel matters - improve semantic segmentation by global convolutional network (2017)
27. Pohlen, T., Hermans, A., Mathias, M., Leibe, B.: Full-resolution residual networks for semantic segmentation in street scenes (2016)
28. Ronneberger, O., Fischer, P., Brox, T.: U-Net: convolutional networks for biomedical image segmentation. In: Navab, N., Hornegger, J., Wells, W.M., Frangi, A.F. (eds.) MICCAI 2015. LNCS, vol. 9351, pp. 234–241. Springer, Cham (2015). https://doi.org/10.1007/978-3-319-24574-4_28
29. Shen, X., Chen, Y.C., Tao, X., Jia, J.: Convolutional neural pyramid for image processing (2017)
30. Shi, W., et al.: Real-time single image and video super-resolution using an efficient sub-pixel convolutional neural network, pp. 1874–1883 (2016)
31. Simonyan, K., Zisserman, A.: Very deep convolutional networks for large-scale image recognition. Computer Science (2014)
32. Szegedy, C., Ioffe, S., Vanhoucke, V., Alemi, A.A.: Inception-v4, inception-ResNet and the impact of residual connections on learning. In: AAAI, pp. 4278–4284 (2017)
33. Szegedy, C., et al.: Going deeper with convolutions. In: Computer Vision and Pattern Recognition, pp. 1–9 (2015)
34. Szegedy, C., Vanhoucke, V., Ioffe, S., Shlens, J., Wojna, Z.: Rethinking the inception architecture for computer vision. In: Proceedings of the IEEE Conference on Computer Vision and Pattern Recognition, pp. 2818–2826 (2016)
35. Wang, P., et al.: Understanding convolution for semantic segmentation (2017)
36. Wu, Z., Shen, C., Hengel, A.V.D.: Wider or deeper: revisiting the ResNet model for visual recognition (2016)
37. Xie, S., Girshick, R., Dollár, P., Tu, Z., He, K.: Aggregated residual transformations for deep neural networks (2016)
38. Yu, F., Koltun, V.: Multi-scale context aggregation by dilated convolutions (2015)
39. Zeiler, M.D., Fergus, R.: Visualizing and understanding convolutional networks. In: Fleet, D., Pajdla, T., Schiele, B., Tuytelaars, T. (eds.) ECCV 2014. LNCS, vol. 8689, pp. 818–833. Springer, Cham (2014). https://doi.org/10.1007/978-3-319-10590-1_53
40. Zhao, H., Shi, J., Qi, X., Wang, X., Jia, J.: Pyramid scene parsing network (2016)

NetAdapt: Platform-Aware Neural Network Adaptation for Mobile Applications

Tien-Ju Yang[1]([✉])[ID], Andrew Howard[2], Bo Chen[2], Xiao Zhang[2], Alec Go[2], Mark Sandler[2], Vivienne Sze[1], and Hartwig Adam[2]

[1] Massachusetts Institute of Technology, Cambridge, USA
{tjy,sze}@mit.edu
[2] Google Inc., Mountain View, CA, USA
{howarda,bochen,andypassion,ago,sandler,hadam}@google.com

Abstract. This work proposes an algorithm, called NetAdapt, that *automatically adapts* a pre-trained deep neural network to a mobile platform given a resource budget. While many existing algorithms simplify networks based on the number of MACs or weights, optimizing those indirect metrics may not necessarily reduce the direct metrics, such as latency and energy consumption. To solve this problem, NetAdapt incorporates direct metrics into its adaptation algorithm. These direct metrics are evaluated using *empirical measurements*, so that detailed knowledge of the platform and toolchain is not required. NetAdapt automatically and progressively simplifies a pre-trained network until the resource budget is met while maximizing the accuracy. Experiment results show that NetAdapt achieves better accuracy versus latency trade-offs on both mobile CPU and mobile GPU, compared with the state-of-the-art automated network simplification algorithms. For image classification on the ImageNet dataset, NetAdapt achieves up to a 1.7× speedup in *measured inference latency* with equal or higher accuracy on MobileNets (V1&V2).

1 Introduction

Deep neural networks (DNNs or networks) have become an indispensable component of artificial intelligence, delivering near or super-human accuracy on common vision tasks such as image classification and object detection. However, DNN-based AI applications are typically too computationally intensive to be deployed on resource-constrained platforms, such as mobile phones. This hinders the enrichment of a large set of user experiences.

A significant amount of recent work on DNN design has focused on improving the efficiency of networks. However, the majority of works are based on optimizing the "indirect metrics", such as the number of multiply-accumulate operations (MACs) or the number of weights, as proxies for the resource consumption of a

---

This work was done while Tien-Ju Yang was an intern at Google.

V. Ferrari et al. (Eds.): ECCV 2018, LNCS 11214, pp. 289–304, 2018.
https://doi.org/10.1007/978-3-030-01249-6_18

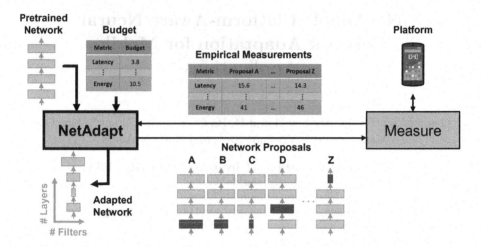

Fig. 1. NetAdapt automatically adapts a pretrained network to a mobile platform given a resource budget. This algorithm is guided by the direct metrics for resource consumption. NetAdapt eliminates the requirement of platform-specific knowledge by using empirical measurements to evaluate the direct metrics. At each iteration, NetAdapt generates many network proposals and measures the proposals on the target platform. The measurements are used to guide NetAdapt to generate the next set of network proposals at the next iteration.

network. Although these indirect metrics are convenient to compute and integrate into the optimization framework, they may not be good approximations to the "direct metrics" that matter for the real applications such as latency and energy consumption. The relationship between an indirect metric and the corresponding direct metric can be highly non-linear and platform-dependent as observed by [15,25,26]. In this work, we will also demonstrate empirically that a network with a fewer number of MACs can be slower when actually running on mobile devices; specifically, we will show that a network of 19% less MACs incurs 29% longer latency in practice (see Table 1).

There are two common approaches to designing efficient network architectures. The first is designing a single architecture with no regard to the underlying platform. It is hard for a single architecture to run optimally on all the platforms due to the different platform characteristics. For example, the fastest architecture on a desktop GPU may not be the fastest one on a mobile CPU with the same accuracy. Moreover, there is little guarantee that the architecture could meet the resource budget (e.g., latency) on all platforms of interest. The second approach is manually crafting architectures for a given target platform based on the platform's characteristics. However, this approach requires deep knowledge about the implementation details of the platform, including the toolchains, the configuration and the hardware architecture, which are generally unavailable given the proprietary nature of hardware and the high complexity of modern systems. Furthermore, manually designing a different architecture for each platform can be taxing for researchers and engineers.

In this work, we propose a platform-aware algorithm, called *NetAdapt*, to address the aforementioned issues and facilitate platform-specific DNN deployment. NetAdapt (Fig. 1) incorporates *direct metrics* in the optimization loop, so it does not suffer from the discrepancy between the indirect and direct metrics. The direct metrics are evaluated by the empirical measurements taken from the target platform. This enables the algorithm to support any platform without detailed knowledge of the platform itself, although such knowledge could still be incorporated into the algorithm to further improve results. In this paper, we use latency as the running example of a direct metric and resource to target even though our algorithm is generalizable to other metrics or a combination of them (Sect. 4.3).

The network optimization of NetAdapt is carried out in an automatic way to gradually reduce the resource consumption of a pretrained network while maximizing the accuracy. The optimization runs iteratively until the resource budget is met. Through this design, NetAdapt can generate not only a network that meets the budget, but also a family of simplified networks with different trade-offs, which allows dynamic network selection and further study. Finally, instead of being a black box, NetAdapt is designed to be easy to interpret. For example, through studying the proposed network architectures and the corresponding empirical measurements, we can understand why a proposal is chosen and this sheds light on how to improve the platform and network design.

The main contributions of this paper are:

- A framework that uses direct metrics when optimizing a pretrained network to meet a given resource budget. Empirical measurements are used to evaluate the direct metrics such that no platform-specific knowledge is required.
- An automated constrained network optimization algorithm that maximizes accuracy while satisfying the constraints (i.e., the predefined resource budget). The algorithm outperforms the state-of-the-art automatic network simplification algorithms by up to 1.7× in terms of reduction in *measured inference latency* while delivering equal or higher accuracy. Moreover, a family of simplified networks with different trade-offs will be generated to allow dynamic network selection and further study.
- Experiments that demonstrate the effectiveness of NetAdapt on different platforms and on real-time-class networks, such as the small MobileNetV1, which is more difficult to simplify than larger networks.

2   Related Work

There is a large body of work that aims to simplify DNNs. We refer the readers to [21] for a comprehensive survey, and summarize the main approaches below.

The most related works are pruning-based methods. [6,14,16] aim to remove individual redundant weights from DNNs. However, most platforms cannot fully take advantage of unstructured sparse filters [26]. Hu et al. [10] and Srinivas et al. [20] focus on removing entire filters instead of individual weights. The draw-back of these methods is the requirement of *manually* choosing the compression rate for each layer. MorphNet [5] leverages the sparsifying regularizers to auto-matically determine the layerwise compression rate. ADC [8] uses reinforcement learning to learn a policy for choosing the compression rates. The crucial dif-ference between all the aforementioned methods and ours is that they are not guided by the direct metrics, and thus may lead to sub-optimal performance, as we see in Sect. 4.3.

Energy-aware pruning [25] uses an energy model [24] and incorporates the estimated energy numbers into the pruning algorithm. However, this requires designing models to estimate the direct metrics of each target platform, which requires detailed knowledge of the platform including its hardware architec-ture [3], and the network-to-array mapping used in the toolchain [2]. NetAdapt does not have this requirement since it can directly use empirical measurements.

DNNs can also be simplified by approaches that involve directly designing efficient network architectures, decomposition or quantization. MobileNets [9,18] and ShuffleNets [27] provide efficient layer operations and reference architecture design. Layer-decomposition-based algorithms [13,23] exploit matrix decompo-sition to reduce the number of operations. Quantization [11,12,17] reduces the complexity by decreasing the computation accuracy. The proposed algorithm, NetAdapt, is complementary to these methods. For example, NetAdapt can adapt MobileNets to further push the frontier of efficient networks as shown in Sect. 4 even though MobileNets are more compact and much harder to simplify than the other larger networks, such as VGG [19].

3   Methodology: NetAdapt

We propose an algorithm, called NetAdapt, that will allow a user to automat-ically simplify a pretrained network to meet the resource budget of a platform while maximizing the accuracy. NetAdapt is guided by direct metrics for resource consumption, and the direct metrics are evaluated by using empirical measure-ments, thus eliminating the requirement of detailed platform-specific knowledge.

3.1   Problem Formulation

NetAdapt aims to solve the following non-convex constrained problem:

$$
\begin{aligned}
&\underset{Net}{\text{maximize}} && Acc(Net) \\
&\text{subject to} && Res_j(Net) \leq Bud_j, \ j = 1, \ldots, m,
\end{aligned}
\tag{1}
$$

where Net is a simplified network from the initial pretrained network, $Acc(\cdot)$ computes the accuracy, $Res_j(\cdot)$ evaluates the direct metric for resource con-sumption of the jth resource, and Bud_j is the budget of the jth resource and the constraint on the optimization. The resource can be latency, energy, memory footprint, etc., or a combination of these metrics.

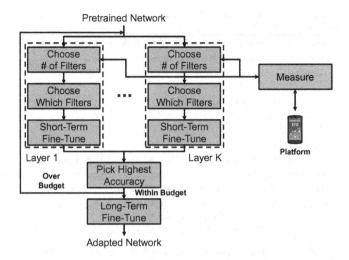

Fig. 2. This figure visualizes the algorithm flow of NetAdapt. At each iteration, NetAdapt decreases the resource consumption by simplifying (i.e., removing filters from) one layer. In order to maximize accuracy, it tries to simplify each layer individually and picks the simplified network that has the highest accuracy. Once the target budget is met, the chosen network is then fine-tuned again until convergence.

Based on an idea similar to progressive barrier methods [1], NetAdapt breaks this problem into the following series of easier problems and solves it iteratively:

$$
\begin{aligned}
&\underset{Net_i}{\text{maximize}} && Acc(Net_i) \\
&\text{subject to} && Res_j(Net_i) \leq Res_j(Net_{i-1}) - \Delta R_{i,j}, \; j = 1, \ldots, m,
\end{aligned}
\tag{2}
$$

where Net_i is the network generated by the ith iteration, and Net_0 is the initial pretrained network. As the number of iterations increases, the constraints (i.e., current resource budget $Res_j(Net_{i-1}) - \Delta R_{i,j}$) gradually become tighter. $\Delta R_{i,j}$, which is larger than zero, indicates how much the constraint tightens for the jth resource in the ith iteration and can vary from iteration to iteration. This is referred to as "resource reduction schedule", which is similar to the concept of learning rate schedule. The algorithm terminates when $Res_j(Net_{i-1}) - \Delta R_{i,j}$ is equal to or smaller than Bud_j for every resource type. It outputs the final adapted network and can also generate a sequence of simplified networks (i.e., the highest accuracy network from each iteration $Net_1, \ldots, Net_i$) to provide the efficient frontier of accuracy and resource consumption trade-offs.

3.2 Algorithm Overview

For simplicity, we assume that we only need to meet the budget of one resource, specifically latency. One method to reduce the latency is to remove filters from the convolutional (CONV) or fully-connected (FC) layers. While there are other ways to reduce latency, we will use this approach to demonstrate NetAdapt.

Algorithm 1. NetAdapt

Input: Pretrained Network: Net_0 (with K CONV and FC layers), Resource
        Budget: Bud, Resource Reduction Schedule: ΔR_i
Output: Adapted Network Meeting the Resource Budget: $\hat{Net}$

1 i = 0;
2 Res_i = TakeEmpiricalMeasurement(Net_i);
3 **while** $Res_i > Bud$ **do**
4   Con = Res_i - ΔR_i;
5   **for** k *from 1 to* K **do**
           /* TakeEmpiricalMeasurement is also called inside
           ChooseNumFilters for choosing the correct number of filters
           that satisfies the constraint (i.e., current budget). */
6   N_Filt_k, Res_Simp_k = ChooseNumFilters(Net_i, k, Con);
7   Net_Simp_k = ChooseWhichFilters(Net_i, k, N_Filt_k);
8   Net_Simp_k = ShortTermFineTune(Net_Simp_k);
9   Net_{i+1}, Res_{i+1} = PickHighestAccuracy($Net\_Simp_.$, $Res\_Simp_.$);
10   i = i + 1;
11 $\hat{Net}$ = LongTermFineTune(Net_i);
12 return $\hat{Net}$;

The NetAdapt algorithm is detailed in pseudo code in Algorithm 1 and in Fig. 2. Each iteration solves Eq. 2 by reducing the number of filters in a *single* CONV or FC layer (the **Choose # of Filters** and **Choose Which Filters** blocks in Fig. 2). The number of filters to remove from a layer is guided by empirical measurements. NetAdapt removes entire filters instead of individual weights because most platforms can take advantage of removing entire filters, and this strategy allows reducing both filters and feature maps, which play an important role in resource consumption [25]. The simplified network is then fine-tuned for a short length of time in order to restore some accuracy (the **Short-Term Fine-Tune** block).

In each iteration, the previous three steps (highlighted in bold) are applied on each of the CONV or FC layers individually[1]. As a result, NetAdapt generates K (i.e., the number of CONV and FC layers) network proposals in one iteration, each of which has a single layer modified from the previous iteration. The network proposal with the highest accuracy is carried over to the next iteration (the **Pick Highest Accuracy** block). Finally, once the target budget is met, the chosen network is fine-tuned again until convergence (the **Long-Term Fine-Tune** block).

---

[1] The algorithm can also be applied to a group of multiple layers as a single unit (instead of a single layer). For example, in ResNet [7], we can treat a residual block as a single unit to speed up the adaptation process.

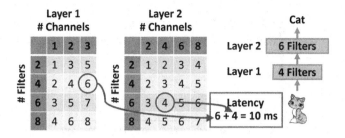

Fig. 3. This figure illustrates how layer-wise look-up tables are used for fast resource consumption estimation.

3.3 Algorithm Details

This section describes the key blocks in the *NetAdapt* algorithm (Fig. 2).

Choose Number of Filters. This step focuses on determining *how many* filters to preserve in a specific layer based on empirical measurements. NetAdapt gradually reduces the number of filters in the target layer and measures the resource consumption of each of the simplified networks. The maximum number of filters that can satisfy the current resource constraint will be chosen. Note that when some filters are removed from a layer, the associated channels in the following layers should also be removed. Therefore, the change in the resource consumption of other layers needs to be factored in.

Choose Which Filters. This step chooses *which* filters to preserve based on the architecture from the previous step. There are many methods proposed in the literature, and we choose the magnitude-based method to keep the algorithm simple. In this work, the N filters that have the largest $\ell 2$-norm magnitude will be kept, where N is the number of filters determined by the previous step. More complex methods can be adopted to increase the accuracy, such as removing the filters based on their joint influence on the feature maps [25].

Short-/Long-Term Fine-Tune. Both the short-term fine-tune and long-term fine-tune steps in NetAdapt involve network-wise end-to-end fine-tuning. Short-term fine-tune has fewer iterations than long-term fine-tune.

At each iteration of the algorithm, we fine-tune the simplified networks with a relatively smaller number of iterations (i.e., short-term) to regain accuracy, in parallel or in sequence. This step is especially important while adapting small networks with a large resource reduction because otherwise the accuracy will drop to zero, which can cause the algorithm to choose the wrong network proposal.

As the algorithm proceeds, the network is continuously trained but does not converge. Once the final adapted network is obtained, we fine-tune the network with more iterations until convergence (i.e., long-term) as the final step.

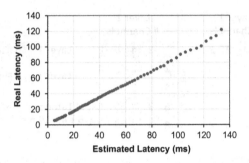

Fig. 4. The comparison between the estimated latency (using layer-wise look-up tables) and the real latency on a single large core of Google Pixel 1 CPU while adapting the 100% MobileNetV1 with the input resolution of 224 [9].

3.4 Fast Resource Consumption Estimation

As mentioned in Sect. 3.3, NetAdapt uses empirical measurements to determine the number of filters to keep in a layer given the resource constraint. In theory, we can measure the resource consumption of each of the simplified networks on the fly during adaptation. However, taking measurements can be slow and difficult to parallelize due to the limited number of available devices. Therefore, it may be prohibitively expensive and become the computation bottleneck.

We solve this problem by building layer-wise look-up tables with pre-measured resource consumption of each layer. When executing the algorithm, we look up the table of each layer, and sum up the layer-wise measurements to estimate the network-wise resource consumption, which is illustrated in Fig. 3. The reason for not using a network-wise table is that the size of the table will grow exponentially with the number of layers, which makes it intractable for deep networks. Moreover, layers with the same shape and feature map size only need to be measured once, which is common for modern deep networks.

Figure 4 compares the estimated latency (the sum of layer-wise latency from the layer-wise look-up tables) and the real latency on a single large core of Google Pixel 1 CPU while adapting the 100% MobileNetV1 with the input resolution of 224 [9]. The real and estimated latency numbers are highly correlated, and the difference between them is sufficiently small to be used by NetAdapt.

4   Experiment Results

In this section, we apply the proposed NetAdapt algorithm to MobileNets [9,18], which are designed for mobile applications, and experiment on the ImageNet dataset [4]. We did not apply NetAdapt on larger networks like ResNet [7] and VGG [19] because networks become more difficult to simplify as they become smaller; these networks are also seldom deployed on mobile platforms. We benchmark NetAdapt against three state-of-the-art network simplification methods:

- **Multipliers** [9] are simple but effective methods for simplifying networks. Two commonly used multipliers are the width multiplier and the resolution multiplier; they can also be used together. Width multiplier scales the number of filters by a percentage across all convolutional (CONV) and fully-connected (FC) layers, and resolution multiplier scales the resolution of the input image. We use the notation "50% MobileNetV1 (128)" to denote applying a width multiplier of 50% on MobileNetV1 with the input image resolution of 128.
- **MorphNet** [5] is an automatic network simplification algorithm based on sparsifying regularization.
- **ADC** [8] is an automatic network simplification algorithm based on reinforcement learning.

We will show the performance of NetAdapt on the small MobileNetV1 (50% MobileNetV1 (128)) to demonstrate the effectiveness of NetAdapt on real-time-class networks, which are much more difficult to simplify than larger networks. To show the generality of NetAdapt, we will also measure its performance on the large MobileNetV1 (100% MobileNetV1 (224)) across different platforms. Lastly, we adapt the large MobileNetV2 (100% MobileNetV2 (224)) to push the frontier of efficient networks.

4.1   Detailed Settings for MobileNetV1 Experiments

We perform most of the experiments and study on MobileNetV1 and detail the settings in this section.

NetAdapt Configuration. MobileNetV1 [9] is based on depthwise separable convolutions, which factorize a $m \times m$ standard convolution layer into a $m \times m$ depthwise layer and a 1×1 standard convolution layer called a pointwise layer. In the experiments, we adapt each depthwise layer with the corresponding pointwise layer and choose the filters to keep based on the pointwise layer. When adapting the small MobileNetV1 (50% MobileNetV1 (128)), the latency reduction ($\Delta R_{i,j}$ in Eq. 2) starts at 0.5 and decays at the rate of 0.96 per iteration. When adapting other networks, we use the same decay rate but scale the initial latency reduction proportional to the latency of the initial pretrained network.

Network Training. We preserve ten thousand images from the training set, ten images per class, as the holdout set. The new training set without the holdout images is used to perform short-term fine-tuning, and the holdout set is used to pick the highest accuracy network out of the simplified networks at each iteration. The whole training set is used for the long-term fine-tuning, which is performed once in the last step of NetAdapt.

Because the training configuration can have a large impact on the accuracy, we apply the same training configuration to all the networks unless otherwise stated to have a fairer comparison. We adopt the same training configuration as MorphNet [5] (except that the batch size is 128 instead of 96). The learning rate for the long-term fine-tuning is 0.045 and that for the short-term fine-tuning is 0.0045. This configuration improves ADC network's top-1 accuracy by 0.3% and

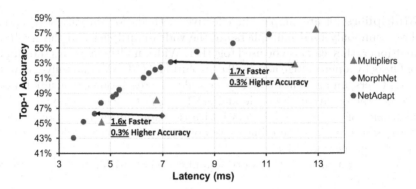

Fig. 5. The figure compares NetAdapt (adapting the small MobileNetV1) with the multipliers [9] and MorphNet [5] on a mobile CPU of Google Pixel 1.

almost all multiplier networks' top-1 accuracy by up to 3.8%, except for one data point, whose accuracy is reduced by 0.2%. We use these numbers in the following analysis. Moreover, all accuracy numbers are reported on the validation set to show the true performance.

Mobile Inference and Latency Measurement. We use Google's TensorFlow Lite engine [22] for inference on a mobile CPU and Qualcomm's Snapdragon Neural Processing Engine (SNPE) for inference on a mobile GPU. For experiments on mobile CPUs, the latency is measured on a single large core of Google Pixel 1 phone. For experiments on mobile GPUs, the latency is measured on the mobile GPU of Samsung Galaxy S8 with SNPE's benchmarking tool. For each latency number, we report the median of 11 latency measurements.

4.2   Comparison with Benchmark Algorithms

Adapting Small MobileNetV1 on a Mobile CPU. In this experiment, we apply NetAdapt to adapt the small MobileNetV1 (50% MobileNetV1 (128)) to a mobile CPU. It is one of the most compact networks and achieves real-time performance. It is more challenging to simplify than other larger networks (include the large MobileNetV1). The results are summarized and compared with the multipliers [9] and MorphNet [5] in Fig. 5. We observe that NetAdapt outperforms the multipliers by up to 1.7× faster with the same or higher accuracy. For MorphNet, NetAdapt's result is 1.6× faster with 0.3% higher accuracy.

Adapting Large MobileNetV1 on a Mobile CPU. In this experiment, we apply NetAdapt to adapt the large MobileNetV1 (100% MobileNetV1 (224)) on a mobile CPU. It is the largest MobileNetV1 and achieves the highest accuracy. Because its latency is approximately 8× higher than that of the small MobileNetV1, we scale the initial latency reduction by 8×. The results are shown and compared with the multipliers [9] and ADC [8] in Fig. 6. NetAdapt achieves

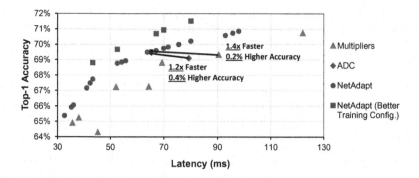

Fig. 6. The figure compares NetAdapt (adapting the large MobileNetV1) with the multipliers [9] and ADC [8] on a mobile CPU of Google Pixel 1. Moreover, the accuracy of the adapted networks can be further increased by up to 1.3% through using a better training configuration (simply adding dropout and label smoothing).

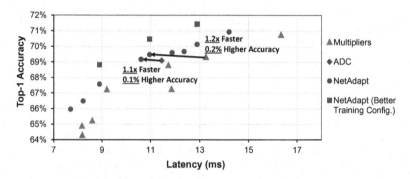

Fig. 7. This figure compares NetAdapt (adapting the large MobileNetV1) with the multipliers [9] and ADC [8] on a mobile GPU of Samsung Galaxy S8. Moreover, the accuracy of the adapted networks can be further increased by up to 1.3% through using a better training configuration (simply adding dropout and label smoothing).

higher accuracy than the multipliers and ADC while increasing the speed by 1.4× and 1.2×, respectively.

While the training configuration is kept the same when comparing to the benchmark algorithms discussed above, we also show in Fig. 6 that the accuracy of the networks adapted using NetAdapt can be further improved with a better training configuration. After simply adding dropout and label smoothing, the accuracy can be increased by 1.3%. Further tuning the training configuration for each adapted network can give higher accuracy numbers, but it is not the focus of this paper.

Adapting Large MobileNetV1 on a Mobile GPU. In this experiment, we apply NetAdapt to adapt the large MobileNetV1 on a mobile GPU to show the generality of NetAdapt. Figure 7 shows that NetAdapt outperforms other

Table 1. The comparison between NetAdapt (adapting the small or large MobileNetV1) and the three benchmark algorithms on image classification when targeting the number of MACs. The latency numbers are measured on a mobile CPU of Google Pixel 1. We roughly match their accuracy and compare their latency.

Network	Top-1 accuracy (%)	# of MACs ($\times 10^6$)	Latency (ms)
25% MobileNetV1 (128) [9]	45.1 (+0)	13.6 (100%)	4.65 (100%)
MorphNet [5]	46.0 (+0.9)	15.0 (110%)	6.52 (140%)
NetAdapt	46.3 (+1.2)	11.0 (81%)	6.01 (129%)
75% MobileNetV1 (224) [9]	68.8 (+0)	325.4 (100%)	69.3 (100%)
ADC [8]	69.1 (+0.3)	304.2 (93%)	79.2 (114%)
NetAdapt	69.1 (+0.3)	284.3 (87%)	74.9 (108%)

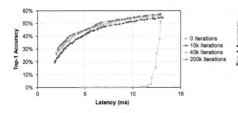

Fig. 8. The accuracy of different short-term fine-tuning iterations when adapting the small MobileNetV1 (without long-term fine-tuning) on a mobile CPU of Google Pixel 1. Zero iterations means no short-term fine-tuning.

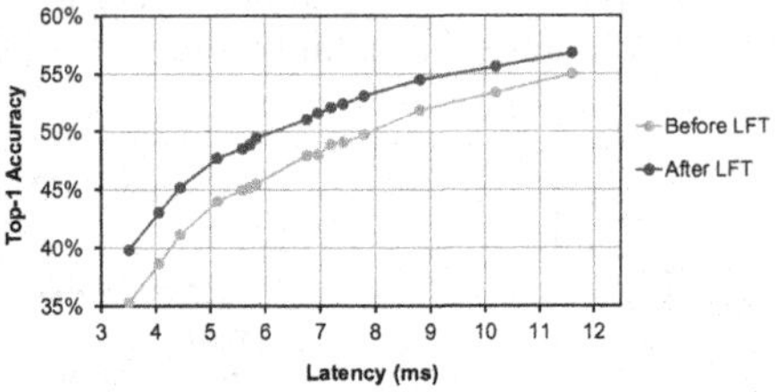

Fig. 9. The comparison between before and after long-term fine-tuning when adapting the small MobileNetV1 on a mobile CPU of Google Pixel 1. Although the short-term fine-tuning preserves the accuracy well, the long-term fine-tuning gives the extra 3.4% on average (from 1.8% to 4.5%).

benchmark algorithms by up to 1.2× speed-up with higher accuracy. Due to the limitation of the SNPE tool, the layerwise latency breakdown only considers the computation time and does not include the latency of other operations, such as feature map movement, which can be expensive [25]. This affects the precision of the look-up tables used for this experiment. Moreover, we observe that there is an approximate 6.2ms (38% of the latency of the network before applying NetAdapt) non-reducible latency. These factors cause a smaller improvement on the mobile GPU compared with the experiments on the mobile CPU. Moreover, when the better training configuration is applied as previously described, the accuracy can be further increased by 1.3%.

4.3 Ablation Studies

Impact of Direct Metrics. In this experiment, we use the indirect metric (i.e., the number of MACs) instead of the direct metric (i.e., the latency) to

Table 2. The influence of resource reduction schedules.

Initialization (ms)	Decay rate	# of total iterations	Top-1 accuracy (%)	Latency (ms)
0.5	0.96	28	47.7	4.63
0.5	1.0	20	47.4	4.71
0.8	0.95	20	46.7	4.65

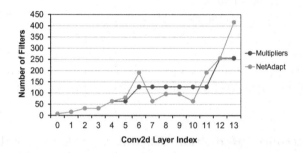

Fig. 10. NetAdapt and the multipliers generate different simplified networks when adapting the small MobileNetV1 to match the latency of 25% MobileNetV1 (128).

guide NetAdapt to investigate the importance of using direct metrics. When computing the number of MACs, we only consider the CONV and FC layers because batch normalization layers can be folded into the corresponding CONV layers, and the other layers are negligibly small. Table 1 shows that NetAdapt outperforms the benchmark algorithms with lower numbers of MACs and higher accuracy. This demonstrates the effectiveness of NetAdapt. However, we also observe that the network with lower numbers of MACs may not necessarily be faster. This shows the necessity of incorporating direct measurements into the optimization flow.

Impact of Short-Term Fine-Tuning. Figure 8 shows the accuracy of adapting the small MobileNetV1 with different short-term fine-tuning iterations (without long-term fine-tuning). The accuracy rapidly drops to nearly zero if no short-term fine-tuning is performed (i.e., zero iterations). In this low accuracy region, the algorithm picks the best network proposal solely based on noise and hence gives poor performance. After fine-tuning a network for a short amount of time (ten thousand iterations), the accuracy is always kept above 20%, which allows the algorithm to make a better decision. Although further increasing the number of iterations improves the accuracy, we find that using forty thousand iterations leads to a good accuracy versus speed trade-off for the small MobileNetV1.

Impact of Long-Term Fine-Tuning. Figure 9 illustrates the importance of performing the long-term fine-tuning. Although the short-term fine-tuning preserves the accuracy well, the long-term fine-tuning can still increase the accuracy by up to another 4.5% or 3.4% on average. Since the short-term fine-tuning has a

Table 3. The comparison between NetAdapt (adapting the large MobileNetV2 (100% MobileNetV2 (224))) and the multipliers [18] on a mobile CPU of Google Pixel 1. We compare the latency at similar accuracy and the accuracy at similar latency.

Network	Top-1 accuracy (%)	Latency (ms)
75% MobileNetV2 (224) [18]	69.8 (+0)	61.4 (100%)
NetAdapt (Similar Latency)	70.9 (+1.1)	61.6 (100%)
NetAdapt (Similar Accuracy)	70.0 (+0.2)	53.5 (87%)

short training time, the training is terminated far before convergence. Therefore, it is not surprising that the final long-term fine-tuning can further increase the accuracy.

Impact of Resource Reduction Schedules. Table 2 shows the impact of using three different resource reduction schedules, which are defined in Sect. 3.1. Empirically, using a larger resource reduction at each iteration increases the adaptation speed (i.e., reducing the total number of adaptation iterations) at the cost of accuracy. With the same number of total iterations, the result suggests that a smaller initial resource reduction with a slower decay is preferable.

4.4   Analysis of Adapted Network Architecture

The network architectures of the adapted small MobileNetV1 by using NetAdapt and the multipliers are shown and compared in Fig. 10. Both of them have similar latency as 25% MobileNetV1 (128). There are two interesting observations.

First, NetAdapt removes more filters in layers 7 to 10, but fewer in layer 6. Since the feature map resolution is reduced in layer 6 but not in layers 7 to 10, we hypothesize that when the feature map resolution is reduced, more filters are needed to avoid creating an information bottleneck.

The second observation is that NetAdapt keeps more filters in layer 13 (i.e. the last CONV layer). One possible explanation is that the ImageNet dataset contains one thousand classes, so more feature maps are needed by the last FC layer to do the correct classification.

4.5   Adapting Large MobileNetV2 on a Mobile CPU

In this section, we show encouraging early results of applying NetAdapt to MobileNetV2 [18]. MobileNetV2 introduces the inverted residual with linear bottleneck into MobileNetV1 and becomes more efficient. Because MobileNetV2 utilizes residual connections, we only adapt individual inner (expansion) layers or reduce all bottleneck layers of the same resolution in lockstep. The main differences between the MobileNetV1 and MobileNetV2 experiment settings are that each network proposal is short-term fine-tuned with ten thousand iterations, the initial latency reduction is .1ms, the latency reduction decay is 0.995, the batch size is 96, and dropout and label smoothing are used. NetAdapt achieves 1.1% higher accuracy or 1.2× faster speed than the multipliers as shown in Table 3.

5   Conclusion

In summary, we proposed an automated algorithm, called NetAdapt, to adapt a pretrained network to a mobile platform given a real resource budget. NetAdapt can incorporate direct metrics, such as latency and energy, into the optimization to maximize the adaptation performance based on the characteristics of the platform. By using empirical measurements, NetAdapt can be applied to any platform as long as we can measure the desired metrics, without any knowledge of the underlying implementation of the platform. We demonstrated empirically that the proposed algorithm can achieve better accuracy versus latency trade-off (by up to 1.7× faster with equal or higher accuracy) compared with other state-of-the-art network simplification algorithms. In this work, we aimed to highlight the importance of using direct metrics in the optimization of efficient networks; we hope that future research efforts will take direct metrics into account in order to further improve the performance of efficient networks.

References

1. Audet, C., Dennis Jr., J.E.: A progressive barrier for derivative-free nonlinear programming. SIAM J. Optim. **20**(1), 445–472 (2009)
2. Chen, Y.H., Emer, J., Sze, V.: Eyeriss: a spatial architecture for energy-efficient dataflow for convolutional neural networks. In: Proceedings of the 43rd Annual International Symposium on Computer Architecture (ISCA) (2016)
3. Chen, Y.H., Krishna, T., Emer, J., Sze, V.: Eyeriss: an energy-efficient reconfigurable accelerator for deep convolutional neural networks. IEEE J. Solid-State Circuits **52**, 127–138 (2016)
4. Deng, J., Dong, W., Socher, R., Li, L.J., Li, K., Fei-Fei, L.: Imagenet: a large-scale hierarchical image database. In: IEEE Conference on Computer Vision and Pattern Recognition (CVPR), pp. 248–255. IEEE (2009)
5. Gordon, A., Eban, E., Nachum, O., Chen, B., Yang, T.J., Choi, E.: Morphnet: fast & simple resource-constrained structure learning of deep networks. In: IEEE Conference on Computer Vision and Pattern Recognition (CVPR) (2018)
6. Han, S., Pool, J., Tran, J., Dally, W.: Learning both weights and connections for efficient neural network. In: Advances in Neural Information Processing Systems, pp. 1135–1143 (2015)
7. He, K., Zhang, X., Ren, S., Sun, J.: Deep residual learning for image recognition. In: IEEE Conference on Computer Vision and Pattern Recognition (CVPR) (2016)
8. He, Y., Han, S.: ADC: automated deep compression and acceleration with reinforcement learning. arXiv preprint arXiv:1802.03494 (2018)
9. Howard, A.G., et al.: Mobilenets: efficient convolutional neural networks for mobile vision applications. arXiv preprint arXiv:1704.04861 (2017)
10. Hu, H., Peng, R., Tai, Y.W., Tang, C.K.: Network trimming: a data-driven neuron pruning approach towards efficient deep architectures. arXiv preprint arXiv:1607.03250 (2016)

11. Hubara, I., Courbariaux, M., Soudry, D., El-Yaniv, R., Bengio, Y.: Binarized neural networks. In: Advances in Neural Information Processing Systems, pp. 4107–4115 (2016)
12. Jacob, B., et al.: Quantization and training of neural networks for efficient integer-arithmetic-only inference. arXiv preprint arXiv:1712.05877 (2017)
13. Kim, Y.D., Park, E., Yoo, S., Choi, T., Yang, L., Shin, D.: Compression of deep convolutional neural networks for fast and low power mobile applications. arXiv preprint arXiv:1511.06530 (2015)
14. Le Cun, Y., Denker, J.S., Solla, S.A.: Optimal brain damage. In: Advances in Neural Information Processing Systems (1990)
15. Lai, L., Suda, N., Chandra, V.: Not all ops are created equal! In: SysML (2018)
16. Molchanov, P., Tyree, S., Karras, T., Aila, T., Kautz, J.: Pruning convolutional neural networks for resource efficient transfer learning. arXiv preprint arXiv:1611.06440 (2016)
17. Rastegari, M., Ordonez, V., Redmon, J., Farhadi, A.: XNOR-Net: imagenet classification using binary convolutional neural networks. In: Leibe, B., Matas, J., Sebe, N., Welling, M. (eds.) ECCV 2016. LNCS, vol. 9908, pp. 525–542. Springer, Cham (2016). https://doi.org/10.1007/978-3-319-46493-0_32
18. Sandler, M., Howard, A.G., Zhu, M., Zhmoginov, A., Chen, L.C.: Inverted residuals and linear bottlenecks: mobile networks for classification, detection and segmentation. In: IEEE Conference on Computer Vision and Pattern Recognition (CVPR) (2018)
19. Simonyan, K., Zisserman, A.: Very deep convolutional networks for large-scale image recognition. In: International Conference on Learning Representations (ICLR) (2014)
20. Srinivas, S., Babu, R.V.: Data-free parameter pruning for deep neural networks. arXiv preprint arXiv:1507.06149 (2015)
21. Sze, V., Chen, Y.H., Yang, T.J., Emer, J.S.: Efficient processing of deep neural networks: a tutorial and survey. Proc. IEEE 105(12), 2295–2329 (2017). https://doi.org/10.1109/JPROC.2017.2761740
22. TensorFlow Lite: https://www.tensorflow.org/mobile/tflite/
23. Yang, Z., et al.: Deep fried convnets. In: Proceedings of the IEEE International Conference on Computer Vision, pp. 1476–1483 (2015)
24. Yang, T.-J., Chen, Y.-H., Emer, J., Sze, V.: A method to estimate the energy consumption of deep neural networks. In: Asilomar Conference on Signals, Systems and Computers (2017)
25. Yang, T.-J., Chen, Y.-H., Sze, V.: Designing energy-efficient convolutional neural networks using energy-aware pruning. In: IEEE Conference on Computer Vision and Pattern Recognition (CVPR) (2017)
26. Yu, J., Lukefahr, A., Palframan, D., Dasika, G., Das, R., Mahlke, S.: Scalpel: customizing DNN pruning to the underlying hardware parallelism. In: Proceedings of the 44th Annual International Symposium on Computer Architecture (2017)
27. Zhang, X., Zhou, X., Lin, M., Sun, J.: Shufflenet: an extremely efficient convolutional neural network for mobile devices. arXiv preprint arXiv:1707.01083 (2017)

Action Anticipation with RBF Kernelized Feature Mapping RNN

Yuge Shi$^{(\boxtimes)}$ (ID), Basura Fernando$^{(\boxtimes)}$ (ID), and Richard Hartley$^{(\boxtimes)}$ (ID)

The Australian National University, Canberra, Australia
u5634555@anu.edu.au, basuraf@gmail.com, Richard.Hartley@anu.edu.au

Abstract. We introduce a novel Recurrent Neural Network-based algorithm for future video feature generation and action anticipation called
feature mapping RNN. Our novel RNN architecture builds upon three
effective principles of machine learning, namely parameter sharing,
Radial Basis Function kernels and adversarial training. Using only some
of the earliest frames of a video, the feature mapping RNN is able to
generate future features with a fraction of the parameters needed in traditional RNN. By feeding these future features into a simple multilayer
perceptron facilitated with an RBF kernel layer, we are able to accurately predict the action in the video.

In our experiments, we obtain 18% improvement on *JHMDB-21*
dataset, 6% on *UCF101-24* and 13% improvement on *UT-Interaction*
datasets over prior state-of-the-art for action anticipation.

Keywords: Human action prediction
novel Recurrent Neural Network · Radial Basis Function kernel
Adversarial training

1 Introduction

Action anticipation (sometimes referred to as action prediction) is gaining a lot
of attention due to its many real world applications such as human-computer
interaction [2,29,32], sports analysis [3,4,55] and pedestrian movement prediction [5,9,18,21,45] especially in the autonomous driving scenarios.

In contrast to most widely studied human action recognition methods, in
action anticipation, we aim to recognize human action as early as possible [22,
27,38,41,48]. This is a challenging task due to the complex nature of video data.
Although a video containing a human action consists of a large number of frames,
many of them are not representative of the action being performed; large amount
of visual data also tend to contain entangled information about variations in
camera position, background, relative movements and occlusions. This results in
cluttered temporal information and makes recognition of the human action a lot
harder. The issue becomes even more significant for action anticipation methods,
as the algorithm has to make a decision using only a fraction of the video at the

© Springer Nature Switzerland AG 2018
V. Ferrari et al. (Eds.): ECCV 2018, LNCS 11214, pp. 305–322, 2018.
https://doi.org/10.1007/978-3-030-01249-6_19

very start. Therefore, finding a good video representation that extracts temporal information relevant to human action is crucial for the anticipation model.

To over come some of these issues, we resort to use deep convolutional neural networks (CNNs) and take the deep feature on the penultimate layer of CNN as video representation. Another motivation to use deep CNNs stems from the difficulty of generating visual appearances for future. Therefore, similar to Vondrick et al. [48], we propose a method to generate future features tailored for action anticipation task: given an observed sequence of deep CNN features, a novel Recurrent Neural Network (RNN) model is used to generate the most plausible future features and thereby predicting the action depicted in video data. An overview of this model can be found in Fig. 1.

The objective of our RNN is to map the feature vector at time t denoted by x_t to the future feature vector at $(t+k)$ denoted by x_{t+k}. Because only a fraction of the frames are observed during inference, the future feature generator should be highly regularized to avoid over-fitting. Furthermore, feature generator needs to model complex dynamics of future frame features.

This can be resolved by parameter sharing. Parameter sharing is a strong machine learning concept that is being used by many modern leaning methods. Typically, CNNs share parameters in the spatial domain and RNNs in the temporal dimension. In our work, we propose to utilize parameter sharing in an unconventional way for RNN models by expanding it to the feature domain. This is based on the intuition that the CNN feature activations are correlated to each other.

By utilizing parameter sharing across feature activations, our proposed RNN is able to learn the temporal mapping from x_t to x_{t+k} with significantly fewer parameters. This greatly boosts the computational efficiency of the prediction model and correspondingly shortens the response time. We call our novel RNN architecture feature mapping RNN.

To model complex dynamic nature of video data, we make use of a novel mapping layer inside our RNN. In principle, the hidden state of the RNN captures the temporal information of observed sequence data. In our method, hidden state of the RNN is processed by a linear combination of Gaussian Radial Basis Function (RBF) kernels to produce the future feature vector. While a linear model defines a simple hyperplane as mapping functions, the kernelized mapping with RBF kernels can model complex surfaces and therefore has the potential of improving the prediction accuracy. In our work, we also implement RBF kernels on the action classification multi-layer perceptron to improve the performance of classifiers.

Ideally, we are interested in learning the probability distribution of future given the past features. To learn this conditional distribution, inspired by the of Generative Adversarial Networks [12], an adversarial approach is used to evaluate the cost of the feature mapping RNN. The RNN is trained with an adversarial loss and re-constrictive L2 loss. In this way, the model is optimized not only with the intention of reducing the Euclidean distance between the prediction

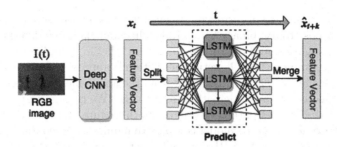

Fig. 1. Overview of Proposed feature mapping RNN: Given a frame extracted from video data, the algorithm first passes the RGB image $I(t)$ through a deep CNN to acquire high level features of the image x_t. The vector is then split into smaller segments x_t^i of equal length. Each scalar element in the segmented vector is used as input to a single LSTM cell that produces the prediction of corresponding feature element in frame $(t + k)$, where $k \geq 1$. After all segments are processed with LSTMs, all the prediction segments $\hat{x}_{t+k}^i$ are concatenated back together to form $\hat{x}_{t+k}$, which contains high level features of $I(t + k)$.

and ground truth, but also taking probability distribution of the feature vector into consideration.

In a summary, our contributions are:

- We propose a novel RNN architecture that share parameters across temporal domain as well as feature space.
- We propose a novel RBF kernel to improve the prediction performance of RNNs.
- We demonstrate the effectiveness of our method for action anticipation task beating state-of-the-art on standard benchmarks.

2   Related Work

The model proposed in this paper focuses on future video content generation for action prediction and action anticipation [10, 20, 22, 26, 28, 34, 35, 38, 41, 48, 49, 54]. In contrast to the widely studied action recognition problem, the action anticipation literature focuses on developing novel loss functions to reduce the predictive generalization error [16, 28, 38] or to improve the generalization capacity of future content such as future appearance [10] and future features [48]. The method propose in this paper also focuses on future content generation and therefore could further benefit from novel loss functions as proposed in [16, 28, 38].

In the early days, Yu *et al.* [54] make use of spatial temporal action matching to tackle early action prediction. Their method relies on spatial-temporal implicit shape models. By explicitly considering all history of observed features, temporal evolution of human actions is used to predict the class label as early as possible by Kong *et al.* [20]. Li *et al.*'s work [26] exploits sequence mining, where a series of actions and object co-occurrences are encoded as symbolic sequences. Soomro et al. [42] propose to use binary SVMs to localize and classify video snippets into sub-action categories, and obtain the final class label in an online manner using dynamic programming. In [49], action prediction is approached using still images with action-scene correlations. Different from the above mentioned methods, our work is focused on action anticipation from videos. We rely on deep CNNs along with a RNN that shares parameters across both feature and time dimensions to generate future features. To model complex dynamics of video data, we are the first to make use of effective RBF kernel functions inside RNNs for the action anticipation task.

On the other hand, feature generation has been studied with the aim of learning video representation, instead of specifically for action anticipation. Inspired by natural language processing technique [1], authors in [33] propose to predict the missing frame or extrapolate future frames from an input video sequence. However, they demonstrate this only for unsupervised video feature leaning. Other popular models include the unsupervised encoder-decoder scheme introduced by [44] for action classification, probabilistic distribution generation model by [24] as well as scene prediction learning using object location and attribute information introduced by [8]. Research in recent years on applications of Generative Adversarial Network on video generation have given rise to models such as MoCoGAN [47], TGAN [39] and Walker et al.'s work [52] on video generation using pose as a conditional information. The mechanisms of these GAN variations are all capable of exploiting both the spatial and temporal information in videos, and therefore have showed promising results in video generation.

Moreover, trajectory prediction [21], optical-flow prediction [51], path prediction [50,53] and motion planning [11,19], sports forecasting [7], activity forecasting of [30] are also related to our work. All these methods generate future aspects of the data. Our novel RNN model, however, focuses on generating future features for action anticipation.

3   Approach

3.1   Overview

Similar to methods adopted by other action anticipation algorithms, our algorithm makes predictions of action by only observing a fraction of video frames at the beginning of a long video. The overall pipeline of our method is shown in Fig. 1. First, we extract some CNN feature vectors from frames and predict the future features based on the past features. Subsequently, a multilayer perceptron (MLP) is used to classify generated features. We aggregate predictions from observed and generated features to recognize the action as early as possible.

3.2   Motivation

Denote observed sequence of feature vectors up to time t by $X = \langle x_1, x_2, x_3, \dots x_t \rangle$ and future feature vector we aim to produce by $\hat{x}_{t+k}$, where

$k \geq 1$ and $\boldsymbol{x}_t \in \mathbb{R}^d$. We are interested in modeling the conditional probability distribution of $P(\boldsymbol{x}_{t+k}|\boldsymbol{x_1},\boldsymbol{x_2},\boldsymbol{x_3},\cdots\boldsymbol{x_t};\Theta)$, where Θ denotes the parameters of the probabilistic model.

It is natural to use RNNs or RNN variants such as Long Short Term Memory (LSTM) [14] to model the temporal evolution of the data. However, learning such a mapping could lead to over-fitting since these methods tend not to utilise the temporal coherence and the evolutionary nature of video data [31].

Furthermore, a naive CNN feature mapping using a LSTM from past to the future is also prone to over-fitting. A LSTM with hidden state of dimensionality H and takes feature vectors of dimensionality d as input uses parameters in the order of $4(dH + d^2)$. As an example, if we use the penultimate activations of Inception V3 [46] as feature vectors ($d = 2048$), a typical LSTM ($H = 512$) would require parameters in the order of 10^7. We believe that the effectiveness of such models can be largely improved by utilising the correlation of high level activations of modern CNN architectures [13,46].

Motivated by these arguments, we propose to train a LSTM model where parameters are not only shared in the time domain, but also across feature activations. By doing so, we aim to self-regularize the feature generation of the algorithm. We name our novel architecture *feature mapping RNN*. Furthermore, to increase the functional capacity of RNNs, we make use of Radial Basis Functions (RBF) to model temporal dynamics of the conditional probability distribution $P(\boldsymbol{x}_{t+k}|\boldsymbol{x_1},\boldsymbol{x_2},\boldsymbol{x_3},\cdots\boldsymbol{x_t};\Theta)$. These mechanisms will be introduced in details in the following subsection.

3.3   Feature Mapping RNN with RBF Kernel Mapping

A traditional feature generation RNN architecture takes a sequence of vectors up to time t as input and predicts the future feature vector $\hat{\boldsymbol{x}}_{t+k}$. Typically, the following recurrent formula is used to model the prediction:

$$h_t = f(\boldsymbol{x}_t, \boldsymbol{h_{t-1}}; \theta) \tag{1}$$

where $\boldsymbol{h}_t$ is the hidden state ($\boldsymbol{h}_t \in \mathbb{R}^H$) which captures the temporal information of the sequence and θ are the parameters of the recurrent formula. Then we utilize this hidden state to predict the future feature vector $\boldsymbol{x}_{t+k}$ using the following formula:

$$\hat{\boldsymbol{x}}_{t+k} = \boldsymbol{h}_t \times \boldsymbol{W} \tag{2}$$

where $\boldsymbol{W} \in \mathbb{R}^{H \times D}$ is the parameter that does the linear mapping to predict the future feature vector.

As introduced previously, in our feature mapping RNN the parameters Θ are shared across several groups of feature activations. This is achieved by segmenting the input feature vector of dimensionality d into equal size sub-vectors of dimensionality D, where D is referred to as *feature step size*.

Now let us denote the ith sub-feature vector of size D by $\boldsymbol{x}_t^i$. Intuitively, if we concatenate all such sub-feature vectors in an end-to-end manner, we will be able to reconstruct the original feature vector $\boldsymbol{x}_t$. The time sequence of data for the

i^{th} sub-feature vector is now denoted by $X^i = \langle x_1^i, x_2^i, x_3^i, \cdots x_t^i \rangle$. If we process each sequence X^i in units of x_t^i with the RNN model in Eqs. 1 and 2, we will be able to predict x_{t+k}^i and by concatenating them end-to-end, generate x_{t+k}. This approach reduces the number of parameters used in the RNN model from $4(dH+d^2)$ to $4(DH+D^2)$, which results in a considerable boost in computational efficiency especially when $D \ll d$. However, the parameter complexity of the model would remain polynomial and is relevant to multiple hyperparameters.

To further improve the efficiency of our model, we adopt an even bolder approach: we propose to convert the sequence of vectors of $X^i = \langle x_1^i, x_2^i, x_3^i, \cdots x_t^i \rangle$ to a sequence of scalars. Let us denote the j-th dimension of sub-vector x_t^i by $x_t^{i(j)}$. Now instead processing sequence of vectors X^i, we convert the sequence X^i to a new sequence of scalars $X'^i = \langle x_1^{i(1)}, x_1^{i(2)}, \cdots x_1^{i(D)}, x_2^{i(1)}, x_2^{i(2)}, \cdots, x_t^{i(k)}, \cdots x_t^{i(D)} \rangle$. Length of the sequence of scalars X'^i is equal to $t \times D$ and we generate $\frac{d}{D}$ number of such sequences from each original sequence of feature vector X.

We then propose to process sequence of scalars using a RNN (LSTM) model. The computation complexity is now linear, with number of parameters used in the recurrent model (LSTM) reduced to $4(H+1)$ and depends only on the hidden state size.

Again, given the current sequence of vectors X, we want to generate future feature vector x_{t+k}. In the our RNN model, this is translated to predicting sequence of scalars $\langle x_{t+k}^{i(1)}, \cdots x_{t+k}^{i(D)} \rangle$ from sequence X'^i for all sub-feature vectors $i = 1$ to $\frac{d}{D}$. Then we merge all predicted scalars for time $t+k$ to obtain x_{t+k}.

Therefore, mathematically our new RNN model that share the parameter over feature activations can be denoted by the following formula:

$$h_t^{i(l)} = f(x_t^{i(l)}, h^{i(l)}{}_{t-1}; \Theta')\tag{3}$$

where Θ' is the new parameter set of the RNN (LSTM) and the future l-th scalar of i-th sub-feature vector is given by:

$$\hat{x}_{t+k}^{i(l)} = h_t^{i(l)} \cdot w'.\tag{4}$$

To further improve the functional capacity of our feature mapping RNN, we make use of Radial Basis Functions (RBF). Instead of using a simple linear projection of the hidden state to the future feature vector, we propose to exploit the more capable Radial Basis Functional mapping. We call this novel RNN architecture the RBF kernelized feature mapping RNN, denoted by the following formula:

$$\hat{x}_{t+k}^{i(l)} = \sum_{j=1}^{n} \alpha_j^l \exp\left[-\frac{(h_t^{i(l)} - \mu_j^l)^2}{\sigma_j^{l^2}} \right]\tag{5}$$

where μ_j^l, σ_j^l and α_j^l are parameters learned during training and n the number of RBF kernels used. These parameters are shared across all sub-feature vectors. The future feature vector $\hat{x}_{t+k}^i$ is calculated as the linear combination of RBF kernels outputs. Since the RBF kernels are better at modeling complex planes in the feature space, this functional mapping is able to accurately capture more complicated dynamics. Implementing the kernalised RBF on our feature mapping RNN enables the model to so with fewer parameters than classical RNNs.

Note that the method we have presented here only uses non-overlapping feature-sub-vectors, *i.e.* no overlapping exists between 2 consecutive sub-vectors. However, overlapping feature-sub-vectors can be used to improve the robustness of feature generation. Therefore, instead of using a non-overlapping *feature stride* of D, we use an overlapping stride of size S. In this case, we take the average between all overlapping parts of 2 consecutive sub-vectors to obtain $\hat{x}_{t+k}^{i(l)}$.

3.4 Training of Feature Mapping RNN

Data generation, especially visual data generation with raw images, has remained a challenging problem for years mainly due to the absence of suitable loss function. The most commonly used function for this task is the $\mathcal{L}_2$ loss. However, it works under the assumption that data is drawn from a Gaussian distribution, which makes the loss function ineffective when dealing with data that follows other distributions. As an example, if there exists only two equally possible value v_1 and v_2 for a pixel, the possibility for $v_{avg} = (v_1 + v_2)/2$ to be the true value for that pixel is minimal. However, v_{avg} will be assigned to the output in a neural network that uses $\mathcal{L}_2$ loss to evaluate the cost. This property of the $\mathcal{L}_2$ loss function causes a "blurry" effect on the generated output. Similar observations can be seen for feature vector generation.

Recent developments in Generative Adversarial Networks address this issue successfully [12]. Traditional GAN consists of 2 CNNs, one of them is named *generator* (denote as $\mathcal{G}$) and the other *discriminator* (denote as $\mathcal{D}$). The GAN effectively learns the probabilistic distribution of the original data, and therefore eliminates the "blockiness" effect caused by $\mathcal{L}_2$ loss function. Here, we propose to train the feature mapping RNN algorithm using a combination of $\mathcal{L}_2$ and adversarial loss, which is realized by implementing the feature mapping RNN as the *generator* denoted by $\mathcal{G} : x_t^i \rightarrow \hat{x}_{t+k}^i$. By doing so, we are able to produce prediction that is both accurate and realistic.

$\mathcal{L}_2$ *loss:* The $\mathcal{L}_2$ loss is defined as the mean squared error between the generated feature and the real feature vector of the future frame given as follows:

$$\mathcal{L}_2^{\mathcal{G}}(x_t) = ||x_{t+k}^i - \hat{x}_{t+k}^i|| = ||x_{t+k}^i - \mathcal{G}(x_t^i)||. \tag{6}$$

Adversarial loss: We use generator adversarial loss proposed by [12] where we train $\mathcal{G}$ so that $\mathcal{D}$ believes $\mathcal{G}(x_t^i)$ comes from the dataset, at which point $\mathcal{D}(\mathcal{G}(x_t^i)) = 1$. The loss function is defined as:

$$\mathcal{L}_{adv}^{\mathcal{G}} = -\log(\mathcal{D}(\mathcal{G}(x_t^i))). \tag{7}$$

By adding this loss to our objective function, the RNN is encouraged to generate feature prediction with probabilistic distribution similar to the original data. Finally, the loss function of our RNN generator $\mathcal{G}$ is given by:

$$\mathcal{L}^{\mathcal{G}} = \lambda_1 \mathcal{L}_2^{\mathcal{G}} + \lambda_2 \mathcal{L}_{adv}^{\mathcal{G}}. \tag{8}$$

The discriminator is trained to judge whether its inputs are real or synthetic. The objective is to output 1 when given input is the real data $\boldsymbol{x}_{t+k}^i$ and 0 when input is generated data $\mathcal{G}(\boldsymbol{x}_t^i)$. Therefore, the discriminator loss is defined as:

$$\mathcal{L}^D = -log(\mathcal{D}(\boldsymbol{x}_{t+k}^i)) - log(1 - \mathcal{D}(\mathcal{G}(\boldsymbol{x}_t^i))). \tag{9}$$

3.5   Action Classifier and Inference

To evaluate the authentication of predicted features generated by the feature matching RNN, we again use the frame features to train a 2-layer MLP appended with a RBF kernel layer (Eq. 5) to classify videos as early as possible. Illustration of our RBF kernelized MLP is shown in Fig. 2. The classification loss is evaluated using a cross-entropy loss. Feature mapping RNN and the action classification MLP is trained separately. One might consider training both MLP and the feature mapping RNN jointly. However, in terms of performance, we did not see that much of advantage.

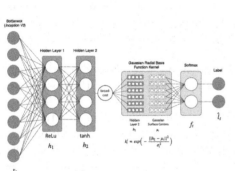

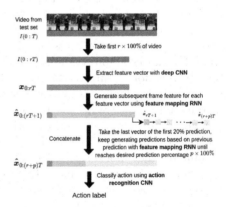

Fig. 2. Illustration of RBF keneralized multilayer perceptron.

Fig. 3. Testing procedure of Feature Mapping RNN

During inference, we take advantage of all observed and generated features to increase the robustness of the results. Accuracy is calculated by performing temporal average pooling on all predictions (see Fig. 3).

4   Experiments

4.1   Datasets

Three datasets are used to evaluate the performance of our model, namely *UT-Interaction* [36], *JHMDB-21* [17] and *UCF101-24* [43]. We follow the standard protocols for each of the datasets in our experiments. We select these datasets because they are the most related to action anticipation task that has been used in prior work [34, 38].

UT-Interaction. The *UT-Interaction* dataset (UTI) is a popular human action recognition dataset with complicated dynamics. The dataset consists of 6 types of human interactions executed under different backgrounds, zoom rates and interference. It has a total of 20 video sequences split into 2 sets. Each video is of approximately 1 min long, depicting 8 interactions on average. The available action classes include handshaking, pointing, hugging, pushing, kicking and punching. The performance evaluation methodology requires the recognition accuracy to be measured using a 10-fold leave-one-out cross validation per set. The accuracy is evaluated for 20 times while changing the test sequence repeatedly and final result is yielded by taking the average of all measurements.

JHMDB-21. *JHMDB-21* is another challenging dataset that contains 928 video clips of 21 types of human actions. Quite different from the *UT-interaction* where video clips of different actions are scripted and shot in relatively noise-free environments, all videos in *JHMDB-21* are collected from either movies or online sources, which makes the dataset a lot more realistic. Each video contains an execution of an action and the dataset is split into 3 sets for training, validation and testing.

UCF101-24. *UCF101-24* is a subset of *UCF101*. The dataset consists of more than 3000 videos from 24 action classes of *UCF101*. Since all the videos are collected from YouTube, the diversity of data in terms of action types, backgrounds, camera motions, lighting conditions etc are guaranteed. In addition, each video depicts up to 12 actions of the same category with different temporal and spatial features, which makes it one of the most challenging dataset to date.

4.2 Implementation Details

Feature Mapping RNN. The Feature Mapping RNN is trained with batch size of 128, using a hidden size (H) of 4 in all experiments unless otherwise specified. The default dimensionality of feature sub vector referred to as *feature step size(D)* is set to 128. We make use of six RBF kernels within the RBF kernelized feature mapping RNN. Feature stride is set to 64 and weight of the adversarial loss (λ_1) is set to 1 and the weight for $\mathcal{L}_2$ loss is set to 10 (*i.e.* λ_2).

Action Classifier MLP. The a simple two layer MLP classifier consists of two hidden layers with 256 and 128 activation respectively. We also use RBF kernels along with the MLP where number of kernels set to 256. MLP is trained with batch size of 256.

Training and Testing Procedures. We use pre-trained Inception V3 [46] penultimate activation as the frame feature representation. The dimensions of each feature vector is 2048 $(d = 2048)$. The action classification MLP is trained on the feature vectors from the training split of the datasets. These features are also used to train our feature mapping RNN to generate future features. Both models are trained with learning rate 0.001 and exponential decay rate 0.9.

Protocols. Following the experimental protocol [34,38], we used only the first $r\%$ (50% for *UT-Interaction* and 20% for *JHMDB-21*) of the video frames to predict action class for each video. To utilise our model, we generate extra $p\%$ (referred to as prediction percentage) of the video features using our RBF kernalized feature mapping RNN. Therefore, we make use of $(r+p)\%$ feature vectors of the original video length to make the final prediction. To generate the next future feature at test time, we recursively apply our feature mapping RNN given all previous features (including the generated ones). We then use our action classification MLP to predict the action label using max pooling or simply average the predictions. This procedure is demonstrated more intuitively in Fig. 3.

4.3   Comparison to State-of-the-Art

We compare our model to the state-of-the-art algorithms for action anticipation task on the *JHMDB-21* dataset. Results are shown in Table 1. Our best algorithm (denoted as *fm+RBF+GAN+Inception V3* in the table) outperforms the state-of-the-art by 18%, and we can clearly see that the implementation of kernel SVM and adversarial training improves the accuracy by around 3 to 4%. In addition, to show the progression of how our method is able to outperform the baseline by such a large margin, we also implemented the Feature Mapping RNN on top of VGG16 so that the deep CNN pre-processing is consistent with other methods in Table 1. The *fm+VGG16* entry in the table shows an 8% improvement from baseline *ELSTM*, which is purely influenced by the implementation of Feature Mapping RNN.

Experiments are also carried out on the two other mentioned datasets, where our best method outperforms the state-of-the-art by 13% on *UT-Interaction* and 6% on *UCF101-24*, as shown in Tables 2 and 3 respectively.

We believe these significant improvements suggests the effectiveness of two main principles, the parameter sharing and expressive capacity of RBF functionals. To further investigate the impact of each component, we perform a series of experiments in the following sections.

4.4   Analysis

In this section we compare the influence of different components of our RBF kernelized feature mapping RNN. As shown in Table 4, we compare following variants of our RNN model, including:

(a) **Feature Mapping RNN:** use only $\mathcal{L}_2$ loss to train the Feature Mapping RNN;
(b) **Feature Mapping RNN + RBF:** our RNN with kernalised RBF, still only using $\mathcal{L}_2$ loss;
(c) **Feature Mapping RNN + RBF + GAN:** RBF kernelized feature mapping RNN with adversarial loss.

Table 1. Comparison of our model against state-of-the-arts on *JHMDB-21* dataset for action anticipation. We follow the protocol of *JHMDB-21* for action anticipation and predictions are made from using only 20% of video sequence.

	Method	Accuracy
Others	ELSTM [38]	55%
	Within-class Loss [27]	33%
	DP-SVM [41]	5%
	S-SVM [41]	5%
	Where/What [42]	10%
	Context-fusion [16]	28%
Ours	fm+VGG16	**63%**
	fm+kSVM+GAN+VGG16	**67%**
	fm+Inception V3	**70%**
	fm+RBF+GAN+Inception V3	**73%**

Table 2. Comparison of our model against state-of-the-arts on *UT-Interaction* dataset for action anticipation. Following protocol of *UT-Interaction*, predictions are made from using only 50% of video sequence.

Method	Accuracy
ELSTM [38]	84%
Within-class Loss [27]	48%
Context-fusion [16]	45%
Cuboid Bayes [34]	25%
I-BoW [34]	65%
D-BoW [34]	70%
Cuboid SVM [37]	32%
BP-SVM [25]	65%
Ours	**97%**

Table 3. Comparison of our model against state-of-the-arts on *UCF101-24* dataset for action anticipation. Again, predictions are made from using only 50% of video sequence.

Method	Accuracy
Temporal Fusion [6]	86%
ROAD [40]	90%
ROAD + BroxFlow [40]	92%
Ours	**98%**

Apart from the Feature Mapping RNN-based models, we also conduct experiments on the following method as comparisons to our model:

(d) **Linear:** a matrix of size $D \times D$ is used for feature generation (D is dimension of input feature);

(e) **Vanilla LSTM:** generate future action features with traditional vanilla LSTM. $\mathcal{L}_2$ loss is used to train it;

(f) **Vanilla LSTM+RBF:** vanilla LSTM with kernalised RBF, using only $\mathcal{L}_2$ loss;

(g) **Vanilla LSTM+RBF+GAN:** RBF kernalized vanilla LSTM with added adversarial loss.

Note that all the results are obtained using features extracted by Inception V3 network, and the accuracy are acquired using max pooling at prediction percentage $p = 50\%$.

Table 4. Comparison of different approach on *JHMDB-21* dataset

Method	Accuracy
Linear	62.7%
Vanilla LSTM	66.3%
Vanilla LSTM + RBF	67.9%
Vanilla LSTM + RBF + GAN	-
Feature Mapping RNN	72.2%
Feature Mapping RNN + RBF	72.8%
Feature Mapping RNN + RBF + GAN	73.4%

The results in Table 4 shows the proposed scheme outperforms the linear model significantly while using fewer parameters. Most interestingly, the feature mapping RNN outperforms vanilla LSTM by almost 6% indicating the impact of parameter sharing in the feature space. We can also conclude from Table 4 that the application of adversarial loss as well as RBF kernel layers encourages the model to generate more realistic future features, which is reflected by the improvement in accuracy with Feature Mapping RNN+RBF and Feature Mapping RNN+RBF+GAN. It is also shown in the Table 4 that vanilla LSTM trained with RBF kernel yields almost 2% higher accuracy than plain vanilla LSTM, which proves further that the RBF layer is something the baseline can benefit from. Regrettably, the vanilla LSTM with adversarial training model failed to stabilise due to large number of parameters needed in the LSTM cells to reconstruct the original feature distribution.

The influence of RBF kernalized feature mapping RNN is quite distinctive. If we compare the red curve to the green one, we can see that the discrepancy between them becomes larger as the prediction percentage increases. This indicates that the RBF kernalized feature mapping RNN generate more accurate future features in the long term, and hence it is a more robust model than plain feature mapping RNN. Comparing the red and green curve to the orange and blue one, we can also conclude that the adversarial loss assist the RNN training in a similar way. Even without the assistance of GAN loss and RBF kernel, the feature mapping RNN still performs better than liner projection RNN (Fig. 4).

4.5 Influence of Hyper-parameters

Feature Step Size. The accuracy of the generated data indicates the existence of strong correlations between the D-dimensional segments of the feature vectors. By default, we resort to feature step size of 128 ($D = 128$). In order to further explore this property, we experimented with different feature step sizes. In Fig. 5, we plot the recognition accuracy against feature step size. We observe that small feature step size guarantees effective feature generation. Specifically, the prediction remains above 70% when feature step size is smaller than 200. This phenomena can be explained by the intuition that when feature step size is

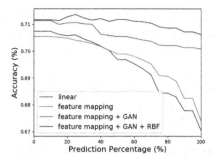

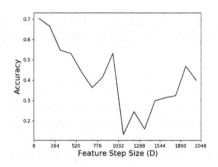

Fig. 4. Prediction accuracy without pooling for JHMDB-21 dataset at different video prediction percentages p. RBF kernalized Feature mapping RNN is trained using adversarial loss is able to achieve the highest stable accuracy. (Color figure online)

Fig. 5. Prediction accuracy evaluated at different feature step sizes on *JHMDB-21* dataset. The accuracy plotted in the image is found by implementing feature step size between $D = 8$ to 2048 with increment of 8 on the model and the rolling average is taken among every 16 measurements. No temporal pooling is used.

Table 5. Prediction accuracy at different feature stride size (S)

Interval size	Accuracy
$S = 4$	74.3%
$S = 8$	73.8%
$S = 16$	74.3%
$S = 32$	73.2%
$S = 64$	73.2%
$S = 128$	72.4%

Table 6. Prediction accuracy using LSTM cells with different state size (H).

Hidden state size	Accuracy
$H = 2$	71.7%
$H = 4$	73.2%
$H = 8$	72.7%
$H = 16$	73.2%
$H = 32$	73.2%
$H = 64$	73.8%

Table 7. Prediction accuracy using different number of RBF kernels.

No. of kernels	Accuracy
$k = 4$	72.7%
$k = 8$	72.7%
$k = 16$	73.3%
$k = 32$	73.3%
$k = 64$	72.7%
$k = 128$	73.8%
$k = 256$	72.2%

large, the model tries to generalize a large set of features with mixed information at one time step, which results in degraded performance.

It is also interesting to note that the prediction accuracy oscillates drastically as the feature step size exceeds 250. This indicates that perhaps the feature vector summarizes information of the original image in fixed-size clusters, and when we attempt to break these clusters by setting different feature step size, the information within each time step lacks continuity and consistency, which subsequently compromises the prediction performance.

Although smaller feature step size builds a more robust model, the training time with feature step size 16 takes only half the amount of time of training with step size 4, with no compromise on prediction accuracy. Therefore, it might be beneficial sometimes to choose a larger feature step size to save computational time.

Interval Size. In this section we experiment the effect of overlapping sub-feature vectors on our RBF kernalized feature mapping RNN. Recall that the feature mapping RNN is denoted by $\mathcal{G} : \boldsymbol{x}_t^i \rightarrow \hat{\boldsymbol{x}}_{t+k}^{i:}$. Instead of incriminating i by the multiple of feature step size D, in an attempt to improve the prediction accuracy, we define an feature stride S that is smaller than D. The prediction accuracy of Feature Mapping RNN with several different feature stride value is shown in Table 5.

LSTM State Size. This section aims at investigating the influence of LSTM cell's hidden state size (H) on the model's performance. Since the hidden state stores essential information of all the input sequence data, it is common to consider it as the "memory" of the RNN. It is intuitive to expect an improvement in performance when we increase the size of the hidden state up to some extent.

However, the results in Table 6 shows that increasing the LSTM state size does not have much effect on the prediction accuracy, especially when the state size becomes larger than 8. This is because in the proposed feature mapping RNN model, each LSTM cell takes only one scalar as input, as opposed to the traditional RNN cells that process entire vectors. As the hidden state size is always greater than the input size (equal to 1), it is not surprising that very large H does not have much influence on the model performance.

Number of RBF Kernels. In this section we study the influence of number of Gaussian surfaces used in feature mapping RNN. We calculate prediction accuracy while increasing the number of Gaussian kernels from 2^1 to 2^8. Results are as shown in Table 7. The results show a general trend of increasing prediction performance as we add more number of kernels, with the highest accuracy achieved at when $k = 128$. However, result obtained when $k = 256$ is worse than when $k = 4$. This phenomena could be explained by over-fitting, resulted from RBF kernel's strong capability of modeling temporal dynamics of data with complex boundaries.

Conclusions for Hyper-parameters Tuning. The conclusion from these experiments is that the model is not too sensitive to the variation of these hyper-parameters in general, which demonstrates its robustness. Results further demonstrated the computational efficiency of our approach. Since it is possible to effectively train the model with very few parameters, it can be stored on mobile devices for fast future action anticipation.

5   Conclusions

The proposed RNN which uses a very few parameters outperforms state-of-the-art algorithms on action anticipation task. Our extensive experiments indicates the model's ability to produce accurate prediction of future features only observing a fraction of the features. Furthermore, our RNN model is fast and consumes fraction of the memory which makes it suitable for real-time execution on mobile devices. Proposed feature mapping RNN can be trained with and without lables to generate future features. Our feature generator does not use class level annotations of video data. Therefore, in principle, we can increase the robustness of the model utilizing large amount of available unlabelled data. The fact that the model is able to generate valid results using very few parameters provides strong proofs for the existence of inner-correlation between deep features, which is a characteristic that can have implications on many related problems such as video tracking, image translation, and metric learning.

In addition, by appending a RBF layer to the RNN, we observe significant improvement in prediction accuracy. However, it was also noted that over-fitting occurs when the model is implemented with too many kernel RBFs. To fully explore functional capacity of RBF function, in future studies, we aim to implement kernel RBFs on fully connected layer of popular deep CNN models such as *ResNet* [13], *AlexNet* [23] and *DenseNet* [15].

In conclusion, proposed RBF kernalized feature mapping RNN demonstrates the power of parameter sharing and RBF functions in a challenging sequence learning task of video action anticipation.

References

1. Bengio, Y., Ducharme, R., Vincent, P., Jauvin, C.: A neural probabilistic language model. J. Mach. Learn. Res. **3**(Feb), 1137–1155 (2003)
2. Dix, A.: Human-computer interaction. In: Liu, L., Özsu, M.T. (eds.) Encyclopedia of Database Systems, pp. 1327–1331. Springer, Bosto (2009). https://doi.org/10.1007/978-0-387-39940-9_192
3. Duan, L.Y., Xu, M., Chua, T.S., Tian, Q., Xu, C.S.: A mid-level representation framework for semantic sports video analysis. In: 2003 ACM International Conference on Multimedia, pp. 33–44. ACM (2003)
4. Ekin, A., Tekalp, A.M., Mehrotra, R.: Automatic soccer video analysis and summarization. IEEE Trans. Image Process. **12**(7), 796–807 (2003)
5. Enzweiler, M., Gavrila, D.M.: Integrated pedestrian classification and orientation estimation. In: 2010 IEEE Conference on Computer Vision and Pattern Recognition, pp. 982–989 (2010)
6. Fan, Z., Lin, T., Zhao, X., Jiang, W., Xu, T., Yang, M.: An online approach for gesture recognition toward real-world applications. In: Zhao, Y., Kong, X., Taubman, D. (eds.) ICIG 2017. LNCS, vol. 10666, pp. 262–272. Springer, Cham (2017). https://doi.org/10.1007/978-3-319-71607-7_23
7. Felsen, P., Agrawal, P., Malik, J.: What will happen next? Forecasting player moves in sports videos. In: 2017 IEEE International Conference on Computer Vision (2017)
8. Fouhey, D.F., Zitnick, C.L.: Predicting object dynamics in scenes. In: 2014 IEEE Conference on Computer Vision and Pattern Recognition, pp. 2027–2034 (2014). https://doi.org/10.1109/CVPR.2014.260
9. Gandhi, T., Trivedi, M.M.: Image based estimation of pedestrian orientation for improving path prediction. In: 2008 IEEE Intelligent Vehicles Symposium, pp. 506–511 (2008)

10. Gao, J., Yang, Z., Nevatia, R.: RED: reinforced encoder-decoder networks for action anticipation. arXiv preprint arXiv:1707.04818 (2017)
11. Gong, H., Sim, J., Likhachev, M., Shi, J.: Multi-hypothesis motion planning for visual object tracking. In: 2011 IEEE International Conference on Computer Vision, pp. 619–626, November 2011. https://doi.org/10.1109/ICCV.2011.6126296
12. Goodfellow, I., et al.: Generative adversarial nets. In: Advances in Neural Information Processing Systems, pp. 2672–2680 (2014)
13. He, K., Zhang, X., Ren, S., Sun, J.: Deep residual learning for image recognition. In: 2016 IEEE Conference on Computer Vision and Pattern Recognition, pp. 770–778 (2016)
14. Hochreiter, S., Schmidhuber, J.: Long short-term memory. Neural Comput. **9**(8), 1735–1780 (1997)
15. Huang, G., Liu, Z., van der Maaten, L., Weinberger, K.Q.: Densely connected convolutional networks. In: 2017 IEEE Conference on Computer Vision and Pattern Recognition (2017)
16. Jain, A., Singh, A., Koppula, H.S., Soh, S., Saxena, A.: Recurrent neural networks for driver activity anticipation via sensory-fusion architecture. In: 2016 IEEE International Conference on Robotics and Automation, pp. 3118–3125 (2016)
17. Jhuang, H., Gall, J., Zuffi, S., Schmid, C., Black, M.J.: Towards understanding action recognition. In: 2013 IEEE International Conference on Computer Vision, pp. 3192–3199 (Dec 2013)
18. Keller, C.G., Gavrila, D.M.: Will the pedestrian cross? A study on pedestrian path prediction. IEEE Trans. Intell. Transp. Syst. **15**(2), 494–506 (2014)
19. Kitani, K.M., Ziebart, B.D., Bagnell, J.A., Hebert, M.: Activity forecasting. In: Fitzgibbon, A., Lazebnik, S., Perona, P., Sato, Y., Schmid, C. (eds.) ECCV 2012. LNCS, vol. 7575, pp. 201–214. Springer, Heidelberg (2012). https://doi.org/10.1007/978-3-642-33765-9_15
20. Kong, Y., Kit, D., Fu, Y.: A discriminative model with multiple temporal scales for action prediction. In: Fleet, D., Pajdla, T., Schiele, B., Tuytelaars, T. (eds.) ECCV 2014. LNCS, vol. 8693, pp. 596–611. Springer, Cham (2014). https://doi.org/10.1007/978-3-319-10602-1_39
21. Kooij, J.F.P., Schneider, N., Flohr, F., Gavrila, D.M.: Context-based pedestrian path prediction. In: Fleet, D., Pajdla, T., Schiele, B., Tuytelaars, T. (eds.) ECCV 2014. LNCS, vol. 8694, pp. 618–633. Springer, Cham (2014). https://doi.org/10.1007/978-3-319-10599-4_40
22. Koppula, H.S., Saxena, A.: Anticipating human activities using object affordances for reactive robotic response. IEEE Trans. Pattern Anal. Mach. Intell. **38**(1), 14–29 (2016). https://doi.org/10.1109/TPAMI.2015.2430335
23. Krizhevsky, A., Sutskever, I., Hinton, G.E.: Imagenet classification with deep convolutional neural networks. In: Pereira, F., Burges, C.J.C., Bottou, L., Weinberger, K.Q. (eds.) Advances in Neural Information Processing Systems 25, pp. 1097–1105. Curran Associates, Inc. (2012)
24. Lampert, C.H.: Predicting the future behavior of a time-varying probability distribution. In: 2015 IEEE Conference on Computer Vision and Pattern Recognition, pp. 942–950 (2015). https://doi.org/10.1109/CVPR.2015.7298696
25. Laviers, K., Sukthankar, G., Aha, D.W., Molineaux, M., Darken, C., et al.: Improving offensive performance through opponent modeling. In: 2009 AAAI Conference on Artificial Intelligence and Interactive Digital Entertainment (2009)
26. Li, K., Fu, Y.: Prediction of human activity by discovering temporal sequence patterns. IEEE Trans. Pattern Anal. Mach. Intell. **36**(8), 1644–1657 (2014)

27. Ma, S., Sigal, L., Sclaroff, S.: Learning activity progression in LSTMs for activity detection and early detection. In: 2016 IEEE Conference on Computer Vision and Pattern Recognition, pp. 1942–1950 (2016). https://doi.org/10.1109/CVPR.2016.214

28. Ma, S., Sigal, L., Sclaroff, S.: Learning activity progression in LSTMs for activity detection and early detection. In: 2016 IEEE Conference on Computer Vision and Pattern Recognition, pp. 1942–1950 (2016)

29. MacKenzie, I.S.: Fitts' law as a research and design tool in human-computer interaction. Hum.-Comput. Interact. 7(1), 91–139 (1992)

30. Mahmud, T., Hasan, M., Roy-Chowdhury, A.K.: Joint prediction of activity labels and starting times in untrimmed videos. In: 2017 IEEE International Conference on Computer Vision, pp. 5784–5793 (2017)

31. Mobahi, H., Collobert, R., Weston, J.: Deep learning from temporal coherence in video. In: 2009 International Conference on Machine Learning, pp. 737–744. ACM (2009)

32. Newell, A., Card, S.K.: The prospects for psychological science in human-computer interaction. Hum.-Comput. Interact. 1(3), 209–242 (1985)

33. Ranzato, M., Szlam, A., Bruna, J., Mathieu, M., Collobert, R., Chopra, S.: Video (language) modeling: a baseline for generative models of natural videos. CoRR abs/1412.6604 (2014)

34. Ryoo, M.S.: Human activity prediction: Early recognition of ongoing activities from streaming videos. In: 2011 International Conference on Computer Vision, pp. 1036–1043, November 2011. https://doi.org/10.1109/ICCV.2011.6126349

35. Ryoo, M.S., Aggarwal, J.K.: Spatio-temporal relationship match: video structure comparison for recognition of complex human activities. In: 2009 IEEE International Conference on Computer Vision, pp. 1593–1600 (2009). https://doi.org/10.1109/ICCV.2009.5459361

36. Ryoo, M.S., Aggarwal, J.K.: UT-Interaction Dataset, ICPR contest on Semantic Description of Human Activities (SDHA) (2010). http://cvrc.ece.utexas.edu/SDHA2010/Human_Interaction.html

37. Ryoo, M.S., Chen, C.-C., Aggarwal, J.K., Roy-Chowdhury, A.: An overview of contest on semantic description of human activities (SDHA) 2010. In: Ünay, D., Çataltepe, Z., Aksoy, S. (eds.) ICPR 2010. LNCS, vol. 6388, pp. 270–285. Springer, Heidelberg (2010). https://doi.org/10.1007/978-3-642-17711-8_28

38. Sadegh Aliakbarian, M., Sadat Saleh, F., Salzmann, M., Fernando, B., Petersson, L., Andersson, L.: Encouraging LSTMs to anticipate actions very early. In: 2017 IEEE International Conference on Computer Vision, October 2017

39. Saito, M., Matsumoto, E., Saito, S.: Temporal generative adversarial nets with singular value clipping. In: 2017 IEEE International Conference on Computer Vision, vol. 2, p. 5 (2017)

40. Singh, G., Saha, S., Sapienza, M., Torr, P., Cuzzolin, F.: Online real time multiple spatiotemporal action localisation and prediction (2017)

41. Soomro, K., Idrees, H., Shah, M.: Online localization and prediction of actions and interactions. CoRR abs/1612.01194 (2016)

42. Soomro, K., Idrees, H., Shah, M.: Predicting the where and what of actors and actions through online action localization. In: 2016 IEEE Conference on Computer Vision and Pattern Recognition, pp. 2648–2657 (2016)

43. Soomro, K., Zamir, A.R., Shah, M.: UCF101: a dataset of 101 human actions classes from videos in the wild. CoRR abs/1212.0402 (2012)

44. Srivastava, N., Mansimov, E., Salakhudinov, R.: Unsupervised learning of video representations using LSTMs. In: 2015 International Conference on Machine Learning. pp. 843–852 (2015)
45. Suard, F., Rakotomamonjy, A., Bensrhair, A., Broggi, A.: Pedestrian detection using infrared images and histograms of oriented gradients. In: 2006 IEEE Intelligent Vehicles Symposium, pp. 206–212. IEEE (2006)
46. Szegedy, C., Vanhoucke, V., Ioffe, S., Shlens, J., Wojna, Z.: Rethinking the inception architecture for computer vision. In: 2016 IEEE Conference on Computer Vision and Pattern Recognition, pp. 2818–2826 (2016). https://doi.org/10.1109/CVPR.2016.308
47. Tulyakov, S., Liu, M.Y., Yang, X., Kautz, J.: MoCoGAN: decomposing motion and content for video generation (2017). arXiv preprint arXiv:1707.04993
48. Vondrick, C., Pirsiavash, H., Torralba, A.: Anticipating visual representations from unlabeled video. In: 2016 IEEE Conference on Computer Vision and Pattern Recognition, pp. 98–106 (2016)
49. Vu, T.-H., Olsson, C., Laptev, I., Oliva, A., Sivic, J.: Predicting actions from static scenes. In: Fleet, D., Pajdla, T., Schiele, B., Tuytelaars, T. (eds.) ECCV 2014. LNCS, vol. 8693, pp. 421–436. Springer, Cham (2014). https://doi.org/10.1007/978-3-319-10602-1_28
50. Walker, J., Gupta, A., Hebert, M.: Patch to the future: Unsupervised visual prediction. In: 2014 IEEE Conference on Computer Vision and Pattern Recognition, pp. 3302–3309 (2014). https://doi.org/10.1109/CVPR.2014.416
51. Walker, J., Gupta, A., Hebert, M.: Dense optical flow prediction from a static image. In: 2015 IEEE International Conference on Computer Vision, pp. 2443–2451, December 2015. https://doi.org/10.1109/ICCV.2015.281
52. Walker, J., Marino, K., Gupta, A., Hebert, M.: The pose knows: Video forecasting by generating pose futures. In: 2017 IEEE International Conference on Computer Vision, pp. 3352–3361 (2017)
53. Xie, D., Todorovic, S., Zhu, S.C.: Inferring dark matter and dark energy from videos. In: 2013 IEEE International Conference on Computer Vision, pp. 2224–2231, December 2013. https://doi.org/10.1109/ICCV.2013.277
54. Yu, G., Yuan, J., Liu, Z.: Predicting human activities using spatio-temporal structure of interest points. In: 2012 ACM International Conference on Multimedia (2012)
55. Zhong, D., Chang, S.F.: Structure analysis of sports video using domain models. In: 2001 IEEE International Conference on Multimedia and Expo. Citeseer (2001)

A-*Contrario* Horizon-First Vanishing Point Detection Using Second-Order Grouping Laws

Gilles Simon[✉], Antoine Fond, and Marie-Odile Berger

Loria, CNRS, Inria Nancy Grand Est, Université de Lorraine, Nancy, France
{gsimon,afond,berger}@loria.fr

Abstract. We show that, in images of man-made environments, the horizon line can usually be hypothesized based on *a-contrario* detections of second-order grouping events. This allows constraining the extraction of the horizontal vanishing points on that line, thus reducing false detections. Experiments made on three datasets show that our method, not only achieves state-of-the-art performance w.r.t. horizon line detection on two datasets, but also yields much less spurious vanishing points than the previous top-ranked methods.

Keywords: Horizon line · Vanishing point detection
A-contrario model · Perceptual grouping · Gestalt theory
Man-made environments

1 Introduction

Accurate detection of *vanishing points* (VPs) is a prerequisite for many computer vision problems such as camera self-calibration [16], single view structure recovery [7], video compass [6], robot navigation [10] and augmented reality [4], among many others. Under the pinhole camera model, a VP is an abstract point on the image plane where 2-D projections of a set of parallel line segments in 3-D space appear to converge. In the Gestalt theory of perception [3], such a spatial arrangement of perceived objects is called a *grouping law*, or a *gestalt*. More specifically, as a 2-D line segment (LS) is in itself a gestalt (grouping of aligned points), a VP is qualified as a *second-order* gestalt [3].

In this paper, we are interested in VP detection from uncalibrated monocular images. As any two parallel lines intersect in a VP, LSs grouping is a difficult problem that often yields a large number of spurious VPs. However, many tasks in computer vision, including the examples mentioned above, only require that the vertical (so-called *zenith*) VP and two or more horizontal VPs (hVPs) are detected. In that case, a lot of spurious VPs may be avoided by first detecting the zenith and the *horizon line* (HL), and then constraining the hVPs on the HL. The zenith is generally easy to detect, as many lines converge towards that point in man-made environments. However, until recently, the HL was detected as an

V. Ferrari et al. (Eds.): ECCV 2018, LNCS 11214, pp. 323–338, 2018.
https://doi.org/10.1007/978-3-030-01249-6_20

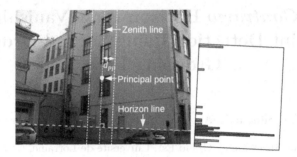

Fig. 1. The horizon line can be detected as a meaningful alignment of image line segments orthogonal to the zenith line. (Color figure online)

alignment of VPs, in other words, a third-order gestalt. This led to a "chicken-and-egg" situation, that motivated e.g. the authors of [14], to minimize an overall energy across the VPs and the HL, at the expense of a high computational cost.

Following [12], we show that, as soon as the HL is inside the image boundaries, this line can usually be detected as an alignment of oriented LSs, that is, a second-order gestalt (at the same perceptive level as the VPs). This comes from a simple observation, that any horizontal LS at the height of the camera's optical center projects to the HL *regardless of its 3-D direction* (red LSs in Fig. 1). In practice, doors, windows, floor separation lines but also man-made objects such as cars, road signs, street furniture, and so on, are often placed at eye level, so that alignments of oriented LSs around the HLs are indeed observed in most images from urban and indoor scenes. Going one step further than [12], we effectively put the HL detection into an *a-contrario* framework. This transposal along with other improvements allows us to obtain top-ranked results in terms of both rapidity of computation and accuracy of the HL, along with more relevant VPs than with the previous top-ranked methods.

2   Related Work and Contributions

There is a vast body of literature on the problem of VP detection in uncalibrated images. [6] use an Expectation-Maximization (EM) algorithm, which iteratively estimates the coordinates of VPs as well as the probabilities of individual LSs belonging to a particular vanishing direction. Although EM is often sensitive to initialization, a very rough procedure is used for this step. Several attempts have been made to obtain a more accurate initialization. [13] estimate VP hypotheses in the image plane using pairs of edges and compute consensus sets using the J-linkage algorithm. The same framework is used in [17], though a probabilistic consistency measure is proposed, which shows better performance. [16] present a RANSAC-based approach using a solution for estimating three orthogonal VPs and focal length from a set of four lines, aligned with either two or three orthogonal directions.

All these methods have been compared on the same datasets (DSs), York Urban (YU) [2] and Eurasian Cities (EC) [14] (see Sect. 5) and with the same protocol of [14]. It is difficult to establish a ground truth (GT) for the VPs, as selecting relevant VPs among hundreds e.g. in an urban scene is a subjective task. For that reason, the evaluation in [14] is focused on the accuracy of the HL. It is easy to show that the HL is orthogonal to the *zenith line* (ZL), which is the line connecting the *principal point* (PP) and the zenith (Fig. 1). The HL can then be found by performing a 1-D search along the ZL, and a weighted least squares fit, where the weight of each detected VP equals the number of corresponding lines. The *horizon error* is then defined as the maximum Euclidean distance between the estimated HL and the GT HL within the image boundaries, divided by the image height. To represent this error over a DS, a cumulative histogram of it is plotted. The plots are reported in Fig. 5. [15] also proposed to report a numerical value as the percentage of area under the curve (AUC) in the subset $[0, 0.25] \times [0, 1]$. These values are also reported in Fig. 5. It can be seen that each new method improves the accuracy, from 74.34% AUC for YU and 68.62% for EC with the earliest method of [6] to 93.45% for YU and 89.15% for EC with the state of the art method in 2013 [17].

A-Contrario Methods. Some authors proposed to detect meaningful VPs in the sense of the Gestalt Theory. This theory was translated by Desolneux et al. into a mathematics and computer vision program [3]. According to the Helmholtz principle, which states that "we immediately perceive whatever could not happen by chance", a universal variable adaptable to many detection problems, the Number of False Alarms (NFA) was defined. The NFA of an event is the expectation of the number of occurrences of this event under a white noise assumption. From this variable, a *meaningful* event in the phenomenological sense can be detected as a so-called ϵ-*meaningful* event, namely an event whose NFA is less than ϵ. Most problems of computer vision have been solved efficiently by simply setting ϵ to 1. When $\epsilon \leq 1$, the event is said *meaningful*. The Helmholtz principle has been applied to the VP detection problem in [1] and [8]. In [1], a practical application of the Santaló's theory [11] is used to partition the infinite image plane into a finite family of so-called *vanishing regions*. Meaningful VPs are then detected from large votes of lines meeting in a vanishing region, thus producing low NFA. Although this method was only qualitatively assessed, it presents interesting matter for the building of our own method, and especially the use of the Santaló's theory. In [8], a point alignment detector based on the Helmholtz principle [9] is used twice: in the image domain, to group LSs into more precise lines, and in dual domains where converging lines become aligned points. This method achieved state-of-the-art accuracy in 2014 (94.51% for YU, 89.20% for EC).

Horizon-First VP Detection. Horizon-first VP detection was simultaneously introduced in two recent works [12,18], both based on the same principle: propose candidate HLs, score them, and keep the best. In [18], a deep convolutional neural network (CNN) is used to extract global image context and guide the generation of a set of candidate HLs. For each candidate, they identify VPs by solving a combinatorial optimization process (see Sect. 5.3) followed by a constrained nonlinear optimization. The final score for each candidate HL is based on the consistency of the lines in the image w.r.t. the selected VPs. This method achieved state-of-the-art accuracy in 2016: 94.78% for YU, 90.80% for EC. In Sect. 5, we closely compare their results with ours and discuss the strengths and weaknesses of each approach. In [12] (our previous work) the ZL is first obtained using a brute force algorithm. Centroids of the LSs orthogonal to the ZL are then projected to the ZL and candidate HLs are taken at the peaks of a histogram of the obtained coordinates. A decreasing density sampling is then performed along each candidate HL. Each sample point is scored by the number of LSs consistent with that point, based on an angular consistency measure, and the VPs are found as peaks in the score curve. The final score for each candidate HL is finally the sum of the best two scores at the peaks (or the best score in case there is only one peak). This method is fast in execution and easy to implement, but middle rank in terms of accuracy (90.40% for YU, 85.64% for EC).

Contributions. In this paper, we build on the advances of several of these works, and especially [1,12,18], to obtain a novel and more accurate HL and VP detection algorithm. In particular: (i) as in [1,8] we put the method into a mathematically, well founded *a-contrario* framework. However, by fractioning the 2-D search of meaningful VPs into three 1-D searches of meaningful events (ZL, HL and VPs), we avoid computationally expensive processes encountered using the previous *a-contrario* approaches; (ii) the ZL itself is obtained based on the Helmholtz principle. One benefit of doing so is to allow considering several orientations for the candidate HLs, therefore succeeding where other methods fail in cases where the vertical of the scene is masked by another near-vertical direction; (iii) As in [18], a set of candidate HLs is sampled around the meaningful HLs. We use a Gaussian mixture model (GMM) for that step, whose modes are the offsets of the meaningful HLs. This step significantly improves the accuracy w.r.t. [12], where no other candidates than the peaks of the histogram are considered; (iv) as in [12] and [18], VPs are hypothesized along the candidate HLs. However, thanks to the Helmholtz principle, we get more meaningful VPs. Moreover, our procedure does not require using any consistency measure, which have proven to be biased [17] and/or expensive to compute. Thanks to these improvements, our approach is top-ranked in terms of accuracy on the usual DSs (95.35% on YU, 91.10% on EC), without compromising neither the easiness of implementation, nor the efficiency of computation. Our method is actually even faster than [12]. It is also much faster than [8] and slightly faster than [18], the two previous state-of-the-art methods. In the next section, we describe how ZLs and HLs are hypothesized based on the Helmholtz principle. VP detection along the candidate HLs and candidate scoring are presented in Sect. 4. Experimental results are finally provided and discussed in Sect. 5.

3   Candidate Horizon Lines

3.1   A-Contrario Zenith Line Detection

As mentioned in introduction, the ZL $\mathcal{L}_z$ is the line connecting the PP and the zenith VP. An initial guess of this line is obtained based on the fact that the vertical LSs in the scene are aligned with $\mathcal{L}_z$ when passing through the PP, and near-parallel to $\mathcal{L}_z$ in a narrow strip around the PP (Fig. 1). This yields a second-order *parallelism* gestalt, which can be detected by finding the *maximal meaningful modes* (MMMs) [3] of an orientation histogram. More specifically, our procedure for detecting hypothesized ZLs consists of the following steps (Fig. 2): (i) a set of M LSs with orientations $\theta_i \in [0, \pi[$ are detected using the LSD algorithm [5], (ii) LSs far from the PP ($|\mathbf{l}_i^T \mathbf{c}| > d_{PP}$, with $\mathbf{l}_i$ the homogeneous coordinates of the LSs normalized so that $\sqrt{l_{i1}^2 + l_{i2}^2} = 1$ and $\mathbf{c}$ the homogeneous coordinates of the PP) or far from being vertical in the image ($|\theta_i - \pi/2| < \theta_v$) are discarded (Fig. 2-A1 shows the LSs remaining at the end of this step), (iii) a L_z-bin orientation histogram of the remaining LSs is built (Fig. 2-A2) and the MMMs of this histogram are computed (blue bins in Fig. 2-A3); the middle orientations of the highest bins of the MMMs are chosen as rough estimates of the hypothesized ZLs (colored circles in Fig. 2-A3), (iv) for each estimate, a set of candidate vertical LSs is selected by thresholding the angles between all image LSs and the estimate ($|\theta_i - \theta_{\mathcal{L}_z}| < \theta_z$, with $\theta_{\mathcal{L}_z} \in [0, \pi[$ the orientation of $\mathcal{L}_z$ (Fig. 2-B1, the LSs are drawn using the same color as the corresponding circles in Fig. 2-A3); the intersection point of these LSs (in direction of the colored dashed lines in Fig. 2-B2) and a set of inlier LSs are obtained using a RANSAC algorithm; finally, the intersection point (the hypothesized zenith VP) is refined from the set of inliers, based on SVD.

Step (iv) is the same as in [18]. MMMs are computed using the large deviation estimate of the NFA[1], with

$$p(a,b) = (b - a + 1)/L \qquad (1)$$

($L = L_z$) the prior probability for a LS to have its orientation in a bin between $[a, b]$ (a uniform distribution is used as null hypothesis). In most cases, only one MMM is detected. However, it can happen, as in Fig. 2, that several modes are obtained (a mean of 1.71 MMMs is obtained in our experiments on YU, 1.66 on EC) while the mode with highest NFA does not correspond to the expected direction. A benefit of using an *a-contrario* approach here, is that all hypotheses

---

[1] Let L be the number of bins of the histogram, M the number of data, $r(a,b)$ the density of data with values in a bin between $[a, b]$, and $p(a, b)$ the prior probability for a data to have its value in a bin between $[a, b]$. An interval $[a, b]$ is said to be a *Meaningful Interval* MI (resp. a *Meaningful Gap* MG) in the large deviation sense if $r(a, b) > p(a, b)$ (resp. $r(a, b) < p(a, b)$) and its relative entropy $H([a, b])$ is greater than $\frac{1}{M} \log \frac{L(L+1)}{2}$. It is said to be a *Meaningful Mode* (MM) if it is a MI and if it does not contain any MG. Finally, an interval I is a *Maximal Meaningful Mode* if it is a MM and if for all MMs $J \subset I, H(J) \leq H(I)$ and for all MMs $J \supsetneq I, H(J) < H(I)$.

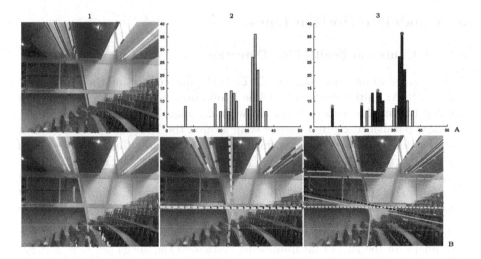

Fig. 2. *A-contrario* detection of the zenith line (see the text). (Color figure online)

can be used to generate candidate HLs, so that the correct solution can still be found in such difficult cases (Fig. 2-B2, the GT HL is drawn in dashed yellow, the estimated HL in cyan). This is a key improvement in comparison with [12] and [18], where only one candidate is obtained at that stage, leading to incorrect results in such cases (e.g. with [18] in Fig. 2-B3). Rarely, a histogram has no MMM. In that case, the vertical direction of the image is taken as an initial guess for the ZL, and refined according to step (iv).

3.2   A-Contrario Horizon Line Detection

The detection of the HL is based on following geometric properties (Fig. 1): (i) the HL is perpendicular to the ZL, (ii) any horizontal LS at the height of the camera's optical center projects to the HL regardless of its 3-D direction. From these properties we get that all horizontal LSs at height of the optical center in the scene accumulate on a line in the image plane, perpendicular to the ZL. This yields a second-order *alignment* gestalt, which is detected by finding the MMMs of an offset histogram. More specifically, our method for detecting the HL is as follows (Fig. 1): (i) LSs far from being perpendicular to the ZL ($||\theta_i - \theta_{\mathcal{L}_z}| - \pi/2| < \theta_h$) are discarded, (ii) the centroids of the remaining LSs are orthogonally projected on the ZL and their offsets are computed relative to the projection of the PP, (iii) a L_h-bin offset histogram is generated and the MMMs of this histogram are computed (red bins in Fig. 1). Again, though more rarely than for the ZL, this procedure can yield several MMMs (a mean of 1.03 MMMs is obtained on YU, 1.06 on EC). The centers of the highest peaks of the N_{init} MMMs are all considered as candidate HLs (blue dashed line in Fig. 1).

3.3   Line Sampling

This estimate of the HL can be inaccurate in some cases, due to the histogram binning and, sometimes, to some offsets between the position of the accumulated LSs and the HL. Following the approach used in [18], we tackle this issue by sampling additional candidate HLs perpendicularly to the ZL, around the initial candidates. In [18], the offset probability density function (PDF) used for this sampling is a Gaussian model, fit from the CNN categorical probability distribution outputs. As we can have several initial candidates, we use a Gaussian mixture model (GMM) where the modes are the offsets of the initial candidates and the standard deviations are identically equal to σH, with H the image height and σ provided in Table 1. We draw $S - N_{init}$ additional candidates, equally divided between the N_{init} initial candidates. In the case where no MMM is found, we have no *a priori* knowledge on the position of the HL along the ZL. The offsets of the S candidate HLs are then sampled linearly between $[-2H, 2H]$.

4   Candidate Vanishing Points

All S candidate HLs are assessed against the success of detecting VPs along the line. Let us assume a line candidate $\mathcal{L}$ with polar coordinates (θ, ρ) is indeed the HL. Then, intersecting all image LSs (extended indefinitely beyond their endpoints) with $\mathcal{L}$ should lead to an accumulation of intersection points around the VPs (Fig. 3-A, B). In the same spirit as previously, these accumulations can be detected by finding the MMMs of a coordinate histogram of the intersection points. However, the prior probability for the coordinates along the HL is not uniform, leading to incorrect or inaccurate MMMs if $p(a, b)$ is taken as in Eq. (1) (e.g. Fig. 3-B, the MMM, shown in red, is very large and its highest bin does not correspond to a VP). In this section, we provide the prior (null hypothesis) suited to this problem and describe how the VPs and the HL are finally obtained.

4.1   Null-Hypothesis

For simplicity, we shall consider the image domain as a circle $\mathcal{C}$ of center O and radius 1 (Fig. 3-A). The polar coordinates of the detected LSs are assumed uniformly distributed over this domain. The prior probability $p(a, b)$ can then be derived from a result obtained by Luis A. Santaló in the late 1970s [11]:

If K_1, K_2 are two bounded convex sets in the plane (which may or may not overlap) and L_1, L_2 the lengths of the boundaries $\partial K_1, \partial K_2$, the probability that a random chord of K_1 intersects K_2 is $p = \frac{L_i - L_e}{L_1}$, where L_e is the length of the external cover C_e of K_1 and K_2, and L_i is the length of the internal cover C_i of K_1 and K_2 if $K_1 \cap K_2 = \emptyset$, or $L_i = L_1 + L_2$ if K_1 and K_2 overlap [2].

---

[2] The external cover C_e is the boundary of the convex hull of $K_1 \cup K_2$. It may be intuitively interpreted as a closed elastic string drawn about K_1 and K_2. The internal cover C_i can also be considered realized by a close elastic string drawn about K_1 and K_2 and crossing over at a point between K_1 and K_2. See [11] for details.

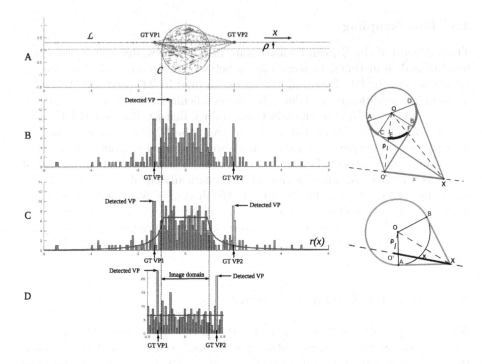

Fig. 3. Left: each line segment gives rise to an intersection point with the horizon line (A). The modes of a coordinate histogram of these intersections (in red and yellow) should appear at the positions of the vanishing points. Different results are shown (B, C, D) depending on the choice of the null hypothesis and the way the histogram is built. Right: computation of p depending on whether the line meets the circle or not. (Color figure online)

This result is applied to our problem as follows. Let O' be the orthogonal projection of O onto the candidate HL $\mathcal{L}$ and let X be a point on $\mathcal{L}$ at a signed distance x from O' (Fig. 3, right). We use $K_1 = \mathcal{C}$ ($L_1 = 2\pi$) and $K_2 = [O'X]$ ($L_2 = 2|x|$). The probability of a LS meeting $\mathcal{L}$ between O' and X depends on whether or not $\mathcal{L}$ meets $\mathcal{C}$.

Case 1: $\mathcal{C} \cap \mathcal{L} = \emptyset$ (Fig. 3, top-right). Let A, B (resp. C, D) be the points of contact of the tangents to the circle $\mathcal{C}$ from point O' (resp. X). We have:

$$L_e = O'X + XD + \widehat{DA} + AO' = O'X + XC + \widehat{DA} + BO',$$
$$L_i = XO' + O'B + \widehat{BD} + \widehat{DA} + \widehat{AC} + CX,$$
$$p = \frac{L_i - L_e}{L_1} = \frac{\widehat{BD} + \widehat{AC}}{2\pi} = \frac{\widehat{EF}}{\pi},$$

where $\frown$ denotes a counterclockwise arc of $\mathcal{C}$, and E, F are the intersection points of the circle $\mathcal{C}$ with lines (OO') and (resp.) $(OX)^3$. Finally:

$$p(x) = \frac{1}{\pi}\tan^{-1}\frac{x}{\rho}. \tag{2}$$

It may be noticed that this expression is similar to the inverse of the sampling function $s(k) = L\tan(k\Delta\theta)$ used in [12], though the term ρ is also involved here.

Case 2: $\mathcal{C} \cap \mathcal{L} \neq \emptyset$. In that case, we have $p = (L_1 + L_2 - L_e)/L_1$ with L_e depending on whether X is inside or outside the circle $\mathcal{C}$. In the sub-case where X is inside the circle, $L_e = L_1$ and

$$p(x) = \frac{x}{\pi}, \tag{3}$$

which is independent from ρ. In the sub-case where X is outside the circle (Fig. 3, bottom-right), $L_e = L1 - \widehat{AB} + AX + BX$ and $p = (2|x| + 2\tan^{-1}(AX) - 2AX)/2\pi$, where A, B denote the points of contact of the tangents to the circle $\mathcal{C}$ from point X. This yields to:

$$p(x) = \frac{1}{\pi}\left(x + \tan^{-1}\left(x\sqrt{1 + \frac{\rho^2 - 1}{x^2}}\right) - x\sqrt{1 + \frac{\rho^2 - 1}{x^2}}\right). \tag{4}$$

Finally, given a coordinate histogram of the intersection points and given a bin range $[a, b]$, the prior probability $p(a, b)$ is given by:

$$p(a, b) = p(r(b)) - p(l(a)), \tag{5}$$

where $l(a), r(a)$ denote the min and (resp.) max values of the histogram bin a.

4.2   A-Contrario VP Detection and Line Scoring

Figure 3-C shows an example of the PDF $r(x) = \frac{\partial p}{\partial x}(x)$, obtained for a line $\mathcal{L}$ in case 2 (purple curve). In this figure, the red and yellow MMMs are obtained using $p(a, b)$ provided by Eq. (5): both VPs are correctly detected. However, the coordinates of the intersection points can be large, depending on the orientations of the detected LSs w.r.t. the HL. For a given bin width, this results in an arbitrary and potentially very large number of bins, yielding poor time performance for the MMM detection. For that reason, we rather use the following approach: (i) the coordinates of the intersection points are transformed using the function $p(x)$, yielding new coordinates, theoretically uniformly distributed (except at the VPs) between $-1/2$ and $1/2$, (ii) a histogram with a fixed number L_{vp} of bins is computed from the new coordinates and the MMMs of this histogram are detected using the prior probability $p(a, b)$ provided by Eq. (1), with $L = L_{vp}$. The histogram and MMMs obtained by following this procedure

---

^{3} $BD = FD - FB = CF - FB = CE + EF - FB = AE - AC + EF - FB =$
$EB - AC + EF - FB \iff AC + BD = EB + EF - FB = EF + EF = 2EF.$

Fig. 4. Horizon lines obtained at the 1st, 25th, 50th, 75th and 100th percentiles of the horizon error (Col. 1–5, resp.) for YU (Row A), EC (Row B) and HLW (Row C). The GT HL is shown in yellow dashed line, the MMMs in blue dashed lines and the estimated HL in cyan solid line. The horizon error is displayed on the top-left corner of each image result. LSs participating to a VP are shown using one color per VP. (Color figure online)

are shown in Fig. 3-D. Both VPs are still detected, while the histogram is much more compact (46 bins against 3630) for the same accuracy (30 bins) inside the image domain. The accuracy may be worse outside the image domain but, as a counterpart, the propagated error e.g. on the inferred 3-D vanishing directions, decreases as the distance between the PP and the VP increases[4]. Finally, an initial set of candidate VPs are extracted at the centers of the highest bins of the MMMs. These candidate VPs are refined using an EM-like algorithm similar to the one used in [18]. This algorithm relies on the consistency measure $f_c(\mathbf{v}_i, \mathbf{l}_j) = \max(\theta_{con} - |\cos^{-1}(\mathbf{v}_i^\top \mathbf{l}_j)|, 0)$, where $\mathbf{l}_j$ is a LS whose consistency with a VP $\mathbf{v}_i$ is measured. At the end of this procedure, we select the two highest weighted VPs $\{\mathbf{v}_i\}_{best}$ (or one if there is only one candidate) and compute the score of the candidate HL as $\sum_{\{\mathbf{v}_i\}_{best}} \sum_{\{\mathbf{l}_j\}} f_c(\mathbf{v}_i, \mathbf{l}_j)$.

It is important to notice that the consistency measure is used to refine the VPs, but *not* to detect them. This is a great difference in comparison with [18], where the consistency measure is used both to detect and refine the VPs, yielding more spurious VPs (see Sect. 5). Moreover, our 1-D search of the VPs has several advantages over the previous *a-contrario* approaches [1,8] that operated in 2-D space. With regard to [1], we avoid computationally expensive local maximization of meaningfulness as well as filtering of spurious vanishing regions, due to artificial mixtures of different segment orientations. With regard to [8], we

---

[4] As the angle θ between the optical axis and a vanishing direction is arc-tangential in the distance d between the VP and the PP, the propagated error $\partial\theta/\partial d$ is inversely proportional to d^2.

Table 1. Algorithm parameters. First row: parameters' values (W is the image width). Second row: parameters' sensitivity.

d_{PP}	θ_v	θ_z	L_z	θ_h	L_h	σ	S	L_{vp}	θ_{con}
$W/8$	22.5°	10°	45	1.5°	64	0.2	300	128	1.5°
0.0%	0.0%	−14.2%	−7.2%	−13.2%	−12.4%	0.0%	−11.4%	−6.4%	−28.7%

avoid highly combinatorial point alignment detection in the dual space, along with tricky parameters tuning (sizes of rectangles, local windows, boxes – see [9] for details).

5   Experimental Results

5.1   Implementation

The source code of our method is available at https://members.loria.fr/GSimon/v/. Algorithm parameters are provided in Table 1. Those were tuned manually using a few images from the DSs. We used the same number of line samples, $S = 300$, as in [18]. The PP is assumed at image center. In order quantify the parameters' sensitivity, we did the following experiment. For each parameter p, we run our method 9 times, multiplying p by $\frac{1}{2}, \frac{5}{8}, \frac{6}{8}, \frac{7}{8}, 1, \frac{5}{4}, \frac{6}{4}, \frac{7}{4}, 2$, respectively, and leaving the other parameters unchanged (the first 20 images of YU and EC were used). For each parameter, we report the relative decrease from the maximum to the minimum AUC obtained over the 9 runs (last row). The consistency thresholds θ_z, θ_h, and particularly θ_{con} (also used in [17]) are the most sensitive parameters. The number of bins in the histograms (L_z, L_h, L_{vp}) are not very sensitive, though L_h is more sensitive than the other two. d_{pp}, θ_v and σ are not sensitive. The number of samples S is not as sensitive as one might expect (from $S = 150$ to $S = 600$, the AUC increases from 93.7% to 94.3%).

5.2   Accuracy of the Horizon Line

Computation of the HL was first evaluated on the two usual DSs: (i) York Urban (YU) [2], consisting of 102 images of resolution 640 × 480, taken indoor and outdoor and mostly following the Manhattan world assumption, and (ii) Eurasian City (EC) [14], consisting of 114 images of resolution 1920 × 1080, including scenes from different parts of the world, more varied viewpoints, and poorer fit to the Manhattan assumption. Example results are provided in Fig. 4, first and second rows (resp. YU and EC). We show the images where the horizon error is the lowest (column 1), the highest (column 5), and at the 25th, 50th and 75th percentiles (columns 2, 3, 4, resp.). The table in Fig. 5 shows the performance of our method, based on the cumulative histogram of the horizon error and the AUC (Sect. 2). We achieve state-of-the-art performance on both DSs. On YU, we improve upon the previous best of Zhai et al. [18] by a relative

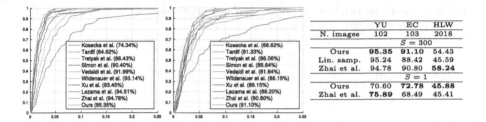

Fig. 5. Performance results w.r.t. HL detection.

improvement $\Delta AUC = (AUC_{new} - AUC_{old})/(1 - AUC_{old}) = 10.9\%$. This is a significant improvement, especially considering their improvement relative to the previous state of the art [8] was 5%. On EC, the relative improvement upon the previous best is 3.3%. To further investigate our results, we replaced our PDF-based sampling method by a linear sampling between $[-2H, 2H]$. The new AUC are shown in the table of Fig. 5 ("Linear samp"). The accuracy is similar to that with our sampling PDF and higher to that with the PDF of [18]. This signifies that YU is a easy DS (two large sets of parallel lines are detected in most images), that does not require fine sampling as long as it covers the range $[-2H, 2H]$ with sufficient density. This tends to attribute the improvement of accuracy w.r.t. to [18] to our scoring procedure. It indeed appears that the method of [18] gets much more spurious VPs than ours on both YU and EC (see Sect. 5.3 below). By contrast, the best result obtained by our method on EC may be interpreted slightly differently, as here both our sampling PDF and the one of [18] improve the accuracy compared to that with a linear sampling, so that both sampling and scoring of the candidate HLs contribute to our performance.

Our method was then evaluated on Horizon Lines in the Wild (HLW), a DS introduced recently by Zhai et al. [18], and consisting of 2018 images of various resolutions. This DS is not only larger but also much more challenging than the previous ones. Most of the photos look like holiday photos, showing man-made environments, but also groups of people, statues occupying a large part of the image, and so on. Furthermore, the roll and tilt angles of the camera have very large range of values, often leading to HLs far from the image boundaries, and ZL angles out of the assumed range (e.g. Fig. 4-C5). Example results and AUCs obtained with our method are shown in Fig. 4-Row C, and (resp.) in the third column of the table in Fig. 5. The approach of Zhai et al. outperforms our method on that DS and we get a relative decrease of 9.1% w.r.t. them. The AUC with a linear sampling is much lower than with our PDF (a relative decrease of 19.4%), which indicates that sampling plays a crucial role on this DS. To closely compare our PDF with the one of [18] and establish which parameters of the PDFs, among the modes and the spreads, are the most critical, we tested both methods using only one sample ($S = 1$), namely the mode of the GMM with highest NFA with our method, and the center of the PDF with the method of Zhai et al. The results are shown in the last two rows of the table in Fig. 5.

The AUC with our method is now quite the same as with [18]. This indicates that, in HLW, the spread of the sampling is the key element of the difference in performance between [18] and our method. In [18], σ is re-estimated each frame from the CNN output, while we take a constant, empirical value in our method. A way to improve our results may be to consider the NFAs of the candidate HLs as uncertainty measures, that may be used to generate more relevant values of σ.

The predictive power of the CNN is interesting in bad images where analytical vision fails, assuming a large DS of similar examples is provided, along with a GT, to the learning process. By contrast, our method may provide accurate results in some images where the CNN fails due to insufficient representation in the learning DS. For instance, Fig. 6-A1 shows an example of an image acquired in an industrial environment. Our method succeeds in predicting the HL, refining it and getting meaningful VPs (Fig. 6-A1), while the method of Zhai et al. poorly estimates the sampling PDF and finally the HL (Fig. 6-A2).

5.3   Relevance of the Vanishing Points

Figure 6-B1, B3, C1, C3 show some example VPs (represented by the LSs consistent with them) obtained by using our method. Performance w.r.t. the previous two best of [8,18] was measured by counting the number of good and spurious VPs obtained on the YU and EC DSs. We chose to use these two DSs, as those are representative of different resolutions (low and high) and get higher accuracy regarding HL detection. In our experiment, a "good VP" is a VP that indeed corresponds to a set of parallel, horizontal lines, while a spurious VP can be of two kinds: "spurious VPs" that correspond to fortuitous convergences of non parallel lines, and "split VPs", issued from undesirable splittings of parallel, horizontal lines normally corresponding to the same VP. In the latter case, one "good VP" plus one "split VP" per added VP are counted. Figure 7-Left shows the total number of good VPs, spurious VPs and split VPs obtained on the two DSs for each method. Our method is the most relevant regarding the three criteria. We obtain the highest number of good VPs, very few spurious VPs and no split VP at all, whatever the DS is.

The method in [18] detects slightly less good VPs than ours (a mean of 2.11 per image–p.i. on the two DSs, against 2.14 with our method) but much more spurious VPs, about one for 2 good VPs, against one for 23 with our method. It also obtains a non-negligible number of split VPs (one for 29 good, against 0 with our method). These relatively poor results are mainly due to the approach used by [18] to initialize VPs along the candidate HLs. This approach consists in randomly selecting a subset of LSs $\{l_j\}$ and computing their intersection with the HL. An optimal subset of VPs $\mathbf{v}_i$ is extracted from the intersections, so that the sum of weights $\sum_{\mathbf{v}_i} \sum_{l_j} f_c(\mathbf{v}_i, l_j)$ is maximal, while ensuring no VPs in the final set are too close. A distance threshold between two VPs has therefore to be fixed, which can lead to split LSs into several groups while they correspond to the same VP (e.g. the blue and yellow LSs on the building's facade in Fig. 6-B2). Moreover, random selection of LSs can prevent detecting a VP represented by few LSs (e.g. the VP consistent with the yellow LSs in Fig. 6-C1, not found

Fig. 6. Qualitative comparisons between our method (Col. 1) and the method of Zhai et al. [18] (Col. 2) on the one hand, and between our method (Col. 3) and the method of Lezama et al. [8] (Col. 4) on the other hand. Plotting conventions are as in Fig. 4. (Color figure online)

in Fig. 6-C2). Finally, as another threshold has to be fixed for the consistency measure, any set of LSs that meet accidentally "near" the same point on the HL can generate a spurious VP (e.g. the yellow LSs in Fig. 6-C2). All these threshold problems are inherently handled when using our *a-contrario* framework.

While also relying on an *a-contrario* framework, the method in [8] gets poor results regarding the detected VPs: the lowest number of found VPs (1.80 p.i.), the second highest number of spurious VPs (one for 3 good) and the highest number of split VPs (one for 4 good). The low number of good VPs (see e.g. the VPs consistent with the orange LSs in Fig. 6-B3 and C3, not found in Fig. 6-B4 and C4, resp.) may be explained by the fact that a VP can appear as meaningful along the HL, but not in the whole image dual domain. The high number of spurious VPs (e.g. the VPs consistent with the cyan, green, red and yellow LSs Fig. 6-C4) is mainly due to accidental intersections of LSs, that appear more frequently in the whole image dual domain than on the HL. Finally, the high number of split VPs is mainly due to the fact that aligned points in the dual domain (meeting LSs in the primal domain) can be scattered in the direction orthogonal to the alignment, producing several meaningful alignments with slightly different orientations (Fig. 6-A4 and B4). Using our method, LSs corresponding to the same VP can meet the HL at coordinates scattered along the HL, but generally in contiguous bins of the coordinate histogram, so that those are fused in a single MMM (Fig. 6-A3 and B3).

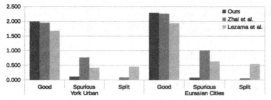

	YU	EC	HLW
$W \times H$ (Mpixels)	0.31	0.81	1.74
Ours (S=300)	**2.07**	**2.44**	**2.88**
Zhai et al. (S=300)	2.08	2.77	3.08
Simon et al.	4.47	12.60	16.04
Lezama et al.	8.11	42.71	108.23
Ours (S=1)	**0.29**	**0.57**	**0.96**
Zhai et al. (S=1)	0.58	0.77	1.12

Fig. 7. Left: performance results w.r.t. VP detection. Right: computation times in sec.

5.4 Computation Times

The method was implemented in Matlab and run on a HP EliteBook 8570p laptop with I7-3520M CPU. Computation times are given in Fig. 7-Right. Our method is faster than the previous methods whose code is available. Moreover, contrary to e.g. [8], it is only slightly affected by increases in the image size, which generally yield larger numbers of LSs. Indeed, our method is in $O(L_z^2 + L_h^2 + S(L_{vp}^2 + M))$, therefore only linearly affected by the number of LSs.

6 Conclusion

As soon as one wishes to detect Manhattan directions, hVPs and/or the HL in an image, which are common tasks in computer vision, our experimental results show that horizon-first strategies are definitely faster and more accurate than all previous methods. In particular, our method achieves state-of-the-art performance w.r.t. HL detection on two over three DSs. Moreover, it provides more relevant VPs than the previous two state-of-the-art approaches, which can be of great interest for any practical use of the VPs (e.g. finding the Manhattan directions). Finally, it performs well in any kind of environment, as soon as man-made objects are visible at eye level. The method of Zhai et al. [18] stays, however, an alternate method that may be more suited to specific environments, learned from large GT DSs, especially when the later condition is not met.

References

1. Almansa, A., Desolneux, A., Vamech, S.: Vanishing point detection without any a priori information. IEEE Trans. Pattern Anal. Mach. Intell. **25**(4), 502–507 (2003)
2. Denis, P., Elder, J.H., Estrada, F.J.: Efficient edge-based methods for estimating Manhattan frames in urban imagery. In: Forsyth, D., Torr, P., Zisserman, A. (eds.) ECCV 2008. LNCS, vol. 5303, pp. 197–210. Springer, Heidelberg (2008). https://doi.org/10.1007/978-3-540-88688-4_15
3. Desolneux, A., Moisan, L., Morel, J.M.: From Gestalt Theory to Image Analysis: A Probabilistic Approach, 1st edn. Springer, New York (2007). https://doi.org/10.1007/978-0-387-74378-3
4. Fond, A., Berger, M.O., Simon, G.: Facade proposals for urban augmented reality. In: IEEE International Symposium on Mixed and Augmented Reality (ISMAR) (2017)

5. Grompone von Gioi, R., Jakubowicz, J., Morel, J.M., Randall, G.: LSD: a line segment detector. Image Process. Line **2**, 35–55 (2012). https://doi.org/10.5201/ipol.2012.gjmr-lsd

6. Košecká, J., Zhang, W.: Video compass. In: Heyden, A., Sparr, G., Nielsen, M., Johansen, P. (eds.) ECCV 2002. LNCS, vol. 2353, pp. 476–490. Springer, Heidelberg (2002). https://doi.org/10.1007/3-540-47979-1_32

7. Lee, D.C., Hebert, M., Kanade, T.: Geometric reasoning for single image structure recovery. In: IEEE Conference on Computer Vision and Pattern Recognition (CVPR) (2009)

8. Lezama, J., Grompone von Gioi, R., Randall, G., Morel, J.M.: Finding vanishing points via point alignments in image primal and dual domains. In: IEEE Conference on Computer Vision and Pattern Recognition (CVPR) (2014)

9. Lezama, J., Morel, J.M., Randall, G., Grompone von Gioi, R.: A contrario 2D point alignment detection. IEEE Trans. Pattern Anal. Mach. Intell. **37**(3), 499–512 (2015). https://doi.org/10.1109/TPAMI.2014.2345389

10. Lu, Y., Song, D., Xu, Y., Perera, A.G.A., Oh, S.: Automatic building exterior mapping using multilayer feature graphs. In: IEEE International Conference on Automation Science and Engineering (CASE) (2013)

11. Santaló, L.: Integral Geometry and Geometric Probability. Cambridge University Press, Cambridge (2004)

12. Simon, G., Fond, A., Berger, M.O.: A simple and effective method to detect orthogonal vanishing points in uncalibrated images of man-made environments. In: EUROGRAPHICS (2016)

13. Tardif, J.P.: Non-iterative approach for fast and accurate vanishing point detection. In: IEEE International Conference on Computer Vision (ICCV) (2009)

14. Tretyak, E., Barinova, O., Kohli, P., Lempitsky, V.: Geometric image parsing in man-made environments. Int. J. Comput. Vis. (IJCV) **97**(3), 305–321 (2012)

15. Vedaldi, A., Zisserman, A.: Self-similar sketch. In: Fitzgibbon, A., Lazebnik, S., Perona, P., Sato, Y., Schmid, C. (eds.) ECCV 2012. LNCS, pp. 87–100. Springer, Heidelberg (2012). https://doi.org/10.1007/978-3-642-33709-3_7

16. Wildenauer, H., Hanbury, A.: Robust camera self-calibration from monocular images of Manhattan worlds. In: IEEE Conference on Computer Vision and Pattern Recognition (CVPR) (2012)

17. Xu, Y., Oh, S., Hoogs, A.: A minimum error vanishing point detection approach for uncalibrated monocular images of man-made environments. In: IEEE Conference on Computer Vision and Pattern Recognition (CVPR) (2013)

18. Zhai, M., Workman, S., Jacobs, N.: Detecting vanishing points using global image context in a non-manhattan world. In: IEEE Conference on Computer Vision and Pattern Recognition (CVPR) (2016)

RT-GENE: Real-Time Eye Gaze Estimation in Natural Environments

Tobias Fischer$^{(\boxtimes)}$ (iD), Hyung Jin Chang (iD), and Yiannis Demiris (iD)

Personal Robotics Laboratory, Department of Electrical and Electronic Engineering,
Imperial College London, London, UK
{t.fischer,hj.chang,y.demiris}@imperial.ac.uk

Abstract. In this work, we consider the problem of robust gaze estimation in natural environments. Large camera-to-subject distances and high variations in head pose and eye gaze angles are common in such environments. This leads to two main shortfalls in state-of-the-art methods for gaze estimation: hindered ground truth gaze annotation and diminished gaze estimation accuracy as image resolution decreases with distance. We first record a novel dataset of varied gaze and head pose images in a natural environment, addressing the issue of ground truth annotation by measuring head pose using a motion capture system and eye gaze using mobile eyetracking glasses. We apply semantic image inpainting to the area covered by the glasses to bridge the gap between training and testing images by removing the obtrusiveness of the glasses. We also present a new real-time algorithm involving appearance-based deep convolutional neural networks with increased capacity to cope with the diverse images in the new dataset. Experiments with this network architecture are conducted on a number of diverse eye-gaze datasets including our own, and in cross dataset evaluations. We demonstrate state-of-the-art performance in terms of estimation accuracy in all experiments, and the architecture performs well even on lower resolution images.

Keywords: Gaze estimation · Gaze dataset
Convolutional neural network · Semantic inpainting
Eyetracking glasses

1 Introduction

Eye gaze is an important functional component in various applications, as it indicates human attentiveness and can thus be used to study their intentions [9] and understand social interactions [41]. For these reasons, accurately estimating gaze is an active research topic in computer vision, with applications in affect analysis [22], saliency detection [42,48,49] and action recognition [31,36], to name

Electronic supplementary material The online version of this chapter (https://doi.org/10.1007/978-3-030-01249-6_21) contains supplementary material, which is available to authorized users.

© Springer Nature Switzerland AG 2018
V. Ferrari et al. (Eds.): ECCV 2018, LNCS 11214, pp. 339–357, 2018.
https://doi.org/10.1007/978-3-030-01249-6_21

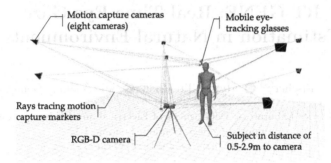

Fig. 1. Proposed setup for recording the gaze dataset. A RGB-D camera records a set of images of a subject wearing Pupil Labs mobile eyetracking glasses [24]. Markers that reflect infrared light are attached to both the camera and the eyetracking glasses, in order to be captured by motion capture cameras. The setup allows accurate head pose and eye gaze annotation in an automated manner.

a few. Gaze estimation has also been applied in domains other than computer vision, such as navigation for eye gaze controlled wheelchairs [12,46], detection of non-verbal behaviors of drivers [16,47], and inferring the object of interest in human-robot interactions [14].

Deep learning has shown successes in a variety of computer vision tasks, where their effectiveness is dependent on the size and diversity of the image dataset [29,51]. However, in deep learning-based gaze estimation, relatively shallow networks are often found to be sufficient as most datasets are recorded in constrained scenarios where the subject is in close proximity to the camera and has a small movement range [15,20,28,60]. In these datasets, ground truth data are typically annotated in an indirect manner by displaying a target on a screen and asking the subject to fixate on this target, with typical recording devices being mobile phones [28], tablets [20,28], laptops [60], desktop screens [15], or TVs [10]. This is due to the difficulty of annotating gaze in scenarios where the subject is far from the camera and allowed to move freely.

To the best of our knowledge, this work is the first to address gaze estimation in natural settings with larger camera-subject distances and less constrained subject motion. In these settings, gaze was previously approximated only by the head pose [30,35]. Our novel approach, RT-GENE, involves automatically annotating ground truth datasets by combining a motion capture system for head pose detection, with mobile eye tracking glasses for eye gaze annotation. As shown in Fig. 1, this setup directly provides the gaze vector in an automated manner under free-viewing conditions (*i.e.* without specifying an explicit gaze target), which allows rapid recording of the dataset.

While our system provides accurate gaze annotations, the eyetracking glasses introduce the problem of unnatural subject appearance when recorded from an external camera. Since we are interested in estimating the gaze of subjects without the use of eyetracking glasses, it is important that the test images

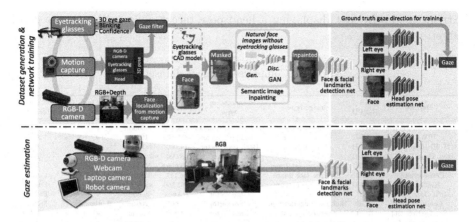

Fig. 2. RT-GENE Architecture overview. During training, a motion capture system is used to find the relative pose between mobile eyetracking glasses and a RGB-D camera (both equipped with motion capture markers), which provides the head pose of the subject. The eyetracking glasses provide labels for the eye gaze vector with respect to the head pose. A face image of the subject is extracted from the camera images, and a semantic image inpainting network is used to remove the eyetracking glasses. We use a landmark detection deep network to extract the positions of five facial landmarks, which are used to generate eye patch images. Finally, our proposed gaze estimation network is trained on the annotated gaze labels.

are not affected by an alteration of the subjects' appearance. For this purpose, we show that semantic image inpainting can be applied in a new scenario, namely the inpainting of the area covered by the eyetracking glasses. The images with removed eyetracking glasses are then used to train a new gaze estimation framework, as shown in Fig. 2, and our experiments validate that the inpainting improves the gaze estimation accuracy. We show that networks with more depth cope well with the large variations of appearance within our new dataset, while also outperforming state-of-the-art methods in traditional datasets[1].

2   Related Work

Gaze Datasets: In Table 1, we compare a range of datasets commonly used for gaze estimation. In the Columbia Gaze dataset [52], subjects have their head placed on a chin rest and are asked to fixate on a dot displayed on a wall whilst their eye gaze is recorded. This setup leads to severely limited appearances: the camera-subject distance is kept constant and there are only a small number of possible head poses and gaze angles. UT Multi-view [53] contains recordings of subjects with multiple cameras, which makes it possible to synthesize additional training images using virtual cameras and a 3D face model. A similar setup wasproposed by Deng and Zhu [10], who captured eye gaze data points at

---

[1] Dataset and code are available to the public: www.imperial.ac.uk/PersonalRobotics.

extreme angles by first displaying a head pose target, followed by an eye gaze target.

Table 1. Comparison of gaze datasets

Dataset	RGB / RGB-D	Image type	Annotation type	#Images	Distance	Head pose annot.	Gaze annot.	Head pose orient.
CMU Multi-Pie [18]	RGB	Camera frame	68 Facial landmarks	755,370	≈300cm	✓	-	All
BIWI [13]	RGB-D	Camera frame	Head pose vector	≈15,500	100cm	✓	-	All
ICT 3D Head pose [2]	RGB-D	Camera frame	Head pose vector	14,000	≈100cm	✓	-	All
Deep Head Pose [38]	RGB-D	Camera frame	Head pose vector	68,000	≈200-800cm	✓	-	All
Vernissage [23]	RGB	(Robot) camera frame	Head pose vector	Unknown	Varying	✓	-	All
Coffeebreak [8]	RGB	Low res. face image	Head pose vector	18,117	Varying	✓	-	All
Eyediap [15]	RGB-D	Face + eye patches	Gaze vector	≈62,500	80-120cm	✓	✓	Frontal
MPII Gaze [60,61]	RGB	Face + eye patches	Gaze vector	213,659	40-60cm	✓	✓	Frontal
Columbia [52]	RGB	High res. camera image	Gaze vector	5,880	200cm	5 orient.	✓	Frontal
SynthesEyes [56]	RGB	Synthesized eye patches	Gaze vector	11,382	Varying	✓	✓	All
UnityEyes [55]	RGB	Synthesized eye patches	Gaze vector	1,000,000	Varying	✓	✓	All
UT Multi-view [53]	RGB	Eye area + eye patches	Gaze vector	1,152,000	60cm	✓	✓	All
Gaze Capture [28]	RGB	Face + eye patches	2D pos on screen	> 2.5M	Close	-	✓	Frontal
Rice TabletGaze [20]	RGB	Tablet camera video	2D pos on screen	≈100,000	30-50cm	-	✓	Frontal
Ours (RT-GENE)	**RGB-D**	**Face + eye patches**	**Gaze vector**	**122,531**	**80-280cm**	**✓**	**✓**	**All**

Recently, several datasets have been collected where subjects are asked to look at pre-defined targets on the screen of a mobile device, with the aim of introducing greater variation in lighting and appearance. Zhang *et al.* [60] presented the MPII Gaze dataset, where 20 target items were displayed on a laptop screen per session. One of the few gaze datasets collected using an RGB-D camera is Eyediap [15]. In addition to targets on a computer screen, the dataset contains a 3D floating target which is tracked using color and depth information. GazeCapture [28] is a crowd-sourced dataset of nearly 1500 subjects looking at gaze targets on a tablet screen. For the aforementioned datasets, the head pose is estimated using landmark positions of the subject and a (generic or subject specific) 3D head model. While these datasets are suitable for situations where a subject is directly facing a screen or mobile device, the distance between subject and camera is relatively small and the head pose is biased towards the screen. In comparison, datasets that capture accurate head pose annotations at larger distances typically do not contain eye gaze labels [2,8,13,18,23,38].

Another way of obtaining annotated gaze data is to create synthetic image patches [32,55–57], which allows arbitrary variations in head and eye poses as well as camera-subject distance. For example, Wood *et al.* [55] proposed a method to render photo-realistic images of the eye region in real-time. However, the domain gap between synthetic and real images makes it hard to apply these trained networks on real images. Shrivastana *et al.* [50] proposed to use a Generative Adversarial Network to refine the synthetic patches to resemble more realistic images, while ensuring that the gaze direction is not affected. However, the appearance and gaze diversity of the refined images is then limited to the variations found in the real images.

A dataset employing a motion capture system and eyetracking glasses was presented by McMurrough *et al.* [37]. It only contains the eye images provided by the eyetracking glasses, but does not contain images from an external camera. Furthermore, the gaze angles are limited as a screen is used to display the targets.

Deep Learning-Based Gaze Estimation: Several works apply Convolutional Neural Networks (CNN) for gaze estimation, as they have been shown to outperform conventional approaches [60], such as k-Nearest Neighbors or random forests. Zhang *et al.* [60] presented a shallow CNN with six layers that takes an eye image as input and fuses this with the head pose in the last fully connected layer of the network. Krafka *et al.* [28] introduced a CNN which estimates the gaze by combining the left eye, right eye and face images, with a face grid, providing the network with information about the location and size of the head in the original image. A spatial weights CNN taking the full face image as input, *i.e.* without any eye patches, was presented in [61]. The spatial weights encode the importance of the different facial areas, achieving state-of-the-art performance on multiple datasets. Recently, Deng and Zhu [10] suggested a two-step training policy, where a head CNN and an eye CNN are trained separately and then jointly fine-tuned with a geometrically constrained "gaze transform layer".

3   Gaze Dataset Generation

One of the main challenges in appearance-based gaze estimation is accurately annotating the gaze of subjects with natural appearance while allowing free movements. We propose RT-GENE, a novel approach which allows the automatic annotation of subjects' ground truth gaze and head pose labels under free-viewing conditions and large camera-subject distances (overall setup shown in Fig. 1). Our new dataset is collected following this approach. The dataset was constructed using mobile eyetracking glasses and a Kinect v2 RGB-D camera, both equipped with motion capture markers, in order to precisely find their poses relative to each other. The eye gaze of the subject is anno-

Fig. 3. Left: 3D model of the eyetracking glasses including the motion capture markers. Right: Eyetracking glasses worn by a subject. The 3D printed yellow parts have been designed to hold the eye cameras of the eyetracking glasses in the same place for each subject. (Color figure online)

tated using the eyetracking glasses, while the Kinect v2 is used as a recording device to provide RGB images at 1920×1080 resolution and depth images at 512×424 resolution. In contrast to the datasets presented in Table 1, our approach allows for accurate annotation of gaze data even when the subject is facing away from the camera.

Eye Gaze Annotation: We use a customized version of the Pupil Labs eyetracking glasses [24], which have a very low average eye gaze error of $0.6°$ in screen base settings. In our dataset with significantly larger distances, we obtain an angular accuracy of $2.58 \pm 0.56°$. The headset consists of a frame with a scene camera facing away from the subject and a 3D printed holder for the eye cameras. This removes the need to adjust the eye camera placement for each subject. The customized glasses provide two crucial advantages over the original headset. Firstly, the eye cameras are mounted further from the subject, which leads to fewer occlusions of the eye area. Secondly, the fixed position of the holder allows the generation of a generic (as opposed to subject-specific) 3D model of the glasses, which is needed for the inpainting process, as described in Sect. 4. The generic 3D model and glasses worn by a subject are shown in Fig. 3.

Head Pose Annotation: We use a commercial OptiTrack motion capture system [39] to track the eyetracking glasses and the RGB-D camera using four markers attached to each object, with an average position error of 1mm for each marker. This allows to infer the pose of the eyetracking glasses with respect to the RGB-D camera, which is used to annotate the head pose as described below.

Coordinate Transforms: The key challenge in our dataset collection setup was to relate the eye gaze $\mathbf{g}$ in the eyetracking reference frame $\mathbf{F}_E$ with the visual frame of the RGB-D camera $\mathbf{F}_C$ as expressed by the transform $\mathbf{T}_{E \to C}$. Using this transform, we can also define the head pose $\mathbf{h}$ as it coincides with $\mathbf{T}_{C \to E}$. However, we cannot directly use the transform $\mathbf{T}_{E^* \to C^*}$ provided by the motion capture system, as the frames perceived by the motion capture system, $\mathbf{F}_{E^*}$ and $\mathbf{F}_{C^*}$, do not match the visual frames, $\mathbf{F}_E$ and $\mathbf{F}_C$.

Therefore, we must find the transforms $\mathbf{T}_{C \to C^*}$ and $\mathbf{T}_{E \to E^*}$. To find $\mathbf{T}_{C \to C^*}$ we use the property of RGB-D cameras which allows to obtain 3D point coordinates of an object in the visual frame $\mathbf{F}_C$. If we equip this object with markers tracked by the motion capture system, we can find the corresponding coordinates in the motion capture frame $\mathbf{F}_{C^*}$. By collecting a sufficiently large number of samples, the Nelder-Mead method [40] can be used to find $\mathbf{T}_{C \to C^*}$. As we have a 3D model of the eyetracking glasses, we use the accelerated iterative closest point algorithm [6] to find the transform $\mathbf{T}_{E \to E^*}$ between the coordinates of the markers within the model and those found using the motion capture system.

Using the transforms $\mathbf{T}_{E^* \to C^*}$, $\mathbf{T}_{C \to C^*}$ and $\mathbf{T}_{E \to E^*}$ it is now possible to convert between any two coordinate frames. Most importantly, we can map the gaze vector $\mathbf{g}$ to the frame of the RGB-D camera using $\mathbf{T}_{E \to C}$.

Data Collection Procedure: At the beginning of the recording procedure, we calibrate the eyetracking glasses using a printed calibration marker, which is shown to the subject in multiple positions covering the subject's field of view while keeping the head fixed. Subsequently, in the first session, subjects are recorded for 10 min while wearing the eyetracking glasses. We instructed the subjects to behave naturally while varying their head poses and eye gazes as much as possible and moving within the motion capture area. In the second

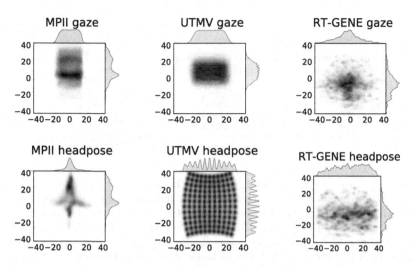

Fig. 4. Top row: Gaze distribution of the MPII Gaze dataset [60] (left), the UT Multi-view dataset [53] (middle) and our proposed RT-GENE dataset (right). Bottom row: Head pose distributions, as above. Our RT-GENE dataset covers a much wider range of gaze angles and head poses, which makes it more suitable for natural scenarios

session, we record unlabeled images of the same subjects without the eyetracking glasses for another 10 min. These images are used for our proposed inpainting method as described in Sect. 4. To increase the variability of appearances for each subject, we change the 3D location of the RGB-D camera, the viewing angle towards the subject and the initial subject-camera distance.

Post-processing: We synchronize the recorded images of the RGB-D camera with the gaze data $\mathbf{g}$ of the eyetracking glasses in a post-processing step. We also filter the training data to only contain head poses $\mathbf{h}$ between $\pm 37.5°$ horizontally and $\pm 30°$ vertically, which allows accurate extraction of the images of both eyes. Furthermore, we filter out blinks and images where the pupil was not detected properly with a confidence threshold of 0.98 (see [24] for details).

Dataset Statistics: The proposed RT-GENE dataset contains recordings of 15 participants (9 male, 6 female, 2 participants recorded twice), with a total of 122,531 labeled training images and 154,755 unlabeled images of the same subjects where the eyetracking glasses are not worn. Figure 4 shows the head pose and gaze angle distribution across all subjects in comparison to other datasets. Compared to [53,60], a much higher variation is demonstrated in the gaze angle distribution, primarily due to the novelty of the presented setup. The free-viewing task leads to a wider spread and resembles natural eye behavior, rather than that associated with mobile device interaction or screen viewing as in [15,20,28,60]. Due to the synthesized images, the UT Multi-view dataset [53] also covers a wide range of head pose angles, however they are not continuous

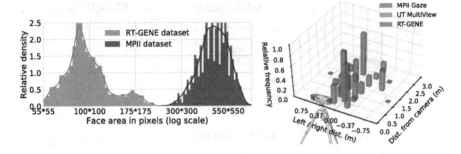

Fig. 5. Left: Face area distribution in the MPII [60] and our proposed RT-GENE datasets. The resolution of the face areas in our dataset is much lower (mean 100 × 100 px) than that of the MPII dataset (mean 485 × 485 px). This is mainly due to the larger camera-subject distance. Right: Distribution of camera-subject distances for various datasets [53,60]. RT-GENE covers significantly more varied camera-to-subject distances than the others, with distances being in the range between 0.5 m and 2.9 m.

due to the fixed placing of the virtual cameras which are used to render the synthesized images.

The camera-subject distances range between 0.5 m and 2.9 m, with a mean distance of 1.82 m as shown in Fig. 5. This compares to a fixed distance of 0.6m for the UT Multi-view dataset [53], and a very narrow distribution of 0.5 m± 0.1 m for the MPII Gaze dataset [60]. Furthermore, the area covered by the subjects' faces is much lower in our dataset (mean: 100 × 100 px) compared to other datasets (MPII Gaze dataset mean: 485 × 485 px). Thus compared to many other datasets, which focus on close distance scenarios [15,20,28,53,60], our dataset captures a more natural real-world setup. Our RT-GENE dataset is the first to provide accurate ground truth gaze annotations in these settings in addition to head pose estimates. This allows application in new scenarios, such as social interactions between multiple humans or humans and robots.

4   Removing Eyetracking Glasses

A disadvantage of using the eyetracking glasses is that they change the subject's appearance. However, when the gaze estimation framework is used in a natural setting, the subject will not be wearing the eyetracking glasses. We propose to semantically inpaint the regions covered by the eyetracking glasses, to remove any discrepancy between training and testing data.

Image inpainting is the process of filling target regions in images by considering the image semantics. Early approaches included diffusion-based texture synthesis methods [1,5,7], where the target area is filled by extending the surrounding textures in a coarse to fine manner. For larger regions, patch-based methods [4,11,19,54] that take a semantic image patch from either the input image or an image database are more successful.

Recently, semantic inpainting has vastly improved in performance through the utilization of Generative Adversarial Network (GAN) architectures [21,44, 58]. In this paper, we adopt this GAN-based image inpainting approach by considering both the textural similarity to the closely surrounding area and the image semantics. To the best of our knowledge, this is the first work using semantic inpainting to improve gaze estimation accuracy.

Masking Eyetracking Glasses Region: The CAD model of the eyetracking glasses is made up of a set of $N = 2662$ vertices $\{\mathbf{v}_n\}_{n=1}^{N}$, with $\mathbf{v}_n \in \mathbb{R}^3$. To find the target region to be inpainted, we use $\mathbf{T}_{E \to C}$ to derive the 3D position of each vertex in the RGB-D camera frame. For extreme head poses, certain parts of the eyetracking glasses may be obscured by the subject's head, thus masking all pixels would result in part of the image being inpainted unnecessarily. To overcome this problem, we design an indicator function $\mathbf{1}_M(\mathbf{p}_n, \mathbf{v}_n) = \{0 \text{ if } \|\mathbf{p}_n - \mathbf{v}_n\| < \tau, \text{ else } 1\}$ which selects vertices $\mathbf{v}_n$ of the CAD model if they are within a tolerance τ of their corresponding point $\mathbf{p}_n$ in the depth field. Each selected vertex is mapped using the camera projection matrix of the RGB-D camera into a 2D image mask $\mathbf{M} = \{m_{i,j}\}$, where each entry $m_{i,j} \in \{0,1\}$ shows whether the pixel at location (i,j) needs to be inpainted.

Semantic Inpainting: To fill the masked regions of the eyetracking glasses, we use a GAN-based image generation approach, similar to that of Yeh *et al.* [58]. There are two conditions to fulfill [58]: the inpainted result should look realistic (perceptual loss $\mathcal{L}_{\text{perception}}$) and the inpainted pixels should be well-aligned with the surrounding pixels (contextual loss $\mathcal{L}_{\text{context}}$). As shown in Fig. 5, the resolution of the face area is larger than the 64×64 px supported in [58]. Our proposed architecture allows the inpainting of images with resolution 224×224 px. This is a crucial feature as reducing the face image resolution for inpainting purposes could impact the gaze estimation accuracy.

We trained a separate inpainting network for each subject i. Let D_i denote a discriminator that takes as input an image $\mathbf{x}_i \in \mathbf{R}^d$ ($d = 224 \times 224 \times 3$) of subject i from the dataset where the eyetracking glasses are not worn, and outputs a scalar representing the probability of input $\mathbf{x}_i$ being a real sample. Let G_i denote the generator that takes as input a latent random variable $\mathbf{z}_i \in \mathbf{R}^z$ ($z = 100$) sampled from a uniform noise distribution $p_{\text{noise}} = \mathcal{U}(-1,1)$ and outputs a synthesized image $G_i(\mathbf{z}_i) \in \mathbf{R}^d$. Ideally, $D_i(\mathbf{x}_i) = 1$ when $\mathbf{x}_i$ is from a real dataset p_i of subject i and $D_i(\mathbf{x}_i) = 0$ when $\mathbf{x}_i$ is generated from G_i. For the rest of the section, we omit subscript i for clarity.

We use a least squares loss [34], which has been shown to be more stable and better performing, while having less chance of mode collapsing [34,62]. The training objective of the GAN is $\min_D \mathcal{L}_{GAN}(D) = \mathbf{E}_{\mathbf{x} \sim p}[(D(\mathbf{x}) - 1)^2] + \mathbf{E}_{\mathbf{z} \sim p_{\text{noise}}}[(D(G(\mathbf{z})))^2]$ and $\min_G \mathcal{L}_{GAN}(G) = \mathbf{E}_{\mathbf{z} \sim p_{\text{noise}}}[(D(G(\mathbf{z})) - 1)^2]$. In particular, $\mathcal{L}_{GAN}(G)$ measures the realism of images generated by G, which we consider as perceptual loss:

Fig. 6. Image pairs showing the original images of the subject wearing the eyetracking glasses (left) and the corresponding inpainted images (right). The inpainted images look very similar to the subjects' appearance at testing time and are thus suited to train an appearance-based gazed estimator. Figure best viewed in color.

$$\mathcal{L}_{\text{perception}}(\mathbf{z}) = \big[D\big(G(\mathbf{z})\big) - 1\big]^2. \tag{1}$$

The contextual loss is measured based on the difference between the real image $\mathbf{x}$ and the generated image $G(\mathbf{z})$ of non-masked regions as follows:

$$\mathcal{L}_{\text{context}}(\mathbf{z}|\mathbf{M}, \mathbf{x}) = |\mathbf{M}' \odot \mathbf{x} - \mathbf{M}' \odot G(\mathbf{z})|, \tag{2}$$

where $\odot$ is the element-wise product and $\mathbf{M}'$ is the complement of $\mathbf{M}$ (*i.e.* to define the region that should not be inpainted).

The latent random variable $\mathbf{z}$ controls the images produced by $G(\mathbf{z})$. Thus, generating the best image for inpainting is equivalent to finding the best $\hat{\mathbf{z}}$ value which minimizes a combination of the perceptual and contextual losses:

$$\hat{\mathbf{z}} = \arg\min_{\mathbf{z}} \big(\lambda\, \mathcal{L}_{\text{perception}}(\mathbf{z}) + \mathcal{L}_{\text{context}}(\mathbf{z}|\mathbf{M}, \mathbf{x})\big) \tag{3}$$

where λ is a weighting parameter. After finding $\hat{\mathbf{z}}$, the inpainted image can be generated by:

$$\mathbf{x}_{\text{inpainted}} = \mathbf{M}' \odot \mathbf{x} + \mathbf{M} \odot G(\hat{\mathbf{z}}). \tag{4}$$

Poisson blending [45] is then applied to $\mathbf{x}_{\text{inpainted}}$ in order to generate the final inpainted images with seamless boundaries between inpainted and not inpainted regions. In Fig. 6 we show the application of inpainting in our scenario.

Network Architecture: We performed hyperparameter tuning to generate high resolution images of high quality. We set the generator with the architecture z-dense(25088)-(256)5d2s-(128)5d2s-(64)5d2s-(32)5d2s-(3)5d2s-x, where "(128)5c2s/(128)5d2s" denotes a convolution /deconvolution layer with 128 output feature maps and kernel size 5 with stride 2. All internal activations use SeLU

[27] while the output layer uses tanh activation function. The discriminator architecture is $\mathbf{x}$-(16)5c2s-(32)5c2s-(64)5c2s-(128)5c2s-(256)5c2s-(512)5c2s-dense(1). We use LeakyReLU [33] with $\alpha = 0.2$ for all internal activations and a sigmoid activation for the output layer. We use the same architecture for all subjects.

Training Hyperparameter Details: To train G and D, we use the Adam optimizer [26] with learning rate 0.00005, $\beta_1 = 0.9$, $\beta_2 = 0.999$ and batch size 128 for 100 epochs. We use the Xavier weight initialization [17] for all layers. To find $\hat{\mathbf{z}}$, we constrain all values in $\mathbf{z}$ to be within $[-1, 1]$, as suggested in [58], and we train for 1000 iterations. The weighting parameter λ is set to 0.1.

5   Gaze Estimation Networks

Overview: As shown in Fig. 2, the gaze estimation is performed using several networks. Firstly, we use Multi-Task Cascaded Convolutional Networks (MTCNN) [59] to detect the face along with the landmark points of the eyes, nose and mouth corners. Using the extracted landmarks, we rotate and scale the face patch so that we minimize the distance between the aligned landmarks and predefined average face point positions to obtain a normalized face image using the accelerated iterative closest point algorithm [6]. We then extract the eye patches from the normalized face images as fixed-size rectangles centered around the landmark points of the eyes. Secondly, we find the head pose of the subject by adopting the state-of-the-art method presented by Patacciola *et al.* [43].

Proposed Eye Gaze Estimation: We then estimate the eye gaze vector using our proposed network. The eye patches are fed separately to VGG-16 networks [51] which perform feature extraction. Each VGG-16 network is followed by a fully connected (FC) layer of size 512 after the last max-pooling layer, followed by batch normalization and ReLU activation. We then concatenate these layers, resulting in a FC layer of size 1024. This layer is followed by another FC layer of size 512. We append the head pose vector to this FC layer, which is followed by two more FC layers of size 256 and 2 respectively[2]. The outputs of the last layer are the yaw and pitch eye gaze angles. For increased robustness, we use an ensemble scheme [29] where the mean of the predictions of the individual networks represents the overall prediction.

Image Augmentation: To increase the robustness of the gaze estimator, we augment the training images in four ways. Firstly, to be robust against slightly off-centered eye patches due to imperfections in the landmark extraction, we perform 10 augmentations by cropping the image on the sides and subsequently resizing it back to its original size. Each side is cropped by a pixel value drawn

---

[2] All layer sizes were determined experimentally.

independently from a uniform distribution $\mathcal{U}(0,5)$. Secondly, for robustness against camera blur, we reduce the image resolution to 1/2 and 1/4 of its original resolution, followed by a bilinear interpolation to retrieve two augmented images of the original image size. Thirdly, to cover various lighting conditions, we employ histogram equalization. Finally, we convert color images to gray-scale images so that gray-scale images can be used as input as well.

Training Details: As loss function, we use the sum of the individual l_2 losses between the predicted and ground truth gaze vectors. The weights for the network estimating the head pose are fixed and taken from a pre-trained model [43]. The weights of the VGG-16 models are initialized using a pre-trained model on ImageNet [51]. As we found that weight sharing results in decreased performance, we do not make use of it. The weights of the FC layers are initialized using the Xavier initialization [17]. We use the Adam optimizer [26] with learning rate 0.001, $\beta_1 = 0.9$, $\beta_2 = 0.95$ and a batch size of 256.

6   Experiments

Dataset Inpainting Validation: We first conduct experiments to validate the effectiveness of our proposed inpainting algorithm. The average pixel error of five facial landmark points (eyes, nose and mouth corners) was compared to manually collected ground truth labels on a set of 100 images per subject before and after inpainting. The results reported in Table 2 confirm that all landmark estimation algorithms benefit from the inpainting, both in increased face detection rate and in lower pixel error ($p < .01$). The performance of our proposed inpainting method is also significantly higher than a method that naively fills the area of the eyetracking glasses uniformly with the mean color ($p < .01$). Importantly however, we found no statistical difference between the inpainted images and images where no eyetracking glasses are worn ($p = .16$).

Gaze Estimation Performance Comparison: We evaluated our method on two de facto standard datasets, MPII Gaze [60] and UT Multi-view [53][3], as well as our newly proposed RT-GENE dataset.

First, we evaluate the performance of our proposed gaze estimation network on the MPII dataset [60]. The MPII dataset uses an evaluation set containing 1500 images of the left and right eye respectively. As our method employs both eyes as input, we directly use the 3000 images without taking the target eye into consideration. The previous state-of-the-art achieves an error of $4.8 \pm 0.7°$ [61] in a leave-one-out setting. We achieve an increased performance of $4.3 \pm 0.9°$ using our method (10.4% improvement), as shown in Fig. 7.

In evaluations on the UT Multi-view dataset [53], we achieve a mean error of $5.1 \pm 0.2°$, outperforming the method of Zhang et al. [60] by 13.6% ($5.9°$

---

[3] We do not compare our method on the Eyediap dataset [15] and the dataset of Deng and Zhu [10] due to licensing restrictions of these datasets.

Table 2. Comparison of various landmark detectors [3, 25] on the original images (with eyetracking glasses), images where the eyetracking glasses are filled with a uniform color (the mean color of the image), and inpainted images as proposed in our method. Both the face detection rate and the landmark error improve significantly when inpainted images are provided as input. The performance of MTCNN [59] is not reported, as it would be a biased comparison (MTCNN was used to extract the face patches).

Landmark detection method	Face detection rate (%)			Landmark error (pixel)		
	Original	Uniformly filled	Inpainted	Original	Uniformly filled	Inpainted
CLNF [3]	54.6 ± 24.7	75.4 ± 20.9	$\mathbf{87.7 \pm 15.6}$	6.0 ± 2.4	5.6 ± 2.3	$\mathbf{5.3 \pm 1.8}$
CLNF in-the-wild [3]	54.6 ± 24.7	75.4 ± 20.9	$\mathbf{87.7 \pm 15.6}$	5.8 ± 2.3	5.3 ± 1.8	$\mathbf{5.2 \pm 1.6}$
ERT [25]	36.7 ± 25.3	59.7 ± 23.0	$\mathbf{84.1 \pm 17.9}$	6.6 ± 2.3	5.8 ± 1.7	$\mathbf{5.1 \pm 1.3}$

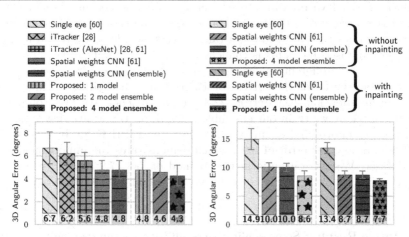

Fig. 7. Left: 3D gaze error on the MPII Gaze dataset. Right: 3D gaze error on our proposed gaze dataset. The inpainting improves the gaze estimation accuracy for all algorithms. Our proposed method performs best with an accuracy of 7.7°.

error). This demonstrates that our proposed method achieves state-of-the-art performance on two existing datasets.

In a third set of experiments, we evaluate the performance on our newly proposed RT-GENE dataset using 3-fold cross validation as shown in Fig. 7. All methods perform worse on our dataset compared to the MPII Gaze and UT Multi-view datasets, which is due to the natural setting with larger appearance variations and lower resolution images due to higher camera-subject distances. We confirm that using inpainted images at training time results in higher accuracy compared to using the original images without inpainting for all algorithms including our own (10.5% performance increase). For the inpainted images, our proposed gaze estimation network achieves the best performance with an error of $7.7 \pm 0.3°$, which compares to [60] with an error of $13.4 \pm 1.0°$ (42.5% improvement) and the previous state-of-the-art network [61] with $8.7 \pm 0.7°$ error (11.5% improvement). These results demonstrate that features obtained using our deeper network architecture are more suitable for this dataset compared to the previous state-of-the-art.

Furthermore, ensemble schemes were found to be particularly effective in our architecture. For a fair comparison, we also applied the ensemble scheme to the state-of-the-art method [61]. However, we did not observe any performance improvement over the single model (see Fig. 7). We assume that this is due to the spatial weights scheme that leads to similar weights in the intermediate layers of the different models. This results in similar gaze predictions of the individual models, and therefore an ensemble does not improve the accuracy for [61].

Cross-Dataset Evaluation: To further validate whether our dataset can be applied in a variety of settings, we trained our proposed ensemble network on samples from our RT-GENE dataset (all subjects included) and tested it on the MPII Gaze dataset [60]. This is challenging, as the face appearance and image resolution is very different as shown in Figs. 5 and 8. We obtained an error of $7.7°$, which outperforms the current best performing method in a similar cross-dataset evaluation [55] ($9.9°$ error, 22.4% improvement). We also conduct an experiment where we train our ensemble network on UT Multi-view instead of RT-GENE as above, and again test the model on MPII Gaze. In this setting, we obtain an angular error of $8.9°$, which demonstrates the importance of our new dataset. We also outperform the method of [50] ($7.9°$ error), which uses unlabeled images of the MPII Gaze dataset at training time, while our method uses none.

Qualitative Results: Some qualitative results of our proposed method applied to MPII Gaze and RT-GENE are displayed in Fig. 8. Our framework can be used for real-time gaze estimation using any RGB or RGB-D camera such as Kinect, webcam and laptop camera, running at 25.3 fps with a latency of 0.12 s. This is demonstrated in the supplementary video. All comparisons are performed on an Intel i7-6900K with a Nvidia 1070 and 64 GB RAM.

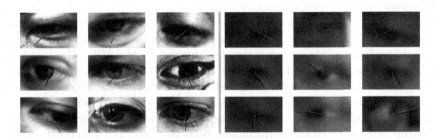

Fig. 8. Sample estimates (red) and ground truth annotations (blue) using our proposed method on the MPII Gaze dataset [60] (left) and our proposed dataset (right). Our dataset is more challenging, as images in our dataset are blurrier due to the higher subject-camera distance and show a higher variation in head pose and gaze angles. Figure best viewed in color.

7 Conclusion and Future Work

Our approach introduces gaze estimation in natural scenarios where gaze was previously approximated by the head pose of the subject. We proposed RT-GENE, a novel approach for ground truth gaze estimation in these natural settings, and we collected a new challenging dataset using this approach. We demonstrated that the dataset covers a wider range of camera-subject distances, head poses and gazes compared to previous in-the-wild datasets. We have shown that semantic inpainting using GAN can be used to overcome the appearance alteration caused by the eyetracking glasses during training. The proposed method could be applied to bridge the gap between training and testing in settings where wearable sensors are attached to a human (*e.g.* EEG/EMG/IMU sensors). Our proposed deep convolutional network achieved state-of-the-art gaze estimation performance on the MPII Gaze dataset (10.4% improvement), UT Multi-view (13.6% improvement), our proposed dataset (11.5% improvement), and in cross dataset evaluation (22.4% improvement).

In future work, we will investigate gaze estimation in situations where the eyes of the participant cannot be seen by the camera, *e.g.* for extreme head poses or when the subject is facing away from the camera. As our dataset allows annotation of gaze even in these diverse conditions, it would be interesting to explore algorithms which can handle these challenging situations. We hypothesize that saliency information of the scene could prove useful in this context.

Acknowledgment. This work was supported in part by the Samsung Global Research Outreach program, and in part by the EU Horizon 2020 Project PAL (643783-RIA). We would like to thank Caterina Buizza, Antoine Cully, Joshua Elsdon and Mark Zolotas for their help with this work, and all subjects who volunteered for the dataset collection.

References

1. Ballester, C., Bertalmio, M., Caselles, V., Sapiro, G., Verdera, J.: Filling-in by joint interpolation of vector fields and gray levels. IEEE Trans. Image Process. **10**(8), 1200–1211 (2001). https://doi.org/10.1109/83.935036
2. Baltrusaitis, T., Robinson, P., Morency, L.P.: 3D constrained local model for rigid and non-rigid facial tracking. In: IEEE Conference on Computer Vision and Pattern Recognition, pp. 2610–2617 (2012). https://doi.org/10.1109/CVPR.2012.6247980
3. Baltrusaitis, T., Robinson, P., Morency, L.P.: Constrained local neural fields for robust facial landmark detection in the wild. In: IEEE International Conference on Computer Vision Workshops, pp. 354–361 (2013). https://doi.org/10.1109/ICCVW.2013.54
4. Barnes, C., Shechtman, E., Finkelstein, A., Goldman, D.B.: Patchmatch: a randomized correspondence algorithm for structural image editing. ACM Trans. Graph. **28**(3), 24:1–24:11 (2009). https://doi.org/10.1145/1531326.1531330
5. Bertalmio, M., Sapiro, G., Caselles, V., Ballester, C.: Image inpainting. In: Annual Conference on Computer Graphics and Interactive Techniques, SIGGRAPH, pp. 417–424 (2000). https://doi.org/10.1145/344779.344972

6. Besl, P.J., McKay, N.D.: A method for registration of 3-D shapes. IEEE Trans. Pattern Anal. Mach. Intell. **14**(2), 239–256 (1992). https://doi.org/10.1109/34.121791

7. Chan, T.F., Shen, J.: Mathematical models for local nontexture inpaintings. SIAM J. Appl. Math. **62**, 1019–1043 (2002). https://doi.org/10.1137/S0036139900368844

8. Cristani, M., et al.: Social interaction discovery by statistical analysis of F-formations. In: British Machine Vision Conference, pp. 23.1–23.12 (2011). https://doi.org/10.5244/C.25.23

9. Demiris, Y.: Prediction of intent in robotics and multi-agent systems. Cogn. Process. **8**(3), 151–158 (2007). https://doi.org/10.1007/s10339-007-0168-9

10. Deng, H., Zhu, W.: Monocular free-head 3D gaze tracking with deep learning and geometry constraints. In: IEEE International Conference on Computer Vision, pp. 3143–3152 (2017). https://doi.org/10.1109/ICCV.2017.341

11. Efros, A., Leung, T.: Texture synthesis by non-parametric sampling. In: International Conference on Computer Vision, pp. 1033–1038 (1999). https://doi.org/10.1109/ICCV.1999.790383

12. Eid, M.A., Giakoumidis, N., El-Saddik, A.: A novel eye-gaze-controlled wheelchair system for navigating unknown environments: case study with a person with ALS. IEEE Access **4**, 558–573 (2016). https://doi.org/10.1109/ACCESS.2016.2520093

13. Fanelli, G., Weise, T., Gall, J., Van Gool, L.: Real time head pose estimation from consumer depth cameras. In: Mester, R., Felsberg, M. (eds.) DAGM 2011. LNCS, vol. 6835, pp. 101–110. Springer, Heidelberg (2011). https://doi.org/10.1007/978-3-642-23123-0_11

14. Fischer, T., Demiris, Y.: Markerless perspective taking for humanoid robots in unconstrained environments. In: IEEE International Conference on Robotics and Automation, pp. 3309–3316 (2016). https://doi.org/10.1109/ICRA.2016.7487504

15. Funes Mora, K.A., Monay, F., Odobez, J.M.: EYEDIAP: a database for the development and evaluation of gaze estimation algorithms from RGB and RGB-D cameras. In: ACM Symposium on Eye Tracking Research and Applications, pp. 255–258 (2014). https://doi.org/10.1145/2578153.2578190

16. Georgiou, T., Demiris, Y.: Adaptive user modelling in car racing games using behavioural and physiological data. User Model. User-Adapt. Interact. **27**(2), 267–311 (2017). https://doi.org/10.1007/s11257-017-9192-3

17. Glorot, X., Bengio, Y.: Understanding the difficulty of training deep feedforward neural networks. In: International Conference on Artificial Intelligence and Statistics, pp. 249–256 (2010), http://proceedings.mlr.press/v9/glorot10a.html

18. Gross, R., Matthews, I., Cohn, J., Kanade, T., Baker, S.: Multi-pie. Image Vis. Comput. **28**(5), 807–813 (2010). https://doi.org/10.1109/AFGR.2008.4813399

19. Hays, J., Efros, A.A.: Scene completion using millions of photographs. ACM Trans. Graph. **26**(3), 4:1–4:7 (2007). https://doi.org/10.1145/1276377.1276382

20. Huang, Q., Veeraraghavan, A., Sabharwal, A.: TabletGaze: dataset and analysis for unconstrained appearance-based gaze estimation in mobile tablets. Mach. Vis. Appl. **28**(5–6), 445–461 (2017). https://doi.org/10.1007/s00138-017-0852-4

21. Iizuka, S., Simo-Serra, E., Ishikawa, H.: Globally and locally consistent image completion. ACM Trans. Graph. **36**(4), 107:1–107:14 (2017). https://doi.org/10.1145/3072959.3073659

22. Jaques, N., Conati, C., Harley, J.M., Azevedo, R.: Predicting affect from gaze data during interaction with an intelligent tutoring system. In: Trausan-Matu, S., Boyer, K.E., Crosby, M., Panourgia, K. (eds.) ITS 2014. LNCS, vol. 8474, pp. 29–38. Springer, Cham (2014). https://doi.org/10.1007/978-3-319-07221-0_4

23. Jayagopi, D.B., et al.: The vernissage corpus: a conversational human-robot-interaction dataset. In: ACM/IEEE International Conference on Human-Robot Interaction, pp. 149–150 (2013). https://doi.org/10.1109/HRI.2013.6483545

24. Kassner, M., Patera, W., Bulling, A.: Pupil: an open source platform for pervasive eye tracking and mobile gaze-based interaction. In: ACM International Joint Conference on Pervasive and Ubiquitous Computing, pp. 1151–1160 (2014). https://doi.org/10.1145/2638728.2641695

25. Kazemi, V., Sullivan, J.: One millisecond face alignment with an ensemble of regression trees. In: IEEE Conference on Computer Vision and Pattern Recognition, pp. 1867–1874 (2014). https://doi.org/10.1109/CVPR.2014.241

26. Kingma, D.P., Ba, J.: Adam: a method for stochastic optimization. In: International Conference on Learning Representations (2015). https://arxiv.org/abs/1412.6980

27. Klambauer, G., Unterthiner, T., Mayr, A., Hochreiter, S.: Self-normalizing neural networks. In: Advances in Neural Information Processing Systems (2017). https://arxiv.org/abs/1706.02515

28. Krafka, K., et al.: Eye tracking for everyone. In: IEEE Conference on Computer Vision and Pattern Recognition, pp. 2176–2184 (2016). https://doi.org/10.1109/CVPR.2016.239

29. Krizhevsky, A., Sutskever, I., Hinton, G.E.: Imagenet classification with deep convolutional neural networks. In: Advances in Neural Information Processing Systems, pp. 1097–1105 (2012). https://doi.org/10.1145/3065386

30. Lemaignan, S., Garcia, F., Jacq, A., Dillenbourg, P.: From real-time attention assessment to with-me-ness in human-robot interaction. In: ACM/IEEE International Conference on Human Robot Interaction, pp. 157–164 (2016). https://doi.org/10.1109/HRI.2016.7451747

31. Liu, Y., Wu, Q., Tang, L., Shi, H.: Gaze-assisted multi-stream deep neural network for action recognition. IEEE Access 5, 19432–19441 (2017). https://doi.org/10.1109/ACCESS.2017.2753830

32. Lu, F., Sugano, Y., Okabe, T., Sato, Y.: Gaze estimation from eye appearance: a head pose-free method via eye image synthesis. IEEE Trans. Image Process. 24(11), 3680–3693 (2015). https://doi.org/10.1109/TIP.2015.2445295

33. Maas, A.L., Hannun, A.Y., Ng, A.Y.: Rectifier nonlinearities improve neural network acoustic models. In: International Conference on Machine Learning (2013). https://sites.google.com/site/deeplearningicml2013/relu_hybrid_icml2013_final.pdf

34. Mao, X., Li, Q., Xie, H., Lau, R.Y., Wang, Z., Paul Smolley, S.: Least squares generative adversarial networks. In: IEEE International Conference on Computer Vision, pp. 2794–2802 (2017). https://doi.org/10.1109/ICCV.2017.304

35. Massé, B., Ba, S., Horaud, R.: Tracking gaze and visual focus of attention of people involved in social interaction. IEEE Trans. Pattern Anal. Mach. Intell. (2017, to appear). https://doi.org/10.1109/TPAMI.2017.2782819

36. Mathe, S., Sminchisescu, C.: Actions in the eye: dynamic gaze datasets and learnt saliency models for visual recognition. IEEE Trans. Pattern Anal. Mach. Intell. 37(7), 1408–1424 (2015). https://doi.org/10.1109/TPAMI.2014.2366154

37. McMurrough, C.D., Metsis, V., Kosmopoulos, D., Maglogiannis, I., Makedon, F.: A dataset for point of gaze detection using head poses and eye images. J. Multimodal User Interfaces 7(3), 207–215 (2013). https://doi.org/10.1007/s12193-013-0121-4

38. Mukherjee, S.S., Robertson, N.M.: Deep head pose: gaze-direction estimation in multimodal video. IEEE Trans. Multimed. 17(11), 2094–2107 (2015). https://doi.org/10.1109/TMM.2015.2482819

39. NaturalPoint: OptiTrack Flex 3. http://optitrack.com/products/flex-3/, http://optitrack.com/products/flex-3/

40. Nelder, J.A., Mead, R.: A simplex method for function minimization. Comput. J. **7**(4), 308–313 (1965)

41. Park, H.S., Jain, E., Sheikh, Y.: Predicting primary gaze behavior using social saliency fields. In: IEEE International Conference on Computer Vision, pp. 3503–3510 (2013). https://doi.org/10.1109/ICCV.2013.435

42. Parks, D., Borji, A., Itti, L.: Augmented saliency model using automatic 3D head pose detection and learned gaze following in natural scenes. Vis. Res. **116**, 113–126 (2015). https://doi.org/10.1016/j.visres.2014.10.027

43. Patacchiola, M., Cangelosi, A.: Head pose estimation in the wild using convolutional neural networks and adaptive gradient methods. Pattern Recognit **71**, 132–143 (2017). https://doi.org/10.1016/j.patcog.2017.06.009

44. Pathak, D., Krähenbühl, P., Donahue, J., Darrell, T., Efros, A.: Context encoders: feature learning by inpainting. In: IEEE Conference on Computer Vision and Pattern Recognition, pp. 2536–2544 (2016). https://doi.org/10.1109/CVPR.2016.278

45. Pérez, P., Gangnet, M., Blake, A.: Poisson image editing. ACM Trans. Graph. **22**(3), 313–318 (2003). https://doi.org/10.1145/882262.882269

46. Philips, G.R., Catellier, A.A., Barrett, S.F., Wright, C.: Electrooculogram wheelchair control. Biomed. Sci. Instrum. **43**, 164–169 (2007). https://europepmc.org/abstract/med/17487075

47. Rasouli, A., Kotseruba, I., Tsotsos, J.K.: Agreeing to cross: how drivers and pedestrians communicate. In: IEEE Intelligent Vehicles Symposium, pp. 264–269 (2017). https://doi.org/10.1109/IVS.2017.7995730

48. Rudoy, D., Goldman, D.B., Shechtman, E., Zelnik-Manor, L.: Learning video saliency from human gaze using candidate selection. In: IEEE Conference on Computer Vision and Pattern Recognition, pp. 1147–1154 (2013). https://doi.org/10.1109/CVPR.2013.152

49. Shapovalova, N., Raptis, M., Sigal, L., Mori, G.: Action is in the eye of the beholder: eye-gaze driven model for spatio-temporal action localization. In: Advances in Neural Information Processing Systems, pp. 2409–2417 (2013). https://dl.acm.org/citation.cfm?id=2999881

50. Shrivastava, A., Pfister, T., Tuzel, O., Susskind, J., Wang, W., Webb, R.: Learning from simulated and unsupervised images through adversarial training. In: IEEE Conference on Computer Vision and Pattern Recognition, pp. 2107–2116 (2017). https://doi.org/10.1109/CVPR.2017.241

51. Simonyan, K., Zisserman, A.: Very deep convolutional networks for large-scale image recognition. In: International Conference on Learning Representations (2015). https://arxiv.org/abs/1409.1556

52. Smith, B.A., Yin, Q., Feiner, S.K., Nayar, S.K.: Gaze locking: passive eye contact detection for human-object interaction. In: ACM Symposium on User Interface Software and Technology, pp. 271–280 (2013). https://doi.org/10.1145/2501988.2501994

53. Sugano, Y., Matsushita, Y., Sato, Y.: Learning-by-synthesis for appearance-based 3D gaze estimation. In: IEEE Conference on Computer Vision and Pattern Recognition, pp. 1821–1828 (2014). https://doi.org/10.1109/CVPR.2014.235

54. Wilczkowiak, M., Brostow, G.J., Tordoff, B., Cipolla, R.: Hole filling through photomontage. In: British Machine Vision Conference, pp. 492–501 (2005). http://www.bmva.org/bmvc/2005/papers/55/paper.pdf

55. Wood, E., Baltrušaitis, T., Morency, L.P., Robinson, P., Bulling, A.: Learning an appearance-based gaze estimator from one million synthesised images. In: ACM Symposium on Eye Tracking Research & Applications, pp. 131–138 (2016). https://doi.org/10.1145/2857491.2857492

56. Wood, E., Baltrusaitis, T., Zhang, X., Sugano, Y., Robinson, P., Bulling, A.: Rendering of eyes for eye-shape registration and gaze estimation. In: IEEE International Conference on Computer Vision, pp. 3756–3764 (2015). https://doi.org/10.1109/ICCV.2015.428

57. Wood, E., Baltrušaitis, T., Morency, L.-P., Robinson, P., Bulling, A.: A 3D morphable eye region model for gaze estimation. In: Leibe, B., Matas, J., Sebe, N., Welling, M. (eds.) ECCV 2016. LNCS, vol. 9905, pp. 297–313. Springer, Cham (2016). https://doi.org/10.1007/978-3-319-46448-0_18

58. Yeh, R.A., Chen, C., Lim, T.Y., G., S.A., Hasegawa-Johnson, M., Do, M.N.: Semantic image inpainting with deep generative models. In: IEEE Conference on Computer Vision and Pattern Recognition, pp. 5485–5493 (2017). https://doi.org/10.1109/CVPR.2017.728

59. Zhang, K., Zhang, Z., Li, Z., Qiao, Y.: Joint face detection and alignment using multitask cascaded convolutional networks. IEEE Signal Process. Lett. **23**(10), 1499–1503 (2016). https://doi.org/10.1109/LSP.2016.2603342

60. Zhang, X., Sugano, Y., Fritz, M., Bulling, A.: Appearance-based gaze estimation in the wild. In: IEEE Conference on Computer Vision and Pattern Recognition, pp. 4511–4520 (2015). https://doi.org/10.1109/CVPR.2015.7299081

61. Zhang, X., Sugano, Y., Fritz, M., Bulling, A.: It's written all over your face: full-face appearance-based gaze estimation. In: IEEE Conference on Computer Vision and Pattern Recognition Workshops, pp. 51–60 (2017). https://doi.org/10.1109/CVPRW.2017.284

62. Zhu, J.Y., Park, T., Isola, P., Efros, A.A.: Unpaired image-to-image translation using cycle-consistent adversarial networks. In: International Conference on Computer Vision, pp. 2223–2232 (2017). https://doi.org/10.1109/ICCV.2017.244

Unsupervised Class-Specific Deblurring

Nimisha Thekke Madam[(✉)] , Sunil Kumar , and A. N. Rajagopalan

Indian Institute of Technology, Madras, Chennai, India
ee13d037@ee.iitm.ac.in
http://www.ee.iitm.ac.in/ipcvlab/

Abstract. In this paper, we present an end-to-end deblurring network designed specifically for a class of data. Unlike the prior supervised deep-learning works that extensively rely on large sets of paired data, which is highly demanding and challenging to obtain, we propose an unsupervised training scheme with unpaired data to achieve the same. Our model consists of a Generative Adversarial Network (GAN) that learns a strong prior on the clean image domain using adversarial loss and maps the blurred image to its clean equivalent. To improve the stability of GAN and to preserve the image correspondence, we introduce an additional CNN module that reblurs the generated GAN output to match with the blurred input. Along with these two modules, we also make use of the blurred image itself to self-guide the network to constrain the solution space of generated clean images. This self-guidance is achieved by imposing a scale-space gradient error with an additional gradient module. We train our model on different classes and observe that adding the reblur and gradient modules helps in better convergence. Extensive experiments demonstrate that our method performs favorably against the state-of-the-art supervised methods on both synthetic and real-world images even in the absence of any supervision.

Keywords: Motion blur · Deblur · Reblur · Unsupervised learning
GAN · CNN

1 Introduction

Blind-image deblurring is a classical image restoration problem which has been an active area of research in image and vision community over the past few decades. With increasing use of hand-held imaging devices, especially mobile phones, motion blur has become a major problem to confront with. In scenarios where the light present in the scene is low, the exposure time of the sensor has to be pumped up to capture a well-lit scene. As a consequence, camera shake becomes inevitable resulting in image blur. Motion blur also occurs when the scene is imaged by fast-moving vehicles such as cars and aircrafts even in

Electronic supplementary material The online version of this chapter (https://doi.org/10.1007/978-3-030-01249-6_22) contains supplementary material, which is available to authorized users.

© Springer Nature Switzerland AG 2018
V. Ferrari et al. (Eds.): ECCV 2018, LNCS 11214, pp. 358–374, 2018.
https://doi.org/10.1007/978-3-030-01249-6_22

low-exposure settings. The problem escalates further in data-deprived situations comprising of only a single blurred frame.

Blind-deblurring can be posed as an image-to-image translation where given a blurred image y in blur domain, we need to learn a non-linear mapping $\mathcal{M}:y \rightarrow x$ that maps the blurred image to its equivalent clean image x in the clean domain. Many recent deep learning based deblurring networks [18,27,28] estimate this mapping when provided with large sets of $\{y_i, x_i\}_{i=1}^{N}$ paired training data. Even though these networks have shown promising results, the basic assumption of availability of paired data is too demanding. In many a situation, collecting paired training data can be difficult, time-consuming and expensive. For example, in applications like scene conversion from day to night and image dehazing, the availability of paired data is scarce or even non-existent.

This debilitating limitation of supervised deep networks necessitates the need for unsupervised learning approaches [21,41,42] from unpaired datasets. In an unsupervised setting, the user collects two sets of images from two marginal distributions in both domains but sans pair-wise correspondences. Then the task is to infer the joint distribution using these images. In this paper, we aim to develop an unsupervised learning framework for blind-deblurring from a single blurred frame *without the need for the corresponding ground truth clean data*. Rather, our network relies on unlabeled image data from blur and clean domains to perform domain-specific deblurring.

Related Works: There is a vast literature on motion deblurring spanning both conventional and deep learning techniques. Similarly, of late there are works on unsupervised image translations gaining popularity due to lack of availability of paired data. We provide a brief description of these two topics below.

Motion deblurring is a long-studied topic in imaging community. To avoid shot noise due to low amount of available photons in low light scenarios, the exposure time is increased. Hence, even a small camera motion is enough to create motion blur in the recorded image due to averaging of light energy from slightly different versions of the same scene. While there are several deblurring works that involve usage of multiple frames [24,35], the problem becomes very ill-posed in data-limited situations where the user ends up with a single blurred frame. This entails the need for single-image blind-deblurring algorithms.

To overcome the ill-posedness of single image-blind deblurring, most of the existing algorithms [11,31,39] rely on image heuristics and assumptions on the sources of the blur. The most widely used image heuristics are sparsity prior, the unnatural l_0 prior [39] and dark channel prior [31]. Assumptions on camera motion are imposed in the form of kernel sparsity and smoothness of trajectory. These heuristics are used as priors and iterative optimization schemes are deployed to solve for camera motion and latent clean frame from a single-blurred input. Even though these methods are devoid of any requirement of paired data, they are highly dependent on the optimization techniques and prior selection.

With deep learning coming to the forefront, several deep networks [18,27,28] have been proposed that perform the task of blind deblurring from a single image. These methods work end-to-end and skip the need for the camera motion estimation and directly provide the clean frame when fed with the blurred image thus overcoming the tedious task of prior selection and parameter tuning. But the main disadvantage with existing deep-learning works is that they require close supervision warranting large amounts of paired datasets for training.

Unsupervised Learning: The recent trend in deep learning is to use unpaired data to achieve domain transfer. With the seminal work of Goodfellow [10], GANs have been used in multiple areas of image-to-image translations. The key to this success is the idea of an adversarial loss that forces the generated images to be indistinguishable from real images thus learning the data domain. Conditional GANs (cGAN) [15,20,40] have made progress recently for cross-domain image-to-image translation in supervised settings. The goal remains the same in unsupervised settings too i.e; to relate the two domains. One way to approach the problem is by enforcing a common representation across the domains by using shared weights with two GANs as in [3,21,22]. The fundamental objective here is to use a pair of coupled GANs, one for the source and one for the target domain, whose generators share their high-layer weights and whose discriminators share their low-layer weights. In this manner, they are able to generate invariant representations which can be used for unsupervised domain transfer.

Following this, the works in [41,42] propose to use a cycle consistency loss on the image space itself rather than asking for invariant feature space. Here too the GANs are used to learn each individual domain and then cross model term with cyclic consistency loss is used to map between domains. Apart from these methods, there are neural style transfer networks [6,7,16] that is also used for image-to-image translation with unsupervised data. The idea here is to combine the 'content' features of one image with the 'style' of another image (like famous paintings). These methods use matching of Gram matrix statistics of pre-trained deep features to achieve image translation between two specific images. On the other hand, our main focus is to learn the mapping between two image collections (rather than two specific images) from different domains by attempting to capture correspondences between higher-level appearance structures.

Class-specific Methods: Of late, domain-specific image restoration methods [1,2,5,33,36,37,40] are gaining relevance and attracting attention due to the inaccuracy of generic algorithms to deal with real-world data. The general priors learned from natural images are not necessarily well-suited for all classes and often lead to deterioration in performance. Recently, class-specific information has been employed in carrying out deblurring which outperforms blanket prior-based approaches. An exemplar-based deblurring for faces was proposed by Pan et al. in [29]. Anwar et al. [1] introduced a method to restore attenuated image frequencies during convolution using class-specific training examples. Deep learning networks too have attempted the task of class-specific deblurring. Text deblurring network in [12] and deep face deblurring network in [5] are a notable few amongst these.

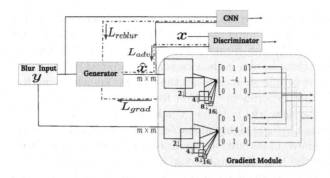

Fig. 1. Our network with GAN, reblur module and scale-space gradient module.

Following these works, we also propose in this paper a domain-specific deblurring architecture focusing mainly on face, text, and checkerboard classes using a single GAN framework. Faces and texts are considered important classes and many restoration techniques have focused on them explicitly. We also included the checkerboard class to study our network performance and to ease the task of parameter tuning akin to [33]. GAN is used in our network to learn a strong class-specific prior on clean data. The discriminator thus learned captures the semantic domain knowledge of a class but fails to capture the content, colors, and structure properly. These are usually corrected with supervised loss functions in regular networks which is not practical in our unsupervised setting. Hence, we introduce self-guidance using the blurred data itself. Our network is trained with unpaired data from clean and blurred domains. A comprehensive diagram of our network is shown in Fig. 1.

The main contributions of our work are

- To the best of our knowledge, this is the first ever data-driven attempt at unsupervised learning for the task of deblurring.
- To overcome the shortcomings of supervision due to unavailability of paired data and to help the network converge to the right solution, we propose self-guidance with two new additional modules
  - A self-supervised reblurring module that guides the generator to produce a deblurred output corresponding to the input blurred image.
  - A gradient module with the key notion that down-sampling decreases gradient matching error and constrains the solution space of generated clean images.

2 Unsupervised Deblurring

A naive approach to unsupervised deblurring would be to adopt existing networks (CoGAN [22], DualGAN [41], CycleGAN [42]) designed for image translations and train them for the task of image restoration. However, a main issue with such an approach is that most of the unsupervised networks discussed thus far are designed for a specific task of domain transformation such as face-to-sketch synthesis, day-to-night etc where the transformations are well-defined. In image deblurring, the transformation from blur to clean domain is a many-to-one mapping while clean to blur is the vice versa depending on the extent and nature of blur. Thus, it is difficult to capture the domain knowledge with these existing architectures (see experiments section for more on this). Also, the underlying idea in all these networks is to use a pair of GANs to learn the domains, but usually training GANs is highly unstable [8,34] and thus using two GANs simultaneously escalates in stability issues in the network. Instead of using a second GAN to learn the blur domain, we use a CNN network for reblurring the output of GAN and a gradient module to constrain the solution space. A detailed description of each module is provided below.

GAN proposed by Goodfellow [10] consists of two networks (a generator and a discriminator) that compete to outperform each other. Given the discriminator D, the generator tries to learn the mapping from noise to real data distribution so as to fool D. Similarly, given the generator G, the discriminator works as a classifier that learns to distinguish between real and generated images. The function of learning GAN is a min-max problem with the cost function

$$E(D, G) = \underset{D}{\mathrm{max}}\,\underset{G}{\mathrm{min}}\,\underset{x \sim P_{data}}{E}\left[\log D(x)\right] + \underset{z \sim P_z}{E}\left[\log(1 - D(G(z)))\right]. \tag{1}$$

where z is random noise and x denotes the real data. This work was followed by conditional GANs (cGAN) [26] that use a conditioning input in the form of image [15], text, class label etc. The objective remains the same in all of these i.e, the discriminator is trained to designate higher probability to real data and lower to the generated data. Hence, the discriminator acts as a data prior that learns clean data domain similar to the heuristics that are used in conventional methods. This motivated us to use GANs for learning the mapping from blur to clean domain using the discriminator as our data prior. In our network, the input to generator G is a blurred image $y \in Y$ and the generator maps it to a clean image $\hat{x}$ such that the generated image $\hat{x} = G(y)$ is indistinguishable from clean data (where clean data statistics are learned from $\tilde{x}s \in X$).

Self-supervision by Reblurring (CNN Module). The goal of GAN in our deblurring framework is to reach an equilibrium where P_{clean} and $P_{generated}$ are close. The alternating gradient update procedure (AGD) is used to achieve this. However, this process is highly unstable and often results in mode collapse [9]. Also, an optimal G that translates from $Y \rightarrow X$ does not guarantee that an individual blurred input y and its corresponding clean output x are paired up in a meaningful way, i.e, there are infinitely many mappings G that will induce the same distribution over $\hat{x}$ [42]. This motivated the use of reconstruction loss ($||\hat{x} - x||^2$) and perceptual loss ($||\Phi_i((\hat{x}) - \Phi_i(x)||^2$, where Φ_i represents VGG module features extracted at the ith layer) along with the adversarial loss in many supervised learning works [15,20,27,38,40], to stabilize the solution and help in better convergence. But, these cost functions require high level of supervision

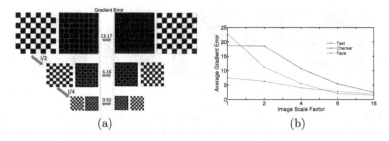

(a)   (b)

Fig. 2. (a) Scale space gradient error. (b) Average decrease in gradient error with respect to down scaling.

in the form of ground truth clean reference images (x) which are not available in our case. This restricts the usage of these supervised cost functions in our network. To account for the unavailability of paired dataset, we use the blurred image y itself as a supervision to guide in deblurring. Ignatov et al. [14] have used a similar reblurring approach with a constant Gaussian kernel to correct for colors in camera mapping. We enforce the generator to produce result ($\hat{x}$) that when reblurred using the CNN module will furnish back the input. Adding such a module ensures that the deblurred result has the same color and texture comparable to the input image thereby constraining the solution to the manifold of images that captures the actual input content.

Gradient Matching Module. With a combined network of GAN and CNN modules, the generator learns to map to clean domain along with color preservation. Now, to enforce the gradients of the generated image to match its corresponding clean image, a **gradient module** is used in our network as given in Fig. 1. Gradient matching resolves the problem of over-sharpening and ringing in the results. However, since we do not have access to the reference image, determining the desired gradient distribution to match with is difficult. Hence, we borrow a heuristic from [25] that takes advantage of the fact that shrinking a blurry image y by a factor of α results in a image y^{α} that is α times sharper than y. Thus, we use the blurred image gradients at different scales to guide the deblurring process. At the highest scales, the gradients of blurred and generated output match the least but improve while going down in scale space. A visual diagram depicting this effect is shown in Fig. 2(a) where the gradients of a blurred and clean checker-board at different scales are provided. Observe that, at the highest scale, the gradients are very different and as we move down in scale the gradients start to look alike and the L_1 error between them decreases. The plot in Fig. 2(b) is the average per pixel L_1 error with respect to scale for 200 images from each of text, checker-board and face datasets. In all these data, the gradient error decreases with scale and hence forms a good guiding input for training our network.

(a)   (b)   (c)   (d)   (e)

Fig. 3. Effect of different cost functions. (a) Input blurred image to the generator, (b) result of unsupervised deblurring with just the GAN cost in Eq. (2), (c) result obtained by adding the reblurring cost in Eq. (3) with (b), (d) result obtained with gradient cost in Eq. (4) with (c), and (e) the target output.

3   Loss Functions

A straightforward way for unsupervised training is by using GAN. Given large unpaired data $\{x_i\}_{i=1}^{M}$ and $\{y_j\}_{j=1}^{N}$ in both domains, train the parameters (θ) of the generator to map from $y \to x$ by minimizing the cost

$$L_{\text{adv}} = \min_{\theta} \frac{1}{N} \sum_i \log(1 - D(G_\theta(y_i))) \tag{2}$$

Training with adversarial cost alone can result in color variations or missing finite details (like eyes and nose in faces or letters in case of texts) in the generated outputs but the discriminator can still end up classifying it as real instead of generated data. This is because discriminating between real and fake does not depend on these small details (see Fig. 3(b), the output of GAN alone wherein eyes and colors are not properly reconstructed).

With the addition of the reblurring module, the generator is more constrained to match the colors and textures of the generated data (see Fig. 3(c)). The generated clean image from generator $\hat{x} = G(y)$ is again passed through the CNN module to obtain back the blurred input. Hence the reblurring cost is given as

$$L_{\text{reblur}} = ||y - \text{CNN}(\hat{x})||_2^2 \tag{3}$$

Along with the above two costs, we also enforce the gradients to match at different scales (s) using the gradient cost defined as

$$L_{\text{grad}} = \sum_{s \in \{1,2,4,8,16\}} \lambda_s |\nabla y_{s\downarrow} - \nabla \hat{x}_{s\downarrow}| \tag{4}$$

where ∇ denotes the gradient operator. A Laplacian operator $\begin{bmatrix} 0 & 1 & 0 \\ 1 & -4 & 1 \\ 0 & 1 & 0 \end{bmatrix}$ is used to calculate the image gradients at different scales and λ_s values are set as $[0.0001, 0.001, 0.01, 0.1, 1]$ for $s = \{1, 2, 4, 8, 16\}$, respectively. Adding the gradient cost removes unwanted ringing artifacts at the boundary of the image and smoothens the result. It is evident from the figure that with inclusion of supporting cost

Table 1. (a) The proposed generator and discriminator network architecture. conv ↓ indicates convolution with stride 2 which in effect reduces the output dimension by half and d/o refers to dropout. (b) Reblurring CNN module architecture

Module	Generator					Discriminator										
Layers	conv	conv	conv	conv	conv	conv	conv	conv	conv	conv	conv↓	conv↓	conv↓	conv↓	conv ↓	fc
Kernel Size	5	5	5	5	5	5	5	5	5	5	4	4	4	4	4	-
Features	64	128	128	256 d/o (0.2)	256 d/o (0.2)	128	128	64	64	3	64	128	256	512	512	-

(a)

Module	CNN					
Layers	conv	conv	conv	conv	conv	tanh
Kernel Size	5	5	5	5	5	
Features	64	64	64	64	3	

(b)

functions corresponding to reblurring and gradient, the output (Fig. 3(d)) of the network becomes comparable with the ground truth (GT) image (Fig. 3(e)). Hence, the generator network is trained with a combined cost function given by

$$L_G = \gamma_{\mathrm{adv}} L_{\mathrm{adv}} + \gamma_{\mathrm{reblur}} L_{\mathrm{reblur}} + \gamma_{\mathrm{grad}} L_{\mathrm{grad}} \tag{5}$$

4   Network Architecture

We followed a similar architecture for our generator and discriminator as proposed in [40], which has shown good performance for blind super-resolution, with slight modification in the feature layers. The network architecture of GAN with filter sizes and the number of feature maps at each stage is provided in Table 1(a). Each convolution (conv) layer in the generator is followed by batch-normalization and non-linearity using Rectified Linear Unit (ReLU) except the last layer. A hyper tangential (Tanh) function is used at the last layer to constrain the output to $[-1, 1]$. The discriminator is a basic 6-layer model with each convolution followed by a Leaky ReLU except the last fully connected (fc) layer which is followed by a Sigmoid. Convolution with stride 2 is used in most layers to go down in dimension and the details of filter size and feature maps are provided in Table 1(a). The reblurring CNN architecture is a simple 5-layer convolutional module provided in Table 1(b). The gradient module is operated on-the-fly for each batch of data using GPU based convolution with the Laplacian operator and downsampling depending on the scaling factor with 'nn' modules.

We used Torch for training and testing with the following options: ADAM optimizer with momentum values $\beta_1 = 0.9$ and $\beta_2 = 0.99$, learning rate of 0.0005, batch-size of 32 and the network was trained with the total cost as provided in Eq. (5). The weights for different costs were initially set as $\gamma_{\mathrm{adv}}=1$, $\gamma_{\mathrm{grad}}=.001$ and $\gamma_{\mathrm{reblur}}=0.01$ to ensure that the discriminator learns the clean data domain. After around 100K iterations the adversarial cost was weighted down and the CNN cost was increased so that the clean image produced corresponds in color and texture to the blurred input. Hence, the weights were readjusted as $\gamma_{\mathrm{adv}}=0.01$, $\gamma_{\mathrm{grad}}=0.1$ and $\gamma_{\mathrm{reblur}}=1$ and the learning rate was reduced

Table 2. Quantitative comparisons on face, text, and checkerboard datasets.

	Method	Face dataset			Text dataset				Checkerboard dataset		
		PSNR	SSIM	KSM	PSNR	SSIM	KSM	CER	PSNR	SSIM	KSM
Conventional methods	Pan et al. [30]	-	-	-	16.19	0.7298	0.8628	0.4716	11.11	0.3701	0.7200
	Pan et al. [31]	19.38	0.7764	0.7436	17.48	0.7713	0.8403	0.3066	13.91	0.5618	0.7027
	Xu et al. [39]	20.28	0.7928	0.7166	14.22	0.5417	0.7991	0.2918	8.18	0.2920	0.6034
	Pan et al.[29]	22.36	0.8523	0.7197	-	-	-	-	-	-	-
Deep learning methods	Nah et al. [27]	24.12	0.8755	0.6229	18.72	0.7521	0.7467	0.2643	18.07	0.6932	0.6497
	Hradiš et al. [12]	-	-	-	24.28	0.9387	0.9435	0.0891	18.09	0.6788	0.6791
Unsupervised technique	Zhu et al. [42]	8.93	0.4406	0.2932	13.19	0.5639	0.8363	0.2306	21.92	0.8264	0.6527
	Ours	22.80	0.8631	0.7536	23.22	0.8792	0.9376	0.126	20.61	0.8109	0.7801

to 0.0001 to continue training. Apart from these, to stabilize the GAN, during training we used drop-out of 0.2 at the fourth and fifth convolution layers of the generator and used a smooth labeling of real and fake labels following [34].

5   Experiments

The experiments section is arranged as follows: (i) training and testing datasets, (ii) comparison methods, (iii) quantitative results, metrics used and comparisons, and (iv) visual results and comparisons.

5.1   Dataset Creation

For all classes, we used 128 × 128 sized images for training and testing. The dataset generation for training and testing of each of these classes is explained below. Note that our network was trained for each of these classes separately.

Camera Motion Generation: In our experiments, to generate the blur kernels required for synthesizing the training and test sets, we used the methodology described by Chakrabarthi in [4]. The blur kernels are generated by randomly sampling six points in a limited size grid (13 × 13), fitting a spline through these points, and setting the kernel values at each pixel on this spline to a value sampled from a Gaussian distribution with mean 1 and standard deviation of 0.5, then clipping these values to be positive, and normalizing the kernel to have unit sum. A total of 100K kernels were used for creating the dataset.

Face Dataset: We use the aligned CelebA face dataset [23] for creating the training data for our case. CelebA is a large-scale face attributes dataset of size 178 × 218 with more than 200K aligned celebrity images. We selected 200K images from it, resized each to 128 × 128 and divided it into two groups of 100K images each. Then, we use the blur kernels generated with [4] to blur one set of images alone and the other set is kept intact. This way, we generate the clean and blur face data (without any correspondence) for training the network.

Table 3. Quantitative comparisons on face and text on real handshake motion [17].

Class	PSNR in (dB)	SSIM	KSM
Text	21.92	0.8968	0.8811
Face	21.40	0.8533	0.7794

Text Dataset: For text images, we use the training dataset of Hradiš et al. [12] which consists of images with both defocus blur generated by anti-aliased disc and motion blur generated by random walk. They have provided a large collection of 66K text images of size 300×300. We use these images for creating the training dataset and use the test data provided by them for testing our network. We first divide the whole dataset into two groups of 33K each with one group containing clean data alone and other containing the blurred data. We took care to avoid any overlapping pairs in the generated set. We then cropped 128×128 patches from these sets to obtain the training set of around 300K images in both clean and blur set.

Checkerboard Dataset: We took a clean checkerboard image of size 256×256 and applied random rotations and translations to it and cropped out 128×128 (avoiding boundary pixels) to generate a set of 100K clean images. The clean images are then partitioned into two sets of 50K images each to ensure that there are no corresponding pairs available during training. To one set we apply synthetic motion blur to create the blurred images by convolving with linear filters and the other set is kept as such. We used a linear approximation of camera motion and parametrized it with length l and rotation angle θ. For the dataset creation, considering the size of input images, we selected the maximum value of l to be in the range $[0, 15]$ and varied θ from $[0, 180]^o$. We use *rand* function of MATLAB to generate 50K such filters. Following similar steps, a test set consisting of 5000 images is also created.

5.2 Comparison Methods

We compare our deblurring results with three classes of approaches, (a) State-of-art conventional deblurring approaches which use prior based optimization, (b) Supervised deep learning based end-to-end deblurring approaches, and (c) latest unsupervised image-to-image translation approaches.

Conventional Single Image Deblurring: We compare with the state-of-the-art conventional deblurring works of Pan et al. [31] and Xu et al. [39] that are proposed for natural images. In addition to this, for face deblurring we used the deblurring work in [29] that is designed specifically for faces. Similarly for text, we compared with the method in [30] that uses prior on text for deblurring. Quantitative results are provided by running their codes on our test dataset.

Deep supervised deblurring: In deep learning, for quantitative analysis on all classes, we compared with end-to-end deblurring work of [27] and additionally for text and checkerboard we also compared with [12]. The work in [27] is a general dynamic scene deblurring framework and [12] is proposed for text deblurring alone. Note that all these methods use paired data for training and hence are supervised. Besides these for visual comparisons on face deblurring, we also compared with [5] on their images since the trained model was not available.

Unsupervised Image-to-Image Translation : We train the cycleGAN [42] network, proposed for unpaired domain translations, for deblurring task. The network is trained from scratch for each class separately and quantitative and visual results are reported for each class in the following sections.

5.3   Quantitative Analysis

For quantitative analysis, we created the test sets for which the ground truth was available to report the metrics mentioned below. For text dataset, we used the test set provided in [12] itself. And for checkerboard, we used synthetic motion parametrized with $\{l, \theta\}$. For faces, we created test sets using the kernels generated from [4].

Quantitative Metrics: We have used PSNR (in dB), SSIM and Kernel Similarity Measure(KSM) values for comparing the performance of different state of art deblurring algorithms on all the classes. For texts, apart from these metrics, we also use Character Error Rate (CER) to evaluate the performance of various deblurring algorithms.

CER [12] is defined as $\frac{i+s+d}{n}$, where, n is total number of characters in the image, i is the minimal number of character insertions, s is the number of substitutions and d is the number of deletions required to transform the reference text into its correct OCR output. We used ABBYY FineReader 11 to recognize the text and its output formed the basis for evaluating the mean CER. Smaller the CER value, better the performance of the method.

Kernel Similarity Measure: In general practice, the deblurring efficiency is evaluated through PSNR, SSIM metric or with visual comparisons. These commonly used measures (MSE) are biased towards smooth outputs due to 2-norm form. Hence, Hu et al. [13] proposed KSM to evaluate deblurring in terms of the camera motion estimation efficiency. KSM effectively compare estimated kernels $(\hat{K})$ evaluated from the deblurred output with the ground truth (K). It is computed as $S(K, \hat{K}) = \max_\gamma \rho(K, \hat{K}, \gamma)$ where $\rho(.)$ is the normalized cross-correlation function given by $(\rho(K, \hat{K}, \gamma) = \frac{\sum_\tau (K(\tau).K(\tau+\gamma))}{||K||.|\hat{K}||})$ and γ is the possible shift between the two kernels. The larger the value, the better the kernel estimate and indirectly the better the deblurring performance.

Results and Comparisons: For fair comparison with other methods, we used the codes provided by the respective authors on their website. Table 2 summarizes the quantitative performance of various competitive methods along with our network results for all the three classes. A set of 30 test images from each class is used to evaluate the performance reported in the table. It is very clear from the results that our unsupervised network performs on par with competitive conventional methods as well as supervised deep networks. Conventional methods are highly influenced by parameter selection. We used the default settings for arriving at the results for conventional methods. The results could perhaps be improved further by fine-tuning the parameters for each image but this is a time-consuming task. Though deep networks perform well for class-specific data, their training is limited by the lack of availability of large collections of paired data. It can be seen from Table 2 that our network (without data pairing) is able to perform equally well when compared to the class-specific supervised deep method [12] for text deblurring. We even outperform the dynamic deblurring network of [27] in most cases. The cycleGAN [42] (though unsupervised) struggles to learn the blur and clean data domains. It can be noted that, for checkerboard, cycleGAN performed better than ours in terms of PSNR and SSIM. This is because checkerboard had simple linear camera motion. Because blur varied for text and faces (general camera motion) the performance of cycleGAN also deteriorated (refer to the reported values).

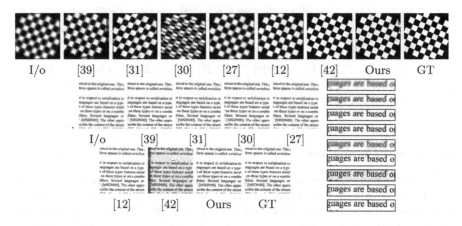

Fig. 4. Visual comparison on checkerboard deblurring. Input blurred image, deblurred results from conventional methods [30,31,39], results from supervised network in [12,27] and unsupervised network [42], our result and the GT clean image are provided in that order.

Real Handshake Motion: In addition, to test the capabilities of our trained network on real camera motion, we also created test sets for face and text classes using the real camera motion dataset from [17]. Camera motion provided in [17] contains 40 trajectories of real camera shake by humans who were asked to take photographs with relatively long exposure times. These camera motions are not confined to translations, but consist of non-uniform blurs, originating from real camera trajectories. The efficiency of our proposed network in deblurring images affected by these real motions is reported in Table 3. Since long exposure leads to heavy motion blur which is not within the scope of this work, we use short segments of the recorded trajectory to introduce small blurs. We generated 40 images for both text and faces using 40 trajectories and used our trained network to deblur them. Table 3 shows the PSNR, SSIM between the clean and deblurred images and KSM between the estimated and original motion. The handshake motion in [17] produces space-varying blur in the image and hence a single kernel cannot be estimated for the entire image. We used patches (32×32) from the image and assumed space-invariant blur over the patch to extract the kernel and computed the KSM. This was repeated on multiple patches and an average KSM is reported for the entire image. The KSM, PSNR, and SSIM are all high for both the classes signifying the effectiveness of our network to deal with real camera motions.

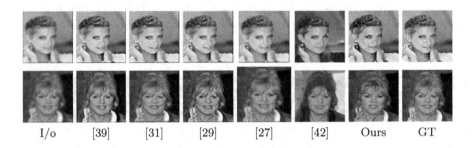

| I/o | [39] | [31] | [29] | [27] | [42] | Ours | GT |

Fig. 5. Visual comparisons on face deblurring.

5.4   Visual Comparisons

The visual results of our network and competitive methods are provided in Figs. 4 and 5. Figure 4 contains the visual results for text and checkerboard data. Comparisons are provided with [31,39] and [30]. The poor performance of these methods can be attributed to the parameter setting (we took the best amongst a set of parameters that gave highest PSNR). Most of these results have ringing artifacts. Now, to analyse the performance of our network over supervised networks, we compared with the dynamic deblurring network of [27] and class-specific deblurring work of [12]. From the visual results it can be clearly observed that even though the method in [27] gave good PSNR in Table 2 it is visually not sharp and some residual blur remains in the output. The supervised text deblurring network [12] result for checkerboard was sharp but the squares were not properly reconstructed. For completeness, we also trained the unsupervised cycleGAN [42] network separately for each of these classes and the results so obtained are also provided in the figure. The inefficiency of cycleGAN to capture the clean and blur domains simultaneously is reflected in the text results. On the contrary, our unsupervised network produces sharp and legible (see the patches of texts) results in both these classes. Our network outperforms existing conventional methods and at the same time works on par with the text-specific deblurring method of [12]. Visual results on face deblurring are provided in Fig. 5. Here too we compared with conventional methods [31,39] as before and the exemplar-based face-specific deblurring method of [29]. Though these results are visually similar to the GT, the effect of ringing is high with default parameter settings. The results from deep learning work of [27] is devoid of any ringing artifacts but are highly oversmoothened. Similarly, CycleGAN [42] fails to learn the domain properly and the results are quite different from the GT. On the other-hand, our results are sharp and visually appealing. While competitive methods failed to reconstruct the eyes of the lady in Fig. 5 (second row), our method reconstructs the eyes and produces sharp outputs comparable to GT.

We also tested our network against the latest deep face deblurring work of [5]. Since the trained model for their network was not available, we ran our network on the images provided in their paper. These are real world blurred images from dataset of Lai et al. [19] and from arbitrary videos. The results obtained are shown in Fig. 6. It can be cleraly seen that our method though unsupervised can perform at par with the supervised method of [5] and even outperforms it in some examples. The results are sharper with our network; it can be clearly noticed that the eyes are eyebrows are reconstructed well with our network (first and second rows last columns) when compared to [5].

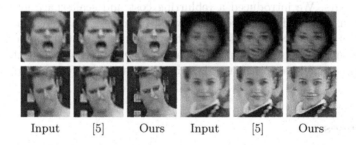

Input   [5]   Ours   Input   [5]   Ours

Fig. 6. Visual comparison with the latest face deblurring work of [5].

Human Perception Ranking: We conducted a survey with 50 users to analyze the visual quality of our deblurring. This was done for face and text datasets separately. The users were provided with 30 sets of images from each class grouped into two sections depending on the presence or absence of reference image. In the first group consisting of 10 sets of images, the users were provided with blurred image, ground truth reference, our deblurred result and output from [29]/[5] or [30]/[12], based on their visual perception. And in the second group

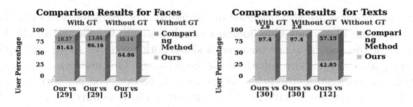

Fig. 7. Summarization of survey: Human rating of our network results against [29] and [5] for faces and [30] and [12] for texts.

with 20 sets of images the references were excluded. From the face survey result provided in Fig. 7, it can be observed that 81% of the time the users preferred our results over the competitive method [29] when GT was provided and 86% of the time our result was preferred when GT was not provided. For texts, the users preferred our output 97% of the time over the conventional method [30] with or without GT. Also, it can be observed that our method matches well with [12]. 43% of the users opted our method while 57% voted for [12]. More results (on testset and real dataset from [32]), discussions on loss functions, details of survey and limitations of the network are provided in the supplementary material.

6   Conclusions

We proposed a deep unsupervised network for deblurring class-specific data. The proposed network does not require any supervision in the form of corresponding data pairs. We introduced a reblurring cost and scale-space gradient cost that were used to self-supervise the network to achieve stable results. The performance of our network was found to be at par with existing supervised deep networks on both real and synthetic datasets. Our method paves the way for unsupervised image restoration, a domain where availability of paired dataset is scarce.

References

1. Anwar, S., Phuoc Huynh, C., Porikli, F.: Class-specific image deblurring. In: Proceedings of the IEEE International Conference on Computer Vision, pp. 495–503 (2015)
2. Anwar, S., Porikli, F., Huynh, C.P.: Category-specific object image denoising. IEEE Trans. Image Process. **26**(11), 5506–5518 (2017)
3. Aytar, Y., Castrejon, L., Vondrick, C., Pirsiavash, H., Torralba, A.: Cross-modal scene networks. IEEE Trans. Pattern Anal. Mach. Intell. (2017)
4. Chakrabarti, A.: A neural approach to blind motion deblurring. In: Leibe, B., Matas, J., Sebe, N., Welling, M. (eds.) ECCV 2016. LNCS, vol. 9907, pp. 221–235. Springer, Cham (2016). https://doi.org/10.1007/978-3-319-46487-9_14
5. Chrysos, G., Zafeiriou, S.: Deep face deblurring. In: 2017 IEEE Conference on Computer Vision and Pattern Recognition Workshops (CVPRW) (2017)

6. Gatys, L.A., Ecker, A.S., Bethge, M.: Image style transfer using convolutional neural networks. In: IEEE Conference on Computer Vision and Pattern Recognition (CVPR), pp. 2414–2423 (2016)
7. Gatys, L.A., Ecker, A.S., Bethge, M., Hertzmann, A., Shechtman, E.: Controlling perceptual factors in neural style transfer. In: IEEE Conference on Computer Vision and Pattern Recognition (CVPR) (2017)
8. Gomez, A.N., Huang, S., Zhang, I., Li, B.M., Osama, M., Kaiser, L.: Unsupervised cipher cracking using discrete gans. arXiv preprint arXiv:1801.04883 (2018)
9. Goodfellow, I.: Nips 2016 tutorial: Generative adversarial networks (2016)
10. Goodfellow, I., et al.: Generative adversarial nets. In: Advances in Neural Information Processing Systems, pp. 2672–2680 (2014)
11. Gupta, A., Joshi, N., Lawrence Zitnick, C., Cohen, M., Curless, B.: Single image deblurring using motion density functions. In: Daniilidis, K., Maragos, P., Paragios, N. (eds.) ECCV 2010. LNCS, vol. 6311, pp. 171–184. Springer, Heidelberg (2010). https://doi.org/10.1007/978-3-642-15549-9_13
12. Hradiš, M., Kotera, J., Zemcík, P., Šroubek, F.: Convolutional neural networks for direct text deblurring. In: Proceedings of BMVC, vol. 10 (2015)
13. Hu, Z., Yang, M.-H.: Good regions to deblur. In: Fitzgibbon, A., Lazebnik, S., Perona, P., Sato, Y., Schmid, C. (eds.) ECCV 2012. LNCS, vol. 7576, pp. 59–72. Springer, Heidelberg (2012). https://doi.org/10.1007/978-3-642-33715-4_5
14. Ignatov, A., Kobyshev, N., Vanhoey, K., Timofte, R., Van Gool, L.: Dslr-quality photos on mobile devices with deep convolutional networks. In: The International Conference on Computer Vision (ICCV) (2017)
15. Isola, P., Zhu, J.Y., Zhou, T., Efros, A.A.: Image-to-image translation with conditional adversarial networks(2016)
16. Johnson, J., Alahi, A., Fei-Fei, L.: Perceptual losses for real-time style transfer and super-resolution. In: Leibe, B., Matas, J., Sebe, N., Welling, M. (eds.) ECCV 2016. LNCS, vol. 9906, pp. 694–711. Springer, Cham (2016). https://doi.org/10.1007/978-3-319-46475-6_43
17. Köhler, R., Hirsch, M., Mohler, B., Schölkopf, B., Harmeling, S.: Recording and playback of camera shake: benchmarking blind deconvolution with a real-world database. In: Fitzgibbon, A., Lazebnik, S., Perona, P., Sato, Y., Schmid, C. (eds.) ECCV 2012. LNCS, vol. 7578, pp. 27–40. Springer, Heidelberg (2012). https://doi.org/10.1007/978-3-642-33786-4_3
18. Kupyn, O., Budzan, V., Mykhailych, M., Mishkin, D., Matas, J.: Deblurgan: blind motion deblurring using conditional adversarial networks. arXiv preprint arXiv:1711.07064 (2017)
19. Lai, W.S., Huang, J.B., Hu, Z., Ahuja, N., Yang, M.H.: A comparative study for single image blind deblurring. In: Proceedings of the IEEE Conference on Computer Vision and Pattern Recognition, pp. 1701–1709 (2016)
20. Ledig, C., et al.: Photo-realistic single image super-resolution using a generative adversarial network. arXiv preprint (2016)
21. Liu, M.Y., Breuel, T., Kautz, J.: Unsupervised image-to-image translation networks. In: Advances in Neural Information Processing Systems, pp. 700–708 (2017)
22. Liu, M.Y., Tuzel, O.: Coupled generative adversarial networks. In: Advances in Neural Information Processing Systems, pp. 469–477 (2016)
23. Liu, Z., Luo, P., Wang, X., Tang, X.: Deep learning face attributes in the wild. In: Proceedings of International Conference on Computer Vision (ICCV) (2015)
24. Ma, Z., Liao, R., Tao, X., Xu, L., Jia, J., Wu, E.: Handling motion blur in multi-frame super-resolution. In: Proceedings of the IEEE Computer Vision and Pattern Recognition (CVPR), pp. 5224–5232 (2015)

25. Michaeli, T., Irani, M.: Blind deblurring using internal patch recurrence. In: Fleet, D., Pajdla, T., Schiele, B., Tuytelaars, T. (eds.) ECCV 2014. LNCS, vol. 8691, pp. 783–798. Springer, Cham (2014). https://doi.org/10.1007/978-3-319-10578-9_51

26. Mirza, M., Osindero, S.: Conditional generative adversarial nets. arXiv preprint arXiv:1411.1784 (2014)

27. Nah, S., Kim, T.H., Lee, K.M.: Deep multi-scale convolutional neural network for dynamic scene deblurring. In: The IEEE Conference on Computer Vision and Pattern Recognition (CVPR), July 2017

28. Nimisha, T., Singh, A.K., Rajagopalan, A.: Blur-invariant deep learning for blind-deblurring. In: Proceedings of the IEEE International Conference on Computer Vision (ICCV) (2017)

29. Pan, J., Hu, Z., Su, Z., Yang, M.-H.: Deblurring face images with exemplars. In: Fleet, D., Pajdla, T., Schiele, B., Tuytelaars, T. (eds.) ECCV 2014. LNCS, vol. 8695, pp. 47–62. Springer, Cham (2014). https://doi.org/10.1007/978-3-319-10584-0_4

30. Pan, J., Hu, Z., Su, Z., Yang, M.H.: Deblurring text images via L0-regularized intensity and gradient prior. In: IEEE Conference on Computer Vision and Pattern Recognition (CVPR), pp. 2901–2908 (2014)

31. Pan, J., Sun, D., Pfister, H., Yang, M.H.: Blind image deblurring using dark channel prior. In: Proceedings of the IEEE Conference on Computer Vision and Pattern Recognition, pp. 1628–1636 (2016)

32. Punnappurath, A., Rajagopalan, A.N., Taheri, S., Chellappa, R., Seetharaman, G.: Face recognition across non-uniform motion blur, illumination, and pose. IEEE Trans. Image Process. **24**(7), 2067–2082 (2015)

33. Rengarajan, V., Balaji, Y., Rajagopalan, A.: Unrolling the shutter: CNN to correct motion distortions. In: Proceedings of the IEEE Conference on Computer Vision and Pattern Recognition, pp. 2291–2299 (2017)

34. Salimans, T., Goodfellow, I., Zaremba, W., Cheung, V., Radford, A., Chen, X.: Improved techniques for training gans. In: Advances in Neural Information Processing Systems, pp. 2234–2242 (2016)

35. Su, S., Delbracio, M., Wang, J., Sapiro, G., Heidrich, W., Wang, O.: Deep video deblurring for hand-held cameras. In: Proceedings of the IEEE Conference on Computer Vision and Pattern Recognition, pp. 1279–1288 (2017)

36. Teodoro, A.M., Bioucas-Dias, J.M., Figueiredo, M.A.: Image restoration with locally selected class-adapted models. In: IEEE International Workshop on Machine Learning for Signal Processing (MLSP), pp. 1–6 (2016)

37. Ulyanov, D., Vedaldi, A., Lempitsky, V.S.: Deep image prior. CoRR abs/1711.10925 (2017). http://arxiv.org/abs/1711.10925

38. Xie, J., Xu, L., Chen, E.: Image denoising and inpainting with deep neural networks. In: Advances in Neural Information Processing Systems, pp. 341–349 (2012)

39. Xu, L., Zheng, S., Jia, J.: Unnatural L0 sparse representation for natural image deblurring. In: 2013 IEEE Conference on Computer Vision and Pattern Recognition (CVPR), pp. 1107–1114. IEEE (2013)

40. Xu, X., Sun, D., Pan, J., Zhang, Y., Pfister, H., Yang, M.H.: Learning to super-resolve blurry face and text images. In: Proceedings of the IEEE Conference on Computer Vision and Pattern Recognition, pp. 251–260 (2017)

41. Yi, Z., Zhang, H., Tan, P., Gong, M.: Dualgan: Unsupervised dual learning for image-to-image translation. arXiv preprint (2017)

42. Zhu, J.Y., Park, T., Isola, P., Efros, A.A.: Unpaired image-to-image translation using cycle-consistent adversarial networks. arXiv preprint arXiv:1703.10593 (2017)

The Unmanned Aerial Vehicle Benchmark: Object Detection and Tracking

Dawei Du[1], Yuankai Qi[2], Hongyang Yu[2], Yifan Yang[1],
Kaiwen Duan[1], Guorong Li[1(✉)], Weigang Zhang[3], Qingming Huang[1],
and Qi Tian[4,5]

[1] University of Chinese Academy of Sciences, Beijing, China
{dawei.du,yifan.yang,kaiwen.duan}@vipl.ict.ac.cn, liguorong@ucas.ac.cn,
qmhuang@ucas.ac.cn
[2] Harbin Institute of Technology, Harbin, China
qykshr@gmail.com, hyang.yu@hit.edu.cn
[3] Harbin Institute of Technology, Weihai, China
wgzhang@hit.edu.cn
[4] Huawei Noah's Ark Lab, Shenzhen, China
tian.qi1@huawei.com
[5] University of Texas at San Antonio, San Antonio, USA
qi.tian@utsa.edu

Abstract. With the advantage of high mobility, Unmanned Aerial Vehicles (UAVs) are used to fuel numerous important applications in computer vision, delivering more efficiency and convenience than surveillance cameras with fixed camera angle, scale and view. However, very limited UAV datasets are proposed, and they focus only on a specific task such as visual tracking or object detection in relatively constrained scenarios. Consequently, it is of great importance to develop an unconstrained UAV benchmark to boost related researches. In this paper, we construct a new UAV benchmark focusing on complex scenarios with new level challenges. Selected from 10 hours raw videos, about 80,000 representative frames are fully annotated with bounding boxes as well as up to 14 kinds of attributes (e.g., weather condition, flying altitude, camera view, vehicle category, and occlusion) for three fundamental computer vision tasks: object detection, single object tracking, and multiple object tracking. Then, a detailed quantitative study is performed using most recent state-of-the-art algorithms for each task. Experimental results show that the current state-of-the-art methods perform relative worse on our dataset, due to the new challenges appeared in UAV based real scenes, e.g., high density, small object, and camera motion. To our knowledge, our work is the first time to explore such issues in unconstrained scenes comprehensively. The dataset and all the experimental results are available in https://sites.google.com/site/daviddo0323/.

Keywords: UAV · Object detection · Single object tracking
Multiple object tracking

© Springer Nature Switzerland AG 2018
V. Ferrari et al. (Eds.): ECCV 2018, LNCS 11214, pp. 375–391, 2018.
https://doi.org/10.1007/978-3-030-01249-6_23

1 Introduction

With the rapid development of artificial intelligence, higher request to efficient and effective intelligent vision systems is putting forward. To tackle with higher semantic tasks in computer vision, such as object recognition, behaviour analysis and motion analysis, researchers have developed numerous fundamental detection and tracking algorithms for the past decades.

To evaluate these algorithms fairly, the community has developed plenty of datasets including detection datasets (*e.g.*, Caltech [14] and DETRAC [46]) and tracking datasets (*e.g.*, KITTI-T [19] and VOT2016 [15]). The common shortcoming of these datasets is that videos are captured by fixed or moving car based cameras, which is limited in viewing angles in surveillance scene.

Benefiting from flourishing global drone industry, Unmanned Aerial Vehicle (UAV) has been applied in many areas such as security and surveillance, search and rescue, and sports analysis. Different from traditional surveillance cameras, UAV with moving camera has several advantages inherently, such as easy to deploy, high mobility, large view scope, and uniform scale. Thus it brings new challenges to existing detection and tracking technologies, such as:

- **High Density.** Since UAV cameras are flexible to capture videos at wider view angle than fixed cameras, leading to large object number.
- **Small Object.** Objects are usually small or tiny due to high altitude of UAV views, resulting in difficulties to detect and track them.
- **Camera Motion.** Objects move very fast or rotate drastically due to the high-speed flying or camera rotation of UAVs.
- **Realtime Issues.** The algorithms should consider realtime issues and maintain high accuracy on embedded UAV platforms for practical application.

To study these problems, limited UAV datasets are collected such as Campus [39] and CARPK [22]. However, they only focus on a specific task such as visual tracking or detection in constrained scenes, for instance, campus or parking lots. The community needs a more comprehensive UAV benchmark in unconstrained scenarios for further boosting research on related tasks.

To this end, we construct a large scale challenging UAV Detection and Tracking (UAVDT) benchmark (*i.e.*, about $80,000$ representative frames from 10 hours raw videos) for 3 important fundamental tasks, *i.e.*, object DETection (DET), Single Object Tracking (SOT) and Multiple Object Tracking (MOT). Our dataset is captured by UAVs[1] in various complex scenarios. Since the current majority of datasets focus on pedestrians, as a supplement, the objects of interest in our benchmark are *vehicles*. Moreover, these frames are manually annotated with bounding boxes and some useful attributes, *e.g.*, vehicle category and occlusion. This paper makes the following contributions: (1) We collect a fully annotated dataset for 3 fundamental tasks applied in UAV surveillance. (2) We provide an extensive evaluation of the most recently state-of-the-art algorithms in various attributes for each task.

---

[1] We use DJI Inspire 2 to collect videos, and more information about the UAV platform can be found in http://www.dji.com/inspire-2.

2   UAVDTBenchmark

The UAVDTbenchmark consists of 100 video sequences, which are selected from over 10 hours of videos taken with an UAV platform at a number of locations in urban areas, representing various common scenes including squares, arterial streets, toll stations, highways, crossings and T-junctions. The average, min, max length of a sequence are 778.69, 83 and 2, 970 respectively. The videos are recorded at 30 frames per seconds (fps), with the resolution of 1080×540 pixels.

Table 1. Summary of existing datasets ($1k = 10^3$). D=DET, M=MOT, S=SOT.

Datasets	Attributes									
	UAV	Frames	Boxes	Tasks	Vehicles	Weather	Occlusion	Altitude	View	Year
MIT-Car [34]		1.1k	1.1k	D	✓					2000
Caltech [14]		132k	347k	D			✓			2012
KAIST [23]		95k	86k	D		✓	✓			2015
KITTI-D [19]		15k	80.3k	D	✓		✓			2014
MOT17Det [1]		11.2k	392.8k	D			✓			2017
CARPK [22]	✓	1.5k	90k	D	✓					2017
Okutama [3]	✓	77.4k	422.1k	D						2017
PETS2009 [18]		1.5k	18.5k	D,M		✓				2009
KITTI-T [19]		19k	> 47.3k	M	✓		✓			2014
MOT15 [26]		11.3k	> 101k	M		✓				2015
DukeMTMC [38]		2852.2k	4077.1k	M			✓			2016
DETRAC [46]		140k	1210k	D,M	✓	✓	✓			2016
Campus [39]	✓	929.5k	19.5k	M	✓					2016
MOT16 [29]		11.2k	> 292k	M		✓	✓			2016
MOT17 [1]		11.2k	392.8k	M		✓	✓			2017
ALOV300 [40]		151.6k	151.6k	S						2015
OTB100 [49]		59k	59k	S						2015
VOT2016 [15]		21.5k	21.5k	S			✓			2016
UAV123 [31]	✓	110k	110k	S	✓					2016
UAVDT	✓	80k	841.5k	D,M,S	✓	✓	✓	✓	✓	2018

2.1   Data Annotation

For annotation, we ask over 10 domain experts to label our dataset using the *vatic* tool[2] for two months. With several rounds of double-check, the annotation errors are reduced as much as possible. Specifically, about 80, 000 frames in the UAVDTbenchmark dataset are annotated over 2, 700 vehicles with 0.84 million bounding boxes. According to PASCAL VOC [16], the regions that cover too small vehicles are ignored in each frame due to low resolution. Figure 1 shows some sample frames with annotated attributes in the dataset.

Based on different shooting conditions of UAVs, we first define 3 attributes for MOT task:

---

[2] http://carlvondrick.com/vatic/.

Fig. 1. Examples of annotated frames in the UAVDTbenchmark. The three rows indicate the DET, MOT and SOT task, respectively. The shooting conditions of UAVs are presented in the lower right corner. The pink areas are ignored regions in the dataset. Different bounding box colors denote different classes of vehicles. For clarity, we only display some attributes. (Color figure online)

- **Weather Condition** indicates illumination when capturing videos, which affects appearance representation of objects. It includes *daylight*, *night* and *fog*. Specifically, videos shot in daylight introduce interference of shadows. Night scene, bearing dim street lamp light, offers scarcely any texture information. In the meantime, frames captured at *fog* lack sharp details so that contours of objects vanish in the background.
- **Flying Altitude** is the flying height of UAVs, affecting the scale variation of objects. Three levels are annotated, *i.e.*, *low-alt*, *medium-alt* and *high-alt*. When shooting in low-altitude ($10m \sim 30m$), more details of objects are captured. Meanwhile the object may occupy larger area, *e.g.*, 22.6% pixels of a frame in an extreme situation. When videos are collected in medium-altitude ($30m \sim 70m$), more view angles are presented. While in much higher altitude ($> 70m$), plentiful vehicles are of less clarity. For example, most tiny objects just contain 0.005% pixels of a frame, yet object numbers can be more than a hundred.
- **Camera View** consists of 3 object views. Specifically, *front-view*, *side-view* and *bird-view* mean the camera shooting along with the road, on the side, and on the top of objects, respectively. Note that the first two views may coexist in one sequence.

To evaluate DET algorithms thoroughly, we also label another 3 attributes including *vehicle category*, *vehicle occlusion* and *out-of-view*. vehicle category consists of *car*, *truck* and *bus*. vehicle occlusion is the fraction of bounding box occlusion, *i.e.*, *no-occ* (0%), *small-occ* ($1\% \sim 30\%$), *medium-occ* ($30\% \sim 70\%$) and *large-occ* ($70\% \sim 100\%$). Out-of-view indicates the degree of vehicle parts outside frame, divided into *no-out* (0%), *small-out* ($1\% \sim 30\%$) and *medium-out* ($30\% \sim 50\%$). The objects are discarded when the out-of-view ratio is larger than 50%. The distribution of the above attributes is shown in Fig. 2. Within an image, objects are defined as "occluded" by other objects or the obstacles in the scenes, *e.g.*, under the bridge; while objects are regarded as "out-of-view" when they are out of the image or in the ignored regions.

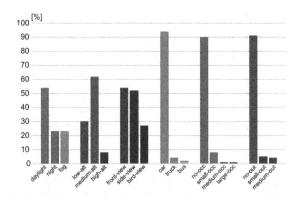

Fig. 2. The distribution of attributes of both DET and MOT tasks in UAVDT.

For SOT task, 8 attributes are annotated for each sequence, *i.e.*, Background Clutter (**BC**), Camera Rotation (**CR**), Object Rotation (**OR**), Small Object (**SO**), Illumination Variation (**IV**), Object Blur (**OB**), Scale Variation (**SV**) and Large Occlusion (**LO**). The distribution of SOT attributes is presented in Table 2. Specifically, 74% videos contain at least 4 visual challenges, and among them 51% have 5 challenges. Meanwhile, 27% of frames contribute to long-term tracking videos. As a consequence, a candidate SOT method can be estimated in various cruel environment, most likely at the same frame, guaranteeing the objectivity and discrimination of the proposed dataset.

Notably, our benchmark is divided into training and testing sets, with 30 and 70 sequences, respectively. The testing set consists of 20 sequences for both DET and MOT tasks, and 50 for SOT task. Besides, training videos are taken at different locations from the testing videos, but share similar scenes and attributes. This setting reduces the overfitting probability to particular scenario.

2.2 Comparison with Existing UAV Datasets

Although new challenges are brought to computer vision by UAVs, limited datasets [22,31,39] have been published to accelerate the improvement and evaluation of various vision tasks. By exploring the flexibility of UAVs flare maneuver in both altitude and plane domain, Matthias *et al.* [31] propose a low-altitude UAV tracking dataset to evaluate ability of SOT methods of tackling with relatively fierce camera movement, scale change and illumination variation, yet it still lacks varieties in weather conditions and camera motions, and its scenes are much less clustered than real circumstances. In [39], several video fragments

Table 2. Distribution of SOT attributes, showing the number of coincident attributes across all videos. The diagonal line denotes the number of sequences with only one attribute.

	BC	CR	OR	SO	IV	OB	SV	LO
BC	**29**	18	20	12	17	9	16	18
CR	18	**30**	21	14	17	12	18	12
OR	20	21	**32**	12	17	13	23	14
SO	12	14	12	**23**	13	13	8	6
IV	17	17	17	13	**28**	18	12	7
OB	9	12	13	13	18	**23**	11	2
SV	16	18	23	8	12	11	**29**	14
LO	18	12	14	6	7	2	14	**20**

are collected to analyze the behaviors of pedestrians in top-view scenes of campus with fixed UAV cameras for the MOT task. Although ideal visual angles benefit trackers to obtain stable trajectories by narrowing down challenges they have to meet, it also risks diversity when evaluating MOT methods. Hsieh *et al.* [22] present a dataset aiming at counting vehicles in parking lots. However, our dataset captures videos in unconstrained areas, resulting in more generalization.

The detailed comparisons of the proposed dataset with other works are summarized in Table 1. Although our dataset is not the largest one compared to existing datasets, it can represent the characteristics of UAV videos more effectively:

- Our dataset provides a higher object density 10.52^3, compared to related works (*e.g.*, UAV123 [31] 1.00, Campus [39] 0.02, DETRAC [46] 8.64 and KITTI [19] 5.35). CARPK [22] is an image based dataset to detect parking vehicles, which is not suitable for visual tracking.
- Compared to related works [22,31,39] just focusing on specified scene, our dataset is collected from various scenarios in different weather conditions, flying altitudes, and camera views, *etc.*

3   Evaluation and Analysis

We run a representative set of state-of-the-art algorithms for each task. Codes for these methods are either available online or from the authors. All the algorithms are trained on the training set and evaluated on the testing set. Interestingly, some high ranking algorithms in other datasets may fail in complex scenarios.

---

[3] The object density indicates the mean number of objects in each frame.

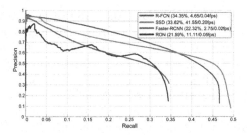

Fig. 3. Precision-Recall plot on the testing set of the UAVDT-DET dataset. The legend presents the AP score and the GPU/CPU speed of each DET method respectively.

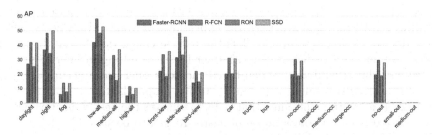

Fig. 4. Quantitative comparison results of DET methods in each attribute.

3.1 Object Detection

The current top deep based object detection frameworks is divided into two main categories: region-based (*e.g.*, Faster-RCNN [37] and R-FCN [8]) and region-free (*e.g.*, SSD [27] and RON [25]). Therefore, we evaluate the above mentioned 4 detectors in the UAVDTdataset.

Metrics. We follow the strategy in the PASCAL VOC challenge [16] to compute the Average Precision (AP) score in the Precision-Recall plot to rank the performance of DET methods. As performed in KITTI-D [19], the hit/miss threshold of the overlap between a pair of detected and groundtruth bounding boxes is set to 0.7.

Implementation Details. We train all DET methods on a machine with CPU i9 7900x and 64G memory, as well as a Nvidia GTX 1080 Ti GPU. Faster-RCNN and R-FCN are fine-tuned on the VGG-16 network and Resnet-50, respectively. We use 0.001 as the learning rate for the first $60k$ iterations and 0.0001 for the next $20k$ iterations. For region-free methods, the batch size is 5 for 512×512 model according to the GPU capacity. For SSD, we use 0.005 as the learning rate for $120k$ iterations. For RON, we use the 0.001 as the learning rate for the first $90k$ iterations, then we decay it to 0.0001 and continue training for the next $30k$ iterations. For all the algorithms, we use a momentum of 0.9 and a weight decay of 0.0005.

Overall Evaluation. Figure 3 shows the quantitative comparisons of DET methods, which shows no promising accuracy. For example, R-FCN obtains 70.06% AP score even in the hard set of KITTI-D[4], but only 34.35% in our dataset. This maybe our dataset contains a large number of small objects due to the shooting perspective, which is a difficult challenge in object detection. Another reason is that higher altitude brings more cluttered background.

To tackle with this problem, SSD combines multi-scale feature maps to handle objects of various sizes. Yet their feature maps are usually extracted from former layers, which lacks enough semantic meanings for small objects. Improved from SSD, RON fuses more semantic information from latter layers using a reverse connection, and performs well on other datasets such as PASCAL VOC [16]. Nevertheless, RON is inferior to SSD on our dataset. It maybe because the later layers are so abstract that represent the appearance of small objects not so effectively due to the low resolution. Thus the reverse connection fusing the latter layers may interfere with features in former layers, resulting in inferior performance. On the other hand, region-based methods offer more accurate initial locations for robust results by generating region proposals from region proposal networks. It is worth mentioning that R-FCN achieves the best result by making the unshared per-ROI computation of Faster-RCNN to be sharable [25].

Attribute-Based Evaluation. To further explore the effectiveness of DET methods on different situations, we also evaluate them on different attributes in Fig. 4. For the first 3 attributes, DET methods perform better on the sequences where objects have more details *e.g.*, *low-alt* and *side-view*. While the object number is bigger and the background is more cluttered in *daylight* than *night*, leading to worse performance in *daylight*. For the remaining attributes, the performance drops very dramatically when detecting large vehicles, as well as handling with occlusion and out-of-view. The results can be attributed to two factors. Firstly, very limited training samples of large vehicles make it hard to train the detector to recognize them. As shown in Fig. 2, the number of *truck* and *bus* is only less than 10% of the whole dataset. Besides, it is even harder to detect small objects with other interference. Much work need to be done for small object detection under occlusions or out-of-view.

Run-time Performance. Although region based methods obtain relative good performance, their running speeds (*i.e.*, < 5fps) are too slow for practical applications especially with constrained computing resources. On the contrary, region free methods save the time of region proposal generation, and proceed at almost realtime speed.

3.2 Multiple Object Tracking

MOT methods are generally grouped into online or batch based. Therefore, we evaluate 8 recent algorithms including online methods (CMOT [2], MDP [50],

---

[4] The detection result is copied from http://www.cvlibs.net/datasets/kitti/eval_object.php?obj_benchmark=2d.

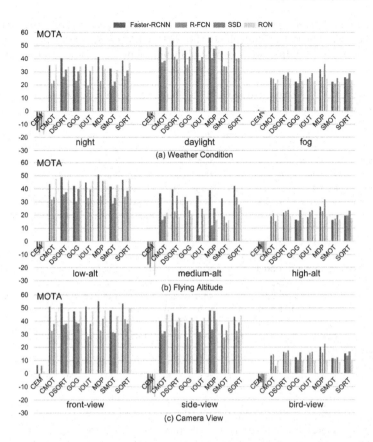

Fig. 5. Quantitative comparison results of MOT methods in each attribute.

SORT [6] and DSORT [48]) and batch based methods (GOG [35], CEM [30], SMOT [13] and IOUT [7]).

Metrics. We use multiple metrics to evaluate the MOT performance. These include identification precision (IDP) [38], identification recall (IDR), and the corresponding F1 score IDF1 (the ratio of correctly identified detections over the average number of ground-truth and computed detections.), Multiple Object Tracking Accuracy (MOTA) [4], Multiple Object Tracking Precision (MOTP) [4], Mostly Track targets (MT, percentage of groundtruth trajectories that are covered by a track hypothesis for at least 80%), Mostly Lost targets (ML, percentage of groundtruth objects whose trajectories are covered by the tracking output less than 20%), the total number of False Positives (FP), the total number of False Negatives (FN), the total number of ID Switches (IDS), and the total number of times a trajectory is Fragmented (FM).

Implementation Details. Since the above MOT algorithms are based on tracking-by-detection framework, all the 4 detection inputs are provided for

Table 3. Quantitative comparison results of MOT methods in the testing set of the UAVDTdataset. The last column shows the GPU/CPU speed. The best performer and realtime methods (> 30fps) are highlighted in bold font. "−" indicates the data is not available.

MOT methods	IDF	IDP	IDR	MOTA	MOTP	MT[%]	ML[%]	FP	FN	IDS	FM	Speed [fps]
Detection Input: Faster-RCNN [37]												
CEM [30]	10.2	19.4	7.0	−7.3	69.6	7.3	68.6	72,378	290,962	2,488	**4,248**	-/14.55
CMOT [2]	52.0	63.9	43.8	36.4	**74.5**	36.5	26.1	53,920	160,963	1,777	5,709	-/2.83
DSORT [48]	58.2	72.2	48.8	40.7	73.2	41.7	23.7	44,868	155,290	2,061	6,432	15.01/2.98
GOG [35]	0.4	0.5	0.3	34.4	72.2	35.5	25.3	41,126	168,194	14,301	12,516	-/436.52
IOUT [7]	23.7	30.3	19.5	36.6	72.1	37.4	25.0	42,245	163,881	9,938	10,463	-/**1438.34**
MDP [50]	**61.5**	**74.5**	**52.3**	**43.0**	73.5	**45.3**	**22.7**	46,151	**147,735**	541	4,299	-/0.68
SMOT [13]	45.0	55.7	37.8	33.9	72.2	36.7	25.7	57,112	166,528	1,752	9,577	-/115.27
SORT [6]	43.7	58.9	34.8	39.0	74.3	33.9	28.0	**33,037**	172,628	2,350	5,787	-/245.79
Detection Input: R-FCN [8]												
CEM [30]	10.3	18.4	7.2	−9.6	70.4	6.0	67.8	81,617	289,683	2,201	3,789	-/9.82
CMOT [2]	50.8	59.4	44.3	27.1	**78.5**	35.9	27.9	80,592	167,043	919	2,788	-/2.65
DSORT [48]	55.5	**67.3**	47.2	**30.9**	77.0	36.6	27.4	66,839	168,409	424	4,746	9.22/1.95
GOG [35]	0.3	0.4	0.3	28.5	77.1	34.4	28.6	60,511	176,256	6,935	6,823	-/433.94
IOUT [7]	44.0	47.5	40.9	26.9	75.9	**44.3**	**22.9**	98,789	**145,617**	4,903	6,129	-/**863.53**
MDP [50]	**55.8**	63.9	**49.5**	28.9	76.7	40.9	25.9	82,540	159,452	411	**2,705**	-/0.67
SMOT [13]	44.0	53.5	37.3	24.5	77.2	33.7	29.2	76,544	179,609	1,370	5,142	-/64.68
SORT [6]	42.6	58.7	33.5	30.2	**78.5**	29.5	31.9	**44,612**	190,999	2,248	4,378	-/209.31
Detection Input: SSD [27]												
CEM [30]	10.1	21.1	6.6	−6.8	70.4	6.6	74.4	64,373	298,090	1,530	**2,835**	-/11.62
CMOT [2]	49.4	53.4	46.0	27.2	75.1	38.3	23.5	98,915	146,418	2,920	6,914	-/0.90
DSORT [48]	51.4	**65.7**	42.2	33.6	**76.7**	27.9	26.9	**51,549**	173,639	**1,143**	8,655	15.00/3.46
GOG [35]	0.3	0.4	0.3	33.6	76.4	36.0	22.4	70,080	148,369	7,964	10,023	-/239.60
IOUT [7]	29.4	34.5	25.6	33.5	76.6	34.3	23.4	65,549	154,042	6,993	8,793	-/**976.47**
MDP [50]	**58.8**	63.2	**55.0**	**39.8**	76.5	**47.3**	**19.5**	79,760	**124,206**	1,310	4,539	-/0.13
SMOT [13]	41.9	45.9	38.6	27.2	76.5	34.9	22.9	95,737	149,777	2,738	9,605	-/11.59
SORT [6]	37.1	45.8	31.1	33.2	**76.7**	27.3	25.4	57,440	166,493	3,918	7,898	-/153.70
Detection Input: RON [25]												
CEM [30]	10.1	18.8	6.9	−9.7	68.8	6.9	72.6	78,265	293,576	2,086	**3,526**	-/9.98
CMOT [2]	57.5	65.7	51.1	36.9	**74.7**	**46.5**	**24.6**	69,109	**144,760**	1,111	3,656	-/0.94
DSORT [48]	58.3	67.9	51.2	35.8	71.5	43.4	25.7	67,090	151,007	698	4,311	17.45/4.02
GOG [35]	0.3	0.3	0.2	35.7	72.0	43.9	26.2	62,929	153,336	3,104	5,130	-/287.97
IOUT [7]	50.1	59.1	43.4	35.6	72.0	43.9	26.2	63,086	153,348	2,991	5,103	-/**1383.33**
MDP [50]	**59.9**	**69.0**	**52.9**	35.3	71.7	45.0	25.5	70,186	149,980	414	3,640	-/0.12
SMOT [13]	52.6	60.8	46.3	32.8	72.0	43.4	27.1	73,226	154,696	1,157	4,643	-/29.37
SORT [6]	54.6	66.9	46.1	**37.2**	72.2	40.8	28.0	**53,435**	159,347	1,369	3,661	-/230.55

MOT task. We run them on test set of the UAVDTdataset on the machine with CPU i7 6700 and 32G memory, as well as a NVIDIA Titan X GPU.

Overall Evaluation. As shown in Table 3, MDP with Faster-RCNN has the best 43.0 MOTA score and 61.5 IDF score among all the combinations. Besides, the MOTA score of SORT in our dataset is much lower than other datasets with Faster-RCNN, *e.g.*, 59.8 ± 10.3 in MOT16 [29]. As object density is large in UAV videos, the FP and FN values on our dataset are also much larger than other datasets for the same algorithm. Meanwhile, IDS and FM appear more frequently. It means the proposed dataset is more challenging than existing ones.

Moreover, the algorithms using only position information (*e.g.*, IOUT, SORT) could keep fewer tracklets combining with higher IDS and FM because of absence of appearance information. GOG has the worst IDF even though the MOTA is well because of the too much IDS and FM. DSORT performs well on IDS among these methods, which means deep feature has an advantage in the aspect of representing appearance of the same target. MDP mostly has the best IDS and FM value because of their individual-wised tracker model. So the trajectories are more complete than others with the higher IDF. Meanwhile, FP values will increase by associating more objects in complex scenes.

Attribute-Based Evaluation. Figure 5 shows the performances of MOT methods on different attributes. Most methods perform better in *daylight* than *night* or *fog* (see Fig. 5(a)). It is fair and reasonable that objects in *daylight* provide clearer appearance clues for tracking. In other illumination conditions, object appearance is confusing so the algorithms considering more motion clues achieve better performance, *e.g.*, SORT, SMOT and GOG. Notably, on the sequences with *night*, the performances of methods are much worse even the provided detections in *night* own a good AP score. This is because objects are hard to track with confusing environment in *night*. In Fig. 5(b), the performance of most MOT methods increases with the decline of height. When UAVs capture videos in a lower height, fewer objects are captured in that view to facilitate object association. In terms of Camera Views as shown in Fig. 5(c), vehicles in *front-view* and *side-view* offer more details to distinguish different targets compared with *bird-view*, leading to better accuracy.

Besides, different detection input can guide MOT methods to focus on different scenes. Specifically, the performance with Faster-RCNN is better on sequences where object details are clearer (*e.g.*, *daylight*, *low-alt* and *side-view*); while R-FCN detection offers more stable inputs for each method when sequences have other challenging attributes, such as *fog* and *high-alt*. SSD and RON offer more accurate detection candidates for tracking such that the performances of MOT methods with these detections are balanced in each attribute.

Run-time Performance. Given different detection inputs, the speed of each method varies with the number of object detection candidates. However, IOUT and SORT using only position information generally proceed at ultra-real-time speed, while DSORT and CMOT using appearance information proceed much slower. As the object number is huge in our dataset, the speed of the method processing each object respectively (*e.g.*, MDP) dramatically declines.

3.3   Single Object Tracking

The SOT field is dominated by correlation filter and deep learning based approaches [15]. We evaluate 18 recent such trackers on our dataset. These trackers can be generally categorized into 3 classes based on their learning strategy

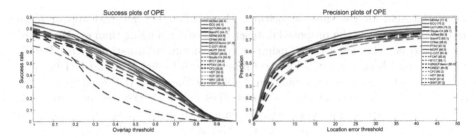

Fig. 6. The precision and success plots on the UAVDT-SOT benchmark using One-pass Evaluation [49].

Table 4. Quantitative comparison results (*i.e.*, overlap score/precision score) of SOT methods in each attribute. The last column shows the GPU/CPU speed. The best performer and realtime methods (> 30fps) are highlighted in bold font. "−" indicates the data is not available.

SOT methods	BC	CR	OR	SO	IV	OB	SV	LO	Speed [fps]
MDNet [33]	**39.7/63.6**	**43.0/69.6**	**42.7/66.8**	44.4/78.4	**48.5**/76.4	**47.0**/72.4	**46.2/68.5**	38.1/54.7	0.89/0.28
ECO [9]	38.9/61.1	42.2/64.4	39.5/62.7	**46.1**/79.1	47.3/76.9	43.7/71.0	43.1/63.2	36.0/50.8	16.95/3.90
GOTURN [20]	38.9/61.1	42.2/64.4	39.5/62.7	**46.1**/79.1	47.3/76.9	43.7/71.0	43.7/63.2	36.0/50.8	**65.29**/11.70
SiamFC [5]	38.6/57.8	40.9/61.6	38.4/60.0	43.9/73.2	47.4/74.2	45.3/**73.8**	42.4/60.4	35.9/47.9	38.20/5.50
ADNet [52]	37.0/60.4	39.9/64.8	36.8/60.1	43.2/77.9	45.8/73.7	42.8/68.9	40.9/61.2	35.8/49.2	5.78/2.42
CFNet [43]	36.0/56.7	39.7/64.3	36.9/59.9	43.5/77.5	45.1/72.7	43.5/71.7	40.9/61.1	33.3/44.7	8.94/6.25
SRDCF [10]	35.3/58.2	39.0/64.2	36.5/60.0	42.2/76.4	45.1/74.7	41.7/70.6	40.2/59.6	32.7/46.0	−/14.25
SRDCFdecon [11]	36.0/57.4	39.0/61.0	36.6/57.8	43.1/73.8	45.5/72.3	42.9/69.5	38.0/54.9	31.5/42.5	−/7.26
C-COT [12]	34.0/55.7	39.0/62.3	34.1/56.1	44.2/79.2	41.6/72.0	37.2/66.2	37.9/55.9	33.5/46.0	0.87/0.79
MCPF [53]	31.0/51.2	36.3/59.2	33.0/55.3	39.7/74.5	42.2/73.1	42.0/73.0	35.9/55.1	30.1/42.5	1.84/0.89
CREST [41]	33.6/56.2	38.7/62.1	35.4/55.8	38.3/74.2	40.5/69.0	37.7/65.6	36.5/56.7	35.1/49.7	2.83/0.36
Staple-CA [32]	32.9/59.2	35.2/65.8	34.6/62.0	38.0/**79.6**	43.1/**77.2**	40.6/71.3	36.7/62.3	32.5/49.6	−/**42.53**
STCT [45]	33.3/56.0	36.0/61.3	34.3/57.5	38.3/71.0	40.8/69.9	37.0/63.3	37.3/59.9	31.7/46.6	1.76/0.09
PTAV [17]	31.2/57.2	35.2/63.9	30.9/56.4	38.0/79.1	38.1/69.6	36.7/66.2	33.3/56.5	32.9/50.3	12.77/0.10
CF2 [28]	29.2/48.6	34.1/56.9	29.7/48.2	35.6/69.5	38.7/67.9	35.8/65.1	29.0/45.3	28.3/38.1	8.07/1.99
HDT [36]	25.1/50.1	27.3/56.2	24.8/48.7	29.8/72.6	31.3/68.6	30.3/65.4	25.0/45.2	25.4/37.6	5.25/1.72
KCF [21]	23.5/45.8	26.7/53.4	24.4/45.4	25.1/58.1	31.1/65.7	29.7/65.2	25.4/49.0	22.8/34.4	−/39.26
SINT [42]	38.9/45.8	26.7/53.4	24.4/45.4	25.1/58.1	31.1/65.7	29.7/65.2	25.4/49.0	22.8/34.4	37.60/−
FCNT [44]	20.6/54.8	21.8/60.2	23.6/54.9	21.9/71.9	25.5/72.1	24.2/70.5	24.6/57.5	22.3/47.2	3.09/−

and utilized features: I) correlation filter (CF) trackers with hand crafted features (KCF [21], Staple-CA [32], and SRDCFdecon [11]); II) CF trackers with deep features (ECO [9], C-COT [12], HDT [36], CF2 [28], CFNet [43], and PTAV [17]); III) Deep trackers (MDNet [33], SiamFC [5], FCNT [44], SINT [42], MCPF [53], GOTURN [20], ADNet [52], CREST [41], and STCT [45]).

Metrics. Following the popular visual tracking benchmark [49], we adopt the success plot and precision plot to evaluate the tracking performance. The success plot shows the percentage of bounding boxes whose intersection over union with their corresponding groundtruth bounding boxes are larger than a given threshold. The trackers in success plot are ranked according to their *success score*, which is defined as the area under the curve (AUC). The precision plot presents the percentage of bounding boxes whose center points are within a given distance (0 ∼ 50 pixels) to the ground truth. Trackers in precision plot are ranked according to their *precision score*, which is the percentage of bounding boxes within a distance threshold of 20 pixels.

Implementation Details. All the trackers are run on the machine with CPU i7 4790k and 16G memory, as well as a NVIDIA Titan X GPU.

Overall Evaluation. The performance for each tracker is reported in Fig. 6. The figure shows that: (I) All the evaluated trackers perform not well on our dataset. Specifically, the state-of-the-art methods such as MDNet only achieves 46.4 success score and 72.5 precision score. Compared to the best results (*i.e.*, 69.4 success score and 92.8 precision score) on OTB100 [49], a significantly large performance gap is formulated. Such performance gap is also observed when compared to the results on UAV-123. For example, KCF achieves a success score of 33.1 on UAV-123 but only 29.0 on our dataset. These results indicate that our dataset poses new challenges for the visual tracking community and more efforts can be devoted to the real-world UAV tracking task. (II) Generally, deep trackers achieves more accurate results than CF trackers with deep features, and then CF trackers with hand-crafted features. Among the top 10 trackers, there are 6 deep trackers (MDNet, GOTURN, SianFC, ADNet, MCFP and CREST), 3 CF trackers with deep features (ECO, CFNet, and C-COT), and one CF tracker with hand-crafted features namely SRDCFdecon.

Attribute-Based Evaluation. As presented in Table 4, the deep tracker MDNet achieves best results on 7 out of 8 tracking attributes, which can be attributed to its multiple domain training and hard sample mining. CF trackers with deep features such as CF2 and HDT fall behind due to no scale adaptation. SINT [42] does not update its models during tracking, which results in a limited performance. Staple-CA performs well on the **SO** and **IV** attributes, as its improved model update strategy can reduce over-fitting to recent samples. Most of the evaluated methods act poorly on the **BC** and **LO** attributes, which may be caused by the decline of discriminative ability of appearance features extracted from cluttered or low resolution image regions.

Run-time Performance. From the last column of Table 4, We note that (I) The top 10 accurate trackers run far from real time even on a high-end CPU. For example, the fastest tracker among top 10 accurate only runs at 11.7fps and the most accurate MDNet runs at 0.28 fps. On the other hand, the realtime trackers on CPU (*e.g.*, Staple-CA and KCF), achieve success scores 39.5 and 29.0, which are intolerant for practical applications. (II) When a high-end GPU card is used, only 3 out of 18 trackers (GOTURN, SiamFC, SINT) can perform in real-time. But again their best success score is just 45.1, which is not accurate enough for real applications. Overall, more work need to be done to develop a faster and more precise tracker.

4   Discussion

Our benchmark, delivering from real-life demand, vividly samples real circumstances. Since algorithms generally perform poorly on it comparing with their plausible performances with other datasets, we think this benchmark dataset can reveal some promising research trends and benefit the community. Based on the above analysis, there are several research directions worth exploring:

Realtime Issues. Running speed is a crucial measurement in practical applications. Although the performance of deep learning methods surpass other methods by a large margin (especially in SOT task), the requirements of computational resources are very harsh in embedded UAV platforms. To achieve high efficiency, some recent methods [47,54] develop an approximate network by pruning, compressing, or low-bit representing. We expect the future works count more realtime constraints not just accuracy.

Scene Priors. Different methods perform the best in different scenarios. When considering scene priors in detection and tracking approaches, more robust performance is expected. For example, MDNet [33] trains a specific object-background classifier for each sequence to handle varies scenarios, which make it rank the first in most datasets. We think along with our dataset this magnificent design may inspired more methods to deal with mutable scenes.

Motion Clues. Since the appearance information is not always reliable, tracking methods would gain more robustness when considering motion clues. Many recently proposed algorithms make their efforts in this trend with the help of LSTM [24,51], but still have not met with expectations. Considering with the fierce motions of both object and background, our benchmark may fruit this research trend in the future.

Small Objects. In our dataset, 27.5% of objects consist of less than 400 pixels, almost 0.07% of a frame. It provides limited textures and contours for feature extraction which causes the accuracy loss of algorithms heavily based on appearance. Meanwhile, generally methods tend to save their time consuming by down-sampling images. It exacerbates the situations harshly, *e.g.*, DET methods mentioned above generally enjoy a 10% accuracy rise due to our parameters adjusting of authors provided codes and settings, mainly dealing with the size of anchors. However their performance still cannot met with expectation. We advise researchers should gain more promotions if they pay more attention on handling with small objects.

5   Conclusion

In this paper, we construct a new and challenging UAV benchmark for 3 foundational visual tasks including DET, MOT and SOT. The dataset consists of 100 videos (80*k* frames) captured with UAV platform from complex scenarios. All frames are annotated with manually labelled bounding boxes and 3 circumstances attributes, *i.e.*, weather condition, flying altitude, and camera view. SOT dataset has additional 8 attributes, *e.g.*, background clutter, camera rotation and small object. Moreover, an extensive evaluation of most recent and state-of-the-art methods is provided. We hope the proposed benchmark will contribute to the community by establishing a unified platform for evaluation of detection and tracking methods for real scenarios. In the future, we expect to extend the current dataset to include more sequences for other high-level tasks applied in computer vision, and richer annotations and more baselines for evaluation.

Acknowledgements. This work was supported in part by National Natural Science Foundation of China under Grant 61620106009, Grant 61332016, Grant U1636214, Grant 61650202, Grant 61772494 and Grant 61429201, in part by Key Research Program of Frontier Sciences, CAS: QYZDJ-SSW-SYS013, in part by Youth Innovation Promotion Association CAS, in part by ARO grants W911NF-15-1-0290 and Faculty Research Gift Awards by NEC Laboratories of America and Blippar.

References

1. Mot17 challenge. https://motchallenge.net/
2. Bae, S.H., Yoon, K.: Robust online multi-object tracking based on tracklet confidence and online discriminative appearance learning. In: CVPR, pp. 1218–1225 (2014)
3. Barekatain, M., et al.: Okutama-action: an aerial view video dataset for concurrent human action detection. In: CVPRW, pp. 2153–2160 (2017)
4. Bernardin, K., Stiefelhagen, R.: Evaluating multiple object tracking performance: The CLEAR MOT metrics. EURASIP J. Image Video Process. **2008**(2008)
5. Bertinetto, L., Valmadre, J., Henriques, J.F., Vedaldi, A., Torr, P.H.S.: Fully-convolutional siamese networks for object tracking. In: Hua, G., Jégou, H. (eds.) ECCV 2016. LNCS, vol. 9914, pp. 850–865. Springer, Cham (2016). https://doi.org/10.1007/978-3-319-48881-3_56
6. Bewley, A., Ge, Z., Ott, L., Ramos, F.T., Upcroft, B.: Simple online and realtime tracking. In: ICIP, pp. 3464–3468 (2016)
7. Bochinski, E., Eiselein, V., Sikora, T.: High-speed tracking-by-detection without using image information. In: AVSS, pp. 1–6 (2017)
8. Dai, J., Li, Y., He, K., Sun, J.: R-FCN: object detection via region-based fully convolutional networks. In: NIPS, pp. 379–387 (2016)
9. Danelljan, M., Bhat, G., Khan, F.S., Felsberg, M.: ECO: efficient convolution operators for tracking. CoRR abs/1611.09224 (2016)
10. Danelljan, M., Häger, G., Khan, F.S., Felsberg, M.: Learning spatially regularized correlation filters for visual tracking. In: ICCV, pp. 4310–4318 (2015)
11. Danelljan, M., Häger, G., Khan, F.S., Felsberg, M.: Adaptive decontamination of the training set: a unified formulation for discriminative visual tracking. In: CVPR, pp. 1430–1438 (2016)
12. Danelljan, M., Robinson, A., Shahbaz Khan, F., Felsberg, M.: Beyond correlation filters: learning continuous convolution operators for visual tracking. In: Leibe, B., Matas, J., Sebe, N., Welling, M. (eds.) ECCV 2016. LNCS, vol. 9909, pp. 472–488. Springer, Cham (2016). https://doi.org/10.1007/978-3-319-46454-1_29
13. Dicle, C., Camps, O.I., Sznaier, M.: The way they move: tracking multiple targets with similar appearance. In: ICCV, pp. 2304–2311 (2013)

14. Dollár, P., Wojek, C., Schiele, B., Perona, P.: Pedestrian detection: an evaluation of the state of the art. TPAMI **34**(4), 743–761 (2012)
15. Kristan, M., et al.: The Visual Object Tracking VOT2016 Challenge Results. In: Hua, G., Jégou, H. (eds.) ECCV 2016. LNCS, vol. 9914, pp. 777–823. Springer, Cham (2016). https://doi.org/10.1007/978-3-319-48881-3_54
16. Everingham, M., Eslami, S.M.A., Gool, L.J.V., Williams, C.K.I., Winn, J.M., Zisserman, A.: The pascal visual object classes challenge: a retrospective. IJCV **111**(1), 98–136 (2015)
17. Fan, H., Ling, H.: Parallel tracking and verifying: a framework for real-time and high accuracy visual tracking. In: ICCV (2017)
18. Ferryman, J., Shahrokni, A.: Pets 2009: dataset and challenge. In: AVSS, pp. 1–6 (2009)
19. Geiger, A., Lenz, P., Urtasun, R.: Are we ready for autonomous driving? the KITTI vision benchmark suite. In: CVPR, pp. 3354–3361 (2012)
20. Held, D., Thrun, S., Savarese, S.: Learning to track at 100 FPS with deep regression networks. In: Leibe, B., Matas, J., Sebe, N., Welling, M. (eds.) ECCV 2016. LNCS, vol. 9905, pp. 749–765. Springer, Cham (2016). https://doi.org/10.1007/978-3-319-46448-0_45
21. Henriques, J.F., Caseiro, R., Martins, P., Batista, J.: High-speed tracking with kernelized correlation filters. TPAMI **37**(3), 583–596 (2015)
22. Hsieh, M., Lin, Y., Hsu, W.H.: Drone-based object counting by spatially regularized regional proposal network. In: ICCV (2017)
23. Hwang, S., Park, J., Kim, N., Choi, Y., Kweon, I.S.: Multispectral pedestrian detection: Benchmark dataset and baseline. In: CVPR, pp. 1037–1045 (2015)
24. Kahou, S.E., Michalski, V., Memisevic, R., Pal, C.J., Vincent, P.: RATM: recurrent attentive tracking model. In: CVPRW, pp. 1613–1622 (2017)
25. Kong, T., Sun, F., Yao, A., Liu, H., Lu, M., Chen, Y.: RON: reverse connection with objectness prior networks for object detection. In: CVPR (2017)
26. Leal-Taixé, L., Milan, A., Reid, I.D., Roth, S., Schindler, K.: Motchallenge 2015: Towards a benchmark for multi-target tracking. CoRR abs/1504.01942 (2015)
27. Liu, W., et al.: SSD: single shot multibox detector. In: Leibe, B., Matas, J., Sebe, N., Welling, M. (eds.) ECCV 2016. LNCS, vol. 9905, pp. 21–37. Springer, Cham (2016). https://doi.org/10.1007/978-3-319-46448-0_2
28. Ma, C., Huang, J., Yang, X., Yang, M.: Hierarchical convolutional features for visual tracking. In: ICCV, pp. 3074–3082 (2015)
29. Milan, A., Leal-Taixé, L., Reid, I.D., Roth, S., Schindler, K.: Mot16: a benchmark for multi-object tracking. CoRR abs/1603.00831 (2016)
30. Milan, A., Roth, S., Schindler, K.: Continuous energy minimization for multitarget tracking. TPAMI **36**(1), 58–72 (2014)
31. Mueller, M., Smith, N., Ghanem, B.: A benchmark and simulator for UAV tracking. In: Leibe, B., Matas, J., Sebe, N., Welling, M. (eds.) ECCV 2016. LNCS, vol. 9905, pp. 445–461. Springer, Cham (2016). https://doi.org/10.1007/978-3-319-46448-0_27
32. Mueller, M., Smith, N., Ghanem, B.: Context-aware correlation filter tracking. In: CVPR (2017)
33. Nam, H., Han, B.: Learning multi-domain convolutional neural networks for visual tracking. In: CVPR, pp. 4293–4302 (2016)
34. Papageorgiou, C., Poggio, T.: A trainable system for object detection. IJCV **38**(1), 15–33 (2000)
35. Pirsiavash, H., Ramanan, D., Fowlkes, C.C.: Globally-optimal greedy algorithms for tracking a variable number of objects. In: CVPR, pp. 1201–1208 (2011)

36. Qi, Y., et al.: Hedged deep tracking. In: CVPR, pp. 4303–4311 (2016)
37. Ren, S., He, K., Girshick, R.B., Sun, J.: Faster R-CNN: towards real-time object detection with region proposal networks. In: NIPS, pp. 91–99 (2015)
38. Ristani, E., Solera, F., Zou, R., Cucchiara, R., Tomasi, C.: Performance measures and a data set for multi-target, multi-camera tracking. In: Hua, G., Jégou, H. (eds.) ECCV 2016. LNCS, vol. 9914, pp. 17–35. Springer, Cham (2016). https://doi.org/10.1007/978-3-319-48881-3_2
39. Robicquet, A., Sadeghian, A., Alahi, A., Savarese, S.: Learning social etiquette: human trajectory understanding in crowded scenes. In: Leibe, B., Matas, J., Sebe, N., Welling, M. (eds.) ECCV 2016. LNCS, vol. 9912, pp. 549–565. Springer, Cham (2016). https://doi.org/10.1007/978-3-319-46484-8_33
40. Smeulders, A.W.M., Chu, D.M., Cucchiara, R., Calderara, S., Dehghan, A., Shah, M.: Visual tracking: an experimental survey. TPAMI 36(7), 1442–1468 (2014)
41. Song, Y., Ma, C., Gong, L., Zhang, J., Lau, R.W.H., Yang, M.: CREST: convolutional residual learning for visual tracking. CoRR abs/1708.00225 (2017)
42. Tao, R., Gavves, E., Smeulders, A.W.M.: Siamese instance search for tracking. In: CVPR, pp. 1420–1429 (2016)
43. Valmadre, J., Bertinetto, L., Henriques, J.F., Vedaldi, A., Torr, P.H.S.: End-to-end representation learning for correlation filter based tracking. In: CVPR (2017)
44. Wang, L., Ouyang, W., Wang, X., Lu, H.: Visual tracking with fully convolutional networks. In: ICCV, pp. 3119–3127 (2015)
45. Wang, L., Ouyang, W., Wang, X., Lu, H.: STCT: sequentially training convolutional networks for visual tracking. In: CVPR, pp. 1373–1381 (2016)
46. Wen, L., et al.: DETRAC: a new benchmark and protocol for multi-object tracking. CoRR abs/1511.04136 (2015)
47. Wen, W., Wu, C., Wang, Y., Chen, Y., Li, H.: Learning structured sparsity in deep neural networks. In: NIPS, pp. 2074–2082 (2016)
48. Wojke, N., Bewley, A., Paulus, D.: Simple online and realtime tracking with a deep association metric. CoRR abs/1703.07402 (2017)
49. Wu, Y., Lim, J., Yang, M.: Object tracking benchmark. TPAMI 37(9), 1834–1848 (2015)
50. Xiang, Y., Alahi, A., Savarese, S.: Learning to track: online multi-object tracking by decision making. In: ICCV, pp. 4705–4713 (2015)
51. Yang, T., Chan, A.B.: Recurrent filter learning for visual tracking. In: ICCVW, pp. 2010–2019 (2017)
52. Yun, S., Choi, J., Yoo, Y., Yun, K., Choi, J.Y.: Action-decision networks for visual tracking with deep reinforcement learning. In: CVPR (2017)
53. Zhang, T., Xu, C., Yang, M.H.: Multi-task correlation particle filter for robust visual tracking. In: CVPR (2017)
54. Zhang, X., Zou, J., Ming, X., He, K., Sun, J.: Efficient and accurate approximations of nonlinear convolutional networks. In: CVPR, pp. 1984–1992 (2015)

Motion Feature Network: Fixed Motion Filter for Action Recognition

Myunggi Lee[1,2], Seungeui Lee[1], Sungjoon Son[1,2], Gyutae Park[1,2],
and Nojun Kwak[1(✉)]

[1] Seoul National University, Seoul, South Korea
{myunggi89,dehlix,sjson,pgt4861,nojunk}@snu.ac.kr
[2] V.DO Inc., Suwon, Korea

Abstract. Spatio-temporal representations in frame sequences play an important role in the task of action recognition. Previously, a method of using optical flow as a temporal information in combination with a set of RGB images that contain spatial information has shown great performance enhancement in the action recognition tasks. However, it has an expensive computational cost and requires two-stream (RGB and optical flow) framework. In this paper, we propose MFNet (Motion Feature Network) containing motion blocks which make it possible to encode spatio-temporal information between adjacent frames in a unified network that can be trained end-to-end. The motion block can be attached to any existing CNN-based action recognition frameworks with only a small additional cost. We evaluated our network on two of the action recognition datasets (Jester and Something-Something) and achieved competitive performances for both datasets by training the networks from scratch.

Keywords: Action recognition · Motion filter · MFNet
Spatio-temporal representation

1 Introduction

Convolutional neural networks (CNNs) [17] are originally designed to represent static appearances of visual scenes well. However, it has a limitation if the underlying structure is characterized by sequential and temporal relations. In particular, since recognizing human behavior in a video requires both spatial appearance and temporal motion as important cues, many previous researches have utilized various modalities that can capture motion information such as optical flow [33] and RGBdiff (temporal difference in consecutive RGB frames) [33]. Methods based on two-stream [7,21,33] and 3D convolutions [2,28] utilizing these input modalities achieve state-of-the-art performances in the field of

---

M. Lee and S. Lee—Equally contributed the paper. This work was supported by the ICT R&D program of MSIP/IITP, Korean Government (2017-0-00306).

V. Ferrari et al. (Eds.): ECCV 2018, LNCS 11214, pp. 392–408, 2018.
https://doi.org/10.1007/978-3-030-01249-6_24

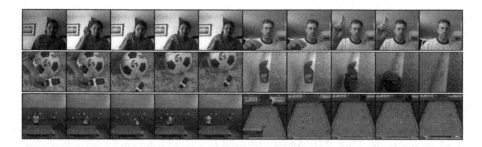

Fig. 1. Some examples of action classes in the three action recognition datasets, Jester (top), Something-Something (middle), and UCF101 (bottom). – top: left *'Sliding Two Fingers Down'*, right *'Sliding Two Fingers Up'*, middle: left *'Dropping something in front of something'*, right *'Removing something, revealing something behind'*, bottom: left *'TableTennisShot'*, right *'Billiards'*. Due to ambiguity of symmetrical pair classes/actions, static images only are not enough to recognize correct labels without sequential information in the former two datasets. However, in case of the bottom UCF101 image frames, the action class can be recognized with only spatial context (*e.g.* background and objects) from a single image.

action recognition. However, even though optical flow is a widely utilized modality that provides short-term temporal information, it takes a lot of time to generate. Likewise, 3D-kernel-based methods such as 3D ConvNets also require heavy computational burden with high memory requirements.

In our view, most previous labeled action recognition datasets such as UCF101 [24], HMDB51 [16], Sports-1M [13] and THUMOS [12] provide highly abstract concepts of human behavior. Therefore they can be mostly recognized without the help of temporal relations of sequential frames. For example, the *'Billiard'* and *'TableTennisShot'* in UCF101 can be easily recognizable by just seeing one frame as shown in the third row of Fig. 1. Unlike these datasets, Jester [1] and Something-Something [8] include more detailed physical aspects of actions and scenes. The appearance information has a very limited usefulness in classifying actions for these datasets. Also, visual objects in the scenes that mainly provide shape information are less important for the purpose of recognizing actions on these datasets. In particular, the Something-Something dataset has little correlation between the object and the action class, as its name implies. The first two rows of Fig. 1 show some examples of these datasets. As shown in Fig. 1, it is difficult to classify the action class with only one image. Also, even if there are multiple images, the action class can be changed according to the temporal order. Thus, it can be easily confused when using the conventional static feature extractors. Therefore, the ability to extract the temporal relationship between consecutive frames is important to classify human behavior in these datasets.

To solve these issues, we introduce a unified model which is named as the Motion Feature Network (MFNet). MFNet contains specially designed motion blocks which represent spatio-temporal relationships from only RGB frames.

Because it extracts temporal information using only RGB, pre-computation time that is typically needed to compute optical flow is not needed compared with the existing optical flow-based approaches. Also, because MFNet is based on a 2D CNN architecture, it has fewer parameters compared to its 3D counterparts.

We perform experiments to verify our model's ability to extract spatio-temporal features on a couple of publicly available action recognition datasets. In these datasets, each video label is closely related to the sequential relationships among frames. MFNet trained using only RGB frames significantly outperforms previous methods. Thus, MFNet can be used as a good solution for an action classification task in videos consisting of sequential relationships of detailed physical entities. We also conduct ablation studies to understand properties of MFNets in more detail.

The rest of this paper is organized as follows. Some related works for action recognition tasks are discussed in Sect. 2. Then in Sect. 3, we introduce our proposed MFNet architecture in detail. After that, experimental results with ablation studies are presented and analyzed in Sect. 4. Finally, the paper is concluded in Sect. 5.

2   Related Works

With the great success of CNNs on various computer vision tasks, a growing number of studies have tried to utilize deeply learned features for action recognition in video datasets. Especially, as the consecutive frames of input data imply sequential contexts, temporal information as well as spatial information is an important cue for classification tasks. There have been several approaches to extract these spatio-temporal features on action recognition problems.

One popular way to learn spatio-temporal features is using 3D convolution and 3D pooling hierarchically [6,9,28,29,36]. In this approach, they usually stack continuous frames of a video clip and feed them into the network. The 3D convolutions have enough capacity to encode spatio-temporal information on densely sampled frames but are inefficient in terms of computational cost. Furthermore, the number of parameters to be optimized are relatively large compared to other approaches. Thus, it is difficult to train on small datasets, such as UCF101 [24] and HMDB51 [15]. In order to overcome these issues, Carreira et al. [2] introduced a new large dataset named Kinetics [14], which facilitates training 3D models. They also suggest inflating 3D convolution filters from 2D convolution filters to bootstrap parameters from the pre-trained ImageNet [4] models. It achieves state-of-the-art performances in action recognition tasks.

Another famous approach is the two-stream-based method proposed by Simonyan et al. [22]. It encodes two kinds of modalities which are raw pixels of an image and the optical flow extracted from two consecutive raw image frames. It predicts action classes by averaging the predictions from both a single RGB frame and a stack of externally computed multiple optical flow frames. A large amount of follow up studies [18,32,35] to improve the performance of action recognition has been proposed based on the two-stream framework [7,21,33]. As an extension to the previous two-stream method, Wang *et al.* [33] proposed the temporal segment network. It samples image frames and optical flow frames on different time segments over the entire video sequences instead of short snippets, then it trains RGB frames and optical flow frames independently. At inference time, it accumulates the results to predict an activity class. While it brings a significant improvement over traditional methods [3,30,31], it still relies on pre-computed optical flows which are computationally expensive.

In order to replace the role of hand-crafted optical flow, there have been some works feeding frames similar to optical flow as inputs to the convolutional networks [33,36]. Another line of works use optical flow only in training phase as ground-truth [20,38]. They trained a network that reconstructs optical flow images from raw images and provide the estimated optical flow information to the action recognition network. Recently, Sun *et al.* [26] proposed a method of optical-flow-guided features. It extracts motion representation using two sets of features from adjacent frames by separately applying temporal subtraction (temporal features) and Sobel filters (spatial features). Our proposed method is highly related to this work. The differences are that we feedforward spatial and temporal features in a unified network instead of separating two features apart. Thus, it is possible to train the proposed MFNet in an end-to-end manner.

3   Model

In this section, we first introduce the overall architecture of the proposed MFNet and then give a detailed description of 'motion filter' and 'motion block' which constitute MFNet. We provide several instantiations of motion filter and motion block to explain the intuition behind it.

3.1   Motion Feature Network

The proposed architecture of MFNet is illustrated in Fig. 2. We construct our architecture based on *temporal segment network* (TSN) [33] which works on a sequence of K snippets sampled from the entire video. Our network is composed of two major components. One is *appearance block* which encodes the spatial information. This can be any of the architectures used in image classification tasks. In our experiments, we use ResNet [10] as our backbone network for appearance blocks. Another component is *motion block* which encodes temporal information. To model the motion representation, it takes two consecutive feature maps of the corresponding consecutive frames from the same hierarchy[1] as inputs and then extracts the temporal information using a set of fixed motion filters which will be described in the next subsection. The extracted spatial and temporal features in each hierarchy should be properly propagated to the next hierarchy. To fully utilize two types of information, we provide several schemes to accumulate them for the next hierarchy.

---

[1] We use the term *hierarchy* to represent the level of abstraction. A layer or a block of layers can correspond to a hierarchy.

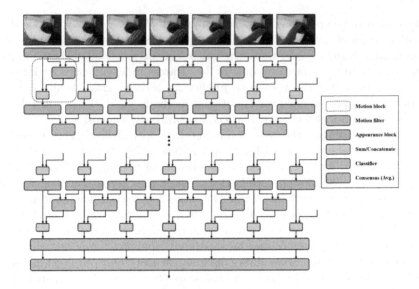

Fig. 2. The overall architecture of MFNet. The proposed network is composed of appearance blocks and motion blocks which encode spatial and temporal information. A motion block takes two consecutive feature maps from respective appearance blocks and extracts spatio-temporal information with the proposed fixed motion filters. The accumulated feature maps from the appearance blocks and motion blocks are used as an input to the next layer. This figure shows the case of $K = 7$.

3.2 Motion Representation

To capture the motion representation, one of the commonly used approaches in action recognition is using optical flow as inputs to a CNN. Despite its important role in the action recognition tasks, optical flow is computationally expensive in practice. In order to replace the role of optical flow and to extract temporal features, we propose motion filters which have a close relationship with the optical flow.

Approximation of Optical Flow. To approximate the feature-level optical flow hierarchically, we propose a modular structure named motion filter. Typically, the brightness consistency constraint of optical flow is defined as follows:

$$I(x + \Delta x, y + \Delta y, t + \Delta t) = I(x, y, t), \tag{1}$$

where $I(x, y, t)$ denotes the pixel value at the location (x, y) of a frame at time t. Here, Δx and Δy denote the spatial displacement in horizontal and vertical axis respectively. The optical flow $(\Delta x, \Delta y)$ that meets (1) is calculated between two consecutive image frames at time t and $t + \Delta t$ at every location of an image.

Originally, solving an optical flow problem is to find the optimal solution $(\Delta x^*, \Delta y^*)$ through an optimization technique. However, it is hard to solve (1)

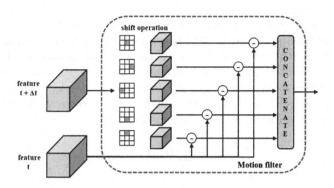

Fig. 3. Motion filter. Motion filter generates spatio-temporal features from two consecutive feature maps. Feature map at time $t + \Delta t$ is shifted by a predefined set of fixed directions and each of them is subtracted from the feature map at time t. With concatenation of features from all directions, motion filter can represent spatio-temporal information.

directly without additional constraints such as spatial or temporal smoothness assumptions. Also, it takes much time to obtain a dense (pixelwise) optical flow.

In this paper, the primary goal is to find the temporal features derived from optical flow to help classifying action recognition rather than finding the optimal solution to optical flow. Thus, we extend (1) to feature space by replacing an image $I(x, y, t)$ with the corresponding feature maps $F(x, y, t)$ and define a residual features R as follows:

$$R_l(x, y, \Delta t) = F_l(x + \Delta x, y + \Delta y, t + \Delta t) - F_l(x, y, t), \qquad (2)$$

where l denotes the index of the layer or hierarchy, F_l is the l-th feature maps from the basic network. R is the residual features produced by two features from the same layer l. Given Δx and Δy, the residual features R can be easily calculated by subtracting two adjacent features at time t and $t + \Delta t$. To fully utilize optical flow constraints in feature level, R tends to have lower absolute intensity. As searching for the lowest absolute value in each location of feature map is trivial but time-consuming, we design a set of predefined fixed directions $\mathbb{D} = \{(\Delta x, \Delta y)\}$ to restrict the search space. For convenience, in our implementation, we restrict $\Delta x, \Delta y \in \{0, \pm 1\}$ and $|\Delta x| + |\Delta y| \leq 1$. Shifting one pixel along each spatial dimension in the image space is responsible for capturing a small amount of optical flow (*i.e.* small movement), while one pixel in the feature space at a higher hierarchy of a CNN can capture larger optical flow (*i.e.* large movement) as it looks at a larger receptive field.

Motion Filter. The motion filter is a modular structure calculated by two feature maps extracted from shared networks feed-forwarded by two consecutive frames as inputs. As shown in Fig. 3, the motion filter takes features $F_l(t)$ and $F_l(t + \Delta t)$ at time t and $t + \Delta t$ as inputs. The predefined set of directions

$\mathbb{D}$ is only applied to the features at time $t + \Delta t$ as illustrated Fig. 3. We follow the shift operation proposed in [34]. It moves each channel of its input tensor in a different spatial direction $\delta \triangleq (\Delta x, \Delta y) \in \mathbb{D}$. This can be alternatively done with widely used depth-wise convolution, whose kernel size is determined by the maximum value of Δx and Δy in $\mathbb{D}$. For example, on our condition, $\Delta x, \Delta y \in \{0, \pm 1\}$, we can implement with 3×3 kernels as shown in Fig. 3. Formally, the shift operation can be formulated as:

$$G^{\delta}_{k,l,m} = \sum_{i,j} K^{\delta}_{i,j} F_{k+\hat{i},l+\hat{j},m}, \tag{3}$$

$$K^{\delta}_{i,j} = \begin{cases} 1 & \text{if } i = \Delta x \text{ and } j = \Delta y, \\ 0 & \text{otherwise.} \end{cases} \tag{4}$$

Here, the subscript indicates the index of a matrix or a tensor, $\delta \triangleq (\Delta x, \Delta y) \in \mathbb{D}$ is a displacement vector, $F \in \mathbb{R}^{W \times H \times C}$ is the input tensor and $\hat{i} = i - \lfloor W/2 \rfloor$, $\hat{j} = j - \lfloor H/2 \rfloor$ are the re-centered spatial indices ($\lfloor \cdot \rfloor$ is the floor operation). The indices k, l and i, j are those along spatial dimensions and m is a channel-wise index. We get a set $\mathbb{G} = \{G^{\delta}_{t+\Delta t} | \delta \in \mathbb{D}\}$, where $G^{\delta}_{t+\Delta t}$ represents the shifted feature map by an amount of δ at time $t + \Delta t$. Then, each of them is subtracted by F_t[2]. Because the concatenated feature map is constructed by temporal subtraction on top of the spatially shifted features, the feature map contains spatio-temporal information suitable for action recognition. As mentioned in Sect. 2, this is quite different from optical-flow-guided features in [26] which use two types of feature maps obtained by temporal subtraction and spatial Sobel filters. Also, it is distinct from 'subtractive correlation layer' in [5] with respect to the implementation and the goal. 'Subtractive correlation layer' is utilized to find correspondences for better reconstruction, while, the proposed motion filter is aimed to encode directional information between two feature maps via learnable parameters.

3.3   Motion Block

As mentioned above, the motion filter is a modular structure which can be adopted to any intermediate layers of two appearance blocks consecutive in time. In order to propagate spatio-temporal information properly, we provide several building blocks. Inspired by the recent success of residual block used in *residual networks* (ResNet) in many challenging image recognition tasks, we develop a new building block named motion block to propagate spatio-temporal information between two adjacent appearance blocks into deeper layers.

---

[2] For convenience, here, we use the notation F_t and $G_{t+\Delta t}$ instead of $F(t)$ and $G(t + \Delta t)$. The meaning of a subscript will be obvious in the context.

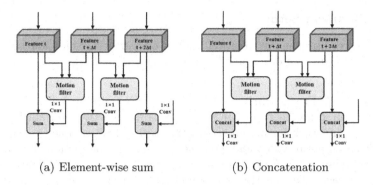

(a) Element-wise sum   (b) Concatenation

Fig. 4. Two ways to aggregate spatial and temporal information from appearance block and motion filter.

Element-Wise Sum. A simple and direct way to aggregate two different characteristics of information is the element-wise sum operation. As illustrated in Fig. 4(a), a set of motion features $R_t^\delta \triangleq F_t - G_{t+\Delta t}^\delta \in \mathbb{R}^{W \times H \times C}$, $\delta \in \mathbb{D}$, generated by motion filter are concatenated along channel dimension to produce a tensor $M_t = [R_t^{\delta_1} | R_t^{\delta_2} | \cdots | R_t^{\delta_S}] \in \mathbb{R}^{W \times H \times N}$, where $[\cdot|\cdot]$ denotes a concatenation operation, $N = S \times C$ and S is the number of the predefined directions in $\mathbb{D}$. It is further compressed by 1×1 convolution filters to produce output $\hat{M}_t$ with the same dimension as F_t. Finally, the features from the appearance block F_t and those from the motion filters $\hat{M}_t$ are summed up to produce inputs to the next hierarchy.

Concatenation. Another popular way to combine the appearance and the motion features is calculated by the concatenation operation. In this paper, the motion features M_t mentioned above are directly concatenated with each of the appearance features F_t as depicted in Fig. 4(b). A set of 1×1 convolution filters is also exploited to encode spatial and temporal information after the concatenation. The 1×1 convolution reduces the channel dimension as we desire. It also implicitly encodes spatio-temporal features to find the relationship between two different types of features: appearance and motion features.

4   Experiments

In this section, the proposed MFNet is applied to action recognition problems and the experimental results of MFNet are compared with those of other action recognition methods. As datasets, Jester [1] and Something-Something [8] are used because these cannot be easily recognized by just seeing a frame as already mentioned in Sect. 1. They also are suitable for observing the effectiveness of the proposed motion blocks. We also perform comprehensive ablation studies to prove the effectiveness of the MFNets.

4.1   Experiment Setup

To conduct comprehensive ablation studies on video classification tasks with motion blocks, first we describe our base network framework.

Base Network Framework. We select the TSN framework [33] as our base network architecture to train MFNet. TSN is an effective and efficient video processing framework for action recognition tasks. TSN samples a sequence of frames from an entire video and aggregates individual predictions into a video-level score. Thus, TSN framework is well suited for our motion blocks because each block directly extracts the temporal relationships between adjacent snippets in a batch manner.

In this paper, we mainly choose ResNet [10] as our base network to extract spatial feature maps. For the sake of clarity, we divide it into 6 stages. Each stage has a number of stacked residual blocks and each block is composed of several convolutional and batch normalization [11] layers with Rectified Linear Unit (ReLU) [19] for non-linearity. The final stage consists of a global pooling layer and a classifier. Our base network differs from the original ResNet in that it contains the max pooling layer in the first stage. Except this, our base network is the same as the conventional ResNet. The backbone network can be replaced by any other network architecture and our motion blocks can be inserted into the network all in the same way regardless of the type of the network used.

Motion Blocks. To form MFNet, we insert our motion blocks into the base network. In case of using ResNet, each motion block is located right after the last residual block of every stage except for the last stage (global pooling and classification layers). Then, MFNet automatically learns to represent spatio-temporal information from consecutive frames, leading the conventional base CNN to extract richer information that combines both appearance and motion features. We also add an 1×1 convolution before each motion block to reduce the number of channels. Throughout the paper, we reduce the number of input channels to motion block by a factor of 16 with the 1×1 convolutional layer. We add a batch normalization layer after the 1×1 convolution to adjust the scale to fit to the features in the backbone network.

Training. In the datasets of Jester and Something-Something, RGB images extracted from videos at 12 frames per second with a height of 100 pixels are provided. To augment training samples, we exploit random cropping method with scale-jittering. The width and height of a cropped image are determined by multiplying the shorter side of the image by a scale which is randomly selected in the set of $\{1.0, 0.875, 0.75, 0.625\}$. Then the cropped image is resized to 112×112, because the width of the original images is relatively small compared to that of other datasets. Note that we do not adopt random horizontal flipping to the cropped images of Jester dataset, because some classes are a symmetrical pair,

Table 1. Top-1 and Top-5 classification accuracies for different networks with different numbers of training segments (3, 5, 7). The compared networks are TSN baseline, MFNet concatenation version (MFNet-C), and MFNet element-wise sum version (MFNet-S) on Jester and Something-Something validation sets. All models use ResNet-50 as a backbone network and are trained from scratch.

Dataset		Jester		Something-Something	
Model	K	top-1 acc.	top-5 acc.	top-1 acc.	top-5 acc.
Baseline	3	82.4%	98.9%	6.6%	21.5%
	5	82.8%	98.9%	9.8%	28.6%
	7	81.0%	98.5%	8.1%	24.7%
MFNet-C50	3	90.4%	99.5%	17.4%	42.6%
	5	95.1%	99.7%	31.5%	61.9%
	7	96.1%	99.7%	37.3%	67.2%
MFNet-S50	3	91.0%	99.6%	15.4%	39.2%
	5	95.6%	99.8%	28.7%	59.1%
	7	96.3%	99.8%	37.1%	67.8%

such as *'Swiping Left'* and *'Swiping Right'*, and *'Sliding Two Fingers Left'* and *'Sliding Two Fingers Right'*.

Since motion block extracts temporal motion features from adjacent feature maps, a frame interval between frames is a very important hyper-parameter. We have trained our model with the fixed-time sampling strategy. However, in our experiments, it leads to worse results than the random sampling strategy in [33]. With a random interval, the method forces the network to learn through frames composed of various intervals. Interestingly, we get better performance on Jester and Something-Something datasets with the temporal sampling interval diversity.

We use the stochastic gradient descent algorithm to learn network parameters. The batch size is set to 128, the momentum is set to 0.9 and weight decay is set to 0.0005. All MFNets are trained from scratch and we train our models with batch normalization layers [11]. The learning rate is initialized as 0.01 and decreases by a factor of 0.1 for every 50 epochs. The training procedure stops after 120 epochs. To mitigate over-fitting effect, we adopt dropout [25] after the global pooling layer with a dropout ratio of 0.5. To speed up training, we employ a multi-GPU data-parallel strategy with 4 NVIDIA TITAN-X GPUs.

Inference. We select equi-distance 10 frames without the random shift. We test our models on sampled frames whose image size is rescaled to 112 × 112. After that, we aggregate separate predictions from each frame and average them before softmax normalization to get the final prediction.

Table 2. Top-1 and Top-5 classification accuracies for different depths of MFNet's base network. ResNet [10] is used as the base network. The values are on JESTER and Something-Something validation sets. All models are trained from scratch, with 10 segments.

Dataset		Jester		Something-Something	
Model	Backbone	top-1 acc.	top-5 acc.	top-1 acc.	top-5 acc.
MFNet-C	ResNet-18	96.3%	99.8%	39.4%	69.1%
	ResNet-50	96.6%	99.8%	40.3%	70.9%
	ResNet-101	96.7%	99.8%	43.9%	73.1%
	ResNet-152	96.5%	99.8%	43.0%	73.2%

4.2 Experimental Results

The Jester [1] is a crowd-acted video dataset for generic human hand gestures recognition. It consists 118,562 videos for training, 14,787 videos for validation, and 14,743 videos for testing. The Something-Something [8] is also a crowd-acted densely labeled video dataset of basic human interactions with daily objects. It contains 86,017 videos for training, 11,522 videos for validation, and 10,960 videos for testing. Each of both datasets is for the action classification task involving 27 and 174 human action categories respectively. We report validation results of our models on the validation sets, and test results from the official leaderboards[3,4].

Evaluation on the Number of Segments. Due to the nature of our MFNet, the number of segments, K, in the training is one of the important parameters. Table 1 shows the comparison results of different models while changing the number of segments from 3 to 7 with the same evaluation strategies. We observe that as the number of segments increases, the performance of overall models increases. The performance of the MFNet-C50 (which means that MFNet concatenate version with ResNet-50 as a backbone network) with 7 segments is by far the better than the same network with 3 segments: 96.1% vs. 90.4% and 37.3% vs. 17.4% on Jester and Something-Something datasets respectively. The trend is the same for MFNet-S50, the network with element-wise sum. Also, unlike baseline TSN, MFNets show significant performance improvement as the number of segments increases from 3 to 5.

These improvements imply that increasing K reduces the interval between sampled frames which allows our model to extract richer information. Interestingly, MFNet-S achieves slightly higher top-1 accuracy (0.2% to 0.6%) than MFNet-C on Jester dataset, and MFNet-C shows better performance (0.2% to 2.8%) than MFNet-S on Something-Something dataset. On the other hand, because the TSN baseline is learned from scratch, performance was worse than

Table 3. Comparison of the top-1 and top-5 validation results of various methods on Jester and Something-something datasets. K denotes the number of training segments. The results of other models are from their respective papers.

Dataset	Jester		Something-Something	
Model	top-1 acc.	top-5 acc.	top-1 acc.	top-5 acc.
Pre-3D CNN + Avg [8]	-	-	11.5%	30.0%
MultiScale TRN [37]	93.70%	99.59%	33.01%	61.27%
MultiScale TRN (10-crop)[37]	95.31%	99.86%	34.44%	63.20%
MFNet-C50, $K = 7$	96.13%	99.65%	37.31%	67.23%
MFNet-S50, $K = 7$	96.31%	99.80%	37.09%	67.78%
MFNet-C50, $K = 10$	96.56%	99.82%	40.30%	70.93%
MFNet-S50, $K = 10$	96.50%	99.86%	39.83%	70.19%
MFNet-C101, $K = 10$	96.68%	99.84%	43.92%	73.12%

Table 4. Selected test results on the Jester and Something-Something datasets from the official leaderboards. Since the test results are continuously updated, some results that are not reported or whose description is missing are excluded. The complete list of test results is available on official public leaderboards. Our results are based on ResNet-101 with $K = 10$ and trained from scratch. For submissions, we use the same evaluation strategies as the validation mode.

Jester		Something-Something	
Model	top-1 acc.	Model	top-1 acc.
BesNet (from [37])	94.23%	BesNet (from [37])	31.66%
MultiScale TRN [37]	94.78%	MultiScale TRN [37]	33.60%
MFNet-C101 (ours)	96.22%	MFNet-C101 (ours)	37.48%

expected. It can be seen that TSN spatial model without pre-training barely generates any action-related visual features in Something-Something dataset.

Comparisons of Network Depths. Table 2 compares the performances as the depths of MFNet's backbone network changes. In the table, we can see that MFNet-C with ResNet-18 achieves comparable performance as the 101-layered ResNet using almost 76% fewer parameters (11.68M vs. 50.23M). It is generally known that as CNNs become deeper, more features can be expressed [10,23,27]. However, one can see that because most of the videos in Jester dataset are composed of almost similar kinds of human appearances, the static visual entities are very little related to action classes. Therefore, the network depth does not appear to have a significant effect on performance. In Something-Something case, accuracy gets also saturated. It could be explained that generalization of a model seems to be difficult without pre-trained weights on other large-scale datasets, such as Imagenet [4] and Kinetics [14].

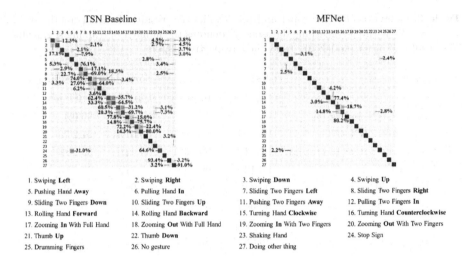

TSN Baseline   MFNet

1. Swiping **Left**   3. Swiping **Down**   4. Swiping **Up**
2. Swiping **Right**
5. Pushing Hand **Away**   6. Pulling Hand **In**   7. Sliding Two Fingers **Left**   8. Sliding Two Fingers **Right**
9. Sliding Two Fingers **Down**   10. Sliding Two Fingers **Up**   11. Pushing Two Fingers **Away**   12. Pulling Two Fingers **In**
13. Rolling Hand **Forward**   14. Rolling Hand **Backward**   15. Turning Hand **Clockwise**   16. Turning Hand **Counterclockwise**
17. Zooming **In** With Full Hand   18. Zooming **Out** With Full Hand   19. Zooming **In** With Two Fingers   20. Zooming **Out** With Two Fingers
21. Thumb **Up**   22. Thumb **Down**   23. Shaking Hand   24. Stop Sign
25. Drumming Fingers   26. No gesture   27. Doing other thing

Fig. 5. Confusion matrices of TSN baseline and our proposed MFNet on Jester dataset. The figure is best viewed in an electronic form.

Comparisons with the State-of-the-Art. Table 3 shows the top-1 and top-5 results on the validation set. Our models outperform Pre-3D CNN + Avg [8] and the MultiScale TRN [37]. Because Jester and Something-Something are recently released datasets in the action recognition research field, we also report the test results on the official leaderboards for each dataset for comparison with previous studies. Table 4 shows that MFNet achieves comparable performance to the state-of-the-art methods with 96.22% and 37.48% top-1 accuracies on Jester and Something-Something test datasets respectively on official leaderboards. Note that we do not introduce any other modalities, ensemble methods or pre-trained initialization weights on large-scale datasets such as ImageNet [4] and Kinetics [14]. We only utilize officially provided RGB images as the input of our final results. Also, without 3D ConvNets and additional complex testing strategies, our method provides competitive performances on the Jester and Something-Something datasets.

4.3 Analysis on the Behavior of MFNet

Confusion Matrix. We analyze the effectiveness of MFNet comparing with the baseline. Figure 5 shows the confusion matrices of TSN baseline (left) and MFNet (right) on Jester dataset. Class numbers and the corresponding class names are listed below. Figure 5 suggests that the baseline model confuses one action class with its counterpart class. That is, it has trouble classifying temporally symmetric action pairs. For example, (*'Swiping Left'*, *'Swiping Right'*) and (*'Two Finger Down'*, *'Two Finger Up'*) are temporally symmetric pairs.

In case of baseline, it predicts an action class by simply averaging the results of sampled frames. Consequently, if there is no optical flow information, it might

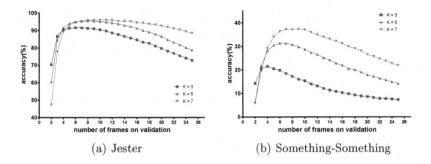

(a) Jester   (b) Something-Something

Fig. 6. Validation accuracies trained with the different number of segments K, while varying the number of validation segments from 2 to 25. The x-axis represents the number of segments at inference time and the y-axis is the validation accuracy of the MFNet-C50 trained with different K.

fail to distinguish some temporal symmetric action pairs. Specifically, we get 62.38% accuracy on *'Rolling Hand Forward'* class among 35.7% of which is misclassified as *'Rolling Hand Backward'*. In contrast, our MFNet showed significant improvement over baseline model as shown in Fig. 5 (right). In our experiments, we get the accuracy of 94.62% on *'Rolling Hand Forward'* class among 4.2% of which is identified as *'Rolling Hand Backward'*. It proves the ability of MFNet in capturing the motion representation.

Varying Number of Segments in the Validation Phase. We evaluated the models which have different numbers of frames in the inference phase. Figure 6 shows the experimental results of MFNet-C50 on Jester (left) and Something-Something (right) datasets. As discussed in Sect. 4.2, K, the number of segments in the training phase is a crucial parameter on performance. As we can see, overall performance for all the number of validation segments is superior on large K (7). Meanwhile, the optimal number of validation segments for each K is different. Interestingly, it does not coincide with K but is slightly larger than K. Using more segments reduces the frame interval which allows extracting more precise spatio-temporal features. It brings the effect of improving performance. However, it does not last if the numbers in the training and the validation phases differ much.

5   Conclusions

In this paper, we present MFNet, a unified network containing appearance blocks and motion blocks which can represent both spatial and temporal information for action recognition problems. Especially, we propose the motion filter that outputs the motion features by performing the shift operation with the fixed set of predefined directional filters and subtracting the resultant feature maps from the feature maps of the preceding frame. This module can be attached to any existing CNN-based network with a small additional cost. We evaluate our model on two datasets, Jester and Something-Something, and obtain outperforming results compared to the existing results by training the network from scratch in an end-to-end manner. Also, we perform comprehensive ablation studies and analysis on the behavior of MFNet to show the effectiveness of our method. In the future, we will validate our network on large-scale action recognition dataset and additionally investigate the usefulness of the proposed motion block.

References

1. The 20bn-jester dataset. https://www.twentybn.com/datasets/jester
2. Carreira, J., Zisserman, A.: Quo vadis, action recognition? A new model and the kinetics dataset. In: 2017 IEEE Conference on Computer Vision and Pattern Recognition (CVPR), pp. 4724–4733. IEEE (2017)
3. Dalal, N., Triggs, B., Schmid, C.: Human detection using oriented histograms of flow and appearance. In: Leonardis, A., Bischof, H., Pinz, A. (eds.) ECCV 2006. LNCS, vol. 3952, pp. 428–441. Springer, Heidelberg (2006). https://doi.org/10.1007/11744047_33
4. Deng, J., Dong, W., Socher, R., Li, L.J., Li, K., Fei-Fei, L.: ImageNet: a large-scale hierarchical image database. In: 2009 IEEE Conference on Computer Vision and Pattern Recognition, CVPR 2009, pp. 248–255. IEEE (2009)
5. Dosovitskiy, A., et al.: Flownet: learning optical flow with convolutional networks. In: Proceedings of the IEEE International Conference on Computer Vision, pp. 2758–2766 (2015)
6. Feichtenhofer, C., Pinz, A., Wildes, R.: Spatiotemporal residual networks for video action recognition. In: Advances in Neural Information Processing Systems, pp. 3468–3476 (2016)
7. Feichtenhofer, C., Pinz, A., Zisserman, A.: Convolutional two-stream network fusion for video action recognition (2016)
8. Goyal, R., et al.: The something something video database for learning and evaluating visual common sense. In: Proceedings of ICCV (2017)
9. Hara, K., Kataoka, H., Satoh, Y.: Learning spatio-temporal features with 3D residual networks for action recognition. In: Proceedings of the ICCV Workshop on Action, Gesture, and Emotion Recognition, vol. 2, p. 4 (2017)
10. He, K., Zhang, X., Ren, S., Sun, J.: Deep residual learning for image recognition. In: Proceedings of the IEEE Conference on Computer Vision and Pattern Recognition, pp. 770–778 (2016)
11. Ioffe, S., Szegedy, C.: Batch normalization: accelerating deep network training by reducing internal covariate shift. In: International Conference on Machine Learning, pp. 448–456 (2015)
12. Jiang, Y., et al.: Thumos challenge: action recognition with a large number of classes (2014)
13. Karpathy, A., Toderici, G., Shetty, S., Leung, T., Sukthankar, R., Fei-Fei, L.: Large-scale video classification with convolutional neural networks. In: Proceedings of the IEEE Conference on Computer Vision and Pattern Recognition, pp. 1725–1732 (2014)
14. Kay, W., et al.: The kinetics human action video dataset. arXiv preprint arXiv:1705.06950 (2017)

15. Kuehne, H., Jhuang, H., Garrote, E., Poggio, T., Serre, T.: HMDB: a large video database for human motion recognition. In: Proceedings of the International Conference on Computer Vision (ICCV) (2011)
16. Kuehne, H., Jhuang, H., Stiefelhagen, R., Serre, T.: HMDB51: a large video database for human motion recognition. In: Nagel, W., Kröner, D., Resch, M. (eds.) High Performance Computing in Science and Engineering '12, pp. 571–582. Springer, Heidelberg (2013). https://doi.org/10.1007/978-3-642-33374-3_41
17. LeCun, Y., Bengio, Y., et al.: Convolutional networks for images, speech, and time series. Handb. Brain Theory Neural Netw. **3361**(10), 1995 (1995)
18. Miech, A., Laptev, I., Sivic, J.: Learnable pooling with context gating for video classification. arXiv preprint arXiv:1706.06905 (2017)
19. Nair, V., Hinton, G.E.: Rectified linear units improve restricted Boltzmann machines. In: Proceedings of the 27th International Conference on Machine Learning (ICML 2010), pp. 807–814 (2010)
20. Ng, J.Y.H., Choi, J., Neumann, J., Davis, L.S.: Actionflownet: learning motion representation for action recognition. arXiv preprint arXiv:1612.03052 (2016)
21. Ng, J.Y.H., Hausknecht, M., Vijayanarasimhan, S., Vinyals, O., Monga, R., Toderici, G.: Beyond short snippets: deep networks for video classification. In: 2015 IEEE Conference on Computer Vision and Pattern Recognition (CVPR), pp. 4694–4702. IEEE (2015)
22. Simonyan, K., Zisserman, A.: Two-stream convolutional networks for action recognition in videos. In: Advances in Neural Information Processing Systems, pp. 568–576 (2014)
23. Simonyan, K., Zisserman, A.: Very deep convolutional networks for large-scale image recognition. arXiv preprint arXiv:1409.1556 (2014)
24. Soomro, K., Zamir, A.R., Shah, M.: UCF101: a dataset of 101 human actions classes from videos in the wild. arXiv preprint arXiv:1212.0402 (2012)
25. Srivastava, N., Hinton, G., Krizhevsky, A., Sutskever, I., Salakhutdinov, R.: Dropout: a simple way to prevent neural networks from overfitting. J. Mach. Learn. Res. **15**(1), 1929–1958 (2014)
26. Sun, S., Kuang, Z., Ouyang, W., Sheng, L., Zhang, W.: Optical flow guided feature: a fast and robust motion representation for video action recognition. CoRR abs/1711.11152 (2017). http://arxiv.org/abs/1711.11152
27. Szegedy, C., et al.: Going deeper with convolutions. In: Cvpr (2015)
28. Tran, D., Bourdev, L., Fergus, R., Torresani, L., Paluri, M.: Learning spatiotemporal features with 3D convolutional networks. In: 2015 IEEE International Conference on Computer Vision (ICCV), pp. 4489–4497. IEEE (2015)
29. Tran, D., Ray, J., Shou, Z., Chang, S.F., Paluri, M.: Convnet architecture search for spatiotemporal feature learning. arXiv preprint arXiv:1708.05038 (2017)
30. Wang, H., Kläser, A., Schmid, C., Liu, C.L.: Action recognition by dense trajectories. In: 2011 IEEE Conference on Computer Vision and Pattern Recognition (CVPR), pp. 3169–3176. IEEE (2011)
31. Wang, H., Schmid, C.: Action recognition with improved trajectories. In: 2013 IEEE International Conference on Computer Vision (ICCV), pp. 3551–3558. IEEE (2013)
32. Wang, L., Li, W., Li, W., Van Gool, L.: Appearance-and-relation networks for video classification. arXiv preprint arXiv:1711.09125 (2017)
33. Wang, L., et al.: Temporal segment networks: towards good practices for deep action recognition. In: Leibe, B., Matas, J., Sebe, N., Welling, M. (eds.) ECCV 2016. LNCS, vol. 9912, pp. 20–36. Springer, Cham (2016). https://doi.org/10.1007/978-3-319-46484-8_2

34. Wu, B., et al.: Shift: a zero flop, zero parameter alternative to spatial convolutions. arXiv preprint arXiv:1711.08141 (2017)
35. Wu, Z., Jiang, Y.G., Wang, X., Ye, H., Xue, X., Wang, J.: Fusing multi-stream deep networks for video classification. arXiv preprint arXiv:1509.06086 (2015)
36. Zhang, B., Wang, L., Wang, Z., Qiao, Y., Wang, H.: Real-time action recognition with enhanced motion vector CNNs. In: 2016 IEEE Conference on Computer Vision and Pattern Recognition (CVPR), pp. 2718–2726. IEEE (2016)
37. Zhou, B., Andonian, A., Torralba, A.: Temporal relational reasoning in videos. arXiv preprint arXiv:1711.08496 (2017)
38. Zhu, Y., Lan, Z., Newsam, S., Hauptmann, A.G.: Hidden two-stream convolutional networks for action recognition. arXiv preprint arXiv:1704.00389 (2017)

Efficient Sliding Window Computation for NN-Based Template Matching

Lior Talker[1]([✉]), Yael Moses[2], and Ilan Shimshoni[1]

[1] The University of Haifa, Haifa, Israel
ltalke01@campus.haifa.ac.il, ishimshoni@mis.haifa.ac.il
[2] The Interdisciplinary Center, Herzliya, Israel
yael@idc.ac.il

Abstract. Template matching is a fundamental problem in computer vision, with many applications. Existing methods use sliding window computation for choosing an image-window that best matches the template. For classic algorithms based on SSD, SAD and normalized cross-correlation, efficient algorithms have been developed allowing them to run in real-time. Current state of the art algorithms are based on nearest neighbor (NN) matching of small patches within the template to patches in the image. These algorithms yield state-of-the-art results since they can deal better with changes in appearance, viewpoint, illumination, non-rigid transformations, and occlusion. However, NN-based algorithms are relatively slow not only due to NN computation for each image patch, but also since their sliding window computation is inefficient. We therefore propose in this paper an efficient NN-based algorithm. Its accuracy is similar (in some cases slightly better) than the existing algorithms and its running time is 43–200 times faster depending on the sizes of the images and templates used. The main contribution of our method is an algorithm for incrementally computing the score of each image window based on the score computed for the previous window. This is in contrast to computing the score for each image window independently, as in previous NN-based methods. The complexity of our method is therefore $O(|I|)$ instead of $O(|I||T|)$, where I and T are the image and the template respectively.

1 Introduction

Template matching is a fundamental problem in computer vision, with applications such as object tracking, object detection and image stitching. The template is a small image and the goal is to detect it in a target image. The challenge is to do so, despite template-image variations caused by changes in the appearance, occlusions, rigid and non-rigid transformations.

Electronic supplementary material The online version of this chapter (https://doi.org/10.1007/978-3-030-01249-6_25) contains supplementary material, which is available to authorized users.

V. Ferrari et al. (Eds.): ECCV 2018, LNCS 11214, pp. 409–424, 2018.
https://doi.org/10.1007/978-3-030-01249-6_25

Given a template we would like to find an image window that contains the same object as the template. Ideally, we would like to find a correct dense correspondence between the image window and the template, where correct correspondence reflects two views of the same world point. In practice, due to template-image variations this may be difficult to obtain and computationally expensive. To overcome these challenges, Bradski *et al.* [9] proposed to collect evidence based on nearest neighbors (NNs) that a given image window contains the same object as the template. In this paper, we follow the same paradigm.

The state-of-the-art algorithms [9,13] compute a matching score for each window of the template size, using a naïve sliding window procedure. The location with the highest score is the result. This is computationally expensive, since the score is computed independently for each window in the image. For an image of size $|I|$ and a template of size $|T|$, the running time complexity is $O(|I||T|)$. For a small image of size 480×320 and a 50×50 template, the running time of the current state-of-the-art algorithm [13] is about one second and for larger images of size 1280×720 and a 200×300 template, it takes ~ 78 s. Thus, even though these NN-based algorithms produce state of the art results, their efficiency should be improved in order for them to be used in practice. The main challenge addressed in this paper is to develop an efficient algorithm for running them.

Our matching score between a template, T, and an image window, τ, is inspired by the one suggested in [13]. However, our algorithm requires only $O(|I|)$ operations, which is a fraction of the running time of [13]. It also marginally improves the accuracy of [13]. Consider, for example, a typical image I of size 1000×1000, a template T of size 100×100, and a SSD score. In this example, $O(|I||T|) = 10^{10}$ operations are required, while in our method it is in the order of $O(|I|) \approx 10^6$.

Our score function, called the Deformable Image Weighted Unpopularity (DIWU), is inspired by the Deformable Diversity Similarity (DDIS) score introduced in [13]. Both scores are based on nearest neighbor (NN) patch-matching between each patch in the image window and the template's patches. The score of an image window is a simple sum of the scores of its pixels. A pixel score consists of the unpopularity measure of its NN, as well as the relative location of the patch in the candidate image window with respect to location of the NN patch in the template. The unpopularity for a pixel in DIWU is defined by the number of (other) pixels in the entire image that choose the same NN as the pixel, while in DDIS only pixels in τ are considered. Moreover, the deformation measure in DIWU is based on the L_1 distance while in DDIS it is based on the L_2 distance. These modifications of DDIS allow us to develop our efficient iterative sliding window algorithm for computing the DIWU score, which also marginally improve the DDIS results.

The main technical contribution of our method[1] is the efficient computation of the DIWU on all possible candidate windows of size $|T|$ of I. The DIWU on a

---

[1] A C++ code (and a Matlab wrapper) for our method is publicly available at http://liortalker.wixsite.com/liortalker/code.

single window τ, can be obtained by a sum of scores that are computed separately for each row and each column of τ. This reduces the problem of computing the score of a 2D window to the problem of computing a set of 1D scores. The score of the window is then obtained using efficient 1D rolling summation. We propose an iterative algorithm for computing the 1D scores of successive windows in only $O(1)$ steps. The algorithm requires an $O(|I|)$ initialization. As a result, we obtain the desired overall complexity of $O(|I|)$ instead of the original complexity of $O(|I||T|)$. We tested our method on two large and challenging datasets and obtained respective runtime speedups of about $43\times$ and $200\times$.

The rest of the paper is organized as follows. After reviewing related work, we present the DDIS score and our new DIWU score in Sect. 3. Then the efficient algorithm for computing DIWU is presented in Sect. 4, and the experiments in Sect. 5. We conclude and propose possible extensions in Sect. 6.

2   Related Work

Since the literature on template matching is vast and the term "template matching" is used for several different problems, we limit our review to template matching where both the template and the image are 2D RGB images. We are interested in "same *instance*" template matching, where the object *instance* that appears in the template also appears in the image. A comprehensive review of template matching is given in [10].

The most common approaches to template matching are the Sum of Squared Differences (SSD), the Sum of Absolute Differences (SAD), and the Normalized Cross-Correlation (NCC), which are very sensitive to deformations or extreme rigid transformations. Other approaches aim to model the transformation between the template and the same object in the image, e.g., using an affine transformation [5,14,19]. In many cases these methods perform well, but they often fail in the presence of occlusions, clutter, and complex non-rigid transformations.

Although deep convolutional neural networks (deep CNNs) have revolutionized the computer vision field (as well as other fields), we are not aware of any work that has used them for template matching (as defined in this paper) despite their success in similar problems. For example, the authors of [6] proposed a window ranking algorithm based on deep CNNs and used it to assist a simple classic template matching algorithm. Similarly, the authors of [11] proposed to use deep CNNs to rule out parts of the image that probably do not match the template. While deep CNN based patch matching algorithms [17,18] might be used for template matching, their goal is to match similar patches (as in stereo matching); hence, they are trained on simple, small changes in patch appearance. In contrast, we consider templates of any size that may undergo extreme changes in appearance, e.g., deformations. Finally, deep CNN based methods for visual object tracking [1,4] do match a template, however, usually for specific object classes known a priori. More importantly, they use video as input, which provides temporal information we do not assume to be available.

Object localization methods such as Deformable Parts Models (DPM) [3] are based on efficient template matching of object parts using the generalized distance transform. However, the root part (e.g., torso in people) still needs to be exhaustively matched as a template, after which the other parts are efficiently aligned with it. An efficient sliding window object detection method proposed in [15] bears some resemblance to our method. The spatial coherency between windows is exploited to incrementally update local histograms. Since the window score is computed using the local histogram, a pixel is assigned with the same score in different windows. This is in contrast to our method, where the deformation score for a pixel is different in different windows.

The works most closely related to ours are [9,13], the latter of which obtains state-of-the-art results and inspired our method. We discuss these methods and the diffrences from our approach in the next sections.

3 Basic Method

The input to our method is an $n \times m$ image I and a $w \times h$ template T. Our goal is to detect a $w \times h$ image window τ that is most similar to the template object. A score $S(\tau_i)$ for each candidate image window τ_i that reflects the quality of this match is defined. A sliding window procedure is used to consider all possible image windows, and the one with the highest score is our output.

As in [9,13], the score $S(\tau)$ is defined based on a nearest neighbor computation performed once for each pixel in I. We denote the nearest neighbor of a pixel $p \in I$ by $N_r(p)$, where the patch around the pixel $N_r(p) \in T$ is the most similar to the patch around $p \in I$. In our implementation we used the FLANN library [8] for efficient approximate nearest neighbor computation. It was used on two different descriptors: 3×3 overlapping patches of RGB, and deep features computed using the VGG net [12].

A score $c^\tau(p)$ ideally reflects the confidence that $N_r(p) \in T$ is the correct match of $p \in \tau$. (We use c^τ since the score of p may be window dependent.) The score $S(\tau)$ of the entire window is the sum of $c^\tau(p)$ values over all $p \in \tau$:

$$S(\tau) = \sum_{p \in \tau} c^\tau(p). \tag{1}$$

The challenge is therefore to define the confidence score $c^\tau(p)$ for $p \in \tau$, such that $S(\tau)$ not only reflects the quality of the match between τ and T but can also be computed efficiently for all candidate windows $\tau \in I$.

3.1 Previous Scores

In [9] the confidence that $p \in \tau$ found a correct match $N_r(p) \in T$ is high if p is also the NN of $N_r(p)$ in τ (dubbed "best-buddies"). In [13] this confidence is defined by the *window-popularity* of $q = N_r(p)$ as a nearest neighbor of other pixels $p' \in \tau$. Formally, the window-popularity of $q \in T$ is defined by:

$$\alpha^\tau(q) = |\{p \mid p \in \tau \ \& \ N_r(p) = q\}|, \tag{2}$$

and the confidence score of a pixel $p \in \tau$ is given by:

$$c_{DIS}^{\tau}(p) = e^{-\alpha^{\tau}(N_r(p))}. \tag{3}$$

Thus, a pixel match is more reliable if its popularity is lower.

To improve robustness, the spatial configuration of the matched pixels is incorporated into the score. The modified score, $c_{DDIS}^{\tau}(p)$, reflects the alignment of p's location in τ and q's location in T ($q = N_r(p)$). Formally, the spatial location of $p \in \tau$ is defined by $p^{\tau} = p - o^{\tau}$, where o^{τ} is the upper left pixel of τ in I. The misalignment of p^{τ} and $q = N_r(p)$ is defined in [13] using the L_2 distance:

$$a_{L_2}^{\tau}(p) = \frac{1}{1 + ||p^{\tau} - q||_2}. \tag{4}$$

The confidence of a pixel p is then given by

$$c_{DDIS}^{\tau}(p) = a_{L_2}^{\tau}(p)c_{DIS}^{\tau}(p). \tag{5}$$

Efficiency: While the NNs are computed only once for each pixel in the image, the values $a_{L_2}^{\tau}(p)$ and $c_{DIS}^{\tau}(p)$ are window dependent. Thus, the computation of $S_{DIS}(\tau)$ and $S_{DDIS}(\tau)$ for each window τ requires $O(|T|)$ operations. Computing the score independently for all windows in I requires $O(|I||T|)$ operations.

3.2   Image Based Unpopularity: The IWU Score

We focus on improving the efficiency of [13], while preserving its accuracy. We do so by modifying the c_{DIS}^{τ} and c_{DDIS}^{τ} to obtain new scores c_{IWU} and c_{DIWU}^{τ}. The window score, computed using these scores, can be efficiently computed for all the windows in I (Sect. 4).

The window-based popularity of $q \in T$ (Eq. 2), is modified to an image-based popularity measure. That is, we consider the set of pixels from the entire image (rather than only pixels in τ) for which q is their NN. The image-based popularity is given by:

$$\alpha(q) = |\{p \mid p \in I \ \& \ N_r(p) = q\}|. \tag{6}$$

If $\alpha(N_r(p))$ is high, it is unlikely that the correspondence between p and $N_r(p)$ is correct. Thus, the confidence score of a pixel p is defined by:

$$c_{IWU}(p) = e^{-\alpha(N_r(p))}. \tag{7}$$

One can argue whether $\alpha(q)$ or $\alpha_{\tau}(q)$ best defines the popularity that should be used for the matching confidence. Our initial motivation was computational efficiency, as we describe below. However, experiments demonstrate that IWU is also slightly more accurate than the DIS while much more efficient to compute (Sect. 5).

There is a subtle difference between IWU and DIS in their response to a template that contains an object that is repeated many times in the image, e.g., windows. Since IWU weights each patch in the context of the entire image, its score is lower than DIS's, which considers only the window context. We argue that it is theoretically beneficial to suppress the score of repeated structures. In practice, however, this difference is rarely reflected in the final output (see Fig. 1 in the supplemental material.)

Efficiency: The values $\alpha(q)$ and $c_{IWU}(p)$ (Eqs. 6 and 7) are independent of the window τ, and therefore computed only once for each pixel in I. The results is the C_{IWU} matrix. To obtain the final score of a single window, we need to sum all its elements in C_{IWU}. Computing the scores for all the windows is done in two steps. For each row in the image we compute the sum of 1D windows using the following rolling summation method. Given the sum of a previous 1D window, one element is subtracted (i.e., the one that is not in the current window) and one element is added (i.e., the one that is not in the previous window). On the result of this step a 1D rolling summation is applied on the columns yielding the final result. The complexity of both steps is $O(|I|)$.

3.3   Deformation: The DIWU Score

We follow [13] and improve the robustness of the c_{IWU} by using a misalignment score. For the sake of efficiency, we use the misalignment in the x and the y components separately, as in the L_1 distance, instead of the L_2 distance used in Eq. 3. Our alignment scores for $q = N_r(p)$ are defined by:

$$a_x^\tau(p) = e^{-|q_x - p_x^\tau|}, \quad a_y^\tau(p) = e^{-|q_y - p_y^\tau|}. \tag{8}$$

Let the confidence $c_D^\tau(p)$ be given by $c_D^\tau(p) = a_x^\tau(p) + a_y^\tau(p)$. The outcome of this definition is that the score $S(\tau)$ that uses $c^\tau(p) = c_D^\tau(p)$ can be separated into two scores, $S_D^x(\tau)$ and $S_D^y(\tau)$, as follows:

$$S_D(\tau) = \sum_{p^\tau \in \tau} (a_x^\tau(p) + a_y^\tau(p)) = \sum_{p^\tau \in \tau} a_x^\tau(p) + \sum_{p^\tau \in \tau} a_y^\tau(p) = S_D^x(\tau) + S_D^y(\tau). \tag{9}$$

The spatial alignment score can be combined with the confidence IWU score (Sect. 3.2) to reflect both the popularity and the spatial configuration. Hence,

$$c_{DIWU}^\tau(p) = a_x^\tau(p)c_{IWU}(p) + a_y^\tau(p)c_{IWU}(p) = c_{DIWU}^{\tau,x}(p) + c_{DIWU}^{\tau,y}(p). \tag{10}$$

Here again the final score can be separated into the sum of two scores:

$$S_{DU}(\tau) = \sum_{p^\tau \in \tau} c_{DIWU}^\tau(p) = S_{DU}^x(\tau) + S_{DU}^y(\tau). \tag{11}$$

The DIWU score is similar to the DDIS score and a similar accuracy is obtained. We next present an algorithm for computing the DIWU score efficiently.

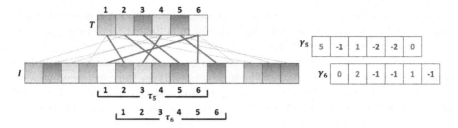

Fig. 1. Illustration of $\gamma_i(p)$ in the 1D case. T and I are the template and the image, respectively. The lines between their pixels represents the NN. Two successive image windows, τ_5 and τ_6, are marked on the image, and the $\gamma_i(p)$ for each of their pixels are presented on the right.

4   Efficient Algorithm

In this section we propose our main technical contribution – an algorithm for efficient computation of $S_{DU}(\tau_i)$ for all candidate windows in I. A naïve sliding window computation requires $O(|I||T|)$ operations, as for computing the DDIS score in [13]. We cannot use a naïve rolling sum algorithm as in Sect. 3.2, since the confidence $c_{IWU}^\tau(p)$ is window dependent. Our algorithm iteratively computes $S_{DU}(\tau_i)$ for each τ in only $O(|I|)$. The NN is computed once for each pixel in I. In addition to C_{IWU}, we store two 2D matrices of size $n \times m$, Q_x and Q_y. The matrices Q_x and Q_y consist of the coordinates of the NN. That is, for $q = N_r(p)$, $Q_x(p) = q_x$ and $Q_y(p) = q_y$. The $C_{IWU}(p)$ consists of the unpopularity of $q = N_r(p)$. For ease of exposition, we first consider the 1D case and then we extend it to the 2D case.

4.1   1D Case

Let T be a $1 \times w$ template and I be a $1 \times n$ image. In this case a pixel p and $N_r(j)$ have a single index, $1 \leq p \leq n$ and $1 \leq N_r(j) \leq w$. The image windows are given by $\{\tau_i\}_{i=1}^{n-w}$, where $\tau_i = (i, \ldots, i + w - 1)$. We first compute $S_D^x(\tau_i)$ and then extend it to $S_{DU}^x(\tau_i)$, defined in Eqs. 9 and 11. That is, we use $c_{DIWU}^\tau(p) = a_x^\tau(p)$ and then we use $c_{DIWU}^\tau(p) = a_x^\tau(p)c_{IWU}(p)$.

Our goal is to iteratively compute $S_D^x(\tau_{i+1})$ given $S_D^x(\tau_i)$, after initially computing $S_D^x(\tau_1)$. This should be done using a fixed small number of operations that are independent of w.

The alignment score in the 1D case is given by $a_x^{\tau_i}(j) = e^{-|\gamma_i(j)|}$, where $\gamma_i(j) = N_r(j) - (j - i)$ is the displacement between j and $N_r(j)$ with respect to τ_i (see Fig. 1). The score of τ_i is then given by:

$$S(\tau_i) = \sum_{j \in \tau_i} e^{-|\gamma_i(j)|} = \sum_{\substack{j \in \tau_i \\ \gamma_i(j) \geq 0}} e^{-|\gamma_i(j)|} + \sum_{\substack{j \in \tau_i \\ \gamma_i(j) < 0}} e^{-|\gamma_i(j)|} = A_x^+(\tau_i) + A_x^-(\tau_i), \quad (12)$$

where $A_x^+(\tau_i)$ and $A_x^-(\tau_i)$ are the sums of the alignments for non-negative and negative values of γ_i, respectively. It is therefore sufficient to show how to iteratively update $A_x^+(\tau_i)$ and $A_x^-(\tau_i)$.

Let us first consider the alignment score of a pixel in the intersection of two successive windows, $j \in \tau_i \cap \tau_{i+1}$. The score depends on the considered window. Since the image window τ_{i+1} is a one-pixel shift relative to τ_i, it follows that $\gamma_{i+1}(j) = N_r(j) - (j - (i+1)) = \gamma_i(j) + 1$. In particular it follows that:

$$e^{-|\gamma_{i+1}(j)|} = \begin{cases} e^{-1}e^{-|\gamma_i(j)|} & \gamma_i(j) \geq 0 \\ e \cdot e^{-|\gamma_i(j)|} & \gamma_i(j) < 0 \end{cases}. \tag{13}$$

We next present an iterative algorithm to update $A_x^+(\tau_{i+1})$ and $A_x^-(\tau_{i+1})$ efficiently given $A_x^+(\tau_i)$ and $A_x^-(\tau_i)$. The following five steps are performed to obtain the updated $A_x^+(\tau_{i+1})$ and $A_x^-(\tau_{i+1})$.

1. Set $A_x^-(\tau_{i+1}) = A_x^-(\tau_i)$ and $A_x^+(\tau_{i+1}) = A_x^+(\tau_i)$.
2. The pixel i is in τ_i but not in τ_{i+1}. Moreover, we have $\gamma_i(i) \geq 0$. Hence, $e^{-|\gamma_i(i)|}$ should be subtracted from $A_x^+(\tau_{i+1})$.
3. Let k be the number of pixels such that $j \in \tau_i \cap \tau_{i+1}$ and $\gamma_i(j) = -1$. Because of the above mentioned shift (Eq. 13), the value of these pixels, $k \cdot e^{-|-1|}$, should be subtracted from $A_x^-(\tau_{i+1})$ and added to $A_x^+(\tau_{i+1})$.
4. Due to the shift (Eq. 13), $A_x^+(\tau_{i+1})$ and $A_x^-(\tau_{i+1})$ are multiplied by e^{-1} and e, respectively.
5. Finally, the pixel $i + w$ is in τ_{i+1} but not in τ_i. Moreover, $\gamma_{i+1}(i + w) \leq 0$. Hence $e^{-|\gamma_{i+1}(i+w)|}$ should be added to either $A_x^+(\tau_{i+1})$ or $A_x^-(\tau_{i+1})$ according to whether $\gamma_{i+1}(i + w) = 0$ or < 0, respectively.

While all these steps can be performed in constant time, the computation of k, the number of pixels in τ_i with displacement -1 (that is, $\gamma_i(j) = -1$), is somewhat tricky in this regard.

To deal with this we use a histogram $hist_i$ with bin values $-w + 1, \ldots, -1$, where $hist_i(-r)$ stores the number of pixels s.t. $j \in \tau_i$ and $\gamma_i(j) = -r$. Positive differences do not have to be maintained in the histogram. The histogram can be iteratively updated by $hist_{i+1}(r) = hist_i(r + 1)$ for $-w + 1 < r < -1$. Hence, $hist_{i+1}$ can be computed by a right-shift of $hist_i$ where the value of $hist_i(-1)$ (defined as k in (3) above) is removed from the histogram. In practice, we store all $hist_i$ in a single $1 \times (w - 1)$ circular-array $hist$ and a single index b, where the index of the first element of $hist_i$ in $hist$ is given by $b(i) = (i \mod (w-1))$. Hence a right-shift corresponds to an increase of one for b. Putting it all together we obtain:

$$A_x^+(\tau_{i+1}) = (A_x^+(\tau_i) - e^{-|\gamma_i(i)|})e^{-1} + hist_i(-1)e^0 + \eta e^{-|\gamma_{i+1}(i+w)|}$$

$$A_x^-(\tau_{i+1}) = A_x^-(\tau_i)e - hist_i(-1)e^0 + (1 - \eta)e^{-|\gamma_{i+1}(i+w)|}, \tag{14}$$

where $\eta = 1$ if $\gamma_{i+1}(i+w) = 0$ and zero otherwise. Finally, the histogram $hist_i$ also has to be updated:

$$
\begin{aligned}
hist_i(-1) &= 0, \\
b(i+1) &= ((i+1) \mod (w-1)).
\end{aligned}
\tag{15}
$$

Algorithm 1. A procedure to compute S_{1DU}

1: **function** COMPUTE1D(Q_x, C_{IWU})
2:     Initialize for $i = 1$: $hist$, $b \leftarrow 1$, A_x^+, A_x^-
3:     **for** i:=2...(m-w) **do**
4:         Define $\gamma_i(j) := Q_x(j) - (j - i)$
5:         $A_x^+ \leftarrow A_x^+ - C_{IWU}(i)e^{-|\gamma_i(i)|}$
6:         $A_x^+ \leftarrow A_x^+ e^{-1} + hist(-1)e^0$
7:         $A_x^- \leftarrow A_x^- e - hist(-1)e^0$
8:         $hist(-1) \leftarrow 0$
9:         $b \leftarrow ((b+1) \mod (w-1))$
10:        **if** $\gamma_{i+1}(i+w) = 0$ **then**
11:            $A_x^+ \leftarrow A_x^+ + C_{IWU}(i+w)e^{-|\gamma_{i+1}(i+w)|}$
12:        **else**
13:            $A_x^- \leftarrow A_x^- + C_{IWU}(i+w)e^{-|\gamma_{i+1}(i+w)|}$
14:            $hist(\gamma(i+w)) \leftarrow hist(\gamma_{i+1}(i+w)) + C_{IWU}(i+w)$
15:        $S_{1DU}(i) = A_x^+ + A_x^-$
16:    **return** S_{1DU}

It is now clear that the number of steps required to iteratively update $S_D^x(\tau_{i+1})$ given $S_D^x(\tau_i)$ is independent of $|T|$. The extension of this algorithm for computing $S_{DU}^x(\tau_{i+1})$ given $S_{DU}^x(\tau_i)$ is straightforward. It is done by adding and subtracting the value of $c_{DIWU}^{\tau}(i) = e^{-|\gamma_i(j)|}c_{IWU}(j)$ into h, A_x^+, and A_x^- instead of only the alignment score, $e^{-|\gamma_i(j)|}$ (see Algorithm 1).

Implementation Details: Due to floating point inaccuracies, each iteration of A_x^- and A_x^+ computation is slightly erroneous. In Eq. 14, the previous, slightly erroneous, values of A_x^- and A_x^+ are used, and are multiplied by e and e^{-1}, respectively. The case for A_x^+ is numerically stable since the error is iteratively reduced ($e^{-1} < 1$). However, the case for A_x^- is numerically unstable, and after tens of iterations the accuracy is reduced considerably. To remedy this, we compute A_x^- as described above, but reversed, starting from τ_{n-w} towards τ_1. This changes the term that multiplies A_x^- from e to e^{-1}. All other details are symmetrical and can be easily deduced. Most importantly the complexity does not change.

4.2   2D Case

Here we consider a 2D image and a 2D template. Since S_{DU} is computed separately for the x and y component, we consider first the x component, S_{DU}^x.

The value of $S_{DU}^x(\tau)$ (see Eq. 11) is given by the sum of $c_{DIWU}^{\tau,x}(p)$ (defined Eq. 10) for all the pixels in τ. We can compute this sum by first summing the $c_{DIWU}^{\tau,x}(p)$ of all pixels in each row, and then computing the summation over all the rows. Formally, let $S_{1DU}^x(\tau_{r=\ell})$ be the sum of row ℓ of τ. Then

$$S_{DU}^x(\tau) = \sum_{\ell=i}^{i+h-1} S_{1DU}^x(\tau_{r=\ell}). \tag{16}$$

Our efficient 1D algorithm (Sect. 4.1) can be applied on each image row separately, where the template is 2D and we consider a single row of τ as a 1D window of I. The result of this algorithm is a matrix S_{1DU}^x, where $S_{1DU}^x(i,j)$ consists of the sum of $c_{DIWU}(p)$ in row i from j up to $j + w - 1$. The following observations justify this computation:

1. The value $a_x(p^\tau)$ is independent of q_y, the y component of $q = N_r(p)$.
2. The value $a_x(p^\tau)$ is independent of o_y^τ, where o^τ is upper-left pixel of τ.

The final result $S_{DU}^x(\tau)$ for all windows in I is obtained by summing all image window rows, using a simple 1D rolling summation on this matrix (see Algorithm 2). In the same manner $S_{DU}^y(\tau)$ can be computed, where the 1D case is first computed for each column.

We can now summarize the complexity of our algorithm for computing $S_{DU}(\tau)$ for all candidate τ in I. Recall that the sizes of I and T are $n \times m$ and $h \times w$, respectively.

- The initialization of the 1D case for each row and each column is given by $O(nw + mh)$ steps.
- Computing the 1D case for each row and each column takes $O(2nm)$ steps.
- 1D rolling summation over the image, once on the columns and once on the rows, takes $O(2nm + hn + wh)$ steps.
- Summing $S_{DU}(\tau) = S_{DU}^x(\tau) + S_{DU}^y(\tau)$ and finding the max takes $O(nm)$ steps.

Hence, the number of steps required for the computation is $O(nm + nh + mw) = O(nm)$, which is linear in $|I|$ and depends on T only in the initialization step of each row and column.

The algorithm naturally lends itself to parallel implementation. This is discussed in the supplementary material.

5   Experiments

We implemented our algorithms in C++ using OpenCV [2] and tested them on an Intel i7 7600U CPU with 16 GB of RAM. We compare IWU and DIWU to the DIS and DDIS [13] since they are currently the state of the art. Following [9,13] we used two types of descriptors to calculate the NNs between I and T: 3×3 overlapping patches of RGB and deep features computed using the VGG net [12].

Algorithm 2. A procedure to compute S_{DU}

1: **function** COMPUTE2D(Q_x, Q_y, C_{IWU})
2: Comment ':' denotes an entire row or column
3: $S^x_{1DU}, S^x_{DU}, S^y_{1DU}, S^y_{DU}, S_{DU} \leftarrow zeros(m,n)$
4: **for** j:=1...n **do**
5:    $S^x_{1DU}(:,j) \leftarrow Compute1D(Q_x(:,j), C_{IWU}(:,j))$
6: **for** i:=1...m **do**
7:    $S^y_{1DU}(i,:) \leftarrow Compute1D(Q_y(i,:), C_{IWU}(i,:))$
8: $S^x_{DU} \leftarrow RollingSum1Dx(S^x_{1DU}, h)$
9: $S^y_{DU} \leftarrow RollingSum1Dy(S^y_{1DU}, w)$
10: **return** $S_{DU} \leftarrow S^x_{DU} + S^y_{DU}$

Datasets: We tested IWU and DIWU on two challenging datasets. The first is BBS [9], which was collected from an object tracking dataset introduced by [16] (Sect. 5.1). This dataset was used by previous methods (including [13]) for evaluation. Since the BBS dataset is composed of only small images (480×320 or smaller), we compiled an additional dataset (TinyTLP) which is based on the shortened version of Track Long and Prosper [7] (Sect. 5.2). This dataset has substantially larger images and templates.

Examples of the results of the four algorithms are shown in Fig. 2. Qualitatively it can be seen that the heat maps for IWU and DIWU are less noisy than the heat maps for DIS and DDIS, respectively.

Quantitative Evaluation: The basic accuracy measure used in our evaluation was the Intersection over Union (IoU) between the estimated window, τ_x, of algorithm x, and the GT window, τ_{GT}. It is given by

$$IoU(\tau_x, \tau_{GT}) = \frac{\tau_x \cap \tau_{GT}}{\tau_x \cup \tau_{GT}}.$$

We use IoU to define two measures of accuracy on an entire dataset: (i) the *Success Rate* (SR) is the ratio between the number of (I,T) pairs with $IoU > 0.5$, and the total number of pairs; (ii) the mean IoU (MIoU) over the entire dataset. We measured the runtime of the methods in seconds. The reported runtime excludes the approximate NN computation (using FLANN [8]), which is the same for all methods and is reported separately.

We also evaluated the accuracy and the runtime of the algorithms as a function of the size of I. This was done by upscaling and downscaling I and T synthetically (Sect. 5.3).

5.1 BBS Dataset

The BBS dataset is composed of three sub-datasets, which we refer to as BBS25, BBS50 and BBS100, with 270, 270, 252 image-template pairs, respectively. The size of the images is 320×480 or 320×240 (relatively small!). The variable X in

Table 1. Results for the BBS datasets. (C) is for RGB features and (D) is for deep VGG net features [12]. All SR and MIoU results are given as normalized percentages and the runtime is given in seconds. The best results in each column are written in bold.

Method	BBS25		BBS50		BBS100		Total		Time
	SR	MIoU	SR	MIoU	SR	MIoU	SR	MIoU	
DIS (C)	0.652	0.564	0.559	0.497	0.484	0.441	0.565	0.501	0.020
IWU (C)	**0.711**	**0.571**	**0.593**	**0.501**	**0.567**	**0.479**	**0.624**	**0.517**	**0.009**
DDIS (C)	0.767	0.649	**0.7**	**0.594**	0.623	**0.539**	0.697	**0.594**	1.030
DIWU (C)	**0.804**	**0.663**	0.693	0.581	**0.627**	0.531	**0.708**	0.592	**0.024**
DIS (D)	**0.755**	**0.634**	0.618	**0.536**	0.611	**0.533**	0.661	**0.568**	0.019
IWU (D)	0.748	0.610	**0.622**	0.532	**0.615**	0.531	**0.662**	0.558	**0.008**
DDIS (D)	**0.833**	**0.682**	**0.696**	**0.592**	0.643	0.558	**0.724**	**0.610**	0.99
DIWU (D)	0.815	0.664	0.674	0.57	**0.675**	**0.584**	0.721	0.606	**0.022**

Table 2. Results for the TinyTLP dataset. All SR and MIoU results are given as normalized percentages and the runtime is given in seconds. (C) is for RGB features and (D) is for deep VGG net features [12]. The best results between each pair of competitors are in bold.

	Method (C)				Method (D)			
	DIS	IWU	DDIS	DIWU	DIS	IWU	DDIS	DIWU
SR	0.538	**0.553**	0.629	**0.681**	0.592	**0.610**	0.651	**0.691**
MIoU	0.459	**0.466**	0.527	**0.555**	0.503	**0.519**	0.562	**0.590**
Time	0.391	**0.059**	42.3	**0.209**	0.412	**0.060**	39.7	**0.222**

BBSX indicates that T and I were taken from two images of the same tracking video with X frames apart. Generally, a larger X indicates a harder dataset.

The results are presented in Table 1. The runtime in seconds of IWU (0.009) is 2.2 times faster than DIS (0.02). However, the significant improvement is obtained for the DIWU (0.024) which runs 43 times faster than DDIS (1.030). Similar improvements are obtained for the deep features. Note that these runtimes do not include the runtime of the NN computation which is common to all algorithms. The NN computations takes about 0.219 s for color features and 4.1 s (!) for the deep features (due to their high dimensionality) on average.

As for the accuracy, as expected the results are improved when the deformation scores are used (DDIS and DIWU v.s. DIS and IWU). In general, when comparing DIS to IWU or DDIS to DIWU, the difference in the results is marginal. For some cases our algorithm perform better and vice versa. It follows that the speedup was achieved without reduction in accuracy.

Fig. 2. Results from BBS (first two) and the TinyTLP (last two) datasets. The left images correspond to the image from which the template was taken (the green rectangle). The middle images are the target. The green, blue, red, black and magenta rectangles correspond to the GT, IWU, DIS, DIWU and DDIS, respectively. The right images correspond to the heat maps, where the top left, top right, bottom left and bottom right correspond to DIS, IWU, DDIS and DIWU, respectively. (Color figure online)

5.2 TinyTLP Dataset

The TinyTLP dataset is composed of 50 shortened video clips with 600 frames each of size 1280×720. (The full version contains the same video clips with thousands of frames each.) The dataset is very challenging with many non-rigid deformations, occlusions, drastic pose changes, etc. To avoid redundant tests, we sample only 50 frames, $1, 11, \ldots, 491$, from which we take the template T from, and the image I is taken from 100 frames ahead, i.e., if x is the frame of T, $x + 100$ is the frame for I. Altogether the dataset contains $50 \cdot 50 = 2500$ image-template pairs.

We present our results in Table 2. The runtime in seconds of IWU (0.059) is 6.6 times faster than DIS (0.391). However, the significant improvement is obtained for the DIWU (0.209) which runs 202 times faster than DDIS (42.3). Similar improvements are obtained for the deep features. Note that these running

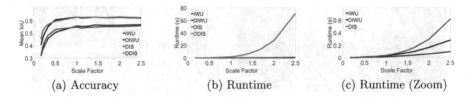

(a) Accuracy   (b) Runtime   (c) Runtime (Zoom)

Fig. 3. The accuracy and the runtime as a function of the resolution. The x-axis corresponds to a relative scale factor (relative to an image of size 480×320). (a) the y-axis corresponds to the accuracy of the algorithms (mean IoU). (b) & (c) the y-axis corresponds to the runtime in seconds. (c) is a zoom-in on the lower part of (b).

times do not include the runtime of the NN computation which is common to all algorithms. The NN computations for the color and deep features takes about 1.37 and 30.56 (!) seconds, respectively.

As for the accuracy, the same behavior as in Sect. 5.1 is obtained where the deformation score improves the results, and the difference of the DIS and IWU's accuracy is marginal. However, our DIWU algorithm not only significantly improves the speed of DDIS, but also its accuracy.

5.3   Accuracy and Runtime as a Function of the Resolution

Our theoretical analysis and the experiments discussed above show that the runtime improvements depend mainly on template size. Here we test the improvement in runtime as a function of the image and template size. For each image in the BBS25 dataset we resized I and T with the same factors. The factors we considered are the in the range of $[1/6, 2.5]$. In addition, we tested whether the results are impaired when the images are downsampled for obtaining faster running time.

The results for the accuracy analysis are presented in Fig. 3(a). The x-axis corresponds to the resize factors defined above. It is evident for all algorithms that the accuracy degrades quickly as I and T are downsampled. For example, when the image is $1/2$ its original size the accuracy is about 10% worse than for the original size. When the image is $1/4$ its original size the accuracy is about 20% worse. When I and T are upsampled the accuracy remains similar to the original resolution.

The runtime analysis is presented in Fig. 3(b) and (c). As for the accuracy, the x-axis corresponds to the resize factors. The runtime increases as I and T are upsampled. For DDIS the increase in runtime as the resolution increases is very rapid (see the magenta curve in Fig. 3(b)). For DIS, IWU and DIWU, the runtime increase is much slower (Fig. 3(c)), where both IWU and DIWU's increase more slowly than that of DIS. It appears that the empirical increase in runtime for DIWU is quadratic as a function of the scale, while the increase for DDIS is quartic, as expected.

6   Summary and Future Work

In this paper we presented an efficient template matching algorithm based on nearest neighbors. The main contribution of this paper is the development of the efficient framework for this task. In particular our new score and algorithm allows to reduce the $O(|I||T|)$ of the state-of-the-art complexity to $O(|I|)$. The improvement in practice depends on the image and template sizes. On the considered datasets, we improve the running time in a factor of 43 up to 200. This rise in efficiency can make NN based template matching feasible for real applications. Given the computed NN, the efficiency of our algorithm may be used to run it several times with only small increase in the overall computation time. For example it can be used to consider several different scales or orientations. However, it is left for future research to determine the best result among the ones obtained from the different runs.

Finally, our algorithm is based on a 1D method extended to 2D templates. It is straightforward to extend our algorithm to k-dimensional templates. Here, the 1D case should be applied to each of the k dimensions and the final score is the sum of all the dimensions. The complexity is still linear in the size of the data and is independent of the template size. It is left to future work to explore this extension.

Acknowledgments. This work was partially supported by the Israel Science Foundation, grant no. 930/12, and by the Israeli Innovation Authority in the Ministry of Economy and Industry.

References

1. Bertinetto, L., Valmadre, J., Henriques, J.F., Vedaldi, A., Torr, P.H.S.: Fully-convolutional siamese networks for object tracking. In: Hua, G., Jégou, H. (eds.) ECCV 2016. LNCS, vol. 9914, pp. 850–865. Springer, Cham (2016). https://doi.org/10.1007/978-3-319-48881-3_56
2. Bradski, G.: The OpenCV Library. Dr. Dobb's Journal of Software Tools (2000)
3. Felzenszwalb, P.F., Huttenlocher, D.P.: Pictorial structures for object recognition. Int. J. Comput. Vis. **61**(1), 55–79 (2005)
4. Held, D., Thrun, S., Savarese, S.: Learning to track at 100 FPS with deep regression networks. In: Leibe, B., Matas, J., Sebe, N., Welling, M. (eds.) ECCV 2016. LNCS, vol. 9905, pp. 749–765. Springer, Cham (2016). https://doi.org/10.1007/978-3-319-46448-0_45
5. Korman, S., Reichman, D., Tsur, G., Avidan, S.: Fast-match: fast affine template matching. In: Proceedings of IEEE Conference on Computer Vision and Pattern Recognition, pp. 2331–2338 (2013)
6. Mercier, J.P., Trottier, L., Giguere, P., Chaib-draa, B.: Deep object ranking for template matching. In: IEEE Winter Conference on Applications of Computer Vision (WACV), pp. 734–742 (2017)
7. Moudgil, A., Gandhi, V.: Long-term visual object tracking benchmark. arXiv preprint arXiv:1712.01358 (2017)
8. Muja, M., Lowe, D.G.: Scalable nearest neighbor algorithms for high dimensional data. IEEE Trans. Pattern Anal. Mach. Intell. **36** (2014)

9. Oron, S., Dekel, T., Xue, T., Freeman, W.T., Avidan, S.: Best-buddies similarity-robust template matching using mutual nearest neighbors. IEEE Trans. Pattern Anal. Mach. Intell. (2017)
10. Ouyang, W., Tombari, F., Mattoccia, S., Di Stefano, L., Cham, W.-K.: Performance evaluation of full search equivalent pattern matching algorithms. IEEE Trans. Pattern Anal. Mach. Intell. **34**(1), 127–143 (2012)
11. Penate-Sanchez, A., Porzi, L., Moreno-Noguer, F.: Matchability prediction for full-search template matching algorithms. In: International Conference on 3D Vision (3DV), pp. 353–361 (2015)
12. Simonyan, K., Zisserman, A.: Very deep convolutional networks for large-scale image recognition. arXiv preprint arXiv:1409.1556 (2014)
13. Talmi, I., Mechrez, R., Zelnik-Manor, L.: Template matching with deformable diversity similarity. In: Proceedings of IEEE Conference on Computer Vision and Pattern Recognition (2017)
14. Tian, Y., Narasimhan, S.G.: Globally optimal estimation of nonrigid image distortion. Int. J. Comput. Vis. **98**(3), 279–302 (2012)
15. Wei, Y., Tao, L.: Efficient histogram-based sliding window. In: Proceedings of IEEE Confernece on Computer Vision Pattern Recognition, pp. 3003–3010 (2010)
16. Wu, Y., Lim, J., Yang, M.H.: Online object tracking: a benchmark. In: Proceedings of the IEEE Conference on Computer Vision and Pattern Recognition, pp. 2411–2418 (2013)
17. Zagoruyko, S., Komodakis, N.: Learning to compare image patches via convolutional neural networks. In: Proceedings of the IEEE Conference on Computer Vision and Pattern Recognition, pp. 4353–4361 (2015)
18. Zbontar, J., LeCun, Y.: Stereo matching by training a convolutional neural network to compare image patches. J. Mach. Learn. Res. **17**(1–32), 2 (2016)
19. Zhang, C., Akashi, T.: Fast affine template matching over Galois field. In: British Machine Vision Conference (BMVC), pp. 121.1–121.11 (2015)

ADVIO: An Authentic Dataset for Visual-Inertial Odometry

Santiago Cortés[1]([✉]) [iD], Arno Solin[1] [iD], Esa Rahtu[2] [iD], and Juho Kannala[1] [iD]

[1] Department of Computer Science, Aalto University, Espoo, Finland
{santiago.cortesreina,arno.solin,juho.kannala}@aalto.fi
[2] Tampere University of Technology, Tampere, Finland
esa.rahtu@tut.fi

Abstract. The lack of realistic and open benchmarking datasets for pedestrian visual-inertial odometry has made it hard to pinpoint differences in published methods. Existing datasets either lack a full six degree-of-freedom ground-truth or are limited to small spaces with optical tracking systems. We take advantage of advances in pure inertial navigation, and develop a set of versatile and challenging real-world computer vision benchmark sets for visual-inertial odometry. For this purpose, we have built a test rig equipped with an iPhone, a Google Pixel Android phone, and a Google Tango device. We provide a wide range of raw sensor data that is accessible on almost any modern-day smartphone together with a high-quality ground-truth track. We also compare resulting visual-inertial tracks from Google Tango, ARCore, and Apple ARKit with two recent methods published in academic forums. The data sets cover both indoor and outdoor cases, with stairs, escalators, elevators, office environments, a shopping mall, and metro station.

Keywords: Visual-inertial odometry · Navigation · Benchmarking

1 Introduction

Various systems and approaches have recently emerged for tracking the motion of hand-held or wearable mobile devices based on video cameras and inertial measurement units (IMUs). There exist both open published methods (*e.g.* [2,12,14,16,21]) and closed proprietary systems. Recent examples of the latter are ARCore by Google and ARKit by Apple which run on the respective manufacturers' flagship smartphone models. Other examples of mobile devices with built-in visual-inertial odometry are the Google Tango tablet device and Microsoft Hololens augmented reality glasses. The main motivation for developing odometry methods for smart mobile devices is to enable augmented reality

Access data and documentation at: https://github.com/AaltoVision/ADVIO.

Electronic supplementary material The online version of this chapter (https://doi.org/10.1007/978-3-030-01249-6_26) contains supplementary material, which is available to authorized users.

© Springer Nature Switzerland AG 2018
V. Ferrari et al. (Eds.): ECCV 2018, LNCS 11214, pp. 425–440, 2018.
https://doi.org/10.1007/978-3-030-01249-6_26

Fig. 1. The custom-built capture rig with a Google Pixel smartphone on the left, a Google Tango device in the middle, and an Apple iPhone 6s on the right.

applications which require precise real-time tracking of ego-motion. Such applications could have significant value in many areas, like architecture and design, games and entertainment, telepresence, and education and training.

Despite the notable scientific and commercial interest towards visual-inertial odometry, the progress of the field is constrained by the lack of public datasets and benchmarks which would allow fair comparison of proposed solutions and facilitate further developments to push the current boundaries of the state-of-the-art systems. For example, since the performance of each system depends on both the algorithms and sensors used, it is hard to compare methodological advances and algorithmic contributions fairly as the contributing factors from hardware and software may be mixed. In addition, as many existing datasets are either captured in small spaces or utilise significantly better sensor hardware than feasible for low-cost consumer devices, it is difficult to evaluate how the current solutions would scale to medium or long-range odometry, or large-scale simultaneous localization and mapping (SLAM), on smartphones.

Further, the availability of realistic sensor data, captured with smartphone sensors, together with sufficiently accurate ground-truth would be beneficial in order to speed up progress in academic research and also lower the threshold for new researchers entering the field. The importance of public datasets and benchmarks as a driving force for rapid progress has been clearly demonstrated in many computer vision problems, like image classification [9,19], object detection [13], stereo reconstruction [10] and semantic segmentation [6,13], to name a few. However, regarding visual-inertial odometry, there are no publicly available datasets or benchmarks that would allow evaluating recent methods in a typical smartphone context. Moreover, since the open-source software culture is not as common in this research area as, for example, it is in image classification and object detection, the research environment is not optimal for facilitating rapid progress. Further, due to the aforementioned reasons, there is a danger that the field could become accessible only for big research groups funded by large corporations, and that would slow down progress and decay open academic research.

(a) View inside mall (b) Tango point cloud (c) Escalator data sets

Fig. 2. Multi-floor environments such as (a) were considered. The point cloud (b) and escalator/elevator paths captured in the mall. The Tango track (red) in (b) has similar shape as the ground-truth in (c). Periodic locomotion can be seen in (c) if zoomed in. (Color figure online)

In this work, we present a dataset that aims to facilitate the development of visual-inertial odometry and SLAM methods for smartphones and other mobile devices with low-cost sensors (*i.e.* rolling-shutter cameras and MEMS based inertial sensors). Our sensor data is collected using a standard iPhone 6s device and contains the ground-truth pose trajectory and the raw synchronized data streams from the following sensors: RGB video camera, accelerometer, gyroscope, magnetometer, platform-provided geographic coordinates, and barometer. In total, the collected sequences contain about 4.5 km of unconstrained hand-held movement in various environments both indoors and outdoors. One example sequence is illustrated in Fig. 2. The data sets are collected in public spaces, conforming the local legislation regarding filming and publishing. The ground-truth is computed by combining a recent pure inertial navigation system (INS) [24] with frequent manually determined position fixes based on a precise floor plan. The quality of our ground-truth is verified and its accuracy estimated.

Besides the benchmark dataset, we present a comparison of visual-inertial odometry methods, including three recent proprietary platforms: ARCore on a Google Pixel device, Apple ARKit on the iPhone, and Tango odometry on a Google Tango tablet device, and two recently published methods, namely ROVIO [1,2] and PIVO [25]. The data for the comparison was collected with a capture rig with the three devices and is illustrated in Fig. 1. Custom applications for data capture were implemented for each device.

The main contributions of our work are summarized in the following:

- A public dataset of iPhone sensor data with 6 degree-of-freedom pose ground-truth for benchmarking monocular visual-inertial odometry in real-life use cases involving motion in varying environments, and also including stairs, elevators and escalators.
- Comparing state-of-the-art visual-inertial odometry platforms and methods.
- A method for collecting ground-truth for smartphone odometry in realistic use cases by combining pure inertial navigation with manual position fixes.

Table 1. An overview of related datasets.

	Rawseeds [5]	KITTI [10]	NCLT [4]	EuRoC [3]	PennCOSYVIO [18]	Proposed
Year	2006	2012	2015	2016	2017	(this paper)
Carrier	Wheeled robot	Car	Segway	MAV	Hand-held device	Hand-held device
Environment	Indoors/Outdoors	Outdoors	Indoors/Outdoors	Indoors	Indoors/Outdoors	Indoors/Outdoors
Scene setup	Campus-scale	City-scale	Campus-scale	2 Rooms	150 m path on campus (walked 4 times)	Multiple levels in 3 buildings + outdoor scenes
Hardware setup	Custom	Custom	Custom	Custom	Custom	Standard smartphone
Distance (total)	~10 km	~39 km	~147 km	~800 m	~600 m	~4.5 km
Long-range use-case	✓	✓	✓	—	✓	✓
3D point cloud	—	✓	✓	✓	—	✓
Ground-truth	GPS/Visual tags	GPS/IMU	GPS/IMU/Laser	MoCap/Laser	Visual tags	IMU + Position fixes
Accuracy	~m	~dm	~dm	~mm	~dm	dm–m

2   Related Work

Despite visual-inertial odometry (VIO) being one of the most promising approaches for real-time tracking of hand-held and wearable devices, there is a lack of good public datasets for benchmarking different methods. A relevant benchmark should include both video and inertial sensor recordings with synchronized time stamps preferably captured with consumer-grade smartphone sensors. In addition, the dataset should be authentic and illustrate realistic use cases. That is, it should contain challenging environments with scarce visual features, both indoors and outdoors, and varying motions, also including rapid rotations without translation as they are problematic for monocular visual-only odometry. Our work is the first one addressing this need.

Regarding pure visual odometry or SLAM, there are several datasets and benchmarks available [6,8,23,26] but they lack the inertial sensor data. Further, many of these datasets are limited because they *(a)* are recorded using ground vehicles and hence do not have rapid rotations [6,23], *(b)* do not contain low-textured indoor scenes [6,23], *(c)* are captured with custom hardware (*e.g.* fisheye lens or global shutter camera) [8], *(d)* lack full 6-degree of freedom ground-truth [8], or *(e)* are constrained to small environments and hence are ideal for SLAM systems but not suitable for benchmarking odometry for medium and long-range navigation [26].

Nevertheless, besides pure vision datasets, there are some public datasets with inertial sensor data included, for example, [3–5,10,18]. Most of these datasets are recorded with sensors rigidly attached to a wheeled ground vehicle. For example, the widely used KITTI dataset [10] contains LIDAR scans and videos from multiple cameras recorded from a moving car. The ground-truth is obtained using a very accurate GPS/IMU localization unit with RTK correction signals. However, the IMU data is captured only with a frequency of 10 Hz, which would not be sufficient for tracking rapidly moving hand-held devices. Further, even if high-frequency IMU data would be available, also KITTI has the constraints *(a)*, *(b)*, and *(c)* mentioned above and this limits its usefulness for smartphone odometry.

Another analogue to KITTI is that we also use pure inertial navigation with external location fixes for determining the ground-truth. In our case, the GPS fixes are replaced with manual location fixes since GPS is not available or accurate indoors. Further, in contrast to KITTI, by utilizing recent advances in inertial navigation [24] we are able to use the inertial sensors of the iPhone for the ground-truth calculation and are therefore not dependent on a high-grade IMU, which would be difficult to attach to the hand-held rig. In our case the manual location fixes are determined from a reference video (Fig. 3a), which views the recorder, by visually identifying landmarks that can be accurately localized from precise building floor plans or aerial images. The benefit of not using optical methods for establishing the ground-truth is that we can easily record long sequences and the camera of the recording device can be temporarily occluded. This makes our benchmark suitable also for evaluating occlusion robustness of VIO methods [25]. Like KITTI, the Rawseeds [5] and NCLT [4] datasets are recorded with a wheeled ground vehicle. Both of them use custom sensors (*e.g.* omnidirectional camera or industrial-grade IMU). These datasets are for evaluating odometry and self-localization of slowly moving vehicles and not suitable for benchmarking VIO methods for hand-held devices and augmented reality.

The datasets that are most related to ours are EuRoC [3] and PennCOSYVIO [18]. EuRoC provides visual and inertial data captured with a global shutter stereo camera and a tactical-grade IMU onboard a micro aerial vehicle (MAV) [17]. The sequences are recorded in two different rooms that are equipped with motion capture system or laser tracker for obtaining accurate ground-truth motion. In PennCOSYVIO, the data acquisition is performed using a hand-held rig containing two Google Tango tablets, three GoPro Hero 4 cameras, and a similar visual-inertial sensor unit as used in EuRoC. The data is collected by walking a 150 m path several times at UPenn campus, and the ground-truth is obtained via optical markers. Due to the need of optic localization for determining ground-truth, both EuRoC and PennCOSYVIO contain data only from a few environments that are all relatively small-scale. Moreover, both datasets use the same high-quality custom sensor with wide field-of-view stereo cameras [17]. In contrast, our dataset contains around 4.5 km of sequences recorded with regular smartphone sensors in multiple floors in several different buildings and different outdoor environments. In addition, our dataset contains motion in stairs, elevators and escalators, as illustrated in Fig. 2, and also temporary occlusions and lack of visual features. We are not aware of any similar public dataset. The properties of different datasets are summarized in Table 1. The enabling factor for our flexible data collection procedure is to utilize recent advances in pure inertial navigation together with manual location fixes [24]. In fact, the methodology for determining the ground-truth is one of the contributions of our work. In addition, as a third contribution, we present a comparison of recent VIO methods and proprietary state-of-the-art platforms based on our challenging dataset.

(a) Reference   (b) Tango (fisheye lens)   (c) iPhone

Fig. 3. Example of simultaneously captured frames from three synchronized cameras. The external reference camera (a) is used for manual position fixes for determining the ground-truth trajectory in a separate post-processing stage.

3   Materials

The data was recorded with the three devices (iPhone 6s, Pixel, Tango) rigidly attached to an aluminium rig (Fig. 1). In addition, we captured the collection process with an external video camera that was viewing the recorder (Fig. 3). The manual position fixes with respect to a 2D map (*i.e.* a structural floor plan image or an aerial image/map) were determined afterwards from the view of the external camera. Since the device was hand-held, in most fix locations the height was given as a constant distance above the floor level (with a reasonable uncertainty estimate), so that the optimization could fit a trajectory that optimally balances the information from fix positions and IMU signals (details in Sect. 4).

The data streams from all the four devices are synchronized using network provided time. That is, the device clock is synchronized over a network time protocol (NTP) request at the beginning of a capture session. All devices were connected to 4G network during recording. Further, in order to enable analysis of the data in the same coordinate frame, we calibrated the internal and external parameters of all cameras by capturing multiple views of a checkerboard. This was performed before each session to account for small movements during transport and storage. The recorded data streams are listed in Table 2.

3.1   Raw iPhone Sensor Capture

An iOS data collection app was developed in Swift 4. It saves inertial and visual data synchronized to the Apple ARKit pose estimation. All individual data points are time stamped internally and then synchronized to global time. The global time is fetched using the Kronos Swift NTP client[1]. The data was cap-

---

[1] https://github.com/lyft/Kronos.

Table 2. Data captured by the devices.

Device	Data	Format	Units	Capture rate
Ground-truth	Pose	Position/orientation	Metric position	100 Hz
iPhone	ARKit pose	Position/orientation	Metric position	60 Hz
	Video	RGB video	Resolution 1280×720	60 Hz
	GNSS	Latitude/Longitude	World coordinates (incl. meta)	∼1 Hz
	Barometer	Pressure	kPa	∼10 Hz
	Gyroscope	Angular rate	rad/s	100 Hz
	Accelerometer	Specific force	g	100 Hz
	Magnetometer	Magnetic field	μT	100 Hz
Pixel	ARCore pose	Position/orientation	Metric position	30 Hz
Tango	Raw pose	Position/orientation	Metric position	60 Hz
	Area learning	Position/orientation	Metric position	60 Hz
	Fisheye video	Grayscale video	Resolution: 640×480	60 Hz
	Point cloud	Array of 3D points	Point coloud	∼5 Hz

tured using an iPhone 6s running iOS 11.0.3. The same software and an identical iPhone was used for collecting the reference video. This model was chosen, because the iPhone 6s (published 2015) is hardware-wise closer to an average smartphone than most recent flagship iPhones and also matches well with the Google Pixel hardware.

During the capture the camera is controlled by the ARKit service. It is performing the usual auto exposure and white balance but the focal length is kept fixed (the camera matrix returned by ARKit is stored during capture). The resolution is also controlled by ARKit and it is 1280×720. The frames are packed into an H.264/MPEG-4 video file. The GNSS/network location data is collected through the CoreLocation API. Locations are requested with the desired accuracy of 'kCLLocationAccuracyBest'. The location service provides latitude and longitude, horizontal accuracy, altitude, vertical accuracy, and speed. The accelerometer, gyroscope, magnetometer, and barometer data are collected through the CoreMotion API and recorded at the maximum rate. The approximate capture rates of the multiple data streams are shown in Table 2. The magnetometer values are uncalibrated. The barometer samples contain both the barometric pressure and associated relative altitude readings.

3.2 Apple ARKit Data

The same application that captures the raw data is running the ARKit framework. It provides a pose estimate associated with every video frame. The pose is saved as a translation vector and a rotation expressed in Euler angles. Each pose is relative to a global coordinate frame created by the phone.

3.3 Google ARCore Data

We wrote an app based on Google's ARCore example[2] for capturing the ARCore tracking result. Like ARKit, the pose data contains a translation to the first

---

[2] https://github.com/google-ar/arcore-android-sdk.

frame of the capture and a rotation to a global coordinate frame. Unlike ARKit, the orientation is stored as a unit quaternion. Note that the capture rate is slower than with ARKit. We do not save the video frames nor the sensor data on the Pixel. The capture was done on a Google Pixel device running Android 8.0.0 Oreo and using the Tango Core AR developer preview (Tango core version 1.57:2017.08.28-release-ar-sdk-preview-release-0-g0ce07954:250018377:stable).

3.4 Google Tango Data

A data collection app developed and published by [11], based on the Paraview project[3], was modified in order to collect the relevant data. The capture includes the position of the device relative to the first frame, the orientation in global coordinates, the fisheye grayscale image, and the point cloud created by the depth sensor. The Tango service was run on a Project Tango tablet running Android 4.4.2 and using Tango Core Argentine (Tango Core version 1.47:2016.11-22-argentine_tango-release-0-gce1d28c8:190012533:stable). The Tango service produces two sets of poses, referred to as *raw odometry* and *area learning*[4]. The raw odometry is built frame to frame without long term memory whereas the area learning uses ongoing map building to close loops and reduce drift. Both tracks are captured and saved.

3.5 Reference Video and Locations

One important contribution of this paper is the flexible data collection framework that enables us to capture realistic use cases in large environments. In such conditions, it is not feasible to use visual markers, motion capture, or laser scanners for ground-truth. Instead, our work takes advantage of pure inertial navigation together with manual location fixes as described in Sect. 4.1.

In order to obtain the location fixes, we record an additional reference video, which is captured by an assisting person who walks within a short distance from the actual collector. Figure 3a illustrates an example frame of such video. The reference video allows us to determine the location of the data collection device with respect to the environment and to obtain the manual location fixes (subject to measurement noise) for the pure inertial navigation approach [24].

In practice, the location fixes are produced as a post-processing step using a location marking tool developed for this paper. In this tool, one can browse the videos, and mark manual location fixes on the corresponding floor plan image. The location fixes are inserted on occasions where it is easy to determine the device position with respect to the floor plan image (*e.g.* in the beginning and the end of escalators, entering and exiting elevator, passing through a door, or walking past a building corner). In all our recordings it was relatively easy to find enough such instances needed to build an accurate ground-truth. Note that it is enough to determine the device location manually, not orientation.

---

[3] https://github.com/Kitware/ParaViewTangoRecorder.

[4] https://developers.google.com/tango/overview/area-learning.

The initial location fixes have to be further transformed from pixel coordinates of floor plan images into metric world coordinates. This is done by first converting pixels to meters by using manually measured reference distances (*e.g.* distance between pillars). Then the floor plan images are registered with respect to each other using manually determined landmark points (*e.g.* pillars or stairs) and floor height measurements.

4 Methods

4.1 Ground-Truth

The ground-truth is an implementation of the purely inertial odometry algorithm presented in [24], with the addition of manual fixation points recorded using the external reference video (see Sec. 3.5). The IMU data used in the inertial navigation system for the ground-truth originated from the iPhone, and is the same data that is shared as part of the dataset. Furthermore, additional calibration data was acquired for the iPhone IMUs accounting for additive gyroscope bias, additive accelerometer bias, and multiplicative accelerometer scale bias.

The inference of the iPhone pose track (position and orientation) was implemented as described in [24] with the addition of fusing the state estimation with both the additional calibration data and the manual fix points. The pose track corresponds to the INS estimates conditional to the fix points and external calibrations,

$$p\left(\mathbf{p}(t_k), \mathbf{q}(t_k) \mid \text{IMU}, \text{calibrations}, \{(t_i, \mathbf{p}_i)\}_{i=1}^{N}\right), \tag{1}$$

where $\mathbf{p}(t_k) \in \mathbb{R}^3$ is the phone position and $\mathbf{q}(t_k)$ is the orientation unit quaternion at time instant t_k. The set of fixpoints consists of time–position pairs $(t_i, \mathbf{p}_i)$, where the manual fixpoint $\mathbf{p}_i \in \mathbb{R}^3$ assigned to a time instant t_i. The 'IMU' refers to all accelerometer and gyroscope data over the entire track.

Accounting for uncertainty and inaccuracy in the fixation point locations is taken into account by not enforcing the phone track to match the points, but including a Gaussian measurement noise term with a standard deviation of 25 cm in the position fixes (in all directions). This allows the estimate track to disagree with the fix. Position fixes are given either as 3D locations or 2D points with unknown altitude while moving between floors.

The inference problem was finally solved with an extended Kalman filter (forward pass) and extended Rauch–Tung–Striebel smoother (backward pass, see [24] for technical details). As real-time computation is not required here, we could have also used batch optimization but that would not have caused noticeable change in the results. Calculated tracks were inspected manually frame by frame and the pose track was refined by additional fixation points until the track matched the movement seen in all three cameras and the floor plan images. Figure 2c shows examples of the estimated ground-truth track. The vertical line is an elevator ride (stopping in each floor). Walking-induced periodic movement can be seen if zoomed in. The obtained accuracy can be checked also from the example video in the supplementary material.

4.2   Evaluation Metrics

For odometry results captured on the fly while collecting the data, we propose the following evaluation metrics. All data was first temporally aligned to the same global clock (acquired by NTP requests while capturing the data), which seemed to give temporal alignments accurate to about 1–2 s. The temporal alignment was further improved by determining a constant time offset by minimizing the median error between the device yaw and roll tracks. This alignment accounts for both temporal registration errors between devices and internal delays in the odometry methods.

After the temporal alignment the tracks provided by the three devices are chopped to the same lengths covering the same time-span as there may be few seconds differences in the starting and stopping times of the recordings with different devices. The vertical direction is already aligned to gravity. To account for the relative poses between the devices, method estimates, and ground-truth, we estimate a planar rigid transform (2D rotation and translation) between estimate tracks and ground-truth based on the first 60 s of estimates in each method (using the entire path would not have had a clear effect on the results, though). The reason for not using the calibrated relative poses is that especially ARCore (and occasionally ARKit) showed wild jumps at the beginning of the tracks, which would have had considerable effects and ruined those datasets for the method.

The aligned tracks all start from origin, and we measure the absolute error to the ground-truth for every output given by each method. The empirical cumulative distribution function for the absolute position error is defined as

$$\hat{F}_n(d) = \frac{\text{number of position errors} \leq d}{n} = \frac{1}{n} \sum_{i=1}^{n} \mathbf{1}_{e_i \leq d}, \qquad (2)$$

where $\mathbf{1}_E$ is an indicator function for the event E, $\mathbf{e} \in \mathbb{R}^n$ is a vector of absolute position errors compared to ground-truth, and n is the number of positions. The function tells the proportion of position estimates being less than d meters from ground-truth.

5   Data and Results

The dataset contains 23 separate recordings captured in six different locations. The total length of all sequences is 4.47 km and the total duration is 1 h 8 min. There are 19 indoor and 4 outdoor sequences. In the indoor sequences there is a manual fix point on average every 3.7 m (or 3.8 s), and outdoors every 14.7 m (or 10 s). The ground-truth 3D trajectories for all the sequences are illustrated in the supplementary material, where also additional details are given. In addition, one of the recordings and its ground-truth are illustrated in the supplementary video. The main characteristics of the dataset sequences and environments are briefly described below.

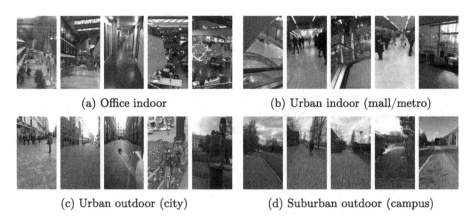

(a) Office indoor   (b) Urban indoor (mall/metro)

(c) Urban outdoor (city)   (d) Suburban outdoor (campus)

Fig. 4. Example frames from datasets. There are 7 sequences from two separate office buildings, 12 sequences from urban indoor scences (malls and metro station), two from urban outdoor scenes, and two from suburban (campus) outdoor scenes.

Our dataset is primarily designed for benchmarking medium and long-range odometry. The most obvious use case is indoor navigation in large spaces, but we have also included outdoor paths for completeness. The indoor sequences were acquired in a 7-storey shopping mall ($\sim$135,000 m^2), in a metro station, and in two different office buildings. The shopping mall and station are in the same building complex. The metro and bus station is located in the bottom floors, and there are plenty of moving people and occasional large vehicles visible in the collected videos, which makes pure visual odometry challenging. Also the lower floors of the mall contain a large number of moving persons. Figure 2 illustrates an overall view of the mall along with ground-truth path examples and a Tango point cloud (Fig. 2b). Figure 4b shows example frames from the mall and station. The use cases were as realistic as possible including motion in stairs, elevators and escalators, and also temporary occlusions and areas lacking visual features. There are ten sequences from the mall and two from the station.

Office building recordings were performed in the lobby and corridors in two office buildings. They contain some people in a static position and a few people moving. The sequences contain stair climbs and elevator rides. There are closed and open (glass) elevator sequences. Example frames are shown in Fig. 4a.

The outdoor sequences were recorded in the city center (urban, two sequences) and university campus (suburban, two sequences). Figures 4c and 4d illustrate example frames from both locations. Urban outdoor captures were performed through city blocks; they contain open spaces, people, and vehicles. Suburban outdoor captures were performed through sparsely populated areas. They contain a few people walking and some vehicle encounters. Most of the spaces are open. The average length of the outdoor sequences is 334.6 m, ranging from 133 to 514 m. The outdoor sequences were acquired in different times of the day illustrating several daylight conditions.

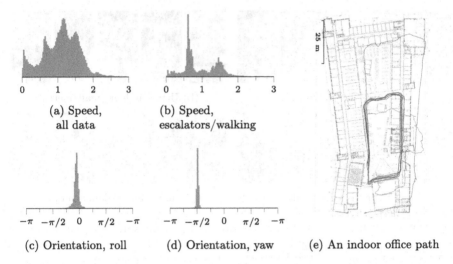

Fig. 5. (a) Speed histograms; peaks correspond to escalators, stairs, and walking. (b) the histogram for one data set with escalator rides/walking. (c–d) the histogram for roll and yaw. (e) the paths for ground-truth (——), ARKit (——), ARCore (——), Tango/Raw (——), Tango/Area learning (——), ROVIO (——), and PIVO (——)

Figure 5a shows the histograms of different motion metrics extracted from the ground-truth. Figure 5a shows the speed histogram which has three peaks that reflect the three main motion modes. From slower to faster they are escalator, stairs, and walking. Figure 5b shows the speed histogram for just one sequence that contained both escalator rides and normal walking. The orientation histograms show that the phone was kept generally in the same position relative to the carrier (portrait orientation, slightly pointing downward). The pitch angle which reflects the heading direction has a close to uniform distribution.

5.1 Benchmark Results

We evaluated two research level VIO systems using the raw iPhone data and the three proprietary solutions run on the respective devices (ARCore on Pixel, ARKit on iPhone, and Tango on the tablet). The research systems used were ROVIO [1,2,20] and PIVO [25]. ROVIO is a fairly recent method, which has been shown to work well on high-quality IMU and large field-of-view camera data. PIVO is a recent method which has shown promising results in comparison with Google Tango [25] using smartphone data. For both methods, implementations (ROVIO as part of maplab[5]) from the original authors were used (in odometry-only mode without map building or loop-closures). We used pre-calibrated camera parameters and rigid transformation from camera to IMU, and pre-estimated the process and measurement noise scale parameters.

---

[5] https://github.com/ethz-asl/maplab.

For testing purposes, we also ran two visual-only odometry methods on the raw data (DSO [7] and ORB-SLAM2 [15]). Both were able to track subsets of the paths, but the small field-of-view, rapid motion with rotations, and challenging environments caused them not to succeed for any of the entire paths.

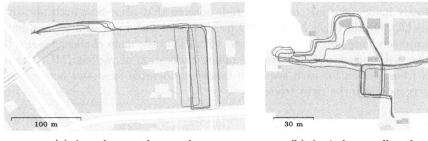

(a) An urban outdoor path   (b) An indoor mall path

Fig. 6. Example paths showing ground-truth (——), ARKit (——), ARCore (——), Tango/Raw (——), and Tango/Area learning (——) that stopped prematurely in (a). Map data © OpenStreetMap. The ground-truth fix points were marked on an architectural drawing. ROVIO and PIVO diverge and are not shown.

In general, the proprietary systems work better than the research methods, as shown in Fig. 7. In indoor sequences, all proprietary systems work well in general (Fig. 7a). Tango has the best performance, ARKit performs well and robustly with only a few clear failure cases (95th percentile ∼10 m), and ARCore occasionally fails, apparently due to incorrect visual loop-closures. Including the outdoor sequences changes the metrics slightly (Fig. 7b). ARKit had severe problems with drifting in the outdoor sequences. In terms of the orientation error all systems were accurate with less than $< 2°$ error from the ground-truth on average. This is due to the orientation tracking by integrating the gyroscope performing well if the gyroscope is well calibrated.

As shown in Fig. 7, the research methods have challenges with our iPhone data which has narrow field-of-view and a low-cost IMU. There are many sequences where both methods diverge completely (*e.g.* Fig. 6). On the other hand, there are also sequences where they work reasonably well. This may be partially explained by the fact that both ROVIO and PIVO estimate the calibration parameters of the IMU (*e.g.* accelerometer and gyroscope biases) internally on the fly and neither software directly supports giving pre-calibrated IMU parameters as input. ROVIO only considers additive accelerometer bias, which shows in many sequences as exponential crawl in position. We provide the ground-truth IMU calibration parameters with our data, and it would hence be possible to evaluate their performance also with pre-calibrated values. Alternatively, part of the sequences could be used for self-calibration and others for testing. Proprietary systems may benefit from factory-calibrated parameters. Figures 5e and 6 show examples of the results. In these cases all commercial solutions worked well.

Still, ARCore had some issues at the beginning of the outdoor path. Moreover, in multi-floor cases drifting was typically more severe and there were sequences where also proprietary systems had clear failures.

In general, ROVIO had problems with long-term occlusions and disagreements between visual and inertial data. Also, in Fig. 5e it has clearly inaccurate scale—most likely due to the not modelled scale bias in the accelerations, which is clearly inadequate for consumer-grade sensors that also show multiplicative biases [22]. On the other hand, PIVO uses a model with both additive and multiplicate accelerometer biases. However, with PIVO the main challenge seems to be that without suitable motion the online calibration of various IMU parameters from scratch for each sequence takes considerable time and hence slows convergence onto the right track.

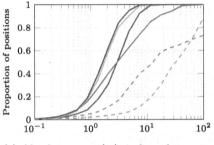
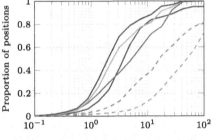

(a) Absolute error (m), indoor data sets   (b) Absolute error (m), all data sets

Fig. 7. Cumulative distributions of position error: ARKit (——), ARCore (——), Tango/Raw (——), Tango/Area learning (——), ROVIO (- - -) and PIVO (- - -).

6   Discussion and Conclusion

We have presented the first public benchmark dataset for long-range visual-inertial odometry for hand-held devices using standard smartphone sensors. The dataset contains 23 sequences recorded both outdoors and indoors on multiple floor levels in varying authentic environments. The total length of the sequences is 4.5 km. In addition, we provide quantitative comparison of three proprietary visual-inertial odometry platforms and two recent academic VIO methods, where we use the raw sensor data. To the best of our knowledge, this is the first back-to-back comparison of ARKit, ARCore, and Tango.

Apple's ARKit performed well in most scenarios. Only in one hard outdoor sequence the ARKit had the classic inertial dead-reckoning failure where the estimated position grew out of control. Google's ARCore showed more aggressive visual loop-closure use than ARKit, which is seen in false positive 'jumps' scattered throughout the tracks (between visually similar areas). The specialized hardware in the Tango gives it a upper hand, which can also be seen in Fig. 7. The area learning was the most robust and accurate system tested. However, all systems performed relatively well in the open elevator where the glass walls let the camera see the open lobby as the elevator moves. In the case of the closed elevator none of the systems were capable of reconciling the inertial motion with the static visual scene. The need for a dataset of this kind is clear from the ROVIO and PIVO results. The community needs challenging narrow field-of-view and low-grade IMU data for developing and testing new VIO methods that generalize to customer-grade hardware.

The collection procedure scales well to new environments. Hence, in future the dataset can be extended with a reasonably small effort. The purpose of the dataset is to enable fair comparison of visual-inertial odometry methods and to speed up development in this area of research. This is relevant because VIO is currently the most common approach for enabling real-time tracking of mobile devices for augmented reality.

Further details of the dataset and the download links can be found on the web page: https://github.com/AaltoVision/ADVIO.

References

1. Bloesch, M., Burri, M., Omari, S., Hutter, M., Siegwart, R.: Iterated extended Kalman filter based visual-inertial odometry using direct photometric feedback. Int. J. Robot. Res. **36**(10), 1053–1072 (2017)
2. Blösch, M., Omari, S., Hutter, M., Siegwart, R.: Robust visual inertial odometry using a direct EKF-based approach. In: Proceedings of the International Conference on Intelligent Robots and Systems (IROS), pp. 298–304, Hamburg, Germany (2015)
3. Burri, M., Nikolic, J., Gohl, P., Schneider, T., Rehder, J., Omari, S., Achtelik, M.W., Siegwart, R.: The EuRoC micro aerial vehicle datasets. Int. J. Robot. Res. **35**, 1157–1163 (2016)
4. Carlevaris-Bianco, N., Ushani, A.K., Eustice, R.M.: University of Michigan north campus long-term vision and LIDAR dataset. Int. J. Robot. Res. **35**, 1023–1035 (2015)
5. Ceriani, S., et al.: Rawseeds ground truth collection systems for indoor self-localization and mapping. Auton. Robots **27**(4), 353–371 (2009)
6. Cordts, M., et al.: The Cityscapes dataset for semantic urban scene understanding. In: Proceedings of the IEEE Conference on Computer Vision and Pattern Recognition (CVPR), pp. 3213–3223, Las Vegas, USA (2016)
7. Engel, J., Koltun, V., Cremers, D.: Direct sparse odometry. IEEE Trans. Pattern Anal. Mach. Intell. **40**(3), 611–625 (2018)
8. Engel, J., Usenko, V.C., Cremers, D.: A photometrically calibrated benchmark for monocular visual odometry. arXiv preprint arXiv:1607.02555 (2016)
9. Everingham, M., Eslami, A., Van Gool, L., Williams, I., Winn, J., Zisserman, A.: The PASCAL visual object classes challenge: a retrospective. Int. J. Comput. Vis. (IJCV) **111**(1), 98–136 (2015)
10. Geiger, A., Lenz, P., Urtasun, R.: Are we ready for autonomous driving? The KITTI vision benchmark suite. In: Proceedings of the IEEE Conference on Computer Vision and Pattern Recognition (CVPR), pp. 3354–3361, Providence, Rhode Island (2012)

11. Laskar, Z., Huttunen, S., Herrera, D., Rahtu, E., Kannala, J.: Robust loop closures for scene reconstruction by combining odometry and visual correspondences. In: Proceedings of the International Conference on Image Processing (ICIP), pp. 2603–2607, Phoenix, AZ, USA (2016)
12. Li, M., Kim, B.H., Mourikis, A.I.: Real-time motion tracking on a cellphone using inertial sensing and a rolling-shutter camera. In: Proceedings of the International Conference on Robotics and Automation (ICRA), pp. 4712–4719 (2013)
13. Lin, T., et al.: Microsoft COCO: common objects in context. In: Proceedings of the European Conference on Computer Vision (ECCV), pp. 740–755, Zurich, Switzerland (2014)
14. Mourikis, A.I., Roumeliotis, S.I.: A multi-state constraint Kalman filter for vision-aided inertial navigation. In: Proceedings of the International Conference on Robotics and Automation (ICRA), pp. 3565–3572, Rome, Italy (2007)
15. Mur-Artal, R., Tardós, J.D.: ORB-SLAM2: an open-source SLAM system for monocular, stereo and RGB-D cameras. IEEE Trans. Robot. **33**(5), 1255–1262 (2017)
16. Mur-Artal, R., Tardós, J.D.: Visual-inertial monocular SLAM with map reuse. Robot. Autom. Lett. **2**(2), 796–803 (2017)
17. Nikolic, J., et al.: A synchronized visual-inertial sensor system with FPGA pre-processing for accurate real-time SLAM. In: Proceedings of the IEEE International Conference on Robotics and Automation (ICRA), pp. 431–437, Hong-Kong, China (2014)
18. Pfrommer, B., Sanket, N., Daniilidis, K., Cleveland, J.: PennCOSYVIO: a challenging visual inertial odometry benchmark. In: Proceedings of the IEEE International Conference on Robotics and Automation (ICRA), pp. 3847–3854, Singapore (2017)
19. Russakovsky, O., et al.: ImageNet large scale visual recognition challenge. Int. J. Comput. Vis. (IJCV) **115**(3), 211–252 (2015)
20. Schneider, T., et al.: Maplab: an open framework for research in visual-inertial mapping and localization. IEEE Robot. Autom. Lett. **3**(3), 1418–1425 (2018)
21. Schöps, T., Engel, J., Cremers, D.: Semi-dense visual odometry for AR on a smartphone. In: Proceedings of the International Symposium on Mixed and Augmented Reality (ISMAR), pp. 145–150 (2014)
22. Shelley, M.A.: Monocular visual inertial odometry on a mobile device. Master's thesis, Technical University of Munich, Germany (2014)
23. Smith, M., Baldwin, I., Churchill, W., Paul, R., Newman, P.: The new college vision and laser data set. Int. J. Robot. Res. **28**(5), 595–599 (2009)
24. Solin, A., Cortes, S., Rahtu, E., Kannala, J.: Inertial odometry on handheld smartphones. In: Proceedings of the International Conference on Information Fusion (FUSION), Cambridge, UK (2018)
25. Solin, A., Cortes, S., Rahtu, E., Kannala, J.: PIVO: probabilistic inertial-visual odometry for occlusion-robust navigation. In: Proceeding of the IEEE Winter Conference on Applications of Computer Vision (WACV), Lake Tahoe, NV, USA (2018)
26. Sturm, J., Engelhard, N., Endres, F., Burgard, W., Cremers, D.: A benchmark for the evaluation of RGB-D SLAM systems. In: Proceedings of the International Conference on Intelligent Robot Systems (IROS), pp. 573–580 (2012)

Extending Layered Models to 3D Motion

Dong Lao$^{(\boxtimes)}$ and Ganesh Sundaramoorthi

KAUST, Thuwal, Saudi Arabia
{dong.lao,ganesh.sundaramoorthi}@kaust.edu.sa

Abstract. We consider the problem of inferring a layered representation, its depth ordering and motion segmentation from video in which objects may undergo 3D non-planar motion relative to the camera. We generalize layered inference to that case and corresponding self-occlusion phenomena. We accomplish this by introducing a flattened 3D object representation, which is a compact representation of an object that contains all visible portions of the object seen in the video, including parts of an object that are self-occluded (as well as occluded) in one frame but seen in another. We formulate the inference of such flattened representations and motion segmentation, and derive an optimization scheme. We also introduce a new depth ordering scheme, which is independent of layered inference and addresses the case of self-occlusion. It requires little computation given the flattened representations. Experiments on benchmark datasets show the advantage of our method over existing layered methods, which do not model 3D motion and self-occlusion.

Keywords: Motion · Video segmentation · Layered models

1 Introduction

Layered models are a powerful way to model a video sequence. Such models aim to explain a video by decomposing it into *layers*, which describe the shapes and appearances of objects, their motion, and a generative means to reconstructing the video. They also relate objects through their occlusion relations and depth ordering, i.e., the ordering of objects in front of each other with respect to the given camera viewpoint. Compared to dense 3D reconstruction from monocular video, which is valid for rigid scenes, layered approaches provide a computationally efficient intermediate 2D representation of (dynamic) scenes, which is still powerful enough for a variety of computer vision problems. Some of these problems include segmentation, motion estimation (e.g., tracking and optical flow), and shape analysis. Since all of the aforementioned problems are coupled,

---

Code available: https://github.com/donglao/layers3Dmotion.

Electronic supplementary material The online version of this chapter (https://doi.org/10.1007/978-3-030-01249-6_27) contains supplementary material, which is available to authorized users.

© Springer Nature Switzerland AG 2018
V. Ferrari et al. (Eds.): ECCV 2018, LNCS 11214, pp. 441–457, 2018.
https://doi.org/10.1007/978-3-030-01249-6_27

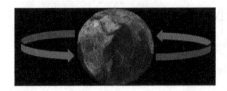

Fig. 1. Example flattened representation of the rotating earth. The video sequence (left) shows the rotating earth. The flattened representation reconstructed by our algorithm is on the right. Notice that the representation compactly captures parts of the earth that are self-occluded in some frames, but visible in others.

layered approaches provide a natural and principled framework to address these problems. Although such models are general in solving a variety of problems and have been successful in these problems, existing layered approaches are fundamentally limited as they are 2D and only model objects moving according to planar motions. Thus, they cannot cope with 3D motions such as rotation in depth and the associated *self-occlusion* phenomena. Here, we define self-occlusion as the part of a 3D object surface that is not visible, in the absence of other objects, due to camera viewpoint. In this paper, we generalize layered models and depth ordering to self-occlusion generated from out-of-plane object motion and non-planar camera viewpoint change.

Specifically, our contributions are as follows. **1.** From a modeling perspective, we introduce *flattened 3D object representations* (see Fig. 1), which are compact 2D representations of the radiance of 3D deforming objects. These representations aggregate parts of the 3D object radiance that are *self-occluded* (and occluded by other objects) in some frames, but are visible in other frames into a compact 2D representation. They generalize layered models to enable modeling of 3D (non-planar) motion and corresponding self-occlusion phenomena. **2.** We derive an optimization algorithm within a variational framework for inferring the flattened representations and segmentation whose complexity grows linearly (as opposed to combinatorially) with the number of layers. **3.** We introduce a new global depth ordering method that treats self-occlusion, in addition to occlusion from other objects. The algorithm requires virtually no computation given the flattened representations and segmentation. It also allows for the depth ordering to change with time. **4.** Finally, we demonstrate the advantage of our approach' in recovering layers, depth ordering and in segmentation on benchmark datasets.

1.1   Related Work

The literature on layered models for segmentation, motion estimation and depth ordering is extensive, and we highlight only some of the advances. Layers relate to video segmentation and motion segmentation (e.g., [1–6]) in that layered models provide a segmentation, and a principled means of dealing with occlusion phenomena. We are interested in more than just segmentation, i.e., a generative *explanation* of the video, which these methods do not provide. Since the problems of segmentation, motion estimation and depth ordering are related, many layered approaches are treated as a joint inference problem where the layers, motion and depth ordering are solved together. As the joint inference problem is difficult and a computationally intensive optimization procedure, early approaches (e.g., [7–15]) for layers employed low dimensional parametric motion models (e.g., translation or affine), which inherently limits them to planar motion.

Later approaches (e.g., [16–19]) to layers model motion of layers with fully non-parametric models based on optical flow (e.g., [20–24]), thus enabling 2D articulated motion and deformation. [16] formulates the problem of inferring layered representations as an extension of the classical Mumford and Shah segmentation problem [25–28], which provides a principled approach to layers. In [16] depth ordering is not formulated, but layers can still be inferred. Optimization, based on gradient descent was employed due to the non-convexity of the problem. While our optimization problem is similar to the framework there, their optimization method does not allow for self-occlusion. Later advances (e.g., [17,18]) improved the optimization in the layer and motion inference. However the depth ordering problem, which is coupled with layered inference, is combinatorial in the number of layers, restricting the number of layers. [29,30] aim to overcome the combinatorial problem by considering localized layers rather than a full global depth ordering. Within local regions there are typically few layers and it is feasible to solve the combinatorial problem. Further advances in optimization were achieved in [19], where the expensive joint optimization problem for segmentation, motion estimation and depth ordering are decoupled, resulting in less expensive optimization. There, depth ordering is solved by a convex optimization problem based on occlusion cues. While the aforementioned layered approaches have modeled complex deformation, they are all 2D and cannot cope with self-occlusion phenomena arising from 3D rotation in depth, which is present in realistic scenes. Thus, segmentation could fail when objects undergo non-planar motion. Our work extends layers to model such self-occlusion, and our depth ordering also accounts for this phenomena. While [3,31] does treat self-occlusion, it only performs video segmentation not layered inference; we show out-performance against that method in experiments in video segmentation.

A recent approach to layers [30] uses semantic segmentation in images (based on the advances in deep learning) to improve optical flow estimation and hence the layered inference. Although our method does not integrate semantic object detectors, as the focus is to address self-occlusion, it does not preclude them, and they can be used to enhance our method, for instance in the initialization.

2   Layered Segmentation with Flattened Object Models

In this section, we formulate the inference of the flattened 3D object representations, and segmentation as an optimization problem.

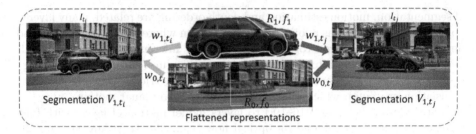

Fig. 2. Schematic of flattened representations and generation of images.

2.1 Energy Formulation

We denote the image sequence by $\{I_t\}_{t=1}^T$ where $I_t : \Omega \to \mathbb{R}^k$ ($k = 3$ for the color channels), $\Omega \subset \mathbb{R}^2$ is the domain of the image, and T is the number of images. Suppose that there are N objects (including the "background" which includes all of the scene except the objects of interest), and denote by $R_i \subset \mathbb{R}^2$ the domain (shape) of the flattened 3D object representation for object i. We denote by $f_i : R_i \to \mathbb{R}^k$ the *radiance function* of object i defined in the flattened object domain. f_i is a compact representation of all the appearances of the object i seen in the image sequence. The object appearance in any image can be obtained from the part of f_i visible in that frame. We define the *warps*, $w_{it} : R_i \to \Omega$, as the mapping from the flattened representation domain of object i to frame t. These will be diffeomorphisms (smooth and invertible maps) from the un-occluded portion of R_i to the segmentation of object i at time t. For convenience, they will be extended diffeomorphically to all of R_i. We denote by $V_{i,t} : \Omega \to [0,1]$ the *visibility functions*, the relaxed indicator functions for the pixels in image t that map to the visible portion of object i. Finally, we let $\tilde{R}_{i,t} = \{V_{i,t} = 1\}$ be the domain of projected flattened object i that is visible in from t. See Fig. 2.

We now define an energy to recover the flattened representation of each the objects, i.e., f_i, R_i, the warps $w_{i,t}$ and the visibility functions. The energy consists of two components, E_{app}, the appearance energy that is driven by the images, and E_{reg}, which contain regularity terms. The main term of the appearance energy aims to choose the flattened representations such that they can as close as possible reconstruct *each* of the images I_t by deforming the flattened representations by smooth warps. Thus, the appearance energy consists of a term that warps the appearances f_i into the image domains via the inverse of w_{it} and compares it via the squared error to the image I_t within $\tilde{R}_{it}$, the segmentations. The first term in the energy to be minimized is thus

$$E_{app} = \sum_{t,i} \int_{\tilde{R}_{it}} |I_t(x) - f_i(w_{it}^{-1}(x))|^2 \, \mathrm{d}x - \int_{\tilde{R}_{it}} \beta_t(x) \log p_i(I_t(x)) \, \mathrm{d}x. \quad (1)$$

The second term above groups pixels by similarity to other image intensities, via local histograms (i.e., a collection of histograms that vary with spatial location) p_i for object i. The spatially varying weight β_t is small when the first term is reliable enough to group the pixel, and small otherwise. This term is needed to cope with noise: if a pixel back projects to a point in the scene that is only visible in few frames, the true appearance that can be recovered is unreliable, and hence more weight is placed on grouping the pixel based on similar intensities in the image. The weighting function β, will be given in the optimization section, as it will be easier to interpret there. Other terms could be used rather than the second one, possibly integrating semantic knowledge, but we choose it for its simplicity, as our main objective is in optimization of the first term.

The regularity energy E_{reg} consists of boundary regularity of the regions defined by the visibility functions and an area penalty on the domains of the flattened object models, and is defined as follows:

$$E_{reg} = \alpha \sum_{i,t} \text{Len}(\partial \tilde{R}_{i,t}) + \gamma \sum_{i} \text{Area}(R_i), \tag{2}$$

where $\alpha, \gamma > 0$ are weights, $\text{Len}(\partial \tilde{R}_{it})$ is the length of the boundary of $\tilde{R}_{it}$, which induces spatially regular regions in the images, and $\text{Area}(R_i)$ is the area of the domain of the object model. The last term, which can be thought of as a measure of compactness of the representation, is needed so that the models are compact as possible. Note that if that term is not included, a trivial (non-useful) solution to the full optimization problem is to simply choose a single object model that is a concatenation of all the images, the warps to be the identity, and the visibility functions to be 1 everywhere, which gives $E_{app} = 0$.

The goal is to optimize the full energy $E = E_{app} + E_{reg}$, which is a joint optimization problem in the shapes R_i and appearances f_i of the flattened objects, the warps w_{it}, and the visibility functions V_{it}.

Occlusion and Self-occlusion: By formulating the energy with flattened object models, we implicitly address issues of both occlusion from one object moving in front of another, *and self-occlusion*, which are both naturally addressed and are not distinguished. The flattened model R_i, f_i contain parts of the projected object that are visible in one frame but not another. The occluded and self-occluded parts of the representation in frame t are the set $R_i \backslash w_{it}^{-1}(\{V_{it} = 1\})$. Considering only the first term of E_{app}, the occluded part of the R_i are the points that map to points x in which the squared error $|I_t(x) - f_i(w_{it}^{-1}(x))|^2$ is not smallest when compared to squared error from other flattened representations that map to the points x.

For the problem of flattened representation inference, distinguishing occlusion and is not needed. However, we eventually want to go beyond segmentation and obtain a depth ordering of objects, which requires distinguishing both occlusion (see Sect. 3). This separation of occlusion and self-occlusion allows one to see behind objects in images. See Fig. 6 where we visualize the flattened representation minus the self-occlusion, which shows the object(s) without other objects occluding them.

Fig. 3. Seeing behind occlusion from other objects. From top to bottom: original image, the flattened representation minus the self-occlusion, which removes occlusion due to other objects, and the object segmentation. Video segmentation datasets label the bottom as the segmentation, but the middle seems to be a natural object segmentation. Which should be considered ground truth?

2.2   Optimization Algorithm

Due to non-convexity, our optimization algorithm will be a joint gradient descent in the flattened shapes, appearances, warps, and the visibility functions. We now show the optimization of each one of these variables, given the others are fixed and then give the full optimization procedure at the end (Fig. 3).

Appearance Optimization: We optimize in f_i given estimates of the other variables. Notice that f_i appears only in the first term of E_{app}. We can perform a change of variables of each of the integrals, and then differentiate the expression in $f_i(x)$, and solve for the global optimum of f_i, which gives that

$$f_i(x) = \frac{\sum_t I_t(w_{it}(x)) V_{it}(w_{it}(x)) J_{it}(x)}{\sum_t V_{it}(w_{it}(x)) J_{it}(x)}, \quad x \in R_i, \tag{3}$$

where $J_{it}(x) = \det \nabla w_{it}(x)$ is the determinant of the Jacobian of the warp. The expression for f_i has a natural interpretation: the appearance at x is a weighted average of the images values at visible projections of x, i.e., $w_{it}(x)$, in the image domain. The weighting is done by area distortion of the mappings.

Shape Optimization: We optimize in the shape of the flattened region R_i by gradient descent, since the energy is non-convex in R_i. We first consider the terms in E_{app} and perform a change of variables so that the integrals are over the domains R_i. The resulting expression fits into a region competition problem [32], and we can use the known gradient computation there. One can show that the gradient with respect to the boundary ∂R_i is given by

$$\nabla_{\partial R_i} E = \sum_t \left[|\tilde{I}_{it} - f_i|^2 - |\tilde{I}_{jt} - \tilde{f}_j|^2 - \beta_t \log \frac{p_i(\tilde{I}_{it})}{p_j(\tilde{I}_{jt})} + \alpha \kappa_i \right] J_{it} \tilde{V}_i N_i + \gamma N_i, \tag{4}$$

Image sequences   2D layer   3D layer

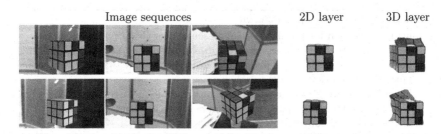

Fig. 4. Layered inference of Rubix cube. Two different video sequences (top and bottom rows) of the same Rubix cube with different camera motion. [Last column]: our flattened 3D representations capture information about the 3D structure (e.g., connectivity between faces of the Rubix cube) and motion, and includes parts of the object that are self-occluded. [Second last column]: existing 2D layered models (result from a modern implementation of [16]) cannot adapt to 3D motion and self-occlusion.

where N_i is the unit outward normal to the boundary of R_i, $\tilde{I}_{it} = I_t \circ w_{it}$, $\tilde{V}_i = V_{it} \circ w_{it}$, $\tilde{f}_j = f_j \circ w_{jt}^{-1} \circ w_{it}$, and j, which is a function of x and t, is the layer adjacent to layer i in I_t. This optimization is needed so that the size and shape of the flattened representation can adapt to new self-occlusion discovered. This is a major distinction over [16], which although has a similar model to ours, by-passes this optimization and instead only optimizes the segmentation, which is equivalent in the case of no self-occlusion, but not otherwise. Thus, it cannot adapt to self-occlusion. See Fig. 4.

Visibility Optimization: We optimize in the visibility functions V_{it}, which form the segmentation, given the other variables. Note that the visibility functions can be determined from the corresponding projected regions $\tilde{R}_{it}$. We thus compute the gradient of the energy with respect to the boundary of the projected regions $\partial \tilde{R}_{it}$. This is a standard region competition problem. One can show that the gradient is then

$$\nabla_{\partial \tilde{R}_{it}} E = \sum_t \left[|I_t - \hat{f}_i|^2 - |I_t - \hat{f}_j|^2 - \beta_t \log \frac{p_i(I_t)}{p_j(I_t)} + \alpha \kappa_i \right] \tilde{N}_i, \quad x \in \partial \tilde{R}_{it} \quad (5)$$

where $\hat{f}_i = f_i(w_{it}^{-1}(x))$, $\tilde{N}_i$ is the normal to $\partial \tilde{R}_{it}$, and j is defined as before: it is the layer adjacent to i in I_t.

Warp Optimization: We optimize in the warps w_{it} given the other variables. Since the energy is non-convex, we use gradient descent. To obtain smooth, diffeomorphic warps, and robustness to local minima, we use Sobolev gradients [33,34]. The only term that involves the warp w_{it} is the first term of the E_{app}. One can show that the Sobolev gradient G_{it} with respect to w_{it}, has a translation component $\text{avg}(G_{it}) = \text{avg}(F_{it})$ and a deformation component that satisfies:

$$\begin{cases} -\Delta \tilde{G}_{it}(x) = F_{it}(x) & x \in w_{it}(R_i) \\ \nabla \tilde{G}_{it}(x) \cdot \tilde{N}_i = |I_t - \hat{f}_i|^2 \tilde{V}_i \tilde{N}_i & x \in \partial w_{it}(R_i) \end{cases}, \quad F_{it} = \nabla \hat{f}_i [I_t - \hat{f}_i]^T \tilde{V}_i \quad (6)$$

Algorithm 1. *Layered optimization*

1: Input: Initialization for the flattened representations R_i, f_i
2: **repeat** // *update the flattened representations, warps and segmentations*
3:     For all i and t, update w_{it} performing gradient descent (6) until convergence
4:     For all i, compute f_i by (3)
5:     For all i, update R_i by one step in negative gradient direction (4)
6:     For all t, update the V_{it} by one step in negative gradient direction (5)
7: **until** the energy E converges

---

where Δ denotes the Laplacian, and ∇ denotes the spatial gradient. The optimization involves updating the warp w_{it} iteratively by the translation until convergence, then one update step of w_{it} by the deformation $\tilde{G}_{it}$, and the process is iterated until convergence.

Initialization: The innovation in our method is the formulation and the optimization for flattened representations and self-occlusion, and we do not focus here on the initialization. Here we provide a simple scheme that we use in experiments, unless otherwise stated. From $\{I_t\}_{t=1}^T$, we compute frame-to-frame optical flow using [23] and then by composing flow, we obtain displacement $v_{t,T/2}$ between t and $T/2$. We use these as components in an edge-detector [35], which gives the number of regions and a segmentation in frame $T/2$. We then choose that segmentation as the initial flattened regions. One could use more sophisticated strategies, for instance, by using semantic object detectors.

Overall Optimization Algorithm: The overall optimization is given by Algorithm 1. Rather than evolving boundaries of regions, we evolve relaxed indicator functions of the regions, described in Supplementary. We now specify β_t in (1) as $\beta_t(x) = [\min_{j \sim i, j=i} \sum_{t'} V_{jt'}(w_{jt'} \circ w_{jt}^{-1}(x)) J_{jt'}(w_{jt}^{-1}(x))]^{-1}$ where $j \sim i$ denotes object j is adjacent to object i at x and $x \in \partial R_i$. β_t is the unreliability of the first term in E_{app}, defined as follows. We compute for each j, the number of frames t' the point x corresponds to a point in the flattened representation j that is visible in frame t'. To deal with distortion effects of the mapping, there is a weighting by $J_{jt'}$. Since the evolution depends on data from all j adjacent to i and i, we define the unreliability $\beta_t(x)$ as the inverse of the least reliable representation. Therefore, more times a point is visible, the more accurate the appearance model will be, and the more dependence on the first term in E_{app}, and the less dependence on local histograms.

3 Depth Ordering

In this section, we show how the depth ordering of the objects in the images can be computed from the segmentation and flattened models determined in the previous section. In the first sub-section, we assume that the object surfaces in 3D, their mapping to the imaging plane, and the segmentation in the image are known, and present a (trivial) algorithm to recover the depth ordering. Of course, in our problem, the objects in 3D are not available. Thus, in the next sub-section, we show how the previous algorithm can be used without 3D object surfaces by using the flattened representations and their mappings to the imaging plane as proxies for the 3D surfaces and their mappings to the image.

3.1   Depth Ordering from 3D Object Surfaces

We first introduce notation for the object surfaces and mappings to the plane, and then formalize *self-occlusion* and *occlusion* induced from other objects. These concepts will be relevant to our depth ordering algorithm, which we present following these formal concepts.

Notation and Definitions: Let $O_1, \ldots, O_N \subset \mathbb{R}^3$ denote N object surfaces in the 3D world that are imaged to form the image $I : \Omega \to \mathbb{R}^k$ at a given viewpoint at a given time. With abuse of notation we let V_i denote the segmentation (points in Ω of object i) in the image I. Based on the given viewpoint, the camera projection from points on the surface O_i to the imaging plane will be denoted $w_{O_i I}$ and $w_{O_i I}^{-1}$ will denote the inverse of the mapping. We can now provide computational definitions for self-occlusion and occlusion induced by other objects, relevant to our algorithms. The **self-occlusion** (formed due to the viewpoint of the camera) is just the points of O_i (when all other objects are removed from the scene) that are not visible from the viewpoint of the camera. $w_{O_i I}(O_i)$ will denote the projection of non self-occluded points on O_i. The **occluded part** of object O_i induced by object O_j is $w_{O_i I}^{-1}(w_{O_i I}(O_i) \cap V_j)$. The **occlusion of** O_i induced by other objects (denoted by $O_{i,occ}$) is just the union of the occluded parts of O_i induced all other objects, which is given by $w_{O_i I}^{-1}(\cup_{j \neq i}(w_{O_i I}(O_i) \cap V_j))$.

Algorithm for Depth Ordering: We now present an algorithm for depth ordering. The algorithm makes the assumption that if any part of object i is occluded by object j, then any part of object j is not occluded by object i. This can be formulated as

Assumption 1. *For $i \neq j$, one of $w_{O_i I}(O_i) \cap V_j$ or $w_{O_j I}(O_j) \cap V_i$ must be empty.*

Under this assumption, we can relate the depth ordering of object i and j; indeed, $Depth(i) < Depth(j)$ (object i is in front of object j) in case $w_{O_j I}(O_j) \cap V_i \neq \emptyset$. This naturally defines the depth ordering of each objects ranging from 1 to N. Note that the depth ordering is not unique due to two cases, when both sets in the assumption above are empty. First, if the projections of two objects do not overlap ($w_{O_i I}(O_i) \cap w_{O_j I}(O_j) = \emptyset$) then no relation can be established and the ordering can be arbitrary. Second, if the overlapping part of the projections of two objects are fully occluded by another object ($w_{O_i I}(O_i) \cap w_{O_j I}(O_j) \subseteq V_k, k \neq i$ or j) then the depth relation between i and j cannot be established.

Under the previous assumption, we can derive a simple algorithm for depth ordering. Note that by definition of depth ordering, for object i satisfying

---

Algorithm 2. *Depth ordering given 3D surfaces*

1: Set $index = 1$;
2: Find i satisfying $V_i = w^i_{OI}(O_i)$, label $Depth(i) = index$;
3: For all objects j not labeled, let $V_j = V_j \cup (w^j_{OI}(O_j) \cap V_i)$;
4: $index = index + 1$, go to Step 2 until all objects are labeled

---

$Depth(i) = 1$, we have that $\cup_{j \neq i} w^i_{OI}(O_i) \cap V_j = \emptyset$, which means that it is not occluded by any other object. Therefore, we can recover the object with depth 1. By removing that object from the scene, we can repeat the same test and identify the object with depth 2. Continuing this way, we can recover the depth ordering of all objects. One can effectively remove an object i from the scene in the image by removing V_i from the segmentation in image I and then augmenting V_j by the occluded part of object j induced by object i. Therefore we can recover the depth ordering by Algorithm 2.

3.2 Depth Ordering from Flattened Representations

We now translate the depth ordering algorithm assuming 3D surfaces in the previous section to the case of depth ordering with flattened representations. We define $w_{O_i R_i}$ to be the mapping from the surface O_i to the flattened representation R_i. Ideally, $w_{O_i R_i}$ is a one-to-one mapping, but in general it will be onto since the video sequence from which the flattened representation is constructed may not observe all parts of the object. By defining the mapping from the flattened representation to the image as $w_{R_i I} := w_{O_i I} \circ w^{-1}_{O_i R}$, the definitions of self-occlusion, occlusion induced by other objects, and the visible part of the object can be naturally extended to the flattened representation. By noting that $w^{-1}_{O_i R_i}(R_i) \subset O_i$, and under Assumption 1, we obtain the following property.

Statement 1. *At least one of $w_{R_i I}(R_i) \cap V_j$ and $w_{R_j I}(R_j) \cap V_i$ must be empty.*

This translates Assumption 1 to the mappings from flattened representations to the image. This statement allows us to similarly define a depth ordering as $w_{R_i I}(R_j) \cap V_i \neq \emptyset$ means $Depth(i) < Depth(j)$, as before. Therefore, we can apply the same algorithm in the previous section with $w_{O_i I}$ replaced by $w_{R_i I}$.

In theory, the mappings $w_{R_i I}$ only map the non-self occluded part of R_i to the image. However, in practice $w_{R_i I}$ is computed from optical flow computation in Sect. 2.2, which maps the entire flattened region R_i to the image. The optical flow computation implicitly ignores data from the occluded (self-occluded as well as occlusion from other objects) part of the flattened representation through robust norms on the data fidelity, and extends the flow into occluded parts by extrapolating the warp from the visible parts. Near the self occluding boundary of the object, the mapping $w_{O_i I}$ maps large surface areas to small ones in the image so that the determinant of the Jacobian of the warp becomes small. Since the warping $w_{R_i I}$ from the flattened representation is a composition with $w_{O_i I}$, near the self-occlusion, the map $w_{R_i I}$ maps large areas to small areas in

---

Algorithm 3. *Depth ordering from flattened representations*

1: Set $index = 1$
2: $i^* = \min_{i \text{ not labeled}} \text{Area}[w_{R_i I}(R_i) \backslash \cup_{j \text{ labeled}} V_j \backslash V_i]$
3: label $Depth(i^*) = index$
4: $index = index + 1$, go to Step 2 until all objects are labeled

---

the image. Since the optical flow algorithm extends the mapping near the self-occlusion into the self-occlusion, the self-occlusion is mapped to a small area (close to zero) in the image. Therefore, in Statement 1 rather than the condition that $w_{R_j I}(R_j) \cap V_i = \emptyset$ (object j is in front of object i), it is reasonable to assume that $w_{R_j I}(R_j) \cap V_i$ has small area (representing the area of the mapping of the self-occluded part of object j to V_i).

We can now extend the algorithm for depth ordering to deal with the case of $w_{R_i I}$ approximated with optical flow computation, based on the fact that self-occlusions are mapped to a small region in the image. To identify the object on top (depth ordering 1), rather than the condition $w_{R_i I}(R_i) \backslash V_i = \emptyset$, we compute the object i_1 such that $\text{Area}(w_{R_i I}(R_i) \backslash V_i)$ is smallest over all i. As in the previous algorithm, we can now remove the object with depth ordering 1, and again find the object i_2 that minimizes $\text{Area}(w_{R_i I}(R_i) \backslash V_{i_1} \backslash V_i)$ over all $i \neq i_1$. We can continue in this way to obtain Algorithm 3. Note that this allows one to compute depth ordering from only a single image, which allows the depth ordering to change with frames in a video sequence.

4   Experiments

In this section, we show the performance of our method on three standard benchmarks, one for layered segmentation, and the others for video segmentation.

MIT Human Annotated Dataset Results: MIT Human Annotated Dataset [36] has 10 sequences, and is used to test layered segmentation approaches and depth ordering. Results are reported visually. Both planar and 3D motion are present in these image sequences. We test our layered framework by using as initialization the human labeled ground truth segmentation of the first frame (not depth ordering). Figure 5 presents the segmentation and depth ordering results. Our algorithm recovers the layers with high accuracy, and the depth ordering of the layers correctly in most of the cases.

DAVIS 2016 Dataset: The DAVIS 2016 dataset [37] dataset is a dataset focusing on video object segmentation tasks. Video segmentation is one output of our method, but our method goes further. The dataset contains 50 sequences ranging from 25 to 100 frames. In each frame the ground truth segmentation of the moving object versus the background is densely annotated. We run our scheme fully automatically initialized by the method described in Sect. 2.2.

Coarse-to-Fine Scheme for DAVIS and FBMS-59: The initialization scheme described in Sect. 2.2 often results in noisy results over time, perhaps

Fig. 5. Segmentation and depth ordering in MIT dataset. Multiple layers are extracted to obtain multi-label segmentation. Based on the segmentation result and extracted layers, Algorithm 3 is applied to compute depth ordering. In most cases the depth ordering are inferred correctly. Note that due to the ambiguity of the depth ordering, in some cases ground truth depth ordering does not exist. Layers in the front are indicated by small values of depth.

missing segmentations in some frames. To clean up this noise, we first run our algorithm with this initialization in small overlapping batches (of size 15 frames) of the video. This fills in missing segmentations. We then run our algorithm with this result as initialization on the whole video. This integrates coarse information across the whole video. Finally, to obtain finer scale details, we again run our algorithm on overlapping small batches (of size 7 frames). We iterate the last two steps to obtain our final result. Table 1 shows the result of these stages (labeled initialization, 1st, 2nd, 3rd, and the final result is labeled "ours") on DAVIS.

Table 1. Evaluation of segmentation results on DAVIS. From left to right: result after our initialization, result after the 1st stage of our coarse-to-fine layered approach (see text for an explanation), result after our 2nd stage, result after our 3rd stage of coarse-to-fine, results of competing methods, and finally our final result after the last stage of our coarse-to-fine scheme.

Method	Initial	1st	2nd	3rd	[16]	[19]	[3]	[38]	Ours
J mean	0.491	0.571	0.644	0.673	0.615	0.514	0.625	0.625	**0.683**
J recall	0.575	0.629	0.745	0.766	0.715	0.581	0.743	0.700	**0.777**
J decay	0.097	0.050	0.064	0.069	**0.041**	0.127	0.110	-	0.069
F mean	0.509	0.575	0.622	0.651	0.593	0.490	0.593	0.593	**0.672**
F recall	0.550	0.637	0.737	0.738	0.695	0.578	0.691	0.662	**0.759**
F decay	0.089	**0.064**	0.075	0.082	0.070	0.128	0.118	-	0.082

Comparison on DAVIS: We compare to a modern implementation of the layered method [16], which is a equivalent to our method if the shape evolution of the flattened representation is not performed. We also compare to [19], which

Fig. 6. Qualitative comparison on DAVIS. From left to right: (images 1–3): sequences with 3D motion inducing self-occlusion, (image 4): sequence with object color similarity to background, and (images 5–8): sequences with occlusion by other objects. Our layered segmentation successfully captures the object all of the sequence cases. In (1–3) [19], a layered approach, fails due lack of 3-D motion modeling; in (4) color similarity leads to wrong labeling in both [3,19] due to reliance on intensity similarities. In (5–8) [3,19] fail due to inability to deal with objects moving behind others. (Color figure online)

is another layered method based on motion. We also include in the comparison non-layered approaches [3], which addresses the problem of self-occlusion in motion segmentation, and [38], which is another motion segmentation approach. Qualitative comparison of the methods can be found in Fig. 6 and quantitative comparison can be found in Table 1. Quantitatively, our method outperforms all comparable motion-based approaches. Note the that the state-of-the-art approaches on this dataset use deep learning and are trained on large datasets (for instance, Pascal), however, they only perform segmentation and do not give a layered interpretation of the video and they are applicable to only binary segmentation, and they cannot be adapted to multiple objects. Our method requires no training data and is low-level, and comes close to the performance of these deep learning approaches. In fact, in 15/50 sequences, our method performs the best more than any other method.

FBMS-59 Dataset: To test our method on inferring more than two layered representations, we test our method on the FBMS-59 Dataset, which is used for benchmarking video segmentation algorithms. The test set of FBMS-59 contains 30 sequences with 69 labeled objects, and the number of frames range from 19 to 800. Ground truth is given on selected frames. We compare to [3] that is a video segmentation that handles self-occlusion but not layers (discussed in the previous section), the layered approach [19], and other motion segmentation approaches. Quantitative results and representative results are shown in Fig. 7. They show that our method has the best results among these methods, and shows a slight improvement over [3], with the additional advantage that our method gives a layered representation, more powerful than just a segmentation.

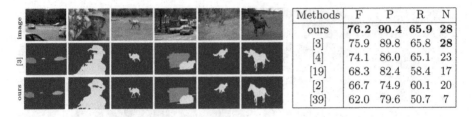

Methods	F	P	R	N
ours	**76.2**	**90.4**	**65.9**	**28**
[3]	75.9	89.8	65.8	**28**
[4]	74.1	86.0	65.1	23
[19]	68.3	82.4	58.4	17
[2]	66.7	74.9	60.1	20
[39]	62.0	79.6	50.7	7

Fig. 7. Results (qualitative and quantitative) and comparison on FBMS-59.

Parameters: Our algorithm has few parameters, i.e., the parameter γ, which is the weight on penalizing the area of the flattened representation, and α, which is the weight on the spatial regularity of the segmentation. These parameters are not sensitive. The values chosen in the experiments were $\gamma = 0.1$ and $\alpha = 2$.

Computational Cost: Our algorithm is linear in the number of layers (due to the optical flow computation for each layer). For 2 layers and 480p video with 30 frames, our entire coarse-to-fine scheme runs in about 10 min with a Matlab implementation, on a standard modern processor.

5   Conclusion

We have generalized layered approaches to 3D planar motions and corresponding self-occlusion phenomena. This was accomplished with an intermediate 2D representation that concatenated all visible parts of an object in a monocular video sequence into a single compact representation. This allowed for representing parts that were self-occluded in one frame but visible in another. Depth ordering was formulated independent of the inference of the flattened representations, and is computationally efficient. Results on benchmark datasets showed that the advantage of this approach over other layered works. Further, increased performance was shown in the problem of motion segmentation over existing layered approaches, which do not account for 3D motion.

A limitation of our method is that is dependent on the initialization, which remains an open problem, although we provided a simple scheme. More advanced schemes could use semantic segmentation. Another limitation is in our representation, in that it does not account for all 3D motions and all self-occlusion phenomena. For instance, a person walking, the crossing of legs cannot be captured with a 2D representation (our method accounted for this case on datasets since the number of frames used was small enough that legs did not fully cross). A solution would be to infer a 3D representation of the object from the monocular video, but this could be expensive computationally, and it is valid for only rigid scenes. Our method trades off between complexity of a full 3D representation and its modeling power: although it does not model all 3D situations, it is a clear advance over existing layered approaches, without the complexity of a 3D representation and its limitation to rigid scenes. Another limitation is when

Assumption 1 is broken (e.g., a hand grasping an object), in which our depth ordering would fail, but the layers are still inferred correctly.

References

1. Cremers, D., Soatto, S.: Motion competition: a variational approach to piecewise parametric motion segmentation. Int. J. Comput. Vis. **62**(3), 249–265 (2005)
2. Ochs, P., Malik, J., Brox, T.: Segmentation of moving objects by long term video analysis. IEEE Trans. Pattern Anal. Mach. Intell. **36**(6), 1187–1200 (2014)
3. Yang, Y., Sundaramoorthi, G., Soatto, S.: Self-occlusions and disocclusions in causal video object segmentation. In: Proceedings of the IEEE International Conference on Computer Vision, pp. 4408–4416 (2015)
4. Keuper, M., Andres, B., Brox, T.: Motion trajectory segmentation via minimum cost multicuts. In: 2015 IEEE International Conference on Computer Vision (ICCV), pp. 3271–3279. IEEE (2015)
5. Tokmakov, P., Alahari, K., Schmid, C.: Learning video object segmentation with visual memory. arXiv preprint arXiv:1704.05737 (2017)
6. Jain, S., Xiong, B., Grauman, K.: FusionSeg: learning to combine motion and appearance for fully automatic segmention of generic objects in videos. arXiv preprint arXiv:1701.05384 (2017)
7. Wang, J.Y., Adelson, E.H.: Representing moving images with layers. IEEE Trans. Image Process. **3**(5), 625–638 (1994)
8. Darrell, T., Pentland, A.: Robust estimation of a multi-layered motion representation. In: 1991 Proceedings of the IEEE Workshop on Visual Motion, pp. 173–178. IEEE (1991)
9. Hsu, S., Anandan, P., Peleg, S.: Accurate computation of optical flow by using layered motion representations. In: Proceedings of the 12th IAPR International Conference on Pattern Recognition 1994, Conference A: Computer Vision & Image Processing, vol. 1, pp. 743–746. IEEE (1994)
10. Ayer, S., Sawhney, H.S.: Layered representation of motion video using robust maximum-likelihood estimation of mixture models and MDL encoding. In: Proceedings of Fifth International Conference on Computer Vision 1995, pp. 777–784. IEEE (1995)
11. Bergen, L., Meyer, F.: Motion segmentation and depth ordering based on morphological segmentation. In: Burkhardt, H., Neumann, B. (eds.) ECCV 1998. LNCS, vol. 1407, pp. 531–547. Springer, Heidelberg (1998). https://doi.org/10.1007/BFb0054763
12. Jojic, N., Frey, B.J.: Learning flexible sprites in video layers. In: Proceedings of the 2001 IEEE Computer Society Conference on Computer Vision and Pattern Recognition, CVPR 2001, vol. 1, pp. I–I. IEEE (2001)
13. Smith, P., Drummond, T., Cipolla, R.: Layered motion segmentation and depth ordering by tracking edges. IEEE Trans. Pattern Anal. Mach. Intell. **26**(4), 479–494 (2004)
14. Kumar, M.P., Torr, P.H., Zisserman, A.: Learning layered motion segmentations of video. Int. J. Comput. Vis. **76**(3), 301–319 (2008)
15. Schoenemann, T., Cremers, D.: A coding-cost framework for super-resolution motion layer decomposition. IEEE Trans. Image Process. **21**(3), 1097–1110 (2012)
16. Jackson, J.D., Yezzi, A.J., Soatto, S.: Dynamic shape and appearance modeling via moving and deforming layers. Int. J. Comput. Vis. **79**(1), 71–84 (2008)

17. Sun, D., Sudderth, E.B., Black, M.J.: Layered segmentation and optical flow estimation over time. In: 2012 IEEE Conference on Computer Vision and Pattern Recognition (CVPR), pp. 1768–1775. IEEE (2012)
18. Sun, D., Wulff, J., Sudderth, E.B., Pfister, H., Black, M.J.: A fully-connected layered model of foreground and background flow. In: 2013 IEEE Conference on Computer Vision and Pattern Recognition (CVPR), pp. 2451–2458. IEEE (2013)
19. Taylor, B., Karasev, V., Soatto, S.: Causal video object segmentation from persistence of occlusions. In: Proceedings of the IEEE Conference on Computer Vision and Pattern Recognition, pp. 4268–4276 (2015)
20. Horn, B.K., Schunck, B.G.: Determining optical flow. Artif. Intell. **17**(1–3), 185–203 (1981)
21. Black, M.J., Anandan, P.: The robust estimation of multiple motions: parametric and piecewise-smooth flow fields. Comput. Vis. Image Underst. **63**(1), 75–104 (1996)
22. Brox, T., Bruhn, A., Papenberg, N., Weickert, J.: High accuracy optical flow estimation based on a theory for warping. In: Pajdla, T., Matas, J. (eds.) ECCV 2004. LNCS, vol. 3024, pp. 25–36. Springer, Heidelberg (2004). https://doi.org/10.1007/978-3-540-24673-2_3
23. Sun, D., Roth, S., Black, M.J.: Secrets of optical flow estimation and their principles. In: 2010 IEEE Conference on Computer Vision and Pattern Recognition (CVPR), pp. 2432–2439. IEEE (2010)
24. Ilg, E., Mayer, N., Saikia, T., Keuper, M., Dosovitskiy, A., Brox, T.: FlowNet 2.0: evolution of optical flow estimation with deep networks. In: IEEE Conference on Computer Vision and Pattern Recognition (CVPR), vol. 2 (2017)
25. Mumford, D., Shah, J.: Optimal approximations by piecewise smooth functions and associated variational problems. Commun. Pure Appl. Math. **42**(5), 577–685 (1989)
26. Tsai, A., Yezzi, A., Willsky, A.S.: Curve evolution implementation of the Mumford-Shah functional for image segmentation, denoising, interpolation, and magnification. IEEE Trans. Image Process. **10**(8), 1169–1186 (2001)
27. Vese, L.A., Chan, T.F.: A multiphase level set framework for image segmentation using the Mumford and Shah model. Int. J. Comput. Vis. **50**(3), 271–293 (2002)
28. Pock, T., Cremers, D., Bischof, H., Chambolle, A.: An algorithm for minimizing the Mumford-Shah functional. In: 2009 IEEE 12th International Conference on Computer Vision, pp. 1133–1140. IEEE (2009)
29. Sun, D., Liu, C., Pfister, H.: Local layering for joint motion estimation and occlusion detection (2014)
30. Sevilla-Lara, L., Sun, D., Jampani, V., Black, M.J.: Optical flow with semantic segmentation and localized layers. In: Proceedings of the IEEE Conference on Computer Vision and Pattern Recognition, pp. 3889–3898 (2016)
31. Yang, Y., Sundaramoorthi, G.: Modeling self-occlusions in dynamic shape and appearance tracking. In: Proceedings of the IEEE International Conference on Computer Vision, pp. 201–208 (2013)
32. Zhu, S.C., Yuille, A.: Region competition: unifying snakes, region growing, and bayes/MDL for multiband image segmentation. IEEE Trans. Pattern Anal. Mach. Intell. **18**(9), 884–900 (1996)
33. Yang, Y., Sundaramoorthi, G.: Shape tracking with occlusions via coarse-to-fine region-based sobolev descent. IEEE Trans. Pattern Anal. Mach. Intell. **37**(5), 1053–1066 (2015)

34. Sundaramoorthi, G., Yezzi, A., Mennucci, A.: Coarse-to-fine segmentation and tracking using sobolev active contours. IEEE Trans. Pattern Anal. Mach. Intell. **30**(5), 851–864 (2008)
35. Dollár, P., Zitnick, C.L.: Fast edge detection using structured forests. IEEE Trans. Pattern Anal. Mach. Intell. **37**(8), 1558–1570 (2015)
36. Liu, C., Freeman, W.T., Adelson, E.H., Weiss, Y.: Human-assisted motion annotation. In: 2008 IEEE Conference on Computer Vision and Pattern Recognition, CVPR 2008, pp. 1–8. IEEE (2008)
37. Perazzi, F., Pont-Tuset, J., McWilliams, B., Van Gool, L., Gross, M., Sorkine-Hornung, A.: A benchmark dataset and evaluation methodology for video object segmentation. In: Computer Vision and Pattern Recognition (2016)
38. Wehrwein, S., Szeliski, R.: Video segmentation with background motion models. In: British Machine Vision Conference (2017)
39. Ayvaci, A., Soatto, S.: Detachable object detection: segmentation and depth ordering from short-baseline video. IEEE Trans. Pattern Anal. Mach. Intell. **34**(10), 1942–1951 (2012)

3DMV: Joint 3D-Multi-view Prediction for 3D Semantic Scene Segmentation

Angela Dai[1(✉)] and Matthias Nießner[2]

[1] Stanford University, Stanford, USA
`adai@cs.stanford.edu`
[2] Technical University of Munich, Munich, Germany

Abstract. We present 3DMV, a novel method for 3D semantic scene segmentation of RGB-D scans in indoor environments using a joint 3D-multi-view prediction network. In contrast to existing methods that either use geometry *or* RGB data as input for this task, we combine both data modalities in a joint, end-to-end network architecture. Rather than simply projecting color data into a volumetric grid and operating solely in 3D – which would result in insufficient detail – we first extract feature maps from associated RGB images. These features are then mapped into the volumetric feature grid of a 3D network using a differentiable back-projection layer. Since our target is 3D scanning scenarios with possibly many frames, we use a multi-view pooling approach in order to handle a varying number of RGB input views. This learned combination of RGB and geometric features with our joint 2D-3D architecture achieves significantly better results than existing baselines. For instance, our final result on the ScanNet 3D segmentation benchmark **increases from 52.8% to 75% accuracy** compared to existing volumetric architectures.

1 Introduction

Semantic scene segmentation is important for a large variety of applications as it enables understanding of visual data. In particular, deep learning-based approaches have led to remarkable results in this context, allowing prediction of accurate per-pixel labels in images [14,22]. Typically, these approaches operate on a single RGB image; however, one can easily formulate the analogous task in 3D on a per-voxel basis [5,13,21,34,40,41], which is a common scenario in the context of 3D scene reconstruction. In contrast to 2D, the third dimension offers a unique opportunity as it not only predicts semantics, but also provides a spatial semantic map of the scene content based on the underlying 3D representation. This is particularly relevant for robotics applications since a robot relies not only on information of *what* is in a scene but also needs to know *where* things are.

---

https://github.com/angeladai/3DMV.

Electronic supplementary material The online version of this chapter (https://doi.org/10.1007/978-3-030-01249-6_28) contains supplementary material, which is available to authorized users.

© Springer Nature Switzerland AG 2018
V. Ferrari et al. (Eds.): ECCV 2018, LNCS 11214, pp. 458–474, 2018.
https://doi.org/10.1007/978-3-030-01249-6_28

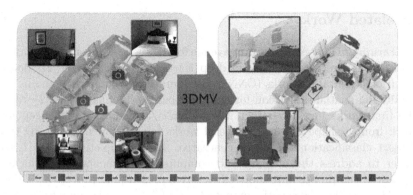

Fig. 1. 3DMV takes as input a reconstruction of an RGB-D scan along with its color images (left), and predicts a 3D semantic segmentation in the form of per-voxel labels (mapped to the mesh, right). The core of our approach is a joint 3D-multi-view prediction network that leverages the synergies between geometric and color features. (Color figure online)

In 3D, the representation of a scene is typically obtained from RGB-D surface reconstruction methods [6,17,26,27] which often store scanned geometry in a 3D voxel grid where the surface is encoded by an implicit surface function such as a signed distance field [4]. One approach towards analyzing these reconstructions is to leverage a CNN with 3D convolutions, which has been used for shape classification [30,43], and recently also for predicting dense semantic 3D voxel maps [5,8,36]. In theory, one could simply add an additional color channel to the voxel grid in order to incorporate RGB information; however, the limited voxel resolution prevents encoding feature-rich image data (Fig. 1).

In this work, we specifically address this problem of how to incorporate RGB information for the 3D semantic segmentation task, and leverage the combined geometric and RGB signal in a joint, end-to-end approach. To this end, we propose a novel network architecture that takes as input the 3D scene representation as well as the input of nearby views in order to predict a dense semantic label set on the voxel grid. Instead of mapping color data directly on the voxel grid, the core idea is to first extract 2D feature maps from 2D images using the full-resolution RGB input. These features are then downsampled through convolutions in the 2D domain, and the resulting 2D feature map is subsequently backprojected into 3D space. In 3D, we leverage a 3D convolutional network architecture to learn from both the backprojected 2D features as well as 3D geometric features. This way, we can join the benefits of existing approaches and leverage all available information, significantly improving on existing approaches.

Our main contribution is the formulation of a joint, end-to-end convolutional neural network which learns to infer 3D semantics from both 3D geometry and 2D RGB input. In our evaluation, we provide a comprehensive analysis of the design choices of the joint 2D-3D architecture, and compare it with current state of the art methods. In the end, our approach increases 3D segmentation accuracy from 52.8% to 75% compared to the best existing volumetric architecture.

2 Related Work

Deep Learning in 3D. An important avenue for 3D scene understanding has been opened through recent advances in deep learning. Similar to the 2D domain, convolutional neural networks (CNNs) can operate in volumetric domains using an additional spatial dimension for the filter banks. 3D ShapeNets [2] was one of the first works in this context; they learn a 3D convolutional deep belief network from a shape database. Several works have followed, using 3D CNNs for object classification [23,30] or generative scene completion tasks [7,8,10]. In order to address the memory and compute requirements, hierarchical 3D CNNs have been proposed to more efficiently represent and process 3D volumes [10,12,32,33,38,42]. The spatial extent of a 3D CNN can also be increased with dilated convolutions [44], which have been used to predict missing voxels and infer semantic labels [36], or by using a fully-convolutional networks, in order to decouple the dimensions of training and test time [8]. Very recently, we have seen also network architectures that operate on an (unstructured) point-based representation [29,31].

Multi-view Deep Networks. An alternative way of learning a classifier on 3D input is to render the geometry, run a 2D feature extractor, and combine the extracted features using max pooling. The multi-view CNN approach by Su et al. [37] was one of the first to propose such an architecture for object classification. However, since the output is a classification score, this architecture does not spatially correlate the accumulated 2D features. Very recently, a multi-view network has been proposed for part-based mesh segmentation [18]. Here, 2D confidence maps of each part label are projected on top of ShapeNet [2] models, where a mesh-based CRF accumulates inputs of multiple images to predict the part labels on the mesh geometry. This approach handles only relatively small label sets (e.g., 2–6 part labels), and its input is 2D renderings of the 3D meshes; i.e., the multi-view input is meant as a replacement input for 3D geometry. Although these methods are not designed for 3D semantic segmentation, we consider them as the main inspiration for our multi-view component.

Multi-view networks have also been proposed in the context of stereo reconstruction. For instance, Choy et al. [3] use an RNN to accumulate features from different views and Tulsiani et al. [39] propose an unsupervised approach that takes multi-view input to learn a latent 3D space for 3D reconstruction. Multi-view networks have also been used in the context of stereo reconstruction [19,20], leveraging feature projection into 3D to produce consistent reconstruction. An alternative way to combine several input views with 3D, is by projecting colors directly into the voxels, maintaining one channel for each input view per voxel [16]. However, due to memory requirements, this becomes impractical for a large number of input views.

3D Semantic Segmentation. Semantic segmentation on 2D images is a popular task and has been heavily explored using cutting-edge neural network approaches [14,22]. The analog task can be formulated in 3D, where the goal is to predict semantic labels on a per-voxel level [40,41]. Although this is a relatively recent task, it is extremely relevant to a large range of applications, in particular, robotics, where a spatial understanding of the inferred semantics is essential. For the 3D semantic segmentation task, several datasets and benchmarks have recently been developed. The ScanNet [5] dataset introduced a 3D semantic segmentation task on approx. 1.5k RGB-D scans and reconstructions obtained with a Structure Sensor. It provides ground truth annotations for training, validation, and testing directly on the 3D reconstructions; it also includes approx. 2.5 mio RGB-D frames whose 2D annotations are derived using rendered 3D-to-2D projections. Matterport3D [1] is another recent dataset of about 90 building-scale scenes in the same spirit as ScanNet; it includes fewer RGB-D frames (approx. 194,400) but has more complete reconstructions.

3 Overview

The goal of our method is to predict a 3D semantic segmentation based on the input of commodity RGB-D scans. More specifically, we want to infer semantic class labels on per-voxel level of the grid of a 3D reconstruction. To this end, we propose a joint 2D-3D neural network that leverages both RGB and geometric information obtained from a 3D scans. For the geometry, we consider a regular volumetric grid whose voxels encode a ternary state (known-occupied, known-free, unknown). To perform semantic segmentation on full 3D scenes of varying sizes, our network operates on a per-chunk basis; i.e., predicting columns of a scene in sliding-window fashion through the xy-plane at test time. For a given xy-location in a scene, the network takes as input the volumetric grid of the surrounding area (chunks of $31 \times 31 \times 62$ voxels). The network then extracts geometric features using a series of 3D convolutions, and predicts per-voxel class labels for the center column at the current xy-location. In addition to the geometry, we select nearby RGB views at the current xy-location that overlap with the associated chunk. For all of these 2D views, we run the respective images through a 2D neural network that extracts their corresponding features. Note that these 2D networks all have the same architecture and share the same weights.

In order to combine the 2D and 3D features, we introduce a differentiable backprojection layer that maps 2D features onto the 3D grid. These projected features are then merged with the 3D geometric information through a 3D convolutional part of the network. In addition to the projection, we add a voxel pooling layer that enables handling a variable number of RGB views associated with a 3D chunk; the pooling is performed on a per-voxel basis. In order to run 3D semantic segmentation for entire scans, this network is run for each xy-location of a scene, taking as input the corresponding local chunks.

In the following, we will first introduce the details of our network architecture (see Sect. 4) and then show how we train and implement our method (see Sect. 5).

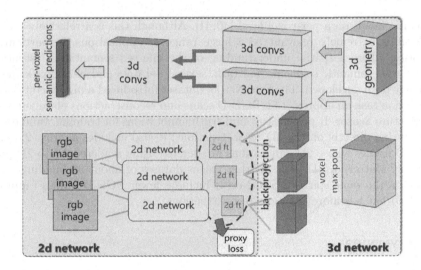

Fig. 2. Network overview: our architecture is composed of a 2D and a 3D part. The 2D side takes as input several aligned RGB images from which features are learned with a proxy loss. These are mapped to 3D space using a differentiable backprojection layer. Features from multiple views are max-pooled on a per-voxel basis and fed into a stream of 3D convolutions. At the same time, we input the 3D geometry into another 3D convolution stream. Then, both 3D streams are joined and the 3D per-voxel labels are predicted. The whole network is trained in an end-to-end fashion.

4   Network Architecture

Our network is composed of a 3D stream and several 2D streams that are combined in a joint 2D-3D network architecture. The 3D part takes as input a volumetric grid representing the geometry of a 3D scan, and the 2D streams take as input the associated RGB images. To this end, we assume that the 3D scan is composed of a sequence of RGB-D images obtained from a commodity RGB-D camera, such as a Kinect or a Structure Sensor; although note that our method generalizes to other sensor types. We further assume that the RGB-D images are aligned with respect to their world coordinate system using an RGB-D reconstruction framework; in the case of ScanNet [5] scenes, the BundleFusion [6] method is used. Finally, the RGB-D images are fused together in a volumetric grid, which is commonly done by using an implicit signed distance function [4]. An overview of the network architecture is provided in Fig. 2.

4.1   3D Network

Our 3D network part is composed of a series of 3D convolutions operating on a regular volumetric gird. The volumetric grid is a subvolume of the voxelized 3D representation of the scene. Each subvolume is centered around a specific xy-location at a size of $31 \times 31 \times 62$ voxels, with a voxel size of 4.8 cm. Hence, we consider a spatial neighborhood of 1.5 m × 1.5 m and 3 m in height. Note that we use a height of 3 m in order to cover the height of most indoor environments, such that we only need to train the network to operate in varying xy-space. The 3D network takes these subvolumes as input, and predicts the semantic labels for the center columns of the respective subvolume at a resolution of $1 \times 1 \times 62$ voxels; i.e., it simultaneously predicts labels for 62 voxels. For each voxel, we encode the corresponding value of the scene reconstruction state: known-occupied (i.e., on the surface), known-free space (i.e., based on empty space carving [4]), or unknown space (i.e., we have no knowledge about the voxel). We represent this through a 2-channel volumetric grid, the first a binary encoding of the occupancy, and the second a binary encoding of the known/unknown space. The 3D network then processes these subvolumes with a series of nine 3D convolutions which expand the feature dimension and reduce the spatial dimensions, along with dropout regularization during training, before a final set of fully connected layers which predict the classification scores for each voxel.

In the following, we show how to incorporate learned 2D features from associated 2D RGB views.

4.2   2D Network

The aim of the 2D part of the network is to extract features from each of the input RGB images. To this end, we use a 2D network architecture based on ENet [28] to learn those features. Note that although we can use a variable of number of 2D input views, all 2D networks share the same weights as they are jointly trained. Our choice to use ENet is due to its simplicity as it is both fast to run and memory-efficient to train. In particular, the low memory requirements are critical since it allows us to jointly train our 2D-3D network in an end-to-end fashion with multiple input images per train sample. Although our aim is 2D-3D end-to-end training, we additionally use a 2D proxy loss for each image that allows us to make the training more stable; i.e., each 2D stream is asked to predict meaningful semantic features for an RGB image segmentation task. Here, we use semantic labels of the 2D images as ground truth; in the case of ScanNet [5], these are derived from the original 3D annotations by rendering the annotated 3D mesh from the camera points of the respective RGB image poses. The final goal of the 2D network is to obtain the features in the last layer before the proxy loss per-pixel classification scores; these features maps are then backprojected into 3D to join with the 3D network, using a differentiable backprojection layer. In particular, from an input RGB image of size 328×256, we obtain a 2D feature map of size $(128\times)41 \times 32$, which is then backprojected into the space of the corresponding 3D volume, obtaining a 3D representation of the feature map of size $(128\times)31 \times 31 \times 62$.

4.3   Backprojection Layer

In order to connect the learned 2D features from each of the input RGB views with the 3D network, we use a differentiable backprojection layer. Since we assume known 6-DoF pose alignments for the input RGB images with respect to each other and the 3D reconstruction, we can compute 2D-3D associations on-the-fly. The layer is essentially a loop over every voxel in 3D subvolume where a given image is associated to. For every voxel, we compute the 3D-to-2D projection based on the corresponding camera pose, the camera intrinsics, and the world-to-grid transformation matrix. We use the depth data from the RGB-D images in order to prune projected voxels beyond a threshold of the voxel size of 4.8 cm; i.e., we compute only associations for voxels close to the geometry of the depth map. We compute the correspondences from 3D voxels to 2D pixels since this allows us to obtain a unique voxel-to-pixel mapping. Although one could pre-compute these voxel-to-pixel associations, we simply compute this mapping on-the-fly in the layer as these computations are already highly memory bound on the GPU; in addition, it saves significant disk storage since this it would involve a large amount of index data for full scenes.

Once we have computed voxel-to-pixel correspondences, we can project the features of the last layer of the 2D network to the voxel grid:

$$n_{feat} \times w_{2d} \times h_{2d} \rightarrow n_{feat} \times w_{3d} \times h_{3d} \times d_{3d}$$

For the backward pass, we use the inverse mapping of the forward pass, which we store in a temporary index map. We use 2D feature maps (feature dim. of 128) of size $(128\times)41 \times 31$ and project them to a grid of size $(128\times)31 \times 31 \times 62$.

In order to handle multiple 2D input streams, we compute voxel-to-pixel associations with respect to each input view. As a result, some voxels will be associated with multiple pixels from different views. In order to combine projected features from multiple input views, we use a voxel max-pooling operation that computes the maximum response on a per feature channel basis. Since the max pooling operation is invariant to the number of inputs, it enables selecting for the features of interest from an arbitrary number of input images.

4.4   Joint 2D-3D Network

The joint 2D-3D network combines 2D RGB features and 3D geometric features using the mapping from the backprojection layer. These two inputs are processed with a series of 3D convolutions, and then concatenated together; the joined feature is then further processed with a set of 3D convolutions. We have experimented with several options as to where to join these two parts: at the beginning (i.e., directly concatenated together without independent 3D processing), approximately 1/3 or 2/3 through the 3D network, and at the end (i.e., directly before the classifier). We use the variant that provided the best results, fusing the 2D and 3D features together at 2/3 of the architectures (i.e., after the 6th 3D convolution of 9); see Table 5 for the corresponding ablation study. Note that the entire network, as shown in Fig. 2, is trained in an end-to-end fashion, which is feasible since all components are differentiable. Table 1 shows an overview of the distribution of learnable parameters of our 3DMV model.

Table 1. Distribution of learnable parameters of our 3DMV model. Note that the majority of the network weights are part of the combined 3D stream just before the per-voxel predictions where we rely on strong feature maps; see top left of Fig. 2.

	2D only	3D (2D input only)	3D (3D geo only)	3D (fused 2D/3D)
# trainable params	146,176	379,744	87,136	10,224,300

4.5   Evaluation in Sliding Window Mode

Our joint 2D-3D network operates on a per-chunk basis; i.e., it takes fixed subvolumes of a 3D scene as input (along with associated RGB views), and predicts labels for the voxels in the center column of the given chunk. In order to perform a semantic segmentation of large 3D environments, we slide the subvolume through the 3D grid of the underlying reconstruction. Since the height of the subvolume (3 m) is sufficient for most indoor environments, we only need to slide over the xy-domain of the scene. Note, however, that for training, the training samples do not need to be spatially connected, which allows us to train on a random set of subvolumes. This de-coupling of training and test extents is particularly important since it allows us to provide a good label and data distribution of training samples (e.g., chunks with sufficient coverage and variety).

5   Training

5.1   Training Data

We train our joint 2D-3D network architecture in an end-to-end fashion. To this end, we prepare correlated 3D and RGB input to the network for the training process. The 3D geometry is encoded in a ternary occupancy grid that encodes known-occupied, known-free, and unknown states for each voxel. The ternary information is split upon 2 channels, where the first channel encodes occupancy and the second channel encodes the known vs. unknown state. To select train subvolumes from a 3D scene, we randomly sample subvolumes as potential training samples. For each potential train sample, we check its label distribution and discard samples containing only structural elements (i.e., wall/floor) with 95% probability. In addition, all samples with empty center columns are discarded as well as samples with less than 70% of the center column geometry annotated.

For each subvolume, we then associate k nearby RGB images whose alignment is known from the 6-DoF camera pose information. We select images greedily based on maximum coverage; i.e., we first pick the image covering the most voxels in the subvolume, and subsequently take each next image which covers the most number of voxels not covered by current set. We typically select 3–5 images since additional gains in coverage become smaller with each added image. For each sampled subvolume, we augment it with 8 random rotations for a total of 1,316,080 train samples. Since existing 3D datasets, such as ScanNet [5] or Matterport3D [1] contain unannotated regions in the ground truth (see Fig. 3, right), we mask out these regions in both our 3D loss and 2D proxy loss. Note that this strategy still allows for making predictions for all voxels at test time.

5.2 Implementation

We implement our approach in PyTorch. While 2D and 3D conv layers are already provided by the PyTorch API, we implement a custom layer for the backprojection layer. We implement this backprojection in python, as a custom PyTorch layer, representing the projection as series of matrix multiplications in order to exploit PyTorch parallelization, and run the backprojection on the GPU through the PyTorch API. For training, we have tried only training parts of the network; however, we found that the end-to-end version that jointly optimizes both 2D and 3D performed best. In the training processes, we use an SGD optimizer with a learning rate of 0.001 and a momentum of 0.9; we set the batch size to 8. Note that our training set is quite biased towards structural classes (e.g., wall, floor), even when discarding most structural-only samples, as these elements are vastly dominant in indoor scenes. In order to account for this data imbalance, we use the histogram of classes represented in the train set to weight the loss during training. We train our network for 200,000 iterations; for our network trained on 3 views, this takes ≈24 h, and for 5 views, ≈48 h.

6 Results

In this section, we provide an evaluation of our proposed method with a comparison to existing approaches. We evaluate on the ScanNet dataset [5], which contains 1513 RGB-D scans composed of 2.5M RGB-D images. We use the public train/val/test split of 1045, 156, 312 scenes, respectively, and follow the 20-class semantic segmentation task defined in the original ScanNet benchmark. We evaluate our results with per-voxel class accuracies, following the evaluations of previous work [5,8,31]. Additionally, we visualize our results qualitatively and in comparison to previous work in Fig. 3, with close-ups shown in Fig. 4. Note that we map the predictions from all methods back onto the mesh reconstruction for ease of visualization.

Comparison to State of the Art. Our main results are shown in Table 2, where we compare to several state-of-the-art volumetric (ScanNet [5], ScanComplete [8]) and point-based approaches (PointNet++[31]) on the ScanNet test set. Additionally, we show an ablation study regarding our design choices in Table 3.

The best variant of our 3DMV network achieves 75% average classification accuracy which is quite significant considering the difficulty of the task and the performance of existing approaches. That is, we improve 22.2% over existing volumetric and 14.8% over the state-of-the-art PointNet++ architecture.

How Much Does RGB Input Help? Table 3 includes a direct comparison between our 3D network architecture when using RGB features against the exact same 3D network without the RGB input. Performance improves from 54.4% to 70.1% with RGB input, even with just a single RGB view. In addition, we tried out the naive alternative of using per-voxel colors rather than a 2D feature extractor. Here, we see only a marginal difference compared to the purely geometric baseline

(54.4% vs. 55.9%). We attribute this relatively small gain to the limited grid resolution ($\approx$5 cm voxels), which is insufficient to capture rich RGB features. Overall, we can clearly see the benefits of RGB input, as well as the design choice to first extract features in the 2D domain.

How Much Does Geometric Input Help? Another important question is whether we actually need the 3D geometric input, or whether geometric information is a redundant subset of the RGB input; see Table 3. The first experiment we conduct in this context is simply a projection of the predicted 2D labels on top of the geometry. If we only use the labels from a single RGB view, we obtain 27% average accuracy (vs. 70.1% with 1 view + geometry); for 3 views, this label backprojection achieves 44.2% (vs. 73.0% with 3 views + geometry). Note that this is related to the limited coverage of the RGB backprojections (see Table 4).

However, the interesting experiment now is what happens if we still run a series of 3D convolutions after the backprojection of the 2D labels. Again, we omit inputting the scene geometry, but we now learn how to combine and propagate the backprojected features in the 3D grid; essentially, we ignore the first part of our 3D network; cf. Fig. 2. For 3 RGB views, this results in an accuracy of 58.2%; this is higher than the 54.4% of geometry only; however, it is much lower than our final 3-view result of 73.0% from the joint network. Overall, this shows that the combination of RGB and geometric information aptly complements each other, and that the synergies allow for an improvement over the individual inputs by 14.8% and 18.6%, respectively (for 3 views).

Table 2. Comparison of our final trained model (5 views, end-to-end) against other state-of-the-art methods on the ScanNet dataset [5]. We can see that our approach makes significant improvements, 22.2% over existing volumetric and approx. 14.8% over state-of-the-art PointNet++ architectures.

	wall	floor	cab	bed	chair	sofa	table	door	wind	bkshf	pic	cntr	desk	curt	fridg	show	toil	sink	bath	other	avg
ScanNet [5]	70.1	90.3	49.8	62.4	69.3	75.7	**68.4**	48.9	20.1	64.6	3.4	32.1	36.8	7.0	66.4	46.8	69.9	39.4	74.3	19.5	50.8
ScanComplete [8]	87.2	96.9	44.5	65.7	75.1	72.1	63.8	13.6	16.9	70.5	10.4	31.4	40.9	49.8	38.7	46.8	72.2	47.4	85.1	26.9	52.8
PointNet++ [31]	**89.5**	**97.8**	39.8	69.7	**86.0**	68.3	59.6	27.5	23.7	84.3	0.0	**37.6**	66.7	48.7	54.7	**85.0**	84.8	62.8	86.1	30.7	60.2
3DMV (ours)	73.9	95.6	**69.9**	**80.7**	85.9	**75.8**	67.8	**86.6**	**61.2**	**88.1**	**55.8**	31.9	**73.2**	**82.4**	**74.8**	82.6	**88.3**	**72.8**	**94.7**	**58.5**	**75.0**

How to Feed 2D Features into the 3D Network? An interesting question is where to join 2D and 3D features; i.e., at which layer of the 3D network do we fuse together the features originating from the RGB images with the features from the 3D geometry. On the one hand, one could argue that it makes more sense to feed the 2D part early into the 3D network in order to have more capacity for learning the joint 2D-3D combination. On the other hand, it might make more sense to keep the two streams separate for as long as possible to first extract strong independent features before combining them.

To this end, we conduct an experiment with different 2D-3D network combinations (for simplicity, always using a single RGB view without end-to-end training); see Table 5. We tried four combinations, where we fused the 2D and

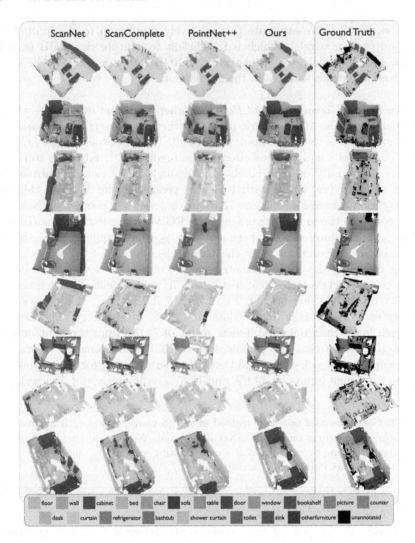

Fig. 3. Qualitative semantic segmentation results on the ScanNet [5] test set. We compare with the 3D-based approaches of ScanNet [5], ScanComplete [8], PointNet++ [31]. Note that the ground truth scenes contain some unannotated regions, denoted in black. Our joint 3D-multi-view approach achieves more accurate semantic predictions.

3D features at the beginning, after the first third of the network, after the second third, and at the very end into the 3D network. Interestingly, the results are relatively similar ranging from 67.6%, 65.4% to 69.1% and 67.5% suggesting that the 3D network can adapt quite well to the 2D features. Across these experiments, the second third option turned out to be a few percentage points higher than the alternatives; hence, we use that as a default in all other experiments.

How Much Do Additional Views Help? In Table 3, we also examine the effect of each additional view on classification performance. For geometry only, we obtain an average classification accuracy of 54.4%; adding only a single view per chunk increases to 70.1% (+15.7%); for 3 views, it increases to 73.1% (+3.0%); for 5 views, it reaches 75.0% (+1.9%). Hence, for every additional view the incremental gains become smaller; this is somewhat expected as a large part of the benefits are attributed to additional coverage of the 3D volume with 2D features. If we already use a substantial number of views, each additional added feature shares redundancy with previous views, as shown in Table 4.

Is End-to-End Training of the Joint 2D-3D Network Useful? Here, we examine the benefits of training the 2D-3D network in an end-to-end fashion, rather than simply using a pre-trained 2D network. We conduct this experiment with 1, 3, and 5 views. The end-to-end variant consistently outperforms the fixed version, improving the respective accuracies by 1.0%, 0.2%, and 0.5%. Although the end-to-end variants are strictly better, the increments are smaller than initially hoped for. We also tried removing the 2D proxy loss that enforces good 2D predictions, which led to a slightly lower performance. Overall, end-to-end training with a proxy loss always performed best and we use it as our default.

Table 3. Ablation study for different design choices of our approach on ScanNet [5]. We first test simple baselines where we backproject 2D labels from 1 and 3 views (rows 1–2), then run set of 3D convs after the backprojections (row 3). We then test a 3D-geometry-only network (row 4). Augmenting the 3D-only version with per-voxel colors shows only small gains (row 5). In rows 6–11, we test our joint 2D-3D architecture with varying number of views, and the effect of end-to-end training. Our 5-view, end-to-end variant performs best.

	wall	floor	cab	bed	chair	sofa	table	door	wind	bkshf	pic	cntr	desk	curt	fridg	show	toil	sink	bath	other	avg
2D only (1 view)	37.1	39.1	26.7	33.1	22.7	38.8	17.5	38.7	13.5	32.6	14.9	7.8	19.1	34.4	33.2	13.3	32.7	29.2	36.3	20.4	27.1
2D only (3 views)	58.6	62.5	40.8	51.6	38.6	59.7	31.1	55.9	25.9	52.9	25.1	14.2	35.0	51.2	57.3	36.0	47.1	44.7	61.5	34.3	44.2
Ours (no geo input)	76.2	92.9	59.3	65.6	80.6	73.9	63.3	75.1	22.6	80.2	13.3	31.8	43.4	56.5	53.4	43.2	82.1	55.0	80.8	9.3	58.2
Ours (3D geo only)	60.4	95.0	54.4	69.5	79.5	70.6	71.3	65.9	20.7	71.4	4.2	20.0	38.5	15.2	59.9	57.3	78.7	48.8	87.0	20.6	54.4
Ours (3D geo+voxel color)	58.8	94.7	55.5	64.3	72.1	80.1	65.5	**70.7**	33.1	69.0	2.9	31.2	49.5	37.2	49.1	54.1	75.9	48.4	85.4	20.5	55.9
Ours (1 view, fixed 2D)	77.3	96.8	**70.0**	78.2	82.6	**85.0**	68.5	88.8	36.0	82.8	15.7	32.6	60.3	71.0	76.7	82.2	74.8	57.6	87.0	58.5	69.1
Ours (1 view)	70.7	96.8	61.4	76.4	84.4	80.3	70.4	83.9	57.9	85.3	41.7	35.0	64.5	75.6	81.3	58.2	85.0	60.5	81.6	51.7	70.1
Ours (3 view, fixed 2D)	**81.1**	96.4	58.0	77.3	84.7	85.2	**74.9**	87.3	51.2	86.3	33.5	**47.0**	52.4	79.5	79.0	72.3	80.8	**76.1**	92.5	**60.7**	72.8
Ours (3 view)	75.2	**97.1**	66.4	77.6	80.6	84.5	66.5	85.8	61.8	87.1	47.6	24.7	68.2	75.2	78.9	73.6	86.9	**76.1**	89.9	57.2	73.0
Ours (5 view, fixed 2D)	77.3	95.7	68.9	**81.7**	**89.6**	84.2	74.8	83.1	**62.0**	87.4	36.0	40.5	55.9	**83.1**	**81.6**	77.0	87.8	70.7	93.5	59.6	74.5
Ours (5 view)	73.9	95.6	69.9	80.7	85.9	75.8	67.8	86.6	61.2	**88.1**	**55.8**	31.9	**73.2**	82.4	74.8	**82.6**	**88.3**	72.8	**94.7**	58.5	**75.0**

Evaluation in 2D Domains Using NYUv2. Although we are predicting 3D per-voxel labels, we can also project the obtained voxel labels into the 2D images. In Table 6, we show such an evaluation on the NYUv2 [35] dataset. For this task, we train our network on both ScanNet data as well as the NYUv2 train annotations projected into 3D. Although this is not the actual task of our method, it can be seen as an efficient way to accumulate semantic information from multiple RGB-D frames by using the 3D geometry as a proxy for the learning framework. Overall, our joint 2D-3D architecture compares favorably against the respective baselines on this 13-class task.

Table 4. Amount of coverage from varying number of views over the annotated ground truth voxels of the ScanNet [5] test scenes.

	1 view	3 views	5 views
Coverage	40.3%	64.4%	72.3%

Table 5. Evaluation of various network combinations for joining the 2D and 3D streams in the 3D architecture (cf. Fig. 2, top). We use the single view variant with a fixed 2D network here for simplicity. Interestingly, performance only changes slightly; however, the 2/3 version performed the best, which is our default for all other experiments.

	wall	floor	cab	bed	chair	sofa	table	door	wind	bkshf	pic	cntr	desk	curt	fridg	show	toil	sink	bath	other	avg
begin	78.8	96.3	63.7	72.8	83.3	81.9	**74.5**	81.6	39.5	89.6	**24.8**	33.9	52.6	**74.8**	76.0	47.5	80.1	**65.4**	85.9	49.4	67.6
1/3	79.3	95.5	65.1	75.2	80.3	81.5	73.8	86.0	30.5	**91.7**	11.3	**35.5**	46.4	66.6	67.9	44.1	**81.7**	55.5	85.9	53.3	65.4
2/3	77.3	**96.8**	**70.0**	**78.2**	82.6	**85.0**	68.5	**88.8**	36.0	82.8	15.7	32.6	**60.3**	71.0	**76.7**	**82.2**	74.8	57.6	87.0	**58.5**	**69.1**
end	**82.7**	96.3	67.1	77.8	**83.2**	80.1	66.0	80.3	**41.0**	83.9	24.3	32.4	57.7	70.1	71.5	58.5	79.6	65.1	**87.2**	45.8	67.5

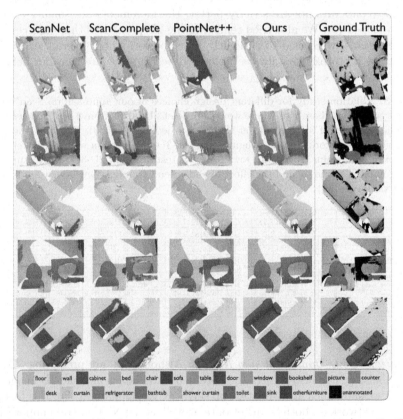

Fig. 4. Additional qualitative semantic segmentation results (close ups) on the ScanNet [5] test set. Note the consistency of our predictions compared to the other baselines.

Table 6. We can also evaluate our method on 2D semantic segmentation tasks by projecting the predicted 3D labels into the respective RGB-D frames. Here, we show a comparison on dense pixel classification accuracy on NYU2 [25]. Note that the reported ScanNet classification is on the 11-class task.

	bed	books	ceil.	chair	floor	furn.	obj.	pic.	sofa	table	tv	wall	wind.	avg.
SceneNet [11]	70.8	5.5	76.2	59.6	95.9	62.3	50.0	18.0	61.3	42.2	22.2	86.1	32.1	52.5
Hermans et al. [15]	68.4	45.4	**83.4**	41.9	91.5	37.1	8.6	35.8	58.5	27.7	38.4	71.8	48.0	54.3
ENet [28]	79.2	35.5	31.6	60.2	82.3	61.8	50.9	43.0	61.2	42.7	30.1	84.1	67.4	56.2
SemanticFusion [24] (RGBD+CRF)	62.0	**58.4**	43.3	59.5	92.7	64.4	**58.3**	65.8	48.7	34.3	34.3	86.3	62.3	59.2
SemanticFusion [24, 9] (Eigen+CRF)	48.3	51.5	79.0	74.7	90.8	63.5	46.9	63.6	46.5	45.9	**71.5**	**89.4**	55.6	63.6
ScanNet [5]	81.4	-	46.2	67.6	**99.0**	65.6	34.6	-	67.2	50.9	35.8	55.8	63.1	60.7
3DMV (ours)	**84.3**	44.0	43.4	**77.4**	92.5	**76.8**	54.6	**70.5**	**86.3**	**58.6**	67.3	84.5	**85.3**	**71.2**

Summary Evaluation.

- RGB and geometric features are orthogonal and help each other.
- More views help, but increments get smaller with every view.
- End-to-end training is strictly better, but the improvement is not that big.
- Variations of where to join the 2D and 3D features change performance to some degree; 2/3 performed best in our tests.
- Our results are significantly better than the best volumetric or PointNet baseline (+22.2% and +14.8%, respectively).

Limitations. While our joint 3D-multi-view approach achieves significant performance gains over previous state of the art in 3D semantic segmentation, there are still several important limitations. Our approach operates on dense volumetric grids, which become quickly impractical for high resolutions; e.g., RGB-D scanning approaches typically produce reconstructions with sub-centimeter voxel resolution; sparse approaches, such as OctNet [33], might be a good remedy. Additionally, we currently predict only the voxels of each column of a scene jointly, while each column is predicted independently, which can give rise to some label inconsistencies in the final predictions since different RGB views might be selected; note, however, that due to the convolutional nature of the 3D networks, the geometry remains spatially coherent.

7 Conclusion and Future Work

We presented 3DMV, a joint 3D-multi-view approach built on the core idea of combining geometric and RGB features in a joint network architecture. We show that our joint approach can achieve significantly better accuracy for semantic 3D scene segmentation. In a series of evaluations, we carefully examine our design choices; for instance, we demonstrate that the 2D and 3D features complement each other rather than being redundant; we also show that our method can successfully take advantage of using several input views from an RGB-D sequence to gain higher coverage, thus resulting in better performance. In the end, we are able to show results at more than **14% higher classification accuracy** than the best existing 3D segmentation approach. Overall, we believe that these improvements will open up new possibilities where not only the semantic content, but also the spatial 3D layout plays an important role.

For the future, we still see many open questions in this area. First, the 3D semantic segmentation problem is far from solved, and semantic instance segmentation in 3D is still at its infancy. Second, there are many fundamental questions about the scene representation for realizing 3D convolutional neural networks, and how to handle mixed sparse-dense data representations. And third, we also see tremendous potential for combining multi-modal features for generative tasks in 3D reconstruction, such as scan completion and texturing.

References

1. Chang, A., et al.: Matterport3D: learning from RGB-D data in indoor environments. In: International Conference on 3D Vision (3DV) (2017)
2. Chang, A.X., et al.: ShapeNet: an information-rich 3D model repository. Technical report, Stanford University – Princeton University – Toyota Technological Institute at Chicago. arXiv:1512.03012 [cs.GR] (2015)
3. Choy, C.B., Xu, D., Gwak, J.Y., Chen, K., Savarese, S.: 3D-R2N2: a unified approach for single and multi-view 3D object reconstruction. In: Leibe, B., Matas, J., Sebe, N., Welling, M. (eds.) ECCV 2016. LNCS, vol. 9912, pp. 628–644. Springer, Cham (2016). https://doi.org/10.1007/978-3-319-46484-8_38
4. Curless, B., Levoy, M.: A volumetric method for building complex models from range images. In: Proceedings of the 23rd Annual Conference on Computer Graphics and Interactive Techniques, pp. 303–312. ACM (1996)
5. Dai, A., Chang, A.X., Savva, M., Halber, M., Funkhouser, T., Nießner, M.: ScanNet: richly-annotated 3D reconstructions of indoor scenes. In: Proceedings of Computer Vision and Pattern Recognition (CVPR). IEEE (2017)
6. Dai, A., Nießner, M., Zollhöfer, M., Izadi, S., Theobalt, C.: BundleFusion: realtime globally consistent 3D reconstruction using on-the-fly surface reintegration. ACM Trans. Gr. (TOG) **36**(3), 24 (2017)
7. Dai, A., Qi, C.R., Nießner, M.: Shape completion using 3D-encoder-predictor CNNs and shape synthesis. In: Proceedings of Computer Vision and Pattern Recognition (CVPR). IEEE (2017)
8. Dai, A., Ritchie, D., Bokeloh, M., Reed, S., Sturm, J., Nießner, M.: ScanComplete: large-scale scene completion and semantic segmentation for 3D scans. arXiv preprint arXiv:1712.10215 (2018)
9. Eigen, D., Fergus, R.: Predicting depth, surface normals and semantic labels with a common multi-scale convolutional architecture. In: Proceedings of the IEEE International Conference on Computer Vision, pp. 2650–2658 (2015)
10. Han, X., Li, Z., Huang, H., Kalogerakis, E., Yu, Y.: High resolution shape completion using deep neural networks for global structure and local geometry inference. In: IEEE International Conference on Computer Vision (ICCV) (2017)
11. Handa, A., Patraucean, V., Badrinarayanan, V., Stent, S., Cipolla, R.: SceneNet: understanding real world indoor scenes with synthetic data. arXiv preprint arXiv:1511.07041 (2015)
12. Häne, C., Tulsiani, S., Malik, J.: Hierarchical surface prediction for 3D object reconstruction. arXiv preprint arXiv:1704.00710 (2017)

13. Hane, C., Zach, C., Cohen, A., Angst, R., Pollefeys, M.: Joint 3D scene reconstruction and class segmentation. In: Proceedings of the IEEE Conference on Computer Vision and Pattern Recognition, pp. 97–104 (2013)
14. He, K., Gkioxari, G., Dollár, P., Girshick, R.: Mask R-CNN. In: 2017 IEEE International Conference on Computer Vision (ICCV), pp. 2980–2988. IEEE (2017)
15. Hermans, A., Floros, G., Leibe, B.: Dense 3D semantic mapping of indoor scenes from RGB-D images. In: 2014 IEEE International Conference on Robotics and Automation (ICRA), pp. 2631–2638. IEEE (2014)
16. Ji, M., Gall, J., Zheng, H., Liu, Y., Fang, L.: SurfaceNet: an end-to-end 3D neural network for multiview stereopsis. arXiv preprint arXiv:1708.01749 (2017)
17. Kähler, O., Prisacariu, V.A., Ren, C.Y., Sun, X., Torr, P., Murray, D.: Very high frame rate volumetric integration of depth images on mobile devices. IEEE Trans. Vis. Comput. Gr. **21**(11), 1241–1250 (2015)
18. Kalogerakis, E., Averkiou, M., Maji, S., Chaudhuri, S.: 3D shape segmentation with projective convolutional networks. In: Proceedings of CVPR. IEEE 2 (2017)
19. Kar, A., Häne, C., Malik, J.: Learning a multi-view stereo machine. In: Advances in Neural Information Processing Systems, pp. 364–375 (2017)
20. Kendall, A., Martirosyan, H., Dasgupta, S., Henry, P., Kennedy, R., Bachrach, A., Bry, A.: End-to-end learning of geometry and context for deep stereo regression. CoRR, abs/1703.04309 (2017)
21. Kundu, A., Li, Y., Dellaert, F., Li, F., Rehg, J.M.: Joint semantic segmentation and 3D reconstruction from monocular video. In: Fleet, D., Pajdla, T., Schiele, B., Tuytelaars, T. (eds.) ECCV 2014. LNCS, vol. 8694, pp. 703–718. Springer, Cham (2014). https://doi.org/10.1007/978-3-319-10599-4_45
22. Long, J., Shelhamer, E., Darrell, T.: Fully convolutional networks for semantic segmentation. In: Proceedings of the IEEE conference on computer vision and pattern recognition, pp. 3431–3440 (2015)
23. Maturana, D., Scherer, S.: VoxNet: A 3D convolutional neural network for real-time object recognition. In: 2015 IEEE/RSJ International Conference on Intelligent Robots and Systems (IROS), pp. 922–928. IEEE (2015)
24. McCormac, J., Handa, A., Davison, A., Leutenegger, S.: SemanticFusion: dense 3D semantic mapping with convolutional neural networks. In: 2017 IEEE International Conference on Robotics and Automation (ICRA), pp. 4628–4635. IEEE (2017)
25. Silberman, N., Hoiem, D., Kohli, P., Fergus, R.: Indoor segmentation and support inference from RGBD images. In: Fitzgibbon, A., Lazebnik, S., Perona, P., Sato, Y., Schmid, C. (eds.) ECCV 2012. LNCS, vol. 7576, pp. 746–760. Springer, Heidelberg (2012). https://doi.org/10.1007/978-3-642-33715-4_54
26. Newcombe, R.A., et al.: KinectFusion: real-time dense surface mapping and tracking. In: 2011 10th IEEE international symposium on Mixed and Augmented Reality (ISMAR), pp. 127–136. IEEE (2011)
27. Nießner, M., Zollhöfer, M., Izadi, S., Stamminger, M.: Real-time 3D reconstruction at scale using voxel hashing. ACM Trans. Gr. (TOG) **32**, 169 (2013)
28. Paszke, A., Chaurasia, A., Kim, S., Culurciello, E.: ENet: a deep neural network architecture for real-time semantic segmentation. arXiv preprint arXiv:1606.02147 (2016)
29. Qi, C.R., Su, H., Mo, K., Guibas, L.J.: PointNet: deep learning on point sets for 3D classification and segmentation. In: Proceedings of Computer Vision and Pattern Recognition (CVPR), vol. 1, no. 2, p. 4. IEEE (2017)
30. Qi, C.R., Su, H., Nießner, M., Dai, A., Yan, M., Guibas, L.: Volumetric and multi-view CNNs for object classification on 3D data. In: Proceedings of Computer Vision and Pattern Recognition (CVPR). IEEE (2016)

31. Qi, C.R., Yi, L., Su, H., Guibas, L.J.: PointNet++: deep hierarchical feature learning on point sets in a metric space. In: Advances in Neural Information Processing Systems, pp. 5105–5114 (2017)
32. Riegler, G., Ulusoy, A.O., Bischof, H., Geiger, A.: OctNetFusion: learning depth fusion from data. arXiv preprint arXiv:1704.01047 (2017)
33. Riegler, G., Ulusoy, A.O., Geiger, A.: OctNet: learning deep 3D representations at high resolutions. In: Proceedings of the IEEE Conference on Computer Vision and Pattern Recognition (2017)
34. Savinov, N., Ladicky, L., Hane, C., Pollefeys, M.: Discrete optimization of ray potentials for semantic 3D reconstruction. In: Proceedings of the IEEE Conference on Computer Vision and Pattern Recognition, pp. 5511–5518 (2015)
35. Silberman, N., Fergus, R.: Indoor scene segmentation using a structured light sensor. In: Proceedings of the International Conference on Computer Vision - Workshop on 3D Representation and Recognition (2011)
36. Song, S., Yu, F., Zeng, A., Chang, A.X., Savva, M., Funkhouser, T.: Semantic scene completion from a single depth image. In: Proceedings of 30th IEEE Conference on Computer Vision and Pattern Recognition (2017)
37. Su, H., Maji, S., Kalogerakis, E., Learned-Miller, E.: Multi-view convolutional neural networks for 3D shape recognition. In: Proceedings of the IEEE International Conference on Computer Vision, pp. 945–953 (2015)
38. Tatarchenko, M., Dosovitskiy, A., Brox, T.: Octree generating networks: efficient convolutional architectures for high-resolution 3D outputs. arXiv preprint arXiv:1703.09438 (2017)
39. Tulsiani, S., Zhou, T., Efros, A.A., Malik, J.: Multi-view supervision for single-view reconstruction via differentiable ray consistency. In: CVPR. vol. 1, p. 3 (2017)
40. Valentin, J., et al.: SemanticPaint: interactive 3D labeling and learning at your fingertips. ACM Trans. Gr. (TOG) **34**(5), 154 (2015)
41. Vineet, V., et al.: Incremental dense semantic stereo fusion for large-scale semantic scene reconstruction. In: 2015 IEEE International Conference on Robotics and Automation (ICRA), pp. 75–82. IEEE (2015)
42. Wang, P.S., Liu, Y., Guo, Y.X., Sun, C.Y., Tong, X.: O-CNN: octree-based convolutional neural networks for 3D shape analysis. ACM Trans. Gr. (TOG) **36**(4), 72 (2017)
43. Wu, Z., et al.: 3D shapeNets: a deep representation for volumetric shapes. In: Proceedings of the IEEE Conference on Computer Vision and Pattern Recognition, pp. 1912–1920 (2015)
44. Yu, F., Koltun, V.: Multi-scale context aggregation by dilated convolutions. arXiv preprint arXiv:1511.07122 (2015)

FishEyeRecNet: A Multi-context Collaborative Deep Network for Fisheye Image Rectification

Xiaoqing Yin[1,2(✉)], Xinchao Wang[3], Jun Yu[4], Maojun Zhang[2],
Pascal Fua[5], and Dacheng Tao[1]

[1] UBTECH Sydney AI Center, SIT, FEIT, University of Sydney, Sydney, Australia
yinxiaoqing89@gmail.com, dacheng.tao@sydney.edu.au
[2] National University of Defense Technology, Changsha, China
zmjbar@163.com
[3] Stevens Institute of Technology, Hoboken, USA
xinchao.w@gmail.com
[4] Hangzhou Dianzi University, Hangzhou, China
yujun@hdu.edu.cn
[5] École Polytechnique Fédérale de Lausanne, Lausanne, Switzerland
pascal.fua@epfl.ch

Abstract. Images captured by fisheye lenses violate the pinhole camera assumption and suffer from distortions. Rectification of fisheye images is therefore a crucial preprocessing step for many computer vision applications. In this paper, we propose an end-to-end multi-context collaborative deep network for removing distortions from single fisheye images. In contrast to conventional approaches, which focus on extracting hand-crafted features from input images, our method learns high-level semantics and low-level appearance features simultaneously to estimate the distortion parameters. To facilitate training, we construct a synthesized dataset that covers various scenes and distortion parameter settings. Experiments on both synthesized and real-world datasets show that the proposed model significantly outperforms current state of the art methods. Our code and synthesized dataset will be made publicly available.

Keywords: Fisheye image rectification
Distortion parameter estimation · Collaborative deep network

1 Introduction

Fisheye cameras have been widely used in varieties of computer vision tasks, including virtual reality [1,2], video surveillance [3,4], automotive applications [5,6] and depth estimation [7], due to their large field of view. Images captured by such cameras however suffer from lens distortion, and thus it is vital to perform rectification as a fundamental pre-processing step for subsequent tasks. In recent years, active research work has been conducted on automatic rectification of

© Springer Nature Switzerland AG 2018
V. Ferrari et al. (Eds.): ECCV 2018, LNCS 11214, pp. 475–490, 2018.
https://doi.org/10.1007/978-3-030-01249-6_29

fisheye images. In spite of the remarkable progress, most existing rectification approaches focus on handcrafted features [8–15], which have limited expressive power and sometimes lead to unsatisfactory results.

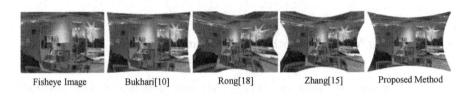

Fisheye Image   Bukhari[10]   Rong[18]   Zhang[15]   Proposed Method

Fig. 1. Our model performs rectification given a single fisheye image.

We devise, to our best knowledge, the first end-to-end trainable deep convolutional neural network (CNN) for fisheye image rectification. Given a single fisheye image as input, our approach outputs the rectified image with distortions corrected, as shown in Fig. 1. Our method explicitly models the formation of fisheye images by first estimating the distortion parameters, during which step the semantic information is also incorporated. The warped images are then produced using the obtained parameters.

We show the proposed model architecture in Fig. 2. We construct a deep CNN model to extract image features and feed the obtained features to a scene parsing network and a distortion parameter estimation network. The former network aims to learn a high-level semantic understanding of the scene, which is then provided to the latter network with the aim of boosting estimation performance. The obtained distortion parameters, together with the input fisheye image and the corresponding scene parsing result, are then fed to a distortion rectification layer to produce the final rectified image and rectified scene parsing result. The whole network is trained end-to-end.

Our motivation for introducing the scene parsing network into the rectification model is that the learned high-level semantics can guide the distortion estimation. Previous methods usually rely on the assumption that straight lines in the 3D space have to be straight after rectification. Nevertheless, given an input image, it is difficult to determine which curved line should be straight in the 3D space. The semantics could help to provide complementary information for this problem. For example, in the case of Fig. 5, semantic segmentation may potentially provide the knowledge that the boundaries of skyscrapers should be straight after rectification but those of the trees should not, and guide the rectification to produce plausible results shown in the last column of Fig. 5. Such high-level semantic supervision is, however, missing in the CNN used for extracting low-level features. By incorporating the scene parsing branch, our model can therefore take advantage of both low-level features and high-level semantics for the rectification process.

To train the proposed deep network, we construct a synthesized dataset of visually high-quality images using the ADE20K [16] dataset. Our dataset consists of fisheye images and corresponding scene parsing labels, as well as rectified images and rectified scene parsing labels from ADE20K. We synthesize both the fisheye images and the corresponding scene parsing labels. Samples are further augmented by adjusting distortion parameters to cover a higher diversity.

We conduct extensive experiments to evaluate the proposed model on both the synthesized and real-world fisheye images. We compare our method with state of the art approaches on our synthesized dataset and also on real-world fisheye images using our model trained on the synthesized dataset. Our proposed model quantitatively and qualitatively outperforms state of the art methods and runs fast.

Our contribution is therefore the first end-to-end deep learning approach for single fisheye image rectification. This is achieved by explicitly estimating the distortion parameters using the learned low-level features and under the guidance of high-level semantics. Our model yields results superior to the current state of the art. More results are provided in the supplementary material. Our synthesized dataset and code will be made publicly available.

2   Related Work

We first briefly review existing fisheye image rectification and other distortion correction methods, and then discuss recent methods for low-level vision tasks with semantic guidance, which we also rely on in this work.

2.1   Distortion Rectification

Previous work has focused on exploiting handcrafted features from distorted fisheye images for rectification. The most commonly used strategy is to utilize lines [8–15,17], the most prevalent entity in man-made scenes, for the correction. The key idea is to recover the curvy lines caused by distortion to straight lines so that the pinhole camera model can be applied.

In the same vein, many methods follow the so-called plumb line assumption. Bukhari et al. [10] proposed a method for radial lens distortion correction using an extended Hough transform of image lines with one radial distortion parameter. Melo et al. [11], on the other hand, used non-overlapping circular arcs for the radial estimation. However, in some cases especially for wide-angle lenses, these approaches yielded unsatisfactory results. Hughes et al. [12] extracted vanishing points from distorted checkerboard images and estimated the image center and distortion parameters. This was, however, unsuitable for images of real-world scenes.

Rosten and Loveland [13] proposed a method that transformed the edges of a distorted image to a 1-D angular Hough space and then optimized the distortion correction parameters by minimizing the entropy of the corresponding normalized histogram. The rectified results were, however, limited by hardware capacity. Ying et al. [14] introduced a universal algorithm for correcting distortion in fisheye images. In this approach, distortion parameters were estimated using at least three conics extracted from the input fisheye image. Brand et al. [17] used a calibration grid to compute the distortion parameters. However, in many cases, it is difficult to obtain feature points whose world coordinates are known a priori. Zhang et al. [15] proposed a multi-label energy optimization method to merge short circular arcs sharing the same or approximately the same circular parameters and selected long circular arcs for camera rectification. These approaches relied on line extractions in the first step, allowing errors to propagate to the final distortion estimation and compromise the results.

The work most related to our method is [18], where CNN was employed for radial lens distortion correction. However, the learning ability of this network was restricted to simulating a simple distortion model with only one parameter, which is not suitable for the more complex fisheye image distortion model. Moreover, this model only estimated the distortion model parameter and could not produce the final output in an end-to-end manner.

All the aforementioned approaches lack semantic information in the finer reconstruction level. Such semantics are, however, important cues for accurate rectification. By contrast, our model explicitly and jointly learns high-level semantics and low-level image features, and incorporates both streams of information in the fisheye image rectification process. The model directly outputs the rectified image and is trainable end-to-end.

2.2 Semantic Guidance

Semantic guidance has been widely adopted in low-level computer vision tasks. Liu et al. [19] proposed a deep CNN solution for image denoising by integrating the modules of image denoising and high-level tasks like segmentation into a unified framework. Semantic information can thus flow into the optimization of the denoising network through a joint loss in the training process. Tsai et al. [20] adopted a joint training scheme to capture both the image context and semantic cues for image harmonization. In their approach, semantic guidance was propagated to the image harmonization decoder, making the final harmonization results more realistic. Qu et al. [21] introduced an end-to-end deep neural network with multi-context architecture for shadow removal from single images, where information from different sources were explored. In their model, one network was used to extract shadow features from a global view, while two complementary networks were used to generate features to obtain both the fine local details and semantic understanding of the input image, leading to state of the art performance.

Inspired by these works, we propose to integrate semantic information to improve fisheye image rectification performance, which has, to our best knowledge, yet to be explored.

3 Methods

In this section, we describe our proposed model in detail. We start by providing a brief review of the fisheye camera model in Sect. 3.1, describe our network architecture in Sect. 3.2, and finally provide the definition of our loss function and training process in Sect. 3.3.

3.1   General Fisheye Camera Model

We start with the pinhole camera projection model, given as:

$$r = f \tan(\theta), \tag{1}$$

where θ denotes the angle between the incoming ray and the optical axis, f is the focal length, and r is the distance between the image point and the principal point.

Unlike the pinhole perspective projection model, images captured by fisheye lenses follow varieties of projections, including stereographic, equidistance, equisolid and orthogonal projection [12,22]. A general model is used for different types of fisheye lenses [22]:

$$r(\theta) = k_1\theta + k_2\theta^3, \tag{2}$$

where $\{k_i\}$ $(i = 1, 2)$ are the coefficients. We adopt the simplified version of the general model. Although Eq. (2) contains few parameters, it is able to approximate all the projection models with high accuracy.

Given pixel coordinates (x, y) in the pinhole projection image, the corresponding image coordinates (x', y') in the fisheye image can be computed: $x' = r(\theta)\cos(\varphi)$, $y' = r(\theta)\sin(\varphi)$, where $\varphi = \arctan((y - y_0)/(x - x_0))$, and (x_0, y_0) are the coordinates of the principal point in the pinhole projection image.

The image coordinates (x', y') are then transformed to pixel coordinates (xf, yf): $x_f = x' + u_0$, $y_f = y' + v_0$, where (u_0, v_0) are the coordinates of the principal point in the fisheye image. We define $P_d = [k_1, k_2, u_0, v_0]$ as the parameters to be estimated, and describe the proposed model as follows.

3.2   Network Architecture

The proposed deep network is shown in Fig. 2. It aims to learn a mapping function from the input fisheye image to the rectified image in an end-to-end manner. Our basic idea is to exploit both the local image features and the contextual semantics for the rectification process. To this end, we build our model by constructing a composite architecture consisting of four cooperative components as shown in Fig. 2: a base network (green box), a distortion parameter estimation network (gray box), a distortion rectification layer (red box) and a scene parsing network (yellow box).

In this unified network architecture, the base network is first used to extract low-level local features from the input image. The obtained features are then fed to the scene parsing network and the distortion parameter estimation network. The scene parsing network decodes the high-level semantic information to generate a scene parsing result for the input fisheye image. Next, the learned

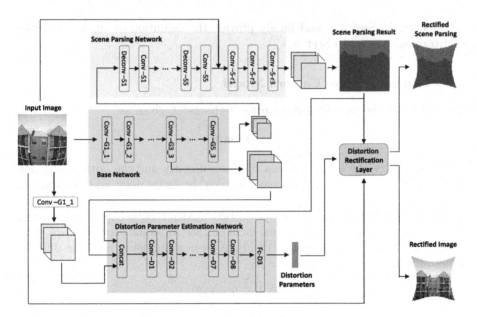

Fig. 2. The overview of the proposed joint network architecture. This composite architecture consists of four cooperative components: a base network, a distortion estimation network, a distortion rectification layer, and a scene parsing network. The distortion parameter estimation network takes as input a concatenation of multiple feature maps from the base network and generates corresponding distortion parameters. Meanwhile, the scene parsing network extracts high-level semantic information to further improve the accuracy of distortion parameter estimation as well as rectification. The estimated parameters are then used by the distortion rectification layer to perform rectification on both the input fisheye image and the corresponding scene parsing results. (Color figure online)

semantics are propagated to the distortion parameter estimation network to produce the estimated parameters. Finally, the estimated parameters, together with the input fisheye image and corresponding scene parsing result, are fed to the distortion rectification layer to generate the final rectified image and rectified scene parsing result. The whole network is trained end-to-end. In what follows, we discuss each component in detail.

Base Network. The base network is built to extract both low- and high-level features for the subsequent fisheye image rectification and scene parsing tasks. Recent work suggests that CNNs trained with large amounts of data for image classification are generalizable to other tasks such as semantic segmentation and depth prediction. To this end, we adopt the VGG-net [23] model for our base network, which is pre-trained on ImageNet for the object recognition task and fine-tuned under the supervision of semantic parsing and rectification.

Distortion Parameter Estimation Network. Our distortion parameter estimation network aims to estimate the distortion parameters P_d discussed in Sect. 3.1. This network takes as input a concatenation of multiple features maps: (1) The output of conv3-3 layer in the base network. Note that a deconvolution step is performed to raise the spatial resolution of feature maps; (2) The input image convolved with 3×3 learnable filters, which aims to preserve raw image information; and (3) The output of the scene parsing network. As shown in Sect. 4, we find that semantic priors help to eliminate the errors in distortion parameters.

In this distortion parameter estimation network, each convolutional layer is followed by a ReLU and a batch normalization [24]. We construct 8 convolutional layers with 3×3 learnable filters, where the number of filters is set as 64, 64, 128, 128, 256, 256, 512, and 512, respectively. Pooling layers with kernel size 2×2 and stride 2 are adopted after every two convolutions. A fully-connected layer with 1024 units is added at the end of the network to produce the parameters. To alleviate over-fitting, drop-out [25] is adopted after the final convolutional layer with a drop probability of 0.5.

Distortion Rectification Layer. The distortion rectification layer takes as input the estimated distortion parameters P_d, the fisheye image, as well as the scene parsing result. It computes the corresponding pixel coordinates and generates the rectified image and the rectified scene parsing result. This makes the network end-to-end trainable. Details of the distortion rectification layer are described as follows.

In the forward propagation, given pixel location (x, y) in the rectified image I_r, the corresponding coordinates (x_f, y_f) in the input fisheye image I_f are computed according to the aforementioned fisheye image model:

$$
\begin{cases}
x_f = u_0 + \frac{x}{\sqrt{x^2+y^2}}(\sum_{i=1}^{2} k_i \theta^{2i-1}) \\
y_f = v_0 + \frac{y}{\sqrt{x^2+y^2}}(\sum_{i=1}^{2} k_i \theta^{2i-1}).
\end{cases}
\tag{3}
$$

The pixel value of location (x, y) in the rectified image is then obtained using the bilinear interpolation:

$$
\begin{aligned}
I_{x,y}^r = \overline{\omega_x}\overline{\omega_y}I_f(\lfloor x_f \rfloor, \lfloor y_f \rfloor) + \omega_x\overline{\omega_y}I_f(\lceil x_f \rceil, \lfloor y_f \rfloor) \\
+\overline{\omega_x}\omega_y I_f(\lfloor x_f \rfloor, \lceil y_f \rceil) + \omega_x\omega_y I_f(\lceil x_f \rceil, \lceil y_f \rceil),
\end{aligned}
\tag{4}
$$

where the coefficients are computed as: $\omega_x = x_f - \lfloor x_f \rfloor$, $\omega_y = y_f - \lfloor y_f \rfloor$ and $\overline{\omega_x} = 1 - \omega_x$, $\overline{\omega_y} = 1 - \omega_y$.

In the back propagation, we need to calculate the derivatives of rectified image with respect to the estimated distortion parameters. For each pixel $I_{x,y}^r$, derivatives with respect to the estimated parameters P_d are computed as follows:

$$
\frac{\partial I_{x,y}^r}{\partial P_i} = \frac{\partial I_{x,y}^r}{\partial x_f} \cdot \frac{\partial x_f}{\partial P_i} + \frac{\partial I_{x,y}^r}{\partial y_f} \cdot \frac{\partial y_f}{\partial P_i},
\tag{5}
$$

where

$$\frac{\partial I^r_{x,y}}{\partial x_f} = -\overline{\omega_y} I_f(\lfloor x_f \rfloor, \lfloor y_f \rfloor) + \overline{\omega_y} I_f(\lceil x_f \rceil, \lfloor y_f \rfloor) \tag{6}$$
$$-\omega_y I_f(\lfloor x_f \rfloor, \lceil y_f \rceil) + \omega_y I_f(\lceil x_f \rceil, \lceil y_f \rceil),$$

and $\partial x_f / \partial P_i$ is obtained according to:

$$\begin{cases} \frac{\partial x_f}{\partial k_i} = \frac{x\theta^{2i-1}}{\sqrt{x^2+y^2}}(i = 1, 2) \\ \frac{\partial x_f}{\partial u_0} = 1. \end{cases} \tag{7}$$

Similarly, we can calculate $\partial I^r_{x,y} / \partial y_f$ and $\partial y_f / \partial P_i$.

Scene Parsing Network. The scene parsing network takes as input the learned local features and is provided with the scene parsing labels for training. Our motivation for introducing this network is that, in many tasks, semantic supervision may benefit low-vision tasks as discussed in Sect. 2.2. In our case, the scene parsing network outputs the semantic segmentations to provide high-level clues including the object contours in the image. Such segmentations provide much richer information compared to straight lines, which are treated as the only clue in many conventional distortion rectification methods. The output scene parsing results are fed to both the distortion paramter estimation network and the distortion rectification layer to provide semantic guidance.

In our implementation, we construct a decoder structure based on the outputs of VGG-Net. The decoder network consists of 5 convolution-deconvolution pairs with kernel size 3×3 for convolution layers and 2×2 for deconvolutions layers. The number of filters is set as 512, 256, 128, 64 and 32. As parts of the fisheye image are compressed due to distortion, the scene parsing results may lose some local details. We find that adding a refinement network can further improve the scene parsing accuracy. This refinement network takes the fisheye image and the initial scene parsing results as input and further refines the final results according to the details in the input image. Three convolutional layers are contained in the refinement network, with number of filters 32, 32, 16 and kernel size 3×3. Note that the architecture of scene parsing module is not restricted to the proposed one. Other scene parsing approaches based on VGG can be applied in our method.

As we will show in Sect. 4, in fact even without the scene parsing network, our deep learning-based fisheye rectification approach already outperforms current state of the art approaches. With the scene parsing network turned on, our semantic-aware rectification yields even higher accuracy. Since we feed to the network distorted segmentations as well as rectified ones, our network can take advantage of such explicit segment-level supervision and potentially learn a segment-to-segment mapping, which helps to achieve better rectification.

3.3   Training Process

We aim to minimize the $L2$ reconstruction loss L_r between the output rectified image I_r and the ground truth image I^{gt}:

$$L_r = \sum_x \sum_y \left\| I^{gt}_{x,y} - I^r_{x,y} \right\|_2^2. \tag{8}$$

In addition to this rectification loss, we also adopt the loss L_{sp} for the scene parsing task introduced by [16] and L2 loss L_p for distortion parameter estimation. The final combined loss for the entire network is:

$$L = \lambda_0 L_p + \lambda_1 L_r + \lambda_2 L_{sp}, \tag{9}$$

where λ_0, λ_1 and λ_2 are the weights to balance the losses of distortion parameters estimation, fisheye image rectification and scene parsing, respectively.

We implement our model in Caffe [26] and apply the adaptive gradient algorithm (ADAGRAD) [27] to optimize the entire network. During the training process, we first pretrain our model using the labels of distortion parameters and scene parsing. We start with training data from the ADE20K dataset to obtain an initial solution for both distortion parameter estimation and scene parsing tasks. Then we add the image reconstruction loss and fine-tune the network in an end-tp-end manner to achieve an optimal solution for fisheye image rectification. We set the initial learning rate as 1e-4 to and reduce it by a factor of 10 every 100K iterations.

Note that, the scene parsing module propagates learned semantic information to the distortion parameter estimation network. By integrating the scene parsing model, the proposed network learns high-level contextual semantics like boundary features and semantic category layout and provides this knowledge to the distortion parameter estimation.

4   Experiments

In this section, we discuss our experimental setup and results. We first introduce our data generation strategies in Sect. 4.1 and then compare our rectification results with those of the state of the art methods quantitatively in Sect. 4.2 and qualitatively in Sect. 4.3. We further show some scene parsing results in Sect. 4.4 and compare the runtime of our method and others in Sect. 4.5. We provide more results in the supplementary material.

4.1   Data Generation

To train the proposed deep network for fisheye image rectification, we must first build a large-scale dataset. Each training sample should consist of a fisheye image, a rectification ground truth, and the scene parsing labels. To this end, we select a subset of the ADE20K dataset [16] with scene parsing labels and then follow the fisheye image model in Sect. 3.1 to create both the fisheye images and the corresponding scene parsing labels. During training, training samples are further augmented by randomly adjusting distortion parameters. The proposed dataset thus covers various scenes and distortion parameter settings, providing a wide range of diversities that potentially prevent over-fitting.

Our training dataset includes 19011 unique simulated fisheye images generated with various distortion parameter settings. Our test dataset contains 1000 samples generated using a similar strategy. We will make our dataset publicly available.

4.2   Quantitative Evaluation

The dataset we constructed enables us to quantitatively assess our method. We run the proposed model and the state of the art ones on our dataset and evaluate them using standard metrics including PSNR and SSIM. All the baseline models were realized according to the implementation details provided in corresponding papers. The model [18] was trained on our simulated dataset, as done for ours.

We show the quantitative comparisons in Table 1. Our method significantly outperforms existing methods in terms of both PSNR and SSIM. To further verify the semantic guidance, we add two experiments for the proposed method: (1) removing both the scene parsing network and the semantic loss, denoted as "Proposed method - SPN - SL", and (2) removing the semantic loss, but keeping the scene parsing network, denoted as "Proposed method - SL". The networks are trained using the same settings. The results indicate that the explicit semantic supervision does play an important role. Robust feature extraction and semantic guidance contribute to more accurate rectification results.

Table 1. PSNR and SSIM scores of different algorithms on our test dataset.

Methods	PSNR	SSIM
Bukhari [10]	11.60	0.2492
Rong [18]	13.12	0.3378
Zhang [15]	12.55	0.2984
Proposed method -SPN -SL	14.43	0.3912
Proposed method - SL	14.56	0.3965
Proposed method	**15.02**	**0.4151**

4.3   Qualitative Evaluation

The qualitative rectification results on our synthesized dataset obtained by our method and the others are shown in Fig. 3. Our method produces results that are overall the most visually plausible and most similar to the ground truths, as evidenced by the fact that we restore the curvy lines to straight, which the other methods fail to do well.

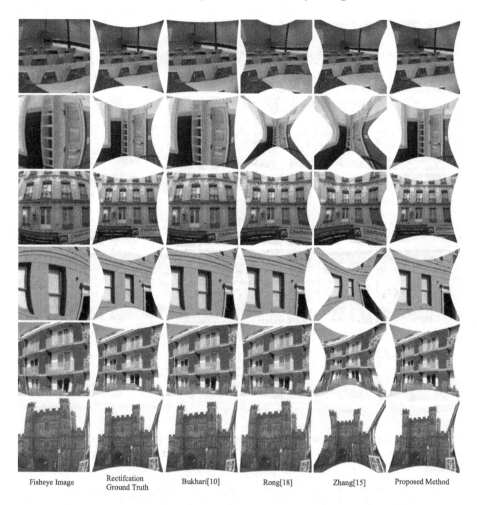

| Fisheye Image | Rectifcation Ground Truth | Bukhari[10] | Rong[18] | Zhang[15] | Proposed Method |

Fig. 3. Qualitative results on our synthesized datasets. From left to right, we show the input, the ground truth, results of three state of the art methods [10,15,18], and the result of our proposed approach. Our method achieves the best overall visual quality of all the compared methods.

To show the effectiveness of our method on real fisheye images, we examine a test set of 650 real fisheye images captured using multiple fisheye cameras with different distortion parameter settings. Samples of different projection types are collected, including stereographic, equidistance, equisolid angle and orthogonal [22]. To cover a wide variety of scenarios, we collect samples from various indoor and outdoor scenes. Selective comparative results are shown in Fig. 4. Our method achieves the most promising visual performance, which indicates our model trained on simululated dataset generalize well to real fisheye images.

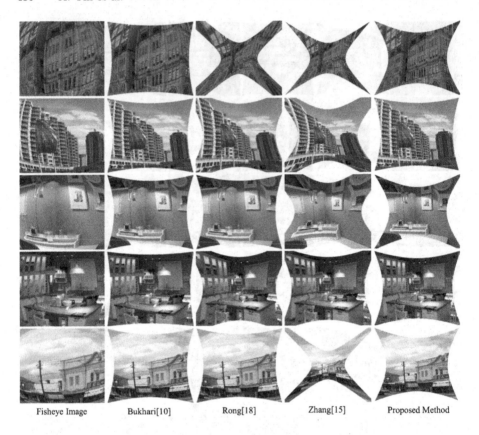

| Fisheye Image | Bukhari[10] | Rong[18] | Zhang[15] | Proposed Method |

Fig. 4. Qualitative results on real fisheye images. From left to right: the input image, results of three state of the art methods [10,15,18], and results using our proposed method.

The results of [10,15] are fragile to the hand-crafted feature extraction. In addition, the rectification of [15] is very sensitive to the initial value provided for the Levenberg-Marquardt (LM) iteration process, making it difficult to be deployed in real-world applications. The approach of [18], on the other hand, is limited to a simple distortion model with one parameter only, and thus it often fails to deal with more complex fisheye image distortion model with multiple types of parameters. Our method, by contrast, is a fully end-to-end trainable approach for fisheye image rectification that learns robust features under the guidance of semantic supervision.

The results from both the synthesized dataset and the real fisheye dataset validate the effectiveness of our model, which uses synthesized data to learn how to perform fisheye image rectification given corresponding ground truth-rectified images. Our network learns both low-level local and high-level semantic features for rectification, which is, to our best knowledge, the first attempt at fisheye distortion rectification.

4.4 Scene Parsing Results

As shown in Table 1, even without the scene parsing module, our method already outperforms the other methods. With the guidance of the semantics, our method yields even better results in terms of PSNR and SSIM as shown in Table 1. To provide more insights into the scene parsing module, we show the parsing results obtained by the network in Fig. 5. It can be seen that the obtained parsing results are visually plausible, indicating that the network can produce semantic segmentation on distorted images, which may be further utilized by the rectification that takes place at a later stage.

We further show in Fig. 5 the rectified images produced by our model without and with the semantic guidance. The results without semantics are generated by removing the scene parsing network from the entire architecture. Our model without semantics, in spite of its already superior performance to other state of the art methods, still produces erroneous results like the distorted boundaries of the skyscraper and the vehicle shown in Fig. 5. With the help of explicit semantic supervision, our final model can potentially learn a segment-to-segment mapping for each semantic category, like the skyscraper or the car, and better guide the rectification during testing.

Regarding the influence of segmentation quality, despite that we indeed observe some erroneous parsings in our experiments, the imperfect segmentation results do help improve rectification for over 90% of the cases. We expect the improvement to be even more significant with better segmentations. As for the model generalization, since the ADE20K benchmark [16] comprises objects of 150 classes and covers most semantic categories in daily life, our model is able to handle most common objects. Handling unseen classes is left for further work.

4.5 Runtime

The run times of our methods and others are compared in Table 2. The methods of [10,15] rely on a minimazing complex objective function and time-consuming iterative optimization. Therefore, these approaches are difficult to accelerate by hardware-based parallelization and require much longer processing time on a 256 × 256 test image. On the contrary, our method can benefit from non-iterative forward process implemented on GPU. For example, when running the experiments on an Intel i5-4200U CPU, methods of [10,15] take over 60 s

Table 2. Run times of different algorithms on our test dataset.

Methods	Average run time (seconds)
Bukhari [10]	62.53 (Intel i5-4200U CPU)
Zhang [15]	80.07 (Intel i5-4200U CPU)
Rong [18]	0.87 (K80 GPU)
Proposed method	1.26 (K80 GPU)

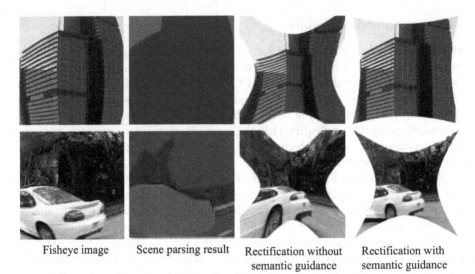

Fisheye image   Scene parsing result   Rectification without   Rectification with
                                            semantic guidance   semantic guidance

Fig. 5. Qualitative rectification results obtained by our model without and with semantic guidance. With semantic supervision, the model can correct distortions that are otherwise neglected by the one without semantics. For example, the straight boundaries of the skyscraper and the shape of the vehicle can be better recovered.

to generate one rectified result. Although our model is slower than [18], the rectification performance is much better in terms of PSNR and SSIM.

5   Conclusions

We devise a multi-context collaborative deep network for single fisheye image rectification. Unlike existing methods that mainly focus on extracting hand-crafted features from the input distorted images, which have limited expressive power and are often unreliable, our method learns both high-level semantic and low-level appearance information for distortion parameter estimation. Our network consists of three collaborative sub-networks and is end-to-end trainable. A distortion rectification layer is designed to perform rectification on both the input fisheye image and corresponding scene parsing results. For training, we construct a synthesized dataset covering a wide range of scenes and distortion parameters. We demonstrate that our approach outperforms state of the art models on the synthesized and real fisheye images, both qualitatively and quantitatively.

In our further work, we will extend this framework to handle other distortion correction tasks like the general radial lens distortion correction. Also, we will explore to handle unseen semantic classes for rectification.

Acknowledgment. This work is partially supported by Australian Research Council Projects (FL-170100117, DP-180103424 and LP-150100671), National Natural Science

Foundation of China (Grant No. 61405252) and State Scholarship Fund of China (Grant No. 201503170310).

References

1. Xiong, Y., Turkowski, K.: Creating image-based VR using a self-calibrating fisheye lens. In: Proceedings of 1997 IEEE Computer Society Conference on Computer Vision and Pattern Recognition, pp. 237–243. IEEE (1997)
2. Orlosky, J., Wu, Q., Kiyokawa, K., Takemura, H., Nitschke, C.: Fisheye vision: peripheral spatial compression for improved field of view in head mounted displays. In: Proceedings of the 2nd ACM Symposium on Spatial User Interaction, pp. 54–61. ACM (2014)
3. Drulea, M., Szakats, I., Vatavu, A., Nedevschi, S.: Omnidirectional stereo vision using fisheye lenses. In: 2014 IEEE International Conference on Intelligent Computer Communication and Processing (ICCP), pp. 251–258. IEEE (2014)
4. DeCamp, P., Shaw, G., Kubat, R., Roy, D.: An immersive system for browsing and visualizing surveillance video. In: Proceedings of the 18th ACM International Conference on Multimedia, pp. 371–380. ACM (2010)
5. Hughes, C., Glavin, M., Jones, E., Denny, P.: Wide-angle camera technology for automotive applications: a review. IET Intell. Transp. Syst. **3**(1), 19–31 (2009)
6. Gehrig, S.K.: Large-field-of-view stereo for automotive applications. In: Proceedings of Workshop on Omnidirectional Vision, Camera Networks and Nonclassical cameras (OMNIVIS 2005) (2005)
7. Shah, S., Aggarwal, J.K.: Depth estimation using stereo fish-eye lenses. In: Proceedings of IEEE International Conference on Image Processing, ICIP 1994, vol. 2, pp. 740–744. IEEE (1994)
8. Sun, J., Zhu, J.: Calibration and correction for omnidirectional image with a fisheye lens. In: Fourth International Conference on Natural Computation, ICNC 2008, vol. 6, pp. 133–137. IEEE (2008)
9. Mei, X., Yang, S., Rong, J., Ying, X., Huang, S., Zha, H.: Radial lens distortion correction using cascaded one-parameter division model. In: 2015 IEEE International Conference on Image Processing (ICIP), pp. 3615–3619. IEEE (2015)
10. Bukhari, F., Dailey, M.N.: Automatic radial distortion estimation from a single image. J. Math. Imaging Vis. **45**(1), 31–45 (2013)
11. Melo, R., Antunes, M., Barreto, J.P., Falcao, G., Goncalves, N.: Unsupervised intrinsic calibration from a single frame using a. In: Proceedings of the IEEE International Conference on Computer Vision, pp. 537–544 (2013)
12. Hughes, C., Denny, P., Glavin, M., Jones, E.: Equidistant fish-eye calibration and rectification by vanishing point extraction. IEEE Trans. Pattern Anal. Mach. Intell. **32**(12), 2289–2296 (2010)
13. Rosten, E., Loveland, R.: Camera distortion self-calibration using the plumb-line constraint and minimal hough entropy. Mach. Vis. Appl. **22**(1), 77–85 (2011)
14. Ying, X., Hu, Z.: Can we consider central catadioptric cameras and fisheye cameras within a unified imaging model. In: Pajdla, T., Matas, J. (eds.) ECCV 2004. LNCS, vol. 3021, pp. 442–455. Springer, Heidelberg (2004). https://doi.org/10.1007/978-3-540-24670-1_34
15. Zhang, M., Yao, J., Xia, M., Li, K., Zhang, Y., Liu, Y.: Line-based multi-label energy optimization for fisheye image rectification and calibration. In: Proceedings of the IEEE Conference on Computer Vision and Pattern Recognition, pp. 4137–4145 (2015)

16. Zhou, B., Zhao, H., Puig, X., Fidler, S., Barriuso, A., Torralba, A.: Semantic understanding of scenes through the ADE20K dataset. arXiv preprint arXiv:1608.05442 (2016)

17. Brand, P., Mohr, R., Bobet, P.: Distorsions optiques: correction dans un modele projectif. 9dine cong~s AFCET RFIA, pp. 87–98 (1993)

18. Rong, J., Huang, S., Shang, Z., Ying, X.: Radial lens distortion correction using convolutional neural networks trained with synthesized images. In: Lai, S.-H., Lepetit, V., Nishino, K., Sato, Y. (eds.) ACCV 2016. LNCS, vol. 10113, pp. 35–49. Springer, Cham (2017). https://doi.org/10.1007/978-3-319-54187-7_3

19. Liu, D., Wen, B., Liu, X., Huang, T.S.: When image denoising meets high-level vision tasks: a deep learning approach. arXiv preprint arXiv:1706.04284 (2017)

20. Tsai, Y.-H., Shen, X., Lin, Z., Sunkavalli, K., Lu, X., Yang, M.-H.: Deep image harmonization. arXiv preprint arXiv:1703.00069 (2017)

21. Qu, L., Tian, J., He, S., Tang, Y., Lau, R.W.: Deshadownet: a multi-context embedding deep network for shadow removal (2017)

22. Kannala, J., Brandt, S.: A generic camera calibration method for fish-eye lenses. In: Proceedings of the 17th International Conference on Pattern Recognition, ICPR 2004, vol. 1, pp. 10–13. IEEE (2004)

23. Simonyan, K., Zisserman, A.: Very deep convolutional networks for large-scale image recognition. arXiv preprint arXiv:1409.1556 (2014)

24. Ioffe, S., Szegedy, C.: Batch normalization: accelerating deep network training by reducing internal covariate shift. In: International Conference on Machine Learning, pp. 448–456 (2015)

25. Srivastava, N., Hinton, G.E., Krizhevsky, A., Sutskever, I., Salakhutdinov, R.: Dropout: a simple way to prevent neural networks from overfitting. J. Mach. Learn. Res. 15(1), 1929–1958 (2014)

26. Jia, Y., et al.: Caffe: convolutional architecture for fast feature embedding. In: Proceedings of the 22nd ACM International Conference on Multimedia, pp. 675–678. ACM (2014)

27. Duchi, J., Hazan, E., Singer, Y.: Adaptive subgradient methods for online learning and stochastic optimization. J. Mach. Learn. Res. 12(Jul), 2121–2159 (2011)

LAPRAN: A Scalable Laplacian Pyramid Reconstructive Adversarial Network for Flexible Compressive Sensing Reconstruction

Kai Xu$^{(\boxtimes)}$ [ID], Zhikang Zhang [ID], and Fengbo Ren [ID]

Arizona State University, Tempe, AZ 85281, USA
{kaixu,zzhan362,renfengbo}@asu.edu

Abstract. This paper addresses the single-image compressive sensing (CS) and reconstruction problem. We propose a scalable Laplacian pyramid reconstructive adversarial network (LAPRAN) that enables high-fidelity, flexible and fast CS images reconstruction. LAPRAN progressively reconstructs an image following the concept of the Laplacian pyramid through multiple stages of reconstructive adversarial networks (RANs). At each pyramid level, CS measurements are fused with a contextual latent vector to generate a high-frequency image residual. Consequently, LAPRAN can produce hierarchies of reconstructed images and each with an incremental resolution and improved quality. The scalable pyramid structure of LAPRAN enables high-fidelity CS reconstruction with a flexible resolution that is adaptive to a wide range of compression ratios (CRs), which is infeasible with existing methods. Experimental results on multiple public datasets show that LAPRAN offers an average 7.47 dB and 5.98 dB PSNR, and an average 57.93% and 33.20% SSIM improvement compared to model-based and data-driven baselines, respectively.

Keywords: Compressive sensing · Reconstruction
Laplacian pyramid · Reconstructive adversarial network
Feature fusion

1 Introduction

Compressive sensing (CS) is a transformative sampling technique that is more efficient than Nyquist Sampling. Rather than sampling at the Nyquist rate and then compressing the sampled data, CS aims to directly sense signals in a compressed form while retaining the necessary information for accurate reconstruction. The trade-off for the simplicity of encoding is the intricate reconstruction

Electronic supplementary material The online version of this chapter (https://doi.org/10.1007/978-3-030-01249-6_30) contains supplementary material, which is available to authorized users.

© Springer Nature Switzerland AG 2018
V. Ferrari et al. (Eds.): ECCV 2018, LNCS 11214, pp. 491–507, 2018.
https://doi.org/10.1007/978-3-030-01249-6_30

process. Conventional CS reconstruction algorithms are based on either convex optimization [2,3,17,26,27] or greedy/iterative methods [5,20,35]. These methods suffer from three major drawbacks limiting their practical usage. First, the iterative nature renders these methods computational intensive and not suitable for hardware acceleration. Second, the widely adopted sparsity constraint assumes the given signal is sparse on a known basis. However, natural images do not have an exactly sparse representation on any known basis (DCT, wavelet, or curvelet) [27]. The strong dependency on the sparsity constraint becomes the performance limiting factor of conventional methods. Constructing over-complete dictionaries with deterministic atoms [37,38] can only moderately relax the constraint, as the learned linear sparsity models are often shallow thus have limited impacts. Third, conventional methods have a rigid structure allowing for reconstruction at a fixed resolution only. The recovery quality cannot be guaranteed when the compression ratio (CR) needs to be compromised due to a limited communication bandwidth or storage space. A better solution is to reconstruct at a compromised resolution while keeping a satisfactory reconstruction signal-to-noise ratio (RSNR) rather than dropping the RSNR for a fixed resolution.

Deep neural networks (DNNs) have been explored recently for learning the inverse mapping of CS [15,16,22,23]. The limitations of existing DNN-based approaches are twofold. First, the reconstruction results tend to be blurry because of the exclusive use of a Euclidean loss. Specifically, the recovery quality of DNN-based methods are usually no better than optimization-based methods when the CR is low, e.g., $CR <= 10$. Second, similar to the optimization-based methods, the existing DNN-based methods all have rigid structures allowing for reconstruction at a fixed and non-adaptive resolution only. The reconstruction will simply fail when the CR is lower than a required threshold.

In this paper, we propose a scalable Laplacian pyramid reconstructive adversarial network (LAPRAN) for flexible CS reconstruction that addresses all the problems mentioned above. LAPRAN does not require sparsity as prior knowledge hence can be potentially used in a broader range of applications, especially where the exact signal sparsity model is unknown. When applied to image signals, LAPRAN progressively reconstruct high-fidelity images following the concept of the Laplacian pyramid through multiple stages of specialized reconstructive adversarial networks (RANs). At each pyramid level, CS measurements are fused with a low-dimensional contextual latent vector to generate a reconstructed image with both higher resolution and reconstruction quality. The non-iterative and high-concurrency natures of LAPRAN make it suitable for hardware acceleration. Furthermore, the scalable pyramid structure of LAPRAN enables high-fidelity CS reconstruction with a flexible resolution that can be adaptive to a wide range of CRs. One can dynamically add or remove RAN stages from LAPRAN to reconstruct images at a higher or lower resolution when the CR becomes lower and higher, respectively. Therefore, a consistently superior recovery quality can be guaranteed across a wide range of CRs.

The contributions of this paper are summarized as follows:

- We propose a novel architecture of the neural network model (LAPRAN) that enables high-fidelity, flexible and fast CS reconstruction.
- We propose to fuse CS measurements with contextual latent vectors of low-resolution images at each pyramid level to enhance the CS recovery quality.
- We illustrate that the progressive learning and reconstruction strategy can mitigate the difficulty of the inverse mapping problem in CS. Such a strategy not only accelerates the training by confining the search space but also improves the recovery quality by eliminating the accumulation of errors.

2 Related Work

CS reconstruction is inherently an under-determined problem. Prior knowledge, i.e., the structure of signals must be exploited to reduce the information loss after reconstruction. According to the way of applying prior knowledge, CS reconstruction methods can be grouped into three categories: (1) model-based methods, (2) data-driven methods, (3) hybrid methods.

2.1 Model-Based Reconstruction Methods

Model-based CS reconstruction methods mostly rely on a sparsity prior. For example, basis pursuit (BP), least absolute shrinkage and selection operator (LASSO), and least angle regression (LARS) are all based on ℓ_1 minimization. Other methods exploit other types of prior knowledge to improve the recovery performance. NLR-CS [17] proposes a non-local low-rank regularization to exploit the group sparsity of similar patches. TVAL3 [26] and EdgeCS [36] use a total variation (TV) regularizer to reconstruct sharper images by preserving edges or boundaries more accurately. D-AMP [27] extends approximate message passing (AMP) to employ denoising algorithms for CS recovery. In general, model-based recovery methods suffer from limited reconstruction quality, especially at high CRs. Because images, though compressible, are not ideally sparse in any commonly used transform domains [27]. Additional knowledge of the image structure is required to further improve the reconstruction quality. Furthermore, when the number of CS measurements available is lower than the theoretical lower bound, the model-based methods will simply fail the reconstruction.

2.2 Data-Driven Reconstruction Methods

Instead of specifying prior knowledge explicitly, data-driven methods have been explored to learn signal characteristics implicitly. Kuldeep *et al.* and Ali *et al.* propose "ReconNet" [23] and "DeepInverse" [29], respectively. Both work aims to reconstruct image blocks from CS measurements via convolutional neural networks (CNNs). Experimental results prove that both models are highly robust to noise and able to recover visually better images than the model-based approaches. However, the major drawback of these methods is the exclusive use of the ℓ_2 reconstruction loss for training. As the ℓ_2 loss cannot reliably generate shape images, additional loss metrics must be introduced to further improve the reconstruction quality. In addition, the direct mapping from the low-dimensional measurement domain to the high-dimensional image domain is highly under-determined. This under-determined mapping problem becomes even more notorious as CR increases since the dimension gap between the two domains is enlarged accordingly.

2.3 Hybrid Reconstruction Methods

Hybrid methods aim to incorporate the benefits of both model-based and data-driven methods. Such methods first utilize expert knowledge to set up a recovery algorithm and then learn additional knowledge from training data while preserving the model interpretability and performance bounds. Inspired by the denoising-based approximate message passing (D-AMP) algorithm, Chris *et al.* propose a learned D-AMP (LDAMP) network for CS image reconstruction. The iterative D-AMP algorithm is unrolled and combined with a denoising convolutional neural network (DnCNN) that serves as the denoiser in each iteration. The major drawback of this method is its sophisticated and iterative structure prohibiting parallel training and efficient hardware acceleration.

Inspired by the success of generative adversarial network (GAN) for image generation, Bora *et al.* propose to use a pre-trained DCGAN [32] for CS reconstruction (CSGM) [6]. This approach finds a latent vector $\hat{z}$ that minimizes the objective $\|AG(z) - y\|^2$, where G, A and z is the generator, sensing matrix, and CS measurements, respectively. The optimal reconstruction result is represented as $G(\hat{z})$. Differently, the proposed LAPRAN directly synthesize an image from CS measurements, which alleviates the exploration of an additional latent space. Although both approaches are GAN-based, they represent two fundamentally different CS reconstruction schemes. CSGM is a sparse-synthesize model [7,8] that approximates an unknown signal as $x = G(z)$, where the sparse coefficient (z) is measured concurrently. While LAPRAN is a co-sparse-analysis model [9,30] that directly synthesize an unknown signal x from the corresponding CS measurements y according to $x = G(y)$. Hence, we call the building block of the proposed model reconstructive adversarial network (RAN) instead of GAN. RAN elegantly approximates the nature image distribution from CS measurement samples, avoiding the detour in the synthesize model. While multiple network propagations are needed to obtain the optimal $\hat{z}$ in CSGM, LAPRAN finishes reconstruction in a single feedforward propagation. Therefore, LAPRAN has lower computational complexity and a faster reconstruction speed.

3   Methodology

The overall structure of the proposed CS system is shown in Fig. 1. It is composed of two functional units, a multi-rate random encoder for sampling and a LAPRAN for reconstruction. The multi-rate random encoder generates multiple CS measurements with different CRs from a single image. LAPRAN takes the

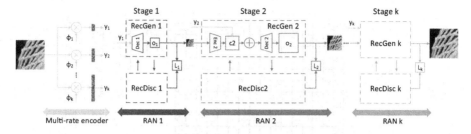

Fig. 1. Overall structure of the proposed LAPRAN. The CS measurement of a high-dimensional image is performed by a multi-rate random encoder. The LAPRAN takes CS measurements as inputs and progressively reconstructs an original image in multiple hierarchies with incremental resolutions and recovery qualities. At each pyramid level, RAN generates an image residual, which is subsequently combined with an upscaled output from the previous level to form a higher-resolution output of the current level (upsampling and upscaling respectively refers to increasing the image resolution with and without new details added). The detailed structure of RAN is shown in Fig. 3.

CS measurements as inputs and progressively reconstructs the original image in multiple hierarchies with incremental resolutions and recovery quality. In the first stage, RAN1 reconstructs a low-resolution thumbnail of the original image (8×8). The following RANs at each stage fuses the low-resolution input generated by the previous stage with CS measurements to produce a reconstructed image upsampled by a factor of 2. Therefore, the resolution of the reconstructed image is progressively improved throughout the cascaded RANs. The proposed LAPRAN architecture is highly scalable. One can concatenate more RANs (just like "LEGO" blocks) to gradually increase the resolution of the reconstructed image. Each building block of LAPRAN is detailed below. Further details about the LAPRAN architecture are provided in the supplementary materials.

3.1 Multi-rate CS Encoder

We propose a multi-rate random encoder for CS sampling. Given an input image, the encoder generates multiple CS measurements $\{\mathbf{y}_1, \cdots, \mathbf{y}_t\}$ simultaneously, each has a different dimension. The generated measurements are fed into each stage of the RANs as input, i.e., $\{\mathbf{y}_1, \cdots, \mathbf{y}_k\}$ is forward to $\{\text{RAN1}, ..., \text{RAN}k\}$, respectively. According to the rate-distortion theory [13], the minimum bit-rate is positively related to the reconstruction quality, which indicates that the i-th RAN requires more information than all the previous RANs in order to improve the image resolution by adding finer details incrementally. The quantitative analysis of the number of measurements required for each RAN is as follows. Let $\mathbf{A}$ be an $m \times n$ sensing matrix that satisfies the restricted isometry property (RIP) of order $2k$, and the isometry constant is $\delta_{2k} \in (0, \frac{1}{2}]$. According to the CS theory [12], the lower bound of the number of CS measurements required for satisfying RIP is defined as: $m \geq Ck \log(\frac{n}{k})$, where $C = \frac{1}{2} \log(\sqrt{24} + 1) \approx 0.28$. In the CS image reconstruction problem, let the number of input measurements

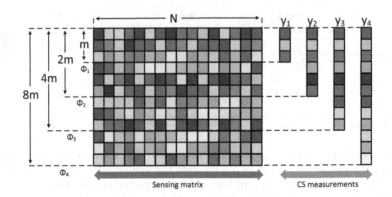

Fig. 2. Illustration of a sensing matrix for multi-rate CS. The four sensing matrices $\Phi_1 \in \mathbb{R}^{m \times N}, \Phi_2 \in \mathbb{R}^{2m \times N}, \Phi_3 \in \mathbb{R}^{4m \times N}, \Phi_4 \in \mathbb{R}^{8m \times N}$ are used to generate the four CS measurements $\{y_1, y_2, y_3, y_4\} \in \mathbb{R}^{\{m,2m,4m,8m\}}$. y_1, y_2, y_3, y_4 is fed into RNN1 to RNN4 as the information source, respectively.

required by two adjacent RANs for accurately reconstructing a $N \times N$ image and a $2N \times 2N$ image is $m1$ and $m2$, respectively, we define the measurement increment ratio as $\beta = \frac{m2}{m1}$. If we assume the sparsity ratio $(\frac{k}{n})$ of the two images remains constant across the two adjacent RANs, then β can be calculated as:

$$\beta = \frac{4k \times \log[(2N \times 2N)/4k]}{k \times \log[(N \times N)/k]} = 4. \tag{1}$$

Equation (1) indicates that the number of CS measurements (as well as CR) required for a former RAN should be at least $1/4$ of a latter one in order to guarantee a satisfactory reconstruction performance. One should note that $\beta = 4$ is the upper bound, lower β values can be used to offer better reconstruction performance at the cost of collecting more CS measurements in early stages. In this work, we adopt $\beta = 2$ to set a gradually increasing CR at different stages instead of using a unified CR. Since the dimension of a measurement vector equals to the number of rows in a sensing matrix, the k sensing matrices in Fig. 1 have the following dimensions: $\Phi_1 \in \mathbb{R}^{m \times N}, \Phi_2 \in \mathbb{R}^{\lfloor \beta m \rfloor \times N}, \cdots, \Phi_k \in \mathbb{R}^{\lfloor \beta^{k-1}m \rfloor \times N}$. An example of the sensing matrix used for the multi-rate encoding of a 4-stage LAPRAN is illustrated in Fig. 2. The generated measurements $y_1 \in \mathbb{R}^m, y_2 \in \mathbb{R}^{2m}, y_3 \in \mathbb{R}^{4m}, y_4 \in \mathbb{R}^{8m}$ is used as the input to RAN1, RAN2, RAN3 and RAN4, respectively. With respect to a k-stage LAPRAN, we only need to generate y_t for training. Since y_i is always a subset of y_{i+1}, we can feed the first $\lfloor \beta^{i-1}m \rfloor$ elements of y_t to the i-th stage in a backward fashion.

The proposed LAPRAN enables CS reconstruction with a flexible resolution, which is not feasible with existing methods. When the number of CS measurements fail to meet the required threshold, the existing methods will fail to reconstruct with no room for maneuver. Alternatively, the proposed method can still reconstruct lower-resolution previews of the image with less detail in the case that the CS measurements are insufficient. The output of each RAN constitutes an image pyramid, providing the user with great flexibility in choosing the desired resolution of reconstructed images.

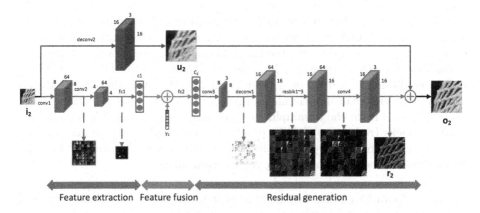

Fig. 3. The structure of RecGen2. A low-resolution input image i_2 is transformed into a high-frequency image residual r_2 by an encoder-decoder network. A high-resolution output image is generated by adding the image residual to the upscaled input image. The dimension of each feature map is denoted in the figure. An example output of each convolutional layer is also shown.

3.2 RAN for CS Image Reconstruction

We propose a RAN at each pyramid level to generate the reconstructed image with a fixed resolution. A RAN is composed of a reconstructive generator denoted as "RecGen", and a discriminator denoted as "RecDisc". RecDisc follows the structure of DCGAN [32], and the structure of RecGen is specially customized for reconstruction. Taking RecGen2 in the 2nd RNN stage as an example (see Fig. 3), $\{i_2, r_2, u_2, o_2\}$ is the contextual input from the previous stage, image residual, upscaled input, and output image, respectively. y_2 is the input measurements generated by the multi-rate CS encoder. RecGen2 is composed of two branches: (1) the upper branch that generates an upscaled input image u_2 via a deconvolutional neural network (deconv1); and (2) the lower branch that generates an image residual r_2 to compensate for the artifacts introduced by the upper branch. Note that u_2 is upscaled from a lower-resolution image, thus u_2 lacks high-frequency components (see Fig. 3) and only provides a coarse approximation to the higher-resolution ground-truth image. It is the addition of the high-frequency residual r_2 that recovers the entire frequency range of the image thus substantially improves the reconstruction quality [14].

The input i_2 is treated as a low-resolution context for generating the residual image r_2. We propose to first use an encoder to extract a contextual latent vector c_1 to represent the low-resolution context i_2. The encoder is composed of two convolutional layers and a fully-connected layer. To guarantee an equal contribution to the feature after fusion, the contextual latent vector c_1 has the same dimension as the CS measurement y_2. It should be noted that by increasing the dimension of c_1, one can expect more image patterns coming from the contextual input appear in the final reconstruction, and vice versa. c_1 is fused with the CS measurement y_2 through concatenation (referred to as "early fusion" in [34]) in a feature space. The fully-connected layer is used to transform the fused vector back to a feature map that has the same dimension as the contextual input i_2. A common practice of upscaling is to use an unpooling layer [41] or interpolation layer (bilinear, bicubic, or nearest neighbor). However, these methods are either non-invertible or non-trainable. Instead, we apply a deconvolutional layer deconv1 [40] to learn the upsampling of the fused feature map. We set up three residual blocks (resblk1~3) [19] to process the upsampled feature map to generate the image residual r_2, which is later combined with u_2 generated by the upper branch (deconv2) to form the final output image.

Learning from Context. Instead of reconstructing the original image from CS measurements directly, we propose to exploit the low-resolution context (i_2 in Fig. 3) to condition for reconstruction. The proposed conditional reconstruction scheme is fundamentally different from the conventional methods that solely rely on CS measurements. The reason is as follows.

Learning the inverse reconstructive mapping is a highly under-determined problem, hence notoriously tricky to solve. We need to accurately predict each pixel value in such an exceptionally high-dimensional space. All the existing data-driven methods directly search in such a vast space and try to establish a direct mapping from the low-dimensional CS measurements to the high-dimensional ground-truth. The intricacy of the problem and the lack of additional constraints make the search process inefficient and untrustworthy. Differently, we delegate the low-resolution context to confine the sub-search space, i.e., the candidates that are far from the context in the search space will be obviated. Besides, the CS measurements supplement the necessary information needed for recovering the entire frequency spectrum of the image. The fusion of the context and CS measurements hence improve both convergence speed and recovery accuracy.

Residual Learning. In LAPRAN, the RecGen of each RAN is similar to a segment of the ResNet in [19]. All the convolutional layers are followed by a spatial batch normalization (BN) layer [21] and a ReLU except for the output layer. The output layer uses a Tanh activation function to ensure the output image has pixel values in the range of [0, 255]. The use of BN and normalized weight initialization [25] alleviates the problem of vanishing or exploding gradients hence improve both convergence accuracy and speed.

3.3   Cascaded RANs for Flexible CS Reconstruction

The existing DNN-based methods all have rigid structures allowing for reconstruction with a fixed CR and at a non-adaptive resolution only. A new model

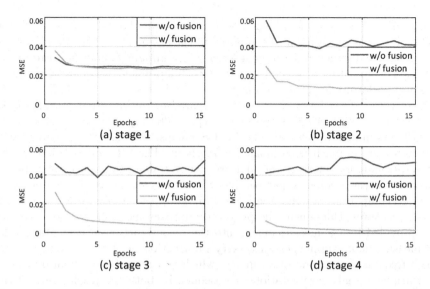

Fig. 4. Convergence analysis. We compare the MSE test error using the CIFAR10 dataset at the CR of 10. The results without measurement fusion can be regarded as the performance of an SR approach. The MSE loss of the SR approach cannot be effectively reduced after stage 1 because of the lack of new information.

must be retrained from scratch when a different CR is used in the encoding process. Inspired by the self-similarity based super resolution (SR) method [10,18], we propose a flexible CS reconstruction approach realized by dynamically cascading multiple RANs (see Fig. 1) at runtime. Upon training, each RAN corresponds to a specific resolution of the reconstructed image as well as an upper bound of the CR needed for accurate reconstruction. The thresholds of CR at different stages should be determined from experiments given a target accuracy metric. At runtime, depending on the CR of inputs, only the RANs with a higher CR threshold will be enabled for reconstruction. As a result, the proposed LAPRAN can perform high-fidelity CS reconstruction with a flexible resolution that is adaptive to a wide range of CRs. This merit is particularly significant to the CS application scenarios, where the CR must be adaptive to the dynamic requirements of storage space or communication bandwidth. When the CR is compromised in such an application scenario, all the existing methods will fail the reconstruction, while the proposed LAPRAN can still reconstruct an accurate preview of the image at a reduced resolution.

Another advantage of the proposed LAPRAN is that its hierarchical structure reduces the difficulty of training. CS reconstruction is a highly under-determined problem that has a humongous space for searching. Therefore, it is very challenging for a single network to approximate the inverse mapping accurately. Adopting a divide-and-conquer strategy, we propose to divide a highly under-determined problem into a series of lightly under-determined problems and conquer them in multiple hierarchies. As the dimensionality gap between the input and output in each sub-problem is significantly reduced, the difficulty for learning each mapping is much reduced compared to the original problem. Besides, since the hierarchical structure leverage a series of upsampling operations, error accumulation occurs at each stage. To alleviate such a problem, we define a loss function and perform back-propagation per stage independently. The training error is effectively reduced after each stage compared to the case that a single back-propagation is performed at the final output. The injected CS measurements at each pyramid level are the key for CS reconstruction, which distinguishes the proposed approach from image SR methods. The SR models [15,16,22,24] are responsible for inferring the high-frequency components non-existed in the input. From the frequency perspective, SR models should be adequately non-linear to compensate for the frequency gap, which inevitably results in complicated structures. Differently, the proposed approach incorporates new information provided by CS measurements into the reconstruction at each stage. The CS measurements supplement necessary information needed for recovering the entire frequency spectrum of an image, which is a powerful information source for learning visual representations. Consequently, both the resolution and the quality of the reconstructed images increase across different stages in the proposed approach. To illustrate this point, we compare LAPRAN with a variant that has no fusion mechanism implemented at each stage (an SR counterpart). The comparison results are shown in Fig. 4. It is obvious that the reconstruction accuracy of the proposed LAPRAN is consistently improved stage by stage, while the SR counterpart suffers from limited performance improvement.

3.4 Reconstruction Loss

We use a pixel-wise ℓ_2 reconstruction loss and an adversarial loss for training. The ℓ_2 loss finds an overall structure of a reconstructed image. The adversarial loss picks up a particular mode from the image distribution and generates a more authentic output [31]. The overall loss function is defined as follows:

$$
\begin{aligned}
\mathbf{z} &\sim \mathrm{Enc}(\mathbf{z}|\mathbf{x_l}), \quad \mathbf{x_h} = G(\mathbf{y}|\mathbf{z}), \\
\mathcal{L}_{adv}(G, D) &= \mathbb{E}_{\mathbf{x_h}}[\log D(\mathbf{x_h}|\mathbf{z})] + \mathbb{E}_{\mathbf{y}}[\log(1 - D(G(\mathbf{y}|\mathbf{z})))], \\
\mathcal{L}_{euc} &= \mathbb{E}_{\mathbf{x_h}}[\|\mathbf{x_h} - \mathbf{x_G}\|_2], \\
\mathcal{L}_{total} &= \lambda_{adv}\mathcal{L}_{adv} + \lambda_{euc}\mathcal{L}_{euc},
\end{aligned}
\tag{2}
$$

where $\mathbf{x_l}$, $\mathbf{x_h}$ and $\mathbf{x_G}, \mathbf{y}$ is the low-resolution input image, the high-resolution output image, the ground-truth image, and the CS measurement, respectively. The encoder function (Enc) maps a low-resolution input $\mathbf{x_l}$ to a distribution over a contextual latent vector $\mathbf{z}$.

3.5 Training

The training of each RAN is performed individually and sequentially. We start by training the first stage and the output is used as the input for the second

Table 1. Summary of the major differences between the proposed and the reference methods.

Name	Model/Data-driven	Iterative?	Reconstruction	Loss
NLR-CS	Model	Yes	Direct	Group sparsity, low rank
TVAL3	Model	Yes	Direct	ℓ_2, TV
D-AMP	Model	Yes	Direct	Denoising
ReconNet	Data	No	Direct	ℓ_2
LDAMP	Hybrid	Yes	Direct	Denoising
CSGM	Data	No	Direct	ℓ_2, Adversarial
LAPRAN	Data	No	Progressive	ℓ_2, Adversarial

stage. The training of all the subsequent stages is performed in such a sequential fashion. Motivated by the fact that the RANs in different stages share a similar structure but with different output dimensionality, we initialize the training of each stage with the pre-trained weights of the previous stage to take advantage of transfer learning. Such a training scheme is shown in experiments to be more stable and has faster convergence than those with static initialization (such as Gaussian or Xavier). Besides, the weight transfer between adjacent stages helps to tackle the notorious mode collapse problem in GAN since the pre-trained weights already cover the diversity existed in training images. It is recommended to leverage weight transfer to facilitate the training of the remaining RANs.

4 Experiments

In this section, we evaluate the performance of the proposed method. We first describe the datasets used for training and testing. Then, the parameters used for training are provided. Finally, we compare our method with state-of-the-art CS reconstruction methods.

4.1 Datasets and Training Setup

We train and evaluate the proposed LAPRAN with three widely used benchmarking datasets. The first two are MNIST and CIFAR10. The third dataset is made following the rule used in prior SR work [22,24,33], which uses 91 images from Yang et al. [39] and 200 images from the Berkeley Segmentation Dataset (BSD) [1]. The 291 images are augmented (rotation and flip) and cut into 228, 688 patches as the training data. Set5 [4] and Set14 [42] are pre-processed using the same method and used for testing.

We implemented a 4-stage LAPRAN for CS image reconstruction. We resize each training image to 64 × 64 and train the LAPRAN with a batch size of 128 for 100 epochs with early stopping. We use Adam solver with a learning rate of 1×10^{-4}. The training takes roughly two days on a single NVidia Titan X GPU.

Table 2. Quantitative evaluation of state-of-the-art CS reconstruction methods.

Algorithm	CR	MNIST		CIFAR10		Set5		Set14	
		SSIM	PSNR	SSIM	PSNR	SSIM	PSNR	SSIM	PSNR
NLR-CS	5	0.408	24.85	0.868	37.91	0.803	30.42	0.794	29.42
D-AMP		0.983	37.78	0.968	41.35	0.852	33.74	0.813	31.17
TVAL-3		0.934	36.39	0.847	32.03	0.812	31.54	0.727	29.48
ReconNet		0.911	29.03	0.871	32.55	0.824	31.78	0.763	29.70
CSGM		0.748	28.94	0.788	30.34	0.619	27.31	0.575	26.18
LDAMP		0.797	31.93	0.971	41.54	0.866	32.26	0.781	30.07
LAPRAN (ours)		0.993	38.46	0.978	42.39	0.895	34.79	0.834	32.71
NLR-CS	10	0.416	21.98	0.840	33.39	0.764	28.89	0.716	27.47
D-AMP		0.963	35.51	0.822	30.78	0.743	27.72	0.649	25.84
TVAL-3		0.715	27.18	0.746	29.21	0.702	28.29	0.615	26.65
ReconNet		0.868	28.98	0.843	29.78	0.779	29.53	0.704	27.45
CSGM		0.589	27.49	0.784	29.83	0.560	25.82	0.514	24.94
LDAMP		0.446	22.40	0.899	34.56	0.796	29.46	0.687	27.70
LAPRAN (ours)		0.990	38.38	0.943	38.13	0.849	32.53	0.775	30.45
NLR-CS	20	0.497	21.79	0.820	31.27	0.729	26.73	0.621	24.88
D-AMP		0.806	28.56	0.402	16.86	0.413	16.72	0.329	15.12
TVAL-3		0.494	21.00	0.623	25.77	0.583	25.18	0.513	24.19
ReconNet		0.898	27.92	0.806	29.08	0.731	27.07	0.623	25.38
CSGM		0.512	27.54	0.751	30.50	0.526	25.04	0.484	24.42
LDAMP		0.346	17.01	0.756	28.66	0.689	27.00	0.591	24.48
LAPRAN (ours)		0.985	37.02	0.896	34.12	0.801	30.08	0.716	28.39
NLR-CS	30	0.339	17.47	0.703	27.26	0.580	22.93	0.581	22.93
D-AMP		0.655	21.47	0.183	10.62	0.230	10.88	0.136	9.31
TVAL-3		0.381	18.17	0.560	24.01	0.536	24.04	0.471	23.20
ReconNet		0.892	25.46	0.777	29.32	0.623	25.60	0.598	24.59
CSGM		0.661	27.47	0.730	27.73	0.524	24.92	0.464	23.97
LDAMP		0.290	15.03	0.632	25.57	0.572	24.75	0.510	22.74
LAPRAN (ours)		0.962	31.28	0.840	31.47	0.693	28.61	0.668	27.09

4.2 Comparisons with State-of-the-Art

We compare the proposed LAPRAN with six state-of-the-art CS reconstruction methods: NLR-CS [17], TVAL3 [26], BM3D-AMP (D-AMP with BM3D denoiser [11]), ReconNet [23], CSGM [6], and learned D-AMP [28]. All methods are summarized in Table 1. Structural similarity (SSIM) and peak signal-to noise ratio (PSNR) are used as the performance metrics in the benchmarking.

The quantitative comparison of reconstruction performance is shown in Table 2. The proposed LAPRAN achieves the best recovery quality on all the testing datasets and at all CRs. Especially, the performance degradation of the LAPRAN at large CRs ($\geq$20) is well bounded. The main reasons are twofold.

Table 3. Runtime (seconds) for reconstructing a 64×64 image patch. Unlike the model-based methods, the runtime of LAPRAN is invariant to CR. LAPRAN is slightly slower than ReconNet because of its large model capacity. CSGM and LDAMP are relatively slow due to their iterative nature.

Name	Device	CR = 5	CR = 10	CR = 20	CR = 30
NLR-CS	CPU	1.869e1	1.867e1	1.833e1	1.822e1
TVAL3	CPU	1.858e1	1.839e1	1.801e1	1.792e1
BM3D-AMP	CPU	4.880e-1	4.213e-1	3.018e-1	2.409e-1
ReconNet	GPU	2.005e-3	1.703e-3	1.524e-3	1.661e-3
CSGM	GPU	1.448e-1	1.125e-1	9.089e-2	8.592e-2
LDAMP	GPU	3.556e-1	2.600e-1	1.998e-1	1.784e-1
LAPRAN	GPU	6.241e-3	6.384e-3	6.417e-3	6.008e-3

First, our approach adopts a progressive reconstruction strategy that greatly mitigates the difficulty of approximating the inverse mapping of CS. In contrast, CSGM tries to generate high-resolution images in a single step thus has a low reconstruction quality due to the difficulty in learning. Second, our approach utilizes a low-resolution image as input to guide the generation process at each stage, which helps to further reduce the search space of the under-determined problem by eliminating irrelevant candidates. The visual comparison of reconstructed images (at the CRs of 5 and 20) from Set 5 and Set 14 is shown in Fig. 5a and b, respectively. It is illustrated that our method can accurately reconstruct high-frequency details, such as the parallel lines, contained in the ground-truth image. In contrast, the reference methods produce noticeable artifacts and start to lose details at the CR of 20.

4.3 Reconstruction Speed

We compare the runtime of each reconstruction method for reconstructing 64×64 image patches to benchmark reconstruction speed. For the optimization-based methods, GPU acceleration is ineffective due to their iterative nature. Thus, we use an Intel Xeon E5-2695 CPU to run the codes provided by the respective authors. For the DNN-based methods, we use a Nvidia GTX TitanX GPU to accelerate the reconstruction process. The average runtime for each method is shown in Table 3. The proposed LAPRAN takes about 6 ms to reconstruct 64×64 image patch, which is four orders of magnitude faster than NLR-CS and TVAL3, and two orders of magnitude faster than BM3D-AMP, LDAMP and CSGM. As illustrated in the Sect. 2.3, both LDAMP and CSGM are hybrid methods that require to solve a convex CS recovery problem. In each iteration, the DNN is propagated to provide a solution for a sub-problem. Therefore, multiple propagations are performed to obtain a single reconstruction, which explains why both LDAMP and CSGM are two orders of magnitude slower than LAPRAN. In comparison with ReconNet, LAPRAN sacrifices minor reconstruction speed for an apparent improvement in recovery quality (improves about 3–10 dB PSNR). The proposed LAPRAN is still sufficiently fast for performing real-time CS reconstruction.

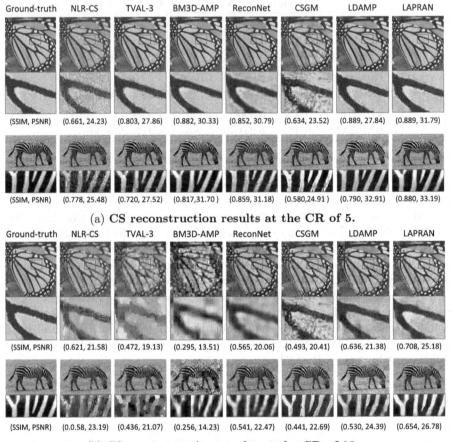

(a) **CS reconstruction results at the CR of 5.**

(b) **CS reconstruction results at the CR of 20.**

Fig. 5. Visual comparison of butterfly (Set 5) and zebra (Set14) at the CR of 5 and 20, respectively. LAPRAN preserves finer details.

5   Conclusions

In this paper, we present a scalable LAPRAN for high-fidelity, flexible, and fast CS image reconstruction. The LAPRAN consists of multiple stages of RANs that progressively reconstruct an image in multiple hierarchies. At each pyramid level, CS measurements are fused with a low-dimensional contextual latent vector to generate a high-frequency image residual, which is subsequently upsampled via a transposed CNN. The generated image residual is then added to a low-frequency image upscaled from the output of the previous level to form the final output of the current level with both higher resolution and reconstruction quality. The hierarchical nature of the LAPRAN is the key to enabling high-fidelity CS reconstruction with a flexible resolution that can be adaptive to a wide range of CRs. Each RAN in the LAPRAN can be trained independently with weight transfer to achieve faster convergence and improved accuracy. Leveraging the contextual input at each stage and the divide-and-conquer strategy in training are the keys to achieving excellent reconstruction performance.

Acknowledgement. This work is supported by NSF grant IIS/CPS-1652038 and Google Faculty Research Award.

References

1. Arbelaez, P., Maire, M., Fowlkes, C., Malik, J.: Contour detection and hierarchical image segmentation. TPAMI **33**(5), 898–916 (2011)
2. Becker, S., Bobin, J., Candès, E.J.: NESTA: a fast and accurate first-order method for sparse recovery. SIAM J. Imaging Sci. **4**(1), 1–39 (2011)
3. Becker, S.R., Candès, E.J., Grant, M.C.: Templates for convex cone problems with applications to sparse signal recovery. Math. Program. Comput. **3**(3), 165–218 (2011)
4. Bevilacqua, M., Roumy, A., Guillemot, C., Alberi-Morel, M.L.: Low-complexity single-image super-resolution based on nonnegative neighbor embedding. In: BMVC, pp. 135.1–135.10 (2012)
5. Blumensath, T., Davies, M.E.: Iterative hard thresholding for compressed sensing. Appl. Comput. Harmonic Anal. **27**(3), 265–274 (2009)
6. Bora, A., Jalal, A., Price, E., Dimakis, A.G.: Compressed sensing using generative models. In: ICML, pp. 537–546 (2017)
7. Candes, E., Romberg, J., Tao, T.: Stable signal recovery from incomplete and inaccurate measurements. Commun. Pure Appl. Math. **59**(8), 1207–1223 (2006)
8. Candès, E.J., Romberg, J., Tao, T.: Robust uncertainty principles: exact signal reconstruction from highly incomplete frequency information. TIT **52**(2), 489–509 (2006)
9. Candès, E.J., Eldar, Y.C., Needell, D., Randall, P.: Compressed sensing with coherent and redundant dictionaries. Appl. Comput. Harmonic Anal. **31**(1), 59–73 (2011)
10. Cui, Z., Chang, H., Shan, S., Zhong, B., Chen, X.: Deep network cascade for image super-resolution. In: Fleet, D., Pajdla, T., Schiele, B., Tuytelaars, T. (eds.) ECCV 2014. LNCS, vol. 8693, pp. 49–64. Springer, Cham (2014). https://doi.org/10.1007/978-3-319-10602-1_4
11. Dabov, K., Foi, A., Katkovnik, V., Egiazarian, K.: Image denoising by sparse 3-D transform-domain collaborative filtering. TIP **16**(8), 2080–2095 (2007)
12. Davenport, M.A.: Random observations on random observations: sparse signal acquisition and processing. Ph.D. thesis, Rice University (2010)
13. Davisson, L.: Rate distortion theory: a mathematical basis for data compression. TCOM **20**(6), 1202 (1972)
14. Denton, E.L., Chintala, S., Szlam, A., Fergus, R.: Deep generative image models using a laplacian pyramid of adversarial networks. In: NIPS, pp. 1486–1494 (2015)

15. Dong, C., Loy, C.C., He, K., Tang, X.: Image super-resolution using deep convolutional networks. TPAMI **38**(2), 295–307 (2016)
16. Dong, C., Loy, C.C., He, K., Tang, X.: Learning a deep convolutional network for image super-resolution. In: Fleet, D., Pajdla, T., Schiele, B., Tuytelaars, T. (eds.) ECCV 2014. LNCS, vol. 8692, pp. 184–199. Springer, Cham (2014). https://doi.org/10.1007/978-3-319-10593-2_13
17. Dong, W., Shi, G., Li, X., Ma, Y., Huang, F.: Compressive sensing via nonlocal low-rank regularization. TIP **23**(8), 3618–3632 (2014)
18. Glasner, D., Bagon, S., Irani, M.: Super-resolution from a single image. In: ICCV, pp. 349–356 (2009)
19. He, K., Zhang, X., Ren, S., Sun, J.: Deep residual learning for image recognition. In: CVPR, pp. 770–778 (2016)
20. Huggins, P.S., Zucker, S.W.: Greedy basis pursuit. TSP **55**(7), 3760–3772 (2007)
21. Ioffe, S., Szegedy, C.: Batch normalization: accelerating deep network training by reducing internal covariate shift. In: ICML, pp. 448–456 (2015)
22. Kim, J., Lee, J.K., Lee, K.M.: Accurate image super-resolution using very deep convolutional networks. In: CVPR, pp. 1646–1654 (2016)
23. Kulkarni, K., Lohit, S., Turaga, P., Kerviche, R., Ashok, A.: Reconnet: non-iterative reconstruction of images from compressively sensed measurements. In: CVPR, pp. 449–458 (2016)
24. Lai, W.S., Huang, J.B., Ahuja, N., Yang, M.H.: Deep laplacian pyramid networks for fast and accurate super-resolution. In: CVPR, pp. 5835–5843 (2017)
25. LeCun, Y.A., Bottou, L., Orr, G.B., Müller, K.-R.: Efficient BackProp. In: Montavon, G., Orr, G.B., Müller, K.-R. (eds.) Neural Networks: Tricks of the Trade. LNCS, vol. 7700, pp. 9–48. Springer, Heidelberg (2012). https://doi.org/10.1007/978-3-642-35289-8_3
26. Li, C., Yin, W., Jiang, H., Zhang, Y.: An efficient augmented Lagrangian method with applications to total variation minimization. Comput. Optim. Appl. **56**(3), 507–530 (2013)
27. Metzler, C.A., Maleki, A., Baraniuk, R.G.: From denoising to compressed sensing. TIT **62**(9), 5117–5144 (2016)
28. Metzler, C., Mousavi, A., Baraniuk, R.: Learned D-AMP: principled neural network based compressive image recovery. In: NIPS, pp. 1772–1783 (2017)
29. Mousavi, A., Baraniuk, R.G.: Learning to invert: signal recovery via deep convolutional networks. In: ICASSP, pp. 2272–2276 (2017)
30. Nam, S., Davies, M., Elad, M., Gribonval, R.: The cosparse analysis model and algorithms. Appl. Comput. Harmonic Anal. **34**(1), 30–56 (2013)
31. Pathak, D., Krähenbühl, P., Donahue, J., Darrell, T., Efros, A.: Context encoders: feature learning by inpainting. In: CVPR, pp. 2536–2544 (2016)
32. Radford, A., Metz, L., Chintala, S.: Unsupervised representation learning with deep convolutional generative adversarial networks. In: ICLR (2015)
33. Schulter, S., Leistner, C., Bischof, H.: Fast and accurate image upscaling with super-resolution forests. In: CVPR, pp. 3791–3799 (2015)
34. Snoek, C.G.M., Worring, M., Smeulders, A.W.M.: Early versus late fusion in semantic video analysis. In: MM, pp. 399–402 (2005)
35. Tropp, J.A., Gilbert, A.C.: Signal recovery from random measurements via orthogonal matching pursuit. TIT **53**(12), 4655–4666 (2007)
36. Weihong Guo, W.Y.: EdgeCS: edge guided compressive sensing reconstruction. SPIE **7744**, 7744 (2010)

37. Xu, K., Li, Y., Ren, F.: An energy-efficient compressive sensing framework incorporating online dictionary learning for long-term wireless health monitoring. In: ICASSP, pp. 804–808 (2016)
38. Xu, K., Li, Y., Ren, F.: A data-driven compressive sensing framework tailored for energy-efficient wearable sensing. In: ICASSP, pp. 861–865 (2017)
39. Yang, J., Wright, J., Huang, T.S., Ma, Y.: Image super-resolution via sparse representation. TIP **19**(11), 2861–2873 (2010)
40. Zeiler, M.D., Taylor, G.W., Fergus, R.: Adaptive deconvolutional networks for mid and high level feature learning. In: ICCV, pp. 1550–5499 (2011)
41. Zeiler, M.D., Fergus, R.: Visualizing and understanding convolutional networks. In: Fleet, D., Pajdla, T., Schiele, B., Tuytelaars, T. (eds.) ECCV 2014. LNCS, vol. 8689, pp. 818–833. Springer, Cham (2014). https://doi.org/10.1007/978-3-319-10590-1_53
42. Zeyde, R., Elad, M., Protter, M.: On single image scale-up using sparse-representations. In: Boissonnat, J.-D., et al. (eds.) Curves and Surfaces 2010. LNCS, vol. 6920, pp. 711–730. Springer, Heidelberg (2012). https://doi.org/10.1007/978-3-642-27413-8_47

3D Face Reconstruction from Light Field Images: A Model-Free Approach

Mingtao Feng[1], Syed Zulqarnain Gilani[2(✉)], Yaonan Wang[1], and Ajmal Mian[2]

[1] College of Electrical and Information Engineering, Hunan University,
Changsha 410006, China
{mintfeng,yaonan}@hnu.edu.cn
[2] Computer Science and Software Engineering, The University of Western Australia,
Perth 6009, Australia
{zulqarnain.gilani,ajmal.mian}@uwa.edu.au

Abstract. Reconstructing 3D facial geometry from a single RGB image has recently instigated wide research interest. However, it is still an ill-posed problem and most methods rely on prior models hence undermining the accuracy of the recovered 3D faces. In this paper, we exploit the Epipolar Plane Images (EPI) obtained from light field cameras and learn CNN models that recover horizontal and vertical 3D facial curves from the respective horizontal and vertical EPIs. Our 3D face reconstruction network (FaceLFnet) comprises a densely connected architecture to learn accurate 3D facial curves from low resolution EPIs. To train the proposed FaceLFnets from scratch, we synthesize photo-realistic light field images from 3D facial scans. The curve by curve 3D face estimation approach allows the networks to learn from only 14K images of 80 identities, which still comprises over 11 Million EPIs/curves. The estimated facial curves are merged into a single pointcloud to which a surface is fitted to get the final 3D face. Our method is model-free, requires only a few training samples to learn FaceLFnet and can reconstruct 3D faces with high accuracy from single light field images under varying poses, expressions and lighting conditions. Comparison on the BU-3DFE and BU-4DFE datasets show that our method reduces reconstruction errors by over 20% compared to recent state of the art.

1 Introduction

Three dimensional face analysis has the potential to address the challenges that confound its two dimensional counterpart such as variations in illumination, pose and scale [4]. This modality has achieved state-of-the-art performances on applications such as face recognition [14,36,39,65], syndrome diagnosis [16,17, 47,55], gender classification [15] and face animation [9,49]. Reconstructing 3D facial geometry from RGB images is, therefore, receiving a significant interest from the research community. However, using a single RGB image to recover the 3D face is an ill-posed problem [31] since the depth information is lost during the projection process. In fact, many different 3D shapes can result in similar 2D projections. The scale and bas-relief ambiguities [6] are common examples.

© Springer Nature Switzerland AG 2018
V. Ferrari et al. (Eds.): ECCV 2018, LNCS 11214, pp. 508–526, 2018.
https://doi.org/10.1007/978-3-030-01249-6_31

Most existing methods have resorted to the use of prior models such as the Basal Face Model (BFM) [43] and the Annotated Face Model(AFM) [12] to generate synthetic data with ground truth to train CNN [11,40] models and to recover the model parameters at test time. However, model-based approaches are inherently biased and constrained to the space of the training data of the prior models.

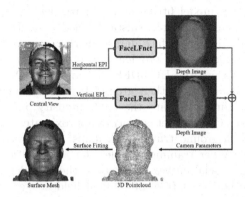

Fig. 1. Proposed pipeline for 3D face reconstruction from a single light field image. Using synthetic light field face images, we train two FaceLFnets for regressing 3D facial curves over their respective horizontal and vertical EPIs. The estimated depth maps are combined, using camera parameters, into a single pointcloud to which a surface is fitted to get the final 3D face.

A 4D light field image captures the RGB color intensities at each pixel as well as the direction of incoming light rays. High resolution plenoptic cameras [2,3] are now commercially available. Plenoptic cameras use an array of micro-lenses to capture many sub-aperture images arranged in an equally spaced rectangular grid. Unlike most 3D scanners that use active light projection and are hence restricted to indoor use, plenoptic cameras are passive and can instantly acquire light field images outdoors as well, in a single photographic exposure. The sub-aperture light field images have been exploited to improve the performance of many applications such as saliency detection [32], hyperspectral light field imaging [57], material classification [53], image segmentation [62] and image restoration [50,56] and in particular, depth estimation [26,34,46,48,52]. This paper focuses on reconstructing 3D faces from light field images under a wide range of pose, expression and illumination variations. Note that unlike stereo, the sub-aperture light field images are captured by the same camera with a single click.

Various methods have been proposed to solve the ill-posed problem of reconstructing 3D facial geometry from a single RGB image [11,29,31,40,44,51]. These methods all use one or more common techniques. For instance, Shape from Shading (SfS) uses the shading variation to reconstruct 3D faces but the caveat is that the method is sensitive to lighting and RGB image texture and even under near ideal conditions, suffers from the bas-relief ambiguity [6]. 3D

Morphable Models (3DMM) [11,40] project the 3D faces in a low-dimensional subspace. However, the models are confined to the linear space of their training data and do not generalize well to all face shapes [13]. Landmark based methods use facial keypoints to guide the reconstruction process but rely heavily on accurate localization of the landmarks.

We propose a model-free approach (see Fig. 1) to reconstruct 3D faces directly from light field images using Convolutional Neural Networks (CNN). Our technique does not rely on model fitting or landmark detection. Training a CNN requires massive amount of photo-realistic labeled data. However, there is no publicly available 4D light field face dataset with corresponding ground truth 3D face models. We address this problem and propose a method of generating the training data. We use the BU-3DFE [58] and BU-4DFE datasets [60] to generate light field images from their ground truth 3D models. Figure 2 shows some examples. We randomly vary the light intensity and pose to make our dataset more realistic. Our dataset comprises approximately 19K photo-realistic light field images with ground truth depth maps[1]. Furthermore, we show that our method requires fewer training samples (facial identities) as it capitalizes on reconstructing 3D facial curves rather than the complete face at once. We believe that our synthesized dataset of 4D light field images with corresponding 3D facial scans can be applied to many other facial analysis problems such as pose estimation, recognition and alignment.

Equipped with a rich light field image dataset, we propose a densely connected CNN architecture (FaceLFnet) to learn 3D facial curves from Epipolar Plane Images (EPIs). We train two networks separately using horizontal and vertical EPIs to increase the accuracy of depth estimation. The densenet architecture is preferred as it can accurately learn the subtle slopes in low resolution EPIs[2]. FaceLFnets are trained using our synthetic light field face images for which the ground truth depth data is available. Once the face curve estimates are obtained independently from the horizontal and vertical FaceLFnets, we merge them into a single pointcloud based on the camera parameters and then use a surface fitting method to recover the final 3D face. The core idea of our work is a model-free approach, where the solution is not restricted to any statistical face space. This is possible by exploiting the shape information present in the Epipolar Plane Images.

Our contribution are: (1) A model-free approach for 3D face reconstruction from a single light field image. Our method does not require face alignment or landmark detection and is robust to facial expressions, pose and illumination variations. Being model-free, our method also estimates the peripheral regions of the face such as hair and neck. (2) A training technique that does not require massive number of facial identities. Exploiting the EPIs, we demonstrate that the proposed FaceLFnet can learn from only a few identities (80) and still outperform the state-of-the-art methods by a margin of 26%. (3) A data syntheses technique

---

[1] We use depth map to represent disparity map as they are related by light field camera parameters [22].

[2] Higher slope of lines in EPI corresponds to lower depth values.

for generating a light field face image dataset which, to the best of our knowledge, is the first of its kind. This dataset will contribute to solving other face analysis problems as well.

2 Related Work

3D face reconstruction from a single image has attracted significant attention recently. Shape-from-shading (SfS) has been a popular approach for this task [18,37,61]. For example, Zhao et al. [61] proposed a symmetric SfS method to obtain illumination-normalized image and developed a face recognition system. Or-El et al. [37] proposed an improved SfS method to enhance the depth map combining the RGB image and rough depth image to create more details. Han et al. [18] estimated lighting variations with both global and local light models. SfS approach was then applied with the estimated lighting models for accurate shape reconstruction. Reconstruction using SfS requires priors of reflectance properties and lighting conditions and suffers from the bas-relief ambiguity [6].

A 3D Morphable Model (3DMM) was introduced by Blanz and Vetter [7] which represents a 3D face as a linear combination of orthogonal basis vectors obtained by PCA over 100 male and 100 female identities. Booth et al. [8] extended the concept and proposed a statistical model combined with a texture model for fitting the 3DMM on face images in *the wild*. 3DMM has also been used in [5,30,38,42] for face reconstruction. The main limitation of such methods is that the 3DMM cannot model every possible face. Moreover, it is unable to extract facial details like wrinkles and folds because such details are not encoded in the linear subspace.

Recently, various attempts were made to integrate 3DMMs with CNN for facial geometry reconstruction from a single image. Richardson et al. [40] employed an iterative CNN trained with synthetic data to estimate 3DMM vectors. The predicted geometry was then refined by the real-time shape-from-shading method. Sela et al. [41] extended the work [40] and introduced an end-to-end CNN framework that recovers the coarse facial shape using a *CoarseNet*, followed by a *FineNet* to refine the facial details. The two net parts are connected by a novel layer that renders the depth image from 3D mesh. Dou et al. [11] proposed an end-to-end 3D face reconstruction method from a single RGB image. They trained a fusion-CNN with multi-task learning loss to simplify 3D face reconstruction into neutral and expressive 3D facial parameters estimation. Jourabloo et al. [29] proposed a 3DMM fitting method for face alignment, which uses a cascaded CNN to regress camera matrix and 3DMM parameters. Tuan Tran et al. [51] used multi image 3DMM estimates as ground truth and then trained a CNN to regress 3DMM shape and texture parameters from an input image.

Kemelmacher el at. [31] used the input image as a guide to build a single reference model to align with the face image and then refined the reference model using SfS method. Hassner et al. [19] used a 3D neutral face as reference model to approximate the RGB image for face frontalization. Sela et al. [44] proposed a translation network that learns two maps (a depth image and a correspondence map), used for non-rigid registration with a template face, from a single RGB image. Fine-tuning is then performed for reconstructing facial details. In contrast to SfS and model fitting based face reconstruction methods, we learn 3D face curves from EPIs of the light field image. Our method does not require face alignment, dense correspondence or model fitting steps and is robust to facial pose, expressions and illumination.

To the best of our knowledge none of the existing methods is model-free and uses a prior face model at some stage of the reconstruction process. On the other hand our method is completely model-free. Similarly, we are unaware of any existing technique that uses light field images for 3D face reconstruction. However, literature points to some research in shape reconstruction from light field images using deep learning. Heber et al. [20] presented a method for reconstructing the shape from light field images that applies a CNN for pixel wise depth estimation from EPI patches. Although this method produces accurate scene depth, it uses a carefully designed dataset containing drastic slope changes in the EPIs. This method is unsuitable for non-rigid facial geometry reconstruction as faces are generally smooth and their EPIs contain only subtle slope variations. Heber et al. [21] proposed a U-shaped network architecture that automatically learns from EPIs to reconstruct their corresponding disparity images. However, training the network requires disparity maps of all the light field sub-views as labels, which is unrealistic for real datasets. Our approach differs in three ways. Firstly, we use one full EPI as input and its corresponding depth values as labels to overcome the problem of inaccurate depth estimation in the presence of subtle slope variations in the EPIs. Secondly, we train networks using horizontal EPIs and vertical EPIs separately to obtain a more accurate combined 3D pointcloud. Finally, our method does not require disparity maps of all the light field sub-views.

3   Facial Light Field Image Dataset Generation

The key to the success of CNN-based 3D face reconstruction from a single RGB image lies in the availability of large training datasets. However, there is no large scale dataset available that provides RGB face images and their corresponding high quality 3D models. Similarly, training a light field face reconstruction network requires a large-scale light field face dataset with corresponding ground truth 3D facial scans. Over the past few years, the computer vision community has made considerable efforts to collect light field images [1,22,33,35,53] for different applications. The only public light field face dataset [45] captured by Lytro Illum[TM] camera consists of 100 identities with 20 samples per person. However, depth maps of this dataset are generated using the Lytro Desktop Software[TM] and have low resolution as well as low depth accuracy. Therefore, this dataset is not suitable for training a network.

In the absence of large-scale 4D light field face datasets, we propose to generate a dataset of light field face images with ground truth 3D models. For this

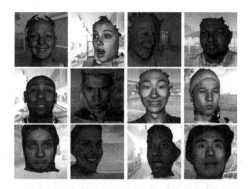

Fig. 2. Central view examples of our rendered light field images. The ground truth 3D scans are aligned with the central view. To make the dataset rich in variations, the generated light field images use random backgrounds and differ extensively in ethnicity, gender, age, pose and illumination.

purpose, we use the public BU-3DFE [58] and BU-4DFE [60] databases to generate light field face images. The former is used for training and testing whereas the latter is used only for testing only. The BU-3DFE dataset consists of 2,500 3D scans from 100 identities (56% female, 44% male), with an age range from 18 to 70 years and multiple ethnicities. Each subject is scanned in one neutral and 6 non-natural expressions each with four intensity levels. The BU-4DFE dataset contains 3D video sequences of 101 identities (58 female and 43 male) in six different facial expressions. We select the most representative frame of each expression sequence. As a result, our dataset contains 606 3D scans. These models contain shape details such as wrinkles of not only the fiducial area, but also the hair, ears and neck area which pose challenges for conventional 3D face reconstruction methods. All 3D models have RGB texture.

To generate plausible synthetic light field face images, it is crucial to control the light field camera parameters, background and illumination properly during rendering. We use the open source Blender[3] software and the light field camera tool proposed by Honauer et al. [22] for this purpose. We place a virtual light field camera in Blender with 15×15 micro-lenses and set its field of view to capture the 3D facial scans. Both BU-3DFE and BU-4DFE databases provide 3D facial models in the near frontal pose. We load the 3D models along with their textures in Blender and apply two rigid rotations ($\pm 15°$) in pitch and four in yaw ($\pm 15°$ and $\pm 30°$). To synthesize photo realistic light field images, we apply randomly selected indoor and outdoor images as backgrounds. We place two lamps at different locations in the scene and randomly change their intensities to achieve lighting variations. The angular resolution of the synthetic light field image is 15×15 and the spatial resolution is 400×400. The ground truth depth maps are aligned with the central view of light field image. Examples of our synthetic light field images are shown in Fig. 2.

---

[3] http://www.blender.org.

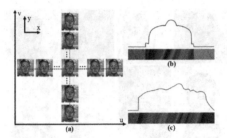

Fig. 3. EPIs corresponding to the 3D face curves. (a) Horizontal and vertical EPIs are obtained between the central view and sub-aperture images that are in the same row and column. (b) and (c) Visualization of the relationship between depth curves and slopes of lines in horizontal and vertical EPIs respectively.

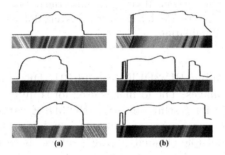

Fig. 4. Examples of EPIs and their corresponding 3D face curves. (a) Horizontal EPIs. (b) Vertical EPIs.

We implement a Python script[4] in Blender on a 3.4 GHz machine with 8GB RAM to automatically generate the light field facial images. The process of synthesizing light field images can be parallelized since each sub-aperture image is rendered independently. In total, we use 80 identities from BU-3DFE dataset to synthesize 14,000 light field images with ground truth disparity maps. The remaining 20 subjects from BU-3DFE and all 101 subjects from the BU-4DFE dataset are used as test data to generate 1,451 light field facial images for evaluation.

4   Proposed Method

An overview of the proposed method for reconstructing facial geometry from light field image is shown in Fig. 1 and the details follow.

4.1   Training Data

A 4D light field image can be parameterized as $L(u, v, x, y)$, where (x, y) and (u, v) represent the spatial and angular coordinates respectively [54]. When we

---

[4] The script for light field facial image synthesis will be made public.

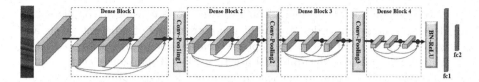

Fig. 5. Our proposed FaceLFnet for learning 3D face curves from EPIs. It contains 4 dense blocks, followed by two fully connected layers. The layers between two neighboring blocks are defined as transition layers and change feature map sizes via convolution and pooling [23].

fix v and y, then $L(u, v^*, x, y^*)$ defines a 2D horizontal EPI. Similarly the 2D vertical EPI can be represented as $L(u^*, v, x^*, y)$ when we keep u and x constant. As shown in Fig. 3, 2D EPIs demonstrate the linear characteristic of the light field image. The orientations of lines within the EPIs can infer the disparity of the corresponding 3D space points [20,21,28,54,59]. Equation (1) shows the relationship between the slope of the line and the disparity value where f is the light field camera parameter and k is the slope of the line.

$$Z = -f \times k, \tag{1}$$

As shown in Fig. 3(b) and (c), EPIs correspond to the 3D facial curves from the ground truth. Different line slopes in the EPI indicate different curve shapes. We use 14,000 synthetic light field images corresponding to the 80 identities of BU-3DFE for training. All together we extract 11.2 Million horizontal and vertical EPIs as training samples. Figure 4 shows some example EPIs and their corresponding curves. Using EPI images as training data removes the need for a huge number of identities. Since each 3D face curve can be learned independently from its corresponding EPI, we are able to generate massive training data from a small number of 3D face scans. Note that we do not need any further data augmentation such as image inversion or multiple crops as our networks learn from the full EPIs.

4.2 FaceLFnet Architecture

Each EPI in our case corresponds to a 3D face curve as shown in Figs. 3 and 4. The goal is to predict the full 3D curve from the EPIs using deep learning. CNNs can learn slope information of the pixels from individual EPIs, however, pixel wise prediction is very challenging. Heber et al. [20] divided each EPI into patches for 3D scene estimation. The authors estimated the depth value from each EPI patch independently as it contained the information pertaining to a single line at the center of the patch. In our case, pixel wise estimation is not practical as our network must learn the inter-relationship between the lines in one full EPI to estimate the complete 3D curve. Furthermore, in case of light field images for faces, some EPI patches especially in the quasi planar facial areas are devoid of lines and hence do not contain enough depth information leading to inaccurate depth estimation. Therefore, we propose using a complete EPI for depth prediction in order to exploit the correlations of adjacent pixels and mitigate the problem of inaccurate depth estimation due to pixel wise prediction.

The dimensions of each input EPI are $15 \times 400 \times 3$ (horizontal/vertical sub-aperture images × horizontal/vertical image pixels × RGB channels). Such a low resolution in the first dimension and size disparity in the first two dimensions pose challenges as the information of the input EPIs will reduce rapidly in one dimension than the other when passed through a deep network. To extenuate this problem and inspired by the success of Huang et al. [23], we propose a light field face network for estimating facial geometry from EPIs. The architecture of our network is illustrated in Fig. 5. It is based on DenseNet that consists of multiple dense blocks and transition layers. We use four dense blocks and change the softmax classifier to a regressor. Before passing the EPIs through the first dense block, a 16 channels convolution layer with 3×3 kernel size is used. For each dense block, we use three convolutional layers and set the growth rate to 12. We also use convolution followed by average pooling as transition layers between two adjacent dense blocks. The sizes of feature-map in the four dense blocks are 15×400, 8×200, 4×100 and 2×50 respectively. The details of network configurations are given in Table 1.

Both horizontal and vertical FaceLFnets are trained from scratch using the Caffe deep learning framework [27]. The initial learning rate is set to 0.0003 which is divided by 10 at 30000 and 50000 iterations. Our networks require only

Table 1. Our proposed FaceLFnet architecture. Note that each convolutional layer in the dense block corresponds to the sequence BN-ReLU. The growth rate of the four blocks is $k = 12$.

Layers	Output size	FaceLFnet
Convolution	15×400	3×3 conv, stride 1
Dense block 1	15×400	[3×3 conv, stride 1]×3
Transition layer 1	15×400	3×3 conv, stride 1
	8×200	2×2 average pool, stride 2
Dense block 2	8×200	[3×3 conv, stride 1]×3
Transition layer 2	8×200	3×3 conv, stride 1
	4×100	2×2 average pool, stride 2
Dense block 3	4×100	[3×3 conv, stride 1]×3
Transition layer 3	4×100	3×3 conv, stride 1
	2×50	2×2 average pool, stride 2
Dense block 4	2×50	[3×3 conv, stride 1]×3
Regression layer	400	4096 fully-connected 400 fully-connected EuclideanLoss

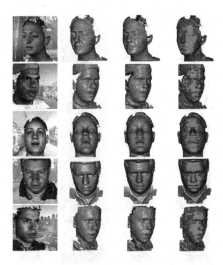

Fig. 6. Pose invariance. Columns one to four in each row respectively depict the input central view of the light field image, the ground truth 3D face, the reconstructed 3D face by our proposed method and the last two overlaid on each other.

one epoch for convergence. The caffe model for the trained networks will be made public.

4.3 3D Face Reconstruction

The output of our horizontal and vertical FaceLFnets are 3D facial curves that together make up a 3D face. We combine all the horizontal and vertical curves (in our case 400 each) of a face to form a horizontal and a vertical depth map separately. The next step is to reconstruct a 3D face from the two depth maps. A naive way to reconstruct the face is to take the average of both depth maps. However, such a methodology results in reconstruction error as each curve was learned independently. To mitigate this problem we propose a technique to project the depth maps on a 2D surface. First of all, we convert both the depth maps to 3D pointclouds, using the camera parameters. Next we give a slight jitter to the horizontal pointcloud by translating it 1 mm to the left on x-axis only. We fit a single surface of the form $z(x, y)$ to both 3D pointclouds simultaneously using the *gridfit* algorithm [10]. Our method ensures that a smooth surface is fitted to the horizontal and vertical pointclouds taking into account the correlation between the curves resulting in a smooth reconstructed 3D face.

5   Experimental Results

To the best of our knowledge, there is no suitable real light field face dataset with accompanying 3D ground truth available in the literature. Hence, we present

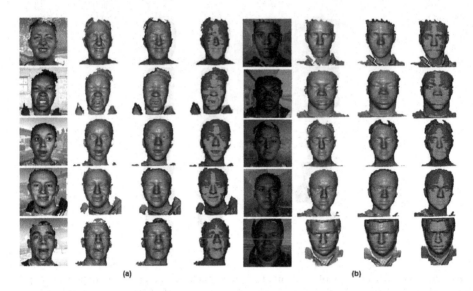

Fig. 7. (a) Expression invariance. As shown, our method can handle exaggerated expressions. (b) Invariance to illumination and skin color. Our method is robust to illumination variations and also works well in the case of dark skin (second row). Columns one to four in each row (in (a) and (b)) respectively depict the input central view of the light field image, the ground truth 3D face, the reconstructed 3D face by our proposed method and the last two overlaid on each other.

the evaluation of our method for 3D face reconstruction on light field images synthesized from the 3D scans of the remaining 20 subjects of BU-3DFE [58] and all 101 subjects from the BU-4DFE [60] dataset. We compare our subjective results with the recent state-of-the-art algorithm [44] for qualitative evaluation. We also present quantitative comparison with VRN-Guided [25] and other state-of-the-art methods [24,31,41,44,63,64] on both datasets. Note that the VRN-Guided method incorporates facial landmarks in their proposed VRN architecture whereas we follow a marker-less strategy.

5.1 Qualitative Evaluation

For qualitative evaluation, we show our reconstruction results on light field images synthesized from BU-3DFE [58] and BU-4DFE [60] databases. We also show the ground truth and predicted 3D face shapes overlaid on each other using the Scanalyze software. Figure 6 shows the reconstructed 3D faces under different poses to demonstrate that our method is robust to pose variations. Unlike model based algorithms for 3D face reconstruction [11,44] from a single RGB image, our method can recover the 3D model of the full head including the peripheral regions such as hair and neck and sometimes even part of the clothing. Figure 6 shows our results under pose invariance while Fig. 7 shows our results

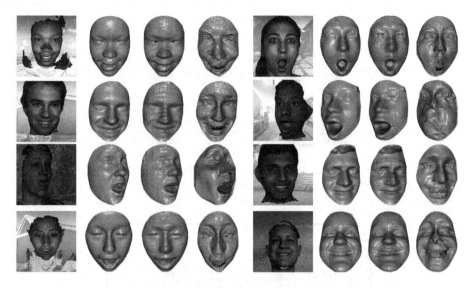

Fig. 8. Qualitative results. The columns contain (in order) central view image, the ground truth 3D face, 3D face reconstructed by our method and 3D face reconstructed by Sela et al. [44].

under exaggerated expressions and illumination changes respectively. Note that our method is robust to variations in pose, expressions and illumination.

We use the code provided by Sela et al. [44] for qualitative comparison of the reconstructed faces. Figure 8 shows 3D faces reconstructed from light field images using our method and 3D faces reconstructed from single central view RGB images using the recent state-of-the-art method proposed by Sela et al. [44]. Since [44] estimate only the facial region, we also crop our reconstructed faces for better visual comparison. As demonstrated, our method produces more visually accurate reconstructions in the global geometry compared to [44]. As compared to methods based on fine-tuning, our method can not capture fine details since we use the output of our network directly without complex post-processing steps. Our proposed method performs better than [44] because, firstly, [44] relies on a face detector and crops the input RGB image based on the detected coordinates while our method does not need any face detection or cropping. Secondly, [44] synthesized their training data from 3DMM parameters and thus their training images do not have the neck and hair regions etc. When the input images are far from the model space, the global face shape will be unsatisfactory at some key facial regions like mouth, nose and eyes as can be seen in Fig. 8. Finally, Sela et al. [44] use non-rigid registration to fit the 3DMM to the coarse output of the proposed network. The model fitting process deforms the facial shape when the model and the coarse shape estimated by the network are quite different.

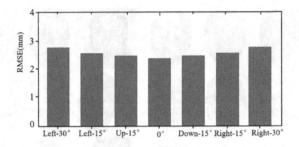

Fig. 9. Reconstruction errors for different facial poses on the BU-3DFE dataset [58]. Note that the RMSE increases from 2.62 to 2.93 (by 0.31 mm only) under extreme pose variations.

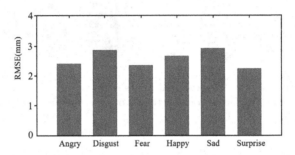

Fig. 10. Reconstruction errors for different facial expressions on the BU-4DFE dataset [60]. The RMSE increases from 2.49 to 2.98 (by only 0.49 mm) under extreme expression variations. Sad has the highest error whereas surprise has the lowest because of more edges around the lips which favors EPI based reconstruction.

5.2 Quantitative Evaluation

For quantitative comparison, we evaluate the 3D reconstruction on 3,500 light field images of 20 subjects from BU-3DFE [58] and 1,400 light field images of 101 subjects from the BU-4DFE dataset. To measure the affect of pose on the reconstruction accuracy, we use the 3,500 light field images from BU-3DFE dataset. There are 500 light field images for each pose. We use the Root Mean Square Error (RMSE) between the 3D point clouds of the estimated and ground truth reconstructions as a quantitative measure. Results of RMSE for different poses are depicted in Fig. 9. Our method is robust to pose variations as the RMSE error increases by only 0.31 mm when the pose is varied by 30°.

To measure the affect of facial expressions on reconstruction accuracy, we synthesize frontal images in different expressions (Angry, Disgust, Fear, Happy, Sad and Surprise) from the BU-4DFE dataset and measure the reconstruction errors. Figure 10 shows that the RMSE of 3D face reconstruction from our method is small even in the presence of exaggerated expressions.

We compare the absolute depth error of our proposed method with the state-of-the-art in Table 2, which shows that our proposed 3D reconstruction outper-

Table 2. Comparative results on the BU-3DFE dataset [58]. The absolute RMSE between ground truth and predicted shapes evaluated by mean, standard deviation, median and the average ninety percent largest error of the different methods are presented.

	Error in mm			
	Mean	SD	Median	90% largest
Kemelmacher et al. [31]	3.89	4.14	2.94	7.34
Zhu et al. [64]	3.85	3.23	2.93	7.91
Richardson et al. [41]	3.61	2.99	2.72	6.82
Sela et al. [44]	3.51	2.69	2.65	6.59
Ours	**2.78**	**2.04**	**1.73**	**5.30**

forms all existing methods. We report depth errors evaluated by mean, standard deviation, median and the average ninety percent largest error. Note that for a fair comparison with Sela et al. [44] we report the results obtained on the same dataset directly from their paper instead of calculating the reconstruction errors from our implementation of their work.

We also compare the results of our method with VRN-Guided [25], 3DDFE [63] and EOS [24] methods using the BU-4DFE dataset [60]. We use the Normalized Mean Error (NME) metric proposed by Aarson [25] to report the results for comparison with existing methods. NME is defined as the average per vertex Euclidean distance between the estimated and the ground truth reconstruction normalized by the outer 3D interocular distance:

$$\text{NME} = \frac{1}{n} \sum_{k=1}^{n} \frac{\|x_k - y_k\|_2}{d}, \tag{2}$$

where n is the total number of vertices per facial mesh and d is the interocular distance. x_k and y_k represent the coordinates of vertices from the estimated and ground truth meshes respectively. The NME is calculated on the face region only. As shown in Table 3, our method outperforms the state-of-the-art.

Table 3. Reconstruction errors on the BU-4DFE dataset [60] in terms of NME defined in Eq. (2). ICP has been used to align the reconstructed face to the ground truth similar to [25].

	3DDFA [63]	EOS [24]	VRN-Guided [25]	Ours
NME	5.14	5.33	4.71	**3.72**

We also compare our results with [20,21] using our own implementation of their model as they did not make their codes/trained models public. We trained the model [20] on synthetic data and then tested it on 10 light field face images of the test data. Figure 11 shows three best facial reconstructions by the model of [20]. These reconstructions are extremely noisy with high RMSE. The average reconstruction error of [20] for these 10 images is 27.23 ± 24.7 mm while ours is 2.79 ± 2.6 mm. The main reason for the poor performance of [20] (and [21]) is that the models were designed for 3D reconstruction of scenes where the textures and EPI slopes are drastic. Hence, these methods [49,50] do not perfrom well at reconstructing 3D faces.

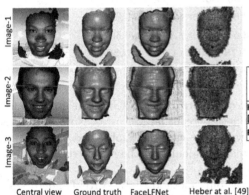

	RMSE $\pm$ SD (mm)		
	Image-1	Image-2	Image-3
Heber at al. [50]	17.39 ± 15.0	20.4 ± 17.4	16.53 ± 13.7
FaceLFNet	2.84 ± 2.4	3.15 ± 2.9	2.69 ± 2.1

Comparison of average and SD of RMSE for 3D reconstruction of each face (shown on left).

Central view   Ground truth   FaceLFNet   Heber at al. [49]

Fig. 11. Qualitative and quantitative comparison of 3D face reconstruction with Heber et al. [20]

6   Conclusion

We presented a model-free approach for recovering the 3D facial geometry from a single light field image. We proposed FaceLFnet, a densely connected network architecture that regresses the 3D facial curves over the Epipolar Plane Images. Using a curve by curve reconstruction approach, our method needs only a few training samples and yet generalizes well to unseen faces. We proposed a photo-realistic light field image synthesis method to generate a large-scale EPI dataset from a relatively small number of real facial identities. Our results show that 3D face reconstruction from light field images is more accurate and allows the use of a model-free approach which is robust to changes in pose, facial expressions, ethnicities and illumination. We conclude that light field cameras are a more appropriate choice as a passive sensor for 3D face reconstruction since they enjoy similar advantages to conventional RGB cameras in that they are point and shoot, portable and have low cost. These cameras are especially a better choice for medical applications where higher accuracy and model-free approaches are desirable. We will make our trained networks and dataset public which will become the first photo-realistic light field face dataset with ground truth 3D facial scans.

Acknowledgments. This research was partly supported by National Natural Science Foundation of China (No. 61401046, 61733004) and Australian Research Council (ARC) Discovery grant DP160101458. We are grateful to NVIDIA Corporation for donating the Titan Xp GPU used for this research.

References

1. http://lightfield.stanford.edu/
2. https://www.lytro.com/
3. https://www.raytrix.com/
4. Abate, A.F., Nappi, M., Riccio, D., Sabatino, G.: 2D and 3D face recognition: a survey. Pattern Recognit. Lett. **28**(14), 1885–1906 (2007)
5. Aldrian, O., Smith, W.A.: Inverse rendering of faces with a 3D morphable model. IEEE Trans. Pattern Anal. Mach. Intell. **35**(5), 1080–1093 (2013)
6. Belhumeur, P.N., Kriegman, D.J., Yuille, A.L.: The bas-relief ambiguity. Int. J. Comput. Vis. **35**(1), 33–44 (1999)
7. Blanz, V., Vetter, T.: A morphable model for the synthesis of 3D faces. In: Proceedings of the 26th Annual Conference on Computer Graphics and Interactive Techniques, pp. 187–194. ACM Press/Addison-Wesley Publishing Co. (1999)
8. Booth, J., Antonakos, E., Ploumpis, S., Trigeorgis, G., Panagakis, Y., Zafeiriou, S.: 3D face morphable models "in-the-wild". In: The IEEE Conference on Computer Vision and Pattern Recognition (CVPR), July 2017
9. Cao, C., Weng, Y., Lin, S., Zhou, K.: 3D shape regression for real-time facial animation. ACM Trans. Graph. (TOG) **32**(4), 41 (2013)
10. DErico, J.: Surface fitting using gridfit. In: MATLAB Central File Exchange (2008)
11. Dou, P., Shah, S.K., Kakadiaris, I.A.: End-to-end 3D face reconstruction with deep neural networks. In: The IEEE Conference on Computer Vision and Pattern Recognition (CVPR), July 2017
12. Fang, T., Zhao, X., Ocegueda, O., Shah, S.K., Kakadiaris, I.A.: 3D/4D facial expression analysis: an advanced annotated face model approach. Image Vis. Comput. **30**(10), 738–749 (2012)
13. Gilani, S.Z., Mian, A., Eastwood, P.: Deep, dense and accurate 3D face correspondence for generating population specific deformable models. Pattern Recognit. **69**, 238–250 (2017)
14. Gilani, S.Z., Mian, A., Shafait, F., Reid, I.: Dense 3D face correspondence. IEEE Trans. Pattern Anal. Mach. Intell. (TPAMI) **40**(7), 1584–1598 (2018)
15. Gilani, S.Z., Rooney, K., Shafait, F., Walters, M., Mian, A.: Geometric facial gender scoring: objectivity of perception. PLoS ONE **9**(6), e99483 (2014)
16. Hammond, P., Forster-Gibson, C., Chudley, A., et al.: Face-brain asymmetry in autism spectrum disorders. Mol. Psychiatry **13**(6), 614–623 (2008)
17. Hammond, P.: The use of 3D face shape modelling in dysmorphology. Arch. Dis. Child. **92**(12), 1120 (2007)
18. Han, Y., Lee, J.Y., So Kweon, I.: High quality shape from a single RGB-D image under uncalibrated natural illumination. In: Proceedings of the IEEE International Conference on Computer Vision, pp. 1617–1624 (2013)
19. Hassner, T., Harel, S., Paz, E., Enbar, R.: Effective face frontalization in unconstrained images. In: Proceedings of the IEEE Conference on Computer Vision and Pattern Recognition, pp. 4295–4304 (2015)

20. Heber, S., Pock, T.: Convolutional networks for shape from light field. In: Proceedings of the IEEE Conference on Computer Vision and Pattern Recognition, pp. 3746–3754 (2016)
21. Heber, S., Yu, W., Pock, T.: U-shaped networks for shape from light field. In: BMVC (2016)
22. Honauer, K., Johannsen, O., Kondermann, D., Goldluecke, B.: A dataset and evaluation methodology for depth estimation on 4D light fields. In: Lai, S.-H., Lepetit, V., Nishino, K., Sato, Y. (eds.) ACCV 2016. LNCS, vol. 10113, pp. 19–34. Springer, Cham (2017). https://doi.org/10.1007/978-3-319-54187-7_2
23. Huang, G., Liu, Z., van der Maaten, L., Weinberger, K.Q.: Densely connected convolutional networks. In: The IEEE Conference on Computer Vision and Pattern Recognition (CVPR), July 2017
24. Huber, P., et al.: A multiresolution 3D morphable face model and fitting framework. In: Proceedings of the 11th International Joint Conference on Computer Vision, Imaging and Computer Graphics Theory and Applications (2016)
25. Jackson, A.S., Bulat, A., Argyriou, V., Tzimiropoulos, G.: Large pose 3D face reconstruction from a single image via direct volumetric CNN regression. In: The IEEE International Conference on Computer Vision (ICCV), October 2017
26. Jeon, H.G., et al.: Accurate depth map estimation from a lenslet light field camera. In: Proceedings of the IEEE Conference on Computer Vision and Pattern Recognition, pp. 1547–1555 (2015)
27. Jia, Y., et al.: Caffe: convolutional architecture for fast feature embedding. In: Proceedings of the 22nd ACM International Conference on Multimedia, pp. 675–678. ACM (2014)
28. Johannsen, O., Sulc, A., Goldluecke, B.: What sparse light field coding reveals about scene structure. In: Proceedings of the IEEE Conference on Computer Vision and Pattern Recognition, pp. 3262–3270 (2016)
29. Jourabloo, A., Liu, X.: Pose-invariant face alignment via CNN-based dense 3D model fitting. Int. J. Comput. Vis. 124(2), 1–17 (2017)
30. Kazemi, V., Keskin, C., Taylor, J., Kohli, P., Izadi, S.: Real-time face reconstruction from a single depth image. In: 2014 2nd International Conference on 3D Vision (3DV), vol. 1, pp. 369–376. IEEE (2014)
31. Kemelmacher-Shlizerman, I., Basri, R.: 3D face reconstruction from a single image using a single reference face shape. IEEE Trans. Pattern Anal. Mach. Intell. 33(2), 394–405 (2011)
32. Li, N., Sun, B., Yu, J.: A weighted sparse coding framework for saliency detection. In: Proceedings of the IEEE Conference on Computer Vision and Pattern Recognition, pp. 5216–5223 (2015)
33. Li, N., Ye, J., Ji, Y., Ling, H., Yu, J.: Saliency detection on light field. In: The IEEE Conference on Computer Vision and Pattern Recognition (CVPR), June 2014
34. Lin, H., Chen, C., Bing Kang, S., Yu, J.: Depth recovery from light field using focal stack symmetry. In: Proceedings of the IEEE International Conference on Computer Vision, pp. 3451–3459 (2015)
35. Marwah, K., Wetzstein, G., Bando, Y., Raskar, R.: Compressive light field photography using overcomplete dictionaries and optimized projections. ACM Trans. Graph. (TOG) 32(4), 46 (2013)
36. Mian, A., Bennamoun, M., Owens, R.: An efficient multimodal 2D–3D hybrid approach to automatic face recognition. IEEE Trans. Pattern Anal. Mach. Intell. 29(11), 1927–1943 (2007)

37. Or-El, R., Rosman, G., Wetzler, A., Kimmel, R., Bruckstein, A.M.: RGBD-fusion: real-time high precision depth recovery. In: Proceedings of the IEEE Conference on Computer Vision and Pattern Recognition, pp. 5407–5416 (2015)
38. Patel, A., Smith, W.A.: 3D morphable face models revisited. In: IEEE Conference on Computer Vision and Pattern Recognition, CVPR 2009, pp. 1327–1334. IEEE (2009)
39. Queirolo, C., Silva, L., Bellon, O., Segundo, M.: 3D face recognition using simulated annealing and the surface interpenetration measure. IEEE TPAMI **32**(2), 206–219 (2010)
40. Richardson, E., Sela, M., Kimmel, R.: 3D face reconstruction by learning from synthetic data. In: 2016 Fourth International Conference on 3D Vision (3DV), pp. 460–469. IEEE (2016)
41. Richardson, E., Sela, M., Or-El, R., Kimmel, R.: Learning detailed face reconstruction from a single image. In: The IEEE Conference on Computer Vision and Pattern Recognition (CVPR), July 2017
42. Roth, J., Tong, Y., Liu, X.: Adaptive 3D face reconstruction from unconstrained photo collections. In: Proceedings of the IEEE Conference on Computer Vision and Pattern Recognition, pp. 4197–4206 (2016)
43. Savran, A., et al.: Bosphorus database for 3D face analysis. In: Schouten, B., Juul, N.C., Drygajlo, A., Tistarelli, M. (eds.) BioID 2008. LNCS, vol. 5372, pp. 47–56. Springer, Heidelberg (2008). https://doi.org/10.1007/978-3-540-89991-4_6
44. Sela, M., Richardson, E., Kimmel, R.: Unrestricted facial geometry reconstruction using image-to-image translation. In: The IEEE International Conference on Computer Vision (ICCV), October 2017
45. Sepas-Moghaddam, A., Chiesa, V., Correia, P.L., Pereira, F., Dugelay, J.L.: The IST-EURECOM light field face database. In: 2017 5th International Workshop on Biometrics and Forensics (IWBF), pp. 1–6. IEEE (2017)
46. Sheng, H., Zhao, P., Zhang, S., Zhang, J., Yang, D.: Occlusion-aware depth estimation for light field using multi-orientation EPIs. Pattern Recognit. **74**, 587–599 (2017)
47. Tan, D.W., et al.: Hypermasculinised facial morphology in boys and girls with autism spectrum disorder and its association with symptomatology. Sci. Rep. **7**(1), 9348 (2017)
48. Tao, M.W., Srinivasan, P.P., Malik, J., Rusinkiewicz, S., Ramamoorthi, R.: Depth from shading, defocus, and correspondence using light-field angular coherence. In: Proceedings of the IEEE Conference on Computer Vision and Pattern Recognition, pp. 1940–1948 (2015)
49. Thies, J., Zollhofer, M., Stamminger, M., Theobalt, C., Nießner, M.: Face2Face: real-time face capture and reenactment of RGB videos. In: Proceedings of the IEEE Conference on Computer Vision and Pattern Recognition, pp. 2387–2395 (2016)
50. Tian, J., Murez, Z., Cui, T., Zhang, Z., Kriegman, D., Ramamoorthi, R.: Depth and image restoration from light field in a scattering medium. In: The IEEE International Conference on Computer Vision (ICCV), October 2017
51. Tuan Tran, A., Hassner, T., Masi, I., Medioni, G.: Regressing robust and discriminative 3D morphable models with a very deep neural network. In: The IEEE Conference on Computer Vision and Pattern Recognition (CVPR), July 2017
52. Wang, T.C., Efros, A.A., Ramamoorthi, R.: Occlusion-aware depth estimation using light-field cameras. In: Proceedings of the IEEE International Conference on Computer Vision, pp. 3487–3495 (2015)

53. Wang, T.-C., Zhu, J.-Y., Hiroaki, E., Chandraker, M., Efros, A.A., Ramamoorthi, R.: A 4D light-field dataset and CNN architectures for material recognition. In: Leibe, B., Matas, J., Sebe, N., Welling, M. (eds.) ECCV 2016. LNCS, vol. 9907, pp. 121–138. Springer, Cham (2016). https://doi.org/10.1007/978-3-319-46487-9_8

54. Wanner, S., Goldluecke, B.: Variational light field analysis for disparity estimation and super-resolution. IEEE Trans. Pattern Anal. Mach. Intell. 36(3), 606–619 (2014)

55. Whitehouse, A.J., et al.: Prenatal testosterone exposure is related to sexually dimorphic facial morphology in adulthood. Proc. R. Soc. B. 282, 20151351 (2015)

56. Wu, G., Zhao, M., Wang, L., Dai, Q., Chai, T., Liu, Y.: Light field reconstruction using deep convolutional network on EPI. In: The IEEE Conference on Computer Vision and Pattern Recognition (CVPR), July 2017

57. Xiong, Z., Wang, L., Li, H., Liu, D., Wu, F.: Snapshot hyperspectral light field imaging. In: The IEEE Conference on Computer Vision and Pattern Recognition (CVPR), July 2017

58. Yin, L., Wei, X., Sun, Y., Wang, J., Rosato, M.J.: A 3D facial expression database for facial behavior research. In: 7th International Conference on Automatic Face and Gesture Recognition, FGR 2006, pp. 211–216. IEEE (2006)

59. Zhang, S., Sheng, H., Li, C., Zhang, J., Xiong, Z.: Robust depth estimation for light field via spinning parallelogram operator. Comput. Vis. Image Underst. 145, 148–159 (2016)

60. Zhang, X., et al.: A high-resolution spontaneous 3D dynamic facial expression database. In: 2013 10th IEEE International Conference and Workshops on Automatic Face and Gesture Recognition (FG), pp. 1–6. IEEE (2013)

61. Zhao, W.Y., Chellappa, R.: Illumination-insensitive face recognition using symmetric shape-from-shading. In: Proceedings of IEEE Conference on Computer Vision and Pattern Recognition, vol. 1, pp. 286–293. IEEE (2000)

62. Zhu, H., Zhang, Q., Wang, Q.: 4D light field superpixel and segmentation. In: The IEEE Conference on Computer Vision and Pattern Recognition (CVPR), July 2017

63. Zhu, X., Lei, Z., Liu, X., Shi, H., Li, S.Z.: Face alignment across large poses: a 3D solution. In: Proceedings of the IEEE Conference on Computer Vision and Pattern Recognition, pp. 146–155 (2016)

64. Zhu, X., Lei, Z., Yan, J., Yi, D., Li, S.Z.: High-fidelity pose and expression normalization for face recognition in the wild. In: Proceedings of the IEEE Conference on Computer Vision and Pattern Recognition, pp. 787–796 (2015)

65. Zulqarnain Gilani, S., Mian, A.: Learning from millions of 3D scans for large-scale 3D face recognition. In: The IEEE Conference on Computer Vision and Pattern Recognition (CVPR), June 2018

"Factual" or "Emotional": Stylized Image Captioning with Adaptive Learning and Attention

Tianlang Chen[1]([✉])[iD], Zhongping Zhang[1], Quanzeng You[3], Chen Fang[2], Zhaowen Wang[2], Hailin Jin[2], and Jiebo Luo[1]

[1] University of Rochester, Rochester, USA
{tchen45,jluo}@cs.rochester.edu, zzhang76@ur.rochester.edu
[2] Adobe Research, San Jose, USA
{cfang,zhawang,hljin}@adobe.com
[3] Microsoft Research, Redmond, USA
quyou@microsoft.com

Abstract. Generating stylized captions for an image is an emerging topic in image captioning. Given an image as input, it requires the system to generate a caption that has a specific style (e.g., humorous, romantic, positive, and negative) while describing the image content semantically accurately. In this paper, we propose a novel stylized image captioning model that effectively takes both requirements into consideration. To this end, we first devise a new variant of LSTM, named style-factual LSTM, as the building block of our model. It uses two groups of matrices to capture the factual and stylized knowledge, respectively, and automatically learns the word-level weights of the two groups based on previous context. In addition, when we train the model to capture stylized elements, we propose an adaptive learning approach based on a reference factual model, it provides factual knowledge to the model as the model learns from stylized caption labels, and can adaptively compute how much information to supply at each time step. We evaluate our model on two stylized image captioning datasets, which contain humorous/romantic captions and positive/negative captions, respectively. Experiments shows that our proposed model outperforms the state-of-the-art approaches, without using extra ground truth supervision.

Keywords: Stylized image captioning · Adaptive learning Attention model

1 Introduction

Automatically generating coherent captions for images has attracted remarkable attention for its strong applicability, such as picture auto-commenting [23] and helping blind people to see [11]. This task is often referred to as image captioning, which combines computer vision, natural language processing and artificial

© Springer Nature Switzerland AG 2018
V. Ferrari et al. (Eds.): ECCV 2018, LNCS 11214, pp. 527–543, 2018.
https://doi.org/10.1007/978-3-030-01249-6_32

intelligence. Most recent image captioning systems focus on generating an objective, neutral and indicative caption without any style characteristics, which is defined as a factual caption. However, the art of language motivates researchers to generate captions with different styles, which can give people different feelings when focusing on a specific image. The "style" can refer to multiple meanings. For example, as shown in Fig. 1, in terms of the fashion of the caption, caption style can be either "romantic" or "humorous". In addition, in terms of the sentiment it brings to people, caption style can be either "positive" or "negative". Without doubt, generating such kinds of captions with different styles will greatly enrich the expressibility of the captions and make them more attractive.

Ideally, a high-performing stylized image captioning model should satisfy two requirements: (1) it generates appropriate stylized words/phrases in appropriate positions of the caption, (2) it still describes the image content accurately. Focused on stylized caption generation, existing state-of-the-art work [9,28] train their captioning models based on two datasets separately, a large dataset with paired images and ground truth factual captions, and a small dataset with paired images and stylized ground truth captions. From the large factual dataset, the model is learned to generate factual captions that can correctly describe the images; from the small stylized dataset, the model is learned to transform factual captions to stylized captions by incorporating suitable non-factual words/phrases at correct positions of the caption. In the training and predicting process, how to effectively take these two aspects into consideration is paramount for the model to generate high quality stylized captions.

To combine and preserve the knowledges learned from both factual and stylized dataset, Gan et al. [9] propose a factored LSTM, which factorizes matrix W_x. into three matrices $(U_{x\cdot}, S_{x\cdot}, V_{x\cdot})$. $U_{x\cdot}$ and $V_{x\cdot}$ are updated by the ground truth factual captions while $S_{x\cdot}$ is updated by ground truth captions with a specific style. In the predicting process, $U_{x\cdot}, S_{x\cdot}$ and $V_{x\cdot}$ are combined to generate the stylized caption. Since $U_{x\cdot}$ and $V_{x\cdot}$ preserve the factual information and $S_{x\cdot}$ preserves the stylized information, the model can thus generate stylized captions that correspond to input images. However, for both the training and predicting processes, factored LSTM cannot differentiate whether paying more attention to the fact-related part (i.e. $U_{x\cdot}$ and $V_{x\cdot}$) or the style-related part (i.e. $S_{x\cdot}$). It is natural that when the model focuses on predicting a stylized word, it should pay more attention to the style-related part, and vice versa. Mathews et al. [28] consider this problem and propose Senticap, which consists of two parallel LSTMs – one updated by the factual captions and one updated by the sentimental captions. When predicting a word, Senticap obtains the result by weighting the predicted word probability distributions of the two LSTMs. However, directly weighting the high level probability distributions can be too "coarse" in that it doesn't consider the low level attention effect on stylized and factual elements. In addition, Senticap obtains the weights of the two distributions by predicting the sentiment strength of the current word. In this step, it uses the extra ground truth word sentiment strength label, which is unavailable for other datasets.

Fig. 1. Examples of stylized image captions. Besides factual captions, there can be four kinds of stylized captions that correspond to humorous, romantic, positive and negative styles, respectively.

In this paper, we propose a novel stylized image captioning model. In particular, we first design a new style-factual LSTM as a core building block of our model. Compared with factored LSTM, it combines fact-related and style-related parts of LSTM in a different way and incorporates self-attention for this two parts. More concretely, for both input word embedding feature and input hidden state of LSTM, we assign two independent groups of matrices to capture the factual and stylized knowledges, respectively. At each time step, it feeds an effective attention mechanism to weight the importance of the two groups of parameters based on previous context information, and combines the two groups of parameters by weighted-sum operation. In addition, to help the model preserve factual information while learning from stylized captions, we develop an adaptive learning approach that feeds a reference factual model as a guidance. At each time step, the model can adaptively learn whether to focus more on the ground truth stylized label or on the factual guidance, based on the similarity between the outputs of the real stylized captioning model and the reference factual model. Overall, both improvements help the model capture and combine the factual and stylized knowledge in a better way.

In summary, the main contributions of this paper are:

- We propose a new stylized image captioning model, with a core building block named style-factual LSTM. Style-factual LSTM incorporates two groups of parameters with dynamic attention weights into an LSTM, to adaptively adjust the relative attention weights between the fact and style-related parts.
- We develop a new learning approach to training the model on stylized captions, which adds the factual output of reference model as a guidance. The model can automatically adjust the strength of guidance based on ground truth stylized caption and reference model output without using additional information.
- Our model outperforms the state-of the-art methods on both image style captioning and image sentiment captioning task, in terms of both the relevance to the image and the appropriateness of the style.
- We visualize the corresponding attention weights for both the style-factual LSTM and the adaptive learning approach, and show explainable improvements in the results.

2 Related Work

Stylized image captioning is mainly related to two research topics: image captioning and style transfer. In this section, we provide the background of image captioning, attention model and style transfer, respectively.

Image Captioning. Image captioning has received much attention in recent years due to the advances in computer vision and natural language processing. Early image captioning methods [6–8,18,19,21,22] generate sentences by combining words which are extracted from corresponding images. A downside of these methods is that their performance is limited by empirical language models. To alleviate the problem, retrieval-based frameworks are developed [14,19,20,31]. They first retrieve similarity images of the input image from a database, then generate new descriptions for the query image by using the captions of retrieved images. However, this kind of approach relies heavily on the image database. Modern approaches [4,5,17,26,27,40,42,44] consider image captioning as a machine translation problem. Vinyals et al. [42] propose an encoder-decoder framework. Many improved approaches [5,17,26,29,40,44] are developed based on this encoder-decoder framework. The differences between these methods often lie in the architecture of recurrent neural network.

Attention Model. Recent successes of attention models [2,13,32,33,38] motivate many researchers to apply visual or language attention models [1,24,29,37,44,45] to the image captioning task. Top-down visual attention models are first widely used [29,39,43,44]. The attention models enable deeper image understanding by assigning different attention weights to different image regions. Bottom-up and top-down combined attention models [1,45] are also proposed to take even one step further. In [24], the authors propose a novel adaptive attention model with a visual sentinel. This model not only can determine where to attend to in images, but also adaptively decide whether it needs to attend the image or to the LSTM decoder according to different words. Motivated by this work, we develop a novel joint style-factual attention architecture to make the model adaptively learns from the factual part and stylized part.

Style Transfer. Most style transfer works [10,16,30,41] focus on image style transfer. These works utilize the Gram matrix of hidden layers to measure the distance between different styles. In the meantime, pure text style transfer is making breakthrough as the development of nature language processing. For example, Shen et al. [35] propose a cross-alignment method to transfer text into different styles by generating a shared latent content space. Hu et al. [15] propose a neural generative model that combines variational auto-encoders (VAEs) and holistic attribute discriminators, to generate sentences while controlling the attributes. Combined with the above topics, in recent years, researchers begin to focus on stylized image captioning. Gan et al. and Mathews et al. propose StyleNet [9] and SentiCap [28] to generate image captions with specific styles and sentiments, respectively. Along the same direction, we propose a novel stylized image captioning model that achieves promising performance on both tasks.

3 Method

In this section, we formally present our stylized image captioning model. Specifically, we introduce the basic encoder-decoder image captioning model in Sect. 3.1. In Sect. 3.2, we present style-factual LSTM as the core building block of our framework. In Sect. 3.3, we present the overall learning strategy of the style-factual LSTM and in Sect. 3.4, we describe an adaptive learning approach to help the model generate stylized captions without deviating from the related image content.

3.1 Encoder-Decoder Image Captioning Model

We first describe the basic encoder-decoder model [42] for image caption generation. Giving an image I and its corresponding caption $\mathbf{y} = \{y_1, ..., y_T\}$, the encoder-decoder model minimizes the following maximum likelihood estimation (MLE) loss function:

$$\theta^* = \arg\min_{\theta} \sum_{I,\mathbf{y}} \log p(\mathbf{y}|I;\theta) \tag{1}$$

where θ denotes the parameters of the model. By applying chain rule, the log likelihood of the joint probability distribution can be expressed as follows:

$$\log p(\mathbf{y}) = \sum_{t=1}^{T} \log p(y_t|y_1, ..., y_{t-1}, I) \tag{2}$$

where we drop the dependency on θ for convenience.

For the encoder-decoder image captioning model, LSTM is commonly used to model $p(y_t|y_1, ..., y_{t-1}, I)$. Specifically, it can be expressed as:

$$\begin{aligned} p(y_{t+1}|y_1, ..., y_t, I) &= f(h_t) \\ h_t &= LSTM(x_t, h_{t-1}) \end{aligned} \tag{3}$$

where h_t is the hidden state of LSTM at time t, $f(\cdot)$ is a non-linear sub-network which maps h_t into word probability distribution. For $t > 0$, x_t is the word embedding feature of word y_t; for $t = 0$, x_0 is the image feature of I.

3.2 Style-Factual LSTM

To make our model capable of generating a stylized caption consistent with the image content, we devise the style-factual LSTM, which feeds two new groups of matrices S_x. and S_h. as the counterparts of W_x. and W_h., to learn to stylize the caption. In addition, at time step t, adaptive weights g_{xt} and g_{ht} are synchronously learned to adjust the relative attention weights between W_x. and S_x.

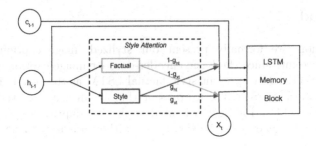

Fig. 2. An illustration of the style-factual LSTM block. Four weights, $1 - g_{ht}$, $1 - g_{xt}$, g_{ht} and g_{xt}, are designed to control the proportions of W_{hi}, W_{xi}, S_{hi} and S_{xi} matrices, respectively.

as well as $W_{h\cdot}$ and $S_{h\cdot}$. The structure of style-factual LSTM is shown as Fig. 2. In particular, the style-factual LSTM are defined as follows:

$$
\begin{aligned}
i_t &= \sigma((g_{xt}S_{xi} + (1 - g_{xt})W_{xi})x_t + (g_{ht}S_{hi} + (1 - g_{ht})W_{hi})h_{t-1} + b_i) \\
f_t &= \sigma((g_{xt}S_{xf} + (1 - g_{xt})W_{xf})x_t + (g_{ht}S_{hf} + (1 - g_{ht})W_{hf})h_{t-1} + b_f) \\
o_t &= \sigma((g_{xt}S_{xo} + (1 - g_{xt})W_{xo})x_t + (g_{ht}S_{ho} + (1 - g_{ht})W_{ho})h_{t-1} + b_o) \\
\tilde{c}_t &= \phi((g_{xt}S_{xc} + (1 - g_{xt})W_{xc})x_t + (g_{ht}S_{hc} + (1 - g_{ht})W_{hc})h_{t-1} + b_c) \\
c_t &= f_t \odot c_{t-1} + i_t \odot \tilde{c}_t \\
h_t &= o_t \odot \phi(c_t)
\end{aligned}
\tag{4}
$$

where $W_{x\cdot}$ and $W_{h\cdot}$ are responsible for generating the factual caption based on the input image, while $S_{x\cdot}$ and $S_{h\cdot}$ are responsible for adding specific style into the caption. At time step t, the style-factual LSTM feeds h_{t-1} into two independent sub-networks with one output node, which in the end figures out g_{xt} and g_{ht} after using the *sigmoid* unit to map the outputs to the range of $(0, 1)$. Intuitively, when the model aims to predict a factual word, g_{xt} and g_{ht} should be close to 0, which encourages the model to predict the word based on $W_{x\cdot}$ and $W_{h\cdot}$. On the other hand, when the model focuses on predicting a stylized word, g_{xt} and g_{ht} should be close to 1, which encourages the model to predict the word based on $S_{x\cdot}$ and $S_{h\cdot}$.

3.3   Overall Learning Strategy

Similar to [9,25], we adopt a two-stage learning strategy to train our model. For each epoch, our model is sequentially trained by two independent stages. In the first stage, we manually fix g_{xt} and g_{ht} to 0, freezing the style-related matrices $S_{x\cdot}$ and $S_{h\cdot}$. We train the model using the paired images and ground truth factual captions. In accordance with [42], for an image-caption pair, we first extract the deep-level feature of the image using a pre-trained CNN, and then map it into an appropriate space by a linear transformation matrix. For each word, we embed its corresponding one-hot vector by a word embedding layer such that each word

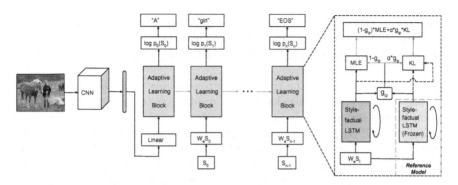

Fig. 3. The framework of our stylized image captioning model. In the adaptive learning block, the style-related matrices in the reference model (yellow) are frozen. It is designed to lead the real style-factual LSTM (blue) to learn from factual information selectively. (Color figure online)

embedding feature has the same dimension as the transformed image feature. During training, the image feature is only fed into the LSTM as an input at the first time step. In this stage, for the style-factual LSTM, only $W_x.$ and $W_h.$ are updated with other layers' parameters so that they focus on generating factual captions without styles. As mentioned in Sect. 3.1, the MLE loss is used to train the model.

In the second stage, g_{xt} and g_{ht} are learned by the two attention sub-networks mentioned in Sect. 3.2, as this activates $S_x.$ and $S_h.$ to participate in generating the stylized caption. For this stage, we use the paired images and ground truth stylized captions to train our model. In particular, different from the first stage, we update $S_x.$ and $S_h.$ for style-factual LSTM, with $W_x.$ and $W_h.$ fixed. Also, the parameters of the two attention sub-networks are updated concurrently with the whole network. Instead of only using the MLE loss, in Sect. 3.4, we will propose a novel approach to training our model in this stage.

For the test stage, to generate a stylized caption based on an image, we still compute g_{xt} and g_{ht} by the attention sub-networks, which activates $S_x.$ and $S_h..$ The classical beam search approach is used to predict the caption.

3.4 Adaptive Learning with Reference Factual Model

Our goal is to generate stylized captions that can accurately describe the image at the same time. Considering our style-factual LSTM, if we directly use the MLE loss to update $S_x.$ and $S_h.$ based on Sect. 3.3, it will only be updated via a few ground truth stylized captions, without learning anything from the much more massive ground truth factual captions. This may lead to the situation where the generated stylized caption cannot describe the images well. Intuitively, in a specific time step, when the generated word is unrelated to style, we encourage the model to learn more from the ground truth factual captions, instead of just a small number of the ground truth stylized captions.

Motivated by this consideration, we propose an adaptive learning approach, for which the model concurrently learns information from the ground truth stylized captions and the reference factual model, and adaptively adjusts their relative learning strengths.

In the second stage of the training process, giving an image and the corresponding ground truth stylized caption, in addition to predicting the stylized caption by the real model as Sect. 3.3, the framework also gives the predicted "factual version" output based on the reference model. Specifically, for reference model, we set g_{xt} and g_{ht} to 0, which freezes S_x and S_h as the first training stage, so that the reference model will generate its output based on W_x and $W_{h\cdot}$. Noted that W_x and W_h are trained by the ground truth factual captions. At time step t, denote the predicted word probability distribution by the real model as P_s^t, and the predicted word probability distribution by the reference model as P_r^t, we first compute their Kullback–Leibler divergence (KL-divergence) as follows:

$$D(P_s^t \| P_r^t) = \sum_{w \in W} P_s^t(w) \log \frac{P_s^t(w)}{P_r^t(w)} \qquad (5)$$

where W is the word vocabulary. Intuitively, if the model focuses on generating a factual word, we aim to decrease $D(P_s^t \| P_r^t)$, which makes P_s^t similar to P_r^t. In contrast, if the model focuses on generating a stylized word, we update the model by the MLE loss based on the corresponding ground truth stylized word.

To judge whether the current predicted word is related to style or not, we compute the inner product of P_s^t and P_r^t as the factual strength of the predicted word, we denote it as g_{ip}^t, and use it to adjust the weight between MLE and KL-divergence losses. In essence, g_{ip}^t represents the similarity between the word probability distributions P_s^t and P_r^t. When g_{ip}^t is close to 0, P_s^t has a higher possibility to correspond to a stylized word, because the reference model does not have the capacity to generate stylized words, which in the end makes g_{ip}^t small. In this situation, a higher attention weight should be given to the MLE loss. On the other hand, when g_{ip}^t is large, P_s^t has a higher possibility to correspond to a factual word, we then give KL-divergence losses higher significance.

The complete framework with the proposed adaptive learning approach is shown in Fig. 3. In the end, the new loss function for the second training stage is expressed as follows:

$$Loss = \sum_{t=1}^{T} -(1 - g_{ip}^t) \log P_s^t(y_t) + \alpha \cdot \sum_{t=1}^{T} g_{ip}^t D(P_s^t \| P_r^t) \qquad (6)$$

where α is a hyper-parameter to control the relative importance of the two loss terms. In the training process, g_{ip}^t and P_r^t do not participate in the back propagation. Still, for the style-factual LSTM, only S_x, S_h and parameters of two attention sub-networks are updated.

4 Experiments

We perform extensive experiments to evaluate the proposed models. Experiments are evaluated by standard image captioning measurements – BLEU, Meteor, Rouge-L and CIDEr. We will first discuss the datasets and model settings used in the experiments. We then compare and analyze the results of the proposed model with the state-of-the-art stylized image captioning models.

4.1 Datasets and Model Settings

At present, there are two datasets related to stylized image captioning. First, Gan et al. [9] collect a FlickrStyle10K dataset that contains 10K Flickr images with stylized captions. It should be noted that only the 7K training set are public. In particular, for the 7K images, each image is labeled with 5 factual captions, 1 humorous caption and 1 romantic caption. We randomly select 6000 of them as the training set, and 1000 of them as the test set. For the training set, we randomly split 10% of them as the validation set to adjust the hyper-parameters. Second, Mathews et al. [28] provide an image sentiment captioning dataset based on MSCOCO images, which contains images that are labeled by positive and negative sentiment captions. The POS subset contains 2,873 positive captions and 998 images for training, and another 2,019 captions over 673 images for testing. The NEG subset contains 2,468 negative captions and 997 images for training, and another 1,509 captions over 503 images for testing. Each of the test images has three positive and/or three negative captions. Following [28], on the training process, this sentiment dataset can be used with MSCOCO training set [3] of 413K+ factual sentences on 82K+ images, as the factual training set.

We extract image features by CNN. To make fair comparisons, for image sentiment captioning, we extract the 4096-dimension image feature by the second to last fully-connected layer of VGG-16 [36]. For stylized image captioning, we extract the 2048-dimension image feature by the last pooling layer of ResNet152 [12]. These settings are consistent with the corresponding works. Same as [28], we set the dimension of both word embedding feature and LSTM hidden state to 512 (this setting applys to all the proposed and baseline models in our experiments). For both style captioning and sentiment captioning, we use the Adam algorithm for model updating with a mini-batch size of 64 for both stages. The learning rate is set to 0.001. For style captioning, the hyper-parameter α mentioned in Sect. 3.4 is set to 1.1, for sentiment captioning, α is set to 0.9 and 1.5 for positive and negative captioning, which leads to the best performance in the validation set. Also, for style captioning, we directly input images into ResNet without normalization, which achieves better performance.

4.2 Performance on Stylized Image Captioning Dataset

Experiment Settings. We first evaluate our proposed model on the style captioning dataset. Consistent with [9], following baselines are used for comparison:

- CaptionBot [40]: the commercial image captioning system released by Microsoft, which is trained on the large-scale factual image-caption pair data.
- Neural Image Caption (NIC) [42]: the standard encoder-decoder model for image captioning. It is trained by factual image-caption pairs of the training dataset and can generate factual captions.
- Fine-tuned: we first train an NIC, and then use the additional stylized image-caption pairs to update the parameters of the LSTM language model.
- StyleNet [9]: we train a StyleNet as [9]. To make fair comparisons, different from the original model that only uses stylized captions to update the parameter in the second stage, we train the model by the complete stylized image-caption pairs. It has two parallel model StyleNet(H) and StyleNet(R), which generate humorous and romantic captions, respectively.

Table 1. BLEU-1, 2, 3, 4, ROUGE, CIDEr, METEOR scores of the proposed model and state-of-the-art methods based on ground truth stylized and factual references. "SF-LSTM" and "Adap" represents style-factual LSTM and adaptive learning approach.

Model	BLEU-1	BLEU-2	BLEU-3	BLEU-4	ROUGE	CIDEr	METEOR
Humorous/Factual generations + Humorous references							
CaptionBot	19.7	9.5	5.1	2.8	22.8	28.1	8.9
NIC	25.4	13.3	7.4	4.2	24.3	34.1	10.4
Fine-tuned(H)	26.5	13.6	7.6	4.3	24.4	35.4	10.6
StyleNet(H)	24.1	11.7	6.5	3.9	22.3	30.7	9.4
SF-LSTM(H) (ours)	26.8	14.2	8.2	4.9	24.8	**39.8**	**11.0**
SF-LSTM + Adap(H) (ours)	**27.4**	**14.6**	**8.5**	**5.1**	**25.3**	39.5	**11.0**
Romantic/Factual generations + Romantic references							
CaptionBot	18.4	8.7	4.5	2.4	22.3	25.0	8.7
NIC	24.3	12.8	7.4	4.4	24.1	33.7	10.2
Fine-tuned(R)	26.8	13.6	7.7	4.6	24.8	36.6	11.0
StyleNet(R)	25.4	11.7	6.1	3.5	23.2	27.9	10.0
SF-LSTM(R) (ours)	27.4	14.2	8.1	**4.9**	25.0	37.4	11.1
SF-LSTM + Adap(R) (ours)	**27.8**	**14.4**	**8.2**	4.8	**25.5**	**37.5**	**11.2**
Humorous generations + Factual references							
Fine-tuned(H)	48.0	31.1	19.9	12.6	39.5	26.2	18.1
StyleNet(H)	45.8	28.5	17.6	11.3	36.3	22.7	16.3
SF-LSTM(H) (ours)	47.8	31.7	20.6	13.1	39.8	28.2	18.7
SF-LSTM + Adap(H) (ours)	**51.5**	**34.6**	**23.1**	**15.4**	**41.7**	**34.2**	**19.3**
Romantic generations + Factual references							
Fine-tuned(R)	46.4	30.4	20.2	13.5	38.5	24.0	18.2
StyleNet(R)	44.2	26.8	16.3	10.4	35.4	15.8	16.3
SF-LSTM(R) (ours)	47.1	30.5	19.8	12.8	38.8	23.5	18.4
SF-LSTM + Adap(R) (ours)	**48.2**	**31.5**	**20.6**	**13.5**	**40.2**	**26.7**	**18.7**

Our goal is to generate captions that are both appropriately stylized and consistent with the image. There are no definite ways to separately measure these two aspects. To measure them comprehensively, for stylized captions generated by different models, we compute the BLEU-1, 2, 3, 4, ROUGE, CIDEr, METEOR scores based on both the ground truth stylized captions and ground truth factual captions. High-performance on both situations will demonstrate the effectiveness of the stylized image captioning model for both requirements. Because we split the dataset in a different way, we re-implement all the models and compute the scores instead of directly citing them from [9].

Experiment Results. Table 1 shows the quantitative results of different models based on different types of ground truth captions. Considering that for each image of the test set, we only have one ground truth stylized caption instead of five, excepts CIDEr, the overall performance of other measures based on the ground truth stylized captions is reasonably lower than [9], because these measures are sensitive to the number of ground truth captions of each image. From the results, we can see that our proposed model achieves the best performance by almost all measures, regardless of testing on stylized or factual references. This demonstrates the effectiveness of our proposed model. In addition, we could see that feeding adaptive learning approach into our model can remarkably improve the scores based on factual references, for both humorous and romantic caption generations. This indicates the improvement for generated captions' affinity toward the images. Compared with directly training the model by stylized references using MLE loss, adaptive learning can guide the model to preserve factual information in a better way, when it focuses on generating a non-stylized word.

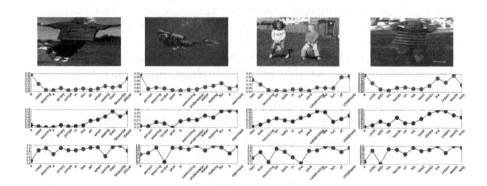

Fig. 4. Visualization of g_{xt}, g_{ht} and $1 - g_{ip}$ on several examples. The *second, third* and *fourth* rows correspond to g_{xt}, g_{ht}. and $1 - g_{ip}$, respectively. The *first* row is the input image. The X-axis shows the ground truth output words and the Y-axis is the weight. The top-4 words with the highest scores are in red color. (Color figure online)

In order to prove that the proposed model is effective, we visualize the attention weights of g_{xt}, g_{ht} and $1 - g_{ip}$ mentioned in Sect. 3 on several examples.

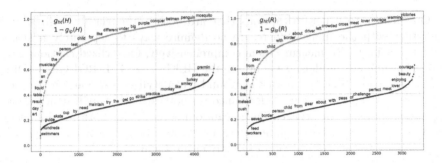

Fig. 5. The mean value of $1 - g_{ip}$ and g_{ht} for different words. *Left*: humorous words. *Right*: romantic words.

Fig. 6. Examples of stylized captions generated by our model for different images.

Specifically, we directly input the ground truth stylized caption into the trained model step by step, so that at each time step, the model will give a predicted word based on the current input word and previous hidden state. This setting simulates the training process. For each time step, Fig. 4 shows the ground truth output word and the corresponding attention weights. From the first example, we could see that when the model aims to predict stylized words, "seeing", "their", "favourite", "player", g_{xt} (red line) and g_{ht} (green line) increase remarkably, indicating that when the model predicts these words, it pays more attention to the $S_x.$ and $S_h.$ matrices, which capture the stylized information. Otherwise, it will focus more on $W_x.$ and $W_h.$, which are learned to generate factual words. On the other hand, from the fourth row, when it aims to generate words "air", "when", "their", "favourite", the predicted word probability distribution similarity between the real and reference models is very low, this encourages the model to directly learn to generate these words by the MLE loss. Otherwise, it will pay considerable attention to the output of the reference model, which contains knowledge learned from ground truth factual captions. For the other three examples, still, when generating stylized phrases (i.e. "looking for a me", "celebrating the fun of childhood" and "thinks ice cream help"), overall, the style-factual LSTM can effectively give more attention to $S_x.$ and $S_h.$, such that it will be trained mostly by corresponding ground truth words. When generating non-stylized words, the model will focus more on the factual part in the training and predicting process. It should be noticed that the first word always gets a relative high value for g_{xt}. This is reasonable because it is usually the same word (i.e. "a") for both factual and stylized captions, the model thus cannot learn to give more attention to fact-related matrices at this very beginning. Also, some articles and prepositions, such as "a", "of", has low $1 - g_{ip}$ even if they belong to a stylized phrase. This is also reasonable and acceptable, because both the real model and reference model can predict it, there is no need to pay all the attention to the corresponding ground truth stylized word.

To further substantiate that our model successfully differentiates between stylized words and factual words, following the visualization process, we compute the mean value of $1-g_{ip}$ and g_{ht} for each word in stylized dataset. As Fig. 5 shows, words that appear frequently in the stylized parts but rarely in the factual parts tend to get higher g_{ht}. Such as "gremlin", "pokeman", "smiley" in humorous sentences and "courage", "beauty", "lover" in romantic sentences. Words that appear in the stylized and factual parts with similar frequencies are likely to hold neutral value, such as "with", "go", "of", "about". Words such as "swimmer", "person", "skate", "cup", which appear mostly in the factual parts rather than the stylized parts, tend to have lower g_{ht} scores. Since g_{ht} represents the stylized weights in the style-factual LSTM, the result of g_{ht} substantiates that the style-factual LSTM is able to differentiate between stylized and factual words. When it comes to $1 - g_{ip}$, the first kind of words we mentioned above still receive high scores. However, we do not observe any clear border between the second and third kinds of words as g_{ht} shows. Still, we attribute it to the fact that predicting a factual noun is overall more difficult than predicting an article or preposition, which makes its corresponding inner product lower, and thus makes $1 - g_{ip}$ higher.

To make our discussion more intuitive, we show several stylized captions generated by our model in Fig. 6. As Fig. 6 shows, our model can generate stylized captions that accurately describe the corresponding images. For different images, the generated captions contain appropriate humorous phrases like "reach outer space", "catch bones", "like a lizard" and appropriate romantic phrases like "to meet his lover", "speed to finish the line", "conquer the high".

4.3   Performance on Image Sentiment Captioning Dataset

We also evaluate our model on the image sentiment caption dataset which is collected by [28]. Following [28], we compare the proposed model with several baselines. Besides NIC, ANP-Replace is based on NIC. For each caption generated by NIC, it randomly chooses a noun and adds the most common adjective of the corresponding sentiment for the chosen noun. In a similar way, ANP-Scoring uses multi-class logistic regression to select the most likely adjective for the chosen noun. LSTM-Transfer earns a fine-tuned LSTM from the sentiment dataset with additional regularization as [34]. Senticap implements a switching LSTM with word-level regularization to generate stylized captions. It should be mentioned that Senticap utilizes ground truth word sentiment strength in their regularization, which are labeled by humans. In contrast, our model only needs ground truth image-caption pairs without extra information.

Table 2. BLEU-1, 2, 3, 4, ROUGE, CIDEr, METEOR scores of the proposed model and the state-of-the-art methods for sentiment captioning.

Model	BLEU-1	BLEU-2	BLEU-3	BLEU-4	ROUGE	CIDEr	METEOR
POS test set							
NIC	48.7	28.1	17.0	10.7	36.6	55.6	15.3
ANP-Replace	48.2	27.8	16.4	10.1	36.6	55.2	16.5
ANP-Scoring	48.3	27.9	16.6	10.1	36.5	55.4	16.6
LSTM-Transfer	49.3	29.5	17.9	10.9	37.2	54.1	**17.0**
SentiCap	49.1	29.1	17.5	10.8	36.5	54.4	16.8
SF-LSTM + Adap (ours)	**50.5**	**30.8**	**19.1**	**12.1**	**38.0**	**60.0**	16.6
NEG test set							
NIC	47.6	27.5	16.3	9.8	36.1	54.6	15.0
ANP-Replace	48.1	28.8	17.7	10.9	36.3	56.5	16.0
ANP-Scoring	47.9	28.7	17.7	11.1	36.2	57.1	16.0
LSTM-Transfer	47.8	29.0	18.7	12.1	36.7	55.9	16.2
SentiCap	50.0	**31.2**	**20.3**	13.1	37.9	**61.8**	**16.8**
SF-LSTM + Adap (ours)	**50.3**	31.0	20.1	**13.3**	**38.0**	59.7	16.2

Fig. 7. Examples of sentiment caption generation based on our model. Positive and negative words are highlighted in red and blue colors. (Color figure online)

Table 2 shows the performance of different models on the sentiment captioning dataset. The performance score of all baselines are directly cited from [28]. We can see that for positive caption generation, the performance of our proposed model remarkably outperforms other baselines, with the highest scores by almost all measures. For negative caption generation, the performance of our model is competitive with Senticap while outperforming all others. Overall, without using extra ground truth information, our model achieves the best performance for generating image captions with sentiment. Figure 7 illustrates several sentiment captions generated by our model, as it can effectively generate captions with the sentiment elements being specified.

5 Conclusions

In this paper, we present a new stylized image captioning model. We design a style-factual LSTM as the core building block of the model, which feeds two groups of matrices into the LSTM to capture both factual and stylized information. To allow the model to preserve factual information in a better way, we leverage the reference model and develop an adaptive learning approach to adaptively adding factual information into the model, based on the prediction similarity between the real and reference models. Experiments on two stylized image captioning datasets demonstrate the effectiveness of our proposed approach. It outperforms the state-of-the-art models for stylized image captioning without using extra ground truth information. Furthermore, visualization of different attention weights demonstrates that our model can indeed differentiate the factual part and stylized part of a caption automatically, and adjust the attention weights adaptively for better learning and prediction.

Acknowledgment. We would like to thank the support of New York State through the Goergen Institute for Data Science, our corporate sponsor Adobe and NSF Award #1704309.

References

1. Anderson, P., et al.: Bottom-up and top-down attention for image captioning and VQA. arXiv preprint arXiv:1707.07998 (2017)
2. Bahdanau, D., Cho, K., Bengio, Y.: Neural machine translation by jointly learning to align and translate. arXiv preprint arXiv:1409.0473 (2014)
3. Chen, X., et al.: Microsoft coco captions: data collection and evaluation server. arXiv preprint arXiv:1504.00325 (2015)
4. Chen, X., Lawrence Zitnick, C.: Mind's eye: a recurrent visual representation for image caption generation. In: Proceedings of the IEEE Conference on Computer Vision and Pattern Recognition, pp. 2422–2431 (2015)
5. Donahue, J., et al.: Long-term recurrent convolutional networks for visual recognition and description. In: Proceedings of the IEEE Conference on Computer Vision and Pattern Recognition, pp. 2625–2634 (2015)
6. Elliott, D., Keller, F.: Image description using visual dependency representations. In: Proceedings of the 2013 Conference on Empirical Methods in Natural Language Processing, pp. 1292–1302 (2013)
7. Fang, H., et al.: From captions to visual concepts and back (2015)
8. Farhadi, A., et al.: Every picture tells a story: generating sentences from images. In: Daniilidis, K., Maragos, P., Paragios, N. (eds.) ECCV 2010. LNCS, vol. 6314, pp. 15–29. Springer, Heidelberg (2010). https://doi.org/10.1007/978-3-642-15561-1_2
9. Gan, C., Gan, Z., He, X., Gao, J., Deng, L.: Stylenet: generating attractive visual captions with styles. In: CVPR (2017)
10. Gatys, L.A., Ecker, A.S., Bethge, M.: Image style transfer using convolutional neural networks. In: 2016 IEEE Conference on Computer Vision and Pattern Recognition (CVPR), pp. 2414–2423. IEEE (2016)
11. Gurari, D., et al.: Vizwiz grand challenge: answering visual questions from blind people. arXiv preprint arXiv:1802.08218 (2018)
12. He, K., Zhang, X., Ren, S., Sun, J.: Deep residual learning for image recognition. In: Proceedings of the IEEE Conference on Computer Vision and Pattern Recognition, pp. 770–778 (2016)

13. Hermann, K.M., et al.: Teaching machines to read and comprehend. In: Advances in Neural Information Processing Systems, pp. 1693–1701 (2015)
14. Hodosh, M., Young, P., Hockenmaier, J.: Framing image description as a ranking task: data, models and evaluation metrics. J. Artif. Intell. Res. **47**, 853–899 (2013)
15. Hu, Z., Yang, Z., Liang, X., Salakhutdinov, R., Xing, E.P.: Toward controlled generation of text. In: International Conference on Machine Learning, pp. 1587–1596 (2017)
16. Johnson, J., Alahi, A., Fei-Fei, L.: Perceptual losses for real-time style transfer and super-resolution. In: Leibe, B., Matas, J., Sebe, N., Welling, M. (eds.) ECCV 2016. LNCS, vol. 9906, pp. 694–711. Springer, Cham (2016). https://doi.org/10.1007/978-3-319-46475-6_43
17. Karpathy, A., Fei-Fei, L.: Deep visual-semantic alignments for generating image descriptions. In: Proceedings of the IEEE Conference on Computer Vision and Pattern Recognition, pp. 3128–3137 (2015)
18. Kulkarni, G., et al.: Baby talk: understanding and generating image descriptions. In: Proceedings of the 24th CVPR. Citeseer (2011)
19. Kuznetsova, P., Ordonez, V., Berg, A.C., Berg, T.L., Choi, Y.: Collective generation of natural image descriptions. In: Proceedings of the 50th Annual Meeting of the Association for Computational Linguistics: Long Papers, vol. 1, pp. 359–368. Association for Computational Linguistics (2012)
20. Kuznetsova, P., Ordonez, V., Berg, T., Choi, Y.: Treetalk: composition and compression of trees for image descriptions. Trans. Assoc. Comput. Linguist. **2**(1), 351–362 (2014)
21. Lebret, R., Pinheiro, P.O., Collobert, R.: Simple image description generator via a linear phrase-based approach. arXiv preprint arXiv:1412.8419 (2014)
22. Li, S., Kulkarni, G., Berg, T.L., Berg, A.C., Choi, Y.: Composing simple image descriptions using web-scale n-grams. In: Proceedings of the Fifteenth Conference on Computational Natural Language Learning, pp. 220–228. Association for Computational Linguistics (2011)
23. Li, Y., Yao, T., Mei, T., Chao, H., Rui, Y.: Share-and-chat: achieving human-level video commenting by search and multi-view embedding. In: Proceedings of the 2016 ACM on Multimedia Conference, pp. 928–937. ACM (2016)
24. Lu, J., Xiong, C., Parikh, D., Socher, R.: Knowing when to look: adaptive attention via a visual sentinel for image captioning. In: Proceedings of the IEEE Conference on Computer Vision and Pattern Recognition (CVPR), vol. 6 (2017)
25. Luong, M.T., Le, Q.V., Sutskever, I., Vinyals, O., Kaiser, L.: Multi-task sequence to sequence learning. arXiv preprint arXiv:1511.06114 (2015)
26. Mao, J., Wei, X., Yang, Y., Wang, J., Huang, Z., Yuille, A.L.: Learning like a child: fast novel visual concept learning from sentence descriptions of images. In: Proceedings of the IEEE International Conference on Computer Vision, pp. 2533–2541 (2015)
27. Mao, J., Xu, W., Yang, Y., Wang, J., Huang, Z., Yuille, A.: Deep captioning with multimodal recurrent neural networks (M-RNN). arXiv preprint arXiv:1412.6632 (2014)
28. Mathews, A.P., Xie, L., He, X.: SentiCap: generating image descriptions with sentiments. In: AAAI, pp. 3574–3580 (2016)
29. Mnih, V., Heess, N., Graves, A., et al.: Recurrent models of visual attention. In: Advances in Neural Information Processing Systems, pp. 2204–2212 (2014)
30. Neumann, L., Neumann, A.: Color style transfer techniques using hue, lightness and saturation histogram matching. In: Computational Aesthetics, pp. 111–122. Citeseer (2005)

31. Ordonez, V., Kulkarni, G., Berg, T.L.: Im2Text: describing images using 1 million captioned photographs. In: Advances in Neural Information Processing Systems, pp. 1143–1151 (2011)
32. Rocktäschel, T., Grefenstette, E., Hermann, K.M., Kočiský, T., Blunsom, P.: Reasoning about entailment with neural attention. arXiv preprint arXiv:1509.06664 (2015)
33. Rush, A.M., Chopra, S., Weston, J.: A neural attention model for abstractive sentence summarization. arXiv preprint arXiv:1509.00685 (2015)
34. Schweikert, G., Rätsch, G., Widmer, C., Schölkopf, B.: An empirical analysis of domain adaptation algorithms for genomic sequence analysis. In: Advances in Neural Information Processing Systems, pp. 1433–1440 (2009)
35. Shen, T., Lei, T., Barzilay, R., Jaakkola, T.: Style transfer from non-parallel text by cross-alignment. In: Advances in Neural Information Processing Systems, pp. 6833–6844 (2017)
36. Simonyan, K., Zisserman, A.: Very deep convolutional networks for large-scale image recognition. arXiv preprint arXiv:1409.1556 (2014)
37. Spratling, M.W., Johnson, M.H.: A feedback model of visual attention. J. Cogn. Neurosci. 16(2), 219–237 (2004)
38. Sutskever, I., Vinyals, O., Le, Q.V.: Sequence to sequence learning with neural networks. In: Advances in Neural Information Processing Systems, pp. 3104–3112 (2014)
39. Tang, Y., Srivastava, N., Salakhutdinov, R.R.: Learning generative models with visual attention. In: Advances in Neural Information Processing Systems, pp. 1808–1816 (2014)
40. Tran, K., He, X., Zhang, L., Sun, J.: Rich image captioning in the wild. In: 2016 IEEE Conference on Computer Vision and Pattern Recognition Workshops (CVPRW), pp. 434–441. IEEE (2016)
41. Ulyanov, D., Lebedev, V., Vedaldi, A., Lempitsky, V.S.: Texture networks: feedforward synthesis of textures and stylized images. In: ICML, pp. 1349–1357 (2016)
42. Vinyals, O., Toshev, A., Bengio, S., Erhan, D.: Show and tell: a neural image caption generator. In: 2015 IEEE Conference on Computer Vision and Pattern Recognition (CVPR), pp. 3156–3164. IEEE (2015)
43. Wu, Z.Y.Y.Y.Y., Cohen, R.S.W.W.: Encode, review, and decode: Reviewer module for caption generation. arXiv preprint arXiv:1605.07912 (2016)
44. Xu, K., et al.: Show, attend and tell: neural image caption generation with visual attention. In: International Conference on Machine Learning, pp. 2048–2057 (2015)
45. You, Q., Jin, H., Wang, Z., Fang, C., Luo, J.: Image captioning with semantic attention. In: Proceedings of the IEEE Conference on Computer Vision and Pattern Recognition, pp. 4651–4659 (2016)

CPlaNet: Enhancing Image Geolocalization by Combinatorial Partitioning of Maps

Paul Hongsuck Seo[1], Tobias Weyand[2], Jack Sim[2], and Bohyung Han[3(✉)]

[1] Department of CSE, POSTECH, Pohang, Korea
hsseo@postech.ac.kr
[2] Google Research, Los Angeles, USA
weyand@google.com, jacksim@google.com
[3] Department of ECE & ASRI, Seoul National University, Seoul, Korea
bhhan@snu.ac.kr

Abstract. Image geolocalization is the task of identifying the location depicted in a photo based only on its visual information. This task is inherently challenging since many photos have only few, possibly ambiguous cues to their geolocation. Recent work has cast this task as a classification problem by partitioning the earth into a set of discrete cells that correspond to geographic regions. The granularity of this partitioning presents a critical trade-off; using fewer but larger cells results in lower location accuracy while using more but smaller cells reduces the number of training examples per class and increases model size, making the model prone to overfitting. To tackle this issue, we propose a simple but effective algorithm, combinatorial partitioning, which generates a large number of fine-grained output classes by intersecting multiple coarse-grained partitionings of the earth. Each classifier votes for the fine-grained classes that overlap with their respective coarse-grained ones. This technique allows us to predict locations at a fine scale while maintaining sufficient training examples per class. Our algorithm achieves the state-of-the-art performance in location recognition on multiple benchmark datasets.

Keywords: Image geolocalization · Combinatorial partitioning
Fine-grained classification

1 Introduction

Image geolocalization is the task of predicting the geographic location of an image based only on its pixels without any meta-information. As the geolocation is an important attribute of an image by itself, it also plays as a proxy to other location attributes such as elevation, weather, and distance to a particular point

Electronic supplementary material The online version of this chapter (https:// doi.org/10.1007/978-3-030-01249-6_33) contains supplementary material, which is available to authorized users.

© Springer Nature Switzerland AG 2018
V. Ferrari et al. (Eds.): ECCV 2018, LNCS 11214, pp. 544–560, 2018.
https://doi.org/10.1007/978-3-030-01249-6_33

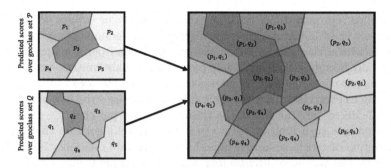

Fig. 1. Visualization of combinatorial partitioning. Two coarse-grained class sets, $\mathcal{P} = \{p_1, p_2, \ldots, p_5\}$ and $\mathcal{Q} = \{q_1, q_2, \ldots, q_5\}$ in the map on the left, are merged to construct a fine-grained partition as shown in the map on the right by a combination of geoclasses in the two class sets. Each resulting fine-grained class is represented by a tuple (p_i, q_j), and is constructed by identifying partially overlapping partitions in $\mathcal{P}$ and $\mathcal{Q}$.

of interest. However, geolocalizing images is a challenging task since input images often contain limited visual information representative of their locations. To handle this issue effectively, the model is required to capture and maintain visual cues of the globe comprehensively.

There exist two main streams to address this task: retrieval and classification based approaches. The former searches for nearest neighbors in a database of geotagged images by matching their feature representations [1–3]. Visual appearance of an image at a certain geolocation is estimated using the representations of the geotagged images in database. The latter treats the task as a classification problem by dividing the map into multiple discrete classes [3,4]. Thanks to recent advances in deep learning, simple classification techniques based on convolutional neural networks handle such complex visual understanding problems effectively.

There are several advantages of formulating the task as classification instead of retrieval. First, classification-based approaches save memory and disk space to store information for geolocalization; they just need to store a set of model parameters learned from training images whereas all geotagged images in the database should be embedded and indexed to build retrieval-based systems. In addition to space complexity, inference of classification-based approaches is faster because a result is given by a simple forward pass computation of a deep neural network while retrieval-based methods undergo significant overhead for online search from a large index given a query image. Finally, classification-based algorithms provide multiple hypotheses of geolocation with no additional cost by presenting multi-modal answer distributions.

On the other hand, the standard classification-based approaches have a few critical limitations. They typically ignore correlation of spatially adjacent or proximate classes. For instance, assigning a photo of Bronx to Queens, which are both within New York city, is treated equally wrong as assigning it to Seoul. Another drawback comes from artificially converting continuous geographic space into discrete class representations. Such an attempt may incur various artifacts since images near class boundaries are not discriminative enough compared to data variations within classes; training converges slowly and performance is affected substantially by subtle changes in map partitioning. This limitation can be alleviated by increasing the number of classes and reducing the area of the region corresponding to each class. However, this strategy increases the number of parameters while decreasing the size of the training dataset per class.

To overcome such limitations, we propose a novel algorithm that enhances the resolution of geoclasses and avoids the training data deficiency issue. This is achieved by *combinatorial partitioning*, which is a simple technique to generate spatially fine-grained classes through a combination of the multiple configurations of classes. This idea has analogy to product quantization [5] since they both construct a lot of quantized regions using relatively few model parameters through a combination of low-bit subspace encodings or coarse spatial quantizations. Our combinatorial partitioning allows the model to be trained with more data per class by considering a relatively small number of classes at a time. Figure 1 illustrates an example of combinatorial partitioning, which enables generating more classes with minimal increase of model size and learning individual classifiers reliably without losing training data per class. Combinatorial partitioning is applied to an existing classification-based image geolocalization technique, PlaNet [4], and our algorithm is referred to as CPlaNet hereafter. Our contribution is threefold:

- We introduce a novel classification-based model for image geolocalization using combinatorial partitioning, which defines a fine-grained class configuration by combining multiple heterogeneous geoclass sets in coarse levels.
- We propose a technique that generates multiple geoclass sets by varying parameters, and design an efficient inference technique to combine prediction results from multiple classifiers with proper normalization.
- The proposed algorithm outperforms the existing techniques in multiple benchmark datasets, especially at fine scales.

The rest of this paper is organized as follows. We review the related work in Sect. 2, and describe combinatorial partitioning for image geolocalization in Sect. 3. The details about training and inference procedures are discussed in Sect. 4. We present experimental results of our algorithm in Sect. 5, and conclude our work in Sect. 6.

2   Related Work

The most common approach of image geolocalization is based on the image retrieval pipeline. Im2GPS [1,2] and its derivative [3] perform image retrieval in a database of geotagged images using global image descriptors. Various visual features can be applied to the image retrieval step. NetVLAD [6] is a global image descriptor trained end-to-end for place recognition on street view data using a ranking loss. Kim et al. [7] learn a weighting mask for the NetVLAD descriptor to focus on image regions containing location cues. While global features have the benefit to retrieve diverse natural scene images based on ambient information, local image features yield higher precision in retrieving structured objects such as buildings and are thus more frequently used [8–16]. DELF [17] is a deeply learned local image feature detector and descriptor with attention for image retrieval.

On the other hand, classification-based image geolocalization formulates the problem as a classification task. In [3,4], a classifier is trained to predict the geolocation of an input image. Since the geolocation is represented in a continuous space, classification-based approaches quantize the map of the entire earth into a set of geoclasses corresponding to partitioned regions. Note that training images are labeled into the corresponding geoclasses based on their GPS tags. At test time, the center of the geoclass with the highest score is returned as the predicted geolocation of an input image. This method is lightweight in terms of space and time complexity compared to retrieval-based methods, but its prediction accuracy highly depends on how the geoclass set is generated. Since every image that belongs to the same geoclass has an identical predicted geolocation, more fine-grained partitioning is preferable to obtain precise predictions. However, it is not always straightforward to increase the number of geoclasses as it linearly increases the number of parameters and makes the network prone to overfitting to training data.

Pose estimation approaches [9,18–23] match query images against 3D models of an area, and employ 2D-3D feature correspondences to identify 6-DOF query poses. Instead of directly matching against a 3D model, [23,24] first perform image retrieval to obtain coarse locations and then estimate poses using the retrieved images. PoseNet [25,26] treats pose estimation as a regression problem based on a convolutional neural network. The accuracy of PoseNet is improved by introducing an intermediate LSTM layer for dimensionality reduction [27].

A related line of research is landmark recognition, where images are clustered by their geolocations and visual similarity to construct a database of popular landmarks. The database serves as the index of an image retrieval system [28–33] or the training data of a landmark classifier [34–36]. Cross-view geolocation recognition makes additional use of satellite or aerial imagery to determine query locations [37–40].

3 Geolocalization Using Multiple Classifiers

Unlike existing classification-based methods [4], CPlaNet relies on multiple classifiers that are all trained with unique geoclass sets. The proposed model predicts more fine-grained geoclasses, which are given by combinatorial partitioning of multiple geoclass sets. Since our method requires a distinct geoclass set for each classifier, we also propose a way to generate multiple geoclass sets.

3.1   Combinatorial Partitioning

Our primary goal is to establish fine-grained geoclasses through a combination of multiple coarse geoclass sets and exploit benefits from both coarse- and fine-grained geolocalization-by-classification approaches. In our model, there are multiple unique geoclass sets represented by partitions $\mathcal{P} = \{p_1, p_2, \ldots, p_5\}$ and $\mathcal{Q} = \{q_1, q_2, \ldots, q_5\}$ as illustrated on the left side of Fig. 1. Since the region boundaries in these geoclass sets are unique, overlapping the two maps constructs a set of fine-grained subregions. This procedure, referred to as combinatorial partitioning, is identical to the Cartesian product of the two sets, but disregards the tuples given by two spatially disjoint regions in the map. For instance, combining two aforementioned geoclass sets in Fig. 1, we obtain fine-grained partitions defined by a tuple (p_i, q_j) as depicted by the map on the right of the figure, while the tuples made by two disjoint regions, $e.g.$, (p_1, q_5), are not considered.

While combinatorial partitioning aggregates results from multiple classifiers, it is conceptually different from ensemble models whose base classifiers predict labels in the same output space. In combinatorial partitioning, while each coarse-grained partition is scored by a corresponding classifier, fine-grained partitions are given different scores by the combinations of multiple unique geoclass sets. Also, combinatorial partitioning is closely related to product quantization [5] for approximate nearest neighbor search in the sense that they both generate a large number of quantized regions by either a Cartesian product of quantized subspaces or a combination of coarse space quantizations. Note that combinatorial partitioning is a general framework and applicable to other tasks, especially where labels have to be defined on the same embedded space as in geographical maps.

3.2   Benefits of Combinatorial Partitioning

The proposed classification model with combinatorial partitioning has the following three major benefits.

Fine-Grained Classes with Fewer Parameters. Combinatorial partitioning generates fine-grained geoclasses using a smaller number of parameters because a single geoclass in a class set can be divided into many subregions by intersections with geoclasses from multiple geoclass sets. For instance in Fig. 1, two sets with 5 geoclasses form 14 distinct classes by the combinatorial partitioning. If we design a single flat classifier with respect to the fine-grained classes, it requires more parameters, $i.e.$, $14 \times F > 2 \times (5 \times F)$, where F is the number of input dimensions to the classification layers.

More Training Data per Class. Training with fine-grained geoclass sets is more desirable for higher resolution of output space, but is not straightforward due to training data deficiency; the more we divide the maps, the less training images remain per geoclass. Our combinatorial partitioning technique enables us to learn models with coarsely divided geoclasses and maintain more training data in each class than a naïve classifier with the same number of classes.

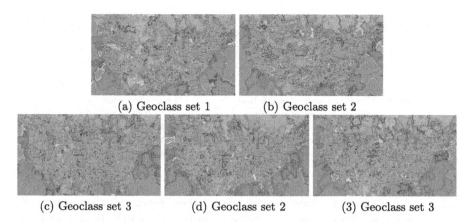

(a) Geoclass set 1   (b) Geoclass set 2

(c) Geoclass set 3   (d) Geoclass set 2   (3) Geoclass set 3

Fig. 2. Visualization of the geoclass sets on the maps of the United States generated by the parameters shown in Table 1. Each distinct region is marked by a different color. The first two sets, (a) and (b), are generated by manually designed parameters while parameters for the others are randomly sampled. (Color figure online)

More Reasonable Class Sets. There is no standard method to define geoclasses for image geolocalization, so that images associated with the same classes have common characteristics. An arbitrary choice of partitioning may incur undesirable artifacts due to heterogeneous images located near class territories; the features trained on loosely defined class sets tend to be insufficiently discriminative and less representative. On the other hand, our framework constructs diverse partitions based on various criteria observed in the images. We can define more tightly-coupled classes through combinatorial partitioning by distilling noisy information from multiple sources.

3.3 Generating Multiple Geoclass Sets

The geoclass set organization is an inherently ill-posed problem as there is no consensus about ideal region boundaries for image geolocalization. Consequently, it is hard to define the optimal class configuration, which motivates the use of multiple random boundaries in our combinatorial partitioning. We therefore introduce a mutable method of generating geoclass sets, which considers both visual and geographic distances between images.

The generation method starts with an initial graph for a map, where a node represents a region in the map and an edge connects two nodes of adjacent regions. We construct the initial graph based on S2 cells[1] at a certain level. Empty S2 cells, which contain no training image, do not construct separate

---

[1] We use Google's S2 library. S2 cells are given by a geographical partitioning of the earth into a hierarchy. The surface of the earth is projected onto six faces of a cube. Each face of the cube is hierarchically subdivided and forms S2 cells in a quad-tree. Refer to https://code.google.com/archive/p/s2-geometry-library/ for more details.

Table 1. Parameters for geoclass set generation. Parameters for geoclass set 1 and 2 are manually given while the ones for rest geoclass sets are randomly sampled.

Parameter group	Parameters	1	2	3	4	5
N/A	Num. of geoclasses	9,969	9,969	12,977	12,333	11,262
	Image feature dimensions	2,048	0	1,187	1,113	14,98
Node score	Weight for num. of images (α_1)	1.000	1.000	0.501	0.953	0.713
	Weight for num. of non-empty S2 cells (α_2)	0.000	0.000	0.490	0.044	0.287
	Weight for num. of S2 cells (α_3)	0.000	0.000	0.009	0.003	0.000
Edge weight	Weight for visual distance (β_1)	1.000	0.000	0.421	0.628	0.057
	Weight for geographical distance (β_2)	0.000	1.000	0.579	0.372	0.943

nodes and are randomly merged with one of their neighboring non-empty S2 cells. This initial graph covers the entire surface of the earth. Both nodes and edges are associated with numbers—scores for nodes and weights for edges. We give a score to each node by a linear combination of three different factors: the number of images in the node and the number of empty and non-empty S2 cells. An edge weight is computed by the weighted sum of geolocational and visual distances between two nodes. The geolocational distance is given by the distance between the centers of two nodes while the visual distance is measured by cosine similarity based on the visual features of nodes, which are computed by averaging the associated image features extracted from the bottleneck layer of a pretrained CNN. Formally, a node score $\omega(\cdot)$ and an edge weight $\nu(\cdot,\cdot)$ are defined respectively as

$$\omega(v_i) = \alpha_1 \cdot n_{\text{img}}(v_i) + \alpha_2 \cdot n_{\text{S2+}}(v_i) + \alpha_3 \cdot n_{\text{S2}}(v_i) \tag{1}$$
$$\nu(v_i, v_j) = \beta_1 \cdot \text{dist}_{\text{vis}}(v_i, v_j) + \beta_2 \cdot \text{dist}_{\text{geo}}(v_i, v_j) \tag{2}$$

where $n_{\text{img}}(v)$, $n_{\text{S2+}}(v)$ and $n_{\text{S2}}(v)$ are functions that return the number of images, non-empty S2 cells and all S2 cells in a node v, respectively, and $\text{dist}_{\text{vis}}(\cdot,\cdot)$ and $\text{dist}_{\text{geo}}(\cdot,\cdot)$ are the visual geolocational distances between two nodes. Note that the weights $(\alpha_1, \alpha_2, \alpha_3)$ and (β_1, β_2) are free parameters in $[0, 1]$.

After constructing the initial graph, we merge two nodes hierarchically in a greedy manner until the number of remaining nodes becomes the desired number of geoclasses. To make each geoclass roughly balanced, we select the node with the lowest score first and merge it with its nearest neighbor in terms of edge weight. A new node is created by the merge process and corresponds to the region given by the union of two merged regions. The score of the new node is set to the sum of the scores of the two merged nodes.

The generated geoclass sets are diversified by the following free parameters: (1) the desired number of final geoclasses, (2) the weights of the factors in the node scores, (3) the weights of the two distances in computing edge weights and (4) the image feature extractor. Each parameter setting constructs a unique geoclass set. Note that multiple geoclass set generation is motivated by the fact that geoclasses are often ill-defined and the perturbation of class boundaries is

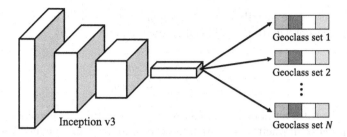

Fig. 3. Network architecture of our model. A single Inception v3 architecture is used as our feature extractor after removing the final classification layer. An image feature is fed to multiple classification branches and classification scores are predicted over multiple geoclass sets.

a natural way to address the ill-posed problem. Figure 2 illustrates generated geoclass sets using different parameters described in Table 1.

4   Learning and Inference

This section describes more details about CPlaNet including network architecture, and training and testing procedure. We also discuss data structures and the detailed inference algorithm.

4.1   Network Architecture

Following [4], we construct our network based on the Inception architecture [41] with batch normalization [42]. Inception v3 without the final classification layer (fc with softmax) is used as our feature extractor, and multiple branches of classification layers are attached on top of the feature extractor as illustrated in Fig. 3. We train the multiple classifiers independently while keeping the weights of the Inception module fixed. Note that, since all classifiers share the feature extractor, our model requires marginal increase of memory to maintain multiple classifiers.

4.2   Inference with Multiple Classifiers

Once the predicted scores in each class set are assigned to the corresponding regions, the subregions overlapped by multiple class sets are given cumulated scores from multiple classifiers. A simple strategy to accumulate geoclass scores is to add the scores to individual S2 cells within the geoclass. Such a simple strategy is inappropriate since it gives favor to classifiers that have geoclasses corresponding to large regions covering more S2 cells. To make each classifier contribute equally to the final prediction regardless of its class configuration, we normalize the scores from individual classifiers with consideration of the number of S2 cells per class before adding them to the current S2 cell scores. Formally, given a geoclass score distributed to S2 cell g_k within a class in a geoclass set $\mathcal{C}^i$, denoted by $\text{geoscore}(g_k; \mathcal{C}^i)$, an S2 cell is given a score $s(\cdot)$ by

$$s(g_k) = \sum_{i=1}^{N} \frac{\text{geoscore}(g_k; \mathcal{C}^i)}{\sum_{t=1}^{K} \text{geoscore}(g_t; \mathcal{C}^i)}, \tag{3}$$

where K is the total number of S2 cells and N is the number of geoclass sets. Note that this process implicitly creates fine-grained partitions because the regions defined by different geoclass combinations are given different scores.

After this procedure, we select the S2 cells with the highest scores and compute their center for the final prediction of geolocation by averaging locations of images in the S2 cells. That is, the predicted geolocation l_{pred} is given by

$$l_{\text{pred}} = \frac{\sum_{k \in \mathcal{G}} \sum_{e \in g_k} \text{geolocation}(e)}{\sum_{k \in \mathcal{G}} |g_k|}, \tag{4}$$

where $\mathcal{G} = \text{argmax}_k s(g_k)$ is an index set of the S2 cells with the highest scores and geolocation($\cdot$) is a function to return the ground-truth GPS coordinates of a training image e. Note that an S2 cell g_k may contain a number of training examples.

In our implementation, all fine-grained partitions are precomputed offline by generating all existing combinations of the multiple geoclass sets, and an index mapping from each geoclass to its corresponding partitions is also constructed offline to accelerate inference. Moreover, we precompute the center of images in each partition. To compute the center of a partition, we convert the latitude and longitude values of GPS tags into 3D Cartesian coordinates. This is because a naïve average of latitude and longitude representations introduces significant errors as the target locations become distant from the equator.

5   Experiments

5.1   Datasets

We train our network using a private dataset collected from Flickr, which has 30.3M geotagged images for training. We have sanitized the dataset by removing noisy examples to weed out unsuitable photos. For example, we disregard unnatural images (e.g., clipart images, product photos, etc.) and accept photos with a minimum size of 0.1 megapixels.

For evaluation, we mainly employ two public benchmark datasets—Im2GPS3k and YFCC4k [3]. The former contains 3,000 images from the Im2GPS dataset whereas the latter has 4,000 random images from the YFCC100m dataset. In addition, we also evaluate on Im2GPS test set [1] to compare with previous work. Note that Im2GPS3k is a different test benchmark from the Im2GPS test set.

Table 2. Geolocational accuracies [%] of models at different scales on Im2GPS3k.

Models	1 km	5 km	10 km	25 km	50 km	100 km	200 km	750 km	2500 km
ImageNetFeat	3.0	5.5	6.4	6.9	7.7	9.0	10.8	18.5	37.5
Deep-Ret [3]	3.7	–	–	19.4	–	–	26.9	38.9	55.9
PlaNet (reprod) [4]	8.5	18.1	21.4	24.8	27.7	30.0	34.3	48.4	**64.6**
ClassSet 1	8.4	18.3	21.7	24.7	27.4	29.8	34.1	47.9	64.5
ClassSet 2	8.0	17.6	20.6	23.8	26.2	29.2	32.7	46.6	63.9
ClassSet 3	8.8	18.9	22.4	25.7	27.9	29.8	33.5	47.8	64.1
ClassSet 4	8.7	18.5	21.4	24.6	26.8	29.6	33.0	47.6	64.4
ClassSet 5	8.8	18.7	21.7	24.7	27.3	29.3	32.9	47.1	64.5
Average[1-2]	8.2	18.0	21.1	24.2	26.8	29.5	33.4	47.3	64.2
Average[1-5]	8.5	18.4	21.5	24.7	27.1	29.5	33.2	47.4	64.3
CPlaNet[1-2]	9.3	19.3	22.7	25.7	27.7	30.1	34.4	47.8	64.5
CPlaNet[1-5]	9.9	20.2	23.3	26.3	28.5	30.4	34.5	**48.8**	**64.6**
CPlaNet[1-5, PlaNet]	**10.2**	**20.8**	**23.7**	**26.5**	**28.6**	**30.6**	**34.6**	48.6	**64.6**

5.2 Parameters and Training Networks

We generate three geoclass sets using randomly generated parameters, which are summarized in Table 1. The number of geoclasses for each set is approximately between 10K and 13K, and the generation parameters for edge weights and node scores are randomly sampled. Specifically, we select random axis-aligned subspaces out of the full 2,048 dimensions for image representations to diversify dissimilarity metrics between image representations. Note that the image representations are extracted by a reproduced PlaNet [4] after removing the final classification layer. In addition to these geoclass sets, we generate two more sets with manually designed parameters; the edge weights in these two cases are given by either visual or geolocational distance exclusively, and their node scores are based on the number of images to mimic the setting of PlaNet. Figure 2 visualizes five geoclass sets generated by the parameters presented in Table 1.

We use S2 cells at level 14 to construct the initial graph, where a total of ~2.8M nodes are obtained after merging empty cells to their non-empty neighbors. To train the proposed model, we employ the pretrained model of the reproduced PlaNet with its parameters fixed while the multiple classification branches are randomly initialized and fine-tuned using our training dataset. The network is trained by RMSprop with a learning rate of 0.005.

5.3 Evaluation Metrics

Following [3,4], we evaluate the models using geolocational accuracies at multiple scales by varying the allowed errors in terms of distances from ground-truth locations as follows: 1 km, 5 km, 10 km, 25 km, 50 km, 100 km, 200 km, 750 km and 2500 km. Our evaluation focuses more on high accuracy range compared

Table 3. Geolocational accuracies [%] on YFCC4k.

Models	1 km	5 km	10 km	25 km	50 km	100 km	200 km	750 km	2500 km
Deep-Ret [3]	2.3	-	-	5.7	-	-	11.0	23.5	42.0
PlaNet (reprod) [4]	5.6	10.1	12.2	14.3	**16.6**	**18.7**	**22.2**	**36.4**	**55.8**
CPlaNet[1-5]	7.3	11.7	13.1	14.7	16.1	18.2	21.7	36.2	55.6
CPlaNet[1-5, PlaNet]	**7.9**	**12.1**	**13.5**	**14.8**	16.3	18.5	21.9	**36.4**	55.5

to the previous papers as we believe that fine-grained geolocalization is more important in practice. A geolocational accuracy a_r at a scale is given by the fraction of images in the test set localized within radius r from ground-truths, which is given by

$$a_r \equiv \frac{1}{M} \sum_{i=1}^{M} u \left[\text{geodist} \left(l_{\text{gt}}^i, l_{\text{pred}}^i \right) < r \right], \tag{5}$$

where M is the number of examples in the test set, $u[\cdot]$ is an indicator function and $\text{geodist}(l_{\text{gt}}^i, l_{\text{pred}}^i)$ is the geolocational distance between the true image location l_{gt}^i and the predicted location l_{pred}^i of the i-th example.

5.4   Results

Benefits of Combinatorial Partitioning. Table 2 presents the geolocational accuracies of the proposed model on the Im2GPS3k dataset. The proposed models outperform the baselines and the existing methods at almost all scales on this dataset. ClassSet 1 through 5 in Table 2 are the models trained with the geoclass sets generated from the parameters presented in Table 1. Using the learned models as the base classifiers, we construct two variants of the proposed method—CPlaNet[1-2] using the first two base classifiers with manual parameter selection and CPlaNet[1-5] using all the base classifiers.

Table 2 presents that both options of our models outperform all the underlying classifiers at every scale. Compared to naïve average of the underlying classifiers denoted by Average[1-5] and Average[1-2], CPlaNet[1-5] and CPlaNet[1-2] have ~16 % and ~13 % of accuracy gains at street level, respectively, compared to their counterparts. We emphasize that CPlaNet achieves substantial improvements by a simple combination of the existing base classifiers and a generation of fine-grained partitions without extra training procedure. The larger performance improvement in CPlaNet[1-5] compared to CPlaNet[1-2] makes sense as using more classifiers constructs more fine-grained geoclasses via combinatorial partitioning and increases prediction resolution. Note that the number of distinct partitions formed by CPlaNet[1-2] is 46,294 while it is 107,593 in CPlaNet[1-5].

The combinatorial partitioning of the proposed model is not limited to geoclass sets from our generation methods, but is generally applicable to any geoclass sets. Therefore, we construct an additional instance of the proposed method,

Table 4. Geolocational accuracies [%] on Im2GPS.

	Models	1 km	5 km	10 km	25 km	50 km	100 km	200 km	750 km	2500 km
Retrieval	Im2GPS [1]	-	-	-	12.0	-	-	15.0	23.0	47.0
	Im2GPS [2]	2.5	12.2	16.9	21.9	25.3	28.7	32.1	35.4	51.9
	Deep-Ret [3]	12.2	-	-	33.3	-	-	44.3	57.4	71.3
	Deep-Ret+ [3]	14.4	-	-	33.3	-	-	**47.7**	61.6	73.4
Classifier	Deep-Cls [3]	6.8	-	-	21.9	-	-	34.6	49.4	63.7
	PlaNet [4]	8.4	19.0	21.5	24.5	27.8	30.4	37.6	53.6	71.3
	PlaNet (reprod) [4]	11.0	23.6	26.6	31.2	35.4	30.5	37.6	**64.6**	**81.9**
	CPlaNet[1-2]	14.8	28.7	31.6	35.4	37.6	40.9	43.9	60.8	80.2
	CPlaNet[1-5]	16.0	**29.1**	33.3	36.7	39.7	42.2	46.4	62.4	78.5
	CPlaNet[1-5, PlaNet]	**16.5**	**29.1**	**33.8**	**37.1**	**40.5**	**42.6**	46.4	62.0	78.5

CPlaNet[1-5, PlaNet], which also incorporates PlaNet (reprod), reproduced version of PlaNet model [4] with our training data, additionally. CPlaNet[1-5, PlaNet] shows extra performance gains over CPlaNet[1-5] and achieves the state-of-the-art performance at all scales. These experiments show that our combinatorial partitioning is a useful framework for image geolocalization through ensemble classification, where multiple classifiers with heterogeneous geoclass sets complement each other.

We also present results on YFCC4k [3] dataset in Table 3. The overall tendency is similar to the one in Im2GPS3k. Our full model outperforms Deep-Ret [3] consistently and significantly. The proposed algorithm also shows substantially better performance compared to PlaNet (reprod) in the low threshold range while two methods have almost identical accuracy at coarse-level evaluation.

On the Im2GPS dataset, our model outperforms other classification-based approaches—Deep-Cls and PlaNet, which are single-classifier models with a different geoclass schema—significantly at every scale, as shown in Table 4. The performance of our models is also better than the retrieval-based models at most scales. Moreover, our model, like other classification-based approaches, requires much less space than the retrieval-based models for inference. Although Deep-Ret+ improves Deep-Ret by increasing the size of the database, it even worsens space and time complexity. In contrast, the classification-based approaches including ours do not require extra space when we have more training images.

Figure 4 presents qualitative results of CPlaNet[1-5] on Im2GPS. It shows how the combinatorial partitioning process improves the geolocalization quality. Given an input image, each map shows an intermediate prediction as we accumulate the scores on different geoclass sets one by one. The region with the highest score is progressively sharded into a smaller region with fewer S2 cells, and the center of the region gradually approaches to the ground-truth location as we integrate more classifiers for inference.

Computational Complexity. Although CPlaNet achieves competitive performance through combinatorial partitioning, one may be concerned about

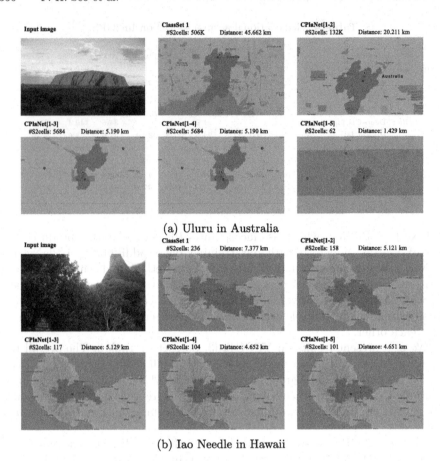

(a) Uluru in Australia

(b) Iao Needle in Hawaii

Fig. 4. Qualitative results of CPlaNet[1-5] on Im2GPS. Each map illustrates the progressive results of combinatorial partitioning by adding classifiers one by one. S2 cells with the highest score and their centers are marked by green area and red pins respectively while the ground-truth location is denoted by the blue dots. We also present the number of S2 cells in the highlighted region and distance between the ground-truth location and the center of the region in each map. (Color figure online)

potential increase of time complexity for its inference due to additional classification layers and overhead in combinatorial partitioning process. However, it turns out that the extra computational cost is negligible since adding few more classification layers on top of the shared feature extractor does not increase inference time substantially and the required information for combinatorial partitioning is precomputed as described in Sect. 4.2. Specifically, when we use 5 classification branches with combinatorial partitioning, theoretical computational costs for multi-head classification and combinatorial partitioning are only 2% and 0.004% of that of feature extraction process. In terms of space complexity, classification based methods definitely have great advantages over retrieval based ones, which

Table 5. Comparisons between the models with and without normalization for combinatorial partitioning on Im2GPS3k. Each number in parentheses denotes the geoclass set size, which varies largely to highlight the effect of normalization for this experiment.

Models	1 km	5 km	10 km	25 km	50 km	100 km	200 km	750 km	2500 km
ClassSet 1 (9969)	8.4	18.3	21.7	24.7	27.4	29.8	34.1	47.9	64.5
ClassSet 2 (9969)	8.0	17.6	20.6	23.8	26.2	29.2	32.7	46.6	63.9
ClassSet 3 (3416)	4.2	15.9	19.1	22.8	24.9	28.0	31.4	46.1	63.5
ClassSet 4 (1444)	1.8	9.5	13.2	16.8	21.2	24.5	29.5	44.4	61.8
ClassSet 5 (10600)	8.2	19.1	22.3	25.2	27.3	29.9	33.6	47.3	**65.5**
SimpleSum	9.7	19.4	23.1	26.6	28.1	30.6	33.8	47.7	64.0
NormalizedSum	**9.8**	**19.8**	**23.6**	**26.8**	**28.8**	**31.1**	**34.9**	**48.3**	65.0

need to maintain the entire image database. Compared to a single-head classifier, our model with five base classifiers requires just four additional classification layers, which incurs moderate increase of memory usage.

Importance of Visual Features. For geoclass set generation, all the parameters of ClassSet 1 and 2 are set to the same values except for the relative importance of two factors for edge weight definition; edge weights for ClassSet 1 are determined by visual distances only whereas those for ClassSet 2 are based on geolocational distances between the cells without any visual information of images. ClassSet 1 presents better accuracies at almost all scales as in Table 2. This result shows how important visual information of images is when defining geoclass sets.

Moreover, we build another model (ImageNetFeat) learned with the same geoclass set with ClassSet 1 but using a different feature extractor pretrained on ImageNet [43]. The large margin between ImageNetFeat and ClassSet 1 indicates importance of feature representation methods, and implies unique characteristics of visual cues required for image geolocalization compared to image classification.

Balancing Classifiers. We normalize the scores assigned to individual S2 cells as discussed in Sect. 4.2, which is denoted by NormalizedSum, to address the artifact that sums of all S2 cell scores are substantially different across classifiers. To highlight the contribution of NormalizedSum, we conduct an additional experiment with classsets that have large variations in number of classes. Table 5 presents that NormalizedSum clearly outperforms the combinatorial partitioning without normalization (SimpleSum) while SimpleSum still illustrates competitive accuracy compared to the base classifiers.

6 Conclusion

We proposed a novel classification-based approach for image geolocalization, referred to as CPlaNet. Our model obtains the final geolocation of an image using a large number of fine-grained regions given by combinatorial partitioning of multiple classifiers. We also introduced an inference procedure appropriate for classification-based image geolocalization. The proposed technique improves image geolocalization accuracy with respect to other methods in multiple benchmark datasets especially at fine scales, and also outperforms the individual coarse-grained classifiers.

Acknowledgment. The part of this work was performed while the first and last authors were with Google, Venice, CA. This research is partly supported by the IITP grant [2017-0-01778], and the Technology Innovation Program [10073166] funded by the Korea government MSIT and MOTIE, respectively.

References

1. Hays, J., Efros, A.A.: Im2GPS: estimating geographic information from a single image. In: CVPR (2008)
2. Hays, J., Efros, A.A.: Large-scale image geolocalization. In: Choi, J., Friedland, G. (eds.) Multimodal Location Estimation of Videos and Images, pp. 41–62. Springer, Cham (2015). https://doi.org/10.1007/978-3-319-09861-6_3
3. Vo, N., Jacobs, N., Hays, J.: Revisiting IM2GPS in the deep learning era. In: ICCV (2017)
4. Weyand, T., Kostrikov, I., Philbin, J.: PlaNet - photo geolocation with convolutional neural networks. In: Leibe, B., Matas, J., Sebe, N., Welling, M. (eds.) ECCV 2016. LNCS, vol. 9912, pp. 37–55. Springer, Cham (2016). https://doi.org/10.1007/978-3-319-46484-8_3
5. Jegou, H., Douze, M., Schmid, C.: Product quantization for nearest neighbor search. TPAMI **33**(1), 117–128 (2011)
6. Arandjelovic, R., Gronat, P., Torii, A., Pajdla, T., Sivic, J.: NetVLAD: CNN architecture for weakly supervised place recognition. In: CVPR (2016)
7. Kim, H.J., Dunn, E., Frahm, J.M.: Learned contextual feature reweighting for image geo-localization. In: CVPR (2017)
8. Baatz, G., Köser, K., Chen, D., Grzeszczuk, R., Pollefeys, M.: Handling urban location recognition as a 2D homothetic problem. In: Daniilidis, K., Maragos, P., Paragios, N. (eds.) ECCV 2010. LNCS, vol. 6316, pp. 266–279. Springer, Heidelberg (2010). https://doi.org/10.1007/978-3-642-15567-3_20
9. Cao, S., Snavely, N.: Graph-based discriminative learning for location recognition. IJCV **112**(2), 239–254 (2015)
10. Chen, D., et al.: City-scale landmark identification on mobile devices. In: CVPR (2011)
11. Kim, H.J., Dunn, E., Frahm, J.M.: Predicting good features for image geolocalization using per-bundle VLAD. In: ICCV (2015)
12. Knopp, J., Sivic, J., Pajdla, T.: Avoiding confusing features in place recognition. In: Daniilidis, K., Maragos, P., Paragios, N. (eds.) ECCV 2010. LNCS, vol. 6311, pp. 748–761. Springer, Heidelberg (2010). https://doi.org/10.1007/978-3-642-15549-9_54
13. Philbin, J., Chum, O., Isard, M., Sivic, J., Zisserman, A.: Object retrieval with large vocabularies and fast spatial matching. In: CVPR (2007)
14. Schindler, G., Brown, M., Szeliski, R.: City-scale location recognition. In: CVPR (2007)

15. Zamir, A.R., Shah, M.: Accurate image localization based on Google maps street view. In: Daniilidis, K., Maragos, P., Paragios, N. (eds.) ECCV 2010. LNCS, vol. 6314, pp. 255–268. Springer, Heidelberg (2010). https://doi.org/10.1007/978-3-642-15561-1_19

16. Zamir, A.R., Shah, M.: Image geo-localization based on multiple nearest neighbor feature matching using generalized graphs. PAMI **36**(8), 1546–1558 (2014)

17. Noh, H., Araujo, A., Sim, J., Weyand, T., Han, B.: Large-scale image retrieval with attentive deep local features. In: ICCV (2017)

18. Irschara, A., Zach, C., Frahm, J.M., Bischof, H.: From structure-from-motion point clouds to fast location recognition. In: CVPR (2009)

19. Li, Y., Snavely, N., Huttenlocher, D.P.: Location recognition using prioritized feature matching. In: Daniilidis, K., Maragos, P., Paragios, N. (eds.) ECCV 2010. LNCS, vol. 6312, pp. 791–804. Springer, Heidelberg (2010). https://doi.org/10.1007/978-3-642-15552-9_57

20. Li, Y., Snavely, N., Huttenlocher, D., Fua, P.: Worldwide pose estimation using 3D point clouds. In: Fitzgibbon, A., Lazebnik, S., Perona, P., Sato, Y., Schmid, C. (eds.) ECCV 2012. LNCS, vol. 7572, pp. 15–29. Springer, Heidelberg (2012). https://doi.org/10.1007/978-3-642-33718-5_2

21. Liu, L., Li, H., Dai, Y.: Efficient global 2D–3D matching for camera localization in a large-scale 3D map. In: ICCV (2017)

22. Sattler, T., Leibe, B., Kobbelt, L.: Fast image-based localization using direct 2D-to-3D matching. In: ICCV (2011)

23. Sattler, T., Weyand, T., Leibe, B., Kobbelt, L.: Image retrieval for image-based localization revisited. In: BMVC (2012)

24. Sattler, T., et al.: Are large-scale 3D models really necessary for accurate visual localization? In: CVPR (2017)

25. Kendall, A., Cipolla, R.: Geometric loss functions for camera pose regression with deep learning. In: CVPR (2017)

26. Kendall, A., Grimes, M., Cipolla, R.: PoseNet: a convolutional network for real-time 6-DOF camera relocalization. In: ICCV (2015)

27. Walch, F., Hazirbas, C., Leal-Taixé, L., Sattler, T., Hilsenbeck, S., Cremers, D.: Image-based localization using LSTMS for structured feature correlation. In: ICCV (2017)

28. Avrithis, Y., Kalantidis, Y., Tolias, G., Spyrou, E.: Retrieving landmark and non-landmark images from community photo collections. In: MM (2010)

29. Gammeter, S., Quack, T., Van Gool, L.: I know what you did last summer: object-level auto-annotation of holiday snaps. In: ICCV (2009)

30. Johns, E., Yang, G.Z.: From images to scenes: compressing an image cluster into a single scene model for place recognition. In: ICCV (2011)

31. Quack, T., Leibe, B., Van Gool, L.: World-scale mining of objects and events from community photo collections. In: CIVR, pp. 47–56 (2008)

32. Zheng, Y.T., et al.: Tour the world: building a web-scale landmark recognition engine. In: CVPR (2009)

33. Weyand, T., Leibe, B.: Visual landmark recognition from internet photo collections: a large-scale evaluation. CVIU **135**, 1–15 (2015)

34. Bergamo, A., Sinha, S.N., Torresani, L.: Leveraging structure from motion to learn discriminative codebooks for scalable landmark classification. In: CVPR (2013)

35. Li, Y., Crandall, D.J., Huttenlocher, D.P.: Landmark classification in large-scale image collections. In: ICCV (2009)

36. Gronat, P., Obozinski, G., Sivic, J., Pajdla, T.: Learning per-location classifiers for visual place recognition. In: CVPR (2013)

37. Workman, S., Souvenir, R., Jacobs, N.: Wide-area image geolocalization with aerial reference imagery. In: ICCV (2015)
38. Lin, T.Y., Belongie, S., Hays, J.: Cross-view image geolocalization. In: CVPR (2013)
39. Lin, T.Y., Cui, Y., Belongie, S., Hays, J.: Learning deep representations for ground-to-aerial geolocalization. In: CVPR (2015)
40. Tian, Y., Chen, C., Shah, M.: Cross-view image matching for geo-localization in urban environments. In: CVPR (2017)
41. Szegedy, C., et al.: Going deeper with convolutions. In: CVPR (2015)
42. Szegedy, C., Vanhoucke, V., Ioffe, S., Shlens, J., Wojna, Z.: Rethinking the inception architecture for computer vision. In: CVPR (2016)
43. Deng, J., Dong, W., Socher, R., Li, L.J., Li, K., Fei-Fei, L.: Imagenet: a large-scale hierarchical image database. In: ICCV (2009)

ESPNet: Efficient Spatial Pyramid of Dilated Convolutions for Semantic Segmentation

Sachin Mehta[1]([⊠])(ID), Mohammad Rastegari[2], Anat Caspi[1], Linda Shapiro[1], and Hannaneh Hajishirzi[1]

[1] University of Washington, Seattle, WA, USA
{sacmehta,caspian,shapiro,hannaneh}@cs.washington.edu
[2] Allen Institute for AI and XNOR.AI, Seattle, WA, USA
mohammadr@allenai.org

Abstract. We introduce a fast and efficient convolutional neural network, ESPNet, for semantic segmentation of high resolution images under resource constraints. ESPNet is based on a new convolutional module, efficient spatial pyramid (ESP), which is efficient in terms of computation, memory, and power. ESPNet is 22 times faster (on a standard GPU) and 180 times smaller than the state-of-the-art semantic segmentation network PSPNet, while its category-wise accuracy is only 8% less. We evaluated ESPNet on a variety of semantic segmentation datasets including Cityscapes, PASCAL VOC, and a breast biopsy whole slide image dataset. Under the same constraints on memory and computation, ESPNet outperforms all the current efficient CNN networks such as MobileNet, ShuffleNet, and ENet on both standard metrics and our newly introduced performance metrics that measure efficiency on edge devices. Our network can process high resolution images at a rate of 112 and 9 frames per second on a standard GPU and edge device, respectively. Our code is open-source and available at https://sacmehta.github.io/ESPNet/.

1 Introduction

Deep convolutional neural network (CNN) models have achieved high accuracy in visual scene understanding tasks [1–3]. While the accuracy of these networks has improved with their increase in depth and width, large networks are slow and power hungry. This is especially problematic on the computationally heavy task of semantic segmentation [4–10]. For example, PSPNet [1] has 65.7 million parameters and runs at about 1 FPS while discharging the battery of a standard laptop at a rate of 77 Watts. Many advanced real-world applications, such as self-driving cars, robots, and augmented reality, are sensitive and demand on-line

Electronic supplementary material The online version of this chapter (https://doi.org/10.1007/978-3-030-01249-6_34) contains supplementary material, which is available to authorized users.

© Springer Nature Switzerland AG 2018
V. Ferrari et al. (Eds.): ECCV 2018, LNCS 11214, pp. 561–580, 2018.
https://doi.org/10.1007/978-3-030-01249-6_34

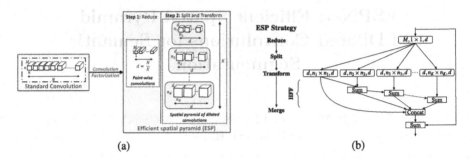

Fig. 1. (a) The standard convolution layer is decomposed into point-wise convolution and spatial pyramid of dilated convolutions to build an efficient spatial pyramid (ESP) module. (b) Block diagram of ESP module. The large effective receptive field of the ESP module introduces gridding artifacts, which are removed using hierarchical feature fusion (HFF). A skip-connection between input and output is added to improve the information flow. See Sect. 3 for more details. Dilated convolutional layers are denoted as (# input channels, effective kernel size, # output channels). The effective spatial dimensions of a dilated convolutional kernel are $n_k \times n_k$, where $n_k = (n-1)2^{k-1}+1$, $k = 1, \cdots, K$. Note that only $n \times n$ pixels participate in the dilated convolutional kernel. In our experiments $n = 3$ and $d = \frac{M}{K}$.

processing of data locally on edge devices. These accurate networks require enormous resources and are not suitable for edge devices, which have limited energy overhead, restrictive memory constraints, and reduced computational capabilities.

Convolution factorization has demonstrated its success in reducing the computational complexity of deep CNNs [11–15]. We introduce an efficient convolutional module, ESP (efficient spatial pyramid), which is based on the convolutional factorization principle (Fig. 1). Based on these ESP modules, we introduce an efficient network structure, ESPNet, that can be easily deployed on resource-constrained edge devices. ESPNet is *fast, small, low power,* and *low latency,* yet still preserves segmentation accuracy.

ESP is based on a convolution factorization principle that decomposes a standard convolution into two steps: (1) ***point-wise convolutions*** and (2) ***spatial pyramid of dilated convolutions***, as shown in Fig. 1. The point-wise convolutions help in reducing the computation, while the spatial pyramid of dilated convolutions re-samples the feature maps to learn the representations from large effective receptive field. We show that our ESP module is more efficient than other factorized forms of convolutions, such as Inception [11–13] and ResNext [14]. Under the same constraints on memory and computation, ESPNet outperforms MobileNet [16] and ShuffleNet [17] (two other efficient networks that are built upon the factorization principle). We note that existing spatial pyramid methods (e.g. the atrous spatial pyramid module in [3]) are computationally expensive and cannot be used at different spatial levels for learning the representations. In contrast to these methods, ESP is computationally efficient and can be used at different spatial levels of a CNN network. Existing models based on dilated convolutions [1, 3, 18, 19] are large and inefficient, but our ESP module generalizes the use of dilated convolutions in a novel and efficient way.

To analyze the performance of a CNN network on edge devices, we introduce several new performance metrics, such as sensitivity to GPU frequency and warp execution efficiency. To showcase the power of ESPNet, we evaluate our model on one of the most expensive tasks in AI and computer vision: semantic segmentation. ESPNet is empirically demonstrated to be more accurate, efficient, and fast than ENet [20], one of the most power-efficient semantic segmentation networks, while learning a similar number of parameters. Our results also show that ESPNet learns generalizable representations and outperforms ENet [20] and another efficient network ERFNet [21] on the unseen dataset. ESPNet can process a *high resolution RGB image* at a rate of 112, 21, and 9 frames per second on the NVIDIA TitanX, GTX-960M, and Jetson TX2 respectively.

2   Related Work

Different techniques, such as convolution factorization, network compression, and low-bit networks, have been proposed to speed up CNNs. We, first, briefly describe these approaches and then provide a brief overview of CNN-based semantic segmentation.

Convolution Factorization: Convolutional factorization decomposes the convolutional operation into multiple steps to reduce the computational complexity. This factorization has successfully shown its potential in reducing the computational complexity of deep CNN networks (e.g. Inception [11–13], factorized network [22], ResNext [14], Xception [15], and MobileNets [16]). ESP modules are also built on this factorization principle. The ESP module decomposes a convolutional layer into a point-wise convolution and spatial pyramid of dilated convolutions. This factorization helps in reducing the computational complexity, while simultaneously allowing the network to learn the representations from a large effective receptive field. **Network Compression:** Another approach for building efficient networks is compression. These methods use techniques such as hashing [23], pruning [24], vector quantization [25], and shrinking [26, 27] to reduce the size of the pre-trained network. **Low-bit networks:** Another approach towards efficient networks is low-bit networks, which quantize the weights to reduce the network size and complexity (e.g. [28–31]). **Sparse CNN:** To remove the redundancy in CNNs, sparse CNN methods, such as sparse decomposition [32], structural sparsity learning [33], and dictionary-based method [34], have been proposed.

We note that compression-based methods, low-bit networks, and sparse CNN methods are equally applicable to ESPNets and are complementary to our work.

Dilated Convolution: Dilated convolutions [35] are a special form of standard convolutions in which the effective receptive field of kernels is increased by inserting zeros (or holes) between each pixel in the convolutional kernel. For a

$n \times n$ dilated convolutional kernel with a dilation rate of r, the effective size of the kernel is $[(n-1)r+1]^2$. The dilation rate specifies the number of zeros (or holes) between pixels. However, due to dilation, only $n \times n$ pixels participate in the convolutional operation, reducing the computational cost while increasing the effective kernel size.

Yu and Koltun [18] stacked dilated convolution layers with increasing dilation rate to learn contextual representations from a large effective receptive field. A similar strategy was adopted in [19,36,37]. Chen et al. [3] introduced an atrous spatial pyramid (ASP) module. This module can be viewed as a parallelized version of [3]. These modules are computationally inefficient (e.g. ASPs have high memory requirements and learn many more parameters; see Sect. 3.2). Our ESP module also learns multi-scale representations using dilated convolutions in parallel; however, it is computationally efficient and can be used at any spatial level of a CNN network.

CNN for Semantic Segmentation: Different CNN-based segmentation networks have been proposed, such as multi-dimensional recurrent neural networks [38], encoder-decoders [20,21,39,40], hypercolumns [41], region-based representations [42,43], and cascaded networks [44]. Several supporting techniques along with these networks have been used for achieving high accuracy, including ensembling features [3], multi-stage training [45], additional training data from other datasets [1,3], object proposals [46], CRF-based post processing [3], and pyramid-based feature re-sampling [1–3].

Encoder-Decoder Networks: Our work is related to this line of work. The encoder-decoder networks first learn the representations by performing convolutional and down-sampling operations. These representations are then decoded by performing up-sampling and convolutional operations. ESPNet first learns the encoder and then attaches a *light-weight decoder* to produce the segmentation mask. This is in contrast to existing networks where the decoder is either an exact replica of the encoder (e.g. [39]) or is relatively small (but not light weight) in comparison to the encoder (e.g. [20,21]).

Feature Re-sampling Methods: The feature re-sampling methods re-sample the convolutional feature maps at the same scale using different pooling rates [1,2] and kernel sizes [3] for efficient classification. Feature re-sampling is computationally expensive and is performed just before the classification layer to learn scale-invariant representations. We introduce a computationally efficient convolutional module that allows feature re-sampling at different spatial levels of a CNN network.

3   ESPNet

We describe ESPNet and its core ESP module. We compare ESP modules with similar CNN modules, Inception [11–13], ResNext [14], MobileNet [16], and ShuffleNet [17].

3.1 ESP Module

ESPNet is based on efficient spatial pyramid (ESP) modules, a factorized form of convolutions that decompose a standard convolution into a point-wise convolution and a spatial pyramid of dilated convolutions (see Fig. 1a). The point-wise convolution applies a 1×1 convolution to project high-dimensional feature maps onto a low-dimensional space. The spatial pyramid of dilated convolutions then re-samples these low-dimensional feature maps using K, $n \times n$ dilated convolutional kernels simultaneously, each with a dilation rate of 2^{k-1}, $k = \{1, \cdots, K\}$. This factorization drastically reduces the number of parameters and the memory required by the ESP module, while preserving a large effective receptive field $\left[(n-1)2^{K-1} + 1\right]^2$. This pyramidal convolutional operation is called a spatial pyramid of dilated convolutions, because each dilated convolutional kernel learns weights with different receptive fields and so resembles a spatial pyramid.

A standard convolutional layer takes an input feature map $\mathbf{F}_i \in \mathbb{R}^{W \times H \times M}$ and applies N kernels $\mathbf{K} \in \mathbb{R}^{m \times n \times M}$ to produce an output feature map $\mathbf{F}_o \in \mathbb{R}^{W \times H \times N}$, where W and H represent the width and height of the feature map, m and n represent the width and height of the kernel, and M and N represent the number of input and output feature channels. For simplicity, we will assume that $m = n$. A standard convolutional kernel thus learns $n^2 MN$ parameters. These parameters are *multiplicatively* dependent on the spatial dimensions of the $n \times n$ kernel and the number of input M and output N channels.

Width Divider K: To reduce the computational cost, we introduce a simple hyper-parameter K. The role of K is to shrink the dimensionality of the feature maps uniformly across each ESP module in the network. *Reduce:* For a given K, the ESP module first reduces the feature maps from M-dimensional space to $\frac{N}{K}$-dimensional space using a point-wise convolution (Step 1 in Fig. 1a). *Split:* The low-dimensional feature maps are split across K parallel branches. *Transform:* Each branch then processes these feature maps simultaneously using $n \times n$ dilated convolutional kernels with different dilation rates given by 2^{k-1}, $k = \{1, \cdots, K-1\}$ (Step 2 in Fig. 1a). *Merge:* The outputs of the K parallel dilated convolutional kernels are concatenated to produce an N-dimensional output feature map Fig. 1b visualizes the *reduce-split-transform-merge* strategy.

The ESP module has $(NM + (Nn)^2)/K$ parameters and its effective receptive field is $((n-1)2^{K-1} + 1)^2$. Compared to the $n^2 NM$ parameters of the standard convolution, factorizing it reduces the number of parameters by a factor of $\frac{n^2 MK}{M + n^2 N}$, while increasing the effective receptive field by $\sim(2^{K-1})^2$. For example, the ESP module learns $\sim 3.6\times$ fewer parameters with an effective receptive field of 17×17 than a standard convolutional kernel with an effective receptive field of 3×3 for $n = 3$, $N = M = 128$, and $K = 4$.

Hierarchical Feature Fusion (HFF) for De-gridding: While concatenating the outputs of dilated convolutions give the ESP module a large effective receptive field, it introduces unwanted checkerboard or gridding artifacts, as shown in Fig. 2. To address the gridding artifact in ESP, the feature maps obtained using

Fig. 2. (a) An example illustrating a gridding artifact with a single active pixel (red) convolved with a 3×3 dilated convolutional kernel with dilation rate $r = 2$. (b) Visualization of feature maps of ESP modules with and without hierarchical feature fusion (HFF). HFF in ESP eliminates the gridding artifact. Best viewed in color.

kernels of different dilation rates are hierarchically added before concatenating them (HFF in Fig. 1b). This simple, effective solution does not increase the complexity of the ESP module, in contrast to existing methods that remove the gridding artifact by learning more parameters using dilated convolutional kernels [19,37]. To improve gradient flow inside the network, the input and output feature maps are combined using an element-wise sum [47].

3.2 Relationship with Other CNN Modules

The ESP module shares similarities with the following CNN modules.

MobileNet Module: The MobileNet module [16], shown in Fig. 3a, uses a depth-wise separable convolution [15] that factorizes a standard convolutions into depth-wise convolutions (*transform*) and point-wise convolutions (*expand*). It learns less parameters, has high memory requirement, and low receptive field than the ESP module. An extreme version of the ESP module (with $K = N$) is almost identical to the MobileNet module, differing only in the order of convolutional operations. In the MobileNet module, the spatial convolutions are followed by point-wise convolutions; however, in the ESP module, point-wise convolutions are followed by spatial convolutions.

ShuffleNet Module: The ShuffleNet module [17], shown in Fig. 3b, is based on the principle of *reduce-transform-expand*. It is an optimized version of the bottleneck block in ResNet [47]. To reduce computation, Shufflenet makes use of grouped convolutions [48] and depth-wise convolutions [15]. It replaces 1×1 and 3×3 convolutions in the bottleneck block in ResNet with 1×1 grouped convolutions and 3×3 depth-wise separable convolutions, respectively. The Shufflenet module learns many less parameters than the ESP module, but has higher memory requirements and a smaller receptive field.

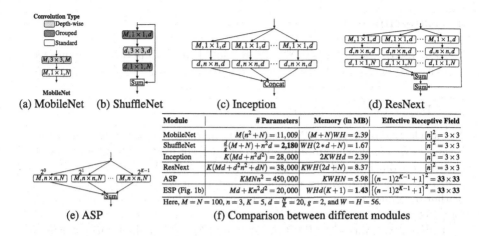

(a) MobileNet   (b) ShuffleNet   (c) Inception   (d) ResNext

(e) ASP

Module	# Parameters	Memory (in MB)	Effective Receptive Field
MobileNet	$M(n^2+N) = 11,009$	$(M+N)WH = 2.39$	$[n]^2 = 3 \times 3$
ShuffleNet	$\frac{d}{g}(M+N)+n^2d = 2,180$	$WH(2*d+N) = 1.67$	$[n]^2 = 3 \times 3$
Inception	$K(Md+n^2d^2) = 28,000$	$2KWHd = 2.39$	$[n]^2 = 3 \times 3$
ResNext	$K(Md+d^2n^2+dN) = 38,000$	$KWH(2d+N) = 8.37$	$[n]^2 = 3 \times 3$
ASP	$KMNn^2 = 450,000$	$KWHN = 5.98$	$[(n-1)2^{K-1}+1]^2 = 33 \times 33$
ESP (Fig. 1b)	$Md+Kn^2d^2 = 20,000$	$WHd(K+1) = 1.43$	$[(n-1)2^{K-1}+1]^2 = 33 \times 33$
Here, $M=N=100$, $n=3$, $K=5$, $d=\frac{N}{K}=20$, $g=2$, and $W=H=56$.			

(f) Comparison between different modules

Fig. 3. Different types of convolutional modules for comparison. We denote the layer as (# input channels, kernel size, # output channels). Dilation rate in (e) is indicated on top of each layer. Here, g represents the number of convolutional groups in grouped convolution [48]. For simplicity, we only report the memory of convolutional layers in (d). For converting the required memory to bytes, we multiply it by 4 (1 float requires 4 bytes for storage).

Inception Module: Inception modules [11–13] are built on the principle of *split-reduce-transform-merge* and are usually heterogeneous in number of channels and kernel size (e.g. some of the modules are composed of standard and factored convolutions). In contrast, ESP modules are straightforward and simple to design. For the sake of comparison, the homogeneous version of an Inception module is shown in Fig. 3c. Figure 3f compares the Inception module with the ESP module. ESP (1) learns fewer parameters, (2) has a low memory requirement, and (3) has a larger effective receptive field.

ResNext Module: A ResNext module [14], shown in Fig. 3d, is a parallel version of the bottleneck module in ResNet [47], based on the principle of *split-reduce-transform-expand-merge*. The ESP module is similar in branching and residual summation, but more efficient in memory and parameters with a larger effective receptive field.

Atrous Spatial Pyramid (ASP) Module: An ASP module [3], shown in Fig. 3e, is built on the principle of *split-transform-merge*. The ASP module involves branching with each branch learning kernel at a different receptive field (using dilated convolutions). Though ASP modules tend to perform well in segmentation tasks due to their high effective receptive fields, ASP modules have high memory requirements and learn many more parameters. Unlike the ASP module, the ESP module is computationally efficient.

4   Experiments

To showcase the power of ESPNet, we evaluate ESPNet's performance on several semantic segmentation datasets and compare to the state-of-the-art networks.

4.1   Experimental Set-Up

Network Structure: ESPNet uses ESP modules for learning convolutional kernels as well as down-sampling operations, except for the first layer: a standard strided convolution. All layers are followed by a batch normalization [49] and a PReLU [50] non-linearity except the last point-wise convolution, which has neither batch normalization nor non-linearity. The last layer feeds into a softmax for pixel-wise classification.

Different variants of ESPNet are shown in Fig. 4. The first variant, ESPNet-A (Fig. 4a), is a standard network that takes an RGB image as an input and learns representations at different spatial levels[1] using the ESP module to produce a segmentation mask. The second variant, ESPNet-B (Fig. 4b), improves the flow of information inside ESPNet-A by sharing the feature maps between the previous strided ESP module and the previous ESP module. The third variant, ESPNet-C (Fig. 4c), reinforces the input image inside ESPNet-B to further improve the flow of information. These three variants produce outputs whose spatial dimensions are $\frac{1}{8}th$ of the input image. The fourth variant, ESPNet (Fig. 4d), adds a light weight decoder (built using a principle of *reduce-upsample-merge*) to ESPNet-C that outputs the segmentation mask of the same spatial resolution as the input image.

To build deeper computationally efficient networks for edge devices without changing the network topology, a hyper-parameter α controls the depth of the network; the ESP module is repeated α_l times at spatial level l. CNNs require more memory at higher spatial levels (at $l = 0$ and $l = 1$) because of the high spatial dimensions of feature maps at these levels. To be memory efficient, neither the ESP nor the convolutional modules are repeated at these spatial levels.

Dataset: We evaluated the ESPNet on the Cityscapes dataset [6], an urban visual scene-understanding dataset that consists of 2,975 training, 500 validation, and 1,525 test high-resolution images. The task is to segment an image into 19 classes belonging to 7 categories (e.g. person and rider classes belong to the same category *human*). We evaluated our networks on the test set using the Cityscapes *online* server.

To study the generalizability, we tested the ESPNet on an unseen dataset. We used the Mapillary dataset [51] for this task because of its diversity. We mapped the annotations (65 classes) in the validation set (# 2,000 images) to seven categories in the Cityscape dataset. To further study the segmentation power of our model, we trained and tested the ESPNet on two other popular

---

[1] At each spatial level l, the spatial dimensions of the feature maps are the same. To learn representations at different spatial levels, a down-sampling operation is performed (see Fig. 4a).

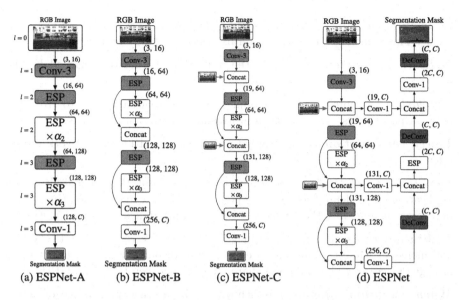

Fig. 4. The path from ESPNet-A to ESPNet. Red and green color boxes represent the modules responsible for down-sampling and up-sampling operations, respectively. Spatial-level l is indicated on the left of every module in (a). We denote each module as (# input channels, # output channels). Here, Conv-n represents $n \times n$ convolution. (Color figure online)

datasets from different domains. First, we used the widely known PASCAL VOC dataset [52] that has 1,464 training images, 1,448 validation images, and 1,456 test images. The task is to segment an image into 20 foreground classes. We evaluate our networks on the test set (comp6 category) using the PASCAL VOC *online* server. Following the convention, we used additional images from [53,54]. Secondly, we used a breast biopsy whole slide image dataset [36], chosen because tissue structures in biomedical images vary in size and shape and because this dataset allowed us to check the potential of learning representations from a large receptive field. The dataset consists of 30 training images and 28 validation images, whose average size is $10,000 \times 12,000$ pixels, much larger than natural scene images. The task is to segment the images into 8 biological tissue labels; details are in [36].

Performance Evaluation Metrics: Most traditional CNNs measure network performance in terms of accuracy, latency, network parameters, and network size [16,17,20,21,55]. These metrics provide high-level insight about the network, but fail to demonstrate the efficient usage of hardware resources with limited availability. In addition to these metrics, we introduce several *system-level metrics* to characterize the performance of a CNN on resource-constrained devices [56,57].

Segmentation accuracy is measured as a mean Intersection over Union (mIOU) score between the ground truth and the predicted segmentation mask.

Latency represents the amount of time a CNN network takes to process an image. This is usually measured in terms of frames per second (FPS).

Network parameters represents the number of parameters learned by the network.

Network size represents the amount of storage space required to store the network parameters. An efficient network should have a smaller network size.

Power consumption is the average power consumed by the network during inference.

Sensitivity to GPU frequency measures the computational capability of an application and is defined as a ratio of percentage change in execution time to the percentage change in GPU frequency. Higher values indicate higher efficiency.

Utilization rates measure the utilization of compute resources (CPU, GPU, and memory) while running on an edge device. In particular, computing units in edge devices (e.g. Jetson TX2) share memory between CPU and GPU.

Warp execution efficiency is defined as the average percentage of active threads in each executed warp. GPUs schedule threads as warps; each thread is executed in *single instruction multiple data* fashion. Higher values represent efficient usage of GPU.

Memory efficiency is the ratio of number of bytes requested/stored to the number of bytes transfered from/to device (or shared) memory to satisfy load/store requests. Since memory transactions are in blocks, this metric measures memory bandwidth efficiency.

Training Details: ESPNet networks were trained using PyTorch [58] with CUDA 9.0 and cuDNN back-ends. ADAM [59] was used with an initial learning rate of 0.0005, and decayed by two after every 100 epochs and with a weight decay of 0.0005. An inverse class probability weighting scheme was used in the cross-entropy loss function to address the class imbalance [20,21]. Following [20,21], the weights were initialized randomly. Standard strategies, such as scaling, cropping and flipping, were used to augment the data. The image resolution in the Cityscape dataset is 2048 × 1024, and all the accuracy results were reported at this resolution. For training the networks, we sub-sampled the RGB images by two. When the output resolution was smaller than 2048 × 1024, the output was up-sampled using bi-linear interpolation. For training on the PASCAL dataset, we used a fixed image size of 512 × 512. For the WSI dataset, the patch-wise training approach was followed [36]. ESPNet was trained in two stages. First, ESPNet-C was trained with down-sampled annotations. Second, a light-weight decoder was attached to ESPNet-C and then, the entire ESPNet network was trained.

Three different GPU devices were used for our experiments: (1) a desktop with a NVIDIA TitanX GPU (3,584 CUDA cores), (2) a laptop with a NVIDIA GTX-960M GPU (640 CUDA cores), and (3) an edge device with a NVIDIA Jetson TX2 (256 CUDA cores). Unless and otherwise stated explicitly, statistics

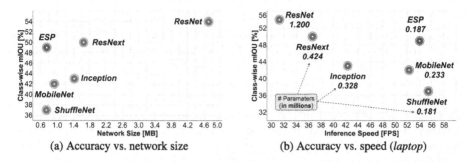

Fig. 5. Comparison between state-of-the-art efficient convolutional modules. For a fair comparison between different modules, we used $K = 5$, $d = \frac{N}{K}$, $\alpha_2 = 2$, and $\alpha_3 = 3$. We used standard strided convolution for down-sampling. For ShuffleNet, we used $g = 4$ and $K = 4$ so that the resultant ESPNet-C network has the same complexity as with the ESP block.

are reported for an RGB image of size 1024×512 averaged over 200 trials. For collecting the hardware-level statistics, NVIDIA's and Intel's hardware profiling and tracing tools, such as NVPROF [60], Tegrastats [61], and PowerTop [62], were used. In our experiments, we will refer to ESPNet with $\alpha_2 = 2$ and $\alpha_3 = 8$ as ESPNet until and otherwise stated explicitly.

4.2 Segmentation Results on the Cityscape Dataset

Comparison with Efficient Convolutional Modules: In order to understand the ESP module, we replaced the ESP modules in ESPNet-C with state-of-the-art efficient convolutional modules, sketched in Fig. 3 (MobileNet [16], ShuffleNet [17], Inception [11–13], ResNext [14], and ResNet [47]) and evaluated their performance on the Cityscape validation dataset. We did not compare with ASP [3], because it is computationally expensive and not suitable for edge devices. Figure 5 compares the performance of ESPNet-C with different convolutional modules. Our ESP module outperformed MobileNet and ShuffleNet modules by 7% and 12%, respectively, while learning a similar number of parameters and having comparable network size and inference speed. Furthermore, the ESP module delivered comparable accuracy to ResNext and Inception more efficiently. A basic ResNet module (stack of two 3×3 convolutions with a skip-connection) delivered the best performance, but had to learn 6.5× more parameters.

Comparison with Segmentation Methods: We compared the performance of ESPNet with state-of-the-art semantic segmentation networks. These networks either use a pre-trained network (*VGG* [63]: FCN-8s [45] and SegNet [39], *ResNet* [47]: DeepLab-v2 [3] and PSPNet [1], and *SqueezeNet* [55]: SQNet [64]) or were trained from scratch (ENet [20] and ERFNet [21]). ESPNet is 2% more accurate than ENet [20], while running 1.27× and 1.16× faster on a desktop and a laptop, respectively (Fig. 6). ESPNet makes some mistakes between classes that belong to the same category, and hence has a lower class-wise accuracy. For example, a rider can be confused with a person. However, ESPNet delivers a good category-wise accuracy. ESPNet had 8% lower category-wise mIOU than PSPNet [1], while learning 180× fewer parameters. ESPNet had lower power consumption, had lower battery discharge rate, and was significantly faster than state-of-the-art methods, while still achieving a competitive category-wise accuracy; this makes ESPNet suitable for segmentation on edge devices. ERFNet, an another efficient segmentation network, delivered good segmentation accuracy, but has 5.5× more parameters, is 5.44× larger, consumes more power, and has a higher battery discharge rate than ESPNet. Also, ERFNet does not utilize limited available hardware resources efficiently on edge devices (Sect. 4.4).

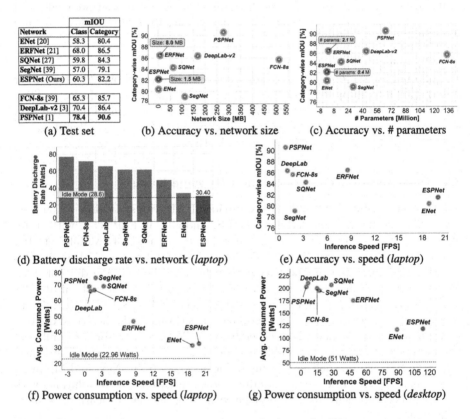

Network	mIOU	
	Class	Category
ENet [20]	58.3	80.4
ERFNet [21]	68.0	86.5
SQNet [27]	59.8	84.3
SegNet [39]	57.0	79.1
ESPNet (Ours)	60.3	82.2
FCN-8s [39]	65.3	85.7
DeepLab-v2 [3]	70.4	86.4
PSPNet [1]	78.4	90.6

(a) Test set

(b) Accuracy vs. network size

(c) Accuracy vs. # parameters

(d) Battery discharge rate vs. network (*laptop*)

(e) Accuracy vs. speed (*laptop*)

(f) Power consumption vs. speed (*laptop*)

(g) Power consumption vs. speed (*desktop*)

Fig. 6. Comparison between segmentation methods on the Cityscape test set on two different devices. All networks (FCN-8s [45], SegNet [39], SQNet [64], ENet [20], DeepLab-v2 [3], PSPNet [1], and ERFNet [21]) were without CRF and converted to PyTorch for a fair comparison.

4.3   Segmentation Results on Other Datasets

Unseen Dataset: Table 1a compares the performance of ESPNet with ENet [20] and ERFNet [21] on an unseen dataset. These networks were trained on the Cityscapes dataset [6] and tested on the Mapillary (unseen) dataset [51]. ENet and ERFNet were chosen, due to the efficiency and power of ENet and high accuracy of ERFNet. Our experiments show that ESPNet learns good generalizable representations of objects and outperforms ENet and ERFNet on the unseen dataset.

PASCAL VOC 2012 Dataset: (Table 1c) On the PASCAL dataset, ESPNet is 4% more accurate than SegNet, one of the smallest network on the PASCAL VOC, while learning 81× fewer parameters. ESPNet is 22% less accurate than PSPNet (one of the most accurate network on the PASCAL VOC) while learning 180× fewer parameters.

Breast Biopsy Dataset: (Table 1d) On the breast biopsy dataset, ESPNet achieved the same accuracy as [36] while learning 9.5× less parameters.

Table 1. Results on different datasets, where ° denotes the values are in millions. * See [66].

	mIOU	# Params°
ENet [20]	0.33	0.364
ERFNet [21]	0.25	2.06
ESPNet	**0.40**	0.364

(a) Mapillary validation set [51]

(b) Mapillary validation set [51] (unseen)

Model	ESPNet (Ours)	SegNet [39]	RefineNet [44]	DeepLab [3]	PSPNet [1]	LRR [65]	Dilation-8 [18]	FCN-8s [45]
# Params°	**0.364**	29.5	42.6	44.04	65.7	48	141.13	134.5
mIOU	63.01	59.10	82.40	79.70	**85.40**	79.30	75.30	67.20

(c) PASCAL VOC test set [52]

Model	Module	mIOU	# Params°
SegNet [39]	VGG	37.6	12.80
Mehta et al. [36]	ResNet	**44.20**	26.03
ESPNet*	ESP	44.03	**2.75**

(d) Breast biopsy validation set [36]

4.4   Performance Analysis on the NVIDIA Jetson TX2 (Edge Device)

Network Size: Figure 7a compares the uncompressed 32-bit network size of ESPNet with ENet and ERFNet. ESPNet had a 1.12× and 5.45× smaller network than ENet and ERFNet, respectively, which reflects well on the architectural design of ESPNet.

Inference Speed and Sensitivity to GPU Frequency: Figure 7b compares the inference speed of ESPNet with ENet and ERFNet. ESPNet had almost the same frame rate as ENet, but it was more sensitive to GPU frequency (Fig. 7c).

As a consequence, ESPNet achieved a higher frame rate than ENet on high-end graphic cards, such as the GTX-960M and TitanX (see Fig. 6). For example, ESPNet is 1.27× faster than ENet on an NVIDIA TitanX. ESPNet is about 3× faster than ERFNet on an NVIDIA Jetson TX2.

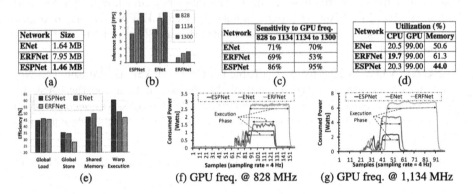

Fig. 7. Performance analysis of ESPNet with ENet and ERFNet on a NVIDIA Jetson TX2: (a) network size, (b) inference speed vs. GPU frequency (in MHz), (c) sensitivity analysis, (d) utilization rates, (e) efficiency rates, and (f, g) power consumption at two different GPU frequencies. In (d), initialization phase statistics were not considered, due to similarity across all networks.

Utilization Rates: Figure 7d compares the CPU, GPU, and memory utilization rates of networks that are throughput intensive; GPU utilization rates are high, while CPU utilization rates are low for these networks. Memory utilization rates are significantly different for these networks. The memory footprint of ESPNet is low in comparison to ENet and ERFNet, suggesting that ESPNet is suitable for memory-constrained devices.

Warp Execution Efficiency: Figure 7e compares the warp execution efficiency of ESPNet with ENet and ERFNet. The warp execution of ESPNet was about 9% higher than ENet and about 14% higher than ERFNet. This indicates that ESPNet has less warp divergence and promotes the efficient usage of limited GPU resources available on edge devices. We note that warp execution efficiency gives a better insight into the utilization of GPU resources than the GPU utilization rate. GPU frequency will be busy even if few warps are active, resulting in a high GPU utilization rate.

Memory Efficiency: (Figure 7e) All networks have similar global load efficiency, but ERFNet has a poor store and shared memory efficiency. This is likely due to the fact that ERFNet spends 20% of the compute power performing memory alignment operations, while ESPNet and ENet spend 4.2% and 6.6% time for this operation, respectively.

Power Consumption: Figure 7f and g compares the power consumption of ESPNet with ENet and ERFNet at two different GPU frequencies. The average power consumption (during network execution phase) of ESPNet, ENet, and ERFNet were 1 W, 1.5 W, and 2.9 W at a GPU frequency of 824 MHz and 2.2 W, 4.6 W, and 6.7 W at a GPU frequency of 1,134 MHz, respectively; suggesting ESPNet is a power-efficient network.

4.5 Ablation Studies on the Cityscapes: The Path from ESPNet-A to ESPNet

Larger networks or ensembling the output of multiple networks delivers better performance [1,3,19], but with ESPNet (sketched in Fig. 4), the goal is an efficient network for edge devices. To improve the performance of ESPNet while maintaining efficiency, a systematic study of design choices was performed. Table 2 summarizes the results.

Table 2. The path from ESPNet-A to ESPNet. Here, ERF represents effective receptive field, * denotes that strided ESP was used for down-sampling, † indicates that the input reinforcement method was replaced with input-aware fusion method [36], and ° denotes the values are in million. All networks in (a–c, e–f) are trained for 100 epochs, while networks in (d, g) are trained for 300 epochs. Here, SPC-s denotes that 3×3 standard convolutions are used instead of dilated convolutions in the spatial pyramid of dilated convolutions (SPC).

(a)

	mIOU	# Params°
ReLU	0.36	0.183
PReLU	0.38	0.183

(b)

Module	mIOU	# Params°
ESP	0.39	0.183
-RL	0.37	0.183

RL - residual learning

(c)

Downsample	mIOU	# Params°
Strided conv.	0.38	0.274
Strided ESP	0.39	0.183

(d)

ESPNet-C configuration	ESP operations Reduce	Transform	# params	Network size	mIOU
C1 - ($\alpha_3 = 3$)	3×3	SPC	0.276	1.2 MB	50.8
C2 - ($\alpha_3 = 3$)	1×1	SPC	0.187	0.8 MB	49.0
C3 - ($\alpha_3 = 3$)	1×1	SPC-s	0.187	0.8 MB	47.4

(e)

Width divider K	2	4	5	6	7	8
mIOU	0.415	0.378	0.381	0.359	0.321	0.303
# Params°	0.358	0.215	0.183	0.165	0.152	0.143
ERF ($n^2 = n \times n$)	5^2	17^2	33^2	65^2	129^2	257^2

(f)

Network	mIOU	# Params°
ESPNet-A*	0.39	0.183
ESPNet-B	0.40	0.186
ESPNet-C	0.42	0.187
ESPNet-C†	0.42	0.206

(g)

α_3	ESPNet-C (Fig. 4c) mIOU	# Params (in million)	Network size	ESPNet (Fig. 4d) mIOU	# Params (in million)	Network size
3	49.0	0.187	0.75 MB	56.3	0.202	0.82 MB
5	51.2	0.252	1.01 MB	57.9	0.267	1.07 MB
8	53.3	0.349	1.40 MB	61.4	0.364	1.46 MB

ReLU vs PReLU: (Table 2a) Replacing ReLU [67] with PReLU [50] in ESPNet-A improved the accuracy by 2%, while having a minimal impact on the network complexity.

Residual Learning in ESP: (Table 2b) The accuracy of ESPNet-A dropped by about 2% when skip-connections in ESP (Fig. 1b) modules were removed. This verifies the effectiveness of the residual learning.

Down-Sampling: (Table 2c) Replacing the standard strided convolution with the strided ESP in ESPNet-A improved accuracy by 1% with 33% parameter reduction.

Width Divider (K): (Table 2e) Increasing K enlarges the effective receptive field of the ESP module, while simultaneously decreasing the number of network parameters. Importantly, ESPNet-A's accuracy decreased with increasing K. For example, raising K from 2 to 8 caused ESPNet-A's accuracy to drop by 11%. This drop in accuracy is explained in part by the ESP module's effective receptive field growing beyond the size of its input feature maps. For an image with size 1024×512, the spatial dimensions of the input feature maps at spatial level $l = 2$ and $l = 3$ are 256×128 and 128×64, respectively. However, some of the kernels have larger receptive fields (257×257 for $K = 8$). The weights of such kernels do not contribute to learning, thus resulting in lower accuracy. At $K = 5$, we found a good trade-off between number of parameters and accuracy, and therefore, we used $K = 5$ in our experiments.

ESPNet-A → ESPNet-C: (Table 2f) Replacing the convolution-based network width expansion operation in ESPNet-A with the concatenation operation in ESPNet-B improved the accuracy by about 1% and did not increase the number of network parameters noticeably. With input reinforcement (ESPNet-C), the accuracy of ESPNet-B further improved by about 2%, while not increasing the network parameters drastically. This is likely due to the fact that the input reinforcement method establishes a direct link between the input image and encoding stage, improving the flow of information.

The closest work to our input reinforcement method is the input-aware fusion method of [36], which learns representations on the down-sampled input image and additively combines them with the convolutional unit. When the proposed input reinforcement method was replaced with the input-aware fusion in [36], no improvement in accuracy was observed, but the number of network parameters increased by about 10%.

ESPNet-C vs ESPNet: (Table 2g) Adding a light-weight decoder to ESPNet-C improved the accuracy by about 6%, while increasing the number of parameters and network size by merely 20,000 and 0.06 MB from ESPNet-C to ESPNet, respectively.

Impact of Different Convolutions in the ESP Block: The ESP block uses point-wise convolutions for reducing the high-dimensional feature maps to low-dimensional space and then transforms those feature maps using a spatial pyramid of dilated convolutions (SPCs) (see Sect. 3). To understand the influence of these two components, we performed the following experiments. *(1) Point-wise convolutions:* We replaced point-wise convolutions with 3×3 standard convolutions in the ESP block (see C1 and C2 in Table 2d), and the resultant network demanded more resources (e.g., 47% more parameters) while improving the mIOU by 1.8%, showing that point-wise convolutions are effective. Moreover, the decrease in number of parameters due to point-wise convolutions in the ESP block enables the construction of deep and efficient networks (see Table 2g). *(2) SPCs:* We replaced 3×3 dilated convolutions with 3×3 standard convolutions in the ESP block. Though the resultant network is as efficient as with dilated convolutions, it is 1.6% less accurate; suggesting SPCs are effective (see C2 and C3 in Table 2d).

5   Conclusion

We introduced a semantic segmentation network, ESPNet, based on an efficient spatial pyramid module. In addition to legacy metrics, we introduced several new system-level metrics that help to analyze the performance of a CNN network. Our empirical analysis suggests that ESPNets are fast and efficient. We also demonstrated that ESPNet learns good generalizable representations of the objects and perform well in the wild.

Acknowledgement. This research was supported by the Intelligence Advanced Research Projects Activity (IARPA) via Interior/Interior Business Center (DOI/IBC) contract number D17PC00343, the Washington State Department of Transportation research grant T1461-47, NSF III (1703166), the National Cancer Institute awards (R01 CA172343, R01 CA140560, and RO1 CA200690), Allen Distinguished Investigator Award, Samsung GRO award, and gifts from Google, Amazon, and Bloomberg. We would also like to acknowledge NVIDIA Corporation for donating the Jetson TX2 board and the Titan X Pascal GPU used for this research. We also thank the anonymous reviewers for their helpful comments. The U.S. Government is authorized to reproduce and distribute reprints for Governmental purposes notwithstanding any copyright annotation thereon. Disclaimer: The views and conclusions contained herein are those of the authors and should not be interpreted as necessarily representing endorsements, either expressed or implied, of IARPA, DOI/IBC, or the U.S. Government.

References

1. Zhao, H., Shi, J., Qi, X., Wang, X., Jia, J.: Pyramid scene parsing network. In: CVPR (2017)
2. He, K., Zhang, X., Ren, S., Sun, J.: Spatial pyramid pooling in deep convolutional networks for visual recognition. In: Fleet, D., Pajdla, T., Schiele, B., Tuytelaars, T. (eds.) ECCV 2014. LNCS, vol. 8691, pp. 346–361. Springer, Cham (2014). https://doi.org/10.1007/978-3-319-10578-9_23
3. Chen, L.C., Papandreou, G., Kokkinos, I., Murphy, K., Yuille, A.L.: DeepLab: semantic image segmentation with deep convolutional nets, atrous convolution, and fully connected CRFs. TPAMI **40**, 834–848 (2018)
4. Ess, A., Müller, T., Grabner, H., Van Gool, L.J.: Segmentation-based urban traffic scene understanding. In: BMVC (2009)
5. Geiger, A., Lenz, P., Stiller, C., Urtasun, R.: Vision meets robotics: the KITTI dataset. Int. J. Robot. Res. **32**, 1231–1237 (2013)
6. Cordts, M., et al.: The cityscapes dataset for semantic urban scene understanding. In: CVPR (2016)
7. Menze, M., Geiger, A.: Object scene flow for autonomous vehicles. In: CVPR (2015)
8. Franke, U., et al.: Making bertha see. In: ICCV Workshops. IEEE (2013)
9. Xiang, Y., Fox, D.: DA-RNN: semantic mapping with data associated recurrent neural networks. In: Robotics: Science and Systems (RSS) (2017)

10. Kundu, A., Li, Y., Dellaert, F., Li, F., Rehg, J.M.: Joint semantic segmentation and 3D reconstruction from monocular video. In: Fleet, D., Pajdla, T., Schiele, B., Tuytelaars, T. (eds.) ECCV 2014. LNCS, vol. 8694, pp. 703–718. Springer, Cham (2014). https://doi.org/10.1007/978-3-319-10599-4_45
11. Szegedy, C., et al.: Going deeper with convolutions. In: CVPR (2015)
12. Szegedy, C., Vanhoucke, V., Ioffe, S., Shlens, J., Wojna, Z.: Rethinking the inception architecture for computer vision. In: CVPR (2016)
13. Szegedy, C., Ioffe, S., Vanhoucke, V.: Inception-v4, inception-resnet and the impact of residual connections on learning. CoRR (2016)
14. Xie, S., Girshick, R., Dollár, P., Tu, Z., He, K.: Aggregated residual transformations for deep neural networks. In: CVPR (2017)
15. Chollet, F.: Xception: deep learning with depthwise separable convolutions. In: CVPR (2017)
16. Howard, A.G., et al.: MobileNets: efficient convolutional neural networks for mobile vision applications. arXiv preprint arXiv:1704.04861 (2017)
17. Zhang, X., Zhou, X., Lin, M., Sun, J.: ShuffleNet: an extremely efficient convolutional neural network for mobile devices. In: CVPR (2018)
18. Yu, F., Koltun, V.: Multi-scale context aggregation by dilated convolutions. In: ICLR (2016)
19. Yu, F., Koltun, V., Funkhouser, T.: Dilated residual networks. In: CVPR (2017)
20. Paszke, A., Chaurasia, A., Kim, S., Culurciello, E.: ENet: a deep neural network architecture for real-time semantic segmentation. arXiv preprint arXiv:1606.02147 (2016)
21. Romera, E., Alvarez, J.M., Bergasa, L.M., Arroyo, R.: ERFNet: efficient residual factorized convnet for real-time semantic segmentation. IEEE Trans. Intell. Transp. Syst. 19, 263–272 (2018)
22. Jin, J., Dundar, A., Culurciello, E.: Flattened convolutional neural networks for feedforward acceleration. arXiv preprint arXiv:1412.5474 (2014)
23. Chen, W., Wilson, J., Tyree, S., Weinberger, K., Chen, Y.: Compressing neural networks with the hashing trick. In: ICML (2015)
24. Han, S., Mao, H., Dally, W.J.: Deep compression: compressing deep neural networks with pruning, trained quantization and Huffman coding. In: ICLR (2016)
25. Wu, J., Leng, C., Wang, Y., Hu, Q., Cheng, J.: Quantized convolutional neural networks for mobile devices. In: CVPR (2016)
26. Zhao, H., Qi, X., Shen, X., Shi, J., Jia, J.: ICNet for real-time semantic segmentation on high-resolution images. arXiv preprint arXiv:1704.08545 (2017)
27. Jaderberg, M., Vedaldi, A., Zisserman, A.: Speeding up convolutional neural networks with low rank expansions. In: BMVC (2014)
28. Rastegari, M., Ordonez, V., Redmon, J., Farhadi, A.: XNOR-Net: imagenet classification using binary convolutional neural networks. In: Leibe, B., Matas, J., Sebe, N., Welling, M. (eds.) ECCV 2016. LNCS, vol. 9908, pp. 525–542. Springer, Cham (2016). https://doi.org/10.1007/978-3-319-46493-0_32
29. Hwang, K., Sung, W.: Fixed-point feedforward deep neural network design using weights 1, 0, and −1. In: 2014 IEEE Workshop on Signal Processing Systems (SiPS) (2014)
30. Courbariaux, M., Hubara, I., Soudry, D., El-Yaniv, R., Bengio, Y.: Binarized neural networks: training neural networks with weights and activations constrained to +1 or −1. arXiv preprint arXiv:1602.02830 (2016)
31. Hubara, I., Courbariaux, M., Soudry, D., El-Yaniv, R., Bengio, Y.: Quantized neural networks: training neural networks with low precision weights and activations. arXiv preprint arXiv:1609.07061 (2016)

32. Liu, B., Wang, M., Foroosh, H., Tappen, M., Pensky, M.: Sparse convolutional neural networks. In: CVPR, pp. 806–814 (2015)
33. Wen, W., Wu, C., Wang, Y., Chen, Y., Li, H.: Learning structured sparsity in deep neural networks. In: NIPS, pp. 2074–2082 (2016)
34. Bagherinezhad, H., Rastegari, M., Farhadi, A.: LCNN: lookup-based convolutional neural network. In: CVPR (2017)
35. Holschneider, M., Kronland-Martinet, R., Morlet, J., Tchamitchian, P.: A real-time algorithm for signal analysis with the help of the wavelet transform. In: Combes, J.M., Grossmann, A., Tchamitchian, P. (eds.) Wavelets, pp. 286–297. Springer, Heidelberg (1990). https://doi.org/10.1007/978-3-642-75988-8_28
36. Mehta, S., Mercan, E., Bartlett, J., Weaver, D.L., Elmore, J.G., Shapiro, L.G.: Learning to segment breast biopsy whole slide images. In: WACV (2018)
37. Wang, P., et al.: Understanding convolution for semantic segmentation. In: WACV (2018)
38. Graves, A., Fernández, S., Schmidhuber, J.: Multi-dimensional recurrent neural networks. In: de Sá, J.M., Alexandre, L.A., Duch, W., Mandic, D. (eds.) ICANN 2007. LNCS, vol. 4668, pp. 549–558. Springer, Heidelberg (2007). https://doi.org/10.1007/978-3-540-74690-4_56
39. Badrinarayanan, V., Kendall, A., Cipolla, R.: SegNet: a deep convolutional encoder-decoder architecture for image segmentation. TPAMI **39**, 2481–2495 (2017)
40. Ronneberger, O., Fischer, P., Brox, T.: U-Net: convolutional networks for biomedical image segmentation. In: Navab, N., Hornegger, J., Wells, W.M., Frangi, A.F. (eds.) MICCAI 2015. LNCS, vol. 9351, pp. 234–241. Springer, Cham (2015). https://doi.org/10.1007/978-3-319-24574-4_28
41. Hariharan, B., Arbeláez, P., Girshick, R., Malik, J.: Hypercolumns for object segmentation and fine-grained localization. In: CVPR (2015)
42. Dai, J., He, K., Sun, J.: Convolutional feature masking for joint object and stuff segmentation. In: CVPR (2015)
43. Caesar, H., Uijlings, J., Ferrari, V.: Region-based semantic segmentation with end-to-end training. In: Leibe, B., Matas, J., Sebe, N., Welling, M. (eds.) ECCV 2016. LNCS, vol. 9905, pp. 381–397. Springer, Cham (2016). https://doi.org/10.1007/978-3-319-46448-0_23
44. Lin, G., Milan, A., Shen, C., Reid, I.: RefineNet: multi-path refinement networks for high-resolution semantic segmentation. In: CVPR (2017)
45. Long, J., Shelhamer, E., Darrell, T.: Fully convolutional networks for semantic segmentation. In: CVPR (2015)
46. Noh, H., Hong, S., Han, B.: Learning deconvolution network for semantic segmentation. In: ICCV (2015)
47. He, K., Zhang, X., Ren, S., Sun, J.: Deep residual learning for image recognition. In: CVPR (2016)
48. Krizhevsky, A., Sutskever, I., Hinton, G.E.: ImageNet classification with deep convolutional neural networks. In: NIPS (2012)
49. Ioffe, S., Szegedy, C.: Batch normalization: accelerating deep network training by reducing internal covariate shift. In: ICML (2015)
50. He, K., Zhang, X., Ren, S., Sun, J.: Delving deep into rectifiers: surpassing human-level performance on imagenet classification. In: ICCV (2015)
51. Neuhold, G., Ollmann, T., Rota Bulò, S., Kontschieder, P.: The mapillary vistas dataset for semantic understanding of street scenes. In: ICCV (2017)
52. Everingham, M., Van Gool, L., Williams, C.K., Winn, J., Zisserman, A.: The pascal visual object classes (VOC) challenge. IJCV **88**, 303–338 (2010)

53. Hariharan, B., Arbeláez, P., Bourdev, L., Maji, S., Malik, J.: Semantic contours from inverse detectors. In: ICCV (2011)
54. Lin, T.-Y., et al.: Microsoft COCO: common objects in context. In: Fleet, D., Pajdla, T., Schiele, B., Tuytelaars, T. (eds.) ECCV 2014. LNCS, vol. 8693, pp. 740–755. Springer, Cham (2014). https://doi.org/10.1007/978-3-319-10602-1_48
55. Iandola, F.N., Han, S., Moskewicz, M.W., Ashraf, K., Dally, W.J., Keutzer, K.: SqueezeNet: AlexNet-level accuracy with 50x fewer parameters and <0.5 MB model size. arXiv preprint arXiv:1602.07360 (2016)
56. Yasin, A., Ben-Asher, Y., Mendelson, A.: Deep-dive analysis of the data analytics workload in cloudsuite. In: 2014 IEEE International Symposium on Workload Characterization (IISWC) (2014)
57. Wu, Y., Wang, Y., Pan, Y., Yang, C., Owens, J.D.: Performance characterization of high-level programming models for GPU graph analytics. In: 2015 IEEE International Symposium on Workload Characterization (IISWC), pp. 66–75. IEEE (2015)
58. PyTorch: Tensors and dynamic neural networks in python with strong GPU acceleration. http://pytorch.org/. Accessed 08 Feb 2018
59. Kingma, D.P., Ba, J.: Adam: a method for stochastic optimization. In: ICLR (2015)
60. NVPROF: CUDA toolkit documentation. http://docs.nvidia.com/cuda/profiler-users-guide/index.html. Accessed 08 Feb 2018
61. TegraTools: NVIDIA embedded computing. https://developer.nvidia.com/embedded/develop/tools. Accessed 08 Feb 2018
62. PowerTop: For PowerTOP saving power on IA isn't everything. It is the only thing! https://01.org/powertop/. Accessed 08 Feb 2018
63. Simonyan, K., Zisserman, A.: Very deep convolutional networks for large-scale image recognition. In: ICLR (2015)
64. Treml, M., et al.: Speeding up semantic segmentation for autonomous driving. In: MLITS, NIPS Workshop (2016)
65. Ghiasi, G., Fowlkes, C.C.: Laplacian pyramid reconstruction and refinement for semantic segmentation. In: Leibe, B., Matas, J., Sebe, N., Welling, M. (eds.) ECCV 2016. LNCS, vol. 9907, pp. 519–534. Springer, Cham (2016). https://doi.org/10.1007/978-3-319-46487-9_32
66. Mehta, S., Mercan, E., Bartlett, J., Weaver, D., Elmore, J., Shapiro, L.: Y-Net: joint segmentation and classification for diagnosis of breast biopsy images. In: MICCAI (2018)
67. Nair, V., Hinton, G.E.: Rectified linear units improve restricted Boltzmann machines. In: ICML (2010)

MVTec D2S: Densely Segmented Supermarket Dataset

Patrick Follmann[1,2](✉) , Tobias Böttger[1,2] , Philipp Härtinger[1] ,
Rebecca König[1] , and Markus Ulrich[1]

[1] MVTec Software GmbH, 80634 Munich, Germany
{follmann,boettger,haertinger,koenig,ulrich}@mvtec.com
[2] Technical University of Munich, 80333 Munich, Germany
https://www.mvtec.com/research

Abstract. We introduce the Densely Segmented Supermarket (D2S) dataset, a novel benchmark for instance-aware semantic segmentation in an industrial domain. It contains 21 000 high-resolution images with pixel-wise labels of all object instances. The objects comprise groceries and everyday products from 60 categories. The benchmark is designed such that it resembles the real-world setting of an automatic checkout, inventory, or warehouse system. The training images only contain objects of a single class on a homogeneous background, while the validation and test sets are much more complex and diverse. To further benchmark the robustness of instance segmentation methods, the scenes are acquired with different lightings, rotations, and backgrounds. We ensure that there are no ambiguities in the labels and that every instance is labeled comprehensively. The annotations are pixel-precise and allow using crops of single instances for articial data augmentation. The dataset covers several challenges highly relevant in the field, such as a limited amount of training data and a high diversity in the test and validation sets. The evaluation of state-of-the-art object detection and instance segmentation methods on D2S reveals significant room for improvement.

Keywords: Instance segmentation dataset · Industrial application

1 Introduction

The task of *instance-aware semantic segmentation* (*instance segmentation* for short) can be interpreted as the combination of *semantic segmentation* and *object*

Electronic supplementary material The online version of this chapter (https://doi.org/10.1007/978-3-030-01249-6_35) contains supplementary material, which is available to authorized users.

V. Ferrari et al. (Eds.): ECCV 2018, LNCS 11214, pp. 581–597, 2018.
https://doi.org/10.1007/978-3-030-01249-6_35

detection. While *semantic segmentation* methods predict a semantic category for each pixel [32], *object detection* focuses on generating bounding boxes for all object instances within an image [27]. As a combination of both, *instance segmentation* methods generate pixel-precise masks for all object instances in an image. While solving this task was considered a distant dream a few years ago, the recent advances in computer vision have made instance segmentation a key focus of current research [9,19,32]. This is especially due to the progress in deep convolutional networks [17] and the development of strong baseline frameworks such as Faster R-CNN [27] and Fully Convolutional Networks (FCN) [32].

Related Work. All top-performing methods in common instance segmentation challenges are based on deep learning and require a large amount of annotated training data. Accordingly, the availability of large-scale datasets, such as *ADE20K* [37], *Cityscapes* [2], *ImageNet* [31], *KITTI* [6], *COCO* [22], *Mapillary Vistas* [25], *VOC* [4], *Places* [36], *The Plant Phenotyping Datasets* [24], or *Youtube-8M* [1], is of paramount importance.

Most of the above datasets focus on everyday photography or urban street scenes, which makes them of limited use for many industrial applications. Furthermore, the amount and diversity of labeled training data is usually much lower in industrial settings. To train a visual warehouse system, for instance, the user typically only has a handful of images of each product in a fixed setting. Nevertheless, at runtime, the products need to be robustly detected in very diverse settings.

With the availability of depth sensors a number of dedicated RGBD datasets have been published [15,16,28,29]: In comparison, these datasets are designed for pose estimation and generally have low resolution images. They often contain fewer scenes (e.g. 111 for [29]) that are captured with video [16] resulting in a high number of frames. Some datasets provide no class annotations [29]. [16] shows fewer, but similar categories to D2S, but only single objects are captured and annotated with lower quality segmentations. In [15], some of these objects occur in real scenes but only box-annotations are provided. The most similar to D2S is [28]: CAD-models and object poses are available and could be used to generate ground truth segmentation masks for non-deformable objects. Compared to D2S, the dataset does not show scenes with more than one instance of the same category and objects appear at a much lower resolution.

Only few datasets focus on industry-relevant challenges in the context of warehouses. The Freiburg Groceries Dataset [13], SOIL-47 [14], and the Supermarket Produce Dataset [30] contain images of supermarket products, but only provide class annotations on image level, and hence no segmentation. The Grocery Products Dataset [7] and GroZi-120 [23] include bounding box annotations that can be used for object detection. However, not all object instances in the images are labeled separately. To the best of our knowledge, none of the existing industrial datasets provides pixel-wise annotations on instance level. In this paper, we introduce the *Densely Segmented Supermarket (D2S) dataset*, which satisfies the industrial requirements described above. The training, validation, and test sets are explicitly designed to resemble the real-world applications of automatic checkout, inventory, or warehouse systems.

Contributions. We present a novel instance segmentation dataset with high-resolution images in a real-world, industrial setting. The annotations for the 60 different object categories were obtained in a meticulous labeling process and are of very high quality. Specific care was taken to ensure that every occurring instance is labeled comprehensively. We show that the high-quality region annotations of the training set can easily be used for artificial data augmentation. Using both the original training data and the augmented data leads to a significant improvement of the average precision (AP) on the test set by about 30% points. In contrast to existing datasets, our setup and the choice of the objects ensures that there is no ambiguity in the labels and an AP of 100% is achievable by an algorithm that performs flawlessly. To evaluate the generalizability of methods, the training set is considerably smaller than the validation and test sets and contains mainly images that show instances of a single category on a homogeneous background. Overall, the dataset serves as a demanding benchmark and resembles real-world applications and their challenges. The dataset is publicly available[1].

Fig. 1. Overview of the 60 different classes within the *D2S* dataset

2   The Densely Segmented Supermarket Dataset

The overall target of the dataset is to realistically cover the real-world applications of an automatic checkout, inventory, or warehouse system. For example,

---

[1] https://www.mvtec.com/research.

existing automatic checkout systems in supermarkets identify isolated products that are conveyed on a belt through a scanning tunnel [3,12]. Even though such systems often provide a semi-controlled environment, external influences (e.g. lighting changes) cannot be completely avoided. Furthermore, the system's efficiency is higher if non-isolated products can be identified as well. Consequently, methods should be able to segment also partly occluded objects. Also, the background behind the products is not constant in many applications because of different types of storage racks in a warehouse system or because of dirt on the conveyer belt of a checkout system in the supermarket, for example.

We acquired a total of 21 000 images in 700 different scenes with various backgrounds, clutter objects, and occlusion levels. In order to obtain systematic test settings and to reduce the amount of manual work, a part of the image acquisition process was automated. Therefore, each scene was rotated ten times with a fixed angle step and acquired under three different illuminations.

Setup. The image acquisition setup is depicted in Fig. 2. A high-resolution (1920 × 1440) industrial color camera was mounted above a turntable. The camera was intentionally mounted off-centered with respect to the rotation center of the turntable to introduce more perspective variations in the rotated images.

Objects. An overview of the 60 different classes is shown in Fig. 1. The object categories cover a selection of common, everyday products such as fruits, vegetables, cereal packets, pasta, and bottles. They are embedded into a class hierarchy tree that splits the classes into groups of different packaging. This results in neighboring leafs being visually very similar, while distant nodes are visually more different, even if they are semantically similar products, e.g. single apples in comparison to a bundle of apples in a cardboard tray. The class hierarchy can

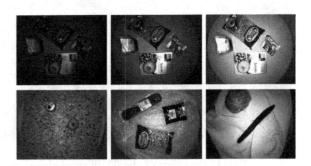

Fig. 2. The *D2S* image acquisition setup. Each scene was rotated ten times using a turntable. For each rotation, three images under different illuminations were acquired

Fig. 3. (*Top*) Each scene was acquired under three different lightings. (*Bottom*) As opposed to the training set (where a single uniform background is used), the test and validation sets include three additional backgrounds. This allows for a detailed evaluation of the robustness of the methods

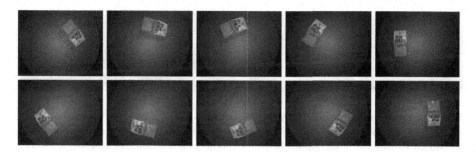

Fig. 4. Each scene was acquired at ten different rotations in steps of 36°. The camera was mounted slightly off-centered in order to introduce more variation in the images

be used, for instance, for advanced training and evaluation strategies similar to those used in [26]. However, it is not used in the scope of this paper.

Rotations. To increase the number of different views and to evaluate the invariance of approaches with respect to rotations [5,38], each scene was rotated ten times in increments of 36°. The turntable allowed automation and ensured precise rotation angles. An example of the ten rotations for a scene from the training set is displayed in Fig. 4.

Lighting. To evaluate the robustness of methods to illumination changes and different amounts of reflection, each scene and rotation was acquired under three different lighting settings. For this purpose an LED ring light was attached to the camera. The illumination was set to span a large spectrum of possible lightings, from under- to overexposure (see *top* of Fig. 3).

Background. The validation and test scenes have a variety of different backgrounds that are shown in Fig. 3 (*bottom*). This allows to evaluate the generalizability of approaches. In contrast, the training set is restricted to images with a single homogeneous background. It is kept constant to imitate the settings of a warehouse system, where new products are mostly imaged within a fixed environment and not in the test scenario.

Occlusion and Clutter. As indicated in Fig. 5, occlusions may arise from objects of the same class, objects of a different class, or from clutter objects. Clutter objects have a category that is not present in the training images. They were added explicitly to the validation and test images to evaluate the robustness to novel objects. Examples of the selected clutter objects are shown in Fig. 6.

Fig. 5. Objects appear with different amounts of occlusion. These may either be caused by objects of the same class, objects of a different class or by clutter objects not within the training set

Fig. 6. To test the robustness of approaches to unseen clutter objects, objects not within the training set were added to the validation and test sets (e.g., a mouse pad and a black foam block)

3   Dataset Splitting

In contrast to existing datasets for instance-aware semantic segmentation, such as *VOC* [4] and *COCO* [22], the *D2S* training set has a different distribution with respect to image and class statistics than the validation and test sets. The complexity of the captured scenes as well as the average number of objects per image are substantially higher in the validation and test sets (see Table 1). The motivation for this choice of split is to follow common industrial requirements, such as: low labelling effort, low complexity of training set acquisition for easy replicability, and the possibility to easily add new classes to the system.

The split is performed on a per-scene basis: all 30 images of a scene, i.e. all combinations of the ten rotations and three lightings, are included in either the training, the validation, or the test set. In the following, we describe the rules for generating the splits.

Training Split. To meet the mentioned industrial requirements, the training scenes are selected to be as simple as possible: They have a homogeneous background, mostly contain only one object and the amount of occlusions is reduced to a minimum. To summarize, we add scenes to the training split that

- contain only objects of one category[2],
- provide new views of an object,
- only contain objects with no or marginal overlap,
- have no clutter and a homogeneous background.

The total number of scenes in the training set is 147, resulting in 4380 images of 6900 objects. The rather small training set should encourage work towards the generation of augmented or synthetic training data, for instance using generative adversarial networks [8, 11, 18, 34, 35].

---

[2] In order to provide similar views of each object class as they are visible in the validation and test set, four scenes were added to the training set that contain two distinct classes.

Table 1. Split statistics. Due to our splitting strategy, the number of images and the number of instances per image is significantly lower for the training set. The complexity of validation and test scenes is approximately the same

Split	all	train	val	test
# scenes	700	146	120	434
# images	21000	4380	3600	13020
# objects	72447	6900	15654	49893
# objects/image	3.45	1.58	4.35	3.83
# scenes w. occlusion	393	10	84	299
# scenes w. clutter	86	0	18	68
Rotations		✓	✓	✓
Lighting variation		✓	✓	✓
Background variation			✓	✓
Clutter			✓	✓

Validation and Test Splits. The remaining scenes are split between the validation and the test set. They consist of scenes with

- single or multiple objects of different classes,
- touching or occluded objects,
- clutter objects and
- varying background.

These scenes were chosen such that the generalization capabilities of approaches can be evaluated. Additionally, current methods struggle with heavy occlusion and novelty detection. These issues are addressed by this choice of splits as well. The split between validation and test set was performed on sub-groups of images containing the same number of total and occluded objects. This ensures that both sets have approximately the same distribution. The ratio of the number of scenes in the validation and test set is chosen to be 1:4. The reasons for this decision are twofold: First, the evaluation of the model on a small validation set is faster. Second, we do not want to encourage training on the validation set, but stimulate work on approaches that require little training data or use augmentation techniques. The statistics of the number of images and objects in the splits are visualized in Table 1.

4   Statistics and Comparison

In this section, we compare our dataset to *VOC* [4] and *COCO* [22]. These datasets have encouraged many researchers to work on instance segmentation and are frequently used to benchmark state-of-the-art methods.

Table 2. Dataset statistics. Number of images and objects per split, average number of objects per image and number of classes for *D2S* (ours), *VOC 2012*, and *COCO*. *For *VOC 2012* and *COCO*, the object numbers are only available for the training and validation set

Dataset		*VOC*	*COCO*	*D2S*
# images	all	4369	163957	21000
	train	1464	118287	4380
	val	1449	5000	3600
	test	1456	40670	13020
# objects	all	-	-	72447
	train	3507	849941	6900
	val	3422	36335	15654
	test	-	-	49893
# obj/img		2.38*	7.19*	3.45
# classes		20	80	60

Dataset Statistics. As summarized in Table 2, *D2S* contains significantly more object instances than *VOC*, but fewer than *COCO*. Specifically, although the *D2S* training set is larger than that of *VOC*, the number of training objects is less than 1% of those in *COCO*. This choice was made intentionally, as in many industrial applications it is desired to use as few training images as possible. In contrast, the proportion of validation images is significantly larger for *D2S* in order to enable a thorough evaluation of the generalization capabilities. On average, there are half as many objects per image in *D2S* as in *COCO*.

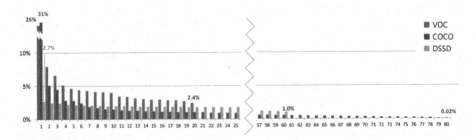

Fig. 7. Ratio of objects per class for *D2S* (*orange*), *VOC* (*green*) and *COCO* (*violet*). In *COCO* and *VOC*, the class *person* is dominant and some classes are underrepresented. In *D2S*, the number of objects per class is uniformly distributed. Note that for *COCO* and *VOC* the diagram was calculated based on train and val splits (Color figure online)

Class Statistics. Since the images of *COCO* and *VOC* were taken from flickr[3], the distribution of object classes is not uniform. In both datasets, the class

---
[3] https://www.flickr.com.

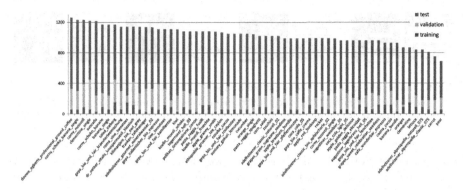

Fig. 8. Number of images per class and split sorted by the total number of images per class for *D2S*. The number of images per class is almost uniformly distributed

person dominates, as visualized in Fig. 7: 31% and 25% of all objects belong to this class for *COCO* and *VOC*, respectively. Moreover, 10% of the classes with the highest number of objects are represented by 51% and 33% of all objects, while only 5.4% and 13.5% of the objects belong to the 25% of classes with the lowest number of objects. This class imbalance is valid since both *COCO* and *VOC* represent the real world where some classes naturally appear more often than others. In the evaluation all classes are weighted uniformly. Therefore, the class imbalance inherently poses a challenge to learn all classes equally well, independent from the number of training samples. For example, the *COCO 2017* validation set contains nine instances of the class *toaster*, but 10 777 instances of *person*. Nevertheless, both categories are equally weighted in the calculation of the mean average precision, which is the metric used for ranking the methods in the *COCO* segmentation challenge.

There is no such class imbalance in *D2S*. In the controlled environment of the supermarket scenario, all classes have the same probability to appear in an image. The class with the highest number of objects is represented by only 2.7% of all objects. Only 14% of the objects represent the 10% of classes with the highest number of objects, while 19% of the objects are from the 25% of classes with the lowest number of objects. The class distribution of *D2S* is visualized in Fig. 8, where the number of images per class is shown in total and for each split. As mentioned above, the number of images for each class is rather low in the training split, especially for classes that have a similar appearance for different views, such as *kiwi* and *orange_single*. Note that, although the split choice between validation and test set is not made on the class level, each class is well represented in both sets. The key challenge of the *D2S* dataset is thus not the handling of underrepresented classes, but the low amount of training data.

Label Consistency. It is difficult to ensure that all object instances in large real-world datasets are labeled consistently. On the one hand, it is hard to establish a reliable review process for the labeling of large datasets, e.g. to avoid unlabeled

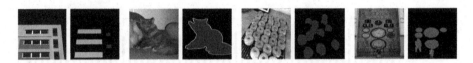

Fig. 9. Large real-world datasets are extremely difficult to label consistently. In the examples from *ADE20K*, *VOC* and *COCO*, some labels are missing (*from left to right*): a window, the sofa, some donuts, and the painting of a person

objects. On the other hand, some labels are ambiguous by nature, for instance a painting of a person. Figure 9 shows examples for label inconsistencies from *ADE20K* [37], *VOC* and *COCO*.

In *D2S*, the object classes are unambiguous and have been labeled by six expert annotators. All present objects are annotated with high quality labels. A perfect algorithm, which flawlessly detects and segments every object in all images of the *D2S* dataset, will achieve an AP of 100%. This is not the case for *COCO*, *VOC*, and *ADE20K*. In these datasets, if an algorithm correctly detects one of the objects that is not labeled, the missing ground truth leads to a false positive. Furthermore, if such an object is not found by an algorithm, the resulting false negative is not accounted for. As algorithms improve, this might prevent better algorithms from obtaining higher scores in the benchmarks. In *COCO*, this problem is addressed using *crowd annotations*, i.e. regions containing many objects of the same class that are ignored in the evaluation. However, crowd annotations are not present in all cases.

5   Benchmark

In this section, we provide first benchmark results for our dataset. We evaluate the performance of state-of-the-art methods for object detection [21,27] and instance segmentation [9,19]. We experiment with various training sets, which differ in the number of rotations and the availability of under- and overexposed images. Furthermore, we evaluate a simple approach for augmenting the training data artificially.

5.1   Evaluated Methods

Object Detection. For the object detection task, we evaluate the performance of Faster R-CNN [27] and RetinaNet [21]. We use the official implementations of both methods, which are provided in the Detectron[4] framework. Both methods use a ResNet-101 [10] backbone with Feature Pyramid Network [20].

Instance Segmentation. For the instance segmentation task, we evaluate the performance of Mask R-CNN [9] and FCIS [19]. We use the official implementation of Mask R-CNN in the Detectron framework and the official implementation of

---

[4] https://github.com/facebookresearch/Detectron.

FCIS provided by the authors[5]. Mask R-CNN uses a ResNet-101 with Feature Pyramid Network as backbone, while FCIS uses a plain ResNet-101. Since both methods output boxes in addition to the segmentation masks, we also include them in the object detection evaluation.

Training. All methods are trained end-to-end. The network weights are initialized with the COCO-pretrained models provided by the respective authors. The input images are resized to have a shorter side of 800 pixels (600 pixels for FCIS, respectively). All methods use horizonal flipping of the images at training time. FCIS uses *online hard example mining* [33] during training.

5.2   Evaluation Metric

The standard metric used for object detection and instance segmentation is *mean average precision* (mAP) [4]. It is used, for instance, for the ranking of state-of-the-art methods in the *COCO* segmentation challenge [22]. We compute the mAP exactly as in the official COCO evaluation tool[6] and give its value in percentage points. The basic average precision (AP) is the area under the precision-recall curve, computed for a specific intersection over union (IoU) threshold. In order to reward algorithms with better localization, the AP is usually averaged over multiple IoU thresholds, typically the interval $[0.5, 0.95]$ in steps of 0.05. The mAP is the mean over APs of all classes in the dataset. In the following, we just use the abbreviation AP for the value averaged over IoUs and classes. When referring to class-averaged AP for a specific IoU threshold, e.g. 0.5, we write AP_{50}.

5.3   Data Augmentation

In order to keep the labeling effort low and still achieve good results, it is crucial to artificially augment the existing training set such that it can be used to train deep neural networks. Hence, we experiment with a simple data augmentation technique, which serves as baseline for more sophisticated approaches. In particular, we simulate the distribution of validation and test set using only the annotations of the training set. For this purpose, we assemble 10 000 new artificial images that contain one to fifteen objects randomly picked from the training split. We denote the augmented data as **aug** in Table 3. For each generated image, we randomly sample the lighting and number of object instances. For each instance, we randomly sample its class, the orientation, and the location in the image. The background of these images is the plain turntable. We make sure that the instances' region centers lie on the turntable and that occluded objects have a visible area larger than 5000 pixels. Figure 10 shows example images of the artificially augmented dataset for all three different lightings. Due to the

---

[5] https://github.com/msracver/FCIS.
[6] https://github.com/cocodataset/cocoapi.

Fig. 10. The artificial augmented training set is generated by randomly assembling objects from the basic training set

high-quality annotations without margins around the object border, the artificially assembled images have an appearance that is very similar to the original test and validation images.

5.4   Results

When trained on the full training set `train` and evaluated on the `test` set, the instance segmentation methods provide solid baseline APs of 49.5% (Mask R-CNN) and 45.6% (FCIS). The object detection results are on a similar level, with APs of 46.5% (Mask R-CNN), 44.0% (FCIS), 46.1% (Faster R-CNN), and 51.0% (RetinaNet). Tables 3 and 4 show the results in full detail.

Ablation Study. As aforementioned, the *D2S* splits are based on scenes, i.e. all rotations and lightings for one placement of objects are included in the same split. To evaluate the importance of these variations and the ability of methods to learn invariance with respect to rotations and illumination, we perform an ablation study. For this purpose, we create three subsets of the full training set `train`. The `train_rot0` set contains all three lightings, but only the first rotation of each scene. The `train_light0` set contains only the default lighting, but all ten rotations of each scene. The `train_rot0_light0` set contains only the default lighting and the first rotation for each scene.

The resulting AP values of the instance segmentation methods Mask R-CNN and FCIS are summarized in Table 3 (top). As expected, we obtain the best results when training on the full `train` set. Training only on the first rotation reduced the AP on the test set by 15.7% and 9.1% for Mask R-CNN and FCIS, respectively. Training only with default lighting reduced the AP slightly by 3.4% for Mask R-CNN and increased the AP by a neglible 0.4% for FCIS. Training on `train_rot0_light0` reduced the AP by 13.2% and 12.9%, respectively. Overall, the results indicate that the models are more invariant to changes in lighting than to rotations of the objects.

Data Augmentation. As shown in Table 3, training on the augmented dataset `aug` boosts the AP on the test set to 76.1% and 69.8% for Mask R-CNN and FCIS, respectively. This is significantly higher than the 49.5% and 45.6% achieved by training on the original `train` set. Combining the sets `train` and `aug` to `train+aug` further improves the AP by 8.3% and 2.7%, respectively.

Table 3. Instance segmentation benchmark results on the test set. Mean average precision values for models trained on different training sets. (*Top*) Training on different subsets of the **train** set. (*Bottom*) Training on augmented data yields the highest AP values

	Mask R-CNN			FCIS		
	AP	AP_{50}	AP_{75}	AP	AP_{50}	AP_{75}
train	49.5	57.6	51.3	45.6	58.3	51.3
train_rot0	33.8	41.6	35.6	36.5	47.5	41.8
train_light0	46.1	54.8	48.0	46.0	59.3	52.0
train_rot0_light0	36.3	45.1	38.6	32.7	43.4	38.1
aug	71.6	86.9	81.7	69.8	87.6	82.4
train+aug	**79.9**	**89.1**	**85.3**	**72.5**	**88.1**	**83.5**

Table 4. Object detection benchmark results on the test set. Mean average precision values for models trained on different training sets

	Mask R-CNN			FCIS			Faster R-CNN			RetinaNet		
	AP	AP_{50}	AP_{75}	AP	AP_{50}	AP_{75}	AP	AP_{50}	AP_{75}	AP	AP_{50}	AP_{75}
train	46.5	58.3	53.5	44.0	59.4	51.7	46.1	55.2	49.7	51.0	61.0	52.8
train_rot0	34.1	42.5	38.3	34.6	48.2	41.3	36.7	46.9	41.5	32.9	39.8	34.5
train_light0	45.5	55.7	49.5	44.0	60.3	51.9	43.7	53.9	47.8	51.7	62.0	53.6
train_rot0_light0	35.7	46.0	40.5	29.9	43.9	35.4	34.3	44.3	39.0	31.6	38.9	33.2
aug	72.9	87.9	82.0	**69.9**	88.1	80.7	73.5	88.4	82.2	74.2	86.9	81.4
train+aug	**78.3**	**89.8**	**84.9**	68.3	**88.5**	**80.9**	**78.0**	**90.3**	**84.8**	**80.1**	**89.6**	**84.5**

Object Detection. We conduct the same ablation study for the task of object detection. The resulting AP values for all training splits of the methods Faster R-CNN and RetinaNet, as well as the results of instance segmentation methods Mask R-CNN and FCIS evaluated on bounding box level, are summarized in Table 4. It is interesting to note, that these AP values are not always better than the AP values obtained for the more difficult task of instance segmentation. On the one hand, we believe that the AP values for object detection and instance segmentation are generally very similar because current instance segmentation methods are based on object detection methods like Faster R-CNN. On the other hand, instance segmentation methods can even outperform object detection methods since a nearly perfect mask can still be generated from a too large underlying box proposal. It is also the case that the box-IoU is a lot more sensitive to the four box coordinates than the final segmentation. A third possible explanation is that the gradients of the mask branch help to learn even more descriptive features. For all methods the overall performance is very similar. Reducing the training set to only one rotation or only one lighting per scene results in worse performance. Analogously, augmenting the dataset by generating artificial training images results in a strong improvement.

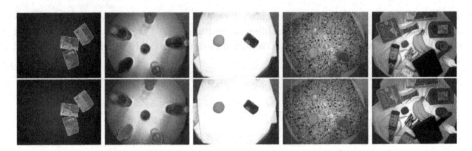

Fig. 11. (*Top*) Ground truth annotations from the *D2S* `val` and `test` sets. (*Bottom*) Results of Mask R-CNN trained on the `train` set. The classes are indicated by different colors (Color figure online)

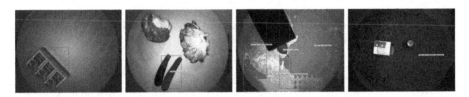

Fig. 12. Typical failure cases of of Mask R-CNN and FCIS on *D2S*. (*From left to right*) (*1*) Nearby objects are detected as a single instance. (*2*) Segmentation mask spans to neighboring objects. (*3 and 4*) Background is falsely detected as object

Qualitative Results. We show qualitative results of the best-performing method Mask R-CNN in Fig. 11. Furthermore, Fig. 12 shows typical failure cases we observed for Mask R-CNN and FCIS on the *D2S* dataset. More qualitative results are provided in the supplementary material.

6   Conclusion

We have introduced *D2S*, a novel dataset for instance-aware semantic segmentation that focuses on real-world industrial applications. The dataset addresses several highly relevant challenges, such as dealing with very limited training data. The training set is intentionally small and simple, while the validation and test sets are much more complex and diverse. As opposed to existing datasets, *D2S* has a very uniform distribution of the samples per class. Furthermore, the fixed acquisition setup prevents ambiguities in the labels, which in turn allows flawless algorithms to achieve an AP of 100%. We showed how the high-quality annotations can easily be utilized for artificial data augmentation to significantly boost the performance of the evaluated methods from an AP of 49.5% and 45.6% to 79.9% and 72.5%, respectively. Overall, the benchmark results indicate a significant room for improvement of the current state-of-the-art. We believe the dataset will help to boost research on instance-aware segmentation and leverage new approaches for artificial data augmentation.

Acknowledgements. We want to thank the students Clarissa Siegfarth, Bela Jugel, Thomas Beraneck, Johannes Köhne, Christoph Ziegler and Bernie Stöffler for their help to acquire and annotate the dataset.

References

1. Abu-El-Haija, S., et al.: Youtube-8m: a large-scale video classification benchmark. CoRR abs/1609.08675 (2016). https://arxiv.org/abs/1609.08675
2. Cordts, M., et al.: The cityscapes dataset for semantic urban scene understanding. In: Proceedings of the IEEE Conference on Computer Vision and Pattern Recognition (CVPR), pp. 3213–3223 (2016). https://doi.org/10.1109/CVPR.2016.350
3. ECRS: RAPTOR. https://www.ecrs.com/products/point-of-sale-pos/accelerated-checkout/. Accessed 7 Mar 2018
4. Everingham, M., Eslami, S.M.A., Gool, L.J.V., Williams, C.K.I., Winn, J.M., Zisserman, A.: The pascal visual object classes challenge: a retrospective. Int. J. Comput. Vis. **111**(1), 98–136 (2015). https://doi.org/10.1007/s11263-014-0733-5
5. Follmann, P., Böttger, T.: A rotationally-invariant convolution module by feature map back-rotation. In: Proceedings of the IEEE Winter Conference on Applications of Computer Vision (WACV), pp. 784–792 (2018). https://doi.org/10.1109/WACV.2018.00091
6. Geiger, A., Lenz, P., Stiller, C., Urtasun, R.: Vision meets robotics: the KITTI dataset. Int. J. Rob. Res. **32**(11), 1231–1237 (2013). https://doi.org/10.1177/0278364913491297
7. George, M., Floerkemeier, C.: Recognizing products: a per-exemplar multi-label image classification approach. In: Fleet, D., Pajdla, T., Schiele, B., Tuytelaars, T. (eds.) ECCV 2014. LNCS, vol. 8690, pp. 440–455. Springer, Cham (2014). https://doi.org/10.1007/978-3-319-10605-2_29
8. Gurumurthy, S., Kiran Sarvadevabhatla, R., Venkatesh Babu, R.: DeLiGAN: generative adversarial networks for diverse and limited data. In: Proceedings of the IEEE Conference on Computer Vision and Pattern Recognition (CVPR), pp. 166–174 (2017). https://doi.org/10.1109/CVPR.2017.525
9. He, K., Gkioxari, G., Dollar, P., Girshick, R.: Mask R-CNN. In: IEEE International Conference on Computer Vision (ICCV), pp. 1059–1067 (2017). https://doi.org/10.1109/ICCV.2017.322
10. He, K., Zhang, X., Ren, S., Sun, J.: Deep residual learning for image recognition. In: Proceedings of the IEEE Conference on Computer Vision and Pattern Recognition (CVPR), pp. 770–778 (2016). https://doi.org/10.1109/CVPR.2016.90
11. Huang, X., Li, Y., Poursaeed, O., Hopcroft, J., Belongie, S.: Stacked generative adversarial networks. In: Proceedings of the IEEE Conference on Computer Vision and Pattern Recognition (CVPR), pp. 5077–5086 (2017). https://doi.org/10.1109/CVPR.2017.202
12. ITAB: HyperFLOW. https://itab.com/en/itab/checkout/self-checkouts/. Accessed 7 Mar 2018
13. Jund, P., Abdo, N., Eitel, A., Burgard, W.: The freiburg groceries dataset. CoRR abs/1611.05799 (2016). https://arxiv.org/abs/1611.05799
14. Koubaroulis, D., Matas, J., Kittler, J.: Evaluating colour-based object recognition algorithms using the SOIL-47 database. In: Asian Conference on Computer Vision, p. 2 (2002)

15. Lai, K., Bo, L., Fox, D.: Unsupervised feature learning for 3D scene labeling. In: 2014 IEEE International Conference on Robotics and Automation (ICRA), pp. 3050–3057. IEEE (2014). https://doi.org/10.1109/ICRA.2014.6907298

16. Lai, K., Bo, L., Ren, X., Fox, D.: A large-scale hierarchical multi-view RGB-D object dataset. In: 2011 IEEE International Conference on Robotics and Automation (ICRA), pp. 1817–1824. IEEE (2011). https://doi.org/10.1109/ICRA.2011.5980382

17. LeCun, Y., Bengio, Y., Hinton, G.: Deep learning. Nature **521**(7553), 436–444 (2015). https://doi.org/10.1038/nature14539

18. Li, J., Liang, X., Wei, Y., Xu, T., Feng, J., Yan, S.: Perceptual generative adversarial networks for small object detection. In: Proceedings of the IEEE Conference on Computer Vision and Pattern Recognition (CVPR), pp. 1222–1230 (2017). https://doi.org/10.1109/CVPR.2017.211

19. Li, Y., Qi, H., Da, J., Ji, X., Wei, Y.: Fully convolutional instance-aware semantic segmentation. In: Proceedings of the IEEE Conference on Computer Vision and Pattern Recognition (CVPR), pp. 2359–2367 (2017). https://doi.org/10.1109/CVPR.2017.472

20. Lin, T.Y., Dollár, P., Girshick, R., He, K., Hariharan, B., Belongie, S.: Feature pyramid networks for object detection. In: Proceedings of the IEEE Conference on Computer Vision and Pattern Recognition (CVPR) (2017). https://doi.org/10.1109/CVPR.2017.106

21. Lin, T.Y., Goyal, P., Girshick, R., He, K., Dollár, P.: Focal loss for dense object detection. In: IEEE International Conference on Computer Vision (ICCV) (2017). https://doi.org/10.1109/ICCV.2017.324

22. Lin, T.-Y., et al.: Microsoft COCO: common objects in context. In: Fleet, D., Pajdla, T., Schiele, B., Tuytelaars, T. (eds.) ECCV 2014. LNCS, vol. 8693, pp. 740–755. Springer, Cham (2014). https://doi.org/10.1007/978-3-319-10602-1_48

23. Merler, M., Galleguillos, C., Belongie, S.: Recognizing groceries in situ using in vitro training data. In: Proceedings of the IEEE Conference on Computer Vision and Pattern Recognition (CVPR), pp. 1–8 (2007). https://doi.org/10.1109/CVPR.2007.383486

24. Minervini, M., Fischbach, A., Scharr, H., Tsaftaris, S.A.: Finely-grained annotated datasets for image-based plant phenotyping. Pattern Recognit. Lett. **81**, 80–89 (2016). https://doi.org/10.1016/j.patrec.2015.10.013

25. Neuhold, G., Ollmann, T., Rota Bulo, S., Kontschieder, P.: The mapillary vistas dataset for semantic understanding of street scenes. In: IEEE International Conference on Computer Vision (ICCV), pp. 4990–4999 (2017). https://doi.org/10.1109/ICCV.2017.534

26. Redmon, J., Farhadi, A.: Yolo9000: better, faster, stronger. In: Proceedings of the IEEE Conference on Computer Vision and Pattern Recognition (CVPR) (2017). https://doi.org/10.1109/CVPR.2017.690

27. Ren, S., He, K., Girshick, R.B., Sun, J.: Faster R-CNN: towards real-time object detection with region proposal networks. IEEE Trans. Pattern Anal. Mach. Intell. **39**(6), 62–66 (2017). https://doi.org/10.1109/TPAMI.2016.2577031

28. Rennie, C., Shome, R., Bekris, K.E., De Souza, A.F.: A dataset for improved RGBD-based object detection and pose estimation for warehouse pick-and-place. IEEE Rob. Autom. Lett. **1**(2), 1179–1185 (2016). https://doi.org/10.1109/LRA.2016.2532924

29. Richtsfeld, A., Mörwald, T., Prankl, J., Zillich, M., Vincze, M.: Segmentation of unknown objects in indoor environments. In: IEEE/RSJ International Conference on Intelligent Robots and Systems (IROS), pp. 4791–4796. IEEE (2012). https://doi.org/10.1109/IROS.2012.6385661

30. Rocha, A., Hauagge, D.C., Wainer, J., Goldenstein, S.: Automatic fruit and vegetable classification from images. Comput. Electron. Agric. **70**(1), 96–104 (2010). https://doi.org/10.1016/j.compag.2009.09.002

31. Russakovsky, O., et al.: ImageNetlarge scale visual recognition challenge. Int. J. Comput. Vis. **115**(3), 211–252 (2015). https://doi.org/10.1007/s11263-015-0816-y

32. Shelhamer, E., Long, J., Darrell, T.: Fully convolutional networks for semantic segmentation. IEEE Trans. Pattern Anal. Mach. Intell. **39**, 640–651 (2015). https://doi.org/10.1109/TPAMI.2016.2572683

33. Shrivastava, A., Gupta, A., Girshick, R.: Training region-based object detectors with online hard example mining. In: Proceedings of the IEEE Conference on Computer Vision and Pattern Recognition (CVPR), pp. 761–769 (2016). https://doi.org/10.1109/CVPR.2016.89

34. Shrivastava, A., Pfister, T., Tuzel, O., Susskind, J., Wang, W., Webb, R.: Learning from simulated and unsupervised images through adversarial training. In: Proceedings of the IEEE Conference on Computer Vision and Pattern Recognition (CVPR), pp. 2107–2116 (2017). https://doi.org/10.1109/CVPR.2017.241

35. Zhang, H., et al.: StackGAN: text to photo-realistic image synthesis with stacked generative adversarial networks. In: IEEE International Conference on Computer Vision (ICCV), pp. 5907–5915 (2017). https://doi.org/10.1109/ICCV.2017.629

36. Zhou, B., Khosla, A., Lapedriza, À., Torralba, A., Oliva, A.: Places: an image database for deep scene understanding. CoRR abs/1610.02055 (2016). http://arxiv.org/abs/1610.02055

37. Zhou, B., Zhao, H., Puig, X., Fidler, S., Barriuso, A., Torralba, A.: Semantic understanding of scenes through the ADE20K dataset. CoRR abs/1608.05442 (2016). http://arxiv.org/abs/1608.05442

38. Zhou, Y., Ye, Q., Qiu, Q., Jiao, J.: Oriented response networks. In: Proceedings of the IEEE Conference on Computer Vision and Pattern Recognition (CVPR), pp. 4961–4970 (2017). https://doi.org/10.1109/CVPR.2017.527

U-PC: Unsupervised Planogram Compliance

Archan Ray[1], Nishant Kumar[2], Avishek Shaw[3],
and Dipti Prasad Mukherjee[4(✉)]

[1] University of Massachusetts, Amherst, MA 01003, USA
ray@cs.umass.edu
[2] Singapore-MIT Alliance for Research and Technology, Singapore
138602, Singapore
nishant@smart.mit.edu
[3] TCS Limited, Mumbai, India
shaw.avishek@tcs.com
[4] Indian Statistical Institute, Kolkata 700108, India
dipti@isical.ac.in

Abstract. We present an end-to-end solution for recognizing merchandise displayed in the shelves of a supermarket. Given images of individual products, which are taken under ideal illumination for product marketing, the challenge is to find these products automatically in the images of the shelves. Note that the images of shelves are taken using hand-held camera under store level illumination. We provide a two-layer hypotheses generation and verification model. In the first layer, the model predicts a set of candidate merchandise at a specific location of the shelf while in the second layer, the hypothesis is verified by a novel graph theoretic approach. The performance of the proposed approach on two publicly available datasets is better than the competing approaches by at least 10%.

Keywords: Planogram compliance · Merchandise recognition

1 Introduction

The display of merchandise on the shelves of a retail store follows a specific strategy, commonly known as planogram. To re-conciliate a planogram, an inspector visits each shelf and manually checks the availability of the merchandise as specified in the planogram. This is an expensive and error-prone exercise. We propose to capture the images of these shelves using hand held camera and provide an end-to-end solution to detect the products available on the shelves from their images. We expect that our tool may be used for planogram compliance. We do not impose any restriction on the camera type and the store lighting condition for wider acceptability of our proposal.

We assume that individual product images, typically used for marketing, are available in an image dataset. In addition we assume that the physical dimensions

© Springer Nature Switzerland AG 2018
V. Ferrari et al. (Eds.): ECCV 2018, LNCS 11214, pp. 598–613, 2018.
https://doi.org/10.1007/978-3-030-01249-6_36

(a)   (b)   (c)   (d)   (e)   (f)   (g)

Fig. 1. (a) An example shelf image. (b)–(e) Sample product images. (f)–(g) Poor quality product images cropped from shelf image. (d)–(e) and (f)–(g) are images of same products, respectively.

of the shelves and the individual products are available in any unit of length. We also assume that the planogram is not available to our software. In other words, we do not have any prior information about the location of products on the shelves. Therefore, for our problem, object recognition and localization are equally important.

A typical shelf image is shown in Fig. 1(a). Individual images of products present on the shelf and available in the dataset of product images are shown in Fig. 1(b) to (d). Notice the variation in illumination, resolution and quality of images between Fig. 1(a) and (b) to (d). Also note that dataset may contain product images (Fig. 1(d) and (e)) which are not available on the shelf.

In this paper we address recognition and localization of multiple objects in a scene at one go. The approaches in [7] propose a set of view-invariant transformations of *rgb* color vector for recognition of consumer products on the shelf. These transformations cannot handle the differences in resolution and illumination between the shelf image and the product image. Further, the unstable imaging conditions may arise from specular reflections, from shiny packages of products, instability in taking images by the shelf inspector. Typical degradation of the quality of product images cropped from a shelf image are shown in Fig. 1(f) and (g).

Zhang *et al.* [17] extract SIFT like features from a region using Harris-Affine interest region detector [13]. Both product image and shelf image are divided into sub-images and matched using histogram of features. We have compared our work with [17]. A combination of SIFT and histogram based matching is used for identifying grocery products in [12].

In [5], George *et al.* present a multi-label image classification approach for localization and recognition of products. They first establish a locality-constraint linear coding (LLC) [15] model using dense SIFT features of product images present in the dataset. A discriminative random forest [16] is then trained with LLC features of product images. Using the trained model, a multi-class ranking of products is estimated at a location by classifying each block of the shelf image.

The authors in [10] perform a deformable spatial pyramid based fast dense pixel matching and genetic algorithm based optimization scheme [8] for localization and recognition of products in the shelf image. In a variation of the above approach in [6], the authors have also integrated text based recognition [9] and features derived from discriminative patches as in [14]. The products are

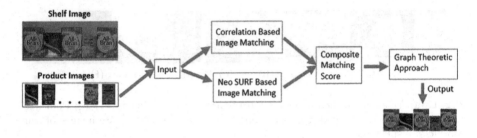

Fig. 2. Overall block diagram of the proposed scheme.

recognized using SVM; the recognition performance is improved using active learning [11] through user feedback.

The approach in [5] looks at the object localization problem more as an image retrieval challenge. Therefore, [5] fails to serve a key challenge that we are addressing is that of simultaneous detection, recognition and localization of multiple products. To explain the challenge further, assume products a and b are neighbors in a shelf. Assume a is identified incorrectly as another product c. The width of c is different from a. Then the region to be cropped to identify b will be incorrect. This is an important issue for retailers who want to locate both a and b instead of retrieving them in isolation. We have handled this problem by introducing a novel graph-theoretic approach to locate all products at the same time.

As mentioned earlier, we have introduced a two-layer approach of hypothesis generation and verification for localization and recognition of multiple objects on the shelf. At the initial stage, our strategy is to allow for exhaustive match of product images with the content of shelf image. This we refer as hypotheses generation. From the set of hypotheses, multiple products are predicted at a particular location on the shelf. In the second layer, one particular product out of these multiple predictions at a particular location is selected based on a graph theoretic approach. The overall block diagram of the proposed scheme is presented in Fig. 2. In the next section, we present the proposed matching scheme. The results are discussed in Sect. 3 followed by conclusions.

2   Image Matching

Multiple product identification in the wild is difficult due to many variabilities. These variables include the unknown scale of the products in the shelf image and color variability due to unconstrained illumination. Images taken from two different brands of cameras may result in variation of color space of images [2]. In a given row of multiple products, identification of a product at a particular location influences identification of neighboring products in the row. We address these variables in our methodology as presented next.

2.1 Hypothesis Generation

Assume images of N products are available in the dataset of product images $\mathcal{D}$. Each such product image is referred as $\mathcal{D}_p$, $p = 1, 2, \cdots, N$. Typical examples of $\mathcal{D}_p$ are shown in Fig. 1(b) to (e). We assume physical dimensions of these individual products in any suitable unit of length are available. Note that different products in $\mathcal{D}_p$ come in different physical and pixel dimensions.

Let the shelf image where multiple products are present, be represented by I_s. An example I_s image is shown in Fig. 1(a). We do not put any restriction on the camera used to capture I_s. But we do have the physical dimension of the shelf in any suitable unit of length. The problem is to find the location of $\mathcal{D}_p$ in I_s.

Dimensions of each image in $\mathcal{D}$ in pixels can be converted to the length-to-pixel scale of I_s. Let the rescaled dataset of product images be $\mathcal{D}'$. To emphasize, pixel dimensions of the pth product, $\mathcal{D}'_p$ is an approximation and does not represent true scale of the product image $\mathcal{D}_p$ in I_s. And this is one of the major challenges of the proposed problem.

Let there be c columns in I_s. For every location i, $i = 1, 2, \cdots, c$, of I_s, N number of images are cropped from I_s. The dimension of each of N crops is same as that of $\mathcal{D}'_p$, $p = 1, 2, \cdots, N$. Each of the N crops are correlated with the corresponding image of $\mathcal{D}'_p$ to calculate the Pearson correlation coefficient. Correlation is done in three separate Lab channels and the average of three correlation coefficients are computed. Therefore, at every location i, $i = 1, 2, \cdots, c$, of I_s, there are N correlation scores.

As mentioned earlier, scaling of $\mathcal{D}_p$ to $\mathcal{D}'_p$ is an approximation. To counter this, we isotropically vary (upscale and downscale) the dimensions of $\mathcal{D}'_p$ within a range $[-l/2, l/2]$ where $l \in \mathbb{R}$. Due to these additional resizes of $\mathcal{D}'_p$, additional l number of transformed images of $\mathcal{D}'_p$ are cropped at location i of I_s.

Combining above two scenarios, at a particular location i, $i = 1, 2, \cdots, c$, of I_s, $(N + N \times l)$ number of crops of I_s equivalent to image size $\mathcal{D}'_p$ and its scaled version are correlated with $\mathcal{D}'_p$. Algorithm 1 sums up this proposed hypothesis generation scheme. Function crop crops a patch at ith column of I_s equivalent to the size of $\mathcal{D}'_p$. In an overloaded version of crop, the k times scaled $\mathcal{D}'_p$ is cropped at ith location. The match_score function computes average of correlation coefficients in Lab channels between the cropped patch and $\mathcal{D}'_p$ or its scaled version. The cumulative score C_r for pth product at ith location of I_s are cumulated for all possible $(N + N \times l)$ values. The top m cumulative scores C_r represent m possible products likely to be present at column i of I_s, $i = 1, 2, \cdots, c$. We refer these m products as top m matches at ith location.

2.2 Matching Strategies

We have explored several image matching strategies between Q and $\mathcal{D}'_p$ or its scaled version other than straightforward correlation. However, we have not seen significant difference in our desired result due to matching strategies. Again, it is not our intention to get an exact match at this stage but to keep the right

---

Algorithm 1. Algorithm for hypothesis generation

1: **procedure** HYPOTHESIS GENERATION($\mathcal{D}', I_s$)
2:    Define $l \in \mathbb{R}^+$
3:    $[h, c] = \text{size}(I_s)$
4:    Initialize $C_r = \text{zeros}(c, N)$
5:    **for** $i \in [1, c]$; $p \in [1, N]$; **do**
6:       $Q = \text{crop}(I_s, \text{size}(\mathcal{D}'_p), i)$
7:       $C_r[i, p]+ = \text{match\_score}(Q, \mathcal{D}'_p)$
8:    **end for**
9:    **for** $i \in [1, c]$; $p \in [1, N]$; $k \in [-l/2, l/2]$ **do**
10:       $Q = \text{crop}(I_s, \text{size}(\mathcal{D}'_p), i, k)$
11:       $C_r[i, p]+ = \text{match\_score}(Q, \mathcal{D}'_p)$
12:    **end for**
13:    **return** C_r
14: **end procedure**

---

product in the list of top m matches. The straightforward correlation based matching proposed in this paper suffices as it always keeps the right product at a particular location within top m matches.

We have observed that complicated matching strategies with a number of tunable parameters do not give any advantage in the choice of the top m possible products at ith location. We have seen that $m = 3$ consistently finds the correct product those are likely to be present at location i. These top m matches are the hypotheses at a particular column location.

Transformation of $\mathcal{D}$ to $\mathcal{D}'$ under store level illumination is a difficult proposition. While the height of the shelf in any unit of length is known, it is impossible to find the exact boundary of the shelf in a shelf image taken by a hand held camera. However, the height of any product cannot be more than the height of the shelf. Therefore, to take care of all possibilities, height of $\mathcal{D}'_p$ is scaled up to the height of the shelf maintaining the aspect ratio of $\mathcal{D}'_p$. This upscaling determines the value of $l/2$. By the same amount $\mathcal{D}'_p$ is downscaled $l/2$ times. This determines the choice of l.

A test suite is designed with 19 product images of $\mathcal{D}$ to calculate C_r for identifying products in Fig. 1(a). C_r values for 19 products at three random locations of the shelf of Fig. 1(a) are shown in Fig. 3. The histogram in Fig. 3 shows that product number 12, 19 and 3 are the top-3 likely candidates based on cumulative score C_r at column 2 of Fig. 1(a). Similarly, for column 32, the likely products are 7, 3 and 12.

This concludes our hypothesis generation step. Next we find the shape based matching scores for top m possible products using SURF [1].

2.3   Neo SURF Based Matching

The Neo SURF (NSURF) introduced for our problem is a speeded up customized version of SURF. The primary motivation of using SURF is to complement our

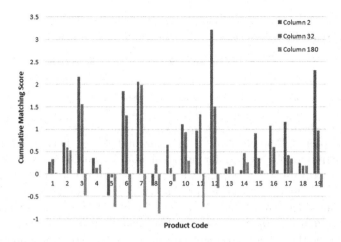

Fig. 3. C_r score of Fig. 1(a) for all 19 products at the 2nd, 32nd and 180th columns.

intensity based correlation score with the matching using shape based features. SURF had been used earlier successfully in similar problems [5]. NSURF differs from SURF in two aspects. First, in our typical use-cases, rotation invariance is not required [1]. The slant of the box on a shelf with respect to its upright position is typically ±15°. Such minor variations in slant do not affect the estimation of key points with SURF. Second, for very small images, the performance of SURF is found to be poor. The larger sized kernels account for this. For our implementation, we have restricted the kernel size to a maximum of 51 × 51. Third, we have used only two lower octaves for NSURF.

NSURF is applied on the cropped patches corresponding to size of $\mathcal{D}'_p$ for top m products at the ith location of I_s. Let the number of keypoints obtained using NSURF on the patch of I_s and $\mathcal{D}'_p$ be $k1$ and $k2$ respectively. Let the feature vector obtained from each keypoints be K_x, $1 \leq x \leq k1$ and K'_y, $1 \leq y \leq k2$, respectively. Each K_x or K'_y is identified by 64 dimensional vector. Let any particular K_x (say, K_d) match best with any particular K'_y (say K'_e) with an Euclidean distance θ. For our implementation, for a potential match between K_d and K'_e, we have chosen a conservative threshold as $\theta \leq 0.04$. In addition we have ensured that the ratio between minimum distance θ and the second minimum distance of K_d from all other K'_y except K'_e should be less than 0.4. This ensures a dominant yet reliable matching of keypoints between the patch of I_s (corresponding to top m products) and $\mathcal{D}'_p$. The total number of such matched keypoints are taken as NSURF score. Next we present the strategy to combine the correlation score derived in Sect. 2.1 with NSURF score.

2.4 Combining Correlation and NSURF Scores

The NSURF score, say U, is significantly higher compared to cumulative correlation score C_r. We design a composite score with a motivation that magnifies the discrimination between top m products at ith location. The designed composite score C_s is given by

$$C_s = U^{C_r}. \tag{1}$$

Similar types of products (for example, breakfast cereals or milk containers), similar in terms of dimension but dissimilar in packaging, are usually available in one given shelf. The packages are rich in content generating a number of NSURF keypoints. Therefore, $U \in \mathbb{Z}^+$ has higher and better discriminatory value compared to C_r, which for an ideal match should be close for similar products. If we raise U to C_r, the value is $\in \mathbb{R}^+$. In other words, (1) helps in magnifying the difference between products and leads to a positive value.

Combining Algorithm 1 and (1), at each column of the shelf image, we have composite scores for top m products. The next task is to select the winning product out of these top m possible products. This choice of winner product should consider all columns in the shelf simultaneously. We employ a directed graph for this purpose which is detailed next.

2.5   Construction of Directed Graph

Given that there are m possible products at a particular column of I_s, one straightforward approach could be to pick up the product with highest C_s. However, the product with highest C_s may not be the correct product. Further if a product $\mathcal{D}'_p$ is chosen at ith column of I_s, no other product should be selected for the width of $\mathcal{D}'_p$. However, within the width of $\mathcal{D}'_p$, there exists other products whose C_s value may be higher than the $\mathcal{D}'_p$ chosen at the ith column. Therefore all possible column locations of I_s should be considered simultaneously in order to find a winner product at the ith column of I_s.

To allow for top m products at all positions of I_s to compete with each other with their C_s score, we construct a DAG, directed acyclic graph, $\mathcal{G}(V,E)$. An arbitrary source node $\mathcal{S}$ and a sink node $\mathcal{T}$ is added to $\mathcal{G}$. Therefore, $\mathcal{G}(V,E)$ has total $(cm + 2)$ nodes. The edges are defined in the matrix E. All nodes in $\mathcal{G} - \mathcal{S}$ have an incoming edge from $\mathcal{S}$ such that $E[\mathcal{S}, \{\mathcal{G} - \mathcal{S}\}] = \epsilon$. Similarly, all nodes have directed edges to $\mathcal{T}$ such that $E[\{\mathcal{G} - \mathcal{T}\}, \mathcal{T}] = \epsilon$. A node $v_{ij} \in V$ represents jth product, $1 \leq j \leq m$ at ith location, $1 \leq i \leq c$.

For any node $v_{ij}, v_{op} \in \mathcal{G} - \{\mathcal{S}, \mathcal{T}\}$, $E[v_{ij}, v_{op}] = C_s[i,j]$, iff $(o - i) \geq width(\mathcal{D}'_j)$. The width of jth product is $width(\mathcal{D}'_j)$. In other words, there is an edge from one product $\mathcal{D}'_j$ to another product $\mathcal{D}'_p$ weighing equivalent to the composite score of $\mathcal{D}'_j$ at position i iff $\mathcal{D}'_p$ is at least as far as the width of $\mathcal{D}'_j$.

A typical $\mathcal{G}$ with some example edge weights is shown in Fig. 4. The red, green and the yellow dots represent products at the first column. These dots represent top m products ($m = 3$ in this case) in terms of score C_s. The black straight lines at the bottom show the width of each product.

We obtain the maximum weighted path in this graph. We expect that the sum of the edge weights or composite scores to be maximum in case the products are identified correctly considering all possible columns of the shelf. Any incorrect

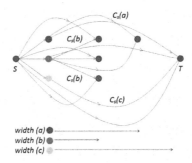

Fig. 4. An example graph $\mathcal{G}$ is shown. The top 3 possible products at the 1st column are a, b and c with composite scores $C_s(a)$, $C_s(b)$ and $C_s(c)$ and widths as $width(a)$, $width(b)$ and $width(c)$, respectively. (Color figure online)

placement of the product(s) should lead to the sum of composite scores being lower than that due to correct placement. Obtaining a maximum weighted path in any graph is an NP-hard problem. Since this is a directed acyclic graph, we have negated the edge weights and obtained the minimum weighted path using Bellman-Ford algorithm [3]. Next we justify our choice of maximum weighted path.

2.6 Justification for Using Maximum Weighted Path

In this section, we prove the following statement: *Solving for detection of multiple products in a shelf image in I_s (problem A) is equivalent to solving for maximum weighted path in a graph $\mathcal{G}$ (problem B).*

Proof. We begin by analyzing the complexity of the graph construction from I_s introduced in Sect. 2.5. Let n be the number of nodes in the graph. The Algorithm 1 is $\mathcal{O}(n^4)$ and the process of calculation of composite score is $\mathcal{O}(n)$. The construction of the graph is a $\mathcal{O}(n)$ algorithm. Thus the overall construction of the graph $\mathcal{G}$ is polynomial in n. We only need to show that if there exists a solution in B, then there will exist a solution in A. For this we first need to understand what is a solution in A.

Define *ideal crop* Q_p of the size of a product $\mathcal{D}'_p$ from I_s as the perfect crop of one instance of $\mathcal{D}'_p$ in I_s. Let product $\mathcal{D}'_p$ appear at the oth location of I_s. Naturally, the composite score for Q_p from I_s would be maximum at column o for the product $\mathcal{D}'_p$.

Now consider another product $\mathcal{D}'_j$ be present in I_s, and its ideal patch be Q_j. Naturally the ideal crop for $\mathcal{D}'_j$ will not be in the range $[o, width(Q_p) + o)$. Without any loss of generality, let the original position of Q_j be at column i, such that $i > o$. The nodes representing products for Q_p and Q_j in $\mathcal{G}$ will be connected by a weighted directed edge from $v_{op} \rightarrow v_{ij}$. Considering the construction of the graph $\mathcal{G}$ detailed in Sect. 2.5, we need to show that the maximum weighted path will have to go through the two nodes v_{op} and v_{ij}.

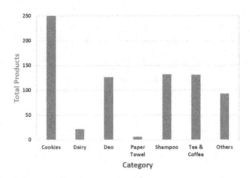

Fig. 5. Categories of product images in the in-house dataset.

Let $\mathcal{P}$ be the maximum weighted path in $\mathcal{G}$ that does not go through $\{v_{op}, v_{ij}\}$. Thus there exist other nodes in the neighborhood of $\{v_{op}, v_{ij}\}$ which has a higher composite score. Let (α, β) be the NSURF scores of the two patches Q_p and Q_j respectively. Since these are ideal patches the correlation score is 1 for both. Thus the composite score for the path through only these two nodes is $(\alpha + \beta)$. It is obvious that,

$$(\alpha + \beta) \geq 2[\min(\alpha, \beta)]. \tag{2}$$

Let the expected value of the NSURF score of falsely matched products around the region $\{o, i\}$ be at most γ. Let ζ be the expected correlation score of incorrectly matched products. Let there be κ such products that can be fit in the region $\{o, i\}$. Then the weight of the path is $\kappa\gamma^\zeta$. Without loss of generality, we know that $\zeta << 1$ and $\gamma << \min(\alpha, \beta)$. Thus $\gamma^\zeta << \min(\alpha, \beta)$.

Given the information above, we would now like to analyze the variation of the total weight of the path $\mathcal{P}$ with respect to the width of each product. Let w be the width of I_s; w_1, w_2 be the minimum and maximum widths of any product in $\mathcal{D}'$ respectively. Thus $\kappa \in [\frac{w}{w_2}, \frac{w}{w_1}]$ and $\kappa \in \mathbb{Z}$. For our assumption to be false, we need to show $\kappa\gamma^\zeta \geq 2\min(\alpha, \beta)$. For the maximum value of κ, we have,

$$\frac{w}{w_1}\gamma^\zeta \geq 2[\min(\alpha, \beta)]. \tag{3}$$

Without loss of generality we can assume that the maximum matched NSURF points, α, are uniformly distributed in the space of an extracted crop Q. We do not assume other distributions because if we are able to show it works in uniform distribution, it can be implied that this would work for other distributions as well. Thus in an ideal case there is a quadratic relationship between an increase in width of Q and the number of matched keypoints for a particular product $\mathcal{D}'_p$. Let us assume that the number of matched keypoints increase at a sub-quadratic rate with the width for incorrect matches of Q. We know, $\frac{w}{w_1}$ decreases linearly with increasing w_1. But α increases with the width of Q, until the ideal crop dimensions are achieved and then becomes constant. Now, γ increases at a sub-quadratic rate, and ζ goes down as the correlation between the crop and the product goes down with the increasing width of the crop.

Since ζ is upper bounded by 1, the function $\frac{\alpha}{\gamma^\zeta}$ is constant for very low values of α, linear for ζ near 1, and increasing otherwise. Thus the $2[\min(\alpha, \beta)]$ always dominates $\frac{w}{w_1}\gamma^\zeta$. This contradicts (3). Thus any maximum path should pass through nodes in $\mathcal{G}$ represented by Q_p and Q_j. This concludes our proof that solving for problem B is equivalent to solving for problem A.

Since by construction our graph $\mathcal{G}$ is a DAG, we can convert the edges to negative weights and solve for the minimum weighted path. The minimum weighted path using Bellman-Ford algorithm considering feed forward edge weights provides the final arrangement of products on the shelf. The result obtained using this proposed scheme is discussed next.

3 Results

The experiment is conducted both with in-house and publicly available datasets of product and shelf images. The in-house dataset consists of images of approximately 750 products in 7 categories. More than 2000 images of shelves are collected both from stores and lab settings. The category wise distributions of image dataset $\mathcal{D}$ are shown in Fig. 5. The proposed approach is also tested and compared using two publicly available datasets [5,17]. We first show some qualitative results of the proposal followed by quantitative analysis.

The reconstructed image of Fig. 1(a), which is the output of DAG of Sect. 2.5 is shown in Fig. 6(a). Another example of reconstruction is shown in Fig. 6(b) where the top row is the shelf and the bottom row is the reconstructed shelf. The correct products are identified in spite of variation in illumination. Notice even minor variations (red stripe at the top of the box instead of green stripe) in the product labels of two consecutive boxes of Chocos cereals (at the right end of the shelf) could be recognized by our approach.

The bottom row of Fig. 7(a) shows yet another reconstruction of the original shelf image in the top row, where the first product, placed behind with respect to others, could not be recognized. Another reconstruction in Fig. 7(b) (bottom

(a)   (b)

Fig. 6. (a) Reconstruction of Fig. 1(a). (b) Correct reconstruction (bottom row) of shelf image (top row). Product with minor variation (two boxes at the right end) is correctly identified.

(a)   (b)   (c)

Fig. 7. (a) Failure case (bottom row) where the first product is incorrectly identified due to displaced position of the product in the shelf image in the top row. (b) Surf bottle and box having identical texture on the cover are identified correctly. (c) Correct reconstruction of the shelf image in spite of extreme specular reflection (top row: original shelf image, bottom row: reconstruction result).

row) shows that even though Surf Excel bottle and Surf pouch has identical dominant texture on the front cover, the bottle and the pouch are identified correctly. The reconstruction of Fig. 7(c) bottom row clearly establishes the superiority of the proposal even under extreme specular reflection on some of the products.

Merler *et al.* [12] have proposed in situ product matching using color histogram. The result following [12] divides both $\mathcal{D}$ and I_s into smaller blocks and matches blocks using a score derived from intersection over union of areas under histograms. The result is shown in Fig. 8(a) whereas the output using proposed approach is shown in Fig. 8(b). Clearly, the accuracy of the proposed approach is better than matching using [12]. The role of integration of NSURF with correlation as opposed to selecting winner product at a location based only on maximum correlation score is shown in Fig. 9. The reconstruction result of Fig. 9(b) is better than that of Fig. 9(a). Similarly, NSURF alone cannot give desired result as opposed to the composite score as shown in Fig. 10. Note that all reconstructed results using proposed approach is the final output of DAG using composite score.

(a)   (b)

Fig. 8. Result using (a) [12], (b) proposed approach (top row: original shelf image, bottom row: reconstruction).

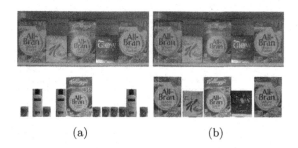

(a)   (b)

Fig. 9. (a) Winner product at a shelf location is selected based on maximum correlation score. (b) Result using composite score (top row: original shelf image, bottom row: reconstruction).

(a)   (b)

Fig. 10. (a) Winner product at a shelf location is selected based on maximum NSURF score. (b) Result using composite score (top row: original shelf image, bottom row: reconstruction).

We start the quantitative analysis of our result by plotting the ROC of the reconstructed result. Assume there are N product images in our dataset where as r products are available in a given shelf. Typically, $r << N$. As mentioned earlier, we are solving both recognition and localization problem. If a product is identified at column i of the shelf and the algorithm predicts the product at a location $i \pm \delta$, we consider that the product is correctly identified. The shift δ is typically considered as 75 mm for approximately 1000 mm wide shelf. Given this, True Positive (TP), False Positive (FP), True Negative (TN) and False Negative (FN) are defined as follows for each of the r products available in the shelf.

If product A is present at column i and the algorithm predicts A at column $i \pm \delta$, TP of product A is counted as 1. If a product other than A is present at column i and the algorithm predicts A at column $i \pm \delta$, FP of product A is counted as 1. If a product other than A is present at column i and the algorithm does not predict A at column $i \pm \delta$, TN of product A is counted as 1. If product A is present at column i and the algorithm predicts a product other than A at column $i \pm \delta$, FN of product A is counted as 1. The true positive rate (TP/(TP+FN)) versus false positive rate (FP/(FP+TN)) for 2000 shelf images is plotted in Fig. 11(a). The area under ROC for the proposed approach is significantly better compared to [12].

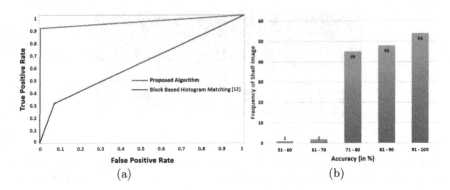

(a)

(b)

Fig. 11. (a) ROC Plot. (b) Accuracy using proposed approach (for example, reconstruction of 45 or 48 rack images has 71–80% or 81–90% accuracy, respectively).

The proposed correlation and NSURF integrated graph based matching is applied on the entire set of shelf images. Approximately 2000 shelf images from lab and stores are organized in 150 racks, each rack containing multiple shelves. The histogram of accuracy values of rack-wise product identification using our approach is shown in Fig. 11(b). The accuracy value is the number of matches between the products of reconstructed result using our algorithm and the products in the ground truth divided by the total number of products present in the rack.

Additionally we have performed stress testing on 500 shelf images of Cookies category. Each of these shelf images is taken after varying camera angle within ±15° and at different camera-to-shelf distances. There are 9 unique products in these shelf images. Therefore, the product image dataset $\mathcal{D}$ initially contains 9 product images. The accuracy of detection of these product images in each of the 500 shelf images are calculated using both the proposed and block based histogram matching [12].

For calculating accuracy, all the product images which are present in the shelf and identified correctly by both the algorithms are divided by the total number of products available in the shelves. The accuracy result averaged for 500 shelf images is reported as accuracy of product identification. The process is now repeated after increasing the size of the product image dataset $\mathcal{D}$ from 9 to 285 in steps of 30. This experiment tests whether the proposed matching algorithm is confused with the additional 30 product images for each subsequent test. Note that these additional product images in multiples of 30 are anyway not present in the 500 shelf images under inspection. The accuracy plot against increasing size of dataset of product images is shown in Fig. 12. The corresponding computation time is also shown in Fig. 12. The experiment is repeated using NMS [4]. Figure 12 shows that our proposal performs better compared to [4]. Further, the proposed image matching is not confused even with large number of spurious potential matches whereas [12] performs poorly with the increase in size of $\mathcal{D}$ containing product images not present in the shelf.

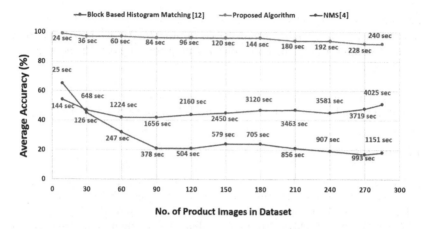

Fig. 12. Accuracy when the number of product images in $\mathcal{D}$ is increased from 9 to 285 in steps of 30. Corresponding computation times are mentioned.

Table 1. Comparison of the proposed approach on publicly available and in-house datasets [5,17].

	Inhouse	WebMarket [17]	Grocery [5]
Proposed	**92.4**	**90.8**	88.51
S1 [17]	41.6	62.03	51.28
S2 [17]	41.2	68.69	53.43
S3 [17]	36	59.29	63.05
MIC [5]	91.2	54.41	69.23
NMS [4]	47.56	51.02	**96.67**

Finally the proposed approach is compared with two related approaches [17], [5]. Subsets of two publicly available datasets of [17], [5] along with in-house data are used for comparison. The approach in [17] has three matching functions $S1$, $S2$ and $S3$ as shown in Table 1. The key difference in our result with respect to competing approaches is that accuracy measure for the proposed approach on our dataset includes accuracy of both recognition and localization (module a shift of $\pm\delta$ from the exact location as mentioned earlier) of products on the shelf. The accuracy using the proposed approach is reported in the top row of the Table 1. For competing approaches [17], [5], the accuracy refers to recognition without any penalization for the inaccuracy of localization of the product.

4 Conclusions

We have provided an end-to-end solution for automatically recognizing products available on the shelf. No a priori information is used to preempt the type of products expected at a particular location of the shelf. Instead of looking at a particular discrete location of the shelf, all columns of the shelf are treated simultaneously using a novel graph based approach. We are now improving the approach by integrating single instance learning technique with the graph based search mechanism.

Acknowledgments. This work is partially supported by TCS Limited. The authors would like to thank Mr. Bikash Santra for his help in preparing the manuscript.

References

1. Bay, H., Tuytelaars, T., Van Gool, L.: SURF: speeded up robust features. In: Leonardis, A., Bischof, H., Pinz, A. (eds.) ECCV 2006. LNCS, vol. 3951, pp. 404–417. Springer, Heidelberg (2006). https://doi.org/10.1007/11744023_32
2. Cheng, D., Prasad, D.K., Brown, M.S.: Illuminant estimation for color constancy: why spatial-domain methods work and the role of the color distribution. JOSA A **31**(5), 1049–1058 (2014)
3. Cormen, T.H., Leiserson, C.E., Rivest, R.L.: Introduction to Algorithms, 3rd edn. MIT Press, Cambridge (2009)
4. Felzenszwalb, P.F., Girshick, R.B., McAllester, D., Ramanan, D.: Object detection with discriminatively trained part-based models. IEEE Trans. Pattern Anal. Mach. Intell. **32**(9), 1627–1645 (2010)
5. George, M., Floerkemeier, C.: Recognizing products: a per-exemplar multi-label image classification approach. In: Fleet, D., Pajdla, T., Schiele, B., Tuytelaars, T. (eds.) ECCV 2014. LNCS, vol. 8690, pp. 440–455. Springer, Cham (2014). https://doi.org/10.1007/978-3-319-10605-2_29
6. George, M., Mircic, D., Soros, G., Floerkemeier, C., Mattern, F.: Fine-grained product class recognition for assisted shopping. In: Proceedings of the IEEE International Conference on Computer Vision Workshops, pp. 154–162 (2015)
7. Gevers, T., Smeulders, A.W.: Color-based object recognition. Pattern Recognit. **32**(3), 453–464 (1999)
8. Goldberg, D.: Genetic Algorithms in Search, Optimization, and Machine Learning. Addison-Wesley, Boston (1989)
9. Jaderberg, M., Vedaldi, A., Zisserman, A.: Deep features for text spotting. In: Fleet, D., Pajdla, T., Schiele, B., Tuytelaars, T. (eds.) ECCV 2014. LNCS, vol. 8692, pp. 512–528. Springer, Cham (2014). https://doi.org/10.1007/978-3-319-10593-2_34
10. Kim, J., Liu, C., Sha, F., Grauman, K.: Deformable spatial pyramid matching for fast dense correspondences. In: Proceedings of the IEEE Conference on Computer Vision and Pattern Recognition, pp. 2307–2314 (2013)
11. MacKay, D.J.: Information-based objective functions for active data selection. Neural Comput. **4**(4), 590–604 (1992)
12. Merler, M., Galleguillos, C., Belongie, S.: Recognizing groceries in situ using in vitro training data. In: CVPR. IEEE Computer Society (2007)
13. Mikolajczyk, K., Schmid, C.: Scale & affine invariant interest point detectors. Int. J. Comput. Vis. **60**(1), 63–86 (2004)
14. Singh, S., Gupta, A., Efros, A.A.: Unsupervised discovery of mid-level discriminative patches. In: Fitzgibbon, A., Lazebnik, S., Perona, P., Sato, Y., Schmid, C. (eds.) ECCV 2012. LNCS, pp. 73–86. Springer, Heidelberg (2012). https://doi.org/10.1007/978-3-642-33709-3_6

15. Wang, J., Yang, J., Yu, K., Lv, F., Huang, T., Gong, Y.: Locality-constrained linear coding for image classification. In: 2010 IEEE Conference on Computer Vision and Pattern Recognition (CVPR), pp. 3360–3367. IEEE (2010)
16. Yao, B., Khosla, A., Fei-Fei, L.: Combining randomization and discrimination for fine-grained image categorization. In: 2011 IEEE Conference on Computer Vision and Pattern Recognition (CVPR), pp. 1577–1584. IEEE (2011)
17. Zhang, Y., Wang, L., Hartley, R., Li, H.: Where's the weet-bix? In: Yagi, Y., Kang, S.B., Kweon, I.S., Zha, H. (eds.) ACCV 2007. LNCS, vol. 4843, pp. 800–810. Springer, Heidelberg (2007). https://doi.org/10.1007/978-3-540-76386-4_76

Recovering Accurate 3D Human Pose in the Wild Using IMUs and a Moving Camera

Timo von Marcard[1]([⊠]), Roberto Henschel[1], Michael J. Black[2],
Bodo Rosenhahn[1], and Gerard Pons-Moll[3]

[1] Leibniz Universität Hannover, Hanover, Germany
{marcard,henschel,rosenhahn}@tnt.uni-hannover.de
[2] MPI for Intelligent Systems, Tübingen, Germany
black@tue.mpg.de
[3] MPI for Informatics, Saarland Informatics Campus, Saarbrücken, Germany
gpons@mpi-inf.mpg.de

Abstract. In this work, we propose a method that combines a single hand-held camera and a set of Inertial Measurement Units (IMUs) attached at the body limbs to estimate accurate 3D poses in the wild. This poses many new challenges: the moving camera, heading drift, cluttered background, occlusions and many people visible in the video. We associate 2D pose detections in each image to the corresponding IMU-equipped persons by solving a novel graph based optimization problem that forces 3D to 2D coherency within a frame and across long range frames. Given associations, we jointly optimize the pose of a statistical body model, the camera pose and heading drift using a continuous optimization framework. We validated our method on the TotalCapture dataset, which provides video and IMU synchronized with ground truth. We obtain an accuracy of 26 mm, which makes it accurate enough to serve as a benchmark for image-based 3D pose estimation in the wild. Using our method, we recorded *3D Poses in the Wild (3DPW)*, a new dataset consisting of more than 51,000 frames with accurate 3D pose in challenging sequences, including walking in the city, going up-stairs, having coffee or taking the bus. We make the reconstructed 3D poses, video, IMU and 3D models available for research purposes at http://virtualhumans.mpi-inf.mpg.de/3DPW.

Keywords: Human pose · Video · IMUs · Sensor fusion · 2D to 3D People tracking · 3D pose dataset

1 Introduction

This paper addresses two inter-related goals. First, we propose a method capable of accurately reconstructing 3D human pose in outdoor scenes, with multiple

Electronic supplementary material The online version of this chapter (https://doi.org/10.1007/978-3-030-01249-6_37) contains supplementary material, which is available to authorized users.

V. Ferrari et al. (Eds.): ECCV 2018, LNCS 11214, pp. 614–631, 2018.
https://doi.org/10.1007/978-3-030-01249-6_37

Fig. 1. We propose Video Inertial Poser (VIP), which enables accurate 3D human pose capture in natural environments. VIP combines video obtained from a hand-held smartphone camera with data coming from body-worn inertial measurement units (IMUs). With VIP we collected *3D Poses in the Wild*, a new dataset of accurate 3D human poses in natural video, containing variations in person identity, activity and clothing.

people interacting with the environment, see Fig. 1. Our method combines data coming from IMUs (attached at the person's limbs) with video obtained from a hand-held phone camera. This allows us to achieve the second goal, which is collecting the first dataset with accurate 3D reconstructions in the wild. Since our system works with a moving camera, we can record people in their everyday environments, for example, walking in the city, having coffee or taking the bus.

3D human pose estimation from un-constrained single images and videos has been a longstanding goal in computer vision. Recently, there has been a significant progress, particularly in 2D human pose estimation [4,23]. This progress has been possible thanks to the availability of large training datasets and benchmarks to compare research methods. While obtaining manual 2D pose annotations in the wild is fairly easy, collecting 3D pose annotations manually is almost impossible. This is probably the main reason there exist very limited datasets with accurate 3D pose in the wild. Datasets such as HumanEva [32] and H3.6M [8] have facilitated progress in the field by providing ground truth 3D poses obtained using a marker-based motion capture system synchronized with video. These datasets, while useful and necessary, are restricted to indoor scenarios with static backgrounds, little variation in clothing and no environmental occlusions. As a result, evaluations of 3D human pose estimation methods in challenging images have been made mainly qualitatively, so far. There exist several options to record humans in outdoor scenes, none of which is satisfactory. Marker-based capture outdoors is limited. Depth sensors like Kinect do not work under strong illumination and can only capture objects near the camera. Using multiple cameras as in [21] requires time consuming set-up and calibration. Most importantly, the fixed recording volume severely limits the kind of activities that can be captured.

Fig. 2. For accurate motion capture in the wild we have to solve several challenges: IMU heading drift has accumulated after a longer recording session and the obtained 3D pose is completely off (left image pair). In order to estimate the heading drift, we combine IMU data and 2D poses detected in the camera view. This requires the association of 2D poses to the person wearing IMUs, which is difficult when several people are in the scene (middle image). Also, 2D pose candidates might be inaccurate and should be automatically rejected during the assignment step (right image pair).

IMU-based systems hold promise because they are not bound to a fixed space since they are worn by the person. In practice, however, accuracy is limited by a number of factors. Inaccuracies in the initial pose introduce sensor-to-bone misalignments. In addition, during continuous operation, IMUs suffer from heading drift, see Fig. 2. This means, that after some time, each IMU does not measure relative to the *same* world coordinate frame. Rather, each sensor provides readings relative to *independent* coordinate frames that slowly drift away from the world frame. Furthermore, global position can not be accurately obtained due to positional drift. Moreover, IMU systems do not provide 3D pose synchronized and aligned with image data.

Therefore, we propose a new method, called *Video Inertial Poser (VIP)*, that jointly estimates the pose of people in the scene by using 6 to 17 IMUs attached at the body limbs and a single hand-held moving phone camera. Using IMUs makes the task less ambiguous but many challenges remain. First, the persons need to be detected in the video and associated with the IMU data, see Fig. 2. Second, IMUs are inaccurate due to heading drift. Third, the estimated 3D poses need to align with the images of the moving camera. Furthermore, the scenes we tackle in this work include complete occlusions, multiple people, tracked persons falling out of the camera view and camera motion. To address these difficulties, we define a novel graph-based association method, and a continuous pose optimization scheme that integrates the measurements from all frames in the sequence. To deal with noise and incomplete data, we exploit SMPL [14], which incorporates anthropometric and kinematic constraints.

Specifically, our approach has three steps: initialization, association and data fusion. During initialization, we compute initial 3D poses by fitting SMPL to the IMU orientations. The association step automatically associates the 3D poses with 2D person detections for the full sequence by solving a single binary quadratic optimization problem. Given those associations, in the data fusion step, we define an objective function and jointly optimize for the 3D poses of the full sequence, the per-sensor heading errors, the camera pose and translation.

Specifically, the objective is minimized when (i) the model orientation and acceleration is close to the IMU readings and (ii) the projected 3D joints of SMPL are close to 2D CNN detections [4] in the image. To further improve results, we repeat association and joint optimization once.

With VIP we can accurately estimate 3D human poses in challenging natural scenes. To validate the accuracy of VIP, we use the recently released 3D dataset Total Capture [39] because it provides video synchronized with IMU data. VIP obtains an average 3D pose error of 26 mm, which makes it accurate enough to benchmark methods that tackle in-the-wild data. Using VIP we created *3D Poses in the Wild (3DPW)*: a dataset consisting of hand-held video with ground-truth 3D human pose and shape in natural videos.

We make 3DPW publicly available for research purposes, including 60 video sequences (51,000 frames or 1700 s of video captured with a phone at 30 Hz), IMU data, 3D scans and 3D people models with 18 clothing variations, and the accurate 3D pose reconstruction results of VIP in all sequences. We anticipate that the dataset will stimulate novel research by providing a platform to quantitatively evaluate and compare methods for 3D human pose estimation.

2 Related Work

Pose Estimation Using IMUs. There exist commercial solutions for MoCap with IMUs. The approach of [30] integrates 17 IMUs in a Kalman Filter to estimate pose. The seminal work of [41] uses a custom made suit to capture pose in everyday surroundings. These approaches require many sensors and do not align the reconstructions with video; therefore they suffer from drift. The approach of [42] fits the SMPL body model to 5–6 IMUs over a full sequence, obtaining realistic results. The method, however, is applied to only 1 person at a time and the motion is not aligned with video. To compensate for drift, 4–8 cameras and 5 IMUs are combined in [17,25]. Using particle-based optimization, in [24] they use 4 cameras and IMUs to sample from a manifold of constrained poses. Other works combine depth data with IMUs [6,47]. In [39] a CNN-based approach fuses information from 8 camera views and IMU data to regress pose. Since these approaches also use multiple static cameras, recordings are restricted to a fixed recording volume. A recent approach [16] also combines IMUs and 2D poses detected in one or two cameras but expects only a single person visible in the cameras and does not account for heading drift.

3D Pose Datasets. The most commonly used datasets for 3D human pose evaluation are HumanEva [32] and H3.6M [8], which provide synchronized video with MoCap. These datasets however are limited to indoor scenes, static backgrounds and limited clothing and activity variation. Recently, a dataset of single people, including outdoor scenes, has been introduced [19]. The approach uses commercial marker-less motion capture from multiple cameras (the accuracy of the marker-less MoCap software used is not reported). The sequences show variation in clothing, but again, since it uses a multi-camera setup, the activities are restricted to a fixed recording volume. Another recent dataset is TotalCapture [39], which features synchronized video, marker-based ground-truth poses and IMUs. In order to collect 3D poses in the wild, in [11] they ask users to pick "acceptable" results obtained using an automatic 3D pose estimation method. The problem is that it is difficult to judge a correct pose visually and it is not clear how accurate automatic methods are with in-the-wild images. We do not see our proposed dataset as an alternative to existing datasets; rather 3DPW complements existing ones with new, more challenging, sequences.

3D Human Pose. Several works lift 2D detections to 3D using learning or geometric reasoning [9,13,18,26,29,33–35,43–45,48,49]. These works aim at recovering the missing depth dimension in single-person images, whereas we focus on directly associating the 3D to the 2D poses in cluttered scenes. For multiple people, the work [1] infers the 3D poses using a tracking formulation that is based on short tracklets of 2D body parts. Recently 2D annotations have been leveraged to train networks for the task of 3D pose estimation [21,28,36,38,50]. Such works typically predict only stick figures or bone skeletons. Some approaches directly predict the parameters of a body model (SMPL) from a single image using 2D supervision [10,22,40]. Closer to our method are the works [2,11], which fit SMPL [14] to 2D detections. The optimization problem we solve, even though it integrates more sensors, is much more involved. Very few approaches tackle multiple-person 3D pose estimation [20,31]. 3DPW allows a quantitative evaluation of all these approaches for in-the-wild images.

3   Background

SMPL Body Model. We utilize the Skinned Multi-Person Linear (SMPL) body model [14], which is a statistical body model parameterized by identity-dependent shape parameters and the skeleton pose. We optimize the shape parameters to the person to be tracked by fitting SMPL to a 3D scan. Holding shape fixed, our aim is to recover the pose $\theta \in \mathbb{R}^{75}$, consisting of 6 parameters for global translation and rotation, and 23 relative rotations represented by axis-angle for each joint. We use the standard forward kinematics to map pose θ to the rigid transformation $\mathbf{G}^{GB}(\theta) : \mathbb{R}^{75} \rightarrow SE(3)$ of bone B. The bone transformation comprises the rotation and translation $\mathbf{G}^{GB} = \{\mathbf{R}^{GB}, \mathbf{t}^{GB}\}$ to map from the local bone coordinate frame F^B to the global SMPL frame F^G.

Coordinate Frames. Ultimately, we want to find the pose θ that produces bone orientations close to the IMU readings. IMUs measure the orientation of the local coordinate frame F^S (of the sensor box) relative to a global coordinate frame F^I. However, this frame F^I is different from the coordinate frame F^G of SMPL, see Fig. 5. The offset $\mathbf{G}^{GI} : F^I \rightarrow F^G$ between coordinate frames is typically assumed constant, and is calibrated at the beginning of a recording session – but that is not enough. We also need to know the offset $\mathbf{R}^{BS}$ from the sensor to the SMPL bone where it is placed. The SMPL bone orientation $\mathbf{R}^{GB}(\theta_0)$ can be obtained in the first frame assuming a known pose θ_0. Using this

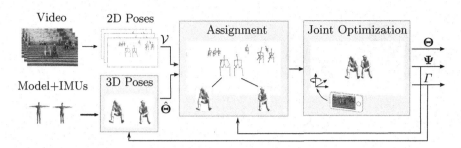

Fig. 3. Method overview: by fitting the SMPL body model to the measured IMU orientations we obtain initial 3D poses $\hat{\Theta}$. Given all 2D poses $\mathcal{V}$ detected in the images we search for a globally consistent assignment of 2D to 3D poses. We jointly optimize camera poses Ψ, heading angles Γ and 3D poses Θ with respect to associated IMU and image data. In a second iteration we feed back camera poses and heading angles which provides additional information further improving the assignment and tracking results.

bone orientation $\mathbf{R}^{GB}(\theta_0)$ and the raw IMU reading $\mathbf{R}^{IS}(0)$ in the first frame, we can trivially find the offset relating them as

$$\mathbf{R}^{BS} = \left(\mathbf{R}^{GB}(\theta_0)\right)^{-1} \mathbf{R}^{GI} \mathbf{R}^{IS}(0) \qquad (1)$$

where the raw IMU reading $\mathbf{R}^{IS}(0)$ needs to be mapped to the SMPL frame first using $\mathbf{R}^{GI}$. We assume that sensors do not move relative to the bones, and hence compute $\mathbf{R}^{BS}$ from the initial pose θ_0 and IMU orientations in the first frame.

Heading Drift. Unfortunately, the orientation measurements of the IMUs are deteriorated by magnetic disturbances, which introduce a time-varying rotational offset to $\mathbf{G}^{GI}$, also commonly known as heading error or heading drift. This drift ($\mathbf{G}^{I'I} : F^I \rightarrow F^{I'}$) shifts the original global inertial frame F^I to a disturbed inertial frame $F^{I'}$. What is even worse, the drift is different for every sensor. While most previous works ignore heading drift or treat it as noise, we model it explicitly and recover it as part of the optimization. Concretely, we model it as a one-parameter rotation $\mathbf{R}(\gamma) \in SO(3)$ about the vertical axis, where γ is the rotation angle. The collection of all angles, one per IMU sensor, is denoted as Γ. Since the heading error commonly varies slowly, we assume it is constant during a single tracking sequence. Recovering heading orientation was crucial in order to be able to perform long recordings without time-consuming re-calibration.

4   Video Inertial Poser (VIP)

In order to perform accurate 3D human motion capture with hand-held video and IMUs we perform three subsequent steps: initialization, pose candidate association and video-inertial fusion. Figure 3 provides an overview of the pipeline and we describe each step in more detail in the following.

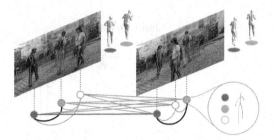
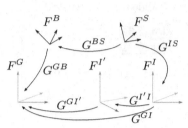

Fig. 4. Every 2D pose represents a node in the graph which can be assigned to a 3D pose corresponding to person 1 or 2 (represented by colors orange and blue). The graph has intra-frame edges (shown in black) activated if two nodes are assigned in a single frame and inter-frame edges (shown in blue and orange) activated for the same person across multiple frames. (Color figure online)

Fig. 5. Coordinate frames: Global tracking frame F^G, global inertial frame F^I, shifted inertial frame $F^{I'}$, bone coordinate frame F^B and IMU sensor coordinate frame F^S.

4.1 Initialization

We obtain initial 3D poses by fitting the SMPL bone orientations to the measured IMU orientations. For an IMU, the *measured bone orientation* $\hat{\mathbf{R}}^{GB}$ is given by

$$\hat{\mathbf{R}}^{GB} = \mathbf{R}^{GI'}\mathbf{R}^{I'I}(\gamma)\mathbf{R}^{IS}\left(\mathbf{R}^{BS}\right)^{-1}, \tag{2}$$

where $\mathbf{R}^{BS}$ represents the constant bone to sensor offset (Eq. (1)), and the concatenation of $\mathbf{R}^{GI'}$, $\mathbf{R}^{I'I}$ and $\mathbf{R}^{IS}$ describes the rotational map from sensor to global frame, see Fig. 5. We define the rotational discrepancy between actual bone orientation $\mathbf{R}^{GB}(\theta)$ and measured bone orientation $\hat{\mathbf{R}}^{GB}$ as

$$\mathbf{e}^{\text{rot}}(\theta) = \log\left(\mathbf{R}^{GB}(\theta)\left(\hat{\mathbf{R}}^{GB}\right)^{-1}\right)^{\vee}, \tag{3}$$

where the log-operation recovers the skew-symmetric matrix from the relative rotation between $\mathbf{R}^{GB}(\theta)$ and $\hat{\mathbf{R}}^{GB}$, and the $^{\vee}$-operator extracts the corresponding axis-angle parameters. We find the 3D initial poses at frame t that minimize the sum of discrepancies for all IMUs

$$\theta_t^* = \arg\min_{\theta} \frac{1}{N_s}\sum_{s=1}^{N_s} ||\mathbf{e}^{\text{rot}}_{s,t}(\theta_t)||^2 + w_{\text{prior}}E_{\text{prior}}(\theta_t), \tag{4}$$

where $E_{\text{prior}}(\theta)$ is a pose prior weighted by w_{prior}. $E_{\text{prior}}(\theta)$ is chosen as defined in [42], enforcing θ to remain close to a multivariate Gaussian distribution of model poses and to stay within joint limits. During the first iteration, we have no information about the heading angles γ. To initialize them, we use the IMU placement as a proxy to know how local sensor axes are aligned with respect to the body. This gives us a rough estimate of the sensor to bone offset $\hat{\mathbf{R}}^{BS}$, which we use to compute initial heading angles by solving Eq. (1) for γ.

In the following, we will refer to this tracking approach simply as the inertial tracker (IT), which outputs initial 3D pose candidates $\theta_{t,l}^*$ for every tracked person l. Such initial 3D poses need to be associated with 2D detections in the video in order to effectively fuse the data – this poses a challenging assignment problem.

4.2 Pose Candidate Assignment

Using the CNN method of Cao *et al.* [4], we obtain 2D pose detections v, which comprise the image coordinates of $N_{\text{joints}} = 18$ landmarks along with corresponding confidence scores. In order to associate each 2D pose v to a 3D pose candidate, we create an undirected weighted graph $G = (\mathcal{V}, \mathcal{E}, c)$, with $\mathcal{V}$ comprising all detected 2D poses in a recording sequence. An assignment hypothesis, denoted as $\mathcal{H}(l, v) = (\theta_t^l, v)$, links the 3D pose θ_t^l of person $l \in \{1, \ldots, P\}$ to the 2D pose $v \in \mathcal{V}$ in the same frame t. We introduce indicator variables x_v^l, which take value 1 if hypothesis $\mathcal{H}(l, v)$ is selected, and 0 otherwise. The basic idea is to assign costs to each hypothesis, and select the assignments for the sequence that minimize the total costs. We cast the selection problem as a graph labeling problem by minimizing the following objective

$$\underset{x \in \mathcal{F} \cap \{0,1\}^{|\mathcal{V}|P}}{\arg\min} \sum_{\substack{v \in \mathcal{V} \\ l \in \{1,\ldots,P\}}} c_v^l x_v^l + \sum_{\substack{\{v,v'\} \in \mathcal{E} \\ l,l' \in \{1,\ldots,P\}}} c_{v,v'}^{l,l'} \, x_v^l x_{v'}^{l'}, \tag{5}$$

where the feasibility set $\mathcal{F}$ is subject to:

$$\text{(a)} \sum_{l=1}^{P} x_v^l \leq 1 \quad \forall v \in \mathcal{V}; \qquad \text{(b)} \sum_{v \in \mathcal{V}_t} x_v^l \leq 1 \quad \forall t, \forall l \in \{1,\ldots,P\}. \tag{6}$$

The edge set $\mathcal{E}$ contains all pairs of 2D poses $\{v, v'\}$ that are considered for the assignment decision. Eq. (6)(a) ensures that a 2D pose v is assigned to at most 1 person, and Eq. (6)(b) ensures that each person is assigned to at most one of the 2D pose detections $v \in \mathcal{V}_t \subset \mathcal{V}$ in frame t. The objective in (5) consists of unary costs c_v^l measuring 2D to 3D consistency, and pairwise costs $c_{v,v'}^{l,l'}$ measuring consistency across different hypothesis. Our formulation automatically outputs a globally consistent assignment and does not require manual initialization.

Next we describe the unaries and pairwise potentials – specifically, we introduce consistency features which are mapped to the costs $c_v^l, c_{v,v'}^{l,l'}$ of the objective in (5) via logistic regression. Details about the training process are described in Sect. 5.1. Figure 4 visualizes the graph for two example frames and also illustrates the corresponding labeling solution.

Unary Costs. To measure 2D to 3D consistency of a hypothesis $\mathcal{H} := \mathcal{H}(l, v)$, we obtain a *hypothesis camera* $\mathbf{M}_{\mathcal{H}}$ by minimizing the re-projection error between 3D landmarks of θ_t^l and the 2D detected ones v. The per landmark re-projection error, denoted by $\mathbf{e}_{\text{img},k}(\mathcal{H}, \mathbf{M}_\mathcal{H})$, is weighted by the confidence scores w_k. The consistency is then measured as the average of all weighted residuals $\mathbf{e}_{\text{img},k}(\mathcal{H}, \mathbf{M}_\mathcal{H})$, denoted by $\mathbf{e}_{\text{img}}(\mathcal{H}, \mathbf{M}_\mathcal{H})$. This measure depends heavily on the distance to the camera. To balance it, we scale it by the average 3D joint distance to the camera center $\mathbf{e}_{\text{cam}}(\mathbf{M}_\mathcal{H})$ and obtain the feature:

$$f_{\text{un}}(\mathcal{H}) = \mathbf{e}_{\text{img}}(\mathcal{H}, \mathbf{M}_\mathcal{H})\mathbf{e}_{\text{cam}}(\mathcal{H}, \mathbf{M}_\mathcal{H}). \tag{7}$$

Pairwise Costs. We define features to measure the consistency of two hypothesis $\mathcal{H} = (\theta_t^l, v)$ and $\mathcal{H}' = (\theta_{t'}^{l'}, v')$ in frames t and t'. In particular, two kinds of edges connect hypothesis: *(a) inter-frame*, and *(b) intra-frame*.

(a) Inter-frame: Consider two hypothesis $\mathcal{H}, \mathcal{H}'$ corresponding to the *same person* and separated by fewer than 30 frames. Then, the respective root joint position $r(\theta_t^l)$ and orientation $\mathbf{R}(\theta_t^l)$ in camera hypothesis $(\mathbf{M}_\mathcal{H})$ coordinates should not vary too much. This variation depends on the temporal distance $|t - t'|$. Consequently, we introduce the following features

$$f_{\text{trans}}(\mathcal{H}, \mathcal{H}') = ||\mathbf{M}_\mathcal{H} r(\theta_t^l) - \mathbf{M}_{\mathcal{H}'} r(\theta_{t'}^{l'})||^2, \tag{8}$$

$$f_{\text{ori}}(\mathcal{H}, \mathcal{H}') = \left|\left| \log\left((\mathbf{R}_\mathcal{H}\mathbf{R}(\theta_t^l))^{-1}(\mathbf{R}_{\mathcal{H}'}\mathbf{R}(\theta_{t'}^{l'})) \right)^\vee \right|\right|^2, \tag{9}$$

$$f_{\text{time}}(\mathcal{H}, \mathcal{H}') = ||t - t'||^2, \tag{10}$$

where f_{trans} and f_{ori} measure root joint translation and orientation consistency, and f_{time} is a feature to accommodate for temporal distance. Here, $\mathbf{R}_\mathcal{H}$ is the rotational part of $\mathbf{M}_\mathcal{H}$, and f_{rot} computes the geodesic distance between $\mathbf{R}(\theta_t^l)$ and $\mathbf{R}(\theta_{t'}^{l'})$, similar to Eq. (3).

(b) Intra-frame: Now consider two hypothesis $\mathcal{H}, \mathcal{H}'$ for *different persons* in the same frame. The resulting camera hypothesis centers should be consistent. To measure coherency, we compute a meta-camera hypothesis $\mathbf{M}_{\underline{\mathcal{H}}}$ by minimizing the re-projection error of both hypothesis at the same time. Then the feature

$$f_{\text{intra}}(\mathcal{H}, \underline{\mathcal{H}}) = ||\mathbf{c}(\theta_t^l, \mathbf{M}_\mathcal{H}) - \mathbf{c}(\theta_t^l, \mathbf{M}_{\underline{\mathcal{H}}})||^2 \tag{11}$$

measures the camera $\mathbf{c}(\theta_t^l, \mathbf{M}_\mathcal{H})$ to meta-camera center $\mathbf{c}(\theta_t^l, \mathbf{M}_{\underline{\mathcal{H}}})$ difference. Accordingly, we also use the feature $f_{\text{intra}}(\mathcal{H}', \underline{\mathcal{H}})$ for intra-frame edges.

Graph Optimization. Although the presented graph labeling problem in (5) is NP-Hard, it can be solved efficiently in practice [7,12]. We use the binary LP solver Gurobi [5] by applying it to the linearized formulation of (5), where we replace each product $x_v^l x_{v'}^{l'}$ by a binary auxiliary variable $y_{v,v'}^{l,l'}$ and add corresponding constraints such that $x_v^l x_{v'}^{l'} = y_{v,v'}^{l,l'}$ for all $v, v' \in \mathcal{V}$, for all $l, l' \in \{1, \ldots, P\}$.

4.3   Video-Inertial Data Fusion

Once the assignment problem is solved we can utilize the associated 2D poses to jointly optimize model poses, camera poses and heading angles by minimizing the following energy:

$$E(\mathbf{\Theta}, \mathbf{\Psi}, \Gamma) = E_{\mathrm{ori}}(\mathbf{\Theta}, \Gamma) + w_{\mathrm{acc}} E_{\mathrm{acc}}(\mathbf{\Theta}, \Gamma) + \\ w_{\mathrm{img}} E_{\mathrm{img}}(\mathbf{\Theta}, \mathbf{\Psi}) + w_{\mathrm{prior}} E_{\mathrm{prior}}(\mathbf{\Theta}), \tag{12}$$

where $\mathbf{\Theta}$ is a vector containing the pose parameters for each actor and frame, Γ is the vector of IMU heading correction angles and $\mathbf{\Psi}$ contains the camera poses for each frame. $E_{\mathrm{ori}}(\mathbf{\Theta}, \Gamma)$, $E_{\mathrm{acc}}(\mathbf{\Theta}, \Gamma)$ and $E_{\mathrm{img}}(\mathbf{\Theta}, \mathbf{\Psi})$ are energy terms related to IMU orientations, IMU accelerations and image information, respectively. $E_{\mathrm{prior}}(\mathbf{\Theta})$ is an energy term related to pose priors. Finally, every term is weighted by a corresponding weight w.

Orientation Term. The orientation term simply extends Eq. (4) by considering all frames N_T of a sequence according to

$$E_{\mathrm{ori}}(\mathbf{\Theta}, \Gamma) = \frac{1}{N_T N_s} \sum_{t=1}^{N_T} \sum_{s=1}^{N_s} ||\mathbf{e}_{s,t}^{\mathrm{rot}}(\theta_t, \gamma_s)||^2. \tag{13}$$

This term also includes the camera IMU, where the camera rotation mapping from camera coordinate system F^C to the global coordinate frame F^G is given by the inverse rotational part of the camera pose M.

Acceleration Term. The acceleration term enforces consistency of the measured IMU acceleration and the acceleration of the corresponding model vertex to which the IMU is attached. The IMU acceleration in world coordinates for sensor s at time t is given by

$$\mathbf{a}_{s,t}^G(\gamma) = \mathbf{R}^{GI'} \mathbf{R}^{I'I}(\gamma_s) \mathbf{R}^{IS} \mathbf{a}_{s,t}^S - \mathbf{g}^G, \tag{14}$$

where $\mathbf{g}^G$ is gravity in global coordinates. The corresponding SMPL vertex acceleration $\hat{\mathbf{a}}(\theta_t)$ is approximated by finite differences. Finally, the acceleration term contains the quadratic norm of the deviation of measured and estimated acceleration for all N_S IMUs over all frames N_T:

$$E_{\mathrm{acc}}(\mathbf{\Theta}, \Gamma) = \frac{1}{N_T N_S} \sum_{t=1}^{N_T} \sum_{s=1}^{N_S} ||\hat{\mathbf{a}}_s(\theta_t) - \mathbf{a}_{s,t}(\gamma_s)||^2. \tag{15}$$

This term also contains the measured acceleration of the camera IMU and the corresponding acceleration of the camera center in global coordinates.

Image Term. The image term simply accumulates the re-projection error over all N_{joints} landmarks and all frames N_T according to

$$E_{\text{img}}(\mathbf{\Theta}, \mathbf{\Psi}) = \frac{1}{N_T N_{\text{coco}}} \sum_{t=1}^{N_T} \sum_{i=k}^{N_{\text{joints}}} w_k \|\mathbf{e}_{\text{img},k}(\theta_t, \mathbf{M}_t)\|^2, \qquad (16)$$

where w_k is the confidence score associated with a landmark.

Prior Term. The prior term is the same as in Eq. (4), now accumulated for all poses Θ and scaled by the number of poses N_Θ.

4.4 Optimization

In order to solve the optimization problems related to obtaining initial 3D poses in Eq. (4), obtaining camera poses to minimize re-projection error and to jointly optimize all variables in Eq. (12), we apply gradient-based Levenberg-Marquardt.

5 Results

To validate our approach quantitatively (Sects. 5.1 and 5.2), we use the recent TotalCapture [39] dataset, which is the only one including IMU data and video synchronized with ground-truth. In Sect. 5.3 we then provide details of the newly recorded 3DPW dataset, demonstrate 3D pose reconstruction of VIP in challenging scenes, and evaluate the accuracy of automatic 2D to 3D pose assignment in multiple-person scenes.

5.1 Tracker Parameters

Pose Assignment: In the graph G, edges $e \in \mathcal{E}$ are created between any two nodes that are at most 30 frames apart. The weights mapping from features to costs are learned using 5 sequences from 3DPW dataset, which have been manually labeled for this purpose. Given the features $\mathbf{f}$ defined in Sect. 4.2 and learned weights α from logistic regression, we turn features into costs via $c = -\langle \mathbf{f}, \alpha \rangle$, making the optimization problem (5) probabilistically motivated [37].

Video Inertial Fusion: Different weighting parameters in Eq. (4) and Eq. (12) produce good results as long as they are balanced. However, rather than setting them by hand, we used Bayesian Optimization [3] in the proposed training set of TotalCapture (seen subjects). The values found are $w_{\text{acc}} = 0.2$, $w_{\text{img}} = 0.0001$ and $w_{\text{prior}} = 0.006$ and are kept fixed for all experiments. Note, that these are very few parameters and therefore, there is very little risk of over-fitting, which is also reflected in the results.

Table 1. Mean Joint Position Error (MPJPE) in mm and Mean Per Joint Angular Error (MPJAE) in degrees evaluated on TotalCapture.

Approach	[39]	[16]	IT	VIP-2D	VIP-Cam	VIP-IMU6	VIP-IT	VIP
MPJPE	70.0	(62)	55.0	15.1	25.3	39.6	28.2	**26.0**
MPJAE	-	-	16.9	10.1	12.1	15.3	12.0	**12.1**

5.2 Tracking Accuracy

We quantitatively evaluate tracking accuracy on the TotalCapture dataset. The dataset consists of 5 subjects performing several activities such as walking, acting, range of motions and freestyle motions – which are recorded using 8 calibrated, static RGB-cameras and 13 IMUs attached to head, sternum, waist, upper arms, lower arms, upper legs, lower legs and feet. Ground-truth poses are obtained using a marker-baser motion capture system. All data is synchronized and operates at a framerate of 60 Hz. The ground truth poses are provided as joint positions, which do not contain information about pronation and supination angles; i.e. rotations about the bone's long axis. To obtain full degree of freedom pose, we fit the SMPL model to the raw ground-truth markers using a method similar to [15].

Error Metrics: We report: Mean Per Joint Position Error (MPJPE) and Mean Per Joint Angular Error (MPJAE). MPJPE is the average Euclidean distance between ground-truth and estimated joint positions of hips, knees, ankles, neck, head, shoulders, elbows and wrists; MPJAE is the average geodesic distance between ground-truth and estimated joint orientations for hips, knees, neck, shoulders and elbows. In order to evaluate pose accuracy independently of absolute camera position and orientation, we align our estimates with the ground-truth. This is standard practice in existing benchmarks [8]. Thus, in our case MPJPE is a measure of pose accuracy independent of global position and orientation.

Results: Our tracking results on TotalCapture are summarized in Table 1. We used only 1 camera and the 13 IMUs provided. The cameras in TotalCapture are rigidly mounted to the building and are not equipped with an IMU – hence we assumed a static camera with *unknown* pose. VIP achieves a remarkably low average MPJPE of 26 mm and a MPJAE of only 12.1°.

Comparisons to State-of-the-Art: We outperform the learning-based approach introduced in the TotalCapture dataset [39] by 44 mm – the approach uses *all 8 cameras* and fuses IMU data with a probabilistic visual hull. We also outperform [16], who report a mean MPJPE of 62 mm using 8 cameras and all 13 IMUs. Admittedly, it is difficult to compare approaches, since [39] and [16] process the data in a frame-by-frame manner which is an advantage w.r.t. VIP, which jointly optimizes over all frames simultaneously. However, VIP uses only a single camera with unknown pose whereas the *competitors use 8 fully calibrated*

Fig. 6. We show example results obtained using VIP for some challenging activities. With VIP we get accurate 3D poses aligning well with the images using the estimated camera poses.

cameras. To understand better the influence of components of VIP we also report the tracking accuracy for five tracker variants in Table 1.

Comparison to IMU Only: The Inertial tracker (IT) corresponds to the single frame approach of Sect. 4.1. It uses only raw IMU orientations and is the initialization for VIP. Over all sequences, IT achieves a MPJPE of 55 mm. VIP decreases this error by more than 50%. This demonstrates the usefulness of fusing image information and optimizing heading angles.

Heading Drift and Misalignments: We report results of VIP-IT to demonstrate the influence of optimizing heading angles, and sensor-to-bone misalignments originating from an inaccurate initial pose. VIP-IT is identical to IT, but uses the heading angles and initial pose obtained with VIP. VIP-IT is only slightly less accurate than VIP validating the importance of inferring drift and accurate initial pose. More evaluations are shown in the supplementary material.

Robustness to 2D Pose Accuracy: VIP-2D is identical to the VIP but utilizes ground-truth 2D poses obtained by projecting ground-truth joint positions to the images. VIP-2D achieves a MPJPE of 15.1 mm which indicates how much VIP can improve if 2D pose estimation methods keep improving.

Robustness to Camera Pose: VIP-Cam is also almost identical to VIP, but uses the ground-truth camera pose instead of estimating it. The MPJPE of VIP-Cam is 25.3 mm, which is only 0.7 mm better compared to VIP.

Fewer Sensors: We report the error of VIP using 6 IMUs similar to [42], denoted as VIP-IMU6. The combination of only 6 IMUs and 2D pose information achieves a MPJPE of 39.6 mm, which is 13.6 mm higher than VIP-13 IMUs but still very accurate. This demonstrates our approach could be used for applications where a minimal number of sensors is required.

This quantitative evaluation demonstrates the accuracy of VIP. Ideally, we would evaluate VIP quantitatively also in challenging scenes, like the ones in 3DPW. However, there exists no dataset with a comparable setting and ground-truth, which was one of the main motivations of this work.

Fig. 7. We show several example frames of sequences in the 3DPW. The dataset contains large variations in person identity, clothing and activities. For a couple of cases we also show animated, textured SMPL body models.

5.3   3D Poses in the Wild Dataset

VIP allowed us to achieve the second goal of this work: recording a dataset with accurate 3D pose in challenging outdoor scenes with a moving camera. A hand-held smartphone camera was used to record one or two IMU-equipped actors performing various activities such as shopping, doing sports, hugging, discussing, capturing selfies, riding bus, playing guitar, relaxing. The dataset includes 60 sequences, more than 51,000 frames and 7 actors in a total of 18 clothing styles. We also scanned subjects and non-rigidly fitted SMPL to obtain 3D models similar to [27,46]. For single subject tracking, we attached 17 IMUs to all major bone segments. We used 9–10 IMUs per person to simultaneously track up to 2 subjects. During all recordings one additional IMU was attached to the smartphone. Video and inertial data was automatically synchronized by a clapping motion at the beginning of a sequence as in [24]. For every sequence, the subjects were asked to start in an upright pose with closed arms. In Fig. 6 we show tracking results illustrating the 3D model alignment with the images. Figure 7 shows more tracking results, where we animated the 3D models with the reconstructed poses. 3DPW is the most challenging dataset (with 3D pose annotation) for state-of-the-art 3D pose estimation methods as evidenced by the results reported in the supplemental material.

Assignment Accuracy: In comparison to TotalCapture, the additional challenges in 3DPW originate from multiple people in the scene. Hence, we assessed the accuracy of our automatic assignment of 2D poses to 3D poses using manually labelled 2D pose candidate IDs. VIP achieves an assignment precision of 99.3% and a recall rate of 92.2% demonstrating the method correctly identifies the tracked persons for the vast majority of frames. This is a strong indication that VIP achieves a 3D pose accuracy on 3DPW comparable to the MPJPE of 26 mm reported for TotalCapture.

6   Conclusions

Combining IMUs and a moving camera, we introduced the first method that can robustly recover pose in challenging scenes. The main challenges we addressed are: person identification and tracking in cluttered scenes, and joint recovery of 3D pose for 2 subjects, camera and IMU heading drift. We combined discrete optimization to find associations, with continuous optimization to effectively fuse the sensor information. Using our method, we collected the *3D Poses in the Wild* dataset, including challenging sequences with accurate 3D poses that we make available for research purposes. With VIP it is possible to record people in natural video easily and we plan to keep adding to the dataset. We anticipate the proposed dataset will provide the means to quantitatively evaluate monocular methods in difficult scenes and stimulate new research in this area.

Acknowledgements. We thank Jorge Márquez, Senya Polikovsky, Matvey Safroshkin and Andrea Keller for the technical support.

References

1. Andriluka, M., Roth, S., Schiele, B.: Monocular 3D pose estimation and tracking by detection. In: The IEEE Conference on Computer Vision and Pattern Recognition (CVPR), pp. 623–630 (2010)
2. Bogo, F., Kanazawa, A., Lassner, C., Gehler, P., Romero, J., Black, M.J.: Keep it SMPL: automatic estimation of 3D human pose and shape from a single image. In: Leibe, B., Matas, J., Sebe, N., Welling, M. (eds.) ECCV 2016. LNCS, vol. 9909, pp. 561–578. Springer, Cham (2016). https://doi.org/10.1007/978-3-319-46454-1_34
3. Bull, A.D.: Convergence rates of efficient global optimization algorithms. J. Mach. Learn. Res. **12**(Oct), 2879–2904 (2011)
4. Cao, Z., Simon, T., Wei, S.E., Sheikh, Y.: Realtime multi-person 2D pose estimation using part affinity fields. In: The IEEE Conference on Computer Vision and Pattern Recognition (CVPR) (2017)
5. Gurobi Optimization Inc.: Gurobi Optimizer Reference Manual (2016)
6. Helten, T., Baak, A., Bharaj, G., Muller, M., Seidel, H.P., Theobalt, C.: Personalization and evaluation of a real-time depth-based full body tracker. In: 3D Vision (3DV) (2013)
7. Henschel, R., Leal-Taixé, L., Cremers, D., Rosenhahn, B.: Fusion of head and full-body detectors for multi-object tracking. In: Computer Vision and Pattern Recognition Workshops (CVPRW) (2018)
8. Ionescu, C., Papava, D., Olaru, V., Sminchisescu, C.: Human3.6M: large scale datasets and predictive methods for 3D human sensing in natural environments. IEEE Trans. Pattern Anal. Mach. Intell. (TPAMI) **36**(7), 1325–1339 (2014)
9. Jahangiri, E., Yuille, A.L.: Generating multiple diverse hypotheses for human 3D pose consistent with 2D joint detections. In: IEEE International Conference on Computer Vision (ICCV) Workshops (PeopleCap) (2017)

10. Kanazawa, A., Black, M.J., Jacobs, D.W., Malik, J.: End-to-end recovery of human shape and pose. In: The IEEE Conference on Computer Vision and Pattern Recognition (CVPR) (2018)
11. Lassner, C., Romero, J., Kiefel, M., Bogo, F., Black, M.J., Gehler, P.V.: Unite the people: closing the loop between 3D and 2D human representations. In: The IEEE Conference on Computer Vision and Pattern Recognition (CVPR), vol. 2 (2017)
12. Levinkov, E., et al.: Joint graph decomposition & node labeling: problem, algorithms, applications. In: CVPR, vol. 7. IEEE (2017)
13. Li, S., Zhang, W., Chan, A.B.: Maximum-margin structured learning with deep networks for 3D human pose estimation. In: IEEE International Conference on Computer Vision (ICCV), pp. 2848–2856 (2015)
14. Loper, M., Mahmood, N., Romero, J., Pons-Moll, G., Black, M.J.: SMPL: a skinned multi-person linear model. ACM Trans. Graph. **34**(6), 248:1–248:16 (2015)
15. Loper, M.M., Mahmood, N., Black, M.J.: MoSh: motion and shape capture from sparse markers. ACM Trans. Graph. (Proc. SIGGRAPH Asia) **33**(6), 220:1–220:13 (2014)
16. Malleson, C., Volino, M., Gilbert, A., Trumble, M., Collomosse, J., Hilton, A.: Real-time full-body motion capture from video and IMUs. In: 2017 Fifth International Conference on 3D Vision (3DV) (2017)
17. von Marcard, T., Pons-Moll, G., Rosenhahn, B.: Human pose estimation from video and IMUs. IEEE Trans. Pattern Anal. Mach. Intell. (TPAMI) **38**(8), 1533–1547 (2016)
18. Martinez, J., Hossain, R., Romero, J., Little, J.J.: A simple yet effective baseline for 3D human pose estimation. In: IEEE International Conference on Computer Vision (ICCV) (2017)
19. Mehta, D., et al.: Monocular 3D human pose estimation in the wild using improved CNN supervision. In: 3D Vision (3DV). IEEE (2017)
20. Mehta, D., et al.: Single-shot multi-person 3D body pose estimation from monocular RGB input. arXiv preprint arXiv:1712.03453 (2017)
21. Mehta, D., et al.: VNect: real-time 3D human pose estimation with a single RGB camera. ACM Trans. Graph. (TOG) **36**(4), 44 (2017)
22. Pavlakos, G., Zhu, L., Zhou, X., Daniilidis, K.: Learning to estimate 3D human pose and shape from a single color image. In: Proceedings of the IEEE Conference on Computer Vision and Pattern Recognition (2018)
23. Pishchulin, L., et al.: DeepCut: joint subset partition and labeling for multi person pose estimation. In: The IEEE Conference on Computer Vision and Pattern Recognition (CVPR) (2016)
24. Pons-Moll, G., et al.: Outdoor human motion capture using inverse kinematics and von mises-fisher sampling. In: Proceedings of the 2011 International Conference on Computer Vision (ICCV), pp. 1243–1250 (2011)
25. Pons-Moll, G., Baak, A., Helten, T., Müller, M., Seidel, H.P., Rosenhahn, B.: Multisensor-fusion for 3D full-body human motion capture. In: The IEEE Conference on Computer Vision and Pattern Recognition (CVPR), pp. 663–670 (2010)
26. Pons-Moll, G., Fleet, D.J., Rosenhahn, B.: Posebits for monocular human pose estimation. In: IEEE Conference on Computer Vision and Pattern Recognition (CVPR), pp. 2337–2344 (2014)
27. Pons-Moll, G., Pujades, S., Hu, S., Black, M.: ClothCap: seamless 4D clothing capture and retargeting. ACM Trans. Graph. (Proc. SIGGRAPH) **36**(4), 73 (2017)
28. Popa, A.I., Zanfir, M., Sminchisescu, C.: Deep multitask architecture for integrated 2D and 3D human sensing. In: The IEEE Conference on Computer Vision and Pattern Recognition (CVPR) (2017)

29. Rhodin, H., et al.: Learning monocular 3D human pose estimation from multi-view images. In: CVPR (2018)
30. Roetenberg, D., Luinge, H., Slycke, P.: Moven: full 6DOF human motion tracking using miniature inertial sensors. Xsen Technologies, December 2007
31. Rogez, G., Weinzaepfel, P., Schmid, C.: LCR-Net++: multi-person 2D and 3D pose detection in natural images. arXiv preprint arXiv:1803.00455 (2018)
32. Sigal, L., Balan, A.O., Black, M.J.: Humaneva: synchronized video and motion capture dataset and baseline algorithm for evaluation of articulated human motion. Int. J. Comput. Vis. (IJCV) **87**(1–2), 4 (2010)
33. Simo-Serra, E., Quattoni, A., Torras, C., Moreno-Noguer, F.: A joint model for 2D and 3D pose estimation from a single image. In: Conference on Computer Vision and Pattern Recognition (CVPR), pp. 3634–3641 (2013)
34. Simo-Serra, E., Ramisa, A., Alenyà, G., Torras, C., Moreno-Noguer, F.: Single image 3D human pose estimation from noisy observations. In: The IEEE Conference on Computer Vision and Pattern Recognition (CVPR), pp. 2673–2680 (2012)
35. Sminchisescu, C., Triggs, B.: Kinematic jump processes for monocular 3D human tracking. In: The IEEE Conference on Computer Vision and Pattern Recognition (CVPR) (2003)
36. Sun, X., Shang, J., Liang, S., Wei, Y.: Compositional human pose regression. arXiv preprint arXiv:1704.00159 (2017)
37. Tang, S., Andres, B., Andriluka, M., Schiele, B.: Subgraph decomposition for multi-target tracking. In: The IEEE Conference on Computer Vision and Pattern Recognition (CVPR), pp. 5033–5041 (2015)
38. Tome, D., Russell, C., Agapito, L.: Lifting from the deep: convolutional 3D pose estimation from a single image. In: The IEEE Conference on Computer Vision and Pattern Recognition (CVPR) (2017)
39. Trumble, M., Gilbert, A., Malleson, C., Hilton, A., Collomosse, J.: Total capture: 3D human pose estimation fusing video and inertial sensors. In: Proceedings of 28th British Machine Vision Conference, pp. 1–13 (2017)
40. Tung, H.Y., Tung, H.W., Yumer, E., Fragkiadaki, K.: Self-supervised learning of motion capture. In: NIPS (2017)
41. Vlasic, D., et al.: Practical motion capture in everyday surroundings. ACM Trans. Graph. (TOG) **26**(3), 35 (2007)
42. von Marcard, T., Rosenhahn, B., Black, M., Pons-Moll, G.: Sparse inertial poser: automatic 3D human pose estimation from sparse IMUs. In: Computer Graphics Forum, Proceedings of the 38th Annual Conference of the European Association for Computer Graphics (Eurographics), vol. 36, no. 2, pp. 349–360 (2017)
43. Wandt, B., Ackermann, H., Rosenhahn, B.: 3D reconstruction of human motion from monocular image sequences. Trans. Pattern Anal. Mach. Intell. (TPAMI) **38**(8), 1505–1516 (2016)
44. Wang, C., Wang, Y., Lin, Z., Yuille, A.L., Gao, W.: Robust estimation of 3D human poses from a single image. In: IEEE Conference on Computer Vision and Pattern Recognition (CVPR), pp. 2361–2368 (2014)
45. Zell, P., Wandt, B., Rosenhahn, B.: Joint 3D human motion capture and physical analysis from monocular videos. In: The IEEE Conference on Computer Vision and Pattern Recognition Workshops (CVPRW) (2017)
46. Zhang, C., Pujades, S., Black, M., Pons-Moll, G.: Detailed, accurate, human shape estimation from clothed 3D scan sequences. In: IEEE Conference on Computer Vision and Pattern Recognition (CVPR) (2017)

47. Zheng, Z., et al.: HybridFusion: real-time performance capture using a single depth sensor and sparse IMUs. In: European Conference on Computer Vision (ECCV) (2018)

48. Zhou, F., De la Torre, F.: Spatio-temporal matching for human detection in video. In: Fleet, D., Pajdla, T., Schiele, B., Tuytelaars, T. (eds.) ECCV 2014. LNCS, vol. 8694, pp. 62–77. Springer, Cham (2014). https://doi.org/10.1007/978-3-319-10599-4_5

49. Zhou, X., Leonardos, S., Hu, X., Daniilidis, K.: 3D shape estimation from 2D landmarks: a convex relaxation approach. In: IEEE Conference on Computer Vision and Pattern Recognition (CVPR), pp. 4447–4455 (2015)

50. Zhou, X., Huang, Q., Sun, X., Xue, X., Wei, Y.: Towards 3D human pose estimation in the wild: a weakly-supervised approach. In: The IEEE Conference on Computer Vision and Pattern Recognition (CVPR), pp. 398–407 (2017)

Deep Bilevel Learning

Simon Jenni[(✉)] and Paolo Favaro

University of Bern, Bern, Switzerland
{jenni,favaro}@inf.unibe.ch

Abstract. We present a novel regularization approach to train neural networks that enjoys better generalization and test error than standard stochastic gradient descent. Our approach is based on the principles of cross-validation, where a validation set is used to limit the model overfitting. We formulate such principles as a bilevel optimization problem. This formulation allows us to define the optimization of a cost on the validation set subject to another optimization on the training set. The overfitting is controlled by introducing weights on each mini-batch in the training set and by choosing their values so that they minimize the error on the validation set. In practice, these weights define mini-batch learning rates in a gradient descent update equation that favor gradients with better generalization capabilities. Because of its simplicity, this approach can be integrated with other regularization methods and training schemes. We evaluate extensively our proposed algorithm on several neural network architectures and datasets, and find that it consistently improves the generalization of the model, especially when labels are noisy.

Keywords: Bilevel optimization · Regularization · Generalization
Neural networks · Noisy labels

1 Introduction

A core objective in machine learning is to build models that generalize well, *i.e.*, that have the ability to perform well on new unseen data. A common strategy to achieve generalization is to employ regularization, which is a way to incorporate additional information about the space of suitable models. This, in principle, prevents the estimated model from overfitting the training data. However, recent work [36] shows that current regularization methods applied to neural networks do not work according to conventional wisdom. In fact, it has been shown that neural networks can learn to map data samples to arbitrary labels despite using regularization techniques such as weight decay, dropout, and data augmentation. While the lone model architecture of a neural network seems to have an implicit regularizing effect [33], experiments show that it can overfit on any dataset, given enough training time. This poses a limitation to the performance of any trained neural network, especially when labels are partially noisy.

In this paper we introduce a novel learning framework that reduces overfitting by formulating training as a *bilevel optimization* problem [5,6]. Although

© Springer Nature Switzerland AG 2018
V. Ferrari et al. (Eds.): ECCV 2018, LNCS 11214, pp. 632–648, 2018.
https://doi.org/10.1007/978-3-030-01249-6_38

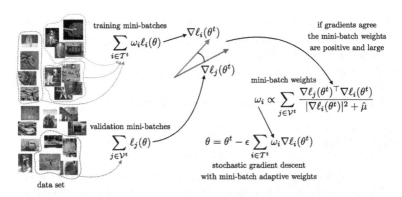

training mini-batches

$$\sum_{i \in \mathcal{T}^t} \omega_i \ell_i(\theta)$$

$\nabla \ell_i(\theta^t)$

$\nabla \ell_j(\theta^t)$

if gradients agree
the mini-batch weights
are positive and large

mini-batch weights

$$\omega_i \propto \sum_{j \in \mathcal{V}^t} \frac{\nabla \ell_j(\theta^t)^\top \nabla \ell_i(\theta^t)}{|\nabla \ell_i(\theta^t)|^2 + \hat{\mu}}$$

validation mini-batches

$$\sum_{j \in \mathcal{V}^t} \ell_j(\theta)$$

$$\theta = \theta^t - \epsilon \sum_{i \in \mathcal{T}^t} \omega_i \nabla \ell_i(\theta^t)$$

stochastic gradient descent
with mini-batch adaptive weights

data set

Fig. 1. The training procedure of our bilevel formulation. At each iteration we sample mini-batches from the data set, which we split into a validation and a training set. The validation is used to define the weights of the loss gradient used in the stochastic gradient descent to update the model parameters. If the gradients of the training set and those of the validation set agree, then the weights are large and positive. Vice versa, if they disagree the weights might be zero or negative.

the mathematical formulation of bilevel optimization is often involved, our final algorithm is a quite straightforward modification of the current training methods. Bilevel optimization differs from the conventional one in that one of the constraints is also an optimization problem. The main objective function is called the *upper-level* optimization task and the optimization problem in the set of constraints is called the *lower-level* optimization task. In our formulation, the lower-level problem is a model parameter optimization on samples from the *training set*, while the upper-level problem works as a performance evaluation on samples from a separate *validation set*. The optimal model is thus the one that is trained on one dataset, but performs well on a different one, a property that closely follows the definition of generalization.

In the optimization procedure we introduce a scalar weight for each sample mini-batch. The purpose of these variables is to find the linear combination of a subset of mini-batches from the training set that can best approximate the validation set error. They can also be seen as a way to: (1) discard noisy samples and (2) adjust the parameter optimization path. Finally, these weights can also be interpreted as hyper-parameters. Hence, bilevel optimization can be seen as an integrated way to continuously optimize for both the model parameters and the hyper-parameters as done in cross-validation.

In its general form, bilevel optimization is known to present computational challenges. To address these challenges, we propose to approximate the loss objectives at every iteration with quadratic functions. These approximations result in closed-form solutions that resemble the well-known stochastic gradient descent (SGD) update rules. Essentially, our bilevel optimization computes loss gradients on the training set and then prescribes adjustments to the learning rates of the SGD iteration so that the updated parameters perform well on the validation set. As we will show later, these adjustments depend on how well the gradients computed on the training set "agree" with the gradients computed on the validation set (see Fig. 1).

Our method can be easily integrated in current training procedures for neural networks and our experiments show that it yields models with better generalization on several network architectures and datasets.

2   Prior Work

We give an overview of prior work relating to three main aspects of the paper: (1) Generalization properties of deep networks and how learning algorithms affect them, (2) memorization of corrupt labels as a special case of overfitting and (3) bilevel optimization in the context of deep learning. Parts of the techniques in our approach can be found also in other work, but with different uses and purposes. Therefore, we do not discuss these cases. For instance, Lopez and Ranzato [20] also use the dot-product between training gradients, but apply it to the context of continual learning with multiple tasks.

Understanding Generalization in Deep Learning. Although convolutional neural networks trained using stochastic gradient descent generalize well in practice, Zhang et al. [36] experimentally demonstrate that these models are able to fit random labelings of the training data. This is true even when using common explicit regularization techniques. Several recent works provide possible explanations for the apparent paradox of good generalization despite the high capacity of the models. The work of Kawaguchi et al. [16] provides an explanation based on model-selection (e.g., network architecture) via cross-validation. Their theoretical analysis also results in new generalization bounds and regularization strategies. Zhang et al. [37] attribute the generalization properties of convolutional neural networks (CNNs) to characteristics of the stochastic gradient descent optimizers. Their results show that SGD favors flat minima, which in turn correspond to large (geometrical) margin classifiers. Smith and Le [29] provide an explanation by evaluating the Bayesian evidence in favor of each model, which penalizes sharp minima. In contrast, we argue that current training schemes for neural networks can avoid overfitting altogether by exploiting cross-validation during the optimization.

Combating Memorization of Noisy Labels. The memorization of corrupted labels is a form of overfitting that is of practical importance since labels are often unreliable. Several works have therefore addressed the problem of learning with noisy labels. Rolnick et al. [28] show that neural networks can be robust to even high levels of noise provided good hyper-parameter choices. They specifically demonstrate that larger batch sizes are beneficial in the case of label noise. Patriani et al. [25] address label noise with a loss correction approach. Nataranjan et al. [22] provide a theoretical study of the binary classification problem under the presence of label noise and provide approaches to modify the loss accordingly. Jindal and Chen [15] use dropout and augment networks with a softmax layer that models the label noise and is trained jointly with the network. Sukhabar *et al.* [31] introduce an extra noise layer into the network that adapts the network output to match the noisy label distribution. Reed *et al.* [27] tackle the problem by augmenting the classification objective with a notion of consistency given similar percepts. Besides approaches that explicitly model the noise distribution, several regularization techniques have proven effective in this scenario. The recent work of Jiang *et al.* [14] introduce a regularization technique to counter label noise. They train a network (MentorNet) to assign weights to each training example. Another recent regularization technique was introduced by Zhang *et al.* [38]. Their method is a form of data augmentation where two training examples are mixed (both images and labels) in a convex combination. Azadi *et al.* [2] propose a regularization technique based on overlapping group norms. Their regularizer demonstrates good performance, but relies on features trained on correctly labeled data. Our method differs from the above, because we avoid memorization by encouraging only model parameter updates that reduce errors on shared sample patterns, rather than example-specific details.

Bilevel Optimization. Bilevel optimization approaches have been proposed by various authors to solve for hyper-parameters with respect to the performance on a validation set [3,4]. Domke [8] introduced a truncated bilevel optimization method where the lower-level is approximated by running an iterative algorithm for a given number of steps and subsequently computing the gradient on the validation loss via algorithmic differentiation. Our method uses the limiting case of using a single step in the lower-level problem. Ochs *et al.* [24] introduce a similar technique to the case of non-smooth lower-level problems by differentiating the iterations of a primal-dual algorithm. Maclaurin *et al.* [21] address the issue of expensive caching required for this kind of optimization by deriving an algorithm to exactly reverse SGD while storing only a minimal amount of information. Kunish *et al.* [19] apply bilevel optimization to learn parameters of a variational image denoising model. We do not use bilevel optimization to solve for existing hyper-parameters, but rather introduce and solve for new hyper-parameters by assigning weights to stochastic gradient samples at each iteration.

Meta Learning. Our proposed algorithm has some similarity to the meta-learning literature [10,23,34]. Most notably, the MAML algorithm by Finn *et al.* [10] also incorporates gradient information of two datasets, but does so in different ways: Their method uses second order derivatives, whereas we only use first-order derivatives. In general, the purpose and data of our approach is quite different to the meta-learning setting: We have only one task while in meta-learning there are multiple tasks.

3   Learning to Generalize

We are given m sample pairs $(x^{(k)}, y^{(k)})_{k=1,\dots,m}$, where $x^{(k)} \in \mathcal{X}$ represents input data and $y^{(k)} \in \mathcal{Y}$ represents targets/labels. We denote with $\phi_\theta : \mathcal{X} \mapsto \mathcal{Y}$ a model that depends on parameters $\theta \in \mathbb{R}^d$ for some positive integer d. In all our experiments this model is a neural network and θ collects all its parameters. To measure the performance of the model, we introduce a loss function $\mathcal{L} : \mathcal{Y} \times \mathcal{Y} \mapsto \mathbb{R}$ per sample. Since we evaluate the loss $\mathcal{L}$ on b mini-batches $\mathcal{B}_i \subset \{1, \ldots, m\}$, $i = 1, \ldots, b$, where $\mathcal{B}_i \cap \mathcal{B}_j = \emptyset$ for $i \neq j$, we redefine the loss as

$$\ell_i(\theta) \triangleq \sum_{k \in \mathcal{B}_i} \mathcal{L}\left(\phi_\theta\left(x^{(k)}\right), y^{(k)}\right). \tag{1}$$

At every iteration, we collect a subset of the mini-batches $\mathcal{U}^t \subset \{1, \ldots, b\}$, which we partition into two separate sets: one for training $\mathcal{T}^t \subset \mathcal{U}^t$ and one for validation $\mathcal{V}^t \subset \mathcal{U}^t$, where $\mathcal{T}^t \cap \mathcal{V}^t = \emptyset$ and $\mathcal{T}^t \cup \mathcal{V}^t = \mathcal{U}^t$. Thus, mini-batches $\mathcal{B}_i$ in the training set have $i \in \mathcal{T}^t$ and those in the validation set have $i \in \mathcal{V}^t$. In all our experiments, the validation set $\mathcal{V}^t$ is always a singleton (one mini-batch).

3.1   Bilevel Learning

At the t-th iteration, Stochastic Gradient Descent (SGD) uses only one mini-batch to update the parameters via

$$\theta^{t+1} = \theta^t - \hat{\epsilon}\nabla\ell_i(\theta^t), \tag{2}$$

where $\hat{\epsilon} > 0$ is the SGD learning rate and $i \in \mathcal{U}^t$. Instead, we consider the subset $\mathcal{T}^t \subset \mathcal{U}^t$ of mini-batches and look for the linear combination of the losses that best approximates the validation error. We introduce an additional coefficient ω_i per mini-batch in $\mathcal{T}^t$, which we estimate during training. Our task is then to find parameters θ of our model by using exclusively mini-batches in the training set $\mathcal{T}^t \subset \mathcal{U}^t$, and to identify coefficients (hyper-parameters) ω_i so that the model performs well on the validation set $\mathcal{V}^t \subset \mathcal{U}^t$. We thus propose to optimize

$$\begin{aligned}\hat{\theta}, \hat{\omega} = \arg\min_{\theta, \omega} & \sum_{j \in \mathcal{V}^t} \ell_j(\theta(\omega)) + \tfrac{\mu}{2}|\omega|^2 \\ \text{subj. to} \quad & \theta(\omega) = \arg\min_{\bar{\theta}} \sum_{i \in \mathcal{T}^t} \omega_i \ell_i(\bar{\theta}) \\ & |\omega|_1 = 1,\end{aligned} \tag{3}$$

where ω is the vector collecting all ω_i, $i \in \mathcal{T}^t$ and $\mu > 0$ is a parameter to regulate the distribution of the weights (large values would encourage a uniform distribution across mini-batches and small values would allow more sparsity). Notice that the solution of the lower-level problem does not change if we multiply all the coefficients ω_i by the same strictly positive constant. Therefore, to fix the magnitude of ω we introduced the L^1 normalization constraint $|\omega|_1 = 1$.

A classical method to solve the above bilevel problem is to solve a linear system in the second order derivatives of the lower-level problem, the so-called *implicit differentiation* [8]. This step leads to solving a very high-dimensional linear system. To avoid these computational challenges, in the next section we introduce a proximal approximation. Notice that when we compare the bilevel formulation (3) with SGD in the experiments, we equalize computational complexity by using the same number of visits per sample.

3.2 A Proximal Formulation

To simplify the bilevel formulation (3) we propose to solve a sequence of approximated problems. The parameters estimated at the t-th approximated problem are denoted θ^{t+1}. Both the upper-level and the lower-level problems are approximated via a first-order Taylor expansion of the loss function based on the previous parameter estimate θ^t, i.e., we let

$$\ell_i(\theta) \simeq \ell_i(\theta^t) + \nabla \ell_i(\theta^t)^\top (\theta - \theta^t). \tag{4}$$

Since the above Taylor expansion holds only in the proximity of the previous parameter estimates θ^t, we also introduce *proximal quadratic* terms $|\theta - \theta^t|^2$. By plugging the linear approximation (4) and the proximal terms in Problem (3) we obtain the following formulation

$$\theta^{t+1}, \hat{\omega} = \arg\min_{\theta, \omega} \sum_{j \in \mathcal{V}^t} \ell_j(\theta^t) + \nabla \ell_j(\theta^t)^\top (\theta(\omega) - \theta^t) + \frac{|\theta(\omega) - \theta^t|^2}{2\lambda} + \frac{\mu}{2}|\omega|^2$$

$$\text{s.t.} \quad \theta(\omega) = \arg\min_{\bar{\theta}} \sum_{i \in \mathcal{T}^t} \omega_i \left[\ell_i(\theta^t) + \nabla \ell_i(\theta^t)^\top (\bar{\theta} - \theta^t) \right] + \frac{|\bar{\theta} - \theta^t|^2}{2\epsilon} \tag{5}$$
$$|\omega|_1 = 1,$$

where the coefficients $\lambda, \epsilon > 0$. The lower-level problem is now quadratic and can be solved in closed-form. This yields an update rule identical to the SGD step (2) when $\omega_i = 1$

$$\theta(\omega) = \theta^t - \epsilon \sum_{i \in \mathcal{T}^t} \omega_i \nabla \ell_i(\theta^t). \tag{6}$$

Now we can plug this solution in the upper-level problem and obtain

$$\hat{\omega} = \arg\min_{\theta, \omega} \sum_{j \in \mathcal{V}^t, i \in \mathcal{T}^t} -\omega_i \nabla \ell_j(\theta^t)^\top \nabla \ell_i(\theta^t) + \frac{|\sum_{i \in \mathcal{T}^t} \omega_i \nabla \ell_i(\theta^t)|^2}{2\lambda/\epsilon} + \frac{\mu}{2\epsilon}|\omega|^2$$
$$\text{s.t.} \quad |\omega|_1 = 1. \tag{7}$$

We simplify the notation by introducing $\hat{\lambda} = \lambda/\epsilon$ and $\hat{\mu} = \mu/\epsilon$. To find the optimal coefficients ω we temporarily ignore the normalization constraint $|\omega|_1 = 1$ and simply solve the unconstrained optimization. Afterwards, we enforce the L^1 normalization to the solution. As a first step, we compute the derivative of the cost functional with respect to w_i and set it to zero, i.e., $\forall i \in \mathcal{T}^t$

$$0 = \sum_{j \in \mathcal{V}^t} -\nabla \ell_j(\theta^t)^\top \nabla \ell_i(\theta^t) + \frac{1}{\hat{\lambda}} \sum_{k \in \mathcal{T}^t} \omega_k \nabla \ell_k(\theta^t)^\top \nabla \ell_i(\theta^t) + \hat{\mu} \omega_i. \tag{8}$$

We now approximate the second sum by ignoring all terms such that $k \neq i$, i.e.,

$$0 = \sum_{j \in \mathcal{V}^t} -\nabla \ell_j(\theta^t)^\top \nabla \ell_i(\theta^t) + \left(\frac{1}{\hat{\lambda}} |\nabla \ell_i(\theta^t)|^2 + \hat{\mu} \right) \omega_i \tag{9}$$

so that we can obtain the weight update rule

$$\forall i \in \mathcal{T}^t, \quad \omega_i \leftarrow \sum_{j \in \mathcal{V}^t} \frac{\nabla \ell_j(\theta^t)^\top \nabla \ell_i(\theta^t)}{|\nabla \ell_i(\theta^t)|^2/\hat{\lambda} + \hat{\mu}}, \qquad \hat{\omega} = \omega/|\omega|_1. \tag{10}$$

Since Eq. (8) describes a linear system, it could be solved exactly via several iterative methods, such as Gauss-Seidel or successive over-relaxations [12]. However, we found that using this level of accuracy does not give a substantial improvement in the model performance to justify the additional computational cost. We can then combine the update rule (10) with the update (6) of the parameters θ and obtain a new gradient descent step

$$\theta(\boldsymbol{\omega}) = \theta^t - \epsilon \sum_{i \in \mathcal{T}^t} \hat{\omega}_i \nabla \ell_i(\theta^t). \tag{11}$$

Notice that $\epsilon \hat{\omega}_i$ can be seen as a learning rate specific to each mini-batch. The update rule for the weights follows a very intuitive scheme: if the gradients of a mini-batch in the training set $\nabla \ell_i(\theta^t)$ agree with the gradients of a mini-batch in the validation set $\nabla \ell_j(\theta^t)$, then their inner product $\nabla \ell_j(\theta^t)^\top \nabla \ell_i(\theta^t) > 0$ and their corresponding weights are also positive and large. This means that we encourage updates of the parameters that also minimize the upper-level problem. When these two gradients disagree, that is, if they are orthogonal $\nabla \ell_j(\theta^t)^\top \nabla \ell_i(\theta^t) = 0$ or in the opposite directions $\nabla \ell_j(\theta^t)^\top \nabla \ell_i(\theta^t) < 0$, then the corresponding weights are also set to zero or a negative value, respectively (see Fig. 1 for a general overview of the training procedure). Moreover, these inner products are scaled by the gradient magnitude of mini-batches from the training set and division by zero is avoided when $\mu > 0$.

Remark 1. Attention must be paid to the sample composition in each mini-batch, since we aim to approximate the validation error with a linear combination of a few mini-batches. In fact, if samples in a mini-batch of the training set are quite independent from samples in mini-batches of the validation set (for example, they belong to very different categories in a classification problem), then their inner product will tend to be very small on average. This would not allow any progress in the estimation of the parameters θ. At each iteration we ensure that samples in each mini-batch from the training set have overlapping labels with samples in mini-batches from the validation set.

4   Implementation

To implement our method we modify SGD with momentum [26]. First, at each iteration t we sample k mini-batches $\mathcal{B}_i$ in such a way that the distributions of labels across the k mini-batches are identical (in the experiments, we consider $k \in \{2, 4, 8, 16, 32\}$). Next, we compute the gradients $\nabla \ell_i(\theta^t)$ of the loss function on each mini-batch $\mathcal{B}_i$. $\mathcal{V}^t$ contains only the index of one mini-batch and $\mathcal{T}^t$ all the remaining indices. We then use $\nabla \ell_j(\theta^t)$, $j \in \mathcal{V}^t$, as the *single* validation gradient and compute the weights ω_i of $\nabla \ell_i(\theta^t)$, $i \in \mathcal{T}^t$, using Eq. (10). The re-weighted gradient $\sum_{i \in \mathcal{T}^t} \omega_i \nabla \ell_i(\theta^t)$ is then fed to the neural network optimizer.

5   Experiments

We perform extensive experiments on several common datasets used for training image classifiers. Section 5.1 shows ablations to verify several design choices. In

Sects. 5.2 and 5.3 we follow the experimental setup of Zhang *et al.* [36] to demonstrate that our method reduces sample memorization and improves performance on noisy labels at test time. In Sect. 5.4 we show improvements on small datasets. The datasets considered in this section are the following:

CIFAR-10 [17]: It contains 50K training and 10K test images of size 32×32 pixels, equally distributed among 10 classes.

CIFAR-100 [17]: It contains 50K training and 10K test images of size 32×32 pixels, equally distributed among 100 classes.

Pascal VOC 2007 [9]: It contains 5,011 training and 4,952 test images (the trainval set) of 20 object classes.

ImageNet [7]: It is a large dataset containing 1.28M training images of objects from 1K classes. We test on the validation set, which has 50K images.

We evaluate our method on several network architectures. On Pascal VOC and ImageNet we use AlexNet [18]. Following Zhang *et al.* [36] we use CifarNet (an AlexNet-style network) and a small Inception architecture adapted to the smaller image sizes of CIFAR-10 and CIFAR-100. We refer the reader to [36] for a detailed description of those architectures. We also train variants of the ResNet architecture [13] to compare to other methods.

5.1   Ablations

We perform extensive ablation experiments on CIFAR-10 using the CifarNet and Inception network. The networks are trained on both clean labels and labels with 50% random noise. We report classification accuracy on the training labels (clean or noisy) and the accuracy on the *clean* test labels. The baseline in all the ablation experiments compares 8 mini-batches and uses $\mu = 0.01$ and $\lambda = 1$. Both networks have a single dropout layer and the baseline configuration uses the same dropping in all the compared mini-batches. The networks are trained for 200 epochs on mini-batches of size 128. We do not use data augmentation for CifarNet, but we use standard augmentations for the Inception network (*i.e.*, random cropping and perturbation of brightness and contrast). The case of the Inception network is therefore closer to the common setup for training neural networks and the absence of augmentation in the case of CifarNet makes overfitting more likely. We use SGD with momentum of 0.9 and an initial learning rate of 0.01 in the case of CifarNet and 0.1 for Inception. The learning rate is reduced by a factor of 0.95 after every epoch. Although in our formulation the validation and training sets split the selected mini-batches into two separate sets, after one epoch, mini-batches used in the validation set could be used in the training set and vice versa. We test the case where we manually enforce that no examples (in mini-batches) used in the validation set are ever used for training, and find no benefit. We explore different sizes of the separate validation and training sets. We define as *validation ratio* the fraction of samples from the dataset used for validation only. Figure 2 demonstrates the influence of the validation ratio (top row), the number of compared mini-batches (second row), the size

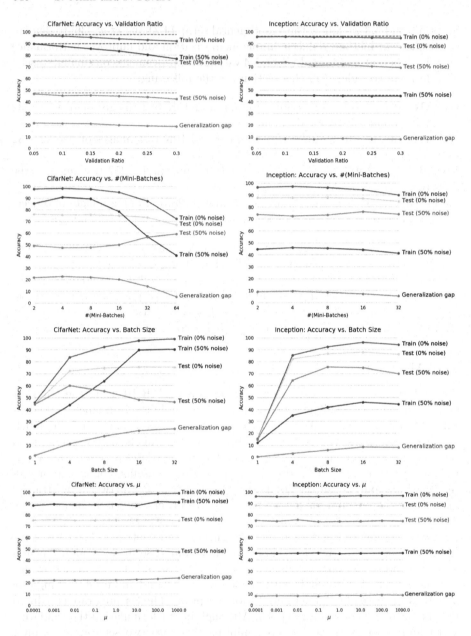

Fig. 2. Ablation experiments on CIFAR-10 with CifarNet (a small AlexNet style network) (*left*) and a small Inception network (*right*). We vary the size of the validation set (*1st row*), the number of mini-batches being compared (*2nd row*), the mini-batch size (*3rd row*) and the hyper-parameter μ (*4th row*). The networks were trained on clean as well as 50% noisy labels. The amount of label noise during training is indicated in parentheses. We show the accuracy on the clean or noisy training data, but always evaluate it on clean data. Note that the baseline of using the full training data as validation set is indicated with dashed lines on the top row.

of the compared mini-batches (third row) and the hyper-parameter μ (bottom row). We can observe that the validation ratio has only a small influence on the performance. We see an overall negative trend in the test accuracy with increasing size of the validation set, probably due to the corresponding reduction of the training set size. The number of mini-batches has a much more pronounced influence on the networks performance, especially in the case of CifarNet, where overfitting is more likely. Note that we keep the number of training steps constant in this experiment. Hence, the case with more mini-batches corresponds to smaller batch sizes. While the performance in case of noisy labels increases with the number of compared mini-batches, we observe a decrease in performance on clean data. We would like to mention that the case of 2 mini-batches is rather interesting, since it amounts to flipping (or not) the sign of the single training gradient based on the dot product with the single validation gradient. To test whether the performance in the case of a growing number of batches is due to the batch sizes, we perform experiments where we vary the batch size while keeping the number of compared batches fixed at 8. Since this modification leads to more iterations we adjust the learning rate schedule accordingly. Notice that all comparisons use the same overall number of times each sample is used. We can observe a behavior similar to the case of the varying number of mini-batches. This suggests that small mini-batch sizes lead to better generalization in the presence of label noise. Notice also the special case where the batch size is 1, which corresponds to per-example weights. Besides inferior performance we found this choice to be computationally inefficient and interfering with batch norm. Interestingly, the parameter μ does not seem to have a significant influence on the performance of both networks. Overall the performance on clean labels is quite robust to hyper-parameter choices except for the size of the mini-batches.

In Table 1, we also summarize the following set of ablation experiments:

(a) **No L^1-Constraint on ω:** We show that using the L^1 constraint $|\omega|_1 = 1$ is beneficial for both clean and noisy labels. We set $\mu = 0.01$ and $\lambda = 1$ for this experiment in order for the magnitude of the weights ω_i to resemble the case with the L^1 constraint. While tuning of μ and λ might lead to an improvement, the use of the L^1 constraint allows plugging our optimization method without adjusting the learning rate schedule of existing models;

(b) **Weights per Layer:** In this experiment we compute a separate $\omega_i^{(l)}$ for the gradients corresponding to each layer l. We then also apply L^1 normalization to the weights $\omega_i^{(l)}$ per layer. While the results on noisy data with CifarNet improve in this case, the performance of CifarNet on clean data and the Inception network on both datasets clearly degrades;

(c) **Mini-Batch sampling:** Here we do not force the distribution of (noisy) labels in the compared mini-batches to be identical. The poor performance in this case highlights the importance of identically distributed labels in the compared mini-batches;

(d) **Dropout:** We remove the restriction of equal dropping in all the compared mini-batches. Somewhat surprisingly, this improves performance in most cases. Note that unequal dropping lowers the influence of gradients in

Table 1. Results of ablation experiments on CIFAR-10 as described in Sect. 5.1. Models were trained on clean labels and labels with 50% random noise. We report classification accuracy on the clean or noisy training labels and clean test labels. The generalization gap (difference between training and test accuracy) on clean data is also included. We also show results of the baseline model and of a model trained with standard SGD.

Experiment	CifarNet					Inception				
	Clean			50% Random		Clean			50% Random	
	Train	Test	Gap	Train	Test	Train	Test	Gap	Train	Test
SGD	99.99	75.68	24.31	96.75	45.15	99.91	88.13	11.78	65.06	47.64
Baseline	97.60	75.52	22.08	89.28	47.62	96.13	87.78	8.35	45.43	73.08
(a) L^1	96.44	74.32	22.12	95.50	45.79	79.46	77.07	2.39	33.86	62.16
(b) ω per layer	97.43	74.36	23.07	81.60	49.62	90.38	85.25	5.13	81.60	49.62
(c) Sampling	72.69	68.19	4.50	16.13	23.93	79.78	78.25	1.53	17.71	27.20
(d) Dropout	95.92	74.76	21.16	82.22	49.23	95.58	87.86	7.72	44.61	75.71

Table 2. Results of the Inception network when trained on data with random pixel permutations (fixed per image). We observe much less overfitting using our method when compared to standard SGD

Model	Train	Test	Gap
SGD	50.0	33.2	16.8
Bilevel	34.8	33.6	1.2

the deep fully-connected layers, therefore giving more weight to gradients of early convolutional layers in the dot-product. Also, dropout essentially amounts to having a different classifier at each iteration. Our method could encourage gradient updates that work well for different classifiers, possibly leading to a more universal representation.

5.2   Fitting Random Pixel Permutations

Zhang *et al.* [36] demonstrated that CNNs are able to fit the training data even when images undergo random permutations of the pixels. Since object patterns are destroyed under such manipulations, learning should be very limited (restricted to simple statistics of pixel colors). We test our method with the Inception network trained for 200 epochs on images undergoing fixed random permutations of the pixels and report a comparison to standard SGD in Table 2. While the test accuracy of both variants is similar, the network trained using our optimization shows a very small generalization gap.

5.3   Memorization of Partially Corrupted Labels

The problem of label noise is of practical importance since the labelling process is in general unreliable and incorrect labels are often introduced in the process.

Table 3. Comparison to state-of-the-art regularization techniques and methods for dealing with label noise on 40% corrupted labels.

Method	Ref.	Network	CIFAR-10	CIFAR-100
Reed *et al.* [27]	[14]	ResNet	62.3%	46.5%
Golderberger *et al.* [11]	[14]	ResNet	69.9%	45.8%
Azadi *et al.* [2]	[2]	AlexNet	75.0%	-
Jilang *et al.* [14]	[14]	ResNet	76.6%	56.9%
Zhang *et al.* [38]	-	PreAct ResNet-18	88.3%	56.4%
Standard SGD	-	PreAct ResNet-18	69.6%	44.9%
Dropout ($p = 0.3$) [30]	-	PreAct ResNet-18	84.5%	50.1%
Label Smoothing (0.1) [32]	-	PreAct ResNet-18	69.3%	46.1%
Bilevel	-	PreAct ResNet-18	87.0%	59.8%
Bilevel + [38]	-	PreAct ResNet-18	89.0%	61.6%

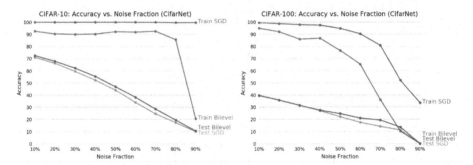

Fig. 3. CifarNet is trained on data from CIFAR-10 and CIFAR-100 with varying amounts of random label noise. We observe that our optimization leads to higher test accuracy and less overfitting in all cases when compared to standard SGD.

Providing methods that are robust to noise in the training labels is therefore of interest. In this section we perform experiments on several datasets (CIFAR-10, CIFAR-100, ImageNet) with different forms and levels of label corruption and using different network architectures. We compare to other state-of-the-art regularization and label-noise methods on CIFAR-10 and CIFAR-100.

Random Label Corruptions on CIFAR-10 and CIFAR-100. We test our method under different levels of synthetic label noise. For a noise level $\pi \in [0, 1]$ and a dataset with c classes, we randomly choose a fraction of π examples per class and uniformly assign labels of the other $c - 1$ classes. Note that this leads to a completely random labelling in the case of 90% label noise on CIFAR-10. Networks are trained on datasets with varying amounts of label noise. We train the networks with our bilevel optimizer using 8 mini-batches and using the training set for validation. The networks are trained for 100 epochs on mini-batches of size 64. Learning schedules, initial learning rates and data augmentation are identical to those in Sect. 5.1. The results using CifarNet are summarized in Fig. 3

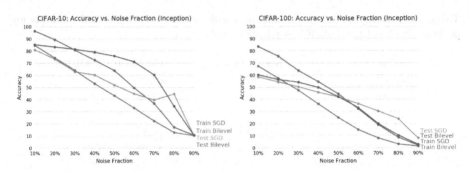

Fig. 4. The Inception network trained on data from CIFAR-10 and CIFAR-100 with varying amounts of random label noise. On CIFAR-10 our optimization leads to substantially higher test accuracy in most cases when compared to standard SGD. Our method also shows more robustness to noise levels up to 50% on CIFAR-100.

Table 4. Experiments with a realistic noise model on ImageNet

Method	44% Noise	Clean
SGD	50.75%	57.4%
Bilevel	52.69%	58.2%

and the results for Inception in Fig. 4. We observe a consistent improvement over standard SGD on CifarNet and significant gains for Inception on CIFAR-10 up to 70% noise. On CIFAR-100 our method leads to better results up to a noise level of 50%. We compare to state-of-the-art regularization methods as well as methods for dealing with label noise in Table 3. The networks used in the comparison are variants of the ResNet architecture [13] as specified in [14] and [38]. An exception is [2], which uses AlexNet, but relies on having a separate large dataset with clean labels for their model. We use the same architecture as the state-of-the-art method by Zhang *et al.* [38] for our results. We also explored the combination of our bilevel optimization with the data augmentation introduced by [38] in the last row. This results in the best performance on both CIFAR-10 and CIFAR-100. We also include results using Dropout [30] with a low keep-probability p as suggested by Arpit *et al.* [1] and results with label-smoothing as suggested by Szegedy *et al.* [32].

Modelling Realistic Label Noise on ImageNet. In order to test the method on more realistic label noise we perform the following experiment: We use the predicted labels of a pre-trained AlexNet to model realistic label noise. Our rationale here is that predictions of a neural network will make similar mistakes as a human annotator would. To obtain a high noise level we leave dropout active when making the predictions on the training set. This results in approximately 44% label noise. We then retrain an AlexNet from scratch on those labels using standard SGD and our bilevel optimizer. The results of this experiment and a comparison on clean data is given in Table 4. The bilevel optimization leads to

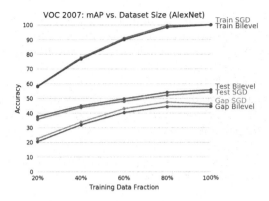

Fig. 5. We train an AlexNet for multi-label classification on varying fractions of the Pascal VOC 2007 `trainval` set and report mAP on the test set as well as the complete `trainval` set. Our optimization technique leads to higher test performance and smaller generalization gap in all cases.

better performance in both cases, improving over standard SGD by nearly 2% in case of noisy labels.

Experiments on Real-World Data with Noisy Labels. We test our method on the Clothing1M dataset introduced by Xiao *et al.* [35]. The dataset consists of fashion images belonging to 14 classes. It contains 1M images with noisy labels and additional smaller sets with clean labels for training (50K), validation (14K) and testing (10K). We follow the same setup as the state-of-the-art by Patrini *et al.* [25] using an ImageNet pre-trained 50-layer ResNet. We achieve 69.9% after training only on the noisy data and 79.9% after fine-tuning on the clean training data. These results are comparable to [25] with 69.8% and 80.4% respectively.

5.4 Generalization on Small Datasets

Small datasets pose a challenge since deep networks will easily overfit in this case. We test our method under this scenario by training an AlexNet on the multi-label classification task of Pascal VOC 2007. Training images are randomly cropped to an area between 30% to 100% of the original and then resized to 227×227. We linearly decay the learning rate from 0.01 to 0 and train for 1K epochs on mini-batches of size 64. We use the bilevel optimization method with 4 mini-batches and without a separate validation set. In Fig. 5 we report the mAP obtained from the average prediction over 10 random crops on varying fractions of the original dataset. We observe a small, but consistent, improvement over the baseline in all cases.

6 Conclusions

Neural networks seem to benefit from additional regularization during training when compared to alternative models in machine learning. However, neural networks still suffer from overfitting and current regularization methods have a limited impact. We introduce a novel regularization approach that implements the principles of cross-validation as a bilevel optimization problem. This formulation is computationally efficient, can be incorporated with other regularizations and is shown to consistently improve the generalization of several neural network architectures on challenging datasets such as CIFAR10/100, Pascal VOC 2007, and ImageNet. In particular, we show that the proposed method is effective in avoiding overfitting with noisy labels.

Acknowledgements. This work was supported by the Swiss National Science Foundation (SNSF) grant number 200021_169622.

References

1. Arpit, D., et al.: A closer look at memorization in deep networks. arXiv preprint arXiv:1706.05394 (2017)
2. Azadi, S., Feng, J., Jegelka, S., Darrell, T.: Auxiliary image regularization for deep CNNs with noisy labels. In: International Conference on Learning Representations (2016)
3. Baydin, A.G., Pearlmutter, B.A.: Automatic differentiation of algorithms for machine learning. arXiv preprint arXiv:1404.7456 (2014)
4. Bengio, Y.: Gradient-based optimization of hyperparameters. Neural Comput. **12**(8), 1889–1900 (2000)
5. Bracken, J., McGill, J.T.: Mathematical programs with optimization problems in the constraints. Oper. Res. **21**(1), 37–44 (1973). https://doi.org/10.1287/opre.21.1.37
6. Colson, B., Marcotte, P., Savard, G.: An overview of bilevel optimization. Ann. Oper. Res. **153**(1), 235–256 (2007). https://doi.org/10.1007/s10479-007-0176-2
7. Deng, J., Dong, W., Socher, R., Li, L.J., Li, K., Fei-Fei, L.: Imagenet: a large-scale hierarchical image database. In: Computer Vision and Pattern Recognition. pp. 248–255. IEEE (2009)
8. Domke, J.: Generic methods for optimization-based modeling. In: Artificial Intelligence and Statistics, pp. 318–326 (2012)
9. Everingham, M., Van Gool, L., Williams, C.K., Winn, J., Zisserman, A.: The pascal visual object classes (VOC) challenge. Int. J. Comput. Vis. **88**(2), 303–338 (2010)
10. Finn, C., Abbeel, P., Levine, S.: Model-agnostic meta-learning for fast adaptation of deep networks. arXiv preprint arXiv:1703.03400 (2017)
11. Goldberger, J., Ben-Reuven, E.: Training deep neural-networks using a noise adaptation layer. In: International Conference on Learning Representations (2016)
12. Hadjidimos, A.: Successive overrelaxation (SOR) and related methods. J. Comput. Appl. Math. **123**(1–2), 177–199 (2000). https://doi.org/10.1016/S0377-0427(00)00403-9
13. He, K., Zhang, X., Ren, S., Sun, J.: Deep residual learning for image recognition. In: Computer Vision and Pattern Recognition, pp. 770–778 (2016)
14. Jiang, L., Zhou, Z., Leung, T., Li, L.J., Fei-Fei, L.: Mentornet: regularizing very deep neural networks on corrupted labels. arXiv preprint arXiv:1712.05055 (2017)
15. Jindal, I., Nokleby, M., Chen, X.: Learning deep networks from noisy labels with dropout regularization. arXiv preprint arXiv:1705.03419 (2017)

16. Kawaguchi, K., Kaelbling, L.P., Bengio, Y.: Generalization in deep learning. arXiv preprint arXiv:1710.05468 (2017)
17. Krizhevsky, A.: Learning multiple layers of features from tiny images (2009)
18. Krizhevsky, A., Sutskever, I., Hinton, G.E.: Imagenet classification with deep convolutional neural networks. In: Advances in Neural Information Processing Systems, pp. 1097–1105 (2012)
19. Kunisch, K., Pock, T.: A bilevel optimization approach for parameter learning in variational models. SIAM J. Imaging Sci. **6**(2), 938–983 (2013)
20. Lopez-Paz, D., et al.: Gradient episodic memory for continual learning. In: Advances in Neural Information Processing Systems, pp. 6470–6479 (2017)
21. Maclaurin, D., Duvenaud, D., Adams, R.: Gradient-based hyperparameter optimization through reversible learning. In: International Conference on Machine Learning, pp. 2113–2122 (2015)
22. Natarajan, N., Dhillon, I.S., Ravikumar, P.K., Tewari, A.: Learning with noisy labels. In: Advances in Neural Information Processing Systems, pp. 1196–1204 (2013)
23. Nichol, A., Schulman, J.: Reptile: a scalable metalearning algorithm. arXiv preprint arXiv:1803.02999 (2018)
24. Ochs, P., Ranftl, R., Brox, T., Pock, T.: Bilevel optimization with nonsmooth lower level problems. In: Aujol, J.-F., Nikolova, M., Papadakis, N. (eds.) SSVM 2015. LNCS, vol. 9087, pp. 654–665. Springer, Cham (2015). https://doi.org/10.1007/978-3-319-18461-6_52
25. Patrini, G., Rozza, A., Menon, A., Nock, R., Qu, L.: Making neural networks robust to label noise: a loss correction approach. In: Computer Vision and Pattern Recognition (2017)
26. Qian, N.: On the momentum term in gradient descent learning algorithms. Neural Netw. **12**(1), 145–151 (1999)
27. Reed, S., Lee, H., Anguelov, D., Szegedy, C., Erhan, D., Rabinovich, A.: Training deep neural networks on noisy labels with bootstrapping. arXiv preprint arXiv:1412.6596 (2014)
28. Rolnick, D., Veit, A., Belongie, S., Shavit, N.: Deep learning is robust to massive label noise. arXiv preprint arXiv:1705.10694 (2017)
29. Smith, S.L., et al.: A Bayesian perspective on generalization and stochastic gradient descent. In: International Conference on Learning Representations (2018)
30. Srivastava, N., Hinton, G., Krizhevsky, A., Sutskever, I., Salakhutdinov, R.: Dropout: a simple way to prevent neural networks from overfitting. J. Mach. Learn. Res. **15**(1), 1929–1958 (2014)
31. Sukhbaatar, S., Bruna, J., Paluri, M., Bourdev, L., Fergus, R.: Training convolutional networks with noisy labels. arXiv preprint arXiv:1406.2080 (2014)
32. Szegedy, C., Vanhoucke, V., Ioffe, S., Shlens, J., Wojna, Z.: Rethinking the inception architecture for computer vision. In: Proceedings of the IEEE Conference on Computer Vision and Pattern Recognition, pp. 2818–2826 (2016)
33. Ulyanov, D., Vedaldi, A., Lempitsky, V.: Deep image prior. In: The IEEE Conference on Computer Vision and Pattern Recognition (CVPR), June 2018
34. Vinyals, O., Blundell, C., Lillicrap, T., Wierstra, D., et al.: Matching networks for one shot learning. In: Advances in Neural Information Processing Systems, pp. 3630–3638 (2016)
35. Xiao, T., Xia, T., Yang, Y., Huang, C., Wang, X.: Learning from massive noisy labeled data for image classification. In: Proceedings of the IEEE Conference on Computer Vision and Pattern Recognition, pp. 2691–2699 (2015)

36. Zhang, C., Bengio, S., Hardt, M., Recht, B., Vinyals, O.: Understanding deep learning requires rethinking generalization. In: International Conference on Learning Representations (2017)
37. Zhang, C., et al.: Theory of deep learning III: generalization properties of SGD. Technical report, Center for Brains, Minds and Machines (CBMM) (2017)
38. Zhang, H., Cisse, M., Dauphin, Y.N., Lopez-Paz, D.: mixup: beyond empirical risk minimization. In: International Conference on Learning Representations (2017)

Joint Optimization for Compressive Video Sensing and Reconstruction Under Hardware Constraints

Michitaka Yoshida[1]([✉])[ID], Akihiko Torii[2], Masatoshi Okutomi[2], Kenta Endo[3], Yukinobu Sugiyama[3], Rin-ichiro Taniguchi[1], and Hajime Nagahara[4][ID]

[1] Kyushu University, Fukuoka, Japan
yoshida@limu.ait.kyushu-u.ac.jp
[2] Tokyo Institute of Technology, Tokyo, Japan
[3] Hamamatsu Photonics K.K., Hamamatsu, Japan
[4] Osaka University, Suita, Japan

Abstract. Compressive video sensing is the process of encoding multiple sub-frames into a single frame with controlled sensor exposures and reconstructing the sub-frames from the single compressed frame. It is known that spatially and temporally random exposures provide the most balanced compression in terms of signal recovery. However, sensors that achieve a fully random exposure on each pixel cannot be easily realized in practice because the circuit of the sensor becomes complicated and incompatible with the sensitivity and resolution. Therefore, it is necessary to design an exposure pattern by considering the constraints enforced by hardware. In this paper, we propose a method of jointly optimizing the exposure patterns of compressive sensing and the reconstruction framework under hardware constraints. By conducting a simulation and actual experiments, we demonstrated that the proposed framework can reconstruct multiple sub-frame images with higher quality.

Keywords: Compressive sensing · Video reconstruction
Deep neural network

1 Introduction

Recording a high-frame video with high spatial resolution has various uses in practical and scientific applications because it essentially provides more information to analyze the recorded events. Such video sensing can be achieved by using a high-speed camera [1] that shortens the readout time from the pixel by employing a buffer for each pixel and reducing the analog-to-digital (AD) conversion time by using parallel AD converters. Since he mass production of these special sensors is not unrealistic, several problems remain unresolved with regard to the replacement of standard complementary metal-oxide-semiconductor (CMOS) sensors. As an example of hardware related problems, a fast readout sensor is larger than

© Springer Nature Switzerland AG 2018
V. Ferrari et al. (Eds.): ECCV 2018, LNCS 11214, pp. 649–663, 2018.
https://doi.org/10.1007/978-3-030-01249-6_39

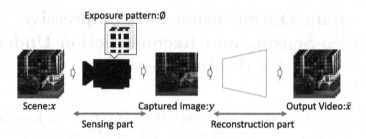

Exposure pattern:Ø

Scene:x   Captured Image:y   Output Video:x̄

Sensing part   Reconstruction part

Fig. 1. Compressive video sensing. A process of encoding multiple sub-frames into a single frame with controlled sensor exposures, and reconstructing the sub-frames from a single compressed frame.

a standard sensor because it is assembled with additional circuits and transistors. To make a high-frame sensor more compact, a smaller phototransistor must be used to lower the sensitivity.

A feasible approach consists of capturing video by using compressive sensing techniques [2–6], *i.e.*, by compressing several sub-frames into a single frame at the time of acquisition, while controlling the exposure of each pixel's position. In contrast to the standard images captured with a global shutter, where all pixels are exposed concurrently, a compressive video sensor samples temporal information and compresses it into a single image, while randomly changing the exposure pattern for each pixel. This non-continuous exposition enables the recovery of high-quality video. Formally, compressive video sensing is expressed as follows:

$$\mathbf{y} = \phi\mathbf{x} \tag{1}$$

where $\mathbf{x}$ is the high-frame video to be compressed, ϕ is the measurement matrix (exposure patterns), and $\mathbf{y}$ is the compressed single image. The following tasks are included in compressive video sensing: reconstruct a high-frame video $\bar{\mathbf{x}}$ from a single image $\mathbf{y}$ by using pattern ϕ; optimize the pattern that enables high-quality video reconstruction (Fig. 1).

Under the assumption that random (theoretically optimal) patterns can be implemented without hardware sensor constraints, numerous studies have investigated a method of reconstructing (decoding) from a single image based on sparse coding [3–5]. In signal recovery theory, the best exposure pattern is random sampling from a uniform distribution. However, this is not an optimal pattern in terms of practical image sensing, because a practical scene does not always maintain the sparsity assumed in compressive sensing theory. Few existing studies [6] have investigated scene adaptive exposure patterns in the context of a target scene.

However, implementing such completely random exposures with a practical CMOS sensor is not realistic, owing to hardware limitations. Achieving compatibility between these special sensors and the sensitivity and resolution is difficult because these sensors typically have more complicated circuits in each pixel, and this decreases the size of the photo-diode [7]. Additionally, standard commercial CMOS sensors, *e.g.*, three-transistor CMOS sensors, do not have a per-pixel frame buffer on the chip. Thus, such sensors are incapable of multiple exposure in a non-destructive manner [3]. There exists an advanced prototype CMOS sensor [2] that can control the exposure time more flexibly. However, its spatial control is limited to per line (column and row) operations. Therefore, it is necessary to optimize the exposure patterns by recognizing the hardware constraints of actual sensors.

Contribution. In this paper, we propose a new pipeline to optimize both the exposure pattern and reconstruction decoder of compressive video sensing by using a deep neural network (DNN) framework [8]. To the best of our knowledge, ours is the first study that considers the actual hardware sensor constraints and jointly optimizes both the exposure patterns and the decoder in an end-to-end manner. The proposed method is a general framework for optimizing the exposure patterns with and without hardware constraints. We demonstrated that the learned exposure pattern can recover high-frame videos with better quality in comparison with existing handcrafted and random patterns. Moreover, we demonstrated the effectiveness of our method with images captured by an actual sensor.

2   Related Studies

Compressive video sensing consists of sensing and reconstruction: sensing pertains to the hardware design of the image sensor for compressing video (subframes) to a single image. Reconstruction pertains to the software design for estimating the original subframes from a single compressed image.

Sensing. Ideal compressive video sensing requires a captured image with random exposure, as expressed in Eq. 1 and shown in Fig. 1. However, conventional charge-coupled device (CCD) and CMOS sensors either have a global or a rolling shutter. A global shutter exposes all of the pixels concurrently, while a rolling shutter exposes every pixel row/column sequentially. A commercial sensor capable of capturing an image with random exposure does not exist. Therefore, most existing studies have only evaluated simulated data [5] or optically emulated implementations [3].

Many studies have investigated the development of sensors for compressive sensing [9]. Robucci et al. [10] proposed the design of a sensor that controls the exposure time by feeding the same signal to pixels located in the same row, *i.e.*, row-wise exposure pattern coding is performed at the sensor level. In an actual sensor implementation, analog computational coding is used before the analog-to-digital (A/D) converter receives the signals. The proposed sensor type is a passive pixel sensor that is not robust to noise, in comparison with an active pixel sensor that is typically used in commercial CMOS image sensors. Dadkhah et al. [11] proposed a sensor with additional exposure control lines connected to the pixel block arrays, each of which was composed of several pixels. The pixel block array shared the same exposure control line. However, each pixel inside the block could be exposed individually. Although the block-wise pattern was repeated, from a global point of view, this sensor could generate a random exposure pattern locally. Because the number of additional exposure control lines was proportional to the number of all pixels in the sensor, the fill factors remained similar to those of a standard CMOS sensor.

Majidzadeh et al. [12] proposed a CMOS sensor with pixel elements equipped with random pattern generators. Because the generator was constructed from a finite state machine sequence, the fill factor of this sensor was extremely low, and this resulted in lower sensor sensitivity. Oike et al. [13] proposed a sensor wherein all pixels were exposed concurrently, as in a regular CMOS image sensor. The exposure information was read out as a sequential signal, which was cloned and blanched to several multiplexers, in a parallel manner. The sequential signal was encoded by using different random patterns.

Through parallel A/D converters, several random measurements, incoherent to each other, can be obtained with a single shot. Relevant studies [10–13] have mainly focused on super-resolution. Because the measured spatial resolution can be reduced, the frame rate can be increased within a certain bandwidth. High frame rate acquisition has not been demonstrated in any actual experiments conducted by these studies.

There have been fewer attempts to implement sensors for compressive video sensing. Spinoulas et al. [14] have demonstrated on-chip compressive sensing. They used an inexpensive commercial development toolkit with flexible readout settings to perform non-uniform sampling from several captured frames in combination with pixel binning, region of interest (ROI) position shifting, and ROI position flipping. Note that this coding was not performed on the sensor chip, but rather during the readout process.

Sonoda et al. [2] used a prototype CMOS sensor with exposure control capabilities. The basic structure of this sensor was similar to that of a standard CMOS sensor, although separate reset and transfer signals controlled the start and end time of the exposure. Because the pixels in a column and row shared the reset and transfer signal, respectively, the exposure pattern had row and column wise dependency. These researchers also proposed to increase the randomness of the exposure pattern. However, the method could not completely solve the pattern's row and column wise dependency.

Reconstruction. There are various methods to reconstruct a video from a single image captured with compressive sensing. Because the video output rank (x in Eq. 1) is higher than the input (y), it is impossible to reconstruct the video deterministically.

One of the major approaches consists of adopting sparse optimization, and assuming that the video x_p can be expressed by a linear combination of sparse bases D, as follows:

$$x_p = D\alpha = \alpha_1 D_1 + \alpha_2 D_2 + \cdots + \alpha_k D_k$$

Fig. 2. Examples of exposure patterns under hardware constraints: (a) random exposure sensor, (b) single bump exposure (SBE) sensor [3], (c) row-column wise exposure (RCE) sensor [2]

where $\alpha = [\alpha_1, .., \alpha_k]^\mathrm{T}$ are the coefficients, and the number of coefficients k is smaller than the dimension of the captured image. In the standard approach, the D bases are pre-computed, $e.g.$, by performing K-SVD [15] on the training data. From Eq. 1, we obtain the following expression:

$$\mathrm{y_p} = \phi_\mathrm{p}\mathrm{D}\alpha. \tag{2}$$

Because $\mathrm{y_p}$, ϕ_p, and D are known, it is possible to reconstruct videos by solving α, $e.g.$, by using the orthogonal matching pursuit (OMP) algorithm [3,16] that optimizes the following equation:

$$\alpha = \arg\min_\alpha ||\alpha||_0 \text{ subject to } ||\phi\mathrm{D}\alpha - \mathrm{y_p}||_2 \le \sigma \tag{3}$$

To solve the sparse reconstruction, L_1 relaxation has been used because L_0 optimization is hard to compute and also computationally expensive. LASSO [17] is a solver for the L_1 minimization problem, as expressed in Eq. 4, and has also been used in the sparse reconstruction of the video.

$$\min_\alpha ||\phi\mathrm{D}\alpha - \mathrm{y_p}||_2 \text{ subject to } ||\phi||_1 \le \sigma \tag{4}$$

Yang et al. [4] proposed a reconstruction method based on Gaussian Mixture Models (GMM). They assumed that the video patch $\{\mathbf{x}_p\}$ could be represented as follows:

$$\mathbf{x}_p \sim \sum_{k=1}^{K} \lambda_k \mathcal{N}(\mathbf{x}_p \mid \mu_k, \Sigma_k) \tag{5}$$

where $\mathcal{N}$ is the Gaussian distribution and K, Σ_k, and λ_k are the number of GMM components, mean, covariance matrix, and weight of the k_{th} Gaussian component ($\lambda_k > 0$ and $\sum_{k=1}^{K} \lambda_k = 1$) Therefore, the video could be reconstructed by computing the conditional expectation value of $\mathbf{x}_p$.

Very recently, Iliadis et al. [5] proposed a decoder based on a DNN. The network was composed by fully connected layers and learned the non-linear mapping between a video sequence and a captured image. The input layer had the size of the captured image, while the hidden and output layers had the size of the video. Because this DNN-based decoder only calculated the convolution with learned weights, the video reconstruction was fast.

3   Hardware Constraints of Exposure Controls

As already discussed in Sect. 2, there exist hardware constraints that prevent
the generation of completely random exposure patterns, which are a theoretical
requirement of compressive video sensing, as shown in Fig. 2a. In this paper, we
describe two examples of hardware constraints, which have been suggested by
[3] and fabricated to control pixel-wise exposures [2] on realistic sensors. In this
section, we detail the hardware constraints resulting from sensor architecture.

Hitomi et al. [3] suggested that CMOS modification is feasible. However, they
did not produce a modified sensor to realize pixel-wise exposure control as shown
in Fig. 3a. Existing CMOS sensors have row addressing, which provides row-wise
exposure such as that of a rolling shutter. These researchers proposed to add a
column addressing decoder to provide pixel-wise exposure. However, a typical
CMOS sensor does not have a per-pixel buffer, but does have the characteristic
of non-destructive readout, which is only a single exposure in a frame, as shown
in Fig. 4a. The exposure should have the same duration in all pixels because
the dynamic range of a pixel is limited. Therefore, we can only control the start
time of a single exposure for each pixel, and cannot split the exposure duration
to multiple exposures in one frame, even though the exposure time would be
controllable. Here, the main hardware restriction is the single bump exposure
(SBE) on this sensor, which is termed as the SBE sensor in this paper. Figure 2b
shows an example of the SBE sensor's space-time exposure pattern.

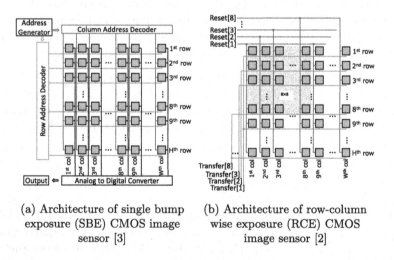

(a) Architecture of single bump
exposure (SBE) CMOS image
sensor [3]

(b) Architecture of row-column
wise exposure (RCE) CMOS
image sensor [2]

Fig. 3. Architecture of single bump exposure (SBE) and row-column wise exposure
(RCE) image sensors. The SEB image sensor in (a) has a row and column address
decoder and can be read out pixel-wise. However, it does not have a per-pixel buffer
and can perform single-bump exposure (Fig. 4). The RCE image sensor shown in (b) has
an additional transistor and exposure control signal line, and can perform multi-bump
exposure. However, it only has row addressing, which provides row wise exposure, such
as that of a rolling shutter.

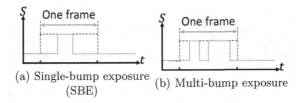

(a) Single-bump exposure (SBE)   (b) Multi-bump exposure

Fig. 4. Exposure bump. Single-bump means that the sensor is exposed only once during the exposure. Conversely, multi-bump means that the sensor is exposed multiple times during the exposure.

Sonoda et al. [2] used the prototype CMOS sensor with additional reset and transfer signal lines to control the exposure time. The sensor's architecture is shown in Fig. 3b. This figure shows the top left of the sensor with a block structure of 8 × 8 pixels. These signal lines are shared by the pixels in the columns and rows. The reset signal lines are shared every eighth column, and the transfer signal lines are shared every eighth row. Therefore, the exposure pattern is cloned block wise. The sensor had a destructive readout and the exposure was more uniquely controllable such that we could use multiple exposures and their different durations in a frame. However, the exposure patterns depended spatially on the rows or columns of the neighboring pixels. In this paper, we termed this sensor as the row-column wise exposure (RCE) sensor. Figure 2c shows an example pattern of the RCE sensor.

Few previous methods [6] of designing and optimizing exposure patterns for compressive video sensing have been reported. However, none of them can be applied to realistic CMOS architectures, because all of these previously reported methods have assumed that exposure is fully controllable. Hence, we propose a new method to optimize patterns under hardware constraints, although we also considered unconstrained sensors in this study.

4   Joint Optimization for Sensing and Reconstruction Under Hardware Constraints

In this section, we describe the proposed optimization method of jointly optimizing the exposure pattern of compressive video sensing, and performing reconstruction by using a DNN. The proposed DNN consists of two main parts. The first part is the sensing layer (encoding) that optimizes the exposure pattern (binary weight) under the constraint imposed by the hardware structure, as described in Sect. 3. The second part is the reconstruction layer that recovers the multiple sub-frames from a single captured image, which was compressed by using the optimized exposure pattern. The overall framework is shown in Fig. 5.

Training was carried out in the following steps:

1. At the time of forward propagation, the binary weight is used for the sensing layer, while the reconstruction layer uses the continuous weights.

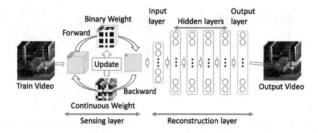

Fig. 5. Network structure. Proposed network structure to jointly optimize the exposure pattern of compressive video sensing, and the reconstruction. The left side represents the sensing layer that compresses video to an image by using the exposure pattern. The right side represents the reconstruction layer that learns non-linear mapping between the compressed image to video reconstruction.

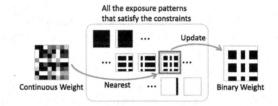

Fig. 6. Binary weight update. Binary weight updated with the most similar patterns in the precomputed binary weights. The similarity between the continuous-value weight and the precomputed binary pattern is computed by the normalized dot product.

2. The gradients are computed by backward propagation.
3. The continuous weights of sensing and reconstruction layers are updated according to the computed gradients.
4. The binary weights of the sensing layer are updated with the continuous weights of the sensing layer.

4.1   Compressive Sensing Layer

We sought an exposure pattern that would be capable of reconstructing video frames with high quality when trained along with the reconstruction (decoding) layer. More importantly, the compressive sensing layer had to be capable of handling the exposure pattern constraints imposed by actual hardware architectures. Because implementing nested spatial pattern constraints (Sect. 3) in the DNN layer was not trivial, we used a binary pattern (weight) chosen from the precomputed binary weights at forward propagation in the training. The binary weight was relaxed to a continuous value [18] to make the network differentiable by backward computation. Next, the weight was binarized for the next forward computation by choosing the most similar patterns in the precomputed binary weights. The similarity between the continuous-value weight and the precomputed binary pattern was computed by the normalized dot product (Fig. 6).

The binary patterns can be readily derived from the hardware constraints. For the SBE sensor [3], we precomputed the patterns from all possible combinations of the single bump exposures with time starting at $t = 0, 1, 2, \cdots, T - d$, where d is the exposure duration.

For the RCE sensor, the possible patterns were computed as follows: (1) generate the possible sets by choosing the reset combinations (8 bits) and transfer (8 bits) signals; (2) simulate the exposure pattern for all signal sets.

For the unconstraint sensor, we applied the same approach to prepare all possible patterns, and then chose the nearest pattern. We used simple thresholding to generate binary patterns, as has been done by Iliadis et al. [6] in experiments, seeing as this approach is not computationally effective.

4.2 Reconstruction Layer

The reconstruction layer decodes high-frame videos from a single image compressed by using the learned exposure pattern, as was described in the previous section. This decoding expands the single image to multiple sub-frames by non-linear mapping, which can be modeled and learned by a multi-layer perceptron (MLP). As illustrated in Fig. 5, the MLP consisted of four hidden layers and each layer was truncated by rectified linear unit (ReLU). The network was trained by minimizing the errors between the training videos and the reconstructed videos. We used the mean squared error (MSE) as the loss function because it was directly related with the peak signal-to-noise ratio (PSNR).

5 Experiments

5.1 Experimental and Training Setup

The network size was determined based on the size of the patch volume to be reconstructed. We used the controllable exposure sensor [2], which exposes the 8 pixel block. Therefore, the volume size of $W_p \times H_p \times T$ was set to $8 \times 8 \times 16$ in the experiments. The reconstruction network had four hidden layers. We trained our network by using the SumMe dataset, which is a public benchmarking video summarization dataset that includes 25 videos. We choose 20 videos out of the available 25. The selected videos contained a relative variety of motion. We randomly cropped the patch volumes from the videos and augmented the directional variety of motions and textures by rotating and flipping the cropped patches. This resulted in 829,440 patch volumes. Subsequently, we used these patches in the end-to-end training of the proposed network to jointly train the sensing and reconstruction layers. In the training, we used 500 epochs with a minibatch size of 200.

5.2 Simulation Experiments

We carried out simulation experiments to evaluate our method. We assumed three different types of hardware constraints for the SBE, RCE, and unconstraint

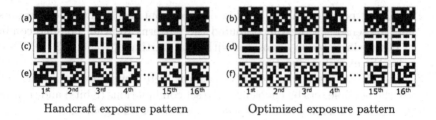

Handcraft exposure pattern   Optimized exposure pattern

Fig. 7. Handcraft and optimized exposure pattern. (a) (b) single bump exposure (SBE) sensor [3] (c) (d) row-column wise exposure (RCE) sensor [2] (e) (f) unconstraint sensor

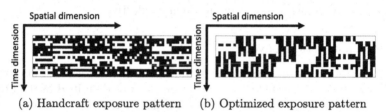

(a) Handcraft exposure pattern   (b) Optimized exposure pattern

Fig. 8. Comparison of exposure patterns. The optimized exposure pattern indicates more smooth and continuous exposures after the training.

sensors. The details of the SBE and RCE sensor constraints are described in Sect. 3. The exposure pattern for an unconstrained sensor can independently control the exposure for each pixel and achieve perfect random exposure, which is ideal in signal recovery. The handcrafted pattern for the unconstrained sensors was random.

Figure 7a shows the handcraft exposure pattern of the SBE sensor. The exposure patterns indicates an exposed pixel in white color and an unexposed pixel in black color. Note that [3] used a patch volume size of $7 \times 7 \times 36$, and an exposure pattern. Instead, we used a size of $8 \times 8 \times 16$ to make a fair comparison with [2] under the same conditions. Figure 7b shows the optimized exposure pattern of the SBE sensor after training. This pattern still satisfies the constraint by which each pixel has a single bump with the same duration as that of other pixels.

Figure 7c shows the handcrafted exposure pattern of the RCE sensor. Figure 7d shows the optimized exposure pattern after training. The optimized pattern satisfied the constraints. Figure 8 compares the exposure patterns. We reshaped the $8 \times 8 \times 16$ exposure patterns to 64×16 to better visualize the space vs. time dimensions. The horizontal and vertical axes represent the spatial and temporal dimension, respectively. The original handcrafted pattern of the RCE sensor indicates that the exposure was not smooth in the temporal direction, while the optimized exposure pattern indicates more temporary, smooth, and continuous exposures after the training. Similar results have been reported by [6], even though our study considered the hardware constraints in pattern optimization.

Figure 7e shows the random exposure pattern, and Fig. 7f shows the optimized exposure pattern of the unconstraint sensor. The optimized patterns were updated by the training and generated differently than the random exposure patterns, which were used as the initial optimization patterns.

We generated a captured image simulated for the SBE, RCE, and unconstraint sensors. We input the simulated images to the reconstruction network to recover the video. We quantitatively evaluated the reconstruction quality by using the peak signal to noise ratio (PSNR). In the evaluation, we used 14 256×256 pixel videos with 16 sub-frames. Figure 9 shows two example results, which are named Car and Crushed can. The upper row (Car) of Fig. 9 shows that, in our result, the edges of the letter mark were reconstructed sharper than in the result of the handcrafted exposure pattern. Additionally, the bottom row (Crushed can) shows that the characters were clearer in the optimized exposure pattern results, in comparison with the results of the handcrafted exposure pattern. The reconstruction qualities were different in each scene. However, the qualities in the optimized exposure pattern were always better than those of the handcrafted exposure pattern, regardless of whether SBE, RCE, or unconstraint sensors were assumed. Hence, the proposed framework effectively determined better exposure patterns under different hardware constraints and jointly optimized the reconstruction layer to suit these patterns. Table 1 shows the average PSNRs of the handcrafted and optimized results for the SBE, RCE, and unconstraint sensors. Owing to the pattern's joint optimization and the reconstruction layers, the proposed method always outperformed the original handcrafted patterns.

We compared our DNN approach with the dictionary-based (OMP) [3] and GMM based [4] approaches. We trained the dictionary for OMP and GMM with the same data used by the DNN, and set the number of dictionary elements to 5,000 for OMP, and the number of components in GMM to 20. These parameters were selected based on preliminary experiments. Additionally, we evaluated

Table 1. Average peak signal-to-noise ratio (PSNR) of video reconstruction with different noise levels.

	Noise level	Handcraft SBE	Optimized SBE	Handcraft RCE	Optimized RCE	Ramdom	Unconstraint
DNN (Ours)	0	29.41	30.05	28.51	29.45	29.17	29.99
	0.01	29.09	29.70	26.76	27.46	28.47	28.88
	0.05	25.61	25.95	19.85	20.22	23.08	22.05
GMM [4]	0	27.69	29.63	28.18	28.82	29.05	29.81
	0.01	27.54	29.29	26.27	26.57	28.13	28.09
	0.05	24.58	25.50	19.18	19.23	22.13	21.25
OMP [3]	0	24.66	26.22	22.96	24.22	24.27	25.83
	0.01	24.46	26.02	22.46	23.46	24.09	25.39
	0.05	21.56	23.32	17.59	17.42	21.21	20.54

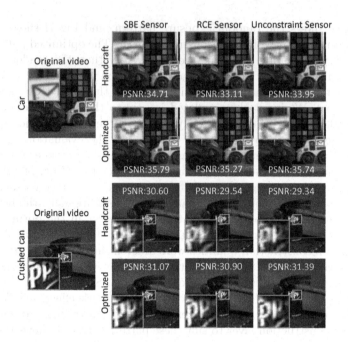

Fig. 9. Reconstruction results of 3rd sub-frame (DNN).

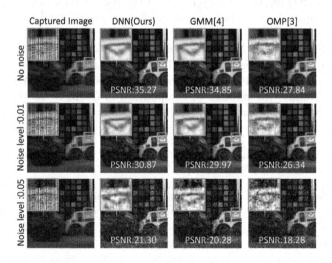

Fig. 10. Reconstruction results of 3rd sub-frame with different noise levels by the deep neural network (DNN), Gaussian mixture models (GMM), and orthogonal matching pursuit (OMP) (exposure pattern: optimized RCE)

the video recovery from a noisy input to validate robustness. We added white Gaussian noise to the simulated captured image with different variances (the mean value was 0). Table 1 shows the average PSNR value between the ground

Fig. 11. Camera used in real experiment.

truth video and the reconstructed video for the variances of 0, 0.01, and 0.05. Figure 10 shows the reconstruction results with different noise levels, as obtained by the DNN, GMM, and OMP. We did not add noise to the training of the DNN. Figure 10 shows that the images were degraded, while the PSNRs decreased when the noise increased by any method. The proposed DNN decoder was affected by the noise, but still achieved the best performance in comparison with the other decoders.

5.3   Real Experiments

We conducted real experiments by using the real compressive image captured by the camera with the sensor reported by [2,19]. Figure 11 shows the camera image used in the real experiment. The compressed video was captured with 15 fps. We set 16 exposure patterns per frame. Thus, the reconstructed video was equivalent to 240 fps after recovering all of the 16 sub-frames. We set the exposure pattern obtained by the sensing layer of the proposed network after the training. Moreover, we reconstructed the video from the captured image by reconstructing the layer of the proposed network. The sensor had a rolling shutter readout and temporal exposure patterns, which were temporally shifted according to the position of the image's row. The shifted exposure pattern was applied every 32 rows (four blocks with a 8 patch), in the case where the resolution of the sensor was 672×512 pixels and the number of exposure patterns was 16 in one frame. For example, the actual sub-exposure pattern was applied to the first four blocks as the 0–15 sub-exposure pattern, the second four blocks were applied as the 1–15, 0 pattern, the third four blocks were applied as the 2–15, 0, 1 pattern, and so on. Hence, we trained 16 different reconstruction networks to apply the variety of shifted exposure patterns. We used these different reconstruction networks every 32 rows in an image. Figure 12 shows the single frame of the real captured image and three of the 16 reconstructed sub-frames. The upper row shows that a moving pendulum appeared at a different position in the reconstructed sub-frames, and the motion and shape were recovered. The second row shows the blinking of an eye, and the bottom row shows a coin dropped into water. Our method successfully recovered very different appearances; namely, the swinging pendulum, closing eye, and moving coin. Because the scene was significantly different from the videos included in the training dataset, these results also demonstrate the generalization of the trained network.

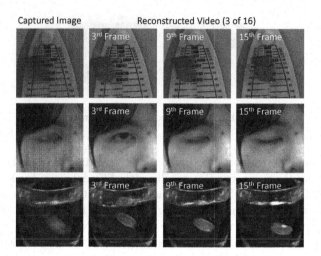

Fig. 12. Reconstruction results. The left column shows the captured image; left of the second column are the 3rd, 9th, and 15th frames of the reconstructed video.

6   Conclusion

In this paper, we first argued that real sensor architectures for developing controllable exposure have various hardware constraints that make non-practical the implementation of compressive video sensing based on completely random exposure patterns. To address this issue, we proposed a general framework that consists of sensing and reconstruction layers by using a DNN. Additionally, we jointly optimized the encoding and decoding models under the hardware constraints. We presented examples of applying the proposed framework to two different constraints of SBE, RCE, and unconstraint sensors. We demonstrated that our optimal patterns and decoding network realized the reconstruction of higher quality video in comparison with handcrafted patterns in simulation and real experiments.

Acknowledgement. This work was supported by JSPS KAKENHI (Grant Number 18K19818).

References

1. Kleinfelder, S., Lim, S., Liu, X., El Gamal, A.: A 10000 frames/s CMOS digital pixel sensor. IEEE J. Solid-State Circ. **36**(12), 2049–2059 (2001)
2. Sonoda, T., Nagahara, H., Endo, K., Sugiyama, Y., Taniguchi, R.: High-speed imaging using CMOS image sensor with quasi pixel-wise exposure. In: International Conference on Computational Photography (ICCP), pp. 1–11 (2016)
3. Hitomi, Y., Gu, J., Gupta, M., Mitsunaga, T., Nayar, S.K.: Video from a single coded exposure photograph using a learned over-complete dictionary. In: International Conference on Computer Vision (ICCV), pp. 287–294 (2011)

4. Yang, J., et al.: Video compressive sensing using Gaussian mixture models. IEEE Trans. Image Process. **23**(11), 4863–4878 (2014)
5. Iliadis, M., Spinoulas, L., Katsaggelos, A.K.: Deep fully-connected networks for video compressive sensing. Digit. Sig. Process. **72**, 9–18 (2018)
6. Iliadis, M., Spinoulas, L., Katsaggelos, A.K.: DeepBinaryMask: learning a binary mask for video compressive sensing. arXiv preprint arXiv:1607.03343 (2016)
7. Sarhangnejad, N., Lee, H., Katic, N., O'Toole, M., Kutulakos, K., Genov, R.: CMOS image sensor architecture for primal-dual coding. In: International Image Sensor Workshop (2017)
8. LeCun, Y., Bengio, Y., Hinton, G.: Deep learning. Nature **521**(7553), 436 (2015)
9. Dadkhah, M., Deen, M.J., Shirani, S.: Compressive sensing image sensors-hardware implementation. Sensors **13**(4), 4961–4978 (2013)
10. Robucci, R., Gray, J.D., Chiu, L.K., Romberg, J., Hasler, P.: Compressive sensing on a CMOS separable-transform image sensor. Proc. IEEE **98**(6), 1089–1101 (2010)
11. Dadkhah, M., Deen, M.J., Shirani, S.: Block-based CS in a CMOS image sensor. IEEE Sens. J. **14**(8), 2897–2909 (2014)
12. Majidzadeh, V., Jacques, L., Schmid, A., Vandergheynst, P., Leblebici, Y.: A (256–256) pixel 76.7 mW CMOS imager/compressor based on real-time in-pixel compressive sensing. In: International Symposium on Circuits and Systems (ISCAS) (2010)
13. Oike, Y., El Gamal, A.: CMOS image sensor with per-column $\sum \Delta$ ADC and programmable compressed sensing. IEEE J. Solid-State Circ. **48**(1), 318–328 (2013)
14. Spinoulas, L., He, K., Cossairt, O., Katsaggelos, A.: Video compressive sensing with on-chip programmable subsampling. In: IEEE Conference on Computer Vision and Pattern Recognition Workshops (2015)
15. Aharon, M., Elad, M., Bruckstein, A.: K-SVD: an algorithm for designing overcomplete dictionaries for sparse representation. IEEE Trans. Sig. Process. **54**(11), 4311–4322 (2006)
16. Pati, Y.C., Rezaiifar, R., Krishnaprasad, P.S.: Orthogonal matching pursuit: recursive function approximation with applications to wavelet decomposition. In: The Twenty-Seventh Asilomar Conference on Signals, Systems and Computers (1993)
17. Tibshirani, R.: Regression shrinkage and selection via the lasso. J. Roy. Stat. Soc. Ser. B (Methodol.) **58**, 267–288 (1996)
18. Courbariaux, M., Hubara, I., Soudry, D., El-Yaniv, R., Bengio, Y.: Binarized neural networks: training deep neural networks with weights and activations constrained to +1 or −1. arXiv preprint arXiv:1602.02830 (2016)
19. Hamamatsu Photonics K.K. Imaging device. Japan patent JP2015-216594A (2015)

Deforming Autoencoders: Unsupervised Disentangling of Shape and Appearance

Zhixin Shu[1]([✉]), Mihir Sahasrabudhe[2], Rıza Alp Güler[2,3], Dimitris Samaras[1], Nikos Paragios[2,4], and Iasonas Kokkinos[5,6]

[1] Stony Brook University, Stony Brook, NY, USA
`zhshu@cs.stonybrook.edu`
[2] CentraleSupélec, Université Paris-Saclay, Gif-sur-Yvette, France
[3] INRIA, Rocquencourt, France
[4] TheraPanacea, Paris, France
[5] Univeristy College London, London, UK
[6] Facebook AI Research, Paris, France

Abstract. In this work we introduce Deforming Autoencoders, a generative model for images that disentangles shape from appearance in an unsupervised manner. As in the deformable template paradigm, shape is represented as a deformation between a canonical coordinate system ('template') and an observed image, while appearance is modeled in deformation-invariant, template coordinates. We introduce novel techniques that allow this approach to be deployed in the setting of autoencoders and show that this method can be used for unsupervised groupwise image alignment. We show experiments with expression morphing in humans, hands, and digits, face manipulation, such as shape and appearance interpolation, as well as unsupervised landmark localization. We also achieve a more powerful form of unsupervised disentangling in template coordinates, that successfully decomposes face images into shading and albedo, allowing us to further manipulate face images.

1   Introduction

Disentangling factors of variation is important for the broader goal of controlling and understanding deep networks, but also for applications such as image manipulation through interpretable operations. Progress in the direction of disentangling the latent space of deep generative models has facilitated the separation of latent image representations into dimensions that account for independent factors of variation, such as identity, illumination, normals, and spatial support [1–4], low-dimensional transformations, such as rotations, translation, or scaling [5–7] or finer-levels of variation, including age, gender, wearing glasses, or other attributes e.g. [2,8] for particular classes, such as faces.

Electronic supplementary material The online version of this chapter (https://doi.org/10.1007/978-3-030-01249-6_40) contains supplementary material, which is available to authorized users.

© Springer Nature Switzerland AG 2018
V. Ferrari et al. (Eds.): ECCV 2018, LNCS 11214, pp. 664–680, 2018.
https://doi.org/10.1007/978-3-030-01249-6_40

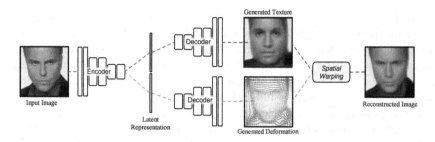

Fig. 1. Deforming Autoencoders follow the deformable template paradigm and model image generation through a cascade of appearance (or, 'texture') synthesis in a canonical coordinate system and a spatial deformation that warps the texture to the observed image coordinates. By keeping the latent vector for texture short, we force the network to model shape variability through the deformation branch. This allows us to train a deep generative image model that disentangles shape and appearance in an entirely unsupervised manner, using solely an image reconstruction loss for training.

Shape variation is more challenging as it is a transformation of a function's domain, rather than its values. Even simple, supervised additive shape models result in complex nonlinear optimization problems [9,10]. Nonetheless, several works in the previous decade aimed at learning shape/appearance factorizations in an unsupervised manner, exploring groupwise image alignment, [11–14].

In a deep learning context, several works incorporated deformations and alignment in supervised settings, including Spatial Transformers [15], Deep Epitomic Networks [16], Deformable CNNs [17], Mass Displacement Networks [18], Mnemonic Descent [19], Densereg [20] or more recently, works that use surface-based 3D face models for accurate face analysis [21,22]. These works have shown that one can improve the accuracy of both classification and localization tasks by injecting deformations and alignment within traditional CNN architectures.

Turning to unsupervised deep learning, even though most works focus on rigid or low-dimensional parametric deformations, e.g. [5,6], several works have attempted to incorporate richer non-rigid deformations within learning. A thread of work aims at dynamically rerouting the processing of information within the network's graph based on the input, starting from neural computation arguments [23–25] and eventually translating into concrete algorithms, such as the 'capsule' works [26,27] that bind neurons on-the-fly. Still, these works lack a transparent, parametric handling of non-rigid deformations. On a more geometric direction, recent work aims at recovering dense correspondences between pairs [28] or sets of RGB images, e.g. [29,30]. These works however do not have the notion of a reference coordinate system ('template') to which images can get mapped - this makes image generation and manipulation harder. More recently, [31] use the equivariance principle to align sets of images to a common coordinate system, but do not develop this into a full-blown generative model of images.

Our work advances this line of research by following the deformable template paradigm [9,10,32–34]. In particular, we consider that object instances are obtained by deforming a prototypical object, or 'template', through dense, diffeomorphic deformation fields. This makes it possible to factor object variability within a category into variations that are associated to spatial transformations, generally linked to the object's 2D/3D shape, and variations that are associated to appearance (or, 'texture' in graphics), e.g. due to facial hair, skin color, or illumination. In particular we model both sources of variation in terms of a low-dimensional latent code that is learnable in an unsupervised manner from images. We achieve disentangling by breaking this latent code into separate parts that are fed into separate decoder networks that deliver appearance and deformation estimates. Even though one could hope that a generic convolutional architecture will learn to represent such effects, we argue that explicitly injecting this inductive bias in a network can help with training, while also yielding control over the generative process. Our main contributions in this work are:

First, we introduce the *Deforming Autoencoder* architecture, bringing together the deformable modeling paradigm with unsupervised deep learning. We treat the template-to-image correspondence task as that of predicting a smooth and invertible transformation. As shown in Fig. 1, our network first predicts a transformation field in tandem with a template-aligned appearance field. It subsequently deforms the synthesized appearance to generate an image similar to its input. This allows us to disentangle shape and appearance by explicitly modelling the effects of image deformation during decoding.

Second, we explore different ways in which deformations can be represented and predicted by the decoder. Instead of building a generic deformation model, we compose a global, affine deformation field, with a non-rigid field that is synthesized as a convolutional decoder network. We develop a method that prevents self-crossings in the synthesized deformation field and show that it simplifies training and improves accuracy. We also show that class-related information can be exploited, when available, to learn better deformation models: this yields sharper images and can be used to learn models that jointly account for multiple classes - e.g. all MNIST digits.

Third, we show that disentangling appearance from deformation has several advantages for modeling and manipulating images. Disentangling leads to clearly better synthesis results for tasks such as expression, pose or identity interpolation, compared to standard autoencoder architectures. Similarly, we show that accounting for deformations facilitates further disentangling of appearance components into intrinsic, shading-albedo decompositions, which allow us to re-shade through simple operations on the latent shading coordinates.

We complement these qualitative results with a quantitative analysis of the learned model in terms of landmark localization accuracy. We show that our method is not too far below supervised methods and outperforms with a margin the latest state-of-the-art works on self-supervised correspondence estimation [31], even though we never explicitly trained our network for correspondence estimation, but rather only aimed at reconstructing pixel intensities.

2   Deforming Autoencoders

Our architecture embodies the deformable template paradigm in an autoencoder architecture. Our premise is that image generation can be interpreted as the combination of two processes: a synthesis of appearance on a deformation-free coordinate system ('template'), followed by a subsequent deformation that introduces shape variability. Denoting by $T(\mathbf{p})$ the value of the synthesized appearance (or, texture) at coordinate $\mathbf{p} = (x, y)$ and by $W(\mathbf{p})$ the estimated deformation field, we reconstruct the observed image, $I(\mathbf{p})$ as follows:

$$I(\mathbf{p}) \simeq T(W(\mathbf{p})), \tag{1}$$

namely the image appearance at position $\mathbf{p}$ is obtained by looking up the synthesized appearance at position $W(\mathbf{p})$. This is implemented in terms of a bilinear sampling layer [15] that allows us to pass gradients through the warping process.

The appearance and deformation functions are synthesized by independent decoder networks. The inputs to the decoders are delivered by a joint encoder network that takes as input the observed image and delivers a low-dimensional latent representation, Z, of shape and appearance. This is split into two parts, $Z = [Z_T, Z_S]$ which feed into the appearance and shape networks respectively, providing us with a clear separation of shape and appearance.

2.1   Deformation Field Modeling

Rather than leave deformation modeling entirely to back-propagation, we use some domain knowledge to simplify and accelerate learning. The first observation is that global aspects can be expressed using low-dimensional linear models. We account for global deformations by an affine Spatial Transformer layer, that uses a six-dimensional input to synthesize a deformation field as an expansion on a fixed basis [15]. This means that the shape representation, Z_S described above is decomposed into two parts, Z_W, Z_A, where Z_A accounts for the affine, and Z_W for the non-rigid, learned part of the deformation field. As is common practice in deformable modeling [9,10], these deformation fields are generated by separate decoders and are composed so that the affine transformation warps the detailed non-rigid warps to the image positions where they should apply.

We note that not every non-rigid deformation field is plausible. Without appropriate regularization the deformation field can amount to a generic permutation matrix. As observed in Fig. 2(f), a non-regularized deformation can spread a connected texture pattern to a disconnected image area.

To prevent this problem, instead of the shape decoder CNN directly predicting the local warping field $W(\mathbf{p}) = (W_x(x, y), W_y(x, y))$, we consider a 'differential decoder' that generates the spatial gradient of the warping field: $\nabla_x W_x$ and $\nabla_y W_y$, where ∇_c denotes the $c - th$ component of the spatial gradient vector. These two quantities measure the displacement of consecutive pixels - for instance $\nabla_x W_x = 2$ amounts to horizontal scaling by a size of 2, while $\nabla_x W_x = -1$ amounts to left-right flipping; a similar behavior is associated with

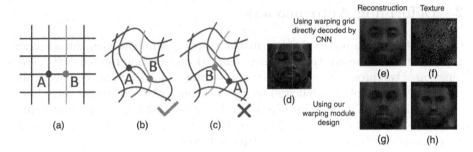

Fig. 2. Our warping module design only permits locally consistent warping, as shown in (b), while the flipping of relative pixel positions, as shown in (c), is not allowed by design. To achieve this, we let the deformation decoder predict the horizontal and vertical increments of the deformation ($\nabla_x W$ and $\nabla_y W$, respectively) and use a ReLU transfer function to remove local flips, caused by going back in the vertical or horizontal direction. A spatial integral module is subsequently applied to generate the grid. This simple mechanism serves as an effective constraint for the deformation generation process, while allowing us to model free-form/non-rigid local deformation.

$\nabla_y W_y$ in the vertical axis. We note that global rotations are handled by the affine warping field, and the $\nabla_x W_y, \nabla_y W_x$ are associated with small local rotations of minor importance - we therefore focus on $\nabla_x W_x, \nabla_y W_y$. Having access to these two values gives us a handle on the deformation field, since we can prevent folding/excessive stretching by controlling $\nabla_x W_x, \nabla_y W_y$.

In particular, we pass the output of our differential decoder through a Rectified Linear Unit (ReLU) layer, which enforces positive horizontal offsets on horizontally adjacent pixels, and positive vertical offsets on vertically adjacent pixels. We subsequently apply a spatial integration layer, implemented as a fixed network layer, on top of the output of the ReLU layer to reconstruct the warping field from its spatial gradient. Thus, the new deformation module enforces the generation of smooth and regular warping fields that avoid self-crossings. In practice we found that clipping the decoded offsets by a maximal value significantly eases training, which amounts to replacing the ReLU layer, $\mathrm{ReLU}(x) = \max(x, 0)$ with a $\mathrm{HardTanh}_{0,\delta}(x) = \min(\max(x, 0), \delta)$ layer. In our experiments we set $\delta = 5/w$, where w denotes the number of pixels along an image dimension.

2.2 Class-Aware Deforming Autoencoder

We can require our network's latent representation to predict not only shape and appearance, but also instance class, if that is available during training. This discrete information may be easier to acquire than the actual deformation field, which requires manual landmark annotation. For instance, for faces such discrete information could represent the expression or a person's identity.

In particular we consider that the latent representation can be decomposed as follows: $Z = [Z_T, Z_C, Z_S]$, where Z_T, Z_S are as previously the appearance-

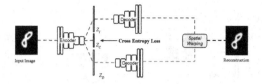

Fig. 3. A *class-aware* model can account for multi-modal deformation distributions by utilizing class information. Introducing a classification loss into latent space helps the model learn a better representation of the input as demonstrated on MNIST.

and shape- related parts of the representation, respectively, while Z_C is fed as input to a sub-network trained to predict the class associated with the input image. Apart from assisting the classification task, the latent vector Z_C is fed into both the appearance and shape decoders, as shown in Fig. 3. Intuitively this allows our decoder network to learn a mixture model that is conditioned on class information, rather than treating the joint, multi-modal distribution through a monolithic model. Even though the class label is only used during training, and not for reconstruction, our experimental results show that a network trained with class supervision can deliver more accurate synthesis results.

2.3 Intrinsic Deforming Autoencoder: Deformation, Albedo and Shading Decomposition

Having outlined Deforming Autoencoders, we now use a Deforming Autoencoder to model complex physical image signals, such as illumination effects, without a supervision signal. For this we design the Intrinsic Deforming-Autoencoder (Intrinsic-DAE) to model shading and albedo for in-the-wild face images. As shown in Fig. 4(a), we introduce two separate decoders for shading S and albedo A, each of which has the same structure as the original texture decoder. The texture is computed by $T = S \circ A$ where $\circ$ denotes the Hadamard product.

In order to model the physical properties of shading and albedo, we follow the intrinsic decomposition regularization loss used in [2]: we apply the L2 smoothness loss on ∇S, meaning that shading is expected to be smooth, while leaving albedo unconstrained. As shown in Fig. 4 and more extensively in the experimental results section, when used in tandem with a Deforming Autoencoder, we can successfully decompose a face image into shape, albedo, and shading components, while a standard Autoencoder completely fails at decomposing unaligned images into shading and albedo. We note that unlike [22], our decomposition is obtained in an entirely unsupervised manner.

2.4 Training

Our objective function is formed as the sum of three losses, combining the reconstruction error with the regularization terms required for the modules described

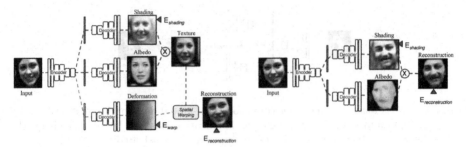

(a) Deforming autoencoder with intrinsic decomposition   (b) Autoencoder with intrinsic decomposition

Fig. 4. Autoencoders with intrinsic decomposition. (a) Deforming Autoencoder with intrinsic decomposition (Intrinsic-DAE): we model the texture by the product of shading and albedo components, each of which is decoded by an individual decoder. The texture is subsequently warped by the predicted deformation field. (b) A plain autoencoder with intrinsic decomposition. Both networks are trained with a reconstruction loss ($E_{\text{Reconstruction}}$) for the final output and a regularization loss on shading (E_{Shading}).

above. Concretely, the loss of the deforming autoencoder can be written as

$$E_{\text{DAE}} = E_{\text{Reconstruction}} + E_{\text{Warp}}, \tag{2}$$

where the reconstruction loss is defined as the standard ℓ_2 loss

$$E_{\text{Reconstruction}} = \|I_{\text{Output}} - I_{\text{Input}}\|^2, \tag{3}$$

and the warping loss is decomposed as follows:

$$E_{\text{Warp}} = E_{\text{Smooth}} + E_{\text{BiasReduce}}. \tag{4}$$

The smoothness cost, E_{smooth}, penalizes quickly-changing deformations encoded by the local warping field. It is measured in terms of the total variation norm of the horizontal and vertical differential warping fields, and is given by:

$$E_{\text{Smooth}} = \lambda_1 \left(\|\nabla W_x(x,y)\|_1 + \|\nabla W_y(x,y)\|_1 \right), \tag{5}$$

where $\lambda_1 = 1e - 6$. Finally, $E_{\text{BiasReduce}}$ is a regularization on (1) the affine parameters defined as the L2-distance between S_A and S_0, S_0 being the identity affine transform and (2) the average of the deformation grid for a random batch of training data being close to identity mapping grid:

$$E_{\text{BiasReduce}} = \lambda_2 \|S_A - S_0\|^2 + \lambda_2' \|\bar{W} - W_0\|^2, \tag{6}$$

where $\lambda_2 = \lambda_2' = 0.01$. $\bar{W}$ denotes the average deformation grid of a mini-batch of training data and W_0 denotes an identity mapping grid. In the class-aware variant described in Sect. 2.2 we augment the loss above with the cross-entropy loss evaluated on the classification network's outputs. We add the following objective function in the training of the Intrinsic-DAE: $E_{\text{Shading}} = \lambda_3 \|\nabla S\|^2$ where $\lambda_3 = 1e - 6$.

We experiment with two architecture types: (1) DAE with a standard convolutional auto-encoder, where both encoder and decoders are CNNs with standard convolution-BatchNorm-ReLU blocks. The number of filters and the texture bottleneck capacity can vary per experiment, image resolution, and dataset, as detailed in the supplemental material; (2) Dense-DAE with a densely connected convolutional network [35] for encoder and decoders respectively (no skip connections over the bottleneck layers). In particular, we follow the architecture of DenseNet-121, but without the 1×1 convolutional layers inside each dense block.

3   Experiments

To demonstrate the properties of our deformation disentangling network, we conduct experiments on MNIST, 11k Hands [36] and Faces-in-the-wild datasets [37, 38]. Our experiments include (1) unsupervised image alignment/appearance inference; (2) learning semantically meaningful manifolds for shape and appearance; (3) unsupervised intrinsic decomposition and (4) unsupervised landmarks detection.

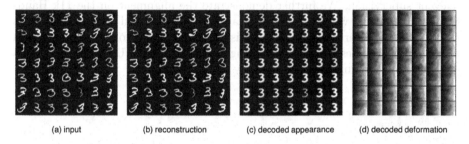

(a) input	(b) reconstruction	(c) decoded appearance	(d) decoded deformation

Fig. 5. Unsupervised deformation-appearance disentangling on a single MNIST digit. Our network learns to reconstruct the input image while automatically deriving a canonical appearance for the input image class. In this experiment, the dimension of the latent representation for appearance Z_T is 1.

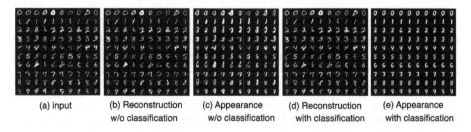

(a) input	(b) Reconstruction w/o classification	(c) Appearance w/o classification	(d) Reconstruction with classification	(e) Appearance with classification

Fig. 6. Class-aware Deforming Autoencoders effectively model the appearance and deformation for multi-class data.

3.1   Unsupervised Appearance Inference

We model canonical appearance and deformation for single category objects. We demonstrate results in the MNIST dataset (Figs. 5 and 6). By limiting the size of Z_T (1 in Fig. 5), we can successfully infer a canonical appearance for a class. In Fig. 5, all different types of digit '3' are aligned to a simple canonical shape.

In cases where the data has a multi-modal distribution exhibiting multiple different canonical appearances, e.g., multi-class MNIST images, learning a single appearance is less meaningful and often challenging (Fig. 6(b)). In such cases, utilizing class information (Sect. 2.2) significantly improves the quality of multi-modal appearance learning (Fig. 6(d)). As the network learns to classify the images implicitly in its latent space, it learns to generate a single canonical appearance for each class. Misclassified data will be decoded into an incorrect class: the image at position (2, 4) in Fig. 6(c, d) is interpreted as a 6.

Moving to a more challenging modeling task, we consider modeling faces in-the-wild. Using the MAFL face dataset we show that our network is able to align the faces to a common texture space under various poses, illumination conditions, or facial expressions (Fig. 9(d)). The aligned textures retain the information of the input image such as lighting, gender, and facial hair, without using any relevant supervision. We further demonstrate the alignment on the 11k Hands dataset [36], where we align palmar images of the left hand of several subjects (Fig. 7). This property of our network is especially useful for applications such as computer graphics, where establishing correspondences (UV map) between a class of objects is important but usually difficult.

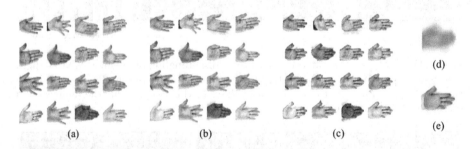

Fig. 7. Unsupervised alignment on images of palms of left hands. (a) The input images; (b) reconstructed images; (c) texture images warped with the average of the decoded deformation; (d) the average input image; and (e) the average texture.

3.2   Autoencoders Vs. Deforming Autoencoders

We now show the ability of our network to learn meaningful deformation representations without supervision. We compare our disentangling network with a plain auto-encoder (Fig. 8). Contrary to our network which disentangles an image into a template texture and a deformation field, the auto-encoder is trained to encode all of the image in a single latent representation.

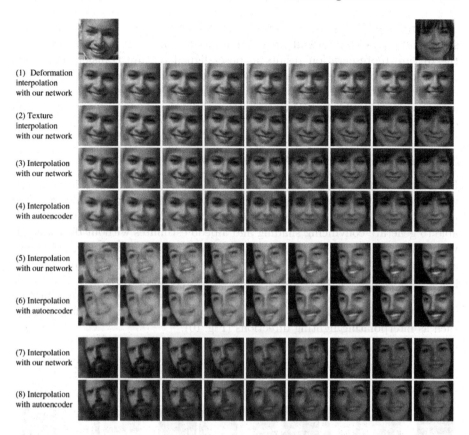

(1) Deformation interpolation with our network

(2) Texture interpolation with our network

(3) Interpolation with our network

(4) Interpolation with autoencoder

(5) Interpolation with our network

(6) Interpolation with autoencoder

(7) Interpolation with our network

(8) Interpolation with autoencoder

Fig. 8. Latent representation interpolation: we embed a face image in the latent space provided by an encoder network. Our network disentangles the texture and deformation in the respective parts of the latent representation vector, allowing a meaningful interpolation between images. Interpolating the deformation-specific part of the latent representation changes the face shape and pose (1); interpolating the latent representation for texture will generate a pose-aligned texture transfer between the images (2); traversing both latent representations will generate smooth and sharp image deformations (3, 5, 7). In contrast, when using a standard auto-encoder (4, 6, 8) such an interpolation often yields artifacts.

We train both networks with the MAFL dataset. To evaluate the learned representation, we conduct manifold traversal (i.e., latent representation interpolation) between two randomly sampled face images: given a source face image I^s and a target image I^t, we first compute their latent representations Zs. We use $Z_T(I^s)$ and $Z_S(I^s)$ to denote the latent representations in our network for I^s, and $Z_{ae}(I^s)$ for the latent representation learned by a plain autoencoder. We then conduct linear interpolation on Z, between Z^s and Z^t: $Z^\lambda = \lambda Z^s + (1 - \lambda)Z^t$. We subsequently reconstruct the image I^λ from Z^λ using the corresponding decoder(s), as shown in Fig. 8.

By traversing the learned deformation representation only, we can change the shape and pose of a face while maintaining its texture (Fig. 8(1)); interpolating the texture representation results in pose-aligned texture transfer (Fig. 8(2)); traversing on both representations will generate a smooth deformation from one image to another (Fig. 8(3, 5, 7)). Compared to the interpolation using the autoencoder (Fig. 8(4, 6, 8)), which often exhibits artifacts, our traversal stays on the semantic manifold of faces and generates sharp facial features.

3.3   Intrinsic Deforming Autoencoders

Having demonstrated the disentanglement abilities of Deforming Autoencoders, we now explore the disentanglement capabilities of the Intrinsic-DAE described in Sect. 2.3. Using only the E_{DA} and regularization losses, the Intrinsic-DAE is able to generate convincing shading and albedo estimates without direct supervision (Fig. 9(b) to (g)). Without the "learning-to-align" property, a baseline autoencoder with an intrinsic decomposition design (Fig. 4(b)) cannot decompose the image into plausible shading and albedo(Fig. 9(h), (i), (j)).

In addition, we show that by manipulating the learned latent representation of S, Intrinsic-DAE allows us to simulate illumination effects for face images, such as interpolating lighting directions (Fig. 10).

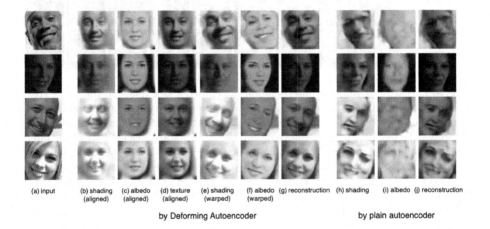

(a) input   (b) shading (aligned)   (c) albedo (aligned)   (d) texture (aligned)   (e) shading (warped)   (f) albedo (warped)   (g) reconstruction   (h) shading   (i) albedo   (j) reconstruction

by Deforming Autoencoder   by plain autoencoder

Fig. 9. Unsupervised intrinsic decomposition with an Intrinsic-DAE. Thanks to the "automatic dense alignment" property of DAE, shading and albedo are faithfully separated (e, f) by the intrinsic decomposition loss. Shading (b) and albedo (c) are learned in an unsupervised manner in the densely aligned canonical space. With the deformation field also learned without supervision, we can recover the intrinsic image components for the original shape and viewpoint (e, f). Without dense alignment, the intrinsic decomposition loss fails to decompose shading and albedo (h, i, j).

As a final demonstration of the potential of the learned models for image synthesis, we note that with $L2$ or $L1$ reconstruction losses, autoencoder-like

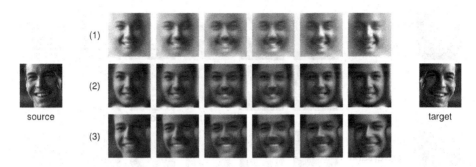

Fig. 10. Lighting interpolation with Intrinsic-DAE. With latent representations learned in an unsupervised manner for shading, albedo, and deformation, the DAE allows us to simulate smooth transitions of the lighting direction. In this example, we interpolate the latent representation of the shading from source (lit from the left) to target (mirrored source, hence lit from the right). The network generates smooth lighting transitions, without explicitly learning geometry, as shown in shading (1) and texture (2). Together with the learned deformation of the source image, DAE enables the relighting of the face in its original pose (3).

architectures are prone to generating smooth images which lack visual realism (Fig. 9). Inspired by generative adversarial networks (GANs) [39], we follow [2] and use an adversarial loss to generate visually realistic images. We train the Intrinsic-DAE with an extra adversarial loss term $E_{\text{Adversarial}}$ applied on the final output, yielding:

$$E_{\text{Intinsic-DAE}} = E_{\text{Reconstruction}} + E_{\text{Warp}} + \lambda_4 E_{\text{Adversarial}}. \tag{7}$$

In practice, we apply a PatchGAN [40,41] as the discriminator and set $\lambda_4 = 0.1$. As shown in Fig. 11, the adversarial loss improves the visual sharpness of the reconstruction while the deformation, shading are still successfully disentangled.

3.4   Unsupervised Alignment Evaluation

Having qualitatively analyzed the disentanglement capabilities of our networks, we now turn to quantifying their performance on the task of unsupervised face landmark localization. We report performance on the MAFL dataset, which contains manually annotated landmark locations (eyes, nose, and mouth corners) for 19,000 training and 1,000 test images. In our experiments, we use a model trained on the CelebA dataset without any form of supervision. Following the evaluation protocol of previous work [31], we train a landmark regressor post-hoc on these deformation fields using the provided training annotations in MAFL. The annotation from the MAFL training set is only used to train the regressor while the DAE is fixed after pre-training. The regressor is a 2-layer MLP. Its inputs are flattened deformation fields (vectors of size $64 \times 64 \times 2$), which are provided as input to a 100-dimensional hidden layer, followed by a ReLU and a

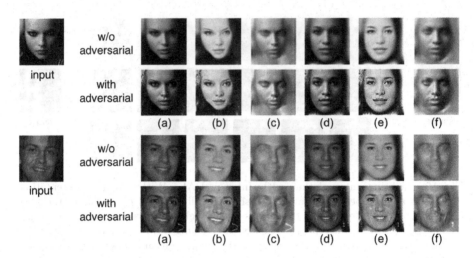

Fig. 11. Intrinsic-DAE with an adversarial loss: (a/d) reconstruction (b/e) albedo, (c/f) shading, in image and template coordinates, respectively. Adding an adversarial loss visually improves the image reconstruction quality of Intrinsic-DAE, while deformation, albedo, and shading can still be successfully disentangled.

Table 1. Landmark localization performance by different types of deformation modeling methods and different training corpus. A indicates affine transformation, I indicates non-rigid transformation by integration, whereas MAFL and CelebA denotes the training set. From columns 1 to 4, we manually annotate landmarks on the average texture, while for column 5, we train a regressor on the deformation fields to predict them. Latent vectors are 32D in these experiments.

A, MAFL	I, MAFL	$A + I$, MAFL	$A + I$, CelebA	$A + I$, CelebA, with regressor
14.13	9.89	8.50	7.54	5.96

10-D output layer to predict the spatial coordinates $((x, y))$ for five landmarks. We use L1 loss as the objective function for regression.

We report the mean error in landmark localization as a percentage of the inter-ocular distance on the MAFL testing set (Tables 1 and 2). As the deformation field determines the alignment in the texture space, it serves as an effective mapping between landmark locations on the aligned texture and those on the original, unaligned faces. Hence, the mean error we report directly quantifies the quality of the (unsupervised) face alignment. In Table 2 we compare with previous state-of-the-art self-supervised image registration [31]. We observe that by better modeling of the deformation space we quickly bridge the gap in performance, even though we never explicitly trained to learn correspondences.

Table 2. Mean error on unsupervised landmark detection on the MAFL test set. Under DAE and Dense-DAE we specify the size of each latent vector. *NR* signifies training without regularization on the estimated deformations, while *Res* signifies training by estimating the residual deformation instead of the integral. Our results outperform the self-supervised method of [31] trained specifically for establishing correspondences.

DAE						Dense-DAE			TCDCN [42]	Thewlis et al. [31]
32-NR	32-Res	16	32	64	96	16	64	96		
10.24	9.93	5.71	5.96	5.70	6.46	6.85	5.50	**5.45**	7.95	5.83

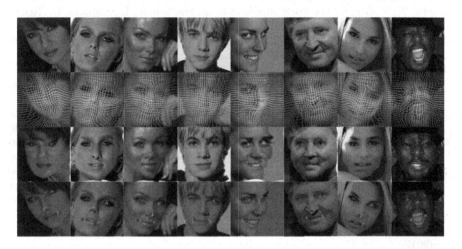

Fig. 12. Row 1: testing images; row 2: estimated deformation grid; row 3: image reverse-transformed to texture space; row 4: semantic landmark locations (green: ground truth, blue: estimation, red: error). (Color figure online)

4   Conclusion and Future Work

In this paper we have developed deforming autoencoders to disentangle shape and appearance in a learned latent representation space. We have shown that this method can be used for unsupervised groupwise image alignment. Our experiments with expression morphing in humans, image manipulation, such as shape and appearance interpolation, as well as unsupervised landmark localization, show the generality of our approach. We have also shown that bringing images in a canonical coordinate system allows for a more extensive form of image disentangling, facilitating the estimation of decompositions into shape, albedo and shading without any form of supervision. We expect that this will lead in the future to a full-fledged disentanglement into normals, illumination, and 3D geometry.

Acknowledgment. This work was supported by a gift from Adobe, NSF grants CNS-1718014 and DMS 1737876, the Partner University Fund, and the SUNY2020 Infrastructure Transportation Security Center. Rıza Alp Güler was supported by the European Horizons 2020 grant no 643666 (I-Support).

References

1. Chen, X., Duan, Y., Houthooft, R., Schulman, J., Sutskever, I., Abbeel, P.: InfoGAN: interpretable representation learning by information maximizing generative adversarial nets. In: NIPS (2016)
2. Shu, Z., Yumer, E., Hadap, S., Sunkavalli, K., Shechtman, E., Samaras, D.: Neural face editing with intrinsic image disentangling. In: CVPR (2017)
3. Worrall, D.E., Garbin, S.J., Turmukhambetov, D., Brostow, G.J.: Interpretable transformations with encoder-decoder networks. In: CVPR (2017)
4. Sengupta, S., Kanazawa, A., Castillo, C.D., Jacobs, D.: SfSNet: learning shape, reflectance and illuminance of faces in the wild. arXiv preprint arXiv:1712.01261 (2017)
5. Memisevic, R., Hinton, G.E.: Learning to represent spatial transformations with factored higher-order Boltzmann machines. Neural Comput. **22**, 1473–1492 (2010)
6. Worrall, D.E., Garbin, S.J., Turmukhambetov, D., Brostow, G.J.: Harmonic networks: deep translation and rotation equivariance (2016)
7. Park, E., Yang, J., Yumer, E., Ceylan, D., Berg, A.C.: Transformation-grounded image generation network for novel 3D view synthesis. In: 2017 IEEE Conference on Computer Vision and Pattern Recognition (CVPR), pp. 702–711. IEEE (2017)
8. Lample, G., Zeghidour, N., Usunier, N., Bordes, A., Denoyer, L., Ranzato, M.: Fader networks: manipulating images by sliding attributes. CoRR abs/1706.00409 (2017)
9. Edwards, G.J., Cootes, T.F., Taylor, C.J.: Face recognition using active appearance models. In: Burkhardt, H., Neumann, B. (eds.) ECCV 1998. LNCS, vol. 1407, pp. 581–595. Springer, Heidelberg (1998). https://doi.org/10.1007/BFb0054766
10. Matthews, I., Baker, S.: Active appearance models revisited. IJCV **60**, 135–164 (2004)
11. Learned-Miller, E.G.: Data driven image models through continuous joint alignment. PAMI **28**, 236–250 (2006)
12. Kokkinos, I., Yuille, A.L.: Unsupervised learning of object deformation models. In: ICCV (2007)
13. Frey, B.J., Jojic, N.: Transformation-invariant clustering using the EM algorithm. IEEE Trans. Pattern Anal. Mach. Intell. **25**(1), 1–17 (2003)
14. Jojic, N., Frey, B.J., Kannan, A.: Epitomic analysis of appearance and shape. In: 9th IEEE International Conference on Computer Vision (ICCV 2003), 14–17 October 2003, Nice, France, pp. 34–43 (2003)
15. Jaderberg, M., Simonyan, K., Zisserman, A., Kavukcuoglu, K.: Spatial transformer networks. CoRR abs/1506.02025 (2015)
16. Papandreou, G., Kokkinos, I., Savalle, P.: Modeling local and global deformations in deep learning: epitomic convolution, multiple instance learning, and sliding window detection. In: CVPR (2015)
17. Dai, J., et al.: Deformable convolutional networks. In: ICCV (2017)
18. Neverova, N., Kokkinos, I.: Mass displacement networks. Arxiv (2017)

19. Trigeorgis, G., Snape, P., Nicolaou, M.A., Antonakos, E., Zafeiriou, S.: Mnemonic descent method: a recurrent process applied for end-to-end face alignment. In: Proceedings of IEEE International Conference on Computer Vision & Pattern Recognition (2016)
20. Güler, R.A., Trigeorgis, G., Antonakos, E., Snape, P., Zafeiriou, S., Kokkinos, I.: DenseReg: fully convolutional dense shape regression in-the-wild. In: CVPR (2017)
21. Cole, F., Belanger, D., Krishnan, D., Sarna, A., Mosseri, I., Freeman, W.T.: Face synthesis from facial identity features (2018)
22. Sengupta, S., Kanazawa, A., Castillo, C.D., Jacobs, D.W.: SfSNet : learning shape, reflectance and illuminance of faces in the wild. In: CVPR (2018)
23. Hinton, G.E.: A parallel computation that assigns canonical object-based frames of reference. In: Proceedings of the 7th International Joint Conference on Artificial Intelligence, IJCAI 1981, 24–28 August 1981, Vancouver, BC, Canada, pp. 683–685(1981)
24. Olshausen, B.A., Anderson, C.H., Essen, D.C.V.: A multiscale dynamic routing circuit for forming size- and position-invariant object representations. J. Comput. Neurosci. 2(1), 45–62 (1995)
25. Malsburg, C.: The correlation theory of brain function. Internal Report 81–2. Gottingen Max-Planck-Institute for Biophysical Chemistry (1981)
26. Hinton, G.E., Krizhevsky, A., Wang, S.D.: Transforming auto-encoders. In: Honkela, T., Duch, W., Girolami, M., Kaski, S. (eds.) ICANN 2011. LNCS, vol. 6791, pp. 44–51. Springer, Heidelberg (2011). https://doi.org/10.1007/978-3-642-21735-7_6
27. Sabour, S., Frosst, N., Hinton, G.E.: Dynamic routing between capsules. CoRR abs/1710.09829 (2017)
28. Bristow, H., Valmadre, J., Lucey, S.: Dense semantic correspondence where every pixel is a classifier. In: ICCV (2015)
29. Zhou, T., Krähenbühl, P., Aubry, M., Huang, Q., Efros, A.A.: Learning dense correspondence via 3D-guided cycle consistency. In: CVPR (2016)
30. Gaur, U., Manjunath, B.S.: Weakly supervised manifold learning for dense semantic object correspondence. In: ICCV (2017)
31. Thewlis, J., Bilen, H., Vedaldi, A.: Unsupervised object learning from dense equivariant image labelling (2017)
32. Amit, Y., Grenander, U., Piccioni, M.: Structural image restoration through deformable templates. J. Am. Stat. Assoc. 86(414), 376–387 (1991)
33. Yuille, A.L.: Deformable templates for face recognition. J. Cogn. Neurosci. 3(1), 59–70 (1991)
34. Blanz, V.T., Vetter, T.: Face recognition based on fitting a 3D morphable model. IEEE Trans. Pattern Anal. Mach. Intell. 25(9), 1063–1074 (2003)
35. Huang, G., Liu, Z., van der Maaten, L., Weinberger, K.Q.: Densely connected convolutional networks. In: Proceedings of the IEEE Conference on Computer Vision and Pattern Recognition (2017)
36. Afifi, M.: Gender recognition and biometric identification using a large dataset of hand images. CoRR abs/1711.04322 (2017)
37. Zhang, Z., Luo, P., Loy, C.C., Tang, X.: Facial landmark detection by deep multitask learning. In: Fleet, D., Pajdla, T., Schiele, B., Tuytelaars, T. (eds.) ECCV 2014. LNCS, vol. 8694, pp. 94–108. Springer, Cham (2014). https://doi.org/10.1007/978-3-319-10599-4_7
38. Liu, Z., Luo, P., Wang, X., Tang, X.: Deep learning face attributes in the wild. In: Proceedings of International Conference on Computer Vision (ICCV) (2015)

39. Goodfellow, I., et al.: Generative adversarial nets. In: Advances in Neural Information Processing Systems, pp. 2672–2680 (2014)
40. Li, C., Wand, M.: Precomputed Real-time texture synthesis with Markovian generative adversarial networks. In: Leibe, B., Matas, J., Sebe, N., Welling, M. (eds.) ECCV 2016. LNCS, vol. 9907, pp. 702–716. Springer, Cham (2016). https://doi.org/10.1007/978-3-319-46487-9_43
41. Isola, P., Zhu, J.Y., Zhou, T., Efros, A.A.: Image-to-image translation with conditional adversarial networks. arxiv (2016)
42. Zhang, Z., Luo, P., Loy, C.C., Tang, X.: Learning deep representation for face alignment with auxiliary attributes. IEEE Trans. Pattern Anal. Mach. Intell. **38**(5), 918–930 (2016)

ExplainGAN: Model Explanation via Decision Boundary Crossing Transformations

Pouya Samangouei[1,2]([envelope]) [ORCID], Ardavan Saeedi[2] [ORCID], Liam Nakagawa[2],
and Nathan Silberman[2] [ORCID]

[1] University of Maryland, College Park, MD 20740, USA
pouya@umiacs.umd.edu
[2] Butterfly Network, New York, NY 10001, USA
{asaeedi,nakagawaliam,nsilberman}@butterflynetinc.com

Abstract. We introduce a new method for interpreting computer vision models: visually perceptible, decision-boundary crossing transformations. Our goal is to answer a simple question: why did a model classify an image as being of class A instead of class B? Existing approaches to model interpretation, including saliency and explanation-by-nearest neighbor, fail to visually illustrate examples of transformations required for a specific input to alter a model's prediction. On the other hand, algorithms for creating decision-boundary crossing transformations (e.g., adversarial examples) produce differences that are visually imperceptible and do not enable insightful explanation. To address this we introduce ExplainGAN, a generative model that produces visually perceptible decision-boundary crossing transformations. These transformations provide high-level conceptual insights which illustrate how a model makes decisions. We validate our model using both traditional quantitative interpretation metrics and introduce a new validation scheme for our approach and generative models more generally.

Keywords: Neural networks · Model interpretation

1 Introduction

Given a classifier, one may ask: What high-level, semantic features of an input is the model using to discriminate between specific classes? Being able to reliably answer this question amounts to an understanding of the classifier's decision boundary at the level of concepts or attributes, rather than pixel-level statistics.

The ability to produce a conceptual understanding of a model's decision boundary would be extremely powerful. It would enable researchers to ensure that a model is extracting relevant, high-level concepts, rather than picking up on spurious features of a dataset. For example, criminal justice systems could determine whether their ethical standards were consistent with that of a model [8]. Additionally, it would provide some measure of validation to consumers (e.g.,

© Springer Nature Switzerland AG 2018
V. Ferrari et al. (Eds.): ECCV 2018, LNCS 11214, pp. 681–696, 2018.
https://doi.org/10.1007/978-3-030-01249-6_41

medical applications, self-driving cars) that a model is making decisions that are difficult to formalize and automatically verify.

Unfortunately, directly visualizing or interpreting decision boundaries in high dimensions is effectively impossible and existing post-hoc interpretation methods fall short of adequately solving this problem. Dimensionality reduction approaches, such as T-SNE [15], are often highly sensitive to their hyperparameters whose values may drastically alter the visualization [27]. Saliency maps are typically designed to highlight the set of pixels that contributed highly to a particular classification. While they can be useful for explaining factors that are present; they cannot adequately describe predictions made due to objects that are missing from the input. Explanation-by-Nearest-Neighbor-Example can indeed demonstrate similar images to a particular query, but there is no guarantee that similar enough images exist to be useful and similarity itself is often ill-defined.

To overcome these limitations, we introduce a novel technique for post-hoc model explanation. Our approach visually explains a model's decisions by producing images on either side of its decision boundary whose differences are perceptually clear. Such an approach makes it possible for a practitioner to conceptualize how a model is making its decisions at the level of semantics or concepts, rather than vectors or pixels.

Our algorithm is motivated by recent successes in both pixel-wise domain adaptation [2,12,30] and style transfer [9] in which generative models are used to transform images from one domain to another. Given a pre-trained classifier, we introduce a second, post-hoc explaining network called ExplainGAN, that takes a query image that falls on one side of the decision boundary and produces a transformed version of this image that falls on the other. ExplainGAN exhibits three important properties that make it ideal for post-hoc model interpretation:

Easily Visualizable Differences: Adversarial example [26] algorithms produce decision boundary crossing images whose differences from the originals are not perceptible, by design. In contrast, our model transforms the input image in a manner that is clearly detectable by the human eye.

Localized Differences: Style transfer [5] and domain adaptation approaches typically produce low-level, global changes. If every pixel in the image changes, even slightly, it is not clear which of those changes actually influenced the classifier to produce a different prediction. In contrast, our model yields changes that are spatially localized. Such sparse changes are more easily interpretable by a viewer as fewer elements change.

Semantically Consistent: Our model must be consistent with the behavior of the pre-trained classifier to be useful: the class predicted for a transformed image must not match with the predicted class of the original image.

We evaluate our model using standard approaches as well as a new metric for evaluating this new style of model interpretation by visualizing boundary-crossing transformations. We also utilize a new medical images dataset where the concept of objectness is not well defined, making it less amenable to domain adaptation approaches that hinge on identifying an object and altering/removing it. Furthermore, this dataset represents a clear and practical use-case for model explanation. To summarize, our work makes several contributions:

1. A new approach to model interpretation: visualizing human-interpretable, decision-boundary crossing images.
2. A new model, ExplainGAN, that produces post-hoc model-explanations via such decision-boundary crossing images.
3. A new metric for evaluating the amount of information retained in decision-boundary crossing transformations.
4. A new and challenging medical image dataset.

2   Related Work

Post-Hoc Model Interpretation methods typically seek to provide some kind of visualization of why a model has made a particular decision in terms of the saliency of local regions of an input image. These approaches broadly fall into two main categories: perturbation-based methods and gradient-based methods.

Perturbation-based methods [3,29], perturb the input image and evaluate the consequent change in the output of the classifier. Such perturbations remove information from specific regions of the input by applying blur or noise, among other pixel manipulations. Perturbation-based methods require multiple iterations and are computationally more costly than activation-based methods.

The perturbation of finer regions also makes these methods vulnerable to the artifacts of the classifier, potentially resulting in the assignment of high saliency to arbitrary, uninterpretable image regions. In order to combat these artifacts, current methods such as [3] are forced to perturb larger, less precise regions of the input.

Gradient-based methods such as [21–25] backpropagate the gradient for a given class label to the input image and estimate how moving along the gradient affects the output. Although these methods are computationally more efficient compared to perturbation-based methods, they rely on heuristics for backpropagation and may not support different network architectures.

A subset of gradient-based methods, which we call activation-based methods, also incorporate neuron activations into their explanations. Methods such as Gradient-weighted Class Activation Mapping Grad-CAM [20], layer-wise Relevance Propagation (LRP) [1] and Deep Taylor Decomposition (DTD) [16] can be considered as activation-based methods. Grad-CAM visualizes the linear combination of (typically) the last convolution layer and class specific gradients. LRP and DTD decompose the activations of each neuron in terms of contributions (i.e. relevances) from its input.

All these explanation methods are based on identifying pixels which contribute the most to the model output. In other words, these methods explain a model's decision by illustrating which pixels most affect a classifier's prediction. This takes the form of an attribution map, a heat map of the same size as the input image, in which each element of the attribution map indicates the degree to which its associated pixel contributed to the model output. In contrast, our model takes a different approach by generating a similar image on the other side of the model's decision boundary.

Adversarial Examples [7,26] are created by performing minute perturbations to image pixels to produce decision-boundary crossing transformations which are visually imperceptible to human observers. Such approaches are extremely useful for exploring ways in which a classifier might be attacked. They do not, however, provide any high-level intuition for why a model is making a particular decision.

Image-to-Image Transformation approaches, such as those used in domain adaptation [2,4,13] have shown increased success in transforming an image in one domain to appear as if drawn from another domain, such as synthetic-to-real or winter-to-summer. These approaches are clearly the most similar to our own in that we seek to transform images predicted as one class to appear to a pre-trained classifier as those from another. These approaches do not, however, constrain the types of transformations allowed and we demonstrate (Sect. 5.3) that significant constraints must be applied (Sect. 4) to ensure that the transformations produced are easily interpretable. Other image-to-image techniques such as Style Transfer [5,6,30] typically produce very low-level and comprehensive transformations to every pixel. In contrast, our own approach seeks highly localized and high-level, semantic changes.

3   Model

The goal of our model is to take a pre-trained binary classifier and a query image and generate both a new, transformed image and a binary mask. The transformed image should be similar to the query image, excepting a visually perceptible difference, such that the pre-trained classifier assigns different labels to the query and transformed image. The binary mask indicates which pixels from the query image where changed in order to produce the transformed image. In this way, our model is able to produce a decision-boundary crossing transformation of the query image and illustrate both *where*, via the binary mask, and *how*, via the transformed image, the transformation occurs.

More formally, given a binary classifier $F(x) \in \{0, 1\}$ operating on an image x, we seek to learn a function which predicts a transformed image t and a mask m such that:

$$F(x) \neq F(t) \tag{1}$$

$$x \odot m \neq t \odot m \tag{2}$$

$$x \odot \neg m = t \odot \neg m \tag{3}$$

where Eq. (1) indicates that the model believes x and t to be of different classes, Eq. (2) indicates that the query and transformed image differ in pixels whose mask values are 1 and Eq. (3) indicates that the query and transformed image match in pixels where mask values are 0 (Fig. 1).

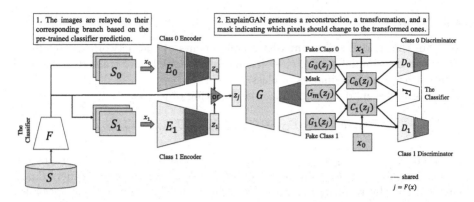

Fig. 1. Model architecture of ExplainGAN. Inference (in blue frame) consists of passing an image x of class j into the appropriate encoder E_j to produce a hidden vector z_j. The hidden vector is decoded to simultaneously create its reconstruction $G_j(z_j)$, a transformed image of the opposite class $G_{1-j}(z_j)$ and a mask showing where the changes were made $G_m(z_j)$. Composite images C_0 and C_1 merge the reconstruction and transformation with the original image x. (Color figure online)

3.1 Prerequisites

Given a dataset of images $S = \{x_i | i \in 1 \ldots N\}$, our pre-trained classifier produces a set of predictions $\{\bar{y}_i | i \in 1 \ldots N\}$. Given these predictions, we now can split the dataset into two groups $S_0 = \{x_i | \bar{y}_i = 0\}$ and $S_1 = \{x_i | \bar{y}_i = 1\}$.

3.2 Inference

Given a query image and a predicted label for that image, our model maps to a reconstructed version of that image, an image of the opposite class and a mask that indicates which pixels it changed. Formally, our model is composed of several components. First, our model uses two class-specific encoders to produce hidden codes:

$$z_j = \mathrm{E}_j(x) \quad j \in \{0, 1\}, \quad x \in S_j \tag{4}$$

Next, a decoder G maps the hidden representation z_j to a reconstructed image $G_j(z_j)$, a transformed image of the opposite class $G_{1-j}(z_j)$ and a mask indicating which pixels changed $G_m(z_j)$. In this manner, images of either class can be transformed into similar looking images of the opposite class with a visually interpretable change.

We also define the concept of a composite image $\mathrm{C}_j(x)$ of class j:

$$\mathrm{C}_j(x_{1-j}) = x_{1-j} \odot (1 - \mathrm{G}_m(z_{1-j})) + \mathrm{G}_j(z_{1-j}) \odot \mathrm{G}_m(z_{1-j}) \tag{5}$$

where z_{1-j} is the code produced by encoding x_{1-j}. The composite image uses the mask to blend the original image x with either the reconstruction or the transformed image.

3.3 Training

To train the model, several auxiliary components of the network are required. First, two discriminators $D_j(x) \to \{\text{real}, \text{fake}\}, j \in \{0, 1\}$ are trained to evaluate between real and fake images of class j.

To train the model we optimize the following objective:

$$\min_{G, E_0, E_1} \max_{D_0, D_1} \mathcal{L}_{\text{GAN}} + \mathcal{L}_{\text{classifier}} + \mathcal{L}_{\text{recon}} + \mathcal{L}_{\text{prior}} \qquad (6)$$

where $\mathcal{L}_{\text{GAN}}$ is a typical GAN loss, $\mathcal{L}_{\text{classifier}}$ is a loss that encourages the generated and composite images to be likely according to the classifier, $\mathcal{L}_{\text{recon}}$ ensures that the reconstructions are accurate, and $\mathcal{L}_{\text{prior}}$ encodes our prior for the types of transformations we want to encourage. $\mathcal{L}_{\text{GAN}}$ is a combination of the GAN losses for each class:

$$\mathcal{L}_{\text{GAN}} = \mathcal{L}_{\text{GAN:0}} + \mathcal{L}_{\text{GAN:1}} \qquad (7)$$

$\mathcal{L}_{\text{GAN}:j}$ for class j discriminates between images x originally classified as class j and reconstructions of x, transformations from x and composites from x. It is defined as:

$$
\begin{aligned}
\mathcal{L}_{GAN:j} = \ & \mathbb{E}_{\mathbf{x} \sim S_j} \log(D_j(x)) \\
& + \mathbb{E}_{x \sim S_j}[\log(1 - D_j(G_j(E_j(x)))] \\
& + \mathbb{E}_{x \sim S_{1-j}}[\log(1 - D_j(G_j(E_{1-j}(x)))] \\
& + \mathbb{E}_{x \sim S_{1-j}}[\log(1 - D_j(C_j(E_{1-j}(x)))]
\end{aligned}
\qquad (8)
$$

Note that this formulation, in which the reconstructions of x are also penalized are part of ensuring that the auto-encoded images are accurate [10] and are included here, rather than as part of $\mathcal{L}$recon out of convenience.

Next, we encourage the composite images to produce images that the classifier correctly predicts:

$$\mathcal{L}_{\text{classifier}} = \mathbb{E}_{x \in S_0} - \log(F(C_1(x))) \qquad (9)$$
$$+ \mathbb{E}_{x \in S_1} - \log(1 - F(C_0(x)) \qquad (10)$$

Finally, we have an auto-encoding loss for the reconstruction:

$$\mathcal{L}_{\text{recon}} = \sum_{j \in 0,1} \mathbb{E}_{x \in S_j} \|G_j(E_j(x)) - x\|^2 \qquad (11)$$

The mask priors are discussed in the following section.

4   Priors for Interpretable Image Transformations

There are many image transformations that will transform an image of one class to appear like an image from another class. Not all of these transformations, however, are equally useful for interpreting a model's behavior at a conceptual level. Adversarial example transformations will change the label but are not perceptible. Style transfer transformations make low-level but not semantic changes. Domain Adaptation approaches may change every pixel in the image which makes it difficult to determine which of these changes actually influenced the classifier. We want to craft set of priors that encourage transformations that are local to a particular part of the image and visually perceptible. To this end, we define our prior loss term as:

$$\mathcal{L}_{\text{prior}} = \mathcal{L}_{\text{const}} + \mathcal{L}_{\text{count}} + \mathcal{L}_{\text{smoothness}} + \mathcal{L}_{\text{entropy}} \tag{12}$$

The **consistency loss** $\mathcal{L}_{\text{const}}$ ensures that if a pixel is not masked, then the transformed image hasn't altered it.

$$\mathcal{L}_{\text{const}} = \sum_{j \in 0,1} \mathbb{E}_{x \in S_j}[\|(1 - G_m(z_j)) \odot x_j - (1 - G_m(z_j)) \odot G_{1-j}(z_j)\|^2] \tag{13}$$

where $z_j = E_j(x)$. The **count loss** $\mathcal{L}_{\text{count}}$ allows us to encode prior information regarding a coarse estimate of the number of pixels we anticipate changing. We approximate the l_0 norm via an l_1 norm:

$$\mathcal{L}_{\text{count}} = \sum_{j \in 0,1} \mathbb{E}_{x \in S_j}[\max(\frac{1}{n}|G_m(z_j)|, \kappa)] \tag{14}$$

where κ is a constant that corresponds to the ratio of number of changed pixels to the total number of the pixels. The **smoothness loss** encourages masks that are localized by penalizing transitions via a total variation [18] penalty:

$$\mathcal{L}_{\text{smoothness}} = \sum_{j \in 0,1} \mathbb{E}_{x \in S_j}|\nabla G_m(z_j)| \tag{15}$$

Finally, we want to encourage the mask to be as binary as possible:

$$\mathcal{L}_{\text{entropy}} = \sum_{j \in 0,1} \mathbb{E}_{x \in S_j}[\|\min_{elementwise}(G_m(z_j), 1 - G_m(z_j))\|] \tag{16}$$

5 Experiments

Our goal is to provide model explainability via visualization of samples on either side of a model's decision boundary. This is an entirely new way of performing model explanation and requires a unique approach to evaluation.

To this end, we first demonstrate qualitative results of our approach and compare to related approaches (Sect. 5.3). Next, we evaluate our model using traditional criteria by demonstrating that our model's inferred masks are highly competitive as saliency maps when compared to state-of-the-art attribution approaches (Sect. 5.4). Next, we introduce two new metrics for evaluating the explainability of decision-boundary crossing examples (Sect. 5.5) and evaluate how our model performs using these quantitative methods.

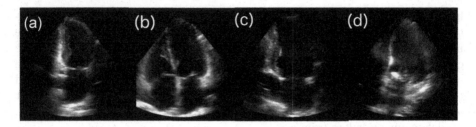

Fig. 2. An example of Ultrasound images from our Medical Ultrasound dataset. (a) A canonical Apical 2 Chamber view. (b) A canonical Apical 4 Chamber view. (c) A difficult Apical 2 Chamber view that is easily confused for a 4 Chamber view. (d) A difficult Apical 4 Chamber view that is easily confused for a 2 Chamber view.

5.1 Datasets

We used four datasets as part of our evaluation: MNIST [11], Fashion-MNIST [28], CelebA [14] and a new Medical Ultrasound dataset that will be released with the publication of this work. For each dataset, 4 splits were used: A classifier-training set used to train the black-box classifier, a training set used to train ExplainGAN, a validation set used to tune hyperparameters and a test set.

MNIST, Fashion-MNIST: We use the standard train/test splits in the following manner: The 60k training set is first split into 3 components: a 2k classifier-training set, a 50k training set and an 8k validation set. We used the standard test set. For MNIST, we used binary class pairs $(3, 8)$, $(4, 9)$ and $(5, 6)$. For Fashion-MNIST, we used binary class pairs (coat, shirt), (pullover, shirt) and (coat, pullover).

CelebA: We use the standard train/validation/test splits in the following manner: 2k images were used from the original validation set as the classifier-training set, all 160k images were used to train ExplainGAN, the remaining 14k validation images were used for validation. We used the standard test set. We used binary class pairs (glasses, no glasses) and (mustache, no mustache).

Medical Ultrasound: Our new medical ultrasound dataset is a collection of 72k cardiac images taken from 5 different views of the heart. Each image was labeled by several cardiac sonographers to determine the correct labels. An example of images from the dataset can be found in Fig. 2. As the Figure illustrates, the dataset is very challenging and is not as amenable to certain senses of 'objectness' found in most standard vision datasets. Of the 72k images, 2k were used as the classifier-training set, 60k were used for training ExplainGAN, 4k were used for validation and 6k were used for testing. We used the binary class pair (Apical 2-Chamber, Apical 4-Chamber).

5.2 Implementation

The model architecture implementation for E, G and D is quite similar to the DCGAN architecture [17]. We share the last few layers of E_0 and E_1 and the last few layers of D_0 and D_1. Each loss term in our objective is scaled by a coefficient whose values were obtained via cross-validation. In practice, the coefficients were quite stable across datasets (we use the same set), other than the κ hyperparameter which controls the effect of the count loss and the scaling coefficient for $\mathcal{L}_{\text{smoothness}}$, the smoothness loss.

5.3   Explanation by Qualitative Evaluation

We evaluated our model qualitatively on a number of datasets. We show results on both the Medical Ultrasound dataset and CelebA dataset in Fig. 3. The use of CelebA and a medical image dataset provides a useful contrast between images whose relationships should be quite familiar to the average reader (glasses vs no-glasses) and relationships that are likely to be foreign to the average reader (apical 2 chamber views versus apical 4 chamber views).

In each block, the "input" column represents images $x \in S_0$, the "transformed" column represents ExplainGAN's transformation, $G_1(z_0)$, to the opposite class. The "mask" column illustrates the model's changes, $G_m(z_0)$, and the "composite" column shows the composite images, $C_1(z_0)$.

The CelebA (top) results in Fig. 3 illustrates that the model's transformations for both "glasses vs no-glasses" and "mustache vs no-mustache" perform highly localized changes and the corresponding mask effectively produces a segmentation of the only visual feature being altered. Furthermore, the model is able to make quite minimal but perceptible changes. For example, in the first row of the "glasses vs no-glasses" task, the mask has preserved the hair over the eyeglasses.

The Ultrasound (bottom) results in Fig. 3 illustrates that the model has both learned to model the anatomy of the heart and is able to transform from one view of the heart to the other with minimal changes. The transformations and masks clearly illustrate that the model is cuing predominantly on the presence of the right ventricle, but interestingly not the right atrium, and the shape of the pericardium.

5.4   Explanation via Pixel-Wise Attribution

Many post-hoc explanation methods that use attribution or saliency rely on visual, qualitative comparisons of attribution maps. Recently, [19] introduced a quantitative approach for comparing attribution maps in which pixels are progressively perturbed in the order of predicted saliency. Performance is judged by evaluating which methods require fewer perturbations to affect the classifier's prediction.

Our model is not designed for attribution/saliency as it produces a binary, rather than continuous mask, which is also paired to a particular transformation image. However, it is possible to loosely interpret our masks as an attribution map in which pixel priority for all pixels in the mask is not known.

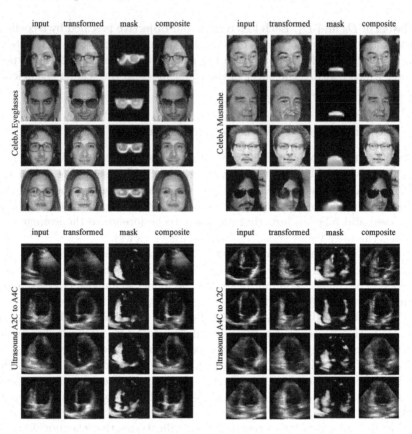

Fig. 3. Qualitative visualization of the ExplainGAN model on two datasets: CelebA and our Medical Ultrasound dataset. The "input" column represents images $x \in S_0$, the "transformed" column represents ExplainGAN's transformation, $G_1(z_0)$, to the opposite class. The "mask" column illustrates the model's changes, $G_m(z_0)$, and the "composite" column shows the composite images, $C_1(z_0)$. The results indicate that in the case of object-related transformations, such as glasses or mustaches, ExplainGAN effectively performs a weakly supervised segmentation of the object. In the ultrasound case, ExplainGAN illustrates which anatomical areas the model is cuing on: the right ventricle and pericardium.

While the work of [19] perturbed individual pixels, we wanted to avoid a comparison in which individual pixel changes, which are neither themselves interpretable, nor plausible as images, might alter the classification results. Consequently, we adapt the approach of [19] by perturbing the image by segments, rather than pixels. To choose the order of perturbation, we normalize the maps to the range $[0, 1]$, threshold them with $t \in [0.5, 0.7, 0.9]$ and segment the resulting binary maps. We then rank the segments based on the average map value within each segment[1]. For perturbation, we replace each pixel in each segment with uniform random noise in the range of the pixel values.

More concretely, we denote the image with k segments perturbed by $x_{SP}^{(k)}$. We compute the area over the segment perturbation curve (AOSPC) as follows:

$$\text{AOSPC} = \frac{1}{K+1} \left\langle \sum_{k=0}^{K} f(x_{SP}^{(0)}) - f(x_{SP}^{(k)}) \right\rangle_{p_x}, \qquad (17)$$

where K is the number of steps, $\langle . \rangle_{p_x}$ denotes the average over all the images, and $f : \mathbb{R}^d \to \mathbb{R}$ is the classification function.

We report AOSPC after 10 steps for the explanation methods of Sect. 2 in Sect. 5.4. We choose the methods to cover the 3 main groups of methods (i.e. perturbation-based, gradient-based and activation-based). A larger AOSPC means that the sensitivity of the segments that are perturbed in 10 steps is higher. To avoid cases where the segmentation assigns all or more than half of the pixels to one segment we choose our threshold from ≥ 0.5 values. Our results demonstrate that, despite not being explicitly optimized for finding the most informative pixels, ExplainGAN performs on par with other explanation methods for classifiers. For qualitative comparison of these methods see Fig. 4 (Table 1).

Table 1. AOSPC value (higher is better, see Eq. (17)) after 10 steps for different segmentation thresholds. Although, ExplainGAN is not directly optimized for this metric, its performance is comparable to reasonable baselines for explanation in classifiers. A larger AOSPC means that the sensitivity of the segments that are perturbed in 10 steps is higher.

Dataset	MNIST			Ultrasound		
Threshold	0.5	0.7	0.9	0.5	0.7	0.9
Grad [22]	1474	1563	240	712	291	81
Grad-CAM [20]	17.2	8	–	–	70	**432**
Saliency [23]	817	718	126	30	63	298
Occlusion [29]	2099	1946	**1486**	**1215**	539	142
LRP [1]	1736	1478	244	700	511	71
ExplainGAN	**2622**	**2083**	1474	1167	**542**	374

5.5   Quantitative Assessment of Explainability

Given two similar images on either side of a model's decision boundary, how can we determine quantitatively whether they provide a conceptual explanation of

---

[1] For ExplainGAN we take the average of the sigmoid outputs over all pixels in a segment.

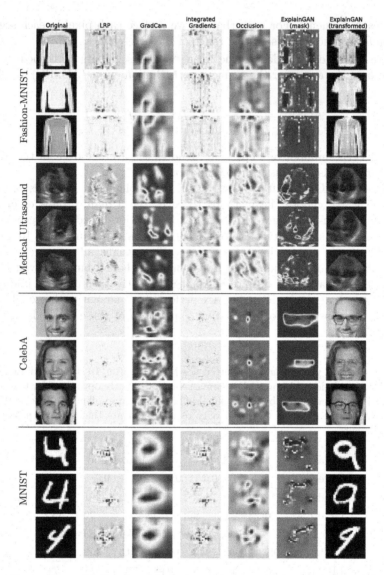

Fig. 4. Comparison of different methods for explaining the model's decision. **Fashion-MNIST**: transforming from pullover to shirt, **Ultrasound**: transforming from A2C to A4C (see Fig. 2 for examples of A2C and A4C views), **CelebA**: transforming from faces without eyeglasses to faces with eyeglasses, **MNIST**: transforming from 4 to 9.

why a model discriminates between them? There are several high-level criteria that must be met in order for people to find such explanatory images useful (Fig. 5).

(a) Input   (b) Substitutable, Localized.   (c) Substitutable, Non-Localized   (d) Non-Substitutable, Non Localized

Fig. 5. Boundary-crossing images have varying explanatory power: images carry more explanatory power if they are (1) Substitutable: they can be used as substitutes in the original dataset without affecting the classifier and (2) Localized: they are different from a query image in small and easily localized ways.

Table 2. Quantitative substitutability experiments across datasets. Class 0 and Class 1 are the classes that the given classifier is trained to identify. Transformed/Composite 0/1 column shows the accuracy of the classifiers when just transformations/compositions of the images used at training time. Ceiling represents the accuracy of the base classifier on the same test set.

Dataset	Class 0	Class 1	Transformed 0	Transformed 1	Composite 0	Composite 1	Ceiling
Ultrasound	A2C	A4C	95.5	94.2	91.4	95.6	99.6
CelebA	W/O Eyeglasses	W/Eyeglasses	93.6	96.2	96.05	96.2	96.5
CelebA	W/O Mustache	W/Mustache	76.65	75.2	74.05	71.4	83.9
CelebA	W/O Black hair	W/Blackhair	75.65	74.8	79.05	77.4	84.3
FMNIST	Coat	Pullover	75.8	73.7	84.8	69.1	94.1
FMNIST	Coat	Shirt	79.7	78.5	71.8	77.2	91.7
MNIST	Three	Eight	99.6	99.1	99.3	98.9	99.9
MNIST	Four	Nine	98.6	99.0	98.6	98.5	99.0
MNIST	Three	Five	98.5	99.3	98.2	98.2	99.2

Localized but not Minimal: In order for the boundary-crossing image to clear demonstrate what pixels caused a label-changing event, it must deviate from the original image in a way that is localized to a clear sub-component of the image, as opposed to every pixel changing or only one or two pixels changing.

Substitutable: If we are explaining a model by comparing an original image from class A, and a boundary-crossing image is produced to appear like it came from class B, then we define *substitutability* to be the property that we can substitute our boundary-crossing image for one of the original images labeled as class B without affecting our classifier's performance.

To this end, we propose two metrics aimed at quantifying such an explanations utility. First, the degree to which changes to a query image are localized can be represented by the number of non-zero elements of the mask. Note that while other measures of locality can be used (cohesiveness, connected components), we make no such assumption as we found empirically that often such specific measures do not correlate well with conveying the set of items changing.

Second, we define the substitutability metric as follows: Let an original training set $\mathcal{D}_{\text{train}} = \{(x_i, y_i | i = 1..N\}$, a test set $\mathcal{D}_{\text{test}}$, and a classifier $\mathcal{F}(x) \rightarrow y$ whose empirical performance on the test set is some score S. Given a new set of model-generated boundary-crossing images $\mathcal{D}_{\text{trans}} = \{(x_i', y_i' | i = 1..N\}$ we say that this set is $R\%$−substitutable if our classifier can be retrained using $\mathcal{D}_{\text{trans}}$ to achieve performance that is $R\%$ of S. For example, if our original dataset and classifier yield 90% performance, and we substitute a generated dataset for our original dataset and a re-trained classifier yields 45%, we would say the new dataset is 50% substitutable.

Table 2 illustrates the substitutability performance of our model on various datasets. These results illustrate that our model produces images that are nearly perfectly substitutable on MNIST, the Ultrasound dataset, and CelebaA for the Eyeglasses attribute. That being said, despite compelling qualitative results (Fig. 4), there is still much room for improvement in terms of substitutability for the other CelebA attributes.(Table 3).

Table 3. Substitutability on Ultrasound Dataset. Transformed/Composite 0/1 shows the accuracy of a classifier on test set when the original samples are replaced with Transformed/Composite 0/1 at training phase. Both Transformed/Composite shows the accuracy of the classifier when all of the images are replaced with Transformed/Composite. Note that PixelDA is a oneway transformer.

	Transformed 0	Transformed 1	Both Transformed	Composite 0	Composite 1	Both composite
PixelDA	87.6	N/A	N/A	N/A	N/A	N/A
CycleGAN	94	64	84.1	N/A	N/A	N/A
ExplainGAN-norec	94.5	83.9	96.1	N/A	N/A	N/A
ExplainGAN-nomask	93.9	97.3	95.1	N/A	N/A	N/A
ExplainGAN-full	95.5	94.2	97.3	91.4	95.6	91.4
Ceiling	99.7	99.7	99.7	99.7	99.7	99.7

6   Conclusion

We introduced ExplainGAN to interpret black box classifiers by visualizing boundary-crossing transformations. These transformations are designed to be interpretable by humans and provide a high-level, conceptual intuition underlying a classifier's decisions. This style of visualization is able to overcome limitations of attribution and example-by-nearest-neighbor methods by making spatially localized changes along with visual examples. While not explicitly trained to act as a saliency map, ExplainGAN's maps are very competitive at demonstrating saliency. We also introduced a new metric, Substitutability, that evaluates how much label-capturing information is retained when performing boundary-crossing image transformations. While our method exhibits a good substitutability score, it is not perfect and we anticipate this metric being used for furthering research in this area.

References

1. Bach, S., Binder, A., Montavon, G., Klauschen, F., Müller, K.R., Samek, W.: On pixel-wise explanations for non-linear classifier decisions by layer-wise relevance propagation. PloS One **10**(7), e0130140 (2015)
2. Bousmalis, K., Silberman, N., Dohan, D., Erhan, D., Krishnan, D.: Unsupervised pixel-level domain adaptation with generative adversarial networks. In: The IEEE Conference on Computer Vision and Pattern Recognition (CVPR), vol. 1, p. 7 (2017)
3. Fong, R.C., Vedaldi, A.: Interpretable explanations of black boxes by meaningful perturbation. arXiv preprint arXiv:1704.03296 (2017)
4. Ganin, Y., et al.: Domain-adversarial training of neural networks. J. Mach. Learn. Res. **17**(1), 1–35 (2016)
5. Gatys, L.A., Ecker, A.S., Bethge, M.: A neural algorithm of artistic style. arXiv preprint arXiv:1508.06576 (2015)
6. Gatys, L.A., Ecker, A.S., Bethge, M.: Image style transfer using convolutional neural networks. In: 2016 IEEE Conference on Computer Vision and Pattern Recognition (CVPR), pp. 2414–2423. IEEE (2016)
7. Goodfellow, I.J., Shlens, J., Szegedy, C.: Explaining and harnessing adversarial examples. arXiv preprint arXiv:1412.6572 (2014)
8. Goodman, B., Flaxman, S.: European union regulations on algorithmic decision-making and a "right to explanation". arXiv preprint arXiv:1606.08813 (2016)
9. Johnson, J., Alahi, A., Fei-Fei, L.: Perceptual losses for real-time style transfer and super-resolution. In: Leibe, B., Matas, J., Sebe, N., Welling, M. (eds.) ECCV 2016. LNCS, vol. 9906, pp. 694–711. Springer, Cham (2016). https://doi.org/10. 1007/978-3-319-46475-6_43
10. Larsen, A.B.L., Sønderby, S.K., Larochelle, H., Winther, O.: Autoencoding beyond pixels using a learned similarity metric. arXiv preprint arXiv:1512.09300 (2015)
11. LeCun, Y., Bottou, L., Bengio, Y., Haffner, P.: Gradient-based learning applied to document recognition. Proc. IEEE **86**(11), 2278–2324 (1998)
12. Liu, M.Y., Breuel, T., Kautz, J.: Unsupervised image-to-image translation networks. In: Advances in Neural Information Processing Systems, pp. 700–708 (2017)
13. Liu, M.Y., Tuzel, O.: Coupled generative adversarial networks. In: Advances in Neural Information Processing Systems, pp. 469–477 (2016)
14. Liu, Z., Luo, P., Wang, X., Tang, X.: Deep learning face attributes in the wild. In: Proceedings of International Conference on Computer Vision (ICCV) (2015)
15. Maaten, L., Hinton, G.: Visualizing data using t-SNE. J. Mach. Learn. Res. **9**(Nov), 2579–2605 (2008)
16. Montavon, G., Lapuschkin, S., Binder, A., Samek, W., Müller, K.R.: Explaining nonlinear classification decisions with deep Taylor decomposition. Pattern Recogn. **65**, 211–222 (2017)
17. Radford, A., Metz, L., Chintala, S.: Unsupervised representation learning with deep convolutional generative adversarial networks. arXiv preprint arXiv:1511.06434 (2015)
18. Rudin, L.I., Osher, S., Fatemi, E.: Nonlinear total variation based noise removal algorithms. Physica D: Nonlinear Phenom. **60**(1–4), 259–268 (1992)
19. Samek, W., Binder, A., Montavon, G., Lapuschkin, S., Müller, K.R.: Evaluating the visualization of what a deep neural network has learned. IEEE Trans. Neural Netw. Learn. Syst. **28**(11), 2660–2673 (2017)

20. Selvaraju, R.R., Cogswell, M., Das, A., Vedantam, R., Parikh, D., Batra, D.: Grad-CAM: visual explanations from deep networks via gradient-based localization, v3, vol. 7, no. 8 (2016). https://arxiv.org/abs/1610.02391

21. Shrikumar, A., Greenside, P., Kundaje, A.: Learning important features through propagating activation differences. arXiv preprint arXiv:1704.02685 (2017)

22. Shrikumar, A., Greenside, P., Shcherbina, A., Kundaje, A.: Not just a black box: learning important features through propagating activation differences. arXiv preprint arXiv:1605.01713 (2016)

23. Simonyan, K., Vedaldi, A., Zisserman, A.: Deep inside convolutional networks: visualising image classification models and saliency maps (2014). arXiv preprint arXiv:1312.6034 (2013)

24. Springenberg, J.T., Dosovitskiy, A., Brox, T., Riedmiller, M.: Striving for simplicity: the all convolutional net. arXiv preprint arXiv:1412.6806 (2014)

25. Sundararajan, M., Taly, A., Yan, Q.: Axiomatic attribution for deep networks. arXiv preprint arXiv:1703.01365 (2017)

26. Szegedy, C., et al.: Intriguing properties of neural networks. arXiv preprint arXiv:1312.6199 (2013)

27. Wattenberg, M., Vigas, F., Johnson, I.: How to use t-SNE effectively. Distill (2016). https://doi.org/10.23915/distill.00002, http://distill.pub/2016/misread-tsne

28. Xiao, H., Rasul, K., Vollgraf, R.: Fashion-MNIST: a novel image dataset for benchmarking machine learning algorithms (2017)

29. Zeiler, M.D., Fergus, R.: Visualizing and understanding convolutional networks. In: Fleet, D., Pajdla, T., Schiele, B., Tuytelaars, T. (eds.) ECCV 2014. LNCS, vol. 8689, pp. 818–833. Springer, Cham (2014). https://doi.org/10.1007/978-3-319-10590-1_53

30. Zhu, J.Y., Park, T., Isola, P., Efros, A.A.: Unpaired image-to-image translation using cycle-consistent adversarial networks. arXiv preprint arXiv:1703.10593 (2017)

Does Haze Removal Help CNN-Based Image Classification?

Yanting Pei[1,2], Yaping Huang[1(✉)], Qi Zou[1], Yuhang Lu[2], and Song Wang[2,3(✉)]

[1] Beijing Key Laboratory of Traffic Data Analysis and Mining,
Beijing Jiaotong University, Beijing, China
{15112073,yphuang,qzou}@bjtu.edu.cn
[2] Department of Computer Science and Engineering, University of South Carolina,
Columbia, SC, USA
yuhang@email.sc.edu, songwang@cec.sc.edu
[3] School of Computer Science and Technology, Tianjin University, Tianjin, China

Abstract. Hazy images are common in real scenarios and many dehazing methods have been developed to automatically remove the haze from images. Typically, the goal of image dehazing is to produce clearer images from which human vision can better identify the object and structural details present in the images. When the ground-truth haze-free image is available for a hazy image, quantitative evaluation of image dehazing is usually based on objective metrics, such as Peak Signal-to-Noise Ratio (PSNR) and Structural Similarity (SSIM). However, in many applications, large-scale images are collected not for visual examination by human. Instead, they are used for many high-level vision tasks, such as automatic classification, recognition and categorization. One fundamental problem here is whether various dehazing methods can produce clearer images that can help improve the performance of the high-level tasks. In this paper, we empirically study this problem in the important task of image classification by using both synthetic and real hazy image datasets. From the experimental results, we find that the existing image-dehazing methods cannot improve much the image-classification performance and sometimes even reduce the image-classification performance.

Keywords: Hazy images · Haze removal · Image classification
Dehazing · Classification accuracy

1 Introduction

Haze is a very common atmospheric phenomenon where fog, dust, smoke and other particles obscure the clarity of the scene and in practice, many images collected outdoors are contaminated by different levels of haze, even on a sunny day and in computer vision society, such images are usually called *hazy images*, as shown in Fig. 1(a). With intensity blurs and lower contrast, it is usually more difficult to identify object and structural details from hazy images, especially

© Springer Nature Switzerland AG 2018
V. Ferrari et al. (Eds.): ECCV 2018, LNCS 11214, pp. 697–712, 2018.
https://doi.org/10.1007/978-3-030-01249-6_42

when the level of haze is strong. To address this issue, many *image dehazing* methods [2,3,9,15,20,21,25,26,33] have been developed to remove the haze and try to recover the original clear version of an image. Those dehazing methods mainly rely on various image prior, such as dark channel prior [9] and color attenuation prior [33]. As shown in Fig. 1, the images after the dehazing are usually more visually pleasing – it can be easier for the human vision to identify the objects and structures in the image. Meanwhile, many objective metrics, such as Peak Signal-to-Noise Ratio (PSNR) [11] and Structural Similarity (SSIM) [30], have been proposed to quantitatively evaluate the performance of image dehazing when the ground-truth haze-free image is available for a hazy image.

Fig. 1. An illustration of image dehazing. (a) A hazy image. (b), (c) and (d) are the images after applying different dehazing methods to the image (a).

However, nowadays large-scale image data are collected not just for visual examination. In many cases, they are collected for high-level vision tasks, such as automatic image classification, recognition and categorization. *One fundamental problem is whether the performance of these high-level vision tasks can be significantly improved if we preprocess all hazy images by applying an image-dehazing method.* On one hand, images after the dehazing are visually clearer with more identifiable details. From this perspective, we might expect the performance improvement of the above vision tasks with image dehazing. On the other hand, most image dehazing methods just process the input images without introducing new information to the images. From this perspective, we may not expect any performance improvement of these vision tasks by using image dehazing since many high-level vision tasks are handled by extracting image information for training classifiers. In this paper, we empirically study this problem in the important task of image classification.

By classifying an image based on its semantic content, *image classification* is an important problem in computer vision and has wide applications in autonomous driving, surveillance and robotics. This problem has been studied for a long time and many well known image databases, such as Caltech-256 [8], PASCAL VOCs [7] and ImageNet [5], have been constructed for evaluating the performance of image classification. Recently, the accuracy of image classification has been significantly boosted by using deep neural networks. In this paper, we will conduct our empirical study by taking Convolutional Neural Network (CNN), one of the most widely used deep neural networks, as the image classifier and then evaluate the image-classification accuracy with and without the preprocessing of image dehazing.

More specifically, in this paper we pick eight state-of-the-art image dehazing methods and examine whether they can help improve the image-classification accuracy. To guarantee the comprehensiveness of empirical study, we use both synthetic data of hazy images and real hazy images for experiments and use AlexNet [14], VGGNet [22] and ResNet [10] for CNN implementation. Note that the goal of this paper is not the development of a new image-dehazing method or a new image-classification method. Instead, we study whether the preprocessing of image dehazing can help improve the accuracy of hazy image classification. We expect this study can provide new insights on how to improve the performance of hazy image classification.

2   Related Work

Hazy images and their analysis have been studied for many years. Many of the existing researches were focused on developing reliable models and algorithms to remove haze and restore the original clear image underlying an input hazy image. Many models and algorithms have been developed for outdoor image haze removal. For example, in [9], dark channel prior was used to remove haze from a single image. In [20], an image dehazing method was proposed with a boundary constraint and contextual regularization. In [33], color attenuation prior was used for removing haze from a single image. In [3], an end-to-end method was proposed for removing haze from a single image. In [21], multi-scale convolutional neural networks were used for haze removal. In [15], a haze-removal method was proposed by directly generating the underlying clean image through a light-weight CNN and it can be embedded into other deep models easily. Besides, researchers also investigated haze removal from the images taken at nighttime hazy scenes. For example, in [16], a method was developed to remove the nighttime haze with glow and multiple light colors. In [32], a fast haze removal method was proposed for nighttime images using the maximum reflectance prior.

Image classification has attracted extensive attention in the community of computer vision. In the early stage, hand-designed features [31] were mainly used for image classification. In recent years, significant progress has been made on image classification, partly due to the creation of large-scale hand-labeled datasets such as ImageNet [5], and the development of deep convolutional neural networks (CNN) [14]. Current state-of-the-art image classification research is focused on training feedforward convolutional neural networks using "very deep" structure [10,22,23]. VGGNet [22], Inception [23] and residual learning [10] have been proposed to train very deep neural networks, resulting in excellent image-classification performances on clear natural images. In [18], a cross-convolutional-layer pooling method was proposed for image classification. In [28], CNN is combined with recurrent neural networks (RNN) for improving the performance of image classification. In [6], three important visual recognition tasks, image classification, weakly supervised point-wise object localization and semantic segmentation, were studied in an integrative way. In [27], a convolutional neural network using attention mechanism was developed for image classification.

Although these CNN-based methods have achieved excellent performance on image classification, most of them were only applied to the classification of clear natural images. Very few of existing works explored the classification of degradation images. In [1], strong classification performance was achieved on corrupted MNIST digits by applying image denoising as an image preprocessing step. In [24], a model was proposed to recognize faces in the presence of noise and occlusion. In [29], classification of very low resolution images was studied by using CNN, with applications to face identification, digit recognition and font recognition. In [12], a preprocessing step of image denoising is shown to be able to improve the performance of image classification under a supervised training framework. In [4], image denoising and classification were tackled by training a unified single model, resulting in performance improvement on both tasks. Image haze studied in this paper is a special kind of image degradations and, to our best knowledge, there is no systematic study on hazy image classification and whether image dehazing can help hazy image classification.

3   Proposed Method

In this section, we elaborate on the hazy image data, image-dehazing methods, image-classification framework and evaluation metrics used in the empirical study. In the following, we first discuss the construction of both synthetic and real hazy image datasets. We then introduce the eight state-of-the-art image-dehazing methods used in our study. After that, we briefly introduce the CNN-based framework used for image classification. Finally, we discuss the evaluation metrics used in our empirical study.

3.1   Hazy-Image Datasets

For this empirical study, we need a large set of hazy images for both image-classifier training and testing. Current large-scale image datasets that are publicly available, such as Caltech-256, PASCAL VOCs and ImageNet, mainly consist of clear images without degradations. In this paper, we use two strategies to get the hazy images. First, we synthesize a large set of hazy images by adding haze to clear images using available physical models. Second, we collect a set of real hazy images from the Internet.

We synthesize hazy images by the following equation [13], where the atmospheric scattering model is used to describe the hazy image generation process:

$$I(x,y) = t(x,y) \cdot J(x,y) + [1 - t(x,y)] \cdot A, \qquad (1)$$

where (x,y) is the pixel coordinate, I is the synthetic hazy image, and J is the original clear image. A is the global atmospheric light. The scene transmission $t(x,y)$ is distance-dependent and defined as

$$t(x,y) = e^{-\beta d(x,y)}, \tag{2}$$

where β is the atmospheric scattering coefficient and $d(x,y)$ is the normalized distance of the scene at pixel (x,y). We compute the depth map $d(x,y)$ of an image by using the algorithm proposed in [17]. An example of such synthetic hazy image, as well as its original clear image and depth map, are shown in Fig. 2. In this paper, we take all the images in Caltech-256 to construct synthetic hazy images and the class label of each synthetic image follow the label of the corresponding original clear image. This way, we can use the synthetic images for image classification.

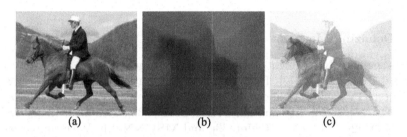

(a)   (b)   (c)

Fig. 2. An illustration of hazy image synthesis. (a) Clear image. (b) Depth map of (a). (c) Synthetic hazy image.

While we can construct synthetic hazy images by following well-acknowledged physical models, real haze models can be much more complicated and a study on synthetic hazy image datasets may not completely reflect what we may encounter on real hazy images. To address this issue, we collect a new dataset of hazy images by collecting images from the Internet. This new dataset contains 4,610 images from 20 classes and we named it as *Haze-20*. These 20 image classes are bird (231), boat (236), bridge (233), building (251), bus (222), car (256), chair (213), cow (227), dog (244), horse (237), people (279), plane (235), sheep (204), sign (221), street-lamp (216), tower (230), traffic-light (206), train (207), tree (239) and truck (223), and in the parenthesis is the number of images collected for each class. The number of images per class varies from 204 to 279. Some examples in Haze-20 are shown in Fig. 3.

In this study, we will try the case of training the image-classifier using clear images and testing on hazy images. For synthetic hazy images, we have their original clear images, which can be used for training. For real images in Haze-20, we do not have their underlying clear images. To address this issue, we collect a new *HazeClear-20* image dataset from the Internet, which consists of haze-free images that fall in the same 20 classes as in Haze-20. HazeClear-20 consists of 3,000 images, with 150 images per class.

Fig. 3. Sample hazy images in our new Haze-20 dataset.

3.2 Dehazing Methods

In this paper we try eight state-of-the-art image-dehazing methods: Dark-Channel Prior (**DCP**) [9], Fast Visibility Restoration (**FVR**) [25], Improved Visibility (**IV**) [26], Boundary Constraint and Contextual Regularization (**BCCR**) [20], Color Attenuation Prior (**CAP**) [33], Non-local Image Dehazing (**NLD**) [2], DehazeNet (**DNet**) [3], and **MSCNN** [21]. We examine each of them to see whether it can help improve the performance of hazy image classification.

- **DCP** removes haze using dark channel prior, which is based on a key observation – most local patches of outdoor haze-free images contain some pixels whose intensity is very low in at least one color channel.
- **FVR** is a fast haze-removal algorithm based on the median filter. Its main advantage is its fast speed since its complexity is just a linear function of the input-image size.
- **IV** enhances the contrast of an input image so that the image visibility is improved. It computes the data cost and smoothness cost for every pixel by using Markov Random Fields.
- **BCCR** is an efficient regularization method for removing haze. In particular, the inherent boundary constraint on the transmission function combined with a weighted L_1-norm based contextual regularization, is modeled into an optimization formulation to recover the unknown scene transmission.
- **CAP** removes haze using color attenuation prior that is based on the difference between the saturation and the brightness of the pixels in the hazy image. By creating a linear model, the scene depth of the hazy image is computed with color attenuation prior, where the parameters are learned by a supervised method.
- **NLD** is a haze-removal algorithm based on a non-local prior, by assuming that colors of a haze-free image are well approximated by a few hundred of distinct colors in the form of tight clusters in RGB space. In a hazy image, these tight color clusters change due to haze and form lines in RGB space that pass through the airlight coordinate.

– **DNet** is an end-to-end haze-removal method based on CNN. The layers of CNN architecture are specially designed to embody the established priors in image dehazing. DNet conceptually consists of four sequential operations – feature extraction, multi-scale mapping, local extremum and non-linear regression, which are constructed by three convolution layers, a max-pooling, a Maxout unit and a bilinear ReLU activation function, respectively.

– **MSCNN** uses a multi-scale deep neural network for image dehazing by learning the mapping between hazy images and their corresponding transmission maps. It consists of a coarse-scale net which predicts a holistic transmission map based on the entire image, and a fine-scale net which refines results locally. The network consists of four operations: convolution, max-pooling, up-sampling and linear combination.

3.3 Image Classification Model

In this paper, we implement CNN-based model for image classification by using AlexNet [14], VGGNet-16 [22] and ResNet-50 [10] on Caffe. The AlexNet [14] has 8 weight layers (5 convolutional layers and 3 fully-connected layers). The VGGNet-16 [22] has 16 weight layers (13 convolutional layers and 3 fully-connected layers). The ResNet-50 [10] has 50 weight layers (49 convolutional layers and 1 fully-connected layer). For those three networks, the last fully-connected layer has N channels (N is the number of classes).

3.4 Evaluation Metrics

We will quantitatively evaluate the performance of image dehazing and the performance of image classification. Other than visual examination, Peak Signal-to-Noise Ratio (PSNR) [11] and Structural Similarity (SSIM) [30] are widely used for evaluating the performance of image dehazing when the ground-truth haze-free image is available for each hazy image. For image classification, classification accuracy is the most widely used performance evaluation metric.

Note that, both PSNR and SSIM are objective metrics based on image statistics. Previous research has shown that they may not always be consistent with the image-dehazing quality perceived by human vision, which is quite subjective. In this paper, what we concern about is the performance of image classification after incorporating image dehazing as preprocessing. Therefore, we will study whether PSNR and SSIM metrics show certain correlation to the image classification performance. In this paper, we simply use the classification accuracy $Accuracy = \frac{R}{N}$ to objectively measure the image-classification performance, where N is the total number of testing images and R is the total number of testing images that are correctly classified by using the trained CNN-based models.

4 Experiments

4.1 Datasets and Experiment Setup

In this section, we evaluate various image-dehazing methods on the hazy images synthesized from Caltech-256 and our newly collected Haze-20 datasets.

We synthesize hazy images using all the images in Caltech-256 dataset, which has been widely used for evaluating image classification algorithms. It contains 30,607 images from 257 classes, including 256 object classes and a clutter class. In our experiment, we select six different hazy levels for generating synthetic images. Specifically, we set the parameter $\beta = 0, 1, 2, 3, 4, 5$ respectively in Eq. (2) for hazy image synthesis where $\beta = 0$ corresponds to original images in Caltech-256. In Caltech-256, we select 60 images randomly from each class as training images, and the rest are used for testing. Among the training images, 20% per class are used as a validation set. We follow this to split the synthetic hazy image data: an image is in training set if it is synthesized from an image in the training set and in testing set otherwise. This way, we have a training set of 60 × 257 = 15,420 images (60 per class) and a testing set of 30,607 − 15,420 = 15,187 images for each hazy level.

For the collected real hazy images in Haze-20, we select 100 images randomly from each class as training images, and the rest are used for testing. Among the training images, 20% per class are used as a validation set. So, we have a training set of $100 \times 20 = 2,000$ images and a testing set of $4,610 - 2,000 = 2,610$ images. For HazeClear-20 dataset, we also select 100 images randomly from each class as training images, and the rest are used for testing. Among the training images, 20% per class are used as a validation set. So, we have a training set of $100 \times 20 = 2,000$ images and a testing set of $50 \times 20 = 1,000$ images.

While the proposed CNN model can use AlexNet, VGGNet, ResNet or another network structures, for simplicity, we use AlexNet, VGGNet-16, ResNet-50 on Caffe in this paper. The CNN architectures are pre-trained on ImageNet dataset that consists of 1,000 classes with 1.2 million training images. We then use the collected images to fine-tune the pre-trained model for image classification, in which we change the number of channels in the last fully connected layer from 1,000 to N, where N is the number of classes in our datasets. To more comprehensively explore the effect of haze-removal to image classification, we study different combinations of the training and testing data, including training and testing on images without applying image dehazing, training and testing on images after dehazing, and training on clear images but testing on hazy images.

4.2   Quantitative Comparisons on Synthetic and Real Hazy Images

To verify whether haze-removal preprocessing can improve the performance of hazy image classification, we test on the synthetic and real hazy images with and without haze removal for quantitative evaluation. The classification results are shown in Fig. 4, where (a–e) are the classification accuracies on testing synthetic hazy images with $\beta = 1, 2, 3, 4, 5$, respectively using different dehazing methods. For these five curve figures, the horizontal axis lists different dehazing methods, where "Clear" indicates the use of the testing images in the original Caltech-256 datasets and this assumes a perfect image dehazing in the ideal case. The case of "Haze" indicates the testing on the hazy images without any dehazing. (f) is the classification accuracy on the testing images in Haze-20 using different dehazing methods, where "Clear" indicates the use of testing images in HazeClear-20 and

"Haze" indicates the use of testing images in Haze-20 without any dehazing. *AlexNet_1*, *VGGNet_1* and *ResNet_1* represent the case of training and testing on the same kinds of images, e.g., training on the training images in Haze-20 after DCP dehazing, then testing on testing images in Haze-20 after DCP dehazing, by using AlexNet, VGGNet and ResNet, respectively. *AlexNet_2*, *VGGNet_2* and *ResNet_2* represent the case of training on clear images, i.e., for (a–e), we train on training images in original Caltech-256, and for (f), we train on training images in HazeClear-20, by using AlexNet, VGGNet and ResNet, respectively.

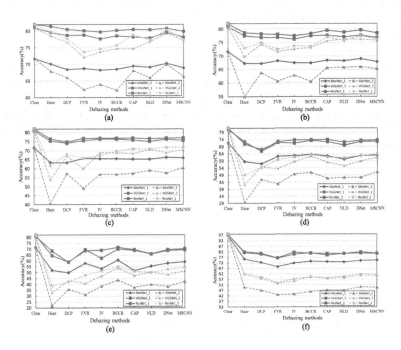

Fig. 4. The classification accuracy on different hazy images. (a–e) Classification accuracies on testing synthetic hazy images with $\beta = 1, 2, 3, 4, 5$, respectively. (f) Classification accuracy on the testing images in Haze-20. (Color figure online)

We can see that when we train CNN models on clear images and test them on hazy images with and without haze removal (e.g., *AlexNet_2*, *VGGNet_2* and *ResNet_2*), the classification performance drop significantly. From Fig. 4(e), image classification accuracy drop from 71.7% to 21.7% when images have a haze level of $\beta = 5$ by using AlexNet. Along the same curve shown in Fig. 4(e), we can see that by applying a dehazing method on the testing images, the classification accuracy can move up to 42.5% (using MSCNN dehazing). But it is still much lower than 71.7%, the accuracy on classifying original clear images. These experiments indicate that haze significantly affects the accuracy of CNN-based image classification when training on original clear images. However, if we directly train the classifiers on the hazy image of the same level, the classification accuracy moves up to 51.9%, as shown in the red curve in Fig. 4(e), where no dehazing is involved in training and testing images. Another choice is to apply the same dehazing methods to both training and testing images: From results shown in all the six subfigures in Fig. 4, we can see that the resulting accuracy is similar to the case where no dehazing is applied to training and testing images. This indicates that the dehazing conducted in this study does not help image classification. We believe this is due to the fact that the dehazing does not introduce new information to the image.

There are also many non-CNN-based image classification methods. While it is difficult to include all of them into our empirical study, we try the one based on sparse coding [31] and the results are shown in Fig. 5, where $\beta = 1, 2, 3, 4, 5$ represent haze levels of synthetic hazy images in Caltech-256 dataset and *Haze-20* represents Haze-20 dataset. For this specific non-CNN-based image classification method, we can get the similar conclusion that the tried dehazing does not help image classification, as shown in Fig. 5. Comparing Figs. 4 and 5, we can see that the classification accuracy of this non-CNN-based method is much lower than the state-of-the-art CNN-based methods. Therefore, we focus on CNN-based image classification in this paper.

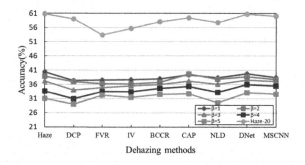

Fig. 5. Classification accuracy (%) on synthetic and real-world hazy images by using a non-CNN-based image classification method. Here the same kinds of images are used for training, i.e., building the basis for sparse coding, and testing, just like the case corresponding to the solid curves (*AlexNet_1, VGGNet_1* and *ResNet_1*) in Fig. 4.

4.3   Training on Mixed-Level Hazy Images

For more comprehensive analysis of dehazing methods, we conduct experiments of training on hazy images with mixed haze levels. For synthetic dataset, we try two cases. In Case 1, we mix all six levels of hazy images by selecting 10 images per class from each level of hazy images as training set and among the training images, two images per class per haze level are taken as validation set. We then test on the testing images of the involved haze levels – actually all six levels for this case – respectively. Results are shown in Fig. 6(a), (b) and (c) when using AlexNet, VGGNet and ResNet respectively. In Case 2, we randomly choose

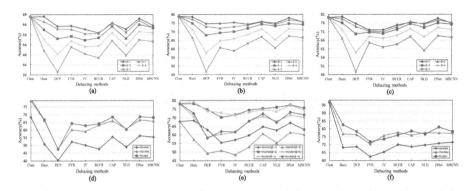

Fig. 6. Classification accuracy when training on mixed-level hazy images. (a, b, c) Mix all six levels of synthetic images. (d) Mix two levels $\beta = 0$ and $\beta = 5$. (e) Mix two levels $\beta = 1$ and $\beta = 4$. (f) Mix Haze-20 and HazeClear-20.

images from two different haze levels and mix them. In this case, 30 images per class per level are taken as training images and among the training images, 6 images per class per level are used as validation images. This way we have 60 images per class for training. Similarly, we then test on the testing images of the involved two haze levels, respectively. Results are shown in Fig. 6(d) and (e) for four different kinds of level combinations, respectively. For real hazy images, we mix clear images in HazeClear-20 and hazy images in Haze-20 by picking 50 images per class for training and then test on the testing images in Haze-20 and HazeClear-20 respectively. Results are shown in Fig. 6(f). Similarly, combining all the results, the use of dehazing does not clearly improve the image classification accuracy, over the case of directly training and testing on hazy images.

4.4 Performance Evaluation of Dehazing Methods

In this section, we study whether there is a correlation between the dehazing metrics PSNR/SSIM and the image classification performance. On the synthetic images, we can compute the metrics PSNR and SSIM on all the dehazing results, which are shown in Fig. 7. In this figure, the PSNR and SSIM values are averaged over the respective testing images. We pick the red curves (*AlexNet_1*) from Fig. 4(a–e) and for each haze level in $\beta = 1, 2, 3, 4, 5$, we rank all the dehazing methods based on the classification accuracy. We then rank these methods based on average PSNR and SSIM at the same haze level. Finally we calculate the rank correlation between image classification and PSNR/SSIM at each haze level. Results are shown in Table 1. Negative values indicate negative correlation, positive values indicate positive correlation and the greater the absolute value, the higher the correlation. We can see that their correlations are actually low, especially when $\beta = 3$.

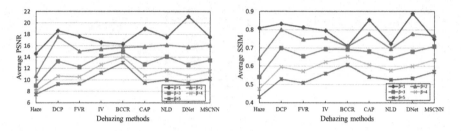

Fig. 7. Average PSNR and SSIM values on synthetic image dataset at different haze levels.

Table 1. The rank correlation between image-classification accuracy and PSNR/SSIM at each haze level.

Correlation	$\beta = 1$	$\beta = 2$	$\beta = 3$	$\beta = 4$	$\beta = 5$
(Accuracy, PSNR)	−0.3095	0.3571	0.0952	−0.2143	0.1905
(Accuracy, SSIM)	−0.2381	−0.5238	−0.0714	0.6905	0.6190

4.5   Subjective Evaluation

In this section, we conduct an experiment for subjective evaluation of the image dehazing. By observing the dehazed images, we randomly select 10 images per class with $\beta = 3$ and subjectively divide them into 5 with better dehazing effect and 5 with worse dehazing effect. This way, we have 2,570 images in total (set M) and 1,285 images each with better dehazing (set A) and worse dehazing (set B). Classification accuracy (%) using VGGNet is shown in Fig. 8 and we can see that there is no significant accuracy difference for these three sets. This indicates that the classification accuracy is not consistent with the human subjective evaluation of the image dehazing quality.

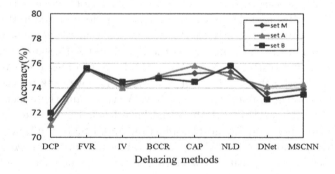

Fig. 8. Classification accuracy of different sets of dehazed images subjectively selected by human.

Input hazy image   Conv1   Conv2   Conv3   Conv4   Conv5   FC6   FC7   FC8

Fig. 9. Sample feature reconstruction results for two images, shown in two rows respectively. The leftmost column shows the input hazy images and the following columns are the images reconstructed from different layers in AlexNet.

4.6 Feature Reconstruction

The CNN networks used for image classification consists of multiple layers to extract deep image features. One interesting question is whether certain layers in the trained CNN actually perform image dehazing implicitly. We picked a reconstruction method [19] to reconstruct the image according to feature maps of all the layers in AlexNet. The reconstruction results are shown in Fig. 9, from which we can see that, for the first several layers, the reconstructed images do not show any dehazing effect. For the last several layers, the reconstructed images have been distorted, let alone dehazing. One possibility of this is that many existing image dehazing methods aim to please human vision system, which may not be good to CNN-based image classification. Meanwhile, many existing image dehazing methods introduce information loss, such as color distortion, and may increase the difficulty of image classification.

4.7 Feature Visualization

In order to further analyze different dehazing methods, we extract and visualize the features at hidden layers using VGGNet. For an input image with size $H \times W$, the activations of a convolution layer is formulated as an order-3 tensor with $H \times W \times D$ elements, where D is the number of channels. The term "activations" is a feature map of all the channels in a convolution layer. The activations in haze-removal images with different dehazing methods are displayed in Fig. 10. From top to bottom are haze-removal images, and the activations at $pool_1$, $pool_3$ and $pool_5$ layers, respectively. We can see that different dehazing methods actually have different activations, such as the activations of $pool_5$ layer of NLD and DNet.

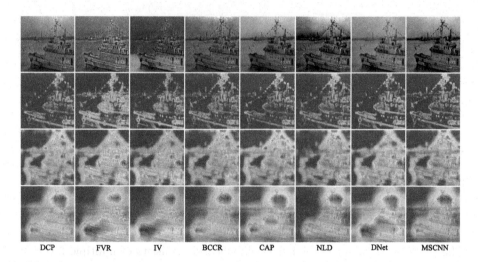

DCP   FVR   IV   BCCR   CAP   NLD   DNet   MSCNN

Fig. 10. Activations of hidden layers of VGGNet on image classification. From top to bottom are the haze-removal images, and the activations at $pool_1$, $pool_3$ and $pool_5$ layers, respectively.

5   Conclusions

In this paper, we conducted an empirical study to explore the effect of image dehazing to the performance of CNN-based image classification on synthetic and real hazy images. We used physical haze models to synthesize a large number of hazy images with different haze levels for training and testing. We also collected a new dataset of real hazy images from the Internet and it contains 4,610 images from 20 classes. We picked eight well-known dehazing methods for our empirical study. Experimental results on both synthetic and real hazy datasets show that the existing dehazing algorithms do not bring much benefit to improve the CNN-based image-classification accuracy, when compared to the case of directly training and testing on hazy images. Besides, we analyzed the current dehazing evaluation measures based on pixel-wise errors and local structural similarities and showed that there is not much correlation between these dehazing metrics and the image-classification accuracy when the images are preprocessed by the existing dehazing methods. While we believe this is due to the fact that image dehazing does not introduce new information to help image classification, we do not exclude the possibility that the existing image-dehazing methods are not sufficiently good in recovering the original clear image and better image-dehazing methods developed in the future may help improve image classification. We hope this study can draw more interests from the community to work on the important problem of haze image classification, which plays a critical role in applications such as autonomous driving, surveillance and robotics.

Acknowledgments. This work is supported, in part, by National Natural Science Foundation of China (NSFC-61273364, NSFC-61672376, NSFC-61473031, NSFC-61472029), Fundamental Research Funds for the Central Universities (2016JBZ005), and US National Science Foundation (NSF-1658987).

References

1. Agostinelli, F., Anderson, M.R., Lee, H.: Adaptive multi-column deep neural networks with application to robust image denoising. In: Advances in Neural Information Processing Systems, pp. 1493–1501 (2013)
2. Berman, D., Treibitz, T., Avidan, S., et al.: Non-local image dehazing. In: IEEE Conference on Computer Vision and Pattern Recognition, pp. 1674–1682 (2016)
3. Cai, B., Xu, X., Jia, K., Qing, C., Tao, D.: DehazeNet: an end-to-end system for single image haze removal. IEEE Trans. Image Process. **25**(11), 5187–5198 (2016)
4. Chen, G., Li, Y., Srihari, S.N.: Joint visual denoising and classification using deep learning. In: IEEE International Conference on Image Processing, pp. 3673–3677 (2016)
5. Deng, J., Dong, W., Socher, R., Li, L.J., Li, K., Fei-Fei, L.: ImageNet: a large-scale hierarchical image database. In: IEEE Conference on Computer Vision and Pattern Recognition, pp. 248–255 (2009)
6. Durand, T., Mordan, T., Thome, N., Cord, M.: WILDCAT: weakly supervised learning of deep convnets for image classification, pointwise localization and segmentation. In: IEEE Conference on Computer Vision and Pattern Recognition (2017)
7. Everingham, M., Van Gool, L., Williams, C.K., Winn, J., Zisserman, A.: The pascal visual object classes (VOC) challenge. Int. J. Comput. Vis. **88**(2), 303–338 (2010)
8. Griffin, G., Holub, A., Perona, P.: Caltech-256 object category dataset (2007)
9. He, K., Sun, J., Tang, X.: Single image haze removal using dark channel prior. IEEE Trans. Pattern Anal. Mach. Intell. **33**(12), 2341–2353 (2011)
10. He, K., Zhang, X., Ren, S., Sun, J.: Deep residual learning for image recognition. In: IEEE Conference on Computer Vision and Pattern Recognition, pp. 770–778 (2016)
11. Huynh-Thu, Q., Ghanbari, M.: Scope of validity of psnr in image/video quality assessment. Electron. Lett. **44**(13), 800–801 (2008)
12. Jalalvand, A., De Neve, W., Van de Walle, R., Martens, J.P.: Towards using reservoir computing networks for noise-robust image recognition. In: International Joint Conference on Neural Networks, pp. 1666–1672 (2016)
13. Koschmieder, H.: Theorie der horizontalen sichtweite. Beitrage zur Physik der freien Atmosphare, pp. 33–53 (1924)
14. Krizhevsky, A., Sutskever, I., Hinton, G.E.: ImageNet classification with deep convolutional neural networks. In: Advances in Neural Information Processing Systems, pp. 1097–1105 (2012)
15. Li, B., Peng, X., Wang, Z., Xu, J., Feng, D.: AOD-Net: all-in-one dehazing network. In: IEEE International Conference on Computer Vision, pp. 4770–4778 (2017)
16. Li, Y., Tan, R.T., Brown, M.S.: Nighttime haze removal with glow and multiple light colors. In: IEEE International Conference on Computer Vision, pp. 226–234 (2015)
17. Liu, F., Shen, C., Lin, G.: Deep convolutional neural fields for depth estimation from a single image. In: IEEE Conference on Computer Vision and Pattern Recognition, pp. 5162–5170 (2015)

18. Liu, L., Shen, C., van den Hengel, A.: The treasure beneath convolutional layers: Cross-convolutional-layer pooling for image classification. In: IEEE Conference on Computer Vision and Pattern Recognition, pp. 4749–4757 (2015)
19. Mahendran, A., Vedaldi, A.: Understanding deep image representations by inverting them. In: IEEE Conference on Computer Vision and Pattern Recognition, pp. 5188–5196 (2015)
20. Meng, G., Wang, Y., Duan, J., Xiang, S., Pan, C.: Efficient image dehazing with boundary constraint and contextual regularization. In: IEEE International Conference on Computer Vision, pp. 617–624 (2013)
21. Ren, W., Liu, S., Zhang, H., Pan, J., Cao, X., Yang, M.-H.: Single image dehazing via multi-scale convolutional neural networks. In: Leibe, B., Matas, J., Sebe, N., Welling, M. (eds.) ECCV 2016. LNCS, vol. 9906, pp. 154–169. Springer, Cham (2016). https://doi.org/10.1007/978-3-319-46475-6_10
22. Simonyan, K., Zisserman, A.: Very deep convolutional networks for large-scale image recognition. arXiv preprint arXiv:1409.1556 (2014)
23. Szegedy, C., et al.: Going deeper with convolutions. In: IEEE Conference on Computer Vision and Pattern Recognition, pp. 1–9 (2015)
24. Tang, Y., Salakhutdinov, R., Hinton, G.: Robust Boltzmann machines for recognition and denoising. In: IEEE Conference on Computer Vision and Pattern Recognition, pp. 2264–2271 (2012)
25. Tarel, J.P., Hautiere, N.: Fast visibility restoration from a single color or gray level image. In: IEEE International Conference on Computer Vision, pp. 2201–2208 (2009)
26. Tarel, J.P., Hautiere, N., Cord, A., Gruyer, D., Halmaoui, H.: Improved visibility of road scene images under heterogeneous fog. In: IEEE Intelligent Vehicles Symposium, pp. 478–485 (2010)
27. Wang, F., et al.: Residual attention network for image classification. arXiv preprint arXiv:1704.06904 (2017)
28. Wang, J., Yang, Y., Mao, J., Huang, Z., Huang, C., Xu, W.: CNN-RNN: a unified framework for multi-label image classification. In: IEEE Conference on Computer Vision and Pattern Recognition, pp. 2285–2294 (2016)
29. Wang, Z., Chang, S., Yang, Y., Liu, D., Huang, T.S.: Studying very low resolution recognition using deep networks. In: IEEE Conference on Computer Vision and Pattern Recognition, pp. 4792–4800 (2016)
30. Wang, Z., Bovik, A.C., Sheikh, H.R., Simoncelli, E.P.: Image quality assessment: from error visibility to structural similarity. IEEE Trans. Image Process. 13(4), 600–612 (2004)
31. Yang, J., Yu, K., Gong, Y., Huang, T.: Linear spatial pyramid matching using sparse coding for image classification. In: IEEE Conference on Computer Vision and Pattern Recognition, pp. 1794–1801 (2009)
32. Zhang, J., Cao, Y., Fang, S., Kang, Y., Chen, C.W.: Fast haze removal for nighttime image using maximum reflectance prior. In: IEEE Conference on Computer Vision and Pattern Recognition, pp. 7418–7426 (2017)
33. Zhu, Q., Mai, J., Shao, L.: A fast single image haze removal algorithm using color attenuation prior. IEEE Trans. Image Process. 24(11), 3522–3533 (2015)

Supervising the New with the Old: Learning SFM from SFM

Maria Klodt$^{(\boxtimes)}$ [iD] and Andrea Vedaldi$^{(\boxtimes)}$ [iD]

Visual Geometry Group, University of Oxford, Oxford, UK
{klodt,vedaldi}@robots.ox.ac.uk

Abstract. Recent work has demonstrated that it is possible to learn deep neural networks for monocular depth and ego-motion estimation from unlabelled video sequences, an interesting theoretical development with numerous advantages in applications. In this paper, we propose a number of improvements to these approaches. First, since such self-supervised approaches are based on the brightness constancy assumption, which is valid only for a subset of pixels, we propose a probabilistic learning formulation where the network predicts distributions over variables rather than specific values. As these distributions are conditioned on the observed image, the network can learn which scene and object types are likely to violate the model assumptions, resulting in more robust learning. We also propose to build on dozens of years of experience in developing handcrafted structure-from-motion (SFM) algorithms. We do so by using an off-the-shelf SFM system to generate a supervisory signal for the deep neural network. While this signal is also noisy, we show that our probabilistic formulation can learn and account for the defects of SFM, helping to integrate different sources of information and boosting the overall performance of the network.

1 Introduction

Visual geometry is one of the few areas of computer vision where traditional approaches have partially resisted the advent of deep learning. However, the community has now developed several deep networks that are very competitive in problems such as ego-motion estimation, depth regression, 3D reconstruction, and mapping. While traditional approaches may still have better absolute accuracy in some cases, these networks have very interesting properties in terms of speed and robustness. Furthermore, they are applicable to cases such as monocular reconstruction where traditional methods cannot be used.

A particularly interesting aspect of the structure-from-motion problem is that it can be used for bootstrapping deep neural networks without the use of manual supervision. Several recent papers have shown in fact that it is possible to learn networks for ego-motion and monocular depth estimation only by

Electronic supplementary material The online version of this chapter (https://doi.org/10.1007/978-3-030-01249-6_43) contains supplementary material, which is available to authorized users.

© Springer Nature Switzerland AG 2018
V. Ferrari et al. (Eds.): ECCV 2018, LNCS 11214, pp. 713–728, 2018.
https://doi.org/10.1007/978-3-030-01249-6_43

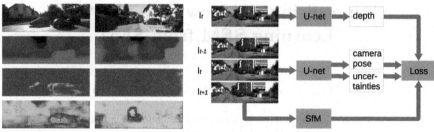

(a) RGB input image and predictions: depth, photometric uncertainty, and depth uncertainty.

(b) proposed network architecture: the depth and pose-uncertainty networks are supervised by traditional SfM.

Fig. 1. (a) Depth and uncertainty prediction on the KITTI dataset: In addition to monocular depth prediction, we propose to predict photometric and depth uncertainty maps in order to facilitate training from monocular image sequences. (b) Overview of the training data flow: two convolutional neural networks are trained under the supervision of a traditional SfM method, and are combined via a joint loss including photo-consistency terms.

watching videos from a moving camera (SfMLearner [1]) or a stereo camera pair (MonoDepth [2]). These methods rely mainly on low-level cues such as brightness constancy and only mild assumptions on the camera motion. This is particularly appealing as it allows to learn models very cheaply, without requiring specialized hardware or setups. This can be used to deploy cheaper and/or more robust sensors, as well as to develop sensors that can automatically learn to operate in new application domains.

In this paper, we build on the SfMLearner approach and consider the problem of learning from scratch a neural network for ego-motion and monocular depth regression using only unlabelled video data from a single, moving camera. Compared to SfMLearner and similar approaches, we contribute three significant improvements to the learning formulation that allows the method to learn better models.

Our first and simplest improvement is to strengthen the brightness constancy loss, importing the structural similarity loss used in MonoDepth in the SfMLearner setup. Despite its simplicity, this change does improve results.

Our second improvement is to incorporate an explicit model of confidence in the neural network. SfMLearner predicts an "explainability map" whose goal is to identify regions in an image where the brightness constancy constraint is likely to be well satisfied. However, the original formulation is heuristic. For example, the explainability maps must be regularized ad-hoc to avoid becoming degenerate. We show that much better results can be obtained by turning explainability into a proper probabilistic model, yielding a self-consistent formulation which measures the likelihood of the observed data. In order to do so, we predict for each pixel a distribution over possible brightnesses, which allows the model to express a degree of confidence on how accurately brightness constancy will be satisfied at a certain image location. For example, this model can learn to expect slight misalignments on objects such as tree branches and cars that could move independently of the camera.

Our third improvement is to integrate another form of cheap supervision in the process. We note that the computer vision community has developed in the past 20 years a treasure trove of high-quality handcrafted structure-from-motion methods (SFM). Thus, it is natural to ask whether these algorithms can be used to teach better deep neural networks. In order to do so, during training we propose to run, in parallel with the forward pass of the network, a standard SFM method. We then require the network to optimize the brightness constancy equation as before *and* to match motion and depth estimates from the SFM algorithm, in a multi-task setting.

Ideally, we would like the network to ultimately perform *better* than traditional SFM methods. The question, then, is how can such an approach train a model that outperforms the teacher. There is clearly an opportunity to do so because, while SFM can provide very high-quality supervision when it works, it can also fail badly. For example, feature triangulation may be off in correspondence of reflections, resulting in inconsistent depth values for certain pixels. Thus, we adopt a probabilistic formulation for the SFM supervisory signal as well. This has the important effect of allowing the model to *learn when and to which extent it can trust the SFM supervision*. In this manner, the deep network can learn failure modalities of traditional SFM, and discount them appropriately while learning.

While we present such improvements in the specific context of 3D reconstruction, we note that the idea of using probabilistic predictions to integrate information from a collection of imperfect supervisory signals is likely to be broadly applicable.

We test our method against SfMLearner, the state of the art in this setting, and show convincing improvements due to our three modifications. The end result is a system that can learn an excellent monocular depth and ego-motion predictor, all without any manual supervision.

2   Related Work

Structure from motion is a well-studied problem in Computer Vision. Traditional approaches such as ORB-SLAM2 [3,4] are based on a pipeline of matching feature points, selecting a set of inlier points, and optimizing with respect to 3D points and camera positions on these points. Typically, the crucial part of these methods is a careful selection of feature points [5–8].

More recently, deep learning methods have been developed for learning 3D structure and/or camera motion from image sequences. In [9] a supervised learning method for estimating depth from a single image has been proposed. For supervision, additional information is necessary, either in form of manual input or as in [9], laser scanner measurements. Supervised approaches for learning camera poses include [10–12].

Unsupervised learning avoids the necessity of additional input by learning from RGB image sequences only. The training is guided by geometric and photometric consistency constraints between multiple images of the same scene. It has been shown that dense depth maps can be robustly estimated from a single image by unsupervised learning [2,13], and furthermore, depth and camera poses [14]. While these methods perform single image depth estimation, they use stereo image pairs for training. This facilitates training, due to a fixed relative geometry between the two stereo cameras and simultaneous image acquisition yielding a static scene.

A more difficult problem is learning structure from motion from monocular image sequences. Here, depth and camera position have to be estimated simultaneously, and moving objects in the scene can corrupt the overall consistency with respect to the world coordinate system. A method for estimating and learning structure from motion from monocular image sequences has been proposed in SfMLearner [1]. Unsupervised learning can be enhanced by supervision in cases where ground truth is partially available in the training data, as has been shown in [15]. Results from traditional SfM methods can be used to guide other methods like 3D localization [16] and prediction of occlusion models [17].

Uncertainty learning for depth and camera pose estimation have been investigated in [18,19] where different types of uncertainties have been investigated for depth map estimation, and in [20] where uncertainties for partially reliable ground truths have been learned.

3   Method

Let $\mathbf{x}_t \in \mathbb{R}^{H \times W \times 3}$, $t \in \mathbb{Z}$ be a video sequence consisting of RGB images captured from a moving camera. Our goal is to train two neural networks. The first $\mathbf{d} = \Phi_{\mathrm{depth}}(\mathbf{x}_t)$ is a *monocular depth estimation network* producing as output a depth map $\mathbf{d} \in \mathbb{R}^{H \times D}$ from a single input frame. The second $(R_t, T_t : t \in \mathcal{T}) = \Phi_{\mathrm{ego}}(\mathbf{x}_t : t \in \mathcal{T})$ is an *ego-motion and uncertainty estimation network*. It takes as input a short time sequence $\mathcal{T} = (-T, \ldots, 0, \ldots, T)$ and estimates 3D camera rotations and translations (R_t, T_t), $t \in \mathcal{T}$ for each of the images $\mathbf{x}_t$ in the sequence. Additionally, it predicts the pose uncertainty, as well as photometric and depth uncertainty maps which help the overall network to learn about outliers and noise caused by occlusions, specularities and other modalities that are hard to handle.

Learning the neural networks Φ_{depth} and Φ_{ego} from a video sequence without any other form of supervision is a challenging task. However, methods such as SfMLearner [1] have shown that this task can be solved successfully using the brightness constancy constraint as a learning cue. We improve over the state of the art in three ways: by improving the photometric loss that captures brightness constancy (Sect. 3.1), by introducing a more robust probabilistic formulation for the observations (Sect. 3.2) and by using the latter to integrate cues from off-the-shelf SFM methods for supervision (Sect. 3.3).

3.1   Photometric Losses

The most fundamental supervisory signal to learn geometry from unlabelled video sequences is the *brightness constancy constraint*. This constraint simply states that pixels in different video frames that correspond to the same scene point must have the same color. While this is only true under certain conditions (Lambertian surfaces, constant illumination, no occlusions, etc.), SfMLearner and other methods have shown it to be sufficient to learn the ego-motion and depth reconstruction networks Φ_{ego} and Φ_{depth}. In fact, the output of these networks can be used to put pixels in different video frames in correspondence and test whether their color match. This intuition can be easily captured in a loss, as discussed below.

Basic Photometric Loss. Let $\mathbf{d}_0$ be the depth map corresponding to image $\mathbf{x}_0$. Let $(u, v) \in \mathbb{R}^2$ be the calibrated coordinate of a pixel in image $\mathbf{x}_0$ (so that $(0, 0)$ is the optical centre and the focal length is unit). Then the coordinates of the 3D point that projects onto (u, v) are given by $\mathbf{d}(u, v) \cdot (u, v, 1)$. If the roto-translation (R_t, T_t) is the motion of the camera from time 0 to time t and $\pi(q_1, q_2, q_3) = (q_1/q_3, q_2/q_3)$ is the perspective projection operator, then the corresponding pixel in image $\mathbf{x}_t$ is given by $(u', v') = g(u, v | \mathbf{d}, R_t, T_t) = \pi(R_t \mathbf{d}(u, v)(u, v, 1)^\top + T_t)$. Due to brightness constancy, the colors $\mathbf{x}_0(u, v) = \mathbf{x}_t(g(u, v | \mathbf{d}, R_t, T_t))$ of the two pixels should match. We then obtain the photometric loss:

$$\mathcal{L} = \sum_{t \in \mathcal{T} - \{0\}} \sum_{(u,v) \in \Omega} |\mathbf{x}_t(g(u, v | \mathbf{d}, R_t, T_t)) - \mathbf{x}_0(u, v)| \tag{1}$$

where Ω is a discrete set of image locations (corresponding to the calibrated pixel centres). The absolute value is used for robustness to outliers.

All quantities in Eq. (1) are known except depth and camera motion, which are estimated by the two neural networks. This means that we can write the loss as a function:

$$\mathcal{L}(\mathbf{x}_t : t \in \mathcal{T} | \Phi_{\text{depth}}, \Phi_{\text{ego}})$$

This expression can then be minimized w.r.t. Φ_{depth} and Φ_{ego} to learn the neural networks.

Structural-Similarity Loss. Comparing pixel values directly may be too fragile. Thus, we complement the simple photometric loss (1) with the more advanced image matching term used in [2] for the case of stereo camera pairs. Given a pair of image patches $\mathbf{a}$ and $\mathbf{b}$, their *structural similarity* [21] SSIM$(\mathbf{a}, \mathbf{b}) \in [0, 1]$ is given by:

$$\text{SSIM}(\mathbf{a}, \mathbf{b}) = \frac{(2\mu_{\mathbf{a}}\mu_{\mathbf{b}})(\sigma_{\mathbf{ab}} + \epsilon)}{(\mu_{\mathbf{a}}^2 + \mu_{\mathbf{b}}^2)(\sigma_{\mathbf{a}}^2 + \sigma_{\mathbf{b}}^2 + \epsilon)}$$

where ϵ is a small constant to avoid division by zero for constant patches, $\mu_{\mathbf{a}} = \frac{1}{n} \sum_{i=1}^{n} a_i$ is the mean of patch $\mathbf{a}$, $\sigma_{\mathbf{a}}^2 = \frac{1}{n-1} \sum_{i=1}^{n} (a_i - \mu_{\mathbf{a}})^2$ is its variance, and $\sigma_{\mathbf{ab}} = \frac{1}{n-1} \sum_{i=1}^{n} (a_i - \mu_{\mathbf{a}})(b_i - \mu_{\mathbf{b}})$ is the correlation of the two patches.

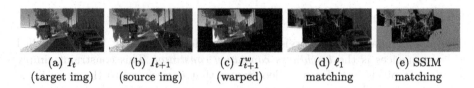

(a) I_t	(b) I_{t+1}	(c) I_{t+1}^w	(d) ℓ_1	(e) SSIM
(target img)	(source img)	(warped)	matching	matching

Fig. 2. Image matching: the photometric loss terms penalize high values in the ℓ_1 difference (d) and SSIM image matching (e) of the target image (a) and the warped source image (c).

This means that the combined structural similarity and photometric loss can be written as $\mathcal{L} = \sum_{(u,v)\in\Omega} \ell(u,v|\mathbf{x}, \mathbf{x}')$ where

$$\ell(u, v|\mathbf{x}, \mathbf{x}') = \alpha\frac{1 - \mathrm{SSIM}(\mathbf{x}|_{\Theta(u,v)}, \mathbf{x}'|_{\Theta(u,v)})}{2} + (1 - \alpha)|\mathbf{x}(u,v) - \mathbf{x}'(u,v)|. \quad (2)$$

The weighting parameter α is set to 0.85.

Multi-scale Loss and Regularization. Figure 2 shows an example for ℓ_1 and SSIM image matching, computed from ground truth depth and poses for two example images of the Virtual KITTI data set [22]. Even with ground truth depth and camera poses, a perfect image matching cannot be guaranteed.

Hence, for added robustness, Eq. (2) is computed at multiple scales. Further robustness is achieved by a suitable smoothness term for regularizing the depth map which is added to the loss function, as in [2].

3.2   Probabilistic Outputs

The brightness constancy constraint fails whenever one of its several assumptions is violated. In practice, common failure cases include occlusions, changes in the field of view, moving objects in the scene, and reflective materials. The key idea to handle such issues is to allow the neural network to *learn to predict such failure modalities*. If done properly, this has the important benefit of extracting as much information as possible from the imperfect supervisory signal while avoiding being disrupted by outliers and noise.

General Approach. Consider at first a simple case in which a predictor estimates a quantity $\hat{y} = \Phi(x)$, where x is a data point and y its corresponding "ground-truth" label. In a standard learning formulation, the predictor Φ would be optimized to minimize a loss such as $\ell = |\hat{y} - y|$. However, if we knew that for this particular example the ground truth is not reliable, we could down-weight the loss as ℓ/σ by dividing it by a suitable coefficient σ. In this manner, the model would be less affected by such noise.

The problem with this idea is how to set the coefficient σ. For example, optimizing it to minimize the loss does not make sense as this has the degenerate solution $\sigma = +\infty$.

An approach is to make σ one of the quantities *predicted by the model* and use it in a probabilistic output formulation. To this end, let the neural network output the parameters $(\hat{y}, \sigma) = \Phi(x)$ of a posterior probability distribution $p(y|\hat{y}, \sigma)$ over possible "ground-truth" labels y. For example, using Laplace's distribution:

$$p(y|\hat{y}, \sigma) = \frac{1}{2\sigma} \exp \frac{-|y - \hat{y}|}{\sigma}.$$

The learning objective is then the negative log-likelihood arising from this distribution:

$$-\log p(y|\hat{y}, \sigma) = \frac{|y - \hat{y}|}{\sigma} + \log \sigma + \text{const.}$$

A predictor that minimises this quantity will try to guess $\hat{y}$ as close as possible to y. At the same time, it will try to set σ to the *fitting error it expects*. In fact, it is easy to see that, for a fixed $\hat{y}$, the loss is minimised when $\sigma = |y - \hat{y}|$, resulting in a log-likelihood value of

$$-\log p(y|\hat{y}, |y - \hat{y}|) = \log |y - \hat{y}| + \text{const.}$$

Note that the model is incentivized to learn σ to reflect as accurately as possible the prediction error. Note also that σ may resemble the threshold in a robust loss such as Huber's. However, there is a very important difference: it is the predictor itself that, after having observed the data point x, estimates on the fly an optimal data-dependent "threshold" σ. This allows the model to perform introspection, thus potentially discounting cases that are too difficult to fit. It also allows the model to learn, and compensate for, cases where the supervisory signal y itself may be unreliable. Furthermore this probabilistic formulation does not have any tunable parameter.

Implementation for the Photometric Loss. For the photometric loss (2), the model above is applied by considering an additional output $(\sigma_t)_{t \in \mathcal{T}-\{0\}}$ to the network Φ_{ego}, to predict, along with the depth map $\mathbf{d}$ and poses (R_t, T_t), an uncertainty map σ_t for photometric matching at each pixel. Then the loss is given by

$$\sum_{t \in \mathcal{T}-\{0\}} \sum_{(u,v) \in \Omega} \frac{\ell(u, v | \mathbf{x}_0, \mathbf{x}_t \circ g_t)}{\sigma_t(u, v)} + \log \sigma_t(u, v),$$

where ℓ is given by Eq. 2 and $g_t(u, v) = g(u, v | \mathbf{d}, R_t, T_t)$ is the warp induced by the estimated depth and camera pose.

3.3   Learning SFM from SFM

In this section, we describe our third contribution: learning a deep neural network that distills as much information as possible from a classical (handcrafted) method for SFM. To this end, for each training subsequence $(\mathbf{x}_t : t \in \mathcal{T})$ a standard high-quality SFM pipeline such as ORB-SLAM2 is used to estimate a depth map $\bar{\mathbf{d}}$ and camera motions $(\bar{R}_t, \bar{T}_t)$. This information can be easily used to supervise the deep neural network by adding suitable losses:

$$\mathcal{L}_{\text{SFM}} = \|\bar{\mathbf{d}} - \mathbf{d}\|_1 + \|\ln \bar{R}_t R_t^\top\|_F + \|\bar{T}_t - T_t\|_2 \tag{3}$$

Here ln denotes the principal matrix logarithm, which maps the residual rotation to its Lie group coordinates which provides a natural metric for small rotations.

While standard SFM algorithms are usually reliable, they are far from perfect. This is particularly true for the depth map $\bar{\mathbf{d}}$. First, since SFM is based on matching discrete features, $\bar{\mathbf{d}}$ will not contain depth information for all image pixels. While missing information can be easily handled in the loss, a more challenging issue is that triangulation will sometimes result in incorrect depth estimates due for example to highlights, objects moving in the scene, occlusion, and other challenging visual effects.

In order to address these issues, as well as to automatically balance the losses in a multi-task setting [19], we propose once more to adopt the probabilistic formulation of Sect. 3.2. Thus loss (3) is replaced with

$$\mathcal{L}_{\text{SFM}}^p = \chi_{\text{SFM}} \left[\sum_{t \in \mathcal{T} - \{t\}} \left[\frac{\|\ln \bar{R}_t R_t^\top\|_F}{\sigma_{\text{SFM}}^{R_t}} + \log \sigma_{\text{SFM}}^{R_t} + \frac{\|\lambda_T \bar{T}_t - T_t\|_2}{\sigma_{\text{SFM}}^{T_t}} + \log \sigma_{\text{SFM}}^{T_t} \right] \right.$$
$$\left. + \sum_{(u,v) \in S} \left[\frac{|(\lambda_{\mathbf{d}} \bar{\mathbf{d}}(u,v))^{-1} - (\mathbf{d}(u,v))^{-1}|}{\sigma_{\text{SFM}}^{\mathbf{d}}(u,v)} + \log \sigma_{\text{SFM}}^{\mathbf{d}}(u,v) \right] \right] \tag{4}$$

where pose uncertainties $\sigma_{\text{SFM}}^R, \sigma_{\text{SFM}}^T$ and pixel-wise depth uncertainty maps $\sigma_{\text{SFM}}^{\mathbf{d}}$ are also estimated as output of the neural network Φ_{ego} from the video sequence. $S \in \Omega$ is a sparse subset of pixels where depth supervision is available.

The translation and depth values from SFM are multiplied by scalars $\lambda_T = \sum_t \|T_t\| / \sum_t \|\bar{T}_t\|$ and $\lambda_{\mathbf{d}} = \text{median}(\mathbf{d}) / \text{median}(\bar{\mathbf{d}})$, respectively, because of the scale ambiguity which is inherent in monocular SFM. Furthermore, the binary variable χ_{SFM} denotes whether a corresponding reconstruction from SFM is available. This allows to include training examples where traditional SFM fails to reconstruct pose and depths. Note that we measure the depth error using inverse depth, in order to get a suitable domain of error values. Thus, small depth values, which correspond to points that are close to the camera, get higher importance in the loss function, and far away points, which are often more unreliable, are down-weighted.

Just as for supervision by the brightness constancy, this allows the neural network to learn about systematic failure modes of the SFM algorithm. Supervision can then avoid to be overly confident about this supervisory signal, resulting in a system which is better able to distill the useful information while discarding noise.

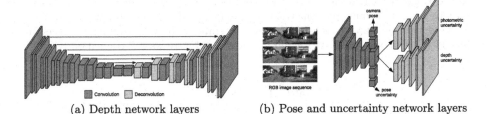

(a) Depth network layers   (b) Pose and uncertainty network layers

Fig. 3. Network architecture: (a) Depth network: the network takes a single RGB image as input and estimates pixel-wise depth through 29 layers of convolution and deconvolution. Skip connections between encoder and decoder allow to recover fine-scale details. (b) Pose and uncertainty network: Input to the network is a short image sequence of variable length. The fourfold output shares a common encoder and splits to pose estimation, pose uncertainty and the two uncertainty maps afterwards. While photometric uncertainty estimates confidence in the photometric image matching, depth uncertainty estimates confidence in depth supervision from SfM.

4   Architecture Learning and Details

Section 3 discussed two neural networks, one for depth estimation (Φ_{depth}) and one for ego-motion and prediction confidence estimation (Φ_{ego}). This section provides the details of these networks. An overview of the network architecture and training data flow with combined pose and uncertainty networks is shown in Fig. 1(b). First, we note that, while two different networks are learned, in practice the pose and uncertainty nets share the majority of their parameters. As a trunk, we consider a U-net [23] architecture similar to the ones used in Monodepth [2] and SfMLearner [1].

Figure 3(a) shows details of the layers of the deep network. The network consists of an encoder and a decoder. The input is a single RGB image, and the output is a map of depth values for each pixel. The encoder is a concatenation of convolutional layers followed by ReLU activations where layers' resolution progressively decreases and the number of feature channels progressively increases. The decoder consists of concatenated deconvolution and convolution layers, with increasing resolution. Skip connections link encoder layers to decoder layers of corresponding size, in order to be able to represent high-resolution details. The last four convolution layers further have a connection to the output layers of the network, with sigmoid activations.

Figure 3(b) shows details of the pose and uncertainty network layers. The input of the network is an image sequence consisting of the target image I_t, which is also the input of the depth network, and n neighboring views before and after I_t in the sequence $\{I_{t-n}, \ldots, I_{t-1}\}$ and $\{I_{t+1}, \ldots, I_{t+n}\}$, respectively. The output of the network is the relative camera pose for each neighboring view with respect to the target view, two uncertainty values for the rotation and translation, respectively, and pixel-wise uncertainties for photo-consistency and depth. The different outputs share a common encoder, which consists of con-

Table 1. Depth evaluation in comparison to SfMLearner: We evaluate the three contributions image matching, photometric uncertainty, and depth and pose from SfM. Each of these show an improvement to the current state of the art. Training datasets are KITTI (K), Virtual KITTI (VK) and Cityscapes (CS). Rows 1–7 trained on KITTI.

	Error measures			Accuracy		
	abs. rel	sq. rel	RMSE	$\delta < 1.25$	$\delta < 1.25^2$	$\delta < 1.25^3$
SfMLearner (paper)	0.208	1.768	6.856	0.678	0.885	0.957
SfMLearner (website)	0.183	1.595	6.709	0.734	0.902	0.959
SfMLearner (reproduced)	0.198	2.423	6.950	0.732	0.903	0.957
+image matching	0.181	2.054	6.771	0.763	0.913	0.963
+photometric uncertainty	0.180	1.970	6.855	0.765	0.913	0.962
+pose from SFM	0.171	1.891	6.588	0.776	**0.919**	0.963
+pose and depth from SFM	**0.166**	**1.490**	**5.998**	**0.778**	**0.919**	**0.966**
Ours, trained on VK	0.270	2.343	7.921	0.546	0.810	0.926
Ours, trained on CS	0.254	2.579	7.652	0.611	0.857	0.942
Ours, trained on CS+K	0.165	1.340	5.764	0.784	0.927	0.970

volution layers, each followed by a ReLU activation. The pose output is of size $2n \times 6$, representing a 6 DoF relative pose for each source view, each consisting of a 3D translation vector and 3 Euler angles representing the camera rotation matrix, as in [1]. The uncertainty output is threefold, consisting of pose, photometric, and depth uncertainty. The pose uncertainty shares weights with the pose estimation, and yields a $2n \times 2$ output representing translational and rotational uncertainty for each source view. The pixel-wise photometric and depth uncertainties each consist of a concatenation of deconvolution layers of increasing width. All uncertainties are activated by a sigmoid activation function.

A complete description of the network architecture is provided in the supplementary material.

5   Experiments

We compare results of the proposed method to SfMLearner [1] which is the only method to our knowledge which estimates monocular depth and relative camera poses from monocular training data only. The experiments show that our method achieves better results that SfMLearner.

5.1   Monocular Depth Estimation

For training and testing monocular depth we use the Eigen split of the KITTI raw dataset [24] as proposed by [9]. This yields a split of 39835 training images, 4387 for validation, and 697 test images. We only use monocular sequences for

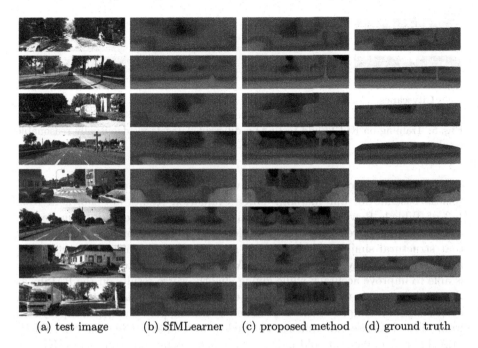

(a) test image   (b) SfMLearner   (c) proposed method   (d) ground truth

Fig. 4. Comparison to SfMLearner and ground truth on test images from KITTI.

training. Training is performed on sequences of three images, where depth is estimated for the centre image.

The state of the art in learning depth maps from a single image using monocular sequences for training only, is SfMLearner [1]. Therefore we compare to this method in our experiments. The laser scanner measurements are used as ground truth for testing only. The predicted depth maps are multiplied by a scalar $s = \mathrm{median}(\mathbf{d}^*)/\mathrm{median}(\mathbf{d})$ before evaluation. This is done in the same way as in [1], in order to resolve scale ambiguity which is inherent to monocular SfM.

Table 1 shows a quantitative comparison of SfMLearner with the different contributions of the proposed method. We compute the error measures used in [9] to compare predicted depth $\mathbf{d}$ with ground truth depth $\mathbf{d}^*$:

- Absolute relative difference (abs. rel.): $\frac{1}{N}\sum_{i=1}^{N}|\mathbf{d}_i - \mathbf{d}_i^*|/\mathbf{d}_i^*$
- Squared relative difference (sq. rel.): $\frac{1}{N}\sum_{i=1}^{N}|\mathbf{d}_i - \mathbf{d}_i^*|^2/\mathbf{d}_i^*$
- Root mean square error (RMSE): $\left(\frac{1}{N}\sum_{i=1}^{N}|\mathbf{d}_i - \mathbf{d}_i^*|^2\right)^{1/2}$

The accuracy measures are giving the percentage of $\mathbf{d}_i$ s.t. $\max\left(\mathbf{d}_i/\mathbf{d}_i^*, \mathbf{d}_i^*/\mathbf{d}_i\right) = \delta$ is less than a threshold, where we use the same thresholds as in [9].

We compare to the error measures given in [1], as well as to a newer version of SfMLearner provided on the website[1]. We also compare to running the

---

[1] https://github.com/tinghuiz/SfMLearner.

| Cityscapes | Virtual KITTI | Oxford RobotCar | Make3D |

Fig. 5. Training on KITTI and testing on different datasets yields visually reasonable results.

code downloaded from this website, as we got slightly different results. We use this as baseline for our method. These evaluation results are shown in rows 1–3 of Table 1. Rows 4–7 refer to our implementation as described in Sect. 3, while changes referred to in each row add to the previous row. The results show that structural similarity based image matching gives an improvement to the brightness constancy loss as used in SfMLearner. The photometric uncertainty is able to improve accuracy while giving slightly worse results on the RMSE, as the method is able to allow for higher errors in parts of the image domain. A more substantial improvement is obtained by adding pose and depth supervision from SFM. In these experiments we used in particular predictions from ORB-SLAM2 [4]. Numbers in bold indicate best performance for training on KITTI. The last three rows show results on the same test set (KITTI eigen split), for the final model with pose and depth from SfM, trained on Virtual KITTI (VK) [22], Cityscapes (CS) [25], and pre-training on Cityscapes with fine-tuning on KITTI (CS+K).

Figure 4 shows a qualitative comparison of depth predicted by SfMlearner against ground truth measurements from a laser scanner. Since the laser scanner measurements are sparse, we densify them for better visualization. While SfMLearner robustly estimates depth, our proposed approach is able to recover many more small-scale details from the images. The last row shows a typical failure case, where the estimated depth is less accurate on regions like car windows. Figure 5 shows a qualitative evaluation of depth prediction for different datasets. The model trained on KITTI was tested on images from Cityscapes [25], Virtual KITTI [22], Oxford RobotCar [26] and Make3D [27], respectively. Test images were cropped to match the ratio of width and height of the KITTI training data. These results show that the method is able to generalize to unknown scenarios and camera settings.

5.2 Uncertainty Estimation

Figure 6 shows example visualizations of the photometric and depth uncertainty maps for some of the images from the KITTI dataset. The color bar indicates high uncertainty at the top and low uncertainty at the bottom. We observe that high photometric uncertainty typically occurs in regions with vegetation, where matching is hard due to repetitive structures, and in regions with specularities which corrupt the brightness constancy assumption, for example car windows

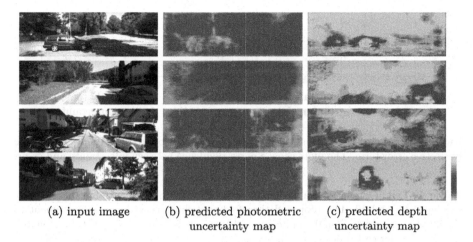

(a) input image	(b) predicted photometric uncertainty map	(c) predicted depth uncertainty map

Fig. 6. Prediction of uncertainty maps: the pixel-wise estimated uncertainty maps allow for higher errors in the image matching at regions with high uncertainty, leading to improved overall network performance. We observe that the photometric uncertainty maps (b) tend to predict high uncertainty for reflective surfaces, lens flares, vegetation, and at the image borders, as these induce high photometric errors when matching subsequent frames. The depth uncertainty maps (c) tend to predict high uncertainties for potentially moving objects, and the sky, where depth values are less reliable. The network seems to be able to discern between moving and stationary cars.

or lens flares. High depth uncertainty occurs typically on moving object as for example cars. We further observe that the network often seems to be able to discern between moving and stationary cars.

Figure 7 shows rotational, translational, depth and photometric uncertainty versus their respective error. The plots show that uncertainties tend to be lower in regions with good matching, and worse in regions with less good matching.

5.3 Camera Pose Estimation

We trained and tested the proposed method on the KITTI odometry dataset [28], using the same split of training and test sequences as in [1]: sequences 00–08 for training and sequences 09–10 for testing, using the left camera images of all sequences only. This gives a split of 20409 training images and 2792 test images. The ground truth odometry provided in the KITTI dataset is used for evaluation purposes only. Again, depth and pose from SFM are obtained from ORB-SLAM2 [4].

Table 2 shows a comparison to SfMLearner with numbers as given in the paper and on the website for the two test sequences 09 and 10. For odometry evaluation, a sequence length of 5 images has been used for training and testing. The error measure is the Absolute Trajectory Error (ATE) [29] on the 5-frame snippets, which are averaged on the whole sequence. The same error measure was used in [1]. We compare results from SfMLearner as stated in the paper and

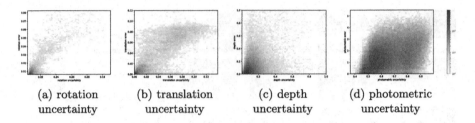

| (a) rotation uncertainty | (b) translation uncertainty | (c) depth uncertainty | (d) photometric uncertainty |

Fig. 7. Uncertainty of rotation, translation, depth, and photo-consistency versus the respective error term. The plots show a correspondence between uncertainty and error.

Table 2. Left: Odometry evaluation in comparison to SfMLearner for the two test sequences 09 and 10. The proposed threefold contributions yield an improvement to the state of the art in Seq. 09 and comparable results in Seq. 10. Right: Concatenated poses with color coded pose uncertainty (green = certain, red = uncertain) for Seq. 09.

	Seq. 09	Seq. 10
ORB-SLAM (full)	0.014 ± 0.008	**0.012 ± 0.011**
ORB-SLAM (short)	0.064 ± 0.141	0.064 ± 0.130
DSO (full)	0.065 ± 0.059	0.047 ± 0.043
SfMLearner (paper)	0.021 ± 0.017	0.020 ± 0.015
SfMLearner (website)	0.016 ± 0.009	0.013 ± 0.009
proposed method	**0.014 ± 0.007**	0.013 ± 0.009

on the website, to the proposed method with uncertainties and depth and pose supervision from SfM. Furthermore we compare to traditional methods ORB-SLAM (results as provided in [1]), and DSO [30]. "Full" refers to reconstruction from all images, and "short" refers to reconstruction from snippets of 5-frames. For DSO we were not able to get results for short sequences, as initialization is based on 5–10 keyframes.

6   Conclusions

In this paper we have presented a new method for simultaneously estimating depth maps and camera positions from monocular image sequences. This method is based on SfMLearning and uses only monocular RGB image sequences for training.

We have improved this baseline in three ways: by improving the image matching loss, by incorporating a probabilistic model of observation confidence and, extending the latter, by leveraging a standard SFM method to help supervising the deep network. Experiments show that our contributions lead to substantial improvements over the current state of the art both for the estimation of depth maps and odometry from monocular image sequences.

Acknowledgements. We are very grateful to Continental Corporation for sponsoring this research.

References

1. Zhou, T., Brown, M., Snavely, N., Lowe, D.G.: Unsupervised learning of depth and ego-motion from video. In: CVPR (2017)
2. Godard, C., Mac Aodha, O., Brostow, G.J.: Unsupervised monocular depth estimation with left-right consistency. In: CVPR (2017)
3. Mur-Artal, R., Montiel, J.M.M., Tardos, J.D.: ORB-SLAM: a versatile and accurate monocular SLAM system. IEEE Trans. Rob. **31**(5), 1147–1163 (2015)
4. Mur-Artal, R., Tardós, J.D.: ORB-SLAM2: an open-source SLAM system for monocular, stereo, and RGB-D cameras. IEEE Trans. Rob. **33**(5), 1255–1262 (2017)
5. Buczko, M., Willert, V.: Monocular outlier detection for visual odometry. In: IEEE Intelligent Vehicles Symposium (IV) (2017)
6. Geiger, A., Ziegler, J., Stiller, C.: StereoScan: dense 3D reconstruction in real-time. In: 2011 IEEE Intelligent Vehicles Symposium (IV), pp. 963–968. IEEE (2011)
7. Klein, G., Murray, D.: Parallel tracking and mapping for small AR workspaces. In: 6th IEEE and ACM International Symposium on Mixed and Augmented Reality, ISMAR 2007, pp. 225–234. IEEE (2007)
8. Moulon, P., Monasse, P., Marlet, R.: Global fusion of relative motions for robust, accurate and scalable structure from motion. In: Proceedings of the IEEE International Conference on Computer Vision, pp. 3248–3255 (2013)
9. Eigen, D., Puhrsch, C., Fergus, R.: Depth map prediction from a single image using a multi-scale deep network. In: Advances in Neural Information Processing Systems, pp. 2366–2374 (2014)
10. Kendall, A., Cipolla, R.: Geometric loss functions for camera pose regression with deep learning. arXiv preprint arXiv:1704.00390 (2017)
11. Kendall, A., Grimes, M., Cipolla, R.: PoseNet: a convolutional network for real-time 6-DOF camera relocalization. In: Proceedings of the IEEE International Conference on Computer Vision, pp. 2938–2946 (2015)
12. Ummenhofer, B., et al.: DeMoN: depth and motion network for learning monocular stereo. arXiv preprint arXiv:1612.02401 (2016)
13. Garg, R., Vijay Kumar, B.G., Carneiro, G., Reid, I.: Unsupervised CNN for single view depth estimation: geometry to the rescue. In: Leibe, B., Matas, J., Sebe, N., Welling, M. (eds.) ECCV 2016. LNCS, vol. 9912, pp. 740–756. Springer, Cham (2016). https://doi.org/10.1007/978-3-319-46484-8_45
14. Wang, S., Clark, R., Wen, H., Trigoni, N.: DeepVO: towards end-to-end visual odometry with deep recurrent convolutional neural networks. In: International Conference on Robotics and Automation (2017)
15. Vijayanarasimhan, S., Ricco, S., Schmid, C., Sukthankar, R., Fragkiadaki, K.: SfM-Net: learning of structure and motion from video. arXiv preprint arXiv:1704.07804 (2017)
16. Song, S., Chandraker, M.: Joint SFM and detection cues for monocular 3D localization in road scenes. In: Proceedings of the IEEE Conference on Computer Vision and Pattern Recognition, pp. 3734–3742 (2015)
17. Dhiman, V., Tran, Q.H., Corso, J.J., Chandraker, M.: A continuous occlusion model for road scene understanding. In: Proceedings of the IEEE Conference on Computer Vision and Pattern Recognition, pp. 4331–4339 (2016)

18. Kendall, A., Gal, Y.: What uncertainties do we need in Bayesian deep learning for computer vision? In: Advances in Neural Information Processing Systems (NIPS) (2017)
19. Kendall, A., Gal, Y., Cipolla, R.: Multi-task learning using uncertainty to weigh losses for scene geometry and semantics. In: Proceedings of the IEEE Conference on Computer Vision and Pattern Recognition (CVPR) (2018)
20. Novotny, D., Larlus, D., Vedaldi, A.: Learning 3D object categories by looking around them. In: IEEE International Conference on Computer Vision (2017)
21. Wang, Z., Bovik, A.C., Sheikh, H.R., Simoncelli, E.P.: Image quality assessment: from error visibility to structural similarity. IEEE Trans. Image Process. **13**(4), 600–612 (2004)
22. Gaidon, A., Wang, Q., Cabon, Y., Vig, E.: Virtual worlds as proxy for multi-object tracking analysis. In: CVPR (2016)
23. Ronneberger, O., Fischer, P., Brox, T.: U-net: convolutional networks for biomedical image segmentation. In: Navab, N., Hornegger, J., Wells, W.M., Frangi, A.F. (eds.) MICCAI 2015. LNCS, vol. 9351, pp. 234–241. Springer, Cham (2015). https://doi.org/10.1007/978-3-319-24574-4_28
24. Geiger, A., Lenz, P., Stiller, C., Urtasun, R.: Vision meets robotics: the KITTI dataset. Int. J. Rob. Res. (IJRR) **32**(11), 1231–1237 (2013)
25. Cordts, M., et al.: The cityscapes dataset for semantic urban scene understanding. In: Proceedings of the IEEE Conference on Computer Vision and Pattern Recognition (CVPR) (2016)
26. Maddern, W., Pascoe, G., Linegar, C., Newman, P.: 1 Year, 1000 km: the Oxford RobotCar dataset. Int. J. Rob. Res. (IJRR) **36**(1), 3–15 (2017)
27. Saxena, A., Sun, M., Ng, A.Y.: Make3D: learning 3D scene structure from a single still image. IEEE Trans. Pattern Anal. Mach. Intell. **31**(5), 824–840 (2009)
28. Geiger, A., Lenz, P., Urtasun, R.: Are we ready for autonomous driving? The KITTI vision benchmark suite. In: Conference on Computer Vision and Pattern Recognition (CVPR) (2012)
29. Sturm, J., Engelhard, N., Endres, F., Burgard, W., Cremers, D.: A benchmark for the evaluation of RGB-D SLAM systems. In: Proceedings of the International Conference on Intelligent Robot Systems (IROS), October 2012
30. Engel, J., Koltun, V., Cremers, D.: Direct sparse odometry. IEEE Trans. Pattern Anal. Mach. Intell. **40**(3), 611–625 (2017)

A Dataset and Architecture for Visual Reasoning with a Working Memory

Guangyu Robert Yang[1,3]($\boxtimes$), Igor Ganichev[2], Xiao-Jing Wang[1], Jonathon Shlens[2], and David Sussillo[2]

[1] Center for Neural Science, New York University, New York, USA
robert.yang@columbia.edu, xjwang@nyu.edu
[2] Google Brain, Mountain View, USA
iga@google.com, shlens@google.com, sussillo@google.com
[3] Department of Neuroscience, Columbia University, New York, USA

Abstract. A vexing problem in artificial intelligence is reasoning about events that occur in complex, changing visual stimuli such as in video analysis or game play. Inspired by a rich tradition of visual reasoning and memory in cognitive psychology and neuroscience, we developed an artificial, configurable visual question and answer dataset (COG) to parallel experiments in humans and animals. COG is much simpler than the general problem of video analysis, yet it addresses many of the problems relating to visual and logical reasoning and memory – problems that remain challenging for modern deep learning architectures. We additionally propose a deep learning architecture that performs competitively on other diagnostic VQA datasets (i.e. CLEVR) as well as easy settings of the COG dataset. However, several settings of COG result in datasets that are progressively more challenging to learn. After training, the network can zero-shot generalize to many new tasks. Preliminary analyses of the network architectures trained on COG demonstrate that the network accomplishes the task in a manner interpretable to humans.

Keywords: Visual reasoning · Visual question answering
Recurrent network · Working memory

1 Introduction

A major goal of artificial intelligence is to build systems that powerfully and flexibly reason about the sensory environment [1]. Vision provides an extremely rich and highly applicable domain for exercising our ability to build systems that

---

G. R. Yang—Work done as an intern at Google Brain.
G. R. Yang and I. Ganichev—Equal contribution.

Electronic supplementary material The online version of this chapter (https://doi.org/10.1007/978-3-030-01249-6_44) contains supplementary material, which is available to authorized users.

© Springer Nature Switzerland AG 2018
V. Ferrari et al. (Eds.): ECCV 2018, LNCS 11214, pp. 729–745, 2018.
https://doi.org/10.1007/978-3-030-01249-6_44

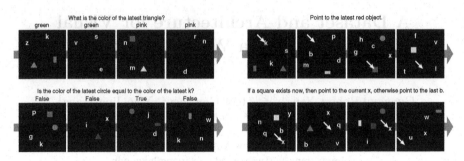

Fig. 1. Sample sequence of images and instruction from the COG dataset. Tasks in the COG dataset test aspects of object recognition, relational understanding and the manipulation and adaptation of memory to address a problem. Each task can involve objects shown in the current image and in previous images. Note that in the final example, the instruction involves the *last* instead of the *latest* "b". The former excludes the current "b" in the image. Target pointing response for each image is shown (white arrow). High-resolution image and proper English are used for clarity.

form logical inferences on complex stimuli [2–5]. One avenue for studying visual reasoning has been Visual Question Answering (VQA) datasets where a model learns to correctly answer challenging natural language questions about static images [6–9]. While advances on these multi-modal datasets have been significant, these datasets highlight several limitations to current approaches. First, it is uncertain the degree to which models trained on VQA datasets merely follow statistical cues inherent in the images, instead of reasoning about the logical components of a problem [10–13]. Second, such datasets avoid the complications of time and memory – both integral factors in the design of intelligent agents [1,14–16] and the analysis and summarization of videos [17–19].

To address the shortcomings related to logical reasoning about spatial relationships in VQA datasets, Johnson and colleagues [10] recently proposed CLEVR to directly test models for elementary visual reasoning, to be used in conjunction with other VQA datasets (e.g. [6–9]). The CLEVR dataset provides artificial, static images and natural language questions about those images that exercise the ability of a model to perform logical and visual reasoning. Recent work has demonstrated networks that achieve impressive performance with near perfect accuracy [4,5,20].

In this work, we address the second limitation concerning time and memory in visual reasoning. A reasoning agent must remember relevant pieces of its visual history, ignore irrelevant detail, update and manipulate a memory based on new information, and exploit this memory at later times to make decisions. Our approach is to create an artificial dataset that has many of the complexities found in temporally varying data, yet also to eschew much of the visual complexity and technical difficulty of working with video (e.g. video decoding, redundancy across temporally-smooth frames). In particular, we take inspiration from decades of research in cognitive psychology [21–25] and modern systems neuroscience (e.g.

[26–31]) – fields which have a long history of dissecting visual reasoning into core components based on spatial and logical reasoning, memory compositionality, and semantic understanding. Towards this end, we build an artificial dataset – termed COG – that exercises visual reasoning in time, in parallel with human cognitive experiments [32–34].

The COG dataset is based on a programmatic language that builds a battery of task triplets: an image sequence, a verbal instruction, and a sequence of correct answers. These randomly generated triplets exercise visual reasoning across a large array of tasks and require semantic comprehension of text, visual perception of each image in the sequence, and a working memory to determine the temporally varying answers (Fig. 1). We highlight several parameters in the programmatic language that allow researchers to modulate the problem difficulty from easy to challenging settings.

Finally, we introduce a multi-modal recurrent architecture for visual reasoning with memory. This network combines semantic and visual modules with a stateful *controller* that modulates visual attention and memory in order to correctly perform a visual task. We demonstrate that this model achieves near state-of-the-art performance on the CLEVR dataset. In addition, this network provides a strong baseline that achieves good performance on the COG dataset across an array of settings. Through ablation studies and an analysis of network dynamics, we find that the network employs human-interpretable, attention mechanisms to solve these visual reasoning tasks. We hope that the COG dataset, corresponding architecture, and associated baseline provide a helpful benchmark for studying reasoning in time-varying visual stimuli[1].

2   Related Work

It is broadly understood in the AI community that memory is a largely unsolved problem and there are many efforts underway to understand this problem, e.g. studied in [35–37]. The ability of sequential models to compute in time is notably limited by memory horizon and memory capacity [37] as measured in synthetic sequential datasets [38]. Indeed, a large constraint in training network models to perform generic Turing-complete operations is the ability to train systems that compute in time [37,39].

Developing computer systems that comprehend time-varying sequence of images is a prominent interest in video understanding [18,19,40] and intelligent video game agents [1,14,15]. While some attempts have used a feed-forward architecture (e.g. [14], baseline model in [16]), much work has been invested in building video analysis and game agents that contain a memory component [16,41]. These types of systems are often limited by the flexibility of network memory systems, and it is not clear the degree to which these systems reason based on complex relationships from past visual imagery.

---

[1] The COG dataset and code for the network architecture are open-sourced at https://github.com/google/cog.

Let us consider Visual Question Answering (VQA) datasets based on single, static images [6–9]. These datasets construct natural language questions to probe the logical understanding of a network about natural images. There has been strong suggestion in the literature that networks trained on these datasets focus on statistical regularities for the prediction tasks, whereby a system may "cheat" to superficially solve a given task [10,11]. Towards that end, several researchers proposed to build an auxiliary diagnostic, synthetic datasets to uncover these potential failure modes and highlight logical comprehension (e.g. attribute identification, counting, comparison, multiple attention, and logical operations) [10,13,42–44]. Further, many specialized neural network architectures focused on multi-task learning have been proposed to address this problem by leveraging attention [45], external memory [35,36], a family of feature-wise transformations [5,46], explicitly parsing a task into executable sub-tasks [2,3], and inferring relations between pairs of objects [4].

Our contribution takes direct inspiration from this previous work on single images but focuses on the aspects of time and memory. A second source of inspiration is the long line of cognitive neuroscience literature that has focused on developing a battery of sequential visual tasks to exercise and measure specific attributes of visual working memory [21,26,47]. Several lines of cognitive psychology and neuroscience have developed multitudes of visual tasks in time that exercise attribute identification, counting, comparison, multiple attention, and logical operations [26,28–34] (see references therein). This work emphasizes compositionality in task generation – a key ingredient in generalizing to unseen tasks [48]. Importantly, this literature provides measurements in humans and animals on these tasks as well as discusses the biological circuits and computations that may underlie and explain the variability in performance [27–31].

3   The COG Dataset

We designed a large set of tasks that requires a broad range of cognitive skills to solve, especially working memory. One major goal of this dataset is to build a compositional set of tasks that include variants of many cognitive tasks studied in humans and other animals [26,28–34] (see also Introduction and Related Work).

The dataset contains triplets of a task instruction, sequences of synthetic images, and sequences of target responses (see Fig. 1 for examples). Each image consists of a number of simple objects that vary in color, shape, and location. There are 19 possible colors and 33 possible shapes (6 geometric shapes and 26 lower-case English letters). The network needs to generate a verbal or pointing response for every image.

To build a large set of tasks, we first describe all potential tasks using a common, unified framework. Each task in the dataset is defined abstractly and constructed compositionally from basic building blocks, namely *operators*. An operator performs a basic computation, such as selecting an object based on attributes (color, shape, etc.) or comparing two attributes (Fig. 2A). The operators are defined abstractly without specifying the exact attributes involved.

A task is formed by a directed acyclic graph of operators (Fig. 2B). Finally, we instantiate a task by specifying all relevant attributes in its graph (Fig. 2C). The task instance is used to generate both the verbal task instruction and minimally-biased image sequences. Many image sequences can be generated from the same task instance.

There are 8 operators, 44 tasks, and more than 2 trillion possible task instances in the dataset (see Appendix for more sample task instances). We vary the number of images (F), the maximum memory duration (M_{max}), and the maximum number of distractors on each image (D_{max}) to explore the memory and capacity of our proposed model and systematically vary the task difficulty. When not explicitly stated, we use a canonical setting with $F = 4$, $M_{max} = 3$, and $D_{max} = 1$ (see Appendix for the rationale).

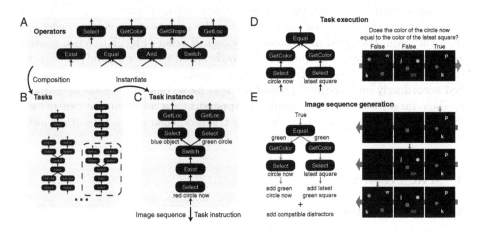

Fig. 2. Generating the compositional COG dataset. The COG dataset is based on a set of operators (A), which are combined to form various task graphs (B). (C) A task is instantiated by specifying the attributes of all operators in its graph. A task instance is used to generate both the image sequence and the semantic task instruction. (D) Forward pass through the graph and the image sequence for normal task execution. (E) Generating a consistent, minimally biased image sequence requires a backward pass through the graph in a reverse topological order and through the image sequence in the reverse chronological order.

The COG dataset is in many ways similar to the CLEVR dataset [10]. Both contain synthetic visual inputs and tasks defined as operator graphs (functional programs). However, COG differs from CLEVR in two important ways. First, all tasks in the COG dataset can involve objects shown in the past, due to the sequential nature of their inputs. Second, in the COG dataset, visual inputs with minimal response bias can be generated on the fly.

An operator is a simple function that receives and produces abstract data types such as an attribute, an object, a set of objects, a spatial range, or a Boolean. There are 8 operators in total: *Select, GetColor, GetShape, GetLoc,*

Exist, Equal, And, and *Switch* (see Appendix for details). Using these 8 operators, the COG dataset currently contains 44 tasks, with the number of operators in each task graph ranging from 2 to 11. Each task instruction is obtained from a task instance by traversing the task graph and combining pieces of text associated with each operator. It is straightforward to extend the COG dataset by introducing new operators.

Response bias is a major concern when designing a synthetic dataset. Neural networks may achieve high accuracy in a dataset by exploiting its bias. Rejection sampling can be used to ensure an *ad hoc* balanced response distribution [10]. We developed a method for the COG dataset to generate minimally-biased synthetic image sequences tailored to individual tasks.

In short, we first determine the minimally-biased responses (target outputs), then we generate images (inputs) that would lead to these specified responses. The images are generated in the reversed order of normal task execution (Fig. 2D, E). During generation, images are visited in the reverse chronological order and the task graph traversed in a reverse topological order (Fig. 2E). When visiting an operator, if its target output is not already specified, we randomly choose one from all allowable outputs. Based on the specified output, the image is modified accordingly and/or the supposed input is passed on to the next operator(s) as their target outputs (see details in Appendix). In addition, we can place a uniformly-distributed $D \sim U(1, D_{\max})$ distractors, then delete those that interfere with the normal task execution.

4   The Network

4.1   General Network Setup

Overall, the network contains four major systems (Fig. 3). The visual system processes the images. The semantic system processes the task instructions. The visual short-term memory system maintains the processed visual information, and provides outputs that guide the pointing response. Finally, the control system integrates converging information from all other systems, uses several attention and gating mechanisms to regulate how other systems process inputs and generate outputs, and provides verbal outputs. Critically, the network is allowed multiple time steps to "ponder" about each image [49], giving it the potential to solve multi-step reasoning problems naturally through iteration.

4.2   Visual Processing System

The visual system processes the raw input images. The visual inputs are 112×112 images and are processed by 4 convolutional layers with 32, 64, 64, 128 feature maps respectively. Each convolutional layer employs 3×3 kernels and is followed by a 2×2 max-pooling layer, batch-normalization [50], and a rectified-linear activation function. This simple and relatively shallow architecture was shown to be sufficient for the CLEVR dataset [4, 10].

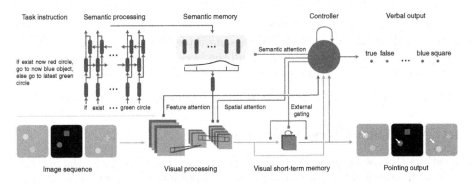

Fig. 3. Diagram of the proposed network. A sequence of images are provided as input into a convolutional neural network (green). An instruction in the form of English text is provided into a sequential embedding network (red). A visual short-term memory (vSTM) network holds visual-spatial information in time and provides the pointing output (teal). The vSTM module can be considered a convolutional LSTM network with external gating. A stateful controller (blue) provides all attention and gating signals directly or indirectly. The output of the network is either discrete (verbal) or 2D continuous (pointing). (Color figure online)

The last two layers of the convolutional network are subject to feature and spatial attention. Feature attention scales and shifts the batch normalization parameters of individual feature maps, such that the activity of all neurons within a feature map are multiplied and added by two scalars. This particular implementation of feature attention has been termed conditional batch-normalization or feature-wise linear modulation (FiLM) [5,46]. FiLM is a critical component for the model that achieved near state-of-the-art performance on the CLEVR dataset [5]. Soft spatial attention [51] is applied to the top convolutional layer following feature attention and the activation function. It multiplies the activity of all neurons with the same spatial preferences using a positive scalar.

4.3 Semantic Processing System

The semantic processing system receives a task instruction and generates a semantic memory that the controller can later attend to. Conceptually, it produces a semantic memory – a contextualized representation of each word in the instruction – before the task is actually being performed. At each pondering step when performing the task, the controller can attend to individual parts of the semantic memory corresponding to different words or phrases.

Each word is mapped to a 64-dimensional trainable embedding vector, then sequentially fed into an 128-unit bidirectional Long Short-Term Memory (LSTM) network [38,52]. The outputs of the bidirectional LSTM for all words form a semantic memory of size $(n_{\text{word}}, n_{\text{rule}}^{(\text{out})})$, where n_{word} is the number of words in the instruction, and $n_{\text{rule}}^{(\text{out})} = 128$ is the dimension of the output vector.

Each $n_{\text{rule}}^{(\text{out})}$-dimensional vector in the semantic memory forms a key. For semantic attention, a query vector of the same dimension $n_{\text{rule}}^{(\text{out})}$ is used to retrieve the semantic memory by summing up all the keys weighted by their similarities to the query. We used Bahdanau attention [53], which computes the similarity between the query $\mathbf{q}$ and a key $\mathbf{k}$ as $\sum_{i=1}^{n_{\text{rule}}^{(\text{out})}} v_i \cdot \tanh(q_i + k_i)$, where $\mathbf{v}$ is trained.

4.4   Visual Short-Term Memory System

To utilize the spatial information preserved in the visual system for the pointing output, the top layer of the convolutional network feeds into a visual short-term memory module, which in turn projects to a group of pointing output neurons. This structure is also inspired by the posterior parietal cortex in the brain that maintains visual-spatial information to guide action [54].

The visual short-term memory (vSTM) module is an extension of a 2-d convolutional LSTM network [55] in which the gating mechanisms are conditioned on external information. The vSTM module consists of a number of 2-D feature maps, while the input and output connections are both convolutional. There is currently no recurrent connections within the vSTM module besides the forget gate. The state c_t and output h_t of this module at step t are

$$c_t = f_t * c_{t-1} + i_t * x_t, \tag{1}$$
$$h_t = o_t * \tanh(c_t), \tag{2}$$

where $*$ indicates a convolution. This vSTM module differs from a convolutional LSTM network mainly in that the input i_t, forget f_t, and output gates o_t are not self-generated. Instead, they are all provided externally from the controller. In addition, the input x_t is not directly fed into the network, but a convolutional layer can be applied in between.

All convolutions are currently set to be 1×1. Equivalently, each feature map of the vSTM module adds its gated previous activity with a weighted combination of the post-attention activity of all feature maps from the top layer of the visual system. Finally, the activity of all vSTM feature maps is combined to generate a single spatial output map h_t.

4.5   Controller

To synthesize information across the entire network, we include a controller that receives feedforward inputs from all other systems and generates feedback attention and gating signals. This architecture is further inspired by the prefrontal cortex of the brain [27]. The controller is a Gated Recurrent Unit (GRU) network. At each pondering step, the post-attention activity of the top visual layer is processed through a 128-unit fully connected layer, concatenated with the retrieved semantic memory and the vSTM module output, then fed into the controller. In addition, the activity of the top visual layer is summed up across space and provided to the controller.

The controller generates queries for the semantic memory through a linear feedforward network. The retrieved semantic memory then generates the feature attention through another linear feedforward network. The controller generates the 49-dimensional soft spatial attention through a two layer feedforward network, with a 10-unit hidden layer and a rectified-linear activation function, followed by a softmax normalization. Finally, the controller state is concatenated with the retrieved semantic memory to generate the input, forget, and output gates used in the vSTM module through a linear feedforward network followed by a sigmoidal activation function.

4.6 Output, Loss, and Optimization

The verbal output is a single word, and the pointing output is the (x, y) coordinates of pointing. Each coordinate is between 0 and 1. A loss function is defined for each output, and only one loss function is used for every task. The verbal output uses a cross-entropy loss. To ensure the pointing output loss is comparable in scale to the verbal output loss, we include a group of pointing output neurons on a 7×7 spatial grid, and compute a cross-entropy loss over this group of neurons. Given a target (x, y) coordinates, we use a Gaussian distribution centered at the target location with $\sigma = 0.1$ as the target probability distribution of the pointing output neurons.

For each image, the loss is based on the output at the last pondering step. No loss is used if there is no valid output for a given image. We use a L2 regularization of strength 2e-5 on all the weights. We clip the gradient norm at 10 for COG and at 80 for CLEVR. We clip the controller state norm at 10000 for COG and 5000 for CLEVR. We also trained all initial states of the recurrent networks. The network is trained end-to-end with Adam [56], combined with a learning rate decay schedule.

5   Results

5.1   Intuitive and Interpretable Solutions on the CLEVR Dataset

To demonstrate the reasoning capability of our proposed network, we trained it on the CLEVR dataset [10], even though there is no explicit need for working memory in CLEVR. The network achieved an overall test accuracy of 96.8% on CLEVR, surpassing human-level performance and comparable with other state-of-the-art methods [4,5,20] (Table 1, see Appendix for more details).

Images were first resized to 128×128, then randomly cropped or resized to 112×112 during training and validation/testing respectively. In the best-performing network, the controller used 12 pondering steps per image. Feature attention was applied to the top two convolutional layers. The vSTM module was disabled since there is no pointing output.

The output of the network is human-interpretable and intuitive. In Fig. 4, we illustrate how the verbal output and various attention signals evolved through

Table 1. CLEVR test accuracies for human, baseline, and top-performing models that relied only on pixel inputs and task instructions during training. (*) denotes use of pretrained models.

Model	Overall	Count	Exist	Compare numbers	Query attribute	Compare attribute
Human [10]	92.6	86.7	96.6	86.5	95.0	96.0
Q-type baseline [10]	41.8	34.6	50.2	51.0	36.0	51.3
CNN+LSTM+SA [4]	76.6	64.4	82.7	77.4	82.6	75.4
CNN+LSTM+RN [4]	95.5	90.1	97.8	93.6	97.9	97.1
CNN+GRU+FiLM [5]	97.6	94.3	99.3	93.4	99.3	99.3
MAC* [20]	98.9	97.2	99.5	99.4	99.3	99.5
Our model	96.8	91.7	99.0	95.5	98.5	98.8

pondering steps for an example image-question pair. The network answered a long question by decomposing it into small, executable steps. Even though training only relies on verbal outputs at the last pondering steps, the network learned to produce interpretable verbal outputs that reflect its reasoning process.

In Fig. 4, we computed effective feature attention as the difference between the normalized activity maps with or without feature attention. To get the post- (or pre-) feature-attention normalized activity map, we average the activity across all feature maps after (or without) feature attention, then divide the activity by its mean. The relative spatial attention is normalized by subtracting the time-averaged spatial attention map. This example network uses 8 pondering steps.

5.2 Training on the COG Dataset

Our proposed model achieved a maximum overall test accuracy of 93.7% on the COG dataset in the canonical setting (see Sect. 3). In the Appendix, we discuss potential strategies for measuring human accuracy on the COG dataset. We noticed a small but significant variability in the final accuracy even for networks with the same hyperparameters (mean $\pm$ std: 90.6 $\pm$ 2.8%, 50 networks). We found that tasks containing more operators tend to take substantially longer to be learned or remain at lower accuracy (see Appendix for more results). We tried many approaches of reducing variance including various curriculum learning regimes, different weight and bias initializations, different optimizers and their hyperparameters. All approaches we tried either did not significantly reduce the variance or degraded performance.

The best network uses 5 pondering steps for each image. Feature attention is applied to the top layer of the visual network. The vSTM module contains 4 feature maps.

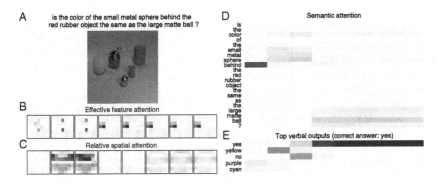

Fig. 4. Pondering process of the proposed network, visualized through attention and output for a single CLEVR example. (A) The example question and image from the CLEVR validation set. (B) The effective feature attention map for each pondering step. (C) The relative spatial attention maps. (D) The semantic attention. (E) Top five verbal outputs. Red and blue indicate stronger and weaker, respectively. After simultaneous feature attention to the "small metal spheres" and spatial attention to "behind the red rubber object", the color of the attended object (yellow) was reflected in the verbal output. Later in the pondering process, the network paid feature attention to the "large matte ball", while the correct answer (yes) emerged in the verbal output. (Color figure online)

5.3 Assessing the Contribution of Model Parts Through Ablation

The model we proposed contains multiple attention mechanisms, a short-term memory module, and multiple pondering steps. To assess the contribution of each component to the overall accuracy, we trained versions of the network on the CLEVR and the COG dataset in which one component was ablated from the full network. We also trained a baseline network with all components ablated. The baseline network still contains a CNN for visual processing, a LSTM network for semantic processing, and a GRU network as the controller. To give each ablated network a fair chance, we re-tuned their hyperparameters, with the total number of parameters limited at 110% of the original network, and reported the maximum accuracy.

We found that the baseline network performed poorly on both datasets (Fig. 5A, B). To our surprise, the network relies on a different combination of mechanisms to solve the CLEVR and the COG dataset. The network depends strongly on feature attention for CLEVR (Fig. 5A), while it depends strongly on spatial attention for the COG dataset (Fig. 5B). One possible explanation is that there are fewer possible objects in CLEVR (96 combinations compared to 608 combinations in COG), making feature attention on ~ 100 feature maps better suited to select objects in CLEVR. Having multiple pondering steps is important for both datasets, demonstrating that it is beneficial to solve multi-step reasoning problems through iteration. Although semantic attention has a rather minor impact on the overall accuracy of both datasets, it is more useful for tasks with more operators and longer task instructions (Fig. 5C).

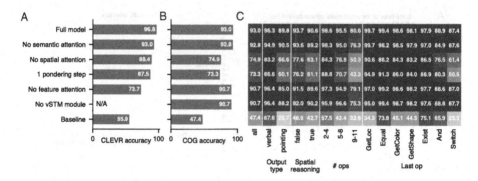

Fig. 5. Ablation studies. Overall accuracies for various ablation models on the CLEVR test set (A) and COG (B). vSTM module is not included in any model for CLEVR. (C) Breaking the COG accuracies down based on the output type, whether spatial reasoning is involved, the number of operators, and the last operator in the task graph.

5.4   Exploring the Range of Difficulty of the COG Dataset

To explore the range of difficulty in visual reasoning in our dataset, we varied the maximum number of distractors on each image ($D_{\max}$), the maximum memory duration ($M_{\max}$), and the number of images in each sequence (F) (Fig. 6). For each setting we selected the best network across 50–80 hyper-parameter settings involving model capacity and learning rate schedules. Out of all models explored, the accuracy of the best network drops substantially with more distractors. When there is a large number of distractors, the network accuracy also drops with longer memory duration. These results suggest that the network has difficulty filtering out many distractors and maintaining memory at the same time. However, doubling the number of images does not have a clear effect on the accuracy, which indicates that the network developed a solution that is invariant to the number of images used in the sequence. The harder setting of the COG dataset with $F = 8$, $D_{\max} = 10$ and $M_{\max} = 7$ can potentially serve as a benchmark for more powerful neural network models.

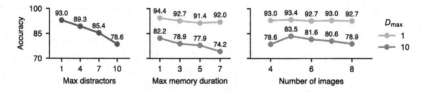

Fig. 6. Accuracies on variants of the COG dataset. From left to right, varying the maximum number of distractors ($D_{\max}$), the maximum memory duration ($M_{\max}$), and the number of images in each sequence (F).

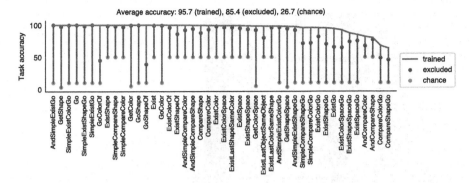

Fig. 7. The proposed network can zero-shot generalize to new tasks. 44 networks were trained on 43 of 44 tasks. Shown are the maximum accuracies of the networks on the 43 trained tasks (gray), the one excluded (blue) task, and the chance levels for that task (red). (Color figure online)

5.5 Zero-Shot Generalization to New Tasks

A hallmark of intelligence is the flexibility and capability to generalize to unseen situations. During training and testing, each image sequence is generated anew, therefore the network is able to generalize to unseen input images. On top of that, the network can generalize to trillions of task instances (new task instructions), although only millions of them are used during training.

The most challenging form of generalization is to completely new tasks not explicitly trained on. To test whether the network can generalize to new tasks, we trained 44 groups of networks. Each group contains 10 networks and is trained on 43 out of 44 COG tasks. We monitored the accuracy of all tasks. For each task, we report the highest accuracy across networks. We found that networks are able to immediately generalize to most untrained tasks (Fig. 7). The average accuracy for tasks excluded during training (85.4%) is substantially higher than the average chance level (26.7%), although it is still lower than the average accuracy for trained tasks (95.7%). Hence, our proposed model is able to perform zero-shot generalization across tasks with some success although not matching the performance as if trained on the task explicitly.

5.6 Clustering and Compositionality of the Controller Representation

To understand how the network is able to perform COG tasks and generalize to new tasks, we carried out preliminary analyses studying the activity of the controller. One suggestion is that networks can perform many tasks by engaging clusters of units, where each cluster supports one operation [57]. To address this question, we examined low-dimensional representations of the activation space of the controller and labeled such points based on the individual tasks. Figure 8A and B highlight the clustering behavior across tasks that emerges from training on the COG dataset (see Appendix for details).

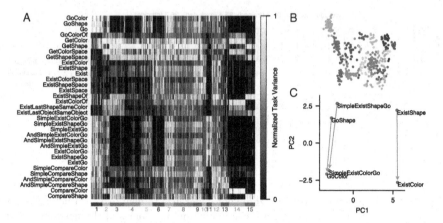

Fig. 8. Clustering and compositionality in the controller. (A) The level of task involvement for each controller unit (columns) in each task (rows). The task involvement is measured by task variance, which quantifies the variance of activity across different inputs (task instructions and image sequences) for a given task. For each unit, task variances are normalized to a maximum of 1. Units are clustered (bottom color bar) according to task variance vectors (columns). Only showing tasks with accuracy higher than 90%. (B) t-SNE visualization of task variance vectors for all units, colored by cluster identity. (C) Example compositional representation of tasks. We compute the state-space representation for each task as its mean controller activity vector, obtained by averaging across many different inputs for that task. The representation of 6 tasks are shown in the first two principal components. The vector in the direction of PC2 is a shared direction for altering a task to change from *Shape* to *Color* (Color figure online).

Previous work has suggested that humans may flexibly perform new tasks by representing learned tasks in a compositional manner [48,57]. For instance, the analysis of semantic embeddings indicates that network may learn shared directions for concepts across word embeddings [58]. We searched for signs of compositional behavior by exploring if directions in the activation space of the controller correspond to common sub-problems across tasks. Figure 8C highlights a direction that was identified that corresponds to axis of `Shape` to `Color` across multiple tasks. These results provide a first step in understanding how neural networks can understand task structures and generalize to new tasks.

6   Conclusions

In this work, we built a synthetic, compositional dataset that requires a system to perform various tasks on sequences of images based on English instructions. The tasks included in our `COG` dataset test a range of cognitive reasoning skills and, in particular, require explicit memory of past objects. This dataset is minimally-biased, highly configurable, and designed to produce a rich array of performance measures through a large number of named tasks.

We also built a recurrent neural network model that harnesses a number of attention and gating mechanisms to solve the COG dataset in a natural, human-interpretable way. The model also achieves near state-of-the-art performance on another visual reasoning dataset, CLEVR. The model uses a recurrent controller to pay attention to different parts of images and instructions, and to produce verbal outputs, all in an iterative fashion. These iterative attention signals provide multiple windows into the model's step-by-step pondering process and provide clues as to how the model breaks complex instructions down into smaller computations. Finally, the network is able to generalize immediately to completely untrained tasks, demonstrating zero-shot learning of new tasks.

References

1. Hassabis, D., Kumaran, D., Summerfield, C., Botvinick, M.: Neuroscience-inspired artificial intelligence. Neuron **95**(2), 245–258 (2017)
2. Hu, R., Andreas, J., Rohrbach, M., Darrell, T., Saenko, K.: Learning to reason: end-to-end module networks for visual question answering. CoRR, abs/1704.05526, vol. 3 (2017)
3. Johnson, J., et al.: Inferring and executing programs for visual reasoning. arXiv preprint arXiv:1705.03633 (2017)
4. Santoro, A., et al.: A simple neural network module for relational reasoning. In: Advances in Neural Information Processing Systems, pp. 4974–4983 (2017)
5. Perez, E., Strub, F., De Vries, H., Dumoulin, V., Courville, A.: Film: visual reasoning with a general conditioning layer. arXiv preprint arXiv:1709.07871 (2017)
6. Antol, S., et al.: VQA: visual question answering. In: Proceedings of the IEEE International Conference on Computer Vision, pp. 2425–2433 (2015)
7. Gao, H., Mao, J., Zhou, J., Huang, Z., Wang, L., Xu, W.: Are you talking to a machine? Dataset and methods for multilingual image question. In: Advances in Neural Information Processing Systems, pp. 2296–2304 (2015)
8. Malinowski, M., Fritz, M.: A multi-world approach to question answering about real-world scenes based on uncertain input. In: Advances in Neural Information Processing Systems, pp. 1682–1690 (2014)
9. Zhu, Y., Groth, O., Bernstein, M., Fei-Fei, L.: Visual7W: grounded question answering in images. In: Proceedings of the IEEE Conference on Computer Vision and Pattern Recognition, pp. 4995–5004 (2016)
10. Johnson, J., Hariharan, B., van der Maaten, L., Fei-Fei, L., Zitnick, C.L., Girshick, R.: CLEVR: a diagnostic dataset for compositional language and elementary visual reasoning. In: 2017 IEEE Conference on Computer Vision and Pattern Recognition (CVPR), pp. 1988–1997. IEEE (2017)
11. Sturm, B.L.: A simple method to determine if a music information retrieval system is a horse. IEEE Trans. Multimed. **16**(6), 1636–1644 (2014)
12. Agrawal, A., Batra, D., Parikh, D.: Analyzing the behavior of visual question answering models. arXiv preprint arXiv:1606.07356 (2016)
13. Winograd, T.: Understanding Natural Language. Academic Press Inc., Orlando (1972)
14. Mnih, V., et al.: Playing atari with deep reinforcement learning. arXiv preprint arXiv:1312.5602 (2013)
15. Mnih, V., et al.: Human-level control through deep reinforcement learning. Nature **518**(7540), 529 (2015)

16. Vinyals, O., et al.: StarCraft II: a new challenge for reinforcement learning. arXiv preprint arXiv:1708.04782 (2017)
17. Karpathy, A., Toderici, G., Shetty, S., Leung, T., Sukthankar, R., Fei-Fei, L.: Large-scale video classification with convolutional neural networks. In: CVPR (2014)
18. Abu-El-Haija, S., et al.: YouTube-8M: a large-scale video classification benchmark. arXiv preprint arXiv:1609.08675 (2016)
19. Caba Heilbron, F., Escorcia, V., Ghanem, B., Carlos Niebles, J.: ActivityNet: a large-scale video benchmark for human activity understanding. In: Proceedings of the IEEE Conference on Computer Vision and Pattern Recognition, pp. 961–970 (2015)
20. Hudson, D.A., Manning, C.D.: Compositional attention networks for machine reasoning. In: International Conference on Learning Representations (2018)
21. Diamond, A.: Executive functions. Ann. Rev. Psychol. **64**, 135–168 (2013)
22. Miyake, A., Friedman, N.P., Emerson, M.J., Witzki, A.H., Howerter, A., Wager, T.D.: The unity and diversity of executive functions and their contributions to complex frontal lobe tasks: a latent variable analysis. Cogn. Psychol. **41**(1), 49–100 (2000)
23. Berg, E.A.: A simple objective technique for measuring flexibility in thinking. J. Gen. Psychol. **39**(1), 15–22 (1948)
24. Milner, B.: Effects of different brain lesions on card sorting: the role of the frontal lobes. Arch. Neurol. **9**(1), 90–100 (1963)
25. Baddeley, A.: Working memory. Science **255**(5044), 556–559 (1992)
26. Miller, E.K., Erickson, C.A., Desimone, R.: Neural mechanisms of visual working memory in prefrontal cortex of the macaque. J. Neurosci. **16**(16), 5154–5167 (1996)
27. Miller, E.K., Cohen, J.D.: An integrative theory of prefrontal cortex function. Ann. Rev. Neurosci. **24**(1), 167–202 (2001)
28. Newsome, W.T., Britten, K.H., Movshon, J.A.: Neuronal correlates of a perceptual decision. Nature **341**(6237), 52 (1989)
29. Romo, R., Salinas, E.: Cognitive neuroscience: flutter discrimination: neural codes, perception, memory and decision making. Nat. Rev. Neurosci. **4**(3), 203 (2003)
30. Mante, V., Sussillo, D., Shenoy, K.V., Newsome, W.T.: Context-dependent computation by recurrent dynamics in prefrontal cortex. Nature **503**(7474), 78 (2013)
31. Rigotti, M., et al.: The importance of mixed selectivity in complex cognitive tasks. Nature **497**(7451), 585 (2013)
32. Yntema, D.B.: Keeping track of several things at once. Hum. Factors **5**(1), 7–17 (1963)
33. Zelazo, P.D., Frye, D., Rapus, T.: An age-related dissociation between knowing rules and using them. Cogn. Dev. **11**(1), 37–63 (1996)
34. Owen, A.M., McMillan, K.M., Laird, A.R., Bullmore, E.: N-back working memory paradigm: a meta-analysis of normative functional neuroimaging studies. Hum. Brain Mapp. **25**(1), 46–59 (2005)
35. Graves, A., Wayne, G., Danihelka, I.: Neural turing machines. CoRR abs/1410.5401 (2014)
36. Joulin, A., Mikolov, T.: Inferring algorithmic patterns with stack-augmented recurrent nets. CoRR abs/1503.01007 (2015)
37. Collins, J., Sohl-Dickstein, J., Sussillo, D.: Capacity and trainability in recurrent neural networks. Stat **1050**, 28 (2017)
38. Hochreiter, S., Schmidhuber, J.: Long short-term memory. Neural Comput. **9**(8), 1735–1780 (1997)
39. Graves, A., et al.: Hybrid computing using a neural network with dynamic external memory. Nature **538**(7626), 471–476 (2016)

40. Kay, W., et al.: The kinetics human action video dataset. arXiv preprint arXiv:1705.06950 (2017)
41. Ng, J.Y.H., Hausknecht, M., Vijayanarasimhan, S., Vinyals, O., Monga, R., Toderici, G.: Beyond short snippets: deep networks for video classification. In: 2015 IEEE Conference on Computer Vision and Pattern Recognition (CVPR), pp. 4694–4702. IEEE (2015)
42. Weston, J., et al.: Towards AI-complete question answering: a set of prerequisite toy tasks. arXiv preprint arXiv:1502.05698 (2015)
43. Zitnick, C.L., Parikh, D.: Bringing semantics into focus using visual abstraction. In: 2013 IEEE Conference on Computer Vision and Pattern Recognition (CVPR), pp. 3009–3016. IEEE (2013)
44. Kuhnle, A., Copestake, A.: ShapeWorld-a new test methodology for multimodal language understanding. arXiv preprint arXiv:1704.04517 (2017)
45. Xu, H., Saenko, K.: Ask, attend and answer: exploring question-guided spatial attention for visual question answering. In: Leibe, B., Matas, J., Sebe, N., Welling, M. (eds.) ECCV 2016. LNCS, vol. 9911, pp. 451–466. Springer, Cham (2016). https://doi.org/10.1007/978-3-319-46478-7_28
46. Dumoulin, V., Shlens, J., Kudlur, M.: A learned representation for artistic style. In: International Conference on Learning Representations (ICLR) (2017)
47. Luck, S.J., Vogel, E.K.: The capacity of visual working memory for features and conjunctions. Nature 390(6657), 279 (1997)
48. Cole, M.W., Laurent, P., Stocco, A.: Rapid instructed task learning: a new window into the human brains unique capacity for flexible cognitive control. Cogn. Affect. Behav. Neurosci. 13(1), 1–22 (2013)
49. Graves, A.: Adaptive computation time for recurrent neural networks. arXiv preprint arXiv:1603.08983 (2016)
50. Ioffe, S., Szegedy, C.: Batch normalization: accelerating deep network training by reducing internal covariate shift. In: International Conference on Machine Learning, pp. 448–456 (2015)
51. Xu, K., et al.: Show, attend and tell: neural image caption generation with visual attention. In: International Conference on Machine Learning, pp. 2048–2057 (2015)
52. Schuster, M., Paliwal, K.K.: Bidirectional recurrent neural networks. IEEE Trans. Sig. Process. 45(11), 2673–2681 (1997)
53. Bahdanau, D., Cho, K., Bengio, Y.: Neural machine translation by jointly learning to align and translate. arXiv preprint arXiv:1409.0473 (2014)
54. Andersen, R.A., Snyder, L.H., Bradley, D.C., Xing, J.: Multimodal representation of space in the posterior parietal cortex and its use in planning movements. Ann. Rev. Neurosci. 20(1), 303–330 (1997)
55. Xingjian, S., Chen, Z., Wang, H., Yeung, D.Y., Wong, W.K., Woo, W.C.: Convolutional LSTM network: a machine learning approach for precipitation nowcasting. In: Advances in Neural Information Processing Systems, pp. 802–810 (2015)
56. Kingma, D.P., Ba, J.: Adam: a method for stochastic optimization. arXiv preprint arXiv:1412.6980 (2014)
57. Yang, G.R., Song, H.F., Newsome, W.T., Wang, X.J.: Clustering and compositionality of task representations in a neural network trained to perform many cognitive tasks. bioRxiv, p. 183632 (2017)
58. Mikolov, T., Sutskever, I., Chen, K., Corrado, G.S., Dean, J.: Distributed representations of words and phrases and their compositionality. In: Advances in Neural Information Processing Systems, pp. 3111–3119 (2013)

Constrained Optimization Based Low-Rank Approximation of Deep Neural Networks

Chong Li[✉] and C. J. Richard Shi

University of Washington, Seattle, WA 98195, USA
{chongli,cjshi}@uw.edu

Abstract. We present COBLA—Constrained Optimization Based Low-rank Approximation—a systematic method of finding an optimal low-rank approximation of a trained convolutional neural network, subject to constraints in the number of multiply-accumulate (MAC) operations and the memory footprint. COBLA optimally allocates the constrained computation resources into each layer of the approximated network. The singular value decomposition of the network weight is computed, then a binary masking variable is introduced to denote whether a particular singular value and the corresponding singular vectors are used in low-rank approximation. With this formulation, the number of the MAC operations and the memory footprint are represented as linear constraints in terms of the binary masking variables. The resulted 0–1 integer programming problem is approximately solved by sequential quadratic programming. COBLA does not introduce any hyperparameter. We empirically demonstrate that COBLA outperforms prior art using the SqueezeNet and VGG-16 architecture on the ImageNet dataset.

Keywords: Low-rank approximation · Resource allocation
Constrained optimization · Integer relaxiation

1 Introduction

The impressive generalization power of deep neural networks comes at the cost of highly complex models that are computationally expensive to evaluate and cumbersome to store in memory. When deploying a trained deep neural network on edge devices, it is highly desirable that the cost of evaluating the network can be reduced without significantly impacting the performance of the network.

In this paper, we consider the following problem: given a set of constraints to the number of multiply-accumulate (MAC) operation and the memory footprint (storage size of the model), the objective is to identify an optimal low-rank approximation of a trained neural network, such that the evaluation of the approximated network respects the constraints. For conciseness, the number of MAC operation and the memory footprint of the approximated network will be referred to as *computation cost* and *memory cost* respectively.

© Springer Nature Switzerland AG 2018
V. Ferrari et al. (Eds.): ECCV 2018, LNCS 11214, pp. 746–761, 2018.
https://doi.org/10.1007/978-3-030-01249-6_45

Our proposed method, named COBLA (**C**onstrained **O**ptimization **B**ased **L**ow-rank **A**pproximation), combines the well-studied low-rank approximation technique in deep neural networks [1,9,11,13,15,21,27,28,30] and sequential quadratic programming (SQP) [2]. Low-rank approximation techniques exploit linear dependency of the network weights, so the computation cost and the memory cost of network evaluation can both be reduced. A major unaddressed obstacle of the low-rank approximation technique is in determining the target rank of each convolutional layer subject to the constraints. In a sense, determining the target rank of each layer can be considered as a *resource allocation* problem, in which constrained resources in terms of computation cost and memory cost are allocated to each layer. Instead of relying on laborious manual tuning or sub-optimal heuristics, COBLA *learns* the optimal target rank of each layer by approximately solving a constrained 0–1 integer program using SQP. COBLA enables the user to freely and optimally trade-off between the evaluation cost and the accuracy of the approximated network.

To the best knowledge of the authors, COBLA is the first systematic method that learns the optimal target ranks (which define the *structure* of the approximated network) subject to constraints in low-rank approximation of neural networks. We empirically demonstrate that COBLA outperforms prior art using SqueezeNet [12] and VGG-16 [26] on the ImageNet (ILSVRC12) dataset [23]. COBLA is independent of how the network weights are decomposed. We performed the experiments using two representative decomposition schemes proposed in [27] and [30]. A distinct advantage of COBLA is that it does not involve any hyperparameter tuning.

2   Low-Rank Approximation and Masking Variable

Matrix multiplication plays a pivotal role in evaluating convolutional neural networks [16]. The time complexity of exactly computing $A \cdot B$ where $A \in \mathbb{R}^{k \times l}$ and $B \in \mathbb{R}^{l \times p}$ is $\mathcal{O}(klp)$. Here A is some transformation of the weight tensor, and B is the input to the layer. With a pre-computed rank r approximation of A, denoted by $\widehat{A}$, it only takes $\mathcal{O}((k + l)pr)$ operations to approximately compute the matrix multiplication. The memory footprint of $\widehat{A}$ is also reduced to $\mathcal{O}((k + l)r)$ from $\mathcal{O}(kl)$.

The focus of this paper is in optimally choosing the target rank r for each layer subject to the constraints. This is a critical issue that was not adequately addressed in the existing literature.

If the target rank r was known, the rank r minimizer of $||A - \widehat{A}||$ (independent of the input data B) could be easily computed by the singular value decomposition (SVD). Let the SVD of A be $A = \sum_{\forall j} \sigma_j \cdot U_j \cdot (V_j)^T$, where σ_j is the jth largest singular value, U_j and V_j are the corresponding singular vectors. The rank r minimizer of $||A - \widehat{A}||$ is simply $\widehat{A} = \sum_{j \leq r} \sigma_j \cdot U_j \cdot (V_j)^T$. Let the set S_σ contain the indices of the singlar values and corresponding singular vectors that are included in the low-rank approximation. In this case $S_\sigma = \{j | j \leq r\}$. Unfortunately, identifying the input data dependent optimal value of $\widehat{A}$ that minimizes $||A \cdot B - \widehat{A} \cdot B||$ is significantly more difficult. As a matter of fact, the general weighted low-rank approximation problem is NP-hard [31].

2.1   Low-Rank Approximation of Neural Networks

Let the kernel of a convolution layer be $W \in \mathbb{R}^{c \times m \times n \times f}$, where c is the number of the input channels, m, n are the size of the filter, and f is the number of output channels. Let an input to the convolution layer be $Z \in \mathbb{R}^{c \times x \times y}$, where $x \times y$ is the size of the image. The output of the convolution layer $T = W * Z$ can be computed as

$$T(x,y,f) = W * Z = \sum_{c'=1}^{c} \sum_{x'=1}^{m} \sum_{y'=1}^{n} W(c',x',y',f) \cdot Z(c',x+x',y+y') \quad (1)$$

Given a trained convolutional neural network, the weight tensor of a convolution layers W can be decomposed into tensors G and H. Essentially, a convolutional layer with weight W is decomposed into two convolutional layers, whose weights are G and H respectively. The *decomposition scheme* defines how a four-dimensional weight tensor is decomposed. We focus on the decomposition schemes described in [27] and [30], which are representative works in low-rank approximation of neural networks. The dimensions of the weights of the decomposed layers are summarized in Table 1.

Table 1. Dimension of the decomposed layers in low-rank approximation of neural networks.

Decomposition scheme	Dimension of G	Dimension of H	Compute decomposed weight with
[27]	$[c,m,1,r]$	$[r,1,n,f]$	Eq. 3
[30]	$[c,m,n,r]$	$[r,1,1,f]$	Eq. 4

r is the target rank, which dictates how much computation cost and memory cost are allocated to a layer.

With the dimension of the decomposed weights defined by the target rank and the decomposition scheme, we now identify the optimal weight of the decomposed layers. The basic idea is to compute the SVD of some matricization of the four-dimensional network weight, and only use a subset of the singular values (together with their corresponding singular vectors) to approximate the network weight. In [27], the following low-rank approximation is applied to the weight tensor $W \in \mathbb{R}^{c \times x \times y \times f}$,

$$W[c',:,:,f'] = \sum_{\forall j} \sigma_j \cdot U_{f'}^j \cdot (V_j^{c'})^T \approx \sum_{j \in S_{\sigma,i}} \sigma_j \cdot U_{f'}^j \cdot (V_j^{c'})^T = \sum_{j \in S_{\sigma,i}} P_{f'}^j \cdot (V_j^{c'})^T \quad (2)$$

For conciseness, scalar σ_j is absorbed into the left singular vector U_j such that $P_j = \sigma_j \cdot U_j$.

Properly choosing S_σ for each layer subject to constraints is critical to the performance of the approximated network. Note that the target rank $r_i = |S_{\sigma,i}|$, where $|\cdot|$ denotes the cardinality of a set. The default technique is truncating the singular values, where $S_{\sigma,i}$ is chosen by adjusting a hyperparameter k_i such that $S_{\sigma,i} = \{j | j \leq k_i\}$ [27,30]. Obviously, truncating the singular values is sub-optimal considering the NP-hardness of the weighted low-rank approximation problem [31]. It is worth emphasizing that k_i is a hyperparameter that has to be individually adjusted for each convolution layer in the network. Given the large number of layers in the network, optimally adjusting the $S_{\sigma,i}$ for each layer constitutes a challenging integer optimization problem by itself. COBLA can be considered as an automatic method to choose $S_{\sigma,i}$ for each layer subject to the constraints.

Equivalently, Eq. 2 can be re-written as

$$W[c', :, :, f'] \approx \sum_{j \in S_{\sigma,i}} P^j_{f'} \cdot (V^{c'}_j)^T = \sum_{\forall j} m_{ij} \cdot (P^j_{f'} \cdot (V^{c'}_j)^T) \tag{3}$$

where $m_{ij} \in \{0, 1\}$ is the *masking variable* of a singular value and its corresponding singular vectors, with $m_{ij} = 1$ indicating the jth singular value of the ith convolutional layer is included in the approximation, and $m_{ij} = 0$ otherwise. Obviously, for the ith convolutional layer $S_{\sigma,i} = \{j \mid m_{ij} = 1\}$. If $m_{ij} = 1$ for all (i, j), then all the singular values and the corresponding singular vectors are included in the approximation. If so, the approximated network would be identical to the original network (subject to numerical error). Let vector $\boldsymbol{m}$ be the concatenation of all m_{ij}. Also, let $\boldsymbol{m}_i$ denote the masking variables of the ith convolutional layer. See Fig. 1 for a small example illustrating how masking variables can be used to select the singular values and the corresponding singular vectors in low-rank approximation.

$$[\, U_1, U_2, \boxed{U_3}, U_4, \boxed{U_5} \,] \cdot \begin{bmatrix} m_1 \cdot \sigma_1 & 0 & 0 & 0 & 0 & 0 \\ 0 & m_2 \cdot \sigma_2 & 0 & 0 & 0 & 0 \\ 0 & 0 & \boxed{m_3 \cdot \sigma_3} & 0 & 0 & 0 \\ 0 & 0 & 0 & m_4 \cdot \sigma_4 & 0 & 0 \\ 0 & 0 & 0 & 0 & \boxed{m_5 \cdot \sigma_5} & 0 \end{bmatrix} \cdot \begin{bmatrix} V_1^T \\ V_2^T \\ \boxed{V_3^T} \\ V_4^T \\ \boxed{V_5^T} \\ V_6^T \end{bmatrix}$$

Fig. 1. An example of utilizing masking variables to select the singular values and the corresponding singular vectors in low-rank approximation. In this example $W \in \mathbb{R}^{5\times 6}$, the SVD of W is $W = U\Sigma V^T$. The values of the masking variables $m_{1..5}$ are [1,1,0,1,0], thus $S_\sigma = \{1, 2, 4\}$. $\widehat{W} = \Sigma_{j\in\{1,2,4\}} \sigma_j \cdot U_j \cdot (V_j)^T$, where $\widehat{W}$ is a rank 3 approximation of W.

We can apply the masking variables formulation to the decomposition scheme described in [30] in a similar fashion. Recall that in most mainstream deep learning frameworks, the convolution operation is substituted by matrix multiplication via the `im2col` subroutine [16]. To compute convolution as matrix multiplication, the network weight $W \in \mathbb{R}^{c \times m \times n \times f}$ is reshaped into a two dimensional matrix $W_M \in \mathbb{R}^{f \times c \cdot m \cdot n}$. In [30], low-rank approximation is applied to W_M. With a slight abuse of notations,

$$W_M = \sum_{\forall j} P_j \cdot (V_j)^T \approx \sum_{j \in S_{\sigma,i}} P_j \cdot (V_j)^T = \sum_{\forall j} m_{ij} \cdot (P_j \cdot (V_j)^T) \qquad (4)$$

It is worth emphasizing that the input to the layer is not considered in Eq. 3 or Eq. 4. Much effort has been made to approximately compute the optimal weight of the decomposed layers (G and H) conditioned on the distribution of the input to the layer [11,28,30]. However, our experiment and prior work [27] indicate that the accuracy improvement enabled by data dependent decomposition vanishes after the fine-tuning process. For this reason, we simply use the data independent decomposition, and focus on identifying an optimal allocation of the constrained computation resources.

3   Problem Statement and Proposed Solution

Let $N_C(m)$ and $N_M(m)$ be the computation cost and the memory cost associated with evaluating the network. Also, let $N_{C,O}$ and $N_{M,O}$ denote the computation cost and the memory cost of the original convolutional neural network.

Consider a general empirical risk minimization problem,

$$E(\mathcal{W}) = \frac{1}{N_S} \sum_{n=1}^{N_S} \{\mathcal{L}(f(I^n, \mathcal{W}), O^n)\} \qquad (5)$$

where $\mathcal{L}(\cdot)$ is the loss function, $f(\cdot)$ is the non-linear function defined by the convolutional neural network, I^n and O^n are the input and output of the nth data sample, N_S is the number of training samples, and $\mathcal{W}$ is the set of weights in the neural network.

Assuming that a convolutional neural network has been trained and low-rank approximation of the weights is performed as in Eq. 3 or Eq. 4, the empirical risk of the approximated neural network is

$$E(m, \mathcal{P}, \mathcal{V}) = \frac{1}{N_S} \sum_{n=1}^{N_S} \{\mathcal{L}(f(I^n, m, \mathcal{P}, \mathcal{V}), O^n)\} \qquad (6)$$

where $\mathcal{P}$ and $\mathcal{V}$ are the sets of P and V vectors of all convolutional layers.

Given a system-level budget defined by the upper limit of computation cost $N_{C,max}$ and the upper limit of memory cost $N_{M,max}$, the problem can be formally stated as

$$\begin{array}{ll} \underset{m,\mathcal{P},\mathcal{V}}{\text{minimize}} & E(m,\mathcal{P},\mathcal{V}) \\ \text{subject to} & N_C(m) \le N_{C,max} \\ & N_M(m) \le N_{M,max} \\ & m_{i,j} \in \{0,1\} \end{array} \qquad (7)$$

In this 0–1 integer program, the computation cost and the memory cost associated with evaluating the approximated network are expressed in terms of m.

If we were given an optimal solution $\{m^*, \mathcal{P}^*, \mathcal{V}^*\}$ to Eq. 7 by an oracle, then the optimal target rank r_i^* for the ith convolutional layer subject to the constraints is simply Σm_i^*. In other words, with the masking variable formulation, we are now able to *learn* the optimal *structure* of the approximated network subject to constraints by solving a constrained optimization problem. This is a key innovation of the proposed method.

However, exactly solving the 0–1 integer program in Eq. 7 is intractable. We propose to approximately solve Eq. 7 in a two-step process: in the first step, we focus on m, while keeping $\mathcal{P}, \mathcal{V}$ as constants. The value of $\mathcal{P}, \mathcal{V}$ are computed using SVD as in Eq. 3 or Eq. 4. To approximately compute m^*, we resort to integer relaxation [22], which is a classic method in approximately solving integer programs. The 0–1 integer variables are relaxed to continuous variables in the interval $[0, 1]$. Essentially, we solve the following program in the first step

$$\begin{array}{ll} \underset{m}{\text{minimize}} & E_{\mathcal{P},\mathcal{V}}(m) \\ \text{subject to} & N_C(m) \le N_{C,max} \\ & N_M(m) \le N_{M,max} \\ & 0 \le m_{i,j} \le 1 \end{array} \qquad (8)$$

A locally optimal solution of Eq. 8, denoted by $\hat{m}^*$, can be identified by a constrained non-linear optimization algorithm such as SQP. Intuitively, $\hat{m}^*$ quantifies the relative importance of each singular value (and its corresponding singular vectors) in the approximation with a scalar between 0 and 1. The resulted target rank of the ith layer $r_i = \lfloor \Sigma \hat{m}_i^* \rceil$, where $\lfloor \cdot \rceil$ operator randomly rounds [25] a real number to an integer, such that

$$\lfloor x \rceil = \begin{cases} \lceil x \rceil & \text{with probability } x - \lfloor x \rfloor \\ \lfloor x \rfloor & \text{otherwise} \end{cases} \qquad (9)$$

Here $\lfloor \Sigma \hat{m}_i^* \rceil$ serves as a surrogate for Σm_i^*. $\hat{m}^*$ scales the corresponding singular values. We therefore let $S_{\sigma,i}$ contain the j index of the r_i largest elements in set $\{\hat{m}_{i,j}^* \cdot \sigma_{i,j} | \forall_j\}$. A binary solution m' due to $\hat{m}^*$ can be expressed as $m'_{i,j} = \mathbb{1}_{S_{\sigma,i}}(j)$ where $\mathbb{1}(\cdot)$ is the indicator function. If m' violates the constraints, the random rounding procedure is repeated until the constraints are satisfied.

In the second step, we incorporate the scaling effect of $\hat{m}^*$ in $\mathcal{P}$ as follows: for the ith convolutional layer, let $P_j \leftarrow \hat{m}_{ij}^* \cdot P_j$. The resulted low-rank approximation of the network is defined by $\{m', \mathcal{P}, \mathcal{V}\}$. With the structure of the approximated network determined by m', $\mathcal{P}$ and $\mathcal{V}$ can be further fine-tuned by simply running back-propagation.

3.1   Sequential Quadratic Programming

In the proposed method, Eq. 8 is solved using the SQP algorithm, which is arguably the most widely adopted method in solving constrained non-linear optimization problems [2]. At each SQP iteration, a linearly constrained quadratic programming (QP) subproblem is constructed and solved to move the current solution closer to a local minimum. To construct the QP subproblem, the gradient of the objective function and the constraints, as well as the Hessian have to be computed. The gradients can be readily computed by an automatic differentiation engine, such as TensorFlow. An approximation of the Hessian is iteratively refined by the BFGS algorithm [3] using the gradient information.

The scalability of the SQP algorithm is not a concern in our method. The number of decision variables (masking variables) in Eq. 8 is generally on the order of thousands, which is significantly smaller than the number of the weight parameters.

With a large training dataset, averaging over the entirety of the dataset to compute the gradient in each SQP iteration can be extremely time-consuming. In such cases, an estimation of the gradient by sub-sampling the training dataset has to be used in lieu of the true gradient. To address the estimation error of the gradients due to sub-sampling, we employed non-monotonic line search [4]. Non-monotonic line search ensures the line search iterations in the SQP algorithm can terminate properly despite the estimation error due to sub-sampled gradients. Note that a properly regularized Hessian estimation due to BFGS is positive semidefinite by construction, even with sub-sampled gradients [18]. Thus the QP subproblem is guaranteed to be convex.

Mathematically rigorous analysis of the convergence property of the SQP algorithm with sub-sampled gradient is the next step of this research. Recent theoretical results [6,7] could potentially provide insights into this problem. We empirically evaluated the numerical stability of SQP with sub-sampled gradients in Sect. 5.2

4   Prior Works

In this section, we thoroughly review the heuristics in the literature that are closely related to our proposed method. These heuristics will serve as the baseline to demonstrate the effectiveness of COBLA.

In [27], the target rank for each layer is identified by trial-and-error. Each trial involves fine-tuning the approximated network, which is highly time-consuming.

The following heuristic is discussed in [27] and earlier works: for the ith convolutional layer $S_{\sigma,i} = \{j | j \leq k_i\}$ is chosen such that the first k_i singular values and their corresponding singular vectors account for a certain percentage of the total variations. Thus, for the ith convolutional layer k_i is chosen to be the largest integer subject to

$$\sum_{j=1}^{k_i} \sigma_{i,j}^2 \le \beta \cdot \sum_{\forall j} \sigma_{i,j}^2 \tag{10}$$

where β is the proportion of the total variations accounted by the low-rank approximation, and $\sigma_{i,j}$ is the jth largest singular value of the ith convolutional layer. It is obvious that the computation cost and the memory cost of the approximated network are monotonic functions of β. The largest β that satisfies the constraints in computation cost and memory cost, denoted by β^*, can be easily computed by bisection. Then the k_i value for each layer can be identified by plugging β^* into Eq. 10. We call this heuristic CPTV (Certain Percentage of Total Variation).

Another heuristics proposed in [30] identifies $S_{\sigma,i} = \{j | j \le k_i\}$ by maximizing the following objective function subject to the constraints in computation cost.

$$\prod_{\forall i} (\sum_{j=1}^{k_i} \sigma_{i,j}^2) \tag{11}$$

In [30], a greedy algorithm is employed to approximately solve this program. We call this heuristic POS-Greedy (Product Of Sum-Greedy). See Sect. 2.4 of [30] for details. Due to the use of the greedy algorithm, only a single constraint can be considered by POS-Greedy.

We can improve the POS-Greedy heuristic by noting that the program in Eq. 11 can be solved with provable optimality and multiple constraints support by using the masking variable formulation. Equation 11 can be equivalently stated as

$$\begin{aligned} \underset{m}{\text{maximize}} \quad & \prod_{\forall i} (\sum_{\forall j} m_{i,j} \cdot \sigma_{i,j}^2) \\ \text{subject to} \quad & N_C(\boldsymbol{m}) \le N_{C,max} \\ & N_M(\boldsymbol{m}) \le N_{M,max} \\ & m_{i,j} \in \{0,1\} \end{aligned} \tag{12}$$

Note that the masking variables and the singular values can only take nonnegative values, thus the objective in Eq. 12 is equivalent to maximizing the *geometric mean*. If the 0–1 integer constraint were omitted, the objective function and the constraints in Eq. 12 are concave in $\boldsymbol{m}$. Even with the 0–1 integer constraint, modern numerical optimization engines can efficiently solve this mixed integer program with provable optimality. The heuristic of exactly solving Eq. 12 is called POS-CVX (Product of Sum-Convex). In our experiment, we observe that the numerical value of the objective function due to POS-CVX is consistently 1.5 to 2 times higher than that due to POS-Greedy.

In [13], variational Bayesian matrix factorization (VBMF) [20] is employed to estimate the target rank. Given an observation V that is corrupted by additive noise $V = U + \sigma Z$, VBMF takes a Bayesian approach to identify a decomposition of matrix U whose rank is no larger than r, such that $U = BA^T$. We refer to this heuristic as R-VBMF (Rank due to VBMF). It is worth emphasizing that with R-VBMF, the user cannot arbitrarily set $N_{C,max}$ or $N_{M,max}$. Rather, the heuristic will decide the computation and the memory cost of the approximated network.

We also experimented with the low-rank signal recovery [5] to estimate the target rank for each layer. This groundbreaking result from the information theory community states that given a low-rank signal of unknown rank r which is contaminated by additive noise, one can optimally recover the low-rank signal in the Minimum-Square-Error (MSE) sense by truncating the singular values of the data matrix to $2.858 \cdot y_{med}$, where y_{med} is the median empirical singular values of the data matrix. This impressive result was not previously applied in the context of low-rank approximation of neural networks.

5   Numerical Experiments

In this section, we compare the performance of COBLA to the previously published heuristics discussed in Sect. 4. Image classification experiments are performed using the SqueezeNet and the VGG-16 architecture on the ImageNet dataset [23]. SqueezeNet is a highly optimized architecture that achieves AlexNet-level accuracy with 50X parameter reduction. Further compressing such a compact and efficient architecture is a challenging task. We report the results using the decomposition scheme in both Eqs. 3 and 4.

The constraints to the computation cost and the memory cost of the approximated network, $N_{C,max}$ and $N_{M,max}$, are expressed in terms of the cost of the original network, denoted by $N_{C,O}$ and $N_{M,O}$. In the experiment $N_{C,max} = \eta \cdot N_{C,O}$ and $N_{M,max} = \eta \cdot N_{M,O}$, for $\eta = \{0.5, 0.6, 0.7\}$. The results in Fig. 2 are compiled by evaluating the approximated network due to each methods, before any fine-tuning is performed.

5.1   Effect of Fine-Tuning

We fine-tune the resulted network approximation due to POS-CVX and COBLA for 50 epochs. The experiment is repeated using the decomposition schemes in Eqs. 3 and 4. The hyperparameters used in the training phase are re-used in the fine-tuning phase, except for learning rate and momentum, which are controlled by the YellowFin optimizer [29]. The fine-tuning results are reported in Table 2.

Before fine-tuning, COBLA performs much better using the decomposition scheme in Eq. 3 (Fig. 2(a)(c)) than Eq. 4 (Fig. 2(b)(d)). Interestingly, the difference is reduced to within 1% after fine-tuning. This observation not only demonstrates that the effectiveness of COBLA is independent of the decomposition scheme, but also suggests that the choice of decomposition scheme is not critical to the success of low-rank approximation techniques.

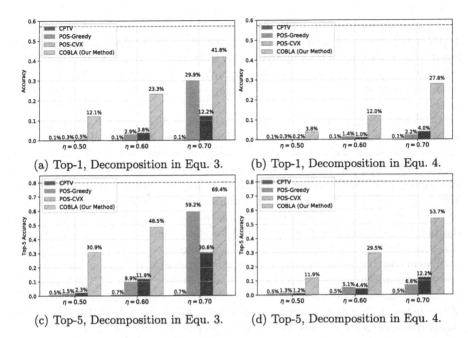

(a) Top-1, Decomposition in Equ. 3.   (b) Top-1, Decomposition in Equ. 4.

(c) Top-5, Decomposition in Equ. 3.   (d) Top-5, Decomposition in Equ. 4.

Fig. 2. Comparison of Top-1 and Top-5 accuracy of the network approximation of SqueezeNet before fine-tuning. The right-hand side of the constraints in Eq. 8 are set to $N_{C,max} = \eta \cdot N_{C,O}$ and $N_{M,max} = \eta \cdot N_{M,O}$, where $N_{C,O}$ and $N_{M,O}$ are the computation cost and the memory cost of the original network without low-rank approximation. The Top-1 and Top-5 accuracy of the original SqueezeNet are 57.2% and 80.0% respectively.

Table 2. Accuracy of the approximated network at various constraint conditions using the SqueezeNet architecture on ImageNet dataset after 50 epochs of fine-tuning. The baseline method is POS-CVX. The Top-1 and Top-5 accuracy of the original SqueezeNet are 57.2% and 80.0% respectively.

	$N_{C,max}$	$N_{M,max}$	Decomposition scheme	Top-1 COBLA	Top-1 baseline	Top-5 COBLA	Top-5 baseline
1	$0.7 \cdot N_{C,O}$	$0.7 \cdot N_{M,O}$	Eq. 3	55.7%	-2.0%	79.2%	-1.1%
2	$0.7 \cdot N_{C,O}$	$0.7 \cdot N_{M,O}$	Eq. 4	55.4%	-2.4%	78.8%	-1.6%
3	$0.6 \cdot N_{C,O}$	$0.6 \cdot N_{M,O}$	Eq. 3	54.4%	-4.1%	78.2%	-2.7%
4	$0.6 \cdot N_{C,O}$	$0.6 \cdot N_{M,O}$	Eq. 4	54.3%	-3.8%	77.9%	-2.7%
5	$0.5 \cdot N_{C,O}$	$0.5 \cdot N_{M,O}$	Eq. 3	52.6%	-7.4%	77.0%	-5.7%
6	$0.5 \cdot N_{C,O}$	$0.5 \cdot N_{M,O}$	Eq. 4	51.7%	-5.5%	76.2%	-4.1%

5.2 Comparison with R-VBMF and Low-Rank Signal Recovery

Section 3.2 of [13] suggests that R-VBMF could function as a general solution for identifying the target rank of each layer in low-rank approximation of neural networks. We compared COBLA to R-VBMF. In our experiment, low-rank approximation is applied to all layers. This is different from the experiment setup in [13], where low-rank approximation is applied to a manually selected subset of layers. The reasoning behind applying R-VBMF to all layers is that if R-VBMF was indeed capable of recovering the true rank of the weight, it would just return the full rank of the weight if no low-rank approximation should be applied to a layer.

R-VBMF returns $N_{C,max} = 0.25 \cdot N_{C,O}$ and $N_{M,max} = 0.19 \cdot N_{M,O}$ on SqueezeNet using the decomposition scheme in Eq. 3. With such tight constraints, the accuracy of the approximated networks due to R-VBMF and COBLA both dropped to chance level before fine-tuning. Even after 10 epochs of fine-tuning, R-VBMF is still stuck close to chance level, while COBLA achieves a Top-1 accuracy of 15.9% and Top-5 accuracy of 36.2%. This experiment demonstrates that COBLA is a more effective method, even with severely constrained computation cost and memory cost. The low-rank signal recovery technique [5] also dramatically underestimated the target ranks.

The ineffectiveness of these rigorous signal processing technique in estimating the target rank in neural networks is not surprising. First of all, the non-linear activation functions between the linear layers are crucial to the overall dynamic of the network, but they cannot be easily considered in R-VBMF or low-rank signal recovery. Also, the low-rank approximation problem is not equivalent to recovering a signal from noisy measurements. Some unjustified assumptions have to be made regarding the distribution of the noise. More importantly, the target rank of each layer should not be analyzed in an isolated and layer-by-layer manner. It would be more constructive to study the approximation error with the dynamic of the entire network in mind. COBLA avoids the aforementioned pitfalls by taking a data-driven approach to address the unique challenges in this constrained optimization problem.

5.3 Effect of Sub-sampled Gradients in SQP Iterations

As discussed in Sect. 3.1, when the dataset is large, it is computationally prohibitive to exactly compute the gradient in each SQP iteration, and a sub-sampled estimation of the gradient has to be used. To investigate the effect of sub-sampled gradients in SQP, we conducted experiments using the NIN architecture [17] on the CIFAR10 dataset [14].

CIFAR10 is a small dataset on which we can afford to exactly compute the gradient in each SQP iteration. Although the CIFAR10 dataset is no longer considered a state-of-the-art benchmark, the 11-layer NIN architecture we used is relatively recent and ensures that the experiment is not conducted on a trivial example.

In Fig. 3, we compare the accuracy of the approximated network due to previously published heuristics and COBLA. The experiment using COBLA is conducted under two conditions. In the first case, labeled COBLA (sub-sampled gradient), 5% of the training dataset is randomly sampled to estimate the gradient in each SQP iteration. In the second case, labeled COBLA (exact gradient), the entire training dataset is used to exactly compute the gradient in each SQP

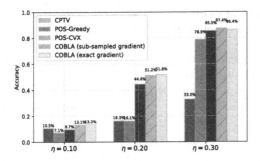

Fig. 3. Comparision of Top-1 accuracy of NIN architecture on the CIFAR10 dataset. The constraints are $N_{C,max} = \eta \cdot N_{C,O}$ and $N_{M,max} = \eta \cdot N_{M,O}$, for $\eta = \{0.1, 0.2, 0.3\}$. The accuracy of the original CIFAR-10 NIN is 91.9%.

iteration. As shown in Fig. 3, accuracies in the two cases are very similar (within 1%). This experiment provides some empirical evidence for the numerical stability of SQP with sub-sampled gradients.

5.4   COBLA on VGG-16

We compared COBLA to [27] using the VGG-16 architecture. We make the note that VGG-16 is an architecture that is over-parameterized by design. Such over-parameterized architectures are not suitable for studying model compression methods, as the intrinsic redundancy of the architecture would allow ineffective methods to achieve significant compression as well [10]. Optimized architectures that are designed to be computationally efficient (e.g. SqueezeNet) are more reasonable benchmarks [10]. The purpose of this experiment is to demonstrate the scalability of COBLA (VGG-16 is 22X larger than SqueezeNet in terms of computation cost). This experiment also provides a side-by-side comparison of COBLA to the results reported in [27].

In [27], the computation cost and the memory cost of the approximated network are $0.33 \cdot N_{C,O}$ and $0.36 \cdot N_{M,O}$ respectively. The resource allocation defined by the target rank of each layer is identified manually by trial-and-error. As shown in Table 3, COBLA *further* reduces the computation *and* the memory cost of the *compressed* VGG-16 in [27] by 12% with no accuracy drop (by 30% with negligible accuracy drop).

6   System Overview of COBLA

In Fig. 4, we present the system overview of COBLA. The centerpiece of COBLA is the SQP algorithm (which solves Eq. 8). The two supporting components are TensorFlow for computing gradients (of the empirical risk w.r.t. the masking variables) and MOSEK [19] for solving the convex QP in each SQP step. Given

Table 3. Comparision of COBLA to [27] using the VGG-16 architecture on ImageNet. The Top-5 accuracy of the original VGG-16 is 89.8%.

	Computation (reduction)	Memory (reduction)	Top-5 accuracy	Target rank of decomposed layers
Baseline [27]	$0.33 \cdot N_{C,O}$ -	$0.36 \cdot N_{M,O}$ -	89.8% -	5, 24, 48, 48, 64, 128, 160 192, 192, 256, 320, 320, 320
COBLA	$0.29 \cdot N_{C,O}$ (−12%)	$0.32 \cdot N_{M,O}$ (−12%)	89.8% (+0.0%)	5, 17, 41, 54, 77, 109, 133 155, 180, 239, 274, 283, 314
COBLA	$0.23 \cdot N_{C,O}$ (−30%)	$0.25 \cdot N_{M,O}$ (−30%)	88.9% (−0.9%)	5, 16, 32, 48, 64, 81, 95 116, 126, 203, 211, 215, 232

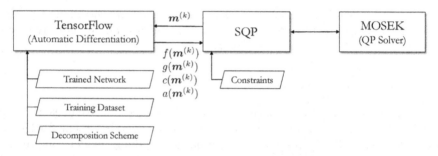

Fig. 4. System overview of COBLA. $m^{(k)}$ is the value of the masking variables at the kth SQP iteration. $f(m^{(k)})$ is the loss, $g(m^{(k)})$ is the gradient of the loss with respect to the masking variables, $c(m^{(k)})$ is the value of the constraint functions, and $a(m^{(k)})$ is the Jacobian of the constraints.

$m^{(k)}$, the value of the masking variables at the kth SQP iteration, Tensor-Flow computes the loss and the gradients based on the trained network and user-defined decomposition scheme. COBLA is available at https://github.com/chongli-uw/cobla.

6.1   Quantifying Parameter Redundancy of Each Layer

Given an approximated network identified by COBLA subject to the constraint of $N_{C,max} = 0.5 \cdot N_{C,O}$ and $N_{M,max} = 0.5 \cdot N_{M,O}$, we visualize the topology of the SqueezeNet and label the reduction of the computation cost of each layer in Fig. 5. For example, 28.9% of the computation cost of layer conv1 is reduced by COBLA, so the computation cost of conv1 in the approximated network is 71.1% of that in the original SqueezeNet network.

In the approximated network identified by COBLA, the allocation of the constrained computation resources is highly inhomogeneous. For most of the 1×1 layers, including the `squeeze` layers and the `expand/1` $\times 1$ layers, the computation cost is not reduced at all. This indicates that there is less linear dependency in the 1×1 layers. However, the output layer `conv10` is an exception. `conv10` is a 1×1 layer that maps the high-dimensional output from previous layers to a vector of size 1000 (the number of classes in ImageNet). As shown in Fig. 5, 66% of the computation in `conv10` can be reduced. This coincides with the design choice that was identified manually in [8], where the author found that the output layer has high parameter redundancy.

In [24], it is hypothesized that the parameter redundancy of a layer is dependent on its relative position in the network and follows certain trends (increasing, decreasing, convex and concave are explored). Figure 5 indicates that the parameter redundancy of each layer is more complex than previously hypothesized and has to be analyzed on a case-by-case basis.

7 Conclusion

In this paper, we presented a systematic method named COBLA, to identify the target rank of each layer in low-rank approximation of a convolutional neural network, subject to the constraints in the computation cost and the memory cost of the approximated network. COBLA optimally allocates constrained computation resources into each layer. The key idea of the COBLA is in applying a binary masking variable to the singular values of the network weights to formulate a constrained 0–1 integer program. We empirically demonstrate that our method outperforms previously published works using the SqueezeNet and VGG-16 on the ImageNet dataset.

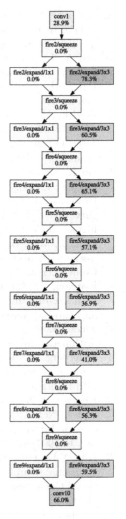

Fig. 5. Per-layer computation cost reduction in the approximated SqueezeNet.

Acknowledgment. The authors would like to thank the anonymous reviewers, particularly Reviewer 3, for their highly constructive advice. This work is supported by an Intel/Semiconductor Research Corporation Ph.D. Fellowship.

References

1. Alvarez, J.M., Salzmann, M.: Compression-aware training of deep networks. In: Neural Information Processing Systems (2017). http://papers.nips.cc/paper/6687-compression-aware-training-of-deep-networks.pdf

2. Boggs, P.T., Tolle, J.W.: Sequential quadratic programming. Acta Num. **4**, 1 (1995). https://doi.org/10.1017/S0962492900002518. http://www.journals.cambri dge.org/abstract_S0962492900002518

3. Dai, Y.H.: Convergence properties of the BFGS algoritm. SIAM J. Optim. **13**(3), 693–701 (2002). https://doi.org/10.1137/S1052623401383455

4. Dai, Y.H., Schittkowski, K.: A sequential quadratic programming algorithm with non-monotone line search. Pac. J. Optim. **4**, 335–351 (2008)

5. Gavish, M., Donoho, D.L.: The optimal hard threshold for singular values is $4/\sqrt{3}$. IEEE Trans. Inf. Theory **60**(8), 5040–5053 (2014). https://doi.org/10. 1109/TIT.2014.2323359. http://ieeexplore.ieee.org/lpdocs/epic03/wrapper.htm? arnumber=6846297

6. Ge, R., Huang, F., Jin, C., Yuan, Y.: Escaping from saddle points - online stochastic gradient for tensor decomposition. J. Mach. Learn. Res. **40** (2015)

7. Gower, R.M., Goldfarb, D., Richtarik, P.: Stochastic block BFGS: squeezing more curvature out of data. In: International Conference on Machine Learning (2016). https://doi.org/10.1016/j.camwa.2005.08.006

8. Han, S., Mao, H., Dally, W.J.: Deep compression - compressing deep neural networks with pruning, trained quantization and huffman coding. In: International Conference on Learning Representations (2016)

9. Ioannou, Y., Robertson, D., Shotton, J., Cipolla, R., Criminisi, A.: Training CNNs with low-rank filters for efficient image classification. In: International Conference on Learning Representations (2016). http://arxiv.org/abs/1511.06744

10. Jacob, B., et al.: Quantization and training of neural networks for efficient integer-arithmetic-only inference. ArXiv (2017). http://arxiv.org/abs/1712.05877

11. Jaderberg, M., Vedaldi, A., Zisserman, A.: Speeding up convolutional neural networks with low rank expansions. In: British Machine Vision Conference (BMVC) (2014). https://doi.org/10.5244/C.28.88, http://arxiv.org/abs/1405.3866

12. Keutzer, F.N.I., Han, S., Moskewicz, M.W., Ashraf, K., Dally, W.J., Kurt: SqueezeNet: AlexNet-level accuracy with 50x fewer parameters and <0.5 MB model size. In: International Conference on Learning Representations (2017). https://doi. org/10.1007/978-3-319-24553-9, http://arxiv.org/abs/1602.07360

13. Kim, Y.D., Park, E., Yoo, S., Choi, T., Yang, L., Shin, D.: Compression of deep convolutional neural networks for fast and low power mobile applications. In: International Conference on Learning Representations (2016). http://arxiv.org/abs/1511. 06530

14. Krizhevsky, A.: Learning multiple layers of features from tiny images. Technical report (2009)

15. Lebedev, V., Ganin, Y., Rakhuba, M., Oseledets, I., Lempitsky, V.: Speeding-up convolutional neural networks using fine-tuned CP-decomposition. In: International Conference on Learning Representations (2015). http://arxiv.org/abs/1412. 6553

16. Lebedev, V., Lempitsky, V.: Fast ConvNets using group-wise brain damage. In: Conference on Computer Vision and Pattern Recognition (2016). https://doi.org/ 10.1109/CVPR.2016.280, http://arxiv.org/abs/1506.02515

17. Lin, M., Chen, Q., Yan, S.: Network in network. In: International Conference on Learning Representations (2013). https://doi.org/10.1109/ASRU.2015.7404828, http://arxiv.org/abs/1312.4400

18. Mokhtari, A.: Efficient methods for large-scale empirical risk minimization. Ph.D. thesis, University of Pennsylvania (2017)

19. MOSEK: the MOSEK optimization toolbox for MATLAB manual. Technical report (2017)

20. Nakajima, S., Tomioka, R., Sugiyama, M., Babacan, S.D.: Condition for perfect dimensionality recovery by variational bayesian PCA. J. Mach. Learn. Reas. **16**, 3757–3811 (2016)
21. Novikov, A., Vetrov, D., Podoprikhin, D., Osokin, A.: Tensorizing neural networks. In: Neural Information Processing Systems (2015), http://arxiv.org/pdf/1509.06569v1.pdf
22. Nowak, I.: Relaxation and Decomposition Methods for Mixed Integer Nonlinear Programming. Birkhäuser Basel (2005). https://doi.org/10.1007/3-7643-7374-1
23. Olga, R., et al.: ImageNet large scale visual recognition challenge. Int. J. Comput. Vis. (2015)
24. Park, E., Ahn, J., Yoo, S.: Weighted-entropy-based quantization for deep neural networks. In: Conference on Computer Vision and Pattern Recognition (2017). https://doi.org/10.1109/CVPR.2017.761
25. Raghavan, P., Tompson, C.: Randomized rounding: a technique for provably good algorithms and algorithmic proofs. Combinatorica **7**(4), 365–374 (1987). https://doi.org/10.1007/BF02579324
26. Simonyan, K., Zisserman, A.: Very deep convolutional networks for large-scale image recognition. In: International Conference on Learning Representations (2015)
27. Tai, C., Xiao, T., Zhang, Y., Wang, X., E, W.: Convolutional neural networks with low-rank regularization. In: International Conference on Learning Representations (2016). http://arxiv.org/abs/1511.06067
28. Yu, X., Liu, T., Wang, X., Tao, D.: On compressing deep models by low rank and sparse decomposition. In: Conference on Computer Vision and Pattern Recognition (CVPR) (2017). https://doi.org/10.1109/CVPR.2017.15
29. Zhang, J., Mitliagkas, I., Ré, C.: YellowFin and the art of momentum tuning. arXiv preprint (2017). http://arxiv.org/abs/1706.03471
30. Zhang, X., Zou, J., Ming, X., He, K., Sun, J.: Efficient and accurate approximations of nonlinear convolutional networks. In: Conference on Computer Vision and Pattern Recognition (2015). http://arxiv.org/abs/1411.4229
31. Zhou, G.: Rank-constrained optimization: a Riemannian manifold approach. Ph.D. thesis, Florida State University (2015)

Human Sensing

Unsupervised Geometry-Aware Representation for 3D Human Pose Estimation

Helge Rhodin$^{(\boxtimes)}$ [ID], Mathieu Salzmann [ID], and Pascal Fua [ID]

CVLab, EPFL, Lausanne, Switzerland
{helge.rhodin,mathieu.salzmann,pascal.fua}@epfl.ch

Abstract. Modern 3D human pose estimation techniques rely on deep networks, which require large amounts of training data. While weakly-supervised methods require less supervision, by utilizing 2D poses or multi-view imagery without annotations, they still need a sufficiently large set of samples with 3D annotations for learning to succeed.

In this paper, we propose to overcome this problem by learning a geometry-aware body representation from multi-view images without annotations. To this end, we use an encoder-decoder that predicts an image from one viewpoint given an image from another viewpoint. Because this representation encodes 3D geometry, using it in a semi-supervised setting makes it easier to learn a mapping from it to 3D human pose. As evidenced by our experiments, our approach significantly outperforms fully-supervised methods given the same amount of labeled data, and improves over other semi-supervised methods while using as little as 1% of the labeled data.

Keywords: 3D reconstruction · Semi-supervised training Representation learning · Monocular human pose reconstruction

1 Introduction

Most current monocular solutions to 3D human pose estimation rely on methods based on convolutional neural networks (CNNs). With networks becoming ever more sophisticated, the main bottleneck now is the availability of sufficiently large training datasets, which typically require a large annotation effort. While such an effort might be practical for a handful of subjects and specific motions such as walking or running, covering the whole range of human body shapes, appearances, and poses is infeasible.

Weakly-supervised methods that reduce the amount of annotation required to achieve a desired level of performance are therefore valuable. For example,

---

Electronic supplementary material The online version of this chapter (https://doi.org/10.1007/978-3-030-01249-6_46) contains supplementary material, which is available to authorized users.

V. Ferrari et al. (Eds.): ECCV 2018, LNCS 11214, pp. 765–782, 2018.
https://doi.org/10.1007/978-3-030-01249-6_46

methods based on articulated 3D skeletons can be trained not only with actual 3D annotations but also using 2D annotations [21,54] and multi-view footage [25, 47]. Some methods dispense with 2D annotations altogether and instead exploit multi-view geometry in sequences acquired by synchronized cameras [31,55]. However, these methods still require a good enough 3D training set to initialize the learning process, which sets limits on the absolute gain that can be achieved from using unlabeled examples.

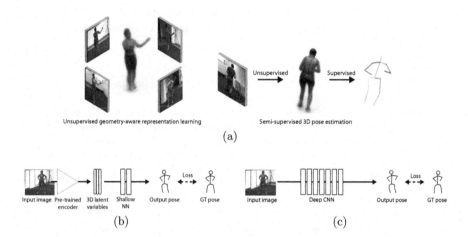

Fig. 1. Approach. (a) During training, we first learn a geometry-aware representation using unlabeled multi-view images. We then use a small amount of supervision to learn a mapping from our representation to actual 3D poses, which only requires a shallow network and therefore a limited amount of supervision. (b) At run-time, we compute the latent representation of the test image and feed it to the shallow network to compute the pose. (c) By contrast, most state-of-the-art approaches train a network to regress directly from the images to the 3D poses, which requires a much deeper network and therefore more training data.

In this paper, we propose to use images of the same person taken from multiple views to learn a latent representation that, as shown on the left side of Fig. 1(a), captures the 3D geometry of the human body. Learning this representation does not require any 2D or 3D pose annotation. Instead, we train an encoder-decoder to predict an image seen from one viewpoint from an image captured from a different one. As sketched on the right side of Fig. 1(a), we can then learn to predict a 3D pose from this latent representation in a supervised manner. The crux of our approach, however, is that because our latent representation already captures 3D geometry, the mapping to 3D pose is much simpler and can be learned using much fewer examples than existing methods that rely on multi-view supervision [31,55], and more generally most state-of-the-art methods that attempt to regress directly from the image to the 3D pose.

As can be seen in Fig. 1, our latent representation resembles a volumetric 3D shape. While such shapes can be obtained from silhouettes [45,50], body outlines are typically difficult to extract from natural images. By contrast, learning our representation does not require any silhouette information. Furthermore, at test time, it can be obtained from a monocular view of the person. Finally, it can also be used for novel view synthesis (NVS) and outperforms existing encoder-decoder algorithms [23,36,37] qualitatively on natural images.

Our contribution is therefore a latent variable body model that can be learned without 2D or 3D annotations, encodes both 3D pose and appearance, and can be integrated into semi-supervised approaches to reduce the required amount of supervised training data. We demonstrate this on the well-known Human3.6Million [13] dataset and show that our method drastically outperforms fully supervised methods in 3D pose reconstruction accuracy when only few labeled examples are available.

2   Related Work

In the following, we first review the literature on semi-supervised approaches to monocular 3D human pose estimation, which is most closely related to our goal. We then discuss approaches that, like us, make use of geometric representations, both in and out of the context of human pose estimation, and finally briefly review the novel view synthesis literature that has inspired us.

Semi-supervised Human Pose Estimation. While most current human pose estimation methods [20,22,24,25,27,33,38,42,54] are fully supervised, relying on large training sets annotated with ground-truth 3D positions coming from multi-view motion capture systems [12,21], several methods have recently been proposed to limit the requirement for labeled data. In this context, foreground and background augmentation [30,32] and the use of synthetic datasets [2,48] focus on increasing the training set size. Unfortunately, these methods do not generalize well to new motions, apparels, and environments that are different from the simulated data. Since larger and less constrained datasets for 2D pose estimation exist, they have been used for transfer learning [22,47] and to provide re-projection constraints [54]. Furthermore, given multiple views of the same person, 3D pose can be triangulated from 2D detections [14,25] and a 2D pose network can be trained to be view-consistent after bootstrapping from annotations. Nevertheless, these methods still require 2D annotation in images capturing the target motion and appearance. By contrast, the methods of [31,55] exploit multi-view geometry in sequences acquired by synchronized cameras, thus removing the need for 2D annotations. However, in practice, they still require a large enough 3D training set to initialize and constrain the learning process. We will show that our geometry-aware latent representation learned from multi-view imagery but without annotations allows us to train a 3D pose estimation network using much less labeled data.

Geometry-Aware Representations. Multi-view imagery has long been used to derive volumetric representations of 3D human pose from silhouettes, for example by carving out the empty space. This approach can be used in conjunction with learning-based methods [44], by defining constraints based on perspective view rays [15,45], orthographic projections [50], or learned projections [29]. It can even be extended to the single-view training-scenario if the distribution of the observed shape can be inferred prior to reconstruction [8,56]. The main drawback of these methods, however, is that accurate silhouettes are difficult to automatically extract in natural scenes, which limits their applicability.

Another approach to encoding geometry relies on a renderer that generates images from a 3D representation [9,16,35,52] and can function as a decoder in an autoencoder setup [1,39]. For simple renderers, the rendering function can even be learned [5,6] and act as an encoder. When put together, such learned encoders and decoders have been used for unsupervised learning, both with GANs [3,43,46] and without them [17]. In [40,41], a CNN was trained to map to and from spherical mesh representations without supervision. While these methods also effectively learn a geometry-aware representation based on images, they have only been applied to well-constrained problems, such as face modeling. As such, it is unclear how they would generalize to the much larger degree of variability of 3D human poses.

Novel View Synthesis. Our approach borrows ideas from the novel view synthesis literature, which is devoted to the task of creating realistic images from previously unseen viewpoints. Most recent techniques rely on encoder-decoder architectures, where the latent code is augmented with view change information, such as yaw angle, and the decoder learns to reconstruct the encoded image from a new perspective [36,37]. Large view changes are difficult. They have been achieved by relying on a recurrent network that performs incremental rotation steps [51]. Optical flow information [23,53] and depth maps [7] have been used to further improve the results. While the above-mentioned techniques were demonstrated on simple objects, methods dedicated to generating images of humans have been proposed. However, most of these methods use additional information as input, such as part-segmentations [18] and 2D poses [19]. Here, we build on the approaches of [4,49] that have been designed to handle large viewpoint changes. We describe these methods and our extensions in more detail in Sect. 3.

3   Unsupervised Geometry-Aware Latent Representation

Our goal is to design a latent representation **L** that encodes 3D pose, along with shape and appearance information, and can be learned without any 2D or 3D pose annotations. To achieve this, we propose to make use of sequences of images acquired from multiple synchronized and calibrated cameras. To be useful, such footage requires care during the setup and acquisition process. However, the amount of effort involved is negligible compared to what is needed to annotate tens of thousands of 2D or 3D poses.

For **L** to be practical, it must be easy to decode into its individual components. To this end, we learn from the images separate representations for the body's 3D pose and geometry, its appearance, and that of the background. We will refer to them as $\mathbf{L}^{3D}$, $\mathbf{L}^{app}$, and $\mathbf{B}$, respectively.

Let us assume that we are given a set, $\mathcal{U} = \{(\mathbf{I}_t^i, \mathbf{I}_t^j)\}_{t=1}^{N_u}$, of N_u image pairs without annotations, where the i and j superscripts refer to the cameras used to capture the images, and the subscript t to the acquisition time. Let $\mathbf{R}^{i\to j}$ be the rotation matrix from the coordinate system of camera i to that of camera j. We now turn to the learning of the individual components of $\mathbf{L}$.

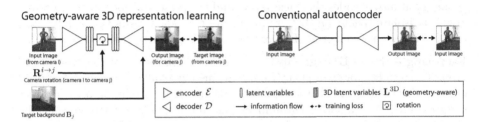

Fig. 2. Representation learning. We learn a representation that encodes geometry and thereby 3D pose information in an unsupervised manner. Our method (Left) extends a conventional auto encoder (Right) with a 3D latent space, rotation operation, and background fusion module. The 3D rotation enforces explicit encoding of 3D information. The background fusion enables application to natural images.

Learning to Encode Multi-view Geometry. For individual images, autoencoders such as the one shown on the right side of Fig. 2 have become standard tools to learn latent representations in unsupervised settings. Let such an autoencoder comprise an encoder $\mathcal{E}_{\theta_e}$ and a decoder $\mathcal{D}_{\theta_d}$, where θ_e and θ_d are the weights controlling their behaviors. For image representation purposes, an autoencoder can be used to encode an image $\mathbf{I}$ into a latent representation $\mathbf{L} = \mathcal{E}_{\theta_e}(\mathbf{I})$, which can then be decoded into a reconstructed image $\hat{\mathbf{I}} = \mathcal{D}_{\theta_d}(\mathbf{L})$. θ_e and θ_d are learned by minimizing $\|\mathbf{I} - \hat{\mathbf{I}}\|^2$ on average over a training set $\mathcal{U}$.

To leverage multi-view geometry, we take our inspiration from Novel View Synthesis methods [4,11,36,37,49] that rely on training encoder-decoders on multiple views of the same object, such as a car or a chair. Let $(\mathbf{I}_t^i, \mathbf{I}_t^j) \in \mathcal{U}$ be two images taken from different viewpoints but at the same time t. Since we are given the rotation matrix $\mathbf{R}^{i\to j}$ connecting the two viewpoints, we could feed this information as an additional input to the encoder and decoder and train them to encode $\mathbf{I}_t^i$ and resynthesize $\mathbf{I}_t^j$, as in [36,37]. Then, novel views of the object could be rendered by varying the rotation parameter $\mathbf{R}^{i\to j}$. However, this does not force the latent representation to encode 3D information explicitly. To this end, we model the latent representation $\mathbf{L}^{3D} \in \mathbb{R}^{3 \times N}$ as a set of N points in 3D space by designing the encoder $\mathcal{E}_{\theta_e}$ and decoder $\mathcal{D}_{\theta_e}$ so that they have a three channel output and input, respectively, as shown on the left side of Fig. 2. This enables us to model the view-change as a proper 3D rotation by matrix multiplication of the encoder output by the rotation matrix before using it as input to the decoder. Formally, the output of the resulting autoencoder $\mathcal{A}_{\theta_e,\theta_d}$ can be written as

$$\mathcal{A}_{\theta_e,\theta_d}(\mathbf{I}_t^i, \mathbf{R}^{i \to j}) = \mathcal{D}_{\theta_d}(\mathbf{R}^{i \to j} \mathbf{L}_{i,t}^{3D}), \text{ with } \mathbf{L}_{i,t}^{3D} = \mathcal{E}_{\theta_e}(\mathbf{I}_t^i) , \qquad (1)$$

and the weights θ_d and θ_e are optimized to minimize $\|\mathcal{A}_{\theta_e,\theta_d}(\mathbf{I}_t^i, \mathbf{R}^{i \to j}) - \mathbf{I}_t^j\|$ over the training set $\mathcal{U}$. In this setup, which was also used in [4,49] and is inspired by [11], the decoder $\mathcal{D}$ does not need to learn how to rotate the input to a new view but only how to decode the 3D latent vector $\mathbf{L}^{3D}$. This means that the encoder is forced to map to a proper 3D latent space, that is, one that can still be decoded by $\mathcal{D}$ after an arbitrary rotation. However, while $\mathbf{L}^{3D}$ now encodes multi-view geometry, it also encodes the background and the person's appearance. Our goal now is to isolate them from $\mathbf{L}^{3D}$ and to create two new vectors $\mathbf{B}$ and $\mathbf{L}^{app}$ that encode the latter two so that $\mathbf{L}^{3D}$ only represents geometry and 3D pose.

Factoring out the Background. Let us assume that we can construct background images $\mathbf{B}_j$, for example by taking the median of all the images taken from a given viewpoint j. To factor them out, we introduce in the decoder a direct connection to the target background $\mathbf{B}_j$, as shown in Fig. 2. More specifically, we concatenate the background image with the output of the decoder and use an additional 1×1 convolutional layer to synthesize the decoded image. This frees the rest of the network from having to learn about the background and ensures that the $\mathbf{L}^{3D}$ vector we learn does not contain information about it anymore.

Appearance representation learning

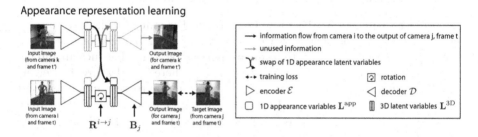

Fig. 3. Appearance representation learning. To encode subject identity, we split the latent space into a 3D geometry part and an appearance part. The latter is not rotated, but swapped between two time frames t and t' depicting the same subject, so as to enforce it not to contain geometric information.

Factoring out Appearance. To separate appearance from geometry in our latent representation, we break up the output of the encoder $\mathcal{E}$ into two separate vectors $\mathbf{L}^{3D}$ and $\mathbf{L}^{app}$ that should describe pose and appearance, respectively. To enforce this separation, we train simultaneously on two frames $\mathbf{I}_t$ and $\mathbf{I}_{t'}$ depicting the same subject at different times, t and t', as depicted in Fig. 3. While the decoder uses $\mathbf{L}_t^{3D}$ and $\mathbf{L}_{t'}^{3D}$, as before, it swaps $\mathbf{L}_t^{app}$ and $\mathbf{L}_{t'}^{app}$. In other words, the decoder uses $\mathbf{L}_t^{3D}$ and $\mathbf{L}_{t'}^{app}$ to resynthesize frame t and $\mathbf{L}_{t'}^{3D}$ and $\mathbf{L}_t^{app}$ for frame t'. Assuming that the person's appearance does not change drastically between t and t' and that differences in the images are caused by 3D pose changes, this results in $\mathbf{L}^{3D}$ encoding pose while $\mathbf{L}^{app}$ encodes appearance.

In practice, the encoder $\mathcal{E}$ has two outputs, that is, $\mathcal{E}_{\theta_e} : \mathbf{I}_t^i \rightarrow (\mathbf{L}_{i,t}^{3D}, \mathbf{L}_{i,t}^{app})$ and the decoder $\mathcal{D}_{\theta_d}$ accepts these plus the background as inputs, after swapping appearance and rotating the geometric representation for two views i and j. We therefore write the output of our encoder-decoder as

$$\mathcal{A}_{\theta_e,\theta_d}(\mathbf{I}_t^i, \mathbf{R}^{i\rightarrow j},\ \mathbf{L}_{k,t'}^{app}, \mathbf{B}_j) = \mathcal{D}_{\theta_d}(\mathbf{R}^{i\rightarrow j}\mathbf{L}_{i,t}^{3D}, \mathbf{L}_{k,t'}^{app}, \mathbf{B}_j) \ . \qquad (2)$$

The viewpoint k can be arbitrary. The critical point is that it was acquired at time $t' \neq t$ such that the poses at t and t' are uncorrelated. Thus, only time-invariant appearance features are encoded into $\mathbf{L}^{app}$. A similar exchange of information has been performed before in [28] for analogy transformations. It is related to works that separate facial identity, pose and illumination [17,26,51].

Combined Optimization. To train $\mathcal{A}$ with sequences featuring several people and backgrounds, we randomly select mini-batches of Z triplets $(\mathbf{I}_t^i, \mathbf{I}_t^j, \mathbf{I}_{t'}^k)$ in $\mathcal{U}$, with $t \neq t'$, from individual sequences. In other words, all three views feature the same person. The first two are taken at the same time but from different viewpoints. The third is taken at a different time and from an arbitrary viewpoint k. For each such mini-batch, we compute the loss

$$E_{\theta_d,\theta_e} = \frac{1}{Z} \sum_{\substack{\mathbf{I}_t^i,\mathbf{I}_t^j,\mathbf{I}_{t'}^k \in \mathcal{U} \\ t \neq t'}} \|\mathcal{A}_{\theta_e,\theta_d}(\mathbf{I}_t^i, \mathbf{R}^{i\rightarrow j}, \mathbf{L}_{k,t'}^{app},\ \mathbf{B}_j) - \mathbf{I}_t^j\| \ , \qquad (3)$$

where $\mathbf{L}_{k,t'} = (\mathbf{L}_{k,t'}^{3D}, \mathbf{L}_{k,t'}^{app})$ is the output of encoder $\mathcal{E}_{\theta_e}$ applied to image $\mathbf{I}_{t'}^k$, $\mathbf{B}_j$ is the background in view j, and $\mathbf{R}^{i\rightarrow j}$ denotes the rotation from view i to view j. Note that we apply $\mathcal{E}$ twice, to obtain $\mathbf{L}_{i,t}^{3D}$ and $\mathbf{L}_{k,t'}^{app}$ in Eq. 3 while ignoring $\mathbf{L}_{i,t}^{app}$ and $\mathbf{L}_{k,t'}^{3D}$ with the swap discussed above.

At training time, we minimize a total loss that is the sum of the pixel-wise error E_{θ_d,θ_e} of Eq. 3 and a second term obtained by first applying a Resnet with 18 layers trained on ImageNet on the output and target image and then computing the feature difference after the second block level, as previously done with VGG by [23]. All individual pixel and feature differences are averaged and their influence is balanced by weighting the feature loss by two. We experiment with L1 and L2 norms. The L1 norm in combination with the additional feature term allows for crisper decodings and improved pose reconstruction.

Translation and Augmentation. Object scale and translation in depth direction are inherently ambiguous for monocular reconstruction and NVS. To make our model invariant instead of ambiguous to these effects, we use the crop information provided in the training datasets. We compute the rotation between two views with respect to the crop center instead of the image center and shear the cropped image so that it appears as if it were taken from a virtual camera pointing in the crop direction. With the human in the same position and scale, these crops remove the need to model object and camera translation. We also apply random in-plane rotations to increase view diversity. As a result, $\mathbf{R}^{i\rightarrow j}$ and $\mathbf{B}_j$ depend on time t, but we neglect this in our notation for readability.

4   3D Human Pose Estimation

Recall that our ultimate goal is to infer the 3D pose of a person from a monocular image. Since $\mathbf{L}^{3D}$ can be rotated and used to generate novel views, we are already part way there. Being a $3 \times N$ matrix, it can be understood as a set of N 3D points, but these do not have any semantic meaning. However, in most practical applications, one has to infer a pre-defined representation, such as a skeleton with K major human body joints, encoded as a vector $\mathbf{p} \in \mathbb{R}^{3K}$.

To instantiate such a representation, we need a mapping $\mathcal{F} : \mathbf{L}^{3D} \rightarrow \mathbb{R}^{3K}$, which can be thought as a different decoder that reconstructs 3D poses instead of images. To learn it, we rely on supervision. However, as we will see in the results section, the necessary amount of human annotations is much smaller than what would have been required to learn the mapping directly from the images, as in many other recent approaches to human pose estimation.

Let $\mathcal{L} = \{(\mathbf{I}_t, \mathbf{p}_t)\}_{t=1}^{N_s}$ be a small set of N_s labeled examples made of image pairs and corresponding ground-truth 3D poses. We model $\mathcal{F}$ as a deep network with parameters θ_f. We train it by minimizing the objective function

$$E_{\theta_f} = \frac{1}{N_s} \sum_{t=1}^{N_s} \| \mathcal{F}_{\theta_f}(\mathbf{L}_t^{3D}) - \mathbf{p}_t \| , \text{ with } (\mathbf{L}_t^{3D}, \cdot) = \mathcal{E}_{\theta_e}(\mathbf{I}_t) . \tag{4}$$

Because our latent representation $\mathbf{L}^{3D}$ already encodes human 3D pose and shape, $\mathcal{F}$ can be implemented as a simple two-layer fully-connected network. Together with the encoder-decoder introduced in Sect. 3, which is trained in an unsupervised manner, they form the semi-supervised setup depicted by Fig. 1(b). In other words, our unsupervised representation does a lot of the hardwork in the difficult task of lifting the image to a 3D representation, which makes the final mapping comparatively easy.

5   Evaluation

In this section, we first evaluate our approach on the task of 3D human pose estimation, which is our main target application, and show that our representation enables us to use far less annotated training data than state-of-the-art approaches to achieve better accuracy. We then evaluate the quality of our latent space itself and show that it does indeed encode geometry, appearance, and background separately.

Dataset. We use the well-known Human3.6M (H36M) [12] dataset. It is recorded in a calibrated multi-view studio and ground-truth human poses are available for all frames. This makes it easy to compare different levels of supervision, unsupervised, semi-supervised, or fully supervised. As in previous approaches [22,27,31,42,54], we use the bounding boxes provided with the dataset to crop images.

5.1   Semi-supervised Human Pose Estimation

Our main focus is semi-supervised human pose estimation. We now demonstrate that, as shown in Fig. 4, recent state-of-the-art methods can do better than us when large amounts of annotated training data are available. However, as we use fewer and fewer of these annotations, the accuracy of the baselines suffers greatly whereas ours does not, which confers a significant advantage in situations where annotations are hard to obtain. We now explain in detail how the graphs of Fig. 4 were produced and further discuss their meaning.

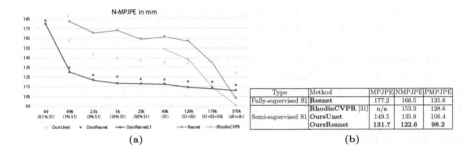

Type	Method	MPJPE	NMPJPE	PMPJPE
Fully-supervised S1	Resnet	177.2	166.5	135.6
	RhodinCVPR [31]	n/a	153.3	128.6
Semi-supervised S1	OursUnet	149.5	135.9	106.4
	OursResnet	131.7	122.6	98.2

(a)   (b)

Fig. 4. (a) Performance as function of the number of training samples. When using all the available annotated 3D data in H36M, that is, 370,000 images, **RhodinCVPR** and **Resnet** yield a better accuracy than our approach. However, when the number of training examples drops below 180'000 the baselines' accuracy degrades significantly, whereas **OursResnet** degrades much more gracefully and our accuracy becomes significantly better. (b) This improvement is consistent across metrics.

Metrics. We evaluate pose prediction accuracy in terms of the mean per joint prediction error (MPJPE), and its normalized variants N-MPJPE and P-MPJPE, where poses are aligned to the ground truth in the least-square sense either in scale only or in scale, rotation and translation, respectively, before computing the MPJPE. The latter is also known as Procrustes alignment. We do this over 16 major human joints and all positions are centered at the pelvis, as in [54]. Our results are consistent across all metrics, as shown in Fig. 4(b).

Baselines. We compare our approach against the state-of-the-art semi-supervised method of [31], which uses the same input as ours and outputs normalized poses. We will refer to it as **RhodinCVPR**. We also use the popular ResNet-based architecture [22] to regress directly from the image to the 3D pose, as shown in Fig. 1(c), we will refer to this as **Resnet**.

Note that even higher accuracies on H36M than those of **RhodinCVPR** and **Resnet** have been reported in the literature [20,24,27,38,54] but they depend both on more complex architectures and using additional information such as labeled 2D poses [20,22,38,54] or semantic segmentation [27], which is not our point here. We want to show that when using *only* 3D annotations and not many of them are available, our representation still allows us to perform well.

Implementation. We base our encoder-decoder architecture on the UNet [34] network, which was used to perform a similar task in [19]. We simply remove the skip connections to force the encoding of all information into the latent spaces and reduce the number of feature channels by half.

Concretely the encoder $\mathcal{E}$ consists of four blocks of two convolutions, where each two convolutions are followed by max pooling. The resulting convolutional features are of dimension $512 \times 16 \times 16$ for an input image resolution of 128×128 pixels. These are mapped to $\mathbf{L}^{app} \in \mathbb{R}^{128}$ and $\mathbf{L}^{3D} \in \mathbb{R}^{200 \times 3}$ by a single fully-connected layer followed by dropout with probability 0.3. The decoder $\mathcal{D}$ maps $\mathbf{L}^{3D}$ to a feature map of dimension $(512 - 128) \times 16 \times 16$ with a fully-connected layer followed by ReLU and dropout and duplicates $\mathbf{L}^{app}$ to form a spatial uniform map of size $128 \times 16 \times 16$. These two maps are concatenated and then reconstructed by four blocks of two convolutions, where the first convolution is preceded by bilinear interpolation and all other pairs by up-convolutions. Each convolution is followed by batch-normalization and ReLU activation functions. We also experimented with a variant in which the encoder $\mathcal{E}$ is an off-the shelf Resnet with fifty layers [10], pre-trained on ImageNet, and the decoder is the same as before. We will refer to these two versions as **OursUnet** and **OursResnet**, respectively.

The pose decoder $\mathcal{F}$ is a fully-connected network with two hidden layers of dimension 2048. The ground-truth poses in the least-squares loss of Eq. 4 are defined as root-centered 3D poses. Poses and images are normalized by their mean and standard deviation on the training set. We use mini-batches of size 32 and the Adam optimizer with learning rate 10^{-3} for optimization of θ_e, θ_d and θ_f.

Dataset Splits. On H36M, we take the unlabeled set $\mathcal{U}$ used to learn our representation to be the complete training set—S1, S5, S6, S7 and S8, where SN refers to all sequences of the Nth subject—but without the available 3D labels. To provide the required supervision to train the shallow network of Fig. 1(b), we then define several scenarios.

- Fully supervised training with the 3D annotation of all five training subjects.
- We use all the 3D annotations for S1; S1 and S5; or S1, S5 and S6.
- We use only 50%, 10%, 5%, 1% or 0.1% of the 3D annotations for S1.

In all cases we used S9 and S11 for testing. We subsampled the test and training videos at 10ps to reduce redundancy and validation time. The resulting numbers of annotated images we used are shown along the x-axis of Fig. 4.

Comparison to the State of the Art. RhodinCVPR is the only method that is designed to leverage unlabeled multi-view footage without using a supplemental 2D dataset [31]. **OursUnet** outperforms it significantly, e.g., on labeled subject S1 by 13.6 mm (8.9% relative improvement) and **OursResnetL1** even attains a gain of 35.7 mm (23.3% relative improvement). The fact that the Resnet architecture, training procedure, and dataset split is the same for our method and **RhodinCVPR** evidences that this gain is due to our new way of exploiting the unlabeled examples, thus showing the effectiveness of learning a geometry-aware latent representation in an unsupervised manner.

Discussion and Ablation Study. As shown in Fig. 4, when more than 300,000 annotated images are used the baselines outperform us. However, their accuracy decreases rapidly when fewer are available and our approach then starts dominating. It only loses accuracy very slowly down to 5,000 images and still performs adequately given only 500.

We used the L2 loss in Eq. 3 by default since our main goal is 3D pose estimation, not NVS quality. Interestingly, however, using the L1 loss makes reconstructions not only crisper but also 3D poses estimates more accurate. It improves pose accuracy consistently by about 5%, shown as **OursResnetL1** in Fig. 4. Unless indicated otherwise, all results are produced with the L2 metric.

To better evaluate different aspects of our approach, we use the **OursUnet** version to conduct an ablation study whose results we report in Table 1. In short, not separating the background and appearance latent spaces reduces N-MPJPE by 14 mm and P-MPJPE by more than 12 mm. Using two hidden layers in $\mathcal{F}$ instead of one increases accuracy by 12 mm. The loss term based on ResNet-18 features not only leads to crisper NVS results but also improves pose estimation by 9 mm. Using bilinear upsampling instead of deconvolution for all decoding layers reduces performance by 4 mm. The largest decrease in accuracy by far, 46.1 mm, occurs when we use our standard **OursUnet** architecture but *without* our geometry-aware 3D latent space. It appears in the last line of the table on the left and strongly suggests that using our latent representation has more impact than tweaking the architecture in various ways.

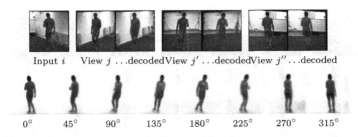

Input i View j ...decodedView j' ...decodedView j'' ...decoded

0°   45°   90°   135°   180°   225°   270°   315°

Fig. 5. Novel viewpoint synthesis. Top row. Each one of the three image pairs of image to the left of it comprise an original image acquired from a different viewpoint and the image synthesized from the input image i. Bottom row. We can also synthesize images for previously unseen viewpoints and remove the background.

Table 1. Ablation study, using S1 for semi-supervised training. The extensions to the NVS methods [36,37] and [4,49] as well as further model choices improve accuracy.

Method	N-MPJPE	P-MPJPE	Method	N-MPJPE	P-MPJPE
OursUnet*	145.6	112.2	OursUnet*	145.6	112.2
OursUnet*, w/o appearance space, as in [4,49]	159.0	117.1	OursUnet*, bilinear upsampling	149.2	114.1
OursUnet*, w/o background handling, as in [4,49]	159.6	124.6	OursUnet*, w/o ImgNet loss	154.1	118.7
OursUnet*, w/o 3D latent space, as in [36,37]	191.7	139.0	OursUnet*, $\mathcal{F}$ with 1 hidden layer	157.4	121.9

* no rotation augmentation. Errors are reported in mm.

5.2   Evaluating the Latent Representation Qualitatively

We now turn to evaluating the quality of our latent representation as such with a number of experiments on **OursUnet**. We show that geometry can be separated from appearance and background and that this improves results. The quality of the synthesized images is best seen in the supplemental videos.

Novel View Synthesis. Recall from Sect. 3 that $\mathcal{E}$ encodes the image into variables $\mathbf{L}^{3D}$ and $\mathbf{L}^{app}$, which are meant to represent geometry and appearance, respectively. To check that this is indeed the case, we multiply $\mathbf{L}^{3D}$ by different rotation matrices $\mathbf{R}$ and feed the result along with the original $\mathbf{L}^{app}$ to $\mathcal{D}$. Figure 5 depicts such synthesized novel views.

For comparison purposes, in Fig. 6, we synthesize rotated images without using our geometry-aware latent space, that is, as in [37]. The resulting images are far blurrier than those of **OursResnet**. Figure 6 further shows that results degrade without the background handling, that is, as in [4,11,49]. Using the L1 instead of L1 loss further improves reconstruction quality. Test subjects wear clothes that differ in color and shape from those seen in the training data. As a result, the geometry in the synthesized images remains correct, but the appearance ends up being a mixture of training appearances that approximates the unseen appearance. Arguably, using more than the five subjects that appear in the training set should result in a better encoding of appearance, which is something we plan to investigate in future work.

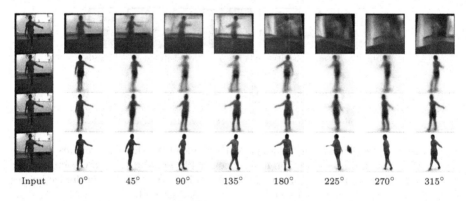

| Input | 0° | 45° | 90° | 135° | 180° | 225° | 270° | 315° |

Fig. 6. Ablation study. First row. Without background handling, as used in [4,49], the synthesized foreground pose appears fuzzy. Second row. Without a geometry-aware latent space, as used by [36,37], results are inaccurate and blurred in new views. Third row. **OursResnet** captures pose and appearance accurately, but contours are still blurred. Fourth row. **OursResnetL1** produces crisper and more accurate results.

Appearance and Background Switching. Let $\mathbf{I}_j$ and $\mathbf{I}_g$ be two images of subjects j and g and $(\mathbf{L}_j^{3D}, \mathbf{L}_j^{app}, \mathbf{B}_j) = \mathcal{E}(\mathbf{I}_j)$ and $(\mathbf{L}_g^{3D}, \mathbf{L}_g^{app}, \mathbf{B}_g) = \mathcal{E}(\mathbf{I}_g)$ their encodings. Re-encoding using $\mathbf{L}^{3D}$ of one and $\mathbf{L}^{app}$ of the other yields results

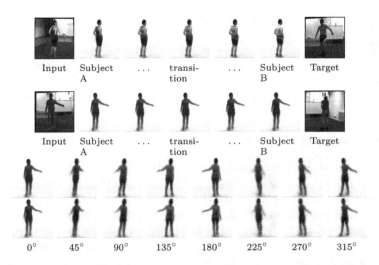

Fig. 7. Appearance separation. Top two rows. The same pose can be decoded to different identities by blending the appearance latent vectors. In the first row, both subjects appear in the training set. In the second row, they are from the test set. Bottom two rows. We generate rotated views of the test subject and its transferred appearance, to demonstrate that appearance can be changed without affecting 3D pose.

such as those depicted by Fig. 7. Note that the appearance of one is correctly transferred to the pose of the other while the geometry remains intact under rotation. This method could be used to generate additional training data, by changing the appearance of an existing multi-view sequence to synthesize images of the same motion being performed by multiple actors.

Similarly, we can switch backgrounds instead of appearances before decoding the latent vectors, as shown in Fig. 8. In one case, we make the background white and in the other we use a natural scene. In the first case, dark patches are visible below the subject, evidently modeling shadowing effects that were learned implicitly. In the second case, the green trees tend to be rendered as orange because our training scenes were mostly reddish—problem a larger training database would almost certainly cure.

Fig. 8. Background separation. The background is handled separately from the foreground an can be chosen arbitrary at decoding time. From left to right, input image, decoded on the input background, on a novel view, on a white, and on a picture. The first row features someone from the training set and the second row from the test set.

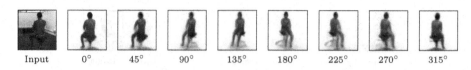

| Input | 0° | 45° | 90° | 135° | 180° | 225° | 270° | 315° |

Fig. 9. Foreground objects are reconstructed too, if seen in training and testing.

5.3 Generalization and Limitations

To analyze the scalability of the unsupervised training we tested using only four out of the five unsupervised training subjects. The additional subject improves OurResnet drastically by 16 N-MPJPE. This indicates that training is not yet saturated and much higher accuracies seem possible by leveraging huge unsupervised sets. These, be it indoors or outdoors, are relatively easy to obtain.

In the data we used, some of the images contain a chair on which the subject sits. Interestingly, as shown in Fig. 9, the chair appearance and 3D position is faithfully reconstructed by our method. This suggests that it is not specific to human poses and can generalize to rigid objects as well as multiple object classes. In future work, we intend to apply it to such more generic problems.

We further tested our method on the MPI-INF-3DHP (3DHP) [21] dataset, which features more diverse clothing and viewpoints, such as low-hanging and ceiling cameras, and is therefore well suited to probe extreme conditions for NVS. Without changing any parameter, **OursResnet** is able to synthesis view transformations in roll, yaw and pitch, as shown in Fig. 10. On H36M, pitch transformation could not be learned due to the solely chest-height training views.

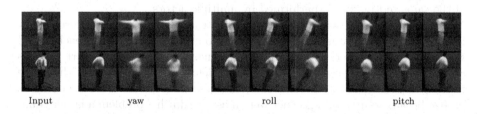

| Input | yaw | roll | pitch |

Fig. 10. Generalization on 3DHP. Our NVS solution generalizes well to the different camera placements in 3DHP, allowing for yaw, pitch and roll transformations.

6   Conclusion

We have introduced an approach to learning a geometry-aware representation of the human body in an unsupervised manner, given only multi-view imagery. Our experiments have shown that this representation is effective both as an intermediate one for 3D pose estimation and for novel view synthesis. For pose estimation, our semi-supervised approach performs much better than state-of-the-art methods when only very little annotated data is available. In future work, we will extend its range by learning an equivalent latent representation for much larger multi-view datasets but still in an unsupervised manner.

Acknowledgment. This work was supported in part by a Microsoft Joint Research Project.

References

1. Bas, A., Huber, P., Smith, W., Awais, M., Kittler, J.: 3D morphable models as spatial transformer networks. arXiv Preprint (2017)
2. Chen, W., et al.: Synthesizing training images for boosting human 3D pose estimation. In: 3DV (2016)
3. Chen, X., Duan, Y., Houthooft, R., Schulman, J., Sutskever, I., Abbeel, P.: Infogan: interpretable representation learning by information maximizing generative adversarial nets. In: Advances in Neural Information Processing Systems, pp. 2172–2180 (2016)
4. Cohen, T., Welling, M.: Transformation properties of learned visual representations. arXiv Preprint (2014)
5. Dosovitskiy, A., Springenberg, J., Brox, T.: Learning to generate chairs with convolutional neural networks. In: Conference on Computer Vision and Pattern Recognition (2015)
6. Dosovitskiy, A., Springenberg, J., Tatarchenko, M., Brox, T.: Learning to generate chairs, tables and cars with convolutional networks. IEEE Trans. Pattern Anal. Mach. Intell. **39**(4), 692–705 (2017)
7. Flynn, J., Neulander, I., Philbin, J., Snavely, N.: Deepstereo: learning to predict new views from the world's imagery. In: Conference on Computer Vision and Pattern Recognition, pp. 5515–5524 (2016)
8. Gadelha, M., Maji, S., Wang, R.: 3D shape induction from 2D views of multiple objects. arXiv preprint arXiv:1612.05872 (2016)
9. Grant, E., Kohli, P., van Gerven, M.: Deep disentangled representations for volumetric reconstruction. In: Hua, G., Jégou, H. (eds.) ECCV 2016. LNCS, vol. 9915, pp. 266–279. Springer, Cham (2016). https://doi.org/10.1007/978-3-319-49409-8_22
10. He, K., Zhang, X., Ren, S., Sun, J.: Deep residual learning for image recognition. In: CVPR, pp. 770–778 (2016)
11. Hinton, G., Krizhevsky, A., Wang, S.: Transforming auto-encoders. In: International Conference on Artificial Neural Networks, pp. 44–51 (2011)
12. Ionescu, C., Carreira, J., Sminchisescu, C.: Iterated second-order label sensitive pooling for 3D human pose estimation. In: Conference on Computer Vision and Pattern Recognition (2014)
13. Ionescu, C., Papava, I., Olaru, V., Sminchisescu, C.: Human3.6M: large scale datasets and predictive methods for 3D human sensing in natural environments. IEEE Trans. Pattern Anal. Mach. Intell. **36**, 1325–1339 (2014)
14. Joo, H., et al.: Panoptic studio: a massively multiview system for social motion capture. In: International Conference on Computer Vision (2015)
15. Kar, A., Häne, C., Malik, J.: Learning a multi-view stereo machine. In: Advances in Neural Information Processing Systems, pp. 364–375 (2017)
16. Kim, H., Zollhöfer, M., Tewari, A., Thies, J., Richardt, C., Theobalt, C.: Inverse-facenet: deep single-shot inverse face rendering from a single image. arXiv Preprint (2017)

17. Kulkarni, T.D., Whitney, W., Kohli, P., Tenenbaum, J.B.: Deep Convolutional Inverse Graphics Network. arXiv (2015)
18. Lassner, C., Pons-Moll, G., Gehler, P.: A generative model of people in clothing. arXiv Preprint (2017)
19. Ma, L., Jia, X., Sun, Q., Schiele, B., Tuytelaars, T., Gool, L.V.: Pose guided person image generation. In: Advances in Neural Information Processing Systems, pp. 405–415 (2017)
20. Martinez, J., Hossain, R., Romero, J., Little, J.: A simple yet effective baseline for 3D human pose estimation. In: International Conference on Computer Vision (2017)
21. Mehta, D., et al.: Monocular 3D human pose estimation in the wild using improved CNN supervision. In: International Conference on 3D Vision (2017)
22. Mehta, D., et al.: Vnect: real-time 3D human pose estimation with a single RGB camera. In: ACM SIGGRAPH (2017)
23. Park, E., Yang, J., Yumer, E., Ceylan, D., Berg, A.: Transformation-grounded image generation network for novel 3D view synthesis. In: Conference on Computer Vision and Pattern Recognition, pp. 702–711 (2017)
24. Pavlakos, G., Zhou, X., Derpanis, K., Konstantinos, G., Daniilidis, K.: Coarse-to-fine volumetric prediction for single-image 3D human pose. In: Conference on Computer Vision and Pattern Recognition (2017)
25. Pavlakos, G., Zhou, X., Konstantinos, K.D.G., Kostas, D.: Harvesting multiple views for marker-less 3D human pose annotations. In: Conference on Computer Vision and Pattern Recognition (2017)
26. Peng, X., Feris, R.S., Wang, X., Metaxas, D.N.: A recurrent encoder-decoder network for sequential face alignment. In: Leibe, B., Matas, J., Sebe, N., Welling, M. (eds.) ECCV 2016. LNCS, vol. 9905, pp. 38–56. Springer, Cham (2016). https://doi.org/10.1007/978-3-319-46448-0_3
27. Popa, A.I., Zanfir, M., Sminchisescu, C.: Deep multitask architecture for integrated 2D and 3D human sensing. In: Conference on Computer Vision and Pattern Recognition (2017)
28. Reed, S., Zhang, Y., Zhang, Y., Lee, H.: Deep visual analogy-making. In: Advances in Neural Information Processing Systems, pp. 1252–1260 (2015)
29. Rezende, D., Eslami, S., Mohamed, S., Battaglia, P., Jaderberg, M., Heess, N.: Unsupervised learning of 3D structure from images. In: Advances in Neural Information Processing Systems, pp. 4996–5004 (2016)
30. Rhodin, H., et al.: Egocap: egocentric marker-less motion capture with two fisheye cameras. ACM SIGGRAPH Asia 35(6), 162 (2016)
31. Rhodin, H., et al.: Learning monocular 3D human pose estimation from multi-view images. In: Conference on Computer Vision and Pattern Recognition (2018)
32. Rogez, G., Schmid, C.: Mocap guided data augmentation for 3D pose estimation in the wild. In: Advances in Neural Information Processing Systems (2016)
33. Rogez, G., Weinzaepfel, P., Schmid, C.: LCR-Net: localization-classification-regression for human pose. In: Conference on Computer Vision and Pattern Recognition (2017)
34. Ronneberger, O., Fischer, P., Brox, T.: U-Net: convolutional networks for biomedical image segmentation. In: Conference on Medical Image Computing and Computer Assisted Intervention (2015)
35. Shu, Z., Yumer, E., Hadap, S., Sunkavalli, K., Shechtman, E., Samaras, D.: Neural face editing with intrinsic image disentangling. In: Conference on Computer Vision and Pattern Recognition (2017)

36. Tatarchenko, M., Dosovitskiy, A., Brox, T.: Single-view to multi-view: reconstructing unseen views with a convolutional network. CoRR abs/1511.06702 **1**, 2 (2015)
37. Tatarchenko, M., Dosovitskiy, A., Brox, T.: Multi-view 3D models from single images with a convolutional network. In: Leibe, B., Matas, J., Sebe, N., Welling, M. (eds.) ECCV 2016. LNCS, vol. 9911, pp. 322–337. Springer, Cham (2016). https://doi.org/10.1007/978-3-319-46478-7_20
38. Tekin, B., Márquez-neila, P., Salzmann, M., Fua, P.: Learning to fuse 2D and 3D image cues for monocular body pose estimation. In: International Conference on Computer Vision (2017)
39. Tewari, A., et al.: Mofa: model-based deep convolutional face autoencoder for unsupervised monocular reconstruction. In: International Conference on Computer Vision (2017)
40. Thewlis, J., Bilen, H., Vedaldi, A.: Unsupervised learning of object frames by dense equivariant image labelling. In: Advances in Neural Information Processing Systems, pp. 844–855 (2017)
41. Thewlis, J., Bilen, H., Vedaldi, A.: Unsupervised learning of object landmarks by factorized spatial embeddings. In: International Conference on Computer Vision (2017)
42. Tome, D., Russell, C., Agapito, L.: Lifting from the deep: convolutional 3D pose estimation from a single image. arXiv preprint, arXiv:1701.00295 (2017)
43. Tran, L., Yin, X., Liu, X.: Disentangled representation learning gan for pose-invariant face recognition. In: CVPR, vol. 3, p. 7 (2017)
44. Tulsiani, S., Efros, A., Malik, J.: Multi-view consistency as supervisory signal for learning shape and pose prediction. arXiv Preprint (2018)
45. Tulsiani, S., Zhou, T., Efros, A., Malik, J.: Multi-view supervision for single-view reconstruction via differentiable ray consistency. In: Conference on Computer Vision and Pattern Recognition, vol. 1, p. 3 (2017)
46. Tung, H.Y., Harley, A., Seto, W., Fragkiadaki, K.: Adversarial inverse graphics networks: learning 2D-to-3D lifting and image-to-image translation from unpaired supervision. In: The IEEE International Conference on Computer Vision (ICCV), vol. 2 (2017)
47. Tung, H.Y., Tung, H.W., Yumer, E., Fragkiadaki, K.: Self-supervised learning of motion capture. In: Advances in Neural Information Processing Systems, pp. 5242–5252 (2017)
48. Varol, G., et al.: Learning from synthetic humans. In: Conference on Computer Vision and Pattern Recognition (2017)
49. Worrall, D., Garbin, S., Turmukhambetov, D., Brostow, G.: Interpretable transformations with encoder-decoder networks. In: International Conference on Computer Vision, vol. 4 (2017)
50. Yan, X., Yang, J., Yumer, E., Guo, Y., Lee, H.: Perspective transformer nets: learning single-view 3D object reconstruction without 3D supervision. In: Advances in Neural Information Processing Systems, pp. 1696–1704 (2016)
51. Yang, J., Reed, S., Yang, M.H., Lee, H.: Weakly-supervised disentangling with recurrent transformations for 3D view synthesis. In: Advances in Neural Information Processing Systems, pp. 1099–1107 (2015)
52. Zhao, B., Wu, X., Cheng, Z.Q., Liu, H., Feng, J.: Multi-view image generation from a single-view. arXiv preprint arXiv:1704.04886 (2017)
53. Zhou, T., Tulsiani, S., Sun, W., Malik, J., Efros, A.A.: View synthesis by appearance flow. In: Leibe, B., Matas, J., Sebe, N., Welling, M. (eds.) ECCV 2016. LNCS, vol. 9908, pp. 286–301. Springer, Cham (2016). https://doi.org/10.1007/978-3-319-46493-0_18

54. Zhou, X., Huang, Q., Sun, X., Xue, X., We, Y.: Weakly-supervised transfer for 3D human pose estimation in the wild. arXiv Preprint (2017)
55. Zhou, X., Karpur, A., Gan, C., Luo, L., Huang, Q.: Unsupervised domain adaptation for 3D keypoint prediction from a single depth scan. arXiv preprint arXiv:1712.05765 (2017)
56. Zhu, J.Y., Park, T., Isola, P., Efros, A.: Unpaired image-to-image translation using cycle-consistent adversarial networks. arXiv preprint arXiv:1703.10593 (2017)

Dual-Agent Deep Reinforcement Learning for Deformable Face Tracking

Minghao Guo, Jiwen Lu$^{(\boxtimes)}$, and Jie Zhou

Tsinghua University, Beijing, China
guomh2014@gmail.com,{lujiwen,jzhou}@tsinghua.edu.cn

Abstract. In this paper, we propose a dual-agent deep reinforcement learning (DADRL) method for deformable face tracking, which generates bounding boxes and detects facial landmarks *interactively* from face videos. Most existing deformable face tracking methods learn models for these two tasks individually, and perform these two procedures subsequently during the testing phase, which ignore the intrinsic connections of these two tasks. Motivated by the fact that the performance of facial landmark detection depends heavily on the accuracy of the generated bounding boxes, we exploit the interactions of these two tasks in probabilistic manner by following a Bayesian model and propose a unified framework for simultaneous bounding box tracking and landmark detection. By formulating it as a Markov decision process, we define two agents to exploit the relationships and pass messages via an adaptive sequence of actions under a deep reinforcement learning framework to iteratively adjust the positions of the bounding boxes and facial landmarks. Our proposed DADRL achieves performance improvements over the state-of-the-art deformable face tracking methods on the most challenging category of the 300-VW dataset.

Keywords: Deformable face tracking · Reinforcement learning
Deep learning

1 Introduction

Deformable face tracking has received considerable attention in computer vision recently with numerous applications such as human computer interaction, facial expression analysis, and person identification. The aim of deformable face tracking is to detect the key points around facial components and facial contours across all frames of a given face video. It is a challenging problem in practice because face samples are usually captured in unconstrained conditions, where large poses, heavy occlusions, illumination variations and motion artifacts usually occur.

Over the past decade, many efforts [1–3] have been devoted to this problem, which usually employ a "tracking-by-detection" strategy to perform deformable face tracking in a *serial* manner. Specifically, these methods first generate a

© Springer Nature Switzerland AG 2018
V. Ferrari et al. (Eds.): ECCV 2018, LNCS 11214, pp. 783–799, 2018.
https://doi.org/10.1007/978-3-030-01249-6_47

high-scored bounding box covering a face region, and then apply face alignment to localize facial landmarks based on the bounding box. Hence, face alignment depends heavily on the generated bounding box. Figure 1(a) shows an example to illustrate the effect of face box generation for facial landmark detection. We see that the bias from the ground-truth bounding box affects the alignment accuracy heavily because the bounding box is generated without considering the face conditions of pose and expression. Especially when face undergoes extreme conditions, the facial region selected by the bounding box usually misses facial landmarks, resulting in limited performance of face alignment. A desirable deformable face tracking approach is to exploit the rich interaction between face bounding box generation and face alignment. Since facial landmarks can effectively represent face pose across frames, they can provide auxiliary information for accurate bounding box generation. However, most existing deformable face tracking methods ignore such interaction, which results in low accuracy fitting for extreme conditions.

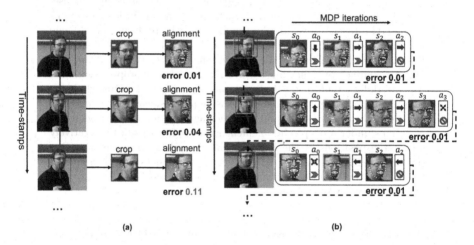

Fig. 1. (a) Existing "tracking-by-detection" methods [1–3] produce deformable face tracking in a *serial* manner. (b) Our DADRL method formulates deformable face tracking as a Markov decision process (MDP) problem, and produces bounding box tracking and landmark detection in an *interactive* manner. Here s_i denotes the MDP state, a_i denotes the MDP action. The dash line represents that initial bounding box of the current frame is the tracked box of previous frame. The blue color and the gray color denote the tracking agent action and the alignment agent action respectively (best viewed in color). (Color figure online)

In this work, we propose a dual-agent deep reinforcement learning (DADRL) method for deformable face tracking, which performs bounding box generation and facial landmark detection in *interactive* manner. Specifically, we exploit the interaction of these two procedures in probabilistic manner by following a Bayesian model. Unlike existing deformable face tracking methods which directly infer the decomposed form of joint probability for bounding boxes and facial landmarks, we train these two models to learn two conditional distributions simultaneously. Then, the connections between these two tasks are formulated as two marginal distributions, and their correlation is explicitly modeled with learnable parameters. Motivated by the observation that the face tracking complexity varies across frames, our method utilizes reinforcement learning as a principled way to learn how to make adaptive decisions during deformable face tracking. We formulate this sequential procedure as a Markov decision process, which models bounding box generation and face alignment as two agents. These dual agents predict a variable-length sequence of actions to position updates of bounding boxes and landmarks. Experiment results show that our proposed DADRL achieves large performance improvements over the state-of-the-art deformable face tracking methods on the 300-VW dataset [4].

2   Related Work

Deformable Face Tracking: Deformable face tracking focuses on tracking a set of facial landmarks across all frames of a given face video. Existing deformable face tracking methods can be mainly classified into two categories: pure shape tracking methods and tracking-by-detection methods. Methods of first category [5–8] perform face detection in the first frame of each face video and then conduct facial landmark localization at each consecutive frame by using the alignment result of the previous frame as the initialization. Based on this fundamental process, recent works focus on exploiting the temporal dependency relationship of landmarks across different frames. For example, the recurrent encoder-decoder network [7] consists of a sequence of spatial and temporal recurrences. The two-stream transformer networks [8] captures both spatial and temporal information by using a couple of networks. These methods partially handle the large variations of pose and expression across the whole video, because the motion between two adjacent frames is usually small. However, these methods struggle with the drifting drawback, as the error accumulates through time across the whole video. Methods in the second category [1,3,9–12] apply face detection/tracking and facial landmark localization successively at each frame, which are also similar to most existing image-based face alignment methods [7,13–18]. While these methods eliminate drifting to some extent, these two models are trained individually and utilized in a serial manner. As a result, the performance of face alignment is restricted, which may cause low accuracy fittings under a poor generated bounding box. To address this, Khan *et al.* [19] proposed a synergistic approach to perform landmark localization by using different detection and tracking initializations, which partially utilizes the correlation between the bounding box generation and the face alignment. However, they only employed a separate tracking model to generate bounding boxes, which is not optimized together with the alignment model during training.

Deep Reinforcement Learning: Reinforcement learning has been originated from humans' decision making process [20], which aims to enable the agent to make decisions from its experiences. Deep reinforcement learning, which is a combination of deep learning and reinforcement learning, can be divided into two classes: deep Q learning [21–23] and policy gradient [24,25]. The goal of deep Q Networks is to learn a state-action value function given by a deep network. Policy gradient methods learn the policy which maximizes the expected future reward using gradient descent. Recently deep reinforcement learning has gained great successes in several computer vision applications. For example, Rao et al. [26] proposed an attention-aware deep reinforcement learning method for keyframe selection in video face recognition. Yu et al. [27] proposed a sequence generative adversarial networks via policy gradient. Yoo et al. [28] proposed a sequential visual tracker learned by policy gradient. Foerster et al. [29] and Sukhbaatar et al. [30] proposed multi-agent deep reinforcement learning methods to communicate message between different agents. Kong et al. [31] proposed a collaborative algorithm to localize multiple objects via multi-agent reinforcement learning. Unlike these methods which have a common network architecture, we propose a dual-agent deep reinforcement learning (DADRL) method which is equipped with a dual-agent process: face bounding box generation and facial landmark detection.

3   Approach

In this section, we first present the Bayesian formulation of deformable face tracking to introduce the dual learning scheme. Then we propose the settings of Markov decision process (MDP) to show how to utilize deep reinforcement learning. Lastly, we detail the architecture of the proposed DADRL and the training procedure.

3.1   Problem Formulation

Suppose we have a face video consisting of K frames, $\{I_k\}_{k=1:K}$. For the k-th frame $I_k \in \mathbb{R}^{w \times h \times 3}$, we have the tracked bounding box $B_{k-1} \in \mathbb{R}^{2 \times 2}$ and the shape vector with L landmarks $V_{k-1} \in \mathbb{R}^{L \times 2}$ of previous frame. The purpose of deformable face tracking is to predict the bounding box B_k and facial shape V_k for the current frame I_k. This task aims to learn a joint probability of face bounding box generation and face landmark detection. Following the Bayesian formulation, the joint probability are derived as follows:

$$p(B_k, V_k | I_k, B_{k-1}, V_{k-1}) = p(B_k | I_k, B_{k-1}, V_{k-1}) p(V_k | B_k, I_k, B_{k-1}, V_{k-1}) \quad (1)$$

Since the joint probability $p(x, y)$ can be computed in two equivalent ways: $p(x, y) = p(x)p(y|x) = p(y)p(x|y)$, ideally the conditional probabilities in deformable face tracking problem should satisfy the following equality (we omit B_{k-1}, V_{k-1} for simplicity):

$$p(B_k | I_k) p(V_k | B_k, I_k) = p(V_k | I_k) p(B_k | V_k, I_k) \quad (2)$$

We call this *probabilistic duality*, which is a necessary condition for the optimality of the learned dual models.

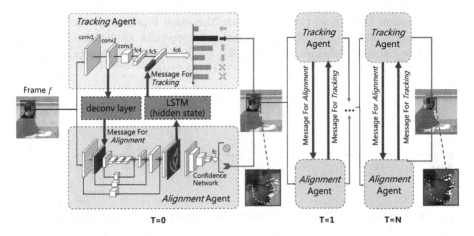

Fig. 2. The architecture of our proposed DADRL. Our DADRL consists of two agents: a tracking agent and an alignment agent. Each agent has a discrete action set. The communicated messages are encoded by a deconvolution layer and a LSTM unit, respectively. These two agents decide a sequence of actions to adjust the target face's bounding box and regress the facial landmarks simultaneously. The agents go to the next frame until the detected facial landmarks are finalized. Note that, T denotes the iteration number of MDP, rather than time-stamps number of the video.

Most existing deformable face tracking methods model the joint probability as the decomposed form in Eq. 1. Since these two models are learned individually, there is no guarantee that the probabilistic duality will hold. To tackle this problem, we propose to explicitly reinforce the empirical probabilistic duality of these two models. We consider the learning objectives of bounding box generation and facial landmark detection as two conditional probabilities. Then the connections between these two tasks can be formulated as two marginal distributions. To satisfy the probabilistic duality during the training, one possible solution is to design a term in the loss function as an appropriate constraint, such as the regularization term in [32], and train the dual models by using standard supervised learning techniques. However, as the ground-truth marginal distributions are not available, the empirical marginal distributions are usually utilized to fulfill the constraint. This is a sub-optimal strategy as the marginal distributions are fixed during training.

Inspired by the observation that marginal distributions should be learned, we propose a deep reinforcement learning framework for deformable face tracking. These two tasks are considered as dual agents. The communicated messages between them are regarded as alternatives of two marginal distributions to satisfy the probabilistic duality. The learning of message channels is facilitated by using the deep Q-learning algorithm.

Our proposed DADRL is different from the following two learning schemes, as illustrated Fig. 3: (1) Tracking-by-detection focuses on single-task learning which has no guarantee to hold the probabilistic duality; (2) Multi-task learning has an assumption that these two tasks share the same input space and coherent feature representation, which is too strong in practical application. Different from these learning schemes, our DADRL disentangles the connection of two tasks and explicitly exploits the synergy between them.

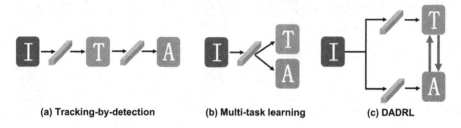

(a) Tracking-by-detection   (b) Multi-task learning   (c) DADRL

Fig. 3. Comparisons of three strategies for deformable face tracking. I, T, and A denote an image frame, bounding box tracking, and face alignment, respectively. (a) Tracking-by-detection processes deformable face tracking in a serial manner, which has no guarantee to hold the probabilistic duality. (b) Multi-task learning assumes that two tasks share the same input space and coherent feature representation, which is too strong in many real applications. (c) Our DADRL explicitly exploits the synergy between these two tasks.

3.2   Dual-Agent Deep Reinforcement Learning

Our DADRL consists of two agents: a tracking agent and an alignment agent. Each agent has a discrete action set. The basic pipeline is as follows: for each frame in the video, firstly the state is initialized by the terminal state of the previous frame. Then, based on the observed state and the received message, these two agents decide a sequence of actions to adjust the target face's bounding box and regress facial landmark coordinates simultaneously. Lastly, the agents go to the next frame until the detected facial landmarks are finalized. Figure 2 illustrates the pipeline of our method.

We formulate our strategy as MDP for each frame in the video. We start by introducing the state definition, which is shared by two agents, followed by the other respective definitions of two agents. We omit the subscript k when we describe MDP in each frame for simplicity.

State: s_t is defined as the current image region extracted by the bounding box, which is resized to a fixed size. Given the frame I and the current bounding box B, the state s_t is formulated as follows:

$$s_t = \phi(B, I) \tag{3}$$

where ϕ denotes the patch-extracting function.

Action: Based on the state s_t, each agent outputs an action a_t. There are totally eight types of actions for two agents, including *movement* actions and *stop/continue* actions, as shown in Fig. 4.

Tracking Agent: The tracking agent aims to produce *movement* actions to change the current observed region. Specifically, the set of actions are defined as: $\{left, right, up, down, scale\,up, scale\,down\}$.

Alignment Agent: The alignment agent produces *stop/continue* actions to determine whether the iteration should be terminated. Thus, the termination of the search process is in light of face alignment quality, rather than the tracked bounding box result.

Fig. 4. The defined actions of two agents. Left: *movement* actions for the tracking agent. Right: *stop/continue* actions for the alignment agent.

State Transition: Having decided the action at the state s_t, the next state s_{t+1} is obtained by the state transition function.

Tracking Agent: For the *movement* actions of the tracking agent, the new state s_{t+1} is obtained by shifting the bounding box with a discrete change, which is relative to the current size of the bounding box as follows:

$$\delta_w = \alpha(x_2 - x_1), \quad \delta_h = \alpha(y_2 - y_1) \tag{4}$$

where $\alpha \in [0, 1]$ denotes a scale vector, $\{x_1, y_1, x_2, y_2\}$ denotes the bounding box coordinates of top-left and bottom-right vertices. The bounding box B is updated by adding or removing δ_w or δ_h to the coordinates according to the output action. For example, if $left$ action is selected, the position of B moves to $\{x_1 - \delta_w, y_1, x_2 - \delta_w, y_2\}$ and *scale up* action changes B into $\{x_1 - \frac{1}{2}\delta_w, y_1 - \frac{1}{2}\delta_h, x_2 + \frac{1}{2}\delta_w, y_2 + \frac{1}{2}\delta_h\}$.

Alignment Agent: For the alignment agent, if a *stop* action is selected, the face alignment result is finalized as the target of the current frame, and the bounding box result is transferred to the initial state of the next frame. The *continue* action continues the iteration of MDP.

Reward: The rewards of the agent depend on the chosen action a_t at state s_t, which are determined by the function r_t.

Tracking Agent: The reward function r_t reflects the landmark detection accuracy improvements. The reward function measures the misalignment descent and is defined as follow:

$$r_t = -sign(d_{t+1} - d_t), \quad d_t = \frac{\sum_{i=1}^{L} \|\hat{V}_{i,t} - V_i^*\|}{L \cdot \zeta} \tag{5}$$

where d_t denotes the normalized point-to-point distance for the t-th iteration of MDP, $\| \cdot \|$ specifies the ℓ_2 norm, ζ denotes the normalizing factor, $\hat{V}$, V^* denote the predicted landmarks points and the ground truth, respectively.

Alignment Agent: For the *continue* action, we use the same reward as the tracking agent. For the *stop* action, we use a different reward scheme because it leads to a terminate state, which is defined as:

$$r_t = \begin{cases} +\eta & \text{if } d_t < \tau \\ -\eta & \text{otherwise} \end{cases} \tag{6}$$

where η is empirically set to 3.0, and τ is a threshold that indicates the maximum error allowed to consider the predicted alignment result as a positive one.

3.3   Network Architecture

The DADRL network consists of three parts: the tracking agent, the alignment agent, and communicated message channels. The tracking agent is a VGG-M model followed by a one-layer Q network. The alignment agent is designed as a combination of stacked hourglass network and a confidence network. Two communicated messages are encoded by a deconvolution layer and a Long Short-Term Memory (LSTM) unit respectively. In this section, we detail communicated message channels and the confidence network, and will detail tracking agent and stacked hourglass network in Sect. 4.2.

Communicated Message Channels: The communicated messages explicitly encode the synergic information flows between these two agents. For the message passed from the tracking agent to the alignment agent, we aim to provide prior additional textural information for the alignment agent to improve the robustness. We select the output feature map of the *conv3* layer in the tracking agent, and concatenate it in depth axis with the feature map which is the output of the first down-sampling step in the hourglass network. We adopt a deconvolution layer as message channel to match the sizes of feature maps.

The message passed from the alignment agent to the tracking agent provides complementary 3D pose information for bounding box tracking. The primary goal is to produce auxiliary knowledge of facial pose for accurate tracking. To achieve this, we take the normalized coordinates of predicted landmark points as a representation of 3D pose information. We also adopt LSTM to memorize the pose variation through time series. The hidden state is not updated until the MDP of one frame is terminated for training stabilization.

Confidence Network: We observe that landmark prediction is usually formulated as a regression problem, which has no confidence score as estimated in classification problems. However, it is necessary for the alignment agent to judge the quality of predicted landmarks and determine whether to continue the adjustment process. For example, in cases that predicted landmarks is obviously implausible due to an inaccurate bounding box, the regression result of the alignment agent should have a low confidence score and be considered as a failure. Inspired by this observation, we propose the confidence network to determine the termination of iterations for these two agents. The proposed confidence network takes the predicted heatmap and shape-indexed local patches as the input, and outputs a $L \times 1$ vector, which represents the confidence of each landmark. Followed by a one-layer fully connected Q-net, Q values of $stop/continue$ actions are predicted for the alignment agent.

3.4   Network Training

As training via reinforcement learning directly from scratch is significantly slow to converge, we exploit a two-stage training procedure: firstly utilize supervised learning to pre-train main branch of the network, then train the other parts via reinforcement learning.

Supervised Learning Stage: For the supervised learning stage, two agents are trained separately and elements of message vectors are set to zero. For the tracking agent, training samples which consist of image patches $\{p_i\}$ and action labels $\{a_i^*\}$ are fed into the network. The image patches are sampled from the training dataset by adding Gaussian noise to the ground truth patches, which are the tightest bounding box of the annotated facial landmarks. The corresponding action label a_i^* is assigned by $a_i^* = \arg\max_a IoU(f(p_i, a), G)$, where $f(p_i, a)$ denotes the moved patch from p_i by the action a from the action set of tracking agent, G denotes the ground truth patch. The loss function for tracking agent is defined as follows,

$$L_{tracking} = CrossEntropy(\hat{a}_i, a_i^*) \tag{7}$$

where $\hat{a}_i$ denotes the predicted action of tracking agent.

For the alignment agent, the loss function of hourglass model is presented as:

$$L_{alignment} = \frac{1}{L} \sum_{n=1}^{L} (\sum_{ij} ||h_n(i, j) - h_n^*(i, j)||_2^2) \tag{8}$$

where $h_n(i, j)$, $h_n^*(i, j)$ represent the predicted and the ground truth heatmap at pixel location (i, j) for the n-th landmark respectively.

Reinforcement Learning Stage: The reinforcement learning stage aims to train parameters of Q-nets, message channels and confidence network simultaneously. Following the Q-learning algorithm, each agent chooses an action according to the current estimation of the Q-function $Q(s, a)$ in an iterative fashion.

Based on $Q(s, a)$, the agent will choose the action that is associated to the highest reward. Q-learning iteratively updates the action-selection policy using the Bellman as follows:

$$Q(s, a) = r + \gamma \max_{a'} Q(s', a') \tag{9}$$

where s and a are the current state and action, γ represents the discount factor.

In our work, we approximate the Q-function by deep Q-network trained with reinforcement learning. In the dual-agent setting, deep Q-network also takes the message received from the other agent as input, formulated as $Q(s, a, m)$. In order to reach the Bellman optimality, we jointly perform sampling to these two agents and the samples are used to update all parameters by jointly minimizing the following loss,

$$L = \mathbb{E}[Q(s_t, a_t) - (r_t + \gamma \max_{a'} Q(s_{t+1}, a'))]^2 \tag{10}$$

The parameters related to message channels between these two agents are also updated because the messages are differential.

4   Experiments and Results

We evaluated the performance of the proposed DADRL on the large-scale face tracking dataset, the 300-VW test set [4], which is one publicly available large scale face tracking dataset. We compared our method with state-of-the-arts, and reported several analyses to investigate the importance of message passing in the dual-agent learning manner in Sect. 4.3. Our results demonstrate the effectiveness of interaction between two tasks.

4.1   Dataset and Settings

The 300-VW dataset consists of 3 categories: 1 (62,135 frames), 2 (32,805 frames), and 3 (26,338 frames). The Category 3 is by far the most challenging, and contains 14 videos in severe wild conditions and each video lasts around one minute (25–30 images per second). We conducted our experiments on Category 3 to study the improved performance of our method on severe conditions including large pose, heavily occlusion, etc. Results were reported for both the 49 inner points and the whole 68 points. Note that, there are several existing evaluation protocols and different versions of annotations for the dataset, such as [3,4]. For fair comparison, we followed the dataset and setting in the original 300VW competition of [4]. The other reported results also follow the same setting.

During supervised learning stage, the two agents were trained separately. We utilized all training data from the 300-W competition [34] to train the alignment agent, and the 300-VW training set to train the tracking agent. During reinforcement learning stage, the whole network was trained with the data of

300-VW training set. We noticed a newly set-up face tracking competition [35] with released 3D projected annotated facial landmarks of 300-VW dataset. We also trained another model with the 3D data and compared it with state-of-the-art methods in Sect. 4.3. For the evaluation protocols, we employed the standard normalized root mean squared error (RMSE) and cumulative error distribution (CED) curves.

4.2 Implementation Details

Our model was built based on the popular accelerated deep learning toolbox TensorFlow [36], which mainly operates on data flow graphs. The network of tracking agent is initialized by the pre-trained VGG-M model. The feature extracted by the pre-trained CNN is trained with ImageNet [37], which helps the parameters of the Q-Network to converge faster. The input fixed size of state s_t is 112×112. As illustrated in Fig. 2, the network consists of three convolutional layers $\{conv1, conv2, conv3\}$, which are identical to the convolutional layers in VGG-M model, and three fully connected layers $\{fc4, fc5, fc6\}$. $\{fc4, fc5\}$ layers are combined with ReLU and dropout layers, and the output of $fc5$ layer is concatenated with the message received from alignment agent. The final $fc6$ layer, without any activation function, predicts the Q value of the six *movement* actions, in order to determine the action of tracking agent for the current iteration.

The basic network of alignment agent is designed based on stacked hourglass network [38]. The original signals are branched out before each down-sampling step and combined before each up-sampling step. Features from the original size to $1/2^n$ size are able to extracted for n scale hourglass model. The output of hourglass model is a set of heatmaps, each of which represents the probability of one keypoint's presence at each pixel. We choose $n = 2$ for the trade-off of accuracy and speed.

For Confidence Network, we concatenate the extracted shape-index patches and the predicted heatmaps, and resize them to 26×26 as input. Then we deploy two convolutional layers (3×3 kernel size, 1×1 stride) with 128 and 512 kernels. By following the convolution layers, we append a two-layer fully connections, where the parameters are 512×512 and $512 \times L$ vector matrices ($L = 68$ for 300-VW dataset). The output vector is fed into a one-layer fully connection to predict the Q value of *stop/continue* actions.

For hyper-parameters during training process, we specified the learning rates to 0.001, the discounted factor to 0.9, and mini-batch size to 20. For parameters in MDP, the scale vector α was set to 0.2, the threshold τ was set to 0.06, ε was set to 0.7. A replay buffer [33] is used for reinforcement learning stage.

4.3 Results and Analysis

Comparison with State-of-the-Arts: In this section, we compared DADRL with state-of-the-arts for both the 49 inner points and 68 points. For 49 inner points, we compared DADRL with 5 state-of-the-art methods including the two

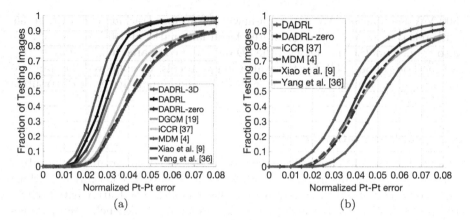

Fig. 5. (a) Comparison between DADRL and state-of-the-arts on Category 3 of 300-VW for 49 inner points. (b) Comparison between DADRL and state-of-the-arts on Category 3 of 300-VW for 68 points.

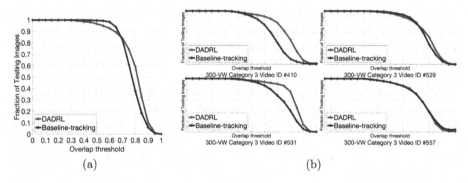

Fig. 6. Bounding box tracking comparison. (a) Success plots for all videos on Category 3 of 300-VW. (b) Success plots for several videos with extreme pose variation on Category 3 of 300-VW.

best performing methods of the 300-VW competition [2,39], the state-of-the-art face alignment method of [16], the state-of-the-art tracker of [40] and a synergy method DGCM of [19]. We introduced a baseline, called 'DADRL-zero', where the communicated messages are set to zero during test phase. As the newly released 3D projected annotated landmarks in [35] has the same inner-points position as the previous 2D annotation, we also reported the result of the model trained by these 3D data, named 'DADRL-3D'. Figure 5(a) shows the obtained results on Category 3. The proposed 'DADRL-3D' is the best performing method, followed by 'DADRL', while the baseline DADRL-zero shows comparable performance with other methods. The large margin between 'DADRL' and other state-of-arts demonstrates the effectiveness of the interactive manner, as the intrinsic correlation between two agents could be held. It is reasonable that 'DADRL-3D' outperforms all state-of-the-arts because the model is more robust to large pose by training with 3D data. The comparison of the proposed 'DADRL' and the baseline 'DADRL-zero' illustrates the importance of the communicated messages.

We also reported our results for the whole 68 points. As the 'DADRL-3D' has an output of 84 points, we did not consider it for the 68-points condition. Compared with 49-inner-points setting, the 68-points setting could better demonstrate the robustness of the methods, as the contour points are more sensitive to extreme conditions. As DGCM of [19] did not report results for 68 points, we did not compare our method with it. As illustrated in Fig. 5(b), our proposed DADRL outperforms other methods by a large margin.

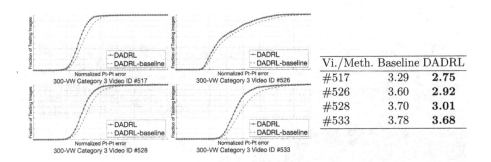

Vi./Meth.	Baseline	DADRL
#517	3.29	**2.75**
#526	3.60	**2.92**
#528	3.70	**3.01**
#533	3.78	**3.68**

Fig. 7. CED curves (left) and averaged errors comparisons (100%) (right) of several videos with heavy occlusions and motion artifacts on Category 3 of 300-VW.

Analysis: In this section, we performed two analyses to illustrate how communicated messages in the dual-agent training manner improve the performance of both bounding box tracking and face alignment. As the comparison between DADRL and the conducted baseline 'DADRL-zero' has already illustrated the importance of communicated messages, we further investigated how two messages assist the respective agent. Two experiments demonstrate that the interaction between two tasks enhances the robustness to extreme conditions for deformable face tracking.

Tracking Experiments: The message passing from alignment agent to tracking agent aims to provide complementary 3D pose information for accuracy bounding box tracking. To verify the effectiveness, we trained another tracking network as baseline. This network has the same architecture as the tracking agent, except the output of the $fc5$ layer is no more concatenated with message code. The network was trained in the same manner as the tracking agent, namely, firstly pretrained by supervised learning, then fine-tuned by reinforcement learning. The baseline tracker also follows MDP and has the same action set as the tracking agent of DADRL. A similar sequence of bounding box shifting is predicted by the baseline network. As there is no *stop* action for this tracker, the selected face region is fed into our DRDAL to determine whether the iteration should stop by our alignment agent. The only difference between this baseline bounding box tracker and our tracking agent is that there is no message input for the baseline. For comparison, we employed success rate as evaluation protocol. As there is no annotated bounding box in 300-VW dataset, we considered the tightest bounding box of the facial landmarks as ground truth. Success plots of Category 3 are shown in Fig. 6(b). We also illustrated success plots of several individual videos, shown in Fig. 6(a). Note that these videos contain faces which undergo extreme pose, even totally turn-around. The results show that the message from alignment agent is an effective complementary 3D information for accurate 2D tracking and can enhance the robustness of tracking agent to large pose. Examples of sequential actions decided by tracking agents are shown in Fig. 8(c).

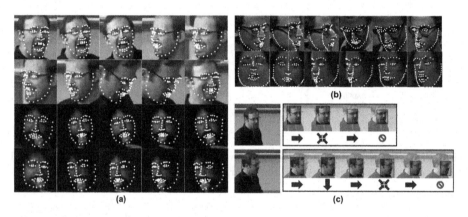

Fig. 8. (a)(b) Examples of alignment results for 68 points and 3D projected 84 points on Category 3 of 300-VW. (c) Sequential actions decided by tracking agent for two frames in Video #533 of 300-VW Category 3.

Alignment Experiments: For better understanding the effect of the message passing to alignment agent, we trained a separated stacked hourglass model as baseline which predicts landmarks without any received message. This baseline model was trained the same way as the supervised learning stage of DADRL. During test phase, we directly used the tightest bounding box of annotated landmarks as the input face region. Two models predicted landmarks with only one feed-forward pass. To verify that this message channel provides prior additional textural information for the alignment agent, we selected several videos which contain frames under occlusions or motion artifacts. The comparison of CED curves and averaged point-to-point error is shown in Fig. 7. We can see the alignment agent with a message input has about 2% performance improvement over the single hourglass model, which demonstrates the robustness to occlusions and motion artifacts of our DADRL. The results further show that the message passing from tracking agent to alignment agent is able to decode the textural information, which is an effective prior information for face alignment under heavy inclusions or motion artifacts. Examples of alignment results are shown in Fig. 8(a) (b), for 68 points and 3D 84 points respectively. In summary, the results of these two experiments suggest that the communicated messages play an important role in our proposed method.

5 Conclusion

In this paper, we have proposed a dual-agent deep reinforcement learning (DADRL) method for deformable face tracking. In our method, we have explicitly exploited the interaction between bounding box generation and face alignment by following a Bayesian model and have proposed a unified framework to simultaneously perform these two tasks. By formulating the problem as MDP, we have defined these two models as dual agents to exploit the relationships and pass messages via an adaptive sequence of actions. The models are trained interactively via deep reinforcement learning. Experimental results have been presented to show the effectiveness of the proposed approach. How to automatically choose the message channels and to further improve the performance of our method seems to be an interesting future work.

Acknowledgements. This work was supported in part by the National Key Research and Development Program of China under Grant 2017YFA0700802, in part by the National Natural Science Foundation of China under Grant 61822603, under Grant 61672306, Grant U1713214, Grant 61572271, and in part by the Shenzhen Fundamental Research Fund (Subject Arrangement) under Grant JCYJ20170412170602564.

References

1. Wang, X., Yang, M., Zhu, S., Lin, Y.: Regionlets for generic object detection. In: ICCV, pp. 17–24 (2013)
2. Xiao, S., Yan, S., Kassim, A.A.: Facial landmark detection via progressive initialization. In: ICCVW, pp. 33–40 (2015)
3. Chrysos, G.G., Antonakos, E., Snape, P., Asthana, A., Zafeiriou, S.: A comprehensive performance evaluation of deformable face tracking "in-the-wild". IJCV **126**(2–4), 198–232 (2018)
4. Shen, J., Zafeiriou, S., Chrysos, G.G., Kossaifi, J., Tzimiropoulos, G., Pantic, M.: The first facial landmark tracking in-the-wild challenge: Benchmark and results. In: ICCVW, pp. 50–58 (2015)
5. Asthana, A., Zafeiriou, S., Cheng, S., Pantic, M.: Incremental face alignment in the wild. In: CVPR, pp. 1859–1866 (2014)
6. Peng, X., Zhang, S., Yang, Y., Metaxas, D.N.: PIEFA: personalized incremental and ensemble face alignment. In: ICCV, pp. 3880–3888 (2015)
7. Peng, X., Feris, R.S., Wang, X., Metaxas, D.N.: A recurrent encoder-decoder network for sequential face alignment. In: Leibe, B., Matas, J., Sebe, N., Welling, M. (eds.) ECCV 2016. LNCS, vol. 9905, pp. 38–56. Springer, Cham (2016). https://doi.org/10.1007/978-3-319-46448-0_3

8. Liu, H., Lu, J., Feng, J., Zhou, J.: Two-stream transformer networks for video-based face alignment. TPAMI (2017). https://doi.org/10.1109/TPAMI.2017.2734779
9. Black, M.J., Yacoob, Y.: Tracking and recognizing rigid and non-rigid facial motions using local parametric models of image motion. In: 1995 Proceedings of Fifth International Conference on Computer Vision, pp. 374–381. IEEE (1995)
10. Chrysos, G.G., Antonakos, E., Zafeiriou, S., Snape, P.: Offline deformable face tracking in arbitrary videos. In: ICCVW, pp. 1–9 (2015)
11. Decarlo, D., Metaxas, D.: Optical flow constraints on deformable models with applications to face tracking. IJCV **38**(2), 99–127 (2000)
12. Tzimiropoulos, G.: Project-out cascaded regression with an application to face alignment. In: CVPR, pp. 3659–3667 (2015)
13. Cao, X., Wei, Y., Wen, F., Sun, J.: Face alignment by explicit shape regression. IJCV **107**(2), 177–190 (2014)
14. Xiong, X., De la Torre, F.: Supervised descent method and its applications to face alignment. In: CVPR, pp. 532–539 (2013)
15. Zhang, Z., Luo, P., Loy, C.C., Tang, X.: Facial landmark detection by deep multi-task learning. In: Fleet, D., Pajdla, T., Schiele, B., Tuytelaars, T. (eds.) ECCV 2014. LNCS, vol. 8694, pp. 94–108. Springer, Cham (2014). https://doi.org/10.1007/978-3-319-10599-4_7
16. Trigeorgis, G., Snape, P., Nicolaou, M.A., Antonakos, E., Zafeiriou, S.: Mnemonic descent method: a recurrent process applied for end-to-end face alignment. In: CVPR, pp. 4177–4187 (2016)
17. Zhang, J., Shan, S., Kan, M., Chen, X.: Coarse-to-fine auto-encoder networks (CFAN) for real-time face alignment. In: Fleet, D., Pajdla, T., Schiele, B., Tuytelaars, T. (eds.) ECCV 2014. LNCS, vol. 8690, pp. 1–16. Springer, Cham (2014). https://doi.org/10.1007/978-3-319-10605-2_1
18. Kumar, A., Chellappa, R.: Disentangling 3D pose in a dendritic cnn for unconstrained 2D face alignment. arXiv preprint arXiv:1802.06713 (2018)
19. Khan, M.H., McDonagh, J., Tzimiropoulos, G.: Synergy between face alignment and tracking via discriminative global consensus optimization. In: ICCV 2017, pp. 3791–3799 (2017)
20. Littman, M.L.: Reinforcement learning improves behaviour from evaluative feedback. Nature **521**(7553), 445 (2015)
21. Gu, S., Lillicrap, T., Sutskever, I., Levine, S.: Continuous deep q-learning with model-based acceleration. In: ICML, pp. 2829–2838 (2016)
22. Mnih, V., et al.: Playing atari with deep reinforcement learning. arXiv preprint arXiv:1312.5602 (2013)
23. Mnih, V., et al.: Human-level control through deep reinforcement learning. Nature **518**(7540), 529 (2015)
24. Ammar, H.B., Eaton, E., Ruvolo, P., Taylor, M.: Online multi-task learning for policy gradient methods. In: ICML, pp. 1206–1214 (2014)
25. Silver, D., Lever, G., Heess, N., Degris, T., Wierstra, D., Riedmiller, M.: Deterministic policy gradient algorithms. In: ICML (2014)
26. Rao, Y., Lu, J., Zhou, J.: Attention-aware deep reinforcement learning for video face recognition. In: CVPR, pp. 3931–3940 (2017)
27. Yu, L., Zhang, W., Wang, J., Seqgan, Y.Y.: Sequence generative adversarial nets with policy gradient. arXiv preprint arXiv:1609.05473 **2**(3), 5 (2016)
28. Yoo, S.Y.J.C.Y., Yun, K., Choi, J.Y.: Action-decision networks for visual tracking with deep reinforcement learning (2017)
29. Foerster, J., Assael, Y., de Freitas, N., Whiteson, S.: Learning to communicate with deep multi-agent reinforcement learning. In: NIPS, pp. 2137–2145 (2016)

30. Sukhbaatar, S., Fergus, R., et al.: Learning multiagent communication with back-propagation. In: NIPS, pp. 2244–2252 (2016)
31. Kong, X., Xin, B., Wang, Y., Hua, G.: Collaborative deep reinforcement learning for joint object search. In: CVPR (2017)
32. Xia, Y., Qin, T., Chen, W., Bian, J., Yu, N., Liu, T.Y.: Dual supervised learning. arXiv preprint arXiv:1707.00415 (2017)
33. Lillicrap, T.P., et al.: Continuous control with deep reinforcement learning. arXiv preprint arXiv:1509.02971 (2015)
34. Sagonas, C., Tzimiropoulos, G., Zafeiriou, S., Pantic, M.: A semi-automatic methodology for facial landmark annotation. In: CVPRW, pp. 896–903 (2013)
35. Zafeiriou, S., Chrysos, G.G., Roussos, A., Ververas, E., Deng, J., Trigeorgis, G.: The 3D menpo facial landmark tracking challenge. In: ICCVW, vol. 5 (2017)
36. Abadi, M., et al.: TensorFlow: large-scale machine learning on heterogeneous systems (2015). tensorflow.org
37. Krizhevsky, A., Sutskever, I., Hinton, G.E.: Imagenet classification with deep convolutional neural networks. In: NIPS, pp. 1097–1105 (2012)
38. Newell, A., Yang, K., Deng, J.: Stacked hourglass networks for human pose estimation. In: Leibe, B., Matas, J., Sebe, N., Welling, M. (eds.) ECCV 2016. LNCS, vol. 9912, pp. 483–499. Springer, Cham (2016). https://doi.org/10.1007/978-3-319-46484-8_29
39. Yang, J., Deng, J., Zhang, K., Liu, Q.: Facial shape tracking via spatio-temporal cascade shape regression. In: ICCVW, pp. 41–49 (2015)
40. Sánchez-Lozano, E., Martinez, B., Tzimiropoulos, G., Valstar, M.: Cascaded continuous regression for real-time incremental face tracking. In: Leibe, B., Matas, J., Sebe, N., Welling, M. (eds.) ECCV 2016. LNCS, vol. 9912, pp. 645–661. Springer, Cham (2016). https://doi.org/10.1007/978-3-319-46484-8_39

Deep Autoencoder for Combined Human Pose Estimation and Body Model Upscaling

Matthew Trumble[1], Andrew Gilbert[1]([✉]), Adrian Hilton[1],
and John Collomosse[1,2]

[1] Centre for Vision Speech and Signal Processing, University of Surrey, Guildford,
UK
a.gilbert@surrey.ac.uk
[2] Creative Intelligence Lab, Adobe Research, San Francisco, USA

Abstract. We present a method for simultaneously estimating 3D human pose and body shape from a sparse set of wide-baseline camera views. We train a symmetric convolutional autoencoder with a dual loss that enforces learning of a latent representation that encodes skeletal joint positions, and at the same time learns a deep representation of volumetric body shape. We harness the latter to up-scale input volumetric data by a factor of $4\times$, whilst recovering a 3D estimate of joint positions with equal or greater accuracy than the state of the art. Inference runs in real-time (25 fps) and has the potential for passive human behaviour monitoring where there is a requirement for high fidelity estimation of human body shape and pose.

Keywords: Deep learning · Pose estimation
Multiple viewpoint video

1 Introduction

Multiple viewpoint video of open spaces (e.g. for sports or surveillance) is often captured using a sparse set of wide-baseline static cameras, in which human subjects are relatively small (tens of pixels in height) due to their physical distance. Nevertheless, it is useful to infer human behavioural data from this limited knowledge for performance analytics or security. In this paper, we explore the possibility of inferring high fidelity three-dimensional (3D) body shape and skeletal pose data from a coarse (low-resolution) volumetric estimate of body shape estimated across a sparse set of camera views (Fig. 1).

The technical contribution of this paper is to explore the possibility of learning a deep representation for volumetric (3D) human body shape driven by a latent encoding for the skeletal pose that can, in turn, be inferred from coarse volumetric shape data. Specifically, we investigate whether convolutional autoencoder architectures, commonly applied to 2D visual content for de-noising and

© Springer Nature Switzerland AG 2018
V. Ferrari et al. (Eds.): ECCV 2018, LNCS 11214, pp. 800–816, 2018.
https://doi.org/10.1007/978-3-030-01249-6_48

Fig. 1. Simultaneous estimation of 3D human pose and 4× upscaled volumetric body shape, from coarse visual hull data derived from a sparse set of wide-baseline views.

up-scaling (super-resolution), may be adapted to up-scale volumetric 3D human shape whilst simultaneously providing high-level information on the 3D human pose from the bottle-neck (latent) representation of the autoencoder. We propose a symmetric autoencoder with 3D convolutional stages capable of refining a probabilistic visual hull (PVH) [1] i.e. voxel occupancy data derived at very coarse scale (grid resolution $32 \times 32 \times 32$ encompassing the subject). We demonstrate that our autoencoder is able to estimate an up-scaled body shape volume at up to $128 \times 128 \times 128$ resolution, whilst able to estimate the skeleton joint positions of the subject to equal or better accuracy than the current state of the art methods due to deep learning.

2   Related Work

Our work makes a dual contribution to two long-standing Computer Vision problems: super-resolution (SR) and human pose estimation (HPE).

Super-Resolution: Data-driven approaches to image SR integrate pixel data e.g. from auxiliary images [2], or from a single image [3,4] to perform image up-scaling or restoration. Model based approaches learn appearance priors from training images, applying these as optimization constraints to solve for SR content [5]. A wide variety of machine learning approaches have been applied to the latter e.g. sparse coding [6], regression trees [7], and stacked autoencoders [8]; many such approaches are surveyed in [9]. Deep learning has more recently applied convolutional autoencoders for up-scaling of images [10–12] and video [13]; our work follows suit, extending symmetric autoencoders commonly used for image restoration to volumetric data using 3D (up-)convolutional layers [14]. Our work is not the first to propose volumetric super-resolution. Data-driven volumetric SR has been explored using multiple image fusion across the depth of field in [15] and across multiple spectral channels in [6]. Very recent work by Brock *et al.* explores deep variational auto-encoders for volumetric SR of objects [16]. However, our work is unique in its ability to upscale to 4× whilst simultaneously estimating human pose to a high accuracy, exploiting a learned latent representation encoding joint positions.

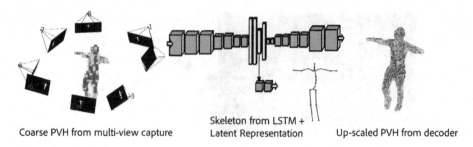

Fig. 2. Overview of the proposed method. A coarse PVH is estimated as input volumetric data (32^3 voxels) and up-scaled via tricubic interpolation to a $(32 * n)^3$ voxel grid (where $n = \{1, 2, 4\}$). The input PVH is deeply encoded to the latent feature representation (3D joint positions). Non-linear decoding of the feature via successive up-convolutional layers yields a higher fidelity PVH of $(32n)^3$ voxels.

Human pose estimation has been classically approached through top-down fitting of models such as Pictorial structures [17], fused with Ada-Boost shape classification in [18]. Conditional dependencies between parts (limbs) during model fitting were explored in [19,20]. Huang [21] tracked 3D mesh deformation over time and attach a skeleton to tracked vertices. The *SMPL* body model [22] provides a rich statistical body model that can be fitted to (possibly incomplete) visual data. Marcard [23] explored the orthogonal modality of IMU measurements using SMPL for HPE without visual data. Malleson [24] used IMUs with a full kinematic solve to estimate 3D pose. SMPL was recently applied to a deep encoder-decoder network to estimate 3D pose from 2D images [25]. Several deep approaches estimate 2D pose or infer 3D pose from intermediate 2D estimations. DeepPose [26] applies a convolutional neural network (CNN) cascade. Descriptors learned via CNN have been used in 2D pose estimation from low-resolution 2D images [27] and real-time multi-subject 2D pose estimates were demonstrated by Cao [28]. Sanzari [29] estimates the location of 2D joints, before predicting 3D pose using appearance and probable 3D pose of parts. Zhou [30] integrates 2D, 3D and temporal information to account for uncertainties in the data.

The challenge of estimating 3D human pose from volumetric data is more sparsely explored. Trumble [31] used a spherical histogram and later voxel input to regress a pose estimate using a CNN [32]. Pavlakos [33] used a simple volumetric representation in a 3D convnet for pose estimation. While Tekin [34] included a pretrained autoencoder within the network to enforce structural constraints. Our work also trains an autoencoder for HPE but simultaneously infers a high resolution body model via a dual loss function.

3   Estimating Human Pose and Body Shape

Our method accepts a coarse resolution volumetric reconstruction of a subject as input, and in a single inference, step estimates both the skeletal joint positions and a higher resolution (up-scaled) volumetric reconstruction of that subject (Fig. 2). Section 3.1 first describes how the input volumetric reconstruction is formed, through a simplified form of Graumann's probabilistic visual hull (PVH) [1]. The architecture of our 3D convolutional autoencoder is then described in Sect. 3.2 including the dual loss function necessary to learn a deep representation of body shape and the latent pose representation. Finally, Sect. 3.3 describes the data augmentation and methodology for training the network.

3.1   Volumetric Representation

The capture volume $\mathcal{V} \in \mathbb{R}^3$ containing the subject is observed by a set of C calibrated cameras $c = [1, C]$ for which camera world position T_c and orientation R_c (both matrices in homogeneous form) are known as are intrinsics: camera focal length (f_c) and optical center $[o_c^x, o_c^y]$. An external process (e.g. a person tracker) is assumed to isolate the bounding sub-volume $X_I \in \mathcal{V}$ corresponding to, and centered upon, a single subject of interest, and which is decimated to a coarse voxel grid $V = \{v_x^i, v_y^i, v_z^i\}$ for $i = [1, \ldots, 32^3]$ where V denotes the coarse voxel volume passed as input to the network in Sect. 3.2. Each voxel $v^i \in V$ projects to coordinates $(x[v^i], y[v^i])$ in each camera view c derived in homogeneous form via pin-hole projection:

$$\begin{bmatrix} \alpha x[v^i] \\ \alpha y[v^i] \\ \alpha \end{bmatrix} = \begin{bmatrix} f_c & 0 & o_c^x & 0 \\ 0 & f_c & o_c^y & 0 \\ 0 & 0 & 1 & 0 \end{bmatrix} (-R_c^{-1}T_c) \begin{bmatrix} v_x^i \\ v_y^i \\ v_z^i \\ 1 \end{bmatrix}. \tag{1}$$

Given a soft matte I_c obtained, for example by background (clean-plate) subtraction, the probability of the voxel being part of the performer in a given view c is:

$$p(v^i|c) = I_c(x[v^i], y[v^i]). \tag{2}$$

The overall probability of occupancy for a given voxel $p(v^i)$ is:

$$p(v^i) = \prod_{i=1}^{C} 1/(1 + e^{p(v^i|c)}). \tag{3}$$

For all voxels $v^i \in V$ we compute $p(v^i)$ to form the coarse input PVH.

3.2   Dual Loss Convolutional Autoencoder

We use a convolutional autoencoder with a symmetrical 'hourglass' (encoder-decoder) architecture. The goal of the network is learn a deep representation given an input tensor $\mathbf{V_I} \in \mathbb{R}^{N \times N \times N \times 1}$ encoding the coarse PVH, V at a given resolution $N = (32n)^3$, where $n = \{1, 2, 4\}$ is a configuration parameter determining the degree of up-scaling required from the network (1x, 2x, 4x) respectively. The coarse PVH input V is scaled via tri-cubic interpolation to fit $\mathbf{V_I}$.

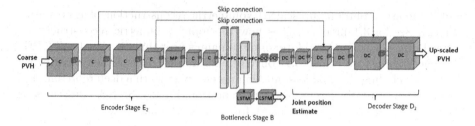

Fig. 3. Proposed convolutional autoencoder structure. The coarse input PVH is encoded into a latent feature representation via 3D (C)onvolutional, (M)ax-(P)ooling and (F)ully-(C)onnected layers. The decoder uses the latent representation to synthesize an up-scaled PVH via (D)e-(C)onvolutional layers. Two skip connections bridge the latent representation which is constrained during training to encode Cartesian joint positions. During inference these are passed through an LSTM to enhance temporal consistency to produce the joint position skeleton estimate. Architecture pictured here is for 2x scale-up – in order to accommodate different receptive field sizes for V_I/V_O (de-)convolutional layer count is adjusted – see Table 1.

We train the deep representation to solve the prediction problem $\mathbf{V_H} = \mathcal{F}(\mathbf{V_I})$ for similarly encoded output tensor $\mathbf{V_O}$, where

$$\mathbf{V_O} = \mathcal{F}(\mathbf{V_I}) = \mathcal{D}(\mathcal{E}(\mathbf{V_I})) \tag{4}$$

for the end to end trained encoder ($\mathcal{E}$) and decoder ($\mathcal{D}$) functions The encoder yields a latent feature representation via a series of 3D convolutions, max-pooling and fully-connected layers. We enforce $J(V_I) = \mathcal{E}(\mathbf{V_I})$ where $J(\mathbf{V_I})$ is a skeletal pose vector corresponding the input PVH; specifically a 78-D vector concatenation of $26\times$ 3D Cartesian joint coordinates in $\{x, y, z\}$. The decoder half of the network inverts this process to output tensor $\mathbf{V_O}$ matching the input resolution but with higher fidelity content. Figure 3 illustrates our architecture which incorporates two skip connections bypassing the network bottleneck to allow the output from a convolutional layer in the encoder to feed into the corresponding up-convolution layer in the decoder. Activations from the preceding layer in the main network and skip connection data are combined via mean average rather than channel augmentation/residuals.

Table 1 describes the parameters (filter count and size) of each layer. We report experiments up-scaling to $n = \{1, 2, 4\}$ requiring varying sizes of receptive field to accommodate $\mathbf{V_I}$ and $\mathbf{V_O}$. For each step up in scale, we add a single additional convolutional layer to the encoder, and two additional de-convolutional layers to the decoder. Max-pooling occurs always at the fourth convolutional layer, and the filter size is $3 \times 3 \times 3$ except for the first two and last two layers, where the filter size is $5 \times 5 \times 5$.

Learning the end-to-end mapping from coarse PVH to both an up-scaled PVH and accurate 3D joint positions requires estimation of the weights ϕ in $\mathcal{F}$ represented by the convolutional and deconvolutional kernels.

Table 1. Convolution layer parameters for the encoder (E_n), bottleneck (B), and decoder (D_n) stages for $n = \{1, 2, 4\}\times$. Suffix $-M$ indicates max-pooling. All E_n and D_n layers learn $3 \times 3 \times 3$ filters, except where indicated by $*$ filters are $5 \times 5 \times 5$. All B layers are fully-connected including the latent representation (3D joint positions) suffixed $-J$.

Network stage	#Layers	#Channels/layer
E_1	5	96* 96* 96 96-M 96
E_2	6	32* 64* 96 96-M 96 96
E_4	7	32* 32* 32 64-M 96 96 96
B	4	1024 1024 78-J 216
D_1	6	96 96 96 96 64* 1*
D_2	8	96 96 96 96 64 64 32* 1*
D_4	10	96 96 96 96 64 64 32 32 32* 1*

Specifically, given a collection of M training triplets $\{\hat{\mathbf{V}}_\mathbf{I}, \hat{\mathbf{V}}_\mathbf{O}, \hat{J}\}$, where $p^i \in \hat{\mathbf{V}}_\mathbf{I}$ is voxel data from a coarse (input) PVH, $q^i \in \hat{\mathbf{V}}_\mathbf{O}$ is voxel data of an ideal up-scaled PVH, and j is a vector of ideal joint positions for the given volume. We minimize the Mean Squared Error (MSE) at the outputs of the bottleneck and decoder stages across $M = N \times N \times N$ voxels:

$$\mathcal{L}(\phi) = \frac{1}{M} \sum_{i=1}^{M} \|\mathcal{F}(p^i : \phi) - q^i\|_2^2 + \lambda \|\mathcal{E}(\hat{\mathbf{V}}_\mathbf{I} : \phi) - j\|_2^2. \quad (5)$$

These training triplets are formed by extracting voxel volumes from exemplar multi-view video footage at resolution $N \times N \times N$ (yielding $\hat{\mathbf{V}}_\mathbf{O}$ and the artificially down-sampling to $32 \times 32 \times 32$ to yield V (from which $\mathbf{V}_\mathbf{I}$ is up-sampled via tri-cubic interpolation). Human pose (joint positions) corresponding to the multi-view video frame is acquired using a commercial (Vicon Blade) human performance capture system run in parallel with video acquisition (such annotations are provided with the *TotalCapture* and *Human3.6M* datasets).

3.3 Training Methodology

To train $\mathcal{F}$ we use Adadelta [35] an extension of Adagrad, with the pose term of the dual loss (Eq. 5) scaled by a factor of λ. We found the approach insensitive to this parameter up to an order of magnitude setting $\lambda = 10^{-3}$ for all experiments. Below 10^{-3}, the bottleneck convergences to a semantic representation of the pose that is stable but does not resemble joint angles—above 10^{-2} the network will not converge. Data is augmented during training with a random rotation around the central vertical axis of the PVH. Before full network training, the encoder stage is trained separately, purely as a pose regression task, up to the latent representation layer. These trained weights initialize the encoder stage to help constrain the latent representation during full, dual-loss network training. Training typically converges within 100 epochs.

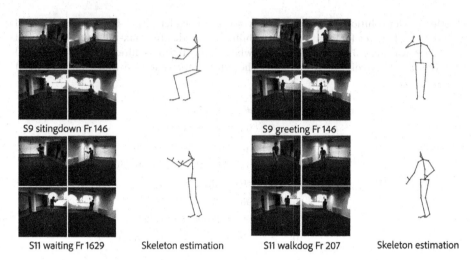

Fig. 4. Representative visual results for pose estimation on Human 3.6M across four test sequences (source footage from four views and inferred 3D skeletal pose).

3.4 Enforcing Temporal Consistency

Given the rich temporal nature of the pose sequences, it is prudent to exploit and enforce the temporal consistency of the otherwise detection based human joint estimation. By enforcing temporal consistency it is possible to smooth noise in individual joint detections that otherwise would cause large estimation errors. To learn a model of the motion over time we employ Long Short Term Memory (LSTM) layers [36], they have been heavily utilized in applications where long term temporal correlation can be exploited such as *e.g.* speech recognition [37], video description [38], and pose estimation [39]. LSTM layers are based on a recurrent neural network (RNN). They can store and access information over long periods of time but are able to mitigate the vanishing gradient problem common in RNNs through a specialized gating mechanism. The input vector from the encoder $\mathbf{J}_i(t) = \mathcal{E}(\mathbf{V_I})$ at time t consisting of concatenated joint spatial coordinates is passed through a series of gates resulting in an output joint vector $\mathbf{J}_o(t)$. The aim is to learn the function that minimizes the loss between the input vector and the output vector $\mathbf{J}_o = o_t \circ tanh(c_t)$ ($\circ$ denotes the Hadamard product) where o_t is the output gate, and c_t is the memory cell, a combination of the previous memory c_{t-1} multiplied by a decay based forget gate, and the input gate. Thus, intuitively the LSTM result is the combination of the previous memory and the new input vector. In the implementation, our model consists of two LSTM layers both with 1024 memory cells, using a look back of $f = 5$.

4 Evaluation and Discussion

To quantify the improvement in both the upscaling of low resolution volumetric representations and human pose estimation, we evaluate over three public multi-

Table 2. A Comparison of our approach to other works on the Human 3.6m dataset

Approach	Direct.	Discus	Eat	Greet.	Phone	Photo	Pose	Purch.
Lin [42]	132.7	183.6	132.4	164.4	162.1	205.9	150.6	171.3
Tekin [43]	85.0	108.8	84.4	98.9	119.4	95.7	98.5	93.8
Tome [44]	65.0	73.5	76.8	86.4	86.3	110.7	68.9	74.8
Trumble [32]	92.7	85.9	72.3	93.2	86.2	101.2	75.1	78.0
Lin [45]	58.0	68.3	63.3	65.8	75.3	93.1	61.2	65.7
Martinez [46]	51.8	56.2	58.1	59.0	69.5	78.4	55.2	58.1
Proposed	41.7	43.2	52.9	70.0	64.9	83.0	57.3	63.5
	Sit.	Sit D	Smke	Wait	W. dog	Walk	W. toget.	Mean
Lin [42]	151.6	243.0	162.1	170.7	177.1	96.6	127.9	162.1
Tekin [43]	73.8	170.4	85.1	116.9	113.7	62.1	94.8	100.1
Tome [44]	110.2	173.9	85.0	85.8	86.3	71.4	73.1	88.4
Trumble [32]	83.5	94.8	85.8	82.0	114.6	94.9	79.7	87.3
Lin [45]	98.7	127.7	70.4	68.2	73.0	50.6	57.7	73.1
Martinez [46]	74.0	94.6	62.3	59.1	65.1	49.5	52.4	62.9
Proposed	61.0	95.0	70.0	62.3	66.2	53.7	52.4	62.5

view video datasets of human actions. For *Human 3.6M* [40] we estimate the 3D human pose, and examine the performance of the skeleton estimation and volume upscaling in the *TotalCapture* [32] dataset. Finally, we visualize the results of the skeleton estimation and upscaling on the dataset *TotalCaptureOutdoor* [41], a challenging collection of multi-view human actions shot outdoors.

4.1 Human 3.6M Evaluation

The 3D human pose estimation dataset *Human3.6M* [40] is a 4 camera view dataset of 10 subjects performing 210 actions at 50 Hz in a 360° arrangement. A 3D ground truth for joint positions (key points) are available via annotation using a commercial marker-based motion capture system, allowing quantification of error. The dataset consists of 3.6 million video frames, balanced over 5 female and 6 male subjects. They perform common activities such as posing, sitting and giving directions. To allow comparison to other approaches we follow the same data partition protocol as in previous works [40, 42–46], and we use the publicly released foreground mattes. The training data consists of subjects S1, S5, S6, S7, S8 and it is tested on unseen subjects S9, S11. We compare our approach to many previously published state of the art methods, using 3D Euclidean (L_2) error to compute accuracy. The error is measured between each ground truth and estimated 3D joint position and is averaged over all frames and all 17 joints in millimetres (mm). The results of our approach are evaluated qualitatively in Fig. 4 and quantitatively in Table 2, drawing a comparison to state of the art approaches.

Table 3. A Comparison of testing on subjects S9 and S11 against a five-fold cross validation of other subject pairs on the Human 3.6m dataset

Approach	Direct.	Discus	Eat	Greet.	Phone	Photo	Pose	Purch.
CrossVal mean	52.2	49.8	53.0	63.1	61.4	76.8	63.2	59.3
CrossVal sd	7.6	5.1	9.1	5.8	3.9	4.7	10.4	6.9
Proposed	41.7	43.2	52.9	70.0	64.9	83.0	57.3	63.5
	Sit.	Sit D	Smke	Wait	W. dog	Walk	W. toget.	Mean
CrossVal mean	64.9	108.3	68.9	63.0	63.6	57.4	55.0	70.2
CrossVal sd	5.2	15.8	5.7	3.2	6.9	5.2	3.0	3.3
Proposed	61.0	95.0	70.0	62.3	66.2	53.7	52.4	62.5

Our approach outperforms with the lowest mean joint error on the challenging Human3.6M dataset, slightly reduced over the state of the art approach by Martinez [46], with a similar mean joint error of just over 6 cm. This is averaged over both test subjects and the 59 sequences. The error decrease over the other approaches is possible due to the dual loss formulation ensuring that the skeleton is kept bounded by realistic 3D volume representations after the decoder. Our approach struggles with the actions Sit Down and Photo, the action sit down contains a chair and given the already poor quality of the PVH it is likely that such incorrect joint estimations occur. In the sequences of *photo* the hands of the subject are close the subject head and it is likely the PVH volume doesn't contain enough discriminative information to correctly estimate their location. However, despite these two sequences, all others have a low error score and are smooth and qualitatively realistic. We show qualitative comparisons with respect to the ground truth in Fig. 4. To illustrate the stability of our approach across different test subjects we performed five rounds of cross-validation using multiple pairs of test subjects with the remaining subjects held out for training the model.Table 3 shows the standard test on S9 and S11 (mean accuracy of 62.5 mm) from Table 2 against the mean and standard deviation from our cross-validation experiment. The mean performance across random pairs of test subjects is similar to that of the official S9/S11 test split, and the σ is low. Thus they serve to show the stability of the approach across different test subject pairings.

4.2   TotalCapture Evaluation

In addition, we evaluate our approach on the TotalCapture dataset [32]. This is also a 3D human pose estimation dataset with the ground truth joint position provided by Vicon markers. It is also captured indoors in a volume roughly measuring 8×4 m with 8 calibration HD video cameras at 60 Hz in a 360°. There are a total of 5 subjects performing 4 actions with 3 repetitions at 60 Hz in a 360° arrangement. There are publicly released foreground mattes that we use as the input to our approach. Note to provide the Vicon groundtruth the subjects in both TotalCapture and Human3.6M are wearing dots visible to infrared cameras.

Table 4. Comparison of our approach on TotalCapture to other human pose estimation approaches, expressed as average per joint error (mm).

Approach	SeenSubjects (S1, 2, 3)			UnseenSubjects (S4, 5)			Mean
	W2	FS3	A3	W2	FS3	A3	
Tri-CPM-LSTM [28]	45.7	102.8	71.9	57.8	142.9	59.6	80.1
2D Matte-LSTM [31]	94.1	128.9	105.3	109.1	168.5	120.6	121.1
Trumble [32]	30.0	90.6	49.0	36.0	112.1	109.2	70.0
AutoEnc-Front-Half	42.0	120.5	59.8	58.4	162.1	103.4	85.4
AutoEnc-x1-LSTM	15.1	54.8	26.6	25.9	76.0	42.7	38.6
AutoEnc-x2-LSTM	13.0	47.0	23.0	21.8	68.5	40.9	34.1
AutoEnc-x4-LSTM	13.4	49.8	24.3	22.0	71.7	40.7	35.5

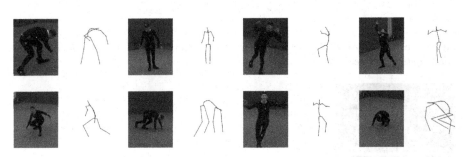

Fig. 5. Representative visual results from *TotalCapture* showing 3D pose estimation (×2 up-scaling). See Table 4 for quantitative results.

However these dots are not used explicitly by our algorithm, and their size is negligible compared to the performance volume. There are five subjects in the dataset, four male, and one female, each performs four diverse performances, that are repeated 3 times: *ROM, Walking, Acting, and Freestyle.* The length of each sequence is between 3000–5000 frames, this results in a total of ~1.9M frames of synchronized groundtruth video data. Especially within the acting and freestyle sequences, there is great diversity in the actions performed, as illustrated in the qualitative results in Fig. 5. To allow for comparison between seen and unseen subjects in the test evaluation, the test consists of sequences Freestyle3 (**FS3**), Acting (**A3**) and Walking2 (**W2**) on subjects 1, 2, 3, 4 and 5. While the training is performed using the sequences of ROM1, 2, 3; Walking1, 3; Freestyle1, 2 and Acting1, 2 on subjects 1, 2 and 3. We compare the pose estimation error for a number of upscale models; x1, x2, and x4 upscaling of the input PVH. Thus at the largest upscaling the PVH volume vector is $v \in \mathbb{R}^{128 \times 128 \times 128}$. Table 4 shows the results of the different upscaling models against the previous state of the art for the dataset.

All three learnt upscaling models reduce the mean error of the joints by over 50% compared to previously published works for this dataset, with the error for

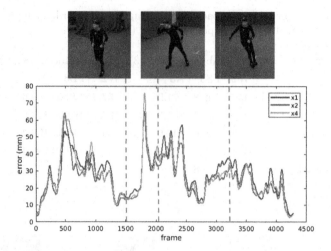

Fig. 6. Per frame skeletal error millimetres (mm) per joint on subject *S3 A3* in the *TotalCapture* test sequence.

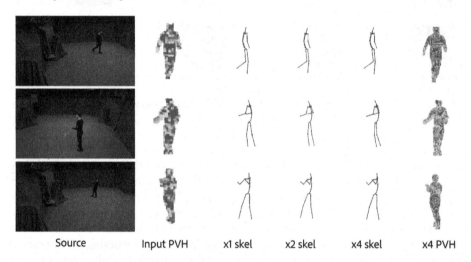

| Source | Input PVH | x1 skel | x2 skel | x4 skel | x4 PVH |

Fig. 7. Results illustrating the x1, x2, x4 upscaled volume for a representative coarse PVH alongside upscaling inferred skeletons.

some subjects sequences being reduced by an order of magnitude. Figure 5 provides some examples of the actions performed by the subjects and the excellent ability of the approach to estimating the pose.

Also, the table presents the *AutoEnc-FrontHalf* results, this shows initial convolutional encoder, without the decoder loss constraints. It provides a far higher error measure, indicating the importance of the dual loss constraining the skeleton pose space during training and inference. It is possible to examine the per frame error for subject 3, sequence Acting3, in Fig. 6. This figure shows how consistently low the error is across the full sequence. Despite a number of challenging poses being performed by the actor. There are a few error peaks, especially at the centre point, and these are generally caused by a failure in the background segmentation from which the input PVH is generated, resulting in, for example, missing or weakly defined limb extremities. This data is under-represented within the training data, however, otherwise the error is low. Use of the symmetrical network and dual loss has provided a large reduction in joint error for the skeleton it is also possible to upscale the initially very coarse and small volume at up to 4× times. Figure 7 displays the initial volume estimate, the 4× upscaled volume and the skeleton estimate for 1x, 2x and 4x for a selection of example frames on the *TotalCapture* dataset. The pose estimate for each upscaled model (1x, 2x and 4x) is nearly identical as born out by the results previously presented in Table 4. However, the volume enhancement from the 4× upscaling is impressive allowing for greater details to be hallucinated without noise or degeneration. Table 5 compares the input and output PVH volumes against a groundtruth high resolution volume generated directly from the camera views. The input volume is a naive tricubic upsampled volume and the error metric is MSE. The table shows that an order of magnitude improvement occurs using our proposed method against a naive tricubic up-sampling method. Comparing the x2 and x4 outputs, the MSE increases only slightly despite the generative doubling of the actor volume. An illustration of the upscaling performance is shown in Fig. 8, where the input and output volumes at up to x4 upscaling are shown for the TotalCapture dataset.

Table 5. Accuracy of generated volumes compared to tri-cubic upsampled input, over TotalCapture dataset. Expressed as mean voxel squared error $\times 10^{-3}$ from ground truth high resolution volume

Approach	SeenSubjects (S1, 2, 3)			UnseenSubjects (S4, 5)			Mean
	W2	FS3	A3	W2	FS3	A3	
AutoEnc-x2 input	9.27	10.14	9.65	9.80	10.66	10.21	9.88
AutoEnc-x2 output	0.34	0.37	0.34	0.40	0.46	0.39	0.37
AutoEnc-x4 input	9.83	10.83	10.19	10.64	11.45	11.03	10.56
AutoEnc-x4 output	0.50	0.55	0.50	0.58	0.68	0.59	0.56

Despite the initial block low-res PVH, we are able to accurately generate a hi-res PVHs at up to 4 times the size, that compare favorably to a natively generated (i.e. $\mathbb{R}^{128 \times 128 \times 128}$) PVH. We are able to maintain extremity and no phantom volumes are formed in the upscaling process. Figure 9 shows the per frame MSE over a sequence, for x2 and x4 upscaling. There is little difference between the two scales despite the greatly increased volume. Table 6 shows the training and inference times (the latter near real-time) of our approach.

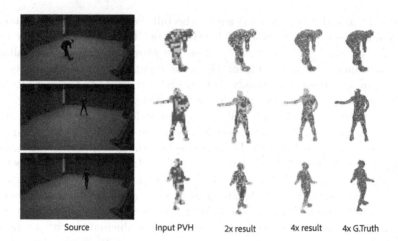

Source   Input PVH   2x result   4x result   4x G.Truth

Fig. 8. Illustration of the upscaling ability of our approach on the TotalCapture dataset together with the native $128 \times 128 \times 128$ groundtruth PVH

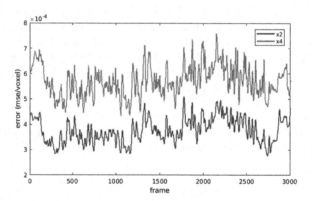

Fig. 9. Plotting volumetric reconstruction error per frame (MSE/voxel) on unseen subject *S4 A3* of the *TotalCapture* test sequence.

Table 6. Computational cost of model training and inference (TotalCapture dataset)

PVH scale	Encoder pre-train		Full training		Inference
	Epochs to converge	Minutes/epoch	Epochs to converge	Minutes/epoch	Millisec
x1	50	34	20	71	15
x2	42	32	40	58	21
x4	13	43	23	180	313

Fig. 10. *TotalCaptureOutdoor* dataset; red box indicates the person in the scene.

4.3   Outdoor Footage Evaluation

To further demonstrate the flexibility of our upscaling and pose estimation approach, we test on a recent challenging dataset, *TotalCaptureOutdoor* [24]. This is
a multi-view video dataset captured outdoors in challenging uncontrolled conditions with a moving and varying background of trees and differing illumination.
There are 6 video cameras placed in a 120° arrangement around the subject,
with a large 10×10 m capture volume used. This large capture volume means
the subjects are small in the scene as shown in Fig. 10 below. For this dataset
there are no released mattes, therefore we background subtraction was performed as a per pixel difference in HSV colour space to provide robust invariance
against illumination change. There is no groundtruth annotation available for
TotalCaptureOutdoor, however, we are present several illustrative results on two
sequences: *Subject1, Freestyle, and Acting1*. Given the small size of the subjects,
a traditional 3D pose estimation or volume reconstruction would be challenging.
However as shown in Fig. 11 we are able to use a small blocky low resolution
PVH volume, that is upscaled by a factor of x4 to produce a smooth approximation of the distant subject together with an accurate estimation of their joints.
Furthermore, despite the camera being arranged in a 120° arc, we are able to
simulate novel viewpoints of the upscaled full volume as shown in Fig. 12, where
complete 360 views are possible. This upscaling enables a future avenue of work,
creating a 3D model of the upscaled volume to produce VR/AR compositions
or for film/sports post-production.

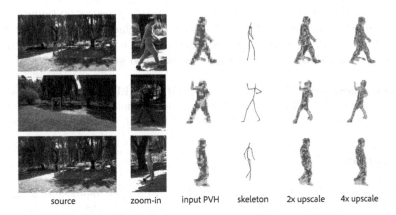

source   zoom-in   input PVH   skeleton   2x upscale   4x upscale

Fig. 11. Representative TotalCaptureOutdoor results showing the low-res input PVH,
and resulting skeleton and upscaled volumes

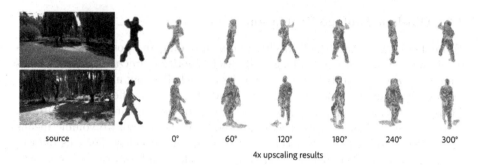

source   0°   60°   120°   180°   240°   300°

4x upscaling results

Fig. 12. Visualising the upscaled volumes from novel viewpoints. 3D reconstruction is of high quality despite the input PVH being captured from just two viewpoints.

5   Conclusion

We proposed a deep representation for volumetric (3D) human body shape driven by a latent encoding for the skeletal pose that can, in turn, be inferred from very coarse ($\mathbb{R}^{32 \times 32 \times 32}$) volumetric shape data. In a single inference pass our convolutional autoencoder both up-scales up the provided volumetric data (demonstrated to a factor of 4×) and predicts 3D human pose (joint positions) with greater or equal accuracy to state of the art deep human pose estimation approaches.

Future work could explore the end-to-end integration of the LSTM to the autoencoder during training since the latter currently learns no temporal prior to aid pose or volume regression. Nevertheless, we achieve state of the art results on very low resolution volumetric input, indicating the technique has potential to enable behavioural analytics using multi-view video footage shot at a distance.

Acknowledgements. The work was supported by an EPSRC doctoral bursary and InnovateUK via the TotalCapture project, grant agreement 102685. The work was supported in part through the donation of GPU hardware by the NVidia corporation.

References

1. Grauman, K., Shakhnarovich, G., Darrell, T.: A Bayesian approach to image-based visual hull reconstruction. In: Proceedings of the CVPR (2003)
2. Fattal, R.: Image upsampling via imposed edge statistics. In: Proceedings of the ACM SIGGRAPH (2007)
3. Glasner, D., Bagon, S., Irani, M.: Super-resolution from a single image. In: Proceedings of the International Conference on Computer Vision (ICCV) (2009)
4. Zhu, Y., Zhang, Y., Yuille, A.L.: Single image super-resolution using deformable patches. In: Proceedings of the Computer Vision and Pattern Recognition (CVPR), pp. 2917–2924 (2014)
5. Freeman, W.T., Jones, T.R., Pasztor, E.C.: Example based super-resolution. IEEE Comput. Graph. Appl. **22**(2), 56–65 (2002)

6. Aydin, V., Foroosh, H.: Volumetric super-resolution of multispectral data. arXiv:1705.05745v1 (2017)
7. Schmidt, U., Jancsary, J., Nowozin, S., Roth, S., Rother, C.: Cascades of regression tree fields for image restoration. IEEE Trans. Pattern Anal. Mach. Intell. **38**(4), 677–689 (2016)
8. Vincent, P., Larochelle, H., Bengio, Y., Manzagol, P.: Extracting and composing robust features with denoising autoencoders. In: Proceedings of the International Conference on Machine Learning (ICML), pp. 1096–1103 (2008)
9. Hayat, K.: Super-resolution via deep learning. CoRR abs/1706.09077 (2017)
10. Xie, J., Xu, L., Chen, E.: Image denoising and inpainting with deep neural networks. In: Proceedings of the Neural Information Processing Systems (NIPS), pp. 350–358 (2012)
11. Wang, Z., Liu, D., Yang, J., Han, W., Huang, T.S.: Deep networks for image super-resolution with sparse prior. In: Proceedings of the International Conference on Computer Vision (ICCV), pp. 370–378 (2015)
12. Dong, C., Loy, C.C., He, K., Tang, X.: Image super-resolution using deep convolutional networks. IEEE Trans. Pattern Anal. Mach. Intell. **38**(2), 295–307 (2016)
13. Shi, W., et al.: Real-time single image and video super-resolution using an efficient sub-pixel convolutional neural network. In: Proceedings of the Computer Vision and Pattern Recognition (CVPR) (2016)
14. Jain, V., Seung, H.: Natural image denoising with convolutional networks. In: Proceedings of the Neural Information Processing Systems (NIPS), pp. 769–776 (2008)
15. Abrahamsson, S., Blom, H., Jans, D.: Multifocus structured illumination microscopy for fast volumetric super-resolution imaging. Biomed. Opt. Express **8**(9), 4135–4140 (2017)
16. Brock, A., Lim, T., Ritchie, J.M., Weston, N.J.: Generative and discriminative voxel modeling with convolutional neural networks (2016)
17. Felzenszwalb, P., Huttenlocher, D.: Pictorial structures for object detection. Int. J. Comput. Vis. **61**, 55–79 (2003)
18. Andriluka, M., Roth, S., Schiele, B.: Pictoral structures revisited: people detection and articulated pose estimation. In: Proceedings of the Computer Vision and Pattern Recognition (2009)
19. Lan, X., Huttenlocher, D.: Beyond trees: common-factor model for 2D human pose recovery. In: Proceedings of the International Conference on Computer Vision, vol. 1, pp. 470–477 (2005)
20. Jiang, H.: Human pose estimation using consistent max-covering. In: International Conference on Computer Vision (2009)
21. Huang, P., Tejera, M., Collomosse, J., Hilton, A.: Hybrid skeletal-surface motion graphs for character animation from 4D performance capture. ACM Trans. Graph. (ToG) **34**, 17 (2015)
22. Loper, M., Mahmood, N., Romero, J., Pons-Moll, G., Black, M.J.: SMPL: a skinned multi-person linear model. ACM Trans. Graph. (ToG) **34**(6), 248 (2015)
23. von Marcard, T., Rosenhahn, B., Black, M., Pons-Moll, G.: Sparse inertial poser: automatic 3D human pose estimation from sparse IMUs. Comput. Graph. Forum **36**(2), 349–360 (2017). Proceedings of the 38th Annual Conference of the European Association for Computer Graphics (Eurographics)
24. Malleson, C., Gilbert, A., Trumble, M., Collomosse, J., Hilton, A.: Real-time full-body motion capture from video and IMUs. In: 3DV (2017)
25. Tan, J., Budvytis, I., Cipolla, R.: Indirect deep structured learning for 3D human body shape and pose prediction. In: BMVC (2017)

26. Toshev, A., Szegedy, C.: Deep pose: human pose estimation via deep neural networks. In: Proceedings of the CVPR (2014)
27. Park, D., Ramanan, D.: Articulated pose estimation with tiny synthetic videos. In: Proceedings of the CHA-LEARN Workshop on Looking at People (2015)
28. Cao, Z., Simon, T., Wei, S.E., Sheikh, Y.: Realtime multi-person 2D pose estimation using part affinity fields. In: ECCV 2016 (2016)
29. Sanzari, M., Ntouskos, V., Pirri, F.: Bayesian image based 3D pose estimation. In: Leibe, B., Matas, J., Sebe, N., Welling, M. (eds.) ECCV 2016. LNCS, vol. 9912, pp. 566–582. Springer, Cham (2016). https://doi.org/10.1007/978-3-319-46484-8_34
30. Zhou, X., Zhu, M., Leonardos, S., Derpanis, K.G., Daniilidis, K.: Sparseness meets deepness: 3D human pose estimation from monocular video. In: Proceedings of the IEEE Conference on Computer Vision and Pattern Recognition, pp. 4966–4975 (2016)
31. Trumble, M., Gilbert, A., Hilton, A., Collomosse, J.: Deep convolutional networks for marker-less human pose estimation from multiple views. In: Proceedings of the 13th European Conference on Visual Media Production (CVMP 2016) (2016)
32. Trumble, M., Gilbert, A., Malleson, C., Hilton, A., Collomosse, J.: Total capture: 3D human pose estimation fusing video and inertial sensors. In: Proceedings of 28th British Machine Vision Conference, pp. 1–13 (2017)
33. Pavlakos, G., Zhou, X., Derpanis, K.G., Daniilidis, K.: Coarse-to-fine volumetric prediction for single-image 3D human pose. In: CVPR (2017)
34. Tekin, B., Katircioglu, I., Salzmann, M., Lepetit, V., Fua, P.: Structured prediction of 3D human pose with deep neural networks. In: BMVC (2016)
35. Zeiler, M.D.: ADADELTA: an adaptive learning rate method. arXiv preprint arXiv:1212.5701 (2012)
36. Hochreiter, S., Schmidhuber, J.: Long short-term memory. Neural Comput. 9, 1735–1780 (1997)
37. Sak, H., Senior, A., Beaufays, F.: Long short-term memory recurrent neural network architectures for large scale acoustic modeling. In: Fifteenth Annual Conference of the International Speech Communication Association (2014)
38. Donahue, J., et al.: Long-term recurrent convolutional networks for visual recognition and description. In: Proceedings of the IEEE Conference on Computer Vision and Pattern Recognition, pp. 2625–2634 (2015)
39. Luo, Y., et al.: LSTM pose machines. arXiv preprint arXiv:1712.06316 (2017)
40. Ionescu, C., Papava, D., Olaru, V., Sminchisescu, C.: Human3.6M: large scale datasets and predictive methods for 3D human sensing in natural environments. IEEE Trans. Pattern Anal. Mach. Intell. 36(7), 1325–1339 (2014)
41. Malleson, C., Volino, M., Gilbert, A., Trumble, M., Collomosse, J., Hilton, A.: Real-time full-body motion capture from video and IMUs. In: 2017 Fifth International Conference on 3D Vision (3DV) (2017)
42. Li, S., Zhang, W., Chan, A.B.: Maximum-margin structured learning with deep networks for 3D human pose estimation. In: Proceedings of the IEEE International Conference on Computer Vision, pp. 2848–2856 (2015)
43. Tekin, B., Márquez-Neila, P., Salzmann, M., Fua, P.: Fusing 2D uncertainty and 3D cues for monocular body pose estimation. arXiv preprint arXiv:1611.05708 (2016)
44. Tome, D., Russell, C., Agapito, L.: Lifting from the deep: convolutional 3D pose estimation from a single image. arXiv preprint arXiv:1701.00295 (2017)
45. Lin, M., Lin, L., Liang, X., Wang, K., Cheng, H.: Recurrent 3D pose sequence machines. In: CVPR (2017)
46. Martinez, J., Hossain, R., Romero, J., Little, J.J.: A simple yet effective baseline for 3D human pose estimation. In: ICCV (2017)

Occlusion-Aware Hand Pose Estimation Using Hierarchical Mixture Density Network

Qi Ye[✉] and Tae-Kyun Kim

Imperial College London, London, UK
q.ye14@imperial.ac.uk

Abstract. Learning and predicting the pose parameters of a 3D hand model given an image, such as locations of hand joints, is challenging due to large viewpoint changes and articulations, and severe self-occlusions exhibited particularly in egocentric views. Both feature learning and prediction modeling have been investigated to tackle the problem. Though effective, most existing discriminative methods yield a single deterministic estimation of target poses. Due to their single-value mapping intrinsic, they fail to adequately handle self-occlusion problems, where occluded joints present multiple modes. In this paper, we tackle the self-occlusion issue and provide a complete description of observed poses given an input depth image by a novel method called hierarchical mixture density networks (HMDN). The proposed method leverages the state-of-the-art hand pose estimators based on Convolutional Neural Networks to facilitate feature learning, while it models the multiple modes in a two-level hierarchy to reconcile single-valued and multi-valued mapping in its output. The whole framework with a mixture of two differentiable density functions is naturally end-to-end trainable. In the experiments, HMDN produces interpretable and diverse candidate samples, and significantly outperforms the state-of-the-art methods on two benchmarks with occlusions, and performs comparably on another benchmark free of occlusions.

Keywords: 3D hand pose estimation · Occlusion
Multi-valued mapping · Convolutional Neural Network
Mixture density network

1 Introduction

3D hand pose estimation has shown an increasing interest with commercial miniaturized RGBD cameras and its ubiquitous applications in virtual/augmented reality (VR/AR) [13], sign language recognition [3,47], activity

---

Electronic supplementary material The online version of this chapter (https://doi.org/10.1007/978-3-030-01249-6_49) contains supplementary material, which is available to authorized users.

© Springer Nature Switzerland AG 2018
V. Ferrari et al. (Eds.): ECCV 2018, LNCS 11214, pp. 817–834, 2018.
https://doi.org/10.1007/978-3-030-01249-6_49

818   Q. Ye and T.-K. Kim

recognition [29], and man-machine interfaces for robots and autonomous vehicles. There are generally two typical camera settings: a third-person viewpoint, where the camera is set in front of the user, and an egocentric (or first-person) viewpoint, where the camera is mounted on the user's head (in VR glasses, for example), or shoulder. While both settings share challenges like the full range of 3D global rotations, complex articulations, self-similar parts of hands, self-occlusions are more dominant in the egocentric viewpoints. Most existing hand benchmarks are collected in the third-person viewpoints, e.g. the two widely used ICVL [38] and NYU [41] have less than 9% occluded finger joints.

Discriminative methods (cf. generative model fitting) in hand pose estimation learn a mapping from an input image to pose parameters from a large training dataset, and have been very successful in the settings of third-person viewpoints. However, they fail to handle occlusions frequently encountered in egocentric viewpoints. They treat the mapping to be single-valued, not being aware of that an input image may have multiple pose hypotheses when occlusions occur. See Fig. 1 where an example image and its multiple pose labels from the BigHand dataset [48] are shown.

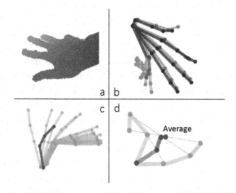

Fig. 1. (a) A hand depth image with the pinky finger occluded. (b) Multiple pose labels (visible joints are in blue and occluded joints in yellow) and the predicted pose (in red) by CNN trained using a mean squared error. (c) A closer look of the multiple labels and the CNN prediction for the occluded joints. (d) The average of two labels yields a physically implausible pose. (Color figure online)

Given a set of hand images and their pose labels i.e. 3D joint locations, discriminative methods such as Convolutional Neural Networks (CNN) minimize a mean squared error function, and the minimization of such error functions typically yields the averages of joint locations conditioned on input images. When all finger joints in the images are visible, the mapping is single-valued and the conditional average is correct, though the average only provides a limited description of the joint locations. However, for the occlusion cases, which happen frequently in the egocentric and hand-object interaction scenarios [7,22–24], the mapping is multi-valued due to occluded joints that exhibit multiple locations given the same images. The conditional average of the joint locations is not necessarily a correct pose, as shown in Fig. 1b and c (The skeletons are shown in a 3D rotated view to better illustrate the problem, same for the other 3D skeletons shown in the paper). The prediction of a CNN trained by the mean squared error function is shown in red. It is interpretable and close to the ground truth for the visible joints, whereas it is physically implausible and not close to any of the given poses for the occluded joints. The example is clearer in Fig. 1d, where we are given two available poses for the same image and CNN trained with the mean squared error function produces the pose estimation in red.

Existing discriminative methods, including the above CNN, are mostly deterministic, i.e. their outputs are single poses, thus lacking the description of all available joint locations. A discriminative method often serves as the initialization of a generative model fitting in the hybrid pose estimation approaches [31,36]. If the discriminative method yields a probability distribution that well fits the data, than a single deterministic output, it would allow sampling pose hypotheses from its distribution. This, in turn, reduces the search space, helping a faster convergence, and avoids local minima from diverse candidates in the model fitting. Such sampling is crucial also for multi-stage pose estimation [36] and hand tracking [21]. Previous methods ignore the pose space to be explored ahead and their optimization frameworks are not aware of occlusions.

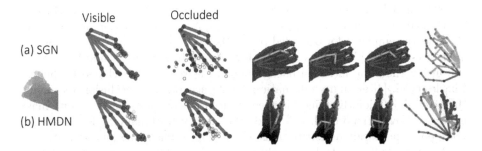

Fig. 2. Samples drawn from the distributions of SGN and HMDN for finger tips.

Fig. 3. Hand images under self-occlusions exhibiting multiple pose labels.

In this paper, hierarchical mixture density networks (HMDN) are proposed to give a complete description of hand poses given images under occlusions. The probability distribution of joint locations is modeled in a two-level hierarchy to consider both single- and multi-valued mapping conditioned on the joint visibility. The first level represents the distribution of a latent variable for the joint visibility, while the second level the distribution of joint locations by a single Gaussian model for visible joints or a Gaussian mixture model for occluded joints. The hierarchical mixture density is topped upon the CNN output layer, and the whole network is trained end-to-end with the differentiable density functions. See Fig. 2. The distribution of the proposed method HMDN captures diverse joint locations in a compact manner, compared to the network that learns a single Gaussian distribution (SGN). To the best of our knowledge, HMDN is the first solution that has its estimation in the form of a conditional probability distribution with the awareness of occlusions in 3D hand pose estimation. The experiments show that the proposed method significantly improves several baselines and state-of-the-art methods under occlusions given the same number of pose hypotheses.

2   Related Work

2.1   Pose Estimation Under Occlusion

For free hand motions, methods explicitly tackling self-occlusions are rare as most existing datasets are collected in third-person viewpoints and the proportion of occluded joints is small. Mueller et al. [16] observed that many existing methods fail to work under occlusions and even some commercial systems claiming for egocentric viewpoints often fail under severe occlusions. Methods developed for hand-object interactions [23,33,42], where occlusions happen frequently, model hands and objects together to resolve the occlusion issues. Jang et al. [13] and Rogez et al. [28] exploit pose priors to refine the estimations. Mueller et al. [16] and Rogez et al. [27] generate synthetic images to train discriminative methods for difficult egocentric views.

In human body pose estimation and object keypoint detection, occlusions are tackled more explicitly [4,5,8,10,12,17,26,32]. Chen et al. [5] and Ghiasi et al. [8] learn templates for occluded parts. Hsiao et al. [12] construct a occlusion model to score the plausibility of occluded regions. Rafi et al. [26] and Wang et al. [44] utilize the information in backgrounds to help localize occluded keypoints. Charles et al. [4] evaluate automatic labeling according to occlusion reasoning. Haque et al. [10] jointly refine the prediction for visible parts and visibility mask in stages. Navaratnam et al. [17] tackle the multi-valued mapping for 3d human body pose via marginal distributions which help estimate the joint density.

The existing methods do not address multi-modalities nor do not model the difference in distributions of visible and occluded joints. For CNN-based hand pose regression [19,20,41,46], the loss function used is the mean squared error, bringing in the aforementioned issues under occlusions. For random forest-based pose regression [31,34,38], the estimation is made from the data in leaf nodes and it is convenient to fit a multi-modal model to the data. However, with no information of which joints are visible or occluded, the data in all leaf nodes is captured either by the mean-shift (a uni-modal distribution) or a Gaussian Mixture Model (GMM) [36].

2.2   Mixture Models

Mixture density networks (MDN) were first proposed in [1] to enable neural networks to overcome the limitation of the mean squared error function by producing a probability distribution. Zen et al. [49] use MDN for acoustic modeling and Kinoshita et al. [15] for speech feature enhancement. Variani [43] proposes to learn the features and the GMM model jointly. All these work apply MDN to model acoustic signals without an adaptation of the mixture density model. In addition to applying MDN to model the hand pose space when multiple modes exist due to occlusion, we extend MDN by a two-level hierarchy to fit the specific mixture of single-valued and multi-valued problems, for the application of hand pose estimation under occlusions. To model data under noise, a similar hierarchical mixture model is proposed in [6] to represent "useful" data and "noise" by different sub-components, and a Bayesian approach is used to learn the parameters of the mixture model. Different from the work, we model a conditional distribution and use CNN to discriminatively learn the model parameters.

3 Hierarchical Mixture Density Network

3.1 Model Representation

The dataset to learn the model consists of $\{x_n, Y_n^d, v_n^d | n = 1, \ldots, N, d = 1, \ldots, D\}$, where x_n, Y_n^d, and v_n^d denote the n-th hand depth image, the multiple pose labels i.e. 3D locations of the d-th joint of the n-th image, and the visibility label of the d-th joint of the n-th image, respectively. The d-th joint is associated with multiple labels $Y_n^d = \{y_{nm}^d\}$, where $y_{nm}^d \in R^3$ is the m-th label i.e. 3D location. See Fig. 3 for examples. Each shows different example labels overlaid on the same depth image (in the first three columns), and all available labels in a 3D rotated view (in the last column). Visible joints are in blue and occluded joints in other colors. The visibility label is binary, indicating whether the d-th joint of the n-th image is visible or not. We treat D joints independently.

To model hand poses under occlusions, a two-level hierarchy is considered. The top-level takes the visibility label, and the bottom-level switches between a uni-modal distribution and a multi-modal distribution, depending on the joint visibility.

The binary label or variable v_n^d follows the Bernoulli distribution,

$$p(v_n^d | w_n^d) = (w_n^d)^{v_n^d}(1 - w_n^d)^{(1-v_n^d)}, \tag{1}$$

where w_n^d is the probability that the joint is visible. As existing hand benchmarks do not provide the joint visibility labels, we use a sphere model similar to [25] to generate the visibility labels from the available pose labels. The sphere centers are obtained from the joint locations and depth image pixels are assigned to the nearest spheres. Hand joints whose spheres have the number of pixels below a threshold are labeled as occluded. See Fig. 4. The visibility labels v_n^d are used for training, and they are inferred at testing.

When $v_n^d = 1$, the joint is visible in the image and the location is deterministic. Considering the label noise, y_{nm}^d is generated from a single Gaussian distribution,

$$p(y_{nm}^d | v_n^d = 1) = \mathcal{N}(y_{nm}^d; \mu_n^d, \sigma_n^d). \tag{2}$$

When the joint is occluded i.e. $v_n^d = 0$, it has multiple labels and they are drawn from a Gaussian Mixture Model (GMM) with J components

$$p(y_{nm}^d | v_n^d = 0) = \sum_{j=1}^{J} \pi_{nj}^d \mathcal{N}(y_{nm}^d; \epsilon_{nj}^d, s_{nj}^d), \tag{3}$$

where ϵ_{nj}^d and s_{nj}^d represent the center and standard deviation of the j-th component. The location y_{nm}^d is drawn from the j-th component dependent on a hidden variable z_{nj}^d, where $z_{nj}^d \in \{0,1\}$ and $\sum_{j=1}^{J} z_{nj}^d = 1$. The hidden variable is under the distribution $p(z_{nj}^d) = \prod_{j=1}^{J} (\pi_{nj}^d)^{(z_{nj}^d)}$, where $0 \leq \pi_{nj}^d \leq 1$, $\sum_{j=1}^{J} \pi_{nj}^d = 1$.

Fig. 4. Left: the hand sphere model; Right: examples with pixels assigned to different parts

With all components defined, the distribution of the joint location conditioned on the visibility is

$$p(y_{nm}^d | v_n^d) = \left[\mathcal{N}(y_{nm}^d; \mu_n^d, \sigma_n^d)\right]^{v_n^d} \left[\sum_{j=1}^{J} \pi_{nj}^d \mathcal{N}(y_{nm}^d; \epsilon_{nj}^d, s_{nj}^d)\right]^{(1-v_n^d)} \tag{4}$$

and the joint distribution of y_{nm}^d and v_n^d is

$$p(y_{nm}^d, v_n^d) = \left[w_n^d \mathcal{N}(y_{nm}^d; \mu_n^d, \sigma_n^d)\right]^{v_n^d} \left[(1 - w_n^d) \sum_{j=1}^{J} \pi_{nj}^d \mathcal{N}(y_{nm}^d; \epsilon_{nj}^d, s_{nj}^d)\right]^{(1-v_n^d)}. \tag{5}$$

Equation (4) shows that the generation of joint locations y_{nm}^d given the input image x_n is in a two-level hierarchy: first, a sample v_n^d is drawn from Eq. (1) and then, depending on v_n^d, a joint location is drawn either from a uni-modal Gaussian distribution or GMM. Thus, the proposed model switches between the two cases and provides a full description of hand poses under occlusions. The joint distribution in Eq. (5) is used to define the loss function in Sect. 3.3.

3.2   Architecture

The formulations in the previous section are presented for the d-th joint y_{nm}^d. For all D joints of hands, the distribution is obtained by multiplying the distributions of independent joints. The observed hand poses and the joint visibility, given x_n, are drawn from $\prod\limits_{d=1}^{D} \prod\limits_{m} p(y_{nm}^d, v_n^d)$.

Note that the hierarchical mixture density in Eq. (4) and the joint distribution in Eq. (5) are conditioned on x_n. All model parameters are in a functional form of x_n and the joint distribution in Eq. (5) is differentiable. We choose to learn these functions by a CNN and the distribution is parameterized by the output of the CNN. As shown in Fig. 5, the input of the CNN is an image x_n and the outputs are the HMDN parameters: $w_n^d, \mu_n^d, \sigma_n^d, \epsilon_{nj}^d, s_{nj}^d, \pi_{nj}^d$, for $d = 1, \ldots, D$ and $j = 1, \ldots, J$. The output parameters consist of three parts. w_n^d is the visibility probability in Eq. (1), μ_n^d, σ_n^d for the uni-modal Gaussian in Eq. (2), and $\epsilon_{nj}^d, s_{nj}^d, \pi_{nj}^d$ for the GMM in Eq. (3). Different activation functions are used to meet the defined ranges of parameters. For instance, the standard deviations σ_n^d and s_{nj}^d are activated by an exponential function to remain positive and π_{nj}^d by a softmax function to be in $[0, 1]$.

The prediction of the visibility, the value of w_n^d, is used to compute the visibility loss over the visibility label v_n^d. See Sect. 3.3. Depending on the visibility label v_n^d, the parameters of the uni-modal Gaussian (for visible joints) or GMM (for occluded joints) are chosen to compute the loss, as shown in blue and in orange respectively in Fig. 5.

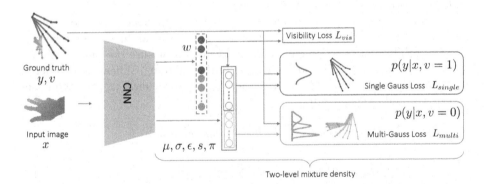

Fig. 5. Hierarchical Mixture Density Network. Hand joint locations y given the input image x are modeled in a two-level hierarchy: in the first level, the visibility is modeled by Bernoulli distribution whose parameter is w; then depending on the visibility, the joint locations are either modeled by uni-modal Gaussian distributions (visible joints, shown in blue) or GMMs (occluded joint, shown in orange). The CNN outputs the parameters of HMDN, i.e. w, μ, σ, ϵ, s, π. (Color figure online)

3.3   Training and Testing

The likelihood for the entire dataset $\{x_n, Y_n^d, v_n^d | n = 1, \ldots, N, d = 1, \ldots, D\}$ is computed as $P = \prod\limits_{n=1}^{N} \prod\limits_{d=1}^{D} \prod\limits_{m} p(y_{nm}^d, v_n^d)$, where $p(y_{nm}^d, v_n^d)$ in (5) has the model parameters dependent on x_n. Thus, our goal is to learn the neural networks that yield the parameters that maximize the likelihood on the dataset. We use the negative logarithmic likelihood as the loss function.

$$L = -logP = \sum_{n=1}^{N}\sum_{d=1}^{D}\sum_{m}\{L_{vis} + L_{single} + L_{multi}\}, \tag{6}$$

where

$$L_{vis} = -v_n^d log(w_n^d) - (1 - v_n^d)log(1 - w_n^d), \tag{7}$$

$$L_{single} = -v_n^d log(\mathcal{N}(y_{nm}^d; \mu_n^d, \sigma_n^d)), \tag{8}$$

$$L_{multi} = -(1 - v_n^d)log(\sum_{j=1}^{J}\pi_{nj}^d\mathcal{N}(y_{nm}^d; \epsilon_{nj}^d, s_{nj}^d)). \tag{9}$$

The three loss functions correspond to the three branches in Fig. 5. The visibility loss L_{vis} is computed using the predicated value of w_n^d. When $v_n^d = 1$, $L_{multi} = 0$ and L_{single} is calculated, and when $v_n^d = 0$, vise versa.

During testing, when an image x_n is fed into the network, the prediction for the d-th joint location is diverted to different branches according to the prediction of the visibility probability w_n^d. If w_n^d is larger than 0.5, the prediction (or sampling) for the location is made by the uni-modal Gaussian distribution in Eq. (2); otherwise, the GMM in Eq. (3).

However, when the prediction for the visibility is erroneous, the prediction for the joint location will be wrong. To help the bias problem, instead of using the binary visibility labels v_n^d to compute the likelihood, we use the samples drawn from the estimated distribution in Eq. (1) during training. When the number of samples is large enough, the mean of these samples becomes w_n^d. So, the losses in Eqs. (8) and (9) change to

$$L_{single} = -w_n^d log(\mathcal{N}(y_{nm}^d; \mu_n^d, \sigma_n^d)), \tag{10}$$

$$L_{multi} = -(1 - w_n^d)log(\sum_{j=1}^{J}\pi_{nj}^d\mathcal{N}(y_{nm}^d; \epsilon_{nj}^d, s_{nj}^d)). \tag{11}$$

The modified losses in Eqs. (10) and (11) can be seen as a soft version of the original ones Eqs. (8) and (9).

3.4   Degradation into Mixture Density Network

HMDN degrades into Mixture Density Network (MDN), without the supervision for learning the visibility variable. The other form of (4) is

$$p(y_{nm}^d|w_n^d) = w_n^d\mathcal{N}(y_{nm}^d; \mu_n^d, \sigma_n^d) + (1 - w_n^d)\left[\sum_{j=1}^{J}\pi_{nj}^d\mathcal{N}(y_{nm}^d; \epsilon_{nj}^d, s_{nj}^d)\right] \tag{12}$$

where the visibility probability w_n^d is learned with visibility labels. When the labels are not available, the above equation becomes

$$p(y_{nm}^d) = \sum_{j=1}^{J+1} \bar{\pi}_{nj}^d \mathcal{N}(y_{nm}^d; \bar{\epsilon}_{nj}^d, \bar{s}_{nj}^d) \tag{13}$$

where $\bar{\pi}_{nJ+1}^d = w_n^d, \bar{\epsilon}_{nJ+1}^d = \mu_n^d, \bar{s}_{nJ+1}^d = \sigma_n^d$, and $\bar{\pi}_{nj}^d = (1 - w_n^d)\pi_{nj}^d, \bar{\epsilon}_{nj}^d = \epsilon_{nj}^d, \bar{s}_{nj}^d = s_{nj}^d$ for $j = 1, \ldots, J$. The visibility probability w_n^d in (12) is absorbed into the GMM mixing coefficients $\bar{\pi}_{nj}^d$, and the distribution becomes a GMM with $J + 1$ components with no dependency on the visibility.

4 Experiments

4.1 Datasets

Public benchmarks for hand pose estimation are mostly collected in third-person viewpoints and do not offer plenty of occluded joints with multiple pose labels. We investigate four datasets, ICVL [37], NYU [41], MSHD [31] and BigHand [48], and exploit those containing a higher portion of occluded joints in the following experiments. The rate of occluded finger joints and the total number of training and testing images are listed in Table 1.

The images in these datasets are paired with pose labels i.e. joint locations, without the visibility information of the finger joints. As explained in Sect. 3.1, we use the sphere model to generate the visibility labels for training HMDN.

Table 1. The rate of occluded finger joints and the total number of frames

Dataset	ICVL	NYU	MSHD	EgoBigHand
Train (rate/total no.)	0.06/16,008	0.09/72,757	0.33/100,000	0.48/969,600
Test (rate/total no.)	0.01/1,596	0.36/8,252	0.16/2,000	0.24/33,468

The BigHand dataset consists of two subparts: the egocentric subset includes lots of self-occlusions but lacks diverse articulations; the third-person viewpoint subset spans the full articulation space while the proportion of occluded joints, especially severe occlusions, is low. We augment the egocentric subset using the articulations of the third-person view dataset, and use it called EgoBigHand for experiments. EgoBigHand includes 8 subjects: frames of 7 subjects are used for training and frames of 1 subject for testing.

More results are also shown on MSHD and NYU datasets.

4.2   Self-comparisons

The baseline of our comparison is Single Gaussian Network (SGN), which is the CNN trained with a uni-modal Gaussian distribution. In [2], it is shown that maximization of the likelihood function under a uni-modal Gaussian distribution for a linear model is equivalent to minimizing the mean squared error errors. In our experiments, we observed that the estimation error of SGN using the Gaussian center is about the same as that of the CNN trained with the mean squared error. For further comparisons under the probabilistic framework, we report the accuracies of SGN.

We also report the experiments of MDN as in the previous section, we showed that HMDN degrades to MDN when there is no visibility label available in training. To compare MDN with HMDN fairly, the number of Gaussian components of MDN is set $J + 1$ and that of GMM branch of HDMN is J.

The CNN network used is the U-net proposed in [30], by adapting the final layers to fully connected layers for regression. All the networks are trained using Adam [14] and the convergence times of all methods above took about 24 h using Geforce GTX 1080Ti.

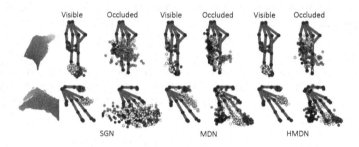

Fig. 6. Samples drawn from the distributions of SGN, MDN and HMDN for finger tips, shown in comparison to a pose label.

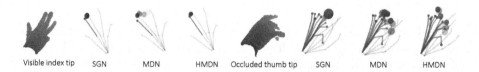

Fig. 7. Distributions predicted by SGN, MDN and HMDN for visible index tip and occluded thumb tip. Each magenta sphere represents a Gaussian component whose radius is the standard deviation and center is the mean. The degree of transparency is in proportion to the mixture coefficients $\{\pi\}$. (Color figure online)

Qualitative Analyses. See Fig. 6. 100 samples for each finger tip are drawn from the distributions of the different methods. HMDN is motivated by the intrinsic mapping difference: single-valued mapping for visible and multi-valued mapping for occluded joints. Our results, shown in Fig. 6, demonstrate its ability of modeling this difference by producing interpretable and diverse candidate samples accordingly. For visible joints, SGN and HMDN produce the samples distributed in a compact region around the ground truth location, while the samples from MDN scatter in a larger area. For occluded joints, while the samples produced by SGN scatter in a broad sphere range, the samples produced by HMDN and MDN form an arc-shaped region, which indicates the movement range of finger tips within the kinematic constraints.

With the aid of visibility supervision, HMDN handles well the self-occlusion problem by tailoring different density functions to the respective cases. The examples of the distributions predicted by SGN, MDN and HMDN for visible and occluded joints are shown in Fig. 7. The resulting compact distributions that fit both visible joints and occluded joints improve the pose prediction accuracies in the following quantitative analyses. Such compact and interpretable distributions are also helpful for hybrid methods [31,36]. For the discriminative-generative pipelines, the distribution largely reduces the space to be explored and produces diverse candidates to avoid being stuck at local minima in the generative part. For hand tracking methods [21], the distributions of occluded joints can be combined with the motion information e.g. speed and direction, to give a sharper i.e. more confident response at a certain location. The model can also find its application in multi-view settings.

Table 2. Estimation errors of different models. *see text for the evaluation metric used.

No. of Gauss. (J)	1	10		20		30	
Model	SGN	MDN	HMDN	MDN	HMDN	MDN	HMDN
Vis. Err. (mm)	32.8	32.2	30.5	34.0	30.7	32.6	30.5
Occ. Err. (mm)	36.5	35.4	34.8	36.4	34.4	35.6	34.2
*Occ. Err. (mm)	38.9	34.8	34.6	35.1	34.2	35.0	34.5

Quantitative Analyses. One hypothesis is drawn from the distribution of each method and is compared with the pose label, i.e. the ground truth joint location to measure the displacement error (in mm). The average errors are reported for visible joints and occluded joints separately in Table 2. Figure 8a presents the comparisons under the commonly used metric, the proportion of joints within a error threshold [31,36,46], using $J = 20$ in MDN/HMDN. HMDN outperforms both MDN and SGN for visible and occluded joints using the different numbers of Gaussian components. For occluded joints, HMDN improves SGN by 10% in the percentage of joints within the error 20 mm (Fig. 8a), and by about 2 mm in the mean displacement error (Table 2). HMDN also outperforms the baselines for visible joints. One can reason that given the limited network capacity, by

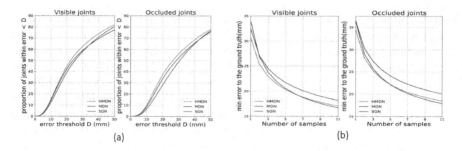

Fig. 8. Comparison of HMDN, SGN, MDN, when $J = 20$.

specifying density functions by data types, HMDN learns to take a better balance between the visible and occluded, while maximizing the likelihood of the entire training data. As shown in Table 2, the estimation errors of HMDN do not change much for $J = 10, 20, 30$. Note, however, the number of model parameters linearly increases with J.

In Fig. 8b, we vary the number of samples drawn from the distributions, and measure the minimum distance error. HMDN consistently achieves lower errors than SGN at all numbers of samples. Compared to MDN, HMDN appears better at the smaller numbers of samples. When the number of samples increases, the error gap between the two methods becomes small.

In both Table 2 and Fig. 8, we repeated the sampling process 100 times and reported the mean accuracies. The standard deviations were fairly small as: 0.03–0.04 mm for occluded joints, and 0.01–0.02 mm for visible joints.

As our motivation is in modeling the distribution of joint locations, we measure how well the predicted distribution aligns with the target distribution. As shown in Fig. 3, multiple pose labels are gathered for the same image with occlusions. We draw multiple samples from the predicted distribution and measure the minimum distance between the set of drawn samples and the set of pose labels. As shown in the last row of Table 2, the improvement is significant. Both MDN and HMDN outperform SGN by about 4 mm, which demonstrates that the arc-shaped distributions produced by MDN/HMDN align better with the target joint locations than the sphere-shaped distribution produced by SGN, as shown in Fig. 6. Instead of the minimum distance, we could use other similarity measures between distributions.

Though the improvement of HMDN over MDN is marginal, the number of parameters for the density is largely reduced by the awareness of occlusion in HMDN when joints are visible.

Bias. In Sect. 3.3, we proposed to mitigate the exposed bias during testing, by sampling from the visibility distribution at training. HMDN trained with the loss functions in Eqs. (8) and (9), is denoted as HMDN$_{hard}$, while the one trained with Eqs. (10) and (11) is HMDN$_{soft}$. In Table 3 HMDN$_{soft}$ consistently achieves lower errors than HMDN$_{hard}$ for different numbers of Gaussian components.

Table 3. Comparison of HMDN$_{hard}$ and HMDN$_{soft}$

No. of Gauss. (J)	10		20		30	
Model	HMDN$_{hard}$	HMDN$_{soft}$	HMDN$_{hard}$	HMDN$_{soft}$	HMDN$_{hard}$	HMDN$_{soft}$
Vis. Err. (mm)	32.2	30.5	32.9	30.7	33.1	30.5
Occ. Err. (mm)	35.8	34.8	35.9	34.4	36.4	34.2

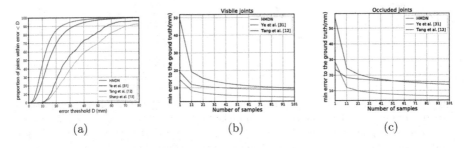

(a)   (b)   (c)

Fig. 9. Comparison of HMDN with prior work.

4.3   Comparison with the State-of-the-Arts

To compete with state-of-the-arts, the following strategies are adopted: first, a CNN network is trained to estimate the global rotation and translation, and conditioned on the estimation, HMDN is then trained; data augmentation, including translation, in-plane rotation, and scaling is used.

MSHD Dataset. MSHD has a considerable number of occluded joints both in training and testing set. We compare HMDN with three methods: Ye et al. [46], Tang et al. [36], Sharp et al. [31]. For [31], the results of its discriminative part are used. Figure 9a shows the proportion of joints within different error thresholds for the four methods, where a single prediction is used from HMDN.

In Fig. 9b and c, we further compare Ye et al. [46] and Tang et al. [36] with HMDN, by varying the number of hypotheses i.e. samples from the output distributions, and measuring the minimum displacement errors. Ye et al. [46] use a deterministic CNN. To produce multiple samples, they jitter around the CNN prediction, which can be treated as a uni-modal Gaussian. Tang et al. [36] use decision forests (3 trees) and the data points in the leaf nodes are modeled by GMM with 3 components. During testing, samples are drawn from GMMs of all trees. We used the original codes from the authors in our experiments.

HMDN significantly outperforms both methods for visible joints. For occluded joints, when the number of samples is 1, the errors of HMDN and Ye et al. [46] are close. However, Ye et al. [46] are not able to produce diverse samples to reach low errors as HMDN when the number of samples increases. Tang et al. [36] provide diverse candidates by GMM in its leaf nodes, but the variance of the distribution is much larger than that of Ye et al. [46] and HMDN for both visible and occluded joints. From the results, HMDN demonstrates its superiority for both the unimodal Gaussian model and GMM: the compact dis-

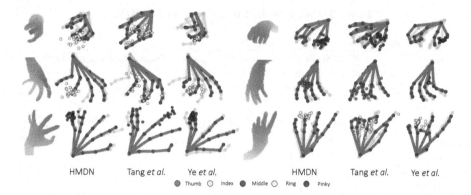

Fig. 10. Comparison of HMDN with Tang et al. [36] and Ye et al. [46]. Ground truth: skeletons in gray. Predictions from the models: skeletons in blue. For each image, samples for one tip joint from the three methods are scattered along the skeletons. Visible joints in the left column and occluded joints in the right column. (Color figure online)

tribution with lower bias for visible joints and the diverse samples yet having smaller variances for occluded joints. See Fig. 10 for example results. The samples from Tang et al. [36] for the finger tips spans a large region; those from Ye et al. [46] are more compact but many deviate from the ground truth.

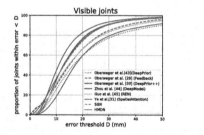 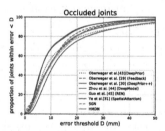

Fig. 11. Comparison with state-of-the-art approaches on NYU dataset.

NYU Dataset. The proposed method has also been evaluated on NYU dataset. Most joints in the training set are visible while on the testing set, there are up to 36% occluded joints. This implies all the joints in the testing dataset will be predicted as visible joints. Despite the ill-setting for HMDN, the method does not fail but degrades into SGN: the performances of SGN and HMDN are similar as shown in Fig. 11, and when compared with various state-of-the-arts based on CNN [9,18–20,46,50], HMDN is in the second place for visible joints and third place for occluded joints. Note the best method [20] uses a 50-layer ResNet model [11] and 21 more CNN models to refine the estimation.

5   Conclusion

This paper addresses the occlusion issues in 3D hand pose estimation. Existing discriminative methods are not aware of the multiple modes of occluded joints and thus do not adequately handle the self-occlusions frequently encountered in egocentric views. The proposed HMDN models the hand pose in a two-level hierarchy to explain visible joints and occluded joints by their unimodal and multi-modal traits respectively. The experimental results show that HMDN successfully captures the distributions of visible and occluded joints, and significantly outperforms prior work in terms of hand pose estimation accuracy. HMDN also produces interpretable and diverse candidate samples, which is useful for hybrid pose estimation, tracking, or multi-stage pose estimation, which require sampling.

In the paper, we assume the outputs are independent and do not exploit the temporal continuity. To sample kinematically valid poses, we can consider modeling hand structural information. One approach is to explicitly learn the dependency on top of part regression, e.g. by deep structured models [45]. Though the pose estimation benefits from the structural models, they usually result in highly interconnected models and thus difficult learning, and exact inference becomes intractable. The other approach exploits the dependency priors to post-process the part regression: e.g. a multivariate normal with correlation priors is used to constrain the pose samples [35,39,40]. We can also further incorporate the temporal dependency using offline priors or learning it with the part regression in the LSTM framework.

Testifying HMDN on hand-object and hand-hand interaction scenarios is interesting. Though it was tested on the datasets with self-occlusions, the generalization to different occlusion types is promising.

References

1. Bishop, C.M.: Mixture density networks (1994)
2. Bishop, C.M.: Pattern Recognition and Machine Learning. Springer, New York (2006)
3. Chang, H., Garcia-Hernando, G., Tang, D., Kim, T.K.: Spatio-temporal hough forest for efficient detection-localisation-recognition of fingerwriting in egocentric camera. CVIU **148**, 87–96 (2016). https://doi.org/10.1016/j.cviu.2016.01.010
4. Charles, J., Pfister, T., Magee, D., Hogg, D., Zisserman, A.: Personalizing human video pose estimation. In: CVPR (2016)
5. Chen, X., Yuille, A.: Parsing occluded people by flexible compositions. In: CVPR (2014)
6. Constantinopoulos, C., Titsias, M.K., Likas, A.: Bayesian feature and model selection for gaussian mixture models. TPAMI **28**(6), 1013–1018 (2006). https://doi.org/10.1109/TPAMI.2006.111
7. Garcia-Hernando, G., Yuan, S., Baek, S., Kim, T.: First-person hand action benchmark with RGB-D videos and 3D hand pose annotations. CoRR abs/1704.02463 (2017). http://arxiv.org/abs/1704.02463

8. Ghiasi, G., Yang, Y., Ramanan, D., Fowlkes, C.C.: Parsing occluded people. In: CVPR (2014)
9. Guo, H., Wang, G., Chen, X., Zhang, C., Qiao, F., Yang, H.: Region ensemble network: improving convolutional network for hand pose estimation. In: ICIP (2017)
10. Haque, A., Peng, B., Luo, Z., Alahi, A., Yeung, S., Fei-Fei, L.: Towards viewpoint invariant 3D human pose estimation. In: Leibe, B., Matas, J., Sebe, N., Welling, M. (eds.) ECCV 2016. LNCS, vol. 9905, pp. 160–177. Springer, Cham (2016). https://doi.org/10.1007/978-3-319-46448-0_10
11. He, K., Zhang, X., Ren, S., Sun, J.: Deep residual learning for image recognition. In: CVPR (2016)
12. Hsiao, E., Hebert, M.: Occlusion reasoning for object detection under arbitrary viewpoint. In: CVPR (2012)
13. Jang, Y., Noh, S.T., Chang, H.J., Kim, T.K., Woo, W.: 3D finger cape: clicking action and position estimation under self-occlusions in egocentric viewpoint. IEEE Trans. Vis. Comput. Graph. (TVCG) 21(4), 501–510 (2015)
14. Kingma, D., Ba, J.: Adam: a method for stochastic optimization. In: ICLR (2014)
15. Kinoshita, K., Delcroix, M., Ogawa, A., Higuchi, T., Nakatani, T.: Deep mixture density network for statistical model-based feature enhancement. In: ICASSP (2017)
16. Mueller, F., Mehta, D., Sotnychenko, O., Sridhar, S., Casas, D., Theobalt, C.: Real-time hand tracking under occlusion from an egocentric RGB-D sensor. In: ICCV (2017)
17. Navaratnam, R., Fitzgibbon, A.W., Cipolla, R.: The joint manifold model for semi-supervised multi-valued regression. In: ICCV (2007)
18. Oberweger, M., Wohlhart, P., Lepetit, V.: Hands deep in deep learning for hand pose estimation. In: Computer Vision Winter Workshop (CVWW) (2015)
19. Oberweger, M., Wohlhart, P., Lepetit, V.: Training a feedback loop for hand pose estimation. In: ICCV (2015)
20. Oberweger, M., Lepetit, V.: Deepprior++: improving fast and accurate 3D hand pose estimation. In: ICCV Workshops (2017)
21. Oikonomidis, I., Kyriazis, N., Argyros, A.: Efficient model-based 3D tracking of hand articulations using Kinect. In: BMVC (2011)
22. Oikonomidis, I., Kyriazis, N., Argyros, A.: Tracking the articulated motion of two strongly interacting hands. In: CVPR (2012)
23. Oikonomidis, I., Kyriazis, N., Argyros, A.A.: Full DOF tracking of a hand interacting with an object by modeling occlusions and physical constraints. In: ICCV (2011)
24. Poier, G., Roditakis, K., Schulter, S., Michel, D., Bischof, H., Argyros, A.: Hybrid one-shot 3D hand pose estimation by exploiting uncertainties. In: BMVC (2015)
25. Qian, C., Sun, X., Wei, Y., Tang, X., Sun, J.: Realtime and robust hand tracking from depth. In: ICCV (2014)
26. Rafi, U., Gall, J., Leibe, B.: A semantic occlusion model for human pose estimation from a single depth image. In: CVPR Workshops (2015)
27. Rogez, G., Supancic, J.S., Ramanan, D.: First-person pose recognition using egocentric workspaces. In: CVPR (2015)
28. Rogez, G., Supancic III, J.S., Khademi, M., Montiel, J.M.M., Ramanan, D.: 3D hand pose detection in egocentric RGB-D images. In: ECCV Workshops (2014)
29. Rohrbach, M., Amin, S., Andriluka, M., Schiele, B.: A database for fine grained activity detection of cooking activities. In: CVPR (2012)

30. Ronneberger, O., Fischer, P., Brox, T.: U-Net: convolutional networks for biomedical image segmentation. In: Navab, N., Hornegger, J., Wells, W.M., Frangi, A.F. (eds.) MICCAI 2015. LNCS, vol. 9351, pp. 234–241. Springer, Cham (2015). https://doi.org/10.1007/978-3-319-24574-4_28
31. Sharp, T., et al.: Accurate, robust, and flexible real-time hand tracking. In: CHI (2015)
32. Sigal, L., Black, M.J.: Measure locally, reason globally: occlusion-sensitive articulated pose estimation. In: CVPR (2006)
33. Sridhar, S., Mueller, F., Zollhöfer, M., Casas, D., Oulasvirta, A., Theobalt, C.: Real-time joint tracking of a hand manipulating an object from RGB-D input. In: Leibe, B., Matas, J., Sebe, N., Welling, M. (eds.) ECCV 2016. LNCS, vol. 9906, pp. 294–310. Springer, Cham (2016). https://doi.org/10.1007/978-3-319-46475-6_19
34. Sun, X., Wei, Y., Liang, S., Tang, X., Sun, J.: Cascaded hand pose regression. In: CVPR (2015)
35. Tan, D.J., et al.: Fits like a glove: rapid and reliable hand shape personalization. In: CVPR (2016)
36. Tang, D., Taylor, J., Kohli, P., Keskin, C., Kim, T.K., Shotton, J.: Opening the black box: hierarchical sampling optimization for estimating human hand pose. In: ICCV (2015)
37. Tang, D., Chang, H.J., Tejani, A., Kim, T.K.: Latent regression forest: structured estimation of 3D hand posture. In: CVPR (2014)
38. Tang, D., Yu, T.H., Kim, T.K.: Real-time articulated hand pose estimation using semi-supervised transductive regression forests. In: ICCV (2013)
39. Taylor, J., et al.: Efficient and precise interactive hand tracking through joint, continuous optimization of pose and correspondences. TOG 35(4), 143 (2016)
40. Tome, D., Russell, C., Agapito, L.: Lifting from the deep: convolutional 3D pose estimation from a single image. In: CVPR (2017)
41. Tompson, J., Stein, M., Lecun, Y., Perlin, K.: Real-time continuous pose recovery of human hands using convolutional networks. TOG 33(5), 169 (2014)
42. Tzionas, D., Ballan, L., Srikantha, A., Aponte, P., Pollefeys, M., Gall, J.: Capturing hands in action using discriminative salient points and physics simulation. IJCV 118(2), 172–193 (2016). https://doi.org/10.1007/s11263-016-0895-4
43. Variani, E., McDermott, E., Heigold, G.: A Gaussian mixture model layer jointly optimized with discriminative features within a deep neural network architecture. In: ICASSP (2015)
44. Wang, T., He, X., Barnes, N.: Learning structured hough voting for joint object detection and occlusion reasoning. In: CVPR (2013)
45. Yang, W., Ouyang, W., Li, H., Wang, X.: End-to-end learning of deformable mixture of parts and deep convolutional neural networks for human pose estimation. In: CVPR (2016)
46. Ye, Q., Yuan, S., Kim, T.-K.: Spatial attention deep net with partial PSO for hierarchical hybrid hand pose estimation. In: Leibe, B., Matas, J., Sebe, N., Welling, M. (eds.) ECCV 2016. LNCS, vol. 9912, pp. 346–361. Springer, Cham (2016). https://doi.org/10.1007/978-3-319-46484-8_21
47. Yin, F., Chai, X., Chen, X.: Iterative reference driven metric learning for signer independent isolated sign language recognition. In: Leibe, B., Matas, J., Sebe, N., Welling, M. (eds.) ECCV 2016. LNCS, vol. 9911, pp. 434–450. Springer, Cham (2016). https://doi.org/10.1007/978-3-319-46478-7_27
48. Yuan, S., Ye, Q., Stenger, B., Kim, T.K.: BigHand2.2M benchmark: hand pose data set and state of the art analysis. In: CVPR (2017)

49. Zen, H., Senior, A.: Deep mixture density networks for acoustic modeling in statistical parametric speech synthesis. In: ICASSP (2014)
50. Zhou, X., Wan, Q., Zhang, W., Xue, X., Wei, Y.: Model-based deep hand pose estimation. In: IJCAI (2016)

GANimation: Anatomically-Aware Facial Animation from a Single Image

Albert Pumarola[1]([✉]), Antonio Agudo[1], Aleix M. Martinez[2], Alberto Sanfeliu[1], and Francesc Moreno-Noguer[1]

[1] Institut de Robòtica i Informàtica Industrial, CSIC-UPC, 08028 Barcelona, Spain
apumarola@iri.upc.edu
[2] The Ohio State University, Columbus, OH 43210, USA

Abstract. Recent advances in Generative Adversarial Networks (GANs) have shown impressive results for task of facial expression synthesis. The most successful architecture is StarGAN, that conditions GANs' generation process with images of a specific domain, namely a set of images of persons sharing the same expression. While effective, this approach can only generate a discrete number of expressions, determined by the content of the dataset. To address this limitation, in this paper, we introduce a novel GAN conditioning scheme based on Action Units (AU) annotations, which describes in a continuous manifold the anatomical facial movements defining a human expression. Our approach allows controlling the magnitude of activation of each AU and combine several of them. Additionally, we propose a fully unsupervised strategy to train the model, that only requires images annotated with their activated AUs, and exploit attention mechanisms that make our network robust to changing backgrounds and lighting conditions. Extensive evaluation show that our approach goes beyond competing conditional generators both in the capability to synthesize a much wider range of expressions ruled by anatomically feasible muscle movements, as in the capacity of dealing with images in the wild.

Keywords: GANs · Face animation · Action-unit condition

1 Introduction

Being able to automatically animate the facial expression from a single image would open the door to many new exciting applications in different areas, including the movie industry, photography technologies, fashion and e-commerce business, to name but a few. As Generative and Adversarial Networks have become more prevalent, this task has experienced significant advances, with architectures such as StarGAN [4], which is able not only to synthesize novel expressions, but also to change other attributes of the face, such as age, hair color or gender. Despite its generality, StarGAN can only change a particular aspect of a face among a discrete number of attributes defined by the annotation granularity of the dataset. For instance, for the facial expression synthesis task, [4] is

© Springer Nature Switzerland AG 2018
V. Ferrari et al. (Eds.): ECCV 2018, LNCS 11214, pp. 835–851, 2018.
https://doi.org/10.1007/978-3-030-01249-6_50

$\mathbf{I_{y_r}}$ $\alpha = .12$ $\alpha = .25$ $\alpha = .37$ $\alpha = .5$ $\alpha = .62$ $\alpha = .75$ $\alpha = .87$ $\alpha = 1$

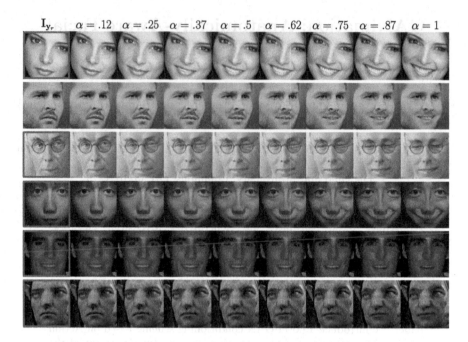

Fig. 1. Facial animation from a single image. We propose an anatomically coherent approach that is not constrained to a discrete number of expressions and can animate a given image and render novel expressions in a continuum. In these examples, we are given solely the left-most input image $\mathbf{I_{y_r}}$ (highlighted by a green square), and the parameter α controls the degree of activation of the target action units involved in a smiling-like expression. Additionally, our system can handle images with unnatural illumination conditions, such as the example in the bottom row.

trained on the RaFD [16] dataset which has only 8 binary labels for facial expressions, namely sad, neutral, angry, contemptuous, disgusted, surprised, fearful and happy.

Facial expressions, however, are the result of the combined and coordinated action of facial muscles that cannot be categorized in a discrete and low number of classes. Ekman and Friesen [6] developed the Facial Action Coding System (FACS) for describing facial expressions in terms of the so-called Action Units (AUs), which are anatomically related to the contractions of specific facial muscles. Although the number of action units is relatively small (30 AUs were found to be anatomically related to the contraction of specific facial muscles), more than 7,000 different AU combinations have been observed [30]. For example, the facial expression for *fear* is generally produced with activations: Inner Brow Raiser (AU1), Outer Brow Raiser (AU2), Brow Lowerer (AU4), Upper Lid Raiser (AU5), Lid Tightener (AU7), Lip Stretcher (AU20) and Jaw Drop (AU26) [5]. Depending on the magnitude of each AU, the expression will transmit the emotion of fear to a greater or lesser extent.

In this paper we aim at building a model for synthetic facial animation with the level of expressiveness of FACS, and being able to generate anatomically-aware expressions in a continuous domain, without the need of obtaining any facial landmarks [36]. For this purpose we leverage on the recent EmotioNet dataset [3], which consists of one million images of facial expressions (we use 200,000 of them) of emotion in the wild annotated with discrete AUs activations[1]. We build a GAN architecture which, instead of being conditioned with images of a specific domain as in [4], it is conditioned on a one-dimensional vector indicating the presence/absence and the magnitude of each action unit. We train this architecture in an unsupervised manner that only requires images with their activated AUs. To circumvent the need for pairs of training images of the same person under different expressions, we split the problem in two main stages. First, we consider an AU-conditioned bidirectional adversarial architecture which, given a single training photo, initially renders a new image under the desired expression. This synthesized image is then rendered-back to the original pose, hence being directly comparable to the input image. We incorporate very recent losses to assess the photorealism of the generated image. Additionally, our system also goes beyond state-of-the-art in that it can handle images under changing backgrounds and illumination conditions. We achieve this by means of an attention layer that focuses the action of the network only in those regions of the image that are relevant to convey the novel expression.

As a result, we build an anatomically coherent facial expression synthesis method, able to render images in a continuous domain, and which can handle images in the wild with complex backgrounds and illumination conditions. As we will show in the results section, it compares favorably to other conditioned-GANs schemes, both in terms of the visual quality of the results, and the possibilities of generation. Figure 1 shows some example of the results we obtain, in which given one input image, we gradually change the magnitude of activation of the AUs used to produce a smile.

2 Related Work

Generative Adversarial Networks. GANs are a powerful class of generative models based on game theory. A typical GAN optimization consists in simultaneously training a generator network to produce realistic fake samples and a discriminator network trained to distinguish between real and fake data. This idea is embedded by the so-called *adversarial loss*. Recent works [1,9] have shown improved stability relaying on the continuous Earth Mover Distance metric, which we shall use in this paper to train our model. GANs have been shown to produce very realistic images with a high level of detail and have been successfully used for image translation [10,13,38], face generation [12,28], super-resolution imaging [18,34], indoor scene modeling [12,33] and human poses editing [27].

---

[1] The dataset was re-annotated with [2] to obtain continuous activation annotations.

Conditional GANs. An active area of research is designing GAN models that incorporate conditions and constraints into the generation process. Prior studies have explored combining several conditions, such as text descriptions [29,37,39] and class information [23,24]. Particularly interesting for this work are those methods exploring image based conditioning as in image super-resolution [18], future frame prediction [22], image in-painting [25], image-to-image translation [10] and multi-target domain transfer [4].

Unpaired Image-to-Image Translation. As in our framework, several works have also tackled the problem of using unpaired training data. First attempts [21] relied on Markov random field priors for Bayesian based generation models using images from the marginal distributions in individual domains. Others explored enhancing GANS with Variational Auto-Encoder strategies [15,21]. Later, several works [19,25] have exploited the idea of driving the system to produce mappings transforming the style without altering the original input image content. Our approach is more related to those works exploiting cycle consistency to preserve key attributes between the input and the mapped image, such as CycleGAN [38], DiscoGAN [13] and StarGAN [4].

Face Image Manipulation. Face generation and editing is a well-studied topic in computer vision and generative models. Most works have tackled the task on attribute editing [17,26,31] trying to modify attribute categories such as adding glasses, changing color hair, gender swapping and aging. The works that are most related to ours are those synthesizing facial expressions. Early approaches addressed the problem using mass-and-spring models to physically approximate skin and muscle movement [7]. The problem with this approach is that is difficult to generate natural looking facial expressions as there are many subtle skin movements that are difficult to render with simple spring models. Another line of research relied on 2D and 3D morphings [35], but produced strong artifacts around the region boundaries and was not able to model illumination changes.

More recent works [4,20,24] train highly complex convolutional networks able to work with images in the wild. However, these approaches have been conditioned on discrete emotion categories (e.g., happy, neutral, and sad). Instead, our model resumes the idea of modeling skin and muscles, but we integrate it in modern deep learning machinery. More specifically, we learn a GAN model conditioned on a continuous embedding of muscle movements, allowing to generate a large range of anatomically possible face expressions as well as smooth facial movement transitions in video sequences.

3   Problem Formulation

Let us define an input RGB image as $\mathbf{I}_{\mathbf{y}_r} \in \mathbb{R}^{H \times W \times 3}$, captured under an arbitrary facial expression. Every gesture expression is encoded by means of a set of N action units $\mathbf{y}_r = (y_1, \ldots, y_N)^\top$, where each y_n denotes a normalized value between 0 and 1 to module the magnitude of the n-th action unit. It is worth

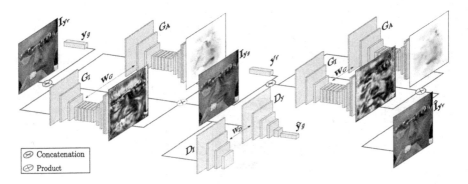

Fig. 2. Overview of our approach to generate photo-realistic conditioned images. The proposed architecture consists of two main blocks: a generator G to regress attention and color masks; and a critic D to evaluate the generated image in its photorealism D_I and expression conditioning fulfillment $\hat{\mathbf{y}}_g$. Note that our systems does not require supervision, i.e., no pairs of images of the same person with different expressions, nor the target image $\mathbf{I}_{\mathbf{y}_g}$ are assumed to be known.

pointing out that thanks to this continuous representation, a natural interpolation can be done between different expressions, allowing to render a wide range of realistic and smooth facial expressions.

Our aim is to learn a mapping $\mathcal{M}$ to translate $\mathbf{I}_{\mathbf{y}_r}$ into an output image $\mathbf{I}_{\mathbf{y}_g}$ conditioned on an action-unit target $\mathbf{y}_g$, i.e., we seek to estimate the mapping $\mathcal{M} : (\mathbf{I}_{\mathbf{y}_r}, \mathbf{y}_g) \rightarrow \mathbf{I}_{\mathbf{y}_g}$. To this end, we propose to train $\mathcal{M}$ in an unsupervised manner, using M training triplets $\{\mathbf{I}_{\mathbf{y}_r}^m, \mathbf{y}_r^m, \mathbf{y}_g^m\}_{m=1}^M$, where the target vectors $\mathbf{y}_g^m$ are randomly generated. Importantly, we neither require pairs of images of the same person under different expressions, nor the expected target image $\mathbf{I}_{\mathbf{y}_g}$.

4 Our Approach

This section describes our novel approach to generate photo-realistic conditioned images, which, as shown in Fig. 2, consists of two main modules. On the one hand, a generator $G(\mathbf{I}_{\mathbf{y}_r}|\mathbf{y}_g)$ is trained to realistically transform the facial expression in image $\mathbf{I}_{\mathbf{y}_r}$ to the desired $\mathbf{y}_g$. Note that G is applied twice, first to map the input image $\mathbf{I}_{\mathbf{y}_r} \rightarrow \mathbf{I}_{\mathbf{y}_g}$, and then to render it back $\mathbf{I}_{\mathbf{y}_g} \rightarrow \hat{\mathbf{I}}_{\mathbf{y}_r}$. On the other hand, we use a WGAN-GP [9] based critic $D(\mathbf{I}_{\mathbf{y}_g})$ to evaluate the quality of the generated image as well as its expression.

4.1 Network Architecture

Generator. Let G be the generator block. Since it will be applied bidirectionally (i.e., to map either input image to desired expression and vice-versa) in the following discussion we use subscripts o and f to indicate *origin* and *final*.

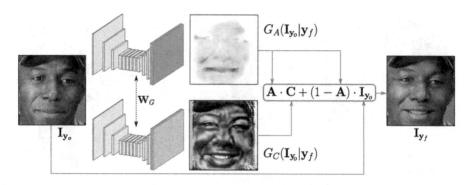

Fig. 3. Attention-based generator. Given an input image and the target expression, the generator regresses and attention mask $\mathbf{A}$ and an RGB color transformation $\mathbf{C}$ over the entire image. The attention mask defines a per pixel intensity specifying to which extend each pixel of the original image will contribute in the final rendered image.

Given the image $\mathbf{I}_{\mathbf{y}_o} \in \mathbb{R}^{H \times W \times 3}$ and the N-vector $\mathbf{y}_f$ encoding the desired expression, we form the input of generator as a concatenation $(\mathbf{I}_{\mathbf{y}_o}, \mathbf{y}_o) \in \mathbb{R}^{H \times W \times (N+3)}$, where $\mathbf{y}_o$ has been represented as N arrays of size $H \times W$.

One key ingredient of our system is to make G focus only on those regions of the image that are responsible of synthesizing the novel expression and keep the rest elements of the image such as hair, glasses, hats or jewelery untouched. For this purpose, we have embedded an attention mechanism to the generator. Concretely, instead of regressing a full image, our generator outputs two masks, a color mask $\mathbf{C}$ and attention mask $\mathbf{A}$. The final image can be obtained as:

$$\mathbf{I}_{\mathbf{y}_f} = \mathbf{A} \cdot \mathbf{C} + (1 - \mathbf{A}) \cdot \mathbf{I}_{\mathbf{y}_o}, \tag{1}$$

where $\mathbf{A} = G_A(\mathbf{I}_{\mathbf{y}_o}|\mathbf{y}_f) \in \{0, \ldots, 1\}^{H \times W}$ and $\mathbf{C} = G_C(\mathbf{I}_{\mathbf{y}_o}|\mathbf{y}_f) \in \mathbb{R}^{H \times W \times 3}$. The mask $\mathbf{A}$ indicates to which extend each pixel of the $\mathbf{C}$ contributes to the output image $\mathbf{I}_{\mathbf{y}_f}$. In this way, the generator does not need to render static elements, and can focus exclusively on the pixels defining the facial movements, leading to sharper and more realistic synthetic images. This process is depicted in Fig. 3.

Conditional Critic. This is a network trained to evaluate the generated images in terms of their photo-realism and desired expression fulfillment. The structure of $D(\mathbf{I})$ resembles that of the PatchGan [10] network mapping from the input image $\mathbf{I}$ to a matrix $\mathbf{Y}_{\mathbf{I}} \in \mathbb{R}^{H/2^6 \times W/2^6}$, where $\mathbf{Y}_{\mathbf{I}}[i, j]$ represents the probability of the overlapping patch ij to be real. Also, to evaluate its conditioning, on top of it we add an auxiliary regression head that estimates the AUs activations $\hat{\mathbf{y}} = (\hat{y}_1, \ldots, \hat{y}_N)^\top$ in the image.

4.2   Learning the Model

The loss function we define contains four terms, namely an *image adversarial loss* [1] with the modification proposed by Gulrajani *et al.* [9] that pushes the distribution of the generated images to the distribution of the training images; the *attention loss* to drive the attention masks to be smooth and prevent them from saturating; the *conditional expression loss* that conditions the expression of the generated images to be similar to the desired one; and the *identity loss* that favors to preserve the person texture identity.

Image Adversarial Loss. In order to learn the parameters of the generator G, we use the modification of the standard GAN algorithm [8] proposed by WGAN-GP [9]. Specifically, the original GAN formulation is based on the Jensen-Shannon (JS) divergence loss function and aims to maximize the probability of correctly classifying real and rendered images while the generator tries to foul the discriminator. This loss is potentially not continuous with respect to the generator's parameters and can locally saturate leading to vanishing gradients in the discriminator. This is addressed in WGAN [1] by replacing JS with the continuous Earth Mover Distance. To maintain a Lipschitz constraint, WGAN-GP [9] proposes to add a gradient penalty for the critic network computed as the norm of the gradients with respect to the critic input.

Formally, let $\mathbf{I_{y_o}}$ be the input image with the initial condition $\mathbf{y}_o$, $\mathbf{y}_f$ the desired final condition, $\mathbb{P}_o$ the data distribution of the input image, and $\mathbb{P}_{\tilde{I}}$ the random interpolation distribution. Then, the *critic loss* $\mathcal{L}_{\mathrm{I}}(G, D_{\mathrm{I}}, \mathbf{I_{y_o}}, \mathbf{y}_f)$ we use is:

$$\mathbb{E}_{\mathbf{I_{y_o}} \sim \mathbb{P}_o}[D_{\mathrm{I}}(G(\mathbf{I_{y_o}}|\mathbf{y}_f))] - \mathbb{E}_{\mathbf{I_{y_o}} \sim \mathbb{P}_o}[D_{\mathrm{I}}(\mathbf{I_{y_o}})] + \lambda_{\mathrm{gp}}\mathbb{E}_{\tilde{I} \sim \mathbb{P}_{\tilde{I}}}\left[(\|\nabla_{\tilde{I}}D_{\mathrm{I}}(\tilde{I})\|_2 - 1)^2\right],$$

where λ_{gp} is a penalty coefficient.

Attention Loss. When training the model we do not have ground-truth annotation for the attention masks $\mathbf{A}$. Similarly as for the color masks $\mathbf{C}$, they are learned from the resulting gradients of the critic module and the rest of the losses. However, the attention masks can easily saturate to 1 which makes that $\mathbf{I_{y_o}} = G(\mathbf{I_{y_o}}|\mathbf{y}_f)$, that is, the generator has no effect. To prevent this situation, we regularize the mask with a l_2-weight penalty. Also, to enforce smooth spatial color transformation when combining the pixel from the input image and the color transformation $\mathbf{C}$, we perform a *Total Variation Regularization* over $\mathbf{A}$. The attention loss $\mathcal{L}_{\mathrm{A}}(G, \mathbf{I_{y_o}}, \mathbf{y}_f)$ can therefore be defined as:

$$\lambda_{\mathrm{TV}}\mathbb{E}_{\mathbf{I_{y_o}} \sim \mathbb{P}_o}\left[\sum_{i,j}^{H,W}\left[(\mathbf{A}_{i+1,j} - \mathbf{A}_{i,j})^2 + (\mathbf{A}_{i,j+1} - \mathbf{A}_{i,j})^2\right]\right] + \mathbb{E}_{\mathbf{I_{y_o}} \sim \mathbb{P}_o}[\|\mathbf{A}\|_2] \quad (2)$$

where $\mathbf{A} = G_A(\mathbf{I_{y_o}}|\mathbf{y}_f)$ and $\mathbf{A}_{i,j}$ is the i,j entry of $\mathbf{A}$. λ_{TV} is a penalty coefficient.

Conditional Expression Loss. While reducing the *image adversarial loss*, the generator must also reduce the error produced by the AUs regression head on top of D. In this way, G not only learns to render realistic samples but also learns to satisfy the target facial expression encoded by $\mathbf{y}_f$. This loss is defined with two components: an AUs regression loss with fake images used to optimize

G, and an AUs regression loss of real images used to learn the regression head on top of D. This loss $\mathcal{L}_y(G, D_y, \mathbf{I}_{\mathbf{y}_o}, \mathbf{y}_o, \mathbf{y}_f)$ is computed as:

$$\mathbb{E}_{\mathbf{I}_{\mathbf{y}_o} \sim \mathbb{P}_o} \left[\| D_y(G(\mathbf{I}_{\mathbf{y}_o} | \mathbf{y}_f))] - \mathbf{y}_f \|_2^2 \right] + \mathbb{E}_{\mathbf{I}_{\mathbf{y}_o} \sim \mathbb{P}_o} \left[\| D_y(\mathbf{I}_{\mathbf{y}_o}) - \mathbf{y}_o \|_2^2 \right]. \quad (3)$$

Identity Loss. With the previously defined losses the generator is enforced to generate photo-realistic face transformations. However, without ground-truth supervision, there is no constraint to guarantee that the face in both the input and output images correspond to the same person. Using a *cycle consistency loss* [38] we force the generator to maintain the identity of each individual by penalizing the difference between the original image $\mathbf{I}_{\mathbf{y}_o}$ and its reconstruction:

$$\mathcal{L}_{\text{idt}}(G, \mathbf{I}_{\mathbf{y}_o}, \mathbf{y}_o, \mathbf{y}_f) = \mathbb{E}_{\mathbf{I}_{\mathbf{y}_o} \sim \mathbb{P}_o} \left[\| G(G(\mathbf{I}_{\mathbf{y}_o} | \mathbf{y}_f) | \mathbf{y}_o) - \mathbf{I}_{\mathbf{y}_o} \|_1 \right]. \quad (4)$$

To produce realistic images it is critical for the generator to model both low and high frequencies. Our *PatchGan* based critic D_I already enforces high-frequency correctness by restricting our attention to the structure in local image patches. To also capture low-frequencies it is sufficient to use l_1-norm. In preliminary experiments, we also tried replacing l_1-norm with a more sophisticated *Perceptual* [11] loss, although we did not observe improved performance.

Full Loss. To generate the target image $\mathbf{I}_{\mathbf{y}_g}$, we build a loss function $\mathcal{L}$ by linearly combining all previous partial losses:

$$\mathcal{L} = \mathcal{L}_\mathrm{I}(G, D_\mathrm{I}, \mathbf{I}_{\mathbf{y}_r}, \mathbf{y}_g) + \lambda_y \mathcal{L}_y(G, D_y, \mathbf{I}_{\mathbf{y}_r}, \mathbf{y}_r, \mathbf{y}_g) \quad (5)$$
$$+ \lambda_\mathrm{A} \left(\mathcal{L}_\mathrm{A}(G, \mathbf{I}_{\mathbf{y}_g}, \mathbf{y}_r) + \mathcal{L}_\mathrm{A}(G, \mathbf{I}_{\mathbf{y}_r}, \mathbf{y}_g) \right) + \lambda_{\text{idt}} \mathcal{L}_{\text{idt}}(G, \mathbf{I}_{\mathbf{y}_r}, \mathbf{y}_r, \mathbf{y}_g),$$

where λ_A, λ_y and λ_{idt} are the hyper-parameters that control the relative importance of every loss term. Finally, we can define the following minimax problem:

$$G^\star = \arg \min_G \max_{D \in \mathcal{D}} \mathcal{L}, \quad (6)$$

where $G^\star$ draws samples from the data distribution. Additionally, we constrain our discriminator D to lie in $\mathcal{D}$, that represents the set of 1-Lipschitz functions.

5   Implementation Details

Our generator builds upon the variation of the network from Johnson *et al.* [11] proposed by [38] as it proved to achieve impressive results for image-to-image mapping. We have slightly modified it by substituting the last convolutional layer with two parallel convolutional layers, one to regress the color mask $\mathbf{C}$ and the other to define the attention mask $\mathbf{A}$. We also observed that changing batch normalization in the generator by instance normalization improved training stability. For the critic we have adopted the *PatchGan* architecture of [10], but removing feature normalization. Otherwise, when computing the gradient penalty, the norm of the critic's gradient would be computed with respect to the entire batch and not with respect to each input independently.

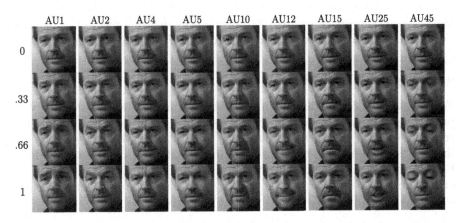

Fig. 4. Single AUs edition. Specific AUs are activated at increasing levels of intensity (from 0.33 to 1). The first row corresponds to a zero intensity application of the AU which correctly produces the original image in all cases.

The model is trained on the EmotioNet dataset [3]. We use a subset of 200,000 samples (over 1 million) to reduce training time. We use Adam [14] with learning rate of 0.0001, beta1 0.5, beta2 0.999 and batch size 25. We train for 30 epochs and linearly decay the rate to zero over the last 10 epochs. Every 5 optimization steps of the critic network we perform a single optimization step of the generator. The weight coefficients for the loss terms in Eq. (5) are set to $\lambda_{gp} = 10$, $\lambda_A = 0.1$, $\lambda_{TV} = 0.0001$, $\lambda_y = 4000$, $\lambda_{idt} = 10$. To improve stability we tried updating the critic using a buffer with generated images in different updates of the generator as proposed in [32] but we did not observe performance improvement. The model takes two days to train with a single GeForce® GTX 1080 Ti GPU.

6   Experimental Evaluation

This section provides a thorough evaluation of our system. We first test the main component, namely the single and multiple AUs editing. We then compare our model against current competing techniques in the task of discrete emotions editing and demonstrate our model's ability to deal with images in the wild and its capability to generate a wide range of anatomically coherent face transformations. Finally, we discuss the model's limitations and failure cases.

It is worth noting that in some of the experiments the input faces are not cropped. In this cases we first use a detector[2] to localize and crop the face, apply the expression transformation to that area with Eq. (1), and finally place the generated face back to its original position in the image. The attention mechanism guaranties a smooth transition between the morphed cropped face and the original image. As we shall see later, this three steps process results on

---

[2] We use the face detector from https://github.com/ageitgey/face_recognition.

higher resolution images compared to previous models. Supplementary material can be found on http://www.albertpumarola.com/research/GANimation/.

6.1   Single Action Units Edition

We first evaluate our model's ability to activate AUs at different intensities while preserving the person's identity. Figure 4 shows a subset of 9 AUs individually transformed with four levels of intensity (0, 0.33, 0.66, 1). For the case of 0 intensity it is desired not to change the corresponding AU. The model properly handles this situation and generates an identical copy of the input image for every case. The ability to apply an identity transformation is essential to ensure that non-desired facial movement will not be introduced.

Fig. 5. Attention model. Details of the intermediate attention mask **A** (first row) and the color mask **C** (second row). The bottom row images are the synthesized expressions. Darker regions of the attention mask **A** show those areas of the image more relevant for each specific AU. Brighter areas are retained from the original image.

For the non-zero cases, it can be observed how each AU is progressively accentuated. Note the difference between generated images at intensity 0 and 1. The model convincingly renders complex facial movements which in most cases are difficult to distinguish from real images. It is also worth mentioning that the independence of facial muscle cluster is properly learned by the generator. AUs relative to the eyes and half-upper part of the face (AUs 1, 2, 4, 5, 45) do not affect the muscles of the mouth. Equivalently, mouth related transformations (AUs 10, 12, 15, 25) do not affect eyes nor eyebrow muscles.

Figure 5 displays, for the same experiment, the attention **A** and color **C** masks that produced the final result $\mathbf{I_{y_g}}$. Note how the model has learned to focus its attention (darker area) onto the corresponding AU in an unsupervised manner. In this way, it relieves the color mask from having to accurately regress each pixel value. Only the pixels relevant to the expression change are carefully estimated, the rest are just noise. For example, the attention is clearly obviating background pixels allowing to directly copy them from the original image. This is a key ingredient to later being able to handle images in the wild (see Sect. 6.5).

6.2   Simultaneous Edition of Multiple AUs

We next push the limits of our model and evaluate it in editing multiple AUs. Additionally, we also assess its ability to interpolate between two expressions. The results of this experiment are shown in Fig. 1, the first column is the original image with expression y_r, and the right-most column is a synthetically generated image conditioned on a target expression y_g. The rest of columns result from evaluating the generator conditioned with a linear interpolation of the original and target expressions: $\alpha y_g + (1 - \alpha)y_r$. The outcomes show a very remarkable smooth an consistent transformation across frames. We have intentionally selected challenging samples to show robustness to light conditions and even, as in the case of the avatar, to non-real world data distributions which were not previously seen by the model. These results are encouraging to further extend the model to video generation in future works.

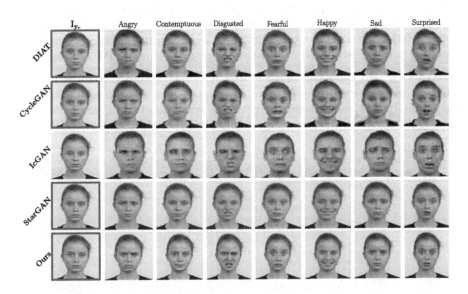

Fig. 6. Qualitative comparison with state-of-the-art. Facial Expression Synthesis results for: DIAT [20], CycleGAN [28], IcGAN [26] and StarGAN [4]; and ours. In all cases, we represent the input image and seven different facial expressions. As it can be seen, our solution produces the best trade-off between visual accuracy and spatial resolution. Some of the results of StarGAN, the best current approach, show certain level of blur. Images of previous models were taken from [4].

6.3   Discrete Emotions Editing

We next compare our approach, against the baselines DIAT [20], CycleGAN [28], IcGAN [26] and StarGAN [4]. For a fair comparison, we adopt the results of these methods trained by the most recent work, StarGAN, on the task of rendering discrete emotions categories (e.g., happy, sad and fearful) in the RaFD dataset [16]. Since DIAT [20] and CycleGAN [28] do not allow conditioning, they were independently trained for every possible pair of source/target emotions. We next briefly discuss the main aspects of each approach:

DIAT [20]. Given an input image $x \in X$ and a reference image $y \in Y$, DIAT learns a GAN model to render the attributes of domain Y in the image x while conserving the person's identity. It is trained with the classic *adversarial loss* and a *cycle loss* $\|x - G_{Y \to X}(G_{X \to Y}(x))\|_1$ to preserve the person's identity.

CycleGAN [28]. Similar to DIAT [20], CycleGAN also learns the mapping between two domains $X \to Y$ and $Y \to X$. To train the domain transfer, it uses a regularization term denoted *cycle consistency loss* combining two cycles: $\|x - G_{Y \to X}(G_{X \to Y}(x))\|_1$ and $\|y - G_{X \to Y}(G_{Y \to X}(y))\|_1$.

IcGAN [26]. Given an input image, IcGAN uses a pretrained encoder-decoder to encode the image into a latent representation in concatenation with an expression vector **y** to then reconstruct the original image. It can modify the expression by replacing **y** with the desired expression before going through the decoder.

StarGAN [4]. An extension of *cycle loss* for simultaneously training between multiple datasets with different data domains. It uses a mask vector to ignore unspecified labels and optimize only on known ground-truth labels. It yields more realistic results when training simultaneously with multiple datasets.

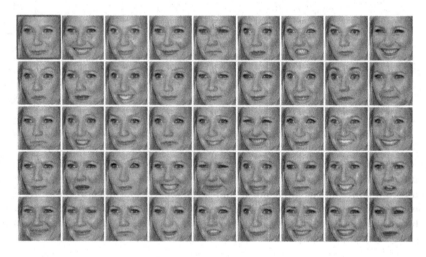

Fig. 7. Sampling the face expression distribution space. As a result of applying our AU-parametrization through the vector $\mathbf{y}_g$, we can synthesize, from the same source image $\mathbf{I}_{\mathbf{y}_r}$, a large variety of photo-realistic images.

Our model differs from these approaches in two main aspects. First, we do not condition the model on discrete emotions categories, but we learn a basis of anatomically feasible warps that allows generating a continuum of expressions. Secondly, the use of the attention mask allows applying the transformation only on the cropped face, and put it back onto the original image without producing any artifact. As shown in Fig. 6, besides estimating more visually compelling images than other approaches, this results on images of higher spatial resolution.

6.4 High Expressions Variability

Given a single image, we next use our model to produce a wide range of anatomically feasible face expressions while conserving the person's identity. In Fig. 7 all faces are the result of conditioning the input image in the top-left corner with a desired face configuration defined by only 14 AUs. Note the large variability of anatomically feasible expressions that can be synthesized with only 14 AUs.

6.5 Images in the Wild

As previously seen in Fig. 5, the attention mechanism not only learns to focus on specific areas of the face but also allows merging the original and generated image background. This allows our approach to be easily applied to images in the wild while still obtaining high resolution images. For these images we follow the detection and cropping scheme we described before. Figure 8 shows two examples on these challenging images. Note how the attention mask allows for a smooth and unnoticeable merge between the entire frame and the generated faces.

Fig. 8. Qualitative evaluation on images in the wild. Top: We represent an image (left) from the film *"Pirates of the Caribbean"* and an its generated image obtained by our approach (right). Bottom: In a similar manner, we use an image frame (left) from the series *"Game of Thrones"* to synthesize five new images with different expressions.

6.6 Pushing the Limits of the Model

We next push the limits of our network and discuss the model limitations. We have split success cases into six categories which we summarize in Fig. 9-top.

The first two examples (top-row) correspond to human-like sculptures and non-realistic drawings. In both cases, the generator is able to maintain the artistic effects of the original image. Also, note how the attention mask ignores artifacts such as the pixels occluded by the glasses. The third example shows robustness to non-homogeneous textures across the face. Observe that the model is not trying to homogenize the texture by adding/removing the beard's hair. The middle-right category relates to anthropomorphic faces with non-real textures. As for the Avatar image, the network is able to warp the face without affecting its texture. The next category is related to non-standard illuminations/colors for which the model has already been shown robust in Fig. 1. The last and most surprising category is face-sketches (bottom-right). Although the generated face suffers from some artifacts, it is still impressive how the proposed method is still capable of finding sufficient features on the face to transform its expression from worried to excited. The second case shows failures with non-previously seen occlusions such as an eye patch causing artifacts in the missing face attributes.

We have also categorized the failure cases in Fig. 9-bottom, all of them presumably due to insufficient training data. The first case is related to errors in the attention mechanism when given extreme input expressions. The attention does not weight sufficiently the color transformation causing transparencies.

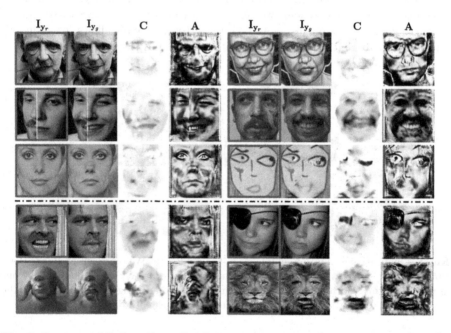

Fig. 9. Success and Failure Cases. In all cases, we represent the source image I_{y_r}, the target one I_{y_g}, and the color and attention masks C and A, respectively. Top: Some success cases in extreme situations. Bottom: Several failure cases.

The model also fails when dealing with non-human anthropomorphic distributions as in the case of cyclopes. Lastly, we tested the model behavior when dealing with animals and observed artifacts like human face features.

7 Conclusions

We have presented a novel GAN model for face animation in the wild that can be trained in a fully unsupervised manner. It advances current works which, so far, had only addressed the problem for discrete emotions category editing and portrait images. Our model encodes anatomically consistent face deformations parameterized by means of AUs. Conditioning the GAN model on these AUs allows the generator to render a wide range of expressions by simple interpolation. Additionally, we embed an attention model within the network which allows focusing only on those regions of the image relevant for every specific expression. By doing this, we can easily process images in the wild, with distracting backgrounds and illumination artifacts. We have exhaustively evaluated the model capabilities and limits in the EmotioNet [3] and RaFD [16] datasets as well as in images from movies. The results are very promising, and show smooth transitions between different expressions. This opens the possibility of applying our approach to video sequences, which we plan to do in the future.

Acknowledgments. This work is partially supported by the Spanish Ministry of Economy and Competitiveness under projects HuMoUR TIN2017-90086-R, ColRob-Transp DPI2016-78957 and María de Maeztu Seal of Excellence MDM-2016-0656; by the EU project AEROARMS ICT-2014-1-644271; and by the Grant R01-DC- 014498 of the National Institute of Health. We also thank Nvidia for hardware donation under the GPU Grant Program.

References

1. Arjovsky, M., Chintala, S., Bottou, L.: Wasserstein GAN. arXiv preprint arXiv:1701.07875 (2017)
2. Baltrušaitis, T., Mahmoud, M., Robinson, P.: Cross-dataset learning and person-specific normalisation for automatic action unit detection. In: FG (2015)
3. Benitez-Quiroz, C.F., Srinivasan, R., Martinez, A.M., et al.: EmotioNet: an accurate, real-time algorithm for the automatic annotation of a million facial expressions in the wild. In: CVPR (2016)
4. Choi, Y., Choi, M., Kim, M., Ha, J.W., Kim, S., Choo, J.: StarGAN: unified generative adversarial networks for multi-domain image-to-image translation. In: CVPR (2018)
5. Du, S., Tao, Y., Martinez, A.M.: Compound facial expressions of emotion. In: Proceedings of the National Academy of Sciences, p. 201322355 (2014)
6. Ekman, P., Friesen, W.: Facial Action Coding System: A Technique for the Measurement of Facial Movement. Consulting Psychologists Press, Palo Alto (1978)
7. Fischler, M.A., Elschlager, R.A.: The representation and matching of pictorial structures. IEEE Trans. Comput. **22**(1), 67–92 (1973)

8. Goodfellow, I., et al.: Generative adversarial nets. In: NIPS (2014)
9. Gulrajani, I., Ahmed, F., Arjovsky, M., Dumoulin, V., Courville, A.C.: Improved training of wasserstein GANs. In: NIPS (2017)
10. Isola, P., Zhu, J.Y., Zhou, T., Efros, A.A.: Image-to-image translation with conditional adversarial networks. In: CVPR (2017)
11. Johnson, J., Alahi, A., Fei-Fei, L.: Perceptual losses for real-time style transfer and super-resolution. In: Leibe, B., Matas, J., Sebe, N., Welling, M. (eds.) ECCV 2016. LNCS, vol. 9906, pp. 694–711. Springer, Cham (2016). https://doi.org/10.1007/978-3-319-46475-6_43
12. Karras, T., Aila, T., Laine, S., Lehtinen, J.: Progressive growing of GANs for improved quality, stability, and variation. In: ICLR (2018)
13. Kim, T., Cha, M., Kim, H., Lee, J., Kim, J.: Learning to discover cross-domain relations with generative adversarial networks. In: ICML (2017)
14. Kingma, D., Ba, J.: ADAM: a method for stochastic optimization. In: ICLR (2015)
15. Kingma, D.P., Welling, M.: Auto-encoding variational bayes. In: ICLR (2014)
16. Langner, O., Dotsch, R., Bijlstra, G., Wigboldus, D.H., Hawk, S.T., Van Knippenberg, A.: Presentation and validation of the radboud faces database. Cogn. Emot. **24**(8), 1377–1388 (2010)
17. Larsen, A.B.L., Sønderby, S.K., Larochelle, H., Winther, O.: Autoencoding beyond pixels using a learned similarity metric. In: ICML (2016)
18. Ledig, C., et al.: Photo-realistic single image super-resolution using a generative adversarial network. In: CVPR (2017)
19. Li, C., Wand, M.: Precomputed real-time texture synthesis with Markovian generative adversarial networks. In: Leibe, B., Matas, J., Sebe, N., Welling, M. (eds.) ECCV 2016. LNCS, vol. 9907, pp. 702–716. Springer, Cham (2016). https://doi.org/10.1007/978-3-319-46487-9_43
20. Li, M., Zuo, W., Zhang, D.: Deep identity-aware transfer of facial attributes. arXiv preprint arXiv:1610.05586 (2016)
21. Liu, M.Y., Breuel, T., Kautz, J.: Unsupervised image-to-image translation networks. In: NIPS (2017)
22. Mathieu, M., Couprie, C., LeCun, Y.: Deep multi-scale video prediction beyond mean square error. In: ICLR (2016)
23. Mirza, M., Osindero, S.: Conditional generative adversarial nets. arXiv preprint arXiv:1411.1784 (2014)
24. Odena, A., Olah, C., Shlens, J.: Conditional image synthesis with auxiliary classifier GANs. In: ICML (2017)
25. Pathak, D., Krahenbuhl, P., Donahue, J., Darrell, T., Efros, A.A.: Context encoders: feature learning by inpainting. In: CVPR (2016)
26. Perarnau, G., van de Weijer, J., Raducanu, B., Álvarez, J.M.: Invertible conditional GANs for image editing. arXiv preprint arXiv:1611.06355 (2016)
27. Pumarola, A., Agudo, A., Sanfeliu, A., Moreno-Noguer, F.: Unsupervised person image synthesis in arbitrary poses. In: CVPR (2018)
28. Radford, A., Metz, L., Chintala, S.: Unpaired image-to-image translation using cycle-consistent adversarial networks. In: ICLR (2016)
29. Reed, S., Akata, Z., Yan, X., Logeswaran, L., Schiele, B., Lee., H.: Generative adversarial text to image synthesis. In: ICML (2016)
30. Scherer, K.R.: Emotion as a process: function, origin and regulation. Soc. Sci. Inf. **21**, 555–570 (1982)
31. Shen, W., Liu, R.: Learning residual images for face attribute manipulation. In: CVPR (2017)

32. Shrivastava, A., Pfister, T., Tuzel, O., Susskind, J., Wang, W., Webb, R.: Learning from simulated and unsupervised images through adversarial training. In: CVPR (2017)

33. Wang, X., Gupta, A.: Generative image modeling using style and structure adversarial networks. In: Leibe, B., Matas, J., Sebe, N., Welling, M. (eds.) ECCV 2016. LNCS, vol. 9908, pp. 318–335. Springer, Cham (2016). https://doi.org/10.1007/978-3-319-46493-0_20

34. Wang, Z., Liu, D., Yang, J., Han, W., Huang, T.: Deep networks for image super-resolution with sparse prior. In: ICCV (2015)

35. Yu, H., Garrod, O.G., Schyns, P.G.: Perception-driven facial expression synthesis. Comput. Graph. 36(3), 152–162 (2012)

36. Zafeiriou, S., Trigeorgis, G., Chrysos, G., Deng, J., Shen, J.: The menpo facial landmark localisation challenge: a step towards the solution. In: CVPRW (2017)

37. Zhang, H., et al.: StackGAN: text to photo-realistic image synthesis with stacked generative adversarial networks. In: ICCV (2017)

38. Zhu, J.Y., Park, T., Isola, P., Efros, A.A.: Unpaired image-to-image translation using cycle-consistent adversarial networks. In: ICCV (2017)

39. Zhu, S., Fidler, S., Urtasun, R., Lin, D., Loy, C.C.: Be your own prada: fashion synthesis with structural coherence. In: ICCV (2017)

Author Index

Printed in the United States
By Bookmasters